The Ante-Nicene Fathers

Volume III
Latin Christianity

**EDITED BY REV. ALEXANDER ROBERTS,
SIR JAMES DONALDSON
& ARTHUR CLEVELAND COXE**

COSIMOCLASSICS

NEW YORK

The Ante-Nicene Fathers: Volume III
Latin Christianity
Cover © 2007 Cosimo, Inc.

For information, address:

Cosimo, P.O. Box 416
Old Chelsea Station
New York, NY 10113-0416

or visit our website at:
www.cosimobooks.com

The Ante-Nicene Fathers: Volume III – Latin Christianity was originally published in 1885.

Cover design by www.kerndesign.net

ISBN: 978-1-60206-473-7

The character of the times in which we live is such as to
call forth from us even this admonition, that we ought not
to be astonished at the heresies (which abound) neither ought
their existence to surprise us, for it was foretold that they
should come to pass; nor the fact that they subvert the faith
of some, for their final cause is, by affording a trial to faith,
to give it also the opportunity of being "approved."

——from *Anti-Marcion: The Prescription Against Heretics*

Contents of Volume III.

THE WRITINGS OF TERTULLIAN.

TERTULLIAN.

PART FIRST.

INTRODUCTORY NOTE.

[A.D. 145–220.] WHEN our Lord repulsed the woman of Canaan (Matt. xv. 22) with apparent harshness, he applied to her people the epithet *dogs*, with which the children of Israel had thought it piety to reproach them. When He accepted her faith and caused it to be recorded for our learning, He did something more: He reversed the curse of the Canaanite and showed that the Church was designed "for all people;" Catholic alike for all time and for all sorts and conditions of men.

Thus the North-African Church was loved before it was born: the Good Shepherd was gently leading those "that were with young." Here was the charter of those Christians to be a Church, who then were Canaanites in the land of their father Ham. It is remarkable indeed that among these pilgrims and strangers to the West the first elements of Latin Christianity come into view. Even at the close of the Second Century the Church in Rome is an inconsiderable, though prominent, member of the great confederation of Christian Churches which has its chief seats in Alexandria and Antioch, and of which the entire Literature is Greek. It is an African presbyter who takes from Latin Christendom the reproach of theological and literary barrenness and begins the great work in which, upon his foundations, Cyprian and Augustine built up, with incomparable genius, that Carthaginian School of Christian thought by which Latin Theology was dominated for centuries. It is important to note (1.) that providentially not one of these illustrious doctors died in Communion with the Roman See, pure though it was and venerable at that time; and (2.) that to the works of Augustine the Reformation in Germany and Continental Europe was largely due; while (3.) the *specialties* of the Anglican Reformation were, in like proportion, due to the writings of Tertullian and Cyprian. The hinges of great and controlling destinies for Western Europe and our own America are to be found in the period we are now approaching.

The merest school-boy knows much of the history of Carthage, and how the North Africans became Roman citizens. How they became Christians is not so clear. A melancholy destiny has enveloped Carthage from the outset, and its glory and greatness as a Christian See were transient indeed. It blazed out all at once in Tertullian, after about a century of missionary labours had been exerted upon its creation : and having given a Minucius Felix, an Arnobius and a Lactantius to adorn the earliest period of Western Ecclesiastical learning, in addition to its nobler luminaries, it rapidly declined. At the beginning of the Third Century, at a council presided over by Agrippinus, Bishop of Carthage, there were present not less than seventy bishops of the Province. A period of cruel persecutions followed, and the African Church received a baptism of blood.

Tertullian was born a heathen, and seems to have been educated at Rome, where he probably practiced as a jurisconsult. We may, perhaps, adopt most of the ideas of Allix, as conjecturally probable, and assign his birth to A.D. 145. He became a Christian about

185, and a presbyter about 190. The period of his strict orthodoxy very nearly expires with the century. He lived to an extreme old age, and some suppose even till A.D. 240. More probably we must adopt the date preferred by recent writers, A.D. 220.

It seems to be the fashion to treat of Tertullian as a Montanist, and only incidentally to celebrate his services to the Catholic Orthodoxy of Western Christendom. Were I his biographer I should reverse this course, as a mere act of justice, to say nothing of gratitude to a man of splendid intellect, to whom the filial spirit of Cyprian accorded the loving tribute of a disciple, and whose genius stamped itself upon the very words of Latin theology, and prepared the language for the labours of a Jerome. In creating the Vulgate, and so lifting the Western Churches into a position of intellectual equality with the East, the latter as well as St. Augustine himself were debtors to Tertullian in a degree not to be estimated by any other than the Providential Mind that inspired his brilliant career as a Christian.

In speaking of Tatian I laid the base for what I wished to say of Tertullian. Let God only be their judge ; let us gratefully recognize the debt we owe to them. Let us read them, as we read the works of King Solomon. We must, indeed, approve of the discipline of the Primitive Age, which allowed of no compromises. The Church was struggling for existence, and could not permit any man to become her master. The more brilliant the intellect, the more dangerous to the poor Church were its perversions of her Testimony. Before the heathen tribunals, and in the market-places, it would not answer to let Christianity appear double-tongued. The orthodoxy of the Church, not less than her children, was undergoing an ordeal of fire. It seems a miracle that her Testimony preserved its unity, and that heresy was branded as such by the instinct of the Faithful. Poor Tertullian was cut off by his own act. The weeping Church might bewail him as David mourned for Absalom, but like David, she could not give the Ark of God into other hands than those of the loyal and the true. I have set the writings of Tertullian in a natural and logical order,[1] so as to aid the student, and to relieve him from the distractions of such an arrangement as one finds in Oehler's edition. Valuable as it is, the practical use of it is irritating and confusing. The reader of that edition may turn to the slightly differing schemes of Neander and Kaye, for a theoretical order of the works; but here he will find a classification which will aid his inquiries. He will find, first, those works which connect with the Apologists of the former volumes of this series: which illustrate the Church's position toward the outside world, the Jews as well as the Gentiles. Next come those works which contend with internal differences and heresies. And then, those which reflect the morals and manners of Christians. These are classed with some reference to their degrees of freedom from the Montanistic taint, and are followed, last of all, by the few tracts which belong to the melancholy period of his lapse, and are directed against the Church's orthodoxy.

Let it be borne in mind, that if this sad close of Tertullian's career cannot be extenuated, the later history of Latin Christianity forbids us to condemn him, in the tones which proceeded from the Virgin Church with authority, and which the law of her testimony and the instinct of self-preservation forced her to utter. Let us reflect that St. Bernard and after him the Schoolmen, whom we so deservedly honour, separated themselves far more absolutely than ever Tertullian did from the orthodoxy of Primitive Christendom. The schism which withdrew the West from Communion with the original seats of Christendom, and from Nicene Catholicity, was formidable beyond all expression, in comparison with Tertullian's entanglements with a delusion which the See of Rome itself had momentarily patronized. Since the Council of Trent, not a theologian of the Latins has been free from organic heresies, compared with which the fanaticism of our author was a trifling aberration. Since the late Council of the Vatican, essential Montanism has become organized in the Latin

---

[1] Elucidation I.

Churches: for what are the new revelations and oracles of the pontiff but the *deliria* of another claimant to the voice and inspiration of the Paraclete? Poor Tertullian! The sad influences of his decline and folly have been fatally felt in all the subsequent history of the West, but, surely subscribers to the Modern Creed of the Vatican have reason to "speak gently of *their father's* fall." To Döllinger, with the "Old Catholic" remnant only, is left the right to name the Montanists heretics, or to upbraid Tertullian as a lapser from Catholicity.[1]

From Dr. Holmes, I append the following INTRODUCTORY NOTICE:[2]

(I.) QUINTUS SEPTIMIUS FLORENS TERTULLIANUS, as our author is called in the MSS. of his works, is thus noticed by Jerome in his *Catalogus Scriptorum Ecclesiasticorum*:[3] "Tertullian, a presbyter, the first Latin writer after Victor and Apollonius, was a native of the province of Africa and city of Carthage, the son of a proconsular centurion: he was a man of a sharp and vehement temper, flourished under Severus and Antoninus Caracalla, and wrote numerous works, which (as they are generally known) I think it unnecessary to particularize. I saw at Concordia, in Italy, an old man named Paulus. He said that when young he had met at Rome with an aged amanuensis of the blessed Cyprian, who told him that Cyprian never passed a day without reading some portion of Tertullian's works, and used frequently to say, *Give me my master*, meaning Tertullian. After remaining a presbyter of the church until he had attained the middle age of life, Tertullian was, by the envy and contumelious treatment of the Roman clergy, driven to embrace the opinions of Montanus, which he has mentioned in several of his works under the title of the New Prophecy. . . . He is reported to have lived to a very advanced age, and to have composed many other works which are not extant." We add Bishop Kaye's notes on this extract, in an abridged shape: "The correctness of some parts of this account has been questioned. Doubts have been entertained whether Tertullian was a presbyter, although these have solely arisen from Roman Catholic objections to a married priesthood; for it is certain that he was married, there being among his works two treatises addressed to his wife. . . . Another question has been raised respecting the place where Tertullian officiated as a presbyter—whether at Carthage or at Rome. That he at one time resided at Carthage may be inferred from Jerome's statement, and is rendered certain by several passages of his own writings. Allix supposes that the notion of his having been a presbyter of the Roman Church owed its rise to what Jerome said of the envy and abuse of the Roman clergy impelling him to espouse the party of Montanus. Optatus,[4] and the author of the work *de Hæresibus*, which Sirmond edited under the title of Prædestinatus, expressly call him a Carthaginian presbyter. Semler, however, in a dissertation inserted in his edition of Tertullian's works,[5] contends that he was a presbyter of the Roman Church. Eusebius[6] tells us that he was accurately acquainted with the Roman laws, and on other accounts a distinguished person at Rome.[7] Tertullian displays, moreover, a knowledge of the

---

[1] The notes of Dr. Holmes were bracketted, and I have been forced to remove this feature, as brackets are tokens in this edition of the contributions of American editors. The perpetual recurrence of brackets in his translations has led me to improve the page by parenthetical marks instead, which answer as well and rarely can be mistaken for the author's *parentheses*, while these disfigure the printer's work much less. I have sometimes substituted italics for brackets, where an inconsiderable word, like *and* or *for*, was bracketted by the translator. In every case that I have noted, an intelligent reader will readily perceive such instances; but a critic who may wish to praise, or condemn, should carefully compare the Edinburgh pages with our own. I found them so painful to the eye and so needlessly annoying to the reader, that I have taken the responsibility of making what seems to me a very great typographical improvement.

[2] (I.) Concerning Tertullian; (II.) Concerning his Work against Marcion, its date, etc.; (III.) Concerning Marcion; (IV.) Concerning Tertullian's Bible; (V.) Influence of his Montanism on his writings.

[3] We quote Bishop Kaye's translation of Jerome's article; see his *Account of the Writings of Tertullian*, pp. 5-8.

[4] *Adv. Parmenianum*, i.   [5] Chap. ii.   [6] *Eccl. Hist.*, ii. 2.

[7] Valesius, however, supposes the historian's words τῶν μάλιστα ἐπὶ Ῥώμης λαμπρῶν to mean, that Tertullian had obtained distinction among Latin writers.

proceedings of the Roman Church with respect to Marcion and Valentinus, who were once members of it, which could scarcely have been obtained by one who had not himself been numbered amongst its presbyters.[1] Semler admits that, after Tertullian seceded from the church, he left and returned to Carthage.   Jerome does not inform us whether Tertullian was born of Christian parents, or was converted to Christianity.   There are passages in his writings[2] which seem to imply that he had been a Gentile; yet he may perhaps mean to describe, not his own condition, but that of Gentiles in general, before their conversion. Allix and the majority of commentators understand them literally, as well as some other passages in which he speaks of his own infirmities and sinfulness.   His writings show that he flourished at the period specified by Jerome—that is, during the reigns of Severus and Antoninus Caracalla, or between the years A.D. 193 and 216; but they supply no precise information respecting the date of his birth, or any of the principal occurrences of his life. Allix places his birth about 145 or 150; his conversion to Christianity about A.D. 185; his marriage about 186; his admission to the priesthood[3] about 192; his adoption of the opinions of Montanus about 199; and his death about A.D. 220.   But these dates, it must be understood, rest entirely on conjecture."[4]

(II.) Tertullian's work against Marcion, as it happens, is, *as to its date*, the best authenticated—perhaps the only well authenticated—particular connected with the author's life. He himself[5] mentions the fifteenth year of the reign of Severus as the time when he was writing the work: "Ad xv. jam Severi imperatoris."   This agrees with Jerome's Chronicle, where occurs this note: "Anno 2223 Severi xv° Tertullianus . . . celebratur."[6]   This year is assigned to the year of our Lord 207;[7] but notwithstanding the certainty of this date, it is far from clear that it describes more than the time of the publication of *the first book.* On the contrary, it is nearly certain that the other books, although connected manifestly enough in the author's argument and purpose (compare the initial and the final chapters of the several books), were yet issued at separate times.   Noesselt[8] shows that between the Book i. and Books ii.–iv. Tertullian issued his *De Præscript. Hæret.*, and previous to Book v. he published his tracts, *De Carne Christi* and *De Resurrectione Carnis.* After giving the incontestable date of the xv. of Severus for the first book, he says it is a mistake to suppose that the other books were published with it.   He adds: "Although we cannot undertake to determine whether Tertullian issued his Books ii., iii., iv., against Marcion, together or separately, or in what year, we yet venture to affirm that Book v. appeared apart from the rest.   For the tract *De Resurr. Carnis* appears from its second chapter to have been published after the tract *De Carne Christi*, in which latter work (chap. vii.) he quotes a passage from the fourth book against Marcion.   But in his Book v. against Marcion (chap. x.), he refers to his work *De Resurr. Carnis;* which circumstance makes it evident that Tertullian published his Book v. at a different time from his Book iv.   In his Book i. he announces his intention (chap. i.) of some time or other completing his tract *De Præscript. Hæret.*, but in his book *De Carne Christi* (chap. ii.), he mentions how he had completed it, —a conclusive proof that his Book i. against Marcion preceded the other books."

[1] See *De Præscript. Hæretic.* xxx.
[2] *De Pœnitentia*, i. Hoc genus hominum, quod et ipsi retro fuimus, cæci, sine Domini lumine, naturâ tenus norunt; *De Fuga in Persecutione*, vi. Nobis autem et via nationum patet, in quâ et inventi sumus; *Adv. Marcionem*, iii. 21. Et nationes, quod sumus nos; *Apolog.* xviii. Hæc et nos risimus aliquando; de vestris fuimus; also *De Spectac.* xix.
[3] [Kaye, p. 9.   A fair view of this point.]
[4] These notes of Bishop Kaye may be found, in their fuller form, in his work on Tertullian, pp. 8–12.
[5] Book i., chap. xv.
[6] Jerome probably took this date as the central period, when Tertullian "flourished," because of its being the only clearly authenticated one, and because also (it may be) of the importance and fame of the Treatise against Marcion.
[7] So Clinton, *Fasti Romani*, i. 204; or 208, Pamelius, *Vita Tertull.*
[8] In his treatise, *De vera ætate ac doctrina script. Tertulliani*, sections 28, 45.

(III.) Respecting Marcion himself, the most formidable heretic who had as yet opposed revealed truth, enough will turn up in this treatise, with the notes which we have added in explanation, to satisfy the reader. It will, however, be convenient to give here a few introductory particulars of him. Tertullian[1] mentions Marcion as being, with Valentinus, in communion with the Church at Rome, "under the episcopate of the blessed Eleutherus." He goes on to charge them with "ever-restless curiosity, with which they infected even the brethren;" and informs us that they were more than once put out of communion—"Marcion, indeed, with the 200 sesterces which he brought into the church."[2] He goes on to say, that "being at last condemned to the banishment of a perpetual separation, they sowed abroad the poisons of their doctrines. Afterwards, when Marcion, having professed penitence, agreed to the terms offered to him, that he should receive reconciliation on condition that he brought back to the church the rest also, whom he had trained up for perdition, he was prevented by death." He was a native of Sinope in Pontus, of which city, according to an account preserved by Epiphanius,[3] which, however, is somewhat doubtful, his father was bishop, and of high character both for his orthodoxy and exemplary practice. He came to Rome soon after the death of Hyginus, probably about A.D. 141 or 142; and soon after his arrival he adopted the heresy of Cerdon.[4]

(IV.) It is an interesting question as to what edition of the Holy Scriptures Tertullian used in his very copious quotations. It may at once be asserted that he did not cite from the Hebrew, although some writers have claimed for him, among his varied learning, a knowledge of the sacred language. Bp. Kaye observes, page 61, n. 1, that "he sometimes speaks as if he was acquainted with Hebrew," and refers to the *Anti-Marcion* iv. 39, the *Adv. Praxeam* v., and the *Adv. Judæos* ix. Be this as it may, it is manifest that Tertullian's Scripture passages never resemble the Hebrew, but in nearly every instance the Septuagint, whenever, as is most frequently the case, that version differs from the original. In the New Testament there is, as might be expected, a tolerably close conformity to the Greek. There is, however, it must be allowed, a sufficiently frequent variation from the letter of both the Greek Testaments to justify Semler's suspicion that Tertullian always quoted from the old Latin version,[5] whatever that might have been, which was current in the African church in the second and third centuries. The most valuable part of Semler's *Dissertatio de varia et incerta indole Librorum Q. S. F. Tertulliani* is his investigation of this very point. In section iv. he endeavours to prove this proposition: "Hic scriptor[6] non in manibus habuit Græcos libros sacros;" and he states his conclusion thus: "Certissimum est nec Tertullianum nec Cyprianum nec ullum scriptorem e Latinis illis ecclesiasticis provocare unquam ad Græcorum librorum auctoritatem si vel maxime obscura aut contraria lectio occurreret;" and again: "Ex his satis certum est, Latinos satis diu secutos fuisse auctoritatem suorum librorum adversus Græcos, nec concessisse nisi serius, cum Augustini et Hieronymi nova auctoritas juvare videretur." It is not ignorance of Greek which is imputed to Tertullian, for he is said to have well understood that language, and even to have composed in it. He probably followed the Latin, as writers now usually quote the authorized English, as being current and best known among their readers. Independent feeling, also, would have weight with such a temper as Tertullian's, to say nothing of the suspicion which largely prevailed in the African branch of the Latin church, that the Greek copies of the Scriptures were much corrupted by the heretics, who were chiefly, if not wholly, Greeks or Greek-speaking persons.

(V.) Whatever perverting effect Tertullian's secession to the sect of Montanus[7] may have

---

[1] *De Præscript. Hæret.* xxx.   [2] Comp. *Adv. Marcionem*, iv. 4.
[3] I., *Adv. Hæret.* xlii. 1.
[4] Dr. Burton's *Lectures on Eccl. Hist. of First Three Centuries*, ii. 105–109.   [5] Or versions.   [6] Tertullianus.
[7] Vincentius Lirinensis, in his celebrated *Commonitorium*, expresses the opinion of Catholic churchmen concerning Tertullian thus: "Tertullian, among the Latins, without controversy, is the chief of all our writers. For who was more learned than he? Who

had on his judgment in his latest writings, it did not vitiate the work against Marcion. With
a few trivial exceptions, this treatise may be read by the strictest Catholic without any feeling of annoyance. His lapse to Montanism is set down conjecturally as having taken place
A.D. 199. Jerome, we have seen, attributed the event to his quarrel with the Roman clergy,
but this is at least doubtful; nor must it be forgotten that Tertullian's mind seems to have
been peculiarly suited by nature[1] to adopt the mystical notions and ascetic principles of
Montanus. It is satisfactory to find that, on the whole, "the authority of Tertullian," as
the learned Dr. Burton says, "upon great points of doctrine is considered to be little,
if at all, affected by his becoming a Montanist." (*Lectures on Eccl. Hist.* vol. ii. p.
234.) Besides the different works which are expressly mentioned in the notes of
this volume, recourse has been had by the translator to Dupin's *Hist. Eccl. Writers*
(trans.), vol. i. pp. 69–86; Tillemont's *Mémoires Hist. Eccl.* iii. 85–103; Dr. Smith's
Greek and Roman Biography, articles "Marcion" and "Tertullian;" Schaff's article, in Herzog's *Cyclopædia*, on "Tertullian;" Munter's *Primordia Eccl. Africanæ*,
pp. 118–150; Robertson's *Church Hist.* vol. i. pp. 70–77; Dr. P. Schaff's *Hist. of
Christian Church* (New York, 1859, pp. 511–519), and Archdeacon Evans' *Biography of the
Early Church*, vol. i. (Lives of "Marcion," pp. 93–122, and "Tertullian," pp. 325–363).
This last work, though of a popular cast, shows a good deal of research and learning, expressed in the pleasant style of the once popular author of *The Rectory of Vale Head*. The
translator has mentioned these works, because they are all quite accessible to the general
reader, and will give him adequate information concerning the subject treated in the present
volume.

     To this introduction of Dr. Holmes must be added that of Mr. Thelwall, the translator
of the Third volume in the Edinburgh Series, as follows:

     To arrange chronologically the works (especially if numerous) of an author whose own
date is known with tolerable precision, is not always or necessarily easy: witness the controversies as to the succession of St. Paul's epistles. To do this in the case of an author
whose own date is itself a matter of controversy may therefore be reasonably expected to
be still less so; and such is the predicament of him who attempts to perform this task for
Tertullian. I propose to give a specimen or two of the difficulties with which the task is
beset; and then to lay before the reader briefly a summary of the results at which eminent
scholars, who have devoted much time and thought to the subject, have arrived. Such a
course, I think, will at once afford him means of judging of the absolute impossibility of
arriving at definite certainty in the matter; and induce him to excuse me if I prefer furnishing him with materials from which to deduce his own conclusions, rather than venturing on
an *ex cathedra* decision on so doubtful a subject.

     1. The book, as Dr. Holmes has reminded us,[2] of the date of which we seem to have the

---

in divinity or humanity more practised ? For, by a certain wonderful capacity of mind, he attained to and understood all philosophy, all the sects of philosophers, all their founders and supporters, all their systems, all sorts of histories and studies. And
for his wit, was he not so excellent, so grave, so forcible, that he scarce ever undertook the overthrow of any position, but either by
quickness of wit he undermined, or by weight of reason he crushed it ? Further, who is able to express the praises which his style of
speech deserves, which is fraught (I know none like it) with that cogency of reason, that such as it cannot persuade, it compels to
assent ; whose so many words almost are as many sentences; whose so many senses, so many victories ? This know Marcion and Apelles, Praxeas and Hermogenes, Jews, Gentiles, Gnostics, and divers others, whose blasphemous opinions he hath overthrown with
his many and great volumes, as it had been thunderbolts. And yet this man after all, this Tertullian, not retaining the Catholic
doctrine—that, is, the old faith—hath discredited with his later error his worthy writings," etc.—Chap. xxiv. (Oxford trans. chap. xviii.)
     [1] Neander's introduction to his *Antignostikus* should be read in connection with this topic. He powerfully delineates the dispo-
sition of Tertullian and the character of Montanism, and attributes his secession to that sect not to outward causes, but to "his
internal congeniality of mind." But, inasmuch as a man's subjective development is very much guided by circumstances, it is
not necessary, in agreeing with Neander, to disbelieve some such account as Jerome has given us of Tertullian (Neander's *Antignostikus*, etc. Bohn's trans., vol. ii. pp. 200–207).
     [2] Introductory Notice to the *Anti-Marcion*, pp. xiii. xiv.

surest evidence, is *adv. Marc.* i. This book was in course of writing, as its author himself
(c. 15) tells us, "in the fifteenth year of the empire of Severus." Now this date would be
clear if there were no doubt as to which year of our era corresponds to Tertullian's fifteenth
of Severus. Pamelius, however, says Dr. Holmes, makes it A.D. 208; Clinton, (whose authority is more recent and better,) 207.

2. Another book which promises to give some clue to its date is the *de Pallio*.[1] The
writer uses these phrases: "præsentis imperii *triplex virtus;*" "Deo *tot Augustis in unum*
favente;" which show that there were at the time *three* persons unitedly bearing the title
Augusti—not *Cæsares* only, but the still higher *Augusti;*—while the remainder of that context, as well as the opening of c. 1, indicates a time of peace of some considerable duration;
a time of plenty; and a time during and previous to which great changes had taken place in
the general aspect of the Roman Empire, and some particular traitor had been discovered
and frustrated. Such a combination of circumstances might seem to fix the date with some
degree of assurance. But unhappily, as Kaye reminds us,[2] commentators cannot agree as
to who the three Augusti are. Some say Severus, Caracalla, and *Albinus;* some say Severus,
Caracalla, and *Geta*. Hence we have a difference of some twelve years or thereabouts in
the computations. For Albinus was defeated by Severus in person, and fell by his own
hand, in A.D. 197; and Geta, Severus' second son, brother of Caracalla, was not associated
by his father with himself and his other son as *Augustus* until A.D. 208, though he had received the title of *Cæsar* ten years before, in the same year in which *Caracalla* had received
that of *Augustus*.[3] For my own part, I may perhaps be allowed to say that I should incline
to agree, like Salmasius, with those who assign the later date. The limits of the present
Introduction forbid my entering at large into my reasons for so doing. I am, however,
supported in it by the authority of Neander.[4] In one point, though, I should hesitate to
agree with Oehler, who appears to follow Salmasius and others herein,—namely, in understanding the expression "et cacto et rubo subdolæ familiaritatis convulso" of *Albinus*. It
seems to me the words might with more propriety be applied to *Plautianus;* and that in the
word "familiaritatis" we may see (after Tertullian's fashion) a play upon the meaning,
with a reference not only to the long-standing but mischievous *intimacy* which existed
between Severus and his countryman (perhaps fellow-townsman) Plautianus, who for his
harshness and cruelty is fitly compared to the prickly *cactus*. He alludes likewise to the
alliance which this ambitious prætorian præfect had contrived to contract with the *family* of
the emperor, by the marriage of his daughter Plautilla to Caracalla,—an event which, as it
turned out, led to his own death. Thus in the "*rubo*" there may be a reference to the
ambitious and conceited "*bramble*" of Jotham's parable,[5] and perhaps, too, to the "thistle"
of Jehoash's.[6] If this be so, the date would be at least approximately fixed, as Plautianus
did not marry his daughter to Caracalla till A.D. 203, and was himself put to death in the
following year, 204, while Geta, as we have seen, was made Augustus in 208.

3. The date of the *Apology*, however, is perhaps at once the most contested, and the
most strikingly illustrative of the difficulties to which allusion has been made. It is not
surprising that its date *should* have been more disputed than that of other pieces, inasmuch
as it is the best known, and (for some reasons) the most interesting and famous, of all our
author's productions. In fact, the dates assigned to it by different authorities vary from
Mosheim's 198 to that suggested by the very learned Allix, who assigns it to 217.[7]

---

[1] In the end of Chapter Second.
[2] *Eccl. Hist. illust. from Tertullian's Writings*, p. 36 sqq. (ed. 3, Lond. 1845).
[3] See Kaye, as above.   [4] *Antignostikus*, p. 424 (Bohn's tr., ed. 1851).
[5] See Judg. ix. 2 sqq.   [6] See 2 Kings (4 Kings in LXX. and Vulg.) xiv. 9.
[7] Here, again, our limits forbid a discussion; but the allusion to the Rhone having "scarcely yet lost the stain of blood" which
we find in the *ad. Natt.* i. 17, compared with *Apol.* 35, seems to favour the idea of those who date the *ad. Natt.* earlier than the

4. Once more.   In the tract *de Monogamia* (c. 3) the author says that since the date of St. Paul's first Epistle to the Corinthians " about 160 years had elapsed."   Here, again, did we only know with certainty the precise date of that epistle, we could ascertain *"about"* the date of the tract.   But (*a*) the date of the epistle is itself variously given, Burton giving it as early as A.D. 52, Michaelis and Mill as late as 57; and (*b*) Tertullian only says, " Armis *circiter* CLX. exinde productis;" while the way in which, in the *ad Natt.*, within the short space of three chapters, he states first[1] that 250, and then (in c. 9) that 300, years had not elapsed since the rise of the Christian name, leads us to think that here again[2] he only desires to speak in round numbers, meaning perhaps *more* than 150, but *less* than 170.

These specimens must suffice, though it might be easy to add to them.   There is, however, another classification of our author's writings which has been attempted.   Finding the hoplessness of strict chronological accuracy, commentators have seized on the idea that peradventure there might be found at all events some internal marks by which to determine which of them were written before, which after, the writer's secession to Montanism.   It may be confessed that this attempt has been somewhat more successful than the other.   Yet even here there are two formidable obstacles standing in our way.   The first and greatest is, that the natural temper of Tertullian was from the first so akin to the spirit of Montanism, that, unless there occur distinct allusions to the " New Prophecy," or expressions specially connected with Montanistic phraseology, the *general tone* of any treatise is not a very safe guide.   The second is, that the subject-matter of *some* of the treatises is not such as to afford much scope for the introduction of the peculiarities of a sect which professed to differ in discipline only, not doctrine, from the church at large.

Still the result of this classification seems to show one important feature of agreement between commentators, however they may differ upon details; and that is, that considerably the larger part of our author's rather voluminous productions[3] must have been subsequent to his lamented secession.   I think the best way to give the reader means for forming his own judgment will be, as I have said, to lay before him in parallel columns a tabular view of the disposition of the books by Dr. Neander and Bishop Kaye.   These two modern writers, having given particular care to the subject, bringing to bear upon it all the advantages derived from wide reading, eminent abilities, and a diligent study of the works of preceding writers on the same questions,[4] have a special right to be heard upon the matter in hand; and I think, if I may be allowed to say so, that, for calm judgment, and minute acquaintance with his author, I shall not be accused of undue partiality if I express my opinion that, as far as my own observation goes, the palm must be awarded to the Bishop. In this view I am supported by the fact that the accomplished Professor Ramsay,[5] follows Dr. Kaye's arrangement.   I premise that Dr. Neander adopts a threefold division, into:

1. Writings which were occasioned by the relation of the Christians to the heathen, and refer to their vindication of Christianity against the heathen; attacks on heathenism; the sufferings and conduct of Christians under persecution; and the intercourse of Christians with heathens:

2. Writings which relate to Christian and church life, and to ecclesiastical discipline:

3. The dogmatic and dogmatico-controversial treatises.

And under each head he subdivides into:

a. Pre-Montanist writings: *b.* Post-Montanist writings:

Apology, and consider the latter as a kind of new edition of the former: while it would fix the date of the *ad. Natt.* as not certainly earlier than 197, in which year (as we have seen) Albinus died.   The fatal battle took place on the banks of the Rhone.
[1] In c. 7.   [2] Viz. in the *de Monog.*
[3] It looks strange to see Tertullian's works referred to as consisting of "about thirty *short treatises*" in Murdock's note on Moshiem.   See the ed. of the *Eccl. Hist.* by Dr. J. Seaton Reid, p. 65, n. 2, Lond. and Bel. 1852.
[4] This last qualification is very specially observable in Dr. Kaye.
[5] In his article on Tertullian in *Smith's Dict. of Biog. and Myth.*

thus leaving no room for what Kaye calls "works respecting which nothing certain can be pronounced." For the sake of clearness, this order has not been followed in the table. On the other side, it will be seen that Dr. Kaye, while not assuming to speak with more than a reasonable probability, is careful so to arrange the treatises under each head as to show the *order*, so far as it is discoverable, in which the books under that head were *published;* i.e., if one book is *quoted* in another book, the book so quoted, if distinctly referred to as *already before the world*, is plainly anterior to that in which it is quoted. Thus, then, we have:

NEANDER.	KAYE.
1. *Pre-Montanist.*	**1. *Pre-Montanist* (probably).**
1. De Pœnitentia.	1. De Pœnitentia.[1]
2. De Oratione.	2. De Oratione.
3. De Baptismo	3. De Baptismo.
4. Ad Uxorem i.	4. Ad Uxorem i.
5. Ad Uxorem ii.	5. Ad Uxorem ii.
6. Ad Martyres.	6. Ad Martyres.
7. De Patientia.	7. De Patientia.
8. De Spectaculis.	8. Adv. Judæos.
9. De Idololatria	9. De Præscr. Hæreticorum.[2]
10. 11. Ad Nationes i. ii.	
12. Apologeticus.	**2. *Montanist* (certainly).**
13. De Testimonio Animæ.	10. Adv. Marc. i.
14. De Præscr. Hæreticorum.	11. Adv. Marc. ii.[3]
15. De Cult. Fem. i.	12. De Anima.[4]
16. De Cult. Fem. ii.	13. Adv. Marc. iii.
	14. Adv. Marc. iv.[5]
2. *Montanist.*	15. De Carne Christi.[6]
17–21. Adv. Marc. i. ii. iii. iv. v.	16. De Resurrectione Carnis.[7]
22. De Anima.	17. Adv. Marc. v.
23. De Carne Christi.	18. Adv. Praxeam.
24. De Res. Carn.	19. Scorpiace.[8]
25. De Cor. Mil.	20. De Corona Militis.
26. De Virg. Vel.	21. De Virginibus Velandis.
27. De Ex. Cast.	22. De Exhortatione Castitatis.
28. De Monog.	23. De Fuga in Persecutione.
29. De Jejuniis.	24. De Monogamia.[9]
30. De Pudicitia.	25. De Jejuniis.
31. De Pallio.	26. De Pudicitia.
32. Scorpiace.	
33. Ad Scapulam.	**3. *Montanist* (probably).**
34. Adv. Valentinianos.	27. Adv. Valentinianos.
35. Adv. Hermogenem.	28. Ad Scapulam.
36. Adv. Praxeam.	29. De Spectaculis.[10]
37. Adv. Judæos.	30. De Idololatria.
38. De Fuga in Persecutione,	31. De Cultu Feminarum i.
	32. De Cultu Feminarum ii.
	4. *Works respecting which nothing certain can be pronounced.*
	33. The Apology.[11]
	34. Ad Nationes i.
	35. Ad Nationes ii.
	36. De Testimonio Animæ.
	37. De Pallio.
	38. Adv. Hermogenem.

---

[1] Referred to apparently in *de Pudic. ad init.*—TR.

[2] The *de Præscr.* is ref. to in *adv. Marc.* i.; *adv. Prax.* 2; *de Carne Christi*, 2; *adv. Hermog.* 1.

[3] Ref. to in *de Res. Carn.* 2, 14; *Scorp.* 5; *de Anima*, 21. The only mark, as the learned Bishop's remarks imply, for fixing the date of *publication* as Montanistic, is the fact that Tertullian alludes, in the opening sentences, to B. i. Hence B. ii. could not, in its present form, have appeared till after B. i. Now B. i. contains evident marks of Montanism : see the last chapter, for instance. But the writer speaks (in the same passage) of B. ii. as being *the* treatise, the ill fate of which *in its unfinished condition* he there relates—at least such seems the legitimate sense of his words—*now remodelled.* Hence, *when originally written*, it may *not* have been Montanistic.—TR.   [4] Ref. to in *de Res. Carn.* 2, 17, 45; comp. cc. 18, 21.   [5] Ref. to in *de Carn. Chr.* 7.

[6] Ref. to in *de Res. Carn.* 2.   [7] See the beginning and end of the *de Carne Christi.*—TR.   Ref. to in *adv. Marc.* v. 10.

[8] In c. 4 Tertullian speaks as if he had already refuted all the heretics.   [9] Ref. to in *de Jej.* c. 1.

[10] Ref. to in *de Idolol.* 13; in *de Cult. Fem.* i. 8. In the *de Cor.* 6 is a reference to the Greek tract *de Spectaculis* by our author.

[11] Archdeacon Evans, in his *Biography of the Early Church* (in the Theological Library), suggests that the success which the

A comparison of these two lists will show that the difference between the two great authorities is, as Kaye remarks, " not great; and with respect to some of the tracts on which we differ, the learned author expresses himself with great diffidence." [1] The main difference, in fact, is that which affects two tracts upon kindred subjects, the *de Spectaculis*, and *Idololatria*, the *de Cultu Feminarum* (a subject akin to the other two), and the *adv. Judæos*. With reference to all these, except the last, to which I believe the Archdeacon does not once refer, the Bishop's opinion appears to have the support of Archdeacon Evans, whose learned and interesting essay, referred to in the note, appears in a volume published in 1837. Dr. Kaye's Lectures, on which his book is founded, were delivered in 1825. Of the date of his first edition I am not aware. Dr. Neander's *Antignostikus* also first appeared in 1825. The preface to his second edition bears date July 1, 1849.[2] As to the *adv. Judæos*, I confess I agree with Neander in thinking that, at all events from the beginning of c. 9, it is spurious. If it be urged that Jerome expressly quotes it as Tertullian's, I reply, Jerome so quotes it, I believe, when he is expounding *Daniel*. Now all that the *adv. Jud.* has to say about *Daniel* ends with the end of c. 8. It is therefore quite compatible with the fact thus stated to recognize the earlier half of the book as genuine, and to reject the rest, *beginning*, as it happens, just *after* the eighth chapter, as spurious. Perhaps Dr. Neander's Jewish birth and training peculiarly fit him to be heard on this question. Nor do I think Professor Ramsay (in the article above alluded to) has quite seen the force of Kaye's own remarks on Neander.[3] What he does say is equally creditable to his candour and his accuracy; namely: " The instances alleged by Dr. Neander, in proof of this position, are undoubtedly very remarkable; but if the concluding chapters of the tract are spurious, no ground seems to be left for asserting that the genuine portion was posterior to the third Book against Marcion,[4] —and none, consequently, for asserting that it was written by a Montanist." With which remark I must draw these observations on the genuine extant works of Tertullian to a close.

The next point to which a brief reference must be made is the *lost works* of Tertullian, lists of these are given both by Oehler and by Kaye, viz.:

1. A Book on Aaron's Robes: mentioned by Jerome, Epist. 128, *ad Fabiolam de Veste Sacerdotali* (tom. ii. p. 586, Opp. ed. Bened.).

2. A Book on the Superstition of the Age.[5]

3. A Book on the Submission of the Soul.

4. A Book on the Flesh and the Soul.

Nos. 2, 3, and 4 are known only by their titles, which are found in the Index to Tertullian's works given in the *Codex Agobardi;* but the tracts themselves are not extant in the MS., which appears to have once contained—

5. A Book on Paradise, named in the Index, and referred to in *de Anima* 55, *adv. Marc.* iii. 12; and

6. A Book on the Hope of the Faithful: also named in the Index, and referred to *adv.*

Apology met with, or at least the fame it brought its author, may have been the occasion of Tertullian's visit to Rome. He rejects entirely the supposition that Tertullian was a presbyter of the Roman church; nor does he think Eusebius' words, καὶ τῶν μάλιστα ἐπὶ Ῥώμης λαμπρῶν (*Eccl. Hist.* ii. 2. 47 *ad fin.*, 48 *ad init.*), sufficiently plain to be relied on. One thing does seem pretty plain, that the rendering of them which Rufinus gives, and Valesius follows, "inter nostros" (*sc.* Latinos) "Scriptores admodum clarus," cannot be correct. That we find a famous Roman lawyer Tertullianus, or Tertyllianus, among the writers fragments of whom are preserved in the Pandects, Neander reminds us; but (as he says) it by no means follows, even if it could be proved that the date of the said lawyer corresponded with the supposed date of our Tertullian, that they were identical. Still it is worth bearing in mind, especially as a similarity of language exists, or has been thought to exist, between the jurist and the Christian author. And the juridical language and tone of our author do seem to point to his having—though Mr. Evans regards that as doubtful—been a trained lawyer.—TR.

[1] Kaye, as above. Pref. to 2d ed. pp. xxi. xxii. incorporated in the 3d ed., which I always quote.
[2] i.e., four years *after* Kaye's *third*.   [3] See Pref. 2d ed. p. xix. n. 9.
[4] It being from that book that the quotations are taken which make up the remainder of the tract, as Semler, worthless as his theories are, has well shown.
[5] Sæculi · " or " of the world," or perhaps " of heathenism."

Marc. iii. 24; and by Jerome in his account of Papias,[1] and on Ezek. xxxvi.;[2] and by Gennadius of Marseilles.[3]

7. Six Books on Ecstasy, with a seventh in reply to Apollonius:[4] see Jerome.[5] See, too, J. A. Fabricius on the words of the unknown author whom the Jesuit Sirmond edited under the name *Prædestinatus;* who gathers thence that " Soter, pope of the City,[6] and Apollonius, bishop[7] of the Ephesians, wrote a book against the Montanists; *in reply to whom* Tertullian, a Carthaginian presbyter, wrote." J. Pamelius thinks these seven books were originally published *in Greek.*

8. A Book in reply to the Apellesites (i.e. the followers of Apelles[8]): referred to in *de Carne Christi,* c. 8.

9. A Book on the Origin[9] of the Soul, in reply to Hermogenes: referred to in *de Anima,* cc. 1, 3, 22, 24.

10. A Book on Fate: referred to by Fulgentius Planciades, p. 562, Merc.; also referred to as either written, or intended to be written, by Tertullian himself, *de Anima,* c. 20. Jerome[10] states that there was extant, or had been extant, a book on Fate under the name of Minucius Felix, written indeed by a perspicuous author, but not in the style of Minucius Felix. This, Pamelius judged, should perhaps be rather ascribed to Tertullian.

11. A Book on the Trinity. Jerome[11] says: " Novatian wrote . . . . . a large volume on the Trinity, *as if making an epitome of a work of Tertullian's, which most men not knowing regard it as Cyprian's.*" Novatian's book stood in Tertullian's name in the MSS. of J. Gangneius, who was the first to edit it; in a Malmesbury MS. which Sig. Gelenius used; and in others.

12. A Book addressed to a Philosophic Friend on the Straits of Matrimony. Both Kaye and Oehler[12] are in doubt whether Jerome's words,[13] by which some have been led to conclude that Tertullian wrote some book or books on this and kindred subjects, really imply as much, or whether they may not refer merely to those tracts and passages in his extant writings which touch upon such matters. Kaye hesitates to think that the " Book to a Philosophic Friend " is the same as the *de Exhortatione Castitatis,* because Jerome says Tertullian wrote on the subject of celibacy " *in his youth;*" but as Cave takes what Jerome elsewhere says of Tertullian's leaving the Church " *about the middle of his age* " to mean his *spiritual age,* the same sense might attach to his words here too, and thus obviate the Bishop's difficulty.

There are some other works which have been attributed to Tertullian—on Circumcision; on Animals Clean and Unclean; on the truth that God is a Judge—which Oehler likewise rejects, believing that the expressions of Jerome refer only to passages in the *Anti-Marcion* and other extant works. To Novatian Jerome does ascribe a distinct work on Circumcision,[14] and this may (comp. 11, just above) have given rise to the view that Tertullian had written one also.

There were, moreover, three treatises at least written by Tertullian *in Greek.* They are:

1. A Book on Public Shows. See *de Cor.* c. 6.
2. A Book on Baptism. See *de Bapt.* c. 15.
3. A Book on the Veiling of Virgins. See *de V.V.* c. 1.

---

[1] *Catal. Scrippt. Eccles.* c. 18.
[2] P. 952, tom. iii. Opp. ed. Bened.
[3] *De Ecclesiæ dogmatibus,* c. 55.
[4] Referred to in *Adv. Marc.* iv. 22. So Kaye thinks; but perhaps the reference is doubtful. See, however, the passage in Dr. Holmes' translation in the present series, with his note thereon. [5] *De Scriptt. Eccles.* 53, 24, 40.
[6] i.e., Rome. [7] Antistes.
[8] A Marcionite at one time: he subsequently set up a sect of his own. He is mentioned in the *adv. omn. Hær.* c. 6.
[9] Censu. [10] *Catal. Scrippt. Eccles.* c. 58.
[11] *Catal. Scrippt. Eccles.* c. 70. [12] Oehler speaks more decidedly than Kaye.
[13] *Epist. ad Eustochium de Custodia Virginitatis,* p. 37, tom. iv. Opp. ed. Bened.; *adv. Jovin.* i. p. 157, tom. iv. Opp. ed. Bened. [14] In the *Catal. Scrippt. Eccles.*

Oehler adds that J. Pamelius, in his epistle dedicatory to Philip II. of Spain, makes mention of a *Greek copy* of Tertullian in the library of that king. This report, however, since nothing has ever been seen or heard of the said copy from that time, Oehler judges to be erroneous.[1]

It remains briefly to notice the confessedly spurious works which the editions of Tertullian generally have appended to them. With these Kaye does not deal. The fragment, *adv. omnes Hæreses*, Oehler attributes to Victorinus Petavionensis, i.e., Victorinus bishop of Pettaw, on the Drave, in Austrian Styria. It was once thought he ought to be called *Pictaviensis, i.e.* of *Poictiers;* but John Launoy[2] has shown this to be an error. Victorinus is said by Jerome to have "understood Greek better than Latin; hence his works are excellent for the sense, but mean as to the style."[3] Cave believes him to have been a Greek by birth. Cassiodorus[4] states him to have been once a professor of rhetoric. Jerome's statement agrees with the style of the tract in question; and Jerome distinctly says Victorinus did write *adversus omnes Hæreses*. Allix leaves the question of its authorship quite uncertain. If Victorinus be the author, the book falls clearly within the ante-Nicene period; for Victorinus fell a martyr in the Diocletian persecution, probably about A.D. 303.

The next fragment—"Of the Execrable Gods of the Heathens"—is of quite uncertain authorship. Oehler would attribute it "to some declaimer not quite ignorant of Tertullian's writings," but certainly not to Tertullian himself.

Lastly we come to the metrical fragments. Concerning these, it is perhaps impossible to assign them to their rightful owners. Oehler has not troubled himself much about them; but he seems to regard the *Jonah* as worthy of more regard than the rest, for he seems to have intended giving more labour to its editing at some future time. Whether he has ever done so, or given us his German version of Tertullian's own works, which, "si Deus adjuverit," he distinctly promises in his preface, I do not know. Perhaps the best thing to be done under the circumstances is to give the judgment of the learned Peter Allix. It may be premised that by the celebrated George Fabricius[5]—who published his great work, *Poetarum Veterum Ecclesiasticorum Opera Christiana*, etc., in 1564—the *Five Books in Reply to Marcion*, and the *Judgment of the Lord*, are ascribed to Tertullian, the *Genesis* and *Sodom* to Cyprian. Pamelius likewise seems to have ascribed the *Five Books*, the *Jonah*, and the *Sodom*[6] to Tertullian; and according to Lardner, Bishop Bull likewise attributed the *Five Books* to him.[7] They have been generally ascribed to the Victorinus above mentioned. Tillemont, among others, thinks they may well enough be his.[8] Rigaltius is content to demonstrate that they are not Tertullian's, but leaves the real authorship without attempting to decide it. Of the others the same eminent critic says, "They seem to have been written at Carthage, at an age not far removed from Tertullian's."[9] Allix, after observing that Pamelius is inconsistent with himself in attributing the *Genesis* and *Sodom* at one time to Tertullian, at another to Cyprian, rejects both views equally, and assigns the *Genesis* with some confidence to Salvian, a presbyter of Marseilles, whose "floruit" Cave gives *cir.* 440, a contemporary of Gennadius, and a copious author. To this it is, Allix thinks, that Gennadius alludes in his *Catalogue of Illustrious Men*, c. 77.

---

[1] "Mendacem" is his word. I know not whether he intends to charge Pamelius with wilful fraud.
[2] Doctor of the Sorbonne, said by Bossuet to have proved himself "a semi-Pelagian and Jansenist!" born in 1603, in Normandy, died in 1678.
[3] Jer. *de Vir. Illust.* c. 74.
[4] B. 470, d. 560.
[5] He must not be confounded with the still more famous John Albert Fabricius of the next century, referred to in p. xv. above.
[6] Whole of these metrical fragments.
[7] Lardner, *Credibility*, vol. iii. p. 169, under "Victorinus of Pettaw," ed. Kippis, Lond. 1838.
[8] See Lardner, as above.
[9] See Migne, who prefixes this judgment of Rig. to the *de Judicio Domini*.

The *Judgment of the Lord* Allix ascribes to one Verecundus, an African bishop, whose date he finds it difficult to decide exactly. He refers to two of the name: one Bishop of Tunis, whom Victor of Tunis in his chronicle mentions as having died in exile at Chalcedon A.D. 552; the other Bishop of Noba, who visited Carthage with many others A.D. 482, at the summons of King Huneric, to answer there for their faith;—and would ascribe the poem to the former, thinking that he finds an allusion to it in the article upon that Verecundus in the *de Viris Illustribus* of Isidore of Seville. Oehler agrees with him. The *Five Books* Allix seems to hint *may* be attributed to some imitator of the Victorinus of Pettaw named above. Oehler attributes them rather to one Victorinus, or Victor, of Marseilles, a rhetorician, who died A.D. 450. He appears in G. Fabricius as Claudius Marius Victorinus, writer of a *Commentary on Genesis*, and an epistle *ad Salomonem Abbata*, both in verse, and of some considerable length.

I.

APOLOGY.

[TRANSLATED BY THE REV. S. THELWALL, LATE SCHOLAR OF CHRIST'S COLLEGE, CANTAB.]

THE APOLOGY.[1]

CHAP. I.

RULERS of the Roman Empire, if, seated for the administration of justice on your lofty tribunal, under the gaze of every eye, and occupying there all but the highest position in the state, you may not openly inquire into and sift before the world the real truth in regard to the charges made against the Christians; if in this case alone you are afraid or ashamed to exercise your authority in making public inquiry with the carefulness which becomes justice; if, finally, the extreme severities inflicted on our people in recently private judgments, stand in the way of our being permitted to defend ourselves before you, you cannot surely forbid the Truth to reach your ears by the secret pathway of a noiseless book.[2] She has no appeals to make to you in regard of her condition, for that does not excite her wonder. She knows that she is but a sojourner on the earth, and that among strangers she naturally finds foes; and more than this, that her origin, her dwelling-place, her hope, her recompense, her honours, are above. One thing, meanwhile, she anxiously desires of earthly rulers—not to be condemned unknown. What harm can it do to the laws, supreme in their domain, to give her a hearing? Nay, for that part of it, will not their absolute supremacy be more conspicuous in their condemning her, even after she has made her plea? But if, unheard, sentence is pronounced against her, besides the odium of an unjust deed, you will incur the merited suspicion of doing it with some idea that it is unjust, as not wishing to hear what you may not be able to hear and condemn.

We lay this before you as the first ground on which we urge that your hatred to the name of Christian is unjust. And the very reason which seems to excuse this injustice (I mean ignorance) at once aggravates and convicts it. For what is there more unfair than to hate a thing of which you know nothing, even though it deserve to be hated? Hatred is only merited when it is *known* to be merited. But without that knowledge, whence is its justice to be vindicated? for that is to be proved, not from the mere fact that an aversion exists, but from acquaintance with the subject. When men, then, give way to a dislike simply because they are entirely ignorant of the nature of the thing disliked, why may it not be precisely the very sort of thing they should not dislike? So we maintain that they are both ignorant while they hate us, and hate us unrighteously while they continue in ignorance, the one thing being the result of the other either way of it. The proof of their ignorance, at once condemning and excusing their injustice, is this, that those who once hated Christianity because they knew nothing about it, no sooner come to know it than they all lay down at once their enmity. From being its haters they become its disciples. By simply getting acquainted with it, they begin now to hate what they had formerly been, and to profess what they had formerly hated; and their numbers are as great as are laid to our charge. The outcry is that the State is filled with Christians—that they are in the fields, in the citadels, in the islands: they make lamentation, as for some calamity, that both sexes, every age and condition, even high rank, are passing over to the profession of the Christian faith; and yet for all, their minds are not awakened to the thought of some good they have failed to notice in it. They must not allow any truer suspicions to cross their minds; they have no

---

[1] [Great diversity exists among the critics as to the date of this Apology; see Kaye, pp. *xvi.* 48, 65. Mosheim says, A.D. 198, Kaye A.D. 204.]

[2] Elucidation II.

2

desire to make closer trial. Here alone the curiosity of human nature slumbers. They like to be ignorant, though to others the knowledge has been bliss. Anacharsis reproved the rude venturing to criticise the cultured; how much more this judging of those who know, by men who are entirely ignorant, might he have denounced! Because they already dislike, they want to know no more. Thus they prejudge that of which they are ignorant to be such, that, if they came to know it, it could no longer be the object of their aversion; since, if inquiry finds nothing worthy of dislike, it is certainly proper to cease from an unjust dislike, while if its bad character comes plainly out, instead of the detestation entertained for it being thus diminished, a stronger reason for perseverance in that detestation is obtained, even under the authority of justice itself. But, says one, a thing is not good merely because multitudes go over to it; for how many have the bent of their nature towards whatever is bad! how many go astray into ways of error! It is undoubted. Yet a thing that is thoroughly evil, not even those whom it carries away venture to defend as good. Nature throws a veil either of fear or shame over all evil. For instance, you find that criminals are eager to conceal themselves, avoid appearing in public, are in trepidation when they are caught, deny their guilt, when they are accused; even when they are put to the rack, they do not easily or always confess; when there is no doubt about their condemnation, they grieve for what they have done. In their self-communings they admit their being impelled by sinful dispositions, but they lay the blame either on fate or on the stars. They are unwilling to acknowledge that the thing is theirs, because they own that it is wicked. But what is there like this in the Christian's case? The only shame or regret he feels, is at not having been a Christian earlier. If he is pointed out, he glories in it; if he is accused, he offers no defence; interrogated, he makes voluntary confession; condemned he renders thanks. What sort of evil thing is this, which wants all the ordinary peculiarities of evil—fear, shame, subterfuge, penitence, lamenting? What! is that a crime in which the criminal rejoices? to be accused of which is his ardent wish, to be punished for which is his felicity? You cannot call it madness, you who stand convicted of knowing nothing of the matter.

CHAP. II.

If, again, it is certain that we are the most wicked of men, why do you treat us so differ-

ently from our fellows, that is, from other criminals, it being only fair that the same crime should get the same treatment? When the charges made against us are made against others, they are permitted to make use both of their own lips and of hired pleaders to show their innocence. They have full opportunity of answer and debate; in fact, it is against the law to condemn anybody undefended and unheard. Christians alone are forbidden to say anything in exculpation of themselves, in defence of the truth, to help the judge to a righteous decision; all that is cared about is having what the public hatred demands—the confession of the name, not examination of the charge: while in your ordinary judicial investigations, on a man's confession of the crime of murder, or sacrilege, or incest, or treason, to take the points of which we are accused, you are not content to proceed at once to sentence,—you do not take that step till you thoroughly examine the circumstances of the confession—what is the real character of the deed, how often, where, in what way, when he has done it, who were privy to it, and who actually took part with him in it. Nothing like this is done in our case, though the falsehoods disseminated about us ought to have the same sifting, that it might be found how many murdered children each of us had tasted; how many incests each of us had shrouded in darkness; what cooks, what dogs had been witness of our deeds. Oh, how great the glory of the ruler who should bring to light some Christian who had devoured a hundred infants! But, instead of that, we find that even inquiry in regard to our case is forbidden. For the younger Pliny, when he was ruler of a province, having condemned some Christians to death, and driven some from their stedfastness, being still annoyed by their great numbers, at last sought the advice of Trajan,[1] the reigning emperor, as to what he was to do with the rest, explaining to his master that, except an obstinate disinclination to offer sacrifices, he found in the religious services nothing but meetings at early morning for singing hymns to Christ and [2] God, and sealing home their way of life by a united pledge to be faithful to their religion, forbidding murder, adultery, dishonesty, and other crimes. Upon this Trajan wrote back that Christians were by no means to be sought after; but if they were brought before him, they should be punished.

---

[1] [For chronological dates in our author's age, see Elucidation III. Tertullian places an interval of 115 years, 6 months and 15 days between Tiberius and Antoninus Pius. See *Answer to the Jews*, cap. vii. *infra*.]
[2] Another reading is " ut Deo," *as God*.

O miserable deliverance,—under the necessities of the case, a self-contradiction! It forbids them to be sought after as innocent, and it commands them to be punished as guilty. It is at once merciful and cruel; it passes by, and it punishes. Why dost thou play a game of evasion upon thyself, O Judgment? If thou condemnest, why dost thou not also inquire. If thou does not inquire, why dost thou not also absolve? Military stations are distributed through all the provinces for tracking robbers. Against traitors and public foes every man is a soldier; search is made even for their confederates and accessories. The Christian alone must not be sought, though he may be brought and accused before the judge; as if a search had any other end than that in view! And so you condemn the man for whom nobody wished a search to be made when he is presented to you, and who even now does not deserve punishment, I suppose, because of his guilt, but because, though forbidden to be sought, he was found. And then, too, you do not in that case deal with us in the ordinary way of judicial proceedings against offenders; for, in the case of others denying, you apply the torture to make them confess—Christians alone you torture, to make them deny; whereas, if we were guilty of any crime, we should be sure to deny it, and you with your tortures would force us to confession. Nor indeed should you hold that our crimes require no such investigation merely on the ground that you are convinced by our confession of the name that the deeds were done,—*you* who are daily wont, though you know well enough what murder is, none the less to extract from the confessed murderer a full account of how the crime was perpetrated. So that with all the greater perversity you act, when, holding our crimes proved by our confession of the name of Christ, you drive us by torture to fall from our confession, that, repudiating the name, we may in like manner repudiate also the crimes with which, from that same confession, you had assumed that we were chargeable. I suppose, though you believe us to be the worst of mankind, you do not wish us to perish. For thus, no doubt, you are in the habit of bidding the murderer deny, and of ordering the man guilty of sacrilege to the rack if he persevere in his acknowledgment! Is that the way of it? But if thus you do not deal with us as criminals, you declare us thereby innocent, when as innocent you are anxious that we do not persevere in a confession which you know will bring on us a condemnation of necessity, not of justice, at your hands. "I am a Christian," the man cries out.

He tells you what he is; you wish to hear from him what he is not. Occupying your place of authority to extort the truth, you do your utmost to get lies from us. "I am," he says, "that which you ask me if I am. Why do you torture me to sin? I confess, and you put me to the rack. What would you do if I denied? Certainly you give no ready credence to others when they deny. When we deny, you believe at once. Let this perversity of yours lead you to suspect that there is some hidden power in the case under whose influence you act against the forms, against the nature of public justice, even against the very laws themselves. For, unless I am greatly mistaken, the laws enjoin offenders to be searched out, and not to be hidden away. They lay it down that persons who own a crime are to be condemned, not acquitted. The decrees of the senate, the commands of your chiefs, lay this clearly down. The power of which you are servants is a civil, not a tyrannical domination. Among tyrants, indeed, torments used to be inflicted even as punishments: with you they are mitigated to a means of questioning alone. Keep to your law in these as necessary till confession is obtained; and if the torture is anticipated by confession, there will be no occasion for it: sentence should be passed; the criminal should be given over to the penalty which is his due, not released. Accordingly, no one is eager for the acquittal of the guilty; it is not right to desire that, and so no one is ever compelled to deny. Well, you think the Christian a man of every crime, an enemy of the gods, of the emperor, of the laws, of good morals, of all nature; yet you compel him to deny, that you may acquit him, which without his denial you could not do. You play fast and loose with the laws. You wish him to deny his guilt, that you may, even against his will, bring him out blameless and free from all guilt in reference to the past! Whence is this strange perversity on your part? How is it you do not reflect that a spontaneous confession is greatly more worthy of credit than a compelled denial; or consider whether, when compelled to deny, a man's denial may not be in good faith, and whether acquitted, he may not, then and there, as soon as the trial is over, laugh at your hostility, a Christian as much as ever? Seeing, then, that in everything you deal differently with us than with other criminals, bent upon the one object of taking from us our name (indeed, it is ours no more if we do what Christians never do), it is made perfectly clear that there is no crime of any kind in the case, but merely a name which a certain system, ever working against the truth, pursues with its enmity, doing this chiefly with the object of securing that men may have no desire to know for certain what they know for certain they are entirely ignorant of. Hence, too, it is that they believe about us things of which they have no proof, and they are disinclined to have them looked into, lest the charges, they would rather take on trust, are all proved to have no foundation, that the name so hostile to that rival power—its crimes presumed, not proved —may be condemned simply on its own confession. So we are put to the torture if we confess, and we are punished if we persevere, and if we deny we are acquitted, because all the contention is about a name. Finally, why do you read out of your tablet-lists that such a man is a Christian? Why not also that he is a murderer? And if a Christian is a murderer, why not guilty, too, of incest, or any other vile thing you believe of us? In our case alone you are either ashamed or unwilling to mention the very names of our crimes. If to be called a "Christian" does not imply any crime, the name is surely very hateful, when that of itself is made a crime.

CHAP. III.

What are we to think of it, that most people so blindly knock their heads against the hatred of the Christian name; that when they bear favourable testimony to any one, they mingle with it abuse of the name he bears? "A good man," says one, "is Gaius Seius, only that he is a Christian." So another, "I am astonished that a wise man like Lucius should have suddenly become a Christian." Nobody thinks it needful to consider whether Gaius is not good and Lucius wise, on this very account that he is a Christian; or a Christian, for the reason that he is wise and good. They praise what they know, they abuse what they are ignorant of, and they inspire their knowledge with their ignorance; though in fairness you should rather judge of what is unknown from what is known, than what is known from what is unknown. Others, in the case of persons whom, before they took the name of Christian, they had known as loose, and vile, and wicked, put on them a brand from the very thing which they praise. In the blindness of their hatred, they fall foul of their own approving judgment! "What a woman she was! how wanton! how gay! What a youth he was! how profligate! how libidinous!—they have become Christians!" So the hated name is given to a reformation of character. Some even barter away their comforts for that hatred, content to bear injury, if they are kept free at home from the

object of their bitter enmity. The wife, now chaste, the husband, now no longer jealous, casts out of his house; the son, now obedient, the father, who used to be so patient, disinherits; the servant, now faithful, the master, once so mild, commands away from his presence; it is a high offence for any one to be reformed by the detested name. Goodness is of less value than hatred of Christians. Well now, if there is this dislike of the name, what blame can you attach to names? What accusation can you bring against mere designations, save that something in the word sounds either barbarous, or unlucky, or scurrilous, or unchaste? But Christian, so far as the meaning of the word is concerned, is derived from anointing. Yes, and even when it is wrongly pronounced by you "Chrestianus" (for you do not even know accurately the name you hate), it comes from sweetness and benignity. You hate, therefore, in the guiltless, even a guiltless name. But the special ground of dislike to the sect is, that it bears the name of its Founder. Is there anything new in a religious sect getting for its followers a designation from its master? Are not the philosophers called from the founders of *their* systems—Platonists, Epicureans, Pythagoreans? Are not the Stoics and Academics so called also from the places in which they assembled and stationed themselves? and are not physicians named from Erasistratus, grammarians from Aristarchus, cooks even from Apicius? And yet the bearing of the name, transmitted from the original institutor with whatever he has instituted, offends no one. No doubt, if it is proved that the sect is a bad one, and so its founder bad as well, that will prove that the name is bad and deserves our aversion, in respect of the character both of the sect and its author. Before, therefore, taking up a dislike to the name, it behoved you to consider the sect in the author, or the author in the sect. But now, without any sifting and knowledge of either, the mere name is made matter of accusation, the mere name is assailed, and a sound alone brings condemnation on a sect and its author both, while of both you are ignorant, because they have such and such a designation, not because they are convicted of anything wrong.

CHAP. IV.

And so, having made these remarks as it were by way of preface, that I might show in its true colours the injustice of the public hatred against us, I shall now take my stand on the plea of our blamelessness; and I shall not only refute the things which are objected to us, but I shall also retort them on the objectors, that in this way all may know that Christians are free from the very crimes they are so well aware prevail among themselves, that they may at the same time be put to the blush for their accusations against us,—accusations I shall not say of the worst of men against the best, but now, as they will have it, against those who are only their fellows in sin. We shall reply to the accusation of all the various crimes we are said to be guilty of in secret, such as we find them committing in the light of day, and as being guilty of which we are held to be wicked, senseless, worthy of punishment, deserving of ridicule. But since, when our truth meets you successfully at all points, the authority of the laws as a last resort is set up against it, so that it is either said that their determinations are absolutely conclusive, or the necessity of obedience is, however unwillingly, preferred to the truth, I shall first, in this matter of the laws, grapple with you as with their chosen protectors. Now first, when you sternly lay it down in your sentences, "It is not lawful for you to exist," and with unhesitating rigour you enjoin this to be carried out, you exhibit the violence and unjust domination of mere tyranny, if you deny the thing to be lawful, simply on the ground that you wish it to be unlawful, not because it ought to be. But if you would have it unlawful because it *ought* not to be lawful, without doubt that should have no permission of law which does harm; and on this ground, in fact, it is already determined that whatever is beneficial is legitimate. Well, if I have found what your law prohibits to be good, as one who has arrived at such a previous opinion, has it not lost its power to debar me from it, though that very thing, if it were evil, it would justly forbid to me? If your law has gone wrong, it is of human origin, I think; it has not fallen from heaven. Is it wonderful that man should err in making a law, or come to his senses in rejecting it? Did not the Lacedæmonians amend the laws of Lycurgus himself, thereby inflicting such pain on their author that he shut himself up, and doomed himself to death by starvation? Are you not yourselves every day, in your efforts to illumine the darkness of antiquity, cutting and hewing with the new axes of imperial rescripts and edicts, that whole ancient and rugged forest of your laws? Has not Severus, that most resolute of rulers, but yesterday repealed the ridiculous Papian laws[1] which compelled

people to have children before the Julian laws allow matrimony to be contracted, and that though they have the authority of age upon their side? There were laws, too, in old times, that parties against whom a decision had been given might be cut in pieces by their creditors; however, by common consent that cruelty was afterwards erased from the statutes, and the capital penalty turned into a brand of shame. By adopting the plan of confiscating a debtor's goods, it was sought rather to pour the blood in blushes over his face than to pour it out. How many laws lie hidden out of sight which still require to be reformed! For it is neither the number of their years nor the dignity of their maker that commends them, but simply that they are just; and therefore, when their injustice is recognized, they are deservedly condemned, even though they condemn. Why speak we of them as unjust? nay, if they punish mere names, we may well call them irrational. But if they punish acts, why in our case do they punish acts solely on the ground of a name, while in others they must have them proved not from the name, but from the wrong done? I am a practiser of incest (so they say); why do they not inquire into it? I am an infant-killer; why do they not apply the torture to get from me the truth? I am guilty of crimes against the gods, against the Cæsars; why am I, who am able to clear myself, not allowed to be heard on my own behalf? No law forbids the sifting of the crimes which it prohibits, for a judge never inflicts a righteous vengeance if he is not well assured that a crime has been committed; nor does a citizen render a true subjection to the law, if he does not know the nature of the thing on which the punishment is inflicted. It is not enough that a law is just, nor that the judge should be convinced of its justice; those from whom obedience is expected should have that conviction too. Nay, a law lies under strong suspicions which does not care to have itself tried and approved: it is a positively wicked law, if, unproved, it tyrannizes over men.

CHAP. V.

To say a word about the origin of laws of the kind to which we now refer, there was an old decree that no god should be consecrated by the emperor till first approved by the senate. Marcus Æmilius had experience of this in reference to his god Alburnus. And this, too, makes for our case, that among you divinity is allotted at the judgment of human beings. Unless gods give satisfaction to men, there will be no deification for them: the god will have to propitiate the man. Ti-

---

[1] [A reference in which Kaye sees no reason to doubt that the Apology was written during the reign under the emperor. See Kaye's *Tertullian*, p. 49.]

berius[1] accordingly, in whose days the Christian name made its entry into the world, having himself received intelligence from Palestine of events which had clearly shown the truth of Christ's divinity, brought the matter before the senate, with his own decision in favour of Christ. The senate, because it had not given the approval itself, rejected his proposal. Cæsar held to his opinion, threatening wrath against all accusers of the Christians. Consult your histories; you will there find that Nero was the first who assailed with the imperial sword the Christian sect, making progress then especially at Rome. But we glory in having our condemnation hallowed by the hostility of such a wretch. For any one who knows him, can understand that not except as being of singular excellence did anything bring on it Nero's condemnation. Domitian, too, a man of Nero's type in cruelty, tried his hand at persecution; but as he had something of the human in him, he soon put an end to what he had begun, even restoring again those whom he had banished. Such as these have always been our persecutors,—men unjust, impious, base, of whom even you yourselves have no good to say, the sufferers under whose sentences you have been wont to restore. But among so many princes from that time to the present day, with anything of divine and human wisdom in them, point out a single persecutor of the Christian name. So far from that, we, on the contrary, bring before you one who was their protector, as you will see by examining the letters of Marcus Aurelius, that most grave of emperors, in which he bears his testimony that that Germanic drought was removed by the rains obtained through the prayers of the Christians who chanced to be fighting under him. And as he did not by public law remove from Christians their legal disabilities, yet in another way he put them openly aside, even adding a sentence of condemnation, and that of greater severity, against their accusers. What sort of laws are these which the impious alone execute against us—and the unjust, the vile, the bloody, the senseless, the insane?—which Trajan to some extent made naught by forbidding Christians to be sought after; which neither a Hadrian, though fond of searching into all things strange and new, nor a Vespasian, though the subjugator of the Jews, nor a Pius, nor a Verus, ever enforced? It should surely be judged more natural for bad men to be eradicated by good princes as being their natural enemies, than by those of a spirit kindred with their own.

CHAP. VI.

I would now have these most religious protectors and vindicators of the laws and institutions of their fathers, tell me, in regard to their own fidelity and the honour, and submission they themselves show to ancestral institutions, if they have departed from nothing —if they have in nothing gone out of the old paths—if they have not put aside whatsoever is most useful and necessary as rules of a virtuous life. What has become of the laws repressing expensive and ostentatious ways of living? which forbade more than a hundred *asses* to be expended on a supper, and more than one fowl to be set on the table at a time, and that not a fatted one; which expelled a patrician from the senate on the serious ground, as it was counted, of aspiring to be too great, because he had acquired ten pounds of silver; which put down the theatres as quickly as they arose to debauch the manners of the people; which did not permit the insignia of official dignities or of noble birth to be rashly or with impunity usurped? For I see the Centenarian suppers must now bear the name, not from the hundred asses, but from the hundred sestertia[1] expended on them; and that mines of silver are made into dishes (it were little if this applied only to senators, and not to freedmen or even mere whip-spoilers[2]). I see, too, that neither is a single theatre enough, nor are theatres unsheltered: no doubt it was that immodest pleasure might not be torpid in the wintertime, the Lacedæmonians invented their woollen cloaks for the plays. I see now no difference between the dress of matrons and prostitutes. In regard to women, indeed, those laws of your fathers, which used to be such an encouragement to modesty and sobriety, have also fallen into desuetude, when a woman had yet known no gold upon her save on the finger, which, with the bridal ring, her husband had sacredly pledged to himself; when the abstinence of women from wine was carried so far, that a matron, for opening the compartments of a wine cellar, was starved to death by her friends,—while in the times of Romulus, for merely tasting wine, Mecenius killed his wife, and suffered nothing for the deed. With reference to this also, it was the custom of women to kiss their relatives, that they might be detected by their breath. Where is that happiness of married life, ever so desirable, which distinguished our earlier manners, and as the result of which for about 600 years there was not among us a single

---

[1] As = 2⅛ farthings. Sestertium = £7, 16s. 3d.
[2] Slaves still bearing the marks of the scourge.

divorce? Now, women have every member of the body heavy laden with gold; wine-bibbing is so common among them, that the kiss is never offered with their will; and as for divorce, they long for it as though it were the natural consequence of marriage. The laws, too, your fathers in their wisdom had enacted concerning the very gods themselves, you their most loyal children have rescinded. The consuls, by the authority of the senate, banished Father Bacchus and his mysteries not merely from the city, but from the whole of Italy. The consuls Piso and Gabinius, no Christians surely, forbade Serapis, and Isis, and Arpocrates, with their dogheaded friend,[1] admission into the Capitol—in the act casting them out from the assembly of the gods—overthrow their altars, and expelled them from the country, being anxious to prevent the vices of their base and lascivious religion from spreading. These, you have restored, and conferred highest honours on them. What has come to your religion—of the veneration due by you to your ancestors? In your dress, in your food, in your style of life, in your opinions, and last of all in your very speech, you have renounced your progenitors. You are always praising antiquity, and yet every day you have novelties in your way of living. From your having failed to maintain what you should, you make it clear, that, while you abandon the good ways of your fathers, you retain and guard the things you ought not. Yet the very tradition of your fathers, which you still seem so faithfully to defend, and in which you find your principal matter of accusation against the Christians—I mean zeal in the worship of the gods, the point in which antiquity has mainly erred—although you have rebuilt the altars of Serapis, now a Roman deity, and to Bacchus, now become a god of Italy, you offer up your orgies,—I shall in its proper place show that you despise, neglect, and overthrow, casting entirely aside the authority of the men of old. I go on meantime to reply to that infamous charge of secret crimes, clearing my way to things of open day.

CHAP. VII.

Monsters of wickedness, we are accused of observing a holy rite in which we kill a little child and then eat it; in which, after the feast, we practise incest, the dogs—our pimps, forsooth, overturning the lights and getting us the shamelessness of darkness for our impious lusts. This is what is constantly laid to our charge, and yet you take no pains to elicit the truth of what we have been so long accused. Either bring, then, the matter to the light of day if you believe it, or give it no credit as having never inquired into it. On the ground of your double dealing, we are entitled to lay it down to you that there is no reality in the thing which you dare not expiscate. You impose on the executioner, in the case of Christians, a duty the very opposite of expiscation: he is not to make them confess what they do, but to make them deny what they are. We date the origin of our religion, as we have mentioned before, from the reign of Tiberius. Truth and the hatred of truth come into our world together. As soon as truth appears, it is regarded as an enemy. It has as many foes as there are strangers to it: the Jews, as was to be looked for, from a spirit of rivalry; the soldiers, out of a desire to extort money; our very domestics, by their nature. We are daily beset by foes, we are daily betrayed; we are oftentimes surprised in our meetings and congregations. Whoever happened withal upon an infant wailing, according to the common story? Whoever kept for the judge, just as he had found them, the gory mouths of Cyclops and Sirens? Whoever found any traces of uncleanness in their wives? Where is the man who, when he had discovered such atrocities, concealed them; or, in the act of dragging the culprits before the judge, was bribed into silence? If we always keep our secrets, when were our proceedings made known to the world? Nay, by whom could they be made known? Not, surely, by the guilty parties themselves; even from the very idea of the thing, the fealty of silence being ever due to mysteries. The Samothracian and Eleusinian make no disclosures—how much more will silence be kept in regard to such as are sure, in their unveiling, to call forth punishment from man at once, while wrath divine is kept in store for the future? If, then, Christians are not themselves the publishers of their crime, it follows of course it must be strangers. And whence have they their knowledge, when it is also a universal custom in religious initiations to keep the profane aloof, and to beware of witnesses, unless it be that those who are so wicked have less fear than their neighbors? Every one knows what sort of thing rumour is. It is one of your own sayings, that " among all evils, none flies so fast as rumour." Why is rumour such an evil thing? Is it because it is fleet? Is it because it carries information? Or is it because it is in the highest degree mendacious?—a thing, not even when it brings some truth to us, without a taint of falsehood, either detracting, or adding, or changing from the simple fact? Nay

---

[1] Anubis.

more, it is the very law of its being to continue only while it lies, and to live but so long as there is no proof; for when the proof is given, it ceases to exist; and, as having done its work of merely spreading a report, it delivers up a fact, and is henceforth held to be a fact, and called a fact. And then no one says, for instance, "They say that it took place at Rome," or, "There is a rumour that he has obtained a province," but, "He has got a province," and, "It took place at Rome." Rumour, the very designation of uncertainty, has no place when a thing is certain. Does any but a fool put his trust in it? For a wise man never believes the dubious. Everybody knows, however zealously it is spread abroad, on whatever strength of asseveration it rests, that some time or other from some one fountain it has its origin. Thence it must creep into propagating tongues and ears; and a small seminal blemish so darkens all the rest of the story, that no one can determine whether the lips, from which it first came forth, planted the seed of falsehood, as often happens, from a spirit of opposition, or from a suspicious judgment, or from a confirmed, nay, in the case of some, an inborn, delight in lying. It is well that time brings all to light, as your proverbs and sayings testify, by a provision of Nature, which has so appointed things that nothing long is hidden, even though rumour has not disseminated it. It is just then as it should be, that fame for so long a period has been alone aware of the crimes of Christians. This is the witness you bring against us—one that has never been able to prove the accusation it some time or other sent abroad, and at last by mere continuance made into a settled opinion in the world; so that I confidently appeal to Nature herself, ever true, against those who groundlessly hold that such things are to be credited.

CHAP. VIII.

See now, we set before you the reward of these enormities. They give promise of eternal life. Hold it meanwhile as your own belief. I ask you, then, whether, so believing, you think it worth attaining with a conscience such as you will have. Come, plunge your knife into the babe, enemy of none, accused of none, child of all; or if that is another's work, simply take your place beside a human being dying before he has really lived; await the departure of the lately given soul, receive the fresh young blood, saturate your bread with it, freely partake. The while as you recline at table, take note of the places which your mother and your sister occupy; mark them well, so that when the dog-made

darkness has fallen on you, you may make no mistake, for you will be guilty of a crime—unless you perpetrate a deed of incest. Initiated and sealed into things like these, you have life everlasting. Tell me, I pray you, is eternity worth it? If it is not, then these things are not to be credited. Even although you had the belief, I deny the will; and even if you had the will, I deny the possibility. Why then can others do it, if you cannot? why cannot you, if others can? I suppose we are of a different nature—are we Cynopæ or Sciapodes?[1] You are a man yourself as well as the Christian: if you cannot do it, you ought not to believe it of others, for a Christian is a man as well as you. But the ignorant, forsooth, are deceived and imposed on. They were quite unaware of anything of the kind being imputed to Christians, or they would certainly have looked into it for themselves, and searched the matter out. Instead of that, it is the custom for persons wishing initiation into sacred rites, I think, to go first of all to the master of them, that he may explain what preparations are to be made. Then, in this case, no doubt he would say, "You must have a child still of tender age, that knows not what it is to die, and can smile under thy knife; bread, too, to collect the gushing blood; in addition to these, candlesticks, and lamps, and dogs—with tid-bits to draw them on to the extinguishing of the lights: above all things, you will require to bring your mother and your sister with you." But what if mother and sister are unwilling? or if there be neither the one nor the other? What if there are Christians with no Christian relatives? He will not be counted, I suppose, a true follower of Christ, who has not a brother or a son. And what now, if these things are all in store for them without their knowledge? At least afterwards they come to know them; and they bear with them, and pardon them. They fear, it may be said, lest they have to pay for it if they let the secret out: nay, but they will rather in that case have every claim to protection; they will even prefer, one might think, dying by their own hand, to living under the burden of such a dreadful knowledge. Admit that they have this fear; yet why do they still persevere? For it is plain enough that you will have no desire to continue what you would never have been, if you had had previous knowledge of it.

CHAP. IX.

That I may refute more thoroughly these charges, I will show that in part openly, in

---

[1] Fabulous monsters.

part secretly, practices prevail among you which have led you perhaps to credit similar things about us. Children were openly sacrificed in Africa to Saturn as lately as the proconsulship of Tiberius, who exposed to public gaze the priests suspended on the sacred trees overshadowing their temple—so many crosses on which the punishment which justice craved overtook their crimes, as the soldiers of our country still can testify who did that very work for that proconsul. And even now that sacred crime still continues to be done in secret. It is not only Christians, you see, who despise you; for all that you do there is neither any crime thoroughly and abidingly eradicated, nor does any of your gods reform his ways. When Saturn did not spare his own children, he was not likely to spare the children of others; whom indeed the very parents themselves were in the habit of offering, gladly responding to the call which was made on them, and keeping the little ones pleased on the occasion, that they might not die in tears. At the same time, there is a vast difference between homicide and parricide. A more advanced age was sacrificed to Mercury in Gaul. I hand over the Tauric fables to their own theatres. Why, even in that most religious city of the pious descendants of Æneas, there is a certain Jupiter whom in their games they lave with human blood. It is the blood of a beast-fighter, you say. Is it less, because of that, the blood of a man?[1] Or is it viler blood because it is from the veins of a wicked man? At any rate it is shed in murder. O Jove, thyself a Christian, and in truth only son of thy father in his cruelty! But in regard to child murder, as it does not matter whether it is committed for a sacred object, or merely at one's own self-impulse—although there is a great difference, as we have said, between parricide and homicide—I shall turn to the people generally. How many, think you, of those crowding around and gaping for Christian blood,—how many even of your rulers, notable for their justice to you and for their severe measures against us, may I charge in their own consciences with the sin of putting their offspring to death? As to any difference in the kind of murder, it is certainly the more cruel way to kill by drowning, or by exposure to cold and hunger and dogs. A maturer age has always preferred death by the sword. In our case, murder being once for all forbidden, we may not destroy even the fœtus in the womb, while as yet the human being derives blood from other parts of the body for

its sustenance. To hinder a birth is merely a speedier man-killing; nor does it matter whether you take away a life that is born, or destroy one that is coming to the birth. That is a man which is going to be one; you have the fruit already in its seed. As to meals of blood and such tragic dishes, read—I am not sure where it is told (it is in Herodotus, I think)—how blood taken from the arms, and tasted by both parties, has been the treaty bond among some nations. I am not sure what it was that was tasted in the time of Catiline. They say, too, that among some Scythian tribes the dead are eaten by their friends. But I am going far from home. At this day, among ourselves, blood consecrated to Bellona, blood drawn from a punctured thigh and then partaken of, seals initiation into the rites of that goddess. Those, too, who at the gladiator shows, for the cure of epilepsy, quaff with greedy thirst the blood of criminals slain in the arena, as it flows fresh from the wound, and then rush off—to whom do they belong? those, also, who make meals on the flesh of wild beasts at the place of combat—who have keen appetites for bear and stag? That bear in the struggle was bedewed with the blood of the man whom it lacerated: that stag rolled itself in the gladiator's gore. The entrails of the very bears, loaded with as yet undigested human viscera, are in great request. And you have men rifting up man-fed flesh? If you partake of food like this, how do your repasts differ from those you accuse us Christians of? And do those, who, with savage lust, seize on human bodies, do less because they devour the living? Have they less the pollution of human blood on them because they only lick up what is to turn into blood? They make meals, it is plain, not so much of infants, as of grown-up men. Blush for your vile ways before the Christians, who have not even the blood of animals at their meals of simple and natural food; who abstain from things strangled and that die a natural death, for no other reason than that they may not contract pollution, so much as from blood secreted in the viscera. To clench the matter with a single example, you tempt Christians with sausages of blood, just because you are perfectly aware that the thing by which you thus try to get them to transgress they hold unlawful.[2] And how unreasonable it is to believe that those, of whom you are convinced that they regard with horror the idea of tasting the blood of oxen, are eager after blood of men; unless, mayhap, you have

---

[1] [Another example of what Christianity was doing for *man* as man.]

[2] [See Elucidation VII., p. 58, *infra* in connection with usages in cap. xxxix.]

tried it, and found it sweeter to the taste! Nay, in fact, there is here a test you should apply to discover Christians, as well as the fire-pan and the censer. They should be proved by their appetite for human blood, as well as by their refusal to offer sacrifice; just as otherwise they should be affirmed to be free of Christianity by their refusal to taste of blood, as by their sacrificing; and there would be no want of blood of men, amply supplied as that would be in the trial and condemnation of prisoners. Then who are more given to the crime of incest than those who have enjoyed the instruction of Jupiter himself? Ctesias tells us that the Persians have illicit intercourse with their mothers. The Macedonians, too, are suspected on this point; for on first hearing the tragedy of Œdipus they made mirth of the incest-doer's grief, exclaiming, ἤλαυνε εἰς τὴν μητέρα. Even now reflect what opportunity there is for mistakes leading to incestuous comminglings—your promiscuous looseness supplying the materials. You first of all expose your children, that they may be taken up by any compassionate passer-by, to whom they are quite unknown; or you give them away, to be adopted by those who will do better to them the part of parents. Well, some time or other, all memory of the alienated progeny must be lost; and when once a mistake has been made, the transmission of incest thence will still go on—the race and the crime creeping on together. Then, further, wherever you are—at home, abroad, over the seas—your lust is an attendant, whose general indulgence, or even its indulgence in the most limited scale, may easily and unwittingly anywhere beget children, so that in this way a progeny scattered about in the commerce of life may have intercourse with those who are their own kin, and have no notion that there is any incest in the case. A persevering and stedfast chastity has protected us from anything like this: keeping as we do from adulteries and all post-matrimonial unfaithfulness, we are not exposed to incestuous mishaps. Some of us, making matters still more secure, beat away from them entirely the power of sensual sin, by a virgin continence, still boys in this respect when they are old. If you would but take notice that such sins as I have mentioned prevail among you, that would lead you to see that they have no existence among Christians. The same eyes would tell you of both facts. But the two blindnesses are apt to go together ; so that those who do not see what is, think they see what is not. I shall show it to be so in everything. But now let me speak of matters which are more clear.

CHAP. X.

"You do not worship the gods," you say; "and you do not offer sacrifices for the emperors." Well, we do not offer sacrifice for others, for the same reason that we do not for ourselves,—namely, that your gods are not at all the objects of our worship. So we are accused of sacrilege and treason. This is the chief ground of charge against us—nay, it is the sum-total of our offending; and it is worthy then of being inquired into, if neither prejudice nor injustice be the judge, the one of which has no idea of discovering the truth, and the other simply and at once rejects it. We do not worship your gods, because we know that there are no such beings. This, therefore, is what you should do: you should call on us to demonstrate their non-existence, and thereby prove that they have no claim to adoration; for only if your gods were truly so, would there be any obligation to render divine homage to them. And punishment even were due to Christians, if it were made plain that those to whom they refused all worship were indeed divine. But you say, They are gods. We protest and appeal from yourselves to your knowledge; let that judge us; let that condemn us, if it can deny that all these gods of yours were but men. If even it venture to deny that, it will be confuted by its own books of antiquities, from which it has got its information about them, bearing witness to this day, as they plainly do, both of the cities in which they were born, and the countries in which they have left traces of their exploits, as well as where also they are proved to have been buried. Shall I now, therefore, go over them one by one, so numerous and so various, new and old, barbarian, Grecian, Roman, foreign, captive and adopted, private and common, male and female, rural and urban, naval and military? It were useless even to hunt out all their names: so I may content myself with a compend; and this not for your information, but that you may have what you know brought to your recollection, for undoubtedly you act as if you had forgotten all about them. No one of your gods is earlier than Saturn: from him you trace all your deities, even those of higher rank and better known. What, then, can be proved of the first, will apply to those that follow. So far, then, as books give us information, neither the Greek Diodorus or Thallus, neither Cassius Severus or Cornelius Nepos, nor any writer upon sacred antiquities, have ventured to say that Saturn was any but a man: so far as the question depends on facts, I find none more trustworthy than those

—that in Italy itself we have the country in which, after many expeditions, and after having partaken of Attic hospitalities, Saturn settled, obtaining cordial welcome from Janus, or, as the Salii will have it, Janis. The mountain on which he dwelt was called Saturnius; the city he founded is called Saturnia to this day; last of all, the whole of Italy, after having borne the name of Oenotria, was called Saturnia from him. He first gave you the art of writing, and a stamped coinage, and thence it is he presides over the public treasury. But if Saturn were a man, he had undoubtedly a human origin; and having a human origin, he was not the offspring of heaven and earth. As his parents were unknown, it was not unnatural that he should be spoken of as the son of those elements from which we might all seem to spring. For who does not speak of heaven and earth as father and mother, in a sort of way of veneration and honour? or from the custom which prevails among us of saying that persons of whom we have no knowledge, or who make a sudden appearance, have fallen from the skies? In this way it came about that Saturn, everywhere a sudden and unlooked-for guest, got everywhere the name of the Heaven-born. For even the common folk call persons whose stock is unknown, sons of earth. I say nothing of how men in these rude times were wont to act, when they were impressed by the look of any stranger happening to appear among them, as though it were divine, since even at this day men of culture make gods of those whom, a day or two before, they acknowledged to be dead men by their public mourning for them. Let these notices of Saturn, brief as they are, suffice. It will thus also be proved that Jupiter is as certainly a man, as from a man he sprung; and that one after another the whole swarm is mortal like the primal stock.

CHAP. XI.

And since, as you dare not deny that these deities of yours once were men, you have taken it on you to assert that they were made gods after their decease, let us consider what necessity there was for this. In the first place, you must concede the existence of one higher God—a certain wholesale dealer in divinity, who has made gods of men. For they could neither have assumed a divinity which was not theirs, nor could any but one himself possessing it have conferred it on them. If there was no one to make gods, it is vain to dream of gods being made when thus you have no god-maker. Most certainly, if they could have deified themselves, with a higher state at their command, they never would have been men. If, then, there be one who is able to make gods, I turn back to an examination of any reason there may be for making gods at all; and I find no other reason than this, that the great God has need of their ministrations and aids in performing the offices of Deity. But first it is an unworthy idea that He should need the help of a man, and in fact a dead man, when, if He was to be in want of this assistance from the dead, He might more fittingly have created some one a god at the beginning. Nor do I see any place for his action. For this entire world-mass—whether self-existent and uncreated, as Pythagoras maintains, or brought into being by a creator's hands, as Plato holds—was manifestly, once for all in its original construction, disposed, and furnished, and ordered, and supplied with a government of perfect wisdom. That cannot be imperfect which has made all perfect. There was nothing waiting on for Saturn and his race to do. Men will make fools of themselves if they refuse to believe that from the very first rain poured down from the sky, and stars gleamed, and light shone, and thunders roared, and Jove himself dreaded the lightnings you put in his hands; that in like manner before Bacchus, and Ceres, and Minerva, nay before the first man, whoever that was, every kind of fruit burst forth plentifully from the bosom of the earth, for nothing provided for the support and sustenance of man could be introduced after his entrance on the stage of being. Accordingly, these necessaries of life are said to have been discovered, not created. But the thing you discover existed before; and that which had a pre-existence must be regarded as belonging not to him who discovered it, but to him who made it, for of course it had a being before it could be found. But if, on account of his being the discoverer of the vine, Bacchus is raised to godship, Lucullus, who first introduced the cherry from Pontus into Italy, has not been fairly dealt with; for as the discoverer of a new fruit, he has not, as though he were its creator, been awarded divine honours. Wherefore, if the universe existed from the beginning, thoroughly furnished, with its system working under certain laws for the performance of its functions, there is, in this respect, an entire absence of all reason for electing humanity to divinity; for the positions and powers which you have assigned to your deities have been from the beginning precisely what they would have been, although you had never deified them. But you turn to another reason, telling us that the conferring of deity was a way of rewarding worth. And hence you grant, I conclude, that the god-making God is of transcendent righteousness,—one who will neither rashly, improperly, nor needlessly bestow a reward so great. I would have you then consider whether the merits of your deities are of a kind to have raised them to the heavens, and not rather to have sunk them down into lowest depths of Tartarus,—the place which you regard, with many, as the prison-house of infernal punishments. For into this dread place are wont to be cast all who offend against filial piety, and such as are guilty of incest with sisters, and seducers of wives, and ravishers of virgins, and boy-polluters, and men of furious tempers, and murderers, and thieves, and deceivers; all, in short, who tread in the footsteps of your gods, not one of whom you can prove free from crime or vice, save by denying that they had ever a human existence. But as you cannot deny that, you have those foul blots also as an added reason for not believing that they were made gods afterwards. For if you rule for the very purpose of punishing such deeds; if every virtuous man among you rejects all correspondence, converse, and intimacy with the wicked and base, while, on the other hand, the high God has taken up their mates to a share of His majesty, on what ground is it that you thus condemn those whose fellow-actors you adore? Your goodness is an affront in the heavens. Deify your vilest criminals, if you would please your gods. You honour them by giving divine honours to their fellows. But to say no more about a way of acting so unworthy, there have been men virtuous, and pure, and good. Yet how many of these nobler men you have left in the regions of doom! as Socrates, so renowned for his wisdom, Aristides for his justice, Themistocles for his warlike genius, Alexander for his sublimity of soul, Polycrates for his good fortune, Crœsus for his wealth, Demosthenes for his eloquence. Which of these gods of yours is more remarkable for gravity and wisdom than Cato, more just and warlike than Scipio? which of them more magnanimous than Pompey, more prosperous than Sylla, of greater wealth than Crassus, more eloquent than Tullius? How much better it would have been for the God Supreme to have waited that He might have taken such men as these to be His heavenly associates, prescient as He must have surely been of their worthier character! He was in a hurry, I suppose, and straightway shut heaven's gates; and now He must surely feel ashamed at these worthies murmuring over their lot in the regions below.

CHAP. XII.

But I pass from these remarks, for I know and I am going to show what your gods are not, by showing what they are. In reference, then, to these, I see only names of dead men of ancient times; I hear fabulous stories; I recognize sacred rites founded on mere myths. As to the actual images, I regard them as simply pieces of matter akin to the vessels and utensils in common use among us, or even undergoing in their consecration a hapless change from these useful articles at the hands of reckless art, which in the transforming process treats them with utter contempt, nay, in the very act commits sacrilege; so that it might be no slight solace to us in all our punishments, suffering as we do because of these same gods, that in their making they suffer as we do themselves. You put Christians on crosses and stakes: [1] what image is not formed from the clay in the first instance, set on cross and stake? The body of your god is first consecrated on the gibbet. You tear the sides of Christians with your claws; but in the case of your own gods, axes, and planes, and rasps are put to work more vigorously on every member of the body. We lay our heads upon the block; before the lead, and the glue, and the nails are put in requisition, your deities are headless. We are cast to the wild beasts, while you attach them to Bacchus, and Cybele, and Cælestis. We are burned in the flames; so, too, are they in their original lump. We are condemned to the mines; from these your gods originate. We are banished to islands; in islands it is a common thing for your gods to have their birth or die. If it is in this way a deity is made, it will follow that as many as are punished are deified, and tortures will have to be declared divinities. But plain it is these objects of your worship have no sense of the injuries and disgraces of their consecrating, as they are equally unconscious of the honours paid to them. O impious words! O blasphemous reproaches! Gnash your teeth upon us—foam with maddened rage against us—ye are the persons, no doubt, who censured a certain Seneca speaking of your superstition at much greater length, and far more sharply! In a word, if we refuse our homage to statues and frigid images, the very counterpart of their dead originals, with which hawks, and mice, and spiders are so well acquainted, does it not merit praise instead of penalty, that we have rejected what we have come to see is error? We cannot surely be made out

---

[1] [Inconsistent this with Gibbon's *minimizing* theory of the number of the Christian martyrs.] Elucidation VIII.

to injure those who we are certain are nonentities. What does not exist, is in its nonexistence secure from suffering.

CHAP. XIII.

"But they are gods to us," you say. And how is it, then, that in utter inconsistency with this, you are convicted of impious, sacrilegious, and irreligious conduct to them, neglecting those you imagine to exist, destroying those who are the objects of your fear, making mock of those whose honour you avenge? See now if I go beyond the truth. First, indeed, seeing you worship, some one god, and some another, of course you give offence to those you do not worship. You cannot continue to give preference to one without slighting another, for selection implies rejection. You despise, therefore, those whom you thus reject; for in your rejection of them, it is plain you have no dread of giving them offence. For, as we have already shown, every god depended on the decision of the senate for his godhead. No god was he whom man in his own counsels did not wish to be so, and thereby condemned. The family deities you call Lares, you exercise a domestic authority over, pledging them, selling them, changing them—making sometimes a cooking-pot of a Saturn, a firepan of a Minerva, as one or other happens to be worn done, or broken in its long sacred use, or as the family head feels the pressure of some more sacred home necessity. In like manner, by public law you disgrace your state gods, putting them in the auction-catalogue, and making them a source of revenue. Men seek to get the Capitol, as they seek to get the herb market, under the voice of the crier, under the auction spear, under the registration of the quæstor. Deity is struck off and farmed out to the highest bidder. But indeed lands burdened with tribute are of less value; men under the assessment of a polltax are less noble; for these things are the marks of servitude. In the case of the gods, on the other hand, the sacredness is great in proportion to the tribute which they yield; nay, the more sacred is a god, the larger is the tax he pays. Majesty is made a source of gain. Religion goes about the taverns begging. You demand a price for the privilege of standing on temple ground, for access to the sacred services; there is no gratuitous knowledge of your divinities permitted—you must buy their favours with a price. What honours in any way do you render to them that you do not render to the dead? You have temples in the one case just as in the other; you have altars in the one case as in

the other. Their statues have the same dress, the same insignia. As the dead man had his age, his art, his occupation, so it is with the deity. In what respect does the funeral feast differ from the feast of Jupiter? or the bowl of the gods from the ladle of the manes? or the undertaker from the soothsayer, as in fact this latter personage also attends upon the dead? With perfect propriety you give divine honours to your departed emperors, as you worship them in life. The gods will count themselves indebted to you; nay, it will be matter of high rejoicing among them that their masters are made their equals. But when you adore Larentina, a public prostitute —I could have wished that it might at least have been Lais or Phryne—among your Junos, and Cereses, and Dianas; when you instal in your Pantheon Simon Magus,[1] giving him a statue and the title of Holy God; when you make an infamous court page a god of the sacred synod, although your ancient deities are in reality no better, they will still think themselves affronted by you, that the privilege antiquity conferred on them alone, has been allowed to others.

CHAP. XIV.

I wish now to review your sacred rites; and I pass no censure on your sacrificing, when you offer the worn-out, the scabbed, the corrupting; when you cut off from the fat and the sound the useless parts, such as the head and the hoofs, which in your house you would have assigned to the slaves or the dogs; when, of the tithe of Hercules you do not lay a third upon his altar (I am disposed rather to praise your wisdom in rescuing something from being lost); but turning to your books, from which you get your training in wisdom and the nobler duties of life, what utterly ridiculous things I find!—that for Trojans and Greeks the gods fought among themselves like pairs of gladiators; that Venus was wounded by a man, because she would rescue her son Æneas when he was in peril of his life from the same Diomede; that Mars was almost wasted away by a thirteen months' imprisonment; that Jupiter was saved by a monster's aid from suffering the same violence at the hands of the other gods; that he now laments the fate of Sarpedon, now foully makes love to his own sister, recounting (to her) former mistresses, now for a long time past not so dear as she. After this, what poet is not found copying the example of his chief, to be a disgracer of the gods? One gives

---

[1] [Confirming the statement of Justin Martyr. See Vol. I., p. 187, note 1, and p. 193, this Series.]

Apollo to king Admetus to tend his sheep; another hires out the building labours of Neptune to Laomedon. A well-known lyric poet, too—Pindar, I mean—sings of Æsculapius deservedly stricken with lightning for his greed in practising wrongfully his art. A wicked deed it was of Jupiter—if he hurled the bolt—unnatural to his grandson, and exhibiting envious feeling to the Physician. Things like these should not be made public if they are true; and if false, they should not be fabricated among people professing a great respect for religion. Nor indeed do either tragic or comic writers shrink from setting forth the gods as the origin of all family calamities and sins. I do not dwell on the philosophers, contenting myself with a reference to Socrates, who, in contempt of the gods, was in the habit of swearing by an oak, and a goat, and a dog. In fact, for this very thing Socrates was condemned to death, that he overthrew the worship of the gods. Plainly, at one time as well as another, that is, always truth is disliked. However, when rueing their judgment, the Athenians inflicted punishment on his accusers, and set up a golden image of him in a temple, the condemnation was in the very act rescinded, and his witness was restored to its former value. Diogenes, too, makes utter mock of Hercules; and the Roman cynic Varro brings forward three hundred Joves, or Jupiters they should be called, all headless.

CHAP. XV.

Others of your writers, in their wantonness, even minister to your pleasures by vilifying the gods. Examine those charming farces of your Lentuli and Hostilii, whether in the jokes and tricks it is the buffoons or the deities which afford you merriment; such farces I mean as Anubis the Adulterer, and Luna of the masculine gender, and Diana under the lash, and the reading the will of Jupiter deceased, and the three famishing Herculeses held up to ridicule. Your dramatic literature, too, depicts all the vileness of your gods. The Sun mourns his offspring [1] cast down from heaven, and you are full of glee; Cybele sighs after the scornful swain,[2] and you do not blush; you brook the stage recital of Jupiter's misdeeds, and the shepherd [3] judging Juno, Venus, and Minerva. Then, again, when the likeness of a god is put on the head of an ignominious and infamous wretch, when one impure and trained up for the art in all effeminacy, represents a Minerva or a Hercules, is

not the majesty of your gods insulted, and their deity dishonored? Yet you not merely look on, but applaud. You are, I suppose, more devout in the arena, where after the same fashion your deities dance on human blood, on the pollutions caused by inflicted punishments, as they act their themes and stories, doing their turn for the wretched criminals, except that these, too, often put on divinity and actually play the very gods. We have seen in our day a representation of the mutilation of Attis, that famous god of Pessinus, and a man burnt alive as Hercules. We have made merry amid the ludicrous cruelties of the noonday exhibition, at Mercury examining the bodies of the dead with his hot iron; we have witnessed Jove's brother,[4] mallet in hand, dragging out the corpses of the gladiators. But who can go into everything of this sort? If by such things as these the honour of deity is assailed, if they go to blot out every trace of its majesty, we must explain them by the contempt in which the gods are held, alike by those who actually do them, and by those for whose enjoyment they are done. This it will be said, however, is all in sport. But if I add—it is what all know and will admit as readily to be the fact—that in the temples adulteries are arranged, that at the altars pimping is practised, that often in the houses of the temple-keepers and priests, under the sacrificial fillets, and the sacred hats,[5] and the purple robes, amid the fumes of incense, deeds of licentiousness are done, I am not sure but your gods have more reason to complain of you than of Christians. It is certainly among the votaries of your religion that the perpetrators of sacrilege are always found, for Christians do not enter your temples even in the day-time. Perhaps they too would be spoilers of them, if they worshipped in them. What then do they worship, since their objects of worship are different from yours? Already indeed it is implied, as the corollary from their rejection of the lie, that they render homage to the truth ; nor continue longer in an error which they have given up in the very fact of recognizing it to be an error. Take this in first of all, and when we have offered a preliminary refutation of some false opinions, go on to derive from it our entire religious system.

CHAP. XVI.

For, like some others, you are under the delusion that our god is an ass's head.[6] Cor-

---

[1] Phaethon.
[2] Atys or Attis.
[3] Paris.

[4] Pluto.
[5] [" Sacred hats and purple robes and incense fumes " have been associated with the same crimes, alas ! in widely different relations.]
[6] [Caricatures of the Crucifixion are extant which show how greedily the heathen had accepted this profane idea.]

nelius Tacitus first put this notion into people's minds. In the fifth book of his histories, beginning the (narrative of the) Jewish war with an account of the origin of the nation ; and theorizing at his pleasure about the origin, as well as the name and the religion of the Jews, he states that having been delivered, or rather, in his opinion, expelled from Egypt, in crossing the vast plains of Arabia, where water is so scanty, they were in extremity from thirst ; but taking the guidance of the wild asses, which it was thought might be seeking water after feeding, they discovered a fountain, and thereupon in their gratitude they consecrated a head of this species of animal. And as Christianity is nearly allied to Judaism, from this, I suppose, it was taken for granted that we too are devoted to the worship of the same image. But the said Cornelius Tacitus (the very opposite of *tacit* in telling lies) informs us in the work already mentioned, that when Cneius Pompeius captured Jerusalem, he entered the temple to see the arcana of the Jewish religion, but found no image there. Yet surely if worship was rendered to any visible object, the very place for its exhibition would be the shrine ; and that all the more that the worship, however unreasonable, had no need there to fear outside beholders. For entrance to the holy place was permitted to the priests alone, while all vision was forbidden to others by an outspread curtain. You will not, however, deny that all beasts of burden, and not parts of them, but the animals entire, are with their goddess Epona objects of worship with you. It is this, perhaps, which displeases you in us, that while your worship here is universal, we do homage only to the ass. Then, if any of you think we render superstitious adoration to the cross, in that adoration he is sharer with us. If you offer homage to a piece of wood at all, it matters little what it is like when the substance is the same : it is of no consequence the form, if you have the very body of the god. And yet how far does the Athenian Pallas differ from the stock of the cross, or the Pharian Ceres as she is put up uncarved to sale, a mere rough stake and piece of shapeless wood ? Every stake fixed in an upright position is a portion of the cross ; we render our adoration, if you will have it so, to a god entire and complete. We have shown before that your deities are derived from shapes modelled from the cross. But you also worship victories, for in your trophies the cross is the heart of the trophy.[1] The camp religion of the Romans is all through a wor-

ship of the standards, a setting the standards above all gods. Well, as those images decking out the standards are ornaments of crosses. All those hangings of your standards and banners are robes of crosses. I praise your zeal : you would not consecrate crosses unclothed and unadorned. Others, again, certainly with more information and greater verisimilitude, believe that the sun is our god. We shall be counted Persians perhaps, though we do not worship the orb of day painted on a piece of linen cloth, having himself everywhere in his own disk. The idea no doubt has originated from our being known to turn to the east in prayer.[1] But you, many of you, also under pretence sometimes of worshipping the heavenly bodies, move your lips in the direction of the sunrise. In the same way, if we devote Sun-day to rejoicing, from a far different reason than Sun-worship, we have some resemblance to those of you who devote the day of Saturn to ease and luxury, though they too go far away from Jewish ways, of which indeed they are ignorant. But lately a new edition of our god has been given to the world in that great city : it originated with a certain vile man who was wont to hire himself out to cheat the wild beasts, and who exhibited a picture with this inscription : The God of the Christians, born of an ass.[2] He had the ears of an ass, was hoofed in one foot, carried a book,[3] and wore a toga. Both the name and the figure gave us amusement. But our opponents ought straightway to have done homage to this biformed divinity, for they have acknowledged gods dog-headed and lionheaded, with horn of buck and ram, with goat-like loins, with serpent legs, with wings sprouting from back or foot. These things we have discussed *ex abundanti*, that we might not seem willingly to pass by any rumor against us unrefuted. Having thoroughly cleared ourselves, we turn now to an exhibition of what our religion really is.

√ CHAP. XVII.

The object of our worship is the One God,[4] He who by His commanding word, His arranging wisdom, His mighty power, brought forth from nothing this entire mass of our world, with all its array of elements, bodies, spirits, for the glory of His majesty ; whence also the Greeks have bestowed on it the name of Κόσμος. The eye cannot see Him, though He is (spiritually) visible. He is incompre-

---

[1] [As noted by Clement of Alexandria. See p. 535, Vol. II., and note.]

[2] Onocoites. If with Oehler, Onochoietes, the meaning is "asinarius sacerdos " (Oehler).

[3] Referring evidently to the Scriptures ; and showing what the Bible was to the early Christians.

[4] [Kaye, p. 168. Remarks on natural religion.]

---

[1] [A premonition of the Labarum.]

hensible, though in grace He is manifested. He is beyond our utmost thought, though our human faculties conceive of Him.   He is therefore equally real and great.   But that which, in the ordinary sense, can be seen and handled and conceived, is inferior to the eyes by which it is taken in, and the hands by which it is tainted, and the faculties by which it is discovered ; but that which is infinite is known only to itself.   This it is which gives some notion of God, while yet beyond all our conceptions—our very incapacity of fully grasping Him affords us the idea of what He really is.   He is presented to our minds in His transcendent greatness, as at once known and unknown.   And this is the crowning guilt of men, that they will not recognize One, of whom they cannot possibly be ignorant. Would you have the proof from the works of His hands, so numerous and so great, which both contain you and sustain you, which minister at once to your enjoyment, and strike you with awe ; or would you rather have it from the testimony of the soul itself ? Though under the oppressive bondage of the body, though led astray by depraving customs, though enervated by lusts and passions, though in slavery to false gods ; yet, whenever the soul comes to itself, as out of a surfeit, or a sleep, or a sickness, and attains something of its natural soundness, it speaks of God ; using no other word, because this is the peculiar name of the true God.   " God is great and good "—" Which may God give," are the words on every lip.   It bears witness, too, that God is judge, exclaiming, " God sees," and, " I commend myself to God," and, " God will repay me."   O noble testimony of the soul by nature [1] Christian !   Then, too, in using such words as these, it looks not to the Capitol, but to the heavens.   It knows that there is the throne of the living God, as from Him and from thence itself came down.

CHAP. XVIII.

But, that we might attain an ampler and more authoritative knowledge at once of Himself, and of His counsels and will, God has added a written revelation for the behoof of every one whose heart is set on seeking Him, that seeking he may find, and finding believe, and believing obey.   For from the first He sent messengers into the world,—men whose stainless righteousness made them worthy to know the Most High, and to reveal Him,— men abundantly endowed with the Holy Spirit, that they might proclaim that there is one

God only who made all things, who formed man from the dust of the ground (for He is the true Prometheus who gave order to the world by arranging the seasons and their course),—these have further set before us the proofs He has given of His majesty in His judgments by floods and fires, the rules appointed by Him for securing His favour, as well as the retribution in store for the ignoring, forsaking and keeping them, as being about at the end of all to adjudge His worshippers to everlasting life, and the wicked to the doom of fire at once without ending and without break, raising up again all the dead from the beginning, reforming and renewing them with the object of awarding either recompense.   Once these things were with us, too, the theme of ridicule.   We are of your stock and nature : men are made, not born, Christians. The preachers of whom we have spoken are called prophets, from the office which belongs to them of predicting the future.   Their words, as well as the miracles which they performed, that men might have faith in their divine authority, we have still in the literary treasures they have left, and which are open to all.   Ptolemy, surnamed Philadelphus, the most learned of his race, a man of vast acquaintance with all literature, emulating, I imagine, the book enthusiasm of Pisistratus, among other remains of the past which either their antiquity or something of peculiar interest made famous, at the suggestion of Demetrius Phalereus, who was renowned above all grammarians of his time, and to whom he had committed the management of these things, applied to the Jews for their writings—I mean the writings peculiar to them and in their tongue, which they alone possessed, for from themselves, as a people dear to God for their fathers' sake, their prophets had ever sprung, and to them they had ever spoken.   Now in ancient times the people we call Jews bare the name of Hebrews, and so both their writings and their speech were Hebrew.   But that the understanding of their books might not be wanting, this also the Jews supplied to Ptolemy ; for they gave him seventy-two interpreters—men whom the philosopher Menedemus, the well-known asserter of a Providence, regarded with respect as sharing in his views.   The same account is given by Aristæus.   So the king left these works unlocked to all, in the Greek language.[2]   To this day, at the temple of Serapis, the libraries of Ptolemy are to be seen, with the identical Hebrew originals in them.   The Jews, too, read them publicly.   Under a tribute-liberty, they are

---

[1] [Though we are not by nature good, in our present estate; this is elsewhere demonstrated by Tertullian, as see cap. xviii.]

[2] [Kaye, p. 291.   See Elucidation I.   Also Vol. II., p. 334.]

in the habit of going to hear them every Sabbath. Whoever gives ear will find God in them ; whoever takes pains to understand, will be compelled to believe.

CHAP. XIX.

Their high antiquity, first of all, claims authority for these writings. With you, too, it is a kind of religion to demand belief on this very ground. Well, all the substances, all the materials, the origins, classes, contents of your most ancient writings, even most nations and cities illustrious in the records of the past and noted for their antiquity in books of annals,—the very forms of your letters, those revealers and custodiers of events, nay (I think I speak still within the mark), your very gods themselves, your very temples and oracles, and sacred rites, are less ancient than the work of a single prophet, in whom you have the *thesaurus* of the entire Jewish religion, and therefore too of ours. If you happen to have heard of a certain Moses, I speak first of him: he is as far back as the Argive Inachus ; by nearly four hundred years—only seven less—he precedes Danaus, your most ancient name ; while he antedates by a millennium the death of Priam. I might affirm, too, that he is five hundred years earlier than Homer, and have supporters of that view. The other prophets also, though of later date, are, even the most recent of them, as far back as the first of your philosophers, and legislators, and historians. It is not so much the difficulty of the subject, as its vastness, that stands in the way of a statement of the grounds on which these statements rest ; the matter is not so arduous as it would be tedious. It would require the anxious study of many books, and the fingers' busy reckoning. The histories of the most ancient nations, such as the Egyptians, the Chaldeans, the Phœnicians, would need to be ransacked ; the men of these various nations who have information to give, would have to be called in as witnesses. Manetho the Egyptian, and Berosus the Chaldean, and Hieromus the Phœnician king of Tyre ; their successors too, Ptolemy the Mendesian, and Demetrius Phalereus, and King Juba, and Apion, and Thallus, and their critic the Jew Josephus, the native vindicator of the ancient history of his people, who either authenticates or refutes the others. Also the Greek censors' lists must be compared, and the dates of events ascertained, that the chronological connections may be opened up, and thus the reckonings of the various annals be made to give forth light. We must go abroad into the histories and literature of all nations. And, in fact, we have already brought the

proof in part before you, in giving those hints as to how it is to be effected. But it seems better to delay the full discussion of this, lest in our haste we do not sufficiently carry it out, or lest in its thorough handling we make too lengthened a digression.

CHAP. XX.

To make up for our delay in this, we bring under your notice something of even greater importance ; we point to the majesty of our Scriptures, if not to their antiquity. If you doubt that they are as ancient as we say, we offer proof that they are divine. And you may convince yourselves of this at once, and without going very far. Your instructors, the world, and the age, and the event, are all before you. All that is taking place around you was fore-announced ; all that you now see with your eye was previously heard by the ear. The swallowing up of cities by the earth ; the theft of islands by the sea ; wars, bringing external and internal convulsions ; the collision of kingdoms with kingdoms ; famines and pestilences, and local massacres, and widespread desolating mortalities ; the exaltation of the lowly, and the humbling of the proud ; the decay of righteousness, the growth of sin, the slackening interest in all good ways ; the very seasons and elements going out of their ordinary course, monsters and portents taking the place of nature's forms— it was all foreseen and predicted before it came to pass. While we suffer the calamities, we read of them in the Scriptures ; as we examine, they are proved. Well, the truth of a prophecy, I think, is the demonstration of its being from above. Hence there is among us an assured faith in regard to coming events as things already proved to us, for they were predicted along with what we have day by day fulfilled. They are uttered by the same voices, they are written in the same books—the same Spirit inspires them. All time is one to prophecy foretelling the future. Among men, it may be, a distinction of times is made while the fulfilment is going on : from being future we think of it as present, and then from being present we count it as belonging to the past. How are we to blame, I pray you, that we believe in things to come as though they already were, with the grounds we have for our faith in these two steps ?

CHAP. XXI.

But having asserted that our religion is supported by the writings of the Jews, the oldest which exist, though it is generally known, and we fully admit that it dates from a comparatively recent period—no further back indeed than the reign of Tiberius—a question may perhaps be raised on this ground about its standing, as if it were hiding something of its presumption under shadow of an illustrious religion, one which has at any rate undoubted allowance of the law, or because, apart from the question of age, we neither accord with the Jews in their peculiarities in regard to food, nor in their sacred days, nor even in their well-known bodily sign, nor in the possession of a common name, which surely behoved to be the case if we did homage to the same God as they. Then, too, the common people have now some knowledge of Christ, and think of Him as but a man, one indeed such as the Jews condemned, so that some may naturally enough have taken up the idea that we are worshippers of a mere human being. But we are neither ashamed of Christ —for we rejoice to be counted His disciples, and in His name to suffer—nor do we differ from the Jews concerning God. We must make, therefore, a remark or two as to Christ's divinity. In former times the Jews enjoyed much of God's favour, when the fathers of their race were noted for their righteousness and faith. So it was that as a people they flourished greatly, and their kingdom attained to a lofty eminence; and so highly blessed were they, that for their instruction God spake to them in special revelations, pointing out to them beforehand how they should merit His favor and avoid His displeasure. But how deeply they have sinned, puffed up to their fall with a false trust in their noble ancestors, turning from God's way into a way of sheer impiety, though they themselves should refuse to admit it, their present national ruin would afford sufficient proof. Scattered abroad, a race of wanderers, exiles from their own land and clime, they roam over the whole world without either a human or a heavenly king, not possessing even the stranger's right to set so much as a simple footstep in their native country. The sacred writers withal, in giving previous warning of these things, all with equal clearness ever declared that, in the last days of the world, God would, out of every nation, and people, and country, choose for Himself more faithful worshippers, upon whom He would bestow His grace, and that indeed in ampler measure, in keeping with the enlarged capacities of a nobler dispensation. Accordingly, He appeared among us, whose coming to renovate and illuminate man's nature was pre-announced by God—I mean Christ, that Son of God. And so the supreme Head and Master of this grace and discipline, the Enlightener and Trainer of the human race, God's own Son, was announced

among us, born—but not so born as to make Him ashamed of the name of Son or of His paternal origin. It was not His lot to have as His father, by incest with a sister, or by violation of a daughter or another's wife, a god in the shape of serpent, or ox, or bird, or lover, for his vile ends transmuting himself into the gold of Danaus. They are your divinities upon whom these base deeds of Jupiter were done. But the Son of God has no mother in any sense which involves impurity; she, whom men suppose to be His mother in the ordinary way, had never entered into the marriage bond.[1] But, first, I shall discuss His essential nature, and so the nature of His birth will be understood. We have already asserted that God made the world, and all which it contains, by His Word, and Reason, and Power. It is abundantly plain that your philosophers, too, regard the Logos—that is, the Word and Reason—as the Creator of the universe. For Zeno lays it down that he is the creator, having made all things according to a determinate plan; that his name is Fate, and God, and the soul of Jupiter, and the necessity of all things. Cleanthes ascribes all this to spirit, which he maintains pervades the universe. And we, in like manner, hold that the Word, and Reason, and Power, by which we have said God made all, have spirit as their proper and essential *substratum*, in which the Word has inbeing to give forth utterances, and reason abides to dispose and arrange, and power is over all to execute. We have been taught that He proceeds forth from God, and in that procession He is generated; so that He is the Son of God, and is called God from unity of substance with God. For God, too, is a Spirit. Even when the ray is shot from the sun, it is still part of the parent mass; the sun will still be in the ray, because it is a ray of the sun—there is no division of substance, but merely an extension. Thus Christ is Spirit of Spirit, and God of God, as light of light is kindled.[2] The material matrix remains entire and unimpaired, though you derive from it any number of shoots possessed of its qualities; so, too, that which has come forth out of God is at once God and the Son of God, and the two are one. In this way also, as He is Spirit of Spirit and God of God, He is made a second in manner of existence —in position, not in nature; and He did not withdraw from the original source, but went forth. This ray of God, then, as it was always foretold in ancient times, descending into a certain virgin, and made flesh in her womb,

---

[1] [That is, by the consummation of her marriage with Joseph.]
[2] [Language common among Christians, and adopted afterwards into the Creed.]

is in His birth God and man united. The flesh formed by the Spirit is nourished, grows up to manhood, speaks, teaches, works, and is the Christ. Receive meanwhile this fable, if you choose to call it so—it is like some of your own—while we go on to show how Christ's claims are proved, and who the parties are with you by whom such fables have been set agoing to overthrow the truth, which they resemble. The Jews, too, were well aware that Christ was coming, as those to whom the prophets spake. Nay, even now His advent is expected by them; nor is there any other contention between them and us, than that they believe the advent has not yet occurred. For two comings of Christ having been revealed to us: a first, which has been fulfilled in the lowliness of a human lot; a second, which impends over the world, now near its close, in all the majesty of Deity unveiled; and, by misunderstanding the first, they have concluded that the second—which, as matter of more manifest prediction, they set their hopes on—is the only one. It was the merited punishment of their sin not to understand the Lord's first advent: for if they had, they would have believed; and if they had believed, they would have obtained salvation. They themselves read how it is written of them that they are deprived of wisdom and understanding—of the use of eyes and ears.[1] As, then, under the force of their pre-judgment, they had convinced themselves from His lowly guise that Christ was no more than man, it followed from that, as a necessary consequence, that they should hold Him a magician from the powers which He displayed,—expelling devils from men by a word, restoring vision to the blind, cleansing the leprous, reinvigorating the paralytic, summoning the dead to life again, making the very elements of nature obey Him, stilling the storms and walking on the sea; proving that He was the Logos of God, that primordial first-begotten Word, accompanied by power and reason, and based on Spirit,—that He who was now doing all things by His word, and He who had done that of old, were one and the same. But the Jews were so exasperated by His teaching, by which their rulers and chiefs were convicted of the truth, chiefly because so many turned aside to Him, that at last they brought Him before Pontius Pilate, at that time Roman governor of Syria; and, by the violence of their outcries against Him, extorted a sentence giving Him up to them to be crucified. He Himself had predicted this; which, however, would have signified little had not the prophets of old

done it as well. And yet, nailed upon the cross, He exhibited many notable signs, by which His death was distinguished from all others. At His own free-will, He with a word dismissed from Him His spirit, anticipating the executioner's work. In the same hour, too, the light of day was withdrawn, when the sun at the very time was in his meridian blaze. Those who were not aware that this had been predicted about Christ, no doubt thought it an eclipse. You yourselves have the account of the world-portent still in your archives.[2] Then, when His body was taken down from the cross and placed in a sepulchre, the Jews in their eager watchfulness surrounded it with a large military guard, lest, as He had predicted His resurrection from the dead on the third day, His disciples might remove by stealth His body, and deceive even the incredulous. But, lo, on the third day there was a sudden shock of earthquake, and the stone which sealed the sepulchre was rolled away, and the guard fled off in terror: without a single disciple near, the grave was found empty of all but the clothes of the buried One. But nevertheless, the leaders of the Jews, whom it nearly concerned both to spread abroad a lie, and keep back a people tributary and submissive to them from the faith, gave it out that the body of Christ had been stolen by His followers. For the Lord, you see, did not go forth into the public gaze, lest the wicked should be delivered from their error; that faith also, destined to a great reward, might hold its ground in difficulty. But He spent forty days with some of His disciples down in Galilee, a region of Judea, instructing them in the doctrines they were to teach to others. Thereafter, having given them commission to preach the gospel through the world, He was encompassed with a cloud and taken up to heaven,—a fact more certain far than the assertions of your Proculi concerning Romulus.[3] All these things Pilate did to Christ; and now in fact a Christian in his own convictions, he sent word of Him to the reigning Cæsar, who was at the time Tiberius. Yes, and the Cæsars too would have believed on Christ, if either the Cæsars had not been necessary for the world, or if Christians could have been Cæsars. His disciples also, spreading over the world, did as their Divine Master bade them; and after suffering greatly themselves from the persecutions of the Jews, and with no unwilling heart, as having faith undoubting in the truth, at last by Nero's cruel sword sowed the seed of Christian blood at

---

[1] Isa. vi. 10.

[2] Elucidation V.
[3] Proculus was a Roman senator who affirmed that Romulus had appeared to him after his death.

Rome.[1] Yes, and we shall prove that even your own gods are effective witnesses for Christ. It is a great matter if, to give you faith in Christians, I can bring forward the authority of the very beings on account of whom you refuse them credit. Thus far we have carried out the plan we laid down. We have set forth this origin of our sect and name, with this account of the Founder of Christianity. Let no one henceforth charge us with infamous wickedness; let no one think that it is otherwise than we have represented, for none may give a false account of his religion. For in the very fact that he says he worships another god than he really does, he is guilty of denying the object of his worship, and transferring his worship and homage to another; and, in the transference, he ceases to worship the god he has repudiated. We say, and before all men we say, and torn and bleeding under your tortures, we cry out, "We worship God through Christ." Count Christ a man, if you please; by Him and in Him God would be known and be adored. If the Jews object, we answer that Moses, who was but a man, taught them their religion; against the Greeks we urge that Orpheus at Pieria, Musæus at Athens, Melampus at Argos, Trophonius in Bœotia, imposed religious rites; turning to yourselves, who exercise sway over the nations, it was the man Numa Pompilius who laid on the Romans a heavy load of costly superstitions. Surely Christ, then, had a right to reveal Deity, which was in fact His own essential possession, not with the object of bringing boors and savages by the dread of multitudinous gods, whose favour must be won, into some civilization, as was the case with Numa; but as one who aimed to enlighten men already civilized, and under illusions from their very culture, that they might come to the knowledge of the truth. Search, then, and see if that divinity of Christ be true. If it be of such a nature that the acceptance of it transforms a man, and makes him truly good, there is implied in that the duty of renouncing what is opposed to it as false; especially and on every ground that which, hiding itself under the names and images of dead, the labours to convince men of its divinity by certain signs, and miracles, and oracles.

CHAP. XXII.

And we affirm indeed the existence of certain spiritual essences; nor is their name unfamiliar. The philosophers acknowledge there are demons; Socrates himself waiting on a

demon's will. Why not? since it is said an evil spirit attached itself specially to him even from his childhood—turning his mind no doubt from what was good. The poets are all acquainted with demons too; even the ignorant common people make frequent use of them in cursing. In fact, they call upon Satan, the demon-chief, in their execrations, as though from some instinctive soul-knowledge of him. Plato also admits the existence of angels. The dealers in magic, no less, come forward as witnesses to the existence of both kinds of spirits. We are instructed, moreover, by our sacred books how from certain angels, who fell of their own free-will, there sprang a more wicked demon-brood, condemned of God along with the authors of their race, and that chief we have referred to. It will for the present be enough, however, that some account is given of their work. Their great business is the ruin of mankind. So, from the very first, spiritual wickedness sought our destruction. They inflict, accordingly, upon our bodies diseases and other grievous calamities, while by violent assaults they hurry the soul into sudden and extraordinary excesses. Their marvellous subtleness and tenuity give them access to both parts of our nature. As spiritual, they can do no harm; for, invisible and intangible, we are not cognizant of their action save by its effects, as when some inexplicable, unseen poison in the breeze blights the apples and the grain while in the flower, or kills them in the bud, or destroys them when they have reached maturity; as though by the tainted atmosphere in some unknown way spreading abroad its pestilential exhalations. So, too, by an influence equally obscure, demons and angels breathe into the soul, and rouse up its corruptions with furious passions and vile excesses; or with cruel lusts accompanied by various errors, of which the worst is that by which these deities are commended to the favour of deceived and deluded human beings, that they may get their proper food of flesh-fumes and blood when that is offered up to idol-images. What is daintier food to the spirit of evil, than turning men's minds away from the true God by the illusions of a false divination? And here I explain how these illusions are managed. Every spirit is possessed of wings. This is a common property of both angels and demons. So they are everywhere in a single moment; the whole world is as one place to them; all that is done over the whole extent of it, it is as easy for them to know as to report. Their swiftness of motion is taken for divinity, because their nature is unknown. Thus they would have themselves thought

---

[1] [Chapter 1. at close. "The blood of Christians is the seed of the Church."]

sometimes the authors of the things which they announce; and sometimes, no doubt, the bad things are their doing, never the good. The purposes of God, too, they took up of old from the lips of the prophets, even as they spoke them; and they gather them still from their works, when they hear them read aloud. Thus getting, too, from this source some intimations of the future, they set themselves up as rivals of the true God, while they steal His divinations. But the skill with which their responses are shaped to meet events, your Crœsi and Pyrrhi know too well. On the other hand, it was in that way we have explained, the Pythian was able to declare that they were cooking a tortoise[1] with the flesh of a lamb; in a moment he had been to Lydia. From dwelling in the air, and their nearness to the stars, and their commerce with the clouds, they have means of knowing the preparatory processes going on in these upper regions, and thus can give promise of the rains which they already feel. Very kind too, no doubt, they are in regard to the healing of diseases. For, first of all, they make you ill; then, to get a miracle out of it, they command the application of remedies either altogether new, or contrary to those in use, and straightway withdrawing hurtful influence, they are supposed to have wrought a cure. What need, then, to speak of their other artifices, or yet further of the deceptive power which they have as spirits: of these Castor apparitions,[2] of water carried by a sieve, and a ship drawn along by a girdle, and a beard reddened by a touch, all done with the one object of showing that men should believe in the deity of stones, and not seek after the only true God?

CHAP. XXIII.

Moreover, if sorcerers call forth ghosts, and even make what seem the souls of the dead to appear; if they put boys to death, in order to get a response from the oracle; if, with their juggling illusions, they make a pretence of doing various miracles; if they put dreams into people's minds by the power of the angels and demons whose aid they have invited, by whose influence, too, goats and tables are made to divine,—how much more likely is this power of evil to be zealous in doing with all its might, of its own inclination, and for its own objects, what it does to serve the ends of others! Or if both angels and demons do just what your gods do, where in that case is the pre-eminence of deity, which we must surely think to be above all in might? Will

it not then be more reasonable to hold that these spirits make themselves gods, giving as they do the very proofs which raise your gods to godhead, than that the gods are the equals of angels and demons? You make a distinction of places, I suppose, regarding as gods in their temple those whose divinity you do not recognize elsewhere; counting the madness which leads one man to leap from the sacred houses, to be something different from that which leads another to leap from an adjoining house; looking on one who cuts his arms and secret parts as under a different furor from another who cuts his throat. The result of the frenzy is the same, and the manner of instigation is one. But thus far we have been dealing only in words: we now proceed to a proof of facts, in which we shall show that under different names you have real identity. Let a person be brought before your tribunals, who is plainly under demoniacal possession. The wicked spirit, bidden to speak by a follower of Christ,[3] will as readily make the truthful confession that he is a demon, as elsewhere he has falsely asserted that he is a god. Or, if you will, let there be produced one of the god-possessed, as they are supposed, who, inhaling at the altar, conceive divinity from the fumes, who are delivered of it by retching, who vent it forth in agonies of gasping. Let that same Virgin Cælestis herself the rain-promiser, let Æsculapius discoverer of medicines, ready to prolong the life of Socordius, and Tenatius, and Asclepiodotus, now in the last extremity, if they would not confess, in their fear of lying to a Christian, that they were demons, then and there shed the blood of that most impudent follower of Christ. What clearer than a work like that? what more trustworthy than such a proof? The simplicity of truth is thus set forth; its own worth sustains it; no ground remains for the least suspicion. Do you say that it is done by magic, or some trick of that sort? You will not say anything of the sort, if you have been allowed the use of your ears and eyes. For what argument can you bring against a thing that is exhibited to the eye in its naked reality? If, on the one hand, they are really gods, why do they pretend to be demons? Is it from fear of us? In that case your divinity is put in subjection to Christians; and you surely can never ascribe deity to that which is under authority of man, nay (if it adds aught to the disgrace) of its very enemies. If, on the other hand, they are demons or angels, why, inconsistently with this, do

---

[1] Herodotus, I. 47. [See Wilberforce's *Five Empires*, p. 67.]
[2] [Castor and Pollux. Imitated in saint worship.]

[3] [This testimony must be noted as something of which Tertullian confidently challenges denial.]

they presume to set themselves forth as acting the part of gods? For as beings who put themselves out as gods would never willingly call themselves demons, if they were gods indeed, that they might not thereby in fact abdicate their dignity; so those whom you know to be no more than demons, would not dare to act as gods, if those whose names they take and use were really divine. For they would not dare to treat with disrespect the higher majesty of beings, whose displeasure they would feel was to be dreaded. So this divinity of yours is no divinity; for if it were, it would not be pretended to by demons, and it would not be denied by gods. But since on both sides there is a concurrent acknowledgment that they are not gods, gather from this that there is but a single race—I mean the race of demons, the real race in both cases. Let your search, then, now be after gods; for those whom you had imagined to be so you find to be spirits of evil. The truth is, as we have thus not only shown from our own gods that neither themselves nor any others have claims to deity, you may see at once who is really God, and whether that is He and He alone whom we Christians own; as also whether you are to believe in Him, and worship Him, after the manner of our Christan faith and discipline. But at once they will say, Who is this Christ with his fables? is he an ordinary man? is he a sorcerer? was his body stolen by his disciples from its tomb? is he now in the realms below? or is he not rather up in the heavens, thence about to come again, making the whole world shake, filling the earth with dread alarms, making all but Christians wail—as the Power of God, and the Spirit of God, as the Word, the Reason, the Wisdom, and the Son of God? Mock as you like, but get the demons if you can to join you in your mocking; let *them* deny that Christ is coming to judge every human soul which has existed from the world's beginning, clothing it again with the body it laid aside at death; let *them* declare it, say, before your tribunal, that this work has been allotted to Minos and Rhadamanthus, as Plato and the poets agree; let them put away from them at least the mark of ignominy and condemnation. They disclaim being unclean spirits, which yet we must hold as indubitably proved by their relish for the blood and fumes and fœtid carcasses of sacrificial animals, and even by the vile language of their ministers. Let them deny that, for their wickedness condemned already, they are kept for that very judgment-day, with all their worshippers and their works. Why, all the authority and power we have over them is from our naming the name of Christ, and recalling to their memory the woes with which God threatens them at the hands of Christ as Judge, and which they expect one day to overtake them. Fearing Christ in God, and God in Christ, they become subject to the servants of God and Christ. So at our touch and breathing, overwhelmed by the thought and realization of those judgment fires, they leave at our command the bodies they have entered, unwilling, and distressed, and before your very eyes put to an open shame. You believe them when they lie; give credit to them, then, when they speak the truth about themselves. No one plays the liar to bring disgrace upon his own head, but for the sake of honour rather. You give a readier confidence to people making confessions against themselves, than denials in their own behalf. It has not been an unusual thing, accordingly, for those testimonies of your deities to convert men to Christianity; for in giving full belief to them, we are led to believe in Christ. Yes, your very gods kindle up faith in our Scriptures, they build up the confidence of our hope. You do homage, as I know, to them also with the blood of Christians. On no account, then, would they lose those who are so useful and dutiful to them, anxious even to hold you fast, lest some day or other as Christians you might put them to the rout,—if under the power of a follower of Christ, who desires to prove to you the Truth, it were at all possible for them to lie.

CHAP. XXIV.

This whole confession of these beings, in which they declare that they are not gods, and in which they tell you that there is no God but one, the God whom we adore, is quite sufficient to clear us from the crime of treason, chiefly against the Roman religion. For if it is certain the gods have no existence, there is no religion in the case. If there is no religion, because there are no gods, we are assuredly not guilty of any offence against religion. Instead of that, the charge recoils on your own head: worshipping a lie, you are really guilty of the crime you charge on us, not merely by refusing the true religion of the true God, but by going the further length of persecuting it. But now, granting that these objects of your worship are really gods, is it not generally held that there is one higher and more potent, as it were the world's chief ruler, endowed with absolute power and majesty? For the common way is to apportion deity, giving an imperial and supreme domination to one, while its offices are put into the hands of many, as Plato describes great Jupiter in the heavens, surrounded by an array at once of deities and demons. It behooves us, therefore, to show equal respect to the procurators, prefects, and governors of the divine empire. And yet how great a crime does he commit, who, with the object of gaining higher favour with the Cæsar, transfers his endeavours and his hopes to another, and does not confess that the appellation of God as of Emperor belongs only to the Supreme Head, when it is held a capital offence among us to call, or hear called, by the highest title any other than Cæsar himself! Let one man worship God, another Jupiter; let one lift suppliant hands to the heavens, another to the altar of Fides ; let one —if you choose to take this view of it—count in prayer the clouds, and another the ceiling panels; let one consecrate his own life to his God, and another that of a goat. For see that you do not give a further ground for the charge of irreligion, by taking away religious liberty,[1] and forbidding free choice of deity, so that I may no longer worship according to my inclination, but am compelled to worship against it. Not even a human being would care to have unwilling homage rendered him; and so the very Egyptians have been permitted the legal use of their ridiculous superstition, liberty to make gods of birds and beasts, nay, to condemn to death any one who kills a god of their sort. Every province even, and every city, has its god. Syria has Astarte, Arabia has Dusares, the Norici have Belenus, Africa has its Cælestis, Mauritania has its own princes. I have spoken, I think, of Roman provinces, and yet I have not said their gods are Roman; for they are not worshipped at Rome any more than others who are ranked as deities over Italy itself by municipal consecration, such as Delventinus of Casinum, Visidianus of Narnia, Ancharia of Asculum, Nortia of Volsinii, Valentia of Ocriculum, Hostia of Satrium, Father Curis of Falisci, in honour of whom, too, Juno got her surname. In, fact, we alone are prevented having a religion of our own. We give offence to the Romans, we are excluded from the rights and privileges of Romans, because we do not worship the gods of Rome. It is well that there is a God of all, whose we all are, whether we will or no. But with you liberty is given to worship any god but the true God, as though He were not rather the God all should worship, to whom all belong.

CHAP. XXV.

I think I have offered sufficient proof upon the question of false and true divinity, having shown that the proof rests not merely on debate and argument, but on the witness of the very beings whom you believe are gods, so that the point needs no further handling. However, having been led thus naturally to speak of the Romans, I shall not avoid the controversy which is invited by the groundless assertion of those who maintain that, as a reward of their singular homage to religion, the Romans have been raised to such heights of power as to have become masters of the world; and that so certainly divine are the beings they worship, that those prosper beyond all others, who beyond all others honour them.[2] This, forsooth, is the wages the gods have paid the Romans for their devotion. The progress of the empire is to be ascribed to Sterculus, the Mutunus, and Larentina! For I can hardly think that foreign gods would have been disposed to show more favour to an alien race than to their own, and given their own fatherland, in which they had their birth, grew up to manhood, became illustrious, and at last were buried, over to invaders from another shore ! As for Cybele, if she set her affections on the city of Rome as sprung of the Trojan stock saved from the arms of Greece, she herself forsooth being of the same race,—if she foresaw her transference[3] to the avenging people by whom Greece the conqueror of Phrygia was to be subdued, let her look to it (in regard of her native country's conquest by Greece). Why, too, even in these days the *Mater Magna* has given a notable proof of her greatness which she has conferred as a boon upon the city; when, after the loss to the State of Marcus Aurelius at Sirmium, on the sixteenth before the Kalends of April, that most sacred high priest of hers was offering, a week after, impure libations of blood drawn from his own arms, and issuing his commands that the ordinary prayers should be made for the safety of the emperor already dead. O tardy messengers ! O sleepy despatches ! through whose fault Cybele had not an earlier knowledge of the imperial decease, that the Christians might have no occasion to ridicule a goddess so unworthy. Jupiter, again, would surely never have permitted his own Crete to fall at once before the Roman Fasces, forgetful of that Idean cave and the Corybantian cymbals, and the sweet odour of her who nursed him there. Would he not have exalted his own tomb above the entire Capitol, that the land which covered the ashes of Jove might rather be the mistress

---

[1] [Observe our author's assertion that in its own nature, worship must be a voluntary act, and note this expression *libertatem religionis*.]

[2] [See Augustine's *City of God*, III. *xvii*. p. 95, *Ed.* Migne.]
[3] Her image was taken from Pessinus to Rome.

of the world? Would Juno have desired the destruction of the Punic city, beloved even to the neglect of Samos, and that by a nation of Æneadæ? As to that I know, " Here were her arms, here was her chariot, this kingdom, if the Fates permit, the goddess tends and cherishes to be mistress of the nations."[1] Jove's hapless wife and sister had no power to prevail against the Fates! " Jupiter himself is sustained by fate." And yet the Romans have never done such homage to the Fates, which gave them Carthage against the purpose and the will of Juno, as to the abandoned harlot Larentina. It is undoubted that not a few of your gods have reigned on earth as kings. If, then, they now possess the power of bestowing empire, when they were kings themselves, from whence had they received their kingly honours? Whom did Jupiter and Saturn worship? A Sterculus, I suppose. But did the Romans, along with the native-born inhabitants, afterwards adore also some who were never kings? In that case, however, they were under the reign of others, who did not yet bow down to them, as not yet raised to godhead. It belongs to others, then, to make gift of kingdoms, since there were kings before these gods had their names on the roll of divinities. But how utterly foolish it is to attribute the greatness of the Roman name to religious merits, since it was after Rome became an empire, or call it still a kingdom, that the religion she professes made its chief progress! Is it the case now? Has its religion been the source of the prosperity of Rome? Though Numa set agoing an eagerness after superstitious observances, yet religion among the Romans was not yet a matter of images or temples. It was frugal in its ways, its rites were simple, and there were no capitols struggling to the heavens; but the altars were offhand ones of turf, and the sacred vessels were yet of Samian earthenware, and from these the odours rose, and no likeness of God was to be seen. For at that time the skill of the Greeks and Tuscans in image-making had not yet overrun the city with the products of their art. The Romans, therefore, were not distinguished for their devotion to the gods before they attained to greatness; and so their greatness was not the result of their religion. Indeed, how could religion make a people great who have owed their greatness to their irreligion? For, if I am not mistaken, kingdoms and empires are acquired by wars, and are extended by victories. More than that, you cannot have wars and victories without the taking, and often

the destruction, of cities. That is a thing in which the gods have their share of calamity. Houses and temples suffer alike ; there is indiscriminate slaughter of priests and citizens ; the hand of rapine is laid equally upon sacred and on common treasure. Thus the sacrileges of the Romans are as numerous as their trophies. They boast as many triumphs over the gods as over the nations ; as many spoils of battle they have still, as there remain images of captive deities. And the poor gods submit to be adored by their enemies, and they ordain illimitable empire to those whose injuries rather than their simulated homage should have had retribution at their hands. But divinities unconscious are with impunity dishonoured, just as in vain they are adored. You certainly never can believe that devotion to religion has evidently advanced to greatness a people who, as we have put it, have either grown by injuring religion, or have injured religion by their growth. Those, too, whose kingdoms have become part of the one great whole of the Roman empire, were not without religion when their kingdoms were taken from them.

CHAP. XXVI.

Examine then, and see if *He* be not the dispenser of kingdoms, who is Lord at once of the world which is ruled, and of man himself who rules ; if He have not ordained the changes of dynasties, with their appointed seasons, who was before all time, and made the world a body of times ; if the rise and the fall of states are not the work of Him, under whose sovereignty the human race once existed without states at all. How do you allow yourselves to fall into such error? Why, the Rome of rural simplicity is older than some of her gods; she reigned before her proud, vast Capitol was built. The Babylonians exercised dominion, too, before the days of the Pontiffs; and the Medes before the Quindecemvirs; and the Egyptians before the Salii; and the Assyrians before the Luperci; and the Amazons before the Vestal Virgins. And to add another point : if the religions of Rome give empire, ancient Judea would never have been a kingdom, despising as it did one and all these idol deities; Judea, whose God you Romans once honoured with victims, and its temple with gifts, and its people with treaties; and which would never have been beneath your sceptre but for that last and crowning offence against God, in rejecting and crucifying Christ

CHAP. XXVII.

Enough has been said in these remarks to confute the charge of treason against your re-

---

[1] [Familiar reference to Virgil, Æneid, I. 15.]

ligion ; for we cannot be held to do harm to that which has no existence. When we are called therefore to sacrifice, we resolutely refuse, relying on the knowledge we possess, by which we are well assured of the real objects to whom these services are offered, under profaning of images and the deification of human names. Some, indeed, think it a piece of insanity that, when it is in our power to offer sacrifice at once, and go away unharmed, holding as ever our convictions, we prefer an obstinate persistence in our confession to our safety. You advise us, forsooth, to take unjust advantage of you; but we know whence such suggestions come, who is at the bottom of it all, and how every effort is made, now by cunning suasion, now by merciless persecution, to overthrow our constancy. No other than that spirit, half devil and half angel, who, hating us because of his own separation from God, and stirred with envy for the favour God has shown us, turns your minds against us by an occult influence, moulding and instigating them to all that perversity in judgment, and that unrighteous cruelty, which we have mentioned at the beginning of our work, when entering on this discussion. For, though the whole power of demons and kindred spirits is subject to us, yet still, as ill-disposed slaves sometimes conjoin contumacy with fear, and delight to injure those of whom they at the same time stand in awe, so is it here. For fear also inspires hatred. Besides, in their desperate condition, as already under condemnation, it gives them some comfort, while punishment delays, to have the usufruct of their malignant dispositions. And yet, when hands are laid on them, they are subdued at once, and submit to their lot; and those whom at a distance they oppose, in close quarters they supplicate for mercy. So when, like insurrectionary workhouses, or prisons, or mines, or any such penal slaveries, they break forth against us their masters, they know all the while that they are not a match for us, and just on that account, indeed, rush the more recklessly to destruction. We resist them, unwillingly, as though they were equals, and contend against them by persevering in that which they assail ; and our triumph over them is never more complete than when we are condemned for resolute adherence to our faith.

CHAP. XXVIII.

But as it was easily seen to be unjust to compel freemen against their will to offer sacrifice (for even in other acts of religious service a willing mind is required), it should be counted quite absurd for one man to compel another to do honour to the gods, when he ought ever voluntarily, and in the sense of his own need, to seek their favour, lest in the liberty which is his right he should be ready to say, "I want none of Jupiter's favours; pray who art thou ? Let Janus meet me with angry looks, with whichever of his faces he likes ; what have you to do with me ?" You have been led, no doubt, by these same evil spirits to compel us to offer sacrifice for the well-being of the emperor; and you are under a necessity of using force, just as we are under an obligation to face the dangers of it. This brings us, then, to the second ground of accusation, that we are guilty of treason against a majesty more august ; for you do homage with a greater dread and an intenser reverence to Cæsar, than Olympian Jove himself. And if you knew it, upon sufficient grounds. For is not any living man better than a dead one, whoever he be ? But this is not done by you on any other ground than regard to a power whose presence you vividly realize; so that also in this you are convicted of impiety to your gods, inasmuch as you show a greater reverence to a human sovereignty than you do to them. Then, too, among you, people far more readily swear a false oath in the name of all the gods, than in the name of the single genius of Cæsar.

CHAP. XXIX.

Let it be made clear, then, first of all, if those to whom sacrifice is offered are really able to protect either emperor or anybody else, and so adjudge us guilty of treason, if angels and demons, spirits of most wicked nature, do any good, if the lost save, if the condemned give liberty, if the dead (I refer to what you know well enough) defend the living. For surely the first thing they would look to would be the protection of their statues, and images, and temples, which rather owe their safety, I think, to the watch kept by Cæsar's guards. Nay, I think the very materials of which these are made come from Cæsar's mines, and there is not a temple but depends on Cæsar's will. Yes, and many gods have felt the displeasure of the Cæsar. It makes for my argument if they are also partakers of his favour, when he bestows on them some gift or privilege. How shall they who are thus in Cæsar's power, who belong entirely to him, have Cæsar's protection in their hands, so that you can imagine them able to give to Cæsar what they more readily get from him ? This, then, is the ground on which we are charged with treason against the imperial majesty, to wit, that we do not put the emperors under their own possessions; that we do not offer a mere mock service on their behalf, as not believing their safety rests in leaden hands. But you are impious in a high degree who look for it where it is not, who seek it from those who have it not to give, passing by Him who has it entirely in His power. Besides this, you persecute those who know where to seek for it, and who, knowing where to seek for it, are able as well to secure it.

CHAP. XXX.

For we offer prayer for the safety of our princes to the eternal, the true, the living God, whose favour, beyond all others, they must themselves desire. They know from whom they have obtained their power; they know, as they are men, from whom they have received life itself; they are convinced that He is God alone, on whose power alone they are entirely dependent, to whom they are second, after whom they occupy the highest places, before and above all the gods. Why not, since they are above all living men, and the living, as living, are superior to the dead? They reflect upon the extent of their power, and so they come to understand the highest; they acknowledge that they have all their might from Him against whom their might is nought. Let the emperor make war on heaven; let him lead heaven captive in his triumph; let him put guards on heaven; let him impose taxes on heaven! He cannot. Just because he is less than heaven, he is great. For he himself is His to whom heaven and every creature appertains. He gets his sceptre where he first got his humanity; his power where he got the breath of life. Thither we lift our eyes, with hands outstretched, because free from sin; with head uncovered, for we have nothing whereof to be ashamed; finally, without a monitor, because it is from the heart we supplicate. Without ceasing, for all our emperors we offer prayer. We pray for life prolonged; for security to the empire; for protection to the imperial house; for brave armies, a faithful senate, a virtuous people, the world at rest, whatever, as man or Cæsar, an emperor would wish. These things I cannot ask from any but the God from whom I know I shall obtain them, both because He alone bestows them and because I have claims upon Him for their gift, as being a servant of His, rendering homage to Him alone, persecuted for His doctrine, offering to Him, at His own requirement, that costly and noble sacrifice of prayer [1] de-

spatched from the chaste body, an unstained soul, a sanctified spirit, not the few grains of incense a farthing buys [2]—tears of an Arabian tree,—not a few drops of wine,—not the blood of some worthless ox to which death is a relief, and, in addition to other offensive things, a polluted conscience, so that one wonders, when your victims are examined by these vile priests, why the examination is not rather of the sacrificers than the sacrifices. With our hands thus stretched out and up to God, rend us with your iron claws, hang us up on crosses, wrap us in flames, take our heads from us with the sword, let loose the wild beasts on us,—the very attitude of a Christian praying is one of preparation for all punishment.[3] Let this, good rulers, be your work : wring from us the soul, beseeching God on the emperor's behalf. Upon the truth of God, and devotion to His name, put the brand of crime.

CHAP. XXXI.

But we merely, you say, flatter the emperor, and feign these prayers of ours to escape persecution. Thank you for your mistake, for you give us the opportunity of proving our allegations. Do you, then, who think that we care nothing for the welfare of Cæsar, look into God's revelations, examine our sacred books, which we do not keep in hiding, and which many accidents put into the hands of those who are not of us. Learn from them that a large benevolence is enjoined upon us, even so far as to supplicate God for our enemies, and to beseech blessings on our persecutors.[4] Who, then, are greater enemies and persecutors of Christians, than the very parties with treason against whom we are charged? Nay, even in terms, and most clearly, the Scripture says, "Pray for kings, and rulers, and powers, that all may be peace with you."[5] For when there is disturbance in the empire, if the commotion is felt by its other members, surely we too, though we are not thought to be given to disorder, are to be found in some place or other which the calamity affects.

CHAP. XXXII.

There is also another and a greater necessity for our offering prayer in behalf of the emperors, nay, for the complete stability of the empire, and for Roman interests in general. For we know that a mighty shock im-

---

[1] Heb. x. 22. [See cap. xlii. *infra* p. 49.]

[2] [Once more this reflection on the use of material incense, which is common to early Christians, as in former volumes noted.]
[3] [A reference to kneeling, which see the *de Corona* cap. 3, *infra*. Christians are represented as standing at prayer, in the delineations of the Catacombs. But, see Nicene Canon, *xx*.]
[4] Matt. v. 44.
[5] 1 Tim. ii. 2.

pending over the whole earth—in fact, the very end of all things threatening dreadful woes—is only retarded by the continued existence of the Roman empire.[1] We have no desire, then, to be overtaken by these dire events; and in praying that their coming may be delayed, we are lending our aid to Rome's duration. More than this, though we decline to swear by the genii of the Cæsars, we swear by their safety, which is worth far more than all your genii. Are you ignorant that these genii are called " Dæmones," and thence the diminutive name " Dæmonia " is applied to them ? We respect in the emperors the ordinance of God, who has set them over the nations. We know that there is that in them which God has willed ; and to what God has willed we desire all safety, and we count an oath by it a great oath. But as for dæmons, that is, your genii, we have been in the habit of exorcising them, not of swearing by them, and thereby conferring on them divine honour.

CHAP. XXXIII.

But why dwell longer on the reverence and sacred respect of Christians to the emperor, whom we cannot but look up to as called by our Lord to his office? So that on valid grounds I might say Cæsar is more ours than yours, for our God has appointed him. Therefore, as having this propriety in him, I do more than you for his welfare, not merely because I ask it of Him who can give it, or because I ask it as one who deserves to get it, but also because, in keeping the majesty of Cæsar within due limits, and putting it under the Most High, and making it less than divine, I commend him the more to the favour of Deity, to whom I make him alone inferior. But I place him in subjection to one I regard as more glorious than himself. Never will I call the emperor God, and that either because it is not in me to be guilty of falsehood; or that I dare not turn him into ridicule ; or that not even himself will desire to have that high name applied to him. If he is but a man, it is his interest as man to give God His higher place. Let him think it enough to bear the name of emperor. That, too, is a great name of God's giving. To call him God, is to rob him of his title. If he is not a man, emperor he cannot be. Even when, amid the honours of a triumph, he sits on that lofty chariot, he is reminded that he is only human. A voice at his back keeps whispering in his ear, " Look behind thee; remember thou art but a man." And it only adds to his exultation,

that he shines with a glory so surpassing as to require an admonitory reference to his condition.[2] It adds to his greatness that he needs such a reminiscence, lest he should think himself divine.

CHAP. XXXIV.

Augustus, the founder of the empire, would not even have the title Lord; for that, too, is a name of Deity. For my part, I am willing to give the emperor this designation, but in the common acceptation of the word, and when I am not forced to call him Lord as in God's place. But my relation to him is one of freedom ; for I have but one true Lord, the God omnipotent and eternal, who is Lord of the emperor as well. How can he, who is truly father of his country, be its lord ? The name of piety is more grateful than the name of power; so the heads of families are called fathers rather than lords. Far less should the emperor have the name of God. We can only profess our belief that he is that by the most unworthy, nay, a fatal flattery ; it is just as if, having an emperor, you call another by the name, in which case will you not give great and unappeasable offence to him who actually reigns?—an offence he, too, needs to fear on whom you have bestowed the title. Give all reverence to God, if you wish Him to be propitious to the emperor. Give up all worship of, and belief in, any other being as divine. Cease also to give the sacred name to him who has need of God himself. If such adulation is not ashamed of its lie, in addressing a man as divine, let it have some dread at least of the evil omen which it bears. It is the invocation of a curse, to give Cæsar the name of god before his apotheosis.

CHAP. XXXV.

This is the reason, then, why Christians are counted public enemies : that they pay no vain, nor false, nor foolish honours to the emperor ; that, as men believing in the true religion, they prefer to celebrate their festal days with a good conscience, instead of with the common wantonness. It is, forsooth, a notable homage to bring fires and couches out before the public, to have feasting from street to street, to turn the city into one great tavern, to make mud with wine, to run in troops to acts of violence, to deeds of shamelessness to lust allurements ! What ! is public joy manifested by public disgrace ? Do things unseemly at other times beseem the festal days of princes ? Do they who observe the rules of virtue out of reverence for Cæsar, for

---

[1] [Cap. xxxix. *infra.* And see Kaye, pp. 20, 348. A subject of which more hereafter.]

[2] [A familiar story of Alexander is alluded to.]

his sake turn aside from them? Shall piety be a license to immoral deeds, and shall religion be regarded as affording the occasion for all riotous extravagance? Poor we, worthy of all condemnation! For why do we keep the votive days and high rejoicings in honour of the Cæsars with chastity, sobriety, and virtue? Why, on the day of gladness, do we neither cover our door-posts with laurels, nor intrude upon the day with lamps? It is a proper thing, at the call of a public festivity, to dress your house up like some new brothel.[1] However, in the matter of this homage to a lesser majesty, in reference to which we are accused of a lower sacrilege, because we do not celebrate along with you the holidays of the Cæsars in a manner forbidden alike by modesty, decency, and purity,—in truth they have been established rather as affording opportunities for licentiousness than from any worthy motive,—in this matter I am anxious to point out how faithful and true *you* are, lest perchance here also those who will not have us counted Romans, but enemies of Rome's chief rulers, be found themselves worse than we wicked Christians! I appeal to the inhabitants of Rome themselves, to the native population of the seven hills: does that Roman vernacular of theirs ever spare a Cæsar? The Tiber and the wild beasts' schools bear witness. Say now if nature had covered our hearts with a transparent substance through which the light could pass, whose hearts, all graven over, would not betray the scene of another and another Cæsar presiding at the distribution of a largess? And this at the very time they are shouting, "May Jupiter take years from us, and with them lengthen like to you,"—words as foreign to the lips of a Christian as it is out of keeping with his character to desire a change of emperor. But this is the rabble, you say; yet, as the rabble, they still are Romans, and none more frequently than they demand the death of Christians.[2] Of course, then, the other classes, as befits their higher rank, are religiously faithful. No breath of treason is there ever in the senate, in the equestrian order, in the camp, in the palace. Whence, then, came a Cassius, a Niger, an Albinus? Whence they who beset the Cæsar[3] between the two laurel groves? Whence they who practised wrestling, that they might acquire skill to strangle him? Whence they who in full armour broke into the palace,[4] more audacious than all your Tigerii and Parthe-

nii.[5] If I mistake not, they were Romans; that is, they were not Christians. Yet all of them, on the very eve of their traitorous outbreak, offered sacrifices for the safety of the emperor, and swore by his genius, one thing in profession, and another in the heart; and no doubt they were in the habit of calling Christians enemies of the state. Yes, and persons who are now daily brought to light as confederates or approvers of these crimes and treasons, the still remnant gleanings after a vintage of traitors, with what verdant and branching laurels they clad their door-posts, with what lofty and brilliant lamps they smoked their porches, with what most exquisite and gaudy couches they divided the Forum among themselves; not that they might celebrate public rejoicings, but that they might get a foretaste of their own votive seasons in partaking of festivities of another, and inaugurate the model and image of their hope, changing in their minds the emperor's name. The same homage is paid, dutifully too, by those who consult astrologers, and soothsayers, and augurs, and magicians, about the life of the Cæsars,—arts which, as made known by the angels who sinned, and forbidden by God, Christians do not even make use of in their own affairs. But who has any occasion to inquire about the life of the emperor, if he have not some wish or thought against it, or some hopes and expectations after it? For consultations of this sort have not the same motive in the case of friends as in the case of sovereigns. The anxiety of a kinsman is something very different from that of a subject.

<h2 style="text-align:center">CHAP. XXXVI.</h2>

If it is the fact that men bearing the name of Romans are found to be enemies of Rome, why are we, on the ground that we are regarded as enemies, denied the name of Romans? *We* may be at once Romans and foes of Rome, when men passing for Romans are discovered to be enemies of their country. So the affection, and fealty, and reverence, due to the emperors do not consist in such tokens of homage as these, which even hostility may be zealous in performing, chiefly as a cloak to its purposes; but in those ways which Deity as cerainly enjoins on us, as they are held to be necessary in the case of all men as well as emperors. Deeds of true heart-goodness are not due by us to emperors alone. We never do good with respect of persons; for in our own interest we conduct ourselves as those who take no payment either of praise or premium

---

[1] [Note this reference to a shameless custom of the heathen in Rome and elsewhere.]
[2] [See cap. l. and Note on cap. xl. *infra*.]
[3] Commodus.
[4] To murder Pertinax.

[5] Tigerius and Parthenius were among the murderers of Commodus.

from man, but from God, who both requires and remunerates an impartial benevolence.[1] We are the same to emperors as to our ordinary neighbors. For we are equally forbidden to wish ill, to do ill, to speak ill, to think ill of all men. The thing we must not do to an emperor, we must not do to any one else: what we would not do to anybody, *a fortiori*, perhaps we should not do to him whom God has been pleased so highly to exalt.

CHAP. XXXVII.

If we are enjoined, then, to love our enemies, as I have remarked above, whom have we to hate? If injured, we are forbidden to retaliate, lest we become as bad ourselves: who can suffer injury at our hands? In regard to this, recall your own experiences. How often you inflict gross cruelties on Christians, partly because it is your own inclination, and partly in obedience to the laws! How often, too, the hostile mob, paying no regard to you, takes the law into its own hand, and assails us with stones and flames! With the very frenzy of the Bacchanals, they do not even spare the Christian dead, but tear them, now sadly changed, no longer entire, from the rest of the tomb, from the asylum we might say of death, cutting them in pieces, rending them asunder. Yet, banded together as we are, ever so ready to sacrifice our lives, what single case of revenge for injury are you able to point to, though, if it were held right among us to repay evil by evil, a single night with a torch or two could achieve an ample vengeance? But away with the idea of a sect divine avenging itself by human fires, or shrinking from the sufferings in which it is tried. If we desired, indeed, to act the part of open enemies, not merely of secret avengers, would there be any lacking in strength, whether of numbers or resources? The Moors, the Marcomanni, the Parthians themselves, or any single people, however great, inhabiting a distinct territory, and confined within its own boundaries, surpasses, forsooth, in numbers, one spread over all the world! We are but of yesterday, and we have filled every place among you—cities, islands, fortresses, towns, market-places, the very camp, tribes, companies, palace, senate, forum,—we have left nothing to you but the temples of your gods. For what wars should we not be fit, not eager, even with unequal forces, we who so willingly yield ourselves to the sword, if in our religion it were not counted better to be slain than to slay? Without arms even, and raising no insurrectionary banner, but simply in enmity to you, we could carry on the contest with you by an ill-willed severance alone. For if such multitudes of men were to break away from you, and betake themselves to some remote corner of the world, why, the very loss of so many citizens, whatever sort they were, would cover the empire with shame; nay, in the very forsaking, vengeance would be inflicted. Why, you would be horror-struck at the solitude in which you would find yourselves, at such an all-prevailing silence, and that stupor as of a dead world. You would have to seek subjects to govern. You would have more enemies than citizens remaining. For now it is the immense number of Christians which makes your enemies so few,—almost all the inhabitants of your various cities being followers of Christ.[2] Yet you choose to call us enemies of the human race, rather than of human error. Nay, who would deliver you from those secret foes, ever busy both destroying your souls and ruining your health? Who would save you, I mean, from the attacks of those spirits of evil, which without reward or hire we exorcise? This alone would be revenge enough for us, that you were henceforth left free to the possession of unclean spirits. But instead of taking into account what is due to us for the important protection we afford you, and though we are not merely no trouble to you, but in fact necessary to your wellbeing, you prefer to hold us enemies, as indeed we are, yet not of man, but rather of his error.

CHAP. XXXVIII.

Ought not Christians, therefore, to receive not merely a somewhat milder treatment, but to have a place among the law-tolerated societies, seeing they are not chargeable with any such crimes as are commonly dreaded from societies of the illicit class? For, unless I mistake the matter, the prevention of such associations is based on a prudential regard to public order, that the state may not be divided into parties, which would naturally lead to disturbance in the electoral assemblies, the councils, the curiæ, the special conventions, even in the public shows by the hostile collisions of rival parties; especially when now, in pursuit of gain, men have begun to consider their violence an article to be bought and sold. But as those in whom all ardour in the pursuit of glory and honour is dead, we have no pressing inducement to take part in your public meetings; nor is there aught more entirely foreign to us than affairs of state. We ac-

---

[1] [Cap. ix. p. 25, note 1 *supra*. Again, Christian democracy, "honouring all men."]

[2] [Elucidation VI.]

knowledge one all-embracing commonwealth —the world. We renounce all your spectacles, as strongly as we renounce the matters originating them, which we know were conceived of superstition, when we give up the very things which are the basis of their representations. Among us nothing is ever said, or seen, or heard, which has anything in common with the madness of the circus, the immodesty of the theatre, the atrocities of the arena, the useless exercises of the wrestling-ground. Why do you take offence at us because we differ from you in regard to your pleasures? If we will not partake of your enjoyments, the loss is ours, if there be loss in the case, not yours. We reject what pleases you. You, on the other hand, have no taste for what is our delight. The Epicureans were allowed by you to decide for themselves one true source of pleasure—I mean equanimity; the Christian, on his part, has many such enjoyments—what harm in that?

CHAP. XXXIX.

I shall at once go on, then, to exhibit the peculiarities of the Christian society, that, as I have refuted the evil charged against it, I may point out its positive good.[1] We are a body knit together as such by a common religious profession, by unity of discipline, and by the bond of a common hope. We meet together as an assembly and congregation, that, offering up prayer to God as with united force, we may wrestle with Him in our supplications. This violence God delights in. We pray, too, for the emperors, for their ministers and for all in authority, for the welfare of the world, for the prevalence of peace, for the delay of the final consummation.[2] We assemble to read our sacred writings, if any peculiarity of the times makes either forewarning or reminiscence needful.[3] However it be in that respect, with the sacred words we nourish our faith, we animate our hope, we make our confidence more stedfast; and no less by inculcations of God's precepts we confirm good habits. In the same place also exhortations are made, rebukes and sacred censures are administered. For with a great gravity is the work of judging carried on among us, as befits those who feel assured that they are in the sight of God; and you have the most notable example of judgment to come when any one has sinned so grievously as to require his severance from us in prayer, in the congregation and in all sacred

intercourse. The tried men of our elders preside over us, obtaining that honour not by purchase, but by established character. There is no buying and selling of any sort in the things of God. Though we have our treasure-chest, it is not made up of purchase-money, as of a religion that has its price. On the monthly day,[4] if he likes, each puts in a small donation; but only if it be his pleasure, and only if he be able: for there is no compulsion; all is voluntary. These gifts are, as it were, piety's deposit fund. For they are not taken thence and spent on feasts, and drinking-bouts, and eating-houses, but to support and bury poor people, to supply the wants of boys and girls destitute of means and parents, and of old persons confined now to the house; such, too, as have suffered shipwreck; and if there happen to be any in the mines, or banished to the islands, or shut up in the prisons, for nothing but their fidelity to the cause of God's Church, they become the nurslings of their confession. But it is mainly the deeds of a love so noble that lead many to put a brand upon us. *See*, they say, *how they love one* [5] *another*, for themselves are animated by mutual hatred; how they are ready even to die for one another, for they themselves will sooner put to death. And they are wroth with us, too, because we call each other brethren; for no other reason, as I think, than because among themselves names of consanguinity are assumed in mere pretence of affection. But we are your brethren as well, by the law of our common mother nature, though you are hardly men, because brothers so unkind. At the same time, how much more fittingly they are called and counted brothers who have been led to the knowledge of God as their common Father, who have drunk in one spirit of holiness, who from the same womb of a common ignorance have agonized into the same light of truth! But on this very account, perhaps, we are regarded as having less claim to be held true brothers, that no tragedy makes a noise about our brotherhood, or that the family possessions, which generally destroy brotherhood among you, create fraternal bonds among us. One in mind and soul, we do not hesitate to share our earthly goods with one another. All things are common among us but our wives. We give up our community where it is practised alone by others, who not only take possession of the wives of their friends, but most tolerantly also accommodate their friends with theirs, following the example, I believe,

1 [Elucidation VII.]
2 [Chap. xxxii. *supra* p. 43.]
3 [An argument for Days of Public Thanksgiving, Fasting and the like.]

4 [On ordinary Sundays, "they laid by in store," apparently: once a month they offered.]
5 [A precious testimony, although the caviller asserts that afterwards the heathen used this expression derisively.]

of those wise men of ancient times, the Greek Socrates and the Roman Cato, who shared with their friends the wives whom they had married, it seems for the sake of progeny both to themselves and to others ; whether in this acting against their partners' wishes, I am not able to say. Why should they have any care over their chastity, when their husbands so readily bestowed it away? O noble example of Attic wisdom, of Roman gravity—the philosopher and the censor playing pimps! What wonder if that great love of Christians towards one another is desecrated by you! For you abuse also our humble feasts, on the ground that they are extravagant as well as infamously wicked. To us, it seems, applies the saying of Diogenes : " The people of Megara feast as though they were going to die on the morrow; they build as though they were never to die!" But one sees more readily the mote in another's eye than the beam in his own. Why, the very air is soured with the eructations of so many tribes, and *curiæ*, and *decuriæ*. The Salii cannot have their feast without going into debt ; you must get the accountants to tell you what the tenths of Hercules and the sacrificial banquets cost ; the choicest cook is appointed for the Apaturia, the Dionysia, the Attic mysteries ; the smoke from the banquet of Serapis will call out the firemen. Yet about the modest supper-room of the Christians alone a great ado is made. Our feast explains itself by its name. The Greeks call it *agapè*, i.e., affection. Whatever it costs, our outlay in the name of piety is gain, since with the good things of the feast we benefit the needy; not as it is with you, do parasites aspire to the glory of satisfying their licentious propensities, selling themselves for a belly-feast to all disgraceful treatment,—but as it is with God himself, a peculiar respect is shown to the lowly. If the object of our feast be good, in the light of that consider its further regulations. As it is an act of religious service, it permits no vileness or immodesty. The participants, before reclining, taste first of prayer to God. As much is eaten as satisfies the cravings of hunger; as much is drunk as befits the chaste. They say it is enough, as those who remember that even during the night they have to worship God; they talk as those who know that the Lord is one of their auditors. After manual ablution, and the bringing in of lights, each[1] is asked to stand forth and sing, as he can, a hymn to God, either one from the holy Scriptures or one of his own composing,—a proof of the measure

of our drinking. As the feast commenced with prayer, so with prayer it is closed. We go from it, not like troops of mischief-doers, nor bands of vagabonds, nor to break out into licentious acts, but to have as much care of our modesty and chastity as if we had been at a school of virtue rather than a banquet. Give the congregation of the Christians its due, and hold it unlawful, if it is like assemblies of the illicit sort: by all means let it be condemned, if any complaint can be validly laid against it, such as lies against secret factions. But who has ever suffered harm from our assemblies? We are in our congregations just what we are when separated from each other ; we are as a community what we are individuals ; we injure nobody, we trouble nobody. When the upright, when the virtuous meet together, when the pious, when the pure assemble in congregation, you ought not to call that a faction, but a *curia*—[i.e., the court of God.]

CHAP. XL.

On the contrary, *they* deserve the name of faction who conspire to bring odium on good men and virtuous, who cry out against innocent blood, offering as the justification of their enmity the baseless plea, that they think the Christians the cause of every public disaster, of every affliction with which the people are visited. If the Tiber rises as high as the city walls, if the Nile does not send its waters up over the fields, if the heavens give no rain, if there is an earthquake, if there is famine or pestilence, straightway the cry[2] is, "Away with the Christians to the lion!" What! shall you give such multitudes to a single beast? Pray, tell me how many calamities befell the world and particular cities before Tiberius reigned—before the coming, that is, of Christ? We read of the islands of Hiera, and Anaphe, and Delos, and Rhodes, and Cos, with many thousands of human beings, having been swallowed up. Plato informs us that a region larger than Asia or Africa was seized by the Atlantic Ocean. An earthquake, too, drank up the Corinthian sea ; and the force of the waves cut off a part of Lucania, whence it obtained the name of Sicily. These things surely could not have taken place without the inhabitants suffering by them. But where—I do not say were Christians, those despisers of your gods—but where were your gods themselves in those days, when the flood poured its destroying waters over all the world, or, as Plato thought, merely the level portion of it? For that they are of later date

---

[1] [Or, perhaps—" One is prompted to stand forth and bring to God, as every one can, whether from the Holy Scriptures, or of his own mind"—i.e. according to his taste.]

[2] [*Christianos ad leonem.* From what class, chiefly, see cap. xxxv. *supra.* Elucidation VIII.]

than that calamity, the very cities in which they were born and died, nay, which they founed, bear ample testimony ; for the cities could have no existence at this day unless as belonging to postdiluvian times. Palestine had not yet received from Egypt its Jewish swarm (of emigrants), nor had the race from which Christians sprung yet settled down there, when its neighbors Sodom and Gomorrah were consumed by fire from heaven. The country yet smells of that conflagration ; and if there are apples there upon the trees, it is only a promise to the eye they give—you but touch them, and they turn to ashes. Nor had Tuscia and Campania to complain of Christians in the days when fire from heaven overwhelmed Vulsinii, and Pompeii was destroyed by fire from its own mountain. No one yet worshipped the true God at Rome, when Hannibal at Cannæ counted the Roman slain by the pecks of Roman rings. Your gods were all objects of adoration, universally acknowledged, when the Senones closely besieged the very Capitol. And it is in keeping with all this, that if adversity has at any time befallen cities, the temples and the walls have equally shared in the disaster, so that it is clear to demonstration the thing was not the doing of the gods, seeing it also overtook themselves. The truth is, the human race has always deserved ill at God's hand. First of all, as undutiful to Him, because when it knew Him in part, it not only did not seek after Him, but even invented other gods of its own to worship ; and further, because, as the result of their willing ignorance of the Teacher of righteousness, the Judge and Avenger of sin, all vices and crimes grew and flourished. But had men sought, they would have come to know the glorious object of their seeking ; and knowledge would have produced obedience, and obedience would have found a gracious instead of an angry God. They ought then to see that the very same God is angry with them now as in ancient times, before Christians were so much as spoken of. It was *His* blessings they enjoyed—created before they made any of their deities : and why can they not take it in, that their evils come from the Being whose goodness they have failed to recognize? They suffer at the hands of Him to whom they have been ungrateful. And, for all that is said, if we compare the calamities of former times, they fall on us more lightly now, since God gave Christians to the world ; for from that time virtue put some restraint on the world's wickedness, and men began to pray for the averting of God's wrath. In a word, when the summer clouds give no rain, and the season is matter of anxiety, you indeed—full of feasting day by day, and ever eager for the banquet, baths and taverns and brothels always busy—offer up to Jupiter your rain-sacrifices ; you enjoin on the people barefoot processions ; you seek heaven at the Capitol ; you look up to the temple-ceilings for the longed-for clouds—God and heaven not in all your thoughts. We, dried up with fastings, and our passions bound tightly up, holding back as long as possible from all the ordinary enjoyments of life, rolling in sackcloth and ashes, assail heaven with our importunities—touch God's heart—and when we have extorted divine compassion, why, Jupiter gets all the honour !

CHAP. XLI.

You, therefore, are the sources of trouble in human affairs ; on you lies the blame of public adversities, since you are ever attracting them—you by whom God is despised and images are worshipped. It should surely seem the more natural thing to believe that it is the neglected One who is angry, and not they to whom all homage is paid ; or most unjustly they act, if, on account of the Christians, they send trouble on their own devotees, whom they are bound to keep clear of the punishments of Christians. But this, you say, hits your God as well, since He permits His worshippers to suffer on account of those who dishonour Him. But admit first of all His providential arrangings, and you will not make this retort. For He who once for all appointed an eternal judgment at the world's close, does not precipitate the separation, which is essential to judgment, before the end. Meanwhile He deals with all sorts of men alike, so that all together share His favours and reproofs. His will is, that outcasts and elect should have adversities and prosperities in common, that we should have all the same experience of His goodness and severity. Having learned these things from His own lips, we love His goodness, we fear His wrath, while both by you are treated with contempt ; and hence the sufferings of life, so far as it is our lot to be overtaken by them, are in our case gracious admonitions, while in yours they are divine punishments. We indeed are not the least put about : for, first, only one thing in this life greatly concerns us, and that is, to get quickly out of it ; and next, if any adversity befalls us, it is laid to the door of your transgressions. Nay, though we are likewise involved in troubles because of our close connection with you, we are rather glad of it, because we recognize in it divine foretellings, which, in fact, go to confirm the confidence and faith of our hope. But if all the evils you endure are inflicted on you by the gods you worship out of spite to us, why do you continue to pay homage to beings so ungrateful, and unjust ; who, instead of being angry with you, should rather have been aiding and abetting you by persecuting Christians —keeping *you* clear of their sufferings ?

CHAP. XLII.

But we are called to account as harm-doers on another[1] ground, and are accused of being useless in the affairs of life. How in all the world can that be the case with people who are living among you, eating the same food, wearing the same attire, having the same habits, under the same necessities of existence ? We are not Indian Brahmins or Gymnosophists, who dwell in woods and exile themselves from ordinary human life. We do not forget the debt of gratitude we owe to God, our Lord and Creator ; we reject no creature of His hands, though certainly we exercise restraint upon ourselves, lest of any gift of His we make an immoderate or sinful use. So we sojourn with you in the world, abjuring neither forum, nor shambles, nor bath, nor booth, nor workshop, nor inn, nor weekly market, nor any other places of commerce. We sail with you, and fight with you,[2] and till the ground with you ; and in like manner we unite with you in your traffickings—even in the various arts we make public property of our works for your benefit. How it is we seem useless in your ordinary business, living with you and by you as we do, I am not able to understand. But if I do not frequent your religious ceremonies, I am still on the sacred day a man. I do not at the Saturnalia bathe myself at dawn, that I may not lose both day and night ; yet I bathe at a decent and healthful hour, which preserves me both in heat and blood. I can be rigid and pallid like you after ablution when I am dead. I do not recline in public at the feast of Bacchus, after the manner of the beast-fighters at their final banquet. Yet of your resources I partake, *wherever* I may chance to eat. I do not buy a crown for my head. What matters it to you how I use them, if nevertheless the flowers are purchased ? I think it more agreeable to have them free and loose, waving all about. Even if they are woven into a crown, we smell the crown with our nostrils : let those look to it who scent the perfume with their hair. We do not go to your spectacles ; yet the articles that are sold there, if I need them, I will ob-

tain more readily at their proper places. We certainly buy no frankincense. If the Arabias complain of this, let the Sabæans be well assured that their more precious and costly merchandise is expended as largely in the burying of Christians[3] as in the fumigating of the gods. At any rate, you say, the temple revenues are every day falling off :[4] how few now throw in a contribution ! In truth, we are not able to give alms both to your human and your heavenly mendicants ; nor do we think that we are required to give any but to those who ask for it. Let Jupiter then hold out his hand and get, for our compassion spends more in the streets than yours does in the temples. But your other taxes will acknowledge a debt of gratitude to Christians ; for in the faithfulness which keeps us from fraud upon a brother, we make conscience of paying all their dues: so that, by ascertaining how much is lost by fraud and falsehood in the census declarations—the calculation may easily be made—it would be seen that the ground of complaint in one department of revenue is compensated by the advantage which others derive.

CHAP. XLIII.

I will confess, however, without hesitation, that there are some who in a sense may complain of Christians that they are a sterile race : as, for instance, pimps, and panders, and bath-suppliers ; assassins, and poisoners, and sorcerers ; soothsayers, too, diviners, and astrologers. But it is a noble fruit of Christians, that they have no fruits for such as these. And yet, whatever loss your interests suffer from the religion we profess, the protection you have from us makes amply up for it. What value do you set on persons, I do not here urge who deliver you from demons, I do not urge who for your sakes present prayers before the throne of the true God, for perhaps you have no belief in that—but from whom you can have nothing to fear ?

CHAP. XLIV.

Yes, and no one considers what the loss is to the common weal,—a loss as great as it is real, no one estimates the injury entailed upon the state, when, men of virtue as we are, we are put to death in such numbers; when so many of the truly good suffer the last penalty. And here we call your own acts to witness, you who are daily presiding at the trials of prisoners, and passing sentence upon crimes. Well, in your long lists of those ac-

---

1 [Elucidation IX. See Kaye, p. 361.]
2 [The occupation of a soldier was regarded as lawful therefore. But see, afterwards, the *De Corona* cap. *xi.*]
3 [An interesting fact as to the burial-rites of Early Christians. As to incense, see cap. xxx. *supra* p, 42.]
4 An index of the growth of Christianity.

cused of many and various atrocities, has any assassin, any cutpurse, any man guilty of sacrilege, or seduction, or stealing bathers' clothes, his name entered as being a Christian too? Or when Christians are brought before you on the mere ground of their name, is there ever found among them an ill-doer of the sort? It is always with your folk the prison is steaming, the mines are sighing, the wild beasts are fed: it is from you the exhibitors of gladiatorial shows always get their herds of criminals to feed up for the occasion. You find no Christian there, except simply as being such; or if one is there as something else, a Christian he is no longer.[1]

CHAP. XLV.

We, then, alone are without crime. Is there ought wonderful in that, if it be a very necessity with us? For a necessity indeed it is. Taught of God himself what goodness is, we have both a perfect knowledge of it as revealed to us by a perfect Master; and faithfully we do His will, as enjoined on us by a Judge we dare not despise. But your ideas of virtue you have got from mere human opinion; on human authority, too, its obligation rests: hence your system of practical morality is deficient, both in the fulness and authority requisite to produce a life of real virtue. Man's wisdom to point out what is good, is no greater than his authority to exact the keeping of it; the one is as easily deceived as the other is despised. And so, which is the ampler rule, to say, "Thou shalt not kill," or to teach, "Be not even angry?" Which is more perfect, to forbid adultery, or to restrain from even a single lustful look? Which indicates the higher intelligence, interdicting evil-doing, or evil-speaking? Which is more thorough, not allowing an injury, or not even suffering an injury done to you to be repaid? Though withal you know that these very laws also of yours, which seem to lead to virtue, have been borrowed from the law of God as the ancient model. Of the age of Moses we have already spoken. But what is the real authority of human laws, when it is in man's power both to evade them, by generally managing to hide himself out of sight in his crimes, and to despise them sometimes, if inclination or necessity leads him to offend? Think of these things, too, in the light of the brevity of any punishment you can inflict—never to last longer than till death. On this ground Epicurus makes light of all suffering and pain, maintaining

that if it is small, it is contemptible; and if it is great, it is not long-continued. No doubt about it, we, who receive our awards under the judgment of an all-seeing God, and who look forward to eternal punishment from Him for sin,—we alone make real effort to attain a blameless life, under the influence of our ampler knowledge, the impossibility of concealment, and the greatness of the threatened torment, not merely long-enduring but everlasting, fearing Him, whom he too should fear who the fearing judges,—even God, I mean, and not the proconsul.

CHAP. XLVI.

We have sufficiently met, as I think, the accusation of the various crimes on the ground of which these fierce demands are made for Christian blood. We have made a full exhibition of our case; and we have shown you how we are able to prove that our statement is correct, from the trustworthiness, I mean, and antiquity of our sacred writings, and from the confession likewise of the powers of spiritual wickedness themselves. Who will venture to undertake our refutation; not with skill of words, but, as we have managed our demonstration, on the basis of reality? But while the truth we hold is made clear to all, unbelief meanwhile, at the very time it is convinced of the worth of Christianity, which has now become well known for its benefits as well as from the intercourse of life, takes up the notion that it is not really a thing divine, but rather a kind of philosophy. These are the very things, it says, the philosophers counsel and profess—innocence, justice, patience, sobriety, chastity. Why, then, are we not permitted an equal liberty and impunity for our doctrines as they have, with whom, in respect of what we teach, we are compared? or why are not they, as so like us, not pressed to the same offices, for declining which our lives are imperilled? For who compels a philosopher to sacrifice or take an oath, or put out useless lamps at midday? Nay, they openly overthrow your gods, and in their writings attack your superstitions; and you applaud them for it. Many of them even, with your countenance, bark out against your rulers, and are rewarded with statues and salaries, instead of being given to the wild beasts. And very right it should be so. For they are called philosophers, not Christians. This name of philosopher has no power to put demons to the rout. Why are they not able to do that too? since philosophers count demons inferior to gods. Socrates used to say, "If the demon grant permission." Yet

---

[1] [An appeal so defiant that its very boldness confirms this tribute to the character of our Christian fathers, p. 42.]

he, too, though in denying the existence of your divinities he had a glimpse of the truth, at his dying ordered a cock to be sacrificed to Æsculapius, I believe in honour of his father,[1] for Apollo pronounced Socrates the wisest of men. Thoughtless Apollo! testifying to the wisdom of the man who denied the existence of his race. In proportion to the enmity the truth awakens, you give offence by faithfully standing by it ; but the man who corrupts and makes a mere pretence of it precisely on this ground gains favour with its persecutors. The truth which philosophers, these mockers and corrupters of it, with hostile ends merely affect to hold, and in doing so deprave, caring for nought but glory, Christians both intensely and intimately long for and maintain in its integrity, as those who have a real concern about their salvation. So that we are like each other neither in our knowledge nor our ways, as you imagine. For what certain information did Thales, the first of natural philosophers, give in reply to the inquiry of Croesus regarding Deity, the delay for further thought so often proving in vain ? There is not a Christian workman but finds out God, and manifests Him, and hence assigns to Him all those attributes which go to constitute a divine being, though Plato affirms that it is far from easy to discover the Maker of the universe ; and when He is found, it is difficult to make Him known to all. But if we challenge you to comparison in the virtue of chastity, I turn to a part of the sentence passed by the Athenians against Socrates, who was pronounced a corrupter of youth. The Christian confines himself to the female sex. I have read also how the harlot Phryne kindled in Diogenes the fires of lust, and how a certain Speusippus, of Plato's school, perished in the adulterous act. The Christian husband has nothing to do with any but his own wife. Democritus, in putting out his eyes, because he could not look on women without lusting after them, and was pained if his passion was not satisfied, owns plainly, by the punishment he inflicts, his incontinence. But a Christian with grace-healed eyes is sightless in this matter ; he is mentally blind against the assaults of passion. If I maintain our superior modesty of behaviour, there at once occurs to me Diogenes with filth-covered feet trampling on the proud couches of Plato, under the influence of another pride : the Christian does not even play the proud man to the pauper. If sobriety of spirit be the virtue in debate, why, there are Pythagoras

at Thurii, and Zeno at Priene, ambitious of the supreme power : the Christian does not aspire to the ædileship. If equanimity be the contention, you have Lycurgus choosing death by self-starvation, because the Lacons had made some emendation of his laws : the Christian, even when he is condemned, gives thanks.[2] If the comparison be made in regard to trustworthiness, Anaxagoras denied the deposit of his enemies : the Christian is noted for his fidelity even among those who are not of his religion. If the matter of sincerity is to be brought to trial, Aristotle basely thrust his friend Hermias from his place : the Christian does no harm even to his foe. With equal baseness does Aristotle play the sycophant to Alexander, instead of exercising to keep him in the right way, and Plato allows himself to be bought by Dionysius for his belly's sake. Aristippus in the purple, with all his great show of gravity, gives way to extravagance ; and Hippias is put to death laying plots against the state : no Christian ever attempted such a thing in behalf of his brethren, even when persecution was scattering them abroad with every atrocity. But it will be said that some of us, too, depart from the rules of our discipline. In that case, however, we count them no longer Christians ; but the philosophers who do such things retain still the name and the honour of wisdom. So, then, where is there any likeness between the Christian and the philosopher? between the disciple of Greece and of heaven? between the man whose object is fame, and whose object is life ? between the talker and he doer? between the man who builds up and the man who pulls down? between the friend and the foe of error? between one who corrupts the truth, and one who restores and teaches it? between its chief and its custodier?

CHAP. XLVII.

Unless I am utterly mistaken, there is nothing so old as the truth; and the already proved antiquity of the divine writings is so far of use to me, that it leads men more easily to take it in that they are the treasure-source whence all later wisdom has been taken. And were it not necessary to keep my work to a moderate size, I might launch forth also into the proof of this. What poet or sophist has not drunk at the fountain of the prophets ? Thence, accordingly, the philosophers watered their arid minds, so that it is the things they

---

[1] [Tertullian's exposition of this enigmatical fact (see the *Phædo*) is better than divers other ingenious theories.]

[2] [John xxi. 19. A pious habit which long survived among Christians, when learning that death was at hand; as in Shakespeare's *Henry IV.*, "Laud be to God, ev'n there my life must end." See 1 Thess. v. 18.]

have from us which bring us into comparison with them. For this reason, I imagine, philosophy was banished by certain states—I mean by the Thebans, by the Spartans also, and the Argives—its disciples sought to imitate our doctrines; and ambitious, as I have said, of glory and eloquence alone, if they fell upon anything in the collection of sacred Scriptures which displeased them, in their own peculiar style of research, they perverted it to serve their purpose: for they had no adequate faith in their divinity to keep them from changing them, nor had they any sufficient understanding of them, either, as being still at the time under veil—even obscure to the Jews themselves, whose peculiar possession they seemed to be. For so, too, if the truth was distinguished by its simplicity, the more on that account the fastidiousness of man, too proud to believe, set to altering it; so that even what they found certain they made uncertain by their admixtures. Finding a simple revelation of God, they proceeded to dispute about Him, not as He had revealed to them, but turned aside to debate about His properties, His nature, His abode. Some assert Him to be incorporeal; others maintain He has a body,—the Platonists teaching the one doctrine, and the Stoics the other. Some think that He is composed of atoms, others of numbers: such are the different views of Epicurus and Pythagoras. One thinks He is made of fire; so it appeared to Heraclitus. The Platonists, again, hold that He administers the affairs of the world; the Epicureans, on the contrary, that He is idle and inactive, and, so to speak, a nobody in human things. Then the Stoics represent Him as placed outside the world, and whirling round this huge mass from without like a potter; while the Platonists place Him within the world, as a pilot is in the ship he steers. So, in like manner, they differ in their views about the world itself, whether it is created or uncreated, whether it is destined to pass away or to remain for ever. So again it is debated concerning the nature of the soul, which some contend is divine and eternal, while others hold that it is dissoluble. According to each one's fancy, He has introduced either something new, or refashioned the old. Nor need we wonder if the speculations of philosophers have perverted the older Scriptures. Some of their brood, with their opinions, have even adulterated our new-given Christian revelation, and corrupted it into a system of philosophic doctrines, and from the one path have struck off many and inexplicable by-roads.[1] And I have alluded

to this, lest any one becoming acquainted with the variety of parties among us, this might seem to him to put us on a level with the philosophers, and he might condemn the truth from the different ways in which it is defended. But we at once put in a plea in bar against these tainters of our purity, asserting that this is the rule of truth which comes down from Christ by transmission through His companions, to whom we shall prove that those devisers of different doctrines are all posterior. Everything opposed to the truth has been got up from the truth itself, the spirits of error carrying on this system of opposition. By them all corruptions of wholesome discipline have been secretly instigated; by them, too, certain fables have been introduced, that, by their resemblance to the truth, they might impair its credibility, or vindicate their own higher claims to faith; so that people might think Christians unworthy of credit because the poets or philosophers are so, or might regard the poets and philosophers as worthier of confidence from their not being followers of Christ. Accordingly, we get ourselves laughed at for proclaiming that God will one day judge the world. For, like us, the poets and philosophers set up a judgment-seat in the realms below. And if we threaten Gehenna, which is a reservoir of secret fire under the earth for purposes of punishment, we have in the same way derision heaped on us. For so, too, they have their Pyriphlegethon, a river of flame in the regions of the dead. And if we speak of Paradise,[2] the place of heavenly bliss appointed to receive the spirits of the saints, severed from the knowledge of this world by that fiery zone as by a sort of enclosure, the Elysian plains have taken possession of their faith. Whence is it, I pray you have all this, so like us, in the poets and philosophers? The reason simply is, that they have been taken from our religion. But if they are taken from our sacred things, as being of earlier date, then ours are the truer, and have higher claims upon belief, since even their imitations find faith among you. If they maintain their sacred mysteries to have sprung from their own minds, in that case ours will be reflections of what are later than themselves, which by the nature of things is impossible, for never does the shadow precede the body which casts it, or the image the reality.[3]

CHAP. XLVIII.

Come now, if some philosopher affirms, as

[See Iræneus, vol. i. p. 377 this Series.]

---

[2] [Elucidation X.]
[3] True, in the sense that a shadow cannot be projected by a body not yet existent.

Laberius holds, following an opinion of Pythagoras, that a man may have his origin from a mule, a serpent from a woman, and with skill of speech twists every argument to prove his view, will he not gain acceptance for it, and work in some the conviction that, on account of this, they should even abstain from eating animal food? May any one have the persuasion that he should so abstain, lest by chance in his beef he eats of some ancestor of his? But if a Christian promises the return of a man from a man, and the very actual Gaius from Gaius,[1] the cry of the people will be to have him stoned; they will not even so much as grant him a hearing. If there is any ground for the moving to and fro of human souls into different bodies, why may they not return into the very substance they have left, seeing this is to be restored, to be that which had been? They are no longer the very things they had been ; for they could not be what they were not, without first ceasing to be what they had been. If we were inclined to give all rein upon this point, discussing into what various beasts one and another might probably be changed, we would need at our leisure to take up many points. But this we would do chiefly in our own defence, as setting forth what is greatly worthier of belief, that a man will come back from a man—any given person from any given person, still retaining his humanity; so that the soul, with its qualities unchanged, may be restored to the same condition, thought not to the same outward framework. Assuredly, as the reason why restoration takes place at all is the appointed judgment, every man must needs come forth the very same who had once existed, that he may receive at God's hands a judgment, whether of good desert or the opposite. And therefore the body too will appear; for the soul is not capable of suffering without the solid substance (that is, the flesh; and for this reason, also) that it is not right that souls should have all the wrath of God to bear : they did not sin without the body, within which all was done by them. But how, you say, can a substance which has been dissolved be made to reappear again? Consider thyself, O man, and thou wilt believe in it ! Reflect on what you were before you came into existence. Nothing. For if you had been anything, you would have remembered it. You, then, who were nothing before you existed, reduced to nothing also when you cease to be, why may you not come into being again out of nothing, at the will of the same Creator whose will created you out of nothing

at the first? Will it be anything new in your case? You who were not, *were* made; when you cease to be again, you *shall* be made. Explain, if you can, your original creation, and then demand to know how you shall be re-created. Indeed, it will be still easier surley to make you what you were once, when the very same creative power made you without difficulty what you never were before. There will be doubts, perhaps, as to the power of God, of Him who hung in its place this huge body of our world, made out of what had never existed, as from a death of emptiness and inanity, animated by the Spirit who quickens all living things, its very self the unmistakable type of the resurrection, that it might be to you a witness—nay, the exact image of the resurrection. Light, every day extinguished, shines out again; and, with like alternation, darkness succeeds light's outgoing. The defunct stars re-live; the seasons, as soon as they are finished, renew their course; the fruits are brought to maturity, and then are reproduced. The seeds do not spring up with abundant produce, save as they rot and dissolve away ;—all things are preserved by perishing, all things are refashioned out of death. Thou, man of nature so exalted, if thou understandest thyself, taught even by the Pythian[2] words, lord of all these things that die and rise,—shalt thou die to perish evermore? Wherever your dissolution shall have taken place, whatever material agent has destroyed you, or swallowed you up, or swept you away, or reduced you to nothingness, it shall again restore you. Even nothingness is His who is Lord of *all*. You ask, Shall we then be always dying, and rising up from death? If so the Lord of all things had appointed, you would have to submit, though unwillingly, to the law of your creation. But, in fact, He has no other purpose than that of which He has informed us. The Reason which made the universe out of diverse elements, so that all things might be composed of opposite substances in unity—of void and solid, of animate and inanimate, of comprehensible and incomprehensible, of light and darkness, of life itself and death—has also disposed time into order, by fixing and distinguishing its mode, according to which this first portion of it, which we inhabit from the beginning of the world, flows down by a temporal course to a close; but the portion which succeeds, and to which we look forward continues forever. When, therefore, the boundary

---

[1] [*i.e.*, Caius, used (like *John Doe* with us) in Roman Law.]

[2] Know thyself. [Juvenal, xi. 27, on which see great wealth of references in J. E. B. Mayor's *Juvenal* (xiii. Satires), and note especially, Bernard, *Serm. de Divers* xl. 3. *In Cant. Cantic.* xxxvi. 5-7.]

and limit, that millennial interspace, has been passed, when even the outward fashion of the world itself—which has been spread like a veil over the eternal economy, equally a thing of time—passes away, then the whole human race shall be raised again, to have its dues meted out according as it has merited in the period of good or evil, and thereafter to have these paid out through the immeasurable ages of eternity. Therefore after this there is neither death nor repeated resurrections, but we shall be the same that we are now, and still unchanged—the servants of God, ever with God, clothed upon with the proper substance of eternity; but the profane, and all who are not true worshippers of God, in like manner shall be consigned to the punishment of everlasting fire—that fire which, from its very nature indeed, directly ministers to their incorruptibility. The philosophers are familiar as well as we with the distinction between a common and a secret fire. Thus that which is in ·common use is far different from that which we see in divine judgments, whether striking as thunderbolts from heaven, or bursting up out of the earth through mountain-tops; for it does not consume what it scorches, but while it burns it repairs. So the mountains continue ever burning; and a person struck by lighting is even now kept safe from any destroying flame. A notable proof this of the fire eternal! a notable example of the endless judgment which still supplies punishment with fuel! The mountains burn, and last. How will it be with the wicked and the enemies of God?[1]

CHAP. XLIX.

These are what are called presumptuous speculations in our case alone; in the philosophers and poets they are regarded as sublime speculations and illustrious discoveries. They are men of wisdom, we are fools. They are worthy of all honour, we are folk to have the finger pointed at; nay, besides that, we are even to have punishments inflicted on us. But let things which are the defence of virtue, if you will, have no foundation, and give them duly the name of fancies, yet still they are necessary; let them be absurd if you will, yet they are of use: they make all who believe them better men and women, under the fear of never-ending punishment and the hope of never-ending bliss. It is not, then, wise to brand as false, nor to regard as absurd, things the truth of which it is expedient to presume. On no ground is it right positively to condemn as bad what beyond all doubt is profitable. Thus, in fact, you are guilty of the very presumption of which you accuse us, in condemning what is useful. It is equally out of the question to regard them as nonsensical; at any rate, if they are false and foolish, they hurt nobody. For they are just (in that case) like many other things on which you inflict no penalties—foolish and fabulous things, I mean, which, as quite innocuous, are never charged as crimes or punished. But in a thing of the kind, if this be so indeed, we should be adjudged to ridicule, not to swords, and flames, and crosses, and wild beasts, in which iniquitous cruelty not only the blinded populace exults and insults over us, but in which some of you too glory, not scrupling to gain the popular favour by your injustice. As though all you can do to us did not depend upon our pleasure. It is assuredly a matter of my own inclination, being a Christian. Your condemnation, then, will only reach me in that case, if I wish to be condemned; but when all you can do to me, you can do only at my will, all you can do is dependent on my will, and is not in your power. The joy of the people in our trouble is therefore utterly reasonless. For it is our joy they appropriate to themselves, since we would far rather be condemned than apostatize from God; on the contrary, our haters should be sorry rather than rejoice, as we have obtained the very thing of our own choice.

CHAP. L.

In that case, you say, why do you complain of our persecutions? You ought rather to be grateful to us for giving you the sufferings you want. Well, it is quite true that it is our desire to suffer, but it is in the way that the soldier longs for war. No one indeed suffers willingly, since suffering necessarily implies fear and danger. Yet the man who objected to the conflict, both fights with all his strength, and when victorious, he rejoices in the battle, because he reaps from it glory and spoil. It is our battle to be summoned to your tribunals that there, under fear of execution, we may battle for the truth. But the day is won when the object of the struggle is gained. This victory of ours gives us the glory of pleasing God, and the spoil of life eternal. But we are overcome. Yes, when we have obtained our wishes. Therefore we conquer in dying;[2] we go forth victorious at the very time we are subdued. Call us, if you like, *Sarmenticii* and *Semaxii*, because, bound to a half-axle stake,

---

[1] [Our author's philosophy may be at fault, but his testimony is not to be mistaken.]

[2] [*Vicimus cum occidimur.*]

we are burned in a circle-heap of fagots. This is the attitude in which we conquer, it is our victory-robe, it is for us a sort of triumphal car. Naturally enough, therefore, we do not please the vanquished; on account of this, indeed, we are counted a desperate, reckless race. But the very desperation and reckless-ness you object to in us, among yourselves lift high the standard of virtue in the cause of glory and of fame. Mucius of his own will left his right hand on the altar : what sublimity of mind ! Empedocles gave his whole body at Catana to the fires of Ætna: what mental resolution ! A certain foundress of Carthage gave herself away in second marriage to the funeral pile: what a noble witness of her chastity! Regulus, not wishing that his one life should count for the lives of many enemies, endured these crosses over all his frame: how brave a man—even in captivity a conqueror ! Anaxarchus, when he was being beaten to death by a barley-pounder, cried out, " Beat on, beat on at the case of Anaxarchus ; no stroke falls on Anaxarchus himself." O mag-nanimity of the philosopher, who even in such an end had jokes upon his lips ! I omit all reference to those who with their own sword, or with any other milder form of death, have bargained for glory. Nay, see how even torture contests are crowned by you. The Athenian courtezan, having wearied out the executioner, at last bit off her tongue and spat it in the face of the raging tyrant, that she might at the same time spit away her power of speech, nor be longer able to confess her fellow-conspirators, if even overcome, that might be her inclination. Zeno the Eleatic, when he was asked by Dionysius what good philosophy did, on answering that it gave con-tempt of death, was all unquailing, given over to the tyrant's scourge, and sealed his opin-ion even to the death. We all know how the Spartan lash, applied with the utmost cruelty under the very eyes of friends en-couraging, confers on those who bear it honor proportionate to the blood which the young men shed. O glory legitimate, because it is human, for whose sake it is counted neither reckless foolhardiness, nor desperate obsti-nacy, to despise death itself and all sorts of savage treatment ; for whose sake you may for your native place, for the empire, for friendship, endure all you are forbidden to do for God! And you cast statues in honour of persons such as these, and you put in-scriptions upon images, and cut out epitaphs on tombs, that their names may never perish. In so far you can by your monuments, you yourselves afford a sort of resurrection to the dead. Yet he who expects the true resurrec-tion from God, is insane, if for God he suffers ! But go zealously on, good presidents, you will stand higher with the people if you sacrifice the Christians at their wish, kill us, torture us, condemn us, grind us to dust ; your injus-tice is the proof that we are innocent. There-fore God suffers that we thus suffer; for but very lately, in condemning a Christian woman to the *leno* rather than to the *leo* you made confession that a taint on our purity is con-sidered among us something more terrible than any punishment and any death.[1] Nor does your cruelty, however exquisite, avail you; it is rather a temptation to us. The oftener we are mown down by you, the more in number we grow; *the blood of Christians is seed.*[2] Many of your writers exhort to the courageous bearing of pain and death, as Cic-ero in the *Tusculans*, as Seneca in his *Chances*, as Diogenes, Pyrrhus, Callinicus; and yet their words do not find so many disciples as Christians do, teachers not by words, but by their deeds. That very obstinacy you rail against is the preceptress. For who that con-templates it, is not excited to inquire what is at the bottom of it ? who, after inquiry, does not embrace our doctrines ? and when he has embraced them, desires not to suffer that he may become partaker of the fulness of God's grace, that he may obtain from God complete forgiveness, by giving in exchange his blood ? For that secures the remission of all offences. On this account it is that we return thanks on the very spot for your sentences. As the divine and human are ever opposed to each other, when we are condemned by you, we are acquitted by the Highest.

---

[1] [Elucidation XI.]
[2] [Elucidation XII.]

ELUCIDATIONS.

I.

(Arrangement, p. 4, *supra*.)

THE arrangement I have adopted in editing these Edinburgh Translations of Tertullian is a practical one. It will be found logical and helpful to the student, who is referred to the Prefatory pages of this volume for an Elucidation of the difficulties, with which any arrangement of these treatises is encumbered. For, *first*, an attempt to place them in chronological order is out of the question;[1] and, *second*, all efforts to separate precisely the Orthodox from the Montanistic or Montanist works of our author have hitherto defied the acumen of critics. It would be mere empiricism for me to attempt an original classification in the face of questions which even experts have been unable to determine.

If we bear in mind, however, a few guiding facts, we shall see that difficulties are less than might appear, assuming our object to be a practical one. (1.) Only *four* of these essays were written against Orthodoxy; (2.) *five* more are reckoned as wholly uncertain, which amounts to saying that they are not positively heretical. (3.) Again, *five* are colourless, as to Montanism, and hence should be reputed Orthodox. (4.) Of others, written after the influences of Montanism had, more or less, tainted his doctrine, the whole are yet valuable and some are noble defences of the Catholic Faith. (5.) Finally eight or ten of his treatises were written while he was a Catholic, and are precious contributions to the testimony of the Primitive Church.

From these facts, we may readily conclude that the mass of Tertullian's writings is Orthodox. Some of them are to be read with caution; others, again, must be rejected for their heresy; but yet all are most instructive historically, and as defining even by errors "the faith once delivered to the Saints." I propose to note those which require caution as we pass them in review. Those written against the Church are classed by themselves, at the end of the list, and all the rest may be read with confidence. A most interesting inquiry arises in connection with the quotations from Scripture to be found in our author. Did a Latin version exist in his day, or does he translate from the Greek of the New Testament and the LXX? A paradoxical writer (Semler) contends that Tertullian "never used a Greek MS." (see Kaye, p. 106.) But Tertullian's rugged Latin betrays everywhere his familiarity with Greek idioms and forms of thought. He wrote, also, in Greek, and there is no reason to doubt that he knew the Greek Scriptures primarily, if he knew any Greek whatever. Possibly we owe to Tertullian the *primordia* of the Old African Latin Versions, some of which seem to have contained the disputed text I. John v. 7; of which more when we come to the *Praxeas*. For the present in the absence of definite evidence we must infer that Tertullian usually translated from the LXX, and from the originals of the New Testament. But Mosheim thinks the progress of the Gospel in the West was now facilitated by the existence of Latin Versions. Observe, also, Kaye's important note, p. 293, and his reference to Lardner, *Cred.* xxvii. 19.

II.

(Address to Magistrates, cap. i., p. 17.)

The Apology comes first in order, on logical grounds. It is classed with our author's orthodox works by Neander, and pronounced colourless by Kaye. It is the noblest of his

---

[1] Kaye, p. 36. Also, p. 8, *supra*.

productions in its purpose and spirit, and it falls in with the Primitive System of Apologetics. I have placed next in order to it several treatises, mostly unblemished, which are of the same character; which defend the cause of Christians against Paganism, against Gentile Philosophy, and against Judaism; closing this portion by the two books *Ad Nationes*, which may be regarded as a recapitulation of the author's arguments, especially those to be found in the Apology. In these successive works, as compared with those of Justin Martyr, we obtain a fair view of the progressive relations of the Church with the Roman Empire and with divers antagonistic systems in the East and West.

III.

(History of Christians, cap. ii., p. 18.)

The following Chronological outline borrowed from the Benedictines and from Bishop Kaye, will prove serviceable here.[1]

		A.D.
Tertullian born (*circa*)		150.
" converted (*surmise*)		185.
" married (*say*)		186.
" ordained presbyter (*circa*)		192.
" lapsed (*circa*)		200.
" deceased (extreme surmise)		240.

The Imperial history of his period may be thus arranged:

	A.D.
Birth of Caracalla	188.
" Geta	189.
Reign of Severus	193.
Defeat of Niger	195.
Caracalla made a *Cæsar*	196.
Capture of Byzantium	196.
Defeat of Albinus	197.
Geta made a *Cæsar*	198.
Caracalla called *Augustus*	198.
Caracalla associated in the Empire	198.
War against the Parthians	198.
Severus returns from the war	203.
Celebration of the Secular Games	204.
Plautianus put to death (*circa*)	205.
Geta called *Augustus*	208.
War in Britain	208.
Wall of Severus	210.
Death of Severus	211.

IV.

(Tiberius, capp. v. and xxiv., pp. 22 and 35.)

A fair examination of what has been said on this subject, *pro* and *con*, may be found in Kaye's *Tertullian*,[2] pp. 102–105. In his abundant candour this author leans to the doubters, but in stating the case he seems to me to fortify the position of Lardner and Mosheim. What the brutal Tiberius may have thought or done with respect to Pilate's report concerning the holy victim of his judicial injustice is of little importance to the believer. Nevertheless, as matter of history it deserves attention. Great stress is to be placed on the fact that Tertullian was probably a jurisconsult, familiar with the Roman archives, and influenced by

[1] Kaye (following *L'Art de verifier les Dates*) pp. 11 and 456.
[2] My references are to the Third Edition, London, Rivingtons, 1845.

them in his own acceptance of Divine Truth. It is not supposable that such a man would have hazarded his bold appeal to the records, in remonstrating with the Senate and in the very faces of the Emperor and his colleagues, had he not known that the evidence was irrefragable.

V.

The darkness at the Crucifixion, cap. xxi., p. 35.)

Kaye disappoints us (p. 150) in his slight notice of this most interesting subject With-out attempting to discuss the story of Phlegon and other points which afford Gibbon an opportunity for misplaced sneering, such as even a Pilate would have rebuked, while it may be well to recall the exposition of Milman,[1] at the close of Gibbon's fifteenth chapter, I must express my own preference for another view. This will be found candidly summed up and stated, in the Speaker's Commentary, in the concise note on St. Matt., xxvii. 45.

VI.

(Numbers of the Faithful, cap. xxxvii., p. 45.)

Kaye, as usual, gives this vexed question a candid survey.[2] Making all allowances, however, I accept the conjecture of some reputable authorities, that there were 2,000,000 of Christians, in the bounds of the Roman Empire at the close of the Second Century. So mightily grew the testimony of Jesus and prevailed. When we reflect that only a century intervened between the times of Tertullian and the conversion of the Roman Emperor, it is not easy to regard our author's language as merely that of fervid genius and of rhetorical hyperbole. He could not have ventured upon exaggeration without courting scorn as well as defeat. What he affirms is probable in the nature of the case. Were it otherwise, then the conditions, which, in a single century rendered it possible for Constantine to effect the greatest revolution in mind and manners that has ever been known among men, would be a miracle compared with which that of his alleged Vision of the Cross sinks into insignificance. To this subject it will be necessary to recur hereafter.

VII.

(Christian usages, cap. xxxix., p. 46.)

A candid review of the matters discussed in this chapter will be found in Kaye (pp. 146, 209.) The important fact is there clearly stated that " the primitive Christians scrupulously complied with the decree pronounced by the Apostles at Jerusalem in abstaining from things strangled and from blood " (Acts xv. 20). On this subject consult the references given in the Speaker's Commentary, *ad locum*. The Greeks, to their honour, still maintain this prohibition, but St. Augustine's great authority relaxed the Western scruples on this matter, for he regarded it is a decree of temporary obligation, while the Hebrew and Gentile Christians were in peril of misunderstanding and estrangement.[3]

On the important question as to the cessation of miracles Kaye takes a somewhat original position. But see his interesting discussion and that of the late Professor Hey, in Kaye's *Tertullian*, pp. 80–102, 151–161. I do not think writers on these subjects have sufficiently distinguished between *miracles* properly so called, and *providences* vouchsafed in answer to prayer. There was no *miracle* in the case of the Thundering Legion, assuming the story to be true; and I dare to affirm that marked answers to prayer, by *providential interpositions*,

---

[1] In his edition of The Decline and Fall, Vol. I., p. 589, American reprint.
[2] pp. 85–88.
[3] Ep. *ad Faust*. xxxii. 13. and see Conybeare and Howson.

but wholly distinct from miraculous agencies, have never ceased among those who "ask in the Son's Name." Such interpositions are often *preternatural* only; that is, they economize certain powers which, though natural in themselves, lie outside of the System of Nature with which we happen to be familiar. This distinction has been overlooked.

VIII.

(Multitudes, cap. xl., p. 47.)

Note the words—"*multitudes* to a single beast." Can it be possible that Tertullian would use such language to the magistrates, if he knew that such sentences were of rare occurrence? The disposition of our times to *minimize* the persecutions of our Christian forefathers calls upon us to note such references, all the more important because occurring *obiter* and mentioned as notorious. Note also, the closing chapter of this Apology, and reference to the outcries of the populace, in Cap. xxxv.[1] See admirable remarks on the benefits derived by the Church from the sufferings of Christian martyrs, with direct reference to Tertullian, Wordsworth, *Church Hist. to Council of Nicæa*, cap. xxiv., p.374.

IX.

(Christian manners, cap. xlii., p. 49.)

A study of the manners of Christians, in the Ante-Nicene Age, as sketched by the unsparing hand of Tertullian, will convince any unprejudiced mind of the mighty power of the Holy Ghost, in framing such characters out of heathen originals. When, under Montanistic influences our severely ascetic author complains of the Church's corruptions, and turns inside-out the whole estate of the faithful, we see all that can be pressed on the other side; but, this very important chapter must be borne in mind, together with the closing sentence of chap. xliv., as evidence that whatever might be said by a rigid disciplinarian, the Church, *as compared with* our day, was still a living embodiment of Philip, iv. 8.

X.

(Paradise, cap. xlvii., p. 52.)

See Kaye, p. 248. Our author seems not always consistent with himself in his references to the Places of departed spirits. Kaye thinks he identifies Paradise with the Heaven of the Most High, in one place (the *De Exhort. Cast.*, xiii.) where he probably confuses the Apostle's ideas, in Galat. v., 12, and Ephes. v., 5. *Commonly*, however, though he is not consistent with himself, this would be his scheme:—

1. The *Inferi*, or *Hades*, where the soul of Dives was in one continent and that of Lazarus in another, with a gulf between. Our author places "Abraham's bosom" in Hades.
2. *Paradise.* In Hades, but in a superior and more glorious region. This more blessed abode was opened to the souls of the martyrs and other greater saints, at our Lord's descent into the place of the dead. After the General Resurrection and Judgment, there remain:
1. *Gehenna*, for the lost, prepared for the devil and his angels.
2. The *Heaven of Heavens*, the eternal abode of the righteous, in the vision of the Lord and His Eternal Joy.

Tertullian's variations on this subject will force us to recur to it hereafter; but, here it may be noted that the confusions of Latin Christianity received their character in this particular, from the genius of our author. Augustine caught from him a certain indecision

---

[1] Compare Kaye on Mosheim, p. 107.

about the terms and places connected with the state of the departed which has continued, to this day, to perplex theologians in the West. Taking advantage of such confusions, the stupendous Roman system of "Purgatory" was fabricated in the middle ages; but the Greeks never accepted it, and it differs fundamentally from what the earlier Latin Fathers, including Tertullian, have given us as speculations.

XI.

(The Leo and the Leno, cap. l., p. 55.)

Here we find the alliterative and epigrammatic genius of Tertullian anticipating a similar poetic charm in Augustine. The Christian maid or matron preferred the *Leo* to the *leno;* to be devoured rather than to be debauched. Our author wrests a tribute to the chastity of Christian women from the cruelty of their judges, who recognizing this fact, were accustomed as a refinement of their injustice to give sentence against them, refusing the mercy of a horrible death, by committing them to the ravisher: "damnando Christianam *ad lenonem* potius quam *ad leonem."*

XII.

(The Seed of the Church, cap. l., p. 55.)

Kaye has devoted a number of his pages [1] to the elucidation of this subject, not only showing the constancy of the martyrs, but illustrating the fact that Christians, like St. Paul, were forced to "die daily," even when they were not subjected to the fiery trial. He who confessed himself a Christian made himself a social outcast. All manner of outrages and wrongs could be committed against him with impunity. Rich men, who had joined themselves to Christ,[2] were forced to accept "the spoiling of their goods." Brothers denounced brothers, and husbands their wives; "a man's foes were they of his own household." But the Church triumphed through suffering, and "out of weakness was made strong."

---

[1] pp. 129-140.   [2] Even under Commodus, vol. ii. p. 598, this series

ON IDOLATRY.

[TRANSLATED BY THE REV. S. THELWALL.]

CHAP. I.—WIDE SCOPE OF THE WORD IDOLATRY.

THE principal crime of the human race, the highest guilt charged upon the world, the whole procuring cause of judgment, is idolatry.[1] For, although each single fault retains its own proper feature, although it is destined to judgment under its own proper name also, yet it is marked off under the *general* account of idolatry. Set aside names, examine works, the idolater is likewise a murderer. Do you inquire whom he has slain? If it contributes ought to the aggravation of the indictment, no stranger nor personal enemy, but his own self. By what snares? Those of his error. By what weapon? The offence done to God. By how many blows? As many as are his idolatries. He who affirms that the idolater *perishes not,*[2] will affirm that the idolater has not committed murder. Further, you may recognize in the same crime[3] *adultery* and *fornication;* for he who serves false gods is doubtless an *adulterer*[4] of truth, because all falsehood is adultery. So, too, he is sunk in fornication. For who that is a fellow-worker with unclean spirits, does not stalk in general pollution and fornication? And thus it is that the Holy Scriptures[5] use the designation of fornication in their upbraiding of idolatry.

---

[1] [This solemn sentence vindicates the place I have given to the *De Idololatria* in the order adopted for this volume. After this and the Apology come three treatises confirming its positions, and vindicating the principles of Christians in conflict with Idolatry, the great generic crime of a world lying in wickedness. These three are the *De Spectaculis*, the *De Corona* and the *Ad Scapulam.* The *De Spectaculis* was written after this treatise, in which indeed it is mentioned,* but logically it follows, illustrates and enforces it. Hence my practical plan: which will be concluded by a scheme (conjectural in part) of chronological order in which precision is affirmed by all critics to be impossible, but, by which we may reach approximate accuracy, with great advantage. The *De Idololatria* is free from Montanism. But see Kaye, p. xvi.]

[2] Lit., "has not perished," as if the perishing were already complete; as, of course, it is *judicially* as soon as the guilt is incurred, though not *actually.*

[3] i.e., in idolatry.

[4] A play on the word: we should say, "an *adulterator.*"

[5] Oehler refers to Ezek. xxiii.; but many other references might be given—in the Pentateuch and Psalms, for instance.

* Cap. xiii.

The essence of *fraud,* I take it, is, that any should seize what is another's, or refuse to another his due; and, of course, fraud done toward *man* is a name of greatest crime. Well, but idolatry does fraud to God, by refusing to Him, and conferring on others, His honours; so that to fraud it also conjoins *contumely.* But if fraud, just as much as fornication and adultery, entails death, then, in these cases, equally with the former, idolatry stands unacquitted of the impeachment of murder. After such crimes, so pernicious, so devouring of salvation, all other crimes also, after some manner, and separately disposed in order, find their own essence represented in idolatry. In it also are the *concupiscences* of the world. For what solemnity of idolatry is without the circumstance of dress and ornament? In it are *lasciviousnesses* and *drunkennesses;* since it is, for the most part, for the sake of food, and stomach, and appetite, that these solemnities are frequented. In it is *unrighteousness.* For what more unrighteous than it, which knows not the Father of righteousness? In it also is *vanity,* since its whole system is vain. In it is *mendacity,* for its whole substance is false. Thus it comes to pass, that in idolatry all crimes are detected, and in all crimes idolatry. Even otherwise, since all faults savour of opposition to God, and there is nothing which savours of opposition to God which is not assigned to demons and unclean spirits, whose property idols are; doubtless, whoever commits a fault is chargeable with idolatry, for he does that which pertains to the proprietors of idols.

CHAP. II.—IDOLATRY IN ITS MORE LIMITED SENSE. ITS COPIOUSNESS.

But let the universal names of crimes withdraw to the specialities of their own works; let idolatry remain in that which it is itself. Sufficient to itself is a name so inimical to God, a substance of crime so copious, which reaches forth so many branches, diffuses so many veins, that from this *name*, for the greatest part, is drawn the material of all the modes in which the expansiveness of idolatry has to be foreguarded against by us, since in manifold wise it subverts the servants of God ; and this not only when unperceived, but also when cloaked over. Most men simply regard idolatry as to be interpreted in these senses alone, viz.: if one burn incense, or immolate *a victim*, or give a sacrificial banquet, or be bound to some sacred functions or priesthoods ; just as if one were to regard adultery as to be accounted in kisses, and in embraces, and in actual fleshly contact ; or murder as to be reckoned only in the shedding forth of blood, and in the actual taking away of life. But how far wider an extent the Lord assigns to those crimes we are sure : when He defines adultery *to consist* even in concupiscence,[1] " if one shall have cast an eye lustfully on," and stirred his soul with immodest commotion ; when He judges murder[2] *to consist* even in a word of curse or of reproach, and in every impulse of anger, and in the neglect of charity toward a brother : just as John teaches,[3] that he who hates his brother is a murderer. Else, both the devil's ingenuity in malice, and God the Lord's in the Discipline by which He fortifies us against the devil's depths,[4] would have but limited scope, if we were judged only in such faults as even the heathen nations have decreed punishable. How will our " righteousness abound above that of the Scribes and Pharisees," as the Lord has prescribed,[5] unless we shall have seen through the abundance of that adversary quality, that is, of *un*righteousness ? But if the head of unrighteousness is idolatry, the first point is, that we be fore-fortified against the abundance of idolatry, while we recognise it not only in its palpable manifestations.

CHAP. III.—IDOLATRY: ORIGIN AND MEANING OF THE NAME.

Idol in ancient times there was none. Before the artificers of this monstrosity had bubbled into being,[6] temples stood solitary and shrines empty, just as to the present day in some places traces of the ancient practice remain permanently. Yet idolatry used to be practised, not under that name, but in that function ; for even at this day it can be prac-

tised outside a temple, and without an idol. But when the devil introduced into the world artificers of statues and of images, and of every kind of likenesses, that former rude business of human disaster attained from idols both a name and a development. Thenceforward every art which in any way produces an idol instantly became a fount of idolatry. For it makes no difference whether a moulder cast, or a carver grave, or an embroiderer weave *the idol;* because neither is it a question of material, whether an idol be formed of gypsum, or of colors, or of stone, or of bronze,[7] or of silver, or of thread. For since even without an idol idolatry is committed, when the idol is there it makes no difference of what kind it be, of what material, or what shape ; lest any should think *that* only to be held an idol which is consecrated in human shape. To establish this point, the interpretation of the word is requisite. *Eidŏs*, in Greek, signifies *form ; eidŏlon*, derived diminutively from that, by an equivalent process in our language, makes *formling*.[8] Every *form* or *formling*, therefore, claims to be called an *idol*. Hence *idolatry* is " all attendance and service about every idol." Hence also, every artificer of an idol is guilty of one and the same crime,[9] unless, the People[10] which consecrated for itself the likeness of a calf, and not of a man, fell short of incurring the guilt of idolatry.[11]

CHAP. IV.—IDOLS NOT TO BE MADE, MUCH LESS WORSHIPPED. IDOLS AND IDOL-MAKERS IN THE SAME CATEGORY.

God prohibits an idol as much to be *made* as to be *worshipped*. In so far as the *making* what may be worshipped is the prior act, so far is the prohibition to *make* (if the worship is unlawful) the prior prohibition. For this cause—the eradicating, namely, of the material of idolatry—the divine law proclaims, " Thou shalt make no idol ;"[12] and by conjoining, " Nor a similitude of the things which are in the heaven, and which are in the earth, and which are in the sea," has interdicted the servants of God from acts of that kind all the universe over. Enoch had preceded, predicting that " the demons, and the spirits of the angelic apostates,[13] would turn into idola-

---

1 Matt. v. 28.
2 Matt. v. 22.
3 1 John, iii. 15.
4 Rev. ii. 24.
5 Matt. v. 20.
6 " Boiled out," " bubbled out."

7 Or, brass.
8 i.e., a little form.
9 Idolatry, namely.
10 [Capitalized to mark its emphatic sense, i.e., the People of God =the Jews.]
11 See Ex. xxxii.; and compare 1 Cor. x. 7, where the latter part of Ex. xxxii. 6 is quoted.
12 Lev. xxvi. 1 ; Ex. xx. 4 ; Deut. v. 8. It must of course be borne in mind that Tertullian has defined the meaning of the word *idol* in the former chapter, and speaks with reference to that definition.
13 Compare *de Oratione*, c. 23, and *de Virg. Vel.* c. 7.

try all the elements, all the garniture of the universe, all things contained in the heaven, in the sea, in the earth, that they might be consecrated as God, in opposition to God." All things, therefore, does human error worship, except the Founder of all Himself. The images of those things are idols; the consecration of the images is idolatry. Whatever guilt idolatry incurs, must necessarily be imputed to every artificer of every idol. In short, the same Enoch fore-condemns in general menace both idol-worshippers and idol-makers together. And again: "I swear to you, sinners, that against the day of perdition of blood [1] repentance is being prepared. Ye who serve stones, and ye who make images of gold, and silver, and wood, and stones and clay, and serve phantoms, and demons, and spirits in fanes, [2] and all errors not according to knowledge, shall find no help from them." But Isaiah [3] says, "Ye are witnesses whether there is a God except Me." "And they who mould and carve out at that time were not : all vain ! who do that which liketh them, which shall not profit them !" And that whole ensuing discourse sets a ban as well on the artificers as the worshippers : the close of which is, "Learn that their heart is ashes and earth, and that none can free his own soul." In which sentence David equally includes the makers too. "Such," says he, "let them become who make them." [4] And why should I, a man of limited memory, suggest anything further? Why recall anything more from the Scriptures? As if either the voice of the Holy Spirit were not sufficient ; or else any further deliberation were needful, whether the Lord cursed and condemned by priority the *artificers* of those things, of which He curses and condemns the *worshippers !*

CHAP. V.[5]—SUNDRY OBJECTIONS OR EXCUSES
DEALT WITH.

We will certainly take more pains in answering the excuses of artificers of this kind, who ought never to be admitted into the house of God, if any have a knowledge of that Discipline.[6] To begin with, that speech, wont

to be cast in our teeth, "I have nothing else whereby to live," may be more severely retorted, "You have, then, whereby to live? If by your own laws, what have you to do with God?"[7] Then, as to the argument they have the hardihood to bring even from the Scriptures, "that the apostle has said, 'As each has been found, so let him persevere.'"[8] We may all, therefore, persevere in *sins*, as the result of *that* interpretation ! for there is not any one of us who has not been found as a *sinner*, since no other cause was the source of Christ's descent than that of setting *sinners* free. Again, they say the same apostle has left a precept, according to his own example, "That each one work with his own hands for a living."[9] If this precept is maintained in respect to *all* hands, I believe even the bath-thieves[10] live by their hands, and robbers themselves gain the means to live by their hands ; forgers, again, execute their evil handwritings, not of course with their feet, but hands ; actors, however, achieve a livelihood not with hands alone, but with their entire limbs. Let the Church, therefore, stand open to *all* who are supported by their hands and by their own work ; if there is no exception of arts which the Discipline of God receives not. But some one says, in opposition to our proposition of "similitude being interdicted," "Why, then, did Moses in the desert make a likeness of a serpent out of bronze?" The figures, which used to be laid as a groundwork for some secret future dispensation, not with a view to the repeal of the law, but as a type of their own final cause, stand in a class by themselves. Otherwise, if we should interpret these things as the adversaries of the law do, do we, too, as the Marcionites do, ascribe inconsistency to the Almighty, whom *they*[11] in this manner destroy as being mutable, while in one place He forbids, in another commands? But if any feigns ignorance of the fact that that effigy of the serpent of bronze, after the manner of one uphung, denoted the shape of the Lord's cross,[12] which

---

[1] "Sanguinis perditionis :" such is the reading of Oehler and others. If it be correct, probably the phrase "perdition of blood" must be taken as equivalent to "bloody perdition," after the Hebrew fashion. Compare, for similar instances, 2 Sam. xvi. 7 ; Ps. v. 6, xxvi. 9, lv. 23; Ezek. xxii. 2, with the marginal readings. But Fr. Junius would read, "Of blood *and* of perdition"—sanguinis et perditionis. Oehler's own interpretation of the reading he gives —"blood-shedding"—appears unsatisfactory.
[2] "In fanis." This is Oehler's reading on conjecture. Other readings are—infamis, infamibus, insanis, infernis.
[3] Isa. xliv. 8 et seqq.
[4] Ps. cxv. 8. In our version, "They that make them are like unto them." Tertullian again agrees with the LXX.
[5] Cf. chaps. viii. and xii.
[6] i.e., the Discipline of the house of God, the Church. Oehler reads, "*eam* disciplinam," and takes the meaning to be that no

artificer of this class should be admitted into the Church, if he applies for admittance, with a knowledge of the law of God referred to in the former chapters, yet persisting in his unlawful craft. Fr. Junius would read, "*ejus* disciplinam."
[7] i.e., If laws of your own, and not the will and law of God, are the source and means of your life, you owe no thanks and no obedience to God, and therefore need not to seek admittance into His house (Oehler).
[8] 1 Cor. vii. 20. In Eng. ver., "Let every man abide in the same calling wherein he was called."
[9] 1 Thess. iv. 11 ; 2 Thess. iii. 6–12.
[10] i.e., thieves who frequented the public baths, which were a favorite resort at Rome.
[11] The Marcionites.
[12] [The argument amounts to this, that *symbols* were not *idols :* yet even so, God only could ordain *symbols* that were innocent. The *Nehushtan* of King Hezekiah teaches us the "peril of Idolatry" (2 Kings, xviii. 4) and that even a divine symbol may be destroyed justly if it be turned to a violation of the Second Commandment.]

was to free us from serpents—that is, from
the devil's angels—while, through itself, it
hanged up the devil slain ; or whatever other
exposition of that figure has been revealed to
worthier men [1] no matter, provided we remember the apostle affirms that all things
happened at that time to the People [2] figuratively. [3] It is enough that the same God, as
by law He forbade the making of similitude,
did, by the extraordinary precept in the case
of the serpent, interdict similitude. [4] If you
reverence the same God, you have His law,
"Thou shalt make no similitude." [5] If you
look back, too, to the precept enjoining the
subsequently made similitude, do you, too,
imitate Moses : make not any likeness in opposition to the law, unless to *you*, too, God
have bidden it. [6]

CHAP. VI.—IDOLATRY CONDEMNED BY BAP-
TISM. TO MAKE AN IDOL IS, IN FACT, TO
WORSHIP IT.

If no law of God had prohibited idols to be
made by us ; if no voice of the Holy Spirit
uttered general menace no less against the
makers than the worshippers of idols ; from
our sacrament itself we would draw our interpretation that arts of that kind are opposed
to the faith. For how have we *renounced* the
devil and his angels, if we *make* them ? What
divorce have we declared from them, I say
not *with* whom, but *dependent on* whom, we
live ? What discord have we entered into with
those to whom we are under obligation for the
sake of our maintenance ? Can you have denied with the tongue what with the hand you
confess ? unmake by word what by deed you
make ? preach one God, you who make so
many ? preach the true God, you who make
false ones ? "I *make*," says one, "but I
worship not ;" as if there were some cause
for which he dare not *worship*, besides that
for which he ought not also to *make*,—the
offence done to God, namely, in either case.
Nay, you who *make*, that they may be able
to be worshipped, *do* worship ; and you worship, not with the spirit of some worthless

perfume, but with your own; nor at the expense of a beast's soul, but of your own. To
them you immolate your ingenuity; to them
you make your sweat a libation; to them you
kindle the torch of your forethought. More
are you to them than a priest, since it is by
your means they *have* a priest ; *your* diligence
is *their* divinity. [7] Do you affirm that you
worship not what you *make ?* Ah ! but *they*
affirm not so, to whom you slay this fatter,
more precious and greater victim, your salvation.

CHAP. VII.—GRIEF OF THE FAITHFUL AT THE
ADMISSION OF IDOL-MAKERS INTO THE
CHURCH; NAY, EVEN INTO THE MINISTRY.

A whole day the zeal of faith will direct its
pleadings to this quarter : bewailing that a
Christian should come from idols into the
Church; should come from an adversary work-
shop into the house of God; should raise to
God the Father hands which are the mothers
of idols; should pray to God with the hands
which, out of doors, are prayed to in opposition to God; should apply to the Lord's
body those hands which confer bodies on
demons. Nor is this sufficient. Grant that
it be a small matter, if from other hands they
receive what they contaminate; but even those
very hands deliver to others what they have
contaminated. Idol-artificers are chosen even
into the ecclesiastical order. Oh wickedness !
Once did the Jews lay hands on Christ ;
these mangle His body daily. Oh hands to
be cut off ! Now let the saying, "If thy hand
make thee do evil, amputate it," [8] see to it
whether it were uttered by way of similitude
merely. What hands more to be amputated
than those in which scandal is done to the
Lord's body ?

CHAP. VIII.—OTHER ARTS MADE SUBSERVIENT
TO IDOLATRY. LAWFUL MEANS OF GAINING
A LIVELIHOOD ABUNDANT.

There are also other species of very many
arts which, although they extend not to the
making of idols, yet, with the same criminality, *furnish the adjuncts* without which
idols have no power. For it matters not
whether you erect or equip: if you have em-
bellished his temple, altar, or niche ; if you
have pressed out gold-leaf, or have wrought
his insignia, or even his house : work of that
kind, which confers not *shape*, but *authority*,
is more important. If the necessity of main-

[1] [On which see Dr. Smith, *Dict. of the Bible, ad vocem* "Serpent."]
[2] i.e., the *Jewish* people, who are generally meant by the expression "the People" in the singular number in Scripture. We
shall endeavour to mark that distinction by writing the word, as
here, with a capital.
[3] See 1 Cor. x. 6, 11.
[4] On the principle that the exception proves the rule. As Oehler
explains it : "By the fact of the extraordinary precept in that particular case, God gave an indication that likeness-making had before been forbidden and interdicted by Him."
[5] Ex. xx. 4, etc. [The absurd "brazen serpent" which I have
seen in the Church of St. Ambrose, in Milan, is with brazen hardihood affirmed to be the identical serpent which Moses lifted up in
the wilderness. But it lacks all *symbolic* character, as it is not
set upon a pole nor in any way fitted to a cross. It greatly resembles a *vane* set upon a pivot.]
[6] [Elucidation I.]

[7] i.e., Unless you *made* them, they would not *exist*, and therefore [would not be regarded as divinities; therefore] your diligence
gives them their divinity.
[8] Matt. xviii. 8.

tenance [1] is urged so much, the arts have other species withal to afford means of livelihood, without outstepping the path of discipline, that is, without the confiction of an idol. The plasterer knows both how to mend roofs, and lay on stuccoes, and polish a cistern, and trace ogives, and draw in relief on party-walls many other ornaments beside likenesses. The painter, too, the marble mason, the bronze-worker, and every graver whatever, knows expansions [2] of his own art, of course much easier of execution. For how much more easily does he who delineates a statue overlay a side-board ! [3] How much sooner does he who carves a Mars out of a lime-tree, fasten together a chest! No art but is either mother or kins-woman of some neighbour [4] art: nothing is independent of its neighbour. The veins of the arts are many as are the concupiscences of men. " But there is difference in wages and the rewards of handicraft;" therefore there is difference, too, in the labour required. Smaller wages are compensated by more frequent earning. How many are the party-walls which require statues ? How many the temples and shrines which are built for idols ? But houses, and official residences, and baths, and tenements, how many are they ? Shoe- and slipper-gilding is daily work ; not so the gilding of Mercury and Serapis. Let that suffice for the gain [5] of handicrafts. Luxury and ostentation have more votaries than all superstition. Ostentation will require dishes and cups more easily than superstition. Luxury deals in wreaths, also, more than ceremony. When, therefore, we urge men generally to such kinds of handicrafts as do not come in contact with an idol indeed, and with the things which are appropriate to an idol ; since, moreover, the things which are common to idols are often common to men too ; of this also we ought to beware, that nothing be, with our knowledge, demanded by any person from our idols' service. For if we shall have made that concession, and shall not have had recourse to the remedies so often used, I think we are not free of the contagion of idolatry, we whose (not unwitting) hands [6] are found busied in the tendence, or in the honour and service, of demons.

CHAP. IX.—PROFESSIONS OF SOME KINDS ALLIED TO IDOLATRY. OF ASTROLOGY IN PARTICULAR.

We observe among the arts [7] also some professions liable to the charge of idolatry. Of astrologers there should be no speaking even ; [8] but since one in these days has challenged us, defending on his own behalf perseverance in that profession, I will use a few words. I allege not that he honours idols, whose names he has inscribed on the heaven, [9] to whom he has attributed all God's power; because men, presuming that we are disposed of by the immutable arbitrament of the stars, think on that account that God is not to be sought after. One proposition I lay down: that those angels, the deserters from God, the lovers of women, [10] were likewise the discoverers of this curious art, on that account also condemned by God. Oh divine sentence, reaching even unto the earth in its vigour, whereto the unwitting render testimony! The astrologers are expelled just like their angels. The city and Italy are interdicted to the astrologers, just as heaven to their angels. [11] There is the same penalty of exclusion for disciples and masters. " But Magi and astrologers came from the east." [12] We know the mutual alliance of magic and astrology. The interpreters of the stars, then, were the first to announce Christ's birth the first to present Him " gifts." By this bond, [must] I imagine, they put Christ under obligation to themselves ? What then ? Shall therefore the religion of those Magi act as patron now also to astrologers ? Astrology now-a-days, forsooth, treats of Christ—is the science of the stars of Christ ; not of Saturn, or Mars, and whomsoever else out of the same class of the dead [13] it pays observance to and preaches ? But, however, that science has been allowed until the Gospel, in order that after Christ's birth no one should thenceforward interpret any one's nativity by the heaven. For they therefore offered to the then infant Lord that frankincense and myrrh and gold, to be, as it were, the close of worldly [14] sacrifice and glory, which Christ was

---

[1] See chaps. v. and xii.
[2] See chap. ii., " The *expansiveness* of idolatry."
[3] Abacum. The word has various meanings ; but this, perhaps, is its most general use : as, for instance, in Horace and Juvenal.
[4] Alterius = ἑτέρου which in the New Testament is = to " neighbour " in Rom. xiii. 8, etc. [Our author must have borne in mind Cicero's beautiful words—" Etenim omnes artes quæ ad humanitatem pertinent habent quoddam commune vinculum," etc. *Pro Archia*, i. tom. x. p. 10. *Ed.* Paris, 1817.]
[5] Quæstum. Another reading is " questum," which would require us to translate " plaint."

[6] " Quorum manus non ignorantium," i.e., " the hands of whom not unwitting;" which may be rendered as above, because in English, as in the Latin, the adjective " unwitting " belongs to the " whose," not to the " hands."
[7] " Ars " in Latin is very generally used to mean " a *scientific* art." [See Titus iii. 14. English margin.]
[8] See Eph. v. 11, 12, and similar passages.
[9] i.e., by naming the stars after them.
[10] Comp. chap. iv., and the references there given. The idea seems founded on an ancient reading found in the Codex Alexandrinus of the LXX. in Gen. vi. 2, " angels of God," for " sons of God."
[11] See Tac. *Ann.* ii. 31, etc. (Oehler.)
[12] See Matt. ii.
[13] Because the names of the heathen divinities, which used to be given to the stars, were in many cases only names of dead men deified.
[14] Or, heathenish.

about to do away. What, then? The dream—
sent, doubtless, of the will of God—suggested
to the same Magi, namely, that they should
go home, but by another way, not that by
which they came. It means this : that they
should not walk in their ancient path.[1] Not
that Herod should not pursue them, who in
fact did not pursue them; unwitting even that
they had departed *by another way*, since he was
withal unwitting by what way they *came*. Just
so we ought to understand by it the right Way
and Discipline. And so the precept was
rather, that thenceforward they should *walk
otherwise*. So, too, that other species of magic
which operates by miracles, emulous even in
opposition to Moses,[2] tried God's patience
until the Gospel. For thenceforward Simon
Magus, just turned believer, (since he was
still thinking somewhat of his juggling sect;
to wit, that among the miracles of his profession he might buy even the gift of the
Holy Spirit through imposition of hands) was
cursed by the apostles, and ejected from the
faith.[3] Both he and that other magician, who
was with Sergius Paulus, (since he began opposing himself to the same apostles) was
mulcted with loss of eyes.[4] The same fate, I
believe, would astrologers, too, have met, if
any had fallen in the way of the apostles.
But yet, when magic is punished, of which
astrology is a species, of course the species
is condemned in the genus. After the
Gospel, you will nowhere find either sophists,
Chaldeans, enchanters, diviners, or magicians,
except as clearly punished. "Where is the
wise, where the grammarian, where the dis-
puter of this age? Hath not God made foolish
the wisdom of this age?"[5] You know nothing, astrologer, if you know not that you
should be a Christian. If you did know it,
you ought to have known this also, that you
should have nothing more to do with that profession of yours which, of itself, fore-chants
the climacterics of others, and might instruct
you of its own danger. There is no part nor
lot for you in that system of yours.[6] He cannot hope for the kingdom of the heavens,
whose finger or wand abuses[7] the heaven.

CHAP. X.—OF SCHOOLMASTERS AND THEIR DIF-
FICULTIES.

Moreover, we must inquire likewise touching schoolmasters ; nor only of them, but

also all other professors of literature. Nay,
on the contrary, we must not doubt that they
are in affinity with manifold idolatry : *first*, in
that it is necessary for them to preach the
gods of the nations, to express their names,
genealogies, honourable distinctions, all and
singular ; and *further*, to observe the solemnities and festivals of the same, as of them
by whose means they compute their revenues. What schoolmaster, without a table
of the seven idols,[8] will yet frequent the Quin-
quatria? The very first payment of every
pupil he consecrates both to the honour and
to the name of Minerva ; so that, even though
he be not said "to eat of that which is sacrificed to idols"[9] *nominally* (not being dedicated
to any particular idol), he is shunned as an
idolater. What less of defilement does he
incur on that ground,[10] than a business brings
which, both nominally and virtually, is consecrated publicly to an idol? The Minervalia
are as much Minerva's, as the Saturnalia
Saturn's ; Saturn's, which must necessarily
be celebrated even by little slaves at the time
of the Saturnalia. New-year's gifts likewise
must be caught at, and the Septimontium
kept; and all the presents of Midwinter and
the feast of Dear Kinsmanship must be exacted ; the schools must be wreathed with
flowers ; the flamens' wives and the ædiles
sacrifice; the school is honoured on the appointed holy-days. The same thing takes
place on an idol's birthday ; every pomp of
the devil is frequented. Who will think that
these things are befitting to a Christian master,[11] unless *it be he* who shall think them
suitable likewise to one who is not a master?
We know it may be said, "If teaching literature is not lawful to God's servants, neither
will learning be likewise ;" and, "How could
one be trained unto ordinary human intelligence, or unto any sense or action whatever,
since literature is the means of training for
all life ? How do we repudiate secular studies,
without which divine studies cannot be pursued ?" Let us see, then, the necessity of
literary erudition ; let us reflect that partly
it cannot be admitted, partly cannot be avoided. Learning literature is allowable for believers, rather than teaching ; for the principle of learning and of teaching is different.
If a believer teach literature, while he is teaching doubtless he commends, while he delivers he affirms, while he recalls he bears
testimony to, the praises of idols interspersed

[1] Or, sect.
[2] See Ex. vii., viii., and comp. 2 Tim. iii. 8.
[3] See Acts viii. 9–24.
[4] See Acts xiii. 6–11.
[5] 1 Cor. i. 20.
[6] See Acts viii. 21.
[7] See 1 Cor. vii. 31, "They that use this world as not abusing it." The astrologer *abuses* the heavens by putting the heavenly bodies to a sinful use.

[8] i.e., the seven planets.
[9] See 1 Cor. viii. 10.
[10] i.e., because "he does not *nominally* eat," etc.
[11] [Note the *Christian* Schoolmaster, already distinguished as such, implying the existence and the character of Christian schools. Of which, learn more from the Emperor Julian, afterwards.]

therein. He seals the gods themselves with this name ;[1] whereas the Law, as we have said, prohibits "the names of gods to be pronounced,"[2] and this name[3] to be conferred on vanity.[4] Hence the devil gets men's early faith built up from the beginnings of their erudition. Inquire whether he who catechizes about idols commit idolatry. But when a believer *learns* these things, if he is already capable of understanding what idolatry is, he neither receives nor allows them ; much more if he is not yet capable. Or, when he *begins* to understand, it behoves him first to understand what he has previously learned, that is, touching God and the faith. Therefore he will reject those things, and will not receive them ; and will be as safe as one who from one who knows it not, knowingly *accepts* poison, but does not *drink* it. To *him* necessity is attributed as an excuse, because he has no other way to learn. Moreover, the not *teaching* literature is as much easier than the not *learning*, as it is easier, too, for the pupil not to attend, than for the master not to frequent, the rest of the defilements incident to the schools from public and scholastic solemnities.

CHAP. XI.—CONNECTION BETWEEN COVETOUSNESS AND IDOLATRY. CERTAIN TRADES, HOWEVER GAINFUL, TO BE AVOIDED.

If we think over the rest of faults, tracing them from their generations, let us begin with covetousness, "a root of all evils,"[5] wherewith, indeed, some having been ensnared, "have suffered shipwreck about faith."[6] Albeit covetousness is by the same apostle called *idolatry*.[7] In the next place *proceeding to* mendacity, the minister of covetousness (of false swearing I am silent, since even swearing is not lawful[8])—is *trade* adapted for a servant of God ? But, covetousness apart, what is the motive for acquiring? When the motive for acquiring ceases, there will be no necessity for trading. Grant now that there be some righteousness in business, secure from the duty of watchfulness against covetousness and mendacity ; I take it that that trade which pertains to the very soul and spirit of idols, which pampers every demon, falls under the charge of idolatry. Rather,

is not that the *principal* idolatry ? If the selfsame merchandises—frankincense, I mean, and all other foreign productions—used as sacrifice to idols, are of use likewise to men for medicinal ointments, to us *Christians* also, over and above, for solaces of sepulture, let them see to it. At all events, while the pomps, while the priesthoods, while the sacrifices of idols, are furnished by dangers, by losses, by inconveniences, by cogitations, by runnings to and fro, or trades, what else are you demonstrated to be but an idols' agent? Let none contend that, in this way, exception may be taken to *all* trades. All graver faults extend the sphere for diligence in watchfulness proportionally to the magnitude of the danger ; in order that we may withdraw not only from the faults, but from the means through which they have being. For although the fault be done by others, it makes no difference if it be *by my means*. In no case ought I to be *necessary* to another, while he is doing what to me is unlawful. Hence I ought to understand that care must be taken by me, lest what I am forbidden to do be done *by my means*. In short, in another cause of no lighter guilt I observe that fore-judgment. In that I am interdicted from fornication, I furnish nothing of help or connivance to others for that purpose; in that I have separated my own flesh itself from stews, I acknowledge that I cannot exercise the trade of pandering, or keep that kind of places for my neighbour's behoof. So, too, the interdiction of murder shows me that a trainer of gladiators also is excluded from the Church ; nor will any one fail to be the means of doing what he subministers to another to do. Behold, here is a more kindred fore-judgment : if a purveyor of the public victims come over to the faith, will you permit him to remain permanently in that trade ? or if one who is already a believer shall have undertaken that business, will you think that he is to be retained in the Church ? No, I take it ; unless any one will dissemble in the case of a frankincense-seller too. In sooth, the agency of *blood* pertains to some, that of *odours* to others. If, before idols were in the world, idolatry, hitherto shapeless, used to be transacted by these wares ; if, even now, the work of idolatry is perpetrated, for the most part, without the idol, by burnings of odours ; the frankincense-seller is a something even more serviceable even toward demons, for idolatry is more easily carried on without the idol, than without the ware of the frankincense-seller.[9] Let us interrogate thoroughly

---

[1] i.e., the name of *gods*.
[2] Ex. xxiii. 13; Josh. xxiii. 7; Ps. xvi. 4; Hos. ii. 17; Zech. xiii. 2.
[3] i.e., the name of *God*.
[4] i.e., on an *idol*, which, as Isaiah says, is "vanity."
[5] 1 Tim. vi. 10.
[6] 1 Tim. i. 19.
[7] Col. iii. 5. It has been suggested that for "quamvis" we should read "quum bis;" *i.e.* "*seeing* covetousness *is twice* called*," etc. The two places are Col. iii. 5, and Eph. v. 5.
[8] Matt. v. 34-37; Jas. v. 12.

[9] [The aversion of the early Christian Fathers *passim* to the ceremonial use of incense finds one explanation here.]

the conscience of the faith itself. With what mouth will a Christian frankincense-seller, if he shall pass through temples, with what mouth will he spit down upon and blow out the smoking altars, for which himself has made provision? With what consistency will he exorcise his own foster-children,[1] to whom he affords his own house as store-room? Indeed, if he shall have ejected a demon,[2] let *him* not congratulate himself on his faith, for he has not ejected an *enemy;* he ought to have had his prayer easily granted by one whom he is daily feeding.[3] No art, then, no profession, no trade, which administers either to equipping or forming idols, can be free from the title of idolatry; unless we interpret idolatry to be altogether something else than the service of idol-tendence.

CHAP. XII.—FURTHER ANSWERS TO THE PLEA, HOW AM I TO LIVE?

In vain do we flatter ourselves as to the necessities of human maintenance, if—after faith sealed[4]—we say, "I have no means to live?"[5] For here I will now answer more fully that abrupt proposition. It is advanced *too late.* For after the similitude of that most prudent builder,[6] who first computes the costs of the work, together with his own means, lest, when he has begun, he afterwards blush to find himself spent, deliberation should have been made *before.* But even now you have the Lord's sayings, as examples taking away from you all excuse. For what is it you say? "I shall be in need." But the Lord calls the needy "happy."[7] "I shall have no food." But "think not," says He, "about food;"[8] and as an example of clothing we have the lilies.[9] "My work was my subsistence." Nay, but "all things are to be sold, and divided to the needy."[10] "But provision must be made for children and posterity." "None, putting his hand on the plough, and looking back, is fit" for work.[11] "But I was under contract." "None can serve two lords."[12] If you wish to be the Lord's disci-

ple, it is necessary you "take your cross, and follow the Lord:"[13] *your cross;* that is, your own *straits* and *tortures,* or your *body* only, which is after the manner of a *cross.* Parents, wives, children, will have to be left behind, for God's sake.[14] Do you hesitate about arts, and trades, and about professions likewise, for the sake of children and parents? Even there was it demonstrated to us, that both "dear pledges,"[15] and handicrafts, and trades, are to be quite left behind for the Lord's sake; while James and John, called by the Lord, do leave quite behind both father and ship;[16] while Matthew is roused up from the toll-booth;[17] while even burying a father was too tardy a business for faith.[18] None of them whom the Lord chose to Him said, "I have no means to live." Faith fears not famine. It knows, likewise, that hunger is no less to be contemned by it for God's sake, than every kind of death. It has learnt not to respect *life;* how much more *food?* [You ask] "How many have fulfilled these conditions?" But what with men is difficult, with God is easy.[19] Let us, however, comfort ourselves about the gentleness and clemency of God in such wise, as not to indulge our "necessities" up to the point of affinities with idolatry, but to avoid even from afar every breath of it, as of a pestilence. [And this] not merely in the cases forementioned, but in the universal series of human superstition; whether appropriated to its gods, or to the defunct, or to kings, as pertaining to the selfsame unclean spirits, sometimes through sacrifices and priesthoods, sometimes through spectacles and the like, sometimes through holy-days.

CHAP. XIII.—OF THE OBSERVANCE OF DAYS CONNECTED WITH IDOLATRY.

But why speak of sacrifices and priesthoods? Of spectacles, moreover, and pleasures of that kind, we have already filled a volume of their own.[20] In this place must be handled the subject of holidays and other extraordinary solemnities, which we accord sometimes to our wantonness, sometimes to our timidity, in opposition to the common faith and Discipline. The first point, indeed, on which I shall join issue is this: whether a servant of God ought to share with the very

---

[1] i.e., the demons, or idols, to whom incense is burned.
[2] i.e., from one possessed.
[3] i.e., The demon, in gratitude for the incense which the man daily feeds him with, ought to depart out of the possessed at his request.
[4] i.e., in baptism.
[5] See above, chaps. v. and viii. [One is reminded here of the famous pleasantry of Dr. Johnson; see *Boswell.*]
[6] See Luke xiv. 28-30.
[7] Luke vi. 20.
[8] Matt. vi. 25, 31, etc.; Luke xii. 22-24.
[9] Matt. vi. 28; Luke xii. 28.
[10] Matt. xix. 21; Luke xviii. 22.
[11] Luke ix. 62, where the words are, "is fit for the kingdom of God."
[12] Matt. vi. 24; Luke xvi. 13.

[13] Matt. xvi. 24; Mark viii. 34; Luke ix. 23, xiv. 27.
[14] Luke xiv. 26; Mark x. 29, 30; Matt xix. 27-30. Compare these texts with Tertullian's words, and see the testimony he thus gives to the deity of Christ.
[15] i.e., any dear relations.
[16] Matt. iv. 21, 22, Mark i. 19, 20; Luke v. 10, 11.
[17] Matt. ix. 9; Mark ii. 14; Luke v. 29.
[18] Luke ix. 59, 60.
[19] Matt. xix. 26; Luke i. 37, xviii. 27.
[20] The treatise *De Spectaculis* [soon to follow, in this volume.]

nations themselves in matters of his kind, either in dress, or in food, or in any other kind of their gladness. "To rejoice with the rejoicing, and grieve with the grieving,"[1] is said about *brethren* by the apostle when exhorting to unanimity. But, for *these* purposes, "There is nought of communion between light and darkness,"[2] between life and death; or else we rescind what is written, "The world shall rejoice, but ye shall grieve."[3] If we rejoice with the world, there is reason to fear that with the world we shall grieve too. But when the world rejoices, let us grieve; and when the world afterward grieves, we shall rejoice. Thus, too, Eleazar[4] in Hades,[5] (attaining refreshment in Abraham's bosom) and the rich man, (on the other hand, set in the torment of fire) compensate, by an answerable retribution, their alternate vicissitudes of evil and good. There are certain gift-days, which with some adjust the claim of honour, with others the debt of wages. "Now, then," you say, "I shall receive back what is mine, or pay back what is another's." If men have consecrated for themselves this custom from superstition, why do you, estranged as you are from all their vanity, participate in solemnities consecrated to idols; as if for you also there were some prescript about a day, short of the observance of a particular day, to prevent your paying or receiving what you owe a man, or what is owed you by a man? Give me the form after which you wish to be dealt with. For why should you skulk withal, when you contaminate your own conscience by your neighbour's ignorance? If you are not unknown to be a Christian, you are tempted, and you act as if you were not a Christian against your neighbour's conscience; if, however, you shall be disguised withal,[6] you are the slave of the temptation. At all events, whether in the latter or the former way, you are guilty of being "ashamed of God."[7] But "whosoever shall be ashamed of Me in the presence of men, of him will I too be ashamed," says He, "in the presence of my Father who is in the heavens."[8]

CHAP. XIV.—OF BLASPHEMY. ONE OF ST. PAUL'S SAYINGS.

But, however, the majority (of Christians) have by this time induced the belief in their mind that it is pardonable if at any time they do what the heathen do, for fear "the Name be blasphemed." Now the blasphemy which must quite be shunned by us in every way is, I take it, this: If any of us lead a heathen into blasphemy with good cause, either by fraud, or by injury, or by contumely, or any other matter of worthy complaint, in which "the Name" is deservedly impugned, so that the Lord, too, be deservedly angry. Else, if of *all* blasphemy it has been said, "By your means My Name is blasphemed,"[9] we all perish at once; since the whole circus, with no desert of ours, assails "the Name" with wicked suffrages. Let us cease (to be Christians) and it will not be blasphemed! On the contrary, while we are, let it be blasphemed: in the observance, not the overstepping, of discipline; while we are being approved, not while we are being reprobated. Oh blasphemy, bordering on martyrdom, which now *at*tests me to be a Christian,[10] while for that very account it *de*tests me! The cursing of well-maintained Discipline is a blessing of the Name. "If," says he, "I wished to please men, I should not be Christ's servant."[11] But the same apostle elsewhere bids us take care to please all: "As I," he says, "please all by all means."[12] No doubt he used to please them by celebrating the Saturnalia and New-year's day! [Was it so] or was it by moderation and patience? by gravity, by kindness, by integrity? In like manner, when he is saying, "I have become all things to all, that I may gain all,"[13] does he mean "to idolaters an idolater?" "to heathens a heathen?" "to the worldly worldly?" But albeit he does not prohibit us from having our conversation with idolaters and adulterers, and the other criminals, saying, "Otherwise ye would go out from the world,"[14] of course he does not so slacken those reins of conversation that, since it is necessary for us both to *live* and to *mingle* with sinners, we may be able to *sin* with them too. Where there is the intercourse of life, which the apostle concedes, there is sinning, which no one permits. To live with heathens is lawful, to die with

---

[1] Rom. xii. 15.
[2] See 2 Cor. vi. 14. In the *De Spect.* xxvi. Tertullian has the same quotation (Oehler). And there, too, he adds, as here, "between life and death."
[3] John xvi. 20. It is observable that Tertullian here translates κόσμος by "seculum."
[4] i.e., Lazarus, Luke xvi. 19-31.
[5] "Apud inferos," used clearly *here* by Tertullian of a place of happiness. Augustine says he never finds it so used in Scripture. See Ussher's "Answer to a Jesuit" on the Article, "He descended into hell." [See Elucid. X. p. 59, *supra*.]
[6] i.e., if you *are* unknown to be a Christian: "dissimulaberis." This is Oehler's reading; but Latinius and Fr. Junius would read "Dissimulaveris," = "if you dissemble the fact" of being a Christian, which perhaps is better.
[7] So Mr. Dodgson renders very well.
[8] Matt. x. 33; Mark viii. 38; Luke ix. 26; 2 Tim. ii. 12.

[9] Isa. lii. 5; Ezek. xxxvi. 20, 23. Cf. 2 Sam. xii. 14; Rom. ii. 24.
[10] [This play on the words is literally copied from the original— "quæ tunc me *testatur* Christianum, cum propter ea me detestatur."]
[11] St. Paul. Gal. i. 10.
[12] 1 Cor. x. 32, 33.
[13] 1 Cor. ix. 22.
[14] 1 Cor. v. 10.

them [1] is not. Let us live with all ; [2] let us be glad with them, out of community of nature, not of superstition. We are peers in soul, not in discipline ; fellow-possessors of the world, not of error. But if we have no right of communion in matters of this kind with strangers, how far more wicked to celebrate them among brethren ! Who can maintain or defend this ? The Holy Spirit upbraids the Jews with their holy-days. "Your Sabbaths, and new moons, and ceremonies," says He, "My soul hateth." [3] By us, to whom Sabbaths are strange, [4] and the new moons and festivals formerly beloved by God, the Saturnalia and New-year's and Midwinter's festivals and Matronalia are frequented —presents come and go—New-year's gifts— games join their noise—banquets join their din ! Oh better fidelity of the nations to their own sect, which claims no solemnity of the Christians for itself ! Not the Lord's day, not Pentecost, even if they had known them, would they have shared with us ; for they would fear lest they should seem to be Christians. We are not apprehensive lest we seem to be *heathens !* If any indulgence is to be granted to the flesh, you have it. I will not say your own days, [5] but more too ; for to the *heathens* each festive day occurs but once annually : *you* have a festive day every eighth day. [6] Call out the individual solemnities of the nations, and set them out into a row, they will not be able to make up a Pentecost. [7]

CHAP. XV.—CONCERNING FESTIVALS IN HONOUR OF EMPERORS, VICTORIES, AND THE LIKE. EXAMPLES OF THE THREE CHILDREN AND DANIEL.

But "let your works shine," saith He ; [8] but now all our shops and gates shine ! You will now-a-days find more doors of heathens without lamps and laurel-wreaths than of Christians. What does the case seem to be with regard to that species (of ceremony) also ? If it is an idol's honour, without doubt an idol's honour is idolatry. If it is for a man's sake, let us again consider that all idolatry is for man's sake ; [9] let us again consider that

all idolatry is a worship done to men, since it is generally agreed even among their worshippers that aforetime the gods themselves of the nations were men ; and so it makes no difference whether that superstitious homage be rendered to men of a former age or of this. Idolatry is condemned, not on account of the persons which are set up for worship, but on account of those its observances, which pertain to demons. "The things which are Cæsar's are to be rendered to Cæsar." [10] It is enough that He set in apposition thereto, "and to God the things which are God's." What things, then, are Cæsar's ? Those, to wit, about which the consultation was then held, whether the poll-tax should be furnished to Cæsar or no. Therefore, too, the Lord demanded that the money should be shown Him, and inquired about the image, whose it was ; and when He had heard it was Cæsar's, said, "Render to Cæsar what are Cæsar's, and what are God's to God ;" that is, the image of Cæsar, which is on the coin, to Cæsar, and the image of God, which is on man, [11] to God ; so as to render to Cæsar indeed money, to God yourself. Otherwise, what will be God's, if all things are Cæsar's ? "Then," do you say, "the lamps before my doors, and the laurels on my posts are an honour to God ?" *They are there* of course, not because they are an honour to God, but to him who is honoured in God's stead by ceremonial observances of that kind, so far as is manifest, saving the religious performance, which is in secret appertaining to demons. For we ought to be sure if there are any whose notice it escapes through ignorance of this world's literature, that there are among the Romans even gods of entrances ; Cardea (Hinge-goddess), called after hinges, and Forculus (Door-god) after doors, and Limentinus (Threshold-god) after the threshold, and Janus himself (Gate-god) after the gate: and of course we know that, though names be empty and feigned, yet, when they are drawn down into superstition, demons and every unclean spirit seize them for themselves, through the bond of consecration. Otherwise demons have no name individually, but they there find a name where they find also a token. Among the Greeks likewise we read of Apollo Thyræus, *i.e.* of the door, and the Antelii, or Anthelii, demons, as presiders over entrances. These things, therefore, the Holy Spirit foreseeing from the beginning, fore-chanted, through the most ancient prophet Enoch, that even entrances would come

[1] i.e., by sinning (Oehler), for "the wages of sin is death."
[2] There seems to be a play on the word "convivere" (whence "convivium," etc.), as in Cic. *de Sen.* xiii.
[3] Isa. i. 14, etc.
[4] [This is noteworthy. In the earlier days sabbaths (Saturdays) were not unobserved, but, it was a concession *pro tempore*, to Hebrew Christians.]
[5] i.e., perhaps your own birthdays. [See cap. xvi. *infra.*] Oehler seems to think it means, "all other Christian festivals beside Sunday."
[6] ["An Easter Day in every week."—*Keble.*]
[7] i.e., a space of fifty days, see Deut. xvi. 10 ; and comp. Hooker, *Ecc. Pol.* iv. 13, 7, ed. Keble.
[8] Matt. v. 16.
[9] See chap. ix. p. 152, note 4.

[10] Matt. xxii. 21 ; Mark xii. 17 ; Luke xx. 25.
[11] See Gen. i. 26, 27, ix. 6 ; and comp. 1 Cor. xi. 7.

into superstitious use. For we see too that other entrances[1] are adored in the baths. But if there are beings which are adored in *entrances*, it is to them that both the lamps and the laurels will pertain. To an idol you will have done whatever you shall have done to an *entrance*. In this place I call a witness on the authority also of God; because it is not safe to suppress whatever may have been shown to *one*, of course for the sake of *all*. I know that a brother was severely chastised, the same night, through a vision, because on the sudden announcement of public rejoicings his servants had wreathed his gates. And yet himself had not wreathed, or commanded them to be wreathed; for he had gone forth *from home* before, and on his return had reprehended the deed. So strictly are we appraised with God in matters of this kind, even with regard to the discipline of our family.[2] Therefore, as to what relates to the honours due to kings or emperors, we have a prescript sufficient, that it behoves us to be in all obedience, according to the apostle's precept,[3] "subject to magistrates, and princes, and powers;"[4] but within the limits of discipline, so long as we keep ourselves separate from idolatry. For it is for this reason, too, that that example of the three brethren has forerun us, who, in other respects obedient toward king Nebuchodonosor, rejected with all constancy the honour to his image,[5] proving that whatever is extolled beyond the measure of human honour, unto the resemblance of divine sublimity, is idolatry. So too, Daniel, in all other points submissive to Darius, remained in his duty so long as it was free from danger to his religion;[6] for, to avoid undergoing *that* danger, *he* feared the royal lions no more than *they* the royal fires. Let, therefore, them who have no light, light their lamps daily; let them over whom the fires of hell are imminent, affix to their posts laurels doomed presently to burn: to them the testimonies of darkness and the omens of their penalties are suitable. *You* are a light of the world,[7] and a tree ever green.[8] If you have renounced temples, make not your own gate a temple. I have said too little. If you have renounced stews, clothe not your own house with the appearance of a new brothel.

CHAP. XVI.—CONCERNING PRIVATE FESTIVALS.

Touching the ceremonies, however, of private and social solemnities—as those of the white toga, of espousals, of nuptials, of name-givings—I should think no danger need be guarded against from the breath of the idolatry which is mixed up with them. For the causes are to be considered to which the ceremony is due. Those above-named I take to be clean in themselves, because neither manly garb, nor the marital ring or union, descends from honours done to any idol. In short, I find no dress cursed by God, except a woman's dress on a man:[9] for "cursed," saith He, "is every man who clothes himself in woman's attire." The toga, however, is a dress of manly *name* as well as *of manly use*.[10] God no more prohibits nuptials to be celebrated than a name to be given. "But there are sacrifices appropriated to these occasions." Let me be invited, and let not the title of the ceremony be "assistance at a sacrifice," and the discharge of my good offices is at the service *of my friends*. Would that it were "at *their* service" indeed, and that we could escape *seeing* what is unlawful for us to *do*. But since the evil one has so surrounded the world with idolatry, it will be lawful for us to be present at some ceremonies which see us doing service to a *man*, not to an *idol*. Clearly, if invited unto priestly function and sacrifice, I will not go, for that is service peculiar to an idol; but neither will I furnish advice, or expense, or any other good office in a matter of *that* kind. If it is on account of the *sacrifice* that I be invited, and stand by, I shall be partaker of idolatry; if any *other* cause conjoins me to the sacrificer, I shall be merely a spectator of the sacrifice.[11]

CHAP. XVII.—THE CASES OF SERVANTS AND OTHER OFFICIALS. WHAT OFFICES A CHRISTIAN MAN MAY HOLD.

But what shall believing servants or children[12] do? officials likewise, when attending on their lords, or patrons, or superiors, when sacrificing? Well, if any one shall have handed the wine to a sacrificer, nay, if by any

---

[1] The word is the same as that for "the mouth" of a river, etc. Hence Oehler supposes the "entrances" or "mouths" *here* referred to to be the mouths of *fountains*, where *nymphs* were supposed to dwell. *Nympha* is supposed to be the same word as *Lympha*. See Hor. *Sat.* i. 5, 97; and Maclean's note.
[2] [He seems to refer to some Providential event, perhaps announced in a dream, not necessarily out of the course of common occurrences.]
[3] Rom. xiii. 1, etc.; 1 Pet. ii, 13, 14.
[4] Tit. iii. 1.
[5] Dan. iii.
[6] Dan. vi.
[7] Matt. v. 14; Phil. ii. 15.
[8] Ps. i. 1-3, xcii. 12-15.

[9] Tertullian should have added, "and a man's on a woman." See Deut. xxii. 5. Moreover, the word "cursed" is not used there, but "abomination" is.
[10] Because it was called *toga virilis*—"the *manly* toga."
[11] [1 Cor. viii. The law of the inspired apostle seems as rigorous here and in 1 Cor. x. 27-29.]
[12] This is Oehler's reading; Regaltius and Fr. Junjus would read "liberti"=freedmen. I admit that in this instance I prefer their reading: among other reasons it answers better to "patronis = "patrons."

single word necessary or belonging to a sacrifice he shall have aided him, he will be held to be a minister of idolatry. Mindful of this rule, we can render service even " to magistrates and powers," after the example of the patriarchs and the other forefathers,[1] who obeyed idolatrous kings up to the confine of idolatry. Hence arose, very lately, a dispute whether a servant of God should take the administration of any dignity or power, if he be able, whether by some special grace, or by adroitness, to keep himself intact from every species of idolatry; after the example that both Joseph and Daniel, clean from idolatry, administered both dignity and power in the livery and purple of the prefecture of entire Egypt or Babylonia. And so let us grant that it is possible for any one to succeed in moving, in whatsoever office, under the mere *name* of the office, neither sacrificing nor lending his authority to sacrifices; not farming out victims; not assigning to others the care of temples; not looking after their tributes; not giving spectacles at his own or the public charge, or presiding over the giving them; making proclamation or edict for no solemnity; not even taking oaths: moreover (what comes under the head of *power*), neither sitting in judgment on any one's life or character, for you might bear with his judging about *money;* neither condemning nor fore-condemning;[2] binding no one, imprisoning or torturing no one—if it is credible that all this is possible.

CHAP. XVIII.—DRESS AS CONNECTED WITH IDOLATRY.

But we must now treat of the garb only and apparatus of office. There is a dress proper to every one, as well for daily use as for office and dignity. That famous purple, therefore, and the gold as an ornament of the neck, were, among the Egyptians and Babylonians, ensigns of dignity, in the same way as bordered, or striped, or palm-embroidered togas, and the golden wreaths of provincial priests, are now; but not on the same terms. For they used only to be conferred, under the name of *honour,* on such as deserved the familiar friendship of kings (whence, too, such used to be styled the "purpled-men"[3] of kings, just as among us,[4] some, from their white toga, are called "candidates"[5]); but *not* on the

understanding that that garb should be tied to *priesthoods* also, or *to any idol-ceremonies.* For if *that* were the case, of course men of such holiness and constancy[6] would instantly have refused the defiled dresses; and it would instantly have appeared that Daniel had been no zealous slave to idols, nor worshipped Bel, nor the dragon, which long after *did* appear. That purple, therefore, was simple, and used not at that time to be a mark of *dignity*[7] among the barbarians, but of *nobility.*[8] For as both Joseph, who had been a slave, and Daniel, who through[9] captivity had changed his state, attained the freedom of the states of Babylon and Egypt through the dress of barbaric nobility;[10] so among us believers also, if need so be, the bordered toga will be proper to be conceded to boys, and the stole to girls,[11] as ensigns of birth, not of power; of race, not of office; of rank, not of superstition. But the purple, or the other ensigns of dignities and powers, dedicated from the beginning to idolatry engrafted on the dignity and the powers, carry the spot of their own profanation; since, moreover, bordered and striped togas, and broad-barred ones, are put even on idols themselves; and *fasces* also, and rods, are borne before them; and deservedly, for demons are the magistrates of this world: they bear the *fasces* and the purples, the ensigns of one college. What end, then, will you advance if you use the garb indeed, but administer not the functions of it? In things unclean, none can appear clean. If you put on a tunic defiled in itself, it perhaps may not be defiled through you; but you, through it, will be unable to be clean. Now by this time, you who argue about "Joseph" and "Daniel," know that things old and new, rude and polished, begun and developed, slavish and free, are not always comparable. For they, even by their circumstances, were slaves; but you, the slave of none,[12] in so far as you are the slave of Christ alone,[13] who has freed you likewise from the captivity of the world, will incur the duty of acting after your Lord's pattern. That Lord walked in humility and obscurity, with no definite home: for "the Son of man," said He, "hath not where to lay His head;"[14] unadorned in dress, for else He had not said,

[1] Majores. Of course the word may be rendered simply "ancients;" but I have kept the common meaning "forefathers."
[2] "The judge condemns, the legislator fore-condemns."—RIGALTIUS.(Oehler.)
[3] Or, "purpurates."
[4] [Not *us* Christians, but *us* Roman citizens.]
[5] Or, "white-men."
[6] Or, "consistency."
[7] i.e., *Official* character.
[8] Or, "free" or "good" "birth.'
[9] Or, "during."
[10] i.e., the dress was the *sign* that they had obtained it.
[11] I have departed from Oehler's reading here, as I have not succeeded in finding that the "*stola*" was a *boy's* garment; and, for grammatical reasons, the reading of Gelenius and Pamelius (which I have taken) seems best.
[12] See 1 Cor. ix. 19.
[13] St. Paul in his epistle glories in the title, "Paul, a slave," or "bondman," "of Christ Jesus."
[14] Luke ix. 58; Matt. viii. 20.

" Behold, they who are clad in soft raiment are in kings' houses :" [1] in short, inglorious in countenance and aspect, just as Isaiah withal had fore-announced.[2] If, also, He exercised no right of power even over His own followers, to whom He discharged menial ministry ; [3] if, in short, though conscious of His own kingdom,[4] He shrank back from being made a king,[5] He in the fullest manner gave His own an example for turning coldly from all the pride and garb, as well of dignity as of power. For *if they were to be used*, who would rather have used them than the Son of God ? What kind and what number of *fasces* would escort Him ? what kind of purple would bloom from His shoulders ? what kind of gold would beam from His head, had He not judged the glory of the world to be alien both to Himself and to His ? Therefore what He was unwilling to accept, He has rejected ; what He rejected, He has condemned ; what He condemned, He has counted as part of the devil's pomp. For He would not have condemned things, except such as were not His ; but things which are not God's, can be no other's but the devil's. If you have forsworn " the devil's pomp," [6] know that whatever there you touch is idolatry. Let even this fact help to remind you that all the powers and dignities of this world are not only alien to, but enemies of, God ; that through them punishments have been determined against God's servants ; through them, too, penalties prepared for the impious are ignored. But " both your birth and your substance are troublesome to you in resisting idolatry." [7] For avoiding it, remedies cannot be lacking ; since, even if they be lacking, there remains that one by which you will be made a happier magistrate, not in the earth, but in the heavens.[8]

CHAP. XIX.—CONCERNING MILITARY SERVICE.

In that last section, decision may seem to have been given likewise concerning military service, which is between dignity and power.[9] But now inquiry is made about this point, whether a believer may turn himself unto military service, and whether the military may be admitted unto the faith, even the rank and file, or each inferior grade, to whom there is no necessity for taking part in sacrifices or capital punishments. There is no agreement between the divine and the human sacrament,[10] the standard of Christ and the standard of the devil, the camp of light and the camp of darkness. One soul cannot be due to two *masters* —God and Cæsar. And yet Moses carried a rod,[11] and Aaron wore a buckle,[12] and John (Baptist) is girt with leather,[13] and Joshua the son of Nun leads a line of march ; and the People warred : if it pleases you to sport with the subject. But how will *a Christian man* war, nay, how will he serve even in peace, without a sword, which the Lord has taken away ? [14] For albeit soldiers had come unto John, and had received the formula of their rule ; [15] albeit, likewise, a centurion had believed; [16] *still* the Lord afterward, in disarming Peter, unbe_d every soldier. No dress is lawful among us, if assigned to any unlawful action.

CHAP. XX.—CONCERNING IDOLATRY IN WORDS.

But, however, since the conduct according to the divine rule is imperilled, not merely by deeds, but likewise by words, (for, just as it is written, " Behold the man and his deeds ; " [17] so, " Out of thy own mouth shalt thou be justified " [18]), we ought to remember that, even in *words*, also the inroad of idolatry must be foreguarded against, either from the defect of custom or of timidity. The law prohibits the gods of the nations from being named,[19] not of course that we are not to pronounce their names, the speaking of which common intercourse extorts from us : for this must very frequently be said, " You find him in the temple of Æsculapius ; " and, " I live in Isis Street ; " and, " He has been made priest of Jupiter ; " and much else after this manner, since even on *men* names of this kind are bestowed. I do not honour Saturnus if I call a man so, by his own name. I honour him no more than I do Marcus, if I call a man Marcus. But it says, " Make not mention of the name of other gods, neither be it heard from thy mouth." [20] The precept it gives is

---

[1] Matt. xi. 8 ; Luke vii. 25.
[2] Isa. liii. 2.
[3] See John xiii. 1–17.
[4] See John xviii. 36.
[5] John vi. 15.
[6] In baptism.
[7] *i.e.* From your birth and means, you will be expected to fill offices which are in some way connected with idolatry.
[8] *i.e.* Martyrdom (La Cerda, quoted by Oehler). For the idea of being " a magistrate in the heavens," [sitting on a throne] compare such passages as Matt. xix. 28 ; Luke xxii. 28, 30 · 1 Cor. vi. 2, 3 ; Rev. ii. 26, 27, iii. 21.
[9] Elucidation II.

[10] " Sacramentum " in Latin is, among other meanings, " a military oath."
[11] Virgam." The vine switch, or rod, in the Roman army was a mark of the centurion's (i.e., captain's) rank.
[12] To fasten the ephod ; hence the buckle worn by soldiers here referred to would probably be the belt buckle. Buckles were sometimes given as military rewards (White and Riddle).
[13] As soldiers with belts.
[14] Matt. xxvi. 52 ; 2 Cor. x. 4 ; St. John xviii. 36.
[15] See Luke iii. 12, 13.
[16] Matt. viii. 5, etc ; Luke vii. 1, etc.
[17] Neither Oehler nor any editor seems to have discovered the passage here referred to.
[18] Matt. xii. 37.
[19] Ex. xxiii. 13 [St. Luke, nevertheless, names Castor and Pollux, Acts xxviii. ii., on our author's principle.]
[20] Ex. xxiii. 13.

this, that we do not call them *gods*. For in the first part of the law, too, " Thou shalt not," saith He, " use the name of the Lord thy God in a vain thing,"[1] that is, in an idol.[2] Whoever, therefore, honours an idol with the name of God, has fallen into idolatry. But if I speak of them as gods, something must be added to make it appear that *I* do not call them gods. For even the Scripture names " gods," but adds " their," viz. " of the nations : " just as David does when he had named " gods," where he says, " But the gods of the nations are demons."[3] But this has been laid by me rather as a foundation for ensuing observations. However, it is a defect of custom to say, " By Hercules, " So help me the god of faith ; "[4] while to the *custom* is added the *ignorance* of some, who are ignorant that it is an oath by Hercules. Further, what will an oath be, in the name of gods whom you have forsworn, but a collusion of faith with idolatry ? For who does not honour them in whose name he swears ?

CHAP. XXI.—OF SILENT ACQUIESCENCE IN HEATHEN FORMULARIES.

But it is a mark of timidity, when some other man binds you in the name of his gods, by the making of an oath, or by some other form of attestation, and you, for fear of discovery,[5] remain quiet. For you equally, by remaining quiet, affirm their majesty, by reason of which *majesty* you will seem to be bound. What matters it, whether you affirm the gods of the nations by calling them gods, or by hearing them so called ? Whether you swear by idols, or, when adjured by another, acquiesce ? Why should we not recognize the subtleties of Satan, who makes it his aim, that, what he cannot effect by *our* mouth, he may effect by the mouth of his servants, introducing idolatry into us through our ears ? At all events, whoever the adjurer is, he binds you to himself either in friendly or unfriendly conjunction. If in unfriendly, you are now challenged unto battle, and know that you must fight. If in friendly, with how far greater security will you transfer your engagement unto the Lord, that you may dissolve the obligation of him through whose means the Evil

One was seeking to annex you to the honour of idols, that is, to idolatry ! All sufferance of that kind is idolatry. You honour those to whom, when imposed as authorities, you have rendered respect. I know that one (whom the Lord pardon !), when it had been said to him in public during a law-suit, " Jupiter be wroth with you," answered, " On the contrary, with *you*." What else would a heathen have done who believed Jupiter to be a god ? For even had he not retorted the malediction by Jupiter (or other such like), yet, *by merely* returning a curse, he would have confirmed the divinity of Jove, shewing himself irritated by a malediction in Jove's name. For what is there to be indignant at, (if cursed) in the name of one whom you know to be nothing ? For if you rave, you immediately affirm his existence, and the profession of your fear will be an act of idolatry. How much more, while you are returning the malediction in the name of Jupiter himself, are you doing honour to Jupiter in the same way as he who provoked you ! But a believer ought to laugh in such cases, not to rave ; nay, according to the precept,[6] not to return a curse in the name of God even, but clearly to *bless* in the name of God, that you may both demolish idols and preach God, and fulfil discipline.

CHAP. XXII.—OF ACCEPTING BLESSING IN THE NAME OF IDOLS.

Equally, one who has been initiated into Christ will not endure to be blessed in the name of the gods of the nations, so as not always to reject the unclean benediction, and to cleanse it out for himself by converting it Godward. To be blessed in the name of the gods of the nations is to be cursed in the name of God. If I have given an alms, or shown any other kindness, and the recipient pray that his gods, or the Genius of the colony, may be propitious to me, my oblation or act will immediately be an honour to idols, in whose name he returns me the favour of blessing. But why should he not know that I have done it for God's sake ; that God may rather be glorified, and demons may not be honoured in that which I have done for the sake of God ? If God sees that I have done it for His sake, He equally sees that I have been unwilling to *show* that I did it for His sake, and have in a manner made His precept[7] a sacrifice to idols. Many say, " No one ought to divulge himself ;" but I think neither ought he to *deny* himself. For whoever dissembles in any cause whatever, by being held as a heathen,

---

[1] Ex. xx. 7.
[2] Because Scripture calls idols "vanities" and "vain things." See 2 Kings xvii. 15, Ps. xxiv. 4, Isa. lix. 4, Deut. xxxii. 21, etc.
[3] Ps. xcvi. 5. The LXX. in whose version ed. Tisch. it is Ps. xcv. read δαιμόνια, like Tertullian. Our version has "idols."
[4] Mehercule. Medius Fidius. I have given the rendering of the latter, which seems preferred by Paley (Ov. *Fast.* vi. 213, note), who considers it = *me dius* (i.e., *Deus*) *fidius juvet*. Smith (*Lat. Dict. s.v.*) agrees with him, and explains it, *me deus fidius servet*. White and Riddle (*s.v.*) take the *me* (which appears to be *short*) as a " demonstrative " particle or prefix, and explain, " By the God of truth !" " As true as heaven," " Most certainly."
[5] i.e., for fear of being discovered to be a Christian (Oehler).

[6] See Matt. v. 44, 1 Pet. iii. 9, etc.
[7] i.e., the precept which enjoins me to " do good and lend."

does deny; and, of course, all denial is idolatry, just as all idolatry is denial, whether in deeds or in words.[1]

CHAP. XXIII.—WRITTEN CONTRACTS IN THE NAME OF IDOLS. TACIT CONSENT.

But there is a certain species of that class, doubly sharpened in deed and word, and mischievous on either side, although it flatter you, as if it were free of danger in each; while it does not seem to be a *deed*, because it is not laid hold of as a *word*. In borrowing money from heathens under pledged[2] securities, *Christians* give a guarantee under oath, and deny themselves *to have done so.* Of course, the time of the prosecution, and the place of the judgment seat, and the person of the presiding judge, decide that they knew themselves *to have so done.*[3] Christ prescribes that there is to be no swearing. "I wrote," says the debtor, "but I said nothing. It is the tongue, not the written letter, which kills." Here I call Nature and Conscience as my witnesses: Nature, because even if the *tongue* in dictating remains motionless and quiet, the hand can write nothing which the *soul* has not dictated; albeit even to the tongue itself the soul may have dictated either something conceived by itself, or else something delivered by another. Now, lest it be said, "Another dictated," I here appeal to Conscience whether, what another dictated, the soul entertains,[4] and transmits unto the hand, whether with the concomitance or the inaction of the tongue. Enough, that the Lord has said faults are committed in the mind and the conscience. If concupiscence or malice have ascended into a man's heart, He saith it is held as a deed.[5] You therefore have given a guarantee; which clearly has "ascended into your heart," which you can neither contend you were ignorant of nor unwilling ; for when you gave the guarantee, you knew *that you did it;* when you knew, of course you were willing : you did it as well in

act as in thought ; nor can you by the lighter charge exclude the heavier,[6] so as to say that it is clearly rendered false, by giving a guarantee I for what you do not actually perform. "Yet I have not denied, because I have not sworn." *But you have sworn,* since, even if you had done no such thing, you would still be said to swear, if you have even *consented* to so doing. Silence of voice is an unavailing plea in a case of *writing* ; and muteness of sound in a case of *letters.* For Zacharias, when punished with a temporary privation of *voice,* holds colloquy with his *mind,* and, passing by his bootless tongue, with the help of his hands dictates from his heart, and without his mouth pronounces the name of his son.[7] Thus, in his pen there speaks a hand clearer than every sound, in his waxen tablet there is heard a letter more vocal that every mouth.[8] Inquire whether a man have *spoken* who is *understood* to have spoken.[9] Pray we the Lord that no necessity for that kind of contract may ever encompass us; and if it *should* so fall out, may He give our brethren the means of helping us, or give us constancy to break off all *such* necessity, lest those denying letters, the substitutes for our mouth, be brought forward against us in the day of judgment, sealed with the seals, not now of witnesses, but of angels !

CHAP. XXIV.—GENERAL CONCLUSION.

Amid these reefs and inlets, amid these shallows and straits of idolatry, Faith, her sails filled by the Spirit of God, navigates; safe if cautious, secure if intently watchful. But to such as are washed overboard is a deep whence is no out-swimming; to such as are run aground is inextricable shipwreck; to such as are engulphed is a whirlpool, where there is no breathing—even in idolatry. All waves thereof whatsoever suffocate; every eddy thereof sucks down unto Hades. Let no one say, "Who will so safely foreguard himself? We shall have to go out of the world !"[10] As if it were not as well worth while to go out, as to stand in the world as an idolater ! Nothing can be easier than caution against idolatry, if the fear of it be our leading fear; any "necessity" whatever

---

[1] Elucidation III.
[2] Or, "mortgaged."
[3] This is, perhaps, the most obscure and difficult passage in the entire treatise. I have followed Oehler's reading, and given what appears to be his sense ; but the readings are widely different, and it is doubtful whether any is correct. I can scarcely, however, help thinking that the "*se negant*" here, and the "*tamen non negavi*" below, are to be connected with the "*puto autem nec negare*" at the end of the former chapter ; and that the true rendering is rather : "And [by so doing] deny themselves," *i.e.* deny their Christian name and faith. "Doubtless a time of persecution," such as the present time is—or "of prosecution," which would make very good sense—"and the place of the tribunal, and the person of the presiding judge, require them to *know* themselves," i.e., to have no shuffling or disguise. I submit this rendering with diffidence ; but it does seem to me to suit the context better, and to harmonize better with the "Yet I have not denied," i.e., my name and faith, which follows, and with the "denying letters" which are mentioned at the end of the chapter.—Tr.
[4] Mr. Dodgson renders "conceiveth ;" and the word is certainly capable of that meaning.
[5] See Matt. v. 28.

[6] Oehler understands "the lighter crime" or "charge" to be "swearing;" the "heavier," to be "denying the Lord Christ."
[7] See Luke i. 20, 22, 62, 63.
[8] This is how Mr. Dodgson renders, and the rendering agrees with Oehler's punctuation. [So obscure however, is Dodgson's rendering that I have slightly changed the punctuation, to clarify it, and subjoin Oehler's text.] But perhaps we may read thus : "He speaks in his pen ; he is heard in his waxen tablet : the hand is clearer than every sound ; the letter is more vocal than every mouth." [Oehler reads thus : "Cum manibus suis a corde dictat et nomen filii sine ore pronuntiat: loquitur in stilo, auditur in cera manus omni sono clarior, littera omni ore vocalior." I see no difficulty here.]
[9] Elucidation IV.
[10] 1 Cor. v. 10.

is too trifling compared to such a peril. The reason why the Holy Spirit did, when the apostles at that time were consulting, relax the bond and yoke for us,[1] was that we might be free to devote ourselves to the shunning of idolatry. This shall be our Law, the more fully to be administered the more ready it is to hand; (a Law) peculiar to Christians, by means whereof we are recognised and examined by heathens. This Law must be set before such as approach unto the Faith, and inculcated on such as are entering 't;

that, in approaching, they may deliberate; observing it, may persevere; not observing it, may renounce their name.[2] We will see to it, if, after the type of the Ark, there shall be in the Church raven, kite, dog, and serpent. At all events, an idolater is not found in the type of the Ark: no animal has been fashioned to represent an idolater. Let not that be in the Church which was not in the Ark.[3]

[1] Acts xv. 1-31.

[2] i.e., cease to be Christians (Rigalt., referred to by Oehler).
[3] [General references to Kaye (3d edition), which will be useful to those consulting that author's Tertullian, for Elucidations of the *De Idololatria*, are as follows: *Preface*, p. xxiii. Then, pp. 56, 141, 206, 231, 300, 360, 343, 360 and 362.]

ELUCIDATIONS

I

(The Second Commandment, p. 64.)

TERTULLIAN's teaching agrees with that of Clement of Alexandria[4] and with all the Primitive Fathers. But compare the Trent Catechism, (chapter ii., quest. 17.)—"Nor let any one suppose that this commandment prohibits the arts of painting, modelling or sculpture, *for*, in the Scriptures we are informed that God himself commanded images of cherubim, and *also of the brazen serpent*, to be made, etc." So far, the comparison is important, because while our author limits any inference from this instance as an *exception*, this Catechism turns it into a *rule:* and so far, we are only looking at the matter with reference to Art. But, the Catechism, (questt. xxiii. xxiv.), goes on to teach that images of the Saints, *etc.* ought to be made and honoured "as a holy practice." It affirms, also, that it is a practice which has been *attended with the greatest advantage to the faithful:* which admits of a doubt, especially when the *honour* thus mentioned is everywhere turned into *worship*, precisely like that offered to the Brazen Serpent, when the People "burned incense to it," and often much more. But even this is not my point; for that Catechism, with what verity need not be argued, affirms, also, that this doctrine "*derives confirmation* from the monuments of the Apostolic age, the general Councils of the Church, and the writings of so many most holy and learned Fathers, *who are of one accord upon the subject.*" Doubtless they are "of one accord," but all the other way.

II.

(Military service, cap. xix., p. 73.)

This chapter must prepare us for a much more sweeping condemnation of the military profession in the *De Spectaculis* and the *De Corona ;* but Neander's judgment seems to me very just. The *Corona*, itself, is rather Montanistic than Montanist, in the opinion of some critics, among whom Gibbon is not to count for much, for the reasons given by Kaye (p. 52), and others hardly less obvious. Surely, if this ascetic opinion and some similar instances were enough to mark a man as a heretic, what are we to say of the thousand crotchets maintained by good Christians, in our day?

---

[4] See vol. II., p. 186, this series.

III.

(Passive idolatry, cap. xxii., pp. 74, 75.)

Neander's opinion as to the freedom of *De Idololatria* from Montanistic taint, is mildly questioned by Bp. Kaye, chiefly on the ground of the agreement of this chapter with the extravagances of the *Scorpiace*. He thinks "the utmost pitch" of such extravagance is reached in the positions here taken. But Neander's judgment seems to me preferable. Lapsers usually give tokens of the bent of their minds, and unconsciously betray their inclinations before they themselves see whither they are tending. Thus they become victims of their own plausible self-deceptions.

IV.

(Tacit consents and reservations, cap. xxiii., p. 75.)

It cannot be doubted that apart from the specific case which Tertullian is here maintaining, his appeal to conscience is maintained by reason, by the Morals of the Fathers and by Holy Scripture. Now compare with this the Morality which has been made dogmatic, among Latins, by the elevation of Liguori to the dignities of a "Saint" and a "Doctor of the Church." Even Cardinal Newman cannot accept it without *reservations*, so thoroughly does it commit the soul to fraud and hyprocrisy. See Liguori, *Opp. Tom.* II., pp. 34–44, and Meyrick, *Moral Theology of the Church of Rome*, London, 1855. Republished, with an Introduction, by the Editor of this Series, Baltimore, 1857. Also Newman, *Apologia*, p. 295 *et seqq.*

THE SHOWS, OR DE SPECTACULIS.[1]

[TRANSLATED BY THE REV. S. THELWALL.]

CHAP. I.

Ye Servants of God, about to draw near to God, that you may make solemn consecration of yourselves to Him,[2] seek well to understand the condition of faith, the reasons of the Truth, the laws of Christian Discipline, which forbid among other sins of the world, the pleasures of the public shows. Ye who have testified and confessed[3] that you have done so already, review the subject, that there may be no sinning whether through real or wilful ignorance. For such is the power of earthly pleasures, that, to retain the opportunity of still partaking of them, it contrives to prolong a willing ignorance, and bribes knowledge into playing a dishonest part. To both things, perhaps, some among you are allured by the views of the heathens who in this matter are wont to press us with arguments, such as these : (1) That the exquisite enjoyments of ear and eye we have in things external are not in the least opposed to religion in the mind and conscience ; and (2) That surely no offence is offered to God, in any human enjoyment, by any of our pleasures, which it is not sinful to partake of in its own time and place, with all due honour and reverence secured to Him. But this is precisely what we are ready to prove : That these things are not consistent with true religion and true obedience to the true God. There are some who

imagine that Christians, a sort of people ever ready to die, are trained into the abstinence they practise, with no other object than that of making it less difficult to despise life, the fastenings to it being severed as it were. *They regard it as an art of* quenching all desire for that which, so far as they are concerned, they have emptied of all that is desirable ; and so it is thought to be rather a thing of human planning and foresight, than clearly laid down by divine command. It were a grievous thing, forsooth, for Christians, while continuing in the enjoyment of pleasures so great, to die for God ! It is not as they say ; though, if it were, even Christian obstinacy might well give all submission to a plan so suitable, to a rule so excellent.

CHAP. II.

Then, again, every one is ready with the argument[4] that all things, as we teach, were created by God, and given to man for his use, and that they must be good, as coming all from so good a source ; but that among them are found the various constituent elements of the public shows, such as the horse, the lion, bodily strength, and musical voice. It cannot, then, be thought that what exists by God's own creative will is either foreign or hostile to Him ; and if it is not opposed to Him, it cannot be regarded as injurious to His worshippers, as certainly it is not foreign to them. Beyond all doubt, too, the very buildings connected with the places of public amusement, composed as they are of rocks, stones, marbles, pillars, are things of God, who has given these various things for the earth's embellishment ; nay, the very scenes are enacted under God's own heaven. How skilful a pleader seems human wisdom to her-

---

[1] [It is the opinion of Dr. Neander that this treatise proceeded from our author before his lapse: but Bp. Kaye (p. xvi.) finds some exaggerated expressions in it, concerning the military life which savour of Montanism. Probably they do, but had he written the tract as a professed Montanist, they would have been much less ambiguous, in all probability. At all events, a work so colourless that doctors can disagree about even its shading, must be regarded as practically orthodox. Exaggerated expressions are but the characteristics of the author's genius. We find the like in all writers of strongly marked individuality. Neander dates this treatise *circa* A.D. 197. That it was written at Carthage is the conviction of Kaye and Dr. Allix; see Kaye, p. 55.]

[2] [He speaks of Catechumens, called elsewhere Novitioli. See Bunsen, *Hippol.* III. Church and House-book, p. 5.]

[3] [Here he addresses the *Fideles* or *Communicants*, as we call them.]

[4] [Kaye (p. 366), declares that all the arguments urged in this tract are comprised in two sentences of the Apology, cap. 38.]

self, especially if she has the fear of losing any of her delights—any of the sweet enjoyments of worldly existence ! In fact, you will find not a few whom the imperilling of their pleasures rather than their life holds back from us. For even the weakling has no strong dread of death *as a debt* he knows is due by him; while the wise man does not look with contempt on pleasure, regarding it as a precious gift—in fact, the one blessedness of life, whether to philosopher or fool. Now nobody denies what nobody is ignorant of—for Nature herself is teacher of it—that God is the Maker of the universe, and that it is good, and that it is man's by free gift of its Maker. But having no intimate acquaintance with the Highest, knowing Him only by natural revelation, and not as His " friends "— afar off, and not as those who have been brought nigh to Him—men cannot but be in ignorance alike of what He enjoins and what He forbids in regard to the administration of His world. They must be ignorant, too, of the hostile power which works against Him, and perverts to wrong uses the things His hand has formed ; for you cannot know either the will or the adversary of a God you do not know. We must not, then, consider merely by whom all things were made, but by whom they have been perverted. We shall find out for what use they were made at first, when we find for what they were not. There is a vast difference between the corrupted state and that of primal purity, just because there is a vast difference between the Creator and the corrupter. Why, all sorts of evils, which as indubitably evils even the heathens prohibit, and against which they guard themselves, come from the works of God. Take, for instance, murder, whether committed by iron, by poison, or by magical enchantments. Iron and herbs and demons are all equally creatures of God. Has the Creator, withal, provided these things for man's destruction? Nay, He puts His interdict on every sort of man-killing by that one summary precept, " Thou shalt not kill." Moreover, who but God, the Maker of the world, put in its gold, brass, silver, ivory, wood, and all the other materials used in the manufacture of idols? Yet has He done this that men may set up a worship in opposition to Himself? On the contrary, idolatry in His eyes is the crowning sin. What is there offensive to God which is not God's? But in offending Him, it ceases to be His ; and in ceasing to be His, it is in His eyes an offending thing. Man himself, guilty as he is of every iniquity, is not only a work of God—he is His image, and yet both in soul and body he has severed himself from his Maker. For we did not get eyes to minister to lust, and the tongue for speaking evil with, and ears to be the receptacle of evil speech, and the throat to serve the vice of gluttony, and the belly to be gluttony's ally, and the genitals for unchaste excesses, and hands for deeds of violence, and the feet for an erring life ; or was the soul placed in the body that it might become a thought-manufactory of snares, and fraud, and injustice ? I think not ; for if God, as the righteous exactor of innocence, hates everything like malignity—if He hates utterly such plotting of evil, it is clear beyond a doubt, that, of all things that have come from His hand, He has made none to lead to works which He condemns, even though these same works may be carried on by things of His making; for, in fact, it is the one ground of condemnation, that the creature misuses the creation. We, therefore, who in our knowledge of the Lord have obtained some knowledge also of His foe—who, in our discovery of the Creator, have at the same time laid hands upon the great corrupter, ought neither to wonder nor to doubt that, as the prowess of the corrupting and God-opposing angel overthrew in the beginning the virtue of man, the work and image of God, the possessor of the world, so he has entirely changed man's nature—created, like his own, for perfect sinlessness—into his own state of wicked enmity against his Maker, that in the very thing whose gift to man, but not to him, had grieved him, he might make man guilty in God's eyes, and set up his own supremacy.[1]

CHAP. III.

Fortified by tnis knowledge against heathen views, let us rather turn to the unworthy reasonings of our own people ; for the faith of some, either too simple or too scrupulous, demands direct authority from Scripture for giving up the shows, and holds out that the matter is a doubtful one, because such abstinence is not clearly and in words imposed upon God's servants. Well, we never find it expressed with the same precision, " Thou shalt not enter circus or theatre, thou shalt not look on combat or show ; " as it is plainly laid down, " Thou shalt not kill; thou shalt not worship an idol ; thou shalt not commit adultery or fraud." [2] But we find that that first word of David bears on this very sort of thing : " Blessed," he says, " is the man who has not gone into the assembly of the impious,

---

[1] [For the demonology of this treatise, compare capp. 10, 12, 13, 23, and see Kaye's full but condensed statement (pp. 201-204), in his *account of the writings*, etc.]
[2] Ex. xx. 14.

nor stood in the way of sinners, nor sat in the seat of scorners."[1] Though he seems to have predicted beforehand of that just man, that he took no part in the meetings and deliberations of the Jews, taking counsel about the slaying of our Lord, yet divine Scripture has ever far-reaching applications : after the immediate sense has been exhausted, in all directions it fortifies the practice of the religious life, so that here also you have an utterance which is not far from a plain interdicting of the shows. If he called those few Jews an assembly of the wicked, how much more will he so designate so vast a gathering of heathens ! Are the heathens less impious, less sinners, less enemies of Christ, than the Jews were then ? And see, too, how other things agree. For at the shows they also stand in the way. For they call the spaces between the seats going round the amphitheatre, and the passages which separate the people running down, ways. The place in the curve where the matrons sit is called a chair. Therefore, on the contrary, it holds, unblessed is he who has entered any council of wicked men, and has stood in any way of sinners, and has sat in any chair of scorners. We may understand a thing as spoken generally, even when it requires a certain special interpretation to be given to it. For some things spoken with a special reference .contain in them general truth. When God admonishes the Israelites of their duty, or sharply reproves them, He has surely a reference to all men ; when He threatens destruction to Egypt and Ethiopia, He surely pre-condemns every sinning nation whatever. If, reasoning from *species* to *genus*, every nation that sins against them is an Egypt and Ethiopia ; so also, reasoning from genus to species, with reference to the origin of shows, every show is an assembly of the wicked.

CHAP. IV.

Lest any one think that we are dealing in mere argumentative subtleties, I shall turn to that highest authority of our " seal " itself. When entering the water, we make profession of the Christian faith in the words of its rule ; we bear public testimony that we have renounced the devil, his pomp, and his angels. Well, is it not in connection with idolatry, above all, that you have the devil with his pomp and his angels? from which, to speak briefly—for I do not wish to dilate—you have every unclean and wicked spirit. If, there-

fore, it shall be made plain that the entire apparatus of the shows is based upon idolatry, beyond all doubt that will carry with it the conclusion that our renunciatory testimony in the laver of baptism has reference to the shows, which, through their idolatry, have been given over to the devil, and his pomp, and his angels. We shall set forth, then, their several origins, in what nursing-places they have grown to manhood ; next the titles of some of them, by what names they are called ; then their apparatus, with what superstitions they are observed; (then their places, to what patrons they are dedicated;) then the arts which minister to them, to what authors they are traced. If any of these shall be found to have had no connection with an idol-god, it will be held as free at once from the taint of idolatry, and as not coming within the range of our baptismal abjuration.[2]

CHAP. V.

In the matter of their origins, as these are somewhat obscure and but little known to many among us, our investigations must go back to a remote antiquity, and our authorities be none other than books of heathen literature. Various authors are extant who have published works on the subject. The origin of the games as given by them is this. Timæus tells us that immigrants from Asia, under the leadership of Tyrrhenus, who, in a contest about his native kingdom, had succumbed to his brother, settled down in Etruria. Well, among other superstitious observances under the name of religion, they set up in their new home public shows. The Romans, at their own request, obtain from them skilled performers—the proper seasons—the name too, for it is said they are called *Ludi*, from *Lydi*. And though Varro derives the name of *Ludi* from *Ludus*, that is, from play, as they called the Luperci also *Ludii*, because they ran about making sport; still that sporting of young men belongs, in his view, to festal days and temples, and objects of religious veneration. However, it is of little consequence the origin of the name, when it is certain that the thing springs from idolatry. The Liberalia, under the general designation of Ludi, clearly declared the glory of Father Bacchus; for to Bacchus these festivities were first consecrated by grateful peasants, in return for the boon he conferred on them, as they say, making known the pleasures of wine.

---

[1] Ps. i. 1. [Kaye's censure of this use of the text, (p. 366) seems to me gratuitous.]

[2] [Neander argues with great force that in referring to Scripture and not at all to the " New Prophecy," our author shows his orthodoxy. We may add " that *highest* authority " to which he appeals in this chapter.]

Then the Consualia were called *Ludi*, and at first were in honour of Neptune, for Neptune has the name of Consus also. Thereafter Romulus dedicated the Equiria to Mars, though they claim the Consualia too for Romulus, on the ground that he consecrated them to Consus, the god, as they will have it, of counsel; of the counsel, forsooth, in which he planned the rape of the Sabine virgins for wives to his soldiers. An excellent counsel truly; and still I suppose reckoned just and righteous by the Romans themselves, I may not say by God. This goes also to taint the origin: you cannot surely hold that to be good which has sprung from sin, from shamelessness, from violence, from hatred, from a fratricidal founder, from a son of Mars. Even now, at the first turning-post in the circus, there is a subterranean altar to this same Consus, with an inscription to this effect: "Consus, great in counsel, Mars, in battle, mighty tutelar deities." The priests of the state sacrifice at it on the nones of July; the priest of Romulus and the Vestals on the twelfth before the Kalends of September. In addition to this, Romulus instituted games in honor of Jupiter Feretrius on the Tarpeian Hill, according to the statement Piso has handed down to us, called both Tarpeian and Capitoline. After him Numa Pompilius instituted games to Mars and Robigo (for they have also invented a goddess of rust); then Tullus Hostilius; then Ancus Martius; and various others in succession did the like. As to the idols in whose honour these games were established, ample information is to be found in the pages of Suetonius Tranquillus. But we need say no more to prove the accusation of idolatrous origin.

CHAP. VI.

To the testimony of antiquity is added that of later games instituted in their turn, and betraying their origin from the titles which they bear even at the present day, in which it is imprinted as on their very face, for what idol and for what religious object games, whether of the one kind or the other, were designed. You have festivals bearing the name of *the great Mother*[1] and Apollo of Ceres too, and Neptune, and Jupiter Latiaris, and Flora, all celebrated for a common end; the others have their religious origin in the birthdays and solemnities of kings, in public successes in municipal holidays. There are also testamentary exhibitions, in which funeral honours are rendered to the memories of private persons; and this according to an insti-

tution of ancient times. For from the first the "Ludi" were regarded as of two sorts, sacred and funereal, that is in honour of the heathen deities and of the dead. But in the matter of idolatry, it makes no difference with us under what name or title it is practised, while it has to do with the wicked spirits whom we abjure. If it is lawful to offer homage to the dead, it will be just as lawful to offer it to their gods: you have the same origin in both cases; there is the same idolatry; there is on our part the same solemn renunciation of all idolatry.

CHAP. VII.

The two kinds of public games, then, have one origin; and they have common names, as owning the same parentage. So, too, as they are equally tainted with the sin of idolatry, their foundress, they must needs be like each other in their pomp. But the more ambitious preliminary display of the circus games to which the name procession specially belongs, is in itself the proof to whom the whole thing appertains, in the many images the long line of statues, the chariots of all sorts, the thrones, the crowns, the dresses. What high religious rites besides, what sacrifices precede, come between, and follow. How many guilds, how many priesthoods, how many offices are set astir, is known to the inhabitants of the great city in which the demon convention has its headquarters. If these things are done in humbler style in the provinces, in accordance with their inferior means, still all circus games must be counted as belonging to that from which they are derived; the fountain from which they spring defiles them. The tiny streamlet from its very spring-head, the little twig from its very budding, contains in it the essential nature of its origin. It may be grand or mean, no matter, any circus procession whatever is offensive to God. Though there be few images to grace it, there is idolatry in one; though there be no more than a single sacred car, it is a chariot of Jupiter: anything of idolatry whatever, whether meanly arrayed or modestly rich and gorgeous, taints it in its origin.

CHAP. VIII.

To follow out my plan in regard to places: the circus is chiefly consecrated to the Sun, whose temple stands in the middle of it, and whose image shines forth from its temple summit; for they have not thought it proper to pay sacred honours underneath a roof to an object they have itself in open space.

---

[1] [Cybele.]

Those who assert that the first spectacle was exhibited by Circe, and in honour of the Sun her father, as they will have it, maintain also the name of circus was derived from her. Plainly, then, the enchantress did this in the name of the parties whose priestess she was —I mean the demons and spirits of evil. What an aggregation of idolatries you see, accordingly, in the decoration of the place! Every ornament of the circus is a temple by itself. The eggs are regarded as sacred to the Castors, by men who are not ashamed to profess faith in their production from the egg of a swan, which was no other than Jupiter himself. The Dolphins vomit forth in honour of Neptune. Images of Sessia, so called as the goddess of sowing; of Messia, so called as the goddess of reaping; of Tutulina, so called as the fruit-protecting deity—load the pillars. In front of these you have three altars to these three gods—Great, Mighty, Victorious. They reckon these of Samo-Thrace. The huge Obelisk, as Hermeteles affirms, is set up in public to the Sun; its inscription, like its origin, belongs to Egyptian superstition. Cheerless were the demon-gathering without their *Mater Magna*; and so she presides there over the Euripus. Consus, as we have mentioned, lies hidden under ground at the Murcian Goals. These two sprang from an idol. For they will have it that Murcia is the goddess of love; and to her, at that spot, they have consecrated a temple. See, Christian, how many impure names have taken possession of the circus! You have nothing to do with a sacred place which is tenanted by such multitudes of diabolic spirits. And speaking of places, this is the suitable occasion for some remarks in anticipation of a point that some will raise. What, then, you say; shall I be in danger of pollution if I go to the circus when the games are not being celebrated? There is no law forbidding the mere places to us. For not only the places for show-gatherings, but even the temples, may be entered without any peril of his religion by the servant of God, if he has only some honest reason for it, unconnected with their proper business and official duties. Why, even the streets, and the market-place, and the baths, and the taverns, and our very dwelling-places, are not altogether free from idols. Satan and his angels have filled the whole world. It is not by merely being in the world, however, that we lapse from God, but by touching and tainting ourselves with the world's sins. I shall break with my Maker, that is, by going to the Capitol or the temple of Serapis to sacrifice or adore, as I shall also do by going as a spectator to the circus and the theatre. The places in themselves do not contaminate, but what is done in them; from this even the places themselves, we maintain, become defiled. The polluted things pollute us. It is on this account that we set before you to whom places of the kind are dedicated, that we may prove the things which are done in them to belong to the idol-patrons to whom the very places are sacred.[1]

CHAP. IX.

Now as to the kind of performances peculiar to the circus exhibitions. In former days equestrianism was practised in a simple way on horseback, and certainly its ordinary use had nothing sinful in it; but when it was dragged into the games, it passed from the service of God into the employment of demons. Accordingly this kind of circus performances is regarded as sacred to Castor and Pollux, to whom, Stesichorus tells us, horses were given by Mercury. And Neptune, too, is an equestrian deity, by the Greeks called Hippius. In regard to the team, they have consecrated the chariot and four to the sun; the chariot and pair to the moon. But, as the poet has it, "Erichthonius first dared to yoke four horses to the chariot, and to ride upon its wheels with victorious swiftness." Erichthonius, the son of Vulcan and Minerva, fruit of unworthy passion upon earth, is a demonmonster, nay, the devil himself, and no mere snake. But if Trochilus the Argive is maker of the first chariot, he dedicated that work of his to Juno. If Romulus first exhibited the four-horse chariot at Rome, he too, I think, has a place given him among idols, at least if he and Quirinus are the same. But as chariots had such inventors, the charioteers were naturally dressed, too, in the colours of idolatry; for at first these were only two, namely white and red,—the former sacred to the winter with its glistening snows, the latter sacred to the summer with its ruddy sun: but afterwards, in the progress of luxury as well as of superstition, red was dedicated by some to Mars, and white by others to the Zephyrs, while green was given to Mother Earth, or spring, and azure to the sky and sea, or autumn. But as idolatry of every kind is condemned by God, that form of it surely shares the condemnation which is offered to the elements of nature.

CHAP. X.

Let us pass on now to theatrical exhibitions, which we have already shown have a common

---

[1] [Very admirable reflections on this chapter may be found in Kaye, pp. 362–3.]

origin with the circus, and bear like idolatrous designations—even as from the first they have borne the name of "Ludi," and equally minister to idols. They resemble each other also in their pomp, having the same procession to the scene of their display from temples and altars, and that mournful profusion of incense and blood, with music of pipes and trumpets, all under the direction of the soothsayer and the undertaker, those two foul masters of funeral rites and sacrifices. So as we went on from the origin of the "Ludi" to the circus games, we shall now direct our course thence to those of the theatre, beginning with the place of exhibition. At first the theatre was properly a temple of Venus; and, to speak briefly, it was owing to this that stage performances were allowed to escape censure, and got a footing in the world. For ofttimes the censors, in the interests of morality, put down above all the rising theatres, foreseeing, as they did, that there was great danger of their leading to a general profligacy; so that already, from this accordance of their own people with us, there is a witness to the heathen, and in the anticipatory judgment of human knowledge even a confirmation of our views. Accordingly Pompey the Great, less only than his theatre, when he had erected that citadel of all impurities, fearing some time or other censorian condemnation of his memory, superposed on it a temple of Venus; and summoning by public proclamation the people to its consecration, he called it not a theatre, but a temple, "under which," said he, "we have placed tiers of seats for viewing the shows." So he threw a veil over a structure on which condemnation had been often passed, and which is ever to be held in reprobation, by pretending that it was a sacred place; and by means of superstition he blinded the eyes of a virtuous discipline. But Venus and Bacchus are close allies. These two evil spirits are in sworn confederacy with each other, as the patrons of drunkenness and lust. So the theatre of Venus is as well the house of Bacchus: for they properly gave the name of Liberalia also to other theatrical amusements— which besides being consecrated to Bacchus (as were the Dionysia of the Greeks), were instituted by him; and, without doubt, the performances of the theatre have the common patronage of these two deities. That immodesty of gesture and attire which so specially and peculiarly characterizes the stage are consecrated to them—the one deity wanton by her sex, the other by his drapery; while its services of voice, and song, and lute, and pipe, belong to Apollos, and Muses, and Minervas, and Mercuries. You will hate, O Christian, the things whose authors must be the objects of your utter detestation. So we would now make a remark about the arts of the theatre, about the things also whose authors in the names we execrate. We know that the names of the dead are nothing, as are their images; but we know well enough, too, who, when images are set up, under these names carry on their wicked work, and exult in the homage rendered to them, and pretend to be divine—none other than spirits accursed, than devils. We see, therefore, that the arts also are consecrated to the service of the beings who dwell in the names of their founders; and that things cannot be held free from the taint of idolatry whose inventors have got a place among the gods for their discoveries. Nay, as regards the arts, we ought to have gone further back, and barred all further argument by the position that the demons, predetermining in their own interests from the first, among other evils of idolatry, the pollutions of the public shows, with the object of drawing man away from his Lord and binding him to their own service, carried out their purpose by bestowing on him the artistic gifts which the shows require. For none but themselves would have made provision and preparation for the objects they had in view; nor would they have given the arts to the world by any but those in whose names, and images, and histories they set up for their own ends the artifice of consecration.

CHAP. XI.

In fulfilment of our plan, let us now go on to consider the combats. Their origin is akin to that of the games (*ludi*). Hence they are kept as either sacred or funereal, as they have been instituted in honour of the idol-gods of the nations or of the dead. Thus, too, they are called Olympian in honour of Jupiter, known at Rome as the Capitoline; Nemean, in honour of Hercules; Isthmian, in honour of Neptune; the rest *mortuarii*, as belonging to the dead. What wonder, then, if idolatry pollutes the combat-parade with profane crowns, with sacerdotal chiefs, with attendants belonging to the various colleges, last of all with the blood of its sacrifices? To add a completing word about the "place"—in the common place for the college of the arts sacred to the Muses, and Apollo, and Minerva, and also for that of the arts dedicated to Mars, they with contest and sound of trumpet emulate the circus in the arena, which is a real temple—I mean of the god whose festivals it celebrates. The gymnastic arts also originated with their Castors, and Herculeses, and Mercuries.

CHAP. XII.

It remains for us to examine the "specta-cle" most noted of all, and in highest favour. It is called a dutiful service (*munus*), from its being an office, for it bears the name of "*offi-cium*" as well as "*munus.*" The ancients thought that in this solemnity they rendered offices to the dead ; at a later period, with a cruelty more refined, they somewhat modified its character. For formerly, in the belief that the souls of the departed were appeased by human blood, they were in the habit of buying captives or slaves of wicked disposition, and immolating them in their funeral obsequies. Afterwards they thought good to throw the veil of pleasure over their iniquity.[1] Those, therefore, whom they had provided for the combat, and then trained in arms as best they could, only that they might learn to die, they, on the funeral day, killed at the places of sepulture. They alleviated death by murders. Such is the origin of the "Munus." But by degrees their refinement came up to their cruelty ; for these human wild beasts could not find pleasure exquisite enough, save in the spectacle of men torn to pieces by wild beasts. Offerings to propitiate the dead then were regarded as belonging to the class of funeral sacrifices ; and these are idolatry : for idolatry, in fact, is a sort of homage to the departed ; the one as well as the other is a service to dead men. Moreover, demons have abode in the images of the dead. To refer also to the matter of names, though this sort of exhibition has passed from honours of the dead to honours of the living, I mean, to quæstorships and magistracies—to priestly offices of different kinds ; yet, since idolatry still cleaves to the dignity's name, whatever is done in its name partakes of its impurity. The same remark will apply to the procession of the "Munus," as we look at that in the pomp which is connected with these honours themselves ; for the purple robes, the fasces, the filiets the crowns, the proclamations too, and edicts, the sacred feasts of the day before, are not without the pomp of the devil, without invitation of demons. What need, then, of dwelling on the place of horrors, which is too much even for the tongue of the perjurer ? For the amphitheatre[2] is consecrated to names more numerous and more dire[3] than is the Capitol itself, temple of all demons as it is. There are as many unclean spirits there as it

holds men. To conclude with a single remark about the arts which have a place in it, we know that its two sorts of amusement have for their patrons Mars and Diana.

CHAP. XIII.

We have, I think, faithfully carried out our plan of showing in how many different ways the sin of idolatry clings to the shows, in re-spect of their origins, their titles, their equip-ments, their places of celebration, their arts ; and we may hold it as a thing beyond all doubt, that for us who have twice[4] renounced all idols, they are utterly unsuitable. "Not that an idol is anything,"[5] as the apostle says, but that the homage they render is to demons, who are the real occupants of these conse-crated images, whether of dead men or (as they think) of gods. On this account, there-fore, because they have a common source— for their dead and their deities are one—we abstain from both idolatries. Nor do we dis-like the temples less than the monuments : we have nothing to do with either altar, we adore neither image ; we do not offer sacrifices to the gods, and we make no funeral oblations to the departed ; nay, we do not partake of what is offered either in the one case or the other, for we cannot partake of God's feast and the feast of devils.[6] If, then, we keep throat and belly free from such defilements, how much more do we withhold our nobler parts, our ears and eyes, from the idolatrous and funereal enjoyments, which are not passed through the body, but are digested in the very spirit and soul, whose purity, much more than that of our bodily organs, God has a right to claim from us.

CHAP. XIV.

Having sufficiently established the charge of idolatry, which alone ought to be reason enough for our giving up the shows, let us now *ex abundanti* look at the subject in an-other way, for the sake of those especially who keep themselves comfortable in the thought that the abstinence we urge is not in so many words enjoined, as if in the condem-nation of the lusts of the world there was not involved a sufficient declaration against all these amusements. For as there is a lust of money, or rank, or eating, or impure enjoy-ment, or glory, so there is also a lust of pleas-ure. But the show is just a sort of pleasure. I think, then, that under the general designa-tion of lusts, pleasures are included ; in like manner, under the general idea of pleasures,

---

[1] [The authority of Tertullian, in this matter, is accepted by the critics, as of historic importance.]
[2] [Though this was probably written at Carthage, his reference to the Flavian theatre in this place is plain from the immediate comparison with the Capitol.]
[3] [To the infernal deities and first of all to Pluto. See vol. I. note 6, p. 131, this Series.]

[4] [Bunsen, *Hippol.* vol. III. pp. 20-22.]
[5] 1 Cor. viii. 4.
[6] 1 Cor. x. 21.

you have as a specific class the " shows." But we have spoken already of how it is with the places of exhibition, that they are not polluting in themselves, but owing to the things that are done in them from which they imbibe impurity, and then spirt it again on others.

CHAP. XV.

Having done enough, then, as we have said, in regard to that principal argument, that there is in them all the taint of idolatry—having sufficiently dealt with that, let us now contrast the other characteristics of the show with the things of God. God has enjoined us to deal calmly, gently, quietly, and peacefully with the Holy Spirit, because these things are alone in keeping with the goodness of His nature, with His tenderness and sensitiveness, and not to vex Him with rage, ill-nature, anger, or grief. Well, how shall this be made to accord with the shows? For the show always leads to spiritual agitation, since where there is pleasure, there is keenness of feeling giving pleasure its zest; and where there is keenness of feeling, there is rivalry giving in turn its zest to that. Then, too, where you have rivalry, you have rage, bitterness, wrath, and grief, with all bad things which flow from them—the whole entirely out of keeping with the religion of Christ. For even suppose one should enjoy the shows in a moderate way, as befits his rank, age or nature, still he is not undisturbed in mind, without some unuttered movings of the inner man. No one partakes of pleasures such as these without their strong excitements; no one comes under their excitements without their natural lapses. These lapses, again, create passionate desire. If there is no desire, there is no pleasure, and he is chargeable with trifling who goes where nothing is gotten; in my view, even that is foreign to us. Moreover, a man pronounces his own condemnation in the very act of taking his place among those with whom, by his disinclination to be like them, he confesses he has no sympathy. It is not enough that we do no such things ourselves, unless we break all connection also with those who do. "If thou sawest a thief," says the Scripture, "thou consentedst with him."[1] Would that we did not even inhabit the same world with these wicked men! But though that wish cannot be realized, yet even now we are separate from them in what is of the world; for the world is God's, but the worldly is the devil's.

---

[1] Ps. xlix. 18. [This chapter bears on modern theatres.]

CHAP. XVI.

Since, then, all passionate excitement is forbidden us, we are debarred from every kind of spectacle, and especially from the circus, where such excitement presides as in its proper element. See the people coming to it already under strong emotion, already tumultuous, already passion-blind, already agitated about their bets. The prætor is too slow for them: their eyes are ever rolling as though along with the lots in his urn; then they hang all eager on the signal; there is the united shout of a common madness. Observe how "out of themselves" they are by their foolish speeches. "He has thrown it!" they exclaim; and they announce each one to his neighbour what all have seen. I have clearest evidence of their blindness; they do not see what is really thrown. They think it a "signal cloth," but it is the likeness of the devil cast headlong from on high. And the result accordingly is, that they fly into rages, and passions, and discords, and all that they who are consecrated to peace ought never to indulge in. Then there are curses and reproaches, with no cause of hatred; there are cries of applause, with nothing to merit them. What are the partakers in all this—not their own masters—to obtain of it for themselves? unless, it may be, that which makes them not their own: they are saddened by another's sorrow, they are gladdened by another's joy. Whatever they desire on the one hand, or detest on the other, is entirely foreign to themselves. So love with them is a useless thing, and hatred is unjust. Or is a causeless love perhaps more legitimate than a causeless hatred? God certainly forbids us to hate even with a reason for our hating; for He commands us to love our enemies. God forbids us to curse, though there be some ground for doing so, in commanding that those who curse us we are to bless. But what is more merciless than the circus, where people do not spare even their rulers and fellow-citizens? If any of its madnesses are becoming elsewhere in the saints of God, they will be seemly in the circus too; but if they are nowhere right, so neither are they there.

CHAP. XVII.

Are we not, in like manner, enjoined to put away from us all immodesty? On this ground, again, we are excluded from the theatre, which is immodesty's own peculiar abode, where nothing is in repute but what elsewhere is disreputable. So the best path to the highest favour of its god is the vileness which the Atellan[1] gesticulates, which the buffoon in woman's clothes exhibits, destroying all natural modesty, so that they blush more readily at home than at the play, which finally is done from his childhood on the person of the pantomime, that he may become an actor. The very harlots, too, victims of the public lust, are brought upon the stage, their misery increased as being there in the presence of their own sex, from whom alone they are wont to hide themselves: they are paraded publicly before every age and every rank— their abode, their gains, their praises, are set forth, and that even in the hearing of those who should not hear such things. I say nothing about other matters, which it were good to hide away in their own darkness and their own gloomy caves, lest they should stain the light of day. Let the Senate, let all ranks, blush for very shame! Why, even these miserable women, who by their own gestures destroy their modesty, dreading the light of day, and the people's gaze, know something of shame at least once a year. But if we ought to abominate all that is immodest, on what ground is it right to hear what we must not speak? For all licentiousness of speech, nay, every idle word, is condemned by God. Why, in the same way, is it right to look on what it is disgraceful to do? How is it that the things which defile a man in going out of his mouth, are not regarded as doing so when they go in at his eyes and ears—when eyes and ears are the immediate attendants on the spirit—and that can never be pure whose servants-in-waiting are impure? You have the theatre forbidden, then, in the forbidding of immodesty. If, again, we despise the teaching of secular literature as being foolishness in God's eyes, our duty is plain enough in regard to those spectacles, which from this source derive the tragic or comic play. If tragedies and comedies are the bloody and wanton, the impious and licentious inventors of crimes and lusts, it is not good even that there should be any calling to remembrance the atrocious or the vile. What you reject in deed, you are not to bid welcome to in word.

CHAP. XVIII.

But if you argue that the racecourse is mentioned in Scripture, I grant it at once. But you will not refuse to admit that the things which are done there are not for you to look upon: the blows, and kicks, and cuffs, and all the recklessness of hand, and every-

thing like that disfiguration of the human countenance, which is nothing less than the disfiguration of God's own image. You will never give your approval to those foolish racing and throwing feats, and yet more foolish leapings; you will never find pleasure in injurious or useless exhibitions of strength; certainly you will not regard with approval those efforts after an artificial body which aim at surpassing the Creator's work; and you will have the very opposite of complacency in the athletes Greece, in the inactivity of peace, feeds up. And the wrestler's art is a devil's thing. The devil wrestled with, and crushed to death, the first human beings. Its very attitude has power in it of the serpent kind, firm to hold—tortures to clasp—slippery to glide away. You have no need of crowns; why do you strive to get pleasures from crowns?

CHAP. XIX.

We shall now see how the Scriptures condemn the amphitheatre. If we can maintain that it is right to indulge in the cruel, and the impious, and the fierce, let us go there. If we are what we are said to be, let us regale ourselves there with human blood. It is good, no doubt, to have the guilty punished. Who but the criminal himself will deny that? And yet the innocent can find no pleasure in another's sufferings: he rather mourns that a brother has sinned so heinously as to need a punishment so dreadful. But who is my guarantee that it is always the guilty who are adjudged to the wild beasts, or to some other doom, and that the guiltless never suffer from the revenge of the judge, or the weakness of the defence, or the pressure of the rack? How much better, then, is it for me to remain ignorant of the punishment inflicted on the wicked, lest I am obliged to know also of the good coming to untimely ends—if I may speak of goodness in the case at all! At any rate, gladiators not chargeable with crime are offered in sale for the games, that they may become the victims of the public pleasure. Even in the case of those who are judicially condemned to the amphitheatre, what a monstrous thing it is, that, in undergoing their punishment, they, from some less serious delinquency, advance to the criminality of manslayers! But I mean these remarks for heathen. As to Christians, I shall not insult them by adding another word as to the aversion with which they should regard this sort of exhibition; though no one is more able than myself to set forth fully the whole subject, unless it be one who is still in the habit

---

[1] [The *ludi Atellani* were so called from Atella, in Campania, where a vast amphitheatre delighted the inhabitants. Juvenal, Sat. vi. 71. The like disgrace our times.]

of going to the shows. I would rather withal be incomplete than set memory a-working.[1]

CHAP. XX.

How vain, then—nay, how desperate—is the reasoning of persons, who, just because they decline to lose a pleasure, hold out that we cannot point to the specific words or the very place where this abstinence is mentioned, and where the servants of God are directly forbidden to have anything to do with such assemblies! I heard lately a novel defence of himself by a certain play-lover. "The sun," said he, "nay, God Himself, looks down from heaven on the show, and no pollution is contracted." Yes, and the sun, too, pours down his rays into the common sewer without being defiled. As for God, would that all crimes were hid from His eye, that we might all escape judgment! But He looks on robberies too; He looks on falsehoods, adulteries, frauds, idolatries, and these same shows; and precisely on that account *we* will not look on them, lest the All-seeing see us. You are putting on the same level, O man, the criminal and the judge; the criminal who is a criminal because he is seen, and the Judge who is a Judge because He sees. Are we set, then, on playing the madman outside the circus boundaries? Outside the gates of the theatre are we bent on lewdness, outside the course on arrogance, and outside the amphitheatre on cruelty, because outside the porticoes, the tiers and the curtains, too, God has eyes? Never and nowhere is that free from blame which God ever condemns; never and nowhere is it right to do what you may not do at all times and in all places. It is the freedom of the truth from change of opinion and varying judgments which constitutes its perfection, and gives it its claims to full mastery, unchanging reverence, and faithful obedience. That which is really good or really evil cannot be ought else. But in all things the truth of God is immutable.

CHAP. XXI.

The heathen, who have not a full revelation of the truth, for they are not taught of God, hold a thing evil and good as it suits self-will and passion, making that which is good in one place evil in another, and that which is evil in one place in another good. So it strangely happens, that the same man who can scarcely in public lift up his tunic, even when necessity of nature presses him, takes it off in the

circus, as if bent on exposing himself before everybody; the father who carefully protects and guards his virgin daughter's ears from every polluting word, takes her to the theatre himself, exposing her to all its vile words and attitudes; he, again, who in the streets lays hands on or covers with reproaches the brawling pugilist, in the arena gives all encouragement to combats of a much more serious kind; and he who looks with horror on the corpse of one who has died under the common law of nature, in the amphitheatre gazes down with most patient eyes on bodies all mangled and torn and smeared with their own blood; nay, the very man who comes to the show, because he thinks murderers ought to suffer for their crime, drives the unwilling gladiator to the murderous deed with rods and scourges; and one who demands the lion for every manslayer of deeper dye, will have the staff for the savage swordsman, and rewards him with the cap of liberty. Yes and he must have the poor victim back again, that he may get a sight of his face—with zest inspecting near at hand the man whom he wished torn in pieces at safe distance from him: so much the more cruel he if that was not his wish.

CHAP. XXII.

What wonder is there in it? Such inconsistencies as these are just such as we might expect from men, who confuse and change the nature of good and evil in their inconstancy of feeling and fickleness in judgment. Why, the authors and managers of the spectacles, in that very respect with reference to which they highly laud the charioteers, and actors, and wrestlers, and those most loving gladiators, to whom men prostitute their souls, women too their bodies, slight and trample on them, though for their sakes they are guilty of the deeds they reprobate; nay, they doom them to ignominy and the loss of their rights as citizens, excluding them from the Curia, and the rostra, from senatorial and equestrian rank, and from all other honours as well as certain distinctions. What perversity! They have pleasure in those whom yet they punish; they put all slights on those to whom, at the same time, they award their approbation; they magnify the art and brand the artist. What an outrageous thing it is, to blacken a man on account of the very things which make him meritorious in their eyes! Nay, what a confession that the things are evil, when their authors, even in highest favour, are not without a mark of disgrace upon them!

---

[1] [See Kaye, p. 11. This expression is thought to confirm the probability of Tertullian's original Gentilism.]

CHAP. XXIII.

Seeing, then, man's own reflections, even in spite of the sweetness of pleasure, lead him to think that people such as these should be condemned to a hapless lot of infamy, losing all the advantages connected with the possession of the dignities of life, how much more does the divine righteousness inflict punishment on those who give themselves to these arts! Will God have any pleasure in the charioteer who disquiets so many souls, rouses up so many furious passions, and creates so many various moods, either crowned like a priest or wearing the colours of a pimp,—decked out by the devil that he may be whirled away in his chariot, as though with the object of taking off Elijah? Will He be pleased with him who applies the razor to himself, and completely changes his features; who, with no respect for his face, is not content with making it as like as possible to Saturn and Isis and Bacchus, but gives it quietly over to contumelious blows, as if in mockery of our Lord? The devil, forsooth, makes it part, too, of his teaching, that the cheek is to be meekly offered to the smiter. In the same way, with their high shoes, he has made the tragic actors taller, because "none can add a cubit to his stature."[1] His desire is to make Christ a liar. And in regard to the wearing of masks, I ask is that according to the mind of God, who forbids the making of every likeness, and especially then the likeness of man who is His own image? The Author of truth hates all the false; He regards as adultery all that is unreal. Condemning, therefore, as He does hypocrisy in every form, He never will approve any putting on of voice, or sex, or age; He never will approve pretended loves, and wraths, and groans, and tears. Then, too, as in His law it is declared that the man is cursed who attires himself in female garments,[2] what must be His judgment of the pantomime, who is even brought up to play the woman! And will the boxer go unpunished? I suppose he received these cæstus-scars, and the thick skin of his fists, and these growths upon his ears, at his creation! God, too, gave him eyes for no other end than that they might be knocked out in fighting! I say nothing of him who, to save himself, thrusts another in the lion's way, that he may not be too little of a murderer when he puts to death that very same man on the arena.

CHAP. XXIV.

In how many other ways shall we yet further

show that nothing which is peculiar to the shows has God's approval, or without that approval is becoming in God's servants? If we have succeeded in making it plain that they were instituted entirely for the devil's sake, and have been got up entirely with the devil's things (for all that is not God's, or is not pleasing in His eyes, belongs to His wicked rival), this simply means that in them you have that pomp of the devil which in the "seal" of our faith we abjure. We should have no connection with the things which we abjure, whether in deed or word, whether by looking on them or looking forward to them; but do we not abjure and rescind that baptismal pledge, when we cease to bear its testimony? Does it then remain for us to apply to the heathen themselves. Let them tell us, then, whether it is right in Christians to frequent the show. Why, the rejection of these amusements is the chief sign to them that a man has adopted the Christian faith. If any one, then, puts away the faith's distinctive badge, he is plainly guilty of denying it. What hope can you possibly retain in regard to a man who does that? When you go over to the enemy's camp, you throw down your arms, desert the standards and the oath of allegiance to your chief: you cast in your lot for life or death with your new friends.

CHAP. XXV.

Seated where there is nothing of God, will one be thinking of his Maker? Will there be peace in his soul when there is eager strife there for a charioteer? Wrought up into a frenzied excitement, will he learn to be modest? Nay, in the whole thing he will meet with no greater temptation than that gay attiring of the men and women. The very intermingling of emotions, the very agreements and disagreements with each other in the bestowment of their favours, where you have such close communion, blow up the sparks of passion. And then there is scarce any other object in going to the show, but to see and to be seen. When a tragic actor is declaiming, will one be giving thought to prophetic appeals? Amid the measures of the effeminate player, will he call up to himself a psalm? And when the athletes are hard at struggle, will he be ready to proclaim that there must be no striking again? And with his eye fixed on the bites of bears, and the sponge-nets of the net-fighters, can he be moved by compassion? May God avert from His people any such passionate eagerness after a cruel enjoyment! For how monstrous it is to go from God's church to the devil's—from

---

[1] Matt. vi. 27.
[2] Deut. xxii.

the sky to the stye,[1] as they say; to raise your hands to God, and then to weary them in the applause of an actor; out of the mouth, from which you uttered Amen over the Holy Thing, to give witness in a gladiator's favour; to cry "for ever" to any one else but God and Christ!

CHAP. XXVI.

Why may not those who go into the temptations of the show become accessible also to evil spirits? We have the case of the woman—the Lord Himself is witness—who went to the theatre, and came back possessed. In the outcasting,[2] accordingly, when the unclean creature was upbraided with having dared to attack a believer, he firmly replied,[3] "And in truth I did it most righteously, for I found her in my domain." Another case, too, is well known, in which a woman had been hearing a tragedian, and on the very night she saw in her sleep a linen cloth—the actor's name being mentioned at the same time with strong disapproval—and five days after that woman was no more. How many other undoubted proofs we have had in the case of persons who, by keeping company with the devil in the shows, have fallen from the Lord! For no one can serve two masters.[4] What fellowship has light with darkness, life with death?[5]

CHAP. XXVII.

We ought to detest these heathen meetings and assemblies, if on no other account than that there God's name is blasphemed—that there the cry "To the lions!" is daily raised against us[6]—that from thence persecuting decrees are wont to emanate, and temptations are sent forth. What will you do if you are caught in that heaving tide of impious judgments? Not that there any harm is likely to come to you from men: nobody knows that you are a Christian; but think how it fares with you in heaven. For at the very time the devil is working havoc in the church, do you doubt that the angels are looking down from above, and marking every man, who speaks and who listens to the blaspheming word, who lends his tongue and who lends his ears to the service of Satan against God? Shall you not then shun those tiers where the enemies

of Christ assemble, that seat of all that is pestilential, and the very superincumbent atmosphere all impure with wicked cries? Grant that you have there things that are pleasant, things both agreeable and innocent in themselves; even some things that are excellent. Nobody dilutes poison with gall and hellebore: the accursed thing is put into condiments well seasoned and of sweetest taste. So, too, the devil puts into the deadly draught which he prepares, things of God most pleasant and most acceptable. Everything there, then, that is either brave, noble, loud-sounding, melodious, or exquisite in taste, hold it but as the honey drop of a poisoned cake; nor make so much of your taste for its pleasures, as of the danger you run from its attractions.

CHAP. XXVIII.

With such dainties as these let the devil's guests be feasted. The places and the times, the inviter too, are theirs. Our banquets, our nuptial joys, are yet to come. We cannot sit down in fellowship with them, as neither can they with us. Things in this matter go by their turns. Now they have gladness and we are troubled. "The world," says Jesus, "shall rejoice; ye shall be sorrowful."[7] Let us mourn, then, while the heathen are merry, that in the day of their sorrow we may rejoice; lest, sharing now in their gladness, we share then also in their grief. Thou art too dainty, Christian, if thou wouldst have pleasure in this life as well as in the next; nay, a fool thou art, if thou thinkest this life's pleasures to be really pleasures. The philosophers, for instance, give the name of pleasure to quietness and repose; in that they have their bliss; in that they find entertainment: they even glory in it. You long for the goal, and the stage, and the dust, and the place of combat! I would have you answer me this question: Can we not live without pleasure, who cannot but with pleasure die? For what is our wish but the apostle's, to leave the world, and be taken up into the fellowship of our Lord?[8] You have your joys where you have your longings.

CHAP. XXIX.

Even as things are, if your thought is to spend this period of existence in enjoyments, how are you so ungrateful as to reckon insufficient, as not thankfully to recognize the many and exquisite pleasures God has bestowed upon you? For what more delightful

---

1 [De Cælo in Cænum: (sic) Oehler.]
2 [The exorcism. For the exorcism in Baptism, see Bunsen, Hippol. iii. 19.]
3 [See Neander's explanation in Kaye, p. xxiii. But, let us observe the entire simplicity with which our author narrates a sort of incident known to the apostles. Acts, xvi. 16.]
4 Matt. vi. 24.
5 2 Cor. iv. 14.
6 [Observe—"daily raised." On this precarious condition of the Christians, in their daily life, see the calm statement of Kaye, pp. 110, 111.]

7 John xvi. 20.
8 Phil. i. 23.

than to have God the Father and our Lord at peace with us, than revelation of the truth, than confession of our errors, than pardon of the innumerable sins of our past life? What greater pleasure than distaste of pleasure itself, contempt of all that the world can give, true liberty, a pure conscience, a contented life, and freedom from all fear of death? What nobler than to tread under foot the gods of the nations—to exorcise evil spirits [1]—to perform cures—to seek divine revealings—to live to God? These are the pleasures, these the spectacles that befit Christian men—holy, everlasting, free. Count of these as your circus games, fix your eyes on the courses of the world, the gliding seasons, reckon up the periods of time, long for the goal of the final consummation, defend the societies of the churches, be startled at God's signal, be roused up at the angel's trump, glory in the palms of martyrdom. If the literature of the stage delight you, we have literature in abundance of our own—plenty of verses, sentences, songs, proverbs; and these not fabulous, but true; not tricks of art, but plain realities. Would you have also fightings and wrestlings? Well, of these there is no lacking, and they are not of slight account. Behold unchastity overcome by chastity, perfidy slain by faithfulness, cruelty stricken by compassion, impudence thrown into the shade by modesty: these are the contests we have among us, and in these *we* win our crowns. Would you have something of blood too? You have Christ's.

CHAP. XXX.

But what a spectacle is that fast-approaching advent [2] of our Lord, now owned by all, now highly exalted, now a triumphant One! What that exultation of the angelic hosts! What the glory of the rising saints! What the kingdom of the just thereafter! What the city New Jerusalem! [3] Yes, and there are other sights: that last day of judgment, with its everlasting issues; that day unlooked for by the nations, the theme of their derision, when the world hoary with age, and all its many products, shall be consumed in one great flame! How vast a spectacle then bursts upon the eye! What there excites my admiration? what my derision? Which sight gives me joy? which rouses me to exultation? —as I see so many illustrious monarchs, whose reception into the heavens was publicly announced, groaning now in the lowest darkness with great Jove himself, and those, too, who bore witness of their exultation; governors of provinces, too, who persecuted the Christian name, in fires more fierce than those with which in the days of their pride they raged against the followers of Christ. What world's wise men besides, the very philosophers, in fact, who taught their followers that God had no concern in ought that is sublunary, and were wont to assure them that either they had no souls, or that they would never return to the bodies which at death they had left, now covered with shame before the poor deluded ones, as one fire consumes them! Poets also, trembling not before the judgment-seat of Rhadamanthus or Minos, but of the unexpected Christ! I shall have a better opportunity then of hearing the tragedians, louder-voiced in their own calamity; of viewing the play-actors, much more "dissolute" in the dissolving flame; of looking upon the charioteer, all glowing in his chariot of fire; of beholding the wrestlers, not in their gymnasia, but tossing in the fiery billows; unless even then I shall not care to attend to such ministers of sin, in my eager wish rather to fix a gaze insatiable on those whose fury vented itself against the Lord. "This," I shall say, "this is that carpenter's or hireling's son, that Sabbath-breaker, that Samaritan and devil-possessed! This is He whom you purchased from Judas! This is He whom you struck with reed and fist, whom you contemptuously spat upon, to whom you gave gall and vinegar to drink! This is He whom His disciples secretly stole away, that it might be said He had risen again, or the gardener abstracted, that his lettuces might come to no harm from the crowds of visitants!'' What quæstor or priest in his munificence will bestow on you the favour of seeing and exulting in such things as these? And yet even now we in a measure have them by faith in the picturings of imagination. But what are the things which eye has not seen, ear has not heard, and which have not so much as dimly dawned upon the human heart? Whatever they are, they are nobler, I believe, than circus, and both theatres, [4] and every race-course.

---

[1] [See cap. 26 *supra*. On this claim to such powers still remaining in the church. See Kaye, p. 89.]

[2] [Kaye, p. 20. He doubtless looked for a speedy appearance of the Lord: and note the apparent expectation of a New Jerusalem, on earth, before the Consummation and Judgment.]

[3] [This *New Jerusalem* gives Bp. Kaye (p. 55) "decisive proof" of Montanism, especially as compared with the Third Book against Marcion. I cannot see it, here.]

[4] Viz., the theatre and amphitheatre. [This concluding chapter, which Gibbon delights to censure, because its fervid rhetoric so fearfully depicts the punishments of Christ's enemies, "appears to Dr. Neander to contain a beautiful specimen of lively faith and Christian confidence." See Kaye, p. *xxix*.]

THE CHAPLET, OR DE CORONA.

CHAP. I.

VERY lately it happened thus: while the bounty of our most excellent emperors[2] was dispensed in the camp, the soldiers, laurel-crowned, were approaching. One of them, more a soldier of God, more stedfast than the rest of his brethren, who had imagined that they could serve two masters, his head alone uncovered, the useless crown in his hand—already even by that peculiarity known to every one as a Christian—was nobly conspicuous. Accordingly, all began to mark him out, jeering him at a distance, gnashing on him near at hand. The murmur is wafted to the tribune, when the person had just left the ranks. The tribune at once puts the question to him, Why are you so different in your attire? He declared that he had no liberty to wear the crown with the rest. Being urgently asked for his reasons, he answered, I am a Christian. O soldier! boasting thyself in God. Then the case was considered and voted on; the matter was remitted to a higher tribunal; the offender was conducted to the prefects. At once he put away the heavy cloak, his disburdening commenced; he loosed from his foot the military shoe, beginning to stand upon holy ground;[3] he gave up the sword, which was not necessary either for the protection of our Lord; from his hand likewise dropped the laurel crown; and now, purple-clad with the hope of his own blood, shod with the preparation of the gospel, girt with the sharper word of God, completely equipped in the apostles' armour, and crowned more worthily with the white crown of martyrdom, he awaits in prison the largess of Christ. Thereafter adverse judgments began to be passed upon his conduct—whether on the part of Christians I do not know, for those of the heathen are not different—as if he were headstrong and rash, and too eager to die, because, in being taken to task about a mere matter of dress, he brought trouble on the bearers of the Name,[4]—he, forsooth, alone brave among so many soldier-brethren, he alone a Christian. It is plain that as they have rejected the prophecies of the Holy Spirit,[5] they are also purposing the refusal of martyrdom. So they murmur that a peace so good and long is endangered for them. Nor do I doubt that some are already turning their back on the Scriptures, are making ready their luggage, are equipped for flight from city to city; for that is all of the gospel they care to remember. I know, too, their pastors are lions in peace, deer in the fight. As to the questions asked for extorting confessions from us, we shall teach elsewhere. Now, as they put forth also the objection—But where are we forbidden to be crowned?—I shall take this point up, as more suitable to be treated of here, being the essence, in fact, of the present contention. So that, on the one hand, the inquirers who are ignorant, but anxious, may be instructed; and on the other, those may be refuted who try to vindicate the sin, especially the laurel-crowned Christians themselves, to whom it is merely a question of debate, as if it might be regarded as either no trespass at all, or at least a doubtful one, because it may be made the subject of investigation. That it is neither sinless nor doubtful, I shall now, however, show.

---

[1] [Kaye, apparently accepting the judgment of Dr. Neander, assigns this treatise to A.D. 204. The bounty here spoken of, then, must be that dispensed in honour of the victories over the Parthians, under Severus.]

[2] "Emperors." The Emperor Severus associated his two sons with him in the possession of the imperial power ; Caracalla in the year 198, Geta in 208.—TR.

[3] [A touch of our author's genius, inspired by the Phrygian enthusiasm for martyrdom. The ground on which a martyr treads begins to be holy, even before the sacrifice, and in loosing his shoe the victim consecrates the spot and at the same time pays it homage.]

[4] [The name of Christ: and the Antiochian name of Christians.]

[5] [Gibbon will have it that the *De Corona* was written while Tertullian was orthodox, but this reference to the Montanist notion of "New Prophecy" seems to justify the decision of critics against Gibbon, who, as Kaye suggests (p. 53) was anxious to make Christianity itself responsible for military insubordination and for offences against Imperial Law.]

CHAP. II.

I affirm that not one of the Faithful has ever a crown upon his head, except at a time of trial. That is the case with all, from catechumens to confessors and martyrs,[1] or (as the case may be) deniers. Consider, then, whence the custom about which we are now chiefly inquiring got its authority. But when the question is raised why it is observed, it is meanwhile evident that it is observed. Therefore that can neither be regarded as no offence, or an uncertain one, which is perpetrated against a practice which is capable of defence, on the ground even of its repute, and is sufficiently ratified by the support of general acceptance. It is undoubted, so that we ought to inquire into the reason of the thing; but without prejudice to the practice, not for the purpose of overthrowing it, but rather of building it up, that you may all the more carefully observe it, when you are also satisfied as to its reason. But what sort of procedure is it, for one to be bringing into debate a practice, when he has fallen from it, and to be seeking the explanation of his having ever had it, when he has left it off? Since, although he may wish to seem on this account desirous to investigate it, that he may show that he has not done wrong in giving it up, it is evident that he nevertheless transgressed previously in its presumptuous observance. If he has done no wrong to-day in accepting the crown, he offended before in refusing it. This treatise, therefore, will not be for those who are not in a proper condition for inquiry, but for those who, with the real desire of getting instruction, bring forward, not a question for debate, but a request for advice. For it is from this desire that a true inquiry always proceeds; and I praise the faith which has believed in the duty of complying with the rule, before it has learned the reason of it. An easy thing it is at once to demand where it is written that we should not be crowned. But is it written that we should be crowned? Indeed, in urgently demanding the warrant of Scripture in a different side from their own, men prejudge that the support of Scripture ought no less to appear on their part. For if it shall be said that it is lawful to be crowned on this ground, that Scripture does not forbid it, it will as validly be retorted that just on this ground is the crown unlawful, because the Scripture does not enjoin it. What shall discipline do? Shall it accept both things, as if neither were forbidden? Or shall it refuse both, as if neither were enjoined? But "the

thing which is not forbidden is freely permitted." I should rather say[2] that what has not been freely allowed is forbidden.

CHAP. III.

And how long shall we draw the saw to and fro through this line, when we have an ancient practice, which by anticipation has made for us the state, i.e., of the question? If no passage of Scripture has prescribed it, assuredly custom, which without doubt flowed from tradition, has confirmed it. For how can anything come into use, if it has not first been handed down? Even in pleading tradition, written authority, you say, must be demanded. Let us inquire, therefore, whether tradition, unless it be written, should not be admitted. Certainly we shall say that it ought not to be admitted, if no cases of other practices which, without any written instrument, we maintain on the ground of tradition alone, and the countenance thereafter of custom, affords us any precedent. To deal with this matter briefly, I shall begin with baptism.[3] When we are going to enter the water, but a little before, in the presence of the congregation and under the hand of the president, we solemnly profess that we disown the devil, and his pomp, and his angels. Hereupon we are thrice immersed, making a somewhat ampler pledge than the Lord has appointed in the Gospel. Then, when we are taken up (as new-born children),[4] we taste first of all a mixture of milk and honey, and from that day we refrain from the daily bath for a whole week. We take also, in congregations before daybreak, and from the hand of none but the presidents, the sacrament of the Eucharist, which the Lord both commanded to be eaten at meal-times, and enjoined to be taken by all alike.[5] As often as the anniversary comes round, we make offerings for the dead as birthday honours. We count fasting or kneeling in worship on the Lord's day to be unlawful. We rejoice in the same privilege also from Easter to Whitsunday. We feel pained should any wine or bread, even though our own, be cast upon the ground. At every forward step and movement, at every going in and out, when we put on our clothes and shoes, when we bathe, when we sit at table, when we light the lamps, on couch, on

[1] [Kaye (p. 231) notes this as a rare instance of classing *Catechumens* among "the Faithful."]

[2] [This is said not absolutely but in contrast with extreme license; but it shows the Supremacy of Scripture. Compare *De Monogam*, cap. 4.]
[3] [Elucidation I, and see Bunsen's *Church and House Book*, pp. 19-24.]
[4] [There is here an allusion to the Roman form of recognizing a lawful child. The father, taking up the new-born infant, gave him adoption into the family, and recognized him as a legitimate son and heir.]
[5] [Men and women, rich and poor.]

seat, in all the ordinary actions of daily life, we trace upon the forehead the sign.[1]

CHAP. IV.

If, for these and other such rules, you insist upon having positive Scripture injunction, you will find none. Tradition will be held forth to you as the originator of them, custom as their strengthener, and faith as their observer. That reason will support tradition, and custom, and faith, you will either yourself perceive, or learn from some one who has. Meanwhile you will believe that there is some reason to which submission is due. I add still one case more, as it will be proper to show you how it was among the ancients also. Among the Jews, so usual is it for their women to have the head veiled, that they may thereby be recognised. I ask in this instance for the law. I put the apostle aside. If Rebecca at once drew down her veil, when in the distance she saw her betrothed, this modesty of a mere private individual could not have made a law, or it will have made it only for those who have the reason which she had. Let virgins alone be veiled, and this when they are coming to be married, and not till they have recognised their destined husband. If Susanna also, who was subjected to unveiling on her trial,[2] furnishes an argument for the veiling of women, I can say here also, the veil was a voluntary thing. She had come accused, ashamed of the disgrace she had brought on herself, properly concealing her beauty, even because now she feared to please. But I should not suppose that, when it was her aim to please, she took walks with a veil on in her husband's avenue. Grant, now, that she was always veiled. In this particular case, too, or, in fact, in that of any other, I demand the dress-law. If I nowhere find a law, it follows that tradition has given the fashion in question to custom, to find subsequently (its authorization in) the apostle's sanction, from the true interpretation of reason. This instances, therefore, will make it sufficiently plain that you can vindicate the keeping of even unwritten tradition established by custom; the proper witness for tradition when demonstrated by long-continued observance.[3] But even in civil matters custom is accepted as law, when positive legal enactment is wanting; and it is the same thing whether it depends on writing or on reason, since reason is, in fact, the basis of law. But, (you say), if reason is the ground of law, all

will now henceforth have to be counted law, whoever brings it forward, which shall have reason as its ground.[4] Or do you think that every believer is entitled to originate and establish a law, if only it be such as is agreeable to God, as is helpful to discipline, as promotes salvation, when the Lord says, "But why do you not even of your own selves judge what is right?"[5] And not merely in regard to a judicial sentence, but in regard to every decision in matters we are called on to consider, the apostle also says, "If of anything you are ignorant, God shall reveal it unto you;"[6] he himself, too, being accustomed to afford counsel though he had not the command of the Lord, and to dictate of himself[7] as possessing the Spirit of God who guides into all truth. Therefore his advice has, by the warrant of divine reason, become equivalent to nothing less than a divine command. Earnestly now inquire of this teacher,[8] keeping intact your regard for tradition, from whomsoever it originally sprang; nor have regard to the author, but to the authority, and especially that of custom itself, which on this very account we should revere, that we may not want an interpreter; so that if reason too is God's gift, you may then learn, not whether custom has to be followed by you, but why.

CHAP. V.

The argument for Christian practices becomes all the stronger, when also nature, which is the first rule of all, supports them. Well, she is the first who lays it down that a crown does not become the head. But I think ours is the God of nature, who fashioned man; and, that he might desire, (appreciate, become partaker of) the pleasures afforded by His creatures, endowed him with certain senses, (acting) through members, which, so to speak, are their peculiar instruments. The sense of hearing he has planted in the ears; that of sight, lighted up in the eyes; that of taste, shut up in the mouth; that of smell, wafted into the nose; that of touch, fixed in the tips of the fingers. By means of these organs of the outer man doing duty to the inner man, the enjoyments of the divine gifts are conveyed by the senses to the soul.[9] What, then, in flowers affords you enjoyment?

---

[1] i.e., of the Cross.
[2] Vulgate, Dan. xiii. 32. [See Apocrypha, *Hist. of Susanna*, v. 32.]
[3] [Observe it must (1.) be based on Apostolic grounds; (2.) must not be a novelty, but derived from a time "to which the memory of men runneth not contrary."]

[4] [I slightly amend the translation to bring out the force of an objection to which our author gives a Montanistic reply.]
[5] Luke xii. 27.
[6] Phil. iii. 15.
[7] [See luminous remarks in Kaye, pp. 371–373.]
[8] [This teacher, i.e., right reason, under the guidance of the Holy Ghost. He is here foisting in a plea for the "New Prophecy," apparently, and this is one of the most decided instances in the Treatise.]
[9] Kaye [p. 187,] has some valuable remarks on this testimony to the senses in Christian Philosophy, and compares Cicero, I. *Tusc.* cap. xx. or xlvi.]

For it is the flowers of the field which are the peculiar, at least the chief, material of crowns. Either smell, you say, or colour, or both together. What will be the senses of colour and smell? Those of seeing and smelling, I suppose. What members have had these senses allotted to them? The eyes and the nose, if I am not mistaken. With sight and smell, then, make use of flowers, for these are the senses by which they are meant to be enjoyed; use them by means of the eyes and nose, which are the members to which these senses belong. You have got the thing from God, the mode of it from the world; but an extraordinary mode does not prevent the use of the thing in the common way. Let flowers, then, both when fastened into each other and tied together in thread and rush, be what they are when free, when loose—things to be looked at and smelt. You count it a crown, let us say, when you have a bunch of them bound together in a series, that you may carry many at one time, that you may enjoy them all at once. Well, lay them in your bosom if they are so singularly pure, and strew them on your couch if they are so exquisitely soft, and consign them to your cup if they are so perfectly harmless. Have the pleasure of them in as many ways as they appeal to your senses. But what taste for a flower, what sense for anything belonging to a crown but its band, have you in the head, which is able neither to distinguish colour, nor to inhale sweet perfumes, nor to appreciate softness? It is as much against nature to long after a flower with the head, as it is to crave food with the ear, or sound with the nostril. But everything which is against nature deserves to be branded as monstrous among all men; but with us it is to be condemned also as sacrilege against God, the Lord and Creator of nature.

CHAP. VI.

Demanding then a law of God, you have that common one prevailing all over the world, engraven on the natural tables to which the apostle too is wont to appeal, as when in respect of the woman's veil he says, " Does not even Nature teach you?"[1]—as when to the Romans, affirming that the heathen do by nature those things which the law requires,[2] he suggests both natural law and a law-revealing nature. Yes, and also in the first chapter of the epistle he authenticates nature, when he asserts that males and females changed among themselves the natural use of the

creature into that which is unnatural,[3] by way of penal retribution for their error. We first of all indeed know God Himself by the teaching of Nature, calling Him God of gods, taking for granted that He is good, and invoking Him as Judge. Is it a question with you whether for the enjoyment of His creatures, Nature should be our guide, that we may not be carried away in the direction in which the rival of God has corrupted, along with man himself, the entire creation which had been made over to our race for certain uses, whence the apostle says that it too unwillingly became subject to vanity, completely bereft of its original character, first by vain, then by base, unrighteous, and ungodly uses? It is thus, accordingly, in the pleasures of the shows, that the creature is dishonoured by those who by nature indeed perceive that all the materials of which shows are got up belong to God, but lack the knowledge to perceive as well that they have all been changed by the devil. But with this topic we have, for the sake of our own play-lovers, sufficiently dealt, and that, too, in a work in Greek.[4]

CHAP. VII.

Let these dealers in crowns then recognize in the meantime the authority of Nature, on the ground of a common sense as human beings, and the certifications of their peculiar religion, as, according to the last chapter, worshippers of the God of nature; and, as it were, thus over and above what is required, let them consider those other reasons too which forbid us wearing crowns, especially on the head, and indeed crowns of every sort. For we are obliged to turn from the rule of Nature, which we share with mankind in general, that we may maintain the whole peculiarity of our Christian discipline, in relation also to other kinds of crowns which seem to have been provided for different uses, as being composed of different substances, lest, because they do not consist of flowers, the use of which nature has indicated (as it does in the case of this military laurel one itself), they may be thought not to come under the prohibition of our sect, since they have escaped any objections of nature. I see, then, that we must go into the matter both with more research, and more fully, from its beginnings on through its successive stages of growth to its more erratic developments. For this we need to turn to heathen literature, for things belonging to the heathen must be proved from their own

---

[1] 1 Cor. xi. 14.
[2] Rom. ii. 14.

[3] Rom. i. 26.
[4] [Plays were regarded as *pomps* renounced in Baptism.]

documents. The little of this I have acquired, will, I believe, be enough. If there really was a Pandora, whom Hesiod mentions as the first of women, hers was the first head the graces crowned, for she received gifts from all *the gods* whence she got *her name* Pandora. But Moses, a prophet, not a poet-shepherd, shows us the first woman Eve having her loins more naturally girt about with leaves than her temples with flowers. Pandora, then, is a myth. And so we have to blush for the origin of the crown, even on the ground of the falsehood connected with it; and, as will soon appear, on the ground no less of its realities. For it is an undoubted fact that certain persons either originated the thing, or shed lustre on it. Pherecydes relates that Saturn was the first who wore a crown; Diodorus, that Jupiter, after conquering the Titans, was honoured with this gift by the rest of the gods. To Priapus also the same author assigns fillets; and to Ariadne a garland of gold and of Indian gems, the gift of Vulcan, afterwards of Bacchus, and subsequently turned into a constellation. Callimachus has put a vine crown upon Juno. So too at Argos, her statue, vine-wreathed, with a lion's skin placed beneath her feet, exhibits the step-mother exulting over the spoils of her two step-sons. Hercules displays upon his head sometimes poplar, sometimes wild-olive, sometimes parsley. You have the tragedy of Cerberus; you have Pindar; and besides Callimachus, who mentions that Apollo, too, when he had killed the Delphic serpent, as a suppliant, put on a laurel garland; for among the ancients suppliants were wont to be crowned. Harpocration argues that Bacchus, the same as Osiris among the Egyptians, was designedly crowned with ivy, because it is the nature of ivy to protect the brain against drowsiness. But that in another way also Bacchus was the originator of the laurel crown, (the crown) in which he celebrated his triumph over the Indians, even the rabble acknowledge, when they call the days dedicated to him the "great crown." If you open, again, the writings of the Egyptian Leo, you learn that Isis was the first who discovered and wore ears of corn upon her head—a thing more suited to the belly. Those who want additional information will find an ample exposition of the subject in Claudius Saturninus, a writer of distinguished talent who treats this question also, for he has a book on crowns, so explaining their beginnings as well as causes, and kinds, and rites, that you find all that is charming in the flower, all that is beautiful in the leafy branch, and every sod or vine-shoot has been dedicated to some head or other;

making it abundantly clear how foreign to us we should judge the custom of the crowned head, introduced as it was by, and thereafter constantly managed for the honour of, those whom the world has believed to be gods. If the devil, a liar from the beginning, is even in this matter working for his false system of godhead (idolatry), he had himself also without doubt provided for his god-lie being carried out. What sort of thing, then, must that be counted among the people of the true God, which was brought in by the nations in honour of the devil's candidates, and was set apart from the beginning to no other than these; and which even then received its consecration to idolatry by idols and in idols yet alive? Not as if an idol were anything, but since the things which *others* offer up to idols belong to demons. But if the things which others offer to them belong to demons how much more what idols offered to themselves, when they were in life! The demons themselves, doubtless, had made provision for themselves by means of those whom they had possessed, while in a state of desire and craving, before provision had been actually made.

<h2 style="text-align:center">CHAP. VIII.</h2>

Hold fast in the meantime this persuasion, while I examine a question which comes in our way. For I already hear it is said, that many other things as well as crowns have been invented by those whom the world believes to be gods, and that they are notwithstanding to be met with both in our present usages and in those of early saints, and in the service of God, and in Christ Himself, who did His work as man by no other than these ordinary instrumentalities of human life. Well, let it be so; nor shall I inquire any further back into the origin of this things. Let Mercury have been the first who taught the knowledge of letters; I will own that they are requisite both for the business and commerce of life, and for performing our devotion to God. Nay, if he also first strung the chord to give forth melody, I will not deny, when listening to David, that this invention has been in use with the saints, and has ministered to God. Let Æsculapius have been the first who sought and discovered cures: Esaias [1] mentions that he ordered Hezekiah medicine when he was sick. Paul, too, knows that a little wine does the stomach good. [2] Let Minerva have been the first who built a ship: I shall see Jonah and the apostles sailing. Nay, there is more than this: for even Christ, we shall find, has ordinary rai-

[1] Isa. xxxviii. 21.
[2] 1 Tim. v. 23.

7

ment; Paul, too, has his cloak.[1] If at once, of every article of furniture and each household vessel, you name some god of the world as the originator, well, I must recognise Christ, both as He reclines on a couch, and when He presents a basin for the feet of His disciples, and when He pours water into it from a ewer, and when He is girt about with a linen towel [2]—a garment specially sacred to Osiris. It is thus in general I reply upon the point, admitting indeed that we use along with others these articles, but challenging that this be judged in the light of the distinction between things agreeable and things opposed to reason, because the promiscuous employment of them is deceptive, concealing the corruption of the creature, by which it has been made subject to vanity. For we affirm that those things only are proper to be used, whether by ourselves or by those who lived before us, and alone befit the service of God and Christ Himself, which to meet the necessities of human life supply what is simply useful and affords real assistance and honourable comfort, so that they may be well believed to have come from God's own inspiration, who first of all no doubt provided for, and taught and ministered to the enjoyment, I should suppose, of His own man. As for the things which are out of this class, they are not fit to be used among us, especially those which on that account indeed are not to be found either with the world, or in the ways of Christ.

CHAP. IX.

In short, what patriarch, what prophet, what Levite, or priest, or ruler, or at a later period what apostle, or preacher of the gospel, or bishop, do you ever find the wearer of a crown?[3] I think not even the temple of God itself was crowned; as neither was the ark of the testament, nor the tabernacle of witness, nor the altar, nor the candlestick crowned; though certainly, both on that first solemnity of the dedication, and in that second rejoicing for the restoration, crowning would have been most suitable if it were worthy of God. But if these things were figures of us (for we are temples of God, and altars, and lights, and sacred vessels), this too they in figure set forth, that the people of God ought not to be crowned. The reality must always correspond with the image. If, perhaps, you object that Christ Himself was crowned, to that you will get the brief reply: Be you too crowned, as He was; you have full permission. Yet even that crown of insolent ungodliness was not of any decree of the Jewish people. It was a device of the Roman soldiers, taken from the practice of the world,—a practice which the people of God never allowed either on the occasion of public rejoicing or to gratify innate luxury: so they returned from the Babylonish captivity with timbrels, and flutes, and psalteries, more suitably than with crowns; and after eating and drinking, uncrowned, they rose up to play. Neither would the account of the rejoicing nor the exposure of the luxury have been silent touching the honour or dishonour of the crown. Thus too Isaiah, as he says, "With timbrels, and psalteries, and flutes they drink wine,"[4] would have added "with crowns," if this practice had ever had place in the things of God.

CHAP. X.

So, when you allege that the ornaments of the heathen deities are found no less with God, with the object of claiming among these for general use the head-crown, you already lay it down for yourself, that we must not have among us, as a thing whose use we are to share with others, what is not to be found in the service of God. Well, what is so unworthy of God indeed as that which is worthy of an idol? But what is so worthy of an idol as that which is also worthy of a dead man? For it is the privilege of the dead also to be thus crowned, as they too straightway become idols, both by their dress and the service of deification, which (deification) is with us a second idolatry. Wanting, then, the sense, it will be theirs to use the thing for which the sense is wanting, just as if in full possession of the sense they wished to abuse it. When there ceases to be any reality in the use, there is no distinction between using and abusing. Who can abuse a thing, when the precipient nature with which he wishes to carry out his purpose is not his to use it? The apostle, moreover, forbids us to abuse, while he would more naturally have taught us not to use, unless on the ground that, where there is no sense for things, there is no wrong use of them. But the whole affair is meaningless, and is, in fact, a dead work so far as concerns the idols; though, without doubt, a living one as respects the demons[5] to whom the religious rite belongs. "The idols of the heathen," says David, "are silver and gold." "They have eyes, and see not; a nose, and

---

[1] 2 Tim. iv. 13. [This is a useful comment as showing what this φαιλόνη was. Our author translates it by *pænula*. Of which more when we reach the *De Pallio*.]

[2] John xiii. 1-5.

[3] [But see Eusebius, *Hist.* B. v., cap. 24, whose story is examined by Lardner, *Cred.*, vol. iv., p. 448.]

[4] Isa. v. 12.

[5] [Compare *De Idololatria*, cap. xv., p. 70, *supra*.]

smell not; hands, and they will not handle."[1] By means of these organs, indeed, we are to enjoy flowers; but if he declares that those who make idols will be like them, they already are so who use anything after the style of idol adornings. "To the pure all things are pure: so, likewise, all things to the impure are impure;"[2] but nothing is more impure than idols. The substances are themselves as creatures of God without impurity, and in this their native state are free to the use of all; but the ministries to which in their use they are devoted, makes all the difference; for I, too, kill a cock for myself, just as Socrates did for Æsculapius; and if the smell of some place or other offends me, I burn the Arabian product myself, but not with the same ceremony, nor in the same dress, nor with the same pomp, with which it is done to idols.[3] If the creature is defiled by a mere word, as the apostle teaches, "But if any one say, This is offered in sacrifice to idols, you must not touch it,"[4] much more when it is polluted by the dress, and rites, and pomp of what is offered to the gods. Thus the crown also is made out to be an offering to idols;[5] for with this ceremony, and dress, and pomp, it is presented in sacrifice to idols, its originators, to whom its use is specially given over, and chiefly on this account, that what has no place among the things of God may not be admitted into use with us as with others. Wherefore the apostle exclaims, "Flee idolatry:"[6] certainly idolatry whole and entire he means. Reflect on what a thicket it is, and how many thorns lie hid in it. Nothing must be given to an idol, and so nothing must be taken from one. If it is inconsistent with faith to recline in an idol temple, what is it to appear in an idol dress? What communion have Christ and Belial? Therefore flee from it; for he enjoins us to keep at a distance from idolatry —to have no close dealings with it of any kind. Even an earthly serpent sucks in men at some distance with its breath. Going still further, John says, "My little children, keep yourselves from idols,"[7]—not now from idolatry, as if from the service of it, but from idols—that is, from any resemblance to them; for it is an unworthy thing that you, the image of the living God, should become the likeness of an idol and a dead man. Thus far we assert, that this attire belongs to idols, both from the history of its origin, and from its use by false religion; on this ground, besides, that while it is not mentioned as connected with the worship of God, it is more and more given over to those in whose antiquities, as well as festivals and services, it is found. In a word, the very doors, the very victims and altars, the very servants and priests, are crowned. You have, in Claudius, the crowns of all the various colleges of priests. We have added also that distinction between things altogether different from each other—things, namely, agreeable, and things contrary to reason—in answer to those who, because there happens to be the use of some things in common, maintain the right of participation in all things. With reference to this part of the subject, therefore, it now remains that the special grounds for wearing crowns should be examined, that while we show these to be foreign, nay, even opposed to our Christian discipline, we may demonstrate that none of them have any plea of reason to support it, on the basis of which this article of dress might be vindicated as one in whose use we can participate, as even some others may whose instances are cast up to us.

CHAP. XI.

To begin with the real ground of the military crown, I think we must first inquire whether warfare is proper at all for Christians. What sense is there in discussing the merely accidental, when that on which it rests is to be condemned? Do we believe it lawful for a human oath[8] to be superadded to one divine, for a man to come under promise to another master after Christ, and to abjure father, mother, and all nearest kinsfolk, whom even the law has commanded us to honour and love next to God Himself, to whom the gospel, too, holding them only of less account than Christ, has in like manner rendered honour? Shall it be held lawful to make an occupation of the sword, when the Lord proclaims that he who uses the sword shall perish by the sword? And shall the son of peace take part in the battle when it does not become him even to sue at law? And shall he apply the chain, and the prison, and the torture, and the punishment, who is not the avenger even of his own wrongs? Shall he, forsooth, either keep watch-service for others more than for Christ, or shall he do it on the Lord's day, when he does not even do it for Christ Himself? And shall he keep guard

---

[1] Ps. cxv. 4–8.
[2] Tit. i. 15.
[3] [He seems to know no use for incense except for burials and for fumigation.]
[4] 1 Cor. x. 28.
[5] [Kaye (p. 362) defends our author against Barbeyrac's animadversions, by the maxim, " put yourself in his place " *i.e.* among the abominations of Paganism.]
[6] 1 Cor. x. 14.
[7] 1 John v. 21.

[8] [He plays on this word *Sacramentum.* Is the military *sacrament* to be added to the Lord's?]

before the temples which he has renounced? And shall he take a meal where the apostle has forbidden him?[1] And shall he diligently protect by night those whom in the day-time he has put to flight by his exorcisms, leaning and resting on the spear the while with which Christ's side was pierced? Shall he carry a flag,[2] too, hostile to Christ? And shall *he* ask a watchword from the emperor who has already received one from God? Shall *he* be disturbed in death by the trumpet of the trumpeter, who expects to be aroused by the angel's trump? And shall the Christian be burned according to camp rule, when he was not permitted to burn incense to an idol, when to him Christ remitted the punishment of fire? Then how many other offences there are involved in the performances of camp offices, which we must hold to involve a transgression of God's law, you may see by a slight survey. The very carrying of the name over from the camp of light to the camp of darkness is a violation of it. Of course, if faith comes later, and finds any preoccupied with military service, their case is different, as in the instance of those whom John used to receive for baptism, and of those most faithful centurions, I mean the centurion whom Christ approves, and the centurion whom Peter instructs; yet, at the same time, when a man has become a believer, and faith has been sealed, there must be either an immediate abandonment of it, which has been the course with many; or all sorts of quibbling will have to be resorted to in order to avoid offending God, and that is not allowed even outside of military service;[3] or, last of all, for God the fate must be endured which a citizen-faith has been no less ready to accept. Neither does military service hold out escape from punishment of sins, or exemption from martyrdom. Nowhere does the Christian change his character. There is one gospel, and the same Jesus, who will one day deny every one who denies, and acknowledge every one who acknowledges God,—who will save, too, the life which has been lost for His sake; but, on the other hand, destroy that which for gain has been saved to His dishonour. With Him the faithful citizen is a soldier, just as the faithful soldier is a citizen.[4] A state of faith admits no plea of necessity; they are under no necessity to sin, whose one necessity is, that they do not sin. For if one is pressed to the offering of sacrifice and the sheer denial of Christ by the necessity of torture or of punishment, yet discipline does not connive even at that necessity; because there is a higher necessity to dread denying and to undergo martyrdom, than to escape from suffering, and to render the homage required. In fact, an excuse of this sort overturns the entire essence of our sacrament, removing even the obstacle to voluntary sins; for it will be possible also to maintain that inclination is a necessity, as involving in it, forsooth, a sort of compulsion. I have, in fact, disposed of this very allegation of necessity with reference to the pleas by which crowns connected with official position are vindicated, in support of which it is in common use, since for this very reason offices must be either refused, that we may not fall into acts of sin, or martyrdoms endured that we may get quit of offices. Touching this primary aspect of the question, as to the unlawfulness even of a military life itself, I shall not add more, that the secondary question may be restored to its place. Indeed, if, putting my strength to the question, I banish from us the military life, I should now to no purpose issue a challenge on the matter of the military crown. Suppose, then, that the military service is lawful, as far as the plea for the crown is concerned.[5]

CHAP. XII.

But I first say a word also about the crown itself. This laurel one is sacred to Apollo or Bacchus—to the former as the god of archery, to the latter as the god of triumphs. In like manner Claudius teaches, when he tells us that soldiers are wont too to be wreathed in myrtle. For the myrtle belongs to Venus, the mother of the Æneadæ, the mistress also of the god of war, who through Ilia and the Romuli is Roman. But I do not believe that Venus is Roman as well as Mars, because of the vexation the concubine gave her.[6] When military service again is crowned with olive, the idolatry has respect to Minerva, who is equally the goddess of arms—but got a crown of the tree referred to, because of the peace she made with Neptune. In these respects, the superstition of the military garland will be everywhere defiled and all-defiling. And it is further defiled, I

---

[1] 1 Cor. viii. 10.
[2] [Vexillum. Such words as these prepared for the *Labarum.*]
[3] "Outside of the military service." By substituting *ex militia* for the corresponding words *extra militiam,* as has been proposed by Rigaltius, the sentence acquires a meaning such that desertion from the army is suggested as one of the methods by which a soldier who has become a Christian may continue faithful to Jesus. But the words *extra militiam* are a genuine part of the text. There is no good ground, therefore, for the statement of Gibbon: "Tertullian (*de Corona Militis,* c. xi.) suggests to them the expedient of deserting; a counsel which, if it had been generally known, was not very proper to conciliate the favour of the emperors toward the Christian sect."—Tr.

[4] "The faithful," etc.; i.e., the kind of occupation which any one has cannot be pleaded by him as a reason for not doing all that Christ has enjoined upon His people.—Tr.
[5] [He was not yet quite a Montanist.]
[6] i.e. Ilia.

should think, also in the grounds of it. Lo! the yearly public pronouncing of vows, what does that bear on its face to be? It takes place first in the part of the camp where the general's tent is, and then in the temples. In addition to the places, observe the words also: "We vow that you, O Jupiter, will then have an ox with gold-decorated horns." What does the utterance mean? Without a doubt the denial (of Christ). Albeit the Christian says nothing in these places with the mouth, he makes his response by having the crown on his head. The laurel is likewise commanded (to be used) at the distribution of the largess. So you see idolatry is not without its gain, selling, as it does, Christ for pieces of gold, as Judas did for pieces of silver. Will it be "Ye cannot serve God and mammon,"[1] to devote your energies to mammon, and to depart from God? Will it be "Render unto Cæsar the things which are Cæsar's, and unto God the things which are God's,"[2] not only not to render the human being to God, but even to take the denarius from Cæsar? Is the laurel of the triumph made of leaves, or of corpses? Is it adorned with ribbons, or with tombs? Is it bedewed with ointments, or with the tears of wives and mothers? It may be of some Christians too;[3] for Christ is also among the barbarians.[4] Has not he who has carried (a crown for) this cause on his head, fought even against himself? Another sort of service belongs to the royal guards. And indeed crowns are called (Castrenses), as belonging to the camp; *Munificæ* likewise, from the Cæsarean functions they perform. But even then you are still the soldier and the servant of another; and if of two masters, of God and Cæsar: but assuredly then not of Cæsar, when you owe yourself to God, as having higher claims, I should think, even in matters in which both have an interest.

CHAP. XIII.

For state reasons, the various orders of the citizens also are crowned with laurel crowns; but the magistrates besides with golden ones, as at Athens, and at Rome. Even to those are preferred the Etruscan. This appellation is given to the crowns which, distinguished by their gems and oak leaves of gold, they put on, with mantles having an embroidery of palm branches, to conduct the chariots containing the images of the gods to the circus.

There are also provincial crowns of gold, needing now the larger heads of images instead of those of men. But your orders, and your magistracies, and your very place of meeting, the church, are Christ's. You belong to Him, for you have been enrolled in the books of life.[6] There the blood of the Lord serves for your purple robe, and your broad stripe is His own cross; there the axe is already laid to the trunk of the tree;[7] there is the branch out of the root of Jesse.[8] Never mind the state horses with their crown. Your Lord, when, according to the Scripture, He would enter Jerusalem in triumph, had not even an ass of His own. These (put their trust) in chariots, and these in horses; but we will seek our help in the name of the Lord our God.[9] From so much as a dwelling in that Babylon of John's Revelation[10] we are called away; much more then from its pomp. The rabble, too, are crowned, at one time because of some great rejoicing for the success of the emperors; at another, on account of some custom belonging to municipal festivals. For luxury strives to make her own every occasion of public gladness. But as for you, you are a foreigner in this world, a citizen of Jerusalem, the city above. Our citizenship, the apostle says, is in heaven.[11] You have your own registers, your own calendar; you have nothing to do with the joys of the world; nay, you are called to the very opposite, for "the world shall rejoice, but ye shall mourn."[12] And I think the Lord affirms, that those who mourn are happy, not those who are crowned. Marriage, too, decks the bridegroom with its crown; and therefore we will not have heathen brides, lest they seduce us even to the idolatry with which among them marriage is initiated. You have the law from the patriarchs indeed; you have the apostle enjoining people to marry in the Lord.[13] You have a crowning also on the making of a freeman; but *you* have been already ransomed by Christ, and that at a great price. How shall the world manumit the servant of another? Though it seems to be liberty, yet it will come to be found bondage. In the world everything is nominal, and nothing real. For even then, as ransomed by Christ, you were under no bondage to man; and now, though man has given you liberty, you are the servant of Christ. If you think freedom of the world to be real, so that you even seal it with a crown, you have returned

---

[1] Matt. vi. 24.
[2] Matt. xxii. 21.
[3] [Such considerations may account for our author's abandonment of what he says in the Apology; which compare in capp. xlii. and xxxix.]
[4] [Et apud barbaros enim Christus. See Kaye's argument, p. 87.]
[6] Phil. iv. 3.
[7] Matt. iii. 10.
[8] Isa. xi. 1.
[9] Ps. xx. 7.
[10] Rev. xviii. 4. [He understands this of Rome.]
[11] Phil. iii. 20.
[12] John xvi. 20.
[13] 1 Cor. vii. 39.

to the slavery of man, imagining it to be free-dom; you have lost the freedom of Christ, fancying it is slavery. Will there be any dis-pute as to the cause of crown-wearing, which contests in the games in their turn supply, and which, both as sacred to the gods and in honour of the dead, their own reason at once condemns? It only remains, that the Olym-pian Jupiter, and the Nemean Hercules, and the wretched little Archemorus, and the hap-less Antinous, should be crowned in a Chris-tian, that he himself may become a spectacle disgusting to behold. We have recounted, as I think, all the various causes of the wearing of the crown, and there is not one which has any place with us: all are foreign to us, un-holy, unlawful, having been abjured already once for all in the solemn declaration of the sacrament. For they were of the pomp of the devil and his angels, offices of the world,[1] honours, festivals, popularity huntings, false vows, exhibitions of human servility, empty praises, base glories, and in them all idolatry, even in respect of the origin of the crowns alone, with which they are all wreathed. Claudius will tell us in his preface, indeed, that in the poems of Homer the heaven also is crowned with constellations, and that no doubt by God, no doubt for man; therefore man himself, too, should be crowned by God. But the world crowns brothels, and baths, and bakehouses, and prisons, and schools, and the very amphitheatres, and the chambers where the clothes are stripped from dead gladiators, and the very biers of the dead. How sacred and holy, how venerable and pure is this ar-ticle of dress, determine not from the heaven of poetry alone, but from the traffickings of the whole world. But indeed a Christian will not even dishonour his own gate with laurel crowns, if so be he knows how many gods the devil has attached to doors; Janus so-called from gate, Limentinus from threshold, Forcus and Carna from leaves and hinges; among the Greeks, too, the Thyræan Apollo, and the evil spirits, the Antelii.

CHAP. XIV.

Much less may the Christian put the service of idolatry on his own head—nay, I might have said, upon Christ, since Christ is the Head of the Christian man—(for his head) is as free as even Christ is, under no obligation to wear a covernig, not to say a band. But even the head which is bound to have the veil, I mean woman's, as already taken possession of by this very thing, is not open also to a band. She has the burden of her own humility to bear. If she ought not to appear with her head uncovered on account of the angels,[2] much more with a crown on it will she offend those (elders) who perhaps are then wearing crowns above.[3] For what is a crown on the head of a woman, but beauty made seductive, but mark of utter wantonness,—a notable casting away of modesty, a setting temptation on fire? Therefore a woman, taking counsel from the apostles' foresight,[4] will not too elaborately adorn herself, that she may not either be crowned with any exquisite arrange-ment of her hair. What sort of garland, how-ever, I pray you, did He who is the Head of the man and the glory of the woman, Christ Jesus, the Husband of the church, submit to in behalf of both sexes? Of thorns, I think, and thistles,—a figure of the sins which the soil of the flesh brought forth for us, but which the power of the cross removed, blunting, in its endurance by the head of our Lord, death's every sting. Yes, and besides the figure, there is contumely with ready lip, and dishonour, and infamy, and the ferocity in-volved in the cruel things which then dis-figured and lacerated the temples of the Lord, that you may now be crowned with laurel, and myrtle, and olive, and any famous branch, and which is of more use, with hundred-leaved roses too, culled from the garden of Midas, and with both kinds of lily, and with violets of all sorts, perhaps also with gems and gold, so as even to rival that crown of Christ which He afterwards obtained. For it was after the gall He tasted the honeycomb,[5] and He was not greeted as King of Glory in heavenly places till He had been condemned to the cross as King of the Jews, having first been made by the Father for a time a little less than the angels, and so crowned with glory and honour. If for these things, you owe your own head to Him, repay it if you can, such as He presented His for yours; or be not crowned with flowers at all, if you cannot be with thorns, because you may not be with flowers.

CHAP. XV.

Keep for God His own property untainted; He will crown it if He choose. Nay, then, He does even choose. He calls us to it. To him who conquers He says, "I will give a crown of life."[6] Be you, too, faithful unto

---

[1] [A suggestive interpretation of the baptismal vow, of which see Bunsen, *Hippol.*, Vol. III., p. 20.]

[2] 1 Cor. xi. 10. [Does he here play on the use of the word *angels* in the Revelation? He seems to make it = *elders*.]
[3] Rev. iv. 4.
[4] 1 Tim. ii. 9; 1 Pet. iii. 3.
[5] [A very striking collocation of Matt. xxvii. 34, and Luke xxiv. 42.]
[6] Rev. ii. 10; Jas. i. 12.

death, and fight *you*, too, the good fight, whose crown the apostle[1] feels so justly confident has been laid up for him. The angel[2] also, as he goes forth on a white horse, conquering and to conquer, receives a crown of victory; and another[3] is adorned with an encircling rainbow (as it were in its fair colours) —a celestial meadow. In like manner, the elders sit crowned around, crowned too with a crown of gold, and the Son of Man Himself flashes out above the clouds. If such are the appearances in the vision of the seer, of what sort will be the realities in the actual manifestation? Look at those crowns. Inhale those odours. Why condemn you to a little chaplet, or a twisted headband, the brow which has been destined for a diadem? For Christ Jesus has made us *you* even kings to God and His Father. What have you in common with the flower which is to die? You have a flower in the Branch of Jesse, upon which the grace of the Divine Spirit in all its fulness rested—a flower undefiled, unfading, everlasting, by choosing which the good soldier, too, has got promotion in the heavenly ranks. Blush, ye fellow-soldiers of his, henceforth not to be condemned even by him, but by some soldier of Mithras, who, at his initiation in the gloomy cavern, in the camp, it may well be said, of darkness, when at the sword's point a crown is presented to him, as though in mimicry of martyrdom, and thereupon put upon his head, is admonished to resist and cast it off, and, if you like, transfer it to his shoulder, saying that Mithras is his crown. And thenceforth he is never crowned; and he has that for a mark to show who he is, if anywhere he be subjected to trial in respect of his religion; and he is at once believed to be a soldier of Mithras if he throws the crown away—if he say that in his god he has his crown. Let us take note of the devices of the devil, who is wont to ape some of God's things with no other design than, by the faithfulness of his servants, to put us to shame, and to condemn us.

[1] 2 Tim. iv. 8.
[2] Rev. vi. 2.
[3] Rev. x. 1.

ELUCIDATIONS.

I.

(Usages, p. 94.)

HERE a reference to Bunsen's Hippolytus, vol. III., so often referred to in the former volume, will be useful. A slight *metaphrase* will bring out the sense, perhaps, of this most interesting portrait of early Christian usages.

In baptism, we use trine immersion, in honour of the trinal Name, after renouncing the devil and his angels and the pomps and vanities of his kingdom.[1] But this trinal rite is a ceremonial amplification of what is actually commanded. It was heretofore tolerated in some places that communicants should take each one his portion, with his own hand, but now we suffer none to receive this sacrament except at the hand of the minister. By our Lord's own precept and example, it may be received at the hour of ordinary meals, and alike by all the faithful whether men or women, yet we usually do this in our gatherings before daybreak. Offerings are made in honour of our departed friends, on the anniversaries of their deaths, which we esteem their true birthdays, as they are born to a better life. We kneel at other times, but on the Lord's day, and from the Paschal Feast to Pentecost we stand in prayer, nor do we count it lawful to fast on Sundays. We are concerned if even a particle of the wine or bread, made ours, in the Lord's Supper, falls to the ground, by our carelessness. In all the ordinary occasions of life we furrow our foreheads with the sign of the Cross, in which we glory none the less because it is regarded as our shame by the heathen in presence of whom it is a profession of our faith.

[1] See Faye, pp. 408–415.

He owns there is no Scripture for any of these usages, in which there was an *amplifying* of the precepts of Christ. Let us note there was yet no *superstitious* usage even of this sign of the Cross. It was an act by which, in suffering "shame for Jesus' name," they fortified themselves against betraying the Master. It took the place, be it remembered, of *innumerable* heathen practices, and was a protest against them. It meant—"God forbid that I should glory, save in the Cross." I express no personal opinion as to this observance, but give the explanation which the early Christians would have given. Tertullian touched with Montanism, but not yet withdrawn from Catholic Communion, pleads the common cause of believers.

II.

(Traditions, cap. iv., p. 95.)

The traditions here argued for respect things in their nature indifferent. And as our author asserts the long continuance of such usages to be their chief justification, it is evident that he supposed them common from the Sub-apostolic age. There is nothing here to justify *amplifications* and traditions which, subsequently, came in like a flood to change principles of the Faith once delivered to the Saints. Even in his little plea for Montanistic revelations of some possible novelties, he pre-supposes that *reason* must be subject to Scripture and Apostolic Law. In a word, his own principle of "Prescription" must be honoured even in things indifferent; if novel they are not Catholic.

V.

TO SCAPULA.[1]

[TRANSLATED BY THE REV. S. THELWALL.]

CHAP. I.

WE are not in any great perturbation or alarm about the persecutions we suffer from the ignorance of men; for we have attached ourselves to this sect, fully accepting the terms of its covenant, so that, as men whose very lives are not their own, we engage in these conflicts, our desire being to obtain God's promised rewards, and our dread lest the woes with which He threatens an unchristian life should overtake us. Hence we shrink not from the grapple with your utmost rage, coming even forth of our own accord to the contest; and condemnation gives us more pleasure than acquittal. We have sent, therefore, this tract to you in no alarm about ourselves, but in much concern for you and for all our enemies, to say nothing of our friends. For our religion commands us to love even our enemies, and to pray for those who persecute us, aiming at a perfection all its own, and seeking in its disciples something of a higher type than the commonplace goodness of the world. For all love those who love them; it is peculiar to Christians alone to love those that hate them. Therefore, mourning over your ignorance, and compassionating human error, and looking on to that future of which every day shows threatening signs, necessity is laid on us to come forth in this way also, that we may set before you the truths you will not listen to openly.

CHAP. II.

We are worshippers of one God, of whose existence and character Nature teaches all men; at whose lightnings and thunders you tremble, whose benefits minister to your happiness. You think that others, too, are gods, whom we know to be devils. However, it is a fundamental human right, a privilege of nature, that every man should worship according to his own convictions: one man's religion neither harms nor helps another man. It is assuredly no part of religion to compel religion—to which free-will and not force should lead us—the sacrificial victims even being required of a willing mind. You will render no real service to your gods by compelling us to sacrifice. For they can have no desire of offerings from the unwilling, unless they are animated by a spirit of contention, which is a thing altogether undivine. Accordingly the true God bestows His blessings alike on wicked men and on His own elect; upon which account He has appointed an eternal judgment, when both thankful and unthankful will have to stand before His bar. Yet you have never detected us—sacrilegious wretches though you reckon us to be —in any theft, far less in any sacrilege. But the robbers of your temples, all of them swear by your gods, and worship them; they are not Christians, and yet it is they who are found guilty of sacrilegious deeds. We have not time to unfold in how many other ways your gods are mocked and despised by their own votaries. So, too, treason is falsely laid to our charge, though no one has ever been able to find followers of Albinus, or Niger, or Cassius, among Christians; while the very men who had sworn by the genii of the emperors, who had offered and vowed sacrifices for their safety, who had often pronounced condemnation on Christ's disciples, are till this day found traitors to the imperial throne. A Christian is enemy to none, least of all to the Emperor of Rome, whom he knows to be appointed by his God, and so cannot but love and honour; and whose well-being moreover, he must needs desire, with that of the empire over which he reigns so long as the world shall stand—for so long as that shall Rome continue.[2] To the emperor, therefore, we render

---

[1] [See Elucidation I. Written late in our author's life, this tract contains no trace of Montanism, and shows that his heart was with the common cause of all Christians. Who can give up such an Ephraim without recalling the words of inspired love for the erring?—Jer. xxxi. 20; Hos. xi. 8.]

[2] [Kaye points out our author's inconsistencies on this matter. If Caractacus ever made the speech ascribed to him (Bede, or Gibbon, cap. lxxi.) it would confirm the opinion of those who make him a convert to Christ: "Quando cadet Roma, cadet et mundus." Elucidation II.]

such reverential homage as is lawful for us and good for him; regarding him as the human being next to God who from God has received all his power, and is less than God alone. And this will be according to his own desires. For thus—as less only than the true God—he is greater than all besides. Thus he is greater than the very gods themselves, even they, too, being subject to him. We therefore sacrifice for the emperor's safety, but to our God and his, and after the manner God has enjoined, in simple prayer. For God, Creator of the universe, has no need of odours or of blood. These things are the food of devils.[1] But we not only reject those wicked spirits: we overcome them; we daily hold them up to contempt; we exorcise them from their victims, as multitudes can testify. So all the more we pray for the imperial well-being, as those who seek it at the hands of Him who is able to bestow it. And one would think it must be abundantly clear to you that the religious system under whose rules we act is one inculcating a divine patience; since, though our numbers are so great—constituting all but the majority in every city—we conduct ourselves so quietly and modestly; I might perhaps say, known rather as individuals than as organized communities, and remarkable only for the reformation of our former vices. For far be it from us to take it ill that we have laid on us the very things we wish, or in any way plot the vengeance at our own hands, which we expect to come from God.

CHAP. III.

However, as we have already remarked, it cannot but distress us that no state shall bear unpunished the guilt of shedding Christian blood; as you see, indeed, in what took place during the presidency of Hilarian, for when there had been some agitation about places of sepulture for our dead, and the cry arose, "No *areæ*—no burial-grounds for the Christians," it came that their own *areæ*,[2] their threshing-floors, were awanting, for they gathered in no harvests. As to the rains of the bygone year, it is abundantly plain of what they were intended to remind men—of the deluge, no doubt, which in ancient times overtook human unbelief and wickedness; and as to the fires which lately hung all night over the walls of Carthage, they who saw them know what they threatened; and what the preceding thunders pealed, *they* who were

hardened by them can tell. All these things are signs of God's impending wrath, which we must needs publish and proclaim in every possible way; and in the meanwhile we must pray it may be only local. Sure are *they* to experience it one day in its universal and final form, who interpret otherwise these samples of it. That sun, too, in the metropolis of Utica,[3] with light all but extinguished, was a portent which could not have occurred from an ordinary eclipse, situated as the lord of day was in his height and house. You have the astrologers, consult them about it. We can point you also to the deaths of some provincial rulers, who in their last hours had painful memories of their sin in persecuting the followers of Christ.[4] Vigellius Saturninus, who first here used the sword against us, lost his eyesight. Claudius Lucius Herminianus in Cappadocia, enraged that his wife had become a Christian, had treated the Christians with great cruelty: well, left alone in his palace, suffering under a contagious malady, he boiled out in living worms, and was heard exclaiming, "Let nobody know of it, lest the Christians rejoice, and Christian wives take encouragement." Afterwards he came to see his error in having tempted so many from their stedfastness by the tortures he inflicted, and died almost a Christian himself. In that doom which overtook Byzantium,[3] Cæcilius Capella could not help crying out, "Christians, rejoice!" Yes, and the persecutors who seem to themselves to have acted with impunity shall not escape the day of judgment. For you we sincerely wish it may prove to have been a warning only, that, immediately after you had condemned Mavilus of Adrumetum to the wild beasts, you were overtaken by those troubles, and that even now for the same reason you are called to a blood-reckoning. But do not forget the future.

CHAP. IV.

We who are without fear ourselves are not seeking to frighten you, but we would save all men if possible by warning them not to fight with God.[5] You may perform the duties of your charge, and yet remember the claims of humanity; if on no other ground than that you are liable to punishment yourself, (you ought to do so). For is not your commission simply to condemn those who confess their guilt, and to give over to the torture those

---

[1] [On this sort of Demonology see Kaye, pp. 203-207, with his useful references. See *De Spectaculis*, p. 80, *supra*.]
[2] [An obvious play on the ambiguity of this word.]
[3] [Notes of the time when this was written. See Kaye, p. 57.]
[4] [Christians remembered Herod (Acts, xii. 23) very naturally; but we may reserve remarks on such instances till we come to Lactantius. But see Kaye (p. 102) who speaks unfavourably of them.]
[5] [Our author uses the Greek (μὴ θεομαχεῖν) but not textually of Acts v. 39.]

who deny? You see, then, how you trespass yourselves against your instructions to wring from the confessing a denial. It is, in fact, an acknowledgment of our innocence that you refuse to condemn us at once when we confess. In doing your utmost to extirpate us, if that is your object, it is innocence you assail. But how many rulers, men more resolute and more cruel than you are, have contrived to get quit of such causes altogether,—as Cincius Severus, who himself suggested the remedy at Thysdris, pointing out how the Christians should answer that they might secure an acquittal; as Vespronius Candidus, who dismissed from his bar a Christian, on the ground that to satisfy his fellow-citizens would break the peace of the community; as Asper, who, in the case of a man who gave up his faith under slight infliction of the torture, did not compel the offering of sacrifice, having owned before, among the advocates and assessors of court, that he was annoyed at having had to meddle with such a case. Pudens, too, at once dismissed a Christian who was brought before him, perceiving from the indictment that it was a case of vexatious accusation; tearing the document in pieces, he refused so much as to hear him without the presence of his accuser, as not being consistent with the imperial commands. All this might be officially brought under your notice, and by the very advocates, who are themselves also under obligations to us, although in court they give their voice as it suits them. The clerk of one of them who was liable to be thrown upon the ground by an evil spirit, was set free from his affliction; as was also the relative of another, and the little boy of a third. How many men of rank (to say nothing of common people) have been delivered from devils, and healed of diseases! Even Severus himself, the father of Antonine, was graciously mindful of the Christians; for he sought out the Christian Proculus, surnamed Torpacion, the steward of Euhodias, and in gratitude for his having once cured him by anointing, he kept him in his palace till the day of his death.[1] Antonine, too, brought up as he was on Christian milk, was intimately acquainted with this man. Both women and men of highest rank, whom Severus knew well to be Christians, were not merely permitted by him to remain uninjured; but he even bore distinguished testimony in their favour, and gave them publicly back to us from the hands of a raging populace. Marcus Aurelius also, in his expedition to Germany, by the prayers his Christian soldiers offered to God, got rain in that well-known thirst.[2] When, indeed, have not droughts been put away by our kneelings and our fastings? At times like these, moreover, the people crying to "the God of gods, the alone Omnipotent," under the name of Jupiter, have borne witness to our God. Then we never deny the deposit placed in our hands; we never pollute the marriage bed; we deal faithfully with our wards; we give aid to the needy; we render to none evil for evil. As for those who falsely pretend to belong to us, and whom we, too, repudiate, let them answer for themselves. In a word, who has complaint to make against us on other grounds? To what else does the Christian devote himself, save the affairs of his own community, which during all the long period of its existence no one has ever proved guilty of the incest or the cruelty charged against it? It is for freedom from crime so singular, for a probity so great, for righteousness, for purity, for faithfulness, for truth, for the living God, that we are consigned to the flames; for this is a punishment you are not wont to inflict either on the sacrilegious, or on undoubted public enemies, or on the treason-tainted, of whom you have so many. Nay, even now our people are enduring persecution from the governors of Legio and Mauritania; but it is only with the sword, as from the first it was ordained that we should suffer. But the greater our conflicts, the greater our rewards.

CHAP. V.

Your cruelty is our glory. Only see you to it, that in having such things as these to endure, we do not feel ourselves constrained to rush forth to the combat, if only to prove that we have no dread of them, but on the contrary, even invite their infliction. When Arrius Antoninus was driving things hard in Asia, the whole Christians of the province, in one united band, presented themselves before his judgment-seat; on which, ordering a few to be led forth to execution, he said to the rest, "O miserable men, if you wish to die, you have precipices or halters." If we should take it into our heads to do the same thing here, what will you make of so many thousands, of such a multitude of men and women, persons of every sex and every age and every rank, when they present themselves before you? How many fires, how many swords will be required? What will be the anguish of Carthage itself, which you will have to decimate,[3] as each one recognises there his rela-

---

[1] [Another note of time. A.D. 211. See Kaye, as before.]

[2] [Compare Vol. I., p. 187, this Series.]
[3] [Compare De Fuga, cap. xii. It is incredible that our author could exaggerate in speaking to the chief magistrate of Carthage.]

tives and companions, as he sees there it may be men of your own order, and noble ladies, and all the leading persons of the city, and either kinsmen or friends of those of your own circle? Spare thyself, if not us poor Christians! Spare Carthage, if not thyself! Spare the province, which the indication of your purpose has subjected to the threats and extortions at once of the soldiers and of private enemies.

We have no master but God. *He is before* you, and cannot be hidden from you, but to Him you can do no injury. But those whom you regard as masters are only men, and one day they themselves must die. Yet still this community will be undying, for be assured that just in the time of its seeming overthrow it is built up into greater power. For all who witness the noble patience of its martyrs, as struck with misgivings, are inflamed with desire to examine into the matter in question;[1] and as soon as they come to know the truth, they straightway enrol themselves its disciples.

---

[1] [Mosheim's strange oversight, in neglecting to include such considerations, in accounting for the growth of the church, is justly censured by Kaye, p. 124.]

ELUCIDATIONS.

I.

(Scapula, cap. i., p. 105.)

SCAPULA was Proconsul of Carthage, and though its date is conjectural (A.D. 217), this work gives valuable *indices* of its time and circumstances. It was composed after the death of Severus, to whom there is an allusion in chapter iv., after the destruction of Byzantium (A.D. 196), to which there is a reference in chapter iii.; and Dr. Allix suggests, after the dark day of Utica (A.D. 210) which he supposes to be referred to in the same chapter. Cincius Severus, who is mentioned in chapter iv., was put to death by Severus, A.D. 198.

II.

(Caractacus, cap. ii., note 2, p. 105.)

Mr. Lewin (*St. Paul*, ii. 397), building on the fascinating theory of Archdeacon Williams, thinks St. Paul's Claudia (*Qu. Gladys?*) may very well have been the daughter of Caradoc, with whose noble character we are made acquainted by Tacitus. (Annals xii. 36.) And Archdeacon Williams gives us very strong reason to believe he was a Christian. He may very well have lived to behold the Coliseum completed. What more natural then, in view of the cruelty against Christians there exercised, for the expressions with which he is credited? In this case his words contain an eloquent ambiguity, which Christians would appreciate, and which may have been in our author's mind when he says—"quousque sæculum stabit." To those who looked for the Second Advent, daily, this did not mean what the heathen might suppose.

Bede's version of the speech (See Du Cange, II., 407.,) is this: "Quandiu stabit Colyseus —stabit et Roma: Quando cadet Colysevs—cadet et Roma: Quando cadet Roma—cadet et mundus."

VI

AD NATIONES.[1]

[TRANSLATED BY DR. HOLMES.]

CHAP. I.[2]—THE HATRED FELT BY THE HEATHEN AGAINST THE CHRISTIANS IS UNJUST, BECAUSE BASED ON CULPABLE IGNORANCE.

ONE proof of that ignorance of yours, which condemns[3] whilst it excuses[4] your injustice, is at once apparent in the fact, that all who once shared in your ignorance and hatred (of the Christian religion), as soon as they have come to know it, leave off their hatred when they cease to be ignorant; nay more, they actually themselves become what they had hated, and take to hating what they had once been. Day after day, indeed, you groan over the increasing number of the Christians. Your constant cry is, that the state is beset (by us); that Christians are in your fields, in your camps, in your islands. You grieve over it as a calamity, that each sex, every age—in short, every rank—is passing over from you to us; yet you do not even after this set your minds upon reflecting whether there be not here some latent good. You do not allow yourselves in suspicions which may prove too true,[5] nor do you like ventures which may be too near the mark.[6] This is the only instance in which human curiosity grows torpid. You love to be ignorant of what other men rejoice to have discovered; you would rather not know it, because you now cherish your hatred as if you were aware that, (with the knowledge,) your hatred would certainly come to an end. Still,[7] if there shall be no just ground for hatred, it will surely be found to be the best course to cease from the past injustice. Should, however, a cause have really existed, there will be no diminution of the hatred, which will indeed accumulate so much the more in the consciousness of its justice; unless it be, forsooth,[8] that you are ashamed to cast off your faults,[9] or sorry to free yourselves from blame.[10] I know very well with what answer you usually meet the argument from our rapid increase.[11] That indeed must not, you say, be hastily accounted a good thing which converts a great number of persons, and gains them over to its side. I am aware how the mind is apt to take to evil courses. How many there are which forsake virtuous living! How many seek refuge in the opposite! Many, no doubt;[12] nay, very many, as the last days approach.[13] But such a comparison as this fails in fairness of application; for all are agreed in thinking thus of the evil-doer, so that not even the guilty themselves, who take the wrong side, and turn away from the pursuit of good to perverse ways, are bold enough to defend evil as good.[14] Base things excite their fear, impious ones their shame. In short, they are eager for concealment, they shrink from publicity, they tremble when caught; when accused, they deny; even when tortured, they do not readily or invariably confess (their crime); at all events,[15] they grieve when they are condemned. They reproach themselves for their past life; their change from innocence to an evil disposition they even attribute to fate. They cannot say that it is not a wrong thing, therefore they will not admit it to be their own act. As for the Christians, however, in what does their case resemble this? No one is ashamed; no one is sorry, except for his former (sins).[16] If he is pointed

---

[1] [As a *recapitulation* I insert this here to close this class of argument for the reasons following.] This treatise resembles *The Apology*, both in its general purport as a vindication of Christianity against heathen prejudice, and in many of its expressions and statements. So great is the resemblance that this shorter work has been thought by some to have been a first draft of the longer and perfect one. Tertullian, however, here addresses his expostulations to the general public, while in *The Apology* it is the rulers and magistrates of the empire whom he seeks to influence. [Dr. Allix conjectures the date of this treatise to be about A.D. 217. See Kaye, p. 50.]
[2] Compare *The Apology*, c. i.
[3] Revincit. "Condemnat" is Tertullian's word in *The Apology*, i.
[4] Defendit. "Excusat" in *Apol.*
[5] Non licet rectius suspicari.
[6] Non lubet propius experiri.
[7] At quin.

[8] Nisi si.
[9] Emendari pudet.
[10] Excusari piget.
[11] Redundantiæ nostræ.
[12] Bona fide.
[13] Pro extremitatibus temporum.
[14] Or perhaps, "to maintain evil in preference to good."
[15] Certe.
[16] Pristinorum. In the corresponding passage (*Apol.* i.) the phrase is, "nisi plane retro non fuisse," i.e., "except that he was not *a Christian* long ago."

at (for his religion), he glories in it; if dragged to trial, he does not resist; if accused, he makes no defence. When questioned, he confesses; when condemned, he rejoices. What sort of evil is this, in which the nature of evil comes to a standstill?[1]

CHAP. II.[2]—THE HEATHEN PERVERTED JUDGMENT IN THE TRIAL OF CHRISTIANS. THEY WOULD BE MORE CONSISTENT IF THEY DISPENSED WITH ALL FORM OF TRIAL. TERTULLIAN URGES THIS WITH MUCH INDIGNATION.

In this case you actually[3] conduct trials contrary to the usual form of judicial process against criminals; for when culprits are brought up for trial, should they deny the charge, you press them for a confession by tortures. When Christians, however, confess without compulsion, you aply the torture to induce them to deny. What great perverseness is this, when you stand out against confession, *and* change the use of the torture, compelling the man who frankly acknowledges the charge[4] to evade it, and him who is unwilling, to deny it? You, who preside for the purpose of extorting truth, demand falsehood from us alone, that we may declare ourselves not to be what we are. I suppose you do not want us to be bad men, and therefore you earnestly wish to exclude us from that character. To be sure,[5] you put others on the rack and the gibbet, to get them to deny what they have the reputation of being. Now, when they deny (the charge against them), you do not believe them; but on our denial, you instantly believe us. If you feel sure that we are the most injurious of men, why, even in processes against us, are we dealt with by you differently from other offenders? I do not mean that you make no account of[6] either an accusation or a denial (for your practice is not hastily to condemn men without an indictment and a defence); but, to take an instance in the trial of a murderer, the case is not at once ended, or the inquiry satisfied, on a man's confessing himself the murderer. However complete his confession,[7] you do not readily believe him; but over and above this, you inquire into accessory circumstances—how often had he committed murder; with what weapons, in what place, with what plunder, accomplices, *and* abettors after the fact[8] (was the crime perpe-

trated)—to the end that nothing whatever respecting the criminal might escape detection, and that every means should be at hand for arriving at a true verdict. In our case, on the contrary,[9] whom you believe to be guilty of more atrocious and numerous crimes, you frame your indictments[10] in briefer and lighter terms. I suppose you do not care to load with accusations men whom you earnestly wish to get rid of, or else you do not think it necessary to inquire into matters which are known to you already. It is, however, all the more perverse that you compel us to deny charges about which you have the clearest evidence. But, indeed,[11] how much more consistent were it with your hatred of us to dispense with all forms of judicial process, and to strive with all your might not to urge us to say "No," and so have to acquit the objects of your hatred; but to confess all and singular the crimes laid to our charge, that your resentments might be the better glutted with an accumulation of our punishments, when it becomes known how many of those feasts each one of us may have celebrated, and how many incests we may have committed under cover of the night! What am I saying? Since your researches for rooting out our society must needs be made on a wide scale, you ought to extend your inquiry against our friends and companions. Let our infanticides and the dressers (of our horrible repasts) be brought out,—ay, and the very dogs which minister to our (incestuous) nuptials;[12] then the business (of our trial) would be without a fault. Even to the crowds which throng the spectacles a zest would be given; for with how much greater eagerness would they resort to the theatre, when one had to fight in the lists who had devoured a hundred babies! For since such horrid and monstrous crimes are reported of us, they ought, of course, to be brought to light, lest they should seem to be incredible, and the public detestation of us should begin to cool. For most persons are slow to believe such things,[13] feeling a horrible disgust at supposing that our nature could have an appetite

[1] Cessat.
[2] Comp. c. ii. of *The Apology.*
[3] Ipsi.
[4] Gratis reum.
[5] Sane.
[6] Neque spatium commodetis.
[7] Quanquam confessis.
[8] Receptoribus, "concealers" of the crime.

[9] Porro.
[10] Elogia.
[11] Immo.
[12] We have for once departed from Oehler's text, and preferred Rigault's: "Perducerentur *infantarii* et coci, ipsi canes pronubi, emendata esset res." The sense is evident from *The Apology,* c. vii.: "It is said that we are guilty of most horrible crimes; that in the celebration of our sacrament we put a child to death, which we afterward devour, and at the end of our banquet revel in incest; that we employ dogs as ministers of our impure delights, to overthrow the candles, and thus to provide darkness, and remove all shame which might interfere with these impious lusts" (Chevalier's translation). These calumnies were very common, and are noticed by Justin Martyr, Minucius Felix, Eusebius, Athenagoras, and Origen, who attributes their origin to the Jews. Oehler reads *infantaria,* after the Agobardine codex and *editio princeps,* and quotes Martial (*Epigr.* iv. 88), where the word occurs in the sense of an inordinate love of children.
[13] Nam et plerique fidem talium temperant.

for the food of wild beasts, when it has pre-cluded these from all concubinage with the race of man.

CHAP. III.[1]—THE GREAT OFFENCE IN THE CHRISTIANS LIES IN THEIR VERY NAME. THE NAME VINDICATED.

Since, therefore, you who are in other cases most scrupulous and persevering in investigating charges of far less serious import, relinquish your care in cases like ours, which are so horrible, and of such surpassing sin that *impiety* is too mild a word for them, by declining to hear confession, which should always be an important process for those who conduct judicial proceedings; and failing to make a full inquiry, which should be gone into by such as sue for a condemnation, it becomes evident that the crime laid to our charge consists not of any sinful conduct, but lies wholly in our *name.* If, indeed,[2] any real crimes were clearly adducible against us, their very names would condemn us, if found applicable,[3] so that distinct sentences would be pronounced against us in this wise: Let that murderer, or that incestuous criminal, or whatever it be that we are charged with, be led to execution, be crucified, or be thrown to the beasts. Your sentences, however,[4] import only that one has confessed himself a Christian. No name of a crime stands against us, but only the crime of a name. Now this in very deed is neither more nor less than[5] the entire odium which is felt against us. The name is the cause: some mysterious force intensified by your ignorance assails it, so that you do not wish to know for certain that which for certain you are sure you know nothing of; and therefore, further, you do not believe things which are not submitted to proof, and, lest they should be easily refuted,[6] you refuse to make inquiry, so that the odious name is punished under the presumption of (real) crimes. In order, therefore, that the issue may be withdrawn from the offensive name, we are compelled to deny it; then upon our denial we are acquitted, with an entire absolution[7] for the past: we are no longer murderers, no longer incestuous, because we have lost that name.[8] But since this point is dealt with in a place of its own,[9] do you tell us plainly why you are pursuing this name even to extirpation? What crime, what offence, what

fault is there in a name? For you are barred by the rule[10] which puts it out of your power to allege crimes (of any man), which no legal action moots, no indictment specifies, no sentence enumerates. In any case which is submitted to the judge,[11] inquired into against the defendant, responded to by him or denied, and cited from the bench, I acknowledge a legal charge. Concerning, then, the merit of a name, whatever offence names may be charged with, whatever impeachment words may be amenable to, I for my part[12] think, that not even a complaint is due to a word or a name, unless indeed it has a barbarous sound, or smacks of ill-luck, or is immodest, or is indecorous for the speaker, or unpleasant to the hearer. These crimes in (mere) words and names are just like barbarous words and phrases, which have their fault, and their solecism, and their absurdity of figure. The name *Christian,* however, so far as its meaning goes, bears the sense of anointing. Even when by a faulty pronunciation you call us " Chrestians " (for you are not certain about even the sound of this noted name), you in fact lisp out the sense of pleasantness and goodness.[13] You are therefore vilifying[14] in harmless men even the harmless name we bear, which is not inconvenient for the tongue, nor harsh to the ear, nor injurious to a single being, nor rude for our country, being a good Greek word, as many others also are, and pleasant in sound and sense. Surely, surely,[15] names are not things which deserve punishment by the sword, or the cross, or the beasts.

CHAP. IV.[16]—THE TRUTH HATED IN THE CHRISTIANS; SO IN MEASURE WAS IT, OF OLD, IN SOCRATES. THE VIRTUES OF THE CHRISTIANS.

But the sect, you say, is punished in the name of its founder. Now in the first place it is, no doubt a fair and usual custom that a sect should be marked out by the name of its founder, since philosophers are called Pythagoreans and Platonists after their masters; in the same way physicians are called after Erasistratus, and grammarians after Aristarchus. If, therefore, a sect has a bad character because its founder was bad, it is punished[17] as the traditional bearer[18] of a bad name. But this would be indulging in a rash assumption.

---

[1] Comp. *The Apology*, cc. i. and ii.
[2] Adeo si.
[3] Si accommodarent.
[4] Porro.
[5] Hæc ratio est.
[6] Reprobentur.
[7] Impunitate.
[8] i.e., the name " Christians."
[9] By the " suo loco," Tertullian refers to *The Apology.*

[10] Præscribitur vobis.
[11] Præsidi.
[12] Ego.
[13] Χρηστός means both "*pleasant*" and "*good;*" and the heathen founded this word with the sacred name Χριστός.
[14] Detinetis.
[15] Et utique.
[16] See *The Apology*, c. iii.
[17] Plectitur.
[18] Tradux.

The first step was to find out what the founder was, that his sect might be understood, instead of hindering[1] inquiry into the founder's character from the sect. But in our case,[2] by being necessarily ignorant of the sect, through your ignorance of its founder, or else by not taking a fair survey of the founder, because you make no inquiry into his sect, you fasten merely on the name, just as if you vilified in it both sect and founder, whom you know nothing of whatever. And yet you openly allow your philosophers the right of attaching themselves to any school, and bearing its founder's name as their own; and nobody stirs up any hatred against them, although both in public and in private they bark out[3] their bitterest eloquence against your customs, rites, ceremonies, and manner of life, with so much contempt for the laws, and so little respect for persons, that they even flaunt their licentious words[4] against the emperors themselves with impunity. And yet it is the truth, which is so troublesome to the world, that these philosophers affect, but which Christians possess: they therefore who have it in possession afford the greater displeasure, because he who affects a thing plays with it; he who possesses it maintains it. For example,[5] Socrates was condemned on that side (of his wisdom) in which he came nearest in his search to the truth, by destroying your gods. Although the name of Christian was not at that time in the world, yet truth was always suffering condemnation. Now you will not deny that he was a wise man, to whom your own Pythian (god) had borne witness. Socrates, he said, was the wisest of men. Truth overbore Apollo, and made him pronounce even against himself; since he acknowledged that he was no god, when he affirmed that that was the wisest man who was denying the gods. However,[6] on your principle he was the less wise because he denied the gods, although, in truth, he was all the wiser by reason of this denial. It is just in the same way that you are in the habit of saying of us: "Lucius Titius is a good man, only he is a Christian;" while another says: "I wonder that so worthy[7] a man as Caius Seius has become a Christian.[8]" According to[9] the blindness of their folly men praise what they know, (and) blame what they are ignorant of; and that which they know, they vitiate by that which they do not know.

It occurs to none (to consider) whether a man is not good and wise because he is a Christian, or therefore a Christian because he is wise and good, although it is more usual in human conduct to determine obscurities by what is manifest, than to prejudice what is manifest by what is obscure. Some persons wonder that those whom they had known to be unsteady, worthless, *or* wicked before they bore this[10] name, have been suddenly converted to virtuous courses; and yet they better know how to wonder (at the change) than to attain to it; others are so obstinate in their strife as to do battle with their own best interests, which they have it in their power to secure by intercourse[11] with that hated name. I know more than one[12] husband, formerly anxious about their wives' conduct, and unable to bear even mice to creep into their bed-room without a groan of suspicion, who have, upon discovering the cause of their new assiduity, and their unwonted attention to the duties of home,[13] offered the entire loan of their wives to others,[14] disclaimed all jealousy, (and) preferred to be the husbands of she-wolves than of Christian women: they could commit themselves to a perverse abuse of nature, but they could not permit their wives to be reformed for the better ! A father disinherited his son, with whom he had ceased to find fault. A master sent his slave to bridewell,[15] whom he had even found to be indispensable to him. As soon as they discovered them to be Christians, they wished they were criminals again; for our discipline carries its own evidence in itself, nor are we betrayed by anything else than our own goodness, just as bad men also become conspicuous[16] by their own evil. Else how is it that we alone are, contrary to the lessons of nature, branded as very evil because of our good ? For what mark do we exhibit except the prime wisdom,[17] which teaches us not to worship the frivolous works of the human hand; the temperance, by which we abstain from other men's goods; the chastity, which we pollute not even with a look; the compassion, which prompts us to help the needy; the truth itself, which makes us give offence; and liberty, for which we have even learned to die ? Whoever wishes to understand who the Christians are, must needs employ these marks for their discovery.

---

[1] Retinere.
[2] At nunc.
[3] Elatrent.
[4] Libertatem suam, "their liberty of speech."
[5] Denique.
[6] Porro.
[7] Gravem, "earnest."
[8] Comp. *The Apology*, c. iii.
[9] Pro.

[10] i.e., the Christian.
[11] De commercio.
[12] Unum atque alium. The sense being *plural*, we have so given it all through.
[13] Captivitatis (as if theirs was a self-inflicted captivity at home).
[14] Omnem uxorem patientiam obtulisse (comp. *Apology*, middle of c. xxxix.).
[15] In ergastulum.
[16] Radiant.
[17] He means the religion of Christ, which he in b. ii. c. ii. contrasts with "*the mere wisdom*" of the philosophers.

CHAP. V.[1]—THE INCONSISTENT LIFE OF ANY FALSE CHRISTIAN NO MORE CONDEMNS TRUE DISCIPLES OF CHRIST, THAN A PASSING CLOUD OBSCURES A SUMMER SKY.

As to your saying of us that we are a most shameful set, and utterly steeped in luxury, avarice, and depravity, we will not deny that this is true of some. It is, however, a sufficient testimonial for our name, that this cannot be said of all, not even of the greater part of us. It must happen even in the healthiest and purest body, that a mole should grow, or a wart arise on it, or freckles disfigure it. Not even the sky itself is clear with so perfect[2] a serenity as not to be flecked with some filmy cloud.[3] A slight spot on the face, because it is obvious in so conspicuous a part, only serves to show purity of the entire complexion. The goodness of the larger portion is well attested by the slender flaw. But although you prove that some of our people are evil, you do not hereby prove that they are Christians. Search and see whether there is any sect to which (a partial shortcoming) is imputed as a general stain.[4] You are accustomed in conversation yourselves to say, in disparagement of us, " Why is so-and-so deceitful, when the Christians are so self-denying ? why merciless, when they are so merciful ? " You thus bear your testimony to the fact that this is not the character of Christians, when you ask, in the way of a retort,[5] how men who are reputed to be Christians can be of such and such a disposition. There is a good deal of difference between an imputation and a name,[6] between an opinion and the truth. For names were appointed for the express purpose of setting their proper limits between mere designation and actual condition.[7] How many indeed are said to be philosophers, who for all that do not fulfil the law of philosophy? All bear the name in respect of their profession; but they hold the designation without the excellence of the profession, and they disgrace the real thing under the shallow pretence of its name. Men are not straightway of such and such a character, because they are said to be so; but when they are not, it is vain to say so of them: they only deceive people who attach reality to a name, when it is its consistency with fact which decides the condition implied in the name.[8] And yet persons of this doubtful stamp do not assemble with us, neither do they belong to our communion: by their delinquency they become yours once more,[9] since we should be unwilling to mix even with them whom your violence and cruelty compelled to recant. Yet we should, of course, be more ready to have included amongst us those who have unwillingly forsaken our discipline than wilful apostates. However, you have no right to call them Christians, to whom the Christians themselves deny that name, and who have not learned to deny themselves.

CHAP. VI.[10]—THE INNOCENCE OF THE CHRISTIANS NOT COMPROMISED BY THE INIQUITOUS LAWS WHICH WERE MADE AGAINST THEM.

Whenever these statements and answers of ours, which truth suggests of its own accord, press and restrain your conscience, which is the witness of its own ignorance, you betake yourselves in hot haste to that poor altar of refuge,[11] the authority of the laws, because these, of course, would never punish the offensive[12] sect, if their deserts had not been fully considered by those who made the laws. Then what is it which has prevented a like consideration on the part of those who put the laws in force, when, in the case of all other crimes which are similarly forbidden and punished by the laws, the penalty is not inflicted[13] until it is sought by regular process?[14] Take,[15] for instance, the case of a murderer or an adulterer. An examination is ordered touching the particulars[16] of the crime, even though it is patent to all what its nature[17] is. Whatever wrong has been done by the Christian ought to be brought to light. No law forbids inquiry to be made; on the contrary, inquiry is made in the interest of the laws.[18] For how are you to keep the law by precautions against that which the law forbids, if you neutralize the carefulness of the precaution by your failing to perceive[19] what it is you have to keep? No law must keep to itself[20] the knowledge of its own righteousness,[21] but (it owes it) to those from whom it claims obedience. The law, however, becomes an object of suspicion when it declines to approve itself. Naturally enough,[22] then, are the laws against

---

1 Compare *The Apology*, cc. ii. xliv. xlvi.
2 *Colata*, " filtered" [or " strained"—*Shaks.*]
3 Ut non alicujus nubiculæ flocculo resignetur. This picturesque language defies translation.
4 Malitiæ.
5 Dum retorquetis.
6 Inter crimen et nomen.
7 Inter dici et esse.
8 Status nominis.

9 Denuo.
10 Compare *The Apology*, c. iv.
11 Ad arulam quandam.
12 Istam.
13 Cessat, " loiters."
14 Requiratur.
15 Lege.
16 Ordo.
17 Genus.
18 Literally, " holding the inquiry makes for the laws."
19 Per defectionem agnoscendi.
20 Sibi debet.
21 Justitiæ suæ.
22 Merito.

the Christians supposed to be just and deserving of respect and observance, just as long as men remain ignorant of their aim and purport; but when this is perceived, their extreme injustice is discovered, and they are deservedly rejected with abhorrence,[1] along with (their instruments of torture)—the swords, the crosses, and the lions. An unjust law secures no respect. In my opinion, however, there is a suspicion among you that some of these laws are unjust, since not a day passes without your modifying their severity and iniquity by fresh deliberations and decisions.

CHAP. VII.[2]—THE CHRISTIANS DEFAMED. A SARCASTIC DESCRIPTION OF FAME; ITS DECEPTION AND ATROCIOUS SLANDERS OF THE CHRISTIANS LENGTHILY DESCRIBED.

Whence comes it to pass, you will say to us, that such a character could have been attributed to you, as to have justified the lawmakers perhaps by its imputation? Let me ask on my side, what voucher they had then, or you now, for the truth of the imputation? (You answer,) Fame. Well, now, is not this—

"Fama malum, quo non aliud velocius ullum?"[3]

Now, why a plague,[4] if it be always true? It never ceases from lying; nor even at the moment when it reports the truth is it so free from the wish to lie, as not to interweave the false with the true, by processes of addition, diminution, or confusion of various facts. Indeed,[5] such is its condition, that it can only continue to exist while it lies. For it lives only just so long as it fails to prove anything. As soon as it proves itself true, it falls; and, as if its office of reporting news were at an end, it quits its post: thenceforward the thing is held to be a fact, and it passes under that name. No one, then, says, to take an instance, "The report is that this happened at Rome," or, "The rumour goes that he has got a province;" but, "He has got a province," and, "This happened at Rome." Nobody mentions a rumour except at an uncertainty, because nobody can be sure of a rumour, but only of certain knowledge; and none but a fool believes a rumour, because no wise man puts faith in an uncertainty. In however wide a circuit[6] a report has been circulated, it must needs have originated some

time or other from one mouth; afterwards it creeps on somehow to ears and tongues which pass it on[7] and so obscures the humble error in which it began, that no one considers whether the mouth which first set it a-going disseminated a falsehood,—a circumstance which often happens either from a temper of rivalry, or a suspicious turn, or even the pleasure of feigning news. It is, however, well that time reveals all things, as your own sayings and proverbs testify; yea, as nature herself attests, which has so ordered it that nothing lies hid, not even that which fame has not reported. See, now, what a witness[8] you have suborned against us: it has not been able up to this time to prove the report it set in motion, although it has had so long a time to recommend it to our acceptance. This name of ours took its rise in the reign of Augustus; under Tiberius it was taught with all clearness and publicity;[9] under Nero it was ruthlessly condemned,[10] and you may weigh its worth and character even from the person of its persecutor. If that prince was a pious man, then the Christians are impious; if he was just, if he was pure, then the Christians are unjust and impure; if he was not a public enemy, we are enemies of our country: what sort of men we are, our persecutor himself shows, since he of course punished what produced hostility to himself.[11] Now, although every other institution which existed under Nero has been destroyed, yet this of ours has firmly remained—righteous, it would seem, as being unlike the author (of its persecution). Two hundred and fifty years, then, have not yet passed since our life began. During the interval there have been so many criminals; so many crosses have obtained immortality;[12] so many infants have been slain; so many loaves steeped in blood; so many extinctions of candles;[13] so many dissolute marriages. And up to the present time it is mere report which fights against the Christians. No doubt it has a strong support in the wickedness of the human mind, and utters its falsehoods with more success among cruel and savage men. For the more inclined you are to maliciousness, the more ready are you to believe evil· in short, men more easily believe the evil that is false, than the good which is true. Now, if injustice has left any place within you for the exercise of prudence in investigating the truth of reports, justice of course demanded

---

[1] Despuuntur.
[2] Comp. *The Apology*, cc. vii, viii.
[3] *Æneid*, iv. 174.
     "Fame, than which never plague that runs
       Its way more swiftly wins."—Conington.
[4] "A plague" = malum.
[5] Quid? quod "Yea more."
[6] Ambitione.

[7] Traduces.
[8] Prodigiam. The word is "indicem" in *The Apology*.
[9] Disciplina ejus illuxit.
[10] Damnatio invaluit.
[11] Æmula sibi.
[12] Divinitatem consecutæ.
[13] See above, c. ii. note.

that you should examine by whom the report could have been spread among the multitude, and thus circulated through the world. For it could not have been by the Christians themselves, I suppose, since by the very constitution and law of all mysteries the obligation of silence is imposed. How much more would this be the case in such (mysteries as are ascribed to us), which, if divulged, could not fail to bring down instant punishment from the prompt resentment of men! Since, therefore, the Christians are not their own betrayers, it follows that it must be strangers. Now I ask, how could strangers obtain knowledge of us, when even true and lawful mysteries exclude every stranger from witnessing them, unless illicit ones are less exclusive? Well, then, it is more in keeping with the character of strangers both to be ignorant (of the true state of a case), and to invent (a false account). Our domestic servants (perhaps) listened, and peeped through crevices and holes, and stealthily got information of our ways. What, then, shall we say when our servants betray them to you?[1] It is better, (to be sure,)[2] for us all not to be betrayed by any; but still, if our practices be so atrocious, how much more proper is it when a righteous indignation bursts asunder even all ties of domestic fidelity? How was it possible for it to endure what horrified the mind and affrighted the eye? This is also a wonderful thing, both that he who was so overcome with impatient excitement as to turn informer,[3] did not likewise desire to prove (what he reported), and that he who heard the informer's story did not care to see for himself, since no doubt the reward[4] is equal both for the informer who proves what he reports, and for the hearer who convinces himself of the credibility[5] of what he hears. But then you say that (this is precisely what has taken place): first came the rumour, then the exhibition of the proof; first the hearsay, then the inspection; and after this, fame received its commission. Now this, I must say,[6] surpasses all admiration, that that was once for all detected and divulged which is being for ever repeated, unless, forsooth, we have by this time ceased from the reiteration of such things[7] (as are alleged of us). But we are called still by the same (offensive) name, and we are supposed to be still engaged in the same prac-

tices, and we multiply from day to day; the more[8] we are, to the more become we objects of hatred. Hatred increases as the material for it increases. Now, seeing that the multitude of offenders is ever advancing, how is it that the crowd of informers does not keep equal pace therewith? To the best of my belief, even our manner of life[9] has become better known; you know the very days of our assemblies; therefore we are both besieged, and attacked, and kept prisoners actually in our secret congregations. Yet who ever came upon a half-consumed corpse (amongst us)? Who has detected the traces of a bite in our blood-steeped loaf? Who has discovered, by a sudden light invading our darkness, any marks of impurity, I will not say of incest, (in our feasts)? If we save ourselves by a bribe[10] from being dragged out before the public gaze with such a character, how is it that we are still oppressed? We have it indeed in our own power not to be thus apprehended at all; for who either sells or buys information about a crime, if the crime itself has no existence? But why need I disparagingly refer to[11] strange spies and informers, when you allege against us such charges as we certainly do not ourselves divulge with very much noise—either as soon as you hear of them, if we previously show them to you, or after you have yourselves discovered them, if they are for the time concealed from you? For no doubt,[12] when any desire initiation in the mysteries, their custom is first to go to the master or father of the sacred rites. Then he will say (to the applicant), You must bring an infant, as a guarantee for our rites, to be sacrificed, as well as some bread to be broken and dipped in his blood; you also want candles, and dogs tied together to upset them, and bits of meat to rouse the dogs. Moreover, a mother too, or a sister, is necessary for you. What, however, is to be said if you have neither? I suppose in that case you could not be a genuine Christian. Now, do let me ask you, Will such things, when reported by strangers, bear to be spread about (as charges against us)? It is impossible for such persons to understand proceedings in which they take no part.[13] The first step of the process is perpetrated with artifice; our feasts and our marriages are invented and detailed[14] by ignorant persons,

[1] i.e., What is the value of *such* evidence?
[2] We have inserted this phrase as the sentence is strongly ironical.
[3] Deferre, an *infinitive* of purpose, of which construction of our author Oehler gives examples.
[4] Fructus.
[5] Si etiam sibi credat.
[6] Quidem.
[7] Talia factitare.
[8] We read "quo," and not "quod," because.
[9] Conversatio.
[10] This refers to a calumny which the heathen frequently spread about the Christians.
[11] Detrectem or simply "treat of," "refer to," like the simple verb "tractare".
[12] The irony of all this passage is evident.
[13] Diversum opus.
[14] Subjiciuntur "are stealthily narrated."

who had never before heard about Christian mysteries. And though they afterwards cannot help acquiring some knowledge of them, it is even then as having to be administered by others whom they bring on the scene.[1] Besides, how absurd is it that the profane know mysteries which the priest knows not! They keep them all to themselves, then,[2] and take them for granted; and so these tragedies, (worse than those) of Thyestes or Œdipus, do not at all come forth to light, nor find their way[3] to the public. Even more voracious bites take nothing away from the credit[4] of such as are initiated, whether servants or masters. If, however, none of these allegations can be proved to be true, how incalculable must be esteemed the grandeur (of that religion) which is manifestly not overbalanced even by the burden of these vast atrocities! O ye heathen, who have and deserve our pity,[5] behold, we set before you the promise which our sacred system offers. It guarantees eternal life to such as follow and observe it; on the other hand, it threatens with the eternal punishment of an unending fire those who are profane and hostile; while to both classes alike is preached a resurrection from the dead. We are not now concerned[6] about the doctrine of these (verities), which are discussed in their proper place.[7] Meanwhile, however, believe them, even as we do ourselves, for I want to know whether you are ready to reach them, as we do, through such crimes. Come, whosoever you are, plunge your sword into an infant; or if that is another's office, then simply gaze at the breathing creature[8] dying before it has lived; at any rate, catch its fresh[9] blood in which to steep your bread; then feed yourself without stint; and whilst this is going on, recline. Carefully distinguish the places where your mother or your sister may have made their bed; mark them well, in order that, when the shades of night have fallen upon them, putting of course to the test the care of every one of you, you may not make the awkward mistake of alighting on somebody else:[10] you

would have to make an atonement, if you failed of the incest. When you have effected all this, eternal life will be in store for you. I want you to tell me whether you think eternal life worth such a price. No, indeed,[11] you do not believe it: even if you did believe it, I maintain that you would be unwilling to give (the fee); or if willing, would be unable. But why should others be able if you are unable? Why should you be able if others are unable? What would you wish impunity (and) eternity to stand you in?[12] Do you suppose that these (blessings) can be bought by us at any price? Have Christians teeth of a different sort from others? Have they more ample jaws?[13] Are they of different nerve for incestuous lust? I trow not. It is enough for us to differ from you in condition[14] by truth alone.

CHAP. VIII.[15]—THE CALUMNY AGAINST THE CHRISTIANS ILLUSTRATED IN THE DISCOVERY OF PSAMMETICHUS. REFUTATION OF THE STORY.

We are indeed said to be the "third race" of men. What, a dog-faced race?[16] Or broadly shadow-footed?[17] Or some subterranean[18] Antipodes? If you attach any meaning to these names, pray tell us what are the first and the second race, that so we may know something of this "third." Psammetichus thought that he had hit upon the ingenious discovery of the primeval man. He is said to have removed certain new-born infants from all human intercourse, and to have entrusted them to a nurse, whom he had previously deprived of her tongue, in order that, being completely exiled from all sound of the human voice, they might form their speech without hearing it; and thus, deriving it from themselves alone, might indicate what that first nation was whose speech was dictated by nature. Their first utterance was BEKKOS, a word which means "*bread*" in the language of Phrygia: the Phrygians, therefore, are supposed to be the first of the human race.[19] But it will not be out of place if we make one observation, with a view to show how your faith abandons itself more to vanities than to verities.

---

[1] Inducunt.
[2] It is difficult to see what this "tacent igitur" means without referring to the similar passage in *The Apology* (end of c. viii.), which supplies a link wanted in the context. "At all events," says he, "they know this afterward, and yet submit to it, and allow it. *They fear to be punished*, while, if they proclaimed the truth, they would deserve universal approbation." Tertullian here states what the enemies of the Christians used to allege against them. After discovering the alleged atrocities of their secret assemblies, they kept their knowledge forsooth to themselves, being afraid of the consequences of a disclosure, etc.
[3] We have for convenience treated "protrahunt" (*q.d.* "nor do they report them") as a neuter verb.
[4] Even worse than Thyestean atrocities would be believed of them.
[5] Miseræ atque miserandæ.
[6] Viderimus.
[7] See below, in c. xix.
[8] Animam.
[9] Rudem, "hardly formed."
[10] Extraneam.

[11] Immo idcirco.
[12] Quanto constare.
[13] "An alii ordines dentium Christianorum, et alii specus faucium?" (literally, "Have Christians other sets of teeth, and other caverns of jaws?") This seems to refer to voracious animals like the shark, whose terrible teeth, lying in several rows, and greediness to swallow anything, however incongruous, that comes in its way, are well-known facts in natural history.
[14] Positione.
[15] Compare *The Apology*, c. viii.
[16] Cynopæ. This class would furnish the unnatural "teeth," and "jaws," just referred to.
[17] Sciapodes with broad feet *producing a large shade;* suited for the "incestuous lust" above mentioned.
[18] Literally, "which come up from under ground."
[19] Tertullian got this story from Herodotus, ii. 2.

Can it be, then, at all credible that the nurse retained her life, after the loss of so important a member, the very organ of the breath of life,[1]—cut out, too, from the very root, with her throat[2] mutilated, which cannot be wounded even on the outside without danger, and the putrid gore flowing back to the chest, and deprived for so long a time of her food? Come, even suppose that by the remedies of a Philomela she retained her life, in the way supposed by wisest persons, who account for the dumbness not by cutting out the tongue, but from the blush of shame; if on such a supposition she lived, she would still be able to blurt out some dull sound. And a shrill inarticulate noise from opening the mouth only, without any modulation of the lips, might be forced from the mere throat, though there were no tongue to help. This, it is probable, the infants readily imitated, and the more so because it was the only sound; only they did it a little more neatly, as they had tongues;[3] and then they attached to it a definite signification. Granted, then, that the Phrygians were the earliest race, it does not follow that the Christians are the third. For how many other nations come regularly after the Phrygians? Take care, however, lest those whom you call the third race should obtain the first rank, since there is no nation indeed which is not Christian. Whatever nation, therefore, was the first, is nevertheless Christian now.[4] It is ridiculous folly which makes you say we are the latest race, and then specifically call us the third. But it is in respect of our religion,[5] not of our nation, that we are supposed to be the third; the series being the Romans, the Jews, and the Christians after them. Where, then, are the Greeks? or if they are reckoned amongst the Romans in regard to their superstition (since it was from Greece that Rome borrowed even her gods), where at least are the Egyptians, since these have, so far as I know, a mysterious religion peculiar to themselves? Now, if they who belong to the third race are so monstrous, what must they be supposed to be who preceded them in the first and the second place?

CHAP. IX.[6]—THE CHRISTIANS ARE NOT THE CAUSE OF PUBLIC CALAMITIES: THERE WERE SUCH TROUBLES BEFORE CHRISTIANITY.

But why should I be astonished at your vain imputations? Under the same natural form, malice and folly have always been associated in one body and growth, and have ever opposed us under the one instigator of error.[7] Indeed, I feel no astonishment; and therefore, as it is necessary for my subject, I will enumerate some instances, that you may feel the astonishment by the enumeration of the folly into which you fall, when you insist on our being the causes of every public calamity or injury. If the Tiber has overflowed its banks, if the Nile has remained in its bed, if the sky has been still, or the earth been in commotion, if death[8] has made its devastations, or famine its afflictions, your cry immediately is, "This is the fault[9] of the Christians!" As if they who fear the true God could have to fear a light thing, or at least anything else (than an earthquake or famine, or such visitations).[10] I suppose it is as despisers of your gods that we call down on us these strokes of theirs. As we have remarked already,[11] three hundred years have not yet passed in our existence; but what vast scourges before that time fell on all the world, on its various cities and provinces! what terrible wars, both foreign and domestic! what pestilences, famines, conflagrations, yawnings, and quakings of the earth has history recorded![12] Where were the Christians, then, when the Roman state furnished so many chronicles of its disasters? Where were the Christians when the islands Hiera, Anaphe, and Delos, and Rhodes, and Cea were desolated with multitudes of men? or, again, when the land mentioned by Plato as larger than Asia or Africa was sunk in the Atlantic Sea? or when fire from heaven overwhelmed Volsinii, and flames from their own mountain consumed Pompeii? when the sea of Corinth was engulphed by an earthquake? when the whole world was destroyed by the deluge? Where then were (I will not say the Christians, who despise your gods, but) your gods themselves, who are proved to be of later origin than that great ruin by the very places and cities in which they were born, sojourned, and were buried, and even those which they founded? For else they would not have remained to the present day, unless they had been more recent than that catastrophe. If you do not care to peruse and reflect upon these testimonies of history, the record of which affects you differently from us,[13] in order

---

[1] Ipsius animæ organo.
[2] Faucibus.
[3] Utpote linguatuli.
[4] This is one of the passages which incidentally show how widely spread was Christianity.
[5] De Superstitione.
[6] Comp. *The Apology*, cc.xl.xli. [And Augustine, *Civ. Dei. iii.*]

[7] By the "manceps erroris" he means the devil.
[8] Libitina.
[9] Christianorum meritum, which with "sit" may be also, "Let the Christians have their due." In *The Apology* the cry is, Christianos ad leonem."
[10] We insert this after Oehler. Tertullian's words are, "Quasi modicum habeant aut aliud metuere qui Deum verum."
[11] See above, c. vii.
[12] Sæculum digessit.
[13] Aliter vobis renuntiata.

especially that you may not have to tax your gods with extreme injustice, since they injure even their worshippers on account of their despisers, do you not then prove yourselves to be also in the wrong, when you hold them to be gods, who make no distinction between the deserts of yourselves and profane persons? If, however, as it is now and then very vainly said, you incur the chastisement of your gods because you are too slack in our extirpation, you then have settled the question [1] of their weakness and insignificance; for they would not be angry with you for loitering over our punishment, if they could do anything themselves,—although you admit the same thing indeed in another way, whenever by inflicting punishment on us you seem to be avenging them. If one interest is maintained by another party, that which defends is the greater of the two. What a shame, then, must it be for gods to be defended by a human being!

CHAP. X.[2]—THE CHRISTIANS ARE NOT THE ONLY CONTEMNERS OF THE GODS. CONTEMPT OF THEM OFTEN DISPLAYED BY HEATHEN OFFICIAL PERSONS. HOMER MADE THE GODS CONTEMPTIBLE.

Pour out now all your venom; fling against this name of ours all your shafts of calumny: I shall stay no longer to refute them; but they shall by and by be blunted, when we come to explain our entire discipline.[3] I shall content myself now indeed with plucking these shafts out of our own body, and hurling them back on yourselves. The same wounds which you have inflicted on us by your charges I shall show to be imprinted on yourselves, that you may fall by your own swords and javelins.[4] Now, first, when you direct against us the general charge of divorcing ourselves from the institutions of our forefathers, consider again and again whether you are not yourselves open to that accusation in common with us. For when I look through your life and customs, lo, what do I discover but the old order of things corrupted, nay, destroyed by you? Of the laws I have already said, that you are daily supplanting them with novel decrees and statutes. As to everything else in your manner of life, how great are the changes you have made from your ancestors—in your style, your dress, your equipage, your very food, and even in your speech; for the old-fashioned you banish, as if it were offensive to you! Everywhere, in your public pursuits and private duties, antiquity is repealed; all the authority of your forefathers your own authority has superseded. To be sure,[5] you are for ever praising old customs; but this is only to your greater discredit, for you nevertheless persistently reject them. How great must your perverseness have been, to have bestowed approbation on your ancestors' institutions, which were too inefficient to be lasting, all the while that you were rejecting the very objects of your approbation! But even that very heir-loom [6] of your forefathers, which you seem to guard and defend with greatest fidelity, in which you actually [7] find your strongest grounds for impeaching us as violators of the law, and from which your hatred of the Christian name derives all its life—I mean the worship of the gods—I shall prove to be undergoing ruin and contempt from yourselves no less than [8] (from us),—unless it be that there is no reason for our being regarded as despisers of the gods like yourselves, on the ground that nobody despises what he knows has absolutely no existence. What certainly exists can be despised. That which *is* nothing, suffers nothing. From those, therefore, to whom it is an existing thing,[9] must necessarily proceed the suffering which affects it. All the heavier, then, is the accusation which burdens you who believe that there are gods and (at the same time) despise them, who worship and also reject them, who honour and also assail them. One may also gather the same conclusion from this consideration, above all: since you worship various gods, some one and some another, you of course despise those which you do not worship. A preference for the one is not possible without slighting the other, and no choice can be made without a rejection. He who selects some *one* out of many, has already slighted the other which he does not select. But it is impossible that so many and so great gods can be worshipped by all. Then you must have exercised your contempt (in this matter) even at the beginning, since indeed you were not then afraid of so ordering things, that all the gods could not become objects of worship to all. For those very wise and prudent ancestors of yours, whose institutions you know not how to repeal, especially in respect of your gods, are themselves found to have been impious. I am much mistaken, if they did not sometimes decree that no general should dedicate a temple, which he may have vowed in battle, before the senate gave its sanction; as in the case of Marcus Æmilius, who had made

---

[1] Absolutum est.
[2] Comp. *The Apology*, cc. xii. xiii. xiv. xv.
[3] See *The Apology* (*passim*), especially cc. xvi.-xxiv. xxx.- xxxvi. and xxxix.
[4] Admentationibus.

[5] Plane.
[6] Traditum.
[7] Vel.
[8] Perinde a vobis.
[9] Quibus est.

a vow to the god Alburnus. Now is it not confessedly the greatest impiety, nay, the greatest insult, to place the honour of the Deity at the will and pleasure of human judgment, so that there cannot be a god except the senate permit him? Many times have the censors destroyed [1] (a god) without consulting the people. Father Bacchus, with all his ritual, was certainly by the consuls, on the seate's authority, cast not only out of the city, but out of all Italy; whilst Varro informs us that Serapis also, and Isis, and Arpocrates, and Anubis, were excluded from the Capitol, and that their altars which the senate had thrown down were only restored by the popular violence. The Consul Gabinius, however, on the first day of the ensuing January, although he gave a tardy consent to some sacrifices, in deference to the crowd which assembled, because he had failed to decide about Serapis and Isis, yet held the judgment of the senate to be more potent than the clamour of the multitude, and forbade the altars to be built. Here, then, you have amongst your own forefathers, if not the name, at all events the procedure,[2] of the Christians, which despises the gods. If, however, you were even innocent of the charge of treason against them in the honour you pay them, I still find that you have made a consistent advance in superstition as well as impiety. For how much more irreligious are you found to be! There are your household gods, the Lares and the Penates, which you possess[3] by a family consecration:[4] you even tread them profanely under foot, you and your domestics, by hawking and pawning them for your wants or your whims. Such insolent sacrilege might be excusable, if it were not practised against your humbler deities; as it is, the case is only the more insolent. There is, however, some consolation for your private household gods under these affronts, that you treat your public deities with still greater indignity and insolence. First of all, you advertise them for auction, submit them to public sale, knock them down to the highest bidder, when you every five years bring them to the hammer among your revenues. For this purpose you frequent the temple of Serapis or the Capitol, hold your sales there,[5] conclude your contracts,[6] as if they were markets, with the well-known[7] voice of the crier, (and) the self-same levy[8] of the quæstor. Now lands become

cheaper when burdened with tribute, and men by the capitation tax diminish in value (these are the well-known marks of slavery). But the gods, the more tribute they pay, become more holy; or rather,[9] the more holy they are, the more tribute do they pay. Their majesty is converted into an article of traffic; men drive a business with their religion; the sanctity of the gods is beggared with sales and contracts. You make merchandise of the ground of your temples, of the approach to your altars, of your offerings,[10] of your sacrifices.[11] You sell the whole divinity (of your gods). You will not permit their gratuitous worship. The auctioneers necessitate more repairs[12] than the priests. It was not enough that you had insolently made a profit of your gods, if we would test the amount of your contempt; and you are not content to have withheld honour from them, you must also depreciate the little you do render to them by some indignity or other. What, indeed, do you do by way of honouring your gods, which you do not equally offer to your dead? You build temples for the gods, you erect temples also to the dead; you build altars for the gods, you build them also for the dead; you inscribe the same superscription over both; you sketch out the same lineaments for their statues—as best suits their genius, or profession, or age; you make an old man of Saturn, a beardless youth of Apollo; you form a virgin from Diana; in Mars you consecrate a soldier, a blacksmith in Vulcan. No wonder, therefore, if you slay the same victims and burn the same odours for your dead as you do for your gods. What excuse can be found for that insolence which classes the dead of whatever sort[13] as equal with the gods? Even to your princes there are assigned the services of priests and sacred ceremonies, and chariots,[14] and cars, and the honours of the *solisternia* and the *lectisternia*, holidays and games. Rightly enough,[15] since heaven is open to them; still it is none the less contumelious to the gods: in the first place, because it could not possibly be decent that other beings should be numbered with them, even if it has been given to them to become divine after their birth; in the second place, because the witness who beheld the man caught up into heaven[16] would not forswear himself so freely and palpably before the people, if it were not for the con-

---

1 Adsolaverunt, "thrown to the ground;" "floored."
2 Sectam. [Rather—"A Christian secession."]
3 Perhibetis.
4 Domestica consecratione, i.e., "for family worship."
5 Addicitur.
6 Conducitur.
7 Eadem.
8 Exactione, "as excise duty for the treasury."

9 Immo.
10 "In money," stipibus.
11 "Victims."
12 Plus refigitur.
13 Utut mortuos.
14 Tensæ.
15 Plane.
16 Rigaltius has the name *Proculus* in his text; but Tertullian refers not merely to that case but to a usual functionary, necessary in all cases of deification.

tempt felt about the objects sworn to both by himself and those[1] who allow the perjury. For these feel of themselves, that what is sworn to is nothing; and more than that, they go so far as to fee the witness, because he had the courage to publicly despise the avengers of perjury. Now, as to that, who among you is pure of the charge of perjury? By this time, indeed, there is an end to all danger in swearing by the gods, since the oath by Cæsar carries with it more influential scruples, which very circumstance indeed tends to the degradation of your gods; for those who perjure themselves when swearing by Cæsar are more readily punished than those who violate an oath to a Jupiter. But, of the two kindred feelings of contempt and derision, contempt is the more honourable, having a certain glory in its arrogance; for it sometimes proceeds from confidence, or the security of consciousness, or a natural loftiness of mind. Derision, however, is a more wanton feeling, and so far it points more directly[2] to a carping insolence. Now only consider what great deriders of your gods you show yourselves to be! I say nothing of your indulgence of this feeling during your sacrificial acts, how you offer for your victims the poorest and most emaciated creatures; or else of the sound and healthy animals only the portions which are useless for food, such as the heads and hoofs, or the plucked feathers and hair, and whatever at home you would have thrown away. I pass over whatever may seem to the taste[3] of the vulgar and profane to have constituted the religion[4] of your forefathers; but then the most learned and serious classes (for seriousness and wisdom to some extent[5] profess[6] to be derived from learning) are always, in fact, the most irreverent towards your gods; and if their learning ever halts, it is only to make up for the remissness by a more shameful invention of follies and falsehoods about their gods. I will begin with that enthusiastic fondness which you show for him from whom every depraved writer gets his dreams, to whom you ascribe as much honour as you derogate from your gods, by magnifying him who has made such sport of them. I mean Homer by this description. He it is, in my opinion, who has treated the majesty of the Divine Being on the low level of human condition, imbuing the gods with the falls[7] and the passions of men; who has pitted them against each other

with varying success, like pairs of gladiators: he wounds Venus with an arrow from a human hand; he keeps Mars a prisoner in chains for thirteen months, with the prospect of perishing;[8] he parades[9] Jupiter as suffering a like indignity from a crowd of celestial (rebels;) or he draws from him tears for Sarpedon; or he represents him wantoning with Juno in the most disgraceful way, advocating his incestuous passion for her by a description and enumeration of his various amours. Since then, which of the poets has not, on the authority of their great prince, calumniated the gods, by either betraying truth or feigning falsehood? Have the dramatists also, whether in tragedy or comedy, refrained from making the gods the authors[10] of the calamities and retributions (of their plays)? I say nothing of your philosophers, whom a certain inspiration of truth itself elevates against the gods, and secures from all fear in their proud severity and stern discipline. Take, for example,[11] Socrates. In contempt of your gods, he swears by an oak, and a dog, and a goat. Now, although he was condemned to die for this very reason, the Athenians afterwards repented of that condemnation, and even put to death his accusers. By this conduct of theirs the testimony of Socrates is replaced at its full value, and I am enabled to meet you with this retort, that in his case you have approbation bestowed on that which is now-a-days reprobated in us. But besides this instance there is Diogenes, who, I know not to what extent, made sport of Hercules; whilst Varro, that Diogenes of the Roman cut,[12] introduces to our view some three hundred Joves, or, as they ought to be called, Jupiters,[13] (and all) without heads. Your other wanton wits[14] likewise minister to your pleasures by disgracing the gods. Examine carefully the sacrilegious[15] beauties of your Lentuli and Hostii; now, is it the players or your gods who become the objects of your mirth in their tricks and jokes? Then, again, with what pleasure do you take up the literature of the stage, which describes all the foul conduct of the gods! Their majesty is defiled in your presence in some unchaste body. The mask of some deity, at your will,[16] covers some infamous paltry head. The Sun mourns for the death of his son by a lightning-flash amid your rude rejoicing.

---

[1] Oehler reads "ei" (of course for "ii"); Rigalt. reads "ii."
[2] Denotatior ad.
[3] Gulæ, "Depraved taste."
[4] Prope religionem convenire, "to have approximated to."
[5] Quatenus.
[6] Credunt, one would expect "creduntur" ("are supposed "), which is actually read by Gothofredus.
[7] Or, "circumstances" (casibus).

[8] Fortasse periturum.
[9] Traducit, perhaps "degrades."
[10] Ut dei præfarentur. Oehler explains the verb "præfari" to mean "auctorem esse et tanquam caput."
[11] Denique.
[12] Stili.
[13] Tertullian gives the comic plural "*Juppiteres.*"
[14] Ingenia.
[15] Because appropriating to themselves the admiration which was due to the gods.
[16] Cujuslibet dei.

Cybele sighs for a shepherd who disdains her, without raising a blush on your cheek; and you quietly endure songs which celebrate[1] the gallantries of Jove. You are, of course, possessed of a more religious spirit in the show of your gladiators, when your gods dance, with equal zest, over the spilling of human blood, (and) over those filthy penalties which are at once their proof and plot for executing your criminals, or else (when) your criminals are punished personating the gods themselves.[2] We have often witnessed in a mutilated criminal your god of Pessinum, Attis; a wretch burnt alive has personated Hercules. We have laughed at the sport of your mid-day game of the gods, when Father Pluto, Jove's own brother, drags away, hammer in hand, the remains of the gladiators; when Mercury, with his winged cap and heated wand, tests with his cautery whether the bodies were really lifeless, or only feigning death. Who now can investigate every particular of this sort, although so destructive of the honour of the Divine Being, and so humiliating to His majesty? They all, indeed, have their origin[3] in a contempt (of the gods), on the part both of those who practise[4] these personations, as well as of those[5] who are susceptible of being so represented.[6] I hardly know, therefore, whether your gods have more reason to complain of yourselves or of us. After despising them on the one hand, you flatter them on the other; if you fail in any duty towards them, you appease them with a fee;[6] in short, you allow yourselves to act towards them in any way you please. We, however, live in a consistent and entire aversion to them.

CHAP. XI.[7]—THE ABSURD CAVIL OF THE ASS'S
HEAD DISPOSED OF.

In this matter we are (said to be) guilty not merely of forsaking the religion of the community, but of introducing a monstrous superstition; for some among you have dreamed that our god is an ass's head,—an absurdity which Cornelius Tacitus first suggested. In the fourth book of his *histories*,[8] where he is treating of the Jewish war, he begins his description with the origin of that nation, and gives his own views respecting both the origin and the name of their religion. He relates that the Jews, in their migration in the desert, when suffering for want of water, escaped by following for guides some wild asses, which they supposed to be going in quest of water after pasture, and that on this account the image of one of these animals was worshipped by the Jews. From this, I suppose, it was presumed that we, too, from our close connection with the Jewish religion, have ours consecrated under the same emblematic form. The same Cornelius Tacitus, however, —who, to say the truth, is most loquacious in falsehood—forgetting his later statement, relates how Pompey the Great, after conquering the Jews and capturing Jerusalem, entered the temple, but found nothing in the shape of an image, though he examined the place carefully. Where, then, should their God have been found? Nowhere else, of course than in so memorable a temple which was carefully shut to all but the priests, and into which there could be no fear of a stranger entering. But what apology must I here offer for what I am going to say, when I have no other object at the moment than to make a passing remark or two in a general way which shall be equally applicable to yourselves?[9] Suppose that our God, then, be an asinine person, will you at all events deny that you possess the same characteristics with ourselves in that matter? (Not their heads only, but) entire asses, are, to be sure, objects of adoration to you, along with their tutelar Epona; and all herds, and cattle, and beasts you consecrate, and their stables into the bargain! This, perhaps, is your grievance against us, that, when surrounded by cattle-worshippers of every kind we are simply devoted to asses!

CHAP. XII.[10]—THE CHARGE OF WORSHIPPING A
CROSS. THE HEATHENS THEMSELVES MADE
MUCH OF CROSSES IN SACRED THINGS; NAY,
THEIR VERY IDOLS WERE FORMED ON A
CRUCIAL FRAME.

As for him who affirms that we are "the

---

[1] Sustinetis modulari.
[2] It is best to add the original of this almost unintelligible passage: "Plane religiosiores estis in gladiatorum cavea, ubi super sanguinem humanum, super inquinamenta pœnarum proinde saltant dei vestri *argumenta et historias nocentibus erogandis, aut in ipsis deis nocentes puniuntur.*" Some little light may be derived from the parallel passage of the *Apology* (c. xv.), which is expressed somewhat less obscurely. Instead of the words in italics, Tertullian there substitutes these: "Argumenta et historias noxiis ministrantes, nisi quod et ipsos deos vestros sæpe noxii induunt" —"whilst furnishing the proofs and the plots for (executing) criminals, only that the said criminals often act the part of your gods themselves." Oehler refers, in illustration of the last clause, to the instance of the notorious robber Laureolus, who personated Prometheus ; others, again, personated Laureolus himself : some criminals had to play the part of Orpheus ; others of Mutius Scævola. It will be observed that these executions were with infamous perverseness set off with scenic show, wherein the criminal enacted some violent death in yielding up his own life. The indignant irony of the whole passage, led off by the "plane religiosiores estis," is evident.
[3] Censentur.
[4] Factitant.
[5] i.e., the gods themselves.
[6] Redimitis.
[7] Comp. *The Apology*, c. xvi.

[8] In *The Apology* (c. xvi.) the reference is to " the fifth book." This is correct. Book v. c. 3, is meant.
[9] In vobis, for " in vos " ex pari transferendorum.
[10] Comp. *The Apology*, c. xvi.

priesthood of a cross,"[1] we shall claim him[2] as our co-religionist.[3] A cross is, in its material, a sign of wood; amongst yourselves also the object of worship is a wooden figure. Only, whilst with you the figure is a human one, with us the wood is its own figure. Never mind[4] for the present what is the shape, provided the material is the same: the form, too, is of no importance,[5] if so be it be the actual body of a god. If, however, there arises a question of difference on this point, what, (let me ask,) is the difference between the Athenian Pallas, or the Pharian Ceres, and wood formed into a cross,[6] when each is represented by a rough stock, without form, and by the merest rudiment of a statue[7] of unformed wood? Every piece of timber[8] which is fixed in the ground in an erect position is a part of a cross, and indeed the greater portion of its mass. But an entire cross is attributed to us, with its transverse beam,[9] of course, and its projecting seat. Now you have the less to excuse you, for you dedicate to religion only a mutilated imperfect piece of wood, while others consecrate to the sacred purpose a complete structure. The truth, however, after all is, that your religion is *all cross*, as I shall show. You are indeed unaware that your gods in their origin have proceeded from this hated cross.[10] Now, every image, whether carved out of wood or stone, or molten in metal, or produced out of any other richer material, must needs have had plastic hands engaged in its formation. Well, then, this modeller,[11] before he did anything else,[12] hit upon the form of a wooden cross, because even our own body assumes as its natural position the latent and concealed outline of a cross. Since the head rises upwards, and the back takes a straight direction, and the shoulders project laterally, if you simply place a man with his arms and hands outstretched, you will make the general outline of a cross. Starting, then, from this rudimental form and prop,[13] as it were, he applies a covering of clay, and so gradually completes the limbs, and forms the body, and covers the cross within with the shape which he meant to impress upon the clay; then from this design, with the help of compasses and leaden

moulds, he has got all ready for his image which is to be brought out into marble, or clay, or whatever the material be of which he has determined to make his god. (This, then, is the process:) after the cross-shaped frame, the clay; after the clay, the god. In a well-understood routine, the cross passes into a god through the clayey medium. The cross then you consecrate, and from it the consecrated (deity) begins to derive his origin.[14] By way of example, let us take the case of a tree which grows up into a system of branches and foliage, and is a reproduction of its own kind, whether it springs from the kernel of an olive, or the stone of a peach, or a grain of pepper which has been duly tempered under ground. Now, if you transplant it, or take a cutting off its branches for another plant, to what will you attribute what is produced by the propagation? Will it not be to the grain, or the stone, or the kernel? Because, as the third stage is attributable to the second, and the second in like manner to the first, so the third will have to be referred to the first, through the second as the mean. We need not stay any longer in the discussion of this point, since by a natural law every kind of produce throughout nature refers back its growth to its original source; and just as the product is comprised in its primal cause, so does that cause agree in character with the thing produced. Since, then, in the production of your gods, you worship the cross which originates them, here will be the original kernel and grain, from which are propagated the wooden materials of your idolatrous images. Examples are not far to seek. Your victories you celebrate with religious ceremony[15] as deities; and they are the more august in proportion to the joy they bring you. The frames on which you hang up your trophies must be crosses: these are, as it were, the very core of your pageants.[16] Thus, in your victories, the religion of your camp makes even crosses objects of worship; your standards it adores, your standards are the sanction of its oaths; your standards it prefers before Jupiter himself. But all that parade[17] of images, and that display of pure gold, are (as so many) necklaces of the crosses. In like manner also, in the banners and ensigns, which your soldiers guard with no less sacred care, you have the streamers (and) vestments of your crosses. You are ashamed, I suppose, to worship unadorned and simple crosses.

---

[1] Crucis antistites.
[2] Erit.
[3] Consacraneus.
[4] Viderint.
[5] Viderit.
[6] Stipite crucis.
[7] Solo staticulo. The use of wood in the construction of an idol is mentioned afterward.
[8] Omne robur.
[9] Antemna. See our *Anti-Marcion*, p. 156. Ed. Edinburgh.
[10] De isto patibulo.
[11] Plasta.
[12] In primo.
[13] Statumini.

[14] Comp. *The Apology*, c. xii.: "Every image of a god has been first constructed on a cross and stake, and plastered with cement. The body of your god is first dedicated upon a gibbet."
[15] Veneramini.
[16] Tropæum, for "tropæorum." We have given the sense rather than the words of this awkward sentence.
[17] Suggestus.

CHAP. XIII.[1]—THE CHARGE OF WORSHIPPING THE SUN MET BY A RETORT.

Others, with greater regard to good manners, it must be confessed, suppose that the sun is the god of the Christians, because it is a well-known fact that we pray towards the east, or because we make Sunday a day of festivity. What then? Do you do less than this? Do not many among you, with an affectation of sometimes worshipping the heavenly bodies likewise, move your lips in the direction of the sunrise? It is you, at all events, who have even admitted the sun into the calendar of the week; and you have selected its day,[2] in preference to the preceding day[3] as the most suitable in the week[4] for either an entire abstinence from the bath, or for its postponement until the evening, or for taking rest and for banqueting. By resorting to these customs, you deliberately deviate from your own religious rites to those of strangers. For the Jewish feasts are the Sabbath and "the Purification,"[5] and Jewish also are the ceremonies of the lamps,[6] and the fasts of unleavened bread, and the "littoral prayers,"[7] all which institutions and practices are of course foreign from your gods. Wherefore, that I may return from this digression, you who reproach us with the sun and Sunday should consider your proximity to us. We are not far off from your Saturn and your days of rest.

CHAP. XIV.[8]—THE VILE CALUMNY ABOUT ONOCOETES RETORTED ON THE HEATHEN BY TERTULLIAN.

Report has introduced a new calumny respecting our God. Not so long ago, a most abandoned wretch in that city of yours,[9] a man who had deserted indeed his own religion—a Jew, in fact, who had only lost his skin, flayed of course by wild beasts,[10] against which he enters the lists for hire day after day with a sound body, and so in a condition to lose his skin[11]—carried about in public a caricature of us with this label: *Onocoetes.*[12] This (figure)

had ass's ears, and was dressed in a *toga* with a book, having a hoof on one of his feet. And the crowd believed this infamous Jew. For what other set of men is the seed-plot[13] of all the calumny against us? Throughout the city, therefore, Onocoetes is all the talk. As, however, it is less then "a nine days' wonder,"[14] and so destitute of all authority from time, and weak enough from the character of its author, I shall gratify myself by using it simply in the way of a retort. Let us then see whether you are not here also found in our company. Now it matters not what their form may be, when our concern is about deformed images. You have amongst you gods with a dog's head, and a lion's head, with the horns of a cow, and a ram, and a goat, goat-shaped or serpent-shaped, and winged in foot, head, and back. Why therefore brand our one God so conspicuously? Many an *Onocoetes* is found amongst yourselves.

CHAP. XV.[15]—THE CHARGE OF INFANTICIDE RETORTED ON THE HEATHEN.

Since we are on a par in respect of the gods, it follows that there is no difference between us on the point of sacrifice, or even of worship,[16] if I may be allowed to make good our comparison from another sort of evidence. We begin our religious service, or initiate our mysteries, with slaying an infant. As for you, since your own transactions in human blood and infanticide have faded from your memory, you shall be duly reminded of them in the proper place; we now postpone most of the instances, that we may not seem to be everywhere[17] handling the selfsame topics. Meanwhile, as I have said, the comparison between us does not fail in another point of view. For if we are infanticides in one sense, you also can hardly be deemed such in any other sense; because, although you are forbidden by the laws to slay new-born infants, it so happens that no laws are evaded with more impunity or greater safety, with the deliberate knowledge of the public, and the suffrages[18] of this entire age.[19] Yet there is no great difference between us, only you do not kill your infants in the way of a sacred rite, nor (as a service) to God. But then you make away with them in a more cruel manner,

---

[1] Comp. *The Apology*, c. xvi.
[2] Sunday.
[3] Saturday.
[4] Ex diebus.
[5] On the "Coena pura," see our *Anti-Marcion*, p. 386, note 4.
[6] See Lev. xxiv. 2; also 2 Chron. xiii. 11. Witsius (*Ægyptiaca*, ii. 16, 17) compares the Jewish with the Egyptian "ritus lucernarum."
[7] Tertullian, in his tract *de Jejun.* xvi., speaks of the Jews praying (after the loss of their temple, and in their dispersion) in the open air, "per omne litus."
[8] Comp. *The Apology*, c. xvi.
[9] In ista civitate, Rome.
[10] This is explained in the passage of *The Apology* (xvi.): "He had for money exposed himself with criminals to fight with wild beasts."
[11] Decutiendus, from a jocular word, "decutire."
[12] This curious word is compounded of ὄνος, *an* ass, and κοιᾶσθαι, which Hesychius explains by ἱερᾶσθαι, *to act as a priest.*

The word therefore means, "asinarius sacerdos," "an *ass* of a priest." Calumnious enough; but suited to the vile occasion, and illustrative of the ribald opposition which Christianity had to encounter.
[13] We take Rigaltius' reading, "seminarium."
[14] Tanquam hesternum.
[15] Comp. *The Apology*, c. ix.
[16] Sacri.
[17] He refers in this passage to his *Apology*, especially c. ix.
[18] Tabellis.
[19] Unius ætatis. This Oehler explains by "per unam jam totam hanc ætatem."

because you expose them to the cold and hunger, and to wild beasts, or else you get rid of them by the slower death of drowning. If, however, there does occur any dissimilarity between us in this matter,[1] you must not overlook the fact that it is your own dear children[2] whose life you quench; and this will supplement, nay, abundantly aggravate, on your side of the question, whatever is defective in us on other grounds. Well, but we are said to sup off our impious sacrifice! Whilst we postpone to a more suitable place[3] whatever resemblance even to this practice is discoverable amongst yourselves, we are not far removed from you in voracity. If in the one case there is unchastity, and in ours cruelty, we are still on the same footing (if I may so far admit our guilt[4]) in nature, where cruelty is always found in concord with unchastity. But, after all, what do you less than we; or rather, what do you not do in excess of us? I wonder whether it be a small matter to you[5] to pant for human entrails, because you devour full-grown men alive? Is it, forsooth, only a trifle to lick up human blood, when you draw out[6] the blood which was destined to live? Is it a light thing in your view to feed on an infant, when you consume one wholly before it is come to the birth?[7]

CHAP. XVI.[8]—OTHER CHARGES REPELLED BY THE SAME METHOD. THE STORY OF THE NOBLE ROMAN YOUTH AND HIS PARENTS.

I am now come to the hour for extinguishing the lamps, and for using the dogs, and practising the deeds of darkness. And on this point I am afraid I must succumb to you; for what similar accusation shall I have to bring against you? But you should at once commend the cleverness with which we make our incest look modest, in that we have devised a spurious night,[9] to avoid polluting the real light and darkness, and have even thought it right to dispense with earthly lights, and to play tricks also with our conscience. For whatever we do ourselves, we suspect in others when we choose (to be suspicious). As for your incestuous deeds, on the contrary,[10] men enjoy them at full liberty, in the face of day, or in the natural night, or before high Heaven; and in proportion to their successful issue is your own ignorance of the result,

since you publicly indulge in your incestuous intercourse in the full cognizance of broad day-light. (No ignorance, however, conceals our conduct from our eyes,) for in the very darkness we are able to recognise our own misdeeds. The Persians, you know very well,[11] according to Ctesias, live quite promiscuously with their mothers, in full knowledge of the fact, and without any horror; whilst of the Macedonians it is well known that they constantly do the same thing, and with perfect approbation: for once, when the blinded[12] Œdipus came upon their stage, they greeted him with laughter and derisive cheers. The actor, taking off his mask in great alarm, said, "Gentlemen, have I displeased you?" "Certainly not," replied the Macedonians, "you have played your part well enough; but either the author was very silly, if he invented (this mutilation as an atonement for the incest), or else Œdipus was a great fool for his pains if he really so punished himself;" and then they shouted out, one to the other, Ἥλαυνε εἰς τὴν μητέρα. But how insignificant, (say you,) is the stain which one or two nations can make on the whole world! As for us, we of course have infected the very sun, polluted the entire ocean! Quote, then, one nation which is free from the passions which allure the whole race of men to incest! If there is a single nation which knows nothing of concubinage through the necessity of age and sex—to say nothing of lust and licentiousness—that nation will be a stranger to incest. If any nature can be found so peculiarly removed from the human state as to be liable neither to ignorance, nor error, nor misfortune, that alone may be adduced with any consistency as an answer to the Christians. Reflect, therefore, on the licentiousness which floats about amongst men's passions[13] as if they were the winds, and consider whether there be any communities which the full and strong tides of passion fail to waft to the commission of this great sin. In the first place, when you expose your infants to the mercy of others, or leave them for adoption to better parents than yourselves, do you forget what an opportunity for incest is furnished, how wide a scope is opened for its accidental commission? Undoubtedly, such of you as are more serious from a principle of self-restraint and careful reflection, abstain from lusts which could produce results of such a kind, in whatever place you may happen to be, at home or abroad, so that no indiscriminate diffusion of seed, or licentious reception thereof, will produce chil-

---

[1] Genere.
[2] Pignora, *scil.* amoris.
[3] See *Apology*, c. ix.
[4] Si forte.
[5] Parum scilicet?
[6] Elicitis.
[7] Infantem totum præcocum.
[8] Comp. *The Apology*, c. ix.
[9] Adulteram noctem.
[10] Ceterum.

[11] Plane.
[12] Trucidatus oculos.
[13] Errores.

dren to you unawares, such as their very parents, or else other children, might encounter in inadvertent incest, for no restraint from age is regarded in (the importunities of) lust. All acts of adultery, all cases of fornication, all the licentiousness of public brothels, whether committed at home or perpetrated out of doors,[1] serve to produce confusions of blood and complications of natural relationship,[2] and thence to conduce to incest; from which consummation your players and buffoons draw the materials of their exhibitions. It was from such a source, too, that so flagrant a tragedy recently burst upon the public as that which the prefect Fuscianus had judicially to decide. A boy of noble birth, who, by the unintentional neglect of his attendants,[3] had strolled too far from home, was decoyed by some passers-by, and carried off. The paltry Greek[4] who had the care of him, or somebody else,[5] in true Greek fashion, had gone into the house and captured him. Having been taken away into Asia, he is brought, when arrived at full age, back to Rome, and exposed for sale. His own father buys him unawares, and treats him as a Greek.[6] Afterwards, as was his wont, the youth is sent by his master into the fields, chained as a slave.[7] Thither the tutor and the nurse had already been banished for punishment. The whole case is represented to them; they relate each other's misfortunes: they, on the one hand, how they had lost their ward when he was a boy; he, on the other hand, that he had been lost from his boyhood. But they agreed in the main, that he was a native of Rome of a noble family; perhaps he further gave sure proofs of his identity. Accordingly, as God willed it for the purpose of fastening a stain upon that age, a presentiment about the time excites him, the periods exactly suit his age, even his eyes help to recall[8] his features, some peculiar marks on his body are enumerated. His master and mistress, who are now no other than his own father and mother, anxiously urge a protracted inquiry. The slave-dealer is examined, the unhappy truth is all discovered. When their wickedness becomes manifest, the parents find a remedy for their despair by hanging themselves; to their son, who survives the miserable calamity, their property is awarded by the prefect, not as an inheritance, but as the wages of infamy and incest. That one case was a sufficient ex-

ample for public exposure[9] of the sins of this sort which are secretly perpetrated among you. Nothing happens among men in solitary isolation. But, as it seems to me, it is only in a solitary case that such a charge can be drawn out against us, even in the mysteries of our religion. You ply us evermore with this charge;[10] yet there are like delinquencies to be traced amongst you, even in your ordinary course of life.[11]

CHAP. XVII.[12]—THE CHRISTIAN REFUSAL TO SWEAR BY THE GENIUS OF CÆSAR. FLIPPANCY AND IRREVERENCE RETORTED ON THE HEATHEN.

As to your charges of obstinacy and presumption, whatever you allege against us, even in these respects, there are not wanting points in which you will bear a comparison with us. Our first step in this contumacious conduct concerns that which is ranked by you immediately after[13] the worship due to God, that is, the worship due to the majesty of the Cæsars, in respect of which we are charged with being irreligious towards them, since we neither propitiate their images nor swear by their genius. We are called enemies of the people. Well, be it so; yet at the same time (it must not be forgotten, that) the emperors find enemies amongst you heathen, and are constantly getting surnames to signalize their triumphs—one becoming *Parthicus*,[14] and another *Medicus* and *Germanicus*.[15] On this head[16] the Roman people must see to it who they are amongst whom[17] there still remain nations which are unsubdued and foreign to their rule. But, at all events, you are of us,[18] and yet you conspire against us. (In reply, we need only state) a well-known fact,[19] that we acknowledge the fealty of Romans to the emperors. No conspiracy has ever broken out from our body: no Cæsar's blood has ever fixed a stain upon us, in the senate or even in the palace; no assumption of the purple has ever in any of the provinces been affected by us. The Syrias still exhale the odours of their corpses; still do the Gauls[20] fail to wash away (their blood) in the waters of their Rhone. Your allegations of our insanity[21] I omit, be-

---

[1] Sive stativo vel ambulatorio titulo.
[2] Compagines generis.
[3] Comitum.
[4] Græculus.
[5] "Aliquis" is nere understood.
[6] Utitur Græco, i.e., cinædo, "for purposes of lust."
[7] Or, "is sent into the country, and put into prison."
[8] Aliquid recordantur.

[9] Publicæ eruptionis.
[10] Intentatis.
[11] Vestris non sacramentis, with a hyphen, ' your non-mysteries."
[12] Comp. *The Apology*, c. xxxv.
[13] Secunda.
[14] Severus, in A.D. 198.
[15] These titles were borne by Caracalla.
[16] Or, "topic"—hoc loco.
[17] i.e., whether among the Christians or the heathen.
[18] A cavil of the heathen.
[19] Sane.
[20] Galliæ.
[21] Vesaniæ.

cause they do not compromise the Roman name. But I will grapple with [1] the charge of sacrilegious vanity, and remind you of [2] the irreverence of your own lower classes, and the scandalous lampoons [3] of which the statues are so cognizant, and the sneers which are sometimes uttered at the public games, [4] and the curses with which the circus resounds. If not in arms, you are in tongue at all events always rebellious. But I suppose it is quite another affair to refuse to swear by the genius of Cæsar? For it is fairly open to doubt as to who are perjurers on this point, when you do not swear honestly [5] even by your gods. Well, we do not call the emperor God; for on this point *sannam facimus*, [6] as the saying is. But the truth is, that you who call Cæsar God both mock him, by calling him what he is not, and curse him, because he does not want to be what you call him. For he prefers living to being made a god. [7]

CHAP. XVIII. [8]—CHRISTIANS CHARGED WITH AN OBSTINATE CONTEMPT OF DEATH. INSTANCES OF THE SAME ARE FOUND AMONGST THE HEATHEN.

The rest of your charge of obstinacy against us you sum up in this indictment, that we boldly refuse neither your swords, nor your crosses, nor your wild beasts, nor fire, nor tortures, such is our obduracy and contempt of death. But (you are inconsistent in your charges); for in former times amongst your own ancestors all these terrors have come in men's intrepidity [9] not only to be despised, but even to be held in great praise. How many swords there were, and what brave men were willing to suffer by them, it were irksome to enumerate. [10] (If we take the torture) of the cross, of which so many instances have occurred, exquisite in cruelty, your own Regulus readily initiated the suffering which up to his day was without a precedent; [11] a queen of Egypt used wild beasts of her own (to accomplish her death); [12] the Carthaginian woman, who in the last extremity of her country was more courageous than her husband Asdrubal, [13]

only followed the example, set long before by Dido herself, of going through fire to her death. Then, again, a woman of Athens defied the tyrant, exhausted his tortures, and at last, lest her person and sex might succumb through weakness, she bit off her tongue and spat out of her mouth the only possible instrument of a confession which was now out of her power. [14] But in your own instance you account such deeds glorious, in ours obstinate. Annihilate now the glory of your ancestors, in order that you may thereby annihilate us also. Be content from henceforth to repeal the praises of your forefathers, in order that you may not have to accord commendation to us for the same (sufferings). Perhaps (you will say) the character of a more robust age may have rendered the spirits of antiquity more enduring. Now, however, (we enjoy) the blessing of quietness and peace; so that the minds and dispositions of men (should be) more tolerant even towards strangers. Well, you rejoin, be it so: *you* may compare *yourselves* with the ancients; *we* must needs pursue with hatred all that we find in you offensive to *ourselves*, because it does not obtain currency [15] among us. Answer me, then, on each particular case by itself. I am not seeking for examples on a uniform scale. [16] Since, forsooth, the sword through their contempt of death produced stories of heroism amongst your ancestors, it is not, of course, [17] from love of life that you go to the trainers sword in hand and offer yourselves as gladiators, [18] (nor) through fear of death do you enrol your names in the army. [19] Since an ordinary [20] woman makes her death famous by wild beasts, it cannot but be of your own pure accord that you encounter wild beasts day after day in the midst of peaceful times. Although no longer any Regulus among you has raised a cross as the instrument of his own crucifixion, yet a contempt of the fire has even now displayed itself, [21] since one of yourselves very lately has offered for a wager [22] to go to any place which may be fixed upon and put on the burning shirt. [23] If a woman once defiantly danced beneath the scourge, the same feat has been very recently performed again by one of your own (circus-) hunters [24] as he traversed the

---

[1] Conveniam.
[2] Recognoscam.
[3] Festivos libellos.
[4] A concilio.
[5] Ex fide.
[6] Literally, "we make faces."
[7] Comp. *The Apology*, c. xxxiii., p. 37, *supra*, and Minucius Felix, *Octavius*, c. xxiii. [Vol. IV. this Series.]
[8] Comp., *The Apology*, c. 50 [p. 54, *infra*.]
[9] A virtute didicerunt.
[10] With the "piget prosequi" to govern the preceding oblique clause, it is unnecessary to suppose (with Oehler) the omission here of some verb like "erogavit."
[11] Novitatem . . . dedicavit.
[12] Tertullian refers to Cleopatra's death also in his tract *ad Mart.* c. iv. [See this Vol. *infra*.]
[13] This case is again referred to in this treatise (p. 138), and in *ad Mart* c. iv. [See this Volume, *infra*.]

[14] Eradicatæ confessionis. [See p. 55, *supra*.]
[15] Non invenitur.
[16] Eadem voce.
[17] Utique. The ironical tone of Tertullian's answer is evident.
[18] Gladio ad lanistas auctoratis.
[19] We follow Oehler in giving the clause this *negative* turn; he renders it: "Tretet nicht aus Furcht vor dem Tode ins Kriegsheer ein."
[20] Alicui.
[21] Jam evasit.
[22] Auctoravit.
[23] Vestiendum incendiale tunica.
[24] Inter venatorios: "venatores circi" (Oehler).

appointed course, not to mention the famous sufferings of the Spartans.[1]

CHAP. XIX.[2]— IF CHRISTIANS AND THE HEATHEN THUS RESEMBLE EACH OTHER, THERE IS GREAT DIFFERENCE IN THE GROUNDS AND NATURE OF THEIR APPARENTLY SIMILAR CONDUCT.

Here end, I suppose, your tremendous charges of obstinacy against the Christians. Now, since we are amenable to them in common with yourselves, it only remains that we compare the grounds which the respective parties have for being personally derided. All our obstinacy, however, is with you a foregone conclusion,[3] based on our strong convictions; for we take for granted[4] a resurrection of the dead. Hope in this resurrection amounts to[5] a contempt of death. Ridicule, therefore, as much as you like the excessive stupidity of such minds as die that they may live; but then, in order that you may be able to laugh more merrily, and deride us with greater boldness, you must take your sponge, or perhaps your tongue, and wipe away those records of yours every now and then cropping out,[6] which assert in not dissimilar terms that souls will return to bodies. But how much more worthy of acceptance is our belief which maintains that they will return to the same bodies! And how much more ridiculous is your inherited conceit,[7] that the human spirit is to reappear in a dog, or a mule, or a peacock! Again, we affirm that a judgment has been ordained by God according to the merits of every man. This you ascribe to Minos and Rhadamanthus, while at the same time _you_ reject Aristides, who was a juster judge than either. By the award of the judgment, we say that the wicked will have to spend an eternity in endless fire, the pious and innocent in a region of bliss. In your view likewise an unalterable condition is ascribed to the respective destinations of Pyriphlegethon[8] and Elysium. Now they are not merely your composers of myth and poetry who write songs of this strain; but your philosophers also speak with all confidence of the return of souls to their former state,[9] and of the twofold award[10] of a final judgment.

CHAP. XX.—TRUTH AND REALITY PERTAIN TO CHRISTIANS ALONE. THE HEATHEN COUNSELLED TO EXAMINE AND EMBRACE IT.

How long therefore, O moſt unjust heathen, will you refuse to acknowledge us, and (what is more) to execrate your own (worthies), since between us no distinction has place, because we are one and the same? Since you do not (of course) hate what you yourselves are, give us rather your right hands in fellowship, unite your salutations,[11] mingle your embraces, sanguinary with the sanguinary, incestuous with the incestuous, conspirators with conspirators, obstinate and vain with those of the selfsame qualities. In company with each other, we have been traitors to the majesty of the gods; and together do we provoke their indignation. You too have your "third race;"[12] not indeed third in the way of religious rite,[13] but a third race in sex, and, made up as it is of male and female in one, it is more fitted to men and women (for offices of lust).[12] Well, then, do we offend you by the very fact of our approximation and agreement? Being on a par is apt to furnish unconsciously the materials for rivalry. Thus "a potter envies a potter, and a smith a smith."[14] But we must now discontinue this imaginary confession.[15] Our conscience has returned to the truth, and to the consistency of truth. For all those points which you allege[16] (against us) will be really found in ourselves alone; and we alone can rebut them, against whom they are adduced, by getting you to listen[17] to the other side of the question, whence that full knowledge is learnt which both inspires counsel and directs judgment. Now it is in fact your own maxim, that no one should determine a cause without hearing both sides of it; and it is only in our own case that you neglect (the equitable principle). You indulge to the full[18] that fault of human nature, that those things which you do not disallow in yourselves you condemn in others, or you boldly charge[19] against others those things the guilt of which[20] you retain a lasting consciousness of[21] in yourselves. The course of life in which you will choose to occupy yourselves ·is different from ours: whilst chaste in the eyes of others, you are

---

[1] "Doubtless the stripes which the Spartans endured with such firmness, aggravated by the presence of their nearest relatives, who encouraged them, conferred honour upon their family."— _Apology_, c. 50. [See p. 55, _supra_.]
[2] Compare _The Apology_, cc. xlvii. xlviii. xlix. [This Vol., _supra_.]
[3] Præstruitur.
[4] Præsumimus.
[5] Est.
[6] Interim.
[7] Traditum.
[8] The heathen hell, _Tartarus_ or _Orcus_.
[9] Reciprocatione.
[10] Distributione.

[11] Compingite oscula.
[12] Eunuchs (Rigalt.).
[13] As the Christians were held to be; coming after (1) the heathen, (2) the Jews. See above, c. viii., and _Scorpiace_, c. x.
[14] An oft-quoted proverb in ancient writers. It occurs in Hesiod (_Opp. et Dies_) 25.
[15] Literally, "cease henceforth, O, simulated confession."
[16] Omnia ista.
[17] This seems to be the force of the "agnitione," which Oehler renders "auditione."
[18] Satisfacitis.
[19] Jactetis.
[20] Quorum reatum.
[21] Memineritis.

unchaste towards your own selves; whilst vigorous against vice out of doors, you succumb to it at home. This is the injustice (which we have to suffer), that, knowing truth, we are condemned by those who know it not; free from guilt, we are judged by those who are implicated in it. Remove the mote, or rather the beam, out of your own eye, that you may be able to extract the mote from the eyes of others. Amend your own lives first, that you may be able to punish the Christians. Only so far as you shall have effected your own reformation, will you refuse to inflict punishment on them—nay, so far will you have become Christians yourselves; and as you shall have become Christians, so far will you have compassed your own amendment of life. Learn what that is which you accuse in us, and you will accuse no longer; search out what that is which you do not accuse in yourselves, and you will become self-accusers. From these very few and humble remarks, so far as we have been able to open out the subject to you, you will plainly get some insight into (your own) error, and some discovery of *our* truth. Condemn that truth if you have the heart,[1] but only after you have examined it; and approve the error still, if you are so minded,[2] only first explore it. But if your prescribed rule is to love error and hate truth, why, (let me ask,) do you not probe to a full discovery the objects both of your love and your hatred?

---

[1] Si potestis.
[2] Si putatis.

AD NATIONES.

BOOK II.[1]

CHAP. I.—THE HEATHEN GODS FROM HEATHEN AUTHORITIES. VARRO HAS WRITTEN A WORK ON THE SUBJECT. HIS THREEFOLD CLASSIFICATION. THE CHANGEABLE CHARACTER OF THAT WHICH OUGHT TO BE FIXED AND CERTAIN.

OUR defence requires that we should at this point discuss with you the character of your gods, O ye heathen, fit objects of our pity,[2] appealing even to your own conscience to determine whether they be truly gods, as you would have it supposed, or falsely, as you are unwilling to have proved.[3] Now this is the material part of human error, owing to the wiles of its author, that it is never free from the ignorance of error,[4] whence your guilt is all the greater. Your eyes are open, yet they see not; your ears are unstopped, yet they hear not; though your heart beats, it is yet dull, nor does your mind understand[5] that of which it is cognizant.[6] If indeed the enormous perverseness (of your worship) could[7] be broken up[8] by a single demurrer, we should have our objection ready to hand in the declaration[9] that, as we know all those gods of yours to have been instituted by men, all belief in the true Deity is by this very circumstance brought to nought;[10] because, of course, nothing which some time or other had a beginning can rightly seem to be divine. But the fact is,[11] there are many things by which tenderness of conscience is hardened into the callousness of wilful error. Truth is beleaguered with the vast force (of the enemy), and yet how secure she is in her own inherent strength! And naturally enough[12] when from her very adversaries she gains to her side whomsoever she will, as her friends and protectors, and prostrates the entire host of her assailants. It is therefore against these things that our contest lies—against the institutions of our ancestors, against the authority of tradition,[13] the laws of our governors, and the reasonings of the wise; against antiquity, custom, submission;[14] against precedents, prodigies, miracles,—all which things have had their part in consolidating that spurious[15] system of your gods. Wishing, then, to follow step by step your own commentaries which you have drawn out of your theology of every sort (because the authority of learned men goes further with you in matters of this kind than the testimony of facts), I have taken and abridged the works of Varro;[16] for he in his treatise *Concerning Divine Things*, collected out of ancient digests, has shown himself a serviceable guide[17] for us. Now, if I inquire of him who were the subtle inventors[18] of the gods, he points to either the philosophers, the peoples, or the poets. For he has made a threefold distinction in classifying the gods: one being the *physical* class, of which the philosophers treat; another the *mythic* class, which is the constant burden of[19] the poets; the third, the *gentile* class, which the nations have adopted each one for itself. When, therefore, the philosophers have ingeniously composed their physical (theology) out of their

---

[1] In this part of his work the author reviews the heathen mythology, and exposes the absurdity of the polytheistic worship in the various classes of the gods, according to the distribution of Varro.
[2] Miserandæ.
[3] Literally, "unwilling to know."
[4] i.e., it does not know that it is error.
[5] Nescit.
[6] Agnoscit.
[7] Liceret.
[8] Discuti, or, in the logical sense, "be tested."
[9] Nunciatio (legally, this is "an information lodged against a wrong.")
[10] Excidere, "falls through."
[11] Sed enim.
[12] Quidni?
[13] Receptorum.
[14] Necessitatem, answering to the "leges dominantium."
[15] Adulterinam.
[16] St. Augustine, in his *de Civit. Dei*, makes similar use of Varro's work on the heathen gods, *Liber Divinarum*.
[17] Scopum, perhaps "mark."
[18] Insinuatores.
[19] Volutetur.

own conjectures, when the poets have drawn their mythical from fables, and the (several) nations have forged their gentile (polytheism) according to their own will, where in the world must truth be placed? In the conjectures? Well, but these are only a doubtful conception. In the fables? But they are at best an absurd story. In the popular accounts?[1] This sort of opinion,[2] however, is only promiscuous[3] and municipal. Now all things with the philosophers are uncertain, because of their variation; with the poets all is worthless, because immoral; with the nations all is irregular and confused, because dependent on their mere choice. The nature of God, however, if it be the true one with which you are concerned, is of so definite a character as not to be derived from uncertain speculations,[4] nor contaminated with worthless fables, nor determined by promiscuous conceits. It ought indeed to be regarded, as it really is, as certain, entire, universal, because it is in truth the property of all. Now, what god shall I believe? One that has been gauged by vague suspicion? One that history[5] has divulged? One that a community has invented? It would be a far worthier thing if I believed no god, than one which is open to doubt, or full of shame, or the object of arbitrary selection.[6]

CHAP. II.—PHILOSOPHERS HAD NOT SUCCEEDED IN DISCOVERING GOD. THE UNCERTAINTY AND CONFUSION OF THEIR SPECULATIONS.

But the authority of the physical philosophers is maintained *among you*[7] as the special property[8] of wisdom. *You mean* of course, that pure and simple wisdom of the philosophers which attests its own weakness mainly by that variety of opinion which proceeds from an ignorance of the truth. Now what wise man is so devoid of truth, as not to know that God is the Father and Lord of wisdom itself and truth? Besides, there is that divine oracle uttered by Solomon: "The fear of the Lord," says he, "is the beginning of wisdom."[9] But[10] fear has its origin in knowledge; for how will a man fear that of which he knows nothing? Therefore he who shall have the fear of God, even if he be ignorant of all things else, if he has attained to the knowledge and truth of

God," will possess full and perfect wisdom. This, however, is what philosophy has not clearly realized. For although, in their inquisitive disposition to search into all kinds of learning, *the philosophers* may seem to have investigated the sacred Scriptures themselves for their antiquity, and to have derived thence some of their opinions; yet because they have interpolated *these deductions* they prove that they have either despised them wholly or have not fully believed them, for in other cases also the simplicity of truth is shaken[12] by the over-scrupulousness of an irregular belief,[13] and that they therefore changed them, as their desire of glory grew, into products of their own mind. The consequence of this is, that even that which they had discovered degenerated into uncertainty, and there arose from one or two drops of truth a perfect flood of argumentation. For after they had simply[14] found God, they did not expound Him as they found Him, but rather disputed about His quality, and His nature, and even about His abode. The Platonists, indeed, (held) Him to care about wordly things, both as the disposer and judge thereof. The Epicureans *regarded* Him as apathetic[15] and inert, and (so to say) a nonentity.[16] The Stoics believed Him to be outside of the world; the Platonists, within the world. The God whom they had so imperfectly admitted, they could neither know nor fear; and therefore they could not be wise, since they wandered away indeed from "the beginning of wisdom," that is, "the fear of God." Proofs are not wanting that among the philosophers there was not only an ignorance, but actual doubt, about the divinity. Diogenes, when asked what was taking place in heaven, answered by saying, "I have never been up there." Again, whether there were any gods, he replied, "I do not know; only there ought to be gods."[17] When Crœsus inquired of Thales of Miletus what he thought of the gods, the latter having taken some time[18] to consider, answered by the word "Nothing." Even Socrates denied with an air of certainty[19] those gods of yours.[20] Yet he with a like certainty requested that a cock should be sacrificed to Æsculapius. And therefore when philosophy, in its practice of defining about God, is detected in such uncertainty and inconsistency,

---

[1] Adoptionibus.
[2] Adoptatio.
[3] Passiva, "a jumble."
[4] Argumentationibus.
[5] Historia. This word seems to refer to the class of *mythical* divinity above mentioned. It therefore means "fable" or "absurd story" (see above).
[6] Adoptivum.
[7] Patrocinatur.
[8] Mancipium.
[9] Prov. ix. 10; Ps. cxi. 10.
[0] Porro.

[11] Deum omnium notitiam et veritatem adsecutus, i.e., "following the God of all as knowledge and truth."
[12] Nutat.
[13] Passivæ fidei.
[14] Solummodo.
[15] Otiosum.
[16] "A nobody."
[17] Nisi ut sint expedire.
[18] Aliquot commeatus.
[19] Quasi certus.
[20] Istos deos.

what " fear " could it possibly have had of Him whom it was not competent[1] clearly to determine ? We have been taught to believe of the world that it is god.[2] For such the physical class of theologizers conclude it to be, since they have handed down such views about the gods that Dionysius the Stoic divides them into three kinds. The first, he supposes, includes those gods which are most obvious, as the Sun, Moon, *and* Stars; the next, those which are not apparent, as Neptune; the remaining one, those which are said to have passed from the human state to the divine, as Hercules *and* Amphiaraus. In like manner, Arcesilaus makes a threefold form of the divinity—the Olympian, the Astral, the Titanian—sprung from Cœlus and Terra; from which through Saturn and Ops came Neptune, Jupiter, and Orcus, and their entire progeny. Xenocrates, of the Academy, makes a twofold division—the Olympian and the Titanian, which descend from Cœlus and Terra. Most of the Egyptians believe that there are four gods—the Sun and the Moon, the Heaven and the Earth. Along with all the supernal fire Democritus conjectures that the gods arose. Zeno, too, will have it that their nature resembles it. Whence Varro also makes fire to be the soul of the world, that in the world fire governs all things, just as the soul does in ourselves. But all this is most absurd. For he says, Whilst it is in us, we have existence; but as soon as it has left us, we die. Therefore, when fire quits the world in lightning, the world comes to its end.

CHAP. III.—THE PHYSICAL PHILOSOPHERS MAINTAINED THE DIVINITY OF THE ELEMENTS; THE ABSURDITY OF THE TENET EXPOSED.

From these developments of opinion, we see that your[3] physical class *of philosophers* are driven to the necessity of contending that the elements are gods, since it alleges that other gods are sprung from them; for it is only from gods that gods could be born. Now, although we shall have to examine these other gods more fully in the proper place, in the mythic section of the poets, yet, inasmuch as we must meanwhile treat of them in their connection with the present class,[4] we shall probably even from their present class,[5] when once we turn to the gods themselves, succeed in showing that they can by no means appear to be gods who are said to be sprung from

the elements; so that we have at once a presumption[6] that the elements are not gods, since they which are born of the elements are not gods. In like manner, whilst we show that the elements are not gods, we shall, according to the law of natural relationship,[7] get a presumptive argument that they cannot rightly be maintained to be gods whose parents (in this case the elements) are not gods. It is a settled point[8] that a god is born of a god, and that what lacks divinity[9] is born of what is not divine. Now, so far as[10] the world of which your philosophers treat[11] (for I apply this term to the *universe* in the most comprehensive sense[12]) contains the elements, ministering to them as its component parts (for whatever its own condition may be, the same of course will be that of its elements and constituent portions), it must needs have been formed either by some being, according to the enlightened view[13] of Plato, or else by none, according to the harsh opinion[14] of Epicurus; and since it was formed, by having a beginning, it must also have an end. That, therefore, which at one time before its beginning had no existence, and will by and by after its end cease to have an existence, cannot of course, by any possibility, seem to be a god, wanting as it does that essential character of divinity, eternity, which is reckoned to be[15] without beginning, and without end. If, however, it[16] is in no wise formed, and therefore ought to be accounted divine—since, as divine, it is subject neither to a beginning nor an end of itself—how is it that some assign generation to the elements, which they hold to be gods, when the Stoics deny that anything can be born of a god? Likewise, how is it that they wish those beings, whom they suppose to be born of the elements, to be regarded as gods, when they deny that a god can be born? Now, what must hold good of the universe[17] will have to be predicated of the elements, I mean of heaven, and of earth, and of the stars, and of fire, which Varro has vainly proposed that you should believe[18] to be gods, and the parents of gods, contrary to that generation and nativity which he had declared to be impossible in a god. Now this same Varro had shown that the earth and the

---

[1] Non tenebat.
[2] De mundo deo didicimus.
[3] Istud.
[4] Ad præsentem speciem, the *physical* class.
[5] Or, classification.

[6] Ut jam hinc præjudicatum sit.
[7] Ad illam agnatorum speciem.
[8] Scitum.
[9] Non-deum.
[10] " Quod," with a subj. mood.
[11] Mundus iste.
[12] Summaliter.
[13] Humanitas.
[14] Duritia.
[15] Censetur.
[16] i.e., " iste mundus."
[17] Mundi, i.e., the universe; see above.
[18] The best reading is " vobis credi; " this is one of Tertullian's " *final* infinitives."

stars were animated.[1] But if this be the case, they must needs be also mortal, according to the condition[2] of animated nature; for although the soul is evidently immortal, this attribute is limited to it alone: it is not extended to that with which it is associated, that is, the body. Nobody, however, will deny that the elements have body, since we both touch them and are touched by them, and we see certain bodies fall down from them. If, therefore, they are animated, laying aside the principle[3] of a soul, as befits their condition as bodies; they are mortal—of course not immortal. And yet whence is it that the elements appear to Varro to be animated? Because, forsooth, the elements have motion. And then, in order to anticipate what may be objected on the other side, that many things else have motion—as wheels, as carriages, as several other machines—he volunteers the statement that he believes only such things to be animated as move of themselves, without any apparent mover or impeller from without, like the apparent mover of the wheel, or propeller of the carriage, or director of the machine. If, then, they are not animated, they have no motion of themselves. Now, when he thus alleges a power which is not apparent, he points to what it was his duty to seek after, even the creator and controller of the motion; for it does not at once follow that, because we do not see a thing, we believe that it does not exist. Rather, it is necessary the more profoundly to investigate what one does not see, in order the better to understand the character of that which is apparent. Besides, if (you admit) only the existence of those things which appear and are supposed to exist simply because they appear, how is it that you also admit them to be gods which do not appear? If, moreover, those things seem to have existence which have none, why may they not have existence also which do not seem to have it? · Such, for instance, as the Mover[4] of the heavenly beings. Granted, then, that things are animated because they move of themselves, and that they move of themselves when they are not moved by another: still it does not follow that they must straightway be gods, because they are animated, nor even because they move of themselves; else what is to prevent all animals whatever being accounted gods, moving as they do of themselves? This, to be sure, is allowed to the Egyptians, but their *superstitious* vanity has another basis.[5]

CHAP. IV.—WRONG DERIVATION OF THE WORD Θεός. THE NAME INDICATIVE OF THE TRUE DEITY. GOD WITHOUT SHAPE AND IMMATERIAL. ANECDOTE OF THALES.

Some affirm that the gods (*i.e.* θεοί) were so called because the verbs θέειν and σείσθαι signify *to run* and *to be moved*.[6] This term, then, is not indicative of any majesty, for it is derived from *running* and *motion*, not from any dominion[7] of godhead. But inasmuch as the Supreme God whom we worship is also designated Θεός, without however the appearance of any *course* or *motion* in Him, because He is not visible to any one, it is clear that that word must have had some other derivation, and that the property of divinity, innate in Himself, must have been discovered. Dismissing, then, that ingenious interpretation, it is more likely that the gods were not called θεοί from *running* and *motion*, but that the term was borrowed from the designation of the true God; so that you gave the name θεοί to the gods, whom you had in like manner forged for yourselves. Now, that this is the case, a plain proof is afforded in the fact that you actually give the common appellation θεοί to all those gods of yours, in whom there is no attribute of *course* or *motion* indicated. When, therefore, you call them both θεοί and *immoveable* with equal readiness, there is a deviation as well from the meaning of the word as from the idea[8] of godhead, which is set aside[9] if measured by the notion of *course* and *motion*. But if that *sacred* name be peculiarly significant of deity, and be simply true and not of a forced interpretation[10] in the case of the *true* God, but transferred in a borrowed sense[11] to those other objects which you choose to call gods, then you ought to show to us[12] that there is also a community of character between them, so that their common designation may rightly depend on their union of essence. But the true God, on the sole ground that He is not an object of sense, is incapable of being compared with those false deities which are cognizable to sight and sense (to sense indeed is sufficient); for this amounts to a clear statement of the difference between an obscure proof and a manifest one. Now, since the elements are obvious to all, (and) since God, on the contrary, is visible to none, how will it be in your power from that part

---

[1] Compare Augustine, *de Civit. Dei*, vii. 6, 23, 24, 28.
[2] Formam.
[3] Ratione.
[4] Motatorem.
[5] Alia sane vanitate.

[6] This seems to mean : "because θέειν has also the sense of σείεσθαι (motion as well as progression)."
[7] "Dominatione" is Oehler's reading, but he approves of "denominatione" (Rigault's reading); this would signify "*designation* of godhead."
[8] Opinione.
[9] Rescinditur.
[10] Interpretatorium.
[11] Reprehensum.
[12] Docete.

which you have not seen to pass to a decision on the objects which you see? Since, therefore, you have not to combine them in your perception or your reason, why do you combine them in name with the purpose of combining them also in power? For see how even Zeno separates the matter of the world from God: he says that the latter has percolated through the former, like honey through the comb. God, therefore, and Matter are two words (and) two things. Proportioned to the difference of the words is the diversity of the things; the condition also of matter follows its designation. Now if matter is not God, because its very appellation teaches us so, how can those things which are inherent in matter—that is, the elements—be regarded as gods, since the component members cannot possibly be heterogeneous from the body? But what concern have I with physiological conceits? It were better for one's mind to ascend above the state of the world, not to stoop down to uncertain speculations. Plato's form for the world was round. Its square, angular shape, such as others had conceived it to be, he rounded off, I suppose, with compasses, from his labouring to have it believed to be simply without a beginning.[1] Epicurus, however, who had said, "What is above us is nothing to us," wished notwithstanding to have a peep at the sky, and found the sun to be a foot in diameter. Thus far you must confess[2] men were niggardly in even celestial objects. In process of time their ambitious conceptions advanced, and so the sun too enlarged its disk.[3] Accordingly, the Peripatetics marked it out as a larger world.[4] Now, pray tell me, what wisdom is there in this hankering after conjectural speculations? What proof is afforded to us, notwithstanding the strong confidence of its assertions, by the useless affectation of a scrupulous curiosity,[5] which is tricked out with an artful show of language? It therefore served Thales of Miletus quite right, when, star-gazing as he walked with all the eyes he had, he had the mortification of falling[6] into a well, and was unmercifully twitted by an Egyptian, who said to him, "Is it because you found nothing on earth to look at, that you think you ought to confine your gaze to the sky?" His fall, therefore, is a figurative picture of the philosophers; of those, I mean,[7] who persist in applying[8] their studies to a vain purpose, since they indulge a stupid curiosity on natural objects, which they ought rather (intelligently to direct) to their Creator and Governor.

CHAP. V.—THE PHYSICAL THEORY CONTINUED. FURTHER REASONS ADVANCED AGAINST THE DIVINITY OF THE ELEMENTS.

Why, then, do we not resort to that far more reasonable[9] opinion, which has clear proof of being derived from men's common sense and unsophisticated deduction?[10] Even Varro bears it in mind, when he says that the elements are supposed to be divine, because nothing whatever is capable, without their concurrence,[11] of being produced, nourished, or applied to the sustenance[12] of man's life and of the earth, since not even our bodies and souls could have sufficed in themselves without the modification[13] of the elements. By this it is that the world is made generally habitable,—a result which is harmoniously secured[14] by the distribution into zones,[15] except where human residence has been rendered impracticable by intensity of cold or heat. On this account, men have accounted as gods —the sun, because it imparts from itself the light of day, ripens the fruit with its warmth, and measures the year with its stated periods; the moon, which is at once the solace of the night and the controller of the months by its governance; the stars also, certain indications as they are of those seasons which are to be observed in the tillage of our fields; lastly, the very heaven also under which, and the earth over which, as well as the intermediate space within which, all things conspire together for the good of man. Nor is it from their beneficent influences only that a faith in their divinity has been deemed compatible with the elements, but from their opposite qualities also, such as usually happen from what one might call[16] their wrath and anger— as thunder, and hail, and drought, and pestilential winds, floods also, and openings of the ground, and earthquakes: these are all fairly enough[17] accounted gods, whether their nature becomes the object of reverence as being favourable, or of fear because terrible—the sovereign dispenser,[18] in fact,[19] both of help and of hurt. But in the practical conduct of

---

[1] Sine capite.
[2] Scilicet.
[3] Aciem.
[4] Majorem orbem. Another reading has "majorem orbe," q.d. "as larger than the world."
[5] Morositatis.
[6] Cecidit turpiter.
[7] Scilicet.
[8] Habituros.
[8] Humaniorem.
[10] Conjectura.
[11] Suffragio.
[12] Sationem.
[13] Temperamento.
[14] Fœderata.
[15] Circulorum conditionibus.
[16] Tanquam.
[16] Jure.
[18] Domina.
[12] Scilicet.

social life, this is the way in which men act and feel: they do not show gratitude or find fault with the very things from which the succour or the injury proceeds, so much as with them by whose strength and power the operation of the things is effected. For even in your amusements you do not award the crown as a prize to the flute or the harp, but to the musician who manages the said flute or harp by the power of his delightful skill.[1] In like manner, when one is in ill-health, you do not bestow your acknowledgments on the flannel wraps,[2] or the medicines, or the poultices, but on the doctors by whose care and prudence the remedies become effectual. So, again, in untoward events, they who are wounded with the sword do not charge the injury on the sword or the spear, but on the enemy or the robber; whilst those whom a falling house covers do not blame the tiles or the stones, but the oldness of the building; as again shipwrecked sailors impute their calamity not to the rocks and waves, but to the tempest. And rightly too; for it is certain that everything which happens must be ascribed not to the instrument with which, but to the agent by whom, it takes place; inasmuch as he is the prime cause of the occurrence,[3] who appoints both the event itself and that by whose instrumentality it comes to pass (as there are in all things these three particular elements—the fact itself, its instrument, and its cause), because he himself who wills the occurrence of a thing comes into notice[4] prior to the thing which he wills, or the instrument by which it occurs. On all other occasions, therefore, your conduct is right enough, because you consider the author; but in physical phenomena your rule is opposed to that natural principle which prompts you to a wise judgment in all other cases, removing out of sight as you do the supreme position of the author, and considering rather the things that happen, than him by whom they happen. Thus it comes to pass that you suppose the power and the dominion to belong to the elements, which are but the slaves and functionaries. Now do we not, in thus tracing out an artificer and master within, expose the artful structure of their slavery[5] out of the appointed functions of those elements to which you ascribe (the attributes) of power?[6] But gods are not

slaves; therefore whatever things are servile in character are not gods. Otherwise[7] they should prove to us that, according to the ordinary course of things, liberty is promoted by irregular licence,[1] despotism by liberty, and that by despotism divine power is meant. For if all the (heavenly bodies) overhead forget not[9] to fulfil their courses in certain orbits, in regular seasons, at proper distances, *and* at equal intervals—appointed in the way of a law for the revolutions of time, and for directing the guidance thereof—can it fail to result[10] from the very observance of their conditions and the fidelity of their operations, that you will be convinced both by the recurrence of their orbital courses and the accuracy of their mutations, when you bear in mind how ceaseless is their recurrence, that a governing power presides over them, to which the entire management of the world[11] is obedient, reaching even to the utility and injury of the human race? For you cannot pretend that these (phenomena) act and care for themselves alone, without contributing anything to the advantage of mankind, when you maintain that the elements are divine for no other reason than that you experience from them either benefit or injury to yourself. For if they benefit themselves only, you are under no obligation to them.

CHAP. VI.—THE CHANGES OF THE HEAVENLY BODIES, PROOF THAT THEY ARE NOT DIVINE. TRANSITION FROM THE PHYSICAL TO THE MYTHIC CLASS OF GODS.

Come now, do you allow that the Divine Being not only has nothing servile in His course, but exists in unimpaired integrity, and ought not to be diminished, or suspended, or destroyed? Well, then, all His blessedness[12] would disappear, if He were ever subject to change. Look, however, at the stellar bodies; they both undergo change, and give clear evidence of the fact. The moon tells us how great has been its loss, as it recovers its full form;[13] its greater losses you are already accustomed to measure in a mirror of water;[15] so that I need not any longer believe in anywise what magians have asserted. The sun, too, is frequently put to the trial of an eclipse. Explain as best you may the modes of these celestial casualties, it is impossible[15] for God

---

[1] Vi suavitatis.
[2] Lanis.
[3] Caput facti.
[4] Invenitur.
[5] Servitutis artem. "Artem" Oehler explains by "artificiose institutum."
[6] We subjoin Oehler's text of this obscure sentence: "Non in ista investigatione alicujus artificis intus et domini servitutis artem ostendimus elementorum certis ex operis" (for "operibus," not unusual in Tertullian) "eorum quas facis potestatis?"

[7] Aut.
[8] De licentia passivitatis libertas approbetur.
[9] Meminerunt.
[10] Num non.
[11] Universa negotiatio mundialis.
[12] Felicitas.
[13] These are the moon's *monthly* changes.
[15] Tertullian refers to the Magian method of watching eclipses, the ἐνοπτρομαντεία.
[16] Instead of "non valet," there is the reading "non volet," "God would not consent," etc.

either to become less or to cease to exist. Vain, therefore, are [1] those supports of human learning, which, by their artful method of weaving conjectures, belie both wisdom and truth. Besides,[2] it so happens, indeed, according to your natural way of thinking, that he who has spoken the best is supposed to have spoken most truly, instead of him who has spoken the truth being held to have spoken the best. Now the man who shall carefully look into things, will surely allow it to be a greater probability that those[3] elements which we have been discussing are under some rule and direction, than that they have a motion of their own, and that being under government they cannot be gods. ·If, however, one is in error in this matter, it is better to err simply than speculatively, like your physical philosophers. But, at the same time,[4] if you consider the character of the *mythic* school, (and compare it with the *physical*,) the error which we have already seen frail men[5] making in the latter is really the more respectable one, since it ascribes a divine nature to those things which it supposes to be *superhuman* in their sensibility, whether in respect of their position, their power, their magnitude, or their divinity. For that which you suppose to be higher than man, you believe to be very near to God.

CHAP. VII.—THE GODS OF THE MYTHIC CLASS. THE POETS A VERY POOR AUTHORITY IN SUCH MATTERS. HOMER AND THE MYTHIC POETS. WHY IRRELIGIOUS.

But to pass to the *mythic* class of gods, which we attributed to the poets,[6] I hardly know whether I must only seek to put them on a par with our own *human* mediocrity, or whether they must be affirmed to be gods, with proofs of divinity, like the African Mopsus and the Bœotian Amphiaraus. I must now indeed but slightly touch on this class, of which a fuller view will be taken in the proper place.[7] Meanwhile, that these were only human beings, is clear from the fact that you do not consistently call them gods, but heroes. Why then discuss the point? Although divine honours had to be ascribed to dead men, it was not to them as such, of course. Look at your own practice, when with similar excess of presumption you sully heaven with the sepulchres of your kings: is

it not such as are illustrious for justice, virtue, piety, and every excellence of this sort, that you honour with the blessedness of deification, contented even to incur contempt if you forswear yourselves[8] for such characters? And, on the other hand, do you not deprive the impious and disgraceful of even the old prizes of human glory, tear up[9] their decrees and titles, pull down their statues, and deface[10] their images on the current coin? Will He, however, who beholds all things, who approves, nay, rewards the good, prostitute before all men[11] the attribute of His own inexhaustible grace and mercy? And shall men be allowed an especial amount of care and righteousness, that they may be wise[12] in selecting and multiplying[13] their deities? Shall attendants on kings and princes be more pure than those who wait on the Supreme God?[14] You turn your back in horror, indeed, on outcasts and exiles, on the poor and weak, on the obscurely born and the low-lived;[15] but yet you honour, even by legal sanctions,[16] unchaste men, adulterers, robbers, and parricides. Must we regard it as a subject of ridicule or indignation, that such characters are believed to be gods who are not fit to be men? Then, again, in this mythic class of yours which the poets celebrate, how uncertain is your conduct as to purity of conscience and the maintenance thereof! For whenever we hold up to execration the wretched, disgraceful and atrocious (examples) of your gods, you defend them as mere fables, on the pretence of poetic licence; whenever you volunteer a silent contempt[17] of this said[18] poetic *licence*, then you are not only troubled with no horror of it, but you go so far as[19] to show it respect, and to hold it as one of the indispensable (fine) arts; nay,[20] you carry out the studies of your higher classes[21] by its means, as the very foundation[22] of your literature. Plato was of opinion that poets ought to be banished, as calumniators of the gods; (he would even have) Homer himself expelled from his republic, although, as you are aware,[23] he was the crowned head of them all. But

---

8 Pejerantes.
9 Lancinatis.
10 Repercutitis.
11 Vulgo.
12 Sapere. The infinitive of *purpose* is frequent in our author.
13 Distribuendis.
14 An allusion to Antinous, who is also referred to in *The Apology*, xiii. ["Court-page." See, p. 29, *Supra*.]
15 Inhoneste institutos.
16 By the "legibus" Tertullian refers to the divine honours ordered to be paid, by decrees of the Senate, to deceased emperors. Comp. Suetonius, *Octav.* 88 ; and Pliny, *Paneg.* 11 (Oehler).
17 Ultro siletur.
18 Ejusmodi.
19 Insuper.
20 Denique.
21 Ingenuitatis
22 Initiatricem
23 Sane.

---

1 Viderint igitur "Let them look to themselves," "never mind them."
2 Alias.
3 Ista.
4 Sedenim.
5 Mortalitas.
6 See above, c. i. [Note 19, p. 129.]
7 See *The Apology*, especially cc. xxii. and xxiii.

while you admit and retain them thus, why should you not believe them when they disclose such things respecting your gods? And if you do believe your poets, how is it that you worship such gods (as they describe)? If you worship them simply because you do not believe the poets, why do you bestow praise on such lying authors, without any fear of giving offence to those whose calumniators you honour? A regard for truth[1] is not, of course, to be expected of poets. But when you say that they only make men into gods after their death, do you not admit that before death the said gods were merely human? Now what is there strange in the fact, that they who were once men are subject to the dishonour[2] of human casualties, or crimes, or fables? Do you not, in fact, put faith in your poets, when it is in accordance with their rhapsodies[3] that you have arranged in some instances your very rituals? How is it that the priestess of Ceres is ravished, if it is not because Ceres suffered a similar outrage? Why are the children of others sacrificed to Saturn,[4] if it is not because he spared not his own? Why is a male mutilated in honour of the Idæan goddess *Cybele,* unless it be that the (unhappy) youth who was too disdainful of her advances was castrated, owing to her vexation at his daring to cross her love?[5] Why was not Hercules "a dainty dish" to the good ladies of Lanuvium, if it was not for the primeval offence which women gave to him? The poets, no doubt, are liars. Yet it is not because *of their telling us that*[6] your gods did such things when they were human beings, nor because they predicated divine scandals[7] of a divine state, since it seemed to you more credible that gods should exist, though not of such a character, than that there should be such characters, although not gods.

CHAP. VIII.—THE GODS OF THE DIFFERENT NATIONS. VARRO'S GENTILE CLASS. THEIR INFERIORITY. A GOOD DEAL OF THIS PERVERSE THEOLOGY TAKEN FROM SCRIPTURE. SERAPIS A PERVERSION OF JOSEPH.

There remains the *gentile* class of gods amongst the several nations:[8] these were adopted out of mere caprice, not from the knowledge of the truth; and our information about them comes from the private notions *of different races.* God, I imagine, is everywhere known, everywhere present, powerful everywhere—an object whom all ought to worship, all ought to serve. Since, then, it happens that even they, whom all the world worships in common, fail in the evidence of their true divinity, how much more must this befall those whom their very votaries[9] have not succeeded in discovering! For what useful authority could possibly precede a theology of so defective a character as to be wholly unknown to fame? How many have either seen or heard of the Syrian Atargatis, the African Cœlestis, the Moorish Varsutina, the Arabian Obodas and Dusaris, or the Norican Belenus, or those whom Varro mentions—Deluentinus of Casinum, Visidianus of Narnia, Numiternus of Atina, *or* Ancharia of Asculum? And who have any clear notions[10] of Nortia of Vulsinii?[11] There is no difference in the worth of even their names, apart from the human surnames which distinguish them. I laugh often enough at the little coteries of gods[12] in each municipality, which have their honours confined within their own city walls. To what lengths this licence of adopting gods has been pushed, the superstitious practices of the Egyptians show us; for they worship even their native[13] animals, *such as* cats, crocodiles, and their snake. It is therefore a small matter that they have also deified a man—him, I mean, whom not Egypt only, or Greece, but the whole world worships, and the Africans swear by; about whose state also all that helps our conjectures and imparts to our knowledge the semblance of truth is stated in our own (sacred) literature. For that Serapis of yours was originally one of our own saints called Joseph.[14] The youngest of his brethren, but superior to them in intellect, he was from envy sold into Egypt, and became a slave in the family of Pharaoh king of the country.[15] Importuned by the unchaste queen, when he refused to comply with her desire, she turned upon him and reported him to the king, by whom he is put into prison. There he displays the power of his divine inspiration, by interpreting aright the dreams of some (fellow-prisoners). Meanwhile the king, too, has some terrible dreams. Joseph being brought

---

[1] Fides.
[2] Polluuntur.
[3] Relationibus.
[4] Comp. *The Apology,* ix. [See, p. 25, *Supra.*]
[5] Comp. Minucius Felix, *Octav.* xxi. ; Arnobius, *adv. Nat.* v. 6, 7; Augustine, *Civ. Dei,* vi. 7.
[6] This is the force of the *subjunctive* verb.
[7] By *divine scandals,* he means such as exceed in their atrocity even human scandals.
[8] See above, c. i. [p. 129.]

[9] Municipes. "Their local worshippers or subjects."
[10] Perceperint.
[11] Literally, "Have men heard of any Nortia belonging to the Vulsinensians?"
[12] Deos decuriones, in allusion to the *small provincial senates* which in the later times spread over the Roman colonies and *municipia.*
[13] Privatas.
[14] Compare Suidas, *s. v.* Σάραπις; Rufinus, *Hist. Eccl.* ii. 23. As Serapis was Joseph in disguise, so was Joseph a type of Christ, according to the ancient Christians, who were fond of subordinating heathen myths to Christian theology.
[15] Tertullian is not the only writer who has made mistakes in citing from memory Scripture narratives. Comp. Arnobius.

before him, according to his summons, was able to expound them. Having narrated the proofs of true interpretation which he had given in the prison, he opens out his dream to the king: those seven fat-fleshed and well-favoured kine signified as many years of plenty; in like manner, the seven lean-fleshed animals predicted the scarcity of the seven following years. He accordingly recommends precautions to be taken against the future famine from the previous plenty. The king believed him. The issue of all that happened showed how wise he was, how invariably holy, and now how necessary. So Pharaoh set him over all Egypt, that he might secure the provision of corn for it, and thenceforth administer its government. They called him Serapis, from the turban[1] which adorned his head. The peck-like[2] shape of this turban marks the memory of his corn-provisioning; whilst evidence is given that the care of the supplies was all on his head,[3] by the very ears of corn which embellish the border of the head-dress. For the same reason, also, they made the sacred figure of a dog,[4] which they regard (as a sentry) in Hades, and put it under his right hand, because the care of the Egyptians was concentrated[5] under his hand. And they put at his side Pharia,[6] whose name shows her to have been the king's daughter. For in addition to all the rest of his kind gifts and rewards, Pharaoh had given him his own daughter in marriage. Since, however, they had begun to worship both wild animals and human beings, they combined both figures under one form Anubis, in which there may rather be seen clear proofs of its own character and condition enshrined[7] by a nation at war with itself, refractory[8] to its kings, despised among foreigners, with even the appetite of a slave and the filthy nature of a dog.

CHAP. IX. THE POWER OF ROME. ROMANIZED ASPECT OF ALL THE HEATHEN MYTHOLOGY. VARRO'S THREEFOLD DISTRIBUTION CRITICISED. ROMAN HEROES (ÆNEAS INCLUDED,) UNFAVOURABLY REVIEWED.

Such are the more obvious or more remarkable points which we had to mention in connection with Varro's threefold distribution of the gods, in order that a sufficient answer might seem to be given touching the physical, the poetic, and the gentile classes. Since, however, it is no longer to the philosohers, nor the poets, nor the nations that we owe the substitution of all (heathen worship for the true religion) although they transmitted the superstition, but to the dominant Romans, who received the tradition and gave it wide authority, another phase of the widespread error of man must now be encountered by us; nay, another forest must be felled *by our axe*, which has obscured the childhood of the degenerate worship[9] with germs of superstitions gathered from all quarters. Well, but even the gods of the Romans have received from (the same) Varro a threefold classification into the *certain*, the *uncertain*, and the *select*. What absurdity! What need had they of uncertain gods, when they possessed certain ones? Unless, forsooth, they wished to commit themselves to[10] such folly as the Athenians did; for at Athens there was an altar with this inscription: "To THE UNKNOWN GODS."[11] Does, then, a man worship that which he knows nothing of? Then, again, as they had certain gods, they ought to have been contented with them, without requiring select ones. In this want they are even found to be irreligious! For if gods are selected as onions are,[12] then such as are not chosen are declared to be worthless. Now we on our part allow that the Romans had two sets of gods, *common* and *proper;* in other words, those which they had in common with other nations, and those which they themselves devised. And were not these called the *public* and the *foreign*[13] gods? Their altars tell us so; there is (a specimen) of the foreign gods at the fane of Carna, of the public gods in the Palatium. Now, since their common gods are comprehended in both the physical and the mythic classes, we have already said enough concerning them. I should like to speak of their particular kinds of deity. We ought then to admire the Romans for that third set of *the gods of their enemies*,[14] because no other nation ever discovered for itself so large a mass of superstition. Their other deities we arrange in two classes: those which have become gods from human beings, and those which have had their origin in some other way. Now, since there is advanced the same colourable pretext for the deification of the dead, that their lives were meritorious, we are compelled to urge the same reply against them, that no one of them was worth so much

---

[1] Suggestu.
[2] Modialis.
[3] Super caput esse, i.e., was entrusted to him.
[4] Canem dicaverunt.
[5] Compressa.
[6] Isis; comp. *The Apology*, xvi. [See p. 31, *supra*.]
[7] Consecrasse.
[8] Recontrans.

[9] Vitii pueritatem.
[10] Recipere (with a dative).
[11] IGNOTIS DEIS. Comp. Acts xvii. 23.
[12] Ut bulbi. This is the passage which Augustine quotes (*de Civit. Dei*, vii. 1) as "too facetious."
[13] Adventicii, "coming from abroad."
[14] Touching these gods of the vanquished nations, compare *The Apology*, xxv.; below, c. xvii.; Minucius Felix, *Octav.* xxv.

pains. Their fond[1] father Æneas, in whom
they believed, was never glorious, and was
felled with a stone[2]—a vulgar weapon, to pelt
a dog withal, inflicting a wound no less ignoble! But this Æneas turns out[3] a traitor
to his country; yes, quite as much as Antenor.
And if they will not believe this to be true of
him, he at any rate deserted his companions
when his country was in flames, and must be
held inferior to that woman of Carthage,[4] who,
when her husband Hasdrubal supplicated the
enemy with the mild pusillanimity of our
Æneas, refused to accompany him, but hurry-
ing her children along with her, disdained to
take her beautiful self and father's noble
heart[5] into exile, but plunged into the flames
of the burning Carthage, as if rushing into
the embraces of her (dear but) ruined country. Is he "pious Æneas" for (rescuing) his
young only son and decrepid old father, but
deserting Priam and Astyanax? But the
Romans ought rather to detest him; for in
defence of their princes and their royal[6]
house, they surrender[7] even children and
wives, and every dearest pledge.[8] They deify
the son of Venus, and this with the full knowledge and consent of her husband Vulcan, and
without opposition from even Juno. Now, if
sons have seats in heaven owing to their piety
to their parents, why are not those noble
youths[9] of Argos rather accounted gods, because they, to save their mother from guilt in
the performance of some sacred rites, with a
devotion more than human, yoked themselves
to her car and dragged her to the temple?
Why not make a goddess, for her exceeding
piety, of that daughter[10] who from her own
breasts nourished her father who was famishing in prison? What other glorious achievement can be related of Æneas, but that he
was nowhere seen in the fight on the field of
Laurentum? Following his bent, perhaps
he fled a second time as a fugitive from the
battle.[11] In like manner, Romulus posthu-
mously becomes a god. Was it because he
founded the city? Then why not others also,
who have built cities, counting even[12] women?
To be sure, Romulus slew his brother in the

bargain, and trickishly ravished some foreign
virgins. Therefore of course he becomes a
god, and therefore a Quirinus ("god of the
spear"), because then their fathers had to
use the spear[13] on his account. What did
Sterculus do to merit deification? If he
worked hard to enrich the fields stercoribus,[14]
(with manure,) Augias had more dung than
he to bestow on them. If Faunus, the son of
Picus, used to do violence to law and right,
because struck with madness, it was more fit
that he should be doctored than deified.[15] If
the daughter of Faunus so excelled in chastity,
that she would hold no conversation with
men, it was perhaps from rudeness, or a consciousness of deformity, or shame for her
father's insanity. How much worthier of divine honour than this "good goddess"[16] was
Penelope, who, although dwelling among so
many suitors of the vilest character, preserved
with delicate tact the purity which they assailed! There is Sanctus, too,[17] who for his
hospitality had a temple consecrated to him
by king Plotius; and even Ulysses had it in
his power to have bestowed one more god
upon you in the person of the most refined
Alcinous.

CHAP. X.—A DISGRACEFUL FEATURE OF THE
ROMAN MYTHOLOGY. IT HONOURS SUCH IN-
FAMOUS CHARACTERS AS LARENTINA.

I hasten to even more abominable cases.
Your writers have not been ashamed to publish
that of Larentina. She was a hired prostitute,
whether as the nurse of Romulus, and therefore called Lupa, because she was a prostitute,
or as the mistress of Hercules, now deceased,
that is to say, now deified. They[18] relate that
his temple-warder[19] happened to be playing at
dice in the temple alone; and in order to represent a partner for himself in the game, in
the absence of an actual one, he began to play
with one hand for Hercules and the other for
himself. (The condition was,) that if he won
the stakes from Hercules, he should with them
procure a supper and a prostitute; if Hercules,
however, proved the winner, I mean his other
hand, then he should provide the same for
Hercules. The hand of Hercules won. That
achievement might well have been added to
his twelve labours! The temple-warden buys
a supper for the hero, and hires Larentina to
play the whore. The fire which dissolved the

---

[1] Diligentem.
[2] See Homer, Il. v. 300.
[3] Invenitur.
[4] Referred to also above, i. 18.
[5] The obscure "formam et patrem" is by Oehler rendered "pulchritudinem et generis nobilitatem."
[6] The word is "eorum" (possessive of "principum"), not "suæ."
[7] Dejerant adversus.
[8] What Tertullian himself thinks on this point, see his de Corona, xi.
[9] Cleobis and Biton; see Herodotus i, 31.
[10] See Valerius Maximus, v. 4, 1.
[11] We need not stay to point out the unfairness of this state-ment, in contrast with the exploits of Æneas against Turnus, as detailed in the last books of the Æneid.
[12] Usque in.

[13] We have thus rendered "quiritatem est," to preserve as far as one could the pun on the deified hero of the Quirites.
[14] We insert the Latin, to show the pun on Sterculus; see The Apology, c. xxv. [See p. 40, supra.]
[15] Curaria quam consecrari.
[16] Bona Dea, i.e., the daughter of Faunus just mentioned.
[17] See Livy, viii. 20, xxxii. 1; Ovid, Fasti, vi. 213, etc. Compare also Augustine, de Civ. Dei, xviii. 19. [Tom, vii. p. 576.]
[18] Compare Augustine, de Civ. Dei, vi. 7. [Tom. vii. p. 184.]
[19] Æditum ejus.

body of even a Hercules [1] enjoyed the supper, and the altar consumed everything. Larentina sleeps alone in the temple; and *she* a woman from the brothel, boasts that in her dreams she had submitted herself to the pleasure of Hercules;[2] and she might possibly have experienced this, as it passed through her mind, in her sleep. In the morning, on going out of the temple very early, she is solicited by a young man—"a third Hercules," so to speak.[3] He invites her home. She complies, remembering that Hercules had told her that it would be for her advantage. He then, to be sure, obtains permission that they should be united in lawful wedlock (for none was allowed to have intercourse with the concubine of a god without being punished for it); the husband makes her his heir. By and by, just before her death, she bequeathed to the Roman people the rather large estate which she had obtained through Hercules. After this she sought deification for her daughters too, whom indeed the divine Larentina ought to have appointed her heirs also. The gods, of the Romans received an accession in her dignity. For she alone of all the wives of Hercules was dear to him, because she alone was rich; and she was even far more fortunate than Ceres, who contributed to the pleasure of the (king of the) dead.[4] After so many examples and *eminent* names among you, who might not have been declared divine? Who, in fact, ever raised a question as to his divinity against Antinous?[5] Was even Ganymede more grateful and dear than he to (the supreme god) who loved him? According to you, heaven is open to the dead. You prepare[6] a way from Hades to the stars. Prostitutes mount it in all directions, so that you must not suppose that you are conferring a great distinction upon your kings.

CHAP. XI.—THE ROMANS PROVIDED GODS FOR BIRTH, NAY, EVEN BEFORE BIRTH, TO DEATH. MUCH INDELICACY IN THIS SYSTEM.

And you are not content to assert the divinity of such as were once known to you, whom you heard and handled, and whose portraits have been painted, and actions recounted, and memory retained amongst you; but men insist upon consecrating with a heavenly life[7] I know not what incorporeal, inanimate shadows, and the *mere* names of things—dividing man's entire existence amongst separate powers even from his conception in the womb: so that there is a god Consevius,[8] to preside over concubital generation; and Fluviona,[9] to preserve the (growth of the) infant in the womb; after these come Vitumnus and Sentinus,[10] through whom the babe begins to have life, and its earliest sensation; then Diespiter,[11] by whose office the child accomplishes its birth. But when women begin their parturition, Candelifera also *comes in* aid, since childbearing requires the light of the candle; and other goddesses there are [12] who get their names from the parts they bear in the stages of travail. There were two Carmentas likewise, according to the general view: to one of them, called Postverta, belonged the function of assisting the birth of the introverted child; while the other, Prosa,[13] executed the like office for the rightly born. The god Farinus was so called from (his inspiring) the first utterance; while others believed in Locutius from his gift of speech. Cunina[14] is present as the protector of the child's deep slumber, and supplies to it refreshing rest. To lift them (when fallen)[15] there is Levana, and along with her Rumina.[16] It is a wonderful oversight that no gods were appointed for cleaning up the filth of children. Then, to preside over their first pap and earliest drink you have Potina and Edula;[17] to teach the child to stand erect is the work of Statina,[18] whilst Adeona helps him to come *to dear Mamma*, and Abeona to toddle off again; then there is Domiduca,[19] (to bring home the bride;) and the goddess Mens, to influence the mind to either good or evil.[20] They have likewise Volumnus and Voleta,[21] to control the will; Paventina, (the goddess) of fear; Venilia, of hope;[22] Volupia, of pleasure;[23] Præstitia, of beauty.[24] Then, again, they give his name to Peragenor,[25] from his teaching men to go through their work; to Consus, from his sug-

---

[1] That is, when he mounted the pyre.
[2] Herculi functam. "Fungi alicui" means to satisfy, or yield to.
[3] The well-known Greek saying, Ἄλλος οὗτος Ἡρακλῆς.
[4] Pluto; Proserpine, the daughter of Ceres, is meant. Oehler once preferred to read, "Hebe, quæ mortuo placuit," i.e., "than Hebe, who gratified Hercules after death."
[5] Tertullian often refers indignantly to this atrocious case.
[6] Subigitus.
[7] Efflagitant cœlo et sanciunt, (i.e., "they insist on deifying.")

[8] Comp. Augustine, *de Civ. Dei*, vi. 9.
[9] A name of Juno, in reference to her office to mothers, "quia eam sanguinis fluorem in conceptu retinere putabant." Comp. August. *de Civ. Dei*, iii. 2.
[10] Comp. August. *de Civ. Dei*, vii. 2, 3.
[11] Comp. August. *de Civ. Dei*, iv. 11.
[12] Such as Lucina, Partula, Nona, Decima, Alemona.
[13] Or, Prosa.
[14] "Quæ infantes *in cunis* (in their cradle) tuetur." Comp. August. *de Civ. Dei*, iv. 11.
[15] Educatrix; Augustine says: "Ipse levet de terra et vocetur dea *Levana*" (*de Civ. Dei*, iv. 11).
[16] From the old word *ruma*, a teat.
[17] Comp. August. *de Civ. Dei*, iv. 9, 11, 36.
[18] See also Tertullian's *de Anima*, xxxix.; and Augustine's *de Civ. Dei*, iv. 21, where the god has the masculine name of *Statilinus*.
[19] See Augustine, *de Civ. Dei*, vi. 9 and vii. 3.
[20] *Ibid.* iv. 21, vii. 3.
[21] *Ibid.* iv. 21.
[22] *Ibid.* iv. 11, vii. 22.
[23] *Ibid.* iv. 11. [N.B.—Augustine's borrowing from our author.]
[24] Arnobius, *adv. Nationes*, iv. 3.
[25] Augustine, *de Civ. Dei*. [iv. 11 and 16] mentions *Agenoria*.

gesting to them counsel. Juventa is their guide on assuming the manly gown, and "bearded Fortune" when they come to full manhood.[1] If I must touch on their nuptial duties, there is Afferenda whose appointed function is to see to the offering of the dower; but fie on you! you have your Mutunus[2] and Tutunus and Pertunda[3] and Subigus and the goddess Prema and likewise Perfica.[4] O spare yourselves, ye impudent gods! No one is present at the secret struggles of married life. Those very few persons who have a wish that way, go away and blush for very shame in the midst of their joy.

CHAP. XII.[5]—THE ORIGINAL DEITIES WERE HUMAN—WITH SOME VERY QUESTIONABLE CHARACTERISTICS. SATURN OR TIME WAS HUMAN. INCONSISTENCIES OF OPINION ABOUT HIM.

Now, how much further need I go in recounting your gods—because I want to descant on the character of such as you have adopted? It is quite uncertain whether I shall laugh at your absurdity, or upbraid you for your blindness. For how many, and indeed what, gods shall I bring forward? Shall it be the greater ones, or the lesser? The old ones, or the novel? The male, or the female? The unmarried, or such as are joined in wedlock? The clever, or the unskilful? The rustic or the town ones? The national or the foreign? For the truth is,[6] there are so many families, so many nations, which require a catalogue[7] (of gods), that they cannot possibly be examined, or distinguished, or described. But the more diffuse the subject is, the more restriction must we impose on it. As, therefore, in this review we keep before us but one object—that of proving that all these gods were once human beings (not, indeed, to instruct you in the fact,[8] for your conduct shows that you have forgotten it)—let us adopt our compendious summary from the most natural method[9] of conducting the examination, even by considering the origin of their race. For the origin characterizes all that comes after it. Now this origin of your gods dates,[10] I suppose, from Saturn. And when Varro men-

tions Jupiter, Juno, and Minerva, as the most ancient of the gods, it ought not to have escaped our notice, that every father is more ancient than his sons, and that Saturn therefore must precede Jupiter, even as Cœlus does Saturn, for Saturn was sprung from Cœlus and Terra. I pass by, however, the origin of Cœlus and Terra. They led in some unaccountable way[11] single lives, and had no children. Of course they required a long time for vigorous growth to attain to such a stature.[12] By and by, as soon as the voice of Cœlus began to break,[13] and the breasts of Terra to become firm,[14] they contract marriage with one another. I suppose either Heaven[15] came down to his spouse, or Earth went up to meet her lord. Be that as it may, Earth conceived seed of Heaven, and when her year was fulfilled brought forth Saturn in a wonderful manner. Which of his parents did he resemble? Well, then, even after parentage began,[16] it is certain[17] that they had no child previous to Saturn, and only one daughter afterwards—Ops; thenceforth they ceased to procreate. The truth is, Saturn castrated Cœlus as he was sleeping. We read this name Cœlus as of the masculine gender. And for the matter of that, how could he be a father unless he were a male? But with what instrument was the castration effected? He had a scythe. What, so early as that? For Vulcan was not yet an artificer in iron. The widowed Terra, however, although still quite young, was in no hurry[18] to marry another. Indeed, there was no second Cœlus for her. What but Ocean offers her an embrace? But he savours of brackishness, and she has been accustomed to fresh water.[19] And so Saturn is the sole male child of Cœlus and Terra. When grown to puberty, he marries his own sister. No laws as yet prohibited incest, nor punished parricide. Then, when male children were born to him, he would devour them; better himself (should take them) than the wolves, (for to these would they become a prey) if he exposed them. He was, no doubt, afraid that one of them might learn the lesson of his father's scythe. When Jupiter was born in course of time, he was removed out of the way:[20] (the father) swallowed a stone instead of the son, as was pretended. This artifice secured his safety for a time; but at length the son, whom

---

[1] On *Fortuna Barbata*, see Augustine, *de Civ. Dei*, iv. 11, where he also names *Consus* and *Juventa.*
[2] Tertullian, in *Apol.* xxv. sarcastically says, "Sterculus, and Mutunus, and Larentina, have raised the empire to its present height."
[3] Arnobius, *adv. Nationes*, iv. 7, 11; August. *de Civ. Dei*, vi. 9.
[4] For these three gods, see Augustine, *de Civ. Dei*, vi. 9; and Arnobius, *adv. Nationes*, iv. 7.
[5] Agrees with *The Apology*, c. x.
[6] Bona fide.
[7] Censum.
[8] There is here an omitted clause, supplied in *The Apology*, "but rather to recall it to your memory."
[9] Ab ipsa ratione.
[10] Signatur.

[11] Undeunde.
[12] Tantam proceritatem.
[13] Insolescere, i.e., at the commencement of puberty.
[14] Lapilliscere, i.e., to indicate maturity.
[15] The nominative "cœlum" is used.
[16] It is not very clear what is the force of "sed et pepererit," as read by Oehler; we have given the clause an impersonal turn.
[17] "Certe" is sometime "certo" in our author.
[18] Distulit.
[19] That is, to rain and cloud.
[20] Abalienato.

he had not devoured, and who had grown up in secret, fell upon him, and deprived him of his kingdom. Such, then, is the patriarch of the gods whom Heaven[1] and Earth produced for you, with the poets officiating as midwives. Now some persons with a refined[2] imagination are of opinion that, by this allegorical fable of Saturn, there is a physiological representation of *Time:* (they think) that it is because all things are destroyed by Time, that Cœlus and Terra were themselves parents without having any of their own, and that the (fatal) scythe was used, and that (Saturn) devoured his own offspring, because he,[3] in fact, absorbs within himself all things which have issued from him. They call in also the witness of his name; for they say that he is called Κρόνος in Greek, meaning the same thing as χρόνος.[4] His Latin name also they derive from *seed-sowing;*[5] for they suppose him to have been the actual procreator—that the seed, in fact, was dropt down from heaven to earth by his means. They unite him with *Ops*, because seeds produce the affluent treasure (*Opem*) of actual life, and because they develope with labour (*Opus*). Now I wish that you would explain this metaphorical[6] statement. It was either Saturn or Time. If it was Time, how could it be Saturn? If he, how could it be Time? For you cannot possibly reckon both these corporeal subjects[7] as co-existing in one person. What, however, was there to prevent your worshipping Time under its proper quality? Why not make a human person, or even a mythic man, an object of your adoration, but each in its proper nature not in the character of Time? What is the meaning of that conceit of your mental ingenuity, if it be not to colour the foulest matters with the feigned appearance of reasonable proofs?[8] Neither, on the one hand, do you mean Saturn to be Time, because you say he is a human being; nor, on the other hand, whilst portraying him as Time, do you on that account mean that he was ever human. No doubt, in the accounts of remote antiquity your god Saturn is plainly described as living on earth in human guise. Anything whatever may obviously be pictured as incorporeal which never had an existence; there is simply no room for such fiction, where there is reality. Since, therefore, there is clear evidence that Saturn once existed, it is in vain that you change his character. He whom you will not

deny to have once been man, is not at your disposal to be treated anyhow, nor can it be maintained that he is either divine or Time. In every page of your literature the origin[9] of Saturn is conspicuous. We read of him in Cassius Severus and in the Corneliuses, Nepos and Tacitus,[10] and, amongst the Greeks also, in Diodorus, and all other compilers of ancient annals.[11] No more faithful records of him are to be traced than in Italy itself. For, after (traversing) many countries, and (enjoying) the hospitality of Athens, he settled in Italy, or, as it was called, Œnotria, having met with a kind welcome from Janus, or Janes,[12] as the Salii call him. The hill on which he settled had the name Saturnius, whilst the city which he founded[13] still bears the name Saturnia; in short, the whole of Italy once had the same designation. Such is the testimony derived from that country which is now the mistress of the world: whatever doubt prevails about the origin of Saturn, his actions tell us plainly that he was a human being. Since, therefore, Saturn was human, he came undoubtedly from a human stock; and more, because he was a man, he, of course, came not of Cœlus and Terra. Some people, however, found it easy enough to call him, whose parents were unknown, the son of those gods from whom all may in a sense seem to be derived. For who is there that does not speak under a feeling of reverence of the heaven and the earth as his own father and mother? Or, in accordance with a custom amongst men, which induces them to say of any who are unknown or suddenly apparent, that "they came from the sky?" Hence it happened that, because a stranger appeared suddenly everywhere, it became the custom to call him a heaven-born man,[14]—just as we also commonly call earth-born all those whose descent is unknown. I say nothing of the fact that such was the state of antiquity, when men's eyes and minds were so habitually rude, that they were excited by the appearance of every newcomer as if it were that of a god: much more would this be the case with a king, and that the primeval one. I will linger some time longer over the case of Saturn, because by fully discussing his primordial history I shall beforehand furnish a compendious answer for all other cases; and I do not wish to omit the more convincing testimony of your sacred literature, the credit of which ought to be the greater in proportion to its antiquity. Now earlier than all litera-

---

[1] The word is "cœlum" here.
[2] Eleganter.
[3] i.e., as representing *Time.*
[4] So Augustine, *de Civ. Dei*, iv. 10; Arnobius, *adv. Nationes*, iii. 29; Cicero, *de Nat. Deor.* ii. 25.
[5] As if from "sero," *satum.*
[6] Translatio.
[7] Utrumque corporale.
[8] Mentitis argumentationibus.

[9] Census.
[10] See his *Histories*, v. 2, 4.
[11] Antiquitatem canos, "hoary antiquity."
[12] Jano sive Jane.
[13] Depalaverat, "marked out with stakes."
[14] Cœlitem.

ture was the Sibyl; that Sibyl, I mean, who was the true prophetess of truth, from whom you borrow their title for the priests of your demons. She in senarian verse expounds the descent of Saturn and his exploits in words to this effect: "In the tenth generation of men, after the flood had overwhelmed the former race, reigned Saturn, and Titan, and Japetus, the bravest of the sons of Terra and Cœlus." Whatever credit, therefore, is attached to your older writers and literature, and much more to those who were the simplest as belonging to that age,[1] it becomes sufficiently certain that Saturn and his family[2] were human beings. We have in our possession, then, a brief principle which amounts to a prescriptive rule about their origin serving for all other cases, to prevent our going wrong in individual instances. The particular character[3] of a posterity is shown by the original founders of the race—mortal beings (come) from mortals, earthly ones from earthly; step after step comes in due relation[4]—marriage, conception, birth—country, settlements, kingdoms, all give the clearest proofs.[5] They, therefore, who cannot deny the birth of men, must also admit their death; they who allow their mortality must not suppose them to be gods.

CHAP: XIII.[6]—THE GODS HUMAN AT FIRST. WHO HAD THE AUTHORITY TO MAKE THEM DIVINE? JUPITER NOT ONLY HUMAN, BUT IMMORAL.

Manifest cases, indeed, like these have a force peculiarly their own. Men like Varro and his fellow-dreamers admit into the ranks of the divinity those whom they cannot assert to have been in their primitive condition anything but men; (and this they do) by affirming that they became gods after their death. Here, then, I take my stand. If your gods were elected[7] to this dignity and deity,[8] just as you recruit the ranks of your senate, you cannot help conceding, in your wisdom, that there must be some one supreme sovereign who has the power of selecting, and is a kind of Cæsar; and nobody is able to confer[9] on others a thing over which he has not absolute control. Besides, if they were able to make gods of themselves after their death, pray tell me why they chose to be in an inferior condition at first? Or, again, if there is no one

who made them gods, how can they be said to have been made such, if they could only have been made by some one else? There is therefore no ground afforded you for denying that there is a certain wholesale distributor[10] of divinity. Let us accordingly examine the reasons for despatching mortal beings to heaven. I suppose you will produce a pair of them. Whoever, then, is the awarder (of the divine honours), exercises his function, either that he may have some supports, or defences, or it may be even ornaments to his own dignity; or from the pressing claims of the meritorious, that he may reward all the deserving. No other cause is it permitted us to conjecture. Now there is no one who, when bestowing a gift on another, does not act with a view to his own interest or the other's. This conduct, however, cannot be worthy of the Divine Being, inasmuch as His power is so great that He can make gods outright; whilst His bringing man into such request, on the pretence that he requires the aid and support of certain, even dead persons, is a strange conceit, since He was able from the very first to create for Himself immortal beings. He who has compared human things with divine will require no further arguments on these points. And yet the latter opinion ought to be discussed, that God conferred divine honours in consideration of meritorious claims. Well, then, if the award was made on such grounds, if heaven was opened to men of the primitive age because of their deserts, we must reflect that after that time no one was worthy of such honour; except it be, that there is now no longer such a place for any one to attain to. Let us grant that anciently men may have deserved heaven by reason of their great merits. Then let us consider whether there really was such merit. Let the man who alleges that it did exist declare his own view of merit. Since the actions of men done in the very infancy of time[11] are a valid claim for their deification, you consistently admitted to the honour the brother and sister who were stained with the sin of incest—Ops and Saturn. Your Jupiter too, stolen in his infancy, was unworthy of both the home and the nutriment accorded to human beings; and, as he deserved for so bad a child, he had to live in Crete.[12] Afterwards, when full-grown, he dethrones his own father, who, whatever his parental character may have been, was most prosperous in his reign, king as he was of the golden age. Under him, a stranger to toil and want,

[1] Magis proximis quoniam illius ætatis.
[2] Prosapia.
[3] Qualitas. [N. B. Our author's use of Præscriptio.]
[4] Comparantur.
[5] Monumenta liquent.
[6] Comp. The Apology, c. xi. [p. 27. Supra.]
[7] Allecti.
[8] This is not so terse as Tertullian's "nomen et numen."
[9] Præstare.

[10] Mancipem.
[11] In cunabulis temporalitatis.
[12] The ill-fame of the Cretans is noted by St. Paul, Tit. i. 12.

peace maintained its joyous and gentle sway; under him—

"Nulli subigebant arva coloni;"[1]
"No swains would bring the fields beneath their sway;"[2]

and without the importunity of any one the earth would bear all crops spontaneously.[3] But he hated a father who had been guilty of incest, and had once mutilated his[4] grandfather. And yet, behold, he himself marries his own sister; so that I should suppose the old adage was made for him: Τοῦ πατρὸς τὸ παιδίον—"Father's own child." There was "not a pin to choose" between the father's piety and the son's. If the laws had been just even at that early time,[5] Jupiter ought to have been "sewed up in both sacks."[6] After this corroboration of his lust with incestuous gratification, why should he hesitate to indulge himself lavishly in the lighter excesses of adultery and debauchery? Ever since[7] poetry sported thus with his character, in some such way as is usual when a runaway slave[8] is posted up in public, we have been in the habit of gossiping without restraint[9] of his tricks[10] in our chat with passers-by;[11] sometimes sketching him out in the form of the very money which was the fee of his debauchery—as when (he personated) a bull, or rather paid the money's worth of one,[12] and showered (gold) into the maiden's chamber, or rather forced his way in with a bribe;[13] sometimes (figuring him) in the very likenesses of the parts which were acted[14]—as the eagle which ravished (the beautiful youth),[15] and the swan which sang (the enchanting song).[16] Well now, are not such fables as these made up of the most disgusting intrigues and the worst of scandals? or would not the morals and tempers of men be likely to become wanton from such examples? In what manner demons, the offspring of evil angels who have been long engaged in their mission, have laboured to turn men[17] aside from the faith to unbelief and to such fables, we must not in this place speak of to any extent. As indeed the general body[18] (of your gods), which took their cue[19] from their

kings, and princes, and instructors,[20] was not of the self-same nature, it was in some other way[21] that similarity of character was exacted by their authority. But how much the worst of them was he who (ought to have been,' but) was not, the best of them? By a title peculiar to him, you are indeed in the habit of calling Jupiter "the Best,"[22] whilst in Virgil he is "Æquus Jupiter."[23] All therefore were *like* him—incestuous towards their own kith and kin, unchaste to strangers, impious, unjust! Now he whom mythic story left untainted with no conspicuous infamy, was not worthy to be made a god.

CHAP. XIV.—GODS, THOSE WHICH WERE CONFESSEDLY ELEVATED TO THE DIVINE CONDITION, WHAT PRE-EMINENT RIGHT HAD THEY TO SUCH HONOUR? HERCULES AN INFERIOR CHARACTER.

But since they will have it that those who have been admitted from the human state to the honours of deification should be kept separate from others, and that the distinction which Dionysius the Stoic drew should be made between the native and the factitious[24] gods, I will add a few words concerning this last class also. I will take Hercules himself for raising the gist of a reply[25] (to the question) whether he deserved heaven and divine honours? For, as men choose to have it, these honours are awarded to him for his merits. If it was for his valour in destroying wild beasts with intrepidity, what was there in that so very memorable? Do not criminals condemned to the games, though they are even consigned to the contest of the vile arena, despatch several of these animals at one time, and that with more earnest zeal? If it was for his world-wide travels, how often has the same thing been accomplished by the rich at their pleasant leisure, or by philosophers in their slave-like poverty?[26] Is it forgotten that the cynic Asclepiades on a single sorry cow,[27] riding on her back, and sometimes nourished at her udder, surveyed[28] the whole world with a personal inspection? Even if Hercules visited the infernal regions, who does not know that the way to Hades is open to all? If you have deified him on account of his much carnage and many battles, a much greater number of victories was gained by the

---

[1] Virgil, *Georg.* i. 125.
[2] Sewell.
[3] Ipsa.
[4] Jupiter's, of course.
[5] The law which prescribed the penalty of the paracide, that he be *sewed up in a sack* with an ape, a serpent, and a cock, and be thrown into the sea.
[6] In duos culleos dividi.
[7] De quo.
[8] De fugitivo.
[9] Abusui nundinare.
[10] The "operam ejus"=*ingenia et artificia* (Oehler).
[11] Percontationi alienæ.
[12] In the case of Europa.
[13] In the case of Danæ.
[14] Similitudines actuum ipsas.
[15] In the case of Ganymede.
[16] In the case of Leda.
[17] Quos.
[18] Plebs.
[19] Morata.

[20] Proseminatoribus.
[21] Alibi.
[22] Optimum.
[23] There would seem to be a 'jest here ; "æquus" is not only *just* but *equal*, i.e., "on a par with" others—in *evil*, of course, as well as *good.*
[24] Inter nativos et factos. See above, c. ii., p. 131.
[25] Summa responsionis.
[26] Famulatoria mendicitas.
[27] Vaccula.
[28] Subegisse oculis, "reduced to his own eyesight."

illustrious Pompey, the conqueror of the pirates who had not spared Ostia itself in their ravages; and (as to carnage), how many thousands, let me ask, were cooped up in one corner of the citadel[1] of Carthage, and slain by Scipio? Wherefore Scipio has a better claim to be considered a fit candidate for deification[2] than Hercules. You must be still more careful to add to the claims of (our) Hercules his debaucheries with concubines *and* wives, and the swathes[3] of Omphale, and his base desertion of the Argonauts because he had lost his beautiful boy.[4] To this mark of baseness add for his glorification likewise his·attacks of madness, adore the arrows which slew his sons and wife. This was the man who, after deeming himself worthy of a funeral pile in the anguish of his remorse for his parricides,[5] deserved rather to die the unhonoured death which awaited him, arrayed in the poisoned robe which his wife sent him on account of his lascivious attachment (to another). You, however, raised him from the pyre to the sky, with the same facility with which (you have distinguished in like manner) another hero[6] also, who was destroyed by the violence of a fire from the gods. He having devised some few experiments, was said to have restored the dead to life by his cures. He was the son of Apollo, half human, although the grandson of Jupiter, and greatgrandson of Saturn (or rather of spurious origin, because his parentage was uncertain, as Socrates of Argos has related; he was exposed also, and found in a worse tutelage than even Jove's, suckled even at the dugs of a dog); nobody can deny that he deserved the end which befell him when he perished by a stroke of lightning. In this transaction, however, your most excellent Jupiter is once more found in the wrong—impious to his grandson, envious of his artistic skill. Pindar, indeed, has not concealed his true desert; according to him, he was punished for his avarice and love of gain, influenced by which he would bring the living to their death, rather than the dead to life, by the perverted use of his medical art which he put up for sale.[7] It is said

that his mother was killed by the same stroke, and it was only right that she, who had bestowed so dangerous a beast on the world,[8] should escape to heaven by the same ladder. And yet the Athenians will not be at a loss how to sacrifice to gods of such a fashion, for they pay divine honours to Æsculapius and his mother amongst their dead (worthies). As if, too, they had not ready to hand[9] their own Theseus to worship, so highly deserving a god's distinction! Well, why not? Did he not on a foreign shore abandon the preserver of his life,[10] with the same indifference, nay heartlessness,[11] with which he became the cause of his father's death?

CHAP. XV.—THE CONSTELLATIONS AND THE GENII VERY INDIFFERENT GODS. THE ROMAN MONOPOLY OF GODS UNSATISFACTORY. OTHER NATIONS REQUIRE DEITIES QUITE AS MUCH.

It would be tedious to take a survey of all those, too, whom you have buried amongst the constellations, and audaciously minister to as gods.[12] I suppose your Castors, and Perseus, and Erigona,[13] have just the same claims for the honours of the sky as Jupiter's own big boy[14] had. But why should we wonder? You have transferred to heaven even dogs, and scorpions, and crabs. I postpone all remarks[15] concerning those whom you worship in your oracles. That this worship exists, is attested by him who pronounces the oracle.[16] Why; you will have your gods to be spectators even of sadness,[17] as is Viduus, who makes a *widow* of the soul, by parting it from the body, and whom you have condemned, by not permitting him to be enclosed within your citywalls; there is Cæculus also, to deprive the eyes of their perception; and Orbana, to bereave seed of its vital power; moreover, there is the goddess of death herself. To pass hastily by all others,[18] you account as gods the sites of places or of the city; such are Father Janus (there being, moreover, the archergoddess[19] Jana[20]), and Septimontius of the seven hills.

Men sacrifice[21] to the same *Genii*, whilst

---

[1] Byrsæ.
[2] Magis obtinendus divinitati deputatur.
[3] Fascias.
[4] Hylas.
[5] Rather murders of children and other kindred.
[6] Æsculapius.
[7] Tertullian does not correctly quote Pindar (*Pyth.* iii. 54–59), who notices the skilful hero's love of reward, but certainly ascribes to him the merit of curing rather than killing : Ἀλλὰ κέρδει καὶ σοφία δέδεται ἔτραπεν καὶ κἀκεῖνον ἀγάνορι μισθῷ χρυσὸς ἐν χερσὶν φανεὶς ἀνδρ ἐκ θανάτου κομίσαι ἤδη ἀλωκότα· χερσὶ δ᾽ ἄρα Κρονίων ῥίψαις δι᾽ ἀμφοῖν ἀμπνοὰν στέρνων καθέλεν ὠκέως, αἴθων δὲ κεραυνὸς ἐνέσκιμψεν μόρον—" Even wisdom has been bound by love of gain, and gold shining in the hand by a magnificent reward induced even him to restore from death a man already seized by it ; and then the son of Saturn, hurling with his hands a bolt through both, speedily took away the breath of their breasts, and the flashing bolt inflicted death " (Dawson Turner).

[8] Tertullian does not follow the legend which is usually received. He wishes to see no good in the object of his hatred, and so takes the worst view, and certainly *improves* upon it. The "bestia" is out of reason. [He doubtless followed some copy now lost.
[9] Quasi non et ipsi.
[10] Ariadne.
[11] Amentia.
[12] Deis ministratis.
[13] The constellation Virgo.
[14] Jovis exoletus, Ganymede, or *Aquarius.*
[15] He makes a similar postponement above, in c. vii., to *The Apology,* cc. xxii. xxiii.
[16] Divini.
[17] Et tristitiæ arbitros.
[18] Transvolem.
[19] Diva arquis.
[20] Perhaps another form of Diana.
[21] Faciunt = ῥίζουσι

they have altars or temples in the same places; but to others besides, when they dwell in a strange place, or live in rented houses.[1] I say nothing about Ascensus, who gets his name for his *climbing* propensity, and Clivicola, from her sloping (haunts); I pass silently by the deities called Forculus from doors, and Cardea from hinges, and Limentinus the god of thresholds, and whatever others are worshipped by your neighbours as tutelar deities of their street doors.[2] There is nothing strange in this, since men have their respective gods in their brothels, their kitchens, and even in their prison. Heaven, therefore, is crowded with innumerable gods of its own, both these and others belonging to the Romans, which have distributed amongst them the functions of one's whole life, in such a way that there is no want of the other[3] gods. Although, it is true,[4] the gods which we have enumerated are reckoned as Roman peculiarly, and as not easily recognised abroad; yet how do all those functions and circumstances, over which men have willed their gods to preside, come about,[5] in every part of the human race, and in every nation, where their guarantees[6] are not only without an official recognition, but even any recognition at all?

CHAP. XVI.—INVENTORS OF USEFUL ARTS UNWORTHY OF DEIFICATION. THEY WOULD BE THE FIRST TO ACKNOWLEDGE A CREATOR. THE ARTS CHANGEABLE FROM TIME TO TIME, AND SOME BECOME OBSOLETE.

Well, but[7] certain men have discovered fruits and sundry necessaries of life, (and hence are worthy of deification).[8] Now let me ask, when you call these persons "discoverers," do you not confess that what they discovered was already in existence? Why then do you not prefer to honour the Author, from whom the gifts really come, instead of converting the Author into *mere* discoverers? Previously he who made the discovery, the inventor himself no doubt expressed his gratitude to the Author; no doubt, too, he felt that He was God, to whom really belonged the religious service,[9] as the Creator (of the gift), by whom also both he who discovered and that which was discovered were alike

created. The green fig of Africa nobody at Rome had heard of when Cato introduced it to the Senate, in order that he might show how near was that province of the enemy[10] whose subjugation he was constantly urging. The cherry was first made common in Italy by Cn. Pompey, who imported it from Pontus. I might possibly have thought the earliest introducers of apples amongst the Romans deserving of the public honour[11] of deification. This, however, would be as foolish a ground for making gods as even the invention of the useful arts. And yet if the skilful men[12] of our own time be compared with these, how much more suitable would deification be to the later generation than to the former! For, tell me, have not all the extant inventions superseded antiquity,[13] whilst daily experience goes on adding to the new stock? Those, therefore, whom you regard as divine because of their arts, you are really injuring by your very arts, and challenging (their divinity) by means of rival attainments, which cannot be surpassed.[14]

CHAP. XVII.[15]—CONCLUSION. THE ROMANS OWE NOT THEIR IMPERIAL POWER TO THEIR GODS. THE GREAT GOD ALONE DISPENSES KINGDOMS. HE IS THE GOD OF THE CHRISTIANS.

In conclusion, without denying all those whom antiquity willed *and* posterity has believed to be gods, to be the guardians of your religion, there yet remains for our consideration that very large assumption of the Roman superstitions which we have to meet in opposition to you, O heathen, viz. that the Romans have become the lords and masters of the whole world, because by their religious offices they have merited this dominion to such an extent that they are within a very little of excelling even their own gods in power. One cannot wonder that Sterculus, and Mutunus, and Larentina, have severally[16] advanced this empire to its height! The Roman people has been by its gods alone ordained to such dominion. For I could not imagine that any foreign *gods* would have preferred doing more for a strange nation than for their own people, and so by such conduct become the deserters and neglecters, nay, the betrayers of the native land wherein they were born and bred, and ennobled and buried. Thus not even Jupiter

---

[1] This seems to be the meaning of an almost unintelligible sentence, which we subjoin: "Geniis eisdem illi faciunt qui in isdem locis aras vel ædes habent; præterea aliis qui in alieno loco aut mercedibus habitant." Oehler, who makes this text, supposes that in each clause the name of some god has dropped out.
[2] Numinum janitorum.
[3] Ceteris.
[4] Immo cum.
[5] Proveniunt.
[6] Prædes.
[7] Sedenim.
[8] We insert this clause at Oehler's suggestion.
[9] Ministerium.

[10] The incident, which was closely connected with the third Punic war, is described pleasantly by Pliny, *Hist. Nat.* xv. 20.
[11] Præconium.
[12] Artifices.
[13] "Antiquitas" is here opposed to "novitas," and therefore means "the arts of old times."
[14] In æmulis. "In," in our author, often marks the instrument.
[15] Compare *The Apology*, xxv. xxvi., pp. 39, 40.
[16] The verb is in the *singular* number.

10

could suffer his own Crete to be subdued by the Roman fasces, forgetting that cave of Ida, and the brazen cymbals of the Corybantes, and the most pleasant odour of *the goat* which nursed him on that *dear* spot. Would he not have made that tomb of his superior to the whole Capitol, so that that land should most widely rule which covered the ashes of Jupiter? Would Juno, *too*, be willing that the Punic city, for the love of which she even neglected Samos, should be destroyed, and that, too, by the fires of the sons of Æneas? Although I am well aware that

> " Hic illius arma,
> Hic currus fuit, hoc regnum dea gentibus esse,
> Si qua fata sinant, jam tunc tenditque fovetque." [1]

> Here were her arms, her chariot here,
> Here goddess-like, to fix one day
> The seat of universal sway,
> Might fate be wrung to yield assent,
> E'en then her schemes, her cares were bent." [2]

Still the unhappy (queen of gods) had no power against the fates! And yet the Romans did not accord as much honour to the fates, although they gave them Carthage, as they did to Larentina. But surely those gods of yours have not the power of conferring empire. For when Jupiter reigned in Crete, and Saturn in Italy, and Isis in Egypt, it was even as men that they reigned, to whom also were assigned many to assist them.[3] Thus he who serves also makes masters, and the bond-slave [4] of Admetus [5] aggrandizes with empire the citizens of Rome, although he destroyed his own liberal votary Crœsus by deceiving him with ambiguous oracles.[6] Being a god, why was he afraid boldly to foretell to him the truth that he must lose his kingdom. Surely those who were aggrandized with the power of wielding empire might always have been able to keep an eye, as it were,[7] on their own cities. If they were strong enough to confer empire on the Romans, why did not Minerva defend Athens from Xerxes? Or why did not Apollo rescue Delphi out of the hand of Pyrrhus? They who lost their own cities preserve the city of Rome, since (forsooth) the religiousness [8] of Rome has merited the protection! But is it not rather the fact that this excessive devotion [9] has been devised since the empire has attained its glory by the in-

crease of its power? No doubt sacred rites were introduced by Numa, but then your proceedings were not marred by a religion of idols and temples. Piety was simple,[10] and worship humble; altars were artlessly reared,[11] and the vessels (thereof) plain, and the incense from them scant, and the god himself nowhere. Men therefore were not religious before they achieved greatness, (nor great) because they were religious. But how can the Romans possibly seem to have acquired their empire by an excessive religiousness and very profound respect for the gods, when that empire was rather increased after the gods had been slighted?[12] Now, if I am not mistaken, every kingdom or empire is acquired and enlarged by wars, whilst they and their gods also are injured by conquerors. For the same ruin affects both city-walls and temples; similar is the carnage both of civilians and of priests; identical the plunder of profane things and of sacred. To the Romans belong as many sacrileges as trophies; and then as many triumphs over gods as over nations. Still remaining are their captive idols amongst them; and certainly, if they can only see their conquerors, they do not give them their love. Since, however, they have no perception, they are injured with impunity; and since they are injured with impunity, they are worshipped to no purpose. The nation, therefore, which has grown to its powerful height by victory after victory, cannot seem to have developed owing to the merits of its religion—whether they have injured the religion by augmenting their power, or augmented their power by injuring the religion. All nations have possessed empire, each in its proper time, as the Assyrians, the Medes, the Persians, the Egyptians; empire is even now also in the possession of some, and yet they that have lost their power used not to behave [13] without attention to religious services and the worship of the gods, even after these had become unpropitious to them,[14] until at last almost universal dominion has accrued to the Romans. It is the fortune of the times that has thus constantly shaken kingdoms with revolution.[15] Inquire who has ordained these changes in the times. It is the same (great Being) who dispenses kingdoms,[16] and has now put the supremacy of them into the hands of the Ro-

---

[1] *Æneid*, i. 16–20.
[2] Conington.
[3] Operati plerique.
[4] Dediticius.
[5] Apollo; comp. *The Apology*, c. xiv., p. 30.
[6] See Herodot. i. 50.
[7] Veluti tueri.
[8] Religiositas.
[9] Superstitio.

[10] Frugi.
[11] Temeraria.
[12] Læsis.
[13] Morabantur. We have taken this word as if from "mores" (character). Tertullian often uses the participle "moratus" in this sense.
[14] Et depropitiorum.
[15] Volutavit.
[16] Compare *The Apology*, c. xxvi.

mans, very much as if[1] the tribute of many nations were after its exaction amassed in one (vast) coffer.　What He has determined con-

cerning it, they know who are the nearest to Him.[2]

---

[1] We have treated this " tanquam " and its clause as something more than a mere simile.　It is, in fact, an integral element of the supremacy which the entire sentence describes as conferred on the Romans by the Almighty.

[2] That is, *the Christians*, who are well aware of God's purposes as declared in prophecy.　St. Paul tells the Thessalonians what the order of the great events subsequent to the Roman power was to be : the destruction of that power was to be followed by the development and reign of Antichrist ; and then the end of the world would come.

APPENDIX.

A FRAGMENT CONCERNING THE EXECRABLE GODS OF THE HEATHEN.

. . . . .

So great blindness has fallen on the Roman race, that they call their enemy Lord, and preach the filcher of blessings as being their very giver, and to him they give thanks. They call those (deities), then, by human names, not by their own, for their own names they know not. That they are dæmons[1] they understand: but they read histories of the old kings, and then, though they see that their character[2] was mortal, they honour them with a deific name.

As for him whom they call Jupiter, and think to be the highest god, when he was born the years (that had elapsed) from the foundation of the world[3] to him[4] were some three thousand. He is born in Greece, from Saturnus and Ops; and, for fear he should be killed by his father (or else, if it is lawful to say so, should be begotten[5] anew), is by the advice of his mother carried down into Crete, and reared in a cave of Ida; is concealed (from his father's search) by (the aid of) Cretans—born men![6]—rattling their arms; sucks a she-goat's dugs; flays her; clothes himself in her hide; and (thus) uses his own nurse's hide, after killing her, to be sure, with his own hand! but he sewed thereon three golden tassels worth the price of an hundred oxen each, as their author Homer[7] relates,

if it is fair to believe it. This Jupiter, in adult age, waged war several years with his father; overcame him; made a parricidal raid on his home; violated his virgin sisters;[8] selected one of them in marriage; drave[9] his father by dint of arms. The remaining scenes, moreover, of that act have been recorded. Of other folks' wives, or else of violated virgins, he begat him sons; defiled freeborn boys; oppressed peoples lawlessly with despotic and kingly sway. The father, whom they erringly suppose to have been the *original* god, was ignorant that this (son of his) was lying concealed in Crete; the son, again, whom they believe the *mightier* god, knows not that the father whom himself had banished is lurking in Italy. If he was in heaven, when would he not see what was doing in Italy? For the Italian land is "not in a corner."[10] And yet, had he been a god, nothing *ought* to have escaped him. But that he whom the Italians call Saturnus did lurk there, is clearly evidenced on the face of it, from the fact that from his lurking[11] the Hesperian[12] tongue is to this day called Latin,[13] as likewise their author Virgil relates.[14] (Jupiter,) then, is said to have been born on earth, while (Saturnus his father) fears lest he be driven by him from his kingdom, and seeks to kill him as being his own rival, and knows not that he has been stealthily carried off, and is in hiding; and afterwards the son-god pursues his father, immortal seeks to slay immortal (is it credible?[15]), and is disappointed by an interval of sea, and is ignorant

---

[1] Dæmons. Gr. δαίμων, which some hold to = δαήμων, "knowing," "skilful," in which case it would come to be used of any superhuman intelligence; others, again, derive from δαίω, "to divide, distribute," in which case it would mean a distributor of destinies; which latter derivation and meaning Liddell and Scott incline to.

[2] Actum: or "career."

[3] Mundi.

[4] i.e., till his time.

[5] Pareretur. As the word seems to be used here with reference to his father, this, although not by any means a usual meaning, would seem to be the sense. [As in the equivalent Greek.]

[6] A Cretibus, hominibus natis. The force seems to be in the absurdity of supposing that, 1st, there should be human beings (hominibus) *born*, (as Jupiter is said to have been "born,") already existing at the time of the "birth" of "the highest god;" 2ndly, that these should have had the power to do him so essential service as to conceal him from the search of his own father, likewise a mighty deity, by the simple expedient of rattling their arms.

[7] See Hom. Il. ii. 446–9; but Homer says there were 100 such tassels.

[8] Oehler's "virgin*is*" must mean "virgin*es*."

[9] So Scott: "He *drave* my cows last Eastern's night."—*Lay of Last Minstrel.*

[10] See Acts xxvi. 26.

[11] Latitatio.

[12] i.e., Western: here=Italian, as being west of Greece.

[13] Latina.

[14] See Virg. Æn. viii. 319–323: see also Ov. *Fast.* i. 234–238.

[15] Oehler does not mark this as a question. If we follow him, we may render, "this can find belief." Above, it seemed necessary to introduce the parenthetical words to make some sense. The Latin is throughout very clumsy and incoherent.

of (his quarry's) flight; and while all this is going on between two gods on earth, heaven is deserted. No one dispensed the rains, no one thundered, no one governed all this mass of world.[1] For they cannot even say that their action and wars took place in heaven; for all this was going on on Mount Olympus in Greece. Well, but heaven is not called Olympus, for heaven is heaven.

These, then, are the actions of theirs, which we will treat of first—nativity, lurking, ignorance, parricide, adulteries, obscenities— things committed not by a god, but by most impure and truculent human beings; beings who, had they been living in these days, would have lain under the impeachment of all laws—laws which are far more just and strict than *their* actions. "He drave his father by dint of arms." The Falcidian and Sempronian law would bind the parricide in a sack with beasts. "He violated his sisters." The Papinian law would punish the outrage with all penalties, limb by limb. "He invaded others' wedlock." The Julian law would visit its adulterous violator capitally. "He defiled freeborn boys." The Cornelian law would condemn the crime of transgressing the sexual bond with novel severities, sacrilegiously guilty as it is of a novel union.[2] This being is shown to have had no divinity either, for he was a human being; his father's flight escaped him. To this human being, of such a character, to so wicked a king, so obscene and so cruel, God's honour has been assigned by men. Now, to be sure, if *on earth* he were born and grew up through the ad-vancing stages of life's periods, and in it committed all these evils, and yet is no more in it, what is thought[3] (of him) but that he is dead? Or else does foolish error think wings were born him in his old age, whence to fly heavenward? Why, even *this* may possibly find credit among men bereft of sense,[4] if indeed they believe, (as they do,) that he turned into a swan, to beget the Castors;[5] an eagle, to contaminate Ganymede; a bull, to violate Europa; gold, to violate Danaë; a horse, to beget Pirithoüs; a goat, to beget Egyppa[6] from a she-goat; a Satyr, to embrace Antiope. Beholding these adulteries, to which sinners are prone, they therefore easily believe that sanctions of misdeed and of every filthiness are borrowed from their feigned god. Do they perceive how void of amendment are the rest of his career's acts which can find credit, which are indeed true, and which, they say, he did without self-transformation? Of Semele, he begets Liber;[7] of Latona, Apollo and Diana; of Maia, Mercury; of Alcmena, Hercules. But the rest of his corruptions, which they themselves confess, I am unwilling to record, lest turpitude, once buried, be again called to men's ears. But of these few (offsprings of his) I have made mention; offsprings whom in their error they believe to be themselves, too, gods—born, to wit, of an incestuous father; adulterous births, supposititious births. And the living,[8] eternal God, of sempiternal divinity, prescient of futurity, immeasurable,[9] they have dissipated (into nothing, by associating Him) with crimes so unspeakable.

---

[1] Orbis.

[2] Lex Cornelia transgressi foederis ammissum novis exemplis novi coitus sacrilegum damnaret. After consulting Dr. Holmes, I have rendered, but not without hesitation, as above. "Foedus" seems to have been technically used, especially in later Latin, of the *marriage compact;* but what "lex Cornelia" is meant I have sought vainly to discover, and whether "lex Cornelia transgressi foederis" ought not to go together I am not sure. For "ammissum" (= admissum) Migne's ed. reads "amissum," a very different word. For "sacrilegus" with a genitive, see *de Res. Carn,* c. xlii. *med.*

[3] Quid putatur (Oehler) putatus (Migne).
[4] Or, "feeling"—"sensu."
[5] The Dioscuri, Castor and Pollux.
[6] Perhaps Ægipana (marginal reading of the MS. as given in Oehler and Migne).
[7] i.e., Bacchus.
[8] Oehler reads "vide etem;" but Migne's "viventem" seems better: indeed, Oehler's is probably a misprint. The punctuation of this treatise in Oehler is very faulty throughout, and has been disregarded.
[9] "Immensum," rendered "incomprehensible" in the "Athanasian Creed."

ELUCIDATION.

This Fragment is noted as spurious, by Oehler who attributes it to somebody only moderately acquainted with Tertullian's style and teaching.[1] I do not find it mentioned by Dupin, nor by Routh. This translation is by Thelwall.

---

[1] See page 14, *supra.*

VII

AN ANSWER TO THE JEWS.[1]

TRANSLATED BY THE REV. S. THELWALL.

CHAP. I.—OCCASION OF WRITING. RELATIVE POSITION OF JEWS AND GENTILES ILLUSTRATED.

It happened very recently a dispute was held between a Christian and a Jewish proselyte. Alternately with contentious cable they each spun out the day until evening. By the opposing din, moreover, of some partisans of the individuals, truth began to be overcast by a sort of cloud. It was therefore our pleasure that that which, owing to the confused noise of disputation, could be less fully elucidated point by point, should be more carefully looked into, and that the pen should determine, for reading purposes, the questions handled

For the occasion, indeed, of claiming Divine grace even for the Gentiles derived a pre-eminent fitness from this fact, that the man who set up to vindicate God's Law as his own was of the Gentiles, and not a Jew " of the stock of the Israelites."[2] For this fact—that Gentiles are admissible to God's Law—is enough to prevent Israel from priding himself on the notion that " the Gentiles are accounted as a little drop of a bucket," or else as " dust out of a threshing-floor:"[3] although we have God Himself as an adequate engager and faithful promiser, in that He promised to Abraham that " in his seed should be blest all nations of the earth;"[4] and that[5] out of the

womb of Rebecca " two peoples and two nations were about to proceed,"[6]—of course those of the Jews, that is, of Israel; and of the Gentiles, that is ours. Each, then, was called a *people* and a *nation*; lest, from the nuncupative appellation, any should dare to claim for himself the privilege of grace. For God ordained " two peoples and two nations " as about to proceed out of the womb of one woman: nor did grace[6] make distinction in the nuncupative appellation, but in the order of birth; to the effect that, which ever was to be prior in proceeding from the womb, should be subjected to " the less," that is, the posterior. For thus unto Rebecca did God speak: " Two nations are in thy womb, and two peoples shall be divided from thy bowels; and people shall overcome people, and the greater shall serve the less."[7] Accordingly, since the *people* or *nation* of the Jews is anterior in time, and " greater " through the grace of primary favour in the Law, whereas ours is understood to be " less " in the age of times, as having in the last era of the world[8] attained the knowledge of divine mercy: beyond doubt, through the edict of the divine utterance, the *prior* and " greater " people—that is, the Jewish—must necessarily serve the " less;" and the " less " people—that is, the Christian—overcome the " greater. " For, withal, according to the memorial records of the divine Scriptures, the *people* of the Jews—that is, the more ancient—quite forsook God, and did degrading service to idols, and, abandoning the Divinity, was surrendered to images; while " the people " said to Aaron, " Make us gods to go before us."[9] And when the gold out of the necklaces of the women and the rings of

---

[1] [This treatise was written while our author was a Catholic. This seems to me the best supported of the theories concerning it. Let us accept Pamelius, for once and date it A.D. 198. Dr. Allix following Baronius, will have it as late as A.D. 208. Neander thinks the work, after the quotation from Isaiah in the beginning of chapter ninth, *is not our author's*, but was finished by another hand, clumsily annexing what is said on the same chapter of Isaiah in the Third Book against Marcion. It is only slightly varied. Bp. Kaye admits the very striking facts instanced by Neander, in support of this theory, but demolishes, with a word any argument drawn from thence that the genuine work was written after the author's lapse. This treatise is sufficiently annotated by Thelwall, and covers ground elsewhere gone over in this Series. My own notes are therefore very few.]
[2] Comp. Phil. iii. 5.
[3] See Isa. xl. 15: " dust of *the balance*," Eng. ver. ; ῥοπὴ ζυγοῦ LXX. For the expression " dust out of a threshing-floor," however, see Ps. i. 4, Dan. ii. 35.
[4] See Gen. xxii. 18 ; and comp. Gal. iii. 16, and the references in both places.

[5] This promise may be said to have been given " to Abraham," because (of course) he was still living at the time ; as we see by comparing Gen. xxi. 5 with xxv. 7 and 26. See, too, Heb. xi. 9.
[6] Or, " nor did He make, by grace, a distinction."
[7] See Gen. xxv. 21–23, especially in the LXX.; and comp. Rom. ix. 10–13.
[8] Sæculi.
[9] Ex. xxxii. 1, 23; Acts vii. 39, 40.

the men had been wholly smelted by fire, and there had come forth a calf-like head, to this figment Israel with one consent (abandoning God) gave honour, saying, " These are the gods who brought us from the land of Egypt."[1] For thus, in the later times in which kings were governing them, did they again, in conjunction with Jeroboam, worship golden kine, and groves, and enslave themselves to Baal.[2] Whence is proved that they have ever been depicted, out of the volume of the divine Scriptures, as guilty of the crime of idolatry; whereas our " less "—that is, posterior—*people*, quitting the idols which formerly it used slavishly to serve, has been converted to the same God from whom Israel, as we have above related, had departed.[3] For thus has the " less "—that is, posterior—*people* overcome the "greater people," while it attains the grace of divine favour, from which Israel has been divorced.

CHAP. II.—THE LAW ANTERIOR TO MOSES.

Stand we, therefore, foot to foot, and determine we the sum and substance of the actual question within definite lists.

For why should God, the founder of the universe, the Governor of the whole world,[4] the Fashioner of humanity, the Sower[5] of universal nations be believed to have given a law through Moses to one people, and not be said to have assigned it to all nations? For unless He had given it to all by no means would He have habitually permitted even proselytes out of the nations to have access to it. But—as is congruous with the goodness of God, and with His equity, as the Fashioner of mankind —He gave to all nations the selfsame law, which at definite and stated times He enjoined should be observed, when He willed, and through whom He willed, and as He willed. For in the beginning of the world He gave to Adam himself and Eve a law, that they were not to eat of the fruit of the tree planted in the midst of paradise; but that, if they did contrariwise, by death they were to die.[6] Which law had continued enough for them, had it been kept. For in this law given to Adam we recognise in embryo[7] all the precepts which afterwards sprouted forth when given through Moses; that is, Thou shalt love the Lord thy God from thy whole heart and out of thy whole soul; Thou shalt love thy

neighbour as thyself;[8] Thou shalt not kill; Thou shalt not commit adultery; Thou shalt not steal; False witness thou shalt not utter; Honour thy father and mother; and, That which is another's, shalt thou not covet. For the primordial law was given to Adam and Eve in paradise, as the womb of all the precepts of God. In short, if they had loved the Lord their God, they would not have contravened His precept; if they had habitually loved their neighbour—that is, themselves[9]—they would not have believed the persuasion of the serpent, and thus would not have committed murder upon themselves,[9] by falling[10] from immortality, by contravening God's precept; from theft also they would have abstained, if they had not stealthily tasted of the fruit of the tree, nor had been anxious to skulk beneath a tree to escape the view of the Lord their God; nor would they have been made partners with the falsehood-asseverating devil, by believing him that they would be " like God;" and thus they would not have offended God either, as their Father, who had fashioned them from clay of the earth, as out of the womb of a mother; if they had not coveted another's, they would not have tasted of the unlawful fruit.

Therefore, in this general and primordial law of God, the observance of which, in the case of the tree's fruit, He had sanctioned, we recognise *en*closed all the precepts specially of the posterior Law, which germinated when *dis*closed at their proper times. For the subsequent superinduction of a law is the work of the same Being who had before premised a precept; since it is His province withal subsequently to train, who had before resolved to form, righteous creatures. For what wonder if He extends a discipline who institutes it? if He advances who begins? In short, before the Law of Moses,[11] written in stone-tables, I contend that there was a law unwritten, which was habitually understood naturally, and by the fathers was habitually kept. For whence was Noah " found righteous,"[12] if in his case the righteousness of a natural law had not preceded? Whence was Abraham accounted " a friend of God,"[13] if not on the ground of equity and righteousness, (in the observance) of a natural law? Whence was Melchizedek named " priest of the most high God,"[14] if,

---

[1] Ex. xxxii. 4 : comp. Acts vii. 38–41 ; 1 Cor. x. 7; Ps. cvi. 19–22.
[2] Comp. 1 Kings xii. 25–33 ; 2 Kings xvii. 7–17 (in LXX. 3 and 4 Kings). The Eng. ver. speaks of "calves;" the LXX. call them " heifers."
[3] Comp. 1 Thess. i. 9, 10
[4] Mundi.
[5] Comp. Jer. xxxi. 27 (in LXX. it is xxxviii. 27) ; Hos. ii. 23 ; Zech. x. 9 ; Matt. xiii. 31–43.
[6] See Gen. ii. 16, 17, iii. 2, 3.
[7] Condita.

[8] Deut. vi. 4, 5 ; Lev. xix. 18 ; comp. Matt. xxii. 34–40 ; Mark xii. 28–34 ; Luke x. 25–28 ; and for the rest, Ex. xx. 12–17 ; Deut. v. 16–21 ; Rom. xiii. 9.
[9] Semetipsos. ? Each other.
[10] Excidendo ; or, perhaps, " by self-excision," or " mutual excision."
[11] Or, " the Law written for Moses in stone-tables."
[12] Gen. vi. 9, vii. 1 ; comp. Heb. xi. 7.
[13] See Isa. xli. 8 ; Jas. ii. 23.
[14] Gen. xiv. 18 · Ps. cx. (cix. in LXX.) 4 ; Heb. v. 10, vii. 1–3, 10, 15, 17

before the priesthood of the Levitical law, there were not levites who were wont to offer sacrifices to God? For thus, after the above-mentioned patriarchs, was the Law given to Moses, at that (well-known) time after their exode from Egypt, after the interval and spaces of four hundred years. In fact, it was after Abraham's "four hundred and thirty years"[1] that the Law was given. Whence we understand that God's law was anterior even to Moses, and was not first (given) in Horeb, nor in Sinai and in the desert, but was more ancient; (existing) first in paradise, subsequently re-formed for the patriarchs, and so again for the Jews, at definite periods: so that we are not to give heed to Moses' Law as to the primitive law, but as to a subsequent, which at a definite period God has set forth to the Gentiles too and, after repeatedly promising so to do through the prophets, has re-formed for the better; and has premonished that it should come to pass that, just as "the law was given through Moses"[2] at a definite time, so it should be believed to have been temporarily observed and kept. And let us not annul this power which God has, which reforms the law's precepts answerably to the circumstances of the times, with a view to man's salvation. In fine, let him who contends that the Sabbath is still to be observed as a balm of salvation, and circumcision on the eighth day because of the threat of death, teach us that, for the time past, righteous men kept the Sabbath, or practised circumcision, and were thus rendered "friends of God." For if circumcision purges a man since God made Adam uncircumcised, why did He not circumcise him, even after his sinning, if circumcision purges? At all events, in settling him in paradise, He appointed one uncircumcised as colonist of paradise. Therefore, since God originated Adam uncircumcised, and inobservant of the Sabbath, consequently his offspring also, Abel, offering Him sacrifices, uncircumcised and inobservant of the Sabbath, was by Him commended; while He accepted[3] what he was offering in simplicity of heart, and reprobated the sacrifice of his brother Cain, who was not rightly dividing what he was offering.[4] Noah also, uncircumcised—yes, and inobservant of the Sabbath—God freed from the deluge.[5] For Enoch, too, most righteous man, uncircumcised and inobservant of the Sabbath, He translated from

this world;[6] who did not first taste[7] death, in order that, being a candidate for eternal life,[8] he might by this time show us that we also may, without the burden of the law of Moses, please God. Melchizedek also, "the priest of the most high God," uncircumcised and inobservant of the Sabbath, was chosen to the priesthood of God.[9] Lot, withal, the brother[10] of Abraham, proves that it was for the merits of righteousness, without observance of the law, that he was freed from the conflagration of the Sodomites.[11]

CHAP. III.—OF CIRCUMCISION AND THE SUPERCESSION OF THE OLD LAW.

But Abraham, (you say,) was circumcised. Yes, but he pleased God before his circumcision;[12] nor yet did he observe the Sabbath. For he had "accepted"[13] circumcision; but such as was to be for "a sign" of that time, not for a prerogative title to salvation. In fact, subsequent patriarchs were uncircumcised, like Melchizedek, who, uncircumcised, offered to Abraham himself, already circumcised, on his return from battle, bread and wine.[14] "But again," (you say) "the son of Moses would upon one occasion have been choked by an angel, if Zipporah[15] had not circumcised the foreskin of the infant with a pebble; whence, "there is the greatest peril if any fail to circumcise the foreskin of his flesh." Nay, but if circumcision altogether brought salvation, even Moses himself, in the case of his own son, would not have omitted to circumcise him on the eighth day; whereas it is agreed that Zipporah did it on the journey, at the compulsion of the angel. Consider we, accordingly, that one single infant's compulsory circumcision cannot have prescribed to every people, and founded, as it were, a law for keeping this precept. For God, foreseeing that He was about to give this circumcision to the people of Israel for "a sign," not for salvation, urges the circumcision of the son of Moses, their future leader, for this reason; that, since He had begun, through him, to give the People the precept of cir-

---

[1] Comp. Gen. xv. 13 with Ex. xii. 40–42 and Acts vii. 6.
[2] John i. 17.
Or, "credited him with."
[4] Gen. iv. 1–7, especially in the LXX.; comp. Heb. xi. 4.
[5] Gen. vi. 18, vii. 23; 2 Pet. ii. 5.

[6] See Gen. v. 22, 24; Heb. xi. 5.
[7] Or, perhaps, "has not yet tasted."
[8] Æternitatis candidatus. Comp. ad Ux. l. i. c. vii., and note 3 there.
[9] See above.
[10] i.e., nephew. See Gen. xi. 31, xii. 5.
[11] See Gen. xix. 1–29; and comp. 2 Pet. ii. 6–9.
[12] See Gen. xii.–xv. compared with xvii. and Rom. iv.
[13] Acceperat. So Tertullian renders, as it appears to me, the ἔλαβε of St. Paul in Rom. iv. 11, q. v.
[14] There is, if the text be genuine, some confusion here. Melchizedek does not appear to have been, in any sense, "subsequent" to Abraham, for he probably was senior to him; and, moreover, Abraham does not appear to have been "already circumcised" carnally when Melchizedek met him. Comp. Gen. xiv. with Gen. xvii.
[15] Tertullian writes Seffora; the LXX. in loco, Σεπφώρα, Ex. iv. 24–26, where the Eng. ver. says, "the Lord met him," etc.; the LXX. ἄγγελος Κυρίου.

cumcision, the people should not despise it, from seeing this example (of neglect) already exhibited conspicuously in their leader's son. For circumcision had to be given; but as "a sign," whence Israel in the last time would have to be distinguished, when, in accordance with their deserts, they should be prohibited from entering the holy city, as we see through the words of the prophets, saying, "Your land is desert; your cities utterly burnt with fire; your country, in your sight, strangers shall eat up; and, deserted and subverted by strange peoples, the daughter of Zion shall be derelict, like a shed in a vineyard, and like a watchhouse in a cucumber-field, and as it were a city which is being stormed." [1] Why so? Because the subsequent discourse of the prophet reproaches them, saying, "Sons have I begotten and upraised, but they have reprobated me;" [2] and again, "And if ye shall have outstretched hands, I will avert my face from you; and if ye shall have multiplied prayers, I will not hear you: for your hands are full of blood;" [3] and again, "Woe! sinful nation; a people full of sins; wicked sons; ye have quite forsaken God, and have provoked unto indignation the Holy One of Israel." [4] This, therefore, was God's foresight,—that of giving circumcision to Israel, for a sign whence they might be distinguished when the time should arrive wherein their above-mentioned deserts should prohibit their admission into Jerusalem: which circumstance, because it was to be, used to be announced; and, because we see it accomplished, is recognised by us. For, as the carnal circumcision, which was temporary, was inwrought for "a sign" in a contumacious people, so the spiritual has been given for salvation to an obedient people; while the prophet Jeremiah says, "Make a renewal for you, and sow not in thorns; be circumcised to God, and circumcise the foreskin of your heart:" [5] and in another place he says, "Behold, days shall come, saith the Lord, and I will draw up, for the house of Judah and for the house of Jacob, [6] a new testament; not such as I once gave their fathers in the day wherein I led them out from the land of Egypt." [7] Whence we understand that the coming cessation of the former circumcision then given, and the coming procession of a new law (not such as He had already given to

the fathers), are announced: just as Isaiah foretold, saying that in the last days the mount of the Lord and the house of God were to be manifest above the tops of the mounts: "And it shall be exalted," he says, "above the hills; and there shall come over it all nations; and many shall walk, and say, Come, ascend we unto the mount of the Lord, and unto the house of the God of *Jacob*," [8]—not of *Esau*, the former son, but of *Jacob*, the second; that is, of *our* "people," whose "mount" is Christ, "præcised without concisors' hands, [9] filling every land," shown in the book of Daniel. [10] In short, the coming procession of a new law out of this "house of the God of Jacob" Isaiah in the ensuing words announces, saying, "For from Zion shall go out a law, and the word of the Lord out of Jerusalem, and shall judge among the nations,"—that is, among *us*, who have been called out of the nations,—"and they shall join to beat their glaives into ploughs, and their lances into sickles; and nations shall not take up glaive against nation, and they shall no more learn to fight." [11] Who else, therefore, are understood but *we*, who, fully taught by the new law, observe these practices,—the old law being obliterated, the coming of whose abolition the action itself [12] demonstrates? For the wont of the old law was to avenge itself by the vengeance of the glaive, and to pluck out "eye for eye," and to inflict retaliatory revenge for injury. [13] But the new law's wont was to point to clemency, and to convert to tranquillity the pristine ferocity of "glaives" and "lances," and to remodel the pristine execution of "war" upon the rivals and foes of the law into the pacific actions of "ploughing" and "tilling" the land. [14] Therefore, as we have shown above that the coming cessation of the old law and of the carnal circumcision was declared, so, too, the observance of the new law and the spiritual circumcision has shone out into the voluntary obediences [15] of peace. For "a people," he says, "whom I knew not hath served me; in obedience of the ear it hath obeyed me." [16] Prophets made the announcement. But what is the "people" which was ignorant of God, but *ours*, who in days bygone knew not God? and who, in the

---

[1] Isa. i. 7, 8. See c. xiii. *sub fin.*
[2] Again an error; for these words *precede* the others. These are found in Isa. i. 2.
[3] Isa. i. 15.
[4] Isa. i. 4.
[5] Jer. iv. 3, 4. In Eng. ver., "Break up your fallow ground;" but comp. *de Pu.* c. vi. *ad init.*
[6] So Tertullian. In Jer. *ibid.* "Israel and . . . Judah."
[7] Jer. xxxi. 31, 32 (in LXX. *ibid.* xxxviii. 31, 32); comp. Heb. viii. 8–13.

[8] Isa. ii. 2, 3.
[9] Perhaps an allusion to Phil. iii. 1, 2.
[10] See Dan. ii. 34, 35, 44, 45. See c. xiv. below.
[11] Isa. ii. 3, 4.
[12] *i.e.*, of beating swords into ploughs, etc.
[13] Comp. Ex. xxi. 24, 25; Lev. xxiv. 17–22; Deut. xix. 11–21; Matt. v. 38.
[14] Especially spiritually. Comp. 1 Cor. iii. 6–9, ix. 9, 10, and similar passages.
[15] Obsequia. See *de Pa.* c. iv. note 1.
[16] See Ps. xviii. 43, 44 (xvii. 44, 45 in LXX.), where the Eng. ver. has the future; the LXX., like Tertullian, the past. Comp. 2 Sam. (in LXX. 2 Kings) xxii. 44, 45, and Rom. x. 14–17.

hearing of the ear, gave heed to Him, but *we*, who, forsaking idols, have been converted to God? For Israel—who *had* been known to God, and who had by Him been "upraised"[1] in Egypt, and was transported through the Red Sea, and who in the desert, fed forty years with manna, was wrought to the semblance of eternity, and not contaminated with human passions,[2] or fed on this world's[3] meats, but fed on "angel's loaves"[4]—the manna—and sufficiently bound to God by His benefits—forgat his Lord and God, saying to Aaron: "Make us gods, to go before us: for that Moses, who ejected us from the land of Egypt, hath quite forsaken us; and what hath befallen him we know not." And accordingly we, who "were not the people of God" in days bygone, have been made His people,[5] by accepting the new law above mentioned, and the new circumcision before foretold.

CHAP. IV.—OF THE OBSERVANCE OF THE SABBATH.

It follows, accordingly, that, in so far as the abolition of carnal circumcision and of the old law is demonstrated as having been consummated at its specific times, so also the observance of the Sabbath is demonstrated to have been temporary.

For the Jews say, that from the beginning God sanctified the seventh day, by resting on it from all His works which He made; and that thence it was, likewise, that Moses said to the People: "REMEMBER the day of the sabbaths, to sanctify it: every servile work ye shall not do therein, except what pertaineth unto life."[6] Whence we (Christians) understand that *we* still more ought to observe a sabbath from all "servile work"[7] always, and not only every seventh day, but through all time. And through this arises the question for us, *what* sabbath God willed us to keep? For the Scriptures point to a sabbath eternal and a sabbath temporal. For Isaiah the prophet says, "*Your* sabbaths my soul hateth;"[8] and in another place he says, "*My* sabbaths ye have profaned."[9] Whence we discern that the temporal sabbath is human, and the eternal sabbath is accounted divine; concerning which He predicts through Isaiah: "And there shall be," He says, "month after month, and day

after day, and sabbath after sabbath; and all flesh shall come to adore in Jerusalem, saith the Lord;"[10] which we understand to have been fulfilled in the times of Christ, when "all flesh"—that is, every nation—"came to adore in Jerusalem" God the Father, through Jesus Christ His Son, as was predicted through the prophet: "Behold, proselytes through me shall go unto Thee."[11] Thus, therefore, before this temporal sabbath, there was withal an eternal sabbath foreshown and foretold; just as before the carnal circumcision there was withal a spiritual circumcision foreshown. In short, let them teach us, as we have already premised, that Adam observed the sabbath; or that Abel, when offering to God a holy victim, pleased Him by a religious reverence for the sabbath; or that Enoch, when translated, had been a keeper of the sabbath; or that Noah the ark-builder observed, on account of the deluge, an immense sabbath; or that Abraham, in observance of the sabbath, offered Isaac his son; or that Melchizedek in his priesthood received the law of the sabbath.

But the Jews are sure to say, that ever since this precept was given through Moses, the observance has been binding. Manifest accordingly it is, that the precept was not eternal nor spiritual, but temporary,[12] which would one day cease. In short, so true is it that it is not in the exemption from work of the sabbath—that is, of the seventh day—that the celebration of this solemnity is to consist, that Joshua the son of Nun, at the time that he was reducing the city Jericho by war, stated that he had received from God a precept to order the People that priests should carry the ark of the testament of God seven days, making the circuit of the city; and thus, when the seventh day's circuit had been performed, the walls of the city would spontaneously fall.[13] Which was so done; and when the space of the seventh day was finished, just as was predicted, down fell the walls of the city. Whence it is manifestly shown, that in the number of the seven days there intervened a sabbath-day. For seven days, whencesoever they may have commenced, must necessarily include within them a sabbath-day; on which day not only must the priests have worked, but the city must have been made a prey by the edge of the sword by all the people of Israel. Nor is it doubtful that they "wrought servile work,"

---

[1] Comp. Isa. i. 2 as above, and Acts xiii. 17.
[2] Sæculi.
[3] Or, perhaps, "not affected, as a body, with human sufferings;" in allusion to such passages as Deut. viii. 4 xxix. 5, Neh. ix. 21.
[4] Ps. lxxviii. (lxxvii. in LXX.) 25; comp. John vi. 31, 32.
[5] See Hos. i. 10; 1 Pet. ii. 10.
[6] Comp. Gal. v. 1, iv. 8, 9.
[7] See Ex. xx. 8-11 and xii. 16 (especially in the LXX.).
[8] Isa. i. 13.
[9] This is not said by Isaiah; it is found in substance in Ezek. xxii. 8.
[10] Isa. lxvi. 23 in LXX.
[11] I am not acquainted with any such passage. Oehler refers to Isa. xlix. in his margin, but gives no verse, and omits to notice this passage of the present treatise in his index.
[12] Or, "temporal."
[13] Josh. vi. 1-20.

when, in obedience to God's precept, they drave the preys of war. For in the times of the Maccabees, too, they did bravely in fighting on the sabbaths, and routed their foreign foes, and recalled the law of their fathers to the primitive style of life by fighting on the sabbaths.[1] Nor should I think it was any other law which they thus vindicated, than the one in which they remembered the existence of the prescript touching "the day of the sabbaths."[2]

Whence it is manifest that the force of such precepts was temporary, and respected the necessity of present circumstances; and that it was not with a view to its observance in perpetuity that God formerly gave them such a law.

CHAP. V.—OF SACRIFICES.

So, again, we show that sacrifices of earthly oblations and of spiritual sacrifices[3] were predicted; and, moreover, that from the beginning the earthly were foreshown, in the person of Cain, to be those of the "elder son," that is, of Israel; and the opposite sacrifices demonstrated to be those of the "younger son," Abel, that is, of *our* people. For the elder, Cain, offered gifts to God from the fruit of the earth; but the younger son, Abel, from the fruit of his ewes. "God had respect unto Abel, and unto his gifts; but unto Cain and unto his gifts He had not respect. And God said unto Cain, Why is thy countenance fallen? hast thou not—if thou offerest indeed aright, but dost not divide aright—sinned? Hold thy peace. For unto thee shall thy conversion be and he shall lord it over thee. And then Cain said unto Abel his brother, Let us go into the field: and he went away with him thither, and he slew him. And then God said unto Cain, Where is Abel thy brother? And he said, I know not: am I my brother's keeper? To whom God said, The voice of the blood of thy brother crieth forth unto me from the earth. Wherefore cursed is the earth, which hath opened her mouth to receive the blood of thy brother. Groaning and trembling shalt thou be upon the earth, and every one who shall have found thee shall slay thee."[4] From this proceeding we gather that the twofold sacrifices of "the peoples" were even from the very beginning foreshown. In short, when the sacerdotal law was being drawn up, through Moses, in Leviticus, we find it prescribed to

the people of Israel that sacrifices should in no other place be offered to God than in the land of promise; which the Lord God was about to give to "the people" Israel and to their brethren, in order that, on Israel's introduction thither, there should there be celebrated sacrifices and holocausts, as well for sins as for souls; and nowhere else but in the holy land.[5] Why, accordingly, does the Spirit afterwards predict, through the prophets, that it should come to pass that in every place and in every land there should be offered sacrifices to God? as He says through the angel Malachi, one of the twelve prophets: "I will not receive sacrifice from your hands; for from the rising sun unto the setting my Name hath been made famous among all the nations, saith the Lord Almighty: and in every place they offer clean sacrifices to my Name."[6] Again, in the Pslams, David says: "Bring to God, ye countries of the nations"—undoubtedly because "unto every land" the preaching of the apostles had to "go out"[7]—"bring to God fame and honour; bring to God the sacrifices of His name: take up[8] victims and enter into His courts."[9] For that it is not by earthly sacrifices, but by spiritual, that offering is to be made to God, we thus read, as it is written, An heart contribulate and humbled is a victim for God;"[10] and elsewhere, "Sacrifice to God a sacrifice of praise, and render to the Highest thy vows."[11] Thus, accordingly, the spiritual "sacrifices of praise" are pointed to, and "an heart contribulate" is demonstrated an acceptable sacrifice to God. And thus, as carnal sacrifices are understood to be reprobated—of which Isaiah withal speaks, saying, "To what end is the multitude of your sacrifices to me? saith the Lord"[12]—so spiritual sacrifices are predicted[13] as accepted, as the prophets announce. For, "even if ye shall have brought me," He says, "the finest wheat flour, it is a vain supplicatory gift: a thing execrable to me;" and again He says, "Your holocausts and sacrifices, and the fat of goats, and blood of bulls, I will not, not even if ye come to be seen by me: for who hath required these things from your hands?"[14] for "from the rising sun unto the setting, my Name hath been made famous among all the nations,

[1] See 1 Macc. ii. 41, etc.
[2] See Ex. xx. 8; Deut. v. 12, 15: in LXX.
[3] This tautology is due to the author, not to the translator: "sacrificia . . . spiritalium sacrificiorum."
[4] See Gen. iv. 2-14. But it is to be observed that the version given in our author differs widely in some particulars from the Heb. and the LXX.
[5] See Lev. xvii. 1-9; Deut. xii. 1-26.
[6] See Mal. i. 10, 11, in LXX.
[7] Comp. Matt. xxviii. 19, 20, Mark xvi. 15, 16, Luke xxiv, 45-48, with Ps. xix. 4 (xviii. 5 in LXX.), as explained in Rom. x. 18.
[8] Tollite = Gr. ἄρατε. Perhaps = "away with."
[9] See Ps. xcvi. (xcv. in LXX.) 7, 8; and comp. xxix. (xxviii. in LXX.) 1, 2.
[10] See Ps. li. 17 (in LXX. l. 19).
[11] Ps. l. (xlix. in LXX.) 14.
[12] Isa. i. 11.
[13] Or, "foretold."
[14] Comp. Isa. i. 11-14, especially in the LXX.

saith the Lord."[1] But of the spiritual sacrifices He adds, saying, "And in every place they offer clean sacrifices to my Name, saith the Lord."[1]

CHAP. VI.—OF THE ABOLITION AND THE ABOLISHER OF THE OLD LAW.

Therefore, since it is manifest that a sabbath temporal was shown, and a sabbath eternal foretold; a circumcision carnal foretold, and a circumcision spiritual pre-indicated; a law temporal and a law eternal formally declared; sacrifices carnal and sacrifices spiritual foreshown; it follows that, after all these precepts had been given carnally, in time preceding, to the people Israel, there was to supervene a time whereat the precepts of the ancient Law and of the old ceremonies would cease, and the promise[2] of the new law, and the recognition of spiritual sacrifices, and the promise of the New Testament, supervene;[3] while the light from on high would beam upon us who were sitting in darkness, and were being detained in the shadow of death.[4] And so there is incumbent on us a necessity[5] binding us, since we have premised that a new law was predicted by the prophets, and that not such as had been already given to their fathers at the time when He led them forth from the land of Egypt,[6] to show and prove, on the one hand, that that old Law has ceased, and on the other, that the promised new law is now in operation.

And, indeed, first we must inquire whether there be expected a giver of the new law, and an heir of the new testament, and a priest of the new sacrifices, and a purger of the new circumcision, and an observer of the eternal sabbath, to suppress the old law, and institute the new testament, and offer the new sacrifices, and repress the ancient ceremonies, and suppress[7] the old circumcision together with its own sabbath,[8] and announce the new kingdom which is not corruptible. Inquire, I say, we must, whether this giver of the new law, observer of the spiritual sabbath, priest of the eternal sacrifices, eternal ruler of the eternal kingdom, be come or no: that, if he is already come, service may have to be rendered him; if he is not yet come, he may have to be awaited, until by his advent it be manifest that the old Law's precepts are suppressed, and that the beginnings of the new law ought to arise. And, primarily, we must lay it down that the ancient Law and the prophets could not have ceased, unless He were come who was constantly announced, through the same Law and through the same prophets, as to come.

CHAP. VII.—THE QUESTION WHETHER CHRIST BE COME TAKEN UP.

Therefore upon this issue plant we foot to foot, whether the Christ who was constantly announced as to come be already come, or whether His coming be yet a subject of hope. For proof of which question itself, the times likewise must be examined by us when the prophets announced that the Christ would come; that, if we succeed in recognising that He has come within the limits of those times, we may without doubt believe Him to be the very one whose future coming was ever the theme of prophetic song, upon whom *we*—the nations, to wit—were ever announced as destined to believe; and that, when it shall have been agreed that He is come, we may undoubtedly likewise believe that the new law has by Him been given, and not disavow the new testament in Him and through Him drawn up for us. For that Christ was to come we know that even the Jews do not attempt to disprove, inasmuch as it is to His advent that they are directing their hope. Nor need we inquire at more length concerning *that* matter, since in days bygone all the prophets have prophesied of it; as Isaiah: "Thus saith the Lord God to my Christ (the) Lord,[9] whose right hand I have holden, that the nations may hear Him: the powers of kings will I burst asunder; I will open before Him the gates, and the cities shall not be closed to Him." Which very thing we see fulfilled. For whose right hand does God the Father hold but Christ's, His Son?—whom all nations have heard, that is, whom all nations have believed,—whose preachers, withal, the apostles, are pointed to in the Psalms of David: "Into the universal earth," says he, "is gone out their sound, and unto the ends of the earth their words."[10] For upon whom else have the universal nations believed, but upon the Christ who is already come? For whom have the nations believed,—Parthians, Medes, Elamites, and they who inhabit Mesopotamia, Armenia, Phrygia, Cappadocia, and they who

---

[1] See Mal. i. as above.
[2] Or, "sending forth"—promissio.
[3] The tautology is again due to the author.
[4] Comp. Luke i. 78, 79, Isa. ix. 1, 2, with Matt. iv. 12–16.
[5] Comp. 1 Cor. ix. 16.
[6] See ch. iii. above.
[7] Here again the repetition is the author's.
[8] Cum suo sibi sabbato. Unless the meaning be—which the context seems to forbid—"together with a sabbath of His own:" the Latinity is plainly incorrect.

[9] The reference is to Isa. xlv. 1. A glance at the LXX. will at once explain the difference between the reading of our author and the genuine reading. One letter—an "ι"—makes all the difference. For Κύρῳ has been read Κυρίῳ. In the Eng. ver. we read "*His Anointed.*"
[10] Ps. xix. 4 (xviii. 5 in LXX.) and Rom. x. 18.

dwell in Pontus, and Asia, and Pamphylia, tarriers in Egypt, and inhabiters of the region of Africa which is beyond Cyrene, Romans and sojourners, yes, and in Jerusalem Jews,[1] and all other nations; as, for instance, by this time, the varied races of the Gætulians, and manifold confines of the Moors, all the limits of the Spains, and the diverse nations of the Gauls, and the haunts of the Britons—inaccessible to the Romans, but subjugated to Christ, and of the Sarmatians, and Dacians, and Germans, and Scythians, and of many remote nations, and of provinces and islands many, to us unknown, and which we can scarce enumerate? In all which places the name of the Christ who is already come reigns, as of Him before whom the gates of all cities have been opened, and to whom none are closed, before whom iron bars have been crumbled, and brazen gates[2] opened. Although there be withal a spiritual sense to be affixed to these expressions,—that the hearts of individuals, blockaded in various ways by the devil, are unbarred by the faith of Christ, —still they have been evidently fulfilled, inasmuch as in all these places dwells the "people" of the Name of Christ. For who *could* have reigned *over all nations* but Christ, God's Son, who was ever announced as destined to reign over all to eternity? For if Solomon "reigned," why, it was within the confines of Judea merely: "from Beersheba unto Dan" the boundaries of his kingdom are marked.[3] If, moreover, Darius "reigned" over the Babylonians and Parthians, he had not power *over all nations;* if Pharaoh, or whoever succeeded him in his hereditary kingdom, over the Egyptians, in that country merely did he possess his kingdom's dominion; if Nebuchadnezzar with his petty kings, "from India unto Ethiopia" he had his kingdom's boundaries;[3] if Alexander the Macedonian, he did not hold more than universal Asia, and other regions, after he had quite conquered them; if the Germans, to this day they are not suffered to cross their own limits; the Britons are shut within the circuit of their own ocean; the nations of the Moors, and the barbarism of the Gætulians, are blockaded by the Romans, lest they exceed the confines of their own regions. What shall I say of the Romans themselves,[5] who fortify their own empire with garrisons of their own legions, nor can extend the might of their kingdom beyond these nations? But Christ's Name is extending everywhere, believed everywhere, worshipped by all the above-enumerated nations, reigning everywhere, adored everywhere, conferred equally everywhere upon all. No king, with Him, finds greater favour, no barbarian lesser joy; no dignities or pedigrees enjoy distinctions of merit; to all He is equal, to all King, to all Judge, to all "God and Lord."[6] Nor would you hesitate to believe what we asseverate, since you see it taking place.

CHAP. VIII.—OF THE TIMES OF CHRIST'S BIRTH AND PASSION, AND OF JERUSALEM'S DESTRUCTION.

Accordingly the times must be inquired into of the predicted and future nativity of the Christ, and of His passion, and of the extermination of the city of Jerusalem, that is, its devastation. For Daniel says, that "both the holy city and the holy place are exterminated together with the coming Leader, and that the pinnacle is destroyed unto ruin."[7] And so the times of the coming Christ, the Leader,[8] must be inquired into, which we shall trace in Daniel; and, after computing them, shall prove Him to be come, even on the ground of the times prescribed, and of competent signs and operations of His. Which matters we prove, again, on the ground of the consequences which were ever announced as to follow His advent; in order that we may believe all to have been as well fulfilled as foreseen.

In such wise, therefore, did Daniel predict concerning Him, as to show both when and in what time He was to set the nations free; and how, after the passion of the Christ, that city had to be exterminated. For he says thus: "In the first year under Darius, son of Ahasuerus, of the seed of the Medes, who reigned over the kingdom of the Chaldees, I Daniel understood in the books the number of the years. . . . And while I was yet speaking in my prayer, behold, the man Gabriel, whom I saw in the vision in the beginning, flying; and he touched me, as it were, at the hour of the evening sacrifice, and made me understand, and spake with me, and said, Daniel I am now come out to imbue thee with understanding; in the beginning of thy supplication went out a word. And I am come to announce to thee, because thou art a man

---

[1] See Acts ii. 9, 10; but comp. ver. 5.
[2] See Isa. xlv. 1, 2 (especially in Lowth's version and the LXX.).
[3] See 1 Kings iv. 25. (In the LXX. it is 3 Kings iv. 25; but the verse is omitted in Tischendorf's text, ed. Lips. 1860, though given in his footnotes there.) The statement in the text differs slightly from Oehler's reading ; where I suspect there is a transposition of a syllable, and that for "in finibus *Judæ* tantum, a *Bersabeæ*," we ought to read "in finibus *Judææ* tantum, a *Bersabe.*" See *de Jej.* c. ix.
[4] See Esth. i. 1, viii. 9.
[5] [Dr. Allix thinks these statements define the Empire after Severus, and hence accepts the date we have mentioned, for this treatise.]
[6] Comp. John xx. 28.
[7] See Dan. ix. 26 (especially in the LXX.).
[8] Comp. Isa. lv. 4.

of desires;[1] and ponder thou on the word, and understand in the vision. Seventy hebdomads have been abridged[2] upon thy commonalty, and upon the holy city, until delinquency be made inveterate, and sins sealed, and righteousness obtained by entreaty, and righteousness eternal introduced; and in order that vision and prophet may be sealed, and an holy one of holy ones anointed. And thou shalt know, and thoroughly see, and understand, from the going forth of a word for restoring and rebuilding Jerusalem unto the Christ, the Leader, hebdomads (seven and an half, and[3]) lxii and an half: and it shall convert, and shall be built into height and entrenchment, and the times shall be renewed: and after these lxii hebdomads shall the anointing be exterminated, and shall not be; and the city and the holy place shall he exterminate together with the Leader, who is making His advent; and they shall be cut short as in a deluge, until (the) end of a war, which shall be cut short unto ruin. And he shall confirm a testament in many. In one hebdomad and the half of the hebdomad shall be taken away my sacrifice and libation, and in the holy place the execration of devastation, (and[4]) until the end of (the) time consummation shall be given with regard to this devastation."[5]

Observe we, therefore, the limit,—how, in truth, he predicts that there are to be lxx hebdomads, *within which* if they receive Him, "it shall be built into height and entrenchment, and the times shall be renewed." But God, foreseeing what was to be—that they will not merely not receive Him, but will both persecute and deliver Him to death—both recapitulated, and said, that in lx and ii and an half of an hebdomad He is born, and an holy one of holy ones is anointed; but that when vii hebdomads[6] and an half were fulfilling, He had to suffer, and the holy city had to be exterminated after one and an half hebdomad, —whereby, namely, the seven and an half hebdomads have been completed. For he says thus: "And the city and the holy place to be exterminated together with the leader

who is to come; and they shall be cut short as in a deluge; and he shall destroy the pinnacle unto ruin."[7] Whence, therefore, do we show that the Christ came within the lxii and an half hebdomads? We shall count, moreover, from the first year of Darius, as at this particular time is shown to Daniel this particular vision; for he says, "And understand and conjecture that at the completion of thy word[8] I make thee these answers." Whence we are bound to compute from the first year of Darius, when Daniel saw this vision.

Let us see, therefore, how the years are filled up until the advent of the Christ:—

For Darius reigned . .	xviiii[9] years (19).
Artaxerxes reigned . .	xl and i years (41).
Then King Ochus (who is also called Cyrus) reigned .	xxiiii years (24).
Argus	one year.
Another Darius, who is also named Melas, . . .	xxi years (21).
Alexander the Macedonian, .	xii years (12).

Then, after Alexander, who had reigned over both Medes and Persians, whom he had reconquered, and had established his kingdom firmly in Alexandria, when withal he called that (city) by his own name;[10] after him reigned, (there, in Alexandria,)

Soter, ...	xxxv years (35).
To whom succeeds Philadelphus, reigning	xxx and viii years (38).
To him succeeds Euergetes, . .	xxv years (25).
Then Philopator . . .	xvii years (17)
After him Epiphanes, . .	xxiiii years (24).
Then another Euergetes, . . .	xxviiii years (29).
Then another Soter, . . .	xxxviii years (38).
Ptolemy . . .	xxxvii years (37).
Cleopatra, . . .	xx years v months (20 5-12).
Yet again Cleopatra reigned jointly with Augustus .	xiii years (13.)
After Cleopatra, Augustus reigned other .	xliii years (43).

For all the years of the empire of Augustus were lvi years (56).

Let us see, moreover, how in the forty-first year of the empire of Augustus, when he has been reigning for xx and viii years after the death of Cleopatra, the Christ is born. (And the same Augustus survived, after Christ is born, xv years; and the remaining times of years to the day of the birth of Christ will

---

[1] Vir desideriorum ; Gr. ἀνὴρ ἐπιθυμιῶν ; Eng. ver. "a man greatly beloved." Elsewhere Tertullian has another rendering—"miserabilis." See *de Jej.* cc. vii, ix.

[2] Or, "abbreviated;" "breviatæ sunt; Gr. συνετμήθησαν. For this rendering, and the interpretations which in ancient and modern days have been founded on it, see G. S. Faber's Dissert. on the prophecy of the seventy weeks, pp. 5, 6, 109-112. (London, 1811.) The whole work will well repay perusal.

[3] These words are given, by Oehler and Rig., on the authority of Pamelius. The mss. and early editions are without them.

[4] Also supplied by Pamelius.

[5] See Dan. ix. 24-27. It seemed best to render with the strictest literality, without regard to anything else ; as an idea will thus be given of ¦the condition of the text, which, as it stands, differs widely, as will be seen, from the Hebrew and also from the LXX., as it stands in the ed. Tisch. Lips. 1860, to which I always adapt my references.

[6] Hebdomad*es* is preferred to Oehler's -*as*, a reading which he follows apparently on slender authority.

[7] There is no trace of these last words in Tischendorf's LXX. here ; and only in his footnotes is the " pinnacle " mentioned.

[8] Or, "speech." The reference seems to be to ver. 23, but there is no such statement in Daniel.

[9] So Oehler ; and I print all these numbers uniformly—as in the former part of the present chapter—exactly in accordance with the Latin forms, for the sake of showing how easily, in such calculations, errors may creep in.

[10] Comp. Ps. xlix. 11 (in LXX. Ps. xlviii. 12).

bring us to the xl first year, which is the xx and viiith of Augustus after the death of Cleopatra.) There are, (then,) made up cccxxx and vii years, v months: (whence are filled up lxii hebdomads and an half: which make up ccccxxxvii years, vi months:) on the day of the birth of Christ. And (then) "righteousness eternal" was manifested, and "an Holy One of holy ones was anointed "— that is, Christ—and "sealed was vision and prophet," and "sins" were remitted, which, through faith in the name of Christ, are washed away[1] for all who believe on Him. But what does he mean by saying that "vision and prophecy *are sealed?*" That all prophets ever announced of Him that He was to come, and had to suffer. Therefore, since the prophecy was fulfilled through His advent, for that reason he said that "vision and prophecy *were sealed;*" inasmuch as He is the signet of all prophets, fulfilling all things which in days bygone they had announced of Him.[2] For after the advent of Christ and His passion there is no longer "vision or prophet" to announce Him as to come. In short, if this is not so, let the Jews exhibit, subsequently to Christ, any volumes of prophets, visible miracles wrought by any angels, (such as those) which in bygone days the patriarchs saw until the advent of Christ, who is now come; since which event "sealed is vision and prophecy," that is, confirmed. And justly does the evangelist[3] write, "The law and the prophets (were) until John" the Baptist. For, on Christ's being baptized, that is, on His sanctifying the waters in His own baptism,[4] all the plenitude of bygone spiritual grace-gifts ceased in Christ, sealing as He did all vision and prophecies, which by His advent He fulfilled. Whence most firmly does he assert that His advent "seals visions and prophecy."

Accordingly, showing, (as we have done,) both the number of the years, and the time of the lx two and an half fulfilled hebdomads, on completion of which, (we have shown) that Christ is come, that is, has been born, let us see what (mean) other "vii and an half hebdomads," which have been subdivided in the abscision of[5] the former hebdomads; (let us see, namely,) in what event they have been fulfilled:—

For, after Augustus who survived after the birth of Christ, are made up . . xv years (15).

To whom succeeded Tiberius Cæsar, and held the empire . . . xx years, vii months, xxviii days (20 etc.).

(In the fiftieth year of his empire Christ suffered. being about xxx years of age when he suffered.)

Again Caius Cæsar, also called Caligula, . . iii years, viii months, xiii days (3 etc.).

Nero Cæsar, . . xi years, ix months, xiii days (11 etc.).

Galba . . . . vii months, vi days. (7 etc.).

Otho . . . . iii days.

Vitellius, . . . viii mos., xxvii days (8mos.)

Vespasian, in the first year of his empire, subdues the Jews in war; and there are made lii years, vi months. For he reigned xi years. And thus, in the day of their storming, the Jews fulfilled the lxx hebdomads predicted in Daniel.

Therefore, when these times also were completed, and the Jews subdued, there afterwards ceased in that place "libations and sacrifices," which thenceforward have not been able to be in that place celebrated; for "the unction," too,[6] was "exterminated" in that place after the passion of Christ. For it had been predicted that the unction *should* be exterminated in that place; as in the Psalms it is prophesied, "They exterminated my hands and feet."[7] And the suffering of this "extermination" was perfected within the times of the lxx hebdomads, under Tiberius Cæsar, in the consulate of Rubellius Geminus and Fufius Geminus, in the month of March, at the times of the passover, on the eighth day before the calends of April,[8] on the first day of unleavened bread, on which they slew the lamb at even, just as had been enjoined by Moses.[9] Accordingly, all the synagogue of Israel *did* slay Him, saying to Pilate, when he was desirous to dismiss Him, "His blood be upon us, and upon our children;"[10] and, "If thou dismiss him, thou art not a friend of Cæsar;"[11] in order that all things might be fulfilled which had been written of Him.[12]

CHAP. IX.—OF THE PROPHECIES OF THE BIRTH AND ACHIEVEMENTS OF CHRIST

Begin we, therefore, to prove that the BIRTH

---

[1] Diluuntur. So Oehler has amended for the reading of the MSS. and edd., "tribuuntur."
[2] Comp. Pusey on Daniel, pp. 178, 179, notes 6, 7, 8, and the passages therein referred to. And for the whole question of the seventy weeks, and of the LXX. version of Daniel, comp. the same book, Lect. iv. and Note E (2d thousand, 1864). See also pp. 376–381 of the same book; and Faber (as above), pp. 293–297.
[3] Or rather, our Lord Himself. See Matt. xi. 13; Luke xvi. 16.
[4] Comp. the very obscure passage in *de Pu.* c. vi., towards the end, on which this expression appears to cast some light.
[5] Or, "in abscision from."

[6] And, without "unction"—i.e. without a priesthood, the head whereof, or high priest, was always anointed—no "sacrifices" were lawful.
[7] See Ps. xxii. 16 (xxi, 17 in LXX.).
[8] i.e., March 25.
[9] Comp. Ex. xii. 6 with Mark xiv. 12, Luke xxii. 7.
[10] See Matt. xxvii. 24, 25, with John xix. 12 and Acts iii. 13.
[11] John xix. 12.
[12] Comp. Luke xxiv. 44, etc.

of Christ was announced by prophets; as Isaiah (*e.g.*,) foretells, "Hear ye, house of David; no petty contest have ye with men, since God is proposing a struggle. Therefore God Himself will give you a sign; Behold, the virgin [1] shall conceive, and bear a son, and ye shall call his name Emmanuel" [2] (which is, interpreted, "God with us" [3]): "butter and honey shall he eat;" [4]: "since, ere the child learn to call father or mother, he shall receive the power of Damascus and the spoils of Samaria, in opposition to the king of the Assyrians." [5]

Accordingly the Jews say: Let us challenge that prediction of Isaiah, and let us institute a comparison whether, in the case of the Christ who is already come, there be applicable to Him, firstly, the name which Isaiah foretold, and (secondly) the signs of it [6] which he announced of Him.

Well, then, Isaiah foretells that it behoves Him to be called Emmanuel; and that subsequently He is to take the power of Damascus and the spoils of Samaria, in opposition to the king of the Assyrians. "Now," say they, "that (Christ) of yours, who is come, neither was called by that name, nor engaged in warfare." But we, on the contrary, have thought they ought to be admonished to recall to mind *the context* of this passage as well. For subjoined is withal the interpretation of Emmanuel—"God with us" [7]—in order that you may regard not the sound only of the name, but the sense too. For the Hebrew sound, which is Emmanuel, has an interpretation, which is, God with us. Inquire, then, whether this speech, "God with us" (which is Emmanuel), be commonly applied to Christ ever since Christ's light has dawned, and I think you will not deny it. For they who out of Judaism believe in Christ, ever since their believing on Him, do, whenever they shall wish to say [8] Emmanuel, signify that God is with us: and thus it is agreed that He who was ever predicted as Emmanuel is already come, because that which Emmanuel signifies is come —that is, "God with us." Equally are they led by the sound of the name when they so understand "the power of Damascus," and "the spoils of Samaria," and "the kingdom of the Assyrians," as if they portended Christ

as a warrior; not observing that Scripture premises, "since, ere the child learn to call father or mother, he shall receive the power of Damascus and the spoils of Samaria, in opposition to the king of the Assyrians." For the first step is to look at the demonstration of His *age*, to see whether the age there indicated can possibly exhibit the Christ as already a *man*, not to say a *general*. Forsooth, by His babyish cry the infant would summon men to arms, and would give the signal of war not with clarion, but with rattle, and point out the foe, not from His charger's back or from a rampart, but from the back or neck of His suckler and nurse, and thus subdue Damascus and Samaria in place of the breast. (It is another matter if, among you, infants rush out into battle,—oiled first, I suppose, to dry in the sun, and then armed with satchels and rationed on butter,—who are to know how to lance sooner than how to lacerate the bosom!) [9] Certainly, if nature nowhere allows this,—(namely,) to serve as a soldier before developing into manhood, to take "the power of Damascus" before knowing your father,— it follows that the pronouncement is visibly figurative. "But again," say they, "nature suffers not a 'virgin' to be a parent; and yet the prophet must be believed." And deservedly so; for he bespoke credit for a thing incredible, by saying that it was to be *a sign*. "Therefore," he says, "shall A SIGN be given you. Behold, a virgin shall conceive in womb, and bear a son." But a sign from God, unless it had consisted in some portentous novelty, would not have appeared a sign. In a word, if, when you are anxious to cast any down from (a belief in) this divine prediction, or to convert whoever are simple, you have the audacity to lie, as if the Scripture contained (the announcement), that not "a virgin," but "a young female," was to conceive and bring forth; you are refuted even by this fact, that a daily occurrence—the pregnancy and parturition of a young female, namely—cannot possibly seem anything of *a sign*. And the setting before us, then, of a virgin-mother is deservedly believed to be *a sign;* but not equally so a warrior-infant. For there would not in this case again be involved the question of a *sign;* but, the *sign* of a novel birth having been awarded, the next step after the *sign* is, that there is enunciated a different ensuing ordering [10] of the infant, who is to eat "honey and butter." Nor is this, of course, for a *sign*. It is natural to infancy. But that he

---

[1] "*A* virgin," Eng. ver.; ἡ παρθένος, LXX.; "*the* virgin," Lowth.
[2] See Isa. vii. 13, 14.
[3] See Matt. i. 23.
[4] See Isa. vii. 15.
[5] See Isa. viii. 4. (All these passages should be read in the LXX.)
[6] i.e., of the predicted name. [Here compare *Against Marcion*, Book III. (vol. vii. Edin. series) Cap. xii. p. 142. See my note (1) on Chapter First; and also Kaye, p. xix.]
[7] In Isa. viii. 8, 10, compared with vii. 14 in the Eng. ver. and the LXX., and also Lowth, introductory remarks on ch. viii.
[8] Or, "to call Him."

[9] See *adv. Marc.* l. iii. c. xiii., which, with the preceding chapter, should be compared throughout with the chapter before us.
[10] Comp. Judg. xiii. 12; Eng. ver., "How shall we *order* the child?"

11

is to receive [1] "the power of Damascus and the spoils of Samaria in opposition to the king of the Assyrians," this is a wondrous *sign*. Keep to the limit of (the infant's) *age*, and inquire into the sense of the prediction; nay, rather, repay to truth what you are unwilling to credit her with, and the prophecy becomes intelligible by the relation of its fulfilment. Let those Eastern magi be believed, dowering with gold and incense the infancy of Christ as a king; [2] and the infant has received "the power of Damascus" without battle and arms. For, besides the fact that it is known to all that the "power"—for that is the "strength"—of the East is wont to abound in gold and odours, certain it is that the divine Scriptures regard "gold" as constituting the "power" also of all other nations; as it says [3] through Zechariah: "And Judah keepeth guard at Jerusalem, and shall amass all the vigour of the surrounding peoples, gold and silver." [4] For of this gift of "gold" David likewise says, "And to Him shall be given of the gold of Arabia;" [5] and again, "The kings of the Arabs and Saba shall bring Him gifts." [6] For the East, on the one hand, generally held the magi (to be) kings; and Damascus, on the other hand, used formerly to be reckoned to Arabia before it was transferred into Syrophœnicia on the division of the Syrias: the "power" whereof Christ then "received" in receiving its ensigns,—gold, to wit, and odours. "The spoils," moreover, "of Samaria" (He received in receiving) the magi themselves, who, on recognising Him, and honouring Him with gifts, and adoring Him on bended knee as Lord and King, on the evidence of the guiding and indicating star, became "the spoils of Samaria," that is, of idolatry—by believing, namely, on Christ. For (Scripture) denoted idolatry by the name of "Samaria," Samaria being ignominious on the score of idolatry; for she had at that time revolted from God under King Jeroboam. For this, again, is no novelty to the Divine Scriptures, figuratively to use a transference of *name* grounded on parallelism of *crimes*. For it [7] calls your rulers "rulers of Sodom," and your people the "people of Gomorrha," [8] when those cities had already long been extinct. [9] And elsewhere it says, through a prophet, to the people of Israel, "Thy father

(was) an Amorite, and thy mother an Hittite;" [10] of whose race they were not begotten, but (were called their sons) by reason of their consimilarity in impiety, whom of old (God) had called *His own sons* through Isaiah the prophet: "I have generated and exalted sons." [11] So, too, Egypt is sometimes understood to mean the whole world [12] in that prophet, on the count of superstition and malediction. [13] So, again, Babylon, in our own John, is a figure of the city Rome, as being equally great and proud of her sway, and triumphant over the saints. [14] On this wise, accordingly, (Scripture) [15] entitled the magi also with the appellation of "Samaritans,"—"despoiled" (of that) which they had had in common with the Samaritans, as we have said —idolatry in opposition to the Lord. (It [16] adds), "in opposition," moreover, "to the king of the Assyrians,"—in opposition to the devil, who to this hour thinks himself to be reigning, if he detrudes the saints from the religion of God.

Moreover, this our interpretation will be supported while (we find that) elsewhere as well the Scriptures designate Christ a warrior, as we gather from the names of certain weapons, and words of that kind. But by a comparison of the remaining senses the Jews shall be convicted. "Gird thee," says David, "the sword upon the thigh." [17] But what do you read above concerning the Christ? "Blooming in beauty above the sons of men; grace is outpoured in thy lips." [18] But very absurd it is if he was complimenting on the bloom of his beauty and the grace of his lips, one whom he was girding for war with a sword; of whom he proceeds subjunctively to say, "Outstretch and prosper, advance and reign!" And he has added, "because of thy lenity and justice." [19] Who will ply the sword without practising the contraries to lenity and justice; that is, guile, and asperity, and injustice, proper (of course) to the business of battles? See we, then, whether that which has another action be not another sword,— that is, the Divine word of God, doubly sharpened [20] with the two Testaments of the ancient law and the new law; sharpened by the equity of its own wisdom; rendering to each one according to his own action. [21] Law-

---

[1] Or, "accept."
[2] See Matt. ii. 1–12.
[3] Of course he ought to have said, "*they say*."
[4] Zech. xiv. 14, omitting the last clause.
[5] Ps. lxxii. 15 (lxxi. 15 in LXX.): "Sheba" in Eng. ver.; "Arabia" in the "Great Bible" of 1539; and so the LXX.
[6] Ps. lxxii. 10, in LXX, and "Great Bible;" "Sheba and Seba," Eng. ver.
[7] Strictly, Tertullian ought to have said "they call," having above said "Divine Scriptures;" as above on the preceding page.
[8] Isa. i. 10.
[9] See Gen. xix. 23–29.

[10] Ezek. xvi. 3, 45.
[11] Isa. i. 2, as before.
[12] Orbis.
[13] Oehler refers to Isa. xix. 1. See, too, Isa. xxx. and xxxi.
[14] See Rev. xvii., etc.
[15] Or we may supply here ["Isaiah"].
[16] Or, "he."
[17] Ps. xlv. 3, clause 1 (in LXX. Ps. xliv. 4).
[18] See Ps. xlv. 2 (xliv. 3 in LXX.).
[19] Ps. xlv. 4 (xliv. 5 in LXX.).
[20] Comp. Heb. iv. 12; Rev. i. 16, ii. 12, xix. 15, 21; also Eph. vi. 17.
[21] Comp. Ps. lxii. 12 (lxi. 13 in LXX.); Rom. ii. 6.

ful, then, it was for the Christ of God to be precinct, in the Psalms, without warlike achievements, with the figurative sword of the word of God; to which sword is congruous the predicated "bloom," together with the "grace of the lips;" with which sword He was then "girt upon the thigh," in the eye of David, when He was announced as about to come to earth in obedience to God the Father's decree. "The greatness of thy right hand, he says, "shall conduct thee"[1] —the virtue to wit, of the spiritual grace from which the recognition of Christ is deduced. "Thine arrows," he says, "are sharp,"[2]—God's everywhere-flying precepts (arrows) threatening the exposure[3] of every heart, and carrying compunction and transfixion to each conscience: "peoples shall fall beneath thee,"[4]—of course, in adoration. Thus mighty in war and weapon-bearing is Christ; thus will He "receive the spoils," not of "Samaria" alone, but of all nations as well. Acknowledge that His "spoils" are figurative whose weapons you have learnt to be allegorical. And thus, so far, the Christ who is come was not a warrior, because He was not predicted as such by Isaiah.

"But if the Christ," say they, "who is believed to be coming is not called Jesus, why is he who is come called Jesus Christ?" Well, each name will meet in the Christ of God, in whom is found likewise the appellation[5] Jesus. Learn the habitual character of your error. In the course of the appointing of a successor to Moses, Oshea[6] the son of Nun[7] is certainly transferred from his pristine name, and begins to be called Jesus.[8] Certainly, you say. This we first assert to have been a figure of the future. For, because Jesus Christ was to introduce the second people (which is composed of us nations, lingering deserted in the world[9] aforetime) into the land of promise, "flowing with milk and honey"[10] (that is, into the possession of eternal life, than which nought is sweeter); and this had to come about, not through Moses (that is, not through the Law's

discipline), but through Joshua (that is, through the new law's grace), after our circumcision with "a knife of rock"[11] (that is, with Christ's precepts, for Christ is in many ways and figures predicted as a rock[12]); therefore the man who was being prepared to act as images of this sacrament was inaugurated under the figure of the Lord's name, even so as to be named Jesus.[13] For He who ever spake to Moses was the Son of God Himself; who, too, was always seen.[14] For God the Father none ever saw, and lived.[15] And accordingly it is agreed that the Son of God Himself spake to Moses, and said to the people, "Behold, I send mine angel before thy"—that is, the people's—"face, to guard thee on the march, and to introduce thee into the land which I have prepared thee: attend to him, and be not disobedient to him; for he hath not escaped[16] thy notice, since my name is upon him."[17] For Joshua was to introduce the people into the land of promise, not Moses. Now He called him an "angel," on account of the magnitude of the mighty deeds which he was to achieve (which mighty deeds Joshua the son of Nun did, and you yourselves read), and on account of his office of prophet announcing (to wit) the divine will; just as withal the Spirit, speaking in the person of the Father, calls the forerunner of Christ, John, a future "angel," through the prophet: "Behold, I send mine angel before Thy"—that is, Christ's—"face, who shall prepare Thy way before Thee."[18] Nor is it a novel practice to the Holy Spirit to call those "angels" whom God has appointed as ministers of His power. For the same John is called not merely an "angel" of Christ, but withal a "lamp" shining before Christ: for David predicts, "I have prepared the lamp for my Christ;"[19] and him Christ Himself, coming "to fulfil the prophets,"[20] called so to the Jews. "He was," He says, "the burning and shining lamp;"[21] as being he who not merely "prepared His ways in the desert,"[22] but withal, by pointing out "the Lamb of God,"[23] illumined the minds of men by his heralding, so that they understood Him

---

[1] See Ps. xlv. 5 (xliv, 6 in LXX.).
[2] Ps. xlv. 5 (xliv. 6 in LXX.).
[3] Traductionem (comp. Heb. iv. 13).
[4] Ps. xlv. 5.
[5] I can find no authority for "appellatus" as a substantive, but such forms are familiar with Tertullian. Or perhaps we may render: "in that He is found to have been likewise called Jesus."
[6] Auses; Αὐσῆ in LXX.
[7] Nave; Ναυή in LXX.
[8] Jehoshua, Joshua, Jeshua, Jesus, are all forms of the same name. But the change from Oshea or Hoshea to Jehoshua appears to have been made when he was sent to spy the land. See Num. xiii. 16 (17 in LXX., who call it a surnaming).
[9] If Oehler's "in sæculo desertæ" is to be retained, this appears to be the construction. But this passage, like others above noted, is but a reproduction of parts of the third book in answer to Marcion; and there the reading is "in sæculi desertis"="in the desert places of the world," or "of heathendom."
[10] See Ex. iii. 8, and the references there.

[11] See Josh. v. 2-9, especially in LXX. Comp. the margin in the Eng. ver. on ver. 2, "flint knives," and Wordsworth in loc., who refers to Ex. iv. 25, for which see ch. iii. above.
[12] See especially 1 Cor. x. 4.
[13] Or, "Joshua."
[14] Comp. Num. xii. 5-8.
[15] Comp. Ex. xxxiii. 20; John i. 18, xiv. 9; Col. i. 15; Heb. i. 3.
[16] Oehler and others read "celavit;" but the correction of Fr. Junius and Rig., "celabit," is certainly more agreeable to the LXX. and the Eng. ver.
[17] Ex. xxiii. 20, 21.
[18] Mal. iii. 1: comp. Matt. xi. 10; Mark i. 2; Luke vii. 27.
[19] See Ps. cxxxii. 17 (cxxi. 17 in LXX.).
[20] Matt. v. 17, briefly; a very favourite reference with Tertullian.
[21] John v. 35, ὁ λύχνος ὁ καιόμενος καὶ φαίνων.
[22] Comp. reference 8, p. 232; and Isa. xl. 3, John i. 23.
[23] See John i. 29, 36.

to be that Lamb whom Moses was wont to announce as destined to suffer. Thus, too, (was the son of Nun called) JOSHUA, on account of the future mystery[1] of his name: for that name (He who spake with Moses) confirmed as His own which Himself had conferred on him, because He had bidden him thenceforth be called, not "angel" nor "Oshea," but "Joshua." Thus, therefore, each name is appropriate to the Christ of God—that He should be called Jesus as well (as Christ).

And that the virgin of whom it behoved Christ to be born (as we have above mentioned) must derive her lineage of the seed of David, the prophet in subsequent passages evidently asserts. "And there shall be born," he says, "a rod from the root of Jesse"—which rod is Mary—"and a flower shall ascend from his root: and there shall rest upon him the Spirit of God, the spirit of wisdom and understanding, the spirit of discernment and piety, the spirit of counsel and truth; the spirit of God's fear shall fill Him."[2] For to none of men was the universal aggregation of spiritual credentials appropriate, except to Christ; paralleled as He is to a "flower" by reason of glory, by reason of grace; but accounted "of the root of Jesse," whence His origin is to be deduced,—to wit, through Mary.[3] For He was from the native soil of Bethlehem, and from the house of David; as, among the Romans, Mary is described in the census, of whom is born Christ.[4]

I demand, again—granting that He who was ever predicted by prophets as destined to come out of Jesse's race, was withal to exhibit all humility, patience, and tranquillity—whether He be come? Equally so (in this case as in the former), the man who is shown to bear that character will be the very Christ who is come. For of Him the prophet says, "A man set in a plague, and knowing how to bear infirmity;" who "was led as a sheep for a victim; and, as a lamb before him who sheareth him, opened not His mouth."[5] If He "neither did contend nor shout, nor was His voice heard abroad," who "crushed not the bruised reed"—Israel's faith, who "quenched not the burning flax"[6]—that is, the momentary glow of the Gentiles—but made it shine more by the rising of His own light,—He can be none other than He who was predicted. The action, therefore, of the Christ who is come must be examined by

being placed side by side with the rule of the Scriptures. For, if I mistake not, we find Him distinguished by a twofold operation,—that of *preaching* and that of *power*. Now, let each count be disposed of summarily. Accordingly, let us work out the order we have set down, teaching that Christ was announced as a *preacher;* as, through Isaiah: "Cry out," he says, "in vigour, and spare not; lift up, as with a trumpet, thy voice, and announce to my commonalty their crimes, and to the house of Jacob their sins. Me from day to day they seek, and to learn my ways they covet, as a people which hath done righteousness, and hath not forsaken the judgment of God," and so forth:[7] that, moreover, He was to do acts of *power* from the Father: "Behold, our God will deal retributive judgment; Himself will come and save us: then shall the infirm be healed, and the eyes of the blind shall see, and the ears of the deaf shall hear, and the mutes' tongues shall be loosed, and the lame shall leap as an hart,"[8] and so on; which works not even you deny that Christ did, inasmuch as you were wont to say that, "on account of the works ye stoned Him not, but because He did them on the Sabbaths."[9]

CHAP. X.—CONCERNING THE PASSION OF CHRIST, AND ITS OLD TESTAMENT PREDICTIONS AND ADUMBRATIONS.

Concerning the last step, plainly, of His passion you raise a doubt; affirming that the passion of the cross was not predicted with reference to Christ, and urging, besides, that it is not credible that God should have exposed His own Son to that kind of death; because Himself said, "Cursed *is* every one who shall have hung on a tree."[10] But the *reason* of the case antecedently explains the sense of this malediction; for He says in Deuteronomy: "If, moreover, (a man) shall have been (involved) in some sin incurring the judgment of death, and shall die, and ye shall suspend him on a tree, his body shall not remain on the tree, but with burial ye shall bury him on the very day; because cursed by God is every one who shall have been suspended on a tree; and ye shall not defile the land which the Lord thy God shall give thee for (thy) lot."[11] Therefore He did not maledictively adjudge Christ to this passion, but drew a distinction, that whoever, *in any sin*, had incurred the judgment of death, and died suspended on a

---

[1] Sacramentum.
[2] See Isa. xi. 1, 2, especially in LXX.
[3] See Luke i. 27.
[4] See Luke ii. 1-7.
[5] See Isa. liii. 3, 7, in LXX.; and comp. Ps. xxxviii. 17 (xxxvii. 18 in LXX.) in the "Great Bible" of 1539.
[6] See Isa. xlii. 2, 3, and Matt. xii. 19, 20.

[7] See Isa. lviii. 1, 2, especially in LXX.
[8] See Isa. xxxv. 4, 5, 6.
[9] See John v. 17, 18, compared with x. 31-33.
[10] Comp. Deut. xxi. 23 with Gal. iii. 13, with Prof. Lightfoot on the latter passage.
[11] Deut. xxi. 22, 23 (especially in the LXX.).

tree, *he* should be "cursed by God," because
his own sins were the cause of his suspension
on the tree. On the other hand, Christ, who
spake not guile from His mouth,[1] and who
exhibited all righteousness and humility, not
only (as we have above recorded it predicted
of Him) was not exposed to that kind of death
for his own deserts, but (was so exposed) in
order that what was predicted by the prophets
as destined to come upon Him through your
means[2] might be fulfilled; just as, in the
Psalms, the Spirit Himself of Christ was
already singing, saying, "They were repaying
me evil for good;"[3] and, "What I had not
seized I was then paying in full;[4]" They exterminated my hands and feet;"[5] and, "They
put into my drink gall, and in my thirst they
slaked me with vinegar;"[6] "Upon my vesture
they did cast (the) lot;"[7] just as the other
(outrages) which you were to commit on Him
were foretold,—all which He, actually and
thoroughly suffering, suffered not for any evil
action of His own, but "that the Scriptures
from the mouth of the prophets might be
fulfilled."[8]

And, of course, it had been meet that the
mystery[9] of the passion itself should be
figuratively set forth in predictions; and the
more incredible (that mystery), the more likely
to be "a stumbling-stone,"[10] if it had been
nakedly predicted; and the more magnificent,
the more to be *adumbrated*, that the difficulty
of its intelligence might seek (help from) the
grace of God.

Accordingly, to begin with, Isaac, when led
by his father as a victim, and himself bearing
his own "wood,"[11] was even at that early period
pointing to Christ's death; conceded, as He
was, as a victim by the Father; carrying, as
He did, the "wood" of His own passion.[12]

Joseph, again, himself was made a figure
of Christ[13] in this point alone (to name no
more, not to delay my own course), that he
suffered persecution at the hands of his brethren, and was sold into Egypt, on account of
the favour of God;[14] just as Christ was sold by
Israel—(and therefore,) "according to the
flesh," by His "brethren"[15]—when He is be-

trayed by Judas.[16] For Joseph is withal blest
by his father[17] after this form: "His glory (is
that) of a bull; his horns, the horns of an
unicorn; on them shall he toss nations alike
unto the very extremity of the earth." Of
course no one-horned rhinoceros was there
pointed to, nor any two-horned minotaur.
But Christ was therein signified: "bull," by
reason of each of His two characters,—to
some fierce, as Judge; to others gentle, as
Saviour; whose "horns" were to be the extremities of the *cross*. For even in a ship's
yard—which is part of a *cross*—this is the
name by which the extremities are called;
while the central pole of the mast is a "unicorn." By this power, in fact, of the cross,
and in this manner horned, He does now, on
the one hand, "toss" universal nations
through *faith*, wafting them away from earth
to heaven; and will one day, on the other,
"toss" them through *judgment*, casting them
down from heaven to earth.

He, again, will be the "bull" elsewhere too
in the same scripture.[18]   When Jacob pronounced a blessing on Simeon and Levi, he
prophesies of the scribes and Pharisees; for
from them[19] is derived their[20] origin. For (his
blessing) interprets spiritually thus: "Simeon
and Levi perfected iniquity out of their sect,"[21]
—whereby, to wit, they persecuted Christ:
"into their counsel come not my soul! and
upon their station rest not my heart! because
in their indignation they slew men"—that is,
prophets—"and in their concupiscence they
hamstrung a bull!"[22]—that is, Christ, whom—
after the slaughter of prophets—they slew,
and exhausted their savagery by transfixing
His sinews with nails. Else it is idle if, after
the murder already committed by them, he
upbraids others, and not them, with butchery.[23]

But, to come now to Moses, why, I wonder,
did he merely at the time when Joshua was
battling against Amalek, pray *sitting* with
hands expanded, when, in circumstances so
critical, he ought rather, surely, to have com-

---

[1] See 1 Pet. ii. 22 with Isa. liii. 9.
[2] Oehler's pointing is disregarded.
[3] Ps. xxxv. (xxxiv. in LXX.) 12.
[4] Ps. lxix. 4 (lxviii. 5 in LXX.).
[5] Ps. xxii. 16 (xxi. 17 in LXX.).
[6] Ps. lxix. 21 (lxviii. 22 in LXX.).
[7] Ps. xxii. 18 (xxi. 19 in LXX.).
[8] See Matt. xxvi. 56, xxvii. 34, 35 ; John xix. 23, 24, 28, 32–37.
[9] Sacramentum.
[10] See Rom. ix. 32, 33, with Isa. xxviii. 16 ; 1 Cor. i. 23 ; Gal. v. 11.
[11] Lignum = ξύλον ; constantly used for the "tree."
[12] Comp. Gen. xxii. 1–10 with John xix. 17.
[13] "Christ*um figuratus*" is Oehler's reading, after the two
MSS. and the Pamelian ed. of 1579 ; the rest read "figu*rans*" or
"figu*ravit*."
[14] Manifested *e.g.*, in his *two dreams*. See Gen. xxxvii.
[15] Comp. Rom. ix. 5.

[16] Or, "Judah."
[17] This is an error. It is not "his father," Jacob, but Moses,
who thus blesses him (see Deut. xxxiii. 17. The same error occurs in *adv. Marc.* l. iii. c. xxiii.
[18] Not strictly "the same ;" for here the reference *is* to Gen.
xlix. 5–7.
[19] i.e., Simeon and Levi.
[20] i.e., the scribes and Pharisees.
[21] Perfecerunt iniquitatem ex sua secta. There seems to be a
play on the word "secta" in connection with the outrage committed by Simeon and Levi, as recorded in Gen. xxxiv. 25–31 ; and
for συνετέλεσαν ἀδικίαν ἐξαιρέσεως αὐτῶν (which is the reading of
the LXX., ed. Tisch. 3, Lips. 1860), Tertullian's Latin seems to
have read, συνετέλεσαν ἀδικίαν ἐξ αἱρέσεως αὐτῶν.
[22] See Gen. xlix. 5–7 in LXX. ; and comp. the margin of Eng.
ver. on ver. 7, and Wordsworth *in loc.*, who incorrectly renders
ταῦρον an "ox" here.
[23] What the sense of this is it is not easy to see. It appears to
have puzzled Pam. and Rig. so effectually that they both, conjecturally and without authority, adopted the reading found in *adv.
Marc.* l. iii. c. xviii. (from which book, as usual, the present passage is borrowed), only altering *illis* to *ipsis*.

mended his prayer by knees bended, and hands beating his breast, and a face prostrate on the ground; except it was that there, where the name of the Lord Jesus was the theme of speech—destined as He was to enter the lists one day singly against the devil—the figure of the *cross* was also necessary, (that figure) through which Jesus was to win the victory?[1] Why, again, did the same Moses, after the prohibition of any "likeness of anything,"[2] set forth a brazen serpent, placed on a "tree," in a hanging posture, for a spectacle of healing to Israel, at the time when, after their idolatry,[3] they were suffering extermination by serpents, except that in this case he was exhibiting the Lord's *cross* on which the "serpent" the devil was "made a show of,"[4] and, for every one hurt by such snakes—that is, his angels[5]—on turning intently from the peccancy of sins to the sacraments of Christ's *cross*, salvation was outwrought? For he who then gazed upon *that (cross)* was freed from the bite of the serpents.[6]

Come, now, if you have read in the utterance of the prophet in the Psalms, "God hath reigned *from the tree*,"[7] I wait to hear what you understand thereby; for fear you may perhaps think some carpenter-king[8] is signified, and not Christ, who has reigned from that time onward when he overcame the death which ensued from His passion of "the tree."

Similarly, again, Isaiah says: "For a child is born to us, and to us is given a son."[9] What novelty is that, unless he is speaking of the "Son" of God?—and one is born to us, the beginning of whose government has been made "on His shoulder." What king in the world wears the ensign of his power *on his shoulder*, and does not bear either diadem on his head, or else sceptre in his hand, or else some mark of distinctive vesture? But the *novel* "King of ages," Christ Jesus, alone reared "on His shoulder" His own *novel* glory, and power, and sublimity,—the *cross*, to wit; that, according to the former prophecy, the Lord thenceforth "might reign *from the tree*." For of this tree likewise it is that God hints, through Jeremiah, that you would say, "Come, let us put *wood*[10] *into his bread*, and let

us wear him away out of the land of the living; and his name shall no more be remembered."[11] Of course on His *body* that "wood" was put;[12] for so Christ has revealed, calling His body "bread,"[13] whose body the prophet in bygone days announced under the term "bread." If you shall still seek for predictions of the Lord's cross, the twenty-first Psalm will at length be able to satisfy you, containing as it does the whole passion of Christ; singing, as He does, even at so early a date, His own glory.[14] "They dug," He says, "my hands and feet"[15]—which is the peculiar atrocity of the cross; and again when He implores the aid of the Father, "Save me," He says, out of the mouth of the lion"—of course, of death —"and from the horn of the unicorns my humility,"[16]—from the ends, to wit, of the cross, as we have above shown; which cross neither David himself suffered, nor any of the kings of the Jews: that you may not think the passion of some other particular man is here prophesied than His who alone was so signally crucified by the People.

Now, if the hardness of your heart shall persist in rejecting and deriding all these interpretations, we will prove that it may suffice that the *death* of the Christ had been prophesied, in order that, from the fact that the *nature* of the death had not been specified, it may be understood to have been effected by means of the *cross*[17] and that the passion of the *cross* is not to be ascribed to any but Him whose *death* was constantly being predicted. For I desire to show, in one utterance of Isaiah, His *death*, and *passion*, and *sepulture*. "By the crimes," he says, "of my people was He led unto death; and I will give the evil for His sepulture, and the rich for His death, because He did not wickedness, nor was guile found in his mouth; and God willed to redeem His soul from death,"[18] and so forth. He says again, moreover: "His sepulture hath been taken away from the midst."[19] For neither was He buried except He were dead, nor was His sepulture removed from the midst except through His resurrection. Finally, he subjoins: "Therefore He shall have many for an heritage, and of many shall He divide spoils:[20]" who else (shall so do) but He who

---

[1] See Ex. xvii. 8-16; and comp. Col. ii. 14, 15.
[2] Ex. xx. 4.
[3] Their sin was "speaking against God and against Moses" (Num. xxi. 4-9).
[4] Comp. Col. ii. 14, 15; Matt. xxv. 41; Rev. xii. 9; also Gen. iii. 1, etc.; 2 Cor. xi. 3; Rev. xii. 9.
[5] Comp. 2 Cor. xi. 14, 15; Matt. xxv. 41; Rev. xii. 9.
[6] Comp. *de Idol.* c. v.; *adv. Marc.* l. iii. c. xviii.
[7] A ligno. Oehler refers us to Ps. xcvi. 10 (xcv. 10 in LXX.); but the special words "a ligno" are wanting there, though the text is often quoted by the Fathers.
[8] Lignarium aliquem regem. It is remarkable, in connection herewith, that our Lord is not only called by the Jews "*the carpenter's son*" (Matt. xiii. 55; Luke iv. 22), but "*the carpenter*" (Mark vi. 3).
[9] See Isa. ix. 6.
[10] Lignum.

[11] See Jer. xi. 19 (in LXX.).
[12] i.e., when they laid on Him the crossbeam to carry. See John xix. 17.
[13] See John vi. *passim*, and the various accounts of the institution of the Holy Supper.
[14] It is Ps. xxii. in our Bibles, xxi. in LXX.
[15] Ver. 16 (17 in LXX.).
[16] Ps. xxii. 21 (xxi. 22 in LXX., who render it as Tertullian does).
[17] i.e., perhaps, because of the extreme ignominy attaching to that death, which prevented its being expressly named.
[18] Isa. liii. 8, 9, 10 (in LXX.).
[19] Isa. lvii. 2 (in LXX.).
[20] Isa. liii. 12 (in LXX.). Comp., too, Bp. Lowth. Oehler's pointing again appears to be faulty.

"was born," as we have above shown?—"in return for the fact that His soul was delivered unto death?" For, the *cause* of the favour accorded Him being shown,—in return, to wit, for the injury of *a death* which had to be recompensed,—it is likewise shown that He, destined to attain these rewards *because of* death, was to attain them *after* death—of course after *resurrection*. For that which happened at His passion, that mid-day grew dark, the prophet Amos announces, saying, "And it shall be," he says, "in that day, saith the Lord, the sun shall set at mid-day, and the day of light shall grow dark over the land: and I will convert your festive days into grief, and all your canticles into lamentation; and I will lay upon your loins sackcloth, and upon every head baldness; and I will make the grief like that for a beloved (son), and them that are with him like a day of mourning." [1] For that you would do thus at the beginning of the first month of your new (years) even Moses prophesied, when he was foretelling that all the community of the sons of Israel was [2] to immolate at eventide a lamb, and were to eat [3] this solemn sacrifice of this day (that is, of the passover of unleavened bread) with bitterness;" and added that "it was the *passover of the Lord*," [4] that is, the *passion of Christ*. Which prediction was thus also fulfilled, that "on the first day of un-leavened bread" [5] you slew Christ; [6] and (that the prophecies might be fulfilled) the day hasted to make an "eventide,"—that is, to cause darkness, which was made at mid-day; and thus "your festive days God converted into grief, and your canticles into lamentation." For after the passion of Christ there overtook you even captivity and dispersion, predicted before through the Holy Spirit.

CHAP. XI.—FURTHER PROOFS, FROM EZEKIEL. SUMMARY OF THE PROPHETIC ARGUMENT THUS FAR.

For, again, it is for these deserts of yours that Ezekiel announces your ruin as about to come: and not only in this age [7]—a ruin which has already befallen—but in the "day of retribution," [8] which will be subsequent. From which ruin none will be freed but he who shall have been frontally sealed [9] with the

passion of the Christ whom you have rejected. For thus it is written: "And the Lord said unto me, Son of man, thou hast seen what the elders of Israel do, each one of them in darkness, each in a hidden bed-chamber: because they have said, The Lord seeth us not; the Lord hath derelinquished the earth. And He said unto me, Turn thee again, and thou shalt see greater enormities which these do. And He introduced me unto the thresholds of the gate of the house of the Lord which looketh unto the north; and, behold, there, women sitting and bewailing Thammuz. And the Lord said unto me, Son of man, hast thou seen? Is the house of Judah *moderate*, to do the enormities which they have done? And yet thou art about to see greater affections of theirs. And He introduced me into the inner shrine of the house of the Lord; and, behold, on the thresholds of the house of the Lord, between the midst of the porch and between the midst of the altar, [10] as it were twenty and five men have turned their backs unto the temple of the Lord, and their faces over against the east; these were adoring the sun. And He said unto me, Seest thou, son of man? Are such deeds trifles to the house of Judah, that they should do the enormities which these have done? because they have filled up (the measure of) their impieties, and, behold, *are* themselves, as it were, grimacing; I will deal with mine indignation, [11] mine eye shall not spare, neither will I pity; they shall cry out unto mine ears with a loud voice, and I will not hear them, nay, I will not pity. And He cried into mine ears with a loud voice, saying, The vengeance of this city is at hand; and each one had vessels of extermination in his hand. And, behold, six men were coming toward the way of the high gate which was looking toward the north, and each one's double-axe of dispersion was in his hand: and one man in the midst of them, clothed with a garment reaching to the feet, [12] and a girdle of sapphire about his loins: and they entered, and took their stand close to the brazen altar. And the glory of the God of Israel, which was over the house, in the open court of it, [13] ascended from the cherubim: and the Lord called the man who was clothed with the garment reaching to the feet, who had upon his loins the girdle; and said unto him,

---

[1] See Amos viii. 9, 10 (especially in the LXX.).
[2] Oehler's "esset" appears to be a mistake for "esse."
[3] The change from singular to plural is due to the Latin, not to the translator.
[4] See Ex. xii. 1-11.
[5] See Matt. xxvi. 17; Mark xiv. 12; Luke xxii. 7; John xviii. 28.
[9] Comp. 1 Cor. v. 7.
[7] Sæculo.
[8] Comp. Isa. lxi. 2.
[9] Or possibly, simply, "sealed"—obsignatus.

[10] Inter mediam elam et inter medium altaris: i.e., probably= "between the porch and the altar," as the Eng. ver. has.
[11] So Oehler points, and Tischendorf in his edition of the LXX. points not very differently. I incline to read: "Because they have filled up the measure of their impieties, and, behold (are) themselves, as it were, grimacing, I will," etc.
[12] Comp. Rev. i. 13.
[13] "Quæ fuit super eam" (i.e. super domum) "in subdivali domûs" is Oehler's reading; but it differs from the LXX.

Pass through the midst of Jerusalem, and write the sign Tau [1] on the foreheads of the men who groan and grieve over all the enormities which are done in their midst. And while these things were doing, He said unto an hearer,[2] Go ye after him into the city, and cut short; and spare not with your eyes, and pity not elder or youth or virgin; and little ones and women slay ye all, that they may be thoroughly wiped away; but all upon whom is the sign Tau approach ye not; and begin with my saints." [3] Now the mystery of this "sign" was in various ways predicted; (a "sign") in which the foundation of life was forelaid for mankind; (a "sign") in which the Jews were not to believe: just as Moses beforetime kept on announcing in Exodus,[4] saying, "Ye shall be ejected from the land into which ye shall enter; and in those nations ye shall not be able to rest; and there shall be instability of the print [5] of thy foot: and God shall give thee a wearying heart, and a pining soul, and failing eyes, that they see not: and thy life shall hang on the tree [6] before thine eyes; and thou shalt not trust thy life."

And so, since prophecy has been fulfilled through His advent—that is, through the nativity, which we have above commemorated, and the passion, which we have evidently explained—that is the reason withal why Daniel said, "Vision and prophet *were sealed;*" because Christ is the "signet" of all prophets, fulfilling all that had in days bygone been announced concerning Him: for, since His advent and personal passion, there is no longer "vision" or "prophet;" whence most emphatically he says that His advent "*seals* vision and prophecy." And thus, by showing "the number of the years, and the time of the lxii and an half fulfilled hebdomads," we have proved that at that specified time Christ came, that is, was born; and, (by showing the time) of the "seven and an half hebdomads," which are subdivided so as to be cut off from the former hebdomads, within which times we have shown Christ to have suffered, and by the consequent conclusion of the "lxx hebdomads," and the extermination of the city, (we have proved) that "sacrifice and unction" thenceforth cease.

Sufficient it is thus far, on these points, to have meantime traced the course of the ordained path of Christ, by which He is proved to be such as He used to be announced, even on the ground of that agreement of Scriptures, which has enabled us to speak out, in opposition to the Jews, on the ground [7] of the prejudgment of the major part. For let them not question or deny the writings we produce; that the fact also that things which were foretold as destined to happen *after* Christ are being recognised as fulfilled may make it impossible for them to deny (these writings) to be on a par with divine Scriptures. Else, unless He were come *after* whom the things which were wont to be announced had to be accomplished, would such as have been completed be proved? [8]

CHAP. XII.—FURTHER PROOFS FROM THE CALLING OF THE GENTILES.

Look at the universal nations thenceforth emerging from the vortex of human error to the Lord God the Creator and His Christ; and if you dare to deny that this was prophesied, forthwith occurs to you the promise of the Father in the Psalms, which says, "My Son art Thou; to-day have I begotten Thee. Ask of Me, and I will give Thee Gentiles *as* Thine heritage, and *as* Thy possession *the* bounds of the earth." [9] For you will not be able to affirm that "son" to be David rather than Christ; or the "bounds of the earth" to have been promised rather to David, who reigned within the single (country of) Judea, than to Christ, who has already taken captive the whole orb with the faith of His gospel; as He says through Isaiah: "Behold, I have given Thee for a covenant [10] of my family, for a light of Gentiles, that Thou mayst open the eyes of the blind"—of course, such as err—"to outloose from bonds the bound"—that is, to free them from sins—"and from the house of prison"—that is, of death—"such as sit in darkness" [11]—of ignorance, to wit. And if these blessings accrue through Christ, they will not have been prophesied of another than Him through whom we consider them to have been accomplished. [12]

CHAP. XIII.—ARGUMENT FROM THE DESTRUCTION OF JERUSALEM AND DESOLATION OF JUDEA.

Therefore, since the sons of Israel affirm

---

[1] The MS. which Oehler usually follows omits "Tau;" so do the LXX.
[2] Et in his dixit ad audientem. But the LXX. reading agrees almost *verbatim* with the Eng. ver.
[3] Ezek. viii. 12–ix. 6 (especially in the LXX.). Comp. *adv. Marc.* l. iii. c. xxii. But our author differs considerably even from the LXX.
[4] Or rather in Deuteronomy. See xxviii. 65 sqq.
[5] Or, "sole."
[6] In ligno. There are no such words in the LXX. If the words be retained, "*thy life*" will mean Christ, who is called "our Life" in Col. iii. 4. See also John i. 4, xiv. 6, xi. 25. And so, again, "Thou shalt not trust (or believe) *thy life*" would mean, "Thou shalt not believe Christ."

[7] Or, "in accordance with."
[8] i.e., Would they have happened? and, *by* happening, have been their own proof?
[9] Ps. ii. 7, 8.
[10] Dispositionem; Gr. διαθήκην.
[11] Isa. xlii. 6, 7, comp. lxi. 1; Luke iv. 14–18
[12] Comp. Luke ii. 25–33.

that we err in receiving the Christ, who is already come, let us put in a demurrer against them out of the Scriptures themselves, to the effect that the Christ who was the theme of prediction *is* come; albeit by the times of Daniel's prediction we *have* proved that the Christ is come already who was the theme of announcement. Now it behoved Him to be born in Bethlehem of Judah. For thus it is written in the prophet: "And thou, Bethlehem, are not the least in the leaders of Judah: for out of thee shall issue a Leader, who shall feed my People Israel."[1] But if hitherto he has not been born, what "leader" was it who was thus announced as to proceed from the tribe of Judah, out of Bethlehem? For it behoves him to proceed from the tribe of Judah and from Bethlehem. But we perceive that *now* none of the race of Israel has remained in Bethlehem; and (so it has been) ever since the interdict was issued forbidding any one of the Jews to linger in the confines of the very district, in order that this prophetic utterance also should be perfectly fulfilled: "Your land is desert, your cities burnt up by fire,"—that is, (he is foretelling) what *will have happened* to them in time of war; "your region strangers shall eat up in your sight, and it shall be desert and subverted by alien peoples."[2] And in another place it is thus said through the prophet: "The King with *His* glory ye shall see,"—that is, Christ, doing deeds of power in the glory of God the Father;[3] "and your eyes shall see the land from afar,"[4]—which is what you do, being prohibited, in reward of your deserts, since the storming of Jerusalem, to enter into your land; it is permitted you merely to see it with your eyes from afar: "your soul," he says, "shall meditate terror,"[5]—namely, at the time when they suffered the ruin of themselves.[6] How, therefore, will a "leader" be born from Judea, and how far will he "proceed from Bethlehem," as the divine volumes of the prophets do plainly announce; since none at all is left there to this day of (the house of) Israel, of whose stock Christ could be born?

Now, if (according to the Jews) He is hitherto not come, when He begins to come whence will He be anointed?[7] For the Law enjoined that, in captivity, it was not lawful for the unction of the royal chrism to be compounded.[8] But, if there is no longer "unction" *there*[9] as Daniel prophesied (for he says, "Unction shall be exterminated"), it follows that *they*[10] no longer have it, because neither have they a *temple* where was the "horn"[11] from which kings were wont to be anointed. If, then, there is no unction, whence shall be anointed the "leader" who shall be born in Bethlehem? or how shall he proceed "from Bethlehem," seeing that of the seed of Israel none at all exists in Bethlehem.

A second time, in fact, let us show that Christ is already come, (as foretold) through the prophets, and has suffered, and is already received back in the heavens, and thence is to come accordingly as the predictions prophesied. For, after His advent, we read, according to Daniel, that the city itself had to be exterminated; and we recognise that so it has befallen. For the Scripture says thus, that "the city and the holy place are simultaneously exterminated together with *the leader*,"[12]—undoubtedly (that Leader) who was to proceed "from Bethlehem," and from the tribe of "Judah." Whence, again, it is manifest that "the city must simultaneously be exterminated" at the time when its "Leader" had to suffer in it, (as foretold) through the Scriptures of the prophets, who say: "I have outstretched my hands the whole day unto a People contumacious and gainsaying Me, who walketh in a way not good, but after their own sins."[13] And in the Psalms, *David* says: "They exterminated my hands and feet: they counted all my bones; they themselves, moreover, contemplated and saw me, and in my thirst slaked me with vinegar."[14] These things *David* did not suffer, so as to seem justly to have spoken of himself; but the Christ who was crucified. Moreover, the "hands and feet," are not "exterminated,"[15] except His who is suspended on a "tree." Whence, again, David said that "the Lord would reign *from the tree:*"[16] for elsewhere, too, the prophet predicts the fruit of this "tree," saying "The earth hath given her blessings,"[17]—of course that virgin-earth, not yet irrigated with rains, nor fertilized by

---

[1] Mic. v. 2 ; Matt. ii. 3–6. Tertullian's Latin agrees rather with the Greek of St. Matthew than with the LXX.
[2] See Isa. i. 7.
[3] Comp. John v. 43, x. 37, 38.
[4] Isa. xxxiii. 17.
[5] Isa. xxxiii. 18.
[6] Comp. the "*failing eyes*" in the passage from Deuteronomy given in c. xi., if "eyes" is to be taken as the subject here. If not, we have another instance of the slipshod writing in which this treatise abounds.
[7] As His name "Christ" or "Messiah" implies.

[8] Comp. Ex. xxx. 22–33.
[9] i.e., in Jerusalem or Judea.
[10] The Jews.
[11] Comp. 1 Kings (3 Kings in LXX.) i. 39, where the Eng. ver. has "*an* horn ;" the LXX. τὸ κέρας, "*the* horn ;" which at that time, of course, was in David's tabernacle (2 Sam.—2 Kings in LXX.—vi. 17,) for "temple" there was yet none.
[12] Dan. ix. 26.
[13] See Isa. lxv. 2 ; Rom. x. 21.
[14] Ps. xxii. 16, 17 (xxi. 17, 18, in LXX.), and lxix. 21 (lxviii. 22 in LXX.).
[15] i.e., displaced, dislocated.
[16] See c. x. above.
[17] See Ps. lxvii. 6 (lxvi. 7 in LXX.), lxxxv. 12 (lxxxiv. 13 in LXX.).

showers, out of which man was of yore first formed, out of which now Christ through the flesh has been born of a virgin; "and *the tree*," [1] he says, "hath brought his fruit," [2]—not that "tree" in paradise which yielded death to the protoplasts, but the "tree" of the passion of Christ, whence life, hanging, was by you not believed ! [3] For this "tree" in a mystery, [4] it was of yore wherewith Moses sweetened the bitter water; whence the People, which was perishing of thirst in the desert, drank and revived; [5] just as we do, who, drawn out from the calamities of the heathendom [6] in which we were tarrying perishing with thirst (that is, deprived of the divine word), drinking, "by the faith which is on Him," [7] the baptismal water of the "tree" of the passion of Christ, have revived,—a faith from which Israel has fallen away, (as foretold) through Jeremiah, who says, "Send, and ask exceedingly whether such things have been done, whether nations will change their gods (and these are not gods !). But My People hath changed their glory: whence no profit shall accrue to them: the heaven turned pale thereat" (and when did it turn pale? undoubtedly when Christ suffered), "and shuddered," he says, "most exceedingly;" [8] and "the sun grew dark at mid-day:" [9] (and when did it "shudder exceedingly" except at the passion of Christ, when the earth also trembled to her centre, and the veil of the temple was rent, and the tombs were burst asunder? [10]) "because these two evils hath My People done; Me," He says, "they have quite forsaken, the fount of water of life, [11] and they have digged for themselves worn-out tanks, which will not be able to contain water." Undoubtedly, by not receiving Christ, the "fount of water of life," they have begun to have "worn-out tanks," that is, synagogues for the use of the "dispersions of the Gentiles," [12] in which the Holy Spirit no longer lingers, as for the time past He was wont to tarry in the temple before the advent of Christ, who is the true temple of God. For, that they should withal suffer this thirst of the Divine Spirit, the prophet Isaiah had said, saying:

"Behold, they who serve Me shall eat, but ye shall be hungry; they who serve Me shall drink, but ye shall thirst, and from general tribulation of spirit shall howl: for ye shall transmit your name for a satiety to Mine elect, but you the Lord shall slay; but for them who serve Me shall be named a new name, which shall be blessed in the lands." [13]

Again, the mystery of this "tree" [14] we read as being celebrated even in the Books of the Reigns. For when the sons of the prophets were cutting "wood" [15] with axes on the bank of the river Jordan, the iron flew off and sank in the stream; and so, on Elisha [16] the prophet's coming up, the sons of the prophets beg of him to extract from the stream the iron which had sunk. And accordingly Elisha, having taken "wood," and cast it into that place where the iron had been submerged, forthwith it rose and swam on the surface," [17] and the "wood" sank, which the sons of the prophets recovered. [18] Whence they understood that Elijah's spirit was presently conferred upon him. [19] What is more manifest than the mystery [20] of this "wood," —that the obduracy of this world [21] had been sunk in the profundity of error, and is freed in baptism by the "wood" of Christ, that is, of His passion; in order that what had formerly perished through the "tree" in Adam, should be restored through the "tree" in Christ? [22] while we, of course, who have succeeded to, and occupy, the room of the prophets, at the present day sustain in the world [23] that treatment which the prophets always suffered on account of divine religion: for some they stoned, some they banished; more, however, they delivered to mortal slaughter, [24]—a fact which they cannot deny. [25]

This "wood," again, Isaac the son of Abraham personally carried for his own sacrifice, when God had enjoined that he should be made a victim to Himself. But, because these had been mysteries [26] which were being kept for perfect fulfilment in the times of Christ, Isaac, on the one hand, with his "wood," was reserved, the ram being of-

---

[1] "Lignum," as before.
[2] See Joel ii. 22.
[3] See c. xi. above, and the note there.
[4] Sacramento.
[5] See Ex. xv. 22–26.
[6] Sæculi.
[7] See Acts xxvi. 18, *ad fin.*
[8] See Jer. ii. 10–12.
[9] See Amos viii. 9, as before, in c. x.
[10] See Matt. xxvii. 45, 50–52 ; Mark xv. 33, 37, 38 , Luke xxiii. 44, 45.
[11] ὕδατος ζωῆς in the LXX. here (ed. Tischendorf, who quotes the Cod. Alex. as reading, however, ὕδατος ζῶντος). Comp. Rev. xxii. 1, 17, and xxi. 6; John vii. 37–39. (The reference, it will be seen, is still to Jer. ii. 10–13 ; but the writer has mixed up words of Amos therewith.)
[12] Comp. the τὴν διασπορὰν τῶν Ἑλλήνων of John vii. 35 ; and see 1 Pet. i. 1.

[13] See Isa. lxv. 13–16 in LXX.
[14] Hujus ligni sacramentum.
[15] Lignum.
[16] Heliszo. Comp. Luke iv. 27.
[17] The careless construction of leaving the nominative "Elisha" with no verb to follow it is due to the original, not to the translator.
[18] See 2 Kings vi. 1–7 (4 Kings vi. 1–7 in LXX). It is not said, however, that the wood sank.
[19] This conclusion they had drawn before, and are not said to have drawn, consequently, upon this occasion. See 2 Kings (4 Kings in LXX.) ii. 16.
[20] Sacramento.
[21] "Sæculi," or perhaps here "heathendom."
[22] For a similar argument, see Anselm's *Cur Deus Homo ?* l. i. c. iii. *sub fin.*
[23] Sæculo.
[24] Mortis necem.
[25] Comp. Acts vii. 51, 52 ; Heb. xi. 32–38
[26] Sacramenta.

fered which was caught by the horns in the bramble;[1] Christ, on the other hand, in His times, carried His "wood" on His own shoulders, adhering to the horns of the cross, with a thorny crown encircling His head. For Him it behoved to be made a sacrifice on behalf of all Gentiles, who "was led as a sheep for a victim, and, like a lamb voiceless before its shearer, so opened not His mouth" (for He, when Pilate interrogated Him, spake nothing[2]); for "in humility His judgment was taken away: His nativity, moreover, who shall declare?" Because no one at all of human beings was conscious of the nativity of Christ at His conception, when as the Virgin Mary was found pregnant by the word of God; and because "His life was to be taken from the land."[3] Why, accordingly, after His resurrection from the dead, which was effected on the third day, did the heavens receive Him back? It was in accordance with a prophecy of Hosea, uttered on this wise: "Before daybreak shall they arise unto Me, saying, Let us go and return unto the Lord our God, because Himself will draw us out and free us. After a space of two days, on the third day"[4]—which is His glorious resurrection—He received back into the heavens (whence withal the Spirit Himself had come to the Virgin[5]) Him whose nativity and passion alike the Jews have failed to acknowledge. Therefore, since the Jews still contend that the Christ is not yet come, whom we have in so many ways approved[6] to be come, let the Jews recognise their own fate,—a fate which they were constantly foretold as destined to incur after the advent of the Christ, on account of the impiety with which they despised and slew Him. For first, from the day when, according to the saying of Isaiah, "a man cast forth his abominations, of gold and silver, which they made to adore with vain and hurtful (rites),"[7]—that is, ever since we Gentiles, with our breast doubly enlightened through Christ's truth, cast forth (let the Jews see it) our idols,—what follows has likewise been fulfilled. For "the Lord of Sabaoth *hath taken away*, among the Jews from Jerusalem," among the other things named, "the wise architect" too,[8] who builds the church, God's temple, and the holy city, and the house of the Lord. For thenceforth God's grace desisted (from working) among

them. And "the clouds were commanded not to rain a shower upon the vineyard of Sorek,"[9]—the clouds being celestial benefits, which were commanded not to be forthcoming to the house of Israel; for it "had borne *thorns*"—whereof that house of Israel had wrought a crown for Christ—and not "*righteousness*, but a *clamour*,"—the clamour whereby it had extorted His surrender to the cross.[10] And thus, the former gifts of grace being withdrawn, "the law and the prophets were until John,"[11] and the fishpool of Bethsaida[12] until the advent of Christ: thereafter it ceased curatively to remove from Israel infirmities of health; since, as the result of their perseverance in their frenzy, the name of the Lord was through them blasphemed, as it is written: "On your account the name of God is blasphemed among the Gentiles:"[13] for it is from them that the infamy (attached to that name) began, and (was propagated during) the interval from Tiberius to Vespasian. And because they had committed these crimes, and had failed to understand that Christ "was to be found"[14] in "the time of their visitation,"[15] their land has been made "desert, and their cities utterly burnt with fire, while strangers devour their region in their sight: the daughter of Sion is derelict, as a watch-tower in a vineyard, or as a shed in a cucumber garden,"—ever since the time, to wit, when "Israel knew not" the Lord, "the People understood Him not;" but rather "quite forsook, and provoked unto indignation, the Holy One of Israel."[16] So, again, we find a *conditional* threat of *the sword:* "If ye shall have been unwilling, and shall not have been obedient, the glaive shall eat you up."[17] Whence we prove that *the sword* was CHRIST, by not hearing whom they perished; who, again, in the Psalm, demands of the Father their dispersion, saying, "Disperse them in Thy power;"[18] who, withal, again through Isaiah prays for their *utter burning.* "On My account," He says, "have these things happened to you; in anxiety shall ye sleep."[19]

Since, therefore, the Jews were predicted as destined to suffer these calamities *on Christ's account*, and we find that they *have* suffered them, and see them sent into dispersion and

---

[1] See Gen. xxii. 1–14.
[2] See Matt. xxvii. 11–14; Mark xv. 1–5; John xix. 8–12.
[3] See Isa. liii. 7, 8.
[4] Oehler refers to Hos. vi. 1; add 2 (*ad init.*).
[5] See Luke i. 35.
[6] For this sense of the word "approve," comp. Acts ii. 22, Greek and English, and Phil. i. 10, Greek and English.
[7] See Isa ii. 20.
[8] See Isa. iii. 1, 3; and comp. 1 Cor. iii. 10, Eph. ii. 20, 21, 1 Pet. ii. 4–8, and many similar passages.

[9] Comp. Isa. v. 2 in LXX. and Lowth.
[10] Comp. Isa v. 6, 7, with Matt. xxvii. 20–25, Mark xv. 8–15, Luke xxiii. 13–25, John xix. 12–16.
[11] Matt. xi. 13; Luke xvi. 16.
[12] See John v. 1–9; and comp. *de Bapt.* c. v., and the note there.
[13] See Isa. lii. 5; Ezek. xxxvi. 20, 23: Rom. ii. 24. (The passage in Isaiah in the LXX. agrees with Rom. ii. 24.)
[14] See Isa. lv. 6, 7.
[15] See Luke xix. 41–44
[16] See Isa. i. 7, 8, 4.
[17] See Isa. i. 20.
[18] See Ps. lix. 11 (lviii. 12 in LXX.)
[19] See Isa. l. 11 in LXX

abiding in it, manifest it is that it is on Christ's account that these things *have* befallen the Jews, the sense of the Scriptures harmonizing with the issue of events and of the order of the times. Or else, if Christ is not yet come, on whose account they were predicted as destined thus to suffer, when He *shall have* come it follows that they *will* thus suffer. And where will then be a daughter of Sion to be derelict, who *now* has no existence? where the cities to be exust, which are already exust and in heaps? where the dispersion of a race which is now in exile? Restore to Judea the condition which Christ is to find; and (then, if you will), contend that some other (Christ) is coming.

CHAP. XIV.—CONCLUSION. CLUE TO THE ERROR OF THE JEWS.

Learn now (over and above the immediate question) the clue to your error. We affirm *two* characters of the Christ demonstrated by the prophets, and as many *advents* of His forenoted: one, in humility (of course the first), when He has to be led " as a sheep for a victim; and, as a lamb voiceless before the shearer, so He opened not His mouth," not even in His aspect comely. For " we have announced," says *the prophet*, " concerning Him, (He is) as a little child, as a root in a thirsty land; and there was not in Him attractiveness or glory. And we saw Him, and He had not attractiveness or grace; but His mien was unhonoured, deficient in comparison of the sons of men," [1] " a man *set* in the plague,[2] and knowing how to bear infirmity: " to wit, as having been set by the Father " for a stone of offence," [3] and " made a little lower " by Him " than angels," [4] He pronounces Himself " a worm, and not a man, an ignominy of man, and *the* refuse of *the* People." [5] Which evidences of ignobility suit the FIRST ADVENT, just as those of sublimity do the SECOND; when He shall be made no longer " a stone of offence nor a rock of scandal," but " the highest corner-stone," [6] after reprobation (on earth) taken up (into heaven) and raised sublime for the purpose of consummation,[7] and that " rock "—so we must admit—which is read of in Daniel as forecut from a mount, which shall crush and crumble the image of secular kingdoms.[8] Of which sec-

ond advent of the same (Christ) Daniel has said: " And, behold, as it were a Son of man, coming with the clouds of the heaven, came unto the Ancient of days, and was present in His sight; and they who were standing by led (Him) unto Him. And there was given Him royal power; and all nations of the earth, according to their race, and all glory, shall serve Him: and His power *is* eternal, which shall not be taken away, and His kingdom *one* which shall not be corrupted." [9] Then, assuredly, is He to have an honourable mien, and a grace not " deficient more than the sons of men;" for (He will then be) " blooming in beauty in comparison with the sons of men." [10] " Grace," says *the Psalmist*, " hath been outpoured in Thy lips: wherefore God hath blessed Thee unto eternity. Gird Thee Thy sword around Thy thigh, most potent in Thy bloom and beauty!" [10] while the Father withal afterwards, after making Him somewhat lower than angels, " crowned Him with glory and honour, and subjected all *things* beneath His feet." [11] And then shall they " learn to know Him whom they pierced, and shall beat their breasts tribe by tribe;" [12] of course because in days bygone they did *not* know Him when conditioned in the humility of human estate. Jeremiah says: " He is a human being, and who will learn to know Him?" [13] because, " His nativity," says Isaiah, " who shall declare?" So, too, in Zechariah, in His own person, nay, in the very mystery [14] of His name withal, the most true Priest of the Father, His own [15] Christ, is delineated in a twofold garb with reference to the TWO ADVENTS.[16] First, He was clad in " sordid attire," that is, in the indignity of passible and mortal flesh, when the devil, withal, was opposing himself to Him—the instigator, to wit, of Judas the traitor [17]—who even after His baptism had tempted Him. In the next place, He was stripped of His former sordid raiment, and adorned with a garment down to the foot, and with a turban and a clean mitre, that is, (with the garb) of the SECOND ADVENT; since He is demonstrated as having attained " glory and honour." Nor

[1] See Isa. liii. 2 in LXX.
[2] See Ps. xxxviii. 17 in the " Great Bible " (xxxvii. 18 in LXX.). Also Isa. liii. 3 in LXX.
[3] See Isa. viii. 14 (where, however, the LXX. rendering is widely different) with Rom. ix. 32, 33; Ps. cxviii 22 (cxvii. 22 in LXX.); 1 Pet. ii. 4.
[4] See Ps. viii. 5 (viii. 6 in LXX.) with Heb. ii. 5-9.
[5] See Ps. xxii. 6 (xxi. 7 in LXX., the Alex. MS. of which here agrees well with Tertullian).
[6] See reference 3 above, with Isa. xxviii. 16.
[7] Comp. Eph. i. 10.
[8] Or, " worldly kingdoms." See Dan. ii. 34, 35, 44, 45.

[9] See Dan. vii. 13, 14.
[10] See c. ix. *med.*
[11] See Ps. viii. 5, 6 (6, 7 in LXX.) ; Heb. ii. 6-9.
[12] See Zech. xii. 10, 12 (where the LXX., as we have it, differs widely from our Eng. ver. in ver. 10) ; Rev. i. 7.
[13] See Jer. xvii. 9 in LXX.
[14] Sacramento.
[15] The reading which Oehler follows, and which seems to have the best authority, is " verissimus sacerdos Patris, Christus Ipsius," as in the text. But Rig., whose judgment is generally very sound, prefers, with some others, to read, " verus summus sacerdos Patris Christus Jesus ;" which agrees better with the previous allusion to " the mystery of His name withal :" comp. c. ix. above, towards the end.
[16] See Zech. iii. " The mystery of His name " refers to the meaning of " Jeshua," for which see c. ix. above.
[17] Comp. John vi. 70 and xiii. 2 (especially in Greek, where the word διάβολος is used in each case).

will you be able to say that the man (there depicted) is "the son of Jozadak,"[1] who was never at all clad in a sordid garment, but was always adorned with the sacerdotal garment, nor ever deprived of the sacerdotal function. But the "Jesus"[2] there alluded to is CHRIST, the Priest of God the most high Father; who at His FIRST ADVENT came in humility, in human form, and passible, even up to the period of His passion; being Himself likewise made, through all (stages of suffering) a victim for us all; who after His resurrection was "clad with a garment down to the foot,"[3] and named the Priest of God the Father unto eternity.[4] So, again, I will make an interpretation of the two goats which were habitually offered on the fast-day.[5] Do not they, too, point to each successive stage in the character of the Christ who is already come? A pair, on the one hand, and consimilar (they were), because of the identity of the Lord's general appearance, inasmuch as He is not to come in some other form, seeing that He has to be recognised by those by whom He was once hurt. But the one of them, begirt with scarlet, amid cursing and universal spitting, and tearing, and piercing, was cast away by the People outside the city into perdition, marked with manifest tokens of Christ's passion; who, after being begirt with scarlet garment, and subjected to universal spitting, and afflicted with all contumelies, was crucified outside the city.[6] The other, however, offered for sins, and given as food *to the priests merely* of the temple,[7] gave signal evidences of the second appearance; in so far as, after the expiation of all sins, the priests of the spiritual temple, that is, of the church, were to enjoy[8] a spiritual public distribution (as it were) of the Lord's grace, while all others are fasting from salvation.

Therefore, since the vaticinations of the FIRST ADVENT obscured it with manifold figures, and debased it with every dishonour, while the SECOND (was foretold as) manifest and wholly worthy of God, it has resulted therefrom, that, by fixing their gaze on that one alone which they could easily understand and believe (that is, the SECOND, which is in honour and glory), they have been (not undeservedly) deceived as to the more obscure —at all events, the more unworthy—that is, the FIRST. And thus to the present moment

they affirm that their Christ is not come, because He is not come in majesty; while they are ignorant of[9] the fact that He was first to come in humility.

Enough it is, meantime, to have thus far followed the stream downward of the order of Christ's course, whereby He is proved such as He was habitually announced: in order that, as a result of this harmony of the Divine Scriptures, we may understand; and that the events which used to be predicted as destined to take place after Christ may be believed to have been accomplished as the result of a divine arrangement. For unless He come *after* whom they had to be accomplished, by no means would the events, the future occurrence whereof was predictively assigned to His advent, have come to pass. Therefore, if you see universal nations thenceforth emerging from the profundity of human error to God the Creator and His Christ (which you dare not assert to have not been prophesied, because, albeit you were so to assert, there would forthwith—as we have already premised[10]—occur to you the promise of the Father saying, "My Son art Thou; I this day have begotten Thee; ask of Me, and I will give Thee Gentiles *as* Thine heritage, and *as* Thy possession the boundaries of the earth." Nor will you be able to vindicate, as the subject of that prediction, rather the son of David, Solomon, than Christ, God's Son; nor "the boundaries of the earth," as promised rather to David's son, who reigned within the single land of Judea, than to Christ the Son of God, who has already illumined the whole world[11] with the rays of His gospel. In short, again, a throne "unto the age"[12] is more suitable to Christ, God's Son, than to Solomon,—a temporal king, to wit, who reigned over Israel alone. For at the present day nations are invoking Christ which used not to know Him; and peoples at the present day are fleeing in a body to the Christ of whom in days bygone they were ignorant[13]), you cannot contend that that is future which you are taking place.[14] Either deny that these events were prophesied, while they are seen before your eyes; or else have been fulfilled, while you hear them read: or, on the other hand, if you fail to deny each position, they will have their fulfilment in Him with respect to whom they were prophesied.

[1] Or "Josedech," as Tertullian here writes, and as we find in Hag. i. 1, 12, ii. 2, 4, Zech. vi. 11, and in the LXX.
[2] Or, "Jeshua."
[3] See Rev. i. 13.
[4] See Ps. cx. (cix. in LXX.) 4 ; Heb. v. 5-10.
[5] See Lev. xvi.
[6] Comp. Heb. xiii. 10-13. It is to be noted, however, that all this spitting, etc., formed no part of the divinely ordained ceremony.
[7] This appears to be an error. See Lev. vi. 30.
[8] Unless Oehler's "fruerentur" is an error for "fruentur" = "will enjoy."
[9] Or, "ignore."
[10] See cc. xi. xii. above.
[11] Orbem.
[12] Or, "unto eternity." Comp. 2 Sam. (2 Kings in LXX.) vii. 13 ; 1 Chron. xvii. 12 ; Ps. lxxxix. 3, 4, 29, 35, 36, 37 (in LXX. Ps. lxxxviii. 4, 5, 30, 36, 37, 38).
[13] See Isa. lv. 5 (especially in the LXX).
[14] Oehler's pointing is discarded. The whole passage, from "which you dare not assert" down to "ignorant," appears to be parenthetical ; and I have therefore marked it as such.

VIII.

THE SOUL'S TESTIMONY.[1]

[BY THE REV S. THELWALL.]

CHAP. I.

IF, with the object of convicting the rivals and persecutors of Christian truth, from their own authorities, of the crime of at once being untrue to themselves and doing injustice to us, one is bent on gathering testimonies in its favour from the writings of the philosophers, or the poets, or other masters of this world's learning and wisdom, he has need of a most inquisitive spirit, and a still greater memory to carry out the research. Indeed, some of our people, who still continued their inquisitive labours in ancient literature, and still occupied memory with it, have published works we have in our hands of this very sort; works in which they relate and attest the nature and origin of their traditions, and the grounds on which their opinions rest, and from which it may be seen at once that we have embraced nothing new or monstrous—nothing for which we cannot claim the support of ordinary and well-known writings, whether in ejecting error from our creed, or admitting truth into it. But the unbelieving hardness of the human heart leads them to slight even their own teachers, otherwise approved and in high renown, whenever they touch upon arguments which are used in defence of Christianity. Then the poets are fools, when they describe the gods with human passions and stories; then the philosophers are without reason, when they knock at the gates of truth. He will thus far be reckoned a wise and sagacious man who has gone the length of uttering sentiments that are almost Christian; while if, in a mere affectation of judgment and wisdom, he sets himself to reject their ceremonies, or to convicting the world of its sin, he is sure to be branded as a Christian. We

will have nothing, then, to do with the literature and the teaching, perverted in its best results, which is believed in its errors rather than its truth. We shall lay no stress on it, if some of their authors have declared that there is one God, and one God only. Nay, let it be granted that there is nothing in heathen writers which a Christian approves, that it may be put out of his power to utter a single word of reproach. For all are not familiar with their teachings; and those who are, have no assurance in regard to their truth. Far less do men assent to our writings, to which no one comes for guidance unless he is already a Christian. I call in a new testimony, yea, one which is better known than all literature, more discussed than all doctrine, more public than all publications, greater than the whole man—I mean all which is man's. Stand forth, O soul, whether thou art a divine and eternal substance, as most philosophers believe—if it be so, thou wilt be the less likely to lie,—or whether thou art the very opposite of divine, because indeed a mortal thing, as Epicurus alone thinks—in that case there will be the less temptation for thee to speak falsely in this case: whether thou art received from heaven, or sprung from earth; whether thou art formed of numbers, or of atoms; whether thine existence begins with that of the body, or thou art put into it at a later stage; from whatever source, and in whatever way, thou makest man a rational being, in the highest degree capable of thought and knowledge,—stand forth and give thy witness. But I call thee not as when, fashioned in schools, trained in libraries, fed in Attic academies and porticoes, thou belchest wisdom. I address thee simple, rude, uncultured and untaught, such as they have thee who have thee only; that very thing of the road, the street, the work-shop, wholly. I want thine inexperience, since in thy small experience no one feels any confidence. I demand of thee the things thou bringest with thee into man, which thou knowest either from

[1] [The tract De Testimonio Animæ is cast into an apologetic form and very properly comes into place here. It was written in Orthodoxy and forms a valuable preface to the De Anima, of which we cannot say that it is quite free from errors. As it refers to the Apology, we cannot place it before that work, and perhaps we shall not greatly err if we consider it a sequel to the Apology. If it proves to others the source of as much enjoyment as it affords to me, it will be treasured by them as one of the most precious testimonies to the Gospel, introducing Man to himself.]

thyself, or from thine author, whoever he may be. Thou art not, as I well know, Christian; for a man becomes a Christian, he is not born one. Yet Christians earnestly press thee for a testimony; they press thee, though an alien, to bear witness against thy friends, that they may be put to shame before thee, for hating and mocking us on account of things which convict thee as an accessory.

CHAP. II.

We give offence by proclaiming that there is one God, to whom the name of God alone belongs, from whom all things come, and who is Lord of the whole universe.[1] Bear thy testimony, if thou knowest this to be the truth; for openly and with a perfect liberty, such as we do not possess, we hear thee both in private and in public exclaim, "Which may God grant," and, "If God so will." By expressions such as these thou declarest that there is one who is distinctively God, and thou confessest that all power belongs to him to whose will, as Sovereign, thou dost look. At the same time, too, thou deniest any others to be truly gods, in calling them by their own names of Saturn, Jupiter, Mars, Minerva; for thou affirmest Him to be God alone to whom thou givest no other name than God; and though thou sometimes callest these others gods, thou plainly usest the designation as one which does not really belong to them, but is, so to speak, a borrowed one. Nor is the nature of the God we declare unknown to thee: "God is good, God does good," thou art wont to say; plainly suggesting further, "But man is evil." In asserting an antithetic proposition, thou, in a sort of indirect and figurative way, reproachest man with his wickedness in departing from a God so good. So, again, as among us, as belonging to the God of benignity and goodness, "Blessing" is a most sacred act in our religion and our life, thou too sayest as readily as a Christian needs, "God bless thee;" and when thou turnest the blessing of God into a curse, in like manner thy very words confess with us that His power over us is absolute and entire. There are some who, though they do not deny the existence of God, hold withal that He is neither Searcher, nor Ruler, nor Judge; treating with especial disdain those of us who go over to Christ out of fear of a coming judgment, as they think, honouring God in freeing Him from the cares of keeping watch, and the trouble of taking note, —not even regarding Him as capable of

anger. For if God, they say, gets angry, then He is susceptible of corruption and passion; but that of which passion and corruption can be affirmed may also perish, which God cannot do. But these very persons elsewhere, confessing that the soul is divine, and bestowed on us by God, stumble against a testimony of the soul itself, which affords an answer to these views. For if either divine or God-given, it doubtless knows its giver; and if it knows Him, it undoubtedly fears Him too, and especially as having been by Him endowed so amply. Has it no fear of Him whose favour it is so desirous to possess, and whose anger it is so anxious to avoid? Whence, then, the soul's natural fear of God, if God cannot be angry? How is there any dread of Him whom nothing offends? What is feared but anger? Whence comes anger, but from observing what is done? What leads to watchful oversight, but judgment in prospect? Whence is judgment, but from power? To whom does supreme authority and power belong, but to God alone? So thou art always ready, O soul, from thine own knowledge, nobody casting scorn upon thee, and no one preventing, to exclaim, "God sees all," and "I commend thee to God," and "May God repay," and "God shall judge between us." How happens this, since thou art not Christian? How is it that, even with the garland of Ceres on the brow, wrapped in the purple cloak of Saturn, wearing the white robe of the goddess Isis, thou invokest God as judge? Standing under the statue of Æsculapius, adorning the brazen image of Juno, arraying the helmet of Minerva with dusky figures, thou never thinkest of appealing to any of these deities. In thine own forum thou appealest to a God who is elsewhere; thou permittest honour to be rendered in thy temples to a foreign god. Oh, striking testimony to truth, which in the very midst of demons obtains a witness for us Christians!

CHAP. III.

But when we say that there are demons—as though, in the simple fact that we alone expel them from the men's bodies,[2] we did not also prove their existence—some disciple of Chrysippus begins to curl the lip. Yet thy curses sufficiently attest that there are such beings, and that they are objects of thy strong dislike.[3] As what comes to thee as a fit expression of thy strong hatred of him, thou callest the man a dæmon who annoys thee with his filthiness,

[1] [The student of Plato will recall such evidences, readily. See *The Laws*, in Jowett's Translation, vol. iv. p. 416. Also Elucidation I.]

[2] [The existence of demoniacal possessions in heathen countries is said to be probable, even in our days. The Fathers unanimously assert the effectual exorcisms of their days.]
[3] [*e.g.* Horace, *Epodes*, Ode V.]

or malice, or insolence, or any other vice which we ascribe to evil spirits. In expressing vexation, contempt, or abhorrence, thou hast Satan constantly upon thy lips;[1] the very same we hold to be the angel of evil, the source of error, the corrupter of the whole world, by whom in the beginning man was entrapped into breaking the commandment of God. And (the man) being given over to death on account of his sin, the entire human race, tainted in their descent from him, were made a channel for transmitting his condemnation. Thou seest, then, thy destroyer; and though he is fully known only to Christians, or to whatever sect[2] confesses the Lord, yet, even thou hast some acquaintance with him while yet thou abhorrest him!

CHAP. IV.

Even now, as the matter refers to thy opinion on a point the more closely belonging to thee, in so far as it bears on thy personal well-being, we maintain that after life has passed away thou still remainest in existence, and lookest forward to a day of judgment, and according to thy deserts art assigned to misery or bliss, in either way of it for ever; that, to be capable of this, thy former substance must needs return to thee, the matter and the memory of the very same human being: for neither good nor evil couldst thou feel if thou wert not endowed again with that sensitive bodily organization, and there would be no grounds for judgment without the presentation of the very person to whom the sufferings of judgment were due. That Christian view, though much nobler than the Pythagorean, as it does not tranfser thee into beasts; though more complete than the Platonic, since it endows thee again with a body; though more worthy of honour than the Epicurean, as it preserves thee from annihilation,—yet, because of the name connected with it, it is held to be nothing but vanity and folly, and, as it is called, a mere presumption. But we are not ashamed of ourselves if our presumption is found to have thy support. Well, in the first place, when thou speakest of one who is dead, thou sayest of him, "Poor man"—poor, surely, not because he has been taken from the good of life, but because he has been given over to punishment and condemnation. But at another time thou speakest of the dead as free from trouble; thou professest to think life a burden, and death a

blessing. Thou art wont, too, to speak of the dead as in repose,[3] when, returning to their graves beyond the city gates[4] with food and dainties, thou art wont to present offerings to thyself rather than to them; or when, coming from the graves again, thou art staggering under the effects of wine. But I want thy sober opinion. Thou callest the dead poor when thou speakest thine own thoughts, when thou art at a distance from them. For at their feast, where in a sense they are present and recline along with thee, it would never do to cast reproach upon their lot. Thou canst not but adulate those for whose sake thou art feasting it so sumptuously. Dost thou then speak of him as *poor* who feels not? How happens it that thou cursest, as one capable of suffering from thy curse, the man whose memory comes back on thee with the sting in it of some old injury? It is thine imprecation that "the earth may lie heavy on him," and that there may be trouble "to his ashes in the realm of the dead." In like manner, in thy kindly feeling to him to whom thou art indebted for favours, thou entreatest "repose to his bones and ashes," and thy desire is that among the dead he may "have pleasant rest." If thou hast no power of suffering after death, if no feeling remains,—if, in a word, severance from the body is the annihilation of thee, what makes thee lie against thyself, as if thou couldst suffer in another state? Nay, why dost thou fear death at all? There is nothing after death to be feared, if there is nothing to be felt. For though it may be said that death is dreadful not for anything it threatens afterwards, but because it deprives us of the good of life; yet, on the other hand, as it puts an end to life's discomforts, which are far more numerous, death's terrors are mitigated by a gain that more than outweighs the loss. And there is no occasion to be troubled about a loss of good things, which is amply made up for by so great a blessing as relief from every trouble. There is nothing dreadful in that which delivers from all that is to be dreaded. If thou shrinkest from giving up life because thy experience of it has been sweet, at any rate there is no need to be in any alarm about death if thou hast no knowledge that it is evil. Thy dread of it is the proof that thou art aware of its evil.

---

[1] [*Satanan*, in omni vexatione . . . *pronuntias*. Does he mean that they used this *word?* Rather, he means the *demon* is none other than Satan.]

[2] [I have been obliged, somewhat, to simplify the translation here.]

12

[3] [This whole passage is useful as a commentary on classic authors who use these poetical expressions. *Cælo Musa beat* (Hor. Ode viii. B. 4.) but the real feeling comes out in such expressions as one finds in Horace's odes to Sextius, (B. i. Ode 4.), or to Postumus, B. ii. Od. 14.]

[4] [The tombs, by the roadside, of which the traveller still sees specimens, used to be scenes of debauchery when the dead were *honoured* in this way. Now, the funeral honours (See *De Corona*, cap. iii.) which Christians substituted for these were Eucharistic alms and oblations: thanking God for their holy lives and perpetuating relations with them in the Communion of Saints.]

Thou wouldst never think it evil—thou wouldst have no fear of it at all—if thou wert not sure that after it there is something to make it evil, and so a thing of terror.[1] Let us leave unnoted at this time that natural way of fearing death. It is a poor thing for any one to fear what is inevitable. I take up the other side, and argue on the ground of a joyful hope beyond our term of earthly life; for desire of posthumous fame is with almost every class an inborn thing.[2] I have not time to speak of the Curtii, and the Reguli, or the brave men of Greece, who afford us innumerable cases of death despised for after renown. Who at this day is without the desire that he may be often remembered when he is dead? Who does not give all endeavour to preserve his name by works of literature, or by the simple glory of his virtues, or by the splendour even of his tomb? How is it the nature of the soul to have these posthumous ambitions and with such amazing effort to prepare the things it can only use after decease? It would care nothing about the future, if the future were quite unknown to it. But perhaps thou thinkest thyself surer, after thy exit from the body, of continuing still to feel, than of any future resurrection, which is a doctrine laid at our door as one of our presumptuous suppositions. But it is also the doctrine of the soul; for if any one inquires about a person lately dead as though he were alive, it occurs at once to say, "He has gone." He is expected to return, then.

CHAP. V.

These testimonies of the soul are simple as true, commonplace as simple, universal as commonplace, natural as universal, divine as natural. I don't think they can appear frivolous or feeble to any one, if he reflect on the majesty of nature, from which the soul derives its authority.[3] If you acknowledge the authority of the mistress, you will own it also in the disciple. Well, nature is the mistress here, and her disciple is the soul. But everything the one has taught or the other learned, has come from God—the Teacher of the teacher. And what the soul may know from the teachings of its chief instructor, thou canst judge from that which is within thee. Think of that which enables thee to think; reflect on that which in forebodings is the prophet, the augur in omens, the foreseer of coming events. Is it a wonderful thing, if, being the gift of God to man, it knows how to divine? Is it anything very strange, if it knows the God by whom it was bestowed? Even fallen as it is, the victim of the great adversary's machinations, it does not forget its Creator, His goodness and law, and the final end both of itself and of its foe. Is it singular then, if, divine in its origin, its revelations agree with the knowledge God has given to His own people? But he who does not regard those outbursts of the soul as the teaching of a congenital nature and the secret deposit of an inborn knowledge, will say that the habit and, so to say, the vice of speaking in this way has been acquired and confirmed from the opinions of published books widely spread among men. Unquestionably the soul existed before letters, and speech before books, and ideas before the writing of them, and man himself before the poet and philosopher.[4] Is it then to be believed, that before literature and its publication no utterances of the sort we have pointed out came from the lips of men? Did nobody speak of God and His goodness, nobody of death, nobody of the dead? Speech went a-begging, I suppose; nay, (the subjects being still awanting, without which it cannot even exist at this day, when it is so much more copious, and rich, and wise), it could not exist at all if the things which are now so easily suggested, that cling to us so constantly, that are so very near to us, that are somehow born on our very lips, had no existence in ancient times, before letters had any existence in the world—before there was a Mercury, I think, at all. And whence was it, I pray, that letters themselves came to know, and to disseminate for the use of speech, what no mind had ever conceived, or tongue put forth, or ear taken in? But, clearly, since the Scriptures of God, whether belonging to Christians or to Jews, into whose olive tree we have been grafted—are much more ancient than any secular literature, (or, let us only say, are of a somewhat earlier date, as we have shown in its proper place when proving their trustworthiness); if the soul have taken these utterances from writings at all, we must believe it has taken them from ours, and not from yours, its instruction coming more naturally from the earlier than the later works. Which latter indeed waited for their own instruction from the former, and though we grant that light has come from you, still it has flowed from the first fountainhead originally; and we claim as

---

[1] [Butler, Analogy, Part I. chap. i.]
[2] [Horace, Book III. Ode 30.]
[3] [This appeal to the universal conscience and consciousness of mankind is unanswerable, and assures us that counter-theories will never prevail. See Bossuet, *De la Connoisance de Dieu* et de Soi-méme. Œuvres, Tom. V. pp. 86 et. seqq. Ed. Paris, 1846.]

[4] [Compare the heathen ideas in Plato: e.g. the story Socrates tells in the Gorgias, (near the close) about death and Judgment.]

entirely ours, all you may have taken from us and handed down. Since it is thus, it matters little whether the soul's knowledge was put into it by God or by His book. Why, then, O man, wilt thou maintain a view so groundless, as that those testimonies of the soul have gone forth from the mere human speculations of your literature, and got hardening of common use?

CHAP. VI.

Believe, then, your own books, and as to our Scriptures so much the more believe writings which are divine, but in the witness of the soul itself give like confidence to Nature. Choose the one of these you observe to be the most faithful friend of truth. If your own writings are distrusted, neither God nor Nature lie. And if you would have faith in God and Nature, have faith in the soul; thus you will believe yourself. Certainly you value the soul as giving you your true greatness,— that to which you belong; which is all things to you; without which you can neither live nor die; on whose account you even put God away from you. Since, then, you fear to become a Christian, call the soul before you, and put her to the question. Why does she worship another? why name the name of God? Why does she speak of demons, when she means to denote spirits to be held accursed? Why does she make her protestations towards the heavens, and pronounce her ordinary execrations earthwards? Why does she render service in one place, in another invoke the Avenger? Why does she pass judgments on the dead? What Christian phrases are those she has got, though Christians she neither desires to see nor hear? Why has she either bestowed them on us, or received them from us? Why has she either taught us them, or learned them as our scholar? Regard with suspicion this accordance in words, while there is such difference in practice. It is utter folly—denying a universal nature—to ascribe this exclusively to our language and the Greek, which are regarded among us as so near akin. The soul is not a boon from heaven to Latins and Greeks alone. Man is the one name belonging to every nation upon earth: there is one soul and many tongues, one spirit and various sounds; every country has its own speech, but the subjects of speech are common to all. God is everywhere, and the goodness of God is everywhere; demons are everywhere, and the cursing of them is everywhere; the invocation of divine judgment is everywhere, death is everywhere, and the sense of death is everywhere, and all the world over is found the witness of the soul. There is not a soul of man that does not, from the light that is in itself, proclaim the very things we are not permitted to speak above our breath. Most justly, then, every soul is a culprit as well as a witness: in the measure that it testifies for truth, the guilt of error lies on it; and on the day of judgment it will stand before the courts of God, without a word to say. Thou proclaimedst God, O soul, but thou didst not seek to know Him: evil spirits were detested by thee, and yet they were the objects of thy adoration; the punishments of hell were foreseen by thee, but no care was taken to avoid them; thou hadst a savour of Christianity, and withal wert the persecutor of Christians.

ELUCIDATIONS.

I.

(Recognition of the Supreme God, cap. ii., p. 176.)

THE passage referred to in the note, begins thus in Jowett's rendering: "The Ruler of the Universe has ordered all things with a view to the preservation and perfection of the whole etc." So, in the same book: "Surely God must not be supposed to have a nature which he himself hates." Again: "Let us not, then, deem God inferior to human workmen, who in proportion to their skill finish and perfect their works . . . . or that God, the wisest of beings, who is willing and able to extend his care to all things, etc." Now, it is a sublime plan which our author here takes up, (making only slight reference to the innumerable citations which were behind his apostrophe to the soul if any one should dispute it) to bid the soul stand forth and confess its consciousness of God.

II.

(Dæmons, cap. vi. p. 176.)

Those who would pursue the subject of Demonology, which Tertullian opens in this admirable treatise, should follow it up in a writer whom Tertullian greatly influenced, in many particulars, even when he presents a remarkable contrast. The Ninth Book of the *City of God* is devoted to inquiries which throw considerable light on some of the startling sayings of our author as to the heathen systems, and their testimony to the Soul's Consciousness of God and of the great enemy of God and the inferior spirit of Evil.

A TREATISE ON THE SOUL.[1]

[TRANSLATED BY PETER HOLMES, D.D.]

CHAP. I.—IT ·IS NOT TO THE PHILOSOPHERS THAT WE RESORT FOR INFORMATION ABOUT THE SOUL BUT TO GOD.[2]

HAVING discussed with Hermogenes the single point of the origin of the soul, so far as his assumption led me, that the soul consisted rather in an adaptation[3] of matter than of the inspiration[4] of God, I now turn to the other questions incidental to the subject; and (in my treatment of these) I shall evidently have mostly to contend with the philosophers. In the very prison of Socrates they skirmished about the state of the soul. I have my doubts at once whether the time was an opportune one for their (great) master—(to say nothing of the place), although *that* perhaps does not much matter. For what could the soul of Socrates then contemplate with clearness and serenity? The sacred ship had returned (from Delos), the hemlock draft to which he had been condemned had been drunk, death was now present before him: (his mind) was,[5] as one may suppose,[6] naturally excited[6] at every emotion; or if nature had lost her influence, it must have been deprived of all power of thought.[7] Or let it have been as placid and tranquil so you please, inflexible, in spite of the claims of natural duty,[8] at the tears of her who was so soon to be his widow, and at the sight of his thenceforward orphan children, yet his soul must have been moved even by its very efforts to suppress emotion; and his constancy itself must have been shaken, as he struggled against the disturbance of the excitement around him. Besides, what other thoughts could any man entertain who had been unjustly condemned to die, but such as should solace him for the injury done to him? Especially would this be the case with that glorious creature, the philosopher, to whom injurious treatment would not suggest a craving for consolation, but rather the feeling of resentment and indignation. Accordingly, after his sentence, when his wife came to him with her effeminate cry, O Socrates, you are unjustly condemned! he seemed already to find joy in answering, Would you then wish me justly condemned? It is therefore not to be wondered at, if even in his prison, from a desire to break the foul hands of Anytus and Melitus, he, in the face of death itself, asserts the immortality of the soul by a strong assumption such as was wanted to frustrate the wrong (they had inflicted upon him). So that all the wisdom of Socrates, at that moment, proceeded from the affectation of an assumed composure, rather than the firm conviction of ascertained truth. For by whom has truth ever been discovered without God? By whom has God ever been found without Christ? By whom has Christ ever been explored without the Holy Spirit? By whom has the Holy Spirit ever been attained without the mysterious gift of faith?[9] Socrates, as none can doubt, was actuated by a different spirit. For they say that a demon clave to

---

[1] [It is not safe to date this treatise before A.D. 203, and perhaps it would be unsafe to assign a later date. The note of the translator, which follows, relieves me from any necessity to add more, just here.]

[2] In this treatise we have Tertullian's speculations on the origin, the nature, and the destiny of the human soul. There are, no doubt, paradoxes startling to a modern reader to be found in it, such as that of the soul's corporeity; and there are weak and inconclusive arguments. But after all such drawbacks (and they are not more than what constantly occur in the most renowned speculative writers of antiquity), the reader will discover many interesting proofs of our author's character for originality of thought, width of information, firm grasp of his subject, and vivacious treatment of it, such as we have discovered in other parts of his writings. If his subject permits Tertullian less than usual of an appeal to his favourite Holy Scripture, he still makes room for occasional illustration from it, and with his characteristic ability; if, however, there is less of this sacred learning in it, the treatise teems with curious information drawn from the secular literature of that early age. Our author often measures swords with Plato in his discussions on the soul, and it is not too much to say that he shows himself a formidable opponent to the great philosopher. See Bp. Kaye, *On Tertullian*, pp. 199, 200.

[3] Suggestu. [Kaye, pp. 60 and 541.]

[4] Flatu "the breath."

[5] Utique.

[6] Consternata.

[7] Externata. "Externatus = ἐκτὸς φρενῶν. Gloss. Philox.

[8] Pietatis.

[9] Fidei sacramento.

him from his boyhood—the very worst teacher certainly, notwithstanding the high place assigned to it by poets and philosophers—even next to, (nay, along with) the gods themselves. The teachings of the power of Christ had not yet been given—(that power) which alone can confute this most pernicious influence of evil that has nothing good in it, but is rather the author of all error, and the seducer from all truth. Now if Socrates was pronounced the wisest of men by the oracle of the Pythian demon, which, you may be sure, neatly managed the business for his friend, of how much greater dignity and constancy is the assertion of the Christian wisdom, before the very breath of which the whole host of demons is scattered! This wisdom of the school of heaven frankly and without reserve denies the gods of this world, and shows no such inconsistency as to order a "cock to be sacrificed to Æsculapius:"[1] no new gods and demons does it introduce, but expels the old ones; it corrupts not youth, but instructs them in all goodness and moderation; and so it bears the unjust condemnation not of one city only, but of all the world, in the cause of that truth which incurs indeed the greater hatred in proportion to its fulness: so that it tastes death not out of a (poisoned) cup almost in the way of jollity; but it exhausts it in every kind of bitter cruelty, on gibbets and in holocausts.[2] Meanwhile, in the still gloomier prison of the world amongst your Cebeses and Phædos, in every investigation concerning (man's) soul, it directs its inquiry according to the rules of God. At all events, you can show us no more powerful expounder of the soul than the Author thereof. From God you may learn about that which you hold of God; but from none else will you get this knowledge, if you get it not from God. For who is to reveal that which God has hidden? To that quarter must we resort in our inquiries whence we are most safe even in deriving our ignorance. For it is really better for us not to know a thing, because He has not revealed it to us, than to know it according to man's wisdom, because *he* has been bold enough to assume it.

CHAP. II.—THE CHRISTIAN HAS SURE AND SIMPLE KNOWLEDGE CONCERNING THE SUBJECT BEFORE US.

Of course we shall not deny that philosophers have sometimes thought the same things as ourselves. The testimony of truth is the issue thereof. It sometimes happens even in a storm, when the boundaries of sky and sea are lost in confusion, that some harbour is stumbled on (by the labouring ship) by some happy chance; and sometimes in the very shades of night, through blind luck alone, one finds access to a spot, or egress from it. In nature, however, most conclusions are suggested, as it were, by that common intelligence wherewith God has been pleased to endow the soul of man. This intelligence has been caught up by philosophy, and, with the view of glorifying her own art, has been inflated (it is not to be wondered at that I use this language) with straining after that facility of language wihch is practised in the building up and pulling down of everything, and which has greater aptitude for persuading men by speaking than by teaching. She assigns to things their forms and conditions; sometimes makes them common and public, sometimes appropriates them to private use; on certainties she capriciously stamps the character of uncertainty; she appeals to precedents, as if all things are capable of being compared together; she describes all things by rule and definition, allotting diverse properties even to similar objects; she attributes nothing to the divine permission, but assumes as her principles the laws of nature. I could bear with her pretensions, if only she were herself true to nature, and would prove to me that she had a mastery over nature as being associated with its creation. She thought, no doubt, that she was deriving her mysteries from sacred sources, as men deem them, because in ancient times most authors were supposed to be (I will not say godlike, but) actually gods: as, for instance, the Egyptian Mercury,[3] to whom Plato paid very great deference;[4] and the Phrygian Silenus, to whom Midas lent his long ears, when the shepherds brought him to him; and Hermotimus, to whom the good people of Clazomenæ built a temple after his death; and Orpheus; and Musæus; and Pherecydes, the master of Pythagoras. But why need we care, since these philosophers have also made their attacks upon those writings which are condemned by us under the title of apocryphal,[5] certain as we are that nothing ought to be received which does not agree with the true system of prophecy, which has arisen in this present age;[6] because we do not forget that there have been false proph-

---

[1] The allusion is to the *inconsistency* of the philosopher, who condemned the gods of the vulgar, and died offering a gift to one of them.
[2] Vivicomburio.

[3] Mentioned below, c. xxxiii.; also *Adv. Valent.* c. xv.
[4] See his *Phædrus*, c. lix. (p. 274); also Augustin, *De. Civ. Dei*, viii. 11; Euseb. *Præp. Evang.* ix. 3.
[5] Or *spurious*; not to be confounded with our so-called *Apocrypha*, which were in Tertullian's days called *Libri Ecclesiastici*.
[6] Here is a touch of Tertullian's Montanism.

ets, and long previous to them fallen spirits, which have instructed the entire tone and aspect of the world with cunning knowledge of this (*philosophic*) cast? It is, indeed, not incredible that any man who is in quest of wisdom may have gone so far, as a matter of curiosity, as to consult the very prophets; (*but be this as it may*), if you take the philosophers, you would find in them more diversity than agreement, since even in their agreement their diversity is discoverable. Whatever things are true *in their systems*, and agreeable to prophetic wisdom, they either recommend as emanating from some other source, or else perversely apply [1] in some other sense. This process is attended with very great detriment to the truth, when they pretend that it is either helped by falsehood, or else that falsehood derives support from it. The following circumstance must needs have set ourselves and the philosophers by the ears, especially in this present matter, that they sometimes clothe sentiments which are common to both sides, in arguments which are peculiar to themselves, but contrary in some points to our rule and standard of faith; and at other times defend opinions which are especially their own, with arguments which both sides acknowledge to be valid, and occasionally conformable to their system of belief. The truth has, at this rate, been well-nigh excluded by the philosophers, through the poisons with which they have infected it; and thus, if we regard both the modes of coalition *which we have now mentioned*, and which are equally hostile to the truth, we feel the urgent necessity of freeing, on the one hand, the sentiments held by us in common with them from the arguments of the philosophers, and of separating, on the other hand, the arguments which both parties employ from the opinions of the same philosophers. *And this we may do* by recalling all questions to God's inspired standard, with the obvious exception of such simple cases as being free from the entanglement of any preconceived conceits, one may fairly admit on mere *human* testimony; because plain evidence of this sort we must sometimes borrow from opponents, when our opponents have nothing to gain from it. Now I am not unaware what a vast mass of literature the philosophers have accumulated concerning the subject before us, in their own commentaries thereon—what various schools of principles there are, what conflicts of opinion, what prolific sources of questions, what perplexing methods of solution. Moreover, I have looked into Medical Science also, the sister (as they

say) of Philosophy, which claims as her function to cure the body, and thereby to have a special acquaintance with the soul. From this circumstance she has great differences with her sister, pretending as the latter does to know more about the soul, through the more obvious treatment, as it were, of her in her domicile *of the body*. But never mind all this contention between them for preeminence! For extending their several researches on the soul, Philosophy, on the one hand, has enjoyed the full scope of her genius; while Medicine, on the other hand, has possessed the stringent demands of her art and practice. Wide are men's inquiries into uncertainties; wider still are their disputes about conjectures. However great the difficulty of adducing proofs, the labour of producing conviction is not one whit less; so that the gloomy Heraclitus was quite right, when, observing the thick darkness which obscured the researches of the inquirers about the soul, and wearied with their interminable questions, he declared that he had certainly not explored the limits of the soul, although he had traversed every road *in her domains*. To the Christian, however, but few words are necessary for the clear understanding of the whole subject. But in the few words there always arises certainty to him; nor is he permitted to give his inquiries a wider range than is compatible with their solution; for "endless questions" the apostle forbids.[2] It must, however, be added, that no solution may be found by any man, but such as is learned from God; and that which is learned of God is the sum and substance of the whole thing.

CHAP. III.—THE SOUL'S ORIGIN DEFINED OUT OF THE SIMPLE WORDS OF SCRIPTURE.

Would to God that no "heresies had been ever necessary, in order that they which are approved may be made manifest!"[3] We should then be never required to try our strength in contests about the soul with philosophers, those patriarchs of heretics, as they may be fairly called.[4] The apostle, so far back as his own time, foresaw, indeed, that philosophy would do violent injury to the truth.[5] This admonition *about false philosophy* he was induced to offer after he had been at Athens, had become acquainted with that *loquacious* city,[6] and had there had a taste of its huckstering wiseacres and talkers. In like manner is the treatment of the soul according to the sophistical doctrines of men which "mix their

[1] Subornant.

[2] 1 Tim. i. 4.
[3] 1 Cor. x. 19.
[4] Compare Tertullian's *Adv. Hermog.* c. viii.
[5] Col. ii. 8.
[6] Linguatam civitatem. Comp. Acts xvii. 21.

wine with water." [1] Some of them deny the immortality of the soul; others affirm that it is immortal, and something more. Some raise disputes about its substance; others about its form; others, again, respecting each of its several faculties. One school of philosophers derives its state from various sources, while another ascribes its departure to different destinations. *The various schools reflect the character of their masters*, according as they have received their impressions from the dignity [2] of Plato, or the vigour [3] of Zeno, or the equanimity [4] of Aristotle, or the stupidity [5] of Epicurus, or the sadness [6] of Heraclitus, or the madness [7] of Empedocles. The fault, I suppose, of the divine doctrine lies in its springing from Judæa [8] rather than from Greece. Christ made a mistake, too, in sending forth fishermen to preach, rather than the sophist. Whatever noxious vapours, accordingly, exhaled from philosophy, obscure the clear and wholesome atmosphere of truth, it will be for Christians to clear away, both by shattering to pieces the arguments which are drawn from the principles of things—I mean those of the philosophers—and by opposing to them the maxims of heavenly wisdom—that is, such as are revealed by the Lord; in order that both the pitfalls wherewith philosophy captivates the heathen may be removed, and the means employed by heresy to shake the faith of Christians may be repressed. We have already decided one point in our controversy with Hermogenes, as we said at the beginning of this treatise, when we claimed the soul to be formed by the breathing [9] of God, and not out of matter. We relied even there on the clear direction of the inspired statement which informs us how that " the Lord God breathed on man's face the breath of life, so that man became a living soul " [10]—by that inspiration of God, of course. On this point, therefore, nothing further need be investigated or advanced by us. It has its own treatise, [11] and its own heretic. I shall regard it as my introduction to the other branches of the subject.

CHAP. IV.—IN OPPOSITION TO PLATO, THE SOUL WAS CREATED AND ORIGINATED AT BIRTH.

After settling the origin of the soul, its condition or state comes up next. For when we

acknowledge that the soul originates in the breath of God, it follows that we attribute a beginning to it. This Plato, indeed, refuses to assign to it, for he will have the soul to be unborn and unmade. [12] We, however, from the very fact of its having had a beginning, as well as from the nature thereof, teach that it had both birth and creation. And when we ascribe both birth and creation to it, we have made no mistake: for being *born*, indeed, is one thing, and being *made* is another,—the former being the term which is best suited to living beings. When distinctions, however, have places and times of their own, they occasionally possess also reciprocity of application among themselves. Thus, the being made admits of being taken in the sense of being brought forth; [13] inasmuch as everything which receives *being* or *existence*, in any way whatever, is in fact generated. For the maker may really be called the parent of the thing that is made: in this sense Plato also uses the phraseology. So far, therefore, as concerns our belief in the souls being made or born, the opinion of the philosopher is overthrown by the authority of prophecy [14] even.

CHAP. V.—PROBABLE VIEW OF THE STOICS, THAT THE SOUL HAS A CORPOREAL NATURE.

Suppose one summons a Eubulus to his assistance, and a Critolaus, and a Zenocrates, and on this occasion Plato's friend Aristotle. They may very possibly hold themselves ready for stripping the soul of its corporeity, unless they happen to see other philosophers opposed to them in their purpose—and this, too, in greater numbers—asserting for the soul a corporeal nature. Now I am not referring merely to those who mould the soul out of manifest bodily substances, as Hipparchus and Heraclitus (do) out of fire; as Hippon and Thales (do) out of water; as Empedocles and Critias (do) out of blood; as Epicurus (does) out of atoms, since even atoms by their coherence form corporeal masses; as Critolaus and his Peripatetics (do) out of a certain indescribable *quintessence*, [15] if that may be called a body which rather includes and embraces bodily substances;—but I call on the Stoics also to help me, who, while declaring almost in our own terms that the soul is a spiritual essence (inasmuch as breath and spirit are in their nature very near akin to each other), will yet have no difficulty in persuading (us) that the soul is a corporeal

[1] Isa. i. 22.
[2] Honor.
[3] Vigor. Another reading has "rigor" (ακληρότηs), harshness.
[4] Tenor.
[5] Stupor.
[6] Mœror.
[7] Furor.
[8] Isa. ii. 3.
[9] Flatu.
[10] Gen. ii. 7.
[11] Titulus.

[12] See his *Phædrus*, c. xxiv.
[13] Capit itaque et facturam provenisse poni.
[14] Or, "inspiration."
[15] Ex quinta nescio qua substantia. Comp. Cicero's *Tuscul.* i. 10.

substance. Indeed, Zeno, defining the soul to be a spirit generated with (the body,[1]) constructs his argument in this way: That substance which by its departure causes the living being to die is a corporeal one. Now it is by the departure of the spirit, which is generated with (the body,) that the living being dies; therefore the spirit which is generated with (the body) is a corporeal substance. But this spirit which is generated with (the body) is the soul: it follows, then, that the soul is a corporeal substance. Cleanthes, too, will have it that family likeness passes from parents to their children not merely in bodily features, but in characteristics of the soul; as if it were out of a mirror of (a man's) manners, and faculties, and affections, that bodily likeness and unlikeness are caught and reflected by the soul also. It is therefore as being corporeal that it is susceptible of likeness and unlikeness. Again, there is nothing in common between things corporeal and things incorporeal as to their susceptibility. But the soul certainly sympathizes with the body, and shares in its pain, whenever it is injured by bruises, and wounds, and sores: the body, too, suffers with the soul, and is united with it (whenever it is afflicted with anxiety, distress, or love) in the loss of vigour which its companion sustains, whose shame and fear it testifies by its own blushes and paleness. The soul, therefore, is (proved to be) corporeal from this intercommunion of susceptibility. Chrysippus also joins hands in fellowship with Cleanthes, when he lays it down that it is not at all possible for things which are endued with body to be separated from things which have not body; because they have no such relation as mutual contact or coherence. Accordingly Lucretius says:[2]

"Tangere enim et tangi nisi corpus nulla potest res."

"For nothing but body is capable of touching or of being touched."

(Such severance, however, is quite natural between the soul and the body); for when the body is deserted by the soul, it is overcome by death. The soul, therefore, is endued with a body; for if it were not corporeal, it could not desert the body.

CHAP. VI.—THE ARGUMENTS OF THE PLATONISTS FOR THE SOUL'S INCORPOREALITY, OPPOSED, PERHAPS FRIVOLOUSLY.

These conclusions the Platonists disturb more by subtilty than by truth. Every body, they say, has necessarily either an animate nature[3] or an inanimate one.[4] If it has the inanimate nature, it receives motion externally to itself; if the animate one, internally. Now the soul receives motion neither externally nor internally: not externally, since it has not the inanimate nature; nor internally, because it is itself rather the giver of motion to the body. It evidently, then, is not a bodily substance, inasmuch as it receives motion neither way, according to the nature and law of corporeal substances. Now, what first surprises us here, is the unsuitableness of a definition which appeals to objects which have no affinity with the soul. For it is impossible for the soul to be called either an animate body or an inanimate one, inasmuch as it is the soul itself which makes the body either animate, if it be present to it, or else inanimate, if it be absent from it. That, therefore, which produces a result, cannot itself be the result, so as to be entitled to the designation of an animate thing or an inanimate one. The soul is so called in respect of its own substance. If, then, that which is the soul admits not of being called an animate body or an inanimate one, how can it challenge comparison with the nature and law of animate and inanimate bodies? Furthermore, since it is characteristic of a body to be moved externally by something else, and as we have already shown that the soul receives motion from some other thing when it is swayed (from the outside, of course, by something else) by prophetic influence or by madness, therefore I must be right in regarding that as bodily substance which, according to the examples we have quoted, is moved by some other object from without. Now, if to receive motion from some other thing is characteristic of a body, how much more is it so to impart motion to something else! But the soul moves the body, all whose efforts are apparent externally, and from without. It is the soul which gives motion to the feet for walking, and to the hands for touching, and to the eyes for sight, and to the tongue for speech—a sort of internal image which moves and animates the surface. Whence could accrue such power to the soul, if it were incorporeal? How could an unsubstantial thing propel solid objects? But in what way do the senses in man seem to be divisible into the corporeal and the intellectual classes? They tell is that the qualities of things corporeal, such as earth and fire, are indicated by the bodily senses—of touch and sight; whilst (the qualities) of incorporeal things—for instance, benevolence and malignity—are

---

[1] Consitum.
[2] *De Nat. Rer.* i. 305.

[3] Animale, "having the nature of soul."
[4] Inanimale.

discovered by the intellectual faculties. And from this (they deduce what is to them) the manifest conclusion, that the soul is incorporeal, its properties being comprehended by the perception not of bodily organs, but of intellectual faculties. Well, (I shall be much surprised) if I do not at once cut away the very ground on which their argument stands. For I show them how incorporeal things are commonly submitted to the bodily senses—sound, for instance, to the organ of hearing; colour, to the organ of sight; smell, to the olfactory organ. And, just as in these instances, the soul likewise has its contact with [1] the body; not to say that the incorporeal objects are reported to us through the bodily organs, for the express reason that they come into contact with the said organs. Inasmuch, then, as it is evident that even incorporeal objects are embraced and comprehended by corporeal ones, why should not the soul, which is corporeal, be equally comprehended and understood by incorporeal faculties? It is thus certain that their argument fails. Among their more conspicuous arguments will be found this, that in their judgment every bodily substance is nourished by bodily substances; whereas the soul, as being an incorporeal essence, is nourished by incorporeal aliments—for instance, by the studies of wisdom. But even this ground has no stability in it, since Soranus, who is a most accomplished authority in medical science, affords us as answer, when he asserts that the soul is even nourished by corporeal aliments; that in fact it is, when failing and weak, actually refreshed oftentimes by food. Indeed, when deprived of all food, does not the soul entirely remove from the body? Soranus, then, after discoursing about the soul in the amplest manner, filling four volumes with his dissertations, and after weighing well all the opinions of the philosophers, defends the corporeality of the soul, although in the process he has robbed it of its immortality. For to all men it is not given to believe the truth which Christians are privileged to hold. As, therefore, Soranus has shown us from facts that the soul is nourished by corporeal aliments, let the philosopher (adopt a similar mode of proof, and) show that it is sustained by an incorporeal food. But the fact is, that no one has even been able to quench this man's [2] doubts and difficulties about the condition of the soul with the honey-water of Plato's subtle eloquence, nor to surfeit them with the crumbs from the minute nostrums of

Aristotle. But what is to become of the souls of all those robust barbarians, which have had no nurture of philosopher's lore indeed, and yet are strong in untaught practical wisdom, and which although very starvelings in philosophy, without your Athenian academies and porches, and even the prison of Socrates, do yet contrive to live? For it is not the soul's actual substance which is benefited by the aliment of learned study, but only its conduct and discipline; such ailment contributing nothing to increase its bulk, but only to enhance its grace. It is, moreover, a happy circumstance that the Stoics affirm that even the arts have corporeality; since at the rate the soul too must be corporeal, since it is commonly supposed to be nourished by the arts. Such, however, is the enormous preoccupation of the philosophic mind, that it is generally unable to see straight before it. Hence (the story of) Thales falling into the well.[3] It very commonly, too, through not understanding even its own opinions, suspects a failure of its own health. Hence (the story of) Chrysippus and the hellebore. Some such hallucination, I take it, must have occurred to him, when he asserted that two bodies could not possibly be contained in one: he must have kept out of mind and sight the case of those pregnant women who, day after day, bear not one body, but even two and three at a time, within the embrace of a single womb. One finds likewise, in the records of the civil law, the instance of a certain Greek woman who gave birth to a quint [4] of children, the mother of all these at one parturition, the manifold parent of a single brood, the prolific produce from a single womb, who, guarded by so many bodies—I had almost said, a people—was herself no less then the sixth person! The whole creation testifies how that those bodies which are naturally destined to issue from bodies, are already (included) in that from which they proceed. Now that which proceeds from some other thing must needs be second to it. Nothing, however, proceeds out of another thing except by the process of generation; but then they are two (things).

CHAP. VII.—THE SOUL'S CORPOREALITY DEMONSTRATED OUT OF THE GOSPELS.

So far as the philosophers are concerned, we have said enough. As for our own teachers, indeed, our reference to them is *ex abundanti*—a surplusage of authority: in the Gospel itself they will be found to have the

[1] Accedit.
[2] We follow Oehler's view of this obscure passage, in preference to Rigaltius'.
[3] See Tertullian's *Ad Nationes* (our translation), p. 33, *Supra.*
[4] Quinionem.

clearest evidence for the corporeal nature of the soul. In hell the soul of a certain man is in torment, punished in flames, suffering excruciating thirst, and imploring from the finger of a happier soul, for his tongue, the solace of a drop of water.[1] Do you suppose that this end of the blessed poor man and the miserable rich man is only imaginary? Then why the name of Lazarus in this narrative, if the circumstance is not in (the category of) a real occurrence? But even if it is to be regarded as imaginary, it will still be a testimony to truth and reality. For unless the soul possessed corporeality, the image of a soul could not possibly contain a finger of a bodily substance; nor would the Scripture feign a statement about the limbs of a body, if these had no existence. But what is that which is removed to Hades[2] after the separation of the body; which is there detained; which is reserved until the day of judgment; to which Christ also, on dying, descended? I imagine it is the souls of the patriarchs. But wherefore (all this), if the soul is nothing in its subterranean abode? For *nothing* it certainly is, if it is not a bodily substance. For whatever is incorporeal is incapable of being kept and guarded in any way; it is also exempt from either punishment or refreshment. That must be a body, by which punishment and refreshment can be experienced. Of this I shall treat more fully in a more fitting place. Therefore, whatever amount of punishment or refreshment the soul tastes in Hades, in its prison or lodging,[3] in the fire or in Abraham's bosom, it gives proof thereby of its own corporeality. For an incorporeal thing suffers nothing, not having that which makes it capable of suffering; else, if it has such capacity, it must be a bodily substance. For in *as* far as every corporeal thing is capable of suffering, in *so* far is that which is capable of suffering also corporeal.[4]

CHAP. VIII.—OTHER PLATONIST ARGUMENTS CONSIDERED.

Besides, it would be a harsh and absurd proceeding to exempt anything from the class of corporeal beings, on the ground that it is not exactly like the other constituents of that class. And where individual creatures possess various properties, does not this variety in works of the same class indicate the great-

ness of the Creator, in making them at the same time different and yet like, amicable yet rivals? Indeed, the philosophers themselves agree in saying that the universe consists of harmonious oppositions, according to Empedocles' (theory of) friendship and enmity. Thus, then, although corporeal essences are opposed to incorporeal ones, they yet differ from each other in such sort as to amplify their species by their variety, without changing their genus, remaining all alike corporeal; contributing to God's glory in their manifold existence by reason of their variety; so various, by reason of their differences; so diverse, in that some of them possess one kind of perception, others another; some feeding on one kind of aliment, others on another; some, again, possessing visibility, while others are invisible; some being weighty, others light. They are in the habit of saying that the soul must be pronounced incorporeal on this account, because the bodies of the dead, after its departure from them, become heavier, whereas they ought to be lighter, being deprived of the weight of a body—since the soul is a bodily substance. But what, says Soranus (in answer to this argument), if men should deny that the sea is a bodily substance, because a ship out of the water becomes a heavy and motionless mass? How much truer and stronger, then, is the soul's corporeal essence, which carries about the body, which eventually assumes so great a weight with the nimblest motion! Again, even if the soul is invisible, it is only in strict accordance with the condition of its own corporeality, and suitably to the property of its own essence, as well as to the nature of even those beings to which its destiny made it to be invisible. The eyes of the owl cannot endure the sun, whilst the eagle is so well able to face his glory, that the noble character of its young is determined by the unblinking strength of their gaze; while the eaglet, which turns away its eye from the sun's ray, is expelled from the nest as a degenerate creature! So true is it, therefore, than to one eye an object is invisible, which may be quite plainly seen by another,—without implying any incorporeality in that which is not endued with an equally strong power (of vision). The sun is indeed a bodily substance, because it is (composed of) fire; the object, however, which the eaglet at once admits the existence of, the owl denies, without any prejudice, nevertheless, to the testimony of the eagle. There is the selfsame difference in respect of the soul's corporeality, which is (perhaps) invisible to the flesh, but perfectly visible to the spirit. Thus John, being " in the Spirit "

[1] Luke xvi. 23, 24.
[2] Ad inferna. [See p. 59, *supra*.]
[3] Diversorio.
[4] Compare *De Resur. Carnis*, xvii. There is, however, some variation in Tertullian's language on this subject. In his *Apol.* xlviii. he speaks as if the soul could not suffer when separated from the body. See also his *De Testimonio Animæ*, ch. iv., p. 177, *supra*; and see Bp. Kaye, p. 183.

of God,[1] beheld plainly the souls of the martyrs.[2]

CHAP. IX.—PARTICULARS OF THE ALLEGED COMMUNICATION TO A MONTANIST SISTER.

When we aver that the soul has a body of a quality and kind peculiar to itself, in this special condition of it we shall be already supplied with a decision respecting all the other accidents of its corporeity; how that they belong to it, because we have shown it to be a body, but that even they have a quality peculiar to themselves, proportioned to the special nature of the body (to which they belong); or else, if any accidents (of a body) are remarkable in this instance for their absence, then this, too, results from the peculiarity of the condition of the soul's corporeity, from which are absent sundry qualities which are present to all other corporeal beings. And yet, notwithstanding all this, we shall not be at all inconsistent if we declare that the more usual characteristics of a body, such as invariably accrue to the corporeal condition, belong also to the soul—such as form[3] and limitation; and that triad of dimensions[4]—I mean length, and breadth, and height—by which philosophers gauge all bodies. What now remains but for us to give the soul a figure?[5] Plato refuses to do this, as if it endangered the soul's immortality.[6] For everything which has figure is, according to him, compound, and composed of parts;[7] whereas the soul is immortal; and being immortal, it is therefore indissoluble; and being indissoluble, it is figureless: for if, on the contrary, it had figure, it would be of a composite and structural formation. He, however, in some other manner frames for the soul an effigy of intellectual forms, beautiful for its just symmetry and tuitions of philosophy, but misshapen by some contrary qualities. As for ourselves, indeed, we inscribe on the soul the lineaments of corporeity, not simply from the assurance which reasoning has taught us of its corporeal nature, but also from the firm conviction which divine grace impresses on us by revelation. For, seeing that we acknowledge spiritual *charismata*, or gifts, we too have merited the attainment of the prophetic gift, although coming after John (the Baptist). We have now amongst us a sister whose lot it has been to be favoured with sundry gifts of revelation, which she experiences in the Spirit by ecstatic vision amidst the sacred rites of the Lord's day in the church: she converses with angels, and sometimes even with the Lord; she both sees and hears mysterious communications;[8] some men's hearts she understands, and to them who are in need she distributes remedies. Whether it be in the reading of Scriptures, or in the chanting of psalms, or in the preaching of sermons, or in the offering up of prayers, in all these religious services matter and opportunity are afforded to her of seeing visions. It may possibly have happened to us, whilst this sister of ours was rapt in the Spirit, that we had discoursed in some ineffable way about the soul. After the people are dismissed at the conclusion of the sacred services, she is in the regular habit of reporting to us whatever things she may have seen in vision (for all her communications are examined with the most scrupulous care, in order that their truth may be probed). "Amongst other things," says she, "there has been shown to me a soul in bodily shape, and a spirit has been in the habit of appearing to me; not, however, a void and empty illusion, but such as would offer itself to be even grasped by the hand, soft and transparent and of an etherial colour, and in form resembling that of a human being in every respect." This was her vision, and for her witness there was God; and the apostle most assuredly foretold that there were to be "spiritual gifts" in the church.[9] Now, can you refuse to believe this, even if indubitable evidence on every point is forthcoming for your conviction? Since, then, the soul is a corporeal substance, no doubt it possesses qualities such as those which we have just mentioned, amongst them the property of *colour*, which is inherent in every bodily substance. Now what colour would you attribute to the soul but an etherial transparent one? Not that its substance is actually the ether or air (although this was the opinion of Ænesidemus and Anaximenes, and I suppose of Heraclitus also, as some say of him), nor transparent light (although Heraclides of Pontus held it to be so). "Thunder-stones,"[10] indeed, are not of igneous substance, because they shine with ruddy redness; nor are beryls composed of aqueous matter, because they are of a pure wavy whiteness. How many things also besides these are there which their colour would associate in the same class, but which nature keeps widely apart! Since, however, everything which is very attenuated and transparent

---

[1] Rev. i. 10.
[2] Rev. vi. 9.
[3] Habitum.
[4] Illud trifariam distantivum (Τριχῶς διαστηματικόν) Fr. Junius.
[5] Effigiem.
[6] See his *Phædo*, pp. 105, 106.
[7] Structile.
[8] Sacramenta.
[9] 1 Cor. xii. 1–11. [A key to our author's
[10] Cerauniis gemmis.

bears a strong resemblance to the air, such would be the case with the soul, since in its material nature[1] it is wind and breath, (or spirit); whence it is that the belief of its corporeal quality is endangered, in consequence of the extreme tenuity and subtilty of its essence. Likewise, as regards the figure of the human soul from your own conception, you can well imagine that it is none other than the human form; indeed, none other than the shape of that body which each individual soul animates and moves about. This we may at once be induced to admit from contemplating man's original formation. For only carefully consider, after God hath breathed upon the face of man the breath of life, and man had consequently become a living soul, surely that breath must have passed through the face at once into the interior structure, and have spread itself throughout all the spaces of the body; and as soon as by the divine inspiration it had become condensed, it must have impressed itself on each internal feature, which the condensation had filled in, and so have been, as it were, congealed in shape, (or stereotyped). Hence, by this densifying process, there arose a fixing of the soul's corporeity; and by the impression its figure was formed and moulded. This is the inner man, different from the outer, but yet one in the twofold condition.[2] It, too, has eyes and ears of its own, by means of which Paul must have heard and seen the Lord;[3] it has, moreover all the other members of the body by the help of which it effects all processes of thinking and all activity in dreams. Thus it happens that the rich man in hell has a tongue and poor (Lazarus) a finger and Abraham a bosom.[4] By these features also the souls of the martyrs under the altar are distinguished and known. The soul indeed which in the beginning was associated with Adam's body, which grew with its growth and was moulded after its form proved to be the germ both of the entire substance (of the human soul) and of that (part of) creation

CHAP. X.—THE SIMPLE NATURE OF THE SOUL IS ASSERTED WITH PLATO. THE IDENTITY OF SPIRIT AND SOUL.

It is essential to a firm faith to declare with Plato[5] that the soul is simple; in other words uniform and uncompounded; simply that is to say in respect of its substance. Never

mind men's artificial views and theories, and away with the fabrications of heresy![6] Some maintain that there is within the soul a natural substance—the spirit—which is different from it:[7] as if to have life—the function of the soul—were one thing; and to emit breath —the alleged[8] function of the spirit—were another thing. Now it is not in all animals that these two functions are found; for there are many which only live but do not breathe in that they do not possess the organs of respiration—lungs and windpipes.[9] But of what use is it, in an examination of the soul of man, to borrow proofs from a gnat or an ant, when the great Creator in His divine arrangements has allotted to every animal organs of vitality suited to its own disposition and nature, so that we ought not to catch at any conjectures from comparisons of this sort? Man, indeed, although organically furnished with lungs and windpipes, will not on that account be proved to *breathe* by one process, and to *live* by another;[10] nor can the ant, although defective in these organs, be on that account said to be without respiration, as if it lived and that was all. For by whom has so clear an insight into the works of God been really attained, as to entitle him to assume that these organic resources are wanting to any living thing? There is that Herophilus, the well-known surgeon, or (as I may almost call him) butcher, who cut up no end of persons,[11] in order to investigate the secrets of nature, who ruthlessly handled[12] human creatures to discover (their form and make): I have my doubts whether he succeeded in clearly exploring all the internal parts of their structure, since death itself changes and disturbs the natural functions of life, especially when the death is not a natural one, but such as must cause irregularity and error amidst the very processes of dissection. Philosophers have affirmed it to be a certain fact, that gnats, and ants, and moths have no pulmonary or arterial organs. Well, then, tell me, you curious and elaborate investigator of these mysteries, have they eyes for seeing withal? But yet they proceed to whatever point they wish, and they both shun and aim at various objects by processes of sight: point out their eyes to me, show me their pupils. Moths also gnaw and eat: demonstrate to me their mandibles, reveal their jaw-teeth. Then,

---

[1] Tradux.
[2] Dupliciter unus.
[3] 2 Cor. xii. 2–4.
[4] Luke xvi. 23, 24.
[5] See his *Phædo*, p. 80 ; *Timæus*, § 12, p. 35 (Bekker, pp. 264, 265)

[6] We have here combined two readings, *effigies* (Oehler's) and *hæreses* (the usual one).
[7] Aliam.
[8] This is the force of the subjunctive *fiat*.
[9] Arterias.
[10] Aliunde spirabit, aliunde vivet. "In the nature of man, life and breath are inseparable." Bp. Kaye, p. 184.
[11] Sexcentos
[12] Odit.

again, gnats hum and buzz, nor even in the dark are they unable to find their way to our ears:[1] point out to me, then, not only the noisy tube, but the stinging lance of that mouth of theirs. Take any living thing whatever, be it the tiniest you can find, it must needs be fed and sustained by some food or other: show me, then, their organs for taking into their system, digesting, and ejecting food. What must we say, therefore? If it is by such instruments that life is maintained, these instrumental means must of course exist in all things which are to live, even though they are not apparent to the eye or to the apprehension by reason of their minuteness. You can more readily believe this, if you remember that God manifests His creative greatness quite as much in small objects as in the very largest. If, however, you suppose that God's wisdom has no capacity for forming such infinitesimal corpuscles, you can still recognise His greatness, in that He has furnished even to the smallest animals the functions of life, although in the absence of the suitable organs,—securing to them the power of sight, even without eyes; of eating, even without teeth; and of digestion, even without stomachs. Some animals also have the ability to move forward without feet, as serpents, by a gliding motion; or as worms, by vertical efforts; or as snails and slugs, by their slimy crawl. Why should you not then believe that respiration likewise may be effected without the bellows of the lungs, and without arterial canals? You would thus supply yourself with a strong proof that the spirit or breath is an adjunct of the human soul, for the very reason that some creatures lack breath, and that they lack it because they are not furnished with organs of respiration. You think it possible for a thing to live without breath; then why not suppose that a thing might breathe without lungs? Pray, tell me, what is it to breathe? I suppose it means to emit breath from yourself. What is it not to live? I suppose it means not to emit breath from yourself. This is the answer which I should have to make, if "to breathe" is not the same thing as "to live." It must, however, be characteristic of a dead man not to respire: to respire, therefore, is the characteristic of a living man. But to respire is likewise the characteristic of a breathing man: therefore also to breathe is the characteristic of a living man. Now, if both one and the other could possibly have been accomplished without the soul, to breathe might not be a function of the soul, but merely to live. But indeed to

live is to breathe, and to breathe is to live. Therefore this entire process, both of breathing and living, belongs to that to which living belongs—that is, to the soul. Well, then, since you separate the spirit (or breath) and the soul, separate their operations also. Let both of them accomplish some act apart from one another—the soul apart, the spirit apart. Let the soul live without the spirit; let the spirit breathe without the soul. Let one of them quit men's bodies, let the other remain; let death and life meet and agree. If indeed the soul and the spirit are two, they may be divided; and thus, by the separation of the one which departs from the one which remains, there would accrue the union and meeting together of life and of death. But such a union never will accrue: therefore they are not two, and they cannot be divided; but divided they might have been, if they had been (two). Still two things may surely coalesce in growth. But the two in question never will coalesce, since to live is one thing, and to breathe is another. Substances are distinguished by their operations. How much firmer ground have you for believing that the soul and the spirit are but one, since you assign to them no difference; so that the soul is itself the spirit, respiration being the function of that of which life also is! But what if you insist on supposing that the day is one thing, and the light, which is incidental to the day, is another thing, whereas day is only the light itself? There must, of course, be also different kinds of light, as (appears) from the ministry of fires. So likewise will there be different sorts of spirits, according as they emanate from God or from the devil. Whenever, indeed, the question is about soul and spirit, the soul will be (understood to be) itself the spirit, just is the day is the light itself. For a thing is itself identical with that by means of which itself exists.

CHAP. XI.—SPIRIT—A TERM EXPRESSIVE OF AN OPERATION OF THE SOUL, NOT OF ITS NATURE. TO BE CAREFULLY DISTINGUISHED FROM THE SPIRIT OF GOD.

But the nature of my present inquiry obliges me to call the soul spirit or breath, because to breathe is ascribed to another substance. We, however, claim this (operation) for the soul, which we acknowledge to be an indivisible simple substance, and therefore we must call it spirit in a definitive sense—not because of its condition, but of its action; not in respect of its nature, but of its operation; because it *respires*, and not because it is spirit

---

[1] Aurium cæci.

in any especial sense.[1] For to blow or breathe is to respire. So that we are driven to describe, by (the term which indicates this respiration—that is to say) *spirit*—the soul which we hold to be, by the propriety of its action, breath. Moreover, we properly and especially insist on calling it breath (or spirit), in opposition to Hermogenes, who derives the soul from matter instead of from the *afflatus* or breath of God. He, to be sure, goes flatly against the testimony of Scripture, and with this view converts breath into spirit, because he cannot believe that the (creature on which was breathed the) Spirit of God fell into sin, and then into condemnation; and therefore he would conclude that the soul came from matter rather than from the Spirit or breath of God. For this reason, we on our side, even from that passage, maintain the soul to be breath and not the spirit, in the scriptural and distinctive sense of the spirit; and here it is with regret that we apply the term spirit at all in the lower sense, in consequence of the identical action of respiring and breathing. In that passage, the only question is about the natural substance; to respire being an act of nature. I would not tarry a moment longer on this point, were it not for those heretics who introduce into the soul some spiritual germ which passes my comprehension: (they make it to have been) conferred upon the soul by the secret liberality of her mother Sophia (*Wisdom*), without the knowledge of the Creator.[2] But (Holy) Scripture, which has a better knowledge of the soul's Maker, or rather God, has told us nothing more than that God breathed on man's face the breath of life, and that man became a living soul, by means of which he was both to live and breathe; at the same time making a sufficiently clear distinction between the spirit and the soul,[3] in such passages as the following, wherein God Himself declares: "My Spirit went forth from me, and I made the breath of each. And the breath of my Spirit became soul."[4] And again: "He giveth breath unto the people that are on the earth, and Spirit to them that walk thereon."[5] First of all there comes the (natural) soul, that is to say, the breath, to the people that are on the earth,—in other words, to those who act carnally in the flesh; then afterwards comes the Spirit to those who walk thereon,—that is, who subdue the works of the flesh; because the apostle also says, that "that is not first which is spiritual, but that which is natural, (or in possession of the natural soul,) and afterward that which is spiritual."[6] For, inasmuch as Adam straightway predicted that "great mystery of Christ and the church,"[7] when he said, "This now is bone of my bones, and flesh of my flesh; therefore shall a man leave his father and his mother, and shall cleave unto his wife, and they two shall become one flesh,"[8] he experienced the influence of the Spirit. For there fell upon him that ecstasy, which is the Holy Ghost's operative virtue of prophecy. And even the evil spirit too is an influence which comes upon a man. Indeed, the Spirit of God not more really "turned Saul into another man,"[9] that is to say, into a prophet, when "people said one to another, What is this which is come to the son of Kish? Is Saul also among the prophets?"[10] than did the evil spirit afterwards turn him into another man—in other words, into an apostate. Judas likewise was for a long time reckoned among the elect (apostles), and was even appointed to the office of their treasurer; he was not yet the traitor, although he was become fraudulent; but afterwards the devil entered into him. Consequently, as the spirit neither of God nor of the devil is naturally planted with a man's soul at his birth, this soul must evidently exist apart and alone, previous to the accession to it of either spirit: if thus apart and alone, it must also be simple and uncompounded as regards its substance; and therefore it cannot respire from any other cause than from the actual condition of its own substance.

CHAP. XII.—DIFFERENCE BETWEEN THE MIND AND THE SOUL, AND THE RELATION BETWEEN THEM.

In like manner the mind also, or *animus*, which the Greeks designate ΝΟΥΣ, is taken by us in no other sense than as indicating that faculty or apparatus[11] which is inherent and implanted in the soul, and naturally proper to it, whereby it acts, whereby it acquires knowledge, and by the possession of which it is capable of a spontaneity of motion within itself, and of thus appearing to be impelled by the mind, as if it were another substance, as is maintained by those who determine the soul to be the moving principle of the universe[12]—the god of Socrates, Valentinus' "only-begotten" of his father[13] *Bythus*, and

---

[1] Proprie "by reason of its nature."
[2] See the tract *Adv. Valentin.* c. xxv. *infra.*
[3] Compare *Adv. Hermog.* xxxii. xxxiii.; also Irenæus, v. 12, 17. [See Vol. I. p. 527, this Series.]
[4] Tertullian's reading of Isa. lvii. 16.
[5] Isa. xlii. 5.
[6] 1 Cor. xv. 46.
[7] Eph. v. 31, 32.
[8] Gen. ii. 24, 25.
[9] 1 Sam. x. 6.
[10] 1 Sam. x. 11.
[11] Suggestum.
[12] Comp. *The Apology,* c. xlviii.; August. *De Civ. Dei,* xiii. 17.
[13] Comp. *Adv. Valentin.* vii. *infra.*

his mother *Sige*. How confused is the opinion of Anaxagoras! For, having imagined the mind to be the initiating principle of all things, and suspending on its axis the balance of the universe; affirming, moreover, that the mind is a simple principle, unmixed, and incapable of admixture, he mainly on this very consideration separates it from all amalgamation with the soul; and yet in another passage he actually incorporates it with[1] the soul. This (inconsistency) Aristotle has also observed; but whether he meant his criticism to be constructive, and to fill up a system of his own, rather than destructive of the principles of others, I am hardly able to decide. As for himself, indeed, although he postpones his definition of the mind, yet he begins by mentioning, as one of the two natural constituents of the mind,[2] that divine principle which he conjectures to be impassible, or incapable of emotion, and thereby removes from all association with the soul. For whereas it is evident that the soul is susceptible of those emotions which it falls to it naturally to suffer, it must needs suffer either by the mind or with the mind. Now if the soul is by nature associated with the mind, it is impossible to draw the conclusion that the mind is impassible; or again, if the soul suffers not either by the mind or with the mind, it cannot possibly have a natural association with the mind, with which it suffers nothing, and which suffers nothing itself. Moreover, if the soul suffers nothing by the mind and with the mind, it will experience no sensation, nor will it acquire any knowledge, nor will it undergo any emotion through the agency of the mind, as they maintain it will. For Aristotle makes even the senses passions, or states of emotion. And rightly too. For to exercise the senses is to suffer emotion, because to suffer is to feel. In like manner, to acquire knowledge is to exercise the senses; and to undergo emotion is to exercise the senses; and the whole of this is a state of suffering. But we see that the soul experiences nothing of these things, in such a manner as that the mind also is not affected by the emotion, by which, indeed, and with which, all is effected. It follows, therefore, that the mind is capable of admixture, in opposition to Anaxagoras; and passible or susceptible of emotion, contrary to the opinion of Aristotle. Besides, if a separate condition between the soul and mind is to be admitted, so that they be two things in substance, then of one of them, emotion and sensation, and every sort of taste, and all action

and motion, will be the characteristics; whilst of the other the natural condition will be calm, and repose, and stupor. There is therefore no alternative: either the mind must be useless and void, or the soul. But if these affections may certainly be all of them ascribed to both, then in that case the two will be one and the same, and Democritus will carry his point when he suppresses all distinction between the two. The question will arise how two can be one—whether by the confusion of two substances, or by the disposition of one? We, however, affirm that the mind coalesces with[3] the soul,—not indeed as being distinct from it in substance, but as being its natural function and agent.[4]

CHAP. XIII.—THE SOUL'S SUPREMACY.

It next remains to examine where lies the supremacy; in other words, which of the two is superior to the other, so that that with which the supremacy clearly lies shall be the essentially superior substance;[5] whilst that over which this essentially superior substance shall have authority shall be considered as the natural functionary of the superior substance. Now who will hesitate to ascribe this entire authority to the soul, from the name of which the whole man has received his own designation in common phraseology? How many *souls*, says the rich man, do I maintain? not how many *minds*. The pilot's desire, also, is to rescue so many *souls* from shipwreck, not so many minds; the labourer, too, in his work, and the soldier on the field of battle, affirms that he lays down his soul (or life), not his mind. Which of the two has its perils or its vows and wishes more frequently on men's lips—the mind or the soul? Which of the two are dying persons, said to have to do with the mind or the soul? In short, philosophers themselves, and medical men, even when it is their purpose to discourse about the mind, do in every instance inscribe on their title-page[6] and table of contents,[7] "*De Anima*" ("*A treatise on the soul*"). And that you may also have God's voucher on the subject, it is the soul which He addresses; it is the soul which He exhorts and counsels, to turn the mind and intellect to Him. It is the soul which Christ came to save; it is the soul which He threatens to destroy in hell; it is the soul (or life) which He forbids being made too much of; it is His soul, too (or life), which the good Shepherd Himself lays down for His

---

[1] Addicit.
[2] Alterum animi genus.

[3] Concretum.
[4] Substantiæ officium.
[5] Substantiæ massa.
[6] Faciem operis.
[7] Fontem materiæ.

sheep. It is to the soul, therefore, that you ascribe the supremacy; in *it* also you possess that union of substance, of which you perceive the mind to be the instrument, not the ruling power.

CHAP. XIV.—THE SOUL VARIOUSLY DIVIDED BY THE PHILOSOPHERS; THIS DIVISION IS NOT A MATERIAL DISSECTION.

Being thus single, simple, and entire in itself, it is as incapable of being composed and put together from external constituents, as it is of being divided in and of itself, inasmuch as it is indissoluble. For if it had been possible to construct it and to destroy it, it would no longer be immortal. Since, however, it is not mortal, it is also incapable of dissolution and division. Now, to be divided means to be dissolved, and to be dissolved means to die. Yet (philosophers) have divided the soul into parts: Plato, for instance, into two; Zeno, into three; Panætius, into five or six; Soranus, into seven; Chrysippus, into as many as eight; and Apollophanes, into as many as nine; whilst certain of the Stoics have found as many as twelve parts in the soul. Posidonius makes even two more than these: he starts with two leading faculties of the soul,—the *directing* faculty, which they designate ἡγεμονικόν; and the *rational* faculty, which they call λογικόν,—and ultimately subdivided these into seventeen [1] parts. Thus variously is the soul dissected by the different schools. Such divisions, however, ought not to be regarded so much as parts of the soul, as powers, or faculties, or operations thereof, even as Aristotle himself has regarded some of them as being. For they are not portions or organic parts of the soul's substance, but functions of the soul —such as those of motion, of action, of thought, and whatsoever others they divide in this manner; such, likewise, as the five senses themselves, so well known to all—seeing, hearing, tasting, touching, smelling. Now, although they have allotted to the whole of these respectively certain parts of the body as their special domiciles, it does not from that circumstance follow that a like distribution will be suitable to the sections of the soul; for even the body itself would not admit of such a partition as they would have the soul undergo. But of the whole number of the limbs one body is made up, so that the arrangement is rather a concretion than a division. Look at that very wonderful piece of organic mechanism by Archimedes,—I mean his hydraulic organ, with its many limbs, parts,

bands, passages for the notes, outlets for their sounds, combinations for their harmony, and the array of its pipes; but yet the whole of these details constitute only one instrument. In like manner the wind, which breathes throughout this organ at the impulse of the hydraulic engine, is not divided into separate portions from the fact of its dispersion through the instrument to make it play: it is whole and entire in its substance, although divided in its operation. This example is not remote from (the illustration) of Strato, and Ænesidemus, and Heraclitus: for these philosophers maintain the unity of the soul, as diffused over the entire body, and yet in every part the same.[2] Precisely like the wind blown in the pipes throughout the organ, the soul displays its energies in various ways by means of the senses, being not indeed divided, but rather distributed in natural order. Now, under what designations these energies are to be known, and by what divisions of themselves they are to be classified, and to what special offices and functions in the body they are to be severally confined, the physicians and the philosophers must consider and decide: for ourselves, a few remarks only will be proper.

CHAP. XV.—THE SOUL'S VITALITY AND INTELLIGENCE. ITS CHARACTER AND SEAT IN MAN.

In the first place, (we must determine) whether there be in the soul some supreme principle of vitality and intelligence [3] which they call "the ruling power of the soul"— τὸ ἡγεμονικόν for if this be not admitted, the whole condition of the soul is put in jeopardy. Indeed, those men who say that there is no such directing faculty, have begun by supposing that the soul itself is simply a nonentity. One Dicæarchus, a Messenian, and amongst the medical profession Andreas and Asclepiades, have thus destroyed the (soul's) directing power, by actually placing in the mind the senses, for which they claim the ruling faculty. Asclepiades rides rough-shod over us with even this argument, that very many animals, after losing those parts of their body in which the soul's principle of vitality and sensation is thought mainly to exist, still retain life in a considerable degree, as well as sensation: as in the case of flies, and wasps, and locusts, when you have cut off their heads; and of she-goats, and tortoises, and eels, when you have pulled out their hearts. (He concludes), therefore, that there is no especial principle or power of the

---

[1] This is Oehler's text ; another reading has *twelve*, which one would suppose to be the right one.

[2] Ubique ipsa.
[3] Sapientialis.

soul; for if there were, the soul's vigour and strength could not continue when it was removed with its domiciles (or corporeal organs). However, Dicæarchus has several authorities against him—and philosophers too—Plato, Strato, Epicurus, Democritus, Empedocles, Socrates, Aristotle; whilst in opposition to Andreas and Asclepiades (may be placed their brother) physicians Herophilus, Erasistratus, Diocles, Hippocrates, and Soranus himself; and better than all others, there are our Christian authorities. We are taught by God concerning both these questions—viz. that there is a ruling power in the soul, and that it is enshrined[1] in one particular recess of the body. For, when one reads of God as being "the searcher and witness of the heart;"[2] when His prophet is reproved by His discovering to him the secrets of the heart;[3] when God Himself anticipates in His people the thoughts of their heart,[4] "Why think ye evil in your hearts?"[5] when David prays, "Create in me a clean heart, O God,"[6] and Paul declares, "With the heart man believeth unto righteousness,"[7] and John says, "By his own heart is each man condemned;"[8] when, lastly, "he who looketh on a woman so as to lust after her, hath already committed adultery with her in his heart,"[9]—then both points are cleared fully up, that there is a directing faculty of the soul, with which the purpose of God may agree; in other words, a supreme principle of intelligence and vitality (for where there is intelligence, there must be vitality), and that it resides in that most precious part[10] of our body to which God especially looks: so that you must not suppose, with Heraclitus, that this sovereign faculty of which we are treating is moved by some external force; nor with Moschion,[11] that it floats about through the whole body; nor with Plato, that it is enclosed in the head; nor with Zenophanes, that it culminates in the crown of the head; nor that it reposes in the brain, according to the opinion of Hippocrates; nor around the basis of the brain, as Herophilus thought; nor in the membranes thereof, as Strato and Erasistratus said; nor in the space between the eyebrows, as Strato the physician held; nor within the enclosure[12] of the breast, according to Epicurus: but rather, as the Egyptians have always taught, especially such of them as were accounted the expounders of sacred truths;[13] in accordance, too, with that verse of Orpheus or Empedocles:

" Namque homini sanguis circumcordialis est sensus."[14]
" Man has his (supreme) sensation in the blood around his heart."

Even Protagoras[15] likewise, and Apollodorus, and Chrysippus, entertain this same view, so that (our friend) Asclepiades may go in quest of his goats bleating without a heart, and hunt his flies without their heads; and let all those (worthies), too, who have predetermined the character of the human soul from the condition of brute animals, be quite sure that it is themselves rather who are alive in a heartless and brainless state.

CHAP. XVI.—THE SOUL'S PARTS. ELEMENTS OF THE RATIONAL SOUL.

That position of Plato's is also quite in keeping with the faith, in which he divides the soul into two parts—the rational and the irrational. To this definition we take no exception, except that we would not ascribe this twofold distinction to the nature (of the soul). It is the rational element which we must believe to be its natural condition, impressed upon it from its very first creation by its Author, who is Himself esentially rational. For how should that be other than rational, which God produced on His own prompting; nay more, which He expressly sent forth by His own *afflatus* or breath? The irrational element, however, we must understand to have accrued later, as having proceeded from the instigation of the serpent—the very achievement of (the first) transgression—which thenceforward became inherent in the soul, and grew with its growth, assuming the manner by this time of a natural development, happening as it did immediately at the beginning of nature. But, inasmuch as the same Plato speaks of the rational element only as existing in the soul of God Himself, if we were to ascribe the irrational element likewise to the nature which our soul has received from God, then the irrational element will be equally derived from God, as being a natural production, because God is the author of nature. Now from the devil proceeds the incentive to sin. All sin, however, is irrational: therefore the irrational proceeds from the devil, from whom sin proceeds; and it is ex-

[1] Consecratum.
[2] Wisd. i. 6.
[3] Prov. xxiv. 12.
[4] Ps. cxxxix. 23.
[5] Matt. ix. 4.
[6] Ps. li. 12.
[7] Rom. x. 10.
[8] 1 John iii. 20.
[9] Matt. v. 28.
[10] In eo thesauro.
[11] Not Suidas' philosopher of that name, but a renowned physician mentioned by Galen and Pliny (Oehler).
[12] Lorica.

[13] The Egyptian *hierophants*.
[14] The original, as given in Stobæus, *Eclog.* i. p. 1026, is this hexameter: Αἷμα γὰρ ἀνθρώποις περικάρδιόν ἐστι νόημα.
[15] Or probably that *Praxagoras* the physician who is often mentioned by Athenæus and by Pliny (Pamel.).

traneous to God, to whom also the irrational is an alien principle. The diversity, then, between these two elements arises from the difference of their authors. When, therefore, Plato reserves the rational element (of the soul) to God alone, and subdivides it into two departments the *irascible*, which they call θυμικόν, and the *concupiscible*, which they designate by the term ἐπιθυμητικόν (in such a way as to make the first common to us and lions, and the second shared between ourselves and flies, whilst the rational element is confined to us and God)—I see that this point will have to to be treated by us, owing to the facts which we find operating also in Christ. For you may behold this triad of qualities in the Lord. There was the *rational* element, by which He taught, by which He discoursed, by which He prepared the way of salvation; there was moreover *indignation* in Him, by which He inveighed against the scribes and the Pharisees; and there was the principle of *desire*, by which He so earnestly desired to eat the passover with His disciples.[1] In our own cases, accordingly, the irascible and the concupiscible elements of our soul must not invariably be put to the account of the irrational (nature), since we are sure that in our Lord these elements operated in entire accordance with reason. God will be angry, with perfect reason, with all who deserve His wrath; and with reason, too, will God desire whatever objects and claims are worthy of Himself. For He will show indignation against the evil man, and for the good man will He desire salvation. To ourselves even does the apostle allow the concupiscible quality. "If any man," says he, "desireth the office of a bishop, he desireth a good work."[2] Now, by saying "a good work," he shows us that the desire is a reasonable one. He permits us likewise to feel indignation. How should he not, when he himself experiences the same? "I would," says he, "that they were even cut off which trouble you."[3] In perfect agreement with reason was that indignation which resulted from his desire to maintain discipline and order. When, however, he says, "We were formerly the children of wrath,"[4] he censures an irrational irascibility, such as proceeds not from that nature which is the production of God, but from that which the devil brought in, who is himself styled the lord or "master" of his own class, "Ye cannot serve two *masters*,"[5] and has the actual designation of "father:" "Ye are of your

father the devil."[6] So that you need not be afraid to ascribe to him the mastery and dominion over that second, later, and deteriorated nature (of which we have been speaking), when you read of him as "the sower of tares," and the nocturnal spoiler of the crop of corn.[7]

CHAP. XVII.—THE FIDELITY OF THE SENSES, IMPUGNED BY PLATO, VINDICATED BY CHRIST HIMSELF.

Then, again, when we encounter the question (as to the veracity of those five senses which we learn with our alphabet; since from this source even there arises some support for our heretics. They are the faculties of seeing, and hearing, and smelling, and tasting, and touching. The fidelity of these senses is impugned with too much severity by the Platonists,[8] and according to some by Heraclitus also, and Diocles, and Empedocles; at any rate, Plato, in the *Timæus*, declares the operations of the senses to be irrational, and vitiated[9] by our opinions or beliefs. Deception is imputed to the sight, because it asserts that oars, when immersed in the water, are inclined or bent, notwithstanding the certainty that they are straight; because, again, it is quite sure that that distant tower with its really quadrangular contour is round; because also it will discredit the fact of the truly parallel fabric of yonder porch or arcade, by supposing it to be narrower and narrower towards its end; and because it will join with the sea the sky which hangs at so great a height above it. In the same way, our hearing is charged with fallacy: we think, for instance, that that is a noise in the sky which is nothing else than the rumbling of a carriage; or, if you prefer it[10] the other way, when the thunder rolled at a distance, we were quite sure that it was a carriage which made the noise. Thus, too, are our faculties of smell and taste at fault, because the selfsame perfumes and wines lose their value after we have used them awhile. On the same principle our touch is censured, when the identical pavement which seemed rough to the hands is felt by the feet to be smooth enough; and in the baths a stream of warm water is pronounced to be quite hot at first, and beautifully temperate afterwards. Thus, according to them, our senses deceive us, when all the while *we* are (the cause of the discrepancies, by) changing our opinions. The Stoics are more moderate in their views;

---

[1] Luke xxii. 15.
[2] 1 Tim. iii. 1.
[3] Gal. v. 12.
[4] Eph. ii. 3.
[5] Matt. vi. 24.

[6] John vi. 44.
[7] Matt. xiii. 25.
[8] Academici.
[9] Coimplicitam "entangled" or "embarrassed." See the *Timæus* pp. 27, 28.
[10] Vel.

for they do not load with the obloquy of deception every one of the senses, and at all times. The Epicureans, again, show still greater consistency, in maintaining that all the senses are equally true in their testimony, and always so—only in a different way. It is not our organs of sensation that are at fault, but our opinion. The senses only experience sensation, they do not exercise opinion; it is the soul that *opines*. They separated opinion from the senses, and sensation from the soul. Well, but whence comes opinion, if not from the senses? Indeed, unless the eye had descried a round shape in that tower, it could have had no idea that it possessed roundness. Again, whence arises sensation if not from the soul? For if the soul had no body, it would have no sensation. Accordingly, sensation comes from the soul, and opinion from sensation; and the whole (process) is the soul. But further, it may well be insisted on that there is a something which causes the discrepancy between the report of the senses and the reality of the facts. Now, since it is possible, (as we have seen), for phenomena to be reported which exist not in the objects, why should it not be equally possible for phenomena to be reported which are caused not by the senses, but by reasons and conditions which intervene, in the very nature of the case? If so, it will be only right that they should be duly recognised. The truth is, that it was the water which was the cause of the oar seeming to be inclined or bent: out of the water, it was perfectly straight in appearance (as well as in fact). The delicacy of the substance or medium which forms a mirror by means of its luminosity, according as it is struck or shaken, by the vibration actually destroys the appearance of the straightness of a right line. In like manner, the condition of the open space which fills up the interval between it and us, necessarily causes the true shape of the tower to escape our notice; for the uniform density of the surrounding air covering its angles with a similar light obliterates their outlines. So, again, the equal breadth of the arcade is sharpened or narrowed off towards its termination, until its aspect, becoming more and more contracted under its prolonged roof, comes to a vanishing point in the direction of its farthest distance. So the sky blends itself with the sea, the vision becoming spent at last, which had maintained duly the boundaries of the two elements, so long as its vigorous glance lasted. As for the (alleged cases of deceptive) hearing, what else could produce the illusion but the similarity of the sounds? And if the perfume afterwards was less strong to the smell, and the wine more flat to the taste, and the water not so hot to the touch, their original strength was after all found in the whole of them pretty well unimpaired. In the matter, however, of the roughness and smoothness of the pavement, it was only natural and right that limbs like the hands and the feet, so different in tenderness and callousness, should have different impressions. In this way, then, there cannot occur an illusion in our senses without an adequate cause. Now if special causes, (such as we have indicated,) mislead our senses and (through our senses) our opinions also, then we must no longer ascribe the deception to the senses, which follow the specific causes of the illusion, nor to the opinions we form; for these are occasioned and controlled by our senses, which only follow the causes. Persons who are afflicted with madness or insanity, mistake one object for another. Orestes in his sister sees his mother; Ajax sees Ulysses in the slaughtered herd; Athamas and Agave descry wild beasts in their children. Now is it their eyes or their phrenzy which you must blame for so vast a fallacy? All things taste bitter, in the redundancy of their bile, to those who have the jaundice. Is it their taste which you will charge with the physical prevarication, or their ill state of health? All the senses, therefore, are disordered occasionally, or imposed upon, but only in such a way as to be quite free of any fault in their own natural functions. But further still, not even against the specific causes and conditions themselves must we lay an indictment of deception. For, since these physical aberrations happen for stated reasons, the reasons do not deserve to be regarded as deceptions. Whatever ought to occur in a certain manner is not a deception. If, then, even these circumstantial causes must be acquitted of all censure and blame, how much more should we free from reproach the senses, over which the said causes exercise a liberal sway! Hence we are bound most certainly to claim for the senses truth, and fidelity, and integrity, seeing that they never render any other account of their impressions than is enjoined on them by the specific causes or conditions which in all cases produce that discrepancy which appears between the report of the senses and the reality of the objects. What mean you, then, O most insolent Academy? You overthrow the entire condition of human life; you disturb the whole order of nature; you obscure the good providence of God Himself: for the senses of man which God has appointed over all His works, that we might understand, inhabit, dispense, and enjoy them, (you reproach) as fallacious and treacherous tyrants ! But is it not from these that all creation receives our services ? Is it not by their means that a second form is impressed even upon the world ?—so many arts, so many industrious resources, so many pursuits, such business, such offices, such commerce, such remedies, counsels, consolations, modes, civilizations, and accomplishments of life ! All these things have produced the very relish and savour of human existence; whilst by these senses of man, he alone of all animated nature has the distinction of being a rational animal, with a capacity for intelligence and knowledge—nay, an ability to form the Academy itself ! But Plato, in order to disparage the testimony of the senses, in the *Phædrus* denies (in the person of Socrates) his own ability to know even himself, according to the injunction of the Delphic oracle; and in the *Theætetus* he deprives himself of the faculties of knowledge and sensation; and again, in the *Phædrus* he postpones till after death the posthumous knowledge, as he calls it, of the truth; and yet for all he went on playing the philosopher even before he died. We may not, I say, we may not call into question the truth of the (poor vilified) senses,[1] lest we should even in Christ Himself, bring doubt upon [2] the truth of their sensation; lest perchance it should be said that He did *not* really " behold Satan as lightning fall from heaven;"[3] that He did *not* really hear the Father's voice testifying of Himself;[4] or that He was deceived in touching Peter's wife's mother;[5] or that the fragrance of the ointment which He afterwards smelled was different from that which He accepted for His burial;[6] and that the taste of the wine was different from that which He consecrated in memory of His blood.[7] On this false principle it was that Marcion actually chose to believe that He was a phantom, denying to Him the reality of a perfect body. Now, not even to His apostles was His nature ever a matter of deception. He was truly both seen and heard upon the mount;[8] true and real was the draught of that wine at the marriage of (Cana in) Galilee;[9] true and real also was the touch of the then believing Thomas.[10] Read the testimony of John: " That which we have seen, which we have heard, which we have looked upon with our eyes, and our hands have handled, of the Word of life."[11] False, of course, and deceptive must have been that testimony, if the witness of our eyes, and ears, and hands be by nature a lie.

CHAP. XVIII.—PLATO SUGGESTED CERTAIN ERRORS TO THE GNOSTICS. FUNCTIONS OF THE SOUL.

I turn now to the department of our intellectual faculties, such as Plato has handed it over to the heretics, distinct from our bodily functions, having obtained the knowledge of them before death.[12] He asks in the *Phædo*, What, then, (do you think) concerning the actual possession of *knowledge?* Will the body be a hindrance to it or not, if one shall admit it as an associate in the search after knowledge ? I have a similar question to ask: Have the faculties of their sight and hearing any truth and reality for human beings or not ? Is it not the case, that even the poets are always muttering against us, that we can never hear or see anything for certain ? He remembered, no doubt, what Epicharmus the comic poet had said: " It is the mind which sees, the mind that hears—all else is blind and deaf." To the same purport he says again, that that man is the wisest whose mental power is the clearest; who never applies the sense of sight, nor adds to his mind the help of any such faculty, but employs the intellect itself in unmixed serenity when he indulges in contemplation for the purpose of acquiring an unalloyed insight into the nature of things; divorcing himself with all his might from his eyes and ears and (as one must express himself) from the whole of his body, on the ground of its disturbing the soul, and not allowing it to possess either truth or wisdom, whenever it is brought into communication with it. We see, then, that in opposition to the bodily senses another faculty is provided of a much more serviceable character, even the powers of the soul, which produce an understanding of that truth whose realities are not palpable nor open to the bodily senses, but are very remote from men's everyday knowledge, lying in secret—in the heights above, and in the presence of God Himself. For Plato maintains that there are certain invisible substances, incorporeal, celestial,[13] divine, and eternal, which they call *ideas*, that is to say, (archetypal) forms, which are the patterns and causes of those objects of nature which are manifest to us, and lie under our corporeal senses: the former, (according to Plato,) are the actual verities, and

---

[1] Sensus istos.
[2] Deliberetur.
[3] Luke x. 18.
[4] Matt. iii. 17.
[5] Matt. viii. 15.
[6] Matt. xxvi. 7–12.
[7] Matt. xxvi. 27, 28 ; Luke xxii. 19, 20 ; 1 Cor. xi. 25.
[8] Matt. xvii. 3–8.
[9] John ii. 1–10.
[10] John xx. 27.

[11] 1 John i. 1.
[12] Said ironicallly, as if rallying Plato for inconsistency between his theory here and the fact.
[13] Supermundiales " placed above this world."

the latter the images and likenesses of them. Well, now, are there not here gleams of the heretical principles of the Gnostics and the Valentinians? It is from this philosophy that they eagerly adopt the difference between the bodily senses and the intellectual faculties,— a distinction which they actually apply to the parable of the ten virgins: making the five foolish virgins to symbolize the five bodily senses, seeing that these are so silly and so easy to be deceived; and the wise virgin to express the meaning of the intellectual faculties, which are so wise as to attain to that mysterious and supernal truth, which is placed in the pleroma. (Here, then, we have) the mystic original of the ideas of these heretics. For in this philosophy lie both their Æons and their genealogies. Thus, too, do they divide sensation, both into the intellectual powers from their spiritual seed, and the sensuous faculties from the animal, which cannot by any means comprehend spiritual things. From the former germ spring invisible things; from the latter, visible things which are grovelling and temporary, and which are obvious to the senses, placed as they are in palpable forms.[1] It is because of these views that we have in a former passage stated as a preliminary fact, that the mind is nothing else than an apparatus or instrument of the soul,[2] and that the spirit is no other faculty, separate from the soul, but is the soul itself exercised in respiration; although that influence which either God on the one hand, or the devil on the other, has breathed upon it, must be regarded in the light of an additional element.[3] And now, with respect to the difference between the intellectual powers and the sensuous faculties, we only admit it so far as the natural diversity between them requires of us. (There is, of course, a difference) between things corporeal and things spiritual, between visible and invisible beings, between objects which are manifest to the view and those which are hidden from it; because the one class are attributed to sensation, and the other to the intellect. But yet both the one and the other must be regarded as inherent in the soul, and as obedient to it, seeing that it embraces bodily objects by means of the body, in exactly the same way that it conceives incorporeal objects by help of the mind, except that it is even exercising sensation when it is employing the intellect. For is it not true, that to employ the senses is to use the intellect? And to employ the intellect amounts to a use of the senses?[4] What

indeed can sensation be, but the understanding of that which is the object of the sensation? And what can the intellect or understanding be, but the seeing of that which is the object understood? Why adopt such excruciating means of torturing simple knowledge and crucifying the truth? Who can show me the sense which does not understand the object of its sensation, or the intellect which perceives not the object which it understands, in so clear a way as to prove to me that the one can do without the other? If corporeal things are the objects of sense, and incorporeal ones objects of the intellect, it is the *classes* of the objects which are different, not the domicile or abode of sense and intellect; in other words, not the soul (*anima*) and the mind (*animus*). By what, in short, are corporeal things perceived? If it is by the soul,[5] then the mind is a sensuous faculty, and not merely an intellectual power; for whilst it understands, it also perceives, because without the perception there is no understanding. If, however, corporeal things are perceived by the soul, then it follows that the soul's power is an intellectual one, and not merely a sensuous faculty; for while it perceives it also understands, because without understanding there is no perceiving. And then, again, by what are incorporeal things understood? If it is by the mind,[6] where will be the soul? If it is by the soul, where will be the mind? For things which differ ought to be mutually absent from each other, when they are occupied in their respective functions and duties. It must be your opinion, indeed, that the mind is absent from the soul on certain occasions; for (you suppose) that we are so made and constituted as not to know that we have seen or heard something, on the hypothesis[7] that the mind was absent at the time. I must therefore maintain that the very soul itself neither saw nor heard, since it was at the given moment absent with its active power— that is to say, the mind. The truth is, that whenever a man is out of his mind,[8] it is his soul that is demented—not because the mind is absent, but because it is a fellow-sufferer (with the soul) at the time.[9] Indeed, it is the soul which is principally affected by casualties of such a kind. Whence is this fact confirmed? It is confirmed from the follow-

[1] Imaginibus.
[2] See above, c. xii. p. 192.
[3] Above, c. xi. p. 191.
[4] Intelligere sentire est.

[5] Oehler has "anima;" we should rather have expected "animo," which is another reading.
[6] "Animo" this time.
[7] Subjunctive verb, "fuerit."
[8] Dementit.
[9] The opposite opinion was held by Tertullian's opponents, who distinguished between the mind and the soul. They said, that when a man was out of his mind, his mind left him, but that his soul remained. (Lactantius, *De Opif.* xviii. ; *Instit. Div.* vii. 12 : La Cerda).

ing consideration: that after the soul's departure, the mind is no longer found in a man: it always follows the soul; nor does it at last remain behind it alone, after death. Now, since it follows the soul, it is also indissolubly attached to it; just as the understanding is attached to the soul, which is followed by the mind, with which the understanding is indissolubly connected. Granted now that the understanding is superior to the senses, and a better discoverer of mysteries, what matters it, so long as it is only a peculiar faculty of the soul, just as the senses themselves are? It does not at all affect my argument, unless the understanding were held to be superior to the senses, for the purpose of deducing from the allegation of such superiority its separate condition likewise. After thus combating their alleged difference, I have also to refute this question of superiority, previous to my approaching the belief (which heresy propounds) in a superior god. On this point, however, of a (superior) god, we shall have to measure swords with the heretics on their own ground.[1] Our present subject concerns the soul, and the point is to prevent the insidious ascription of a superiority to the intellect or understanding. Now, although the objects which are touched by the intellect are of a higher nature, since they are spiritual, than those which are embraced by the senses, since these are corporeal, it will still be only a superiority in the *objects*—as of lofty ones contrasted with humble—not in the *faculties* of the intellect against the senses. For how can the intellect be superior to the senses, when it is these which educate it for the discovery of various truths? It is a fact, that these truths are learned by means of palpable forms; in other words, invisible things are discovered by the help of visible ones, even as the apostle tells us in his epistle: "For the invisible things of Him are clearly seen from the creation of the world, being understood by the things that are made;"[2] and as Plato too might inform our heretics: "The things which appear are the image[3] of the things which are concealed from view,"[4] whence it must needs follow that this world is by all means an image of some other: so that the intellect evidently uses the senses for its own guidance, and authority, and mainstay; and without the senses truth could not be attained. How, then, can a thing be superior to that which is instrumental to its existence, which is also indispensable to it, and

to whose help it owes everything which it acquires? Two conclusions therefore follow from what we have said: (1) That the intellect is not to be preferred above the senses, on the (supposed) ground that the agent through which a thing exists is inferior to the thing itself; and (2) that the intellect must not be separated from the senses, since the instrument by which a thing's existence is sustained is associated with the thing itself.

CHAP. XIX.—THE INTELLECT COEVAL WITH THE SOUL IN THE HUMAN BEING. AN EXAMPLE FROM ARISTOTLE CONVERTED INTO EVIDENCE FAVOURABLE TO THESE VIEWS.

Nor must we fail to notice those writers who deprive the soul of the intellect even for a short period of time. *They do this* in order to prepare the way of introducing the intellect —and the mind also—at a subsequent time of life, even at the time when intelligence appears in a man. They maintain that the stage of infancy is supported by the soul alone, simply to promote vitality, without any intention of acquiring knowledge also, because not all things have knowledge which possess life. Trees, for instance, to quote Aristotle's example,[5] have vitality, but have not knowledge; and *with him agrees* every one who gives a share to all animated beings of the animal substance, which, according to our view, exists in man alone as his special property,—not because it is the work of God, which all other creatures are likewise, but because it is the breath of God, which this (human soul) alone is, which we say is born with the full equipment of its proper faculties. Well, let them meet us with the example of the trees: we will accept their challenge, (nor shall we find in it any detriment to our own argument;) for it is an undoubted fact, that whilst trees are yet but twigs and sprouts, and before they even reach the sapling stage, there is in them their own proper faculty of life, as soon as they spring out of their native beds. But then, as time goes on, the vigour of the tree slowly advances, as it grows and hardens into its woody trunk, until its mature age completes the condition which nature destines for it. Else what resources would trees possess in due course for the inoculation of grafts, and the formation of leaves, and the swelling of their buds, and the graceful shedding of their blossom, and the softening of their sap, were there not in them the quiet growth of the full provision of their nature, and the distribution of this life over all their branches for the accomplishment of their maturity?

---

[1] See his treatise, *Against Marcion.*
[2] Rom. i. 20.
[3] Facies.
[4] *Timæus*, pp. 29, 30, 37, 38.

[5] His *De Anima.* ii. 2. 3.

Trees, therefore, have ability or knowledge; and they derive it from whence they also derive vitality—that is, from the one source of vitality and knowledge which is peculiar to their nature, and *that* from the infancy which they, too, begin with. For I observe that even the vine, although yet tender and immature, still understands its own natural business, and strives to cling to some support, that, leaning on it, and lacing through it,[1] it may so attain its growth. Indeed, without waiting for the husbandman's training, without an espalier, without a prop, whatever its tendrils catch, it will fondly cling to,[2] and embrace with really greater tenacity and force by its own inclination than by your volition. It longs and hastens to be secure. Take also ivy-plants, never mind how young: I observe their attempts from the very first to grasp objects above them, and outrunning everything else, to hang on to the highest thing, preferring as they do to spread over walls with their leafy web and woof rather than creep on the ground and be trodden under by every foot that likes to crush them. On the other hand, in the case of such trees as receive injury from contact with a building, how do they hang off as they grow and avoid what injures them! You can see that their branches were naturally meant to take the opposite direction, and can very well understand the vital instincts[3] of such a tree from its avoidance of the wall. It is contented (if it be only a little shrub) with its own insignificant destiny, which it has in its foreseeing instinct thoroughly been aware of from its infancy, only it still fears even a ruined building. On my side, then, why should I not contend for these wise and sagacious natures of trees? Let them have vitality, as the philosophers permit it; but let them have knowledge too, although the philosophers disavow it. Even the infancy of a log, then, may have an intellect (suitable to it): how much more may that of a human being, whose soul (which may be compared with the nascent sprout of a tree) has been derived from Adam as its root, and has been propagated amongst his posterity by means of woman, to whom it has been entrusted for transmission, and thus has sprouted into life with all its natural apparatus, both of intellect and of sense! I am much mistaken if the human person, even from his infancy, when he saluted life with his infant cries, does not testify to his actual possession of the faculties of sensation and intellect by the fact of his birth, vindicating at one and the same time the use of all his senses—that of seeing by the light, that of hearing by sounds, that of taste by liquids, that of smell by the air, that of touch by the ground. This earliest voice of infancy, then, is the first effort of the senses, and the initial impulse of mental perceptions.[4] There is also the further fact, that some persons understand this plaintive cry of the infant to be an augury of affliction in the prospect of our tearful life, whereby from the very moment of birth (the soul) has to be regarded as endued with prescience, much more with intelligence. Accordingly by this intuition[5] the babe knows his mother, discerns the nurse, and even recognises the waiting-maid; refusing the breast of another woman, and the cradle that is not his own, and longing only for the arms to which he is accustomed. Now from what source does he acquire this discernment of novelty and custom, if not from instinctive knowledge? How does it happen that he is irritated and quieted, if not by help of his initial intellect? It would be very strange indeed that infancy were naturally so lively, if it had not mental power; and naturally so capable of impression and affection, if it had no intellect. But (we hold the contrary): for Christ, by "accepting praise out of the mouth of babes and sucklings,"[6] has declared that neither childhood nor infancy is without sensibility,[7]—the former of which states, when meeting Him with approving shouts, proved its ability to offer Him testimony;[8] while the other, by being slaughtered, for His sake of course, knew what violence meant.[9]

CHAP. XX.—THE SOUL, AS TO ITS NATURE UNIFORM, BUT ITS FACULTIES VARIOUSLY DEVELOPED. VARIETIES ONLY ACCIDENTAL.

And here, therefore, we draw our conclusion, that all the natural properties of the soul are inherent in it as parts of its substance; and that they grow and develope along with it, from the very moment of its own origin at birth. Just as Seneca says, whom we so often find on our side:[10] "There are implanted within us the seeds of all the arts and periods of life. And God, our Master, secretly produces our mental dispositions;" that is, from the germs which are implanted and hidden in us by means of infancy, and these are the intellect: for from these our natural dispositions are

---

[1] Innixa et innexa.
[2] Amabit.
[3] Animationem. The possession and use of an "ánima."
[4] Intellectuam.
[5] Spiritu. The mental instinct, just mentioned.
[6] Ps. viii. 2 ; Matt. xxi. 16.
[7] Hebetes.
[8] Matt. xxi. 15.
[9] Matt. ii. 16–18.
[10] Sæpe noster.

evolved. Now, even the seeds of plants have one form in each kind, but their development varies: some open and expand in a healthy and perfect state, while others either improve or degenerate, owing to the conditions of weather and soil, and from the appliance of labour and care; also from the course of the seasons, and from the occurrence of casual circumstances. In like manner, the soul may well be [1] uniform in its seminal origin, although multiform by the process of nativity.[2] And here local influences, too, must be taken into account. It has been said that dull and brutish persons are born at Thebes; and the most accomplished in wisdom and speech at Athens, where in the district of Colythus [3] children speak—such is the precocity of their tongue—before they are a month old. Indeed, Plato himself tells us, in the *Timæus*, that Minerva, when preparing to found her great city, only regarded the nature of the country which gave promise of mental dispositions of this kind; whence he himself in *The Laws* instructs Megillus and Clinias to be careful in their selection of a site for building a city. Empedocles, however, places the cause of a subtle or an obtuse intellect in the quality of the blood, from which he derives progress and perfection in learning and science. The subject of national peculiarities has grown by this time into proverbial notoriety. Comic poets deride the Phrygians for their cowardice; Sallust reproaches the Moors for their levity, and the Dalmatians for their cruelty; even the apostle brands the Cretans as "liars."[4] Very likely, too, something must be set down to the score of bodily condition and the state of the health. Stoutness hinders knowledge, but a spare form stimulates it; paralysis prostrates the mind, a decline preserves it. How much more will those accidental circumstances have to be noticed, which, in addition to the state of one's body or one's health, tend to sharpen or to dull the intellect! It is sharpened by learned pursuits, by the sciences, the arts, by experimental knowledge, business habits, and studies; it is blunted by ignorance, idle habits, inactivity, lust, inexperience, listlessness, and vicious pursuits. Then, besides these influences, there must perhaps [5] be added the supreme powers. Now these are the supreme powers: according to our (Christian) notions, they are the Lord God and His adversary the devil; but according to men's general opinion about providence, they are fate and necessity; and about fortune, it is man's freedom of will. Even the philosophers allow these distinctions; whilst on our part we have already undertaken to treat of them, on the principles of the (Christian) faith, in a separate work.[6] It is evident how great must be the influences which so variously affect the one nature of the soul, since they are commonly regarded as separate "*natures.*" Still they are not different species, but casual incidents of one nature and substance—even of that which God conferred on Adam, and made the mould of all (subsequent ones). Casual incidents will they always remain, but never will they become specific differences. However great, too, at present is the variety of men's manners, it was not so in Adam, the founder of their race. But all these discordances ought to have existed in him as the fountainhead, and thence to have descended to us in an unimpaired variety, if the variety had been due to nature.

CHAP. XXI.—AS FREE-WILL ACTUATES AN INDIVIDUAL SO MAY HIS CHARACTER CHANGE.

Now, if the soul possessed this uniform and simple nature from the beginning in Adam, previous to so many mental dispositions (being developed out of it), it is not rendered multiform by such various development, nor by the triple [7] form predicated of it in "*the Valentinian trinity*" (that we may still keep the condemnation of that heresy in view), for not even this nature is discoverable in Adam. What had he that was spiritual? Is it because he prophetically declared "the great mystery of Christ and the church?"[8] "This is bone of my bone, and flesh of my flesh: she shall be called Woman. Therefore shall a man leave his father and mother, and he shall cleave unto his wife; and they two shall be one flesh."[9] But this (gift of prophecy) only came on him afterwards, when God infused into him the ecstasy, or spiritual quality, in which prophecy consists. If, again, the evil of sin was developed in him, this must not be accounted as a *natural* disposition: it was rather produced by the instigation of the (old) serpent as far from being incidental to his nature as it was from being *material* in him, for we have already excluded belief in "Matter."[10] Now, if neither the spiritual element, nor what the heretics call the material element, was properly inherent in him

---

[1] Licebit.
[2] Fetu.
[3] Tertullian perhaps mentions this "demus" of Athens as the birthplace of Plato (Oehler).
[4] Tit. i. 12.
[5] Si et alia.

[6] Tertullian wrote a work *De Fato*, which is lost. Fulgentius, p. 561, gives a quotation from it.
[7] i.e., the carnal, the animal, and the spiritual. Comp. *Adv. Valentin.* xxv., and *De Resur. Carnis*, lv.
[8] Eph. v. 32.
[9] Gen. ii. 23, 24.
[10] See *Adv. Hermog.* xiii.

(since, if he had been created out of matter, the germ of evil must have been an integral part of his constitution), it remains that the one only original element of his nature was what is called the *animal* (the principle of vitality, the soul), which we maintain to be simple and uniform in its condition. Concerning this, it remains for us to inquire whether, as being called natural, it ought to be deemed subject to change. (The heretics whom we have referred to) deny that nature is susceptible of any change,[1] in order that they may be able to establish and settle their threefold theory, or "trinity," in all its characteristics as to the several natures, because "a good tree cannot produce evil fruit, nor a corrupt tree good fruit; and nobody gathers figs of thorns, nor grapes of brambles."[2] If so, then "God will not be able any longer to raise up from the stones children unto Abraham; nor to make a generation of vipers bring forth fruits of repentance."[3] And if so, the apostle too was in error when he said in his epistle, "Ye were at one time darkness, (but now are ye light in the Lord;)"[4] and, "We also were by nature children of wrath;"[5] and, "Such were some of you, but ye are washed."[6] The statements, however, of holy Scripture will never be discordant with truth. A corrupt tree will never yield good fruit, unless the better nature be grafted into it; nor will a good tree produce evil fruit, except by the same process of cultivation. Stones also will become children of Abraham, if educated in Abraham's faith; and a generation of vipers will bring forth the fruits of penitence, if they reject the poison of their malignant nature. This will be the power of the grace of God, more potent indeed than nature, exercising its sway over the faculty that underlies itself within us—even the freedom of our will, which is described as αὐτεξούσιος (of independent authority); and inasmuch as this faculty is itself also natural and mutable, in whatsoever direction it turns, it inclines of its own nature. Now, that there does exist within us naturally this independent authority (τὸ αὐτεξούσιον), we have already shown in opposition both to Marcion[7] and to Hermogenes.[8] If, then, the natural condition has to be submitted to a definition, it must be determined to be twofold —there being the category of the born and the unborn, the made and not-made. Now that

which has received its constitution by being made or by being born, is by nature capable of being changed, for it can be both born again and re-made; whereas that which is not-made and unborn will remain for ever immoveable. Since, however, this state is suited to God alone, as the only Being who is unborn and not-made (and therefore immortal and unchangeable), it is absolutely certain that the nature of all other existences which are born and created is subject to modification and change; so that if the threefold state is to be ascribed to the soul, it must be supposed to arise from the mutability of its accidental circumstances, and not from the appointment of nature.

CHAP. XXII.—RECAPITULATION. DEFINITION OF THE SOUL.

Hermogenes has already heard from us what are the other natural faculties of the soul, as well as their vindication and proof; whence it may be seen that the soul is rather the offspring of God than of matter. The names of these faculties shall here be simply repeated, that they may not seem to be forgotten and passed out of sight. We have assigned, then, to the soul both that freedom of the will which we just now mentioned, and its dominion over the works of nature, and its occasional gift of divination, independently of that endowment of prophecy which accrues to it expressly from the grace of God. We shall therefore now quit this subject of the soul's disposition, in order to set out fully in order its various qualities.[9] The soul, then, we define to be sprung from the breath of God, immortal, possessing body, having form, simple in its substance, intelligent in its own nature, developing its power in various ways, free in its determinations, subject to be changes of accident, in its faculties mutable, rational, supreme, endued with an instinct of presentiment, evolved out of one (archetypal soul). It remains for us now to consider how it is developed out of this one original source; in other words, whence, and when, and how it is produced.

---

[1] See *Adv. Valentin.* xxix.
[2] Luke vi. 43, 44.
[3] Matt. iii. 7-9.
[4] Eph. v. 8.
[5] Eph. ii. 3.
[6] 1 Cor. vi. 11.
[7] See our *Anti-Marcion*, ii. 5-7.
[8] In his work against this man, entitled *De Censu Animæ*, not now extant.

[9] Tertullian had shown that "the soul is the breath or *afflatus* of God," in ch. iv. and xi. above. He demonstrated its "*immortality*" in ch. ii.-iv., vi., ix., xiv.; and he will repeat his proof hereafter, in ch. xxiv., xxxviii., xlv., li., liii., liv. Moreover, he illustrates the soul's "*corporeity*" in ch. v.-viii.; its "endowment with *form or figure*," in ch. ix.; its "*simplicity*" in substance" in ch. x. and xi.; its "inherent *intelligence*," in ch. xii.; its varied development, in ch. xiii.-xv. The soul's "*rationality*," "*supremacy*," and "instinctive *divination*," Tertullian treated of in his treatise *De Censu Animæ* against Hermogenes (as he has said in the text); but he has treated somewhat of the soul's "rational nature" in the sixteenth chapter above; in the fourteenth and fifteenth chapters he referred to the soul's "supremacy or *hegemony*;" whilst we have had a hint about its "*divining* faculty," even in infants, in ch. xix. The propagation of souls from the one archetypal soul is the subject of the chapter before us, as well as of the five succeeding ones (La Cerda).

CHAP. XXIII.—THE OPINIONS OF SUNDRY HERE-
TICS WHICH ORIGINATE ULTIMATELY WITH
PLATO.

Some suppose that they came down from heaven, with as firm a belief as they are apt to entertain, when they indulge in the prospect of an undoubted return thither. Saturninus, the disciple of Menander, who belonged to Simon's sect, introduced this opinion: he affirmed that man was made by angels. A futile, imperfect creation at first, weak and unable to stand, he crawled upon the ground like a worm, because he wanted the strength to maintain an erect posture; but afterwards having, by the compassion of the Supreme Power (in whose image, which had not been fully understood, he was clumsily formed), obtained a slender spark of life, this roused and righted his imperfect form, and animated it with a higher vitality, and provided for its return, on its relinquishment of life, to its original principle. Carpocrates, indeed, claims for himself so extreme an amount of the supernal qualities, that his disciples set their own souls at once on an equality with Christ (not to mention the apostles); and sometimes, when it suits their fancy, even give them the superiority—deeming them, forsooth, to have partaken of that sublime virtue which looks down upon the principalities that govern this world. Apelles tells us that our souls were enticed by earthly baits down from their supercelestial abodes by a fiery angel, Israel's God and ours, who then enclosed them firmly within our sinful flesh. The hive of Valentinus fortifies the soul with the germ of *Sophia*, or Wisdom; by means of which germ they recognise, in the images of visible objects, the stories and Milesian fables of their own Æons. I am sorry from my heart that Plato has been the caterer in all these heretics. For in the *Phædo* he imagines that souls wander from this world to that, and thence back again hither; whilst in the *Timæus* he supposes that the children of God, to whom had been assigned the production of mortal creatures, having taken for the soul the germ of immortality, congealed around it a mortal body,—thereby indicating that this world is the figure of some other. Now, to procure belief in all this—that the soul had formerly lived with God in the heavens above, sharing His *ideas* with Him, and afterwards came down to live with us on earth, and whilst here recollects the eternal patterns of things which it had learnt before—he elaborated his new formula, μαθήσεις ἀναμνήσεις, which means that "learning is reminiscence;" implying that the souls which come to us from thence forget the things amongst which they formerly lived, but that they afterwards recall them, instructed by the objects they see around them. Forasmuch, therefore, as the doctrines which the heretics borrow from Plato are cunningly defended by this kind of argument, I shall sufficiently refute the heretics if I overthrow the argument of Plato.

CHAP. XXIV.—PLATO'S INCONSISTENCY. HE
SUPPOSES THE SOUL SELF-EXISTENT, YET
CAPABLE OF FORGETTING WHAT PASSED IN A
PREVIOUS STATE.

In the first place, I cannot allow that the soul is capable of a failure of memory; because he has conceded to it so large an amount of divine quality as to put it on a par with God. He makes it *unborn*, which single attribute I might apply as a sufficient attestation of its perfect divinity; he then adds that the soul is immortal, incorruptible, incorporeal—since he believed God to be the same—invisible, incapable of delineation, uniform, supreme, rational, and intellectual. What more could he attribute to the soul, if he wanted to call it God? We, however, who allow no appendage to God[1] (in the sense of equality), by this very fact reckon the soul as very far below God: for we suppose it to be born, and hereby to possess something of a diluted divinity and an attenuated felicity, as the breath (of God), though not His spirit; and although immortal, as this is an attribute of divinity, yet for all that passible, since this is an incident of a born condition, and consequently from the first capable of deviation from perfection and right,[2] and by consequence susceptible of a failure in memory. This point I have discussed sufficiently with Hermogenes.[3] But it may be further observed, that if the soul is to merit being accounted a god, by reason of all its qualities being equal to the attributes of God, it must then be subject to no passion, and therefore to no loss of memory; for this defect of oblivion is as great an injury to that of which you predicate it, as memory is the glory thereof, which Plato himself deems the very safeguard of the senses and intellectual faculties, and which Cicero has designated the treasury of all the sciences. Now we need not raise the doubt whether so divine a faculty as the soul was capable of losing memory: the question rather is, whether it is able to recover afresh that which it has lost. I could not decide whether that, which ought to have lost memory, if it once incurred the loss, would be powerful enough to recollect itself. Both alternatives,

[1] Nihil Deo appendimus.
[2] Exorbitationis.
[3] In his, now lost, treatise, *De Censu Animæ*.

indeed, will agree very well with my soul, but not with Plato's. In the second place, my objection to him will stand thus: (Plato,) do you endow the soul with a natural competency for understanding those well-known *ideas* of yours? Certainly I do, will be your answer. Well, now, no one will concede to you that the knowledge, (which you say is) the gift of nature, of the natural sciences can fail. But the knowledge of the sciences fails; the knowledge of the various fields of learning and of the arts of life fails; and so perhaps the knowledge of the faculties and affections of our minds fails, although they seem to be inherent in our nature, but really are not so: because, as we have already said,[1] they are affected by accidents of place, of manners and customs, of bodily condition, of the state of man's health—by the influences of the Supreme Powers, and the changes of man's free-will. Now the instinctive knowledge of natural objects never fails, not even in the brute creation. The lion, no doubt, will forget his ferocity, if surrounded by the softening influence of training; he may become, with his beautiful mane, the plaything of some Queen Berenice, and lick her cheeks with his tongue. A wild beast may lay aside his habits, but his natural instincts will not be forgotten. He will not forget his proper food, nor his natural resources, nor his natural alarms; and should the queen offer him fishes or cakes, he will wish for flesh; and if, when he is ill, any antidote be prepared for him, he will still require the ape; and should no hunting-spear be presented against him, he will yet dread the crow of the cock. In like manner with man, who is perhaps the most forgetful of all creatures, the knowledge of everything natural to him will remain ineradicably fixed in him,—but this alone, as being alone a natural instinct. He will never forget to eat when he is hungry; or to drink when he is thirsty; or to use his eyes when he wants to see; or his ears, to hear; or his nose, to smell; or his mouth, to taste; or his hand, to touch. These are, to be sure, the senses, which philosophy depreciates by her preference for the intellectual faculties. But if the natural knowledge of the sensuous faculties is permanent, how happens it that the knowledge of the intellectual faculties fails, to which the superiority is ascribed? Whence, now, arises that power of forgetfulness itself which precedes recollection? From long lapse of time, he says. But this is a shortsighted answer. Length of time cannot be incidental to that which, according to him, is unborn,

and which therefore must be deemed most certainly eternal. For that which is eternal, on the ground of its being unborn, since it admits neither of beginning nor end of time, is subject to no *temporal* criterion. And that which time does not measure, undergoes no change in consequence of time; nor is long lapse of time at all influential over it. If time is a cause of oblivion, why, from the time of the soul's entrance into the body, does memory fail, as if thenceforth the soul were to be affected by time? for the soul, being undoubtedly prior to the body, was of course not irrespective of time. Is it, indeed, immediately on the soul's entrance into the body that oblivion takes place, or some time afterwards? If immediately, where will be the long lapse of the time which is as yet inadmissible in the hypothesis?[2] Take, for instance, the case of the infant. If some time afterwards, will not the soul, during the interval previous to the moment of oblivion, still exercise its powers of memory? And how comes it to pass that the soul subsequently forgets, and then afterwards again remembers? How long, too, must the lapse of the time be regarded as having been, during which the oblivion oppressed the soul? The whole course of one's life, I apprehend, will be insufficient to efface the memory of an age which endured so long before the soul's assumption of the body. But then, again, Plato throws the blame upon the body, as if it were at all credible that a born substance could extinguish the power of one that is unborn. There exist, however, among bodies a great many differences, by reason of their rationality, their bulk, their condition, their age, and their health. Will there then be supposed to exist similar differences in obliviousness? Oblivion, however, is uniform and identical. Therefore bodily peculiarity, with its manifold varieties, will not become the cause of an effect which is an invariable one. There are likewise, according to Plato's own testimony, many proofs to show that the soul has a divining faculty, as we have already advanced against Hermogenes. But there is not a man living, who does not himself feel his soul possessed with a presage and augury of some omen, danger, or joy. Now, if the body is not prejudicial to divination, it will not, I suppose, be injurious to memory. One thing is certain, that souls in the same body both forget and remember. If any corporeal condition engenders forgetfulness, how will it admit the opposite state of recollection? Because recollection, after forgetfulness, is

---

[1] Above, in ch. xix, xx. pp. 200, 201.

[2] Or, " which has been too short for calculation."

actually the resurrection of the memory. Now, how should not that which is hostile to the memory at first, be also prejudicial to it in the second instance? Lastly, who have better memories than little children, with their fresh, unworn souls, not yet immersed in domestic and public cares, but devoted only to those studies the acquirement of which is itself a reminiscence? Why, indeed, do we not all of us recollect in an equal degree, since we are equal in our forgetfulness? But this is true only of philosophers! But not even of the whole of them. Amongst so many nations, in so great a crowd of sages, Plato, to be sure, is the only man who has combined the oblivion and the recollection of ideas. Now, since this main argument of his by no means keeps its ground, it follows that its entire superstructure must fall with it,—namely, that souls are supposed to be unborn, and to live in the heavenly regions, and to be instructed in the divine mysteries thereof; moreover, that they descend to this earth, and here recall to memory their previous existence, for the purpose, of course, of supplying to our heretics the fitting materials for their systems.

CHAP. XXV.—TERTULLIAN REFUTES, PHYSIO-LOGICALLY, THE NOTION THAT THE SOUL IS INTRODUCED AFTER BIRTH.

I shall now return to the cause of this digression, in order that I may explain how all souls are derived from one, when and where and in what manner they are produced. Now, touching this subject, it matters not whether the question be started by the philosopher, by the heretic, or by the crowd. Those who profess the truth care nothing about their opponents, especially such of them as begin by maintaining that the soul is not conceived in the womb, nor is formed and produced at the time that the flesh is moulded, but is impressed from without upon the infant before his complete vitality, but after the process of parturition. They say, moreover, that the human seed having been duly deposited *ex concubiter* in the womb, and having been by natural impulse quickened, it becomes condensed into the mere substance of the flesh, which is in due time born, warm from the furnace of the womb, and then released from its heat. (This flesh) resembles the case of hot iron, which is in that state plunged into cold water; for, being smitten by the cold air (into which it is born), it at once receives the power of animation, and utters vocal sound. This view is entertained by the Stoics, along with Æne-sidemus, and occasionally by Plato himself,

when he tells us that the soul, being quite a separate formation, originating elsewhere and externally to the womb, is inhaled [1] when the new-born infant first draws breath, and by and by exhaled [2] with the man's latest breath. We shall see whether this view of his is merely fictitious. Even the medical profession has not lacked its Hicesius, to prove a traitor both to nature and his own calling. These gentlemen, I suppose, were too modest to come to terms with women on the mysteries of childbirth, so well known to the latter. But how much more is there for them to blush at, when in the end they have the women to refute them, instead of commending them. Now, in such a question as this, no one can be so useful a teacher, judge, or witness, as the sex itself which is so intimately concerned. Give us your testimony, then, ye mothers, whether yet pregnant, or after delivery (let barren women and men keep silence),—the truth of your own nature is in question, the reality of your own suffering is the point to be decided. (Tell us, then,) whether you feel in the embryo within you any vital force [3] other than your own, with which your bowels tremble, your sides shake, your entire womb throbs, and the burden which oppresses you constantly changes its position? Are these movements a joy to you, and a positive removal of anxiety, as making you confident that your infant both possesses vitality and enjoys it? Or, should his restlessness cease, your first fear would be for him; and he would be aware of it within you, since he is disturbed at the novel sound; and you would crave for injurious diet,[4] or would even loathe your food—all on his account; and then you and he, (in the closeness of your sympathy,) would share together your common ailments —so far that with your contusions and bruises would he actually become marked,—whilst within you, and even on the selfsame parts of the body, taking to himself thus peremptorily [5] the injuries of his mother! Now, whenever a livid hue and redness are incidents of the blood, the blood will not be without the vital principle,[6] or soul; or when disease attacks the soul or vitality, (it becomes a proof of its real existence, since) there is no disease where there is no soul or principle of life. Again, inasmuch as sustenance by food, and the want thereof, growth and decay, fear and motion, are conditions of the soul or life, he who experiences them must be alive.

---

[1] "Inhaled" is Bp. Kaye's word for *adduci*, "taken up."
[2] Educi.
[3] Vivacitas.
[4] Ciborum vanitates.
[5] Rapiens.
[6] Anima.

And, so, he at last ceases to live, who ceases to experience them. And thus by and by infants are still-born; but how so, unless they had had life? For how could any die, who had not previously lived? But sometimes by a cruel necessity, whilst yet in the womb, an infant is put to death, when lying awry in the orifice of the womb he impedes parturition, and kills his mother, if he is not to die himself. Accordingly, among surgeons' tools there is a certain instrument, which is formed with a nicely-adjusted flexible frame for opening the *uterus* first of all, and keeping it open; it is further furnished with an annular blade,[1] by means of which the limbs within the womb are dissected with anxious but unfaltering care; its last appendage being a blunted or covered hook, wherewith the entire *fœtus* is extracted[2] by a violent delivery. There is also (another instrument in the shape of) a copper needle or spike, by which the actual death is managed in this furtive robbery of life: they give it, from its infanticide function, the name of ἐμβρυοσφάκτης, the slayer of the infant, which was of course alive. Such apparatus was possessed both by Hippocrates, and Asclepiades, and Erasistratus, and Herophilus, that dissector of even adults, and the milder Soranus himself, who all knew well enough that a living being had been conceived, and pitied this most luckless infant state, which had first to be put to death, to escape being tortured alive. Of the necessity of such harsh treatment I have no doubt even Hicesius was convinced, although he imported their soul into infants after birth from the stroke of the frigid air, because the very term for soul, forsooth, in Greek answered to such a refrigeration![3] Well, then, have the barbarian and Roman nations received souls by some other process, (I wonder;) for they have called the soul by another name than ψυχή? How many nations are there who commence life[4] under the broiling sun of the torrid zone, scorching their skin into its swarthy hue? Whence do they get their souls, with no frosty air to help them? I say not a word of those well-warmed bed-rooms, and all that apparatus of heat which ladies in childbirth so greatly need, when a breath of cold air might endanger their life. But in the very bath almost a babe will slip into life, and at once his cry is heard! If, however, a good frosty air is to the soul so indispensable a treasure, then beyond the German and the Scythian tribes, and the Alpine and the Argæan heights, nobody ought ever to be born! But the fact really is,

that population is greater within the temperate regions of the East and the West, and men's minds are sharper; whilst there is not a Sarmatian whose wits are not dull and humdrum. The minds of men, too, would grow keener by reason of the cold, if their souls came into being amidst nipping frosts; for as the substance is, so must be its active power. Now, after these preliminary statements, we may also refer to the case of those who, having been cut out of their mother's womb, have breathed and retained life—your Bacchuses[5] and Scipios.[6] If, however, there be any one who, like Plato,[7] supposes that two souls cannot, more than two bodies could, co-exist in the same individual, I, on the contrary, could show him not merely the co-existence of two souls in one person, as also of two bodies in the same womb, but likewise the combination of many other things in natural connection with the soul—for instance, of demoniacal possession; and *that* not of one only, as in the case of Socrates' own demon; but of seven spirits as in the case of the Magdalene;[8] and of a legion in number, as in the Gadarene.[9] Now one soul is naturally more susceptible of conjunction with another soul, by reason of the identity of their substance, than an evil spirit is, owing to their diverse natures. But when the same philosopher, in the sixth book of *The Laws*, warns us to beware lest a vitiation of seed should infuse a soil into both body and soul from an illicit or debased concubinage, I hardly know whether he is more inconsistent with himself in respect of one of his previous statements, or of that which he had just made. For he here shows us that the soul proceeds from human seed (and warns us to be on our guard about it), not, (as he had said before,) from the first breath of the new-born child. Pray, whence comes it that from similarity of soul we resemble our parents in disposition, according to the testimony of Cleanthes,[10] if we are not produced from this seed of the soul? Why, too, used the old astrologers to cast a man's nativity from his first conception, if his soul also draws not its origin from that moment? To this (nativity) likewise belongs the inbreathing of the soul, whatever that is.

CHAP. XXVI.—SCRIPTURE ALONE OFFERS CLEAR KNOWLEDGE ON THE QUESTIONS WE HAVE BEEN CONTROVERTING.

Now there is no end to the uncertainty and

---

[1] Anulocultro. [To be seen in the Museum at Naples.]
[2] Or, " the whole business (totum facinus) is despatched.
[3] So Plato, *Cratylus*, p. 399, c. 17.
[4] Censentur.
[5] Liberi aliqui.
[6] See Pliny, *Natural History*, vii. 9.
[7] See above, ch. x.
[8] Mark xvi. 9.
[9] Mark vi. 1-9.
[10] See above, ch. v.

irregularity of human opinion, until we come to the limits which God has prescribed. I shall at last retire within our own lines and firmly hold my ground there, for the purpose of proving to the Christian (the soundness of) my answers to the Philosophers and the Physicians. Brother (in Christ), on your own foundation[1] build up your faith. Consider the wombs of the most sainted women instinct with the life within them, and their babes which not only breathed therein, but were even endowed with prophetic intuition. See how the bowels of Rebecca are disquieted,[2] though her child-bearing is as yet remote, and there is no impulse of (vital) air. Behold, a twin offspring chafes within the mother's womb, although she has no sign as yet of the twofold nation. Possibly we might have regarded as a prodigy the contention of this infant progeny, which struggled before it lived, which had animosity previous to animation, if it had simply disturbed the mother by its restlessness within her. But when her womb opens, and the number of her offspring is seen, and their presaged condition known, we have presented to us a proof not merely of the (separate) souls of the infants, but of their hostile struggles too. He who was the first to be born was threatened with detention by him who was anticipated in birth, who was not yet fully brought forth, but whose hand only had been born. Now if he actually imbibed life, and received his soul, in Platonic style, at his first breath; or else, after the Stoic rule, had the earliest taste of animation on touching the frosty air; what was the other about, who was so eagerly looked for, who was still detained within the womb, and was trying to detain (the other) outside? I suppose he had not yet breathed when he seized his brother's heel;[3] and was still warm with his mother's warmth, when he so strongly wished to be the first to quit the womb. What an infant! so emulous, so strong, and already so contentious; and all this, I suppose, because even now full of life! Consider, again, those extraordinary conceptions, which were more wonderful still, of the barren woman and the virgin: these women would only be able to produce imperfect offspring against the course of nature, from the very fact that one of them was too old to bear seed, and the other was pure from the contact of man. If there was to be bearing at all in the case, it was only fitting that they should be born without a soul, (as the philosopher would say,) who had been irregularly conceived. How-

ever, even these have life, each of them in his mother's womb. Elizabeth exults with joy, (for) John had leaped in her womb;[4] Mary magnifies the Lord, (for) Christ had instigated her within.[5] The mothers recognise each their own offspring, being moreover each recognised by their infants, which were therefore of course alive, and were not souls merely, but spirits also. Accordingly you read the word of God which was spoken to Jeremiah, "Before I formed thee in the belly, I knew thee."[6] Since God forms us in the womb, He also breathes upon us, as He also did at the first creation, when "the Lord God formed man, and breathed into him the breath of life."[7] Nor could God have known man in the womb, except in his entire nature: "And before thou camest forth out of the womb, I sanctified thee."[8] Well, was it then a dead body at that early stage? Certainly not. For "God is not the God of the dead, but of the living."

CHAP. XXVII.—SOUL AND BODY CONCEIVED, FORMED AND PERFECTED IN ELEMENT SIMULTANEOUSLY.

How, then, is a living being conceived? Is the substance of both body and soul formed together at one and the same time? Or does one of them precede the other in natural formation? We indeed maintain that both are conceived, and formed, and perfectly simultaneously, as well as born together; and that not a moment's interval occurs in their conception, so that a prior place can be assigned to either.[9] Judge, in fact, of the incidents of man's earliest existence by those which occur to him at the very last. As death is defined to be nothing else than the separation of body and soul,[10] life, which is the opposite of death, is susceptible of no other definition than the conjunction of body and soul. If the severance happens at one and the same time to both substances by means of death, so the law of their combination ought to assure us that it occurs simultaneously to the two substances by means of life. Now we allow that life begins with conception, because we contend that the soul also begins from conception; life taking its commencement at the same moment and place that the soul does. Thus, then, the processes which act together to produce separation by death, also combine in a simultaneous action to produce

---

[1] Of the Scriptures.
[2] Gen. xxv. 22, 23.
[3] Gen. xxv. 26.

[4] Luke i. 41-45.
[5] Luke i. 46.
[6] Jer. i. 5.
[7] Gen. ii. 7.
[8] Jer. i. 5.
[9] Comp. De Resurr. Carnis, xlv.
[10] So Plato, Phædo. p. 64.

life. If we assign priority to (the formation of) one of the natures, and a subsequent time to the other, we shall have further to determine the precise times of the semination, according to the condition and rank of each. And that being so, what time shall we give to the seed of the body, and what to the seed of the soul? Besides, if different periods are to be assigned to the seminations then arising out of this difference in time, we shall also have different substances.[1] For although we shall allow that there are two kinds of seed—that of the body and that of the soul—we still declare that they are inseparable, and therefore contemporaneous and simultaneous in origin. Now let no one take offence or feel ashamed at an interpretation of the processes of nature which is rendered necessary (by the defence of the truth). Nature should be to us an object of reverence, not of blushes. It is lust, not natural usage, which has brought shame on the intercourse of the sexes. It is the excess, not the normal state, which is immodest and unchaste: the normal condition has received a blessing from God, and is blest by Him: "Be fruitful, and multiply, (and replenish the earth.)"[2] Excess, however, has He cursed, in adulteries, and wantonness, and chambering.[3] Well, now, in this usual function of the sexes which brings together the male and the female in their common intercourse, we know that both the soul and the flesh discharge a duty together: the soul supplies desire, the flesh contributes the gratification of it; the soul furnishes the instigation, the flesh affords the realization. The entire man being excited by the one effort of both natures, his seminal substance is discharged, deriving its fluidity from the body, and its warmth from the soul. Now if *the soul* in Greek is a word which is synonymous with *cold*,[4] how does it come to pass that the body grows cold after the soul has quitted it? Indeed (if I run the risk of offending modesty even, in my desire to prove the truth), I cannot help asking, whether we do not, in that very heat of extreme gratification when the generative fluid is ejected, feel that somewhat of our soul has gone from us? And do we not experience a faintness and prostration along with a dimness of sight? This, then, must be the soul-producing seed, which arises at once from the out-drip of the soul, just as that fluid is the body-producing seed which proceeds from the drainage of the flesh. Most true are the examples of the first crea-

tion. Adam's flesh was formed of clay. Now what is clay but an excellent moisture, whence should spring the generating fluid? From the breath of God first came the soul. But what else is the breath of God than the vapour of the spirit, whence should spring that which we breathe out through the generative fluid? Forasmuch, therefore, as these two different and separate substances, the clay and the breath, combined at the first creation in forming the individual man, they then both amalgamated and mixed their proper seminal rudiments in one, and ever afterwards communicated to the human race the normal mode of its propagation, so that even now the two substances, although diverse from each other, flow forth simultaneously in a united channel; and finding their way together into their appointed seed-plot, they fertilize with their combined vigour the human fruit out of their respective natures. And inherent in this human product is his own seed, according to the process which has been ordained for every creature endowed with the functions of generation. Accordingly from the one (primeval) man comes the entire outflow and redundance of men's souls—nature proving herself true to the commandment of God, "Be fruitful, and multiply."[5] For in the very preamble of this one production, "Let us make man,"[6] man's whole posterity was declared and described in a plural phrase, "Let *them* have dominion over the fish of the sea," etc.[7] And no wonder: in the seed lies the promise and earnest of the crop.

CHAP. XXVIII.—THE PYTHAGOREAN DOCTRINE OF TRANSMIGRATION SKETCHED AND CENSURED.

What, then, by this time means that ancient saying, mentioned by Plato,[8] concerning the reciprocal migration of souls; how they remove hence and go thither, and then return hither and pass through life, and then again depart from this life, and afterwards become alive from the dead? Some will have it that this is a saying of Pythagoras; Albinus supposes it to be a divine announcement, perhaps of the Egyptian Mercury.[9] But there is no divine saying, except of the one true God, by whom the prophets, and the apostles, and Christ Himself declared their grand message. More ancient than Saturn a good deal (by some nine hundred years or so), and even than his grandchildren, is Moses; and he is certainly much more divine, recounting and tracing out,

---

[1] Materiæ.
[2] Gen. i. 28.
[3] Lupanaria.
[4] See above, c. xxv. p. 206.

[5] Gen. i. 28.
[6] Ver. 26.
[7] Ver. 26.
[8] *Phædo*, p. 70.
[9] [Hermes. See Bacon, *De Aug.* i. p. 99.]

as he does, the course of the human race from the very beginning of the world, indicating the several births (of the fathers of mankind) according to their names and their epochs; giving thus plain proof of the divine character of his work, from its divine authority and word. If, indeed, the sophist of Samos is Plato's authority for the eternally revolving migration of souls out of a constant alternation of the dead and the living states, then no doubt did the famous Pythagoras, however excellent in other respects, for the purpose of fabricating such an opinion as this, rely on a falsehood, which was not only shameful, but also hazardous. Consider it, you that are ignorant of it, and believe with us. He feigns death, he conceals himself underground, he condemns himself to that endurance for some seven years, during which he learns from his mother, who was his sole accomplice and attendant, what he was to relate for the belief of the world concerning those who had died since his seclusion;[1] and when He thought that he had succeeded in reducing the frame of his body to the horrid appearance of a dead old man, he comes forth from the place of his concealment and deceit, and pretends to have returned from the dead. Who would hesitate about believing that the man, whom he had supposed to have died, was come back again to life? especially after hearing from him facts about the recently dead,[1] which he evidently could only have discovered in Hades itself ! Thus, that men are made alive after death, is rather an old statement. But what if it be rather a recent one also? The truth does not desire antiquity, nor does falsehood shun novelty. This notable saying I hold to be plainly false, though ennobled by antiquity. How should that not be false, which depends for its evidence on a falsehood?—How can I help believing Pythagoras to be a deceiver, who practises deceit to win my belief? How will he convince me that, before he was Pythagoras, he had been Æthalides, and Euphorbus, and the fisherman Pyrrhus, and Hermotimus, to make us believe that men live again after they have died, when he actually perjured himself afterwards as Pythagoras. In proportion as it would be easier for me to believe that he had returned once to life in his own person, than so often in the person of this man and that, in the same degree has he deceived me in things which are too hard to be credited, because he has played the impostor in matters which might be readily believed. Well, but he recognised the shield of Euphorbus, which had been formerly conse-

crated at Delphi, and claimed it as his own, and proved his claim by signs which were generally unknown. Now, look again at his subterranean lurking-place, and believe his story, if you can. For, as to the man who devised such a tricksty scheme, to the injury of his health, fraudulently wasting his life, and torturing it for seven years underground, amidst hunger, idleness, and darkness—with a profound disgust for the mighty sky—what reckless effort would he not make, what curious contrivance would he not attempt, to arrive at the discovery of this famous shield ? Suppose now, that he found it in some of those hidden researches; suppose that he recovered some slight breath of report which survived the now obsolete tradition; suppose him to have come to the knowledge of it by an inspection which he had bribed the beadle to let him have,—we know very well what are the resources of magic skill for exploring hidden secrets: there are the *catabolic* spirits,[2] which floor their victims; and the *paredral* spirits, which are ever at their side[3] to haunt them; and the *pythonic* spirits, which entrance them by their divination and ventriloquistic[4] arts. For was is not likely that Pherecydes also, the master of our Pythagoras, used to divine, or I would rather say rave and dream, by such arts and contrivances as these? Might not the self-same demon have been in him, who, whilst in Euphorbus, transacted deeds of blood ? But lastly, why is it that the man, who proved himself to have been Euphorbus by the evidence of the shield, did not also recognise any of his former Trojan comrades ? For they, too, must by this time have recovered life, since men were rising again from the dead.

CHAP. XXIX.—THE PYTHAGOREAN DOCTRINE REFUTED BY ITS OWN FIRST PRINCIPLE, THAT LIVING MEN ARE FORMED FROM THE DEAD.

It is indeed, manifest that dead men are formed from living ones; but it does not follow from that, that living men are formed from dead ones. For from the beginning the living came first in the order of things, and therefore also from the beginning the dead came afterwards in order. But these proceeded from no other source except from the living. The living had their origin in any other source (you please) than in the dead; whilst the dead had no source whence to derive their beginning, except from the living.

---

[1] De posteris defunctis.

[2] From καταβάλλειν, to knock down.
[3] From πάρεδος, sitting by one.
[4] From πυθωνικός, an attribute of *Pythius* Apollo ; this class were sometimes called ἐγγαστρίμυθοι, ventriloquists.

If, then, from the very first the living came not from the dead, why should they afterwards (be said to) come from the dead? Had that original source, whatever it was, come to an end? Was the form or law thereof a matter for regret? Then why was it preserved in the case of the dead? Does it not follow that, because the dead came from the living at the first, therefore they always came from the living? For either the law which obtained at the beginning must have continued in both of its relations, or else it must have changed in both; so that, if it had become necessary for the living afterwards to proceed from the dead, it would be necessary, in like manner, for the dead also not to proceed from the living. For if a faithful adherence to the institution was not meant to be perpetuated in each respect, then contraries cannot in due alternation continue to be re-formed from contraries. We, too, will on our side adduce against you certain contraries, of the born and the unborn, of vision [1] and blindness, of youth and old age, of wisdom and folly. Now it does not follow that the unborn proceeds from the born, on the ground that a contrary issues from a contrary; nor, again, that vision proceeds from blindness, because blindness happens to vision; nor, again, that youth revives from old age, because after youth comes the decrepitude of senility; nor that folly [2] is born with its obtuseness from wisdom, because wisdom may possibly be sometimes sharpened out of folly. Albinus has some fears for his (master and friend) Plato in these points, and labours with much ingenuity to distinguish different kinds of contraries; as if these instances did not as absolutely partake of the nature of contrariety as those which are expounded by him to illustrate his great master's principle—I mean, life and death. Nor is it, for the matter of that, true that life is restored out of death, because it happens that death succeeds [3] life.

CHAP. XXX.—FURTHER REFUTATION OF THE PYTHAGOREAN THEORY. THE STATE OF CONTEMPORARY CIVILISATION.

But what must we say in reply to what follows? For, in the first place, if the living come from the dead, just as the dead proceed from the living, then there must always remain unchanged one and the selfsame number of mankind, even the number which originally introduced (human) life. The living preceded the dead, afterwards the dead issued from the living, and then again the living

from the dead. Now, since this process was evermore going on with the same persons, therefore they, issuing from the same, must always have remained in number the same. For they who emerged (into life) could never have become more nor fewer than they who disappeared (in death). We find, however, in the records of the Antiquities of Man, [4] that the human race has progressed with a gradual growth of population, either occupying different portions of the earth as aborigines, or as nomade tribes, or as exiles, or as conquerors —as the Scythians in Parthia, the Temenidæ in Peloponnesus, the Athenians in Asia, the Phrygians in Italy, and the Phœnicians in Africa; or by the more ordinary methods of emigration, which they call ἀποικίαι or *colonies*, for the purpose of throwing off redundant population, disgorging into other abodes their overcrowded masses. The aborigines remain still in their old settlements, and have also enriched other districts with loans of even larger populations. Surely it is obvious enough, if one looks at the whole world, that it is becoming daily better cultivated and more fully peopled than anciently. All places are now accessible, all are well known, all open to commerce; most pleasant farms have obliterated all traces of what were once dreary and dangerous wastes; cultivated fields have subdued forests; flocks and herds have expelled wild beasts; sandy deserts are sown; rocks are planted; marshes are drained; and where once were hardly solitary cottages, there are now large cities. No longer are (savage) islands dreaded, nor their rocky shores feared; everywhere are houses, and inhabitants, and settled government, and civilised life. What most frequently meets our view (and occasions complaint), is our teeming population: our numbers are burdensome to the world, which can hardly supply us from its natural elements; our wants grow more and more keen, and our complaints more bitter in all mouths, whilst Nature fails in affording us her usual sustenance. In very deed, pestilence, and famine, and wars, and earthquakes have to be regarded as a remedy for nations, as the means of pruning the luxuriance of the human race; and yet, when the hatchet has once felled large masses of men, the world has hitherto never once been alarmed at the sight of a restitution of its dead coming back to life after their millennial exile. [5] But such a spectacle would have become quite obvious by the balance of mortal

---

[1] Visualitatis.
[2] Insipientiam. " Imbecility " is the meaning here, though the word takes the more general sense in the next clause.
[3] Deferatur.

[4] A probable allusion to Varro's work, *De Antiqq. Rerum Humanarum.*
[5] An allusion to Plato's notion that, at the end of a thousand years, such a restoration of the dead, took place. See his *Phædrus*, p. 248, and *De Republ.* x. p. 614.

loss and vital recovery, if it were true that the dead came back again to life. Why, however, is it after a thousand years, and not at the moment, that this return from death is to take place, when, supposing that the loss is not at once supplied, there must be a risk of an utter extinction, as the failure precedes the compensation? Indeed, this furlough of our present life would be quite disproportioned to the period of a thousand years; so much briefer is it, and on that account so much more easily is its torch extinguished than re-kindled. Inasmuch, then, as the period which, on the hypothesis we have discussed, ought to intervene, if the living are to be formed from the dead, has not actually oc-curred, it will follow that we must not believe that men come back to life from the dead (in the way surmised in this philosophy).

CHAP. XXXI.—FURTHER EXPOSURE OF TRANSMI-
    GRATION.   ITS INEXTRICABLE EMBARRASS-
    MENT.

Again, if this recovery of life from the dead take place at all, individuals must of course resume their own individuality. Therefore the souls which animated each several body must needs have returned separately to their several bodies. Now, whenever two, or three, or five souls are re-enclosed (as they constantly are) in one womb, it will not amount in such cases to life from the dead, because there is not the separate restitution which individuals ought to have; although at this rate, (no doubt,) the law of the primeval creation is signally kept,[1] by the production still of sev-eral souls out of only one! Then, again, if souls depart at different ages of human life, how is it that they come back again at one uniform age? For all men are imbued with an *infant* soul at their birth. But how hap-pens it that a man who dies in old age returns to life as an infant? If the soul, whilst dis-embodied, decreases thus by retrogression of its age, how much more reasonable would it be, that it should resume its life with a richer progress in all attainments of life after the lapse of a thousand years! At all events, it should return with the age it had attained at its death, that it might resume the precise life which it had relinquished. But even if, at this rate, they should reappear the same evermore in their revolving cycles, it would be proper for them to bring back with them, if not the selfsame forms of body, at least their original peculiarities of character, taste, and disposition, because it would be hardly

possible[2] for them to be regarded as the same, if they were deficient in those characteristics by means of which their identity should be proved. (You, however, meet me with this question): How can you possibly know, you ask, whether all is not a secret process? may not the work of a thousand years take from you the power of recognition, since they re-turn unknown to you? But I am quite cer-tain that such is not the case, for you yourself present Pythagoras to me as (the restored) Euphorbus. Now look at Euphorbus: he was evidently possessed of a military and warlike soul, as is proved by the very renown of the sacred shields. As for Pythagoras, however, he was such a recluse, and so un-warlike, that he shrank from the military ex-ploits of which Greece was then so full, and preferred to devote himself, in the quiet re-treat of Italy, to the study of geometry, and astrology, and music—the very opposite to Euphorbus in taste and disposition. Then, again, the Pyrrhus (whom he represented) spent his time in catching fish; but Pythagoras, on the contrary, would never touch fish, ab-staining from even the taste of them as from animal food. Moreover, Æthalides and Her-motimus had included the bean amongst the common esculents at meals, while Pythagoras taught his disciples not even to pass through a plot which was cultivated with beans. I ask, then, how the same souls are resumed, which can offer no proof of their identity, either by their disposition, or habits, or living? And now, after all, (we find that) only four souls are mentioned as recovering life[3] out of all the multitudes of Greece. But limiting our-selves merely to Greece, as if no transmigra-tions of souls and resumptions of bodies oc-curred, and *that* every day, in every nation, and amongst all ages, ranks, and sexes, how is it that Pythagoras alone experiences these changes into one personality and another? Why should not I too undergo them? Or if it be a privilege monopolized by philosophers —and Greek philosophers only, as if Scythians and Indians had no philosophers—how is it that Epicurus had no recollection that he had been once another man, nor Chrysippus, nor Zeno, nor indeed Plato himself, whom we might perhaps have supposed to have been Nestor, from his honeyed eloquence?

CHAP. XXXII.—EMPEDOCLES INCREASED THE
    ABSURDITY OF PYTHAGORAS BY DEVELOPING
    THE POSTHUMOUS CHANGE OF MEN INTO
    VARIOUS ANIMALS.

But the fact is, Empedocles, who used to

---

[1] Signatur. Rigaltius reads "singulatur, after the *Codex Agobard.*, as meaning, "The *single* origin of the human race is in principle maintained," etc.

[2] Temere.
[3] Recensentur.

dream that he was a god, and on that account, I suppose, disdained to have it thought that he had ever before been merely some hero, declares in so many words: "I once was Thamnus, and a fish." Why not rather a melon, seeing that he was such a fool; or a cameleon, for his inflated brag? It was, no doubt, as a fish (and a queer one too!) that he escaped the corruption of some obscure grave, when he preferred being roasted by a plunge into Ætna; after which accomplishment there was an end for ever to his μετενσω-μάτωσις or putting himself into another body —(fit only now for) a light dish after the roast-meat. At this point, therefore, we must likewise contend against that still more monstrous presumption, that in the course of the transmigration beasts pass from human beings, and human beings from beasts. Let (Empedocles') Thamnuses alone. Our slight notice of them in passing will be quite enough: (to dwell on them longer will inconvenience us,) lest we should be obliged to have recourse to raillery and laughter instead of serious instruction. Now our position is this: that the human soul cannot by any means at all be transferred to beasts, even when they are supposed to originate, according to the philosophers, out of the substances of the elements. Now let us suppose that the soul is either fire, or water, or blood, or spirit, or air, or light; we must not forget that all the animals in their several kinds have properties which are opposed to the respective elements. There are the cold animals which are opposed to fire—water-snakes, lizards, salamanders, and what things soever are produced out of the rival element of water. In like manner, those creatures are opposite to water which are in their nature dry and sapless; indeed, locusts, butterflies, and chameleons rejoice in droughts. So, again, such creatures are opposed to blood which have none of its purple hue, such as snails, worms, and most of the fishy tribes. Then opposed to spirit are those creatures which seem to have no respiration, being unfurnished with lungs and wind-pipes, such as gnats, ants, moths, and minute things of this sort. Opposed, moreover, to air are those creatures which always live under ground and under water, and never imbibe air—things of which you are more acquainted with the existence than with the names. Then opposed to light are those things which are either wholly blind, or possess eyes for the darkness only, such as moles, bats, and owls. These examples (have I adduced), that I might illustrate my subject from clear and palpable natures. But even if I could take in my hand the "atoms" of Epicurus, or if

my eye could see the "numbers" of Pythagoras, or if my foot could stumble against the "ideas" of Plato, or if I could lay hold of the "entelechies" of Aristotle, the chances would be, that even in these (impalpable) classes I should find such animals as I must oppose to one another on the ground of their contrariety. For I maintain that, of whichsoever of the before-mentioned natures the human soul is composed, it would not have been possible for it to pass for new forms into animals so contrary to each of the separate natures, and to bestow an origin by its passage on those beings, from which it would have to be excluded and rejected rather than to be admitted and received, by reason of that original contrariety which we have supposed it to possess,[1] and which commits the bodily substance receiving it to an interminable strife; and then again by reason of the subsequent contrariety, which results from the development inseparable from each several nature. Now it is on quite different conditions[2] that the soul of man has had assigned to it (in individual bodies[3]) its abode, and aliment, and order, and sensation, and affection, and sexual intercourse, and procreation of children; also (on different conditions has it, in individual bodies, received especial) dispositions, as well as duties to fulfil, likings, dislikes, vices, desires, pleasures, maladies, remedies—in short, its own modes of living, its own outlets of death. How, then, shall that (human) soul which cleaves to the earth, and is unable without alarm to survey any great height, or any considerable depth, and which is also fatigued if it mounts many steps, and is suffocated if it is submerged in a fish-pond,—(how, I say, shall a soul which is beset with such weaknesses) mount up at some future stage into the air in an eagle, or plunge into the sea in an eel? How, again, shall it, after being nourished with generous and delicate as well as exquisite viands, feed deliberately on, I will not say husks, but even on thorns, and the wild fare of bitter leaves, and beasts of the dung-hill, and poisonous worms, if it has to migrate into a goat or into a quail? —nay, it may be, feed on carrion, even on human corpses in some bear or lion? But how indeed (shall it stoop to this), when it remembers its own (nature and dignity)? In the same way, you may submit all other instances to this criterion of incongruity, and so save us from lingering over the distinct consideration of each of them in turn. Now,

---

[1] Hujus.
[2] Alias.
[3] This is the force of the objective nouns, which are all put in the *plural* form.

whatever may be the measure and whatever the mode of the human soul, (the question is forced upon us,) what it will do in far larger animals, or in very diminutive ones? It must needs be, that every individual body of whatever size is filled up by the soul, and that the soul is entirely covered by the body. How, therefore, shall a man's soul fill an elephant? How, likewise, shall it be contracted within a gnat? If it be so enormously extended or contracted, it will no doubt be exposed to peril. And this induces me to ask another question: If the soul is by no means capable of this kind of migration into animals, which are not fitted for its reception, either by the habits of their bodies or the other laws of their being, will it then undergo a change according to the properties of various animals, and be adapted to their life, notwithstanding its contrariety to human life—having, in fact, become contrary to its human self by reason of its utter change? Now the truth is, if it undergoes such a transformation, and loses what it once was, the human soul will not be what it was; and if it ceases to be its former self, the *metensomatosis*, or adaptation of some other body, comes to nought, and is not of course to be ascribed to the soul which will cease to exist, on the supposition of its complete change. For only then can a soul be said to experience this process of the *metensomatosis*, when it undergoes it by remaining unchanged in its own (primitive) condition. Since, therefore, the soul does not admit of change, lest it should cease to retain its identity; and yet is unable to remain unchanged in its original state, because it fails then to receive contrary (bodies),—I still want to know some credible reason to justify such a transformation as we are discussing. For although some men are compared to the beasts because of their character, disposition, and pursuits (since even God says, "Man is like the beasts that perish"[1]), it does not on this account follow that rapacious persons become kites, lewd persons dogs, ill-tempered ones panthers, good men sheep, talkative ones swallows, and chaste men doves, as if the selfsame substance of the soul everywhere repeated its own nature in the properties of the animals (into which it passed). Besides, a substance is one thing, and the nature of that substance is another thing; inasmuch as the substance is the special property of one given thing, whereas the nature thereof may possibly belong to many things. Take an example or two. A stone or a piece of iron is the substance: the hardness of the stone and

the iron is the nature of the substance. Their hardness combines objects by a common quality; their substances keep them separate. Then, again, there is softness in wool, and softness in a feather: their natural qualities are alike, (and put them on a par;) their substantial qualities are not alike, (and keep them distinct.) Thus, if a man likewise be designated a wild beast or a harmless one, there is not for all that an identity of soul. Now the similarity of nature is even then observed, when dissimilarity of substance is most conspicuous: for, by the very fact of your judging that a man resembles a beast, you confess that their soul is not identical; for you say that they *resemble* each other, not that they are the *same*. This is also the meaning of the word of God (which we have just quoted): it likens man to the beasts in nature, but not in substance. Besides, God would not have actually made such a comment as this concerning man, if He had known him to be in substance only bestial

CHAP. XXXIII.—THE JUDICIAL RETRIBUTION OF THESE MIGRATIONS REFUTED WITH RAILLERY.

Forasmuch as this doctrine is vindicated even on the principle of judicial retribution, on the pretence that the souls of men obtain as their partners the kind of animals which are suited to their life and deserts,—as if they ought to be, according to their several characters, either slain in criminals destined to execution, or reduced to hard work in menials, or fatigued and wearied in labourers, or foully disgraced in the unclean; or, again, on the same principle, reserved for honour, and love, and care, and attentive regard in characters most eminent in, rank and virtue, usefulness, and tender sensibility,—I must here also remark, that if souls undergo a transformation, they will actually not be able to accomplish and experience the destinies which they shall deserve; and the aim and purpose of judicial recompense will be brought to nought, as there will be wanting the sense and consciousness of merit and retribution. And there must be this want of consciousness, if souls lose their condition; and there must ensue this loss, if they do not continue in one stay. But even if they should have permanency enough to remain unchanged until the judgment,—a point which Mercurius Ægyptius recognised, when he said that the soul, after its separation from the body, was not dissipated back into the soul of the universe, but retained permanently its distinct individuality, "in order that it might render," to use his own words, "an account to the Father of those things which it has done in the body;"

[1] Ps. xlix. 20.

—(even supposing all this, I say,) I still want to examine the justice, the solemnity, the majesty, and the dignity of this reputed judgment of God, and see whether human judgment has not too elevated a throne in it—exaggerated in both directions, in its office both of punishments and rewards, too severe in dealing out its vengeance, and too lavish in bestowing its favour. What do you suppose will become of the soul of the murderer? (It will animate), I suppose, some cattle destined for the slaughter-house and the shambles, that it may itself be killed, even as it has killed; and be itself flayed, since it has fleeced others; and be' itself used for food, since it has cast to the wild beasts the ill-fated victims whom it once slew in woods and lonely roads. Now, if such be the judicial retribution which it is to receive, is not such a soul likely to find more of consolation than of punishment, in the fact that it receives its *coup de grâce* from the hands of most expert practitioners—is buried with condiments served in the most piquant styles of an Apicius or a Lurco, is introduced to the tables of your exquisite Ciceros, is brought up on the most splendid dishes of a Sylla, finds its obsequies in a banquet, is devoured by respectable (mouths) on a par with itself, rather than by kites and wolves, so that all may see how it has got a man's body for its tomb, and has risen again after returning to its own kindred race—exulting in the face of human judgments, if it has experienced them? For these barbarous sentences of death consign to various wild beasts, which are selected and trained even against their nature for their horrible office, the criminal who has committed murder, even while yet alive; nay, hindered from too easily dying, by a contrivance which retards his last moment in order to aggravate his punishment. But even if his soul should have anticipated by its departure the sword's last stroke, his body at all events must not escape the weapon: retribution for his own crime is yet exacted by stabbing his throat and stomach, and piercing his side. After that he is flung into the fire, that his very grave may be cheated.[1] In no other way, indeed, is a sepulture allowed him. Not that any great care, after all, is bestowed on his pyre, so that other animals light upon his remains. At any rate, no mercy is shown to his bones, no indulgence to his ashes, which must be punished with exposure and nakedness. The vengeance which is inflicted among men upon the homicide is really as great as that which is imposed by nature. Who would not prefer the justice of the world, which, as

the apostle himself testifies, "beareth not the sword in vain,"[2] and which is an institute of religion when it severely avenges in defence of human life? When we contemplate, too, the penalties awarded to other crimes—gibbets, and holocausts, and sacks, and harpoons, and precipices—who would not think it better to receive his sentence in the courts of Pythagoras and Empedocles? For even the wretches whom they will send into the bodies of asses and mules to be punished by drudgery and slavery, how will they congratulate themselves on the mild labour of the mill and the water-wheel, when they recollect the mines, and the convict-gangs, and the public works, and even the prisons and black-holes, terrible in their idle, do-nothing routine? Then, again, in the case of those who, after a course of integrity, have surrendered their life to the Judge, I likewise look for rewards, but I rather discover punishments. To be sure, it must be a handsome gain for good men to be restored to life in any animals whatsoever! Homer, so dreamt Ennius, remembered that he was once a peacock; however, I cannot for my part believe poets, even when wide awake A peacock, no doubt, is a very pretty bird, pluming itself, at will, on its splendid feathers; but then its wings do not make amends for its voice, which is harsh and unpleasant; and there is nothing that poets like better than a good song. His transformation, therefore, into a peacock was to Homer a penalty, not an honour. The world's remuneration will bring him a much greater joy, when it lauds him as the father of the liberal sciences; and he will prefer the ornaments of his fame to the graces of his tail! But never mind! let poets migrate into peacocks, or into swans, if you like, especially as swans have a respectable voice: in what animal will you invest that righteous hero Æacus? In what beast will you clothe the chaste and excellent Dido? What bird shall fall to the lot of Patience? what animal to the lot of Holiness? what fish to that of Innocence? Now all creatures are the servants of man; all are his subjects, all his dependants. If by and by he is to become one of these creatures, he is by such a change debased and degraded he to whom, for his virtues, images, statues, and titles are freely awarded as public honours and distinguished privileges, he to whom the senate and the people vote even sacrifices! Oh, what judicial sentences for gods to pronounce, as men's recompense after death! They are more mendacious than any human judgments; they are contemptible as punishments, dis-

---

[1] Or, "that he may be punished even in his sepulture."

[2] Rom. xiii. 4.

gusting as rewards; such as the worst of men could never fear, nor the best desire; such indeed, as criminals will aspire to, rather than saints,—the former, that they may escape more speedily the world's stern sentence,—the latter that they may more tardily incur it. How well, (forsooth), O ye philosophers do you teach us, and how usefully do you advise us, that after death rewards and punishments fall with lighter weight! whereas, if any judgment awaits souls at all, it ought rather to be supposed that it will be heavier at the conclusion of life than in the conduct [1] thereof, since nothing is more complete than that which comes at the very last—nothing, moreover, is more complete than that which is especially divine. Accordingly, God's judgment will be more full and complete, because it will be pronounced at the very last, in an eternal irrevocable sentence, both of punishment and of consolation, (on men whose) souls are not to transmigrate into beasts, but are to return into their own proper bodies. And all this once for all, and on "that day, too, of which the Father only knoweth;"[2] (only knoweth,) in order that by her trembling expectation faith may make full trial of her anxious sincerity, keeping her gaze ever fixed on that day, in her perpetual ignorance of it, daily fearing that for which she yet daily hopes.

CHAP. XXXIV.—THESE VAGARIES STIMULATED SOME PROFANE CORRUPTIONS OF CHRISTIANITY. THE PROFANITY OF SIMON MAGUS CONDEMNED.

No tenet, indeed, under cover of any heresy has as yet burst upon us, embodying any such extravagant fiction as that the souls of human beings pass into the bodies of wild beasts; but yet we have deemed it necessary to attack and refute this conceit, as a consistent sequel to the preceding opinions, in order that Homer in the peacock might be got rid of as effectually as Pythagoras in Euphorbus; and in order that, by the demolition of the *metempsychosis* and *metensomatosis* by the same blow, the ground might be cut away which has furnished no inconsiderable support to our heretics. There is the (infamous) Simon of Samaria in the Acts of the Apostles, who chaffered for the Holy Ghost: after his condemnation by *Him*, and a vain remorse that he and his money must perish together,[3] he applied his energies to the destruction of the truth, as if to console himself with revenge. Besides the support with which his own magic arts fur-

nished him, he had recourse to imposture, and purchased a Tyrian woman of the name of Helen out of a brothel, with the same money which he had offered for the Holy Spirit,—a traffic worthy of the wretched man. He actually feigned himself to be the Supreme Father, and further pretended that the woman was his own primary conception, wherewith he had purposed the creation of the angels and the archangels; that after she was possessed of this purpose she sprang forth from the Father and descended to the lower spaces, and there anticipating the Father's design had produced the angelic powers, which knew nothing of the Father, the Creator of this world; that she was detained a prisoner by these from a (rebellious) motive very like her own, lest after her departure from them they should appear to be the offspring of another being; and that, after being on this account exposed to every insult, to prevent her leaving them anywhere after her dishonour, she was degraded even to the form of man, to be confined, as it were, in the bonds of the flesh. Having during many ages wallowed about in one female shape and another, she became the notorious Helen who was so ruinous to Priam, and afterwards to the eyes of Stesichorus, whom, she blinded in revenge for his lampoons, and then restored to sight to reward him for his eulogies. After wandering about in this way from body to body, she, in her final disgrace, turned out a viler Helen still as a professional prostitute. This wench, therefore, was the lost sheep, upon whom the Supreme Father, even Simon, descended, who, after he had recovered her and brought her back—whether on his shoulders or loins I cannot tell—cast an eye on the salvation of man, in order to gratify his spleen by liberating them from the angelic powers. Moreover, to deceive these he also himself assumed a visible shape; and feigning the appearance of a man amongst men, he acted the part of the Son in Judea, and of the Father in Samaria. O hapless Helen, what a hard fate is yours between the poets and the heretics, who have blackened your fame sometimes with adultery, sometimes with prostitution! Only her rescue from Troy is a more glorious affair than her extrication from the brothel. There were a thousand ships to remove her from Troy; a thousand pence were probably more than enough to withdraw her from the stews. Fie on you, Simon, to be so tardy in seeking her out, and so inconstant in ransoming her! How different from Menelaus! As soon as he has lost her, he goes in pursuit of her; she is no sooner ravished than he begins his search; after a ten years' conflict he boldly

---

rescues her: there is no lurking, no deceiving, no cavilling. I am really afraid that he was a much better "Father," who laboured so much more vigilantly, bravely, and perseveringly, about the recovery of his Helen.

CHAP. XXXV.—THE OPINIONS OF CARPOCRATES, ANOTHER OFFSET FROM THE PYTHAGOREAN DOGMAS, STATED AND CONFUTED.

However, it is not for you alone, (Simon), that the transmigration philosophy has fabricated this story. Carpocrates also makes equally good use of it, who was a magician and a fornicator like yourself, only he had not a Helen.[1] And why should he not? since he asserted that souls are reinvested with bodies, in order to ensure the overthrow by all means of divine and human truth. For, (according to his miserable doctrine,) this life became consummated to no man until all those blemishes which are held to disfigure it have been fully displayed in its conduct; because there is nothing which is accounted evil by nature, but simply as men think of it. The transmigration of human souls, therefore, into any kind of heterogeneous bodies, he thought by all means indispensable, whenever any depravity whatever had not been fully perpetrated in the early stage of life's passage. Evil deeds (one may be sure) appertain to life. Moreover, as often as the soul has fallen short as a defaulter in sin, it has to be recalled to existence, until it "pays the utmost farthing,"[2] thrust out from time to time into the prison of the body. To this effect does he tamper with the whole of that allegory of the Lord which is extremely clear and simple in its meaning, and ought to be from the first understood in its plain and natural sense. Thus our "adversary" (therein mentioned[3]) is the heathen man, who is walking with us along the same road of life which is common to him and ourselves. Now "we must needs go out of the world,"[4] if it be not allowed us to have conversation with them. He bids us, therefore, show a kindly disposition to such a man. "Love your enemies," says He, "pray for them that curse you,"[5] lest such a man in any transaction of business be irritated by any unjust conduct of yours, and "deliver thee to the judge" of his own (nation[6]), and you be thrown into prison, and be detained in its close and narrow cell until you have liquidated all your debt against him.[7] Then,

again, should you be disposed to apply the term "adversary" to the devil, you are advised by the (Lord's) injunction, "while you are in the way with him," to make even with him such a compact as may be deemed compatible with the requirements of your true faith. Now the compact you have made respecting him is to renounce him, and his pomp, and his angels. Such is your agreement in this matter. Now the friendly understanding you will have to carry out must arise from your observance of the compact: you must never think of getting back any of the things which you have abjured, and have restored to him, lest he should summon you as a fraudulent man, and a transgressor of your agreement, before God the Judge (for in this light do we read of him, in another passage, as "the accuser of the brethren,"[8] or saints, where reference is made to the actual practice of legal prosecution); and lest this Judge deliver you over to the angel who is to execute the sentence, and *he* commit you to the prison of hell, out of which there will be no dismissal until the smallest even of your delinquencies be paid off in the period before the resurrection.[9] What can be a more fitting sense than this? What a truer interpretation? If, however, according to Carpocrates, the soul is bound to the commission of all sorts of crime and evil conduct, what must we from his system understand to be its "adversary" and foe? I suppose it must be that better mind which shall compel it by force to the performance of some act of virtue, that it may be driven from body to body, until it be found in none a debtor to the claims of a virtuous life. This means, that a good tree is known by its bad fruit—in other words, that the doctrine of truth is understood from the worst possible precepts. I apprehend[10] that heretics of this school seize with especial avidity the example of Elias, whom they assume to have been so reproduced in John (the Baptist) as to make our Lord's statement sponsor for their theory of transmigration, when He said, "Elias is come already, and they knew him not;"[11] and again, in another passage, "And if ye will receive it, this is Elias, which was for to come."[12] Well, then, was it really in a Pythagorean sense that the Jews approached John with the inquiry, "Art thou Elias?"[13] and not rather in the sense of the divine pre-

---

[1] For Carpocrates, see Irenæus, i. 24; Eusebius, *H. E.* iv. 7; Epiphan. *Hær.* 27.
[2] Matt. v. 26.
[3] Ver. 25.
[4] 1 Cor. v. 10.
[5] Luke vi. 27.
[6] Matt. v. 25.
[7] Ver. 26.

[8] Rev. xii. 10.
[9] Morâ resurrectionis. For the force of this phrase, as apparently implying a doctrine of *purgatory*, and an explanation of Tertullian's teaching on this point, see Bp. Kaye on *Tertullian*, pp. 328, 329. [See p. 59, *supra.*]
[10] Spero.
[11] Matt. xvii. 12.
[12] Matt. xi. 14.
[13] John i. 21.

diction, " Behold, I will send you Elijah" the Tisbite?[1] The fact, however, is, that their metempsychosis, or transmigration theory, signifies the recall of the soul which had died long before, and its return to some other body. But Elias is to come again, not after quitting life (in the way of dying), but after his translation (or removal without dying); not for the purpose of being restored to the body, from which he had not departed, but for the purpose of revisiting the world from which he was translated; not by way of resuming a life which he had laid aside, but of fulfilling prophecy,— really and truly the same man, both in respect of his name and designation, as well as of his unchanged humanity. How, therefore, could John be Elias? You have your answer in the angel's announcement: "And he shall go before the people," says he, " in the spirit and power of Elias "—not (observe) in his soul and his body. These substances are, in fact, the natural property of each individual; whilst " the spirit and power" are bestowed as external gifts by the grace of God, and so may be transferred to another person according to the purpose and will of the Almighty, as was anciently the case with respect to the spirit of Moses.[2]

CHAP. XXXVI.—THE MAIN POINTS OF OUR AUTHOR'S SUBJECT. ON THE SEXES OF THE HUMAN RACE.

For the discussion of these questions we abandoned, if I remember rightly, ground to which we must now return. We had established the position that the soul is seminally placed in man, and by human agency, and that its seed from the very beginning is uniform, as is that of the soul also, to the race of man; (and this we settled) owing to the rival opinions of the philosophers and the heretics, and that ancient saying mentioned by Plato (to which we referred above).[3] We now pursue in their order the points which follow from them. The soul, being sown in the womb at the same time as the body, receives likewise along with it its sex; and this indeed so simultaneously, that neither of the two substances can be alone regarded as the cause of the sex. Now, if in the semination of these substances any interval were admissible in their conception, in such wise that either the flesh or the soul should be the first to be conceived, one might then ascribe an especial sex to one of the substances, owing to the difference in the time of the impregnations, so that either the flesh would impress its sex

upon the soul, or the soul upon the sex ; even as Apelles (the heretic, not the painter[4]) gives the priority over their bodies to the souls of men and women, as he had been taught by Philumena, and in consequence makes the flesh, as the later, receive its sex from the soul. They also who make the soul supervene after birth on the flesh predetermine, of course, the sex of the previously formed soul to be male or female, according to (the sex of) the flesh. But the truth is, the seminations of the two substances are inseparable in point of time, and their effusion is also one and the same, in consequence of which a community of gender is secured to them; so that the course of nature, whatever that be, shall draw the line (for the distinct sexes). Certainly in this view we have an attestation of the method of the first two formations, when the male was moulded and tempered in a completer way, for Adam was first formed; and the woman came far behind him, for Eve was the later formed. So that her flesh was for a long time without specific form (such as she afterwards assumed when taken out of Adam's side); but she was even then herself a living being, because I should regard her at that time in soul as even a portion of Adam. Besides, God's *afflatus* would have animated her too, if there had not been in the woman a transmission from Adam of his soul also as well as of his flesh.

CHAP. XXXVII.—ON THE FORMATION AND STATE OF THE EMBRYO. ITS RELATION WITH THE SUBJECT OF THIS TREATISE.

Now the entire process of sowing, forming, and completing the human embryo in the womb is no doubt regulated by some power, which ministers herein to the will of God, whatever may be the method which it is appointed to employ. Even the superstition of Rome, by carefully attending to these points, imagined the goddess *Alemona* to nourish the fœtus in the womb; as well as (the goddesses) *Nona* and *Decima*, called after the most critical months of gestation; and *Partula*, to manage and direct parturition; and *Lucina*, to bring the child to the birth and light of day. We, on our part, believe the angels to officiate herein for God. The embryo therefore becomes a human being in the womb from the moment that its form is completed. The law of Moses, indeed, punishes with due penalties the man who shall cause abortion, inasmuch as there exists already the rudiment of a human being,[5] which has imputed to it even

---

[1] Mal. iv. 5.
[2] Num. xii. 2.
[3] In ch. xxviii. at the beginning.

[4] See above, ch. xxiii. [Also p. 246, *infra*.]
[5] Causa hominis.

now the condition of life and death, since it is already liable to the issues of both, although, by living still in the mother, it for the most part shares its own state with the mother. I must also say something about the period of the soul's birth, that I may omit nothing incidental in the whole process. A mature and regular birth takes place, as a general rule, at the commencement of the tenth month. They who theorize respecting numbers, honour the number ten as the parent of all the others, and as imparting perfection to the human nativity. For my own part, I prefer viewing this measure of time in reference to God, as if implying that the ten months rather initiated man into the ten commandments; so that the numerical estimate of the time needed to consummate our natural birth should correspond to the numerical classification of the rules of our regenerate life. But inasmuch as birth is also completed with the seventh month, I more readily recognize in this number than in the eighth the honour of a numerical agreement with the sabbatical period; so that the month in which God's image is sometimes produced in a human birth, shall in its number tally with the day on which God's creation was completed and hallowed. Human nativity has sometimes been allowed to be premature, and yet to occur in fit and perfect accordance with an *hebdomad* or sevenfold number, as an auspice of our resurrection, and rest, and kingdom. The *ogdoad*, or eightfold number, therefore, is not concerned in our formation;[1] for in the time it represents there will be no more marriage.[2] We have already demonstrated the conjunction of the body and the soul, from the concretion of their very seminations to the complete formation of the *fœtus*. We now maintain their conjunction likewise from the birth onwards; in the first place, because they both grow together, only each in a different manner suited to the diversity of their nature— the flesh in magnitude, the soul in intelligence —the flesh in material condition, the soul in sensibility. We are, however, forbidden to suppose that the soul increases in substance, lest it should be said also to be capable of diminution in substance, and so its extinction even should be believed to be possible; but its inherent power, in which are contained all its natural peculiarities, as originally implanted in its being, is gradually developed along with the flesh, without impairing the germinal basis of the substance, which it re-

ceived when breathed at first into man. Take a certain quantity of gold or of silver—a rough mass as yet: it has indeed a compact condition, and one that is more compressed at the moment than it will be; yet it contains within its contour what is throughout a mass of gold or of silver. When this mass is afterwards extended by beating it into leaf, it becomes larger than it was before by the elongation of the original mass, but not by any addition thereto, because it is extended in space, not increased in bulk; although in a way it is even increased when it is extended: for it may be increased in form, but not in state. Then, again, the sheen of the gold or the silver, which when the metal was only in block was inherent in it no doubt really, but yet only obscurely, shines out in developed lustre. Afterwards various modifications of shape accrue, according to the feasibility in the material which makes it yield to the manipulation of the artisan, who yet adds nothing to the condition of the mass but its configuration. In like manner, the growth and developments of the soul are to be estimated, not as enlarging its substance, but as calling forth its powers.

CHAP. XXXVIII.—ON THE GROWTH OF THE SOUL. ITS MATURITY COINCIDENT WITH THE MATURITY OF THE FLESH IN MAN.

Now we have already[3] laid down the principle, that all the natural properties of the soul which relate to sense and intelligence are inherent in its very substance, and spring from its native constitution, but that they advance by a gradual growth through the stages of life and develope themselves in different ways by accidental circumstances, according to men's means and arts, their manners and customs their local situations, and the influences of the Supreme Powers;[4] but in pursuance of that aspect of the association of body and soul which we have now to consider, we maintain that the *puberty* of the soul coincides with that of the body, and that they attain both together to this full growth at about the fourteenth year of life, speaking generally,—the former by the suggestion of the senses, and the latter by the growth of the bodily members; and (we fix on this age) not because, as Asclepiades supposes, reflection then begins, nor because the civil laws date the commencement of the real business of life from this period, but because this was the appointed order from the very first. For as Adam and Eve felt that they must cover their naked-

---

[1] The *ogdoad*, or number *eight*, mystically representing "*heaven*," where they do not marry.
[2] Beyond the *hebdomad* comes the resurrection, on which see Matt. xxii. 30.

[3] See above, in ch. xx.
[4] See above, in ch. xxiv.

ness after their knowledge of good and evil, so we profess to have the same discernment of good and evil from the time that we experience the same sensation of shame. Now from the before-mentioned age (of fourteen years) sex is suffused and clothed with an especial sensibility, and concupiscence employs the ministry of the eye, and communicates its pleasure to another, and understands the natural relations between male and female, and wears the fig-tree apron to cover the shame which it still excites, and drives man out of the paradise of innocence and chastity, and in its wild pruriency falls upon sins and unnatural incentives to delinquency; for its impulse has by this time surpassed the appointment of nature, and springs from its vicious abuse. But the strictly natural concupiscence is simply confined to the desire of those aliments which God at the beginning conferred upon man. "Of every tree of the garden," He says, "ye shall freely eat;" [1] and then again to the generation which followed next after the flood He enlarged the grant: "Every moving thing that liveth shall be meat for you; behold, as the green herb have I given you all these things," [2]—where He has regard rather to the body than to the soul, although it be in the interest of the soul also. For we must remove all occasion from the caviller, who, because the soul apparently wants aliments, would insist on the soul's being from this circumstance deemed mortal, since it is sustained by meat and drink and after a time loses its vigour when they are withheld, and on their complete removal ultimately droops and dies. Now the point we must keep in view is not merely which particular faculty it is which desires these (aliments), but also for what end; and even if it be for its own sake, still the question remains, Why this desire, and when felt, and how long? Then again there is the consideration, that it is one thing to desire by natural instinct, and another thing to desire through necessity; one thing to desire as a property of being, another thing to desire for a special object. The soul, therefore, will desire meat and drink—for itself indeed, because of a special necessity; for the flesh, however, from the nature of its properties. For the flesh is no doubt the house of the soul, and the soul is the temporary inhabitant of the flesh. The desire, then, of the lodger will arise from the temporary cause and the special necessity which his very designation suggests,—with a view to benefit and improve the place of his temporary abode, while sojourning in it; not

with the view, certainly, of being himself the foundation of the house, or himself its walls, or himself its support and roof, but simply and solely with the view of being accommodated and housed, since he could not receive such accommodation except in a sound and well-built house. (Now, applying this imagery to the soul,) if it be not provided with this accommodation, it will not be in its power to quit its dwelling-place, and for want of fit and proper resources, to depart safe and sound, in possession, too, of its own supports, and the aliments which belong to its own proper condition,—namely immortality, rationality, sensibility, intelligence, and freedom of the will.

CHAP. XXXIX.—THE EVIL SPIRIT HAS MARRED THE PURITY OF THE SOUL FROM THE VERY BIRTH.

All these endowments of the soul which are bestowed on it at birth are still obscured and depraved by the malignant being who, in the beginning, regarded them with envious eye, so that they are never seen in their spontaneous action, nor are they administered as they ought to be. For to what individual of the human race will not the evil spirit cleave, ready to entrap their souls from the very portal of their birth, at which he is invited to be present in all those superstitious processes which accompany childbearing? Thus it comes to pass that all men are brought to the birth with idolatry for the midwife, whilst the very wombs that bear them, still bound with the fillets that have been wreathed before the idols, declare their offspring to be consecrated to demons: for in parturition they invoke the aid of Lucina and Diana; for a whole week a table is spread in honour of Juno; on the last day the fates of the horoscope [3] are invoked; and then the infant's first step on the ground is sacred to the goddess Statina. After this does any one fail to devote to idolatrous service the entire head of his son, or to take out a hair, or to shave off the whole with a razor, or to bind it up for an offering, or seal it for sacred use—in behalf of the clan, of the ancestry, or for public devotion? On this principle of early possession it was that Socrates, while yet a boy, was found by the spirit of the demon. Thus, too, is it that to all persons their *genii* are assigned, which is only another name for *demons*. Hence in no case (I mean of the heathen, of course) is there any nativity which is pure of idolatrous superstition. It was from this circumstance that the apostle said, that when either of the

[1] Gen. ii. 16.
[2] Gen. ix. 3.

[3] Fata Scribunda.

parents was sanctified, the children were holy;[1] and this as much by the prerogative of the (Christian) seed as by the discipline of the institution (by baptism and Christian education). "Else," says he, "were the children unclean" by birth:[1] as if he meant us to understand that the children of believers were designed for holiness, and thereby for salvation; in order that he might by the pledge of such a hope give his support to matrimony, which he had determined to maintain in its integrity. Besides, he had certainly not forgotten what the Lord had so definitively stated: "Except a man be born of water and of the Spirit, he cannot enter into the kingdom of God;"[2] in other words, he cannot be holy.

CHAP. XL.—THE BODY OF MAN ONLY ANCILLARY TO THE SOUL IN THE COMMISSION OF EVIL.

Every soul, then, by reason of its birth, has its nature in Adam until it is born again in Christ; moreover, it is unclean all the while that it remains without this regeneration;[3] and because unclean, it is actively sinful, and suffuses even the flesh (by reason of their conjunction) with its own shame. Now although the flesh is sinful, and we are forbidden to walk in accordance with it,[4] and its works are condemned as lusting against the spirit,[5] and men on its account are censured as carnal,[6] yet the flesh has not such ignominy on its own account. For it is not of itself that it thinks anything or feels anything for the purpose of advising or commanding sin. How should it, indeed? It is only a ministering thing, and its ministration is not like that of a servant or familiar friend—animated and human beings; but rather that of a vessel, or something of that kind: it is body, not soul. Now a cup may minister to a thirsty man; and yet, if the thirsty man will not apply the cup to his mouth, the cup will yield no ministering service. Therefore the *differentia*, or distinguishing property, of man by no means lies in his earthy element; nor is the flesh the human person, as being some faculty of his soul, and a personal quality; but it is a thing of quite a different substance and different condition, although annexed to the soul as a chattel or as an instrument for the offices of life. Accordingly the flesh is blamed in the Scriptures, because nothing is done by the soul without the flesh in operations of con-

cupiscence, appetite, drunkenness, cruelty, idolatry, and other works of the flesh,—operations, I mean, which are not confined to sensations, but result in effects. The emotions of sin, indeed, when not resulting in effects, are usually imputed to the soul: "Whosoever looketh on a woman to lust after, hath already in his heart committed adultery with her."[7] But what has the flesh alone, without the soul, ever done in operations of virtue, righteousness, endurance, or chastity? What absurdity, however, it is to attribute sin and crime to that substance to which you do not assign any good actions or character of its own ! Now the party which aids in the commission of a crime is brought to trial, only in such a way that the principal offender who actually committed the crime may bear the weight of the penalty, although the abettor too does not escape indictment. Greater is the odium which falls on the principal, when his officials are punished through his fault. He is beaten with more stripes who instigates and orders the crime, whilst at the same time he who obeys such an evil command is not acquitted.

CHAP. XLI.—NOTWITHSTANDING THE DEPRAVITY OF MAN'S SOUL BY ORIGINAL SIN, THERE IS YET LEFT A BASIS WHEREON DIVINE GRACE CAN WORK FOR ITS RECOVERY BY SPIRITUAL REGENERATION.

There is, then, besides the evil which supervenes on the soul from the intervention of the evil spirit, an antecedent, and in a certain sense natural, evil which arises from its corrupt origin. For, as we have said before, the corruption of our nature is another nature having a god and father of its own, namely the author of (that) corruption. Still there is a portion of good in the soul, of that original, divine, and genuine good, which is its proper nature. For that which is derived from God is rather obscured than extinguished. It can be obscured, indeed, because it is not God; extinguished, however, it cannot be, because it comes from God. As therefore light, when intercepted by an opaque body, still remains, although it is not apparent, by reason of the interposition of so dense a body; so likewise the good in the soul, being weighed down by the evil, is, owing to the obscuring character thereof, either not seen at all, its light being wholly hidden, or else only a stray beam is there visible where it struggles through by an accidental outlet. Thus some men are very bad, and some very good; but yet the souls of all form but one genus: even in the worst there is something good, and in the best

[1] 1 Cor. vii. 14.
[2] John iii. 5.
[3] Rom. vi. 4.
[4] Gal. v. 16.
[5] Ver. 17.
[6] Rom. viii. 5.
[7] Matt. v. 28.

there is something bad. For God alone is without sin; and the only man without sin is Christ, since Christ is also God. Thus the divinity of the soul bursts forth in prophetic forecasts in consequence of its primeval good; and being conscious of its origin, it bears testimony to God (its author) in exclamations such as: *Good God! God knows!* and *Good-bye!*[1] Just as no soul is without sin, so neither is any soul without seeds of good. Therefore, when the soul embraces the faith, being renewed in its second birth by water and the power from above, then the veil of its former corruption being taken away, it beholds the light in all its brightness. It is also taken up (in its second birth) by the Holy Spirit, just as in its first birth it is embraced by the unholy spirit. The flesh follows the soul now wedded to the Spirit, as a part of the bridal portion—no longer the servant of the soul, but of the Spirit. O happy marriage, if in it there is committed no violation of the nuptial vow!

CHAP. XLII.—SLEEP, THE MIRROR OF DEATH, AS INTRODUCTORY TO THE CONSIDERATION OF DEATH.

It now remains (that we discuss the subject) of death, in order that our subject-matter may terminate where the soul itself completes it; although Epicurus, indeed, in his pretty widely known doctrine, has asserted that death does not appertain to us. That, says he, which is dissolved lacks sensation; and that which is without sensation is nothing to us. Well, but it is not actually death which suffers dissolution and lacks sensation, but the human person who experiences death. Yet even *he* has admitted suffering to be incidental to the being to whom action belongs. Now, if it is in man to suffer death, which dissolves the body and destroys the senses, how absurd to say that so great a susceptibility belongs not to man! With much greater precision does Seneca say: "After death all comes to an end, even (death) itself." From which position of his it must needs follow that death will appertain to its own self, since itself comes to an end; and much more to man, in the ending of whom amongst the "*all*," itself also ends. Death, (says Epicurus) belongs not to us; then at that rate, life belongs not to us. For certainly, if that which causes our dissolution have no relation to us, that also which compacts and composes us must be unconnected with us. If the deprivation of our sensation be nothing to us, neither can the acquisition of sensation have anything to do with us.

The fact, however, is, he who destroys the very soul, (as Epicurus does), cannot help destroying death also. As for ourselves, indeed, (Christians as we are), we must treat of death just as we should of the posthumous life and of some other province of the soul, (assuming) that we at all events belong to death, if it does not pertain to us. And on the same principle, even *sleep*, which is the very mirror of death, is not alien from our subject-matter.

CHAP. XLIII.—SLEEP A NATURAL FUNCTION AS SHOWN BY OTHER CONSIDERATIONS, AND BY THE TESTIMONY OF SCRIPTURE.

Let us therefore first discuss the question of sleep, and afterwards in what way the soul encounters[2] death. Now sleep is certainly not a supernatural thing, as some philosophers will have it be, when they suppose it to be the result of causes which appear to be above nature. The Stoics affirm sleep to be "a temporary suspension of the activity of the senses;"[3] the Epicureans define it as an intermission of the animal spirit; Anaxagoras and Xenophanes as a weariness of the same; Empedocles and Parmenides as a cooling down thereof; Strato as a separation of the (soul's) connatural spirit; Democritus as the soul's indigence; Aristotle as the interruption[4] of the heat around the heart. As for myself, I can safely say that I have never slept in such a way as to discover even a single one of these conditions. Indeed, we cannot possibly believe that sleep is a weariness; it is rather the opposite, for it undoubtedly removes weariness, and a person is refreshed by sleep instead of being fatigued. Besides, sleep is not always the result of fatigue; and even when it is, the fatigue continues no longer. Nor can I allow that sleep is a cooling or decaying of the animal heat, for our bodies derive warmth from sleep in such a way that the regular dispersion of the food by means of sleep could not so easily go on if there were too much heat to accelerate it unduly, or cold to retard it, if sleep had the alleged refrigerating influence. There is also the further fact that perspiration indicates an over-heated digestion; and digestion is predicated of us as a process of concoction, which is an operation concerned with heat and not with cold. In like manner, the immortality of the soul precludes belief in the theory that sleep is an intermission of the animal spirit, or an indigence of the spirit, or a separation of the (soul's) connatural spirit. The soul perishes if it undergoes diminution or intermis-

---

[1] Deo commendo = *God be wi' ye. De Test.* c. ii. p. 176, *supra.*

[2] Decurrat.
[3] So Bp. Kaye, p. 195.
[4] Marcorem, "the decay."

sion. Our only resource, indeed, is to agree with the Stoics, by determining the soul to be a temporary suspension of the activity of the senses, procuring rest for the body only, not for the soul also. For the soul, as being always in motion, and always active, never succumbs to rest,—a condition which is alien to immortality: for nothing immortal admits any end to its operation; but sleep is an end of operation. It is indeed on the body, which is subject to mortality, and on the body alone, that sleep graciously bestows[1] a cessation from work. He, therefore, who shall doubt whether sleep is a natural function, has the dialectical experts calling in question the whole difference between things natural and supernatural—so that what things he supposed to be beyond nature he may, (if he likes,) be safe in assigning to nature, which indeed has made such a disposition of things, that they may seemingly be accounted as beyond it; and so, of course, all things are natural or none are natural, (as occasion requires.) With us (Christians), however, only that can receive a hearing which is suggested by contemplating God, the Author of all the things which we are now discussing. For we believe that nature, if it is anything, is a reasonable work of God. Now reason presides over sleep; for sleep is so fit for man, so useful, so necessary, that were it not for it, not a soul could provide agency for recruiting the body, for restoring its energies, for ensuring its health, for supplying suspension from work and remedy against labour, and for the legitimate enjoyment of which day departs, and night provides an ordinance by taking from all objects their very colour. Since, then, sleep is indispensable to our life, and health, and succour, there can be nothing pertaining to it which is not reasonable, and which is not natural. Hence it is that physicians banish beyond the gateway of nature everything which is contrary to what is vital, healthful, and helpful to nature; for those maladies which are inimical to sleep—maladies of the mind and of the stomach—they have decided to be contrariant to nature, and by such decision have determined as its corollary that sleep is perfectly natural. Moreover, when they declare that sleep is not natural in the lethargic state, they derive their conclusion from the fact that it is natural when it is in its due and regular exercise. For every natural state is impaired either by defect or by excess, whilst it is maintained by its proper measure and amount. That, therefore, will be natural in its condition which may be rendered non-natural by defect or by excess. Well, now, what if you were to remove eating and drinking from the conditions of nature? if in them lies the chief incentive to sleep. It is certain that, from the very beginning of his nature, man was impressed with these instincts (of sleep).[2] If you receive your instruction from God, (you will find) that the fountain of the human race, Adam, had a taste of drowsiness before having a draught of repose; slept before he laboured, or even before he ate, nay, even before he spoke; in order that men may see that sleep is a natural feature and function, and one which has actually precedence over all the natural faculties. From this primary instance also we are led to trace even then the image of death in sleep. For as Adam was a figure of Christ, Adam's sleep shadowed out the death of Christ, who was to sleep a mortal slumber, that from the wound inflicted on His side might, in like manner (as Eve was formed), be typified the church, the true mother of the living. This is why sleep is so salutary, so rational, and is actually formed into the model of that death which is general and common to the race of man. God, indeed, has willed (and it may be said in passing that He has, generally, in His dispensations brought nothing to pass without such types and shadows) to set before us, in a manner more fully and completely than Plato's example, by daily recurrence the outlines of man's state, especially concerning the beginning and the termination thereof; thus stretching out the hand to help our faith more readily by types and parables, not in words only, but also in things. He accordingly sets before your view the human body stricken by the friendly power of slumber, prostrated by the kindly necessity of repose immoveable in position, just as it lay previous to life, and just as it will lie after life is past: there it lies as an attestation of its form when first moulded, and of its condition when at last buried—awaiting the soul in both stages, in the former previous to its bestowal, in the latter after its recent withdrawal. Meanwhile the soul is circumstanced in such a manner as to seem to be elsewhere active, learning to bear future absence by a dissembling of its presence for the moment. We shall soon know the case of Hermotimus. But yet it dreams in the interval. Whence then its dreams? The fact is, it cannot rest or be idle altogether, nor does it confine to the still hours of sleep the nature of its immortality. It proves itself to possess a constant motion; it travels over land

---

[1] Adulatur.

[2] Gen. ii. 21.

and sea, it trades, it is excited, it labours, it plays, it grieves, it rejoices, it follows pursuits lawful and unlawful; it shows what very great power it has even without the body, how well equipped it is with members of its own, although betraying at the same time the need it has of impressing on some body its activity again. Accordingly, when the body shakes off its slumber, it asserts before your eye the resurrection of the dead by its own resumption of its natural functions. Such, therefore, must be both the natural reason and the reasonable nature of sleep. If you only regard it as the image of death, you initiate faith, you nourish hope, you learn both how to die and how to live, you learn watchfulness, even while you sleep.

CHAP. XLIV.—THE STORY OF HERMOTIMUS, AND THE SLEEPLESSNESS OF THE EMPEROR NERO. NO SEPARATION OF THE SOUL FROM THE BODY UNTIL DEATH.

With regard to the case of Hermotimus, they say that he used to be deprived of his soul in his sleep, as if it wandered away from his body like a person on a holiday trip. His wife betrayed the strange peculiarity. His enemies, finding him asleep, burnt his body, as if it were a corpse: when his soul returned too late, it appropriated (I suppose) to itself the guilt of the murder. However the good citizens of Clazomenæ consoled poor Hermotimus with a temple, into which no woman ever enters, because of the infamy of this wife. Now why this story? In order that, since the vulgar belief so readily holds sleep to be the separation of the soul from the body, credulity should not be encouraged by this case of Hermotimus. It must certainly have been a much heavier sort of slumber: one would presume it was the nightmare, or perhaps that diseased languor which Soranus suggests in opposition to the nightmare, or else some such malady as that which the fable has fastened upon Epimenides, who slept on some fifty years or so. Suetonius, however, informs us that Nero never dreamt, and Theopompus says the same thing about Thrasymedes; but Nero at the close of his life did with some difficulty dream after some excessive alarm. What indeed would be said, if the case of Hermotimus were believed to be such that the repose of his soul was a state of actual idleness during sleep, and a positive separation from his body? You may conjecture it to be anything but such a licence of the soul as admits of flights away from the body without death, and that by continual recurrence, as if habitual to its state and constitution.

If indeed such a thing were told me to have happened at any time to the soul—resembling a total eclipse of the sun or the moon—I should verily suppose that the occurrence had been caused by God's own interposition, for it would not be unreasonable for a man to receive admonition from the Divine Being either in the way of warning or of alarm, as by a flash of lightning, or by a sudden stroke of death; only it would be much the more natural conclusion to believe that this process should be by a dream, because if it must be supposed to be, (as the hypothesis we are resisting assumes it to be,) not a dream, the occurrence ought rather to happen to a man whilst he is wide awake.

CHAP. XLV.—DREAMS, AN INCIDENTAL EFFECT OF THE SOUL'S ACTIVITY. ECSTASY.

We are bound to expound at this point what is the opinion of Christians respecting dreams, as incidents of sleep, and as no slight or trifling excitements of the soul, which we have declared to be always occupied and active owing to its perpetual movement, which again is a proof and evidence of its divine quality and immortality. When, therefore, rest accrues to human bodies, it being their own especial comfort, the soul, disdaining a repose which is not natural to it, never rests; and since it receives no help from the limbs of the body, it uses its own. Imagine a gladiator without his instruments or arms, and a charioteer without his team, but still gesticulating the entire course and exertion of their respective employments: there is the fight, there is the struggle; but the effort is a vain one. Nevertheless the whole procedure seems to be gone through, although it evidently has not been really effected. There is the act, but not the effect. This power we call *ecstasy*, in which the sensuous soul stands out of itself, in a way which even resembles madness.[1] Thus in the very beginning sleep was inaugurated by ecstasy: "And God sent an ecstasy upon Adam, and he slept."[2] The sleep came on his body to cause it to rest, but the ecstasy fell on his soul to remove rest: from that very circumstance it still happens ordinarily (and from the order results the nature of the case) that sleep is combined with ecstasy. In fact, with what real feeling, and anxiety, and suffering do we experience joy, and sorrow, and alarm in our dreams! Whereas we should not be moved by any such emotions, by what would be the merest fan-

---

[1] We had better give Tertullian's own succinct definition: "Excessus sensûs et amentiæ instar."
[2] Gen. ii. 21.

tasies of course, if when we dream we were masters of ourselves, (unaffected by ecstasy.) In these dreams, indeed, good actions are useless, and crimes harmless; for we shall no more be condemned for visionary acts of sin, than we shall be crowned for imaginary martyrdom. But how, you will ask, can the soul remember its dreams, when it is said to be without any mastery over its own operations? This memory must be an especial gift of the ecstatic condition of which we are treating, since it arises not from any failure of healthy action, but entirely from natural process; nor does it expel mental function—it withdraws it for a time. It is one thing to shake, it is another thing to move; one thing to destroy, another thing to agitate. That, therefore, which memory supplies betokens soundness of mind; and that which a sound mind ecstatically experiences whilst the memory remains unchecked, is a kind of madness. We are accordingly not said to be mad, but to dream, in that state; to be in the full possession also of our mental faculties,[1] if we are at any time. For although the power to exercise these faculties[2] may be dimmed in us, it is still not extinguished; except that it may seem to be itself absent at the very time that the ecstasy is energizing in us in its special manner, in such wise as to bring before us images of a sound mind and of wisdom, even as it does those of aberration.

CHAP. XLVI. — DIVERSITY OF DREAMS AND VISIONS. EPICURUS THOUGHT LIGHTLY OF THEM, THOUGH GENERALLY MOST HIGHLY VALUED. INSTANCES OF DREAMS.

We now find ourselves constrained to express an opinion about the character of the dreams by which the soul is excited. And when shall we arrive at the subject of death? And on such a question I would say, When God shall permit: that admits of no long delay which must needs happen at all events. Epicurus has given it as his opinion that dreams are altogether vain things; (but he says this) when liberating the Deity from all sort of care, and dissolving the entire order of the world, and giving to all things the aspect of merest chance, casual in their issues, fortuitous in their nature. Well, now, if such be the nature of things, there must be some chance even for truth, because it is impossible for it to be the only thing to be exempted from the fortune which is due to all things. Homer has assigned two gates to dreams,[3]—the *horny* one of truth, the *ivory* one of error

and delusion. For, they say, it is possible to see through horn, whereas ivory is untransparent. Aristotle, while expressing his opinion that dreams are in most cases untrue, yet acknowledges that there is some truth in them. The people of Telmessus will not admit that dreams are in any case unmeaning, but they blame their own weakness when unable to conjecture their signification. Now, who is such a stranger to human experience as not sometimes to have perceived some truth in dreams? I shall force a blush from Epicurus, if I only glance at some few of the more remarkable instances. Herodotus[4] relates how that Astyages, king of the Medes, saw in a dream issuing from the womb of his virgin daughter a flood which inundated Asia; and again, in the year which followed her marriage, he saw a vine growing out from the same part of her person, which overspread the whole of Asia. The same story is told prior to Herodotus by Charon of Lampsacus. Now they who interpreted these visions did not deceive the mother when they destined her son for so great an enterprise, for Cyrus both inundated and overspread Asia. Philip of Macedon, before he became a father, had seen imprinted on the pudenda of his consort Olympias the form of a small ring, with a lion as a seal. He had concluded that an offspring from her was out of the question (I suppose because the lion only becomes once a father), when Aristodemus or Aristophon happened to conjecture that nothing of an unmeaning or empty import lay under that seal, but that a son of very illustrious character was portended. They who know anything of Alexander recognise in him the lion of that small ring. Ephorus writes to this effect. Again, Heraclides has told us, that a certain woman of Himera beheld in a dream Dionysius' tyranny over Sicily. Euphorion has publicly recorded as a fact, that, previous to giving birth to Seleucus, his mother Laodice foresaw that he was destined for the empire of Asia. I find again from Strabo, that it was owing to a dream that even Mithridates took possession of Pontus; and I further learn from Callisthenes that it was from the indication of a dream that Baraliris the Illyrian stretched his dominion from the Molossi to the frontiers of Macedon. The Romans, too, were acquainted with dreams of this kind. From a dream Marcus Tullius (Cicero) had learnt how that one, who was yet only a little boy, and in a private station, who was also plain Julius Octavius, and personally unknown to (Cicero) himself, was the destined Augustus,

[1] Prudentes.
[2] Sapere.
[3] See the *Odyssey*, xix. 562, etc. [Also, *Æneid*, vi. 894.]

[4] See i. 107, etc.

and the suppressor and destroyer of (Rome's) civil discords. This is recorded in the Commentaries of Vitellius. But visions of this prophetic kind were not confined to predictions of supreme power; for they indicated perils also, and catastrophes: as, for instance, when Cæsar was absent from the battle of Philippi through illness, and thereby escaped the sword of Brutus and Cassius, and then although he expected to encounter greater danger still from the enemy in the field, he quitted his tent for it, in obedience to a vision of Artorius, and so escaped (the capture by the enemy, who shortly after took possession of the tent) ; as, again, when the daughter of Polycrates of Samos foresaw the crucifixion which awaited him from the anointing of the sun and the bath of Jupiter.[1] So likewise in sleep revelations are made of high honours and eminent talents; remedies are also discovered, thefts brought to light, and treasures indicated. Thus Cicero's eminence, whilst he was still a little boy, was foreseen by his nurse. The swan from the breast of Socrates soothing men, is his disciple Plato. The boxer Leonymus is cured by Achilles in his dreams. Sophocles the tragic poet discovers, as he was dreaming, the golden crown, which had been lost from the citadel of Athens. Neoptolemus the tragic actor, through intimations in his sleep from Ajax himself, saves from destruction the hero's tomb on the Rhoetean shore before Troy; and as he removes the decayed stones, he returns enriched with gold. How many commentators and chroniclers vouch for this phenomenon? There are Artemon, Antiphon, Strato, Philochorus, Epicharmus, Serapion, Cratippus, and Dionysius of Rhodes, and Hermippus—the entire literature of the age. I shall only laugh at all, if indeed I ought to laugh at the man who fancied that he was going to persuade us that Saturn dreamt before anybody else; which we can only believe if Aristotle, (who would fain help us to such an opinion,) lived prior to any other person. Pray forgive me for laughing. Epicharmus, indeed, as well as Philochorus the Athenian, assigned the very highest place among divinations to dreams. The whole world is full of oracles of this description: there are the oracles of Amphiaraus at Oropus, of Amphilochus at Mallus, of Sarpedon in the Troad, of Trophonius in Bœotia, of Mopsus in Cilicia, of Hermione in Macedon, of Pasiphäe in Laconia. Then, again, there are others, which with their original foundations, rites, and historians, together with the entire litera-

ture of dreams, Hermippus of Berytus in five portly volumes will give you all the account of, even to satiety. But the Stoics are very fond of saying that God, in His most watchful providence over every institution, gave us dreams amongst other preservatives of the arts and sciences of divination, as the especial support of the natural oracle. So much for the dreams to which credit has to be ascribed even by ourselves, although we must interpret them in another sense. As for all other oracles, at which no one ever dreams, what else must we declare concerning them, than that they are the diabolical contrivance of those spirits who even at that time dwelt in the eminent persons themselves, or aimed at reviving the memory of them as the mere stage of their evil purposes, going so far as to counterfeit a divine power under their shape and form, and, with equal persistence in evil, deceiving men by their very boons of remedies, warnings, and forecasts,—the only effect of which was to injure their victims the more they helped them; while the means whereby they rendered the help withdrew them from all search after the true God, by insinuating into their minds ideas of the false one? And of course so pernicious an influence as this is not shut up nor limited within the boundaries of shrines and temples: it roams abroad, it flies through the air, and all the while is free and unchecked. So that nobody can doubt that our very homes lie open to these diabolical spirits, who beset their human prey with their fantasies not only in their chapels but also in their chambers.

CHAP. XLVII.—DREAMS VARIOUSLY CLASSIFIED. SOME ARE GOD-SENT, AS THE DREAMS OF NEBUCHADNEZZAR ; OTHERS SIMPLY PRODUCTS OF NATURE.

We declare, then, that dreams are inflicted on us mainly by demons, although they sometimes turn out true and favourable to us. When, however, with the deliberate aim after evil, of which we have just spoken, they assume a flattering and captivating style, they show themselves proportionately vain, and deceitful, and obscure, and wanton, and impure. And no wonder that the images partake of the character of the realities. But from God—who has promised, indeed, " to pour out the grace of the Holy Spirit upon all flesh, and has ordained that His servants and His handmaids should see visions as well as utter prophecies "[2]—must all those visions be regarded as emanating, which may be compared to the actual grace of God, as being honest, holy, prophetic, inspired, instructive, inviting

---

[1] See an account of her vision and its interpretation in Herodot. iv. 124.

[2] Joel iii. 1.

to virtue, the bountiful nature of which causes them to overflow even to the profane, since God, with grand impartiality, "sends His showers and sunshine on the just and on the unjust." [1] It was, indeed by an inspiration from God that Nebuchadnezzar dreamt his dreams; [2] and almost the greater part of mankind get their knowledge of God from dreams. Thus it is that, as the mercy of God superabounds to the heathen, so the temptation of the evil one encounters the saints, from whom he never withdraws his malignant efforts to steal over them as best he may in their very sleep, if unable to assault them when they are awake. The third class of dreams will consist of those which the soul itself apparently creates for itself from an intense application to special circumstances. Now, inasmuch as the soul cannot dream of its own accord (for even Epicharmus is of this opinion), how can it become to itself the cause of any vision? Then must this class of dreams be abandoned to the action of nature, reserving for the soul, even when in the ecstatic condition, the power of enduring whatever incidents befall it? Those, moreover, which evidently proceed neither from God, nor from diabolical inspiration, nor from the soul, being beyond the reach as well of ordinary expectation, usual interpretation, or the possibility of being intelligibly related, will have to be ascribed in a separate category to what is purely and simply the ecstatic state and its peculiar conditions.

CHAP. XLVIII.—CAUSES AND CIRCUMSTANCES OF DREAMS. WHAT BEST CONTRIBUTES TO EFFICIENT DREAMING.

They say that dreams are more sure and clear when they happen towards the end of the night, because then the vigour of the soul emerges, and heavy sleep departs. As to the seasons of the year, dreams are calmer in spring, since summer relaxes, and winter somehow hardens, the soul; while autumn, which in other respects is trying to health, is apt to enervate the soul by the lusciousness of its fruits. Then, again, as regards the position of one's body during sleep, one ought not to lie on his back, nor on his right side, nor so as to wrench [3] his intestines, as if their cavity were reversely stretched: a palpitation of the heart would ensue, or else a pressure on the liver would produce a painful disturbance of the mind. But however this be, I take it that it all amounts to ingenious conjecture rather than certain proof (although

the author of the conjecture be no less a man than Plato); [4] and possibly all may be no other than the result of chance. But, generally speaking, dreams will be under control of a man's will, if they be capable of direction at all; for we must not examine what *opinion* on the one hand, and *superstition* on the other, have to prescribe for the treatment of dreams, in the matter of distinguishing and modifying different sorts of food. As for the *superstition*, we have an instance when fasting is prescribed for such persons as mean to submit to the sleep which is necessary for receiving the oracle, in order that such abstinence may produce the required purity; while we find an instance of the *opinion* when the disciples of Pythagoras, in order to attain the same end, reject the bean as an aliment which would load the stomach, and produce indigestion. But the three brethren, who were the companions of Daniel, being content with pulse alone, to escape the contamination of the royal dishes, [5] received from God, besides other wisdom, the gift especially of penetrating and explaining the sense of dreams. For my own part, I hardly know whether fasting would not simply make me dream so profoundly, that I should not be aware whether I had in fact dreamt at all. Well, then, you ask, has not sobriety something to do in this matter? Certainly it is as much concerned in this as it is in the entire subject: if it contributes some good service to superstition, much more does it to religion. For even demons require such discipline from their dreamers as a gratification to their divinity, because they know that it is acceptable to God, since Daniel (to quote him again) "ate no pleasant bread" for the space of three weeks. [6] This abstinence, however, he used in order to please God by humiliation, and not for the purpose of producing a sensibility and wisdom for his soul previous to receiving communication by dreams and visions, as if it were not rather to effect such action in an ecstatic state. This *sobriety*, then, (in which our question arises,) will have nothing to do with exciting ecstasy, but will rather serve to recommend its being wrought by God.

CHAP. XLIX.—NO SOUL NATURALLY EXEMPT FROM DREAMS.

As for those persons who suppose that infants do not dream, on the ground that all the functions of the soul throughout life are accomplished according to the capacity of age, they ought to observe attentively their

---

[1] Matt. v. 45.
[2] Dan. ii. 1, etc.
[3] Conresupinatis.

[4] See his *Timæus*, c. xxxii. p. 71.
[5] Dan. i. 8–14.
[6] Dan. x. 2.

tremors, and nods, and bright smiles as they sleep, and from such facts understand that they are the emotions of their soul as it dreams, which so readily escape to the surface through the delicate tenderness of their infantine body. The fact, however, that the African nation of the Atlantes are said to pass through the night in a deep lethargic sleep, brings down on them the censure that something is wrong in the constitution of their soul. Now either report, which is occasionally calumnious against barbarians, deceived Herodotus,[1] or else a large force of demons of this sort domineers in those barbarous regions. Since, indeed, Aristotle remarks of a certain hero of Sardinia that he used to withhold the power of visions and dreams from such as resorted to his shrine for inspiration, it must lie at the will and caprice of the demons to take away as well as to confer the faculty of dreams; and from this circumstance may have arisen the remarkable fact (which we have mentioned[2]) of Nero and Thrasymedes only dreaming so late in life. We, however, derive dreams from God. Why, then, did not the Atlantes receive the dreaming faculty from God, because there is really no nation which is now a stranger to God, since the gospel flashes its glorious light through the world to the ends of the earth? Could it then be that rumour deceived Aristotle, or is this caprice still the way of demons? (Let us take any view of the case), only do not let it be imagined that any soul is by its natural constitution exempt from dreams.

CHAP. L.—THE ABSURD OPINION OF EPICURUS AND THE PROFANE CONCEITS OF THE HERETIC MENANDER ON DEATH. EVEN ENOCH AND ELIJAH RESERVED FOR DEATH.

We have by this time said enough about sleep, the mirror and image of death; and likewise about the occupations of sleep, even dreams. Let us now go on to consider the cause of our departure hence—that is, the appointment and course of death—because we must not leave even it unquestioned and unexamined, although it is itself the very end of all questions and investigations. According to the general sentiment of the human race, we declare death to be " the debt of nature." So much has been settled by the voice of God;[3] such is the contract with everything which is born: so that even from this the frigid conceit of Epicurus is refuted, who says that no such debt is due from us; and not only so, but the insane opinion of the Samari-

tan heretic Menander is also rejected, who will have it that death has not only nothing to do with his disciples, but in fact never reaches them. He pretends to have received such a commission from the secret power of One above, that all who partake of his baptism become immortal, incorruptible and instantaneously invested with resurrection-life. We read, no doubt, of very many wonderful kinds of waters: how, for instance, the vinous quality of the stream intoxicates people who drink of the Lyncestis; how at Colophon the waters of an oracle-inspiring fountain[4] affect men with madness; how Alexander was killed by the poisonous water from Mount Nonacris in Arcadia. Then, again, there was in Judea before the time of Christ a pool of medicinal virtue. It is well known how the poet has commemorated the marshy Styx as preserving men from death; although Thetis had, in spite of the preservative, to lament her son. And for the matter of that, were Menander himself to take a plunge into this famous Styx, he would certainly have to die after all; for you must come to the Styx, placed as it is by all accounts in the regions of the dead. Well, but what and where are those blessed and charming waters which not even John Baptist ever used in his preministrations, nor Christ after him ever revealed to His disciples? What was this wondrous bath of Menander? He is a comical fellow, I ween.[5] But why (was such a font) so seldom in request, so obscure, one to which so very few ever resorted for their cleansing? I really see something to suspect in so rare an occurrence of a sacrament to which is attached so very much security and safety, and which dispenses with the ordinary law of dying even in the service of God Himself, when, on the contrary, all nations have " to ascend to the mount of the Lord and to the house of the God of Jacob," who demands of His saints in martyrdom that death which He exacted even of His Christ. No one will ascribe to magic such influence as shall exempt from death, or which shall refresh and vivify life, like the vine by the renewal of its condition. Such power was not accorded to the great Medea herself— over a human being at any rate, if allowed her over a silly sheep. Enoch no doubt was translated,[6] and so was Elijah;[7] nor did they experience death: it was postponed, (and only postponed,) most certainly: they are reserved for the suffering of death, that by their blood

---

[1] Who mentions this story of the *Atlantes* in iv. 184.
[2] In ch. xliv. p. 223.
[3] Gen. ii. 17. [Not *ex natura*, but as penalty.]

[4] Scaturigo dæmonica.
[5] It is difficult to say what Tertullian means by his " comicum credo." Is it a playful parody on the heretic's name, the same as the comic poet's (Menander) ?
[6] Gen. v. 24 ; Heb. xi. 5.
[7] 2 Kings ii. 11.

they may extinguish Antichrist.[1] Even John underwent death, although concerning him there had prevailed an ungrounded expectation that he would remain alive until the coming of the Lord.[2] Heresies, indeed, for the most part spring hurriedly into existence, from examples furnished by ourselves: they procure their defensive armour from the very place which they attack. The whole question resolves itself, in short, into this challenge: Where are to be found the men whom Menander himself has baptized? whom he has plunged into his Styx? Let them come forth and stand before us—those apostles of his whom he has made immortal? Let my (doubting) Thomas see them, let him hear them, let him handle them—and he is convinced.

CHAP. LI.—DEATH ENTIRELY SEPARATES THE SOUL FROM THE BODY.

But the operation of death is plain and obvious: it is the separation of body and soul. Some, however, in reference to the soul's immortality, on which they have so feeble a hold through not being taught of God, maintain it with such beggarly arguments, that they would fain have it supposed that certain souls cleave to the body even after death. It is indeed in this sense that Plato, although he despatches at once to heaven such souls as he pleases,[3] yet in his *Republic*[4] exhibits to us the corpse of an unburied person, which was preserved a long time without corruption, by reason of the soul remaining, as he says, unseparated from the body. To the same purport also Democritus remarks on the growth for a considerable while of the human nails and hair in the grave. Now, it is quite possible that the nature of the atmosphere tended to the preservation of the above-mentioned corpse. What if the air were particularly dry, and the ground of a saline nature? What, too, if the substance of the body itself were unusually dry and arid? What, moreover, if the mode of the death had already eliminated from the corpse all corrupting matter? As for the nails, since they are the commencement of the nerves, they may well seem to be prolonged, owing to the nerves themselves being relaxed and extended, and to be protruded more and more as the flesh fails. The hair, again, is nourished from the brain, which would cause it endure for a long time as its secret aliment and defence. Indeed, in the case of living persons themselves, the whole head of hair is copious or scanty in proportion

to the exuberance of the brain. You have medical men (to attest the fact). But not a particle of the soul can possibly remain in the body, which is itself destined to disappear when time shall have abolished the entire scene on which the body has played its part. And yet even this partial survival of the soul finds a place in the opinions of some men; and on this account they will not have the body consumed at its funeral by fire, because they would spare the small residue of the soul. There is, however, another way of accounting for this pious treatment, not as if it meant to favour the relics of the soul, but as if it would avert a cruel custom ·in the interest even of the body; since, being human, it is itself undeserving of an end which is also inflicted upon murderers. The truth is, the soul is indivisible, because it is immortal; (and this fact) compels us to believe that death itself is an indivisible process, accruing indivisibly to the soul, not indeed because it is immortal, but because it is indivisible. Death, however, would have to be divided in its operation, if the soul were divisible into particles, any one of which has to be reserved for a later stage of death. At this rate, a part of death will have to stay behind for a portion of the soul. I am not ignorant that some vestige of this opinion still exists. I have found it out from one of my own people. I am acquainted with the case of a woman, the daughter of Christian parents,[5] who in the very flower of her age and beauty slept peacefully (in Jesus), after a singularly happy though brief married life. Before they laid her in her grave, and when the priest began the appointed office, at the very first breath of his prayer she withdrew her hands from her side, placed them in an attitude of devotion, and after the holy service was concluded restored them to their lateral position. Then, again, there is that well-known story among our own people, that a body voluntarily made way in a certain cemetery, to afford room for another body to be placed near to it. If, as is the case, similar stories are told amongst the heathen, (we can only conclude that) God everywhere manifests signs of His own power—to His own people for their comfort, to strangers for a testimony unto them. I would indeed much rather suppose that a portent of this kind happened form the direct agency of God than from any relics of the soul: for if there were a residue of these, they would be certain to move the other limbs; and even if they moved the hands, this still would not have been for the purpose of a prayer. Nor would the corpse hav been simply content to have made way

---

[1] Rev. xi. 3.
[2] John xxi. 23.
[3] See below, ch. liv.
[4] Ch. x. p. 614.

[5] Vernaculam ecclesiæ.

for its neighbour: it would, besides, have benefited its own self also by the change of its position. But from whatever cause proceeded these phenomena, which you must put down amongst signs and portents, it is impossible that they should regulate nature. Death, if it once falls short of totality in operation, is not death. If any fraction of the soul remain, it makes a living state. Death will no more mix with life, than will night with day.

CHAP. LII.—ALL KINDS OF DEATH A VIOLENCE TO NATURE, ARISING FROM SIN.—SIN AN INTRUSION UPON NATURE AS GOD CREATED IT.

Such, then, is the work of death—the separation of the soul from the body. Putting out of the question fates and fortuitous circumstances, it has been, according to men's views, distinguished in a twofold form—the ordinary and the extraordinary. The ordinary they ascribe to nature, exercising its quiet influence in the case of each individual decease; the extraordinary is said to be contrary to nature, happening in every violent death. As for our own views, indeed, we know what was man's origin, and we boldly assert and persistently maintain that death happens not by way of natural consequence to man, but owing to a fault and defect which is not itself natural; although it is easy enough, no doubt, to apply the term *natural* to faults and circumstances which seem to have been (though from the emergence of an external cause[1]) inseparable to us from our very birth. If man had been directly appointed to die as the condition of his creation,[2] then of course death must be imputed to nature. Now, that he was not thus appointed to die, is proved by the very law which made his condition depend on a warning, and death result from man's arbitrary choice. Indeed, if he had not sinned, he certainly would not have died. That cannot be nature which happens by the exercise of volition after an alternative has been proposed to it, and not by necessity—the result of an inflexible and unalterable condition. Consequently, although death has various issues, inasmuch as its causes are manifold, we cannot say that the easiest death is so gentle as not to happen by violence (to our nature). The very law which produces death, simple though it be, is yet violence. How can it be otherwise, when so close a companionship of soul and body, so inseparable a growth together from their very conception of two sister substances, is sundered and divided? For although a man may breathe his last for joy,

like the Spartan Chilon, while embracing his son who had just conquered in the Olympic games; or for glory, like the Athenian Clidemus, while receiving a crown of gold for the excellence of his historical writings; or in a dream, like Plato; or in a fit of laughter, like Publius Crassus,—yet death is much too violent, coming as it does upon us by strange and alien means, expelling the soul by a method all its own, calling on us to die at a moment when one might live a jocund life in joy and honour, in peace and pleasure. That is still a violence to ships: although far away from the Capharean rocks, assailed by no storms, without a billow to shatter them, with favouring gale, in gliding course, with merry crews, they founder amidst some internal shock, suddenly, owing to some internal shock. Not dissimilar are the shipwrecks of life,—the issues of even a tranquil death. It matters not whether the vessel of the human body goes with unbroken timbers or shattered with storms, if the navigation of the soul be overthrown.

CHAP. LIII.—THE ENTIRE SOUL BEING INDIVISIBLE REMAINS TO THE LAST ACT OF VITALITY; NEVER PARTIALLY OR FRACTIONALLY WITHDRAWN FROM THE BODY.

But where at last will the soul have to lodge, when it is bare and divested of the body? We must certainly not hesitate to follow it thither, in the order of our inquiry. We must, however, first of all fully state what belongs to the topic before us, in order that no one, because we have mentioned the various issues of death, may expect from us a special description of these, which ought rather to be left to medical men, who are the proper judges of the incidents which appertain to death, or its causes, and the actual conditions of the human body. Of course, with the view of preserving the truth of the soul's immortality, whilst treating this topic, I shall have, on mentioning death, to introduce phrases about dissolution of such a purport as seems to intimate that the soul escapes by degrees, and piece by piece; for it withdraws (from the body) with all the circumstances of a decline, seeming to suffer consumption, and suggests to us the idea of being annihilated by the slow process of its departure. But the entire reason of this phenomenon is in the body, and arises from the body. For whatever be the kind of death (which operates on man), it undoubtedly produces the destruction either of the matter, or of the region, or of the passages of vitality: of the matter, such as the gall and the blood; of the region, such as the heart and the liver; of the passages, such as the veins and the ar-

---

[1] Ex accidentia.
[2] In mortem directo institutus est. [See p. 227, *supra*.]

teries. Inasmuch, then, as these parts of the body are severally devastated by an injury proper to each of them, even to the very last ruin and annulling of the vital powers—in other words, of the ends, the sites, and the functions of nature—it must needs come to pass, amidst the gradual decay of its instruments, domiciles, and spaces, that the soul also itself, being driven to abandon each successive part, assumes the appearance of being lessened to nothing; in some such manner as a charioteer is assumed to have himself failed, when his horses, through fatigue, withdraw from him their energies. But this assumption applies only to the circumstances of the despoiled person, not to any real condition of suffering. Likewise the body's charioteer, the animal spirit, fails on account of the failure of its vehicle, not of itself—abandoning its work, but not its vigour—languishing in operation, but not in essential condition—bankrupt in solvency, not in substance—because ceasing to put in an appearance, but not ceasing to exist. Thus every rapid death —such as a decapitation, or a breaking of the neck,[1] which opens at once a vast outlet for the soul; or a sudden ruin, which at a stroke crushes every vital action, like that inner ruin apoplexy—retards not the soul's escape, nor painfully separates its departure into successive moments. Where, however, the death is a lingering one, the soul abandons its position in the way in which it is itself abandoned. And yet it is not by this process severed in fractions: it is slowly drawn out; and whilst thus extracted, it causes the last remnant to seem to be but a part of itself. No portion, however, must be deemed separable, because it is the last; nor, because it is a small one, must it be regarded as susceptible of dissolution. Accordant with a series is its end, and the middle is prolonged to the extremes; and the remnants cohere to the mass, and are waited for, but never abandoned by it. And I will even venture to say, that the last of a whole is the whole; because while it is less, and the latest, it yet belongs to the whole, and completes it. Hence, indeed, many times it happens that the soul in its actual separation is more powerfully agitated with a more anxious gaze, and a quickened loquacity; whilst from the loftier and freer position in which it is now placed, it enunciates, by means of its last remnant still lingering in the flesh, what it sees, what it hears, and what it is beginning to know. In Platonic phrase, indeed, the body is a prison,[2] but in the apos-

tle's it is " the temple of God,"[3] because it is in Christ. Still, (as must be admitted,) by reason of its enclosure it obstructs and obscures the soul, and sullies it by the concretion of the flesh; whence it happens that the light which illumines objects comes in upon the soul in a more confused manner, as if through a window of horn. Undoubtedly, when the soul, by the power of death, is released from its concretion with the flesh, is by the very release cleansed and purified: it is, moreover, certain that it escapes from the veil of the flesh into open space, to its clear, and pure, and intrinsic light; and then finds itself enjoying its enfranchisement from matter, and by virtue of its liberty it recovers its divinity, as one who awakes out of sleep passes from images to verities. Then it tells out what it sees; then it exults or it fears, according as it finds what lodging is prepared for it, as soon as it sees the very angel's face, that arraigner of souls, the Mercury of the poets.

CHAP. LIV.—WHITHER DOES THE SOUL RETIRE WHEN IT QUITS THE BODY? OPINIONS OF PHILOSOPHERS ALL MORE OR LESS ABSURD. THE HADES OF PLATO.

To the question, therefore, whither the soul is withdrawn, we now give an answer. Almost all the philosophers, who hold the soul's immortality, notwithstanding their special views on the subject, still claim for it this (eternal condition), as Pythagoras, and Empedocles, and Plato, and as they who indulge it with some delay from the time of its quitting the flesh to the conflagration of all things, and as the Stoics, who place only their own souls, that is, the souls of the wise, in the mansions above. Plato, it is true, does not allow this destination to all the souls, indiscriminately, of even all the philosophers, but only of those who have cultivated their philosophy out of love to boys. So great is the privilege which impurity obtains at the hands of philosophers! In his system, then, the souls of the wise are carried up on high into the ether: according to Arius,[4] into the air; according to the Stoics, into the moon. I wonder, indeed, that they abandon to the earth the souls of the unwise, when they affirm that even these are instructed by the wise, so much their superiors. For where is the school where they can have been instructed in the vast space which divides them? By what means can the pupil-souls have resorted to their teachers, when they are parted from each other by so distant an interval? What

---

[1] We have made Tertullian's " cervicum messis " include both these modes of instantaneous death.
[2] *Phædo*, p. 62, c. 6.

[3] 1 Cor. iii. 16, vi. 19 ; 2 Cor. vi. 16.
[4] An Alexandrian philosopher in great repute with the Emperor Augustus.

profit, too, can any instruction afford them at all in their posthumous state, when they are on the brink of perdition by the universal fire? All other souls they thrust down to Hades, which Plato, in his *Phædo*,[1] describes as the bosom of the earth, where all the filth of the world accumulates, settles, and exhales, and where every separate draught of air only renders denser still the impurities of the seething mass.

CHAP. LV.—THE CHRISTIAN IDEA OF THE POSITION OF HADES; THE BLESSEDNESS OF PARADISE IMMEDIATELY AFTER DEATH. THE PRIVILEGE OF THE MARTYRS.

By ourselves the lower regions (of Hades) are not supposed to be a bare cavity, nor some subterranean sewer of the world, but a vast deep space in the interior of the earth, and a concealed recess in its very bowels; inasmuch as we read that Christ in His death spent three days in the heart of the earth,[2] that is, in the secret inner recess which is hidden in the earth, and enclosed by the earth, and superimposed on the abysmal depths which lie still lower down. Now although Christ is God, yet, being also man, "He died according to the Scriptures,"[3] and "according to the same Scriptures was buried."[4] With the same law of His being He fully complied, by remaining in Hades in the form and condition of a dead man; nor did He ascend into the heights of heaven before descending into the lower parts of the earth, that He might there make the patriarchs and prophets partakers of Himself.[5] (This being the case), you must suppose Hades to be a subterranean region, and keep at arm's length those who are too proud to believe that the souls of the faithful deserve a place in the lower regions.[6] These persons, who are "servants above their Lord, and disciples above their Master,"[7] would no doubt spurn to receive the comfort of the resurrection, if they must expect it in Abraham's bosom. But it was for this purpose, say they, that Christ descended into hell, that we might not ourselves have to descend thither. Well, then, what difference is there between heathens and Christians, if the same prison awaits them all when dead? How, indeed, shall the soul mount up to heaven, where Christ is already sitting at the Father's right hand, when as yet the archangel's trumpet has not been heard by the command of God,[8]—when as yet those whom the coming of the Lord is to find on the earth, have not been caught up into the air to meet Him at His coming,[9] in company with the dead in Christ, who shall be the first to arise?[10] To no one is heaven opened; the earth is still safe for him, I would not say it is shut against him. When the world, indeed, shall pass away, then the kingdom of heaven shall be opened. Shall we then have to sleep high up in ether, with the boy-loving worthies of Plato; or in the air with Arius; or around the moon with the Endymions of the Stoics? No, but in Paradise, you tell me, whither already the patriarchs and prophets have removed from Hades in the retinue of the Lord's resurrection. How is it, then, that the region of Paradise, which as revealed to John in the Spirit lay under the altar,[11] displays no other souls as in it besides the souls of the martyrs? How is it that the most heroic martyr Perpetua on the day of her passion saw only her fellow-martyrs there, in the revelation which she received of Paradise, if it were not that the sword which guarded the entrance permitted none to go in thereat, except those who had died in Christ and not in Adam? A new death for God, even the extraordinary one for Christ, is admitted into the reception-room of mortality, specially altered and adapted to receive the new-comer. Observe, then, the difference between a heathen and a Christian in their death: if you have to lay down your life for God, as the Comforter[12] counsels, it is not in gentle fevers and on soft beds, but in the sharp pains of martyrdom: you must take up the cross and bear it after your Master, as He has Himself instructed you.[13] The sole key to unlock Paradise is your own life's blood.[14] You have a treatise by us,[15] (on Paradise), in which we have established the position that every soul is detained in safe keeping in Hades until the day of the Lord.

CHAP. LVI.—REFUTATION OF THE HOMERIC VIEW OF THE SOUL'S DETENTION FROM HADES OWING TO THE BODY'S BEING UNBURIED. THAT SOULS PREMATURELY SEPARATED FROM THE BODY HAD TO WAIT FOR ADMISSION INTO HADES ALSO REFUTED.

There arises the question, whether this takes place immediately after the soul's de-

---

[1] *Phædo*, pp. 112–114.
[2] Matt. xii. 40.
[3] 1 Cor. xv. 3.
[4] Ver. 4.
[5] 1 Pet. iii. 19.
[6] See Irenæus, *adv. Hares.* v. [Vol. I. p. 566, this Series.]
[7] Matt. x. 24.

[8] 1 Cor. xv. 52 and 1 Thess. iv. 16.
[9] 1 Thess. iv. 17.
[10] Ver. 16.
[11] Rev. vi. 9.
[12] Paracletus.
[13] Matt. xvi. 24.
[14] The souls of the martyrs were, according to Tertullian, at once removed to Paradise (Bp. Kaye, p. 249).
[15] *De Paradiso.* [Compare, p. 216, note 9, *supra.*]

parture from the body; whether some souls are detained for special reasons in the meantime here on earth; and whether it is permitted them of their own accord, or by the intervention of authority, to be removed from Hades[1] at some subsequent time? Even such opinions as these are not by any means lacking persons to advance them with confidence. It was believed that the unburied dead were not admitted into the infernal regions before they had received a proper sepulture; as in the case of Homer's Patroclus, who earnestly-asks for a burial of Achilles in a dream, on the ground that he could not enter Hades through any other portal, since the souls of the sepulchred dead kept thrusting him away.[2] We know that Homer exhibited more than a poetic licence here; he had in view the rights of the dead. Proportioned, indeed, to his care for the just honours of the tomb, was his censure of that delay of burial which was injurious to souls. (It was also his purpose to add a warning), that no man should, by detaining in his house the corpse of a friend, only expose himself, along with the deceased, to increased injury and trouble, by the irregularity[3] of the consolation which he nourishes with pain and grief. He has accordingly kept a twofold object in view in picturing the complaints of an unburied soul: he wished to maintain honour to the dead by promptly attending to their funeral, as well as to moderate the feelings of grief which their memory excited. But, after all, how vain is it to suppose that the soul could bear the rites and requirements of the body, or carry any of them away to the infernal regions! And how much vainer still is it, if injury be supposed to accrue to the soul from that neglect of burial which it ought to receive rather as a favour! For surely the soul which had no willingness to die might well prefer as tardy a removal to Hades as possible. It will love the undutiful heir, by whose means it still enjoys the light. If, however, it is certain that injury accrues to the soul from a tardy interment of the body —and the gist of the injury lies in the neglect of the burial—it is yet in the highest degree unfair, that that should receive all the injury to which the faulty delay could not possibly be imputed, for of course all the fault rests on the nearest relations of the dead. They also say that those souls which are taken away by a premature death wander about hither and thither until they have completed the residue of the years which they would have lived through, had it not been for their untimely fate. Now either their days are appointed to all men severally, and if so appointed, I cannot suppose them capable of being shortened; or if, notwithstanding such appointment, they may be shortened by the will of God, or some other powerful influence, then (I say) such shortening is of no validity, if they still may be accomplished in some other way. If, on the other hand, they are not appointed, there cannot be any residue to be fulfilled for unappointed periods. I have another remark to make. Suppose it be an infant that dies yet hanging on the breast; or it may be an immature boy; or it may be, once more, a youth arrived at puberty: suppose, moreover, that the life in each case ought to have reached full eighty years, how is it possible that the soul of either could spend the whole of the shortened years here on earth after losing its body by death? One's age cannot be passed without one's body, it being by help of the body that the period of life has its duties and labours transacted. Let our own people, moreover, bear this in mind, that souls are to receive back at the resurrection the self-same bodies in which they died. Therefore our bodies must be expected to resume the same conditions and the same ages, for it is these particulars which impart to bodies their especial modes. By what means, then, can the soul of an infant so spend on earth its residue of years, that it should be able at the resurrection to assume the state of an octogenarian, although it had barely lived a month? Or if it shall be necessary that the appointed days of life be fulfilled here on earth, must the same course of life in all its vicissitudes, which has been itself ordained to accompany the appointed days, be also passed through by the soul along with the days? Must it employ itself in school studies in its passage from infancy to boyhood; play the soldier in the excitement and vigour of youth and earlier manhood; and encounter serious and judicial responsibilities in the graver years between ripe manhood and old age? Must it ply trade for profit, turn up the soil with hoe and plough, go to sea, bring actions at law, get married, toil and labour, undergo illnesses, and whatever casualties of weal and woe await it in the lapse of years? Well, but how are all these transactions to be managed without one's body? Life (spent) without life? But (you will tell me) the destined period in question is to be bare of all incident whatever, only to be accomplished by merely elapsing. What, then, is to prevent its being fulfilled in Hades, where there is absolutely no use to which you can apply it? We therefore maintain that every soul, whatever be its age on quitting the

[1] Ab inferis.
[2] *Iliad*, xxiii. 72, etc.
[3] Enormitate.

body, remains unchanged in the same, until the time shall come when the promised perfection shall be realized in a state duly tempered to the measure of the peerless angels. Hence those souls must be accounted as passing an exile in Hades, which people are apt to regard as carried off by violence, especially by cruel tortures, such as those of the cross, and the axe, and the sword, and the lion; but we do not account those to be violent deaths which justice awards, that avenger of violence. So then, you will say, it is all the wicked souls that are banished in Hades. (Not quite so fast, is my answer.) I must compel you to determine (what you mean by Hades), which of its two regions, the region of the good or of the bad. If you mean the bad, (all I can say is, that) even now the souls of the wicked deserve to be consigned to those abodes; if you mean the good why should you judge to be unworthy of such a resting-place the souls of infants and of virgins, and [1] those which, by reason of their condition in life were pure and innocent?

CHAP. LVII.—MAGIC AND SORCERY ONLY APPARENT IN THEIR EFFECTS.　GOD ALONE CAN RAISE THE DEAD.

It is either a very fine thing to be detained in these infernal regions with the *Aori*, or souls which were prematurely hurried away; or else a very bad thing indeed to be there associated with the *Biaeothanati*, who suffered violent deaths. I may be permitted to use the actual words and terms with which magic rings again, that inventor of all these odd opinions—with its Ostanes, and Typhon, and Dardanus, and Damigeron, and Nectabis, and Berenice. There is a well-known popular bit of writing,[2] which undertakes to summon up from the abode of Hades the souls which have actually slept out their full age, and had passed away by an honourable death, and had even been buried with full rites and proper ceremony. What after this shall we say about magic? Say, to be sure, what almost everybody says of it—that it is an imposture. But it is not we Christians only whose notice this system of imposture does not escape. We, it is true, have discovered these spirits of evil, not, to be sure, by a complicity with them, but by a certain knowledge which is hostile to them; nor is it by any procedure which is attractive to them, but by a power which subjugates them that we handle (their wretched system)—that manifold pest of the mind of man, that artificer of all error, that destroyer of our salvation and our soul at one swoop:[3] In this way, even by magic, which is indeed only a second idolatry, wherein they pretend that after death they become demons, just as they were supposed in the first and literal idolatry to become gods (and why not? since the gods are but dead things), the before-mentioned *Aori Biaeothanati* are actually invoked,—and not unfairly,[4] if one grounds his faith on this principle, that it is clearly credible for those souls to be beyond all others addicted to violence and wrong, which with violence and wrong have been hurried away by a cruel and premature death and which would have a keen appetite for reprisals. Under cover, however, of these souls, demons operate, especially such as used to dwell in them when they were in life, and who had driven them, in fact, to the fate which had at last carried them off. For, as we have already suggested,[5] there is hardly a human being who is unattended by a demon; and it is well known to many, that premature and violent deaths, which men ascribe to accidents, are in fact brought about by demons. This imposture of the evil spirit lying concealed in the persons of the dead, we are able, if I mistake not, to prove by actual facts, when in cases of exorcism (the evil spirit) affirms himself sometimes to be one of the relatives [6] of the person possessed by him, sometimes a gladiator or a *bestiarius*,[7] and sometimes even a god; always making it one of his chief cares to extinguish the very truth which we are proclaiming, that men may not readily believe that all souls remove to Hades, and that they may overthrow faith in the resurrection and the judgment. And yet for all that, the demon, after trying to circumvent the bystanders, is vanquished by the pressure of divine grace, and sorely against his will confesses all the truth. So also in that other kind of magic, which is supposed to bring up from Hades the souls now resting there, and to exhibit them to public view, there is no other expedient of imposture ever resorted to which operates more powerfully. Of course, why a phantom becomes visible, is because a body is also attached to it; and it is no difficult matter to delude the external vision of a man whose mental eye it is so easy to blind. The serpents which emerged from the magicians' rods, certainly appeared to Pharaoh and to the Egyptians as bodily substances. It is true

---

[1] We have treated this particle as a conjunction · but it may only be an intensive particle introducing an explanatory clause : "*even* those which were pure," etc. [a better rendering.]
[2] Litteratura.
[3] Oehler takes these descriptive clauses as meant of *Satan*, instead of being synonymes of *magic*, as the context seems to require.
[4] Æque.
[5] Above, in ch. XXXIX. p. 219.
[6] Aliquem ex parentibus.
[7] One who fought with wild beasts in the public games, only without the weapons allowed to the gladiator.

that the verity of Moses swallowed up their lying deceit.[1] Many attempts were also wrought against the apostles by the sorcerers Simon and Elymas,[2] but the blindness which struck (them) was no enchanter's trick. What novelty is there in the effort of an unclean spirit to counterfeit the truth? At this very time, even, the heretical dupes of this same Simon (Magus) are so much elated by the extravagant pretensions of their art, that they undertake to bring up from Hades the souls of the prophets themselves. And I suppose that they can do so under cover of a lying wonder. For, indeed, it was no less than this that was anciently permitted to the Pythonic (or ventriloquistic) spirit[3]—even to represent the soul of Samuel, when Saul consulted the dead, after (losing the living) God.[3] God forbid, however, that we should suppose that the soul of any saint, much less of a prophet, can be dragged out of (its resting-place in Hades) by a demon. We know that "Satan himself is transformed into an angel of light"[5] —much more into a man of light—and that at last he will "show himself to be even God,"[6] and will exhibit "great signs and wonders, insomuch that, if it were possible, he shall deceive the very elect."[7] He hardly[8] hesitated on the before-mentioned occasion to affirm himself to be a prophet of God, and especially to Saul, in whom he was then actually dwelling. You must not imagine that he who produced the phantom was one, and he who consulted it was another; but that it was one and the same spirit, both in the sorceress and in the apostate (king), which easily pretended an apparition of that which it had already prepared them to believe as real— (even the spirit) through whose evil influence Saul's heart was fixed where his treasure was, and where certainly God was not. Therefore it came about, that he saw him through whose aid he believed that he was going to see, because he believed him through whose help he saw. But we are met with the objection, that in visions of the night dead persons are not unfrequently seen, and that for a set purpose.[9] For instance, the Nasamones consult private oracles by frequent and lengthened visits to the sepulchres of their relatives, as one may find in Heraclides, or Nymphodorus, or Herodotus;[10] and the Celts, for the same purpose, stay away all night at the tombs of their brave chieftains, as Nicander affirms. Well, we admit apparitions of dead persons in dreams to be not more really true than those of living persons; but we apply the same estimate to all alike—to the dead and to the living, and indeed to all the phenomena which are seen. Now things are not true because they appear to be so, but because they are fully proved to be so. The truth of dreams is declared from the realization, not the aspect. Moreover, the fact that Hades is not in any case opened for (the escape of) any soul, has been firmly established by the Lord in the person of Abraham, in His representation of the poor man at rest and the rich man in torment.[11] No one, (he said,) could possibly be despatched from those abodes to report to us how matters went in the nether regions,—a purpose which, (if any could be,) might have been allowable on such an occasion, to persuade a belief in Moses and the prophets. The power of God has, no doubt, sometimes recalled men's souls to their bodies, as a proof of His own transcendent rights; but there must never be, because of this fact, any agreement supposed to be possible between the divine faith and the arrogant pretensions of sorcerers, and the imposture of dreams, and the licence of poets. But yet in all cases of a true resurrection, when the power of God recalls souls to their bodies, either by the agency of prophets, or of Christ, or of apostles, a complete presumption is afforded us, by the solid, palpable, and ascertained reality (of the revived body), that its true form must be such as to compel one's belief of the fraudulence of every incorporeal apparition of dead persons.

CHAP. LVIII.—CONCLUSION. POINTS POSTPONED. ALL SOULS ARE KEPT IN HADES UNTIL THE RESURRECTION, ANTICIPATING THEIR ULTIMATE MISERY OR BLISS.

All souls, therefore, are shut up within Hades: do you admit this? (It is true, whether) you say yes or no: moreover, there are already experienced there punishments and consolations; and there you have a poor man and a rich. And now, having postponed some stray questions[12] for this part of my work, I will notice them in this suitable place, and then come to a close. Why, then, cannot you suppose that the soul undergoes punishment and consolation in Hades in the interval, while it awaits its alternative of judgment, in a certain anticipation either of gloom or of glory? You reply: Because in the judgment of God its matter ought to be sure and safe,

---

[1] Ex. vii. 12.
[2] Acts viii. 9, xiii. 8.
[3] See above in ch. xxviii. p. 209, *supra*.
[4] 1 Sam. xxviii. 6-16.
[5] 2 Cor. xi. 14.
[6] 2 Thess. ii. 4.
[7] Matt. xxiv. 24.
[8] Si forte.
[9] Non frustra.
[10] In iv. 172.

[11] Luke xvi. 26. [Compare note 15. p. 231, *supra*.
[12] Nescio quid.

nor should there be any inkling beforehand of the award of His sentence; and also because (the soul) ought to be covered first by its vestment[1] of the restored flesh, which, as the partner of its actions, should be also a sharer in its recompense. What, then, is to take place in that interval? Shall we sleep? But souls do not sleep even when men are alive : it is indeed the business of *bodies* to sleep, to which also belongs death itself, no less than its mirror and counterfeit sleep. Or will you have it, that nothing is there done whither the whole human race is attracted, and whither all man's expectation is postponed for safe keeping? Do you think this state is a foretaste of judgment, or its actual commencement? a premature encroachment on it, or the first course in its full ministration? Now really, would it not be the highest possible injustice, even[2] in Hades, if all were to be still well with the guilty even there, and not well with the righteous even yet? What, would you have hope be still more confused after death? would you have it mock us still more with uncertain expectation? or shall it now become a review of past life, and an arranging of judgment, with the inevitable feeling of a trembling fear? But, again, must the soul always tarry for the body, in order to experience sorrow or joy? Is it not sufficient, even of itself, to suffer both one and the other of these sensations? How often, without any pain to the body, is the soul alone tortured by ill-temper, and anger, and fatigue, and very often unconsciously, even to itself? How often, too, on the other hand, amidst bodily suffering, does the soul seek out for itself some furtive joy, and withdraw for the moment from the body's importunate society? I am mistaken if the soul is not in the habit, indeed, solitary and alone, of rejoicing and glorying over the very tortures of the body. Look for instance, at the soul of Mutius *Scævola* as he melts his right hand over the fire ; look also at Zeno's, as the torments of Dionysius pass over it.[3] The bites of wild beasts are a glory to young heroes, as on Cyrus were the scars of the bear.[4] Full well, then, does the soul even in Hades know how to joy and to sorrow even without the body; since when in the flesh it feels pain when it likes, though the body is unhurt; and when it likes it feels joy though the body is in pain. Now if such sensations occur at its will during life, how much rather may they not happen after death by the judicial appointment of God ! Moreover, the soul executes not all its operations with the ministration of the flesh; for the judgment of God pursues even simple cogitations and the merest volitions. "Whosoever looketh on a woman to lust after her, hath committed adultery with her already in his heart."[5] Therefore, even for this cause it is most fitting that the soul, without at all waiting for the flesh, should be punished for what it has done without the partnership of the flesh. So, on the same principle, in return for the pious and kindly thoughts in which it shared not the help of the flesh, shall it without the flesh receive its consolation. Nay more,[6] even in matters done through the flesh the soul is the first to conceive them, the first to arrange them, the first to authorize them, the first to precipitate them into acts. And even if it is sometimes unwilling to act, it is still the first to treat the object which it means to effect by help of the body. In no case, indeed, can an accomplished fact be prior to the mental conception[7] thereof. It is therefore quite in keeping with this order of things, that that part of our nature should be the first to have the recompense and reward to which they are due on account of its priority. In short, inasmuch as we understand "the prison" pointed out in the Gospel to be Hades,[8] and as we also interpret "the uttermost farthing"[9] to mean the very smallest offence which has to be recompensed there before the resurrection,[10] no one will hesitate to believe that the soul undergoes in Hades some compensatory discipline, without prejudice to the full process of the resurrection, when the recompense will be administered through the flesh besides. This point the Paraclete has also pressed home on our attention in most frequent admonitions, whenever any of us has admitted the force of His words from a knowledge of His promised spiritual disclosures.[11] And now at last having, as I believe, encountered every human opinion concerning the soul, and tried its character by the teaching of (our holy faith,) we have satisfied the curiosity which is simply a reasonable and necessary one. As for that which is extravagant and idle, there will evermore be as great a defect in its information, as there has been exaggeration and self-will in its researches.

---

[1] "Operienda" is Oehler's text ; another reading gives "opperienda," *q.d.* "the soul must *wait for* the restored body."
[2] This "etiam" is "otium" in the Agobardine MS., a good reading ; *q.d.* "a most iniquitous *indifference* to justice," etc.
[3] Comp. *The Apology*, last chapter.
[4] Xen. *Cyropæd.* p. 6.
[5] Matt. v. 28.
[6] Quid nunc si.
[7] Conscientia.
[8] Matt. v. 25.
[9] Ver. 26.
[10] Morâ resurrectionis. See above, on this opinion of Tertullian, in ch. xxxv.
[11] [A symptom of Montanism.]

TERTULLIAN.

PART SECOND.

INTRODUCTION, BY THE AMERICAN EDITOR.

THE Second Class of Tertullian's works, according to the logical method I have endeavoured to carry out, is that which includes his treatises against the heresies of his times. In these, the genius of our author is brilliantly illustrated, while, in melancholy fact, he is demonstrating the folly of his own final lapse and the wickedness of that schism and heresy into which he fell away from Truth. Were it not that history abounds in like examples of the frailty of the human intellect and of the insufficiency of "man that walketh to direct his steps," we should be forced to a theory of mental decay to account for inconsistencies so gross and for delusions so besotted. "Genius to madness is *indeed* allied," and who knows but something like that imbecility which closed the career of Swift [1] may have been the fate of this splendid wit and versatile man of parts? Charity, admiration and love force this inquiry upon my own mind continually, as I explore his fascinating pages. And the order in which the student will find them in this series, will lead, I think, to similar reflections on the part of many readers. We observe a natural bent and turn of mind, even in his Catholic writings, which indicate his perils. These are more and more apparent in his recent works, as his enthusiasm heats itself into a frenzy which at last becomes a rage. He breaks down by degrees, as in orthodoxy so also in force and in character. It is almost like the collapse of Solomon or of Bacon. And though our own times have produced no example of stars of equal magnitude, to become falling-stars, we have seen illustrations the most humiliating, of those calm words of Bishop Kaye: "Human nature often presents the curious phenomenon of an union of the most opposite qualities in the same mind; of vigour, acuteness and discrimination on some subjects, with imbecility, dulness and bigotry on others." Milton, himself another example of his own threnode, breaks forth in this splendid utterance of lyrical confession:

> "God of our fathers what is man?
>   Nor do I name of men the common rout,
>   That, wandering loose about,
> Grow up and perish as the summer fly,
> Heads without name, no more remembered,
> But such as thou hast solemnly elected,
> With gifts and graces eminently adorned,
> To some great work, thy glory
> And people's safety, *which in part they effect.*"

And here, I must venture a remark on the ambiguity of the expressions concerning our author's Montanism. In the treatise against Marcion, written late in his career, Tertullian identifies himself with the Church and strenuously defends its faith and its apostolic order. In only rare instances does his weakness for the "new prophecy" crop out, and then, it is only as one identifies himself with a school within the church. Precisely so Fenelon maintained his milder Montanism, without a thought of deserting the Latin Church. Afterwards Fenelon drew back, but at last poor Tertullian fell away. So with the Jansenists. They credited the *miracles* and the *convulsions* (or ecstasies) of their school,[2] and condemned those

---

[1] "From Marlboro's eyes the tears of dotage flow,
  And Swift expires a driveller and a show."

[2] See the story of the Abbé Paris, Guettée, *Histoire de l'Eglise de France*, Tom. xii. p. 12. Also, Parton, *Voltaire*, Vol. I. pp. 236, 261, etc.

who rejected them, as Tertullian condemns the *Psychics*. The great expounder of the Nicene
Faith (Bp. Bull) does indeed speak very decidedly of Tertullian as a *lapser*, even when he
wrote his first book against Marcion. His semi-schismatic position must be allowed. But,
was it a *formal* lapse at that time? The English non-jurors were long in communion with
the Church, even while they denounced their brethren and the "Erastianizing" clergy, much
as Tertullian does the *Psychics*. St. Augustine speaks of *Tertullianists*[1] with great moderation,
and notes the final downfall of our author as something distinct from Tertullianism. When we
reflect, therefore, that only four of all his varied writings (now extant) are proofs of an
accomplished lapse, ought we not carefully to maintain the distinction between the Montanistic Tertullian and Tertullian the Montanist? Bishop Bull, it seems to me would not object
to this way of putting it, when we consider his own discrimination in the following weighty
words. He says:

"A clear distinction must be made between those works which Tertullian, when already a
Montanist, wrote specifically in defence of Montanism *against the church*, and those which
he composed, as a Montanist indeed, yet *not in defence of Montanism against the church*, but
rather, *in defence of the common doctrines of the church*—and of Montanus, in opposition to
other heretics."

Now in arranging the works of this second class, *the Prescription* comes logically first,
because, written in Orthodoxy, it forcibly upholds the Scriptural Rule of Faith, the Catholic
touchstone of all professed verity. It is also a necessary Introduction to the great work
against Marcion which I have placed next in order; giving it the precedence to which it is
entitled in part on chronological ground, in part because of the general purity of its material
with the exhibition it presents of the author's mental processes and of his very gradual decline from Truth.

Very fortunate were the Edinburgh Editors in securing for this work and some others,
the valuable labours of Dr. Holmes, of whom I have elsewhere given some biographical particulars. The merit and fulness of his annotations are so marked, that I have been spared
a great deal of work, such as I was forced to bestow on the former volumes of this American
Edition. But on the other hand these pages have given me much patient study and toil as
an editor, because of the "shreds and patches" in which Tertullian comes to us, in the
Edinburgh Series; and because of some typographical peculiarities, exceptional in that Series
itself, and presenting complications, when transferred to a new form of mechanical arrangement. For example, apart from some valuable material which belongs to the General Preface,
and which I have transferred accordingly, the following dislocations confronted me to begin
with: The *Marcion* is presented to us in Volume VII. apart from the other writings of Tertullian. At the close of Vol. XI. we reach the *Ad Nationes*, of which Dr. Holmes is the
translator, another hand (Mr. Thelwall's) having been employed on former pages of that volume. It is not till we reach Volume XV. that Tertullian again appears, but this volume is
wholly the work of Dr. Holmes. Finally, in Volume XVIII., we meet Tertullian again,
(Mr. Thelwall the able translator), but, here is placed the "Introduction" to all the works of
Tertullian, which, of course, I have, transferred to its proper place. I make these explanations by no means censoriously, but to point out at once the nature of my own task, and
the advantage that accrues to the reader, by the order in which the works of the great Tertullian appear in this edition, enabling him to compare different or parallel passages, all
methodically arranged in consecutive pages, without a minute's search, or delay.

Now, as to typographical difficulties to which I have referred, Dr. Holmes marks all his
multiplied and useful notes with *brackets*, which are almost always superfluous, and which in

[1] See opp. Tom. viii. p. 46, Ed. Migne.

this American Edition are used to designate my own contributions, when printed with the text, or apart from Preface and Elucidations. These, therefore, I have removed necessarily and with no appreciable loss to the work, but great gain to the beauty of the page. But, again, Dr. Holmes' translations are all so heavily bracketed as to become an eyesore, and the disfigured pages have been often complained of as afflictive to the reader. Many words strictly implied by the original Latin, and which should therefore be ummarked, are yet put between brackets. Even minute words (*and,* or *to wit,* or *again,*) when, in the nature of the case the English idiom requires them, are thus marked. I have not retained these blemishes; but when an inconsiderable word or a repetition does add to the sense, or qualify it, I have italicized such words, throwing more important interpolations into parenthetical marks, which are less painful to the sight than brackets. I have found them quite as serviceable to denote the auxiliary word or phrase; and where the author himself uses a parenthesis, I have observed very few instances in which a sensible reader would confound it with the translator's efforts to eke out the sense. Sometimes, an awkward interpolation has been thrown into a footnote. Occasionally the crabbed sentences of the great Carthaginian are so obscure that Dr. Holmes has been unable to make them lucid, although, with the original in hand, he probably felt a force in his own rendering which the mere English reader must fail to perceive. In a few such instances, noting the fact in the margin, I have tried to bring out the sense, by slight modifications of punctuation and arrangement. Occasionally too I have dropped a superfluous interpolation (such *e.g.* as *to conclude,* or let me say again,) when I have found that it only served to clog and overcharge a sentence. Last of all, Dr. Holmes' *headings* have sometimes been condensed, to avoid phrases and sentences immediately recurring in the chapter.[1] These purely mechanical parts require a terse form of statement, like those in the English Bible, and I have frequently reduced them on that model, dropping redundant adverbs and adjectives to bring out the catchwords.

---

[1] Take e. g. the heading to chapter xxiv. of the *De Præscriptione.* It reads thus : "*St. Peter's further vindication. St. Paul was not at all superior to St. Peter in teaching Nothing was imparted to the former, in the* "*third heaven,*" *to enable him to add to the faith—however foolishly the heretics may boast of him as if they had, forsooth, been favoured with some of the secrets so imparted to him in paradise.*" If the reader will turn to the chapter referred to, he will observe an instance of condensation by which nothing is forfeited that is requisite to a *heading,* though redundancies are dropped.

16

THE PRESCRIPTION AGAINST HERETICS.[1]

[TRANSLATED BY THE REV. PETER HOLMES, D.D., F.R.A.S., ETC., ETC.]

CHAP. I.—INTRODUCTORY. HERESIES MUST EXIST, AND EVEN ABOUND; THEY ARE A PROBATION TO FAITH.

The character of the times in which we live is such as to call forth from us even this admonition, that we ought not to be astonished at the heresies (which abound)[2] neither ought their existence to surprise us, for it was foretold that they should come to pass;[3] nor the fact that they subvert the faith of some, for their final cause is, by affording a trial to faith, to give it also the opportunity of being "approved."[4] Groundless, therefore, and inconsiderate is the offence of the many[5] who are scandalized by the very fact that heresies prevail to such a degree. How great (might their offence have been) if they had not existed.[6] When it has been determined that a thing must by all means be, it receives the (final) cause for which it has its being. This secures the power through which it exists, in such a way that it is impossible for it not to have existence.

CHAP. II.—ANALOGY BETWEEN FEVERS AND HERESIES. HERESIES NOT TO BE WONDERED AT: THEIR STRENGTH DERIVED FROM WEAKNESS OF MEN'S FAITH. THEY HAVE NOT THE TRUTH. SIMILE OF PUGILISTS AND GLADIATORS IN ILLUSTRATION.

Taking the similar case[7] of fever, which is appointed a place amongst all other deadly and excruciating issues (of life) for destroying man: we are not surprised either that it exists, for there it is, or that it consumes man, for that is the purpose of its existence. In like manner, with respect to heresies, which are produced for the weakening and the extinction of faith, since we feel a dread because they have this power, we should first dread the fact of their existence; for as long as they exist, they have they have their power; and as long as they have their power, they have their existence. But still fever, as being an evil both in its cause[8] and in its power, as all know, we rather loathe than wonder at, and to the best of our power guard against, not having its extirpation in our power. Some men prefer wondering at heresies, however, which bring with them eternal death and the heat of a stronger fire, for possessing this power, instead of avoiding their power when they have the means of escape: but heresies would have no power, if (men) would cease to wonder that they have such power. For it either happens that, while men wonder, they fall into a snare, or, because they are ensnared, they cherish their surprise, as if heresies

---

[1] Of the various forms of the title of this treatise, *de Præscriptione Hæreticorum, de Præscriptionibus Hæreticorum, de Præscriptionibus adversus Hæreticos*, the first is adopted by Oehler after the oldest authorities, such as the Liber Agobardinus and the Codex Paterniacensis (or Seletstadiensis), and the Editio Princeps of Rhenanus. The term *præscriptio* is a legal one, meaning a *demurrer*, or formal objection. The genitive *hæreticorum* is used in an objective sense, as if *adversus hæreticos*. Tertullian himself, in *de Carne Christi*, ii. says, "Sed plenius ejusmodi præscriptionibus adversus omnes hæreses alibi jam usi sumus. The title therefore means, "On the Church's Prescriptive Rule against Heresies of all kinds." [Elucidation I.]
[2] Istas.
[3] Matt. vii. 15, xxiv. 4, 11, 24 ; 1 Tim. iv. 1–3 ; 2 Pet. ii. 1.
[4] 1 Cor. xi. 19.
[5] Plerique, "the majority."
[6] The Holy Ghost having foretold that they should exist. (Rigalt.)

[7] Denique has in Tertullian sometimes the meaning of *proinde*.
[8] Causam " purpose," " final cause."

were so powerful because of some truth which belonged to them. It would no doubt be a wonderful thing that evil should have any force of its own, were it not that heresies are strong in those persons who are not strong in faith. In a combat of boxers and gladiators, generally speaking, it is not because a man is strong that he gains the victory, or loses it because he is not strong, but because he who is vanquished was a man of no strength ; and indeed this very conqueror, when afterwards matched against a really powerful man, actually retires crest-fallen from the contest. In precisely the same way, heresies derive such strength as they have from the infirmities of individuals—having no strength whenever they encounter a really powerful faith.

CHAP. III.—WEAK PEOPLE FALL AN EASY PREY TO HERESY, WHICH DERIVES STRENGTH FROM THE GENERAL FRAILTY OF MANKIND. EMINENT MEN HAVE FALLEN FROM FAITH: SAUL, DAVID, SOLOMON. THE CONSTANCY OF CHRIST.

It is usual, indeed, with persons of a weaker character, to be so built up (in confidence) by certain individuals who are caught by heresy, as to topple over into ruin themselves. How comes it to pass, (they ask), that this woman or that man, who were the most faithful, the most prudent, and the most approved[1] in the church, have gone over to the other side ? Who that asks such a question does not in fact reply to it himself, to the effect that men whom heresies have been able to pervert[2] ought never to have been esteemed prudent, or faithful, or approved ? This again is, I suppose, an extraordinary thing, that one who has been approved should afterwards fall back ? Saul, who was good beyond all others, is afterwards subverted by envy.[3] David, a good man "after the Lord's own heart,"[4] is guilty afterwards of murder and adultery.[5] Solomon, endowed by the Lord with all grace and wisdom, is led into idolatry by women.[6] For to the Son of God alone was it reserved to persevere to the last without sin.[7] But what if a bishop, if a deacon, if a widow, if a virgin, if a doctor, if even a martyr,[8] have fallen from the rule (of faith), will heresies on that account appear to possess[9] the truth ?

Do we prove the faith[10] by the persons, or the persons by the faith ? No one is wise, no one is faithful, no one excels in dignity,[11] but the Christian ; and no one is a Christian but he who perseveres even to the end.[12] You, as a man, know any other man from the outside appearance. You think as you see. And you see as far only as you have eyes. But says (the Scripture), "the eyes of the Lord are lofty."[13] " Man looketh at the outward appearance, but God looketh at the heart."[14] " The Lord (beholdeth and) knoweth them that are His;"[15] and " the plant which (my heavenly Father) hath not planted, He rooteth up;"[16] and "the first shall," as He shows, "be last ;"[17] and He carries " His fan in His hand to purge His threshing-floor."[18] Let the chaff of a fickle faith fly off as much as it will at every blast of temptation, all the purer will be that heap of corn which shall be laid up in the garner of the Lord. Did not certain of the disciples turn back from the Lord Himself,[19] when they were offended ? Yet the rest did not therefore think that they must turn away from following Him,[20] but because they knew that He was the Word of Life, and was come from God,[21] they continued in His company to the very last, after He had gently inquired of them whether they also would go away.[22] It is a comparatively small thing,[23] that certain men, like Phygellus, and Hermogenes, and Philetus, and Hymenæus, deserted His apostle:[24] the betrayer of Christ was himself one of the apostles. We are surprised at seeing His churches forsaken by some men, although the things which we suffer after the example of Christ Himself, show us to be Christians. " They went out from us," says (St. John,) " but they were not of us. If they had been of us, they would no doubt have continued with us."[25]

CHAP. IV.—WARNINGS AGAINST HERESY GIVEN US IN THE NEW TESTAMENT. SUNDRY PASSAGES ADDUCED. THESE IMPLY THE POSSIBILITY OF FALLING INTO HERESY.

But let us rather be mindful of the sayings of the Lord, and of the letters of the apostles;

---

[1] Usitatissimi, " most experienced."
[2] Demutare.
[3] 1 Sam. xviii. 8, 9.
[4] 1 Sam. xiii. 14.
[5] 2 Sam. xi.
[6] 1 Kings xi. 4.
[7] Heb. iv. 15. [See p. 221, supra.]
[8] [Here the word martyr means no more than a witness or confessor, and may account for what are called exaggerated statements as to the number of primitive martyrs. See Kaye p. 128.]
[9] Obtinere.

[10] Fidem, " The Creed."
[11] Major.
[12] Matt. x. 22.
[13] Jer. xxxii. 19.
[14] 1 Sam. xvi. 7.
[15] 2 Tim. ii. 19.
[16] Matt. xv. 13.
[17] Matt. xx. 16.
[18] Matt. iii. 12.
[19] John vi. 66.
[20] A vestigiis ejus.
[21] John i. 1, vi. 68, and xvi. 30.
[22] John vi. 67.
[23] Minus.
[24] 2 Tim. i. 15, ii. 17 ; 1 Tim. i. 20.
[25] 1 John ii. 19. [i.e., with the Apostolic Churches. See Cap. XX. infra.]

for they have both told us beforehand that there shall be heresies, and have given us, in anticipation, warnings to avoid them; and inasmuch as we are not alarmed because they exist, so we ought not to wonder that they are capable of doing that, on account of which they must be shunned. The Lord teaches us that many "ravening wolves shall come in sheep's clothing."[1] Now, what are these sheep's clothings, but the external surface of the Christian profession? Who are the ravening wolves but those deceitful senses and spirits which are lurking within to waste the flock of Christ? Who are the false prophets but deceptive predictors of the future? Who are the false apostles but the preachers of a spurious gospel?[2] Who also are the Antichrists, both now and evermore, but the men who rebel against Christ?[3] Heresies, at the present time, will no less rend the church by their perversion of doctrine, than will Antichrist persecute her at that day by the cruelty of his attacks,[4] except that persecution makes even martyrs, (but) heresy only apostates. And therefore "heresies must needs be in order that they which are approved might be made manifest,[5] both those who remained stedfast under persecution, and those who did not wander out of their way[6] into heresy. For *the apostle* does not mean[7] that those persons should be deemed *approved* who exchange their creed for heresy; although they contrariously interpret his words to their own side, when he says in another passage, "Prove all things; hold fast that which is good;"[8] as if, after proving all things amiss, one might not through error make a determined choice of some evil thing.

CHAP. V.—HERESY, AS WELL AS SCHISM AND DISSENSION, DISAPPROVED BY ST. PAUL, WHO SPEAKS OF THE NECESSITY OF HERESIES, NOT AS A GOOD, BUT, BY THE WILL OF GOD, SALUTARY TRIALS FOR TRAINING AND APPROVING THE FAITH OF CHRISTIANS.

Moreover, when he blames dissensions and schisms, which undoubtedly are evils, he immediately adds *heresies* likewise. Now, that which he subjoins to evil things, he of course confesses to be itself an evil; and all the greater, indeed, because he tells us that his belief of their schisms and dissensions was grounded on his knowledge that "there must be heresies also."[9] For he shows us that it was owing to the prospect of the greater evil that he readily believed the existence of the lighter ones; and so far indeed was he from believing, in respect of evils (of such a kind), that heresies were good, that his object was to forewarn us that we ought not to be surprised at temptations of even a worse stamp, since (he said) they tended "to make manifest all such as were approved;"[10] in other words, those whom they were unable to pervert.[11] In short, since the whole passage[12] points to the maintenance of unity and the checking of divisions, inasmuch as heresies sever men from unity no less than schisms and dissensions, no doubt he classes heresies under the same head of censure as he does schisms also and dissensions. And by so doing, he makes those to be "not approved," who have fallen into heresies; more especially when with reproofs he exhorts[13] men to turn away from such, teaching them that they should "all speak and think the selfsame thing,"[14] the very object which heresies do not permit.

CHAP. VI.—HERETICS ARE SELF-CONDEMNED. HERESY IS SELF-WILL, WHILST FAITH IS SUBMISSION OF OUR WILL TO THE DIVINE AUTHORITY. THE HERESY OF APELLES.

On this point, however, we dwell no longer, since it is the same Paul who, in his Epistle to the Galatians, counts "heresies" among "the sins of the flesh,"[15] who also intimates to Titus, that "a man who is a heretic" must be "rejected after the first admonition," on the ground that "he that is such is perverted, and committeth sin, as a self-condemned man."[16] Indeed, in almost every epistle, when enjoining on us (the duty) of avoiding false doctrines, he sharply condemns[17] heresies. Of these the practical effects[18] are false doctrines, called in Greek *heresies*,[19] a word used in the sense of that *choice* which a man makes when he either teaches them (to others)[20] or takes up with them (for himself).[21] For this reason it is that he calls the heretic *self-condemned*,[22] because he has himself chosen that

---

[1] Matt. vii. 15.
[2] Adulteri evangelizatores, the spurious preachers of the gospel. [Galat. i. 8, 9, an example of Apostolic præscription.]
[3] Hoc *scil.* "tempore."
[4] Oehler's "persecutionem" ought of course to be "persecutionum."
[5] 1 Cor. xi. 19.
[6] Exorbitaverint.
[7] Juvat.
[8] 1 Thess. v. 21. [But Truth is to be demonstrated as a *theorem*, not treated as a *problem* of which we must seek the solution.]

[9] 1 Cor. xi. 19.
[10] 1 Cor. xi. 18.
[11] Depravare.
[12] Capitulum.
[13] Objurget.
[14] 1 Cor. i. 10.
[15] Gal. v. 20.
[16] Tit. iii. 10, 11.
[17] Taxat.
[18] Opera.
[19] Αἱρέσεις.
[20] Instituendas.
[21] Suscipiendas.
[22] [A remarkable word is subjoined by the Apostle (ἐξέστραπται) which signifies *turned inside out*, and so self-condemned, as exhibiting his inward contentiousness and pravity.]

for which he is condemned. We, however, are not permitted to cherish any object[1] after our own will, nor yet to make choice of that which another has introduced of his private fancy. In the Lord's apostles we possess our authority; for even they did not of themselves choose to introduce anything, but faithfully delivered to the nations (of mankind) the doctrine[2] which they had received from Christ. If, therefore, even "an angel from heaven should preach any other gospel" (than theirs), he would be called accursed[3] by us. The Holy Ghost had even then foreseen that there would be in a certain virgin (called) Philumene[4] an angel of deceit, "transformed into an angel of light,"[5] by whose miracles and illusions[6] Apelles was led (when) he introduced his new heresy.

CHAP. VII.—PAGAN PHILOSOPHY THE PARENT OF HERESIES. THE CONNECTION BETWEEN DEFLECTIONS FROM CHRISTIAN FAITH AND THE OLD SYSTEMS OF PAGAN PHILOSOPHY.

These are "the doctrines" of men and "of demons"[7] produced for itching ears of the spirit of this world's wisdom: this the Lord called "foolishness,"[8] and "chose the foolish things of the world" to confound even philosophy itself. For (philosophy) it is which is the material of the world's wisdom, the rash interpreter of the nature and the dispensation of God. Indeed[9] heresies are themselves instigated[10] by philosophy. From this source came the Æons, and I known not what infinite forms,[11] and the trinity of man[12] in the system of Valentinus, who was of Plato's school. From the same source came Marcion's better god, with all his tranquillity; he came of the Stoics. Then, again, the opinion that the soul dies is held by the Epicureans; while the denial of the restoration of the body is taken from the aggregate school of all the philosophers; also, when matter is made equal to God, then you have the teaching of Zeno; and when any doctrine is alleged touching a god of fire, then Heraclitus comes in. The same subject-matter is discussed over and over

again[13] by the heretics and the philosophers; the same arguments[14] are involved. Whence comes evil? Why is it permitted? What is the origin of man? and in what way does he come? Besides the question which Valentinus has very lately proposed—Whence comes God? Which he settles with the answer: From *enthymesis* and *ectroma*.[15] Unhappy Aristotle! who invented for these men dialectics, the art of building up and pulling down; an art so evasive in its propositions,[16] so far-fetched in its conjectures, so harsh, in its arguments, so productive of contentions—embarrassing[17] even to itself, retracting everything, and really treating of[18] nothing! Whence spring those "fables and endless genealogies,"[19] and "unprofitable questions,"[20] and "words which spread like a cancer?"[21] From all these, when the apostle would restrain us, he expressly names *philosophy* as that which he would have us be on our guard against. Writing to the Colossians, he says, "See that no one beguile you through philosophy and vain deceit, after the tradition of men, and contrary to the wisdom of the Holy Ghost."[22] He had been at Athens, and had in his interviews (with its philosophers) become acquainted with that human wisdom which pretends to know the truth, whilst it only corrupts it, and is itself divided into its own manifold heresies, by the variety of its mutually repugnant sects. What indeed has Athens to do with Jerusalem? What concord is there between the Academy and the Church? what between heretics and Christians? Our instruction comes from "the porch of Solomon,"[23] who had himself taught that "the Lord should be sought in simplicity of heart."[24] Away with[25] all attempts to produce a mottled Christianity of Stoic, Platonic, and dialectic composition! We want no curious disputation after possessing Christ Jesus, no inquisition after enjoying the gospel! With our faith, we desire no further belief. For this is our palmary faith, that there is nothing which we ought to believe besides.

---

[1] Nihil, any *doctrine.*
[2] Disciplinam, including both the principles and practice of the Christian religion.
[3] Anathema. See Gal. i. 8.
[4] Concerning Philumene, see below, chap. xxv.; Eusebius, *Hist. Eccl.* v. 13; Augustine, *de Hæres.* chap. xlii.; Jerome, *Epist. adv. Ctesiph.* (*Works,* ed. Ben.) iv. 477, and in his Commentary on Galatians, ii. See also Tertullian, *Against Marcion,* p. 139. Edinb. Edition.
[5] 2 Cor. xi. 14.
[6] Præstigiis.
[7] 1 Tim. iv. 1.
[8] 1 Cor. iii. 18 and 25.
[9] Denique.
[10] Subornantur.
[11] Formæ, "*Ideæ*" (Oehler).
[12] See Tertullian's treatises, *adversus Valentinum,* xxv., and *de Anima,* xxi.; also Epiphanius, *Hær.* xxxi. 23.

[13] Volutatur.
[14] Retractatus.
[15] "De enthymesi;" for this word Tertullian gives *animationem* (in his tract against Valentinus, ix.), which seems to mean, "the mind in operation." (See the same treatise, x. xi.) With regard to the other word, Jerome (on Amos. iii.) adduces Valentinus as calling Christ ἔκτρωμα, that is, *abortion.*
[16] Sententiis.
[17] Molestam.
[18] Tractaverit, in the sense of *conclusively settling.*
[19] 1 Tim. i. 4.
[20] Tit. iii. 9.
[21] 2 Tim. ii. 17.
[22] Col. ii. 8. The last clause, "præter providentiam Spiritus Sancti," is either Tertullian's reading, or his gloss of the *apostle's* οὐ κατὰ Χριστόν—"not after Christ."
[23] Because in the beginning of the church the apostles taught in Solomon's porch, Acts iii. 5.
[24] Wisdom of Solomon, i. 1.
[25] Viderint.

CHAP. VIII.—CHRIST'S WORD, SEEK, AND YE SHALL FIND, NO WARRANT FOR HERETICAL DEVIATIONS FROM THE FAITH. ALL CHRIST'S WORDS TO THE JEWS ARE FOR US, NOT INDEED AS SPECIFIC COMMANDS, BUT AS PRINCIPLES TO BE APPLIED.

I come now to the point which (is urged both by our own brethren and by the heretics). Our brethren adduce *it* as a pretext for entering on curious inquiries,[1] and the heretics insist on it for importing the scrupulosity (of their unbelief).[2] It is written, they say, "Seek, and ye shall find."[3] Let us remember at what time the Lord said this. I think it was at the very outset of His teaching, when there was still a doubt felt by all whether He were the Christ, and when even Peter had not yet declared Him to be the Son of God, and John (Baptist) had actually ceased to feel assurance about Him.[4] With good reason, therefore, was it then said, "Seek, and ye shall find," when inquiry was still be to made of Him who was not yet become known. Besides, this *was said* in respect of the Jews. For it is to them that the whole matter[5] of this reproof[6] pertains, seeing that they had (a revelation) where they might seek Christ. "They have," says He, "Moses and Elias,"[7] —in other words, the law and the prophets, which preach Christ; as also in another place He says plainly, "Search the Scriptures, in which ye expect (to find) salvation; for they testify of me;"[8] which will be the meaning of "Seek, and ye shall find." For it is clear that the next words also apply to the Jews: "Knock, and it shall be opened unto you."[9] The Jews had formerly been in covenant with[10] God; but being afterwards cast off on account of their sins, they began to be[11] without God. The Gentiles, on the contrary, had never been in covenant with God; they were only as "a drop from a bucket," and "as dust from the threshing-floor,"[12] and were ever outside the door. Now, how shall he who was always outside knock at the place where he never was? What door does he know of, when he has passed through none, either by entrance or ejection? Is it not rather he who is aware that he once lived within and was thrust out, that (probably) found the door and knocked thereat? In like manner, "Ask, and ye shall receive,"[13] is suitably said[14] to one who was aware from whom he ought to ask,—by whom also some promise had been given; that is to say, "the God of Abraham, of Isaac, and of Jacob." Now, the Gentiles knew nothing either of Him, or of any of His promises. Therefore it was to Israel that he spake when He said, "I am not sent but to the lost sheep of the house of Israel."[15] Not yet had He "cast to the dogs the children's bread;"[16] not yet did He charge them to "go into the way of the Gentiles."[17] It is only at the last that He instructs them to "go and teach all nations, and baptize them,"[18] when they were so soon to receive "the Holy Ghost, the Comforter, who should guide them into all the truth."[19] And this, too, makes towards the the same conclusion. If the apostles, who were ordained[20] to be teachers to the Gentiles, were themselves to have the Comforter for their teacher, far more needless[21] was it to say to us, "Seek, and ye shall find," to whom was to come, without research,[22] our instruction[23] by the apostles, and to the apostles themselves by the Holy Ghost. All the Lord's sayings, indeed, are set forth for all men; through the ears of the Jews have they passed on to us. Still most of them were addressed to *Jewish* persons;[24] they therefore did not constitute instruction properly designed[25] for ourselves, but *rather* an example.[26]

CHAP. IX.—THE RESEARCH AFTER DEFINITE TRUTH ENJOINED ON US. WHEN WE HAVE DISCOVERED THIS, WE SHOULD BE CONTENT.

I now purposely[27] relinquish this ground of argument. Let it be granted, that the words, "Seek, and ye shall find," were addressed to all men (equally). Yet even here one's aim is[28] carefully to determine[29] the sense of the words[30] consistently with[31] (that reason),[32] which is the guiding principle[33] in all interpretation. (Now) no divine saying is so unconnected[34]

---

[1] Curiositatem.
[2] Scrupulositatem, "hair-splitting."
[3] Matt. vii. 7.
[4] See our translation of the *Anti-Marcion*, iv. 18 (*infra*), and Tertullian's treatise, *de Bapt.* x.
[5] Sermo.
[6] Suggillationis.
[7] Luke xvi. 29.
[8] John v. 39.
[9] Matt. vii. 7.
[10] Penes.
[11] Or, "were for the first time."
[12] Isa. xl. 15.
[13] Matt. vii. 7.
[14] Competit.
[15] Matt. xv. 24.
[16] Ver. 26.
[17] Matt. x. 5.
[18] Matt. xxviii. 19.
[19] John xvi. 13.
[20] Destinati.
[21] Multo magis vacabat.
[22] Ultro.
[23] Doctrina.
[24] In personas, i.e. *Judæorum* (Oehler).
[25] Proprietatem admonitionis.
[26] "That is, not a specific command" primarily meant for us, but a principle "to be applied by us" (Dodgson).
[27] Sponte.
[28] Expetit.
[29] Certare.
[30] Sensus.
[31] Cum.
[32] See Oehler's note.
[33] Gubernaculo. See Irenæus, ii. 46, for a similar view (Rigalt.). Surely Dodgson's version, if intelligible in itself even, incorrectly represents Tertullian's sense.
[34] Dissoluta.

and diffuse, that its *words* only are to be insisted on, and their *connection* left undetermined. But at the outset I lay down (this position) that there is some one, and therefore definite, thing taught by Christ, which the Gentiles are by all means bound to believe, and for that purpose to " seek," in order that they may be able, when they have " found " it, to believe. However,[1] there can be no indefinite seeking for that which has been taught as one only definite thing. You must " seek " until you " find," and believe when you have found; nor have you anything further to do but to keep what you have believed, provided you believe this besides, that nothing else is to be believed, and therefore nothing else is to be sought, after you have found and believed what has been taught by Him who charges you to seek no other thing than that which He has taught.[2] When, indeed, any man doubts about this, proof will be forthcoming,[3] that we have in our possession[4] that which was taught by Christ. Meanwhile, such is my confidence in our proof, that I anticipate it, in the shape of an admonition to certain persons, not " to seek " anything beyond what they have believed—that this is what they ought to have sought, how to avoid[5] interpreting, " Seek, and ye shall find," without regard to the rule of reason.

CHAP. X.—ONE HAS SUCCEEDED IN FINDING
    DEFINITE TRUTH, WHEN HE BELIEVES. HERET-
    ICAL WITS ARE ALWAYS OFFERING MANY
    THINGS FOR VAIN DISCUSSION, BUT WE ARE
    NOT TO BE ALWAYS SEEKING.

Now the reason of this saying is comprised in three points: in the matter, in the time, in the limit.[6] In the matter, so that you must consider *what it is* you have to seek; in the time, *when* you have to seek; in the limit, *how long*. What you have " to seek," then, is that which Christ has taught,[7] (and you must go on seeking) of course for such time as you fail to find,[8]—until indeed you find[9] it. But you have succeeded in finding[10] when you have believed. For you would not have believed if you had not found; as neither would you have sought except with a view to find. Your object, therefore, in seeking *was* to find; and

your object in finding *was* to believe. All further delay for seeking and finding you have prevented[11] by believing. The very fruit of your seeking has determined for you this limit. This boundary[12] has He set for you Himself, who is unwilling that you should believe anything else than what He has taught, or, therefore, even seek for it. If, however, because so many other things have been taught by one and another, we are on that account bound to go on seeking, so long as we are able to find anything, we must (at that rate) be ever seeking, and never believe anything at all. For where shall be the end of seeking ? where the stop[13] in believing ? where the completion in finding ? (Shall it be) with Marcion ? But even Valentinus proposes (to us the) maxim, " Seek, and ye shall find." (Then shall it be) with Valentinus ? Well, but Apelles, too, will assail me with the same quotation; Hebion also, and Simon, and all in turn, have no other argument wherewithal to·entice me, and draw me over to their side. Thus I shall be nowhere, and still be encountering[14] (that challenge), " Seek, and ye shall find," precisely as if I had no resting-place;[15] as if (indeed) I had never found that which Christ has taught—that which ought[16] to be sought, that which must needs[17] be believed.

CHAP. XI.—AFTER WE HAVE BELIEVED, SEARCH
    SHOULD CEASE; OTHERWISE IT MUST END IN
    A DENIAL OF WHAT WE HAVE BELIEVED. NO
    OTHER OBJECT PROPOSED FOR OUR FAITH.

There is impunity in erring, if there is no delinquency; although indeed to err it is itself an act of delinquency.[18] With impunity, I repeat, does a man ramble,[19] when he (purposely) deserts nothing. But yet, if I have believed what I was bound to believe, and then afterwards think that there is something new to be sought after, I of course expect that there is something else to be found, although I should by no means entertain such

---

[1] Porro.
[2] [Not to be contented with Truth, once known, is a sin preceding that against the Holy Spirit, and this state of mind explains the judicial blindness inflicted on Lapsers, as asserted by St. Paul, 2 Thess. ii. 10, 13, where note—" they received not the *love* of the truth." They had it and were not content with it.]
[3] Constabit.
  Penes nos.
[5] Ne.
[6] In modo.
[7] This is, " *the matter*."
[8] " The time."
[9] " The limit."
[10] Invenisti.

[11] Fixisti, " determined."
[12] Fossam.
[13] Statio, " resting-place."
[14] Dum convenero.
[15] This is the rendering of Oehler's text, " et velut si nusquam. There are other readings of this obscure passage, of which we add the two most intelligible. The *Codex Agobardinus* has, " et velim si nunquam ;" that is, " and I would that I were nowhere," with no fixed belief—in such wise as never to have had the truth ; not, as must now be, to have forfeited it. (Dodgson). This seems far-fetched, and inferior to the reading of Pamelius and his MSS.: " et velint me sic esse nusquam "—or (as Semler puts it) " velint sic nusquam ;" i.e., " and they (the heretics) would wish me to be nowhere "—without the fixed faith of the Catholic. This makes good sense. [Semler is here mentioned, and if anybody wishes to understand what sort of editor he was, he may be greatly amused by Kaye's examination of some of his positions, pp. 64–84. Elucidation II.]
[16] Oportet.
[17] Necesse est. Observe these degrees of obligation.
[18] Quamvis et errare delinquere est.
[19] Vagatur.

expectation, unless it were because I either had not believed, although I apparently had become a believer, or else have ceased to believe. If I thus desert my faith, I am found to be a denier thereof. Once for all I would say, No man seeks, except him who either never possessed, or else has lost (what he sought). The old woman (in the Gospel)[1] had lost one of her ten pieces of silver, and therefore she sought it;[2] when, however, she found it, she ceased to look for it. The neighbour was without bread, and therefore he knocked; but as soon as the door was opened to him, and he received the bread, he discontinued knocking.[3] The widow kept asking to be heard by the judge, because she was not admitted; but when her suit was heard, thenceforth she was silent.[4] So that there is a limit both to seeking, and to knocking, and to asking. "For to every one that asketh," says He, "it shall be given, and to him that knocketh it shall be opened, and by him that seeketh it shall be found."[5] Away with the man[6] who is ever seeking because he never finds; for he seeks there where nothing can be found. Away with him who is always knocking because it will never be opened to him; for he knocks where there is none (to open). Away with him who is always asking because he will never be heard; for he asks of one who does not hear.

CHAP. XII.—A PROPER SEEKING AFTER DIVINE KNOWLEDGE, WHICH WILL NEVER BE OUT OF PLACE OR EXCESSIVE, IS ALWAYS WITHIN THE RULE OF FAITH.

As for us, although we must still seek, and *that* always, yet where ought our search to be made? Amongst the heretics, where all things are foreign[7] and opposed to our own verity, and to whom we are forbidden to draw near? What slave looks for food from a stranger, not to say an enemy of his master? What soldier expects to get bounty and pay from kings who are unallied, I might almost say hostile—unless forsooth he be a deserter, and a runaway, and a rebel? Even that old woman[8] searched for the piece of silver within her own house. It was also at his neighbour's door that the persevering assailant kept knocking. Nor was it to a hostile judge, although a severe one, that the widow made her appeal. No man gets instruction[9] from that which

tends to destruction.[10] No man receives illumination from a quarter where all is darkness. Let our "seeking," therefore be in that which is our own, and from those who are our own, and concerning that which is our own,—that, and only that,[11] which can become an object of inquiry without impairing the rule of faith.

CHAP. XIII.—SUMMARY OF THE CREED, OR RULE OF FAITH. NO QUESTIONS EVER RAISED ABOUT IT BY BELIEVERS. HERETICS ENCOURAGE AND PERPETUATE THOUGHT INDEPENDENT OF CHRIST'S TEACHING.

Now, with regard to this rule of faith—that we may from this point[12] acknowledge what it is which we defend—it is, you must know, that which prescribes the belief that there is one only God, and that He is none other than the Creator of the world, who produced all things out of nothing through His own Word, first of all sent forth;[13] that this Word is called His Son, *and*, under the name of God, was seen "in diverse manners" by the patriarchs, heard at all times in the prophets, at last brought down by the Spirit and Power of the Father into the Virgin Mary, was made flesh in her womb, and, being born of her, went forth as Jesus Christ; thenceforth He preached the new law and the new promise of the kingdom of heaven, worked miracles; having been crucified, He rose again the third day; (then) having ascended[14] into the heavens, He sat at the right hand of the Father; sent instead of Himself[15] the Power of the Holy Ghost to lead such as believe; will come with glory to take the saints to the enjoyment of everlasting life and of the heavenly promises, and to condemn the wicked to everlasting fire, after the resurrection of both these classes shall have happened, together with the restoration of their flesh. This rule, as it will be proved, was taught by Christ, and raises amongst ourselves no other questions than those which heresies introduce, and which make men heretics.[16]

CHAP. XIV.—CURIOSITY OUGHT NOT RANGE BEYOND THE RULE OF FAITH. RESTLESS CURIOSITY, THE FEATURE OF HERESY.

So long, however, as its form exists in its proper order, you may seek and discuss as

---

[1] Anus illa.
[2] Luke xv. 8.
[3] Luke xi. 5.
[4] Luke xviii. 2, 3.
[5] Luke xi. 9.
[6] Viderit.
[7] Extranea.
[8] Although Tertullian calls her "anus," St. Luke's word is γυνή, not γραῦς.
[9] Instrui potest.

[10] Unde destruitur.
[11] Idque dumtaxat.
[12] Jam hinc.
[13] Primo omnium demissum. Literally, "sent down." See on this *procession of the Son of God* to create the world, Bishop Bull's *Defence of the Nicene Creed, etc.*, by the translator of this work, pp. 445 and following.
[14] Ereptum, having been taken away.
[15] Vicariam. [Scott's *Christian Life*, Vol. III. p. 64.]
[16] [See Bunsen (Hippol. III. Notes, etc., p. 129.) for a castigated form of the Latin Creed, as used in Rome. Observe it lacks the word *Catholic*. But a much better study of these formulas may be found in Dupin's comparative Table. First Cent. pp. 9–12.]

much as you please, and give full rein to [1] your curiosity, in whatever seems to you to hang in doubt, or to be shrouded in obscurity. You have at hand, no doubt, some learned [2] brother gifted with the grace of knowledge, some one of the experienced class, some one of your close acquaintance who is curious like yourself; although with yourself, a seeker, he will, after all,[3] be quite aware [4] that it is better for you to remain in ignorance, lest you should come to know what you ought not, because you have acquired the knowledge of what you ought to know.[5] "Thy faith," He says, "hath saved thee"[6] not *observe* your skill [7] in the Scriptures. Now, faith has been deposited in the rule; it has a law, and (in the observance thereof) salvation. Skill,[7] however, consists in curious art, having for its glory simply the readiness that comes from knack.[8] Let such curious art give place to faith; let such glory yield to salvation. At any rate, let them either relinquish their noisiness,[9] or else be quiet. To know nothing in opposition to the rule (of faith), is to know all things. (Suppose) that heretics were not enemies to the truth, so that we were not forewarned to avoid them, what sort of conduct would it be to agree with men who do themselves confess that they are still seeking? For if they are still seeking, they have not as yet found anything amounting to certainty; and therefore, whatever they seem for a while [10] to hold, they betray their own scepticism,[11] whilst they continue seeking. You therefore, who seek after their fashion, looking to those who are themselves ever seeking, a doubter to doubters, a waverer to waverers, must needs be "led, blindly by the blind, down into the ditch."[12] But when, for the sake of deceiving us, they pretend that they are still seeking, in order that they may palm [13] their essays [14] upon us by the suggestion of an anxious sympathy,[15]—when, in short (after gaining an access to us), they proceed at once to insist on the necessity of our inquiring into such points as they were in the habit of advancing, then it is high time for us in moral obligation [16] to repel [17] them, so that they may know that it is not Christ, but themselves, whom we disavow. For since they are still seekers, they have no fixed tenets yet; [18] and being not fixed in tenet, they have not yet believed; and being not yet believers, they are not Christians. But even though they have their tenets and their belief, they still say that inquiry is necessary in order to discussion.[19] Previous, however, to the discussion, they deny what they confess not yet to have believed, so long as they keep it an object of inquiry. When men, therefore, are not Christians even on their own admission,[20] how much more (do they fail to appear such) to us! What sort of truth is that which they patronize,[21] when they commend it to us with a lie? Well, but they actually [22] treat of the Scriptures and recommend (their opinions) out of the Scriptures! To be sure they do.[23] From what other source could they derive arguments concerning the things of the faith, except from the records of the faith?

CHAP. XV.—HERETICS NOT TO BE ALLOWED TO ARGUE OUT OF THE SCRIPTURES. THE SCRIPTURES, IN FACT, DO NOT BELONG TO THEM.[24]

We are therefore come to (the gist of) our position; for at this point we were aiming, and for this we were preparing in the preamble of our address (which we have just completed),—so that we may now join issue on the contention to which our adversaries challenge us. They put forward [25] the Scriptures, and by this insolence [26] of theirs they at once influence some. In the encounter itself, however, they weary the strong, they catch the weak, and dismiss waverers with a doubt. Accordingly, we oppose to them this step above all others, of not admitting them to any discussion of the Scriptures.[27]

If in these lie their resources, before they can use them, it ought to be clearly seen to whom belongs the possession of the Scriptures, that none may be admitted to the use thereof who has no title at all to the privilege.

---

[1] Omnem libidinem effundas, " pour out the whole desire for."
[2] Doctor, literally, " teacher." See Eph. iv. 11 ; also above ; chap. iii. p. 244.
[3] This seems to be the more probable meaning of *novissime* in this rather obscure sentence. Oehler treats it adverbially as " postremo," and refers to a similar use of the word below in chap. xxx. Dr. Routh (and, after him, the translator in *The Library of the Fathers*, Tertullian, p. 448) makes the word a noun, " thou newest of novices," and refers to Tertullian's work, *against Praxeas*, chap. xxvii., for a like use. This seems to us too harsh for the present context.
[4] Sciet.
[5] See 1 Cor. xii. 8.
[6] Luke xviii. 42.
[7] Exercitatio.
[8] De peritiæ studio.
[9] Non obstrepant.
[10] Interim.
[11] Dubitationem.
[12] Matt. xv. 14.
[13] Insinuent.
[14] Tractatus.
[15] Or, " by instilling an anxiety into us " (Dodgson).

[16] Jam debemus.
[17] Refutare.
[18] Nondum tenent.
[19] Ut defendant.
[20] Nec sibi sunt.
[21] Patrocinantur.
[22] Ipsi.
[23] Scilicet.
[24] [See *Marcion*, B. I. Cap. xxii. *infra*, note.]
[25] Obtendunt.
[26] Audacia.
[27] De Scripturis. But as this preposition is often the sign of the *instrument* in Tertullian, this phrase may mean "*out of*," or " *by means of* the Scriptures." See the last chapter.

CHAP. XVI.—APOSTOLIC SANCTION TO THIS EXCLUSION OF HERETICS FROM THE USE OF THE SCRIPTURES. HERETICS, ACCORDING TO THE APOSTLE, ARE NOT TO BE DISPUTED WITH, BUT TO BE ADMONISHED.

I might be thought to have laid down this position to remedy distrust in my case,[1] or from a desire of entering on the contest[2] in some other way, were there not reasons on my side, especially this, that our faith owes deference[3] to the apostle, who forbids us to enter on "questions," or to lend our ears to new-fangled statements,[4] or to consort with a heretic "after the first and second admonition,"[5] not, (be it observed,) after discussion. Discussion he has inhibited in this way, by designating *admonition* as the purpose of dealing with a heretic, and the *first* one too, because he is not a Christian; in order that he might not, after the manner of a Christian, seem to require correction again and again, and "before two or three witnesses,"[6] seeing that he ought to be corrected, for the very reason that he is not to be disputed with; and in the next place, because a controversy over the Scriptures can, clearly,[7] produce no other effect than help to upset either the stomach or the brain.

CHAP. XVII.—HERETICS, IN FACT, DO NOT USE, BUT ONLY ABUSE, SCRIPTURE. NO COMMON GROUND BETWEEN THEM AND YOU.

Now this heresy of yours[8] does not receive certain Scriptures; and whichever of them it does receive, it perverts by means of additions and diminutions, for the accomplishment of it own purpose; and such as it does receive, it receives not in their entirety; but even when it does receive any up to a certain point[9] as entire, it nevertheless perverts even these by the contrivance of diverse interpretations. Truth is just as much opposed by an adulteration of its meaning as it is by a corruption of its text.[10] Their vain presumptions must needs refuse to acknowledge the (writings) whereby they are refuted. They rely on those which they have falsely put together, and which they have selected, because of[11] their ambiguity. Though most skilled[12] in the Scriptures, you will make no progress,[13] when everything which you maintain is denied

on the other side, and whatever you deny is (by them) maintained. As for yourself, indeed, you will lose nothing but your breath, and gain nothing but vexation from their blasphemy.

CHAP. XVIII.—GREAT EVIL ENSUES TO THE WEAK IN FAITH, FROM ANY DISCUSSION OUT OF THE SCRIPTURES. CONVICTION NEVER COMES TO THE HERETIC FROM SUCH A PROCESS.

But with respect to the man for whose sake you enter on the discussion of the Scriptures,[14] with the view of strengthening him when afflicted with doubts, (let me ask) will it be to the truth, or rather to heretical opinions that he will lean? Influenced by the very fact that he sees you have made no progress, whilst the other side is on an equal footing[15] (with yourself) in denying and in defence, or at any rate on a like standing[16] he will go away confirmed in his uncertainty[17] by the discussion, not knowing which side to adjudge heretical. For, no doubt, they too are able[18] to retort these things on us. It is indeed a necessary consequence that they should go so far as to say that adulterations of the Scriptures, and false expositions thereof, are rather introduced by ourselves, inasmuch as they, no less than we[19] maintain that truth is on their side.

CHAP. XIX. APPEAL, IN DISCUSSION OF HERESY, LIES NOT TO THE SCRIPTURES. THE SCRIPTURES BELONG ONLY TO THOSE WHO HAVE THE RULE OF FAITH

Our appeal, therefore, must not be made to the Scriptures; nor must controversy be admitted on points in which victory will either be impossible,[20] or uncertain, or not certain enough.[21] But even if a discussion from the Scriptures[22] should not turn out in such a way as to place both sides on a par, (yet) the natural order of things would require that this point should be first proposed, which is now the only one which we must discuss: "With whom lies that very faith to which the Scriptures belong.[23] From what and through whom, and when, and to whom, has been handed down that rule,[24] by which men become Christians?" For wherever it shall be manifest that the true Christian rule and faith shall be,

---

[1] De consilio diffidentiæ.
[2] Constitutionis, "prima causarum conflictio,"—a term of the law courts.
[3] Obsequium.
[4] 1 Tim. vi. 3, 4.
[5] Tit. iii. 10.
[6] Matt. xviii. 16.
[7] Plane, ironical.
[8] Ista hæresis.
[9] Aliquatenus.
[10] Stilus.
[11] "De" has often the sense of "propter" in our author.
[12] Literally, "O most skilled.
[13] Quid promovebis.

[14] Or, "from the Scriptures."
[15] Æquo gradu.
[16] Statu certe pari.
[17] Incertior.
[18] Habent.
[19] Proinde.
[20] Nulla.
[21] Parum certa.
[22] Conlatio scripturarum, or, "a polemical comparison of the Scriptures."
[23] Quibus competat fides ipsa cujus sint Scripturæ.
[24] Disciplina [or, where was the guide-post set?]

there will likewise be the true Scriptures and expositions thereof, and all the Christian traditions.

CHAP. XX.—CHRIST FIRST DELIVERED THE FAITH. THE APOSTLES SPREAD IT ; THEY FOUNDED CHURCHES AS THE DEPOSITORIES THEREOF. THAT FAITH, THEREFORE, IS APOSTOLIC, WHICH DESCENDED FROM THE APOSTLES, THROUGH APOSTOLIC CHURCHES.

Christ Jesus our Lord (may He bear with me a moment in thus expressing myself!), whosoever He is, of what God soever He is the Son, of what substance soever He is man and God, of what faith soever He is the teacher, of what reward soever He is the Promiser, did, whilst He lived on earth, Himself declare what He was, what He had been, what the Father's will was which He was administering, what the duty of man was which He was prescribing; (and this declaration He made,) either openly to the people, or privately to His disciples, of whom He had chosen the twelve chief ones to be at His side,[1] and whom He destined to be the teachers of the nations. Accordingly, after one of these had been struck off, He commanded the eleven others, on His departure to the Father, to "go and teach *all* nations, who were to be baptized into the Father, and into the Son, and into the Holy Ghost."[2] Immediately, therefore, so did the apostles, whom this designation indicates as "*the sent.*" Having, on the authority of a prophecy, which occurs in a psalm of David,[3] chosen Matthias by lot as the twelfth, into the place of Judas, they obtained the promised power of the Holy Ghost for the gift of miracles and of utterance; and after first bearing witness to the faith in Jesus Christ throughout Judæa, and founding churches (there), they next went forth into the world and preached the same doctrine of the same faith to the nations. They then in like manner founded churches in every city, from which all the other churches, one after another, derived the tradition of the faith,[4] and the seeds of doctrine, and are every day deriving them,[5] that they may become churches. Indeed, it is on this account only that they will be able to deem themselves apostolic, as being the offspring of apostolic churches. Every sort of thing[6] must necessarily revert to its original for its classification.[7] Therefore the churches, although they are so many and so great, comprise but the one primitive church, (founded) by the apostles, from which they all (spring). In this way all are primitive, and all are apostolic, whilst they are all proved to be one, in (unbroken) unity, by their peaceful communion,[8] and title of brotherhood, and bond[9] of hospitality,—privileges[10] which no other rule directs than the one tradition of the selfsame mystery.[11]

CHAP. XXI.—ALL DOCTRINE TRUE WHICH COMES THROUGH THE CHURCH FROM THE APOSTLES, WHO WERE TAUGHT BY GOD THROUGH CHRIST. ALL OPINION WHICH HAS NO SUCH DIVINE ORIGIN AND APOSTOLIC TRADITION TO SHOW, IS IPSO FACTO FALSE.

From this, therefore, do we draw up our rule. Since the Lord Jesus Christ sent the apostles to preach, (our rule is) that no others ought to be received as preachers than those whom Christ appointed; for "no man knoweth the Father save the Son, and he to whomsoever the Son will reveal Him."[12] Nor does the Son seem to have revealed Him to any other than the apostles, whom He sent forth to preach—that, of course, which He revealed to them. Now, what that was which they preached—in other words, what it was which Christ revealed to them—can, as I must here likewise prescribe, properly be proved in no other way than by those very churches which the apostles founded in person, by declaring the gospel to them directly themselves, both *vivâ voce*, as the phrase is, and subsequently by their epistles. If, then, these things are so, it is in the same degree[13] manifest that all doctrine which agrees with the apostolic churches—those moulds[14] and original sources of the faith must be reckoned for truth, as undoubtedly containing that which the (said) churches received from the apostles, the apostles from Christ, Christ from God. Whereas all doctrine must be prejudged[15] as false[16] which savours of contrariety to the truth of the churches and apostles of Christ and God. It remains, then, that we demonstrate whether this doctrine of ours, of which we have now given the rule, has its origin[17] in the tradition of the apostles, and whether all other *doctrines* do not *ipso facto*[18] proceed from falsehood. We hold communion with the apostolic churches because our doctrine is in no respect

---

[1] Mark iv. 34.
[2] Matt. xxviii. 19.
[3] Ps. cix. 8 ; comp. with Acts i. 15-20.
[4] Traducem fidei.
[5] Mutuantur, " borrowing."
[6] Omne genus.
[7] Censeatur or, " for its origin."

[8] Communicatio pacis.
[9] Contesseratio. [III. John 8.]
[10] Jura, " rights."
[11] That is, of the faith, or Christian creed.
[12] Matt. xi. 27.
[13] Perinde.
[14] Matricibus.
[15] Præjudicandam. [This then is *Præscription*.]
[16] De mendacio.
[17] Censeatur.
[18] Ex hoc ipso, " from this very circumstance."

different *from theirs*. This is *our* witness of truth.

CHAP. XXII.—ATTEMPT TO INVALIDATE THIS RULE OF FAITH REBUTTED. THE APOSTLES SAFE TRANSMITTERS OF THE TRUTH. SUFFICIENTLY TAUGHT AT FIRST, AND FAITHFUL IN THE TRANSMISSION.

But inasmuch as the proof is so near at hand,[1] that if it were at once produced there would be nothing left to be dealt with, let us give way for a while to the opposite side, if they think that they can find some means of invalidating this rule, just as if no proof were forthcoming from us. They usually tell us that the apostles did not know all things: (but herein) they are impelled by the same madness, whereby they turn round to the very opposite point,[2] and declare that the apostles certainly knew all things, but did not deliver all things to all persons,—in either case exposing Christ to blame for having sent forth apostles who had either too much ignorance, or too little simplicity. What man, then, of sound mind can possibly suppose that they were ignorant of anything, whom the Lord ordained to be masters (or teachers),[3] keeping them, as He did, inseparable (from Himself) in their attendance, in their discipleship, in their society, to whom, "when they were alone, He used to expound" all things[4] which were obscure, telling them that "to them it was given to know those mysteries,"[5] which it was not permitted the people to understand? Was anything withheld from the knowledge of Peter, who is called "the rock on which the church should be built,"[6] who also obtained "the keys of the kingdom of heaven,"[7] with the power of "loosing and binding in heaven and on earth?"[8] Was anything, again, concealed from John, the Lord's most beloved disciple, who used to lean on His breast[9] to whom alone the Lord pointed Judas out as the traitor,[10] whom He commended to Mary as a son in His own stead?[11] Of what could He have meant those to be ignorant, to whom He even exhibited His own glory with Moses and Elias, and the Father's voice moreover, from heaven?[12] Not as if He thus disapproved[13] of all the rest, but because "by three witnesses

must every word be established."[14] After the same fashion,[15] too, (I suppose) were they ignorant to whom, after His resurrection also, He vouchsafed, as they were journeying together, "to expound all the Scriptures."[16] No doubt[17] He had once said, "I have yet many things to say unto you, but ye cannot hear them now;" but even then He added, "When He, the Spirit of truth, shall come, He will lead you into all truth."[18] He (thus) shows that there was nothing of which they were ignorant, to whom He had promised the future attainment of all truth by help of the Spirit of truth. And assuredly He fulfilled His promise, since it is proved in the Acts of the Apostles that the Holy Ghost did come down. Now they who reject that Scripture[19] can neither belong to the Holy Spirit, seeing that they cannot acknowledge that the Holy Ghost has been sent as yet to the disciples, nor can they presume to claim to be a church themselves[20] who positively have no means of proving when, and with what swaddling-clothes[21] this body was established. Of so much importance is it to them not to have any proofs for the things which they maintain, lest along with them there be introduced damaging exposures[22] of those things which they mendaciously devise.

CHAP. XXIII.—THE APOSTLES NOT IGNORANT. THE HERETICAL PRETENCE OF ST. PETER'S IMPERFECTION BECAUSE HE WAS REBUKED BY ST. PAUL. ST. PETER NOT REBUKED FOR ERROR IN TEACHING.

Now, with the view of branding[23] the apostles with some mark of ignorance, they put forth the case of Peter and them that were with him having been rebuked by Paul. "Something therefore," they say, "was wanting in them." (This they allege,) in order that they may from this construct that other position of theirs, that a fuller knowledge may possibly have afterwards come over (the apostles,) such as fell to the share of Paul when he rebuked those who preceded him. I may here say to those who reject *The Acts of the Apostles:* "It is first necessary that you shows us who this Paul was,—both what he was before he was an apostle, and how he became an apostle,"—so very great is the use which they make of him in respect of other

1 Expedita.
2 Susum rursus convertun
3 Magistros.
4 Mark iv. 34.
5 Matt. xiii. 11.
6 Matt. xvi. 18. [See Kaye p. 222, also Elucidation II.]
7 Ver. 19.
8 Ver. 19
9 John xxi. 20.
10 John xiii. 25. [N.B. loco suo.]
11 John xix. 26.
12 Matt. xvii. 1–8.
13 Reprobans.
14 Deut. xix. 15, and 2 Cor. xiii. 1.
15 Itaque, ironical.
16 Luke xxiv. 27.
17 Plane.
18 John xvi. 12, 13.
19 See Tertullian's *Anti-Marcion*, iv. 5, and v. 2 (*Trans.* pp. 187 and 377.
20 Nec ecclesiam se dicant defendere.
21 Incunabulis, infant nursing.
22 Traductiones.
23 Suggillandam.

questions also. It is true that he tells us himself that he was a persecutor before he became an apostle,[1] still this is not enough for any man who examines before he believes, since even the Lord Himself did not bear witness of Himself.[2] But let them believe without the Scriptures, if their object is to believe contrary to the Scriptures.[3] Still they should show, from the circumstance which they allege of Peter's being rebuked by Paul, that Paul added yet another form of the gospel besides that which Peter and the rest had previously set forth. But the fact is,[4] having been converted from a persecutor to a preacher, he is introduced as one of the brethren to brethren, by brethren—to them, indeed, by men who had put on faith from the apostles' hands. Afterwards, as he himself narrates, he "went up to Jerusalem for the purpose of seeing Peter,"[5] because of his office, no doubt,[6] and by right of a common belief and preaching. Now they certainly would not have been surprised at his having become a preacher instead of a persecutor, if his preaching were of something contrary; nor, moreover, would they have "glorified the Lord,"[7] because Paul had presented himself as an adversary to Him. They accordingly even gave him "the right hand of fellowship,"[8] as a sign of their agreement with him, and arranged amongst themselves a distribution of office, not a diversity of gospel, so that they should severally preach not a different gospel, but (the same), to different persons,[9] Peter to the circumcision, Paul to the Gentiles. Forasmuch, then, as Peter was rebuked because, after he had lived with the Gentiles, he proceeded to separate himself from their company out of respect for persons, the fault surely was one of conversation, not of preaching.[10] For it does not appear from this, that any other God than the Creator, or any other Christ than (the son) of Mary, or any other hope than the resurrection, was (by him) announced.

CHAP. XXIV.—ST. PETER'S FURTHER VINDICATION. ST. PAUL NOT SUPERIOR TO ST. PETER IN TEACHING. NOTHING IMPARTED TO THE FORMER IN THE THIRD HEAVEN ENABLED HIM TO ADD TO THE FAITH. HERETICS BOAST AS IF FAVOURED WITH SOME OF THE SECRETS IMPARTED TO HIM.

I have not the good fortune,[11] or, as I must rather say,[12] I have not the unenviable task,[13] of setting apostles by the ears.[14] But, inasmuch as our very perverse cavillers obtrude the rebuke in question for the set purpose of bringing the earlier[15] doctrine into suspicion, I will put in a defence, as it were, for Peter, to the effect that even Paul said that he was "made all things to all men—to the Jews a Jew," to those who were not Jews as one who was not a Jew—"that he might gain all."[16] Therefore it was according to times and persons and causes that they used to censure certain practices, which they would not hesitate themselves to pursue, in like conformity to times and persons and causes. Just (e.g.) as if Peter too had censured Paul, because, whilst forbidding circumcision, he actually circumcised Timothy himself. Never mind[17] those who pass sentence on apostles! It is a happy fact that Peter is on the same level with Paul in the very glory[18] of martyrdom. Now, although Paul was carried away even to the third heaven, and was caught up to paradise,[19] and heard certain revelations there, yet these cannot possibly seem to have qualified him for (teaching) another doctrine, seeing that their very nature was such as to render them communicable to no human being.[20] If, however, that unspeakable mystery[21] did leak out,[22] and become known to any man, and if any heresy affirms that it does itself follow the same, (then) either Paul must be charged with having betrayed the secret, or some other man must actually[23] be shown to have been afterwards "caught up into paradise," who had permission to speak out plainly what Paul was not allowed (even) to mutter.

CHAP. XXV.—THE APOSTLES DID NOT KEEP BACK ANY OF THE DEPOSIT OF DOCTRINE WHICH CHRIST HAD ENTRUSTED TO THEM. ST. PAUL OPENLY COMMITTED HIS WHOLE DOCTRINE TO TIMOTHY.

But here is, as we have said,[24] the same madness, in their allowing indeed that the apostles were ignorant of nothing, and preached not any (doctrines) which contradicted one another, but at the same time insisting that they did not reveal all to all men, for that they proclaimed some openly and to

---

[1] Gal. i. 13.
[2] John v. 31.
[3] Ut credunt contra Scripturas.
[4] Atquin.
[5] Gal. i. 18.
[6] Scilicet.
[7] Gal. i. 24.
[8] Gal. ii. 9.
[9] The same verse. [Note Peter's restriction to Jews.]
[10] Vers. 12, 13. See also Anti-Marcion, iv. 3 (Trans. p. 182).
[11] Non mihi tam bene est.

[12] Immo.
[13] Non mihi tam male est.
[14] Ut committam.
[15] Superiorem, "that which Peter had preached."
[16] 1 Cor. ix. 20, 22.
[17] Viderint.
[18] Et in martyrio.
[19] 2 Cor. xii. 4.
[20] Nulli hominum.
[21] Nescio quid illud.
[22] Emanavit.
[23] Et.
[24] Above, in chap. xxii. [Note the Gnostic madness of such a plea. Kaye, p. 235 and Elucidation IV.]

all the world, whilst they disclosed others (only) in secret and to a few, because Paul addressed even this expression to Timothy: "O Timothy, guard that which is entrusted to thee;"[1] and again: "That good thing which was committed unto thee keep."[2] What is this deposit? Is it so secret as to be supposed to characterize[3] a new doctrine? or is it a part of that charge of which he says, "This charge I commit unto thee, son Timothy?"[4] and also of that precept of which he says, "I charge thee in the sight of God, who quickeneth all things, and before Jesus Christ, who witnessed a good confession under Pontius Pilate, that thou keep this commandment?"[5] Now, what is (this) commandment, and what is (this) charge? From the preceding and the succeeding contexts, it will be manifest that there is no mysterious[6] hint darkly suggested in this expression about (some) far-fetched[7] doctrine, but that a warning is rather given against receiving any other (doctrine) than that which *Timothy* had heard from himself, *as I take it* publicly: "Before many witnesess" is his phrase.[8] Now, if they refuse to allow that the church is meant by these "many witnesses," it matters nothing, since nothing could have been secret which was produced "before many witnesses." Nor, again, must the circumstance of his having wished him to "commit these things to faithful men, who should be able to teach others also,"[9] be construed into a proof of there being some occult doctrine. For, when he says "these things," he refers to the things of which he is writing at the moment. In reference, however, to occult subjects, he would have called them, as being absent, *those things*, not *these things*, to one who had a joint knowledge of them with himself.[10]

CHAP. XXVI.—THE APOSTLES DID IN ALL CASES TEACH THE WHOLE TRUTH TO THE WHOLE CHURCH. NO RESERVATION, NOR PARTIAL COMMUNICATION TO FAVOURITE FRIENDS.

Besides which, it must have followed, that, for the man to whom he committed the ministration of the gospel, he would add the injunction that it be not ministered in all places,[11] and without respect to persons,[12] in accordance with the Lord's saying, "Not to cast one's pearls before swine, nor that which is holy unto dogs."[13] Openly did the Lord speak,[14] without any intimation of a hidden mystery. He had Himself commanded that, "whatsoever they had heard in darkness" and in secret, they should "declare in the light and on the house-tops."[15] He had Himself foreshown, by means of a parable, that they should not keep back in secret, fruitless of interest,[16] a single pound, that is, one word of His. He used Himself to tell them that a candle was not usually "pushed away under a bushel, but placed on a candlestick," in order to "give light to all who are in the house."[17] These things the apostles either neglected, or failed to understand, if they fulfilled them not, by concealing any portion of the light, that is, of the word of God and the mystery of Christ. Of no man, I am quite sure, were they afraid,—neither of Jews nor of Gentiles in their violence;[18] with all the greater freedom, then, would they certainly preach in the church, who held not their tongue in synagogues and public places. Indeed they would have found it impossible either to convert Jews or to bring in Gentiles, unless they "set forth in order"[19] that which they would have them believe. Much less, when churches were advanced in the faith, would they have withdrawn from them anything for the purpose of committing it separately to some few others. Although, even supposing that among intimate friends,[20] so to speak, they did hold certain discussions, yet it is incredible that these could have been such as to bring in some other rule of faith, differing from and contrary to that which they were proclaiming through the Catholic churches,[21]—as if they spoke of one God in the Church, (and) another at home, and described one substance of Christ, publicly, (and) another secretly, and announced one hope of the resurrection before all men, (and) another before the few; although they themselves, in their epistles, besought men that they would all speak one and the same thing, and that there should be no divisions and dissensions in the church,[22] seeing that

---

[1] 1 Tim. vi. 20.
[2] 2 Tim. i. 14.
[3] Ut alterius doctrinæ deputetur.
[4] 1 Tim. i. 18.
[5] 1 Tim. vi. 13.
[6] Nescis quid.
[7] Remotiore.
[8] 2 Tim. ii. 2.
[9] 2 Tim. ii. 2.
[10] Apud conscientiam. [Clement of Alexandria is to be interpreted by *Tertullian*, with whom he does not essentially differ. For Clement's Esoteric Doctrine (See Vol. II. pp. 302, 313, etc.) is defined as *perfecting* the type of the Christian by the *strong meat* of Truth, of which *the entire deposit* is presupposed as common to all Christians. We must not blame Clement for the abuse of his teaching by perverters of Truth itself.]

[11] Passim.
[12] Inconsiderate.
[13] Matt. vii. 6.
[14] John xviii. 20.
[15] Matt. x. 27.
[16] Luke xix. 20-24.
[17] Matt. v. 15.
[18] Literally, "the violence of neither Jew nor Gentile."
[19] Luke i. 1.
[20] Domesticos. [All this interprets Clement and utterly deprives the Trent System of its appeal to a secret doctrine, against our *Præscription*.]
[21] Catholice, or, "which they were bringing before the public in a catholic way."
[22] 1 Cor. i. 10.

they, whether Paul or others, preached the same things. Moreover, they remembered (the words): "Let your communication be yea, yea; nay, nay; for whatsoever is more than this cometh of evil;" [1] so that they were not to handle the gospel in a diversity of treatment.

CHAP. XXVII.—GRANTED THAT THE APOSTLES TRANSMITTED THE WHOLE DOCTRINE OF TRUTH, MAY NOT THE CHURCHES HAVE BEEN UNFAITHFUL IN HANDING IT ON? INCONCEIVABLE THAT THIS CAN HAVE BEEN THE CASE.

Since, therefore, it is incredible that the apostles were either ignorant of the whole scope of the message which they had to declare,[2] or failed to make known to all men the entire rule of faith, let us see whether, while the apostles proclaimed it, perhaps, simply and fully, the churches, through their own fault, set it forth otherwise than the apostles had done. All these suggestions of distrust[3] you may find put forward by the heretics. They bear in mind how the churches were rebuked by the apostle: "O foolish Galatians, who hath bewitched you?"[4] and, "Ye did run so well; who hath hindered you?"[5] and how the epistle actually begins: "I marvel that ye are so soon removed from Him, who hath called you as His own in grace, to another gospel."[6] That they likewise (remember), what was written to the Corinthians, that they "were yet carnal," who "required to be fed with milk," being as yet "unable to bear strong meat;"[7] who also "thought that they knew somewhat, whereas they knew not yet anything, as they ought to know."[8] When they raise the objection that the churches were rebuked, let them suppose that they were also corrected; let them also remember those (churches), concerning whose faith and knowledge and conversation the apostle "rejoices and gives thanks to God," which nevertheless, even at this day, unite with those which were rebuked in the privileges of one and the same institution.

CHAP. XXVIII.—THE ONE TRADITION OF THE FAITH, WHICH IS SUBSTANTIALLY ALIKE IN THE CHURCHES EVERYWHERE, A GOOD PROOF THAT THE TRANSMISSION HAS BEEN TRUE AND HONEST IN THE MAIN.

Grant, then, that all have erred; that the apostle was mistaken in giving his testimony; that the Holy Ghost had no such respect to any one (church) as to lead it into truth, although sent with this view by Christ,[9] and for this asked of the Father that He might be the teacher of truth;[10] grant, also, that He, the Steward of God, the Vicar of Christ,[11] neglected His office, permitting the churches for a time to understand differently, (and) to believe differently, what He Himself was preaching by the apostles,—is it likely that so many churches, and they so great, should have gone astray into one and the same faith? No casualty distributed among many men issues in one and the same result. Error of doctrine in the churches must necessarily have produced various issues. When, however, that which is deposited among many is found to be one and the same, it is not the result of error, but of tradition. Can any one, then, be reckless[12] enough to say that they were in error who handed on the tradition?

CHAP. XXIX.—THE TRUTH NOT INDEBTED TO THE CARE OF THE HERETICS; IT HAD FREE COURSE BEFORE THEY APPEARED. PRIORITY OF THE CHURCH'S DOCTRINE A MARK OF ITS TRUTH.

In whatever manner error came, it reigned of course[13] only as long as there was an absence of heresies? Truth had to wait for certain Marcionites and Valentinians to set it free. During the interval the gospel was wrongly[14] preached; men wrongly believed; so many thousands were wrongly baptized; so many works of faith were wrongly wrought; so many miraculous gifts,[15] so many spiritual endowments,[16] were wrongly set in operation; so many priestly functions, so many ministries,[17] were wrongly executed; and, to sum up the whole, so many martyrs wrongly received their crowns! Else, if not wrongly done, and to no purpose, how comes it to pass that the things of God were on their course before it was known to what God they belonged? that there were Christians before Christ was found? that there were heresies before true doctrine? Not so; for in all cases truth precedes its copy, the likeness succeeds the reality. Absurd enough, however, is it, that heresy should be deemed to have preceded its own prior doctrine, even on this account, because it is that (doctrine) itself which foretold that there

---

[1] Matt. v. 37.
[2] Plenitudinem prædicationis.
[3] Scrupulositatis.
[4] Gal. iii. 1.
[5] Gal. v. 7.
[6] Gal. i. 6.
[7] 1 Cor. iii. 1, and following verses.
[8] 1 Cor. viii. 2.

[9] John xiv. 26.
[10] John xv. 26.
[11] [Tertullian knows no other Vicar of Christ than the Holy Spirit. They who attribute infallibility to any mortal man become Montanists; they attribute the Paraclete's voice to their oracle.]
[12] Audeat.
[13] Utique, ironical.
[14] Perperam.
[15] Virtutes, "potestatem edendi miracula" (Oehler).
[16] Charismata.
[17] Ministeria. Another reading has *mysteria*, "mysteries" or "sacraments."

should be heresies against which men would have to guard! To a church which possessed this doctrine, it was written—yea, the doctrine itself writes to its own church—"Though an angel from heaven preach any other gospel than that which we have preached, let him be accursed."[1]

CHAP. XXX.—COMPARATIVE LATENESS OF HERESIES. MARCION'S HERESY. SOME PERSONAL FACTS ABOUT HIM. THE HERESY OF APELLES. CHARACTER OF THIS MAN; PHILUMENE; VALENTINUS; NIGIDIUS, AND HERMOGENES.

Where was Marcion *then*, that shipmaster of Pontus, the zealous student of Stoicism? Where was Valentinus *then*, the disciple of Platonism? For it is evident that those men lived not so long ago,—in the reign of Antoninus, for the most part,[2]—and that they at first were believers in the doctrine of the Catholic Church, in the church of Rome under the episcopate of the blessed Eleutherus,[3] until on account of their ever restless curiosity, with which they even infected the brethren, they were more than once expelled. Marcion, indeed, [went] with the two hundred sesterces which he had brought into the church, and,[4] when banished at last to a permanent excommunication, they scattered abroad the poisons of their doctrines. Afterwards, it is true, Marcion professed repentance, and agreed to the conditions granted to him—that he should receive reconciliation if he restored to the church all the others whom he had been training for perdition: he was prevented, however, by death. It was indeed[5] necessary that there should be heresies;[6] and yet it does not follow from that necessity, that heresies are a good thing. As if it has not been necessary also that there should be evil! It was even necessary that the Lord should be betrayed; but woe to the traitor![7] So that no man may from this defend heresies. If we must likewise touch the descent[8] of Apelles, he is far from being "one of the old school,"[9] like his instructor and moulder, Marcion; he rather forsook the continence of Marcion, by resorting to the company of a woman, and withdrew to Alexandria, out of sight of his most abstemious[10] master. Returning therefrom, after some years, unimproved, except that he was no longer a Marcionite, he clave[11] to another woman, the maiden Philumene (whom we have already[12] mentioned), who herself afterwards became an enormous prostitute. Having been imposed on by her vigorous spirit,[13] he committed to writing *the revelations* which he had learned of her. Persons are still living who remember them,—their own actual disciples and successors,—who cannot therefore deny the lateness of their date. But, in fact, by their own works they are convicted, even as the Lord said.[14] For since Marcion separated the New Testament from the Old, he is (necessarily) subsequent to that which he separated, inasmuch as it was only in his power to separate what was (previously) united. Having then been united previous to its separation, the fact of its subsequent separation proves the subsequence also of the man who effected the separation. In like manner Valentinus, by his different expositions and acknowledged[15] emendations, makes these changes on the express ground of previous faultiness, and therefore demonstrates the difference[16] of the documents. These corrupters of the truth we mention as being more notorious and more public[17] than others. There is, however, a certain man[18] named Nigidius, and Hermogenes, and several others, who still pursue the course[19] of perverting the ways of the Lord. Let them show me by what authority they come! If it be some other God they preach, how comes it that they employ the things and he writings and the names of that God against whom they preach? If it be the same God, why treat Him in some other way? Let them prove themselves to be new apostles![20] Let them maintain that Christ has come down a second time, taught in person a second time, has been twice crucified, twice dead, twice raised! For thus has the apostle described (the order of events in the life of Christ); for thus, too, is He[21] accustomed to make His apostles—to give them, (that is), power besides of working the same miracles which He worked Himself.[22] I would therefore have their mighty deeds also brought forward; except that I allow their

[1] Gal. i. 8. [In this chapter (xxix.) the principle of *Prescription* is condensed and brought to the needle-point—*Quod semper.* If you can't show that your doctrine was *always* taught, it is false: and this is "Prescription."]
[2] Fere.
[3] [Kaye, p. 226.]
[4] See *adv. Marcion*, iv. 4 *infra*.
[5] Enim, profecto (Oehler).
[6] 1 Cor. xi. 19.
[7] Mark xiv. 21.
[8] Stemma. The reading of the *Cod. Agobard.* is "stigma," which gives very good sense.
[9] Vetus.
[10] Sanctissimi. This may be an *ironical* allusion to Marcion's repudiation of marriage.

[11] Impegit.
[12] In chap. vi. p. 246 above.
[13] Energemate. Oehler defines this word, "vis et efficacia dæmonum, quibus agebatur." [But see Lardner, *Credib.* viii. p. 540.]
[14] Matt. vii. 16.
[15] Sine dubio.
[16] Alterius fuisse. One reading is *anterius*; i.e., "demonstrates the *priority*" of the book he alters.
[17] Frequentiores.
[18] Nescio qui.
[19] Ambulant.
[20] Compare *de Carne Christi*, chap. ii. [Elucidation IV.]
[21] Christ: so Routh.
[22] We add Oehler's reading of this obscure passage: "Sic enim apostolus descripsit, sic enim apostolos solet facere, dare præterea illis virtutem eadem signa edendi quæ et ipse." ["It is worthy of remark" (says Kaye, p. 95), "that he does not appeal *to any instance* of the exercise of miraculous powers in his own day."]

mightiest deed to be that by which they perversely vie with the apostles. For whilst they used to raise men to life from the dead, these consign men to death from their living state.

CHAP. XXXI.—TRUTH FIRST, FALSEHOOD AFTERWARDS, AS ITS PERVERSION. CHRIST'S PARABLE PUTS THE SOWING OF THE GOOD SEED BEFORE THE USELESS TARES.

Let me return, however, from this digression[1] to discuss[2] the priority of truth, and the comparative lateness[3] of falsehood, deriving support for my argument even from that parable which puts in the first place the sowing by the Lord of the good seed of the wheat, but introduces at a later stage the adulteration of the crop by its enemy the devil with the useless weed of the wild oats. For herein is figuratively described the difference of doctrines, since in other passages also the word of God is likened unto seed. From the actual order, therefore, it becomes clear, that that which was first delivered is of the Lord and is true, whilst that is strange and false which was afterwards introduced. This sentence will keep its ground in opposition to all later heresies, which have no consistent quality of kindred knowledge[4] inherent in them—to claim the truth as on their side.

CHAP. XXXII.—NONE OF THE HERETICS CLAIM SUCCESSION FROM THE APOSTLES. NEW CHURCHES STILL APOSTOLIC, BECAUSE THEIR FAITH IS THAT WHICH THE APOSTLES TAUGHT AND HANDED DOWN. THE HERETICS CHALLENGED TO SHOW ANY APOSTOLIC CREDENTIALS.

But if there be any (heresies) which are bold enough to plant themselves in the midst of the apostolic age, that they may thereby seem to have been handed down by the apostles, because they existed in the time of the apostles, we can say: Let them produce the original records[5] of their churches; let them unfold the roll of their bishops, running down in due succession from the beginning in such a manner that [that first bishop of theirs[6]] bishop shall be able to show for his ordainer and predecessor some one of the apostles or of apostolic men,—a man, moreover, who continued stedfast with the apostles. For this is the manner in which the apostolic churches

transmit[7] their registers:[8] as the church of Smyrna, which records that Polycarp was placed therein by John; as also the church of Rome, which makes Clement to have been ordained in like manner by Peter.[9] In exactly the same way the other churches likewise exhibit (their several worthies), whom, as having been appointed to their episcopal places by apostles, they regard as transmitters of the apostolic seed. Let the heretics contrive[10] something of the same kind. For after their blasphemy, what is there that is unlawful for them (to attempt)? But should they even effect the contrivance, they will not advance a step. For their very doctrine, after comparison with that of the apostles, will declare, by its own diversity and contrariety, that it had for its author neither an apostle nor an apostolic man ; because, as the apostles would never have taught things which were self-contradictory, so the apostolic men would not have inculcated teaching different from the apostles, unless they who received their instruction from the apostles went and preached in a contrary manner. To this test, therefore will they be submitted for proof[11] by those churches, who, although they derive not their founder from apostles or apostolic men (as being of much later date, for they are in fact being founded daily), yet, since they agree in the same faith, they are accounted as not less apostolic because they are akin in doctrine.[12] Then let all the heresies, when challenged to these two[13] tests by our apostolic church, offer their proof of how they deem themselves to be apostolic. But in truth they neither are so, nor are they able to prove themselves to be what they are not. Nor are they admitted to peaceful relations and communion by such churches as are in any way connected with apostles, inasmuch as they are in no sense themselves apostolic because of their diversity as to the mysteries of the faith.[14]

CHAP. XXXIII.—PRESENT HERESIES (SEEDLINGS OF THE TARES NOTED BY THE SACRED WRITERS) ALREADY CONDEMNED IN SCRIPTURE. THIS DESCENT OF LATER HERESY FROM THE EARLIER TRACED IN SEVERAL INSTANCES.

Besides all this, I add a review of the doctrines themselves, which, existing as they did

---

[1] Ab excessu.
[2] Disputandam. Another reading has *deputandam*, i.e., "to attribute."
[3] Posteritatem.
[4] Nulla constantia de conscientia, "no conscientious ground of confidence" (Dodgson).
[5] Origines, "the originals" (Dodgson).
[6] Ille. A touch of irony occurs in the phrase "primus ille episcopus."
[7] Deferunt.
[8] Fastos.
[9] [Linus and Cletus must have died, or been martyred, therefore, almost as soon as appointed. Our author had seen these registers, no doubt.]
[10] Confingant.
[11] Probabuntur. Another reading is *provocabuntur*, "will be challenged." [Not to one particular See, but to all the Apostolic churches : *Quod ubique*.]
[12] Pro consanguinitate doctrinæ.
[13] That is, the succession of bishops from the apostles, and the identity of doctrine with the apostolic.
[14] Sacramenti.

in the days of the apostles, were both exposed and denounced by the said apostles. For by this method they will be more easily reprobated,[1] when they are detected to have been even then in existence, or at any rate to have been seedlings[2] of the (tares) which then were. Paul, in his first epistle to the Corinthians, sets his mark on certain who denied and doubted the resurrection.[3] This opinion was the especial property of the Sadducees.[4] A part of it, however, is maintained by Marcion and Apelles and Valentinus, and all other impugners of the resurrection. Writing also to the Galatians, he inveighs against such men as observed and defend circumcision and the (Mosaic) law.[5] Thus runs Hebion's heresy. Such also as "forbid to marry" he reproaches in his instructions to Timothy.[6] Now, this is the teaching of Marcion and his follower Apelles. (The apostle) directs a similar blow[7] against those who said that "the resurrection was past already."[8] Such an opinion did the Valentinians assert of themselves. When again he mentions "endless genealogies,"[9] one also recognises Valentinus, in whose system a certain Æon, whosoever he be,[10] of a new name, and that not one only, generates of his own grace[11] Sense and Truth ; and these in like manner produce of themselves Word[12] and Life, while these again afterwards beget Man and the Church. From these primary eight[13] ten other Æons after them spring, and then the twelve others arise with their wonderful names, to complete the mere story of the thirty Æons. The same apostle, when disapproving of those who are "in bondage to elements,"[14] points us to some dogma of Hermogenes, who introduces matter as having no beginning,[15] and then compares it with God, who has no beginning.[16] By thus making the mother of the elements a goddess, he has it in his power "to be in bondage" to a being which he puts on a par with[17] God. John, however, in the Apocalypse is charged to chastise those "who eat things sacrificed to idols," and "who commit fornication."[18] There are even now another sort of Nicolaitans.

Theirs is called the Gaian[19] heresy. But in his epistle he especially designates those as "Antichrists" who "denied that Christ was come in the flesh,"[20] and who refused to think that Jesus was the Son of God. The one dogma Marcion maintained; the other, Hebion.[21] The doctrine, however, of Simon's sorcery, which inculcated the worship of angels,[22] was itself actually reckoned amongst idolatries and condemned by the Apostle Peter in Simon's own person.

CHAP. XXXIV.—NO EARLY CONTROVERSY RESPECTING THE DIVINE CREATOR; NO SECOND GOD INTRODUCED AT FIRST. HERESIES CONDEMNED ALIKE BY THE SENTENCE AND THE SILENCE OF HOLY SCRIPTURE.

These are, as I suppose, the different kinds of spurious doctrines, which (as we are informed by the apostles themselves) existed in their own day. And yet we find amongst so many various perversions of truth, not one school[23] which raised any controversy concerning God as the Creator of all things. No man was bold enough to surmise a second god. More readily was doubt felt about the Son than about the Father, until Marcion introduced, in addition to the Creator, another god of goodness only. Apelles made the Creator of some nondescript[24] glorious angel, who belonged to the superior God, the god (according to him,) of the law and of Israel, affirming that he was fire.[25] Valentinus disseminated his Æons, and traced the sin of one Æon[26] to the production of God the Creator. To none, forsooth, except these, nor prior to these, was revealed the truth of the Divine Nature; and they obtained this especial honour and fuller favour from the devil, we cannot doubt,[27] because he wished even in this respect to rival God, that he might succeed, by the poison of his doctrines, in doing himself what the Lord said could not be done—making "the disciples above their Master."[28] Let the entire mass[29] of heresies choose, therefore, for themselves the times when they should appear; provided that the *when* be an unimportant point; allowing, too, that they be not of the truth, and (as a matter of course[30]) that such as had no exist-

---

[1] Traducentur.
[2] Semina sumpsisse.
[3] 1 Cor. xv. 12.
[4] Comp. Tertull. *de Resur. Carnis*, xxxvi.
[5] Gal. v. 2.
[6] 1 Tim. iv. 3.
[7] Æque tangit.
[8] 2 Tim. ii. 3.
[9] 1 Tim. i. 4.
[10] Nescio qui.
[11] Charite.
[12] Sermonem.
[13] De qua prima ogdoade. [See Irenæus, Vol. I. p. 316, *etc* this Series.]
[14] Gal. iv. 9.
[15] Non natam, literally, "as being unbegotten."
[16] Deo non nato.
[17] Comparat.
[18] Rev. ii. 14.

[19] Gaiana. So Oehler ; the common reading being " *Caiana.*"
[20] 1 John iv. 3.
[21] Comp. Epiphanius, i. 30.
[22] Referred to perhaps in Col. ii. 18.
[23] Institutionem.
[24] Nescio quem.
[25] Igneum, " consisted of fire."
[26] "The *ectroma*, or fall of Sophia from the Pleroma, from whom the Creator was fabled to be descended " (Dodgson).
[27] Scilicet.
[28] Luke vi. 40.
[29] Universæ.
[30] Utique.

ence in the time of the apostles could not possibly have had any connection with the apostles. If indeed they had then existed, their names would be extant,[1] with a view to their own repression likewise. Those (heresies) indeed which did exist in the days of the apostles, are condemned in their very mention.[2] If it be true, then, that those heresies, which in the apostolic times were in a rude form, are now found to be the same, only in a much more polished shape, they derive their condemnation from this very circumstance. Or if they were not the same, but arose afterwards in a different form, and merely assumed from them certain tenets, then, by sharing with them an agreement in their teaching,[3] they must needs partake in their condemnation, by reason of the above-mentioned definition,[4] of lateness of date, which meets us on the very threshold.[5] Even if they were free from any participation in condemned doctrine, they would stand already judged[6] on the mere ground of time, being all the more spurious because they were not even named by the apostles. Whence we have the firmer assurance, that these were (the heresies) which even then,[7] were announced as about to arise.

CHAP. XXXV.—LET HERETICS MAINTAIN THEIR CLAIMS BY A DEFINITE AND INTELLIGIBLE EVIDENCE. THIS THE ONLY METHOD OF SOLVING THEIR QUESTIONS. CATHOLICS APPEAL ALWAYS TO EVIDENCE TRACEABLE TO APOSTOLIC SOURCES.

Challenged and refuted by us, according to these definitions, let all the heresies boldly on their part also advance similar rules to these against our doctrine, whether they be later than the apostles or contemporary with the apostles, provided they be different from them; provided also they were, by either a general or a specific censure, precondemned by them. For since they deny the truth of (our doctrine), they ought to prove that it also is heresy, refutable by the same rule as that by which they are themselves refuted; and at the same time to show us where we must seek the truth, which it is by this time evident has no existence amongst them. Our system[8] is not behind any in date; on the contrary, it is earlier than all; and this fact will be the evidence of that truth which everywhere occupies the first place. The apostles, again, nowhere con-

demn it; they rather defend it,—a fact which will show that it comes from themselves.[9] For that doctrine which they refrain from condemning, when they have condemned every strange opinion, they show to be their own, and on that ground too they defend it.

CHAP. XXXVI.—THE APOSTOLIC CHURCHES THE VOICE OF THE APOSTLES. LET THE HERETICS EXAMINE THEIR APOSTOLIC CLAIMS, IN EACH CASE, INDISPUTABLE. THE CHURCH OF ROME DOUBLY APOSTOLIC; ITS EARLY EMINENCE AND EXCELLENCE. HERESY, AS PERVERTING THE TRUTH, IS CONNECTED THEREWITH.

Come now, you who would indulge a better curiosity, if you would apply it to the business of your salvation, run over the apostolic churches, in which the very thrones[10] of the apostles are still pre-eminent in their places,[11] in which their own authentic writings[12] are read, uttering the voice and representing the face of each of them severally. Achaia is very near you, (in which) you find Corinth. Since you are not far from Macedonia, you have Philippi; (and there too) you have the Thessalonians. Since you are able to cross to Asia, you get Ephesus. Since, moreover, you are close upon Italy,[13] you have Rome, from which there comes even into our own hands the very authority (of apostles themselves).[14] How happy is its church, on which apostles poured forth all their doctrine along with their blood! where Peter endures a passion like his Lord's! where Paul wins his crown in a death like John's![15] where the Apostle John was first plunged, unhurt, into boiling oil, and thence remitted to his island-exile! See what she has learned, what taught, what fellowship has had with even (our) churches in Africa![16] One Lord God does she acknowledge, the Creator of the universe, and Christ Jesus (born) of the Virgin Mary, the Son of God the Creator; and the Resurrection of the flesh; the law and the prophets she unites[17] in one volume with the writings of evangelists and apostles, from which she drinks in her faith. This she seals with the water (of baptism), arrays with the Holy

---

1 Nominarentur et ipsæ.
2 Nominatione, i.e. by the apostles.
3 Prædicationis.
4 Fine.
5 Præcedente.
6 Præjudicarentur. [i.e. by Præscription.]
7 i.e., in the days of the apostles, and by their mouth.
8 Res.

9 Indicium proprietatis, a proof of its being their own.
10 Cathedræ.
11 Suis locis præsident.
12 Authenticæ. This much disputed phrase may refer to the *autographs* or the Greek *originals* (rather than the Latin translations), or full *unmutilated* copies as opposed to the garbled ones of the heretics. The second sense is probably the correct one.
13 [Note, *those near by* may resort to this ancient and glorious church; not as any better than Corinth, or Philippi, or having any higher Apostolic throne. See Irenæus, Vol. I. p. 415, (note) and Elucid. p. 460.]
14 Compare our *Anti-Marcion*, iv. 5, p. 186.
15 The Baptist's.
16 [Observe—" even with us in Africa." If this implies noteworthy love, it proves that there was no organic relation requiring such particular fellowship, even in the West.]
17 Miscet.

Ghost, feeds with the Eucharist, cheers with martyrdom,[1] and against such a discipline thus (maintained) she admits no gainsayer. This is the discipline which I no longer say foretold that heresies should come, but from[2] which they proceeded. However, they were not of her, because they were opposed to her.[3] Even the rough wild-olive arises from the germ[4] of the fruitful, rich, and genuine[5] olive; also from the seed[6] of the mellowest and sweetest fig there springs the empty and useless wild-fig. In the same way heresies, too, come from our plant,[7] although not of our kind; (they come) from the grain of truth,[8] but, owing to their falsehood, they have only wild leaves to show.[9]

CHAP. XXXVII.—HERETICS NOT BEING CHRISTIANS, BUT RATHER PERVERTERS OF CHRIST'S TEACHING, MAY NOT CLAIM THE CHRISTIAN SCRIPTURES. THESE ARE A DEPOSIT, COMMITTED TO AND CAREFULLY KEPT BY THE CHURCH.

Since this is the case, in order that the truth may be adjudged to belong to us, "as many as walk according to the rule," which the church has handed down from the apostles, the apostles from Christ, and Christ from God, the reason of our position is clear, when it determines that heretics ought not to be allowed to challenge an appeal to the Scriptures, since we, without the Scriptures, prove that they have nothing to do with the Scriptures. For as they are heretics, they cannot be true Christians, because it is not from Christ that they get that which they pursue of their own mere choice, and from the pursuit incur and admit the name of heretics.[10] Thus, not being Christians, they have acquired[11] no right to the Christian Scriptures; and it may be very fairly said to them, "Who are you? When and whence did you come? As you are none of mine, what have you to do with that which is mine? Indeed, Marcion, by what right do you hew my wood? By whose permission, Valentinus, are you diverting the streams of my fountain? By what power, Apelles, are you removing my landmarks? This is my property. Why are you, the rest, sowing and feeding here at your own pleasure? This (I say) is my property. I have long possessed it; I possessed it before you. I hold sure title-deeds from the original owners themselves, to whom the estate belonged. I am the heir of the apostles. Just as they carefully prepared their will and testament, and committed it to a trust, and adjured (the trustees to be faithful to their charge),[12] even so do I hold it. As for you, they have, it is certain, always held you as disinherited, and rejected you as strangers—as enemies. But on what ground are heretics strangers and enemies to the apostles, if it be not from the difference of their teaching, which each individual of his own mere will has either advanced or received in opposition to the apostles?"

CHAP. XXXVIII.—HARMONY OF THE CHURCH AND THE SCRIPTURES. HERETICS HAVE TAMPERED WITH THE SCRIPTURES, AND MUTILATED, AND ALTERED THEM. CATHOLICS NEVER CHANGE THE SCRIPTURES, WHICH ALWAYS TESTIFY FOR THEM.

Where diversity of doctrine is found, there, then, must the corruption both of the Scriptures and the expositions thereof be regarded as existing. On those whose purpose it was to teach differently, lay the necessity of differently arranging the instruments of doctrine.[13] They could not possibly have effected their diversity of teaching in any other way than by having a difference in the means whereby they taught. As in their case, corruption in doctrine could not possibly have succeeded without a corruption also of its instruments, so to ourselves also integrity of doctrine could not have accrued, without integrity in those means by which doctrine is managed. Now, what is there in our Scriptures which is contrary to us?[14] What of our own have we introduced, that we should have to take it away again, or else add to it, or alter it, in order to restore to its natural soundness anything which is contrary to it, and contained in the Scriptures?[15] What we are ourselves, that also the Scriptures are, (and have been) from the beginning.[16] Of

---

[1] We have taken Oehler's hint in favour of "martyrio." The usual reading "martyrium" (meaning "she exhorts to martyrdom") is stiff, and unsuited to the context.
[2] De.
[3] Or, "they were not of it, because they were opposed to it," i.e., the discipline or teaching.
[4] Nucleo.
[5] Necessariæ.
[6] Papavere. "Ego cum aliis papaver ficus interpretor de seminalibus ficus, non de ipso fructu" (Oehler).
[7] Frutice.
[8] We again follow Oehler's hint, who would like to read "de grano veritatis." The texts are obscure, and vary much here.
[9] Silvestres.
[10] "That is, in following out their own choice (αἵρεσις) of opinions, they both receive and admit the name of heretics," αἱρετικοί, "self-choosers" (Dodgson). [In Theology, technically, one must be a baptized Christian in order to be a heretic. The Mohammedans, e. g., are not heretics but pagans. But, our author speaks rhetorically.]
[11] Capiunt.
[12] Compare 1 Tim. v. 21, and vi. 13; 2 Tim. ii. 14, and iv. 1-4.
[13] By the instrumenta doctrinæ he here means the writings of the New Testament.
[14] [Our author insists on the precise agreement of Catholic Tradition with Holy Scripture. See valuable remarks on Schleiermacher, in Kaye, pp. 279-284.]
[15] We add the original of this sentence, which is obscured by its terseness: "Quid de proprio intulimus, ut aliquid contrarium ei et in Scripturis deprehensum detractione vel adjectione vel transmutatione remediaremus?"
[16] That is, teaching the same faith and conversation (De la Cerda).

them we have our being, before there was any other way, before they were interpolated by you. Now, inasmuch as all interpolation must be believed to be a later process, for the express reason that it proceeds from rivalry which is never in any case previous to nor home-born[1] with that which it emulates, it is as incredible to every man of sense that we should seem to have introduced any corrupt text into the Scriptures, existing, as we have been, from the very first, and being the first, as it is that they have not in fact introduced it, who are both later in date and opposed (to the Scriptures). One man perverts the Scriptures with his hand, another their meaning by his exposition. For although Valentinus seems to use the entire volume,[2] he has none the less laid violent hands on the truth only with a more cunning mind and skill[3] than Marcion. Marcion expressly and openly used the knife, not the pen, since he made such an excision of the Scriptures as suited his own subject-matter.[4] Valentinus, however, abstained from such excision, because he did not invent Scriptures to square with his own subject-matter, but adapted his matter to the Scriptures; and yet he took away more, and added more, by removing the proper meaning of every particular word, and adding fantastic arrangements of things which have no real existence.[5]

CHAP. XXXIX.—WHAT ST. PAUL CALLS SPIRITUAL WICKEDNESSES DISPLAYED BY PAGAN AUTHORS, AND BY HERETICS, IN NO DISSIMILAR MANNER. HOLY SCRIPTURE ESPECIALLY LIABLE TO HERETICAL MANIPULATION. AFFORDS MATERIAL FOR HERESIES, JUST AS VIRGIL HAS BEEN THE GROUNDWORK OF LITERARY PLAGIARISMS, DIFFERENT IN PURPORT FROM THE ORIGINAL.

These were the ingenious arts of "spiritual wickednesses,"[6] wherewith we also, my brethren, may fairly expect to have "to wrestle," as necessary for faith, that the elect may be made manifest, (and) that the reprobate may be discovered. And therefore they possess influence, and a facility in thinking out and fabricating[7] errors, which ought not to be wondered at as if it were a difficult and inexplicable process, seeing that in profane writings also an example comes ready to hand of a similar facility. You see in our own day, composed out of Virgil,[8] a story of a wholly different character, the subject-matter being arranged according to the verse, and the verse according to the subject-matter. In short,[9] Hosidius Geta has most completely pilfered his tragedy of *Medea* from Virgil. A near relative of my own, among some leisure productions[10] of his pen, has composed out of the same poet *The Table of Cebes*. On the same principle, those *poetasters* are commonly called *Homerocentones*, "collectors of Homeric odds and ends," who stitch into one piece, patchwork fashion, works of their own from the lines of Homer, out of many scraps put together from this passage and from that (in miscellaneous confusion). Now, unquestionably, the Divine Scriptures are more fruitful in resources of all kinds for this sort of facility. Nor do I risk contradiction in saying[11] that the very Scriptures were even arranged by the will of God in such a manner as to furnish materials for heretics, inasmuch as I read that "there must be heresies,"[12] which there cannot be without the Scriptures.

CHAP. XL.—NO DIFFERENCE IN THE SPIRIT OF IDOLATRY AND OF HERESY. IN THE RITES OF IDOLATRY, SATAN IMITATED AND DISTORTED THE DIVINE INSTITUTIONS OF THE OLDER SCRIPTURES. THE CHRISTIAN SCRIPTURES CORRUPTED BY HIM IN THE PERVERSIONS OF THE VARIOUS HERETICS.

The question will arise, By whom is to be interpreted[13] the sense of the passages which make for heresies? By the devil, of course, to whom pertain those wiles which pervert the truth, and who, by the mystic rites of his idols, vies even with the essential portions[14] of the sacraments of God.[15] He, too, baptizes some —that is, his own believers and faithful followers;[17] he promises the putting away[17] of sins by a laver (of his own); and if my memory still serves me, Mithra there, (in the kingdom of Satan,) sets his marks on the foreheads of his soldiers; celebrates also the oblation of bread, and introduces an image of a resurrec-

---

[1] Domestica.
[2] Integro instrumento.
[3] Callidiore ingenio.
[4] That is, cutting out whatever did not fall in with it (Dodgson).
[5] Non comparentium rerum. [Note, he says above " of *them*, the Scriptures, we, Catholics, *have our being." Præscription* does not undervalue Scripture as the food and life of the Church, but supplies a short and decisive method with innovaters.]
[6] See Eph. vi. 12, and 1 Cor. xi. 18.
[7] Instruendis.

[8] Oehler reads ex Vergilio, although the *Codex Agobard.* has ex Virgilio.
[9] Denique. [" Getica lyra."]
[10] Otis.
[11] Nec periclitor dicere. [Truly, a Tertullianic paradox; but compare 2 Pet. iii. 16. N.B. Scripture the test of heresy.]
[12] 1 Cor. xi. 19.
[13] " Interpretur " is here a passive verb.
[14] Res.
[15] Sacramentorum divinorum. The form, however, of this phrase seems to point not only to the *specific sacraments* of the gospel, but to the *general mysteries* of our religion.
[16] Compare Tertullian's treatises, de Bapt. v. and de Corona, last chapter.
[17] Expositionem.

tion, and before a sword wreathes a crown.[1] What also must we say to (Satan's) limiting his chief priest[2] to a single marriage? He, too, has his virgins; he, too, has his proficients in continence.[3] Suppose now we revolve in our minds the superstitions of Numa Pompilius, and consider his priestly offices and badges and privileges, his sacrificial services, too, and the instruments and vessels of the sacrifices themselves, and the curious rites of his expiations and vows: is it not clear to us that the devil imitated the well-known[4] moroseness of the Jewish law? Since, therefore, he has shown such emulation in his great aim of expressing, in the concerns of his idolatry, those very things of which consists the administration of Christ's sacraments, it follows, of course, that the same being, possessing still the same genius, both set his heart upon,[5] and succeeded in, adapting[6] to his profane and rival creed the very documents of divine things and of the Christian saints[7]—his interpretation from their interpretations, his words from their words, his parables from their parables. For this reason, then, no one ought to doubt, either that "spiritual wickednesses," from which also heresies come, have been introduced by the devil, or that there is any real difference between heresies and idolatry, seeing that they appertain both to the same author and the same work that idolatry does. They either pretend that there is another god in opposition to the Creator, or, even if they acknowledge that the Creator is the one only God, they treat of Him as a different being from what He is in truth. The consequence is, that every lie which they speak of God is in a certain sense a sort of idolatry

CHAP. XLI.—THE CONDUCT OF HERETICS: ITS FRIVOLITY, WORLDLINESS, AND IRREGULARITY. THE NOTORIOUS WANTONNESS OF THEIR WOMEN.

I must not omit an account of the conduct[8] also of the heretics—how frivolous it is, how worldly, how merely human, without seriousness, without authority, without discipline, as suits their creed. To begin with, it is doubtful who is a catechumen, and who a believer;

they have all access alike, they hear alike, they pray alike—even heathens, if any such happen to come among them. "That which is holy they will cast to the dogs, and their pearls," although (to be sure) they are not real ones, "they will fling to the swine."[9] Simplicity they will have to consist in the overthrow of discipline, attention to which on our part they call brotherly.[10] Peace also they huddle up[11] anyhow with all comers; for it matters not to them, however different be their treatment of subjects, provided only they can conspire together to storm the citadel of the one only Truth. All are puffed up, all offer you knowledge. Their catechumens are perfect before they are full-taught.[12] The very women of these heretics, how wanton they are! For they are bold enough to teach, to dispute, to enact exorcisms, to undertake[13] cures—it may be even to baptize.[14] Their ordinations, are carelessly administered,[15] capricious, changeable.[16] At one time they put *novices* in office; at another time, men who are bound to some secular employment;[17] at another, persons who have apostatized from us, to bind them by vainglory, since they cannot by the truth. Nowhere is promotion easier than in the camp of rebels, where the mere fact of being there is a foremost service.[18] And so it comes to pass that to-day one man is their bishop, to-morrow another; to-day he is a deacon who to-morrow is a reader; to-day he is a presbyter who to-morrow is a layman. For even on laymen do they impose the functions of priesthood.

CHAP. XLII.—HERETICS WORK TO PULL DOWN AND TO DESTROY, NOT TO EDIFY AND ELEVATE. HERETICS DO NOT ADHERE EVEN TO THEIR OWN TRADITIONS, BUT HARBOUR DISSENT EVEN FROM THEIR OWN FOUNDERS.

But what shall I say concerning the ministry of the word, since they make it their business not to convert the heathen, but to subvert our people? This is rather the glory which they catch at, to compass the fall of those who stand, not the raising of those who are down. Accordingly, since the very work which they purpose to themselves comes not from the building up of their own society, but from the demolition of the truth, they undermine our edifices, that they may erect their own. Only

---

[1] "Et sub gladio redimit coronam" is the text of this obscure sentence, which seems to allude to a pretended *martyrdom.* Compare Tertullian's tract, *de Corona*, last chapter.
[2] The *Flamen Dialis.* See Tertullian's tract, *ad Uxorem*, i. 7.
[3] [*Corruptio optimi pessima.* Compare the surprising parallels of M. Huc between debased Christianity and the Paganism of Thibet, etc. *Souvenirs d'un voyage*, etc. Hazlitt's translation, 1867.]
[4] Morositatem Illam. [He refers to the minute and vexatious ordinances complained of by St. Peter (Acts xiv. 10,) which Latin Christianity has ten-folded, in his name.]
[5] Gestiit.
[6] Attemperare.
[7] i.e., the Scriptures of the New Testament.
[8] Conversationis.

[9] See Matt. vii. 6.
[10] Lenocinium. "Pandering" is Archdeacon Dodgson's word.
[11] Miscent.
[12] Edocti.
[13] Repromittere.
[14] Compare Tertullian's tract, *de Bapt.* i. and *de Veland. Virg.* viii. [Also, Epiphan. iv. p. 453, Ed. Oehler.]
[15] Temerariæ.
[16] They were constantly changing their ministers. It was a saying of the heretics, "Alius hodie episcopus, cras alius" (Rigalt.).
[17] Sæculo obstrictos.
[18] Promereri est.

deprive them of the law of Moses, and the prophets, and the divinity of the Creator, and they have not another objection to talk about. The consequence is, that they more easily accomplish the ruin of standing houses than the erection of fallen ruins. It is only when they have such objects in view that they show themselves humble and bland and respectful. Otherwise they know no respect even for their own leaders. Hence it is [supposed] that schisms seldom happen among heretics, because, even when they exist, they are not obvious.[1] Their very unity, however,[2] is schism. I am greatly in error if they do not amongst themselves swerve even from their own regulations, forasmuch as every man, just as it suits his own temper, modifies the traditions he has received after the same fashion as the man who handed them down did, when he moulded them according to his own will. The progress of the matter is an acknowledgment at once of its character and of the manner of its birth. That was allowable to the Valentinians which had been allowed to Valentinus; that was also fair for the Marcionites which had been done by Marcion—even to innovate on the faith, as was agreeable to their own pleasure. In short, all heresies, when throughly looked into, are detected harbouring dissent in many particulars even from their own founders. The majority of them have not even churches.[3] Motherless, houseless, creedless, outcasts, they wander about in their own essential worthlessness.[4]

CHAP. XLIII.—LOOSE COMPANY PREFERRED BY HERETICS. UNGODLINESS THE EFFECT OF THEIR TEACHING THE VERY OPPOSITE OF CATHOLIC TRUTH, WHICH PROMOTES THE FEAR OF GOD, BOTH IN RELIGIOUS ORDINANCES AND PRACTICAL LIFE.

It has also been a subject of remark, how extremely frequent is the intercourse which heretics hold with magicians, with mountebanks, with astrologers, with philosophers; and the reason is,[5] that they are men who devote themselves to curious questions. "Seek, and ye shall find," is everywhere in their minds. Thus, from the very nature of their conduct, may be estimated the quality of their faith. In their discipline we have an index of their doctrine. They say that God is not to be feared; therefore all things are in their

view free and unchecked. Where, however is God not feared, except where He *is* not? Where God is not, there truth also is not. Where there is no truth, then, naturally enough, there is also such a discipline as theirs. But where God is, there exists "the fear of God, which is the beginning of wisdom."[6] Where the fear of God is, there is seriousness, an honourable and yet thoughtful[7] diligence, as well as an anxious carefulness and a well-considered admission (to the sacred ministry)[8] and a safely-guarded[9] communion, and promotion after good service, and a scrupulous submission (to authority), and a devout attendance,[10] and a modest gait, and a united church, and God *in* all things.

CHAP. XLIV.—HERESY LOWERS RESPECT FOR CHRIST, AND DESTROYS ALL FEAR OF HIS GREAT JUDGMENT. THE TENDENCY OF HERETICAL TEACHING ON THIS SOLEMN ARTICLE OF THE FAITH. THE PRESENT TREATISE AN INTRODUCTION TO CERTAIN OTHER ANTI-HERETICAL WORKS OF OUR AUTHOR.

These evidences, then, of a stricter discipline existing among us, are an additional proof of truth, from which no man can safely turn aside, who bears in mind that future judgment, when "we must all stand before the judgment-seat of Christ,"[11] to render an account of our faith itself before all things. What, then, will they say who shall have defiled it, even the virgin which Christ committed to them with the adultery of heretics? I suppose they will allege that no injunction was ever addressed to them by Him or by His apostles concerning depraved[12] and perverse doctrines assailing them,[13] or about their avoiding and abhorring the same. (He and His apostles, perhaps,) will acknowledge[14] that the blame rather lies with themselves and their disciples, in not having given us previous warning and instruction! They[15] will, besides, add a good deal respecting the high authority of each doctor of heresy,—how that these mightily strengthened belief in their own doctrine; how that they raised the dead,

---

[1] Non parent.
[2] Enim. [E.g. The Trent system of Unity, alas! is of this sort.]
[3] Hence the saying, "Wasps make combs, so Marcionites make churches" (see our *Anti-Marcion*, p. 187); describing the strangeness and uselessness of the societies, not (as Gibbon said) their number (Dodgson).
[4] Sua in vilitate. Another reading, pronounced corrupt by Oehler, has "quasi sibi latæ vagantur," *q.d.* "All for themselves, as it were, they wander" etc. (Dodgson).
[5] Scilicet.

[6] Ps. cxi. 10; Prov. i. 7.
[7] Attonita, as if in fear that it might go wrong (Rigalt.).
[8] In contrast to the opposite fault of the heresies exposed above.
[9] Deliberata, where the character was *well weighed* previous to admission to the eucharist.
[10] Apparitio, the duty and office of an *apparitor*, or attendant on men of higher rank, whether in church or state.
[11] 2 Cor. v. 10.
[12] Scævis.
[13] Futuris.
[14] It seems to us, that this is the force of the strong irony, indicated by the "credo," which pervades this otherwise unintelligible passage. Dodgson's version seems untenable: "Let them (the heretics) acknowledge that the fault is with themselves rather than with those who prepared us so long beforehand."
[15] Christ and His apostles, as before, in continuation of the strong irony.

restored the sick, foretold the future, that so they might deservedly be regarded as apostles. As if this caution were not also in the written record: that many should come who were to work even the greatest miracles, in defence of the deceit of their corrupt preaching. So, forsooth, they will deserve to be forgiven! If, however, any, being mindful of the writings and the denunciations of the Lord and the apostles, shall have stood firm in the integrity of the faith, I suppose *they* will run great risk of missing pardon, when the Lord answers: I plainly forewarned you that there should be teachers of false doctrine in my name, as well as that of the prophets and apostles also; and to my own disciples did I give a charge, that they should preach the same things to you. But as for you, it was not, of course, to be supposed[1] that you would believe me! I once gave the gospel and the doctrine of the said rule (of life and faith) to my apostles; but afterwards it was my pleasure to make considerable changes in it! I had promised a resurrection, even of the flesh; but, on second thoughts, it struck me[2] that I might not be able to keep my promise! I had shown my-

self to have been born of a virgin; but this seemed to me afterwards to be a discreditable thing.[3] I had said that He was my Father, who is the Maker of the sun and the showers; but another and better father has adopted me! I had forbidden you to lend an ear to heretics; but in this I erred! Such (blasphemies), it is possible,[4] do enter the minds of those who go out of the right path,[5] and who do not defend[6] the true faith from the danger which besets it. On the present occasion, indeed, our treatise has rather taken up a general position against heresies, (showing that they must) all be refuted on definite, equitable, and necessary rules, without[7] any comparison with the Scriptures. For the rest, if God in His grace permit, we shall prepare answers to certain of these heresies in separate treatises.[8] To those who may devote their leisure in reading through these (pages), in the belief of the truth, be peace, and the grace of our God Jesus Christ for ever.[9]

[3] Turpe.
[4] Capit.
[5] Exorbitant.
[6] Cavent.
[7] This sense comes from the "repellendas" and the "a collatione Scripturarum."
[8] Specialiter. He did this, indeed, in his treatises against Marcion, Hermogenes, the Valentinians, Praxeas, and others. [These are to follow in this Series. Kaye (p. 47) justly considered this sentence as proving the *De Præscript.* a preface to all his treatises against particular heresies.]
[9] Elucidation V.

[1] This must be the force of a sentence which is steeped in irony: "Scilicet cum vos non crederetis." We are indebted to Oehler for restoring the sentence thus.
[2] Recogitavi.

ELUCIDATIONS.

I.

(Prescription, Chap. I., p. 243, *Supra.*)

In adopting this expression from the Roman Law, Tertullian has simply puzzled beginners to get at his idea. Nor do they learn much when it is called a *demurrer,* which, if I comprehend the word as used in law-cases, is a rejoinder to the testimony of the other parts, amounting to—"Well, what of it? It does not prove your case." Something like this is indeed in Tertullian's use of the term *præscription;* but Dr. Holmes furnishes what seems to me the best explanation, (though he only half renders it,) "the Prescriptive Rule against Heresies." In word, it means "*the Rule of Faith* asserted against Heresies." And his practical point is, it is useless to discuss Scripture with convicted (Titus, iii. 10, 11,) heretics; every one of them is ready with "his psalm, his doctrine, his interpretation," and you may argue fruitlessly till Doomsday. But bring them to the test of (*Quod Semper,* etc.), the apostolic *præscription,* (I. Cor. xi. 16).—*We have no such custom neither the Churches of God.* State this *Rule of Faith,* viz. Holy Scripture, as interpreted from the apostolic day, proves the doctrine or custom a *novelty;* then it has no foundation, and even if it be harmless, it cannot be innocently professed against the order and peace of the churches.

II.

(Semler, cap. x., note 15, p. 248.)

The extent to which Bp. Kaye has stretched his notice of this critic is to be accounted for by the fact that, for a time, the German School of the last century exerted a sad influence in England. In early life Dr. Pusey came near to being led away by it, and Hugh James Rose was raised up to resist it. Semler lived (at Halle and elsewhere) from A.D. 1725 to 1791. Kahnis in his invaluable manual, named below, thus speaks of his Patristic theories: "The history of the Kingdom of God became, under his hands, a world of atoms, which crossed each other as chaotically as the masses of notes which lay heaped up in the memory of Semler. . . . Under his pragmatical touches the halo of the martyrs faded, etc." *Internal Hist. of German Protestantism* (since *circa* 1750,) by Ch. Fred. Aug. Kahnis, D.D. (Lutheran) Professor at Leipzig. Translated. T. and F. Clark, Edinburgh, 1856.

III.

(Peter, cap. xxii. note 6, p. 253.)

In the treatise of Cyprian, *De Unitate*, we shall have occasion to speak fully on this interesting point. The reference to Kaye may suffice, here. But, since the inveterate confusion of all that is said of Peter with all that is claimed by a modern bishop for himself promotes a false view of this passage, it may be well to note (1) that St. Peter's name is expounded by himself (I. Peter, ii. 4, 5,) so as to make Christ the Rock and *all believers* "lively stones"—or *Peters*—by faith in Him. St. Peter is often called *the rock*, most justly, in this sense, by a rhetorical play on his name: Christ the Rock and all believers "*lively stones*," being cemented with Him by the Spirit. But, (2.) this *specialty* of St. Peter, as such, belongs to him (*Cephas*) only. (3.) So far as transmitted it belongs to no particular See. (4.) The claim of Rome is disproved by *Præscription*. (5.) Were it otherwise, it would not justify that See in making new articles of Faith. (6.) Nor in its Schism with the East. (7.) When it restores St. Peter's Doctrine and Holiness, to the Latin Churches, there will be no quarrel about pre-eminence. Meantime, Rome's *fallibility* is expressly taught in Romans xi. 18–21.

IV.

(The Apostles, cap. xxv. p. 254.)

Nothing less than a new incarnation of Christ and a new commission to new apostles can give us anything new in religion. This *præscription* is our Catholic answer to the Vatican oracles of our own time. These give us a new revelation, prefacing the Gospels (1) by defining the *immaculate conception* of Mary in the womb of her mother; and (2) adding a new chapter to the Acts of the Apostles, in defining the infallibility of a single bishop.

Clearly, had Tertullian known anything of this last dogma of Latin Novelty, he would not have taken the trouble to write this treatise. He would have said to heretics, We can neither discuss Scripture nor Antiquity with you. Rome is the touchstone of dogma, and to its bishop we refer you.

V.

(Truth and Peace, cap. xliv. p. 265.)

The famous appeal of Bishop Jewel, known as "the Challenge at Paul's Cross," which he made in a sermon preached there on Passion Sunday, A.D. 1560, is an instance of "Præscription against heresies," well worthy of being recalled, in a day which has seen Truth and Peace newly sacrificed to the ceaseless innovations of Rome. It is as follows:—"If any learned man of all our adversaries, or, if all the learned men that be alive, be able to bring *any one sufficient sentence* out of any old Catholic doctor or father; or out of any old general Council; or out of the Holy Scriptures of God;[1] or, any *one example* of the primitive Church, whereby it may be clearly and plainly proved, that—1. There was any private mass in the whole world at that time, for the space of six hundred years after Christ; or that—2. There was then any communion ministered unto the people under one kind; or that—3. The people had their common prayers, then, in a strange tongue that they understood not; or that—4. The bishop of Rome was then called an universal bishop, or the head of the universal Church; or that—5. The people was then taught to believe that Christ's body is really, substantially, corporally, carnally or naturally in the Sacrament; or that—6. His body is, or may be, in a thousand places or more, at one time; or that—7. The priest did then hold up the Sacrament over his head; or that—8. The people did then fall down and worship it with godly honour; or that—9. The Sacrament was then, or now ought to be, hanged up under a canopy; or that—10. In the Sacrament after the words of consecration there remaineth only the *accidents* and shews, without the *substance* of bread and wine; or that—11. The priest then divided the Sacrament in three parts and afterwards received himself, alone; or that—12. Whosoever had said the Sacrament is a pledge, a token, or a remembrance of Christ's body, had therefore been judged a heretic; or that—13. It was lawful, then, to have thirty, twenty, fifteen, ten, or five masses said in one Church, in one day; or that—14. Images were then set up in churches to the intent the people might worship them; or that—15. The lay people was then forbidden to read the word of God, in their own tongue:

"If any man alive be able to prove any of these articles, by any one clear or plain clause or sentence, either of the Scriptures, or of the old doctors, or of any old General Council, or by any Example of the Primitive Church; I promise, then, that I will give over and subscribe unto him."

All this went far beyond the concession of *præscription* which makes little of *any one saying of any one Father*, and demands the general consent of Antiquity; but, it is needless to say that Jewel's challenge has remained unanswered for more than three hundred years, and so it will be to all Eternity

With great erudition Jewel enlarged his propositions and maintained all his points. See his works, vol. I., p. 20 *et seqq.* Cambridge University Press, 1845.

---

[1] It must be remembered that an appeal to Scripture lies behind Tertullian's *Præscription :* only he will not discuss Holy Scripture with heretics.

II.

THE FIVE BOOKS AGAINST MARCION.

[TRANSLATED BY DR. HOLMES.]

DEDICATION.

To the Right Rev. the Lord Bishop of Chester.

My Dear Lord,

I am gratified to have your permission to dedicate this volume to your Lordship. It is the fruit of some two years' leisure labour. Every man's occupation spares to him some λείψανα χρόνου; and thirty years ago you taught me, at Oxford, how to husband these opportunities in the pleasant studies of Biblical and Theological Science. For that and many other kindnesses I cannot cease to be thankful to you.

But, besides this private motive, I have in your Lordship's own past course an additional incentive for resorting to you on this occasion. You, until lately, presided over the theological studies of our great University; and you have given great encouragement to patristic literature by your excellent edition of the Apostolic Fathers.[1] To whom could I more becomingly present this humble effort to make more generally known the great merits of perhaps the greatest work of the first of the Latin Fathers than to yourself?

I remain, with much respect,

My dear Lord,

Very faithfully yours,

PETER HOLMES.

Mannamead, Plymouth,[2]
March, 1868.

---

[1] [The name of Bishop Jacobson was often introduced in our first volume, in notes to the Apostolic Fathers. He has recently "fallen asleep," after a life of exemplary labour "with good report of all men and of the Truth itself." His learning and piety were adorned by a profound humility, which gave a primitive cast to his character. At the Lambeth Conference, having the honour to sit at his side, I observed his extreme modesty. He rarely rose to speak, though he sometimes honoured me with words in a whisper, which the whole assembly would have rejoiced to hear. Like his great predecessor, Pearson, in many respects, the mere filings and clippings of his thought were gold-dust.]

[2] [Dr. Holmes is described, in the Edinburgh Edition, as "Domestic Chaplain to the Rt. Hon. the Countess of Rothes." He was B. A. (Oxon.) in 1840, and took orders that year. Was Head-Master of Plymouth Grammar School at one time, and among his very valuable and learned works should be mentioned, as very useful to the reader of this series, his Translation of Bull's *Defensio Fidei Nicænæ* (two vols. 8vo. Oxford, 1851), and of the same great author's *Judicium Ecclesiæ Catholicæ*, 8vo. Oxford, 1855.]

PREFACE BY THE TRANSLATOR.[3]

The reader has, in this volume a translation (attempted for the first time in English) of the largest of the extant works of the earliest Latin Fathers. The most important of Tertullian's writings have always been highly valued in the church, although, as was natural from their varied character, for different reasons. Thus his two best-known treatises, *The Apology* and *The Prescription against Heretics*, have divided between them for more than sixteen centuries the admiration of all intelligent readers,—the one for its masterly defence of the Christian religion against its heathen persecutors, and the other for its lucid vindication of the church's rule of faith against its heretical assailants. The present work has equal claims on the reader's appreciation, in respect of those qualities of vigorous thought, close reasoning, terse expression, and earnest purpose, enlivened by sparkling wit and impassioned eloquence, which have always secured for Tertullian, in spite of many drawbacks, the esteem which is given to a great and favourite author. If these books against Marcion have received, as indeed it must be allowed they have, less attention from the general reader than their intrinsic merit deserves, the neglect is mainly due to the fact that the interesting character of their contents is concealed by the usual title-page, which points only to a heresy supposed to be extinct and inapplicable, whether in the materials of its defence or confutation, to any modern circumstances. But many treatises of great authors, which have outlived their literal occasion, retain a value from their collateral arguments, which is not inferior to that effected by their primary subject. Such is the case with the work before us. If Marcionism is in the letter obsolete, there is its spirit still left in the church, which in more ways than one develops its ancient

---

[3] [This preface and the frequent annotations of our author relieve the American editor, save very sparingly, from adding notes of his own.]

characteristics. What these were, the reader will soon discover in this volume; but reference may be made even here, in passing, to that prominent aim of the heresy which gave Tertullian his opportunity of proving the essential coherence of the Old and the New Testaments, and of exhibiting both his great knowledge of the details of Holy Scripture, and his fine intelligence of the progressive nature of God's revelation as a whole. This constitutes the charm of the present volume, which might almost be designated a *Treatise on the Connection between the Jewish and the Christian Scriptures*. How interesting this subject is to earnest men of the present age, is proved by the frequent treatment of it in our religious literature.[1] In order to assist the reader to a more efficient use of this volume, in reference to its copiousness of Scripture illustration, a full *Index of Scriptural Passages* has been drawn up. Another satisfactory result will, it is believed, accompany the reading of this volume, in the evidence which it affords of the venerable catholicity of that system of biblical and dogmatic truth which constitutes the belief of what is called the " *orthodox* " Christian of the present day. Orthodoxy has been impugned of late, as if it had suffered much deterioration in its transmission to us; and an advanced school of thinkers has demanded its reform by a manipulation which they have called " free handling." To such readers, then, as prize the deposit of the Christian creed which they have received, in the light of St. Jude's description, as " *the faith once for all delivered to the saints*," it cannot but prove satisfactory to be able to trace in Tertullian, writing more than sixteen centuries ago, the outlines of their own cherished convictions—held by one who cannot be charged with too great an obsequiousness to traditional authority, and who at the same time possessed honesty, earnestness, and intelligence enough to make him an unexceptionable witness to facts of such a kind. The translator would only add, that he has, in compliance with the wise canon laid down by the editors of this series, endeavoured always to present to the reader the meaning of the author in readable English, keeping as near as idiomatic rules allowed to the sense and even style of the original. Amidst the many well-known difficulties of Tertullian's writings (and his *Anti-Marcion* is not exempt from any of these difficulties,[2]) the translator cannot hope that he has accomplished his labour without mistakes, for which he would beg the reader's indulgence. He has, however, endeavoured to obviate the inconvenience of faulty translation by quoting in foot-notes all words, phrases, and passages which appeared to him difficult.[3] He has also added such notes as seemed necessary to illustrate the author's argument, or to explain any obscure allusions. The translation has been made always from Oehler's edition, with the aid of his scholarly Index Verborum. Use has also been made of Semler's edition, and the *variorum* reprint of the Abbé Migne, the chief result of which recension has been to convince the translator of the great superiority and general excellence of Oehler's edition. When he had completed two-thirds of his work, he happened to meet with the French translation of Tertullian by Mon[r]. Denain, in Genoude's series, *Les Pères de l'Eglise*, published some twenty-five years ago. This version, which runs in fluent language always, is very unequal in its relation to the original: sometimes it has the brevity of an abridgment, sometimes the fulness of a paraphrase. Often does it miss the author's point, and never does it keep his style. The Abbé Migne correctly describes it: " Elegans potius quam fidissimus interpres, qui Africanæ loquelæ asperitatem splendenti ornavit sermone, egregiaque interdum et ad vivum expressa interpretatione recreavit."

---

[1] Two works are worth mentioning in connection with this topic for their succinct and handy form, as well as satisfactory treatment of their argument : Mr. Perowne's Norrisian prize essay, entitled *The Essential Coherence of the Old and New Testaments* (1858), and Sir William Page Wood's recent work, *The Continuity of Scripture*, as declared by the testimony of our Lord, and of the evangelists and apostles.

[2] Bishop Kaye says of Tertullian (page 62) : " He is indeed the harshest and most obscure of writers, and the least capable of being accurately represented in a translation ;" and he quotes the learned Ruhnken's sentence of our author : " Latinitatis certè pessimum auctorem esse aio et confirmo." This is surely much too sweeping. To the careful student Tertullian's style commends itself, by and by, as suited exactly to his subject—as the terse and vigorous expression of terse and vigorous thought. Bishop Butler has been often censured for an awkward style ; whereas it is a fairer criticism to say, that the arguments of the *Analogy* and the *Sermons on Human Nature* have been delivered in the language best suited to their character. This adaptation of style to matter is probably in all great authors a real characteristic of genius. A more just and favourable view is taken of Tertullian's Latin by Niebuhr, *Hist. Rom.* (Schmitz), vol. v. p. 271, and his *Lectures on Ancient Hist.* (Schmitz), vol. ii. p. 54.

[3] He has also, as the reader will observe, endeavoured to distinguish, by the help of type, between the true God and Marcion's god, printing the initials of the former, and of the pronouns referring to Him, in capitals, and those of the latter in small letters. To do this was not always an easy matter, for in many passages the argument amalgamates the two. Moreover, in the earlier portion of the work the translator fears that he may have occasionally neglected to make the distinction.

THE FIVE BOOKS AGAINST MARCION.

Book I.[1]

WHEREIN IS DESCRIBED THE GOD OF MARCION. HE IS SHOWN TO BE UTTERLY WANTING IN ALL THE ATTRIBUTES OF THE TRUE GOD.

CHAP. I.—PREFACE. REASON FOR A NEW WORK. PONTUS LENDS ITS ROUGH CHARACTER TO THE HERETIC MARCION, A NATIVE. HIS HERESY CHARACTERIZED IN A BRIEF INVECTIVE.

WHATEVER in times past[1] we have wrought in opposition to Marcion, is from the present moment no longer to be accounted of.[3] It is a new work which we are undertaking in lieu of the old one.[4] My original tract, as too hurriedly composed, I had subsequently superseded by a fuller treatise. This latter I lost, before it was completely published, by the fraud of a person who was then a brother,[5] but became afterwards an apostate. He, as it happened, had transcribed a portion of it, full of mistakes, and then published it. The necessity thus arose for an amended work; and the occasion of the new edition induced me to make a considerable addition to the treatise. This present text,[6] therefore, of my work—which is the third as superseding[7] the second, but henceforward to be considered the first instead of the third—renders a preface necessary to this issue of the tract itself that no reader may be perplexed, if he should by chance fall in with the various forms of it which are scattered about.

The Euxine Sea, as it is called, is self-contradictory in its nature, and deceptive in its name.[8] As you would not account it hospitable from its situation, so is it severed from our more civilised waters by a certain stigma which attaches to its barbarous character. The fiercest nations inhabit it, if indeed it can be called *habitation*, when life is passed in waggons. They have no fixed abode; their life has[9] no germ of civilisation; they indulge their libidinous desires without restraint, and for the most part naked. Moreover, when they gratify secret lust, they hang up their quivers on their car-yokes,[10] to warn off the curious and rash observer. Thus without a blush do they prostitute their weapons of war. The dead bodies of their parents they cut up with their sheep, and devour at their feasts. They who have not died so as to become food for others, are thought to have died an accursed death. Their women are not by their sex softened to modesty. They uncover the breast, from which they suspend their battle-axes, and prefer warfare to marriage. In their climate, too, there is the same rude nature.[11] The day-time is never clear, the sun never cheerful;[12] the sky is uniformly cloudy; the whole year is wintry; the only wind that blows is the angry North. Waters melt only by fires; their rivers flow not by reason of the ice; their mountains are covered[13] with heaps of snow. All things are torpid, all stiff with cold. Nothing there has the glow[14] of life, but that ferocity which has given to scenic plays their stories of the sacrifices[15] of the Taurians, and the loves[16] of the Colchians, and the torments[17] of the Caucasus. Nothing, however, in Pontus is so barbarous

---

[1] [Written A.D. 207. See Chapter xv. *infra*. In cap. xxix. is the token of Montanism which denotes his impending lapse.]
[2] Retro.
[3] Jam hinc viderit.
[4] Ex vetere.
[5] Fratris.
[6] Stilus.
[7] De.
[8] [Euxine=hospitable. One recalls Shakspeare:
    —" Like to the Pontick Sea
    Whose icy current and compulsive force
    Ne'er feels retiring ebb."—*Othel.*]

[9] Cruda.
[10] De jugo. See Strabo (Bohn's trans.), vol. i. p. 247.
[11] Duritia.
[12] Libens.
[13] Exaggerantur.
[14] Calet.
[15] [*Iphigenia* of Euripides.]
[16] [See the *Medea* of Euripides.]
[17] [*Prometheus* of Æschylus.]

and sad as the fact that Marcion was born there, fouler than any Scythian, more roving than the waggon-life [1] of the Sarmatian, more inhuman than the Massagete, more audacious than an Amazon, darker than the cloud, [2] (of Pontus) colder than its winter, more brittle than its ice, more deceitful than the Ister, more craggy than Caucasus. Nay [3] more, the true Prometheus, Almighty God, is mangled [4] by Marcion's blasphemies. Marcion is more savage than even the beasts of that barbarous region. For what beaver was ever a greater emasculator [5] than he who has abolished the nuptial bond? What Pontic mouse ever had such gnawing powers as he who has gnawed the Gospels to pieces? Verily, O Euxine, thou hast produced a monster more credible to philosophers than to Christians. For the cynic Diogenes used to go about, lantern in hand, at mid-day to find a man; whereas Marcion has quenched the light of his faith, and so lost the God whom he had found. His disciples will not deny that his first faith he held along with ourselves; a letter of his own [6] proves this; so that for the future [7] a heretic may from his case [8] be designated as one who, forsaking that which was prior, afterwards chose out for himself that which was not in times past. [9] For in *as* far as what was delivered in times past and from the beginning will be held as truth, in *so* far will that be accounted heresy which is brought in later. But another brief treatise [10] will maintain this position against heretics, who ought to be refuted even without a consideration of their doctrines, on the ground that they are heretical by reason of the novelty of their opinions. Now, so far as any controversy is to be admitted, I will for the time [11] (lest our compendious principle of novelty, being called in on all occasions to our aid, should be imputed to want of confidence) begin with setting forth our adversary's rule of belief, that it may escape no one what our main contention is to be.

---

[1] Hamaxobio. This Sarmatian clan received its name Ἀμαξόβιοι from its gypsy kind of life.
[2] [I fancy there is point in this singular, the sky of Pontus being always overcast. Cowper says:
"There is but one cloud in the sky,
But that doth the welkin invest," etc.
[3] Quidni.
[4] Lancinatur.
[5] Castrator carnis. See Pliny, *N. H.* viii. 47 (Bohn's trans. vol. ii. p. 297).
[6] Ipsius litteris.
[7] Jam.
[8] Hinc.
[9] Retro.
[10] He alludes to his book *De Præscriptione Hæreticorum.* Was this work then already written? Dr. Allix thinks not. But see Kaye, p. 47.]
[11] Interdum. [Can it be that when all this was written (speaking of *ourselves*) our author had fully lapsed from Communion with the Catholic Church?]

CHAP. II.—MARCION, AIDED BY CERDON, TEACHES A DUALITY OF GODS; HOW HE CONSTRUCTED THIS HERESY OF AN EVIL AND A GOOD GOD.

The heretic of Pontus introduces two Gods, like the twin Symplegades of his own shipwreck: One whom it was impossible to deny, *i.e.* our Creator; and one whom he will never be able to prove, *i.e.* his own *god.* The unhappy man gained [12] the first idea [13] of this conceit from the simple passage of our Lord's saying, which has reference to human beings and not divine ones, wherein He disposes of those examples of a good tree and a corrupt one; [14] how that "the good tree bringeth not forth corrupt fruit, neither the corrupt tree good fruit." Which means, that an honest mind and good faith cannot produce evil deeds, any more than an evil disposition can produce good deeds. Now (like many other persons now-a-days, especially those who have an heretical proclivity), while morbidly brooding [15] over the question of the origin of evil, his perception became blunted by the very irregularity of his researches; and when he found the Creator declaring, "I am He that createth evil," [16] inasmuch as he had already concluded from other arguments, which are satisfactory to every perverted mind, that God is the author of evil, so he now applied to the Creator the figure of the corrupt tree bringing forth evil fruit, that is, moral evil, [17] and then presumed that there ought to be another god, after the analogy of the good tree producing its good fruit. Accordingly, finding in Christ a different disposition, as it were—one of a simple and pure benevolence [18] —differing from the Creator, he readily argued that in his Christ had been revealed a new and strange [19] divinity; and then with a little leaven he leavened the whole lump of the faith, flavouring it with the acidity of his own heresy.

He had, moreover, in one [20] Cerdon an abettor of this blasphemy,—a circumstance which made them the more readily think that they saw most clearly their two gods, blind though they were; for, in truth, they had not seen the one God with soundness of faith. [21] To men of diseased vision even one lamp looks like many. One of his gods, therefore, whom he was obliged to acknowledge, he destroyed by defaming his attributes in the

---

[12] Passus.
[13] Instinctum.
[14] St. Luke, vi. 43 sq.
[15] Languens.
[16] Isa. xlv. 7.
[17] Mala.
[18] [This purely good or *goodish* divinity is an idea of the Stoics. *De Præscript.* chap. 7.]
[19] Hospitam.
[20] Quendam. [See Irenæus, Vol. I. p. 352, this Series.]
[21] Integre.

matter of evil; the other, whom he laboured so hard to devise, he constructed, laying his foundation[1] in the principle of good. In what articles[2] he arranged these natures, we show by our own refutations of them.

CHAP. III.—THE UNITY OF GOD. HE IS THE SUPREME BEING, AND THERE CANNOT BE A SECOND SUPREME.

The principal, and indeed[3] the whole, contention lies in the point of *number:* whether two Gods may be admitted, by poetic licence (if they must be),[4] or pictorial fancy, or by the third process, as we must now add,[5] of heretical pravity. But the Christian verity has distinctly declared this principle, "God is not, if He is not one;" because we more properly believe that that has no existence which is not as it ought to be. In order, however, that you may know that God is one, ask what God is, and you will find Him to be not otherwise than one. So far as a human being can form a definition of God, I adduce one which the conscience of all men will also acknowledge,—that God is the great Supreme, existing in eternity, unbegotten, unmade, without beginning, without end. For such a condition as this must needs be ascribed to that eternity which makes God to be the great Supreme, because for such a purpose as this is this very attribute[6] in God; and so on as to the other qualities: so that God is the great Supreme in form and in reason, and in might and in power.[7] Now, since all are agreed on this point (because nobody will deny that God is in some sense[8] the great Supreme, except the man who shall be able to pronounce the opposite opinion, that God is but some inferior being, in order that he may deny God by robbing Him of an attribute of God), what must be the condition of the great Supreme Himself? Surely it must be that nothing is equal to Him, *i.e.* that there is no other great supreme; because, if there were, He would have an equal; and if He had an equal, He would be no longer the great Supreme, now that the condition and (so to say) our law, which permits nothing to be equal to the great Supreme, is subverted. That Being, then, which is the great Supreme, must needs be *unique*,[9] by having no equal, and so not ceasing to be

the great Supreme. Therefore He will not otherwise exist than by the condition whereby He has His being; that is, by His absolute uniqueness. Since, then, God is the great Supreme, our *Christian* verity has rightly declared,[10] "God is not, if He is not one." Not as if we doubted His being God, by saying, He is not, if He is not one; but because we define Him, in whose being we thoroughly believe, to be that without which He is not God; that is to say, the great Supreme. But then[11] the great Supreme must needs be unique. This Unique Being, therefore, will be God—not otherwise God than as the great Supreme; and not otherwise the great Supreme than as having no equal; and not otherwise having no equal than as being Unique. Whatever other god, then, you may introduce, you will at least be unable to maintain his divinity under any other guise,[12] than by ascribing to him too the property of Godhead—both eternity and supremacy over all. How, therefore, can two great Supremes co-exist, when this is the attribute of the Supreme Being, to have no equal,—an attribute which belongs to One alone, and can by no means exist in two?

CHAP. IV.—DEFENCE OF THE DIVINE UNITY AGAINST OBJECTION. NO ANALOGY BETWEEN HUMAN POWERS AND GOD'S SOVEREIGNTY. THE OBJECTION OTHERWISE UNTENABLE, FOR WHY STOP AT TWO GODS?

But some one may contend that two great Supremes may exist, distinct and separate in their own departments; and may even adduce, as an example, the kingdoms of the world, which, though they are so many in number, are yet supreme in their several regions. Such a man will suppose that human circumstances are always comparable with divine ones. Now, if this mode of reasoning be at all tolerable, what is to prevent our introducing, I will not say a third god or a fourth, but as many as there are kings of the earth? Now it is God that is in question, whose main property it is to admit of no comparison with Himself. Nature itself, therefore, if not an Isaiah, or rather God speaking by Isaiah, will deprecatingly ask, "To whom will ye liken me?"[13] Human circumstances may perhaps be compared with divine ones, but they may not be with God. God is one thing, and what belongs to God is another thing. Once more:[14] you who apply the example of a king, as a great

---

[1] Præstruendo.
[2] Or sections.
[3] Et exinde.
[4] Si Forte.
[5] Jam.
[6] Of eternity.
[7] We subjoin the original of this difficult passage: Hunc enim statum æternitati censendum, quæ summum magnum deum efficiat, dum hoc est in deo ipsa, atque ita et cetera, ut sit deus summum magnum et forma et ratione et vi et potestate.
[8] Quid.
[9] Unicus. [Alone of His kind.]

[10] As its first principle.
[11] Porro.
[12] Forma.
[13] Isa. xl. 18, 25.
[14] Denique.

supreme, take care that you can use it properly. For although a king is supreme on his throne next to God, he is still inferior to God; and when he is compared with God, he will be dislodged[1] from that great supremacy which is transferred to God. Now, this being the case, how will you employ in a comparison with God an object as your example, which fails[2] in all the purposes which belong to a comparison? Why, when supreme power among kings cannot evidently be multifarious, but only unique and singular, is an exception made in the case of Him (of all others)[3] who is King of kings, and (from the exceeding greatness of His power, and the subjection of all other ranks[4] to Him) the very summit,[5] as it were, of dominion? But even in the case of rulers of that other form of government, where they one by one preside in a union of authority, if with their petty[6] prerogatives of royalty, so to say, they be brought on all points[7] into such a comparison with one another as shall make it clear which of them is superior in the essential features[8] and powers of royalty, it must needs follow that the supreme majesty will redound[9] to one alone,— all the others being gradually, by the issue of the comparison, removed and excluded from the supreme authority. Thus, although, when spread out in several hands, supreme authority seems to be multifarious, yet in its own powers, nature, and condition, it is unique. It follows, then, that if two gods are compared, as two kings and two supreme authorities, the concentration of authority must necessarily, according to the meaning of the comparison, be conceded to one of the two; because it is clear from his own superiority that he is the supreme, his rival being now vanquished, and proved to be not the greater, however great. Now, from this failure of his rival, the other is unique in power, possessing a certain solitude, as it were, in his singular pre-eminence. The inevitable conclusion at which we arrive, then, on this point is this: either we must deny that God is the great Supreme, which no wise man will allow himself to do; or say that God has no one else with whom to share His power.

CHAP. V.—THE DUAL PRINCIPLE FALLS TO THE GROUND; PLURALITY OF GODS, OF WHATEVER NUMBER, MORE CONSISTENT. ABSURDITY AND INJURY TO PIETY RESULTING FROM MARCION'S DUALITY.

But on what principle did Marcion confine his supreme powers to *two*? I would first ask, If there be two, why not more? Because if *number* be compatible with the substance of Deity, the richer you make it in number the better. Valentinus was more consistent and more liberal; for he, having once imagined two deities, Bythos and Sige,[10] poured forth a swarm of divine essences, a brood of no less than thirty Æons, like the sow of Æneas.[11] Now, whatever principle refuses to admit several supreme begins, the same must reject even two, for there is plurality in the very lowest number after one. After unity, *number* commences. So, again, the same principle which could admit two could admit more. After two, *multitude* begins, now that one is exceeded. In short, we feel that reason herself expressly[12] forbids the belief in more gods than one, because the self-same rule lays down one God and not two, which declares that God must be a Being to which, as the great Supreme, nothing is equal; and that Being to which nothing is equal must, moreover, be unique. But further, what can be the use or advantage in supposing two supreme beings, two co-ordinate[13] powers? What numerical difference could there be when two equals differ not from one? For that thing which is the same in two is one. Even if there were several equals, all would be just as much one, because, as equals, they would not differ one from another. So, if of two beings neither differs from the other, since both of them are on the supposition[14] supreme, both being gods, neither of them is more excellent than the other; and so, having no pre-eminence, their numerical distinction[15] has no reason in it. Number, moreover, in the Deity ought to be consistent with the highest reason, or else His worship would be brought into doubt. For consider[16] now, if, when I saw two Gods before me (who, being both Supreme Beings, were equal to each other), I were to worship them both, what should I be doing? I should be much afraid that the abundance of my homage would be deemed superstition rather than piety. Because, as both of them are so equal and are both included in either of the

[1] Excidet.
[2] Amittitur. "Tertullian" (who thinks lightly of the analogy of earthly monarchs) "ought rather to have contended that the illustration strengthened his argument. In each kingdom there is only one supreme power; but the universe is God's kingdom: there is therefore only one Supreme Power in the universe."—BP. KAYE, *On the Writings of Tertullian*, Third edition, p. 453, note 2.
[3] Scilicet.
[4] Graduum.
[5] Culmen.
[6] Minutalibus regnis.
[7] Undique.
[8] Substantiis.
[9] Eliquetur.

[10] Depth and silence.
[11] See Virgil, *Æneid*, viii. 43, etc.
[12] Ipso termino.
[13] Paria.
[14] Jam.
[15] Numeri sui.
[16] Ecce.

two, I might serve them both acceptably in only one; and by this very means I should attest their equality and unity, provided that I worshipped them mutually the one in the other, because in the one both are *present* to me. If I were to worship one of the two, I should be equally conscious of seeming to pour contempt on the uselessness of a numerical distinction, which was superfluous, because it indicated no difference; in other words, I should think it the safer course to worship neither of these two Gods than one of them with some scruple of conscience, or both of them to none effect.

CHAP. VI.—MARCION UNTRUE TO HIS THEORY. HE PRETENDS THAT HIS GODS ARE EQUAL, BUT HE REALLY MAKES THEM DIVERSE. THEN, ALLOWING THEIR DIVINITY, DENIES THIS DIVERSITY.

Thus far our discussion seems to imply that Marcion makes his two gods equal. For while we have been maintaining that God ought to be believed as the one only great Supreme Being, excluding from Him every possibility[1] of equality, we have treated of these topics on the assumption of two equal *Gods;* but nevertheless, by teaching that *no* equals can exist according to the law[2] of the Supreme Being, we have sufficiently affirmed the impossibility that *two* equals should exist. For the rest, however,[3] we know full well[4] that Marcion makes his gods unequal: one judicial, harsh, mighty in war; the other mild, placid, and simply[5] good and excellent. Let us with similar care consider also this aspect of the question, whether *diversity* (in the Godhead) can at any rate contain two, since *equality* therein failed to do so. Here again the same rule about the great Supreme will protect us, inasmuch as it settles[6] the entire condition of the Godhead. Now, challenging, and in a certain sense arresting[7] the meaning of our adversary, who does not deny that the Creator is God, I most fairly object[8] against him that he has no room for any diversity in his gods, because, having once confessed that they are on a par,[9] he cannot now pronounce them different; not indeed that human beings may not be very different under the same designation, be because the Divine Being can be neither said nor believed to be God, except as the great Supreme. Since, therefore, he is

obliged to acknowledge that the God whom he does not deny is the great Supreme, it is inadmissible that he should predicate of the Supreme Being such a diminution as should subject Him to another Supreme Being. For He ceases (to be Supreme), if He becomes subject to any. Besides, it is not the characteristic of God to cease from any attribute[10] of His divinity—say, from His supremacy. For at this rate the supremacy would be endangered even in Marcion's more powerful god, if it were capable of depreciation in the Creator. When, therefore, two gods are pronounced to be two great Supremes, it must needs follow that neither of them is greater or less than the other, neither of them loftier or lowlier than the other. If you deny[11] him to be God whom you call inferior, you deny[11] the supremacy of this inferior being. But when you confessed both gods to be divine, you confessed then both to be supreme. Nothing will you be able to take away from either of them; nothing will you be able to add. By allowing their divinity, you have denied their diversity.

CHAP. VII.—OTHER BEINGS BESIDES GOD ARE IN SCRIPTURE CALLED GOD. THIS OBJECTION FRIVOLOUS, FOR IT IS NOT A QUESTION OF NAMES. THE DIVINE ESSENCE IS THE THING AT ISSUE. HERESY, IN ITS GENERAL TERMS, THUS FAR TREATED.

But this argument you will try to shake with an objection from the name of God, by alleging that that name is a vague[12] one, and applied to other beings also; as it is written, " God standeth in the congregation of the mighty;[13] He judgeth among the gods." And again, " I have said, Ye are gods."[14] As therefore the attribute of supremacy would be inappropriate to these, although they are called gods, so is it to the Creator. This is a foolish objection; and my answer to it is, that its author fails to consider that quite as strong an objection might be urged against the (superior) god of Marcion: he too is called god, but is not on that account proved to be divine, as neither are angels nor men, the Creator's *handiwork*. If an identity of names affords a presumption in support of equality of condition, how often do worthless menials strut insolently in the names of kings—your Alexanders, Cæsars, and Pompeys![15] This fact,

---

[1] Parilitatem.
[2] Formam.
[3] Alioquin.
[4] Certi (sumus).
[5] Tantummodo.
[6] Vindicet.
[7] Injecta manu detinens.
[8] Præscribo.
[9] Ex æquo deos confessus.

[10] De statu suo.
[11] Nega.
[12] Passivo.
[13] בַּעֲדַתאֵל. Tertullian's version is: *In ecclesia deorum.*
The Vulgate: *In synagoga deorum.*
[14] Ps. lxxxii. 1, 6.
[15] The now less obvious nicknames of " Alex. Darius and Olofernes," are in the text.

however, does not detract from the real attributes of the royal persons. Nay more, the very idols of the Gentiles are called gods. Yet not one of them is divine because he is called a god. It is not, therefore, for the name of god, for its sound or its written form, that I am claiming the supremacy in the Creator, but for the essence [1] to which the name belongs; and when I find that essence alone is unbegotten and unmade—alone eternal, and the maker of all things—it is not to its name, but its state, not to its designation, but its condition, that I ascribe and appropriate the attribute of the supremacy. And so, because the essence to which I ascribe it has come [2] to be called god, you suppose that I ascribe it to the name, because I must needs use a name to express the essence, of which indeed that Being consists who is called God, and who is accounted the great Supreme because of His essence, not from His name. In short, Marcion himself, when he imputes this character to his god, imputes it to the nature,[3] not to the word. That supremacy, then, which we ascribe to God in consideration of His essence, and not because of His name, ought, as we maintain, to be equal [4] in both the beings who consist of that substance for which the name of God is given; because, in as far as they are called gods (i.e. supreme beings, on the strength, of course, of their unbegotten and eternal, and therefore great and supreme essence), in so far the attribute of being the great Supreme cannot be regarded as less or worse in one than in another great Supreme. If the happiness, and sublimity, and perfection [5] of the Supreme Being shall hold good of Marcion's god, it will equally so of ours; and if not of ours, it will equally not *hold* of Marcion's. Therefore two supreme beings will be neither equal nor unequal: not equal, because the principle which we have just expounded, that the Surpeme Being admits of no comparison with Himself, forbids it; not unequal, because another principle meets us respecting the Supreme Being, that He is capable of no diminution. So, Marcion, you are caught [6] in the midst of your own Pontic tide. The waves of truth overwhelm you on every side. You can neither set up equal gods nor unequal ones. For there are not two; so far as the question of *number* is properly concerned. Although the whole matter of the two gods is at issue, we have yet confined our discussion to certain bounds, within

which we shall now have to contend about separate peculiarities.

CHAP. VIII.—SPECIFIC POINTS. THE NOVELTY OF MARCION'S GOD FATAL TO HIS PRETENSIONS. GOD IS FROM EVERLASTING, HE CANNOT BE IN ANY WISE NEW.

In the first place, how arrogantly do the Marcionites build up their stupid system,[7] bringing forward a new god, as if we were ashamed of the old one! So schoolboys are proud of their new shoes, but their old master beats their strutting vanity out of them. Now when I hear of a new god,[8] who, in the old world and in the old time and under the old god was unknown and unheard of; whom, (*accounted as* no one through such long centuries back, and ancient in men's very ignorance of him),[9] a certain "Jesus Christ," and none else revealed; whom Christ revealed, *they say* —Christ himself new, *according to them, even,* in ancient names—I feel grateful for this conceit [10] of theirs. For by its help I shall at once be able to prove the heresy of their tenet of a new deity. It will turn out to be such a novelty [11] as has made gods even for the heathen by some new and yet again and ever new title [12] for each several deification. What new god is there, except a false one? Not even Saturn will be proved to be a god by all his ancient fame, because it was a novel pretence which some time or other produced even him, when it first gave him godship.[13] On the contrary, living and perfect [14] Deity has its origin [15] neither in novelty nor in antiquity, but in its own true nature. Eternity has no time. It is itself all time. It acts; it cannot then suffer. It cannot be born, therefore it lacks age. God, if old, forfeits the eternity that is to come; if new, the eternity which is past.[16] The newness bears witness to a beginning; the oldness threatens an end. God, moreover, is as independent of beginning and end as He is of time, which is only the arbiter and measurer of a beginning and an end.

---

[1] Substantiæ.
[2] Vocari obtinuit.
[3] Statum.
[4] Ex pari.
[5] Integritas.
[6] Hæsisti.

[7] Stuporem suum.
[8] [Cap. xix. *infra*.]
[9] The original of this obscure passage is: "Novum igitur audiens deum, in vetere mundo et in vetere ævo et sub vetere deo inauditum quem tantis retro seculis neminem, et ipsa ignorantia antiquum, quidam Jesus Christus, et ille in veteribus nominibus novus, revelaverit, nec alius antehac." The harsh expression, "quidam Jesus Christus," bears, of course, a sarcastic reference to the capricious and inconsistent novelty which Marcion broached in his heresy about Christ. [By some slight change in punctuation and arrangement, I have endeavoured to make it a little clearer.]
[10] Gloriæ. [*Qu.* boast?]
[11] Hæc erit novitas quæ.
[12] Novo semper ac novo titulo.
[13] Consecravit.
[14] Germana.
[15] Censetur. A frequent meaning in Tertullian. See *Apol.* 7 and 12.
[16] We cannot preserve the terseness of the Latin · Deus, si est vetus, non erit ; si est novus, non fuit.

CHAP. IX.—MARCION'S GNOSTIC PRETENSIONS VAIN, FOR THE TRUE GOD IS NEITHER UNKNOWN NOR UNCERTAIN. THE CREATOR, WHOM HE OWNS TO BE GOD, ALONE SUPPLIES AN INDUCTION, BY WHICH TO JUDGE OF THE TRUE GOD.

Now I know full well by what perceptive faculty they boast of their new god; even their knowledge.[1] It is, however, this very discovery of a novel thing—so striking to common minds—as well as the natural gratification which is inherent in novelty, that I wanted to refute, and thence further to challenge a proof of this unknown god. For him whom by their knowledge[2] they present to us as new, they prove to have been unknown previous to that knowledge. Let us keep within the strict limits and measure of our argument. Convince me there could have been an unknown god. I find, no doubt,[3] that altars have been lavished on unknown gods; that, however, is the idolatry of Athens. And on uncertain gods; but that, too, is only Roman superstition. Furthermore, uncertain gods are not well known, because no certainty about them exists; and because of this uncertainty they are therefore unknown. Now, which of these two titles shall we carve for Marcion's god? Both, I suppose, as for a being who is still *uncertain*, and was formerly *unknown*. For inasmuch as the Creator, being a known God, caused him to be unknown; so, as being a certain God, he made him to be uncertain. But I will not go so far out of my way, as to say:[4] If God was unknown and concealed, He was overshadowed in such a region of darkness, as must have been itself new and unknown, and be even now likewise uncertain—some immense region indeed, one undoubtedly greater than the God whom it concealed. But I will briefly state my subject, and afterwards most fully pursue it, premising that God neither could have been, nor ought to have been, unknown. *Could* not have been, because of His greatness; *ought* not to have been, because of His goodness, especially as He is (supposed, by Marcion) more excellent in both these attributes than our Creator. Since, however, I observe that in some points the proof of every new and heretofore unknown god ought, for its test,[5] to be compared to the form of the Creator, it will be my duty[6] first of all to show that this very course is adopted by me in a settled plan,[7] such as I might with greater confidence[8] use in support of my argument. Before every other consideration, (let me ask) how it happens that you,[9] who acknowledge[10] the Creator to be God, and from your knowledge confess Him to be prior in existence, do not know that the other *god* should be examined by you in exactly the same course of investigation which has taught you how to find out a god in the first case? Every prior thing has furnished the rule for the latter. In the present question two gods are propounded, the unknown and the known. Concerning the known there is no[11] question. It is plain that He exists, else He would not be known. The dispute is concerning the unknown god. Possibly he has no existence; because, if he had, he would have been known. Now that which, so long as it is unknown, is an object to be questioned, is an uncertainty so long as it remains thus questionable; and all the while is in this state of uncertainty, it possibly has no existence at all. You have a god who is so far certain, as he is known; and uncertain, as unknown. This being the case, does it appear to you to be justly defensible, that uncertainties should be submitted for proof to the rule, and form, and standard of certainties? Now, if to the subject before us, which is in itself full of uncertainty thus far, there be applied also arguments[12] derived from uncertainties, we shall be involved in such a series of questions arising out of our treatment of these same uncertain arguments, as shall by reason of their uncertainty be dangerous to the faith, and we shall drift into those insoluble questions which the apostle has no affection for. If, again,[13] in things wherein there is found a diversity of condition, they shall prejudge, as no doubt they will,[14] uncertain, doubtful, and intricate points, by the certain, undoubted, and clear sides[15] of their rule, it will probably happen that[16] (those points) will not be submitted to the standard of certainties for determination, as being freed by the diversity of their essential condition[17] from the application of such a standard in all other respects. As, therefore, it is two gods which are the subject of our proposition, their essential condition must be the same in both. For, as concerns their divinity, they are both unbegotten, unmade, eternal. This will be their essential condition. All other points Marcion

---

[1] Agnitione. The distinctive term of the *Gnostic* pretension was the Greek equivalent Γνῶσις.
[2] Agnitione.
[3] Plane.
[4] Non evagabor, ut dicam.
[5] Provocari.
[6] Debebo.
[7] Ratione.
[8] Constantius.
[9] Quale est ut.
[10] Agnoscis.
[11] Vacat.
[12] Argumenta = " proofs."
[13] Sin.
[14] Plane.
[15] Regulæ partibus.
[16] Fortasse an.
[17] Status principalis.

himself seems to have made light of,[1] for he has placed them in a different[2] category. They are subsequent in the order of treatment; indeed, they will not have to be brought into the discussion,[3] since on the essential condition there is no dispute. Now there is this absence of our dispute, because they are both of them gods. Those things, therefore, whose community of condition is evident, will, when brought to a test on the ground of that common condition,[4] have to be submitted, although they are uncertain, to the standard[5] of those certainties with which they are classed in the community of their essential condition, so as on this account to share also in their manner of proof. I shall therefore contend[6] with the greatest confidence that he is not God who is to-day uncertain, because he has been hitherto unknown; for of whomsoever it is evident that he is God, from this very fact it is (equally) evident, that he never has been unknown, and therefore never uncertain.

CHAP. X.—THE CREATOR WAS KNOWN AS THE TRUE GOD FROM THE FIRST BY HIS CREATION. ACKNOWLEDGED BY THE SOUL AND CONSCIENCE OF MAN BEFORE HE WAS REVEALED BY MOSES.

For indeed, as the Creator of all things, He was from the beginning discovered equally with them, they having been themselves manifested that He might become known as God. For although Moses, some long while afterwards, seems to have been the first to introduce the knowledge of[7] the God of the universe in the temple of his writings, yet the birthday of that knowledge must not on that account be reckoned from the Pentateuch. For the volume of Moses does not at all initiate[8] the knowledge of the Creator, but from the first gives out that it is to be traced from Paradise and Adam, not from Egypt and Moses. The greater part, therefore,[9] of the human race, although they knew not even the name of Moses, much less his writings, yet knew the God of Moses; and even when idolatry overshadowed the world with its extreme prevalence, men still spoke of Him separately by His own name as God, and the God of gods, and said, "If God grant," and, "As God pleases," and, "I commend you to God."[10] Reflect, then, whether they knew

Him, of whom they testify that He can do all things. To none of the writings of Moses do they owe this. The soul was before prophecy.[11] From the beginning the knowledge of God is the dowry of the soul, one and the same amongst the Egyptians, and the Syrians, and the tribes of Pontus. For their souls call the God of the Jews their God. Do not, O barbarian heretic, put Abraham before the world. Even if the Creator had been the God of one family, He was yet not later than your god; even in Pontus was He known before him. Take then your standard from Him who came first: from the Certain (must be judged) the uncertain; from the Known the unknown. Never shall God be hidden, never shall God be wanting. Always shall He be understood, always be heard, nay even seen, in whatsoever way He shall wish. God has for His witnesses this whole being of ours, and this universe wherein we dwell. He is thus, because not unknown, proved to be both God and the only One, although another still tries hard to make out his claim.

CHAP. XI.—THE EVIDENCE FOR GOD EXTERNAL TO HIM; BUT THE EXTERNAL CREATION WHICH YIELDS THIS EVIDENCE IS REALLY NOT EXTRANEOUS, FOR ALL THINGS ARE GOD'S. MARCION'S GOD, HAVING NOTHING TO SHOW FOR HIMSELF, NO GOD AT ALL. MARCION'S SCHEME ABSURDLY DEFECTIVE, NOT FURNISHING EVIDENCE FOR HIS NEW GOD'S EXISTENCE, WHICH SHOULD AT LEAST BE ABLE TO COMPETE WITH THE FULL EVIDENCE OF THE CREATOR.

And justly so, they say. For who is there that is less well known by his own (inherent) qualities than by strange[12] ones? No one. Well, I keep to this statement. How could anything be strange[12] to God, to whom, if He were personally existent, nothing would be strange? For this is the attribute of God, that all things are His, and all things belong to Him; or else this question would not so readily be heard from us: What has He to do with things strange to Him?—a point which will be more fully noticed in its proper place. It is now sufficient to observe, that no one is proved to exist to whom nothing is proved to belong. For as the Creator is shown to be God, God without any doubt, from the fact that all things are His, and nothing is strange to Him; so the rival[14] god is seen to be no god, from the circumstance that nothing is his, and all things are therefore strange to

---

[1] Viderit.
[2] In diversitate.
[3] Nec admittentur.
[4] Sub eo.
[5] Formam.
[6] Dirigam.
[7] Dedicasse.
[8] Instituat.
[9] Denique.
[10] See also *De test. anim.* 2, and *De anima*, 41. [Bp. Kaye refers (p. 166.) to Profr. Andrews Norton of Harvard, with great respect: specially to a Note on this usage of the Heathen, in his *Evidences*, etc. *Vol. III.*]

[11] Prophetia, inspired Scripture.
[12] Extraneous.
[13] Extraneum.
[14] Alius.

him. Since, then, the universe belongs to the Creator, I see no room for any other god. All things are full of their Author, and occupied by Him. If in created beings there be any portion of space anywhere void of Deity, the void will be of a false deity clearly.[1] By falsehood the truth is made clear. Why cannot the vast crowd of false gods somewhere find room for Marcion's god? This, therefore, I insist upon, from the character[2] of the Creator, that God must have been known from the works of some world peculiarly His own, both in its human constituents, and the rest of its organic life;[3] when even the error of the world has presumed to call gods those men whom it sometimes acknowledges, on the ground that in every such case something is seen which provides for the uses and advantages of life.[4] Accordingly, this also was believed from the character of God to be a divine function; namely, to teach or point out what is convenient and needful in human concerns. So completely has the authority which has given influence to a false divinity been borrowed from that source, whence it had previously flowed forth to the true one. One stray vegetable[5] at least Marcion's god ought to have produced as his own; so might he be preached up as a new Triptolemus.[6] Or else state some reason which shall be worthy of a God, why he, supposing him to exist, created nothing; because he must, on supposition of his existence, have been a creator, on that very principle on which it is clear to us that our God is no otherwise existent, than as having been the Creator of this universe of ours. For, once for all, the rule[7] will hold good, that they cannot both acknowledge the Creator to be God, and also prove him divine whom they wish to be equally believed in as God, except they adjust him to the standard of Him whom they and all men hold to be God; which is this, that whereas no one doubts the Creator to be God on the express ground of His having made the universe, so, on the self-same ground, no one ought to believe that he also is God who has made nothing—except, indeed, some good reason be forthcoming. And this must needs be limited to one of two: he was either *unwilling* to create, or else *unable*. There is no third reason.[8] Now, that he was unable, is a reason unworthy of God. Whether to have been unwilling to be a worthy one, I want to inquire. Tell me, Marcion, did your

god wish himself to be recognised at any time or not? With what other purpose did he come down from heaven, and preach, and having suffered rise again from the dead, if it were not that he might be acknowledged? And, doubtless, since he was acknowledged, he willed it. For no circumstance could have happened to him, if he had been unwilling. What indeed tended so greatly to the knowledge of himself, as his appearing in the humiliation of the flesh,—a degradation all the lower indeed if the flesh were only illusory?[9] For it was all the more shameful if he, who brought on himself the Creator's curse by hanging on a tree, only pretended the assumption of a bodily substance. A far nobler foundation might he have laid for the knowledge of himself in some evidences of a creation of his own, especially when he had to become known in opposition to Him in whose territory[10] he had remained unknown by any works from the beginning. For how happens it that the Creator, although unaware, as the Marcionites aver, of any god being above Himself, and who used to declare even with an oath that He existed alone, should have guarded by such mighty works the knowledge of Himself, about which, on the assumption of His being alone without a rival, He might have spared Himself all care; while the Superior God, knowing all the while how well furnished in power His inferior rival was, should have made no provision at all towards getting Himself acknowledged? Whereas He ought to have produced works more illustrious and exalted still, in order that He might, after the Creator's standard, both be acknowledged as God from His works, and even by nobler deeds show Himself to be more potent and more gracious than the Creator.

CHAP. XII.—IMPOSSIBILITY OF ACKNOWLEDGING GOD WITHOUT THIS EXTERNAL EVIDENCE[11] OF HIS EXISTENCE. MARCION'S REJECTION OF SUCH EVIDENCE FOR HIS GOD SAVOURS OF IMPUDENCE AND MALIGNITY.

But even if we were able to allow that he exists, we should yet be bound to argue that he is without a cause.[11] For he who had nothing (to show for himself as proof of his existence), would be without a cause, since (such) proof[12] is the whole cause that there exists

---

[1] Plane falsæ vacabit.
[2] Forma.
[3] Proprii sui mundi, et hominis et sæculi.
[4] [Kaye, p. 206.]
[5] Cicerculam.
[6] [—"uncique puer monstrator aratri," Virg. *Georg.* i. 19, and see Heyne's note.]
[7] Præscriptio.
[8] Tertium cessat.

[9] Falsæ. An allusion to the *Docetism* of Marcion.
[10] Apud quem.
[11] The word *cause* throughout this chapter is used in the popular, inaccurate sense, which almost confounds it with *effect*, the "causa cognoscendi," as distinguished from the "causa essendi," the strict *cause*.
[12] The word "*res*" is throughout this argument used strictly by Tertullian; it refers to "*the thing*" made by God—that product of His creative energy which affords to us evidence of His existence. We have translated it "*proof*" for want of a better word.

some person to whom the proof belongs. Now, in *as* far as nothing ought to be without a cause, that is, without a proof (because if it be without a cause, it is all one as if it be not, not having the very proof which is the cause of a thing), in *so* far shall I more worthily believe that God does not exist, than that He exists without a cause. For he is without a cause who has not a cause by reason of not having a proof. God, however, ought not to be without a cause, that is to say, without a proof. Thus, as often as I show that He exists without a cause, although (I allow[1] that) He exists, I do really determine this, that He does not exist; because, if He had existed, He could not have existed altogether without a cause.[2] So, too, even in regard to faith itself, I say that he[3] seeks to obtain it[4] with out cause from man, who is otherwise accustomed to believe in God from the idea he gets of Him from the testimony of His works:[5] (without cause, I repeat,) because he has provided no such proof as that whereby man has acquired the knowledge of God. For although most persons believe in Him, they do not believe at once by unaided reason,[6] without having some token of Deity in works worthy of God. And so upon this ground of inactivity and lack of works he[7] is guilty both of impudence and malignity: of impudence, in aspiring after a belief which is not due to him, and for which he has provided no foundation;[8] of malignity, in having brought many persons under the charge of unbelief by furnishing to them no groundwork for their faith.

CHAP. XIII.—THE MARCIONITES DEPRECIATE THE CREATION, WHICH, HOWEVER, IS A WORTHY WITNESS OF GOD. THIS WORTHINESS ILLUSTRATED BY REFERENCES TO THE HEATHEN PHILOSOPHERS, WHO WERE APT TO INVEST THE SEVERAL PARTS OF CREATION WITH DIVINE ATTRIBUTES.

While we are expelling from this rank (of Deity) a god who has no evidence to show for himself which is so proper and God-worthy as the testimony of the Creator, Marcion's most shameless followers with haughty impertinence fall upon the Creator's works to destroy them. To be sure, say they, the world is a grand work, worthy of a God.[9] Then is the Creator not at all a God? By all means

He is God.[10] Therefore[11] the world is not unworthy of God, for God has made nothing unworthy of Himself; although it was for man, and not for Himself, that He made the world (and) although every work is less than its maker. And yet, if to have been the author of our creation, such as it is, be unworthy of God, how much more unworthy of Him is it to have created absolutely nothing at all!—not even a production which, although unworthy, might yet have encouraged the hope of some better attempt. To say somewhat, then, concerning the alleged[12] unworthiness of this world's fabric, to which among the Greeks also is assigned a name of ornament and grace,[13] not of sordidness, those very professors of wisdom,[14] from whose genius every heresy derives its spirit,[15] called the said unworthy elements divine; as Thales did water, Heraclitus fire, Anaximenes air, Anaximander all the heavenly bodies, Strato the sky and earth, Zeno the air and ether, and Plato the stars, which he calls a fiery kind of gods; whilst concerning the world, when they considered indeed its magnitude, and strength, and power, and honour, and glory,—the abundance, too, the regularity, and law of those individual elements which contribute to the production, the nourishment, the ripening, and the reproduction of all things,—the majority of the philosophers hesitated[16] to assign a beginning and an end to the said world, lest its constituent elements,[17] great as they undoubtedly are, should fail to be regarded as divine,[18] which are objects of worship with the Persian magi, the Egyptian hierophants, and the Indian gymnosophists. The very superstition of the crowd, inspired by the common idolatry, when ashamed of the names and fables of their ancient dead borne by their idols, has recourse to the interpretation of natural objects, and so with much ingenuity cloaks its own disgrace, figuratively reducing Jupiter to a heated substance, and Juno to an aërial one (according to the literal sense of the Greek words);[19] Vesta, in like manner, to fire, and the Muses to waters, and the Great Mother[20] to the earth, mowed as to its crops, ploughed up with lusty arms, and watered

---

[1] The "tanquam sit," in its subjunctive form, seems to refer to the concession indicated at the outset of the chapter.
[2] Omnino sine causa.
[3] Illum, i.e., Marcion's god.
[4] Captare.
[5] Deum ex operum auctoritate formatum.
[6] Non statim ratione, on *a priori* grounds.
[7] i.e., Marcion's god.
[8] Compare Rom. i. 20, a passage which is quite subversive of Marcion's theory.
[9] This is an ironical concession from the Marcionite side

[10] Another concession.
[11] Tertullian's rejoinder.
[12] De isto.
[13] They called it κόσμος.
[14] By *sapientiæ professores* he means the heathen philosophers; see *De Præscript. Hæret.* c. 7.
[15] In his book *adv. Hermogenem*, c. 8, Tertullian calls the philosophers "hæreticorum patriarchæ."
[16] Formidaverint.
[17] Substantiæ.
[18] Dei.
[19] The Greek name of Jupiter, Ζεύς, is here derived from ζέω, ferveo, *I glow*. Juno's name, Ἥρα, Tertullian connects with ἀήρ, the air; παρὰ τὸ ἀὴρ καθ᾽ ὑπέρθεσιν Ἥρα. These names of the two great deities suggest a connection with fire and air.
[20] i.e., Cybele.

with baths.[1] Thus Osiris also, whenever he is buried, and looked for to come to life again, and with joy recovered, is an emblem of the regularity wherewith the fruits of the ground return, and the elements recover life, and the year comes round; as also the lions of Mithras[2] are philosophical sacraments of arid and scorched nature. It is, indeed, enough for me that natural elements, foremost in site and state, should have been more readily regarded as divine than as unworthy of God. I will, however, come down to[3] humbler objects. A single floweret from the hedgerow, I say not from the meadows; a single little shellfish from any sea, I say not from the Red Sea; a single stray wing of a moorfowl, I say nothing of the peacock,—will, I presume, prove to you that the Creator was but a sorry[4] artificer!

CHAP. XIV.—ALL PORTIONS OF CREATION AT-
TEST THE EXCELLENCE OF THE CREATOR,
WHOM MARCION VILIFIES. HIS INCONSISTENCY
HEREIN EXPOSED. MARCION'S OWN GOD DID
NOT HESITATE TO USE THE CREATOR'S WORKS
IN INSTITUTING HIS OWN RELIGION.

Now, when you make merry with those minuter animals, which their glorious Maker has purposely endued with a profusion of instincts and resources,[5]—thereby teaching us that greatness has its proofs in lowliness, just as (according to the apostle) there is power even in infirmity,[6]—imitate, if you can, the cells of the bee, the hills of the ant, the webs of the spider, and the threads of the silkworm; endure, too, if you know how, those very creatures[7] which infest your couch and house, the poisonous ejections of the blister-beetle,[8] the spikes of the fly, and the gnat's sheath and sting. What of the greater animals, when the small ones so affect you with pleasure or pain, that you cannot even in their case despise their Creator? Finally, take a circuit round your own self; survey man within and without. Even this handiwork of our God will be pleasing to you, inasmuch as your own lord, that better god, loved it so well,[9] and for your sake was at the pains[10] of descending from the third heaven to these poverty-

stricken[11] elements, and for the same reason was actually crucified in this sorry[12] apartment of the Creator. Indeed, up to the present time, he has not disdained the water which the Creator made wherewith he washes his people; nor the oil with which he anoints them; nor that union of honey and milk wherewithal he gives them the nourishment[13] of children; nor the bread by which he represents his own proper body, thus requiring in his very sacraments the "beggarly[14] elements" of the Creator. You, however, are a disciple above his master, and a servant above his lord; you have a higher reach of discernment than his; you destroy what he requires. I wish to examine whether you are at least honest in this, so as to have no longing for those things which you destroy. You are an enemy to the sky, and yet you are glad to catch its freshness in your houses. You disparage the earth, although the elemental parent[15] of your own flesh, as if it were your undoubted enemy, and yet you extract from it all its fatness[16] for your food. The sea, too, you reprobate, but are continually using its produce, which you account the more sacred diet.[17] If I should offer you a rose, you will not disdain its Maker. You hypocrite, however much of abstinence you use to show yourself a Marcionite, that is, a repudiator of your Maker (for if the world displeased you, such abstinence ought to have been affected by you as a martyrdom), you will have to associate yourself with[18] the Creator's material production, into what element soever you shall be dissolved. How hard is this obstinacy of yours! You vilify the things in which you both live and die.

CHAP. XV.—THE LATENESS OF THE REVELATION
OF MARCION'S GOD. THE QUESTION OF THE
PLACE OCCUPIED BY THE RIVAL DEITIES.
INSTEAD OF TWO GODS, MARCION REALLY
(ALTHOUGH, AS IT WOULD SEEM, UNCON-
SCIOUSLY) HAD NINE GODS IN HIS SYSTEM.

After all, or, if you like,[19] before all, since you have said that he has a creation[20] of his own, and his own world, and his own sky; we shall see,[21] indeed, about that third heaven, when we come to discuss even your own apos-

---

[1] The earth's irrigations, and the washings of the image of Cybele every year in the river Almo by her priests, are here confusedly alluded to. For references to the pagan custom, see White and Riddle's large *Lat. Dict. s. v.* ALMO.
[2] Mithras, the Persian sun-god, was symbolized by the image of a lion. The sun entering the zodiacal sign *Leo* amidst summer heat may be glanced at.
[3] Deficiam ad.
[4] Sordidum. [Well and nobly said.]
[5] De industria ingeniis aut viribus ampliavit.
[6] 2 Cor. xii. 5.
[7] Tertullian, it should be remembered, lived in *Africa*.
[8] Cantharidis.
[9] Adamavit.
[10] Laboravit.

[11] Paupertina. This and all such phrases are, of course, in imitation of Marcion's contemptuous view of the Creator's work.
[12] Cellula.
[13] Infantat.
[14] Mendicitatibus.
[15] Matricem.
[16] Medullas.
[17] [The use of fish for fasting-days has no better warrant than Marcion's example.]
[18] Uteris.
[19] Vel.
[20] Conditionem.
[21] *Adv. Marcionem*, v. 12.

tle.[1]   Meanwhile, whatever is the (created) substance, it ought at any rate to have made its appearance in company with its own god.   But now, how happens it that the Lord has been revealed since the twelfth year of Tiberius Cæsar, while no creation of His at all has been discovered up to the fifteenth of the Emperor Severus;[2] although, as being more excellent than the paltry works[3] of the Creator, it should certainly have ceased to conceal itself, when its lord and author no longer lies hid?   I ask, therefore,[4] if it was unable to manifest itself in this world, how did its Lord appear in this world?   If this world received its Lord, why was it not able to receive the created substance, unless perchance it was greater than its Lord?   But now there arises a question about place, having reference both to the world above and to the God thereof.   For, behold, if he[5] has his own world beneath him, above the Creator, he has certainly fixed it in a position, the space of which was empty between his own feet and the Creator's head. Therefore God both Himself occupied local space, and caused the world to occupy local space; and this local space, too, will be greater than God and the world together.   For in no case is that which contains not greater than that which is contained.   And indeed we must look well to it that no small patches[6] be left here and there vacant, in which some third god also may be able with a world of his own to foist himself in.[7]   Now, begin to reckon up your gods.   There will be local space for a god, not only as being greater than God, but as being also unbegotten and unmade, and therefore eternal, and equal to God, in which God has ever been.   Then, inasmuch as He too has fabricated[8] a world out of some underlying material which is unbegotten, and unmade, and contemporaneous with God, just as Marcion holds of the Creator, you reduce this likewise to the dignity of that local space which has enclosed two gods, both God and matter. For matter also is a god according to the rule of Deity, being (to be sure) unbegotten, and unmade, and eternal.   If, however, it was out of nothing that he made his world, this also

(our heretic) will be obliged to predicate[9] of the Creator, to whom he subordinates[10] matter in the substance of the world.   But it will be only right that he[11] too should have made his world out of matter, because the same process occurred to him as God which lay before the Creator as equally God.   And thus you may, if you please, reckon up so far,[12] three gods as Marcion's,—the Maker, local space, and matter.   Furthermore,[13] he in like manner makes the Creator a god in local space, which is itself to be appraised on a precisely identical scale of dignity; and to Him as its lord he subordinates matter, which is notwithstanding unbegotten, and unmade, and by reason hereof eternal.   With this matter he further associates evil, an unbegotten principle with an unbegotten object, an unmade with an unmade, and an eternal with an eternal; so here he makes a fourth God.   Accordingly you have three substances of Deity in the higher instances, and in the lower ones four. When to these are added their Christs—the one which appeared in the time of Tiberius, the other which is promised by the Creator— Marcion suffers a manifest wrong from those persons who assume that he holds two gods, whereas he implies[14] no less than nine,[15] though he knows it not.

CHAP. XVI.—MARCION ASSUMES THE EXISTENCE OF TWO GODS FROM THE ANTITHESIS BETWEEN THINGS VISIBLE AND THINGS INVISIBLE.   THIS ANTITHETICAL PRINCIPLE IN FACT CHARACTERISTIC OF THE WORKS OF THE CREATOR, THE ONE GOD—MAKER OF ALL THINGS VISIBLE AND INVISIBLE.

Since, then, that other world does not appear, nor its god either, the only resource left[16] to them is to divide things into the two classes of visible and invisible, with two gods for their authors, and so to claim[17] the invisible for their own, (the supreme) God.   But who, except an heretical spirit, could ever bring his mind to believe that the invisible part of creation belongs to him who had previously displayed no visible thing, rather than to Him who, by His operation on the visible world, produced a belief in the invisible also, since it is far more

---

[1] For Marcion's exclusive use, and consequent abuse, of St. *Paul*, see Neander's *Antignostikus* (Bohn), vol. ii. pp. 491, 505, 506.

[2] [This date not merely settles the time of our author's work against Marcion, but supplies us with evidence that his total lapse must have been very late in life. For the five books, written at intervals and marked by progressive tokens of his spiritual decline, are as a whole, only slightly offensive to Orthodoxy. This should be borne in mind.]

[3] Frivolis.   Again in reference to Marcion undervaluing the creation as the work of the Demiurge.

[4] Et ideo.

[5] In this and the following sentences, the reader will observe the distinction which is drawn between the Supreme and good God of Marcion and his " Creator," or Demiurge.

[6] Subsciva.

[7] Stipare se.

[8] Molitus est.

[9] Sentire.

[10] Subicit.

[11] The Supreme and good God.   Tertullian here gives it as one of Marcion's tenets, that the Demiurge created the World out of pre-existent matter.

[12] Interim.

[13] Proinde et.

[14] Assignet.

[15] Namely, (1) the supreme and good God ; (2) His Christ ; (3) the *space* in which He dwells ; (4) the *matter* of *His* creation ; (5) the Demiurge (or Marcion's " Creator ") ; (6) his promised Christ ; (7) the *space* which contains him ; (8) this world, his creation ; (9) evil, inherent in it.

[16] Consequens est ut.

[17] Defendant.

reasonable to give one's assent after some samples (of a work) than after none? We shall see to what author even (your favourite) apostle attributes[1] the invisible creation, when we come to examine him. At present (we withhold his testimony), for[2] we are for the most part engaged in preparing the way, by means of common sense and fair arguments, for a belief in the future support of the Scriptures also. We affirm, then, that this diversity of things visible and invisible must on this ground be attributed to the Creator, even because the whole of His work consists of diversities—of things corporeal and incorporeal; of animate and inanimate; of vocal and mute; of moveable and stationary; of productive and sterile; of arid and moist; of hot and cold. Man, too, is himself similarly tempered with diversity, both in his body and in his sensation. Some of his members are strong, others weak; some comely, others uncomely; some twofold, others unique; some like, others unlike. In like manner there is diversity also in his sensation: now joy, then anxiety; now love, then hatred; now anger, then calmness. Since this is the case, inasmuch as the whole of this creation of ours has been fashioned[3] with a reciprocal rivalry amongst its several parts, the invisible ones are due to the visible, and not to be ascribed to any other author than Him to whom their counterparts are imputed, marking as they do diversity in the Creator Himself, who orders what He forbade, and forbids what He ordered; who also strikes and heals. Why do they take Him to be uniform in one class of things alone, as the Creator of visible things, and only them; whereas He ought to be believed to have created both the visible and the invisible, in just the same way as life and death, or as evil things and peace?[4] And verily, if the invisible creatures are greater than the visible, which are in their own sphere great, so also is it fitting that the greater should be His to whom the great belong; because neither the great, nor indeed the greater, can be suitable property for one who seems to possess not even the smallest things.

CHAP. XVII.—NOT ENOUGH, AS THE MARCIONITES PRETEND, THAT THE SUPREME GOD SHOULD RESCUE MAN; HE MUST ALSO HAVE CREATED HIM. THE EXISTENCE OF GOD PROVED BY HIS CREATION, A PRIOR CONSIDERATION TO HIS CHARACTER.

Pressed by these arguments, they exclaim: One work is sufficient for our god; he has de-livered man by his supreme and most excellent goodness, which is preferable to (the creation of) all the locusts.[5] What superior god is this, of whom it has not been possible to find any work so great as *the man* of the lesser god! Now without doubt the first thing you have to do is to prove that he exists, after the same manner that the existence of God must ordinarily be proved—by his works; and only after that by his good deeds. For the first question is, Whether he exists? and then, What is his character? The former is to be tested[6] by his works, the other by the beneficence of them. It does not simply follow that he exists, because he is said to have wrought deliverance for man; but only after it shall have been settled that he exists, will there be room for saying that he has affected this liberation. And even this point also must have its own evidence, because it may be quite possible both that he has existence, and yet has not wrought the alleged deliverance. Now in that section of our work which concerned the question of the unknown god, two points were made clear enough—both that he had created nothing, and that he ought to have been a creator, in order to be known by his works; because, if he had existed, he ought to have been known, and that too from the beginning of things; for it was not fit that God should have lain hid. It will be necessary that I should revert to the very trunk of that question of the unknown god, that I may strike off into some of its other branches also. For it will be first of all proper to inquire, Why he, who afterwards brought himself into notice, did so—so late, and not at the very first? From creatures, with which as God he was indeed so closely connected (and the closer this connection was,[7] the greater was his goodness), he ought never to have been hidden. For it cannot be pretended that there was not either any means of arriving at the knowledge of God, or a good reason for it, when from the beginning man was in the world, for whom the deliverance is now come; as was also that malevolence of the Creator, in opposition to which the good God has wrought the deliverance. He was therefore either ignorant of the good reason for and means of his own necessary manifestation, or doubted them; or else was either unable or unwilling to encounter them. All these alternatives are unworthy of God, especially the supreme

---

[1] Col. i. 16.
[2] Nunc enim. The elliptical νῦν γάρ of Greek argumentation.
[3] Modulata.
[4] "I make peace, and create evil," Isa. xlv. 7.

[5] To depreciate the Creator's work the more, Marcion (and Valentinus too) used to attribute to Him the formation of all the lower creatures—worms, locusts, etc.—reserving the mightier things to the good and supreme God. See St. Jerome's *Proem. in Epist. ad Philem.* [See, Stier, *Words of Jesus*, Vol. vi. p. 81.]
[6] Dinoscetur.
[7] Quo necessarior.

and best.   This topic,[1] however, we shall afterwards[2] more fully treat, with a condemnation of the tardy manifestation; we at present simply point it out.

CHAP. XVIII.—NOTWITHSTANDING THEIR CONCEITS, THE GOD OF THE MARCIONITES FAILS IN THE VOUCHERS BOTH OF CREATED EVIDENCE AND OF ADEQUATE REVELATION.

Well, then,[3] he has now advanced into notice, just when he willed, when he could, when the destined hour arrived.   For perhaps he was hindered hitherto by his leading star,[4] or some weird malignants, or Saturn in quadrature,[5] or Mars at the trine.[6]   The Marcionites are very strongly addicted to astrology; nor do they blush to get their livelihood by help of the very stars which were made by the Creator (whom they depreciate). We must here also treat of the quality[7] of the (new) revelation; whether Marcion's supreme god has become known *in a way worthy of him*, so as to secure the proof of his existence; and *in the way of truth*, so that he may be believed to be the very being who had been already proved to have been revealed in a manner worthy of his character.   For things which are worthy of God will prove the existence of God.   We maintain[8] that God must first be known[9] from *nature*, and afterwards authenticated[10] by *instruction*: from nature, by His *works*; by instruction,[11] through His revealed announcements.[12]   Now, in a case where nature is excluded, no natural means (of knowledge) are furnished.   He ought, therefore, to have carefully supplied[13] a revelation of himself, even by announcements, especially as he had to be revealed in opposition to One who, after so many and so great works, both of creation and revealed announcement, had with difficulty succeeded in satisfying[14] men's faith.   In what manner, therefore, has the revelation been made?   If by man's conjectural guesses, do not say that God can possibly become known in any other way than by Himself, and appeal not only to the standard of the Creator, but to the conditions both of God's greatness and man's littleness; so that

man seem not by any possibility to be greater than God, by having somehow drawn Him out into public recognition, when He was Himself unwilling to become known by His own energies, although man's littleness has been able, according to experiments all over the world, more easily to fashion for itself gods, than to follow the true God whom men now understand by nature.   As for the rest,[15] if man shall be thus able to devise a god,—as Romulus did Consus, and Tatius Cloacina, and Hostilius Fear, and Metellus Alburnus, and a certain authority[16] some time since Antinous,—the same accomplishment may be allowed to others.   As for us, we have found our pilot in Marcion, although not a king nor an emperor.

CHAP. XIX.—JESUS CHRIST, THE REVEALER OF THE CREATOR, COULD NOT BE THE SAME AS MARCION'S GOD, WHO WAS ONLY MADE KNOWN BY THE HERETIC SOME CXV. YEARS AFTER CHRIST, AND THAT, TOO, ON A PRINCIPLE UTTERLY UNSUITED TO THE TEACHING OF JESUS CHRIST, I.E., THE OPPOSITION BETWEEN THE LAW AND THE GOSPELS.

Well, but our god, say the Marcionites, although he did not manifest himself from the beginning and by means of the creation, has yet revealed himself in Christ Jesus.   A book will be devoted[17] to Christ, treating of His entire state; for it is desirable that these subject-matters should be distinguished one from another, in order that they may receive a fuller and more methodical treatment.   Meanwhile it will be sufficient if, at this stage of the question, I show—and that but briefly—that Christ Jesus is the revealer[18] of none other god but the Creator.   In the fifteenth year of Tiberius,[19] Christ Jesus vouchsafed to come down from heaven, as the spirit of saving health.[20]   I cared not to inquire, indeed, in what particular year of the elder Antoninus. He who had so gracious a purpose did rather, like a pestilential sirocco,[21] exhale this health or salvation, which Marcion teaches from his Pontus.   Of this teacher there is no doubt that he is a heretic of the Antonine period, impious under the pious.   Now, from Tiberius to Antoninus Pius, there are about 115 years and 6½ months.   Just such an interval do they place between Christ and Marcion.   Inasmuch, then, as Marcion, as we have shown,

---

[1] Locum.
[2] In chap. xxii.
[3] Age.
[4] Anabibazon.   The ἀναβιβάζων was the most critical point in the ecliptic, in the old astrology, for the calculation of stellar influences.
[5] Quadratus.
[6] Trigonus.   Saturn and Mars were supposed to be malignant planets.   See Smith, *Greek and Rom. Ant.* p. 144, c. 2.
[7] Qualitate.
[8] Definimus.
[9] Cognoscendum.
[10] Recognoscendum.
[11] Doctrina.
[12] Ex prædicationibus.
[13] Operari.
[14] Vix impleverat.

[15] Alioquin.
[16] He means the Emperor Hadrian ; comp. *Apolog.* c. 13.
[17] The third of these books against Marcion.
[18] Circumlatorem.
[19] The author says this, not as his own, but as Marcion's opinion ; as is clear from his own words in his fourth book against Marcion, c. 7, (Pamelius).
[20] Spiritus salutaris.
[21] Aura canicularis.

first introduced this god to notice in the time of Antoninus, the matter becomes at once clear, if you are a shrewd observer. The dates already decide the case, that he who came to light for the first time[1] in the reign of Antoninus, did not appear in that of Tiberius; in other words, that the God of the Antonine period was not the God of the Tiberian; and consequently, that he whom Marcion has plainly preached for the first time, was not revealed by Christ (who announced His revelation as early as the reign of Tiberius). Now, to prove clearly what remains of the argument, I shall draw materials from my very adversaries. Marcion's special and principal work is the separation of the law and the gospel; and his disciples will not deny that in this point they have their very best pretext for initiating and confirming themselves in his heresy. These are Marcion's *Antitheses*, or contradictory propositions, which aim at committing the gospel to a variance with the law, in order that from the diversity of the two documents which contain them,[2] they may contend for a diversity of gods also. Since, therefore, it is this very opposition between the law and the gospel which has suggested that the God of the gospel is different from the God of the law, it is clear that, before the said separation, that god could not have been known who became known[3] from the argument of the separation itself. He therefore could not have been revealed by Christ, who came before the separation, but must have been devised by Marcion, the author of the breach of peace between the gospel and the law. Now this peace, which had remained unhurt and unshaken from Christ's appearance to the time of Marcion's audacious doctrine, was no doubt maintained by that way of thinking, which firmly held that the God of both law and gospel was none other than the Creator, against whom after so long a time a separation has been introduced by the heretic of Pontus.

CHAP. XX.—MARCION, JUSTIFYING HIS ANTITHESIS BETWEEN THE LAW AND THE GOSPEL BY THE CONTENTION OF ST. PAUL WITH ST. PETER, SHOWN TO HAVE MISTAKEN ST. PAUL'S POSITION AND ARGUMENT. MARCION'S DOCTRINE CONFUTED OUT OF ST. PAUL'S TEACHING, WHICH AGREES WHOLLY WITH THE CREATOR'S DECREES.

This most patent conclusion requires to be defended by us against the clamours of the opposite side. For they allege that Marcion

did not so much innovate on the rule (of faith) by his separation of the law and the gospel, as restore it after it had been previously adulterated. O Christ,[4] most enduring Lord, who didst bear so many years with this interference with Thy revelation, until Marcion forsooth came to Thy rescue! Now they adduce the case of Peter himself, and the others, who were pillars of the apostolate, as having been blamed by Paul for not walking uprightly, according to the truth of the gospel—that very Paul indeed, who, being yet in the mere rudiments of grace, and trembling, in short, lest he should have run or were still running in vain, then for the first time held intercourse with those who were apostles before himself. Therefore because, in the eagerness of his zeal against Judaism as a neophyte, he thought that there was something to be blamed in their conduct—even the promiscuousness of their conversation[5]—but afterwards was himself to become in his practice all things to all men, that he might gain all,—to the Jews, as a Jew, and to them that were under the law, as under the law,—you would have his censure, which was merely directed against conduct destined to become acceptable even to their accuser, suspected of prevarication against God on a point of public doctrine.[6] Touching their public doctrine, however, they had, as we have already said, joined hands in perfect concord, and had agreed also in the division of their labour in their fellowship of the gospel, as they had indeed in all other respects:[7] "Whether it were I or they, so we preach."[8] When, again, he mentioned "certain false brethren as having crept in unawares," who wished to remove the Galatians into another gospel,[9] he himself shows that that adulteration of the gospel was not meant to transfer them to the faith of another god and christ, but rather to perpetuate the teaching of the law; because he blames them for maintaining circumcision, and observing times, and days, and months, and years, according to those Jewish ceremonies which they ought to have known were now abrogated, according to the new dispensation purposed by the Creator Himself, who of old foretold this very thing by His prophets. Thus He says by Isaiah: Old things have passed away. "Behold, I will do a new thing."[10] And in another passage: "I will make a new covenant, not according to the covenant that I made with their fathers, when I brought them out of the land of

[1] Primum processit.
[2] Utriusque instrumenti.
[3] Innotuit.
[4] Tertullian's indignant reply.
[5] Passivum scilicet convictum.
[6] Prædicationis. [Largely *ad hominem*, this argument.]
[7] Et alibi.
[8] 1 Cor. xv. 11.
[9] See Gal. i. 6, 7, and ii. 4.
[10] Isa. xliii. 19.

Egypt." [1] In like manner by Jeremiah: Make to yourselves a new covenant, "circumcise yourselves to the Lord, and take away the foreskins of your heart." [2] It is this circumcision, therefore, and this renewal, which the apostle insisted on, when he forbade those ancient ceremonies concerning which their very founder announced that they were one day to cease ; thus by Hosea : " I will also cause all her mirth to cease, her feast-days, her new moons, and her Sabbaths, and all her solemn feasts." [3] So likewise by Isaiah : " The new moons, and Sabbaths, the calling of assemblies, I cannot away with ; your holy days, and fasts, and feast-days, my soul hateth." [4] Now, if even the Creator had so long before discarded all these things, and the apostle was now proclaiming them to be worthy of renunciation, the very agreement of the apostle's meaning with the decrees of the Creator proves that none other God was preached by the apostle than He whose purposes he now wished to have recognised, branding as false both apostles and brethren, for the express reason that they were pushing back the gospel of Christ the Creator from the new condition which the Creator had foretold, to the old one which He had discarded.

CHAP. XXI.—ST. PAUL PREACHED NO NEW GOD, WHEN HE ANNOUNCED THE REPEAL OF SOME OE GOD'S ANCIENT ORDINANCES. NEVER ANY HESITATION ABOUT BELIEF IN THE CREATOR, AS THE GOD WHOM CHRIST REVEALED, UNTIL MARCION'S HERESY.

Now if it was with the view of preaching a new god that he was eager to abrogate the law of the old God, how is it that he prescribes no rule about [5] the new god, but solely about the old law, if it be not because faith in the Creator [6] was still to continue, and His law alone was to come to an end ? [7]—just as the Psalmist had declared: " Let us break their bands asunder, and cast away their cords from us. Why do the heathen rage, and the people imagine a vain thing ? The kings of the earth stand up, and the rulers take counsel together against the Lord, and against His Anointed." [8] And, indeed, if another god were preached by Paul, there could be no doubt about the law, whether it were to be kept or not, because of course it would not belong to the new lord, the enemy [9] of the law. The very newness and difference of the god

would take away not only all question about the old and alien law, but even all mention of it. But the whole question, as it then stood, was this, that although the God of the law was the same as was preached in Christ, yet there was a disparagement [10] of His law. Permanent still, therefore, stood faith in Creator and in His Christ; manner of life and discipline alone fluctuated. [11] Some disputed about eating idol sacrifices, others about the veiled dress of women, others again about marriage and divorce, and some even about the hope of the resurrection; but about God no one disputed. Now, if this question also had entered into dispute, surely it would be found in the apostle, and that too as a great and vital point. No doubt, after the time of the apostles, the truth respecting the belief of God suffered corruption, but it is equally certain that during the life of the apostles their teaching on this great article did not suffer at all; so that no other teaching will have the right of being received as apostolic than that which is at the present day proclaimed in the churches of apostolic foundation. You will, however, find no church of apostolic origin [12] but such as reposes its Christian faith in the Creator. [13] But if the churches shall prove to have been corrupt from the beginning, where shall the pure ones be found ? Will it be amongst the adversaries of the Creator ? Show us, then, one of your churches, tracing its descent from an apostle, and you will have gained the day. [14] Forasmuch then as it is on all accounts evident that there was from Christ down to Marcion's time no other God in the rule of sacred truth [15] than the Creator, the proof of our argument is sufficiently established, in which we have shown that the god of our heretic first became known by his separation of the gospel and the law. Our previous position [16] is accordingly made good, that no god is to be believed whom any man has devised out of his own conceits; except indeed the man be a prophet, [17] and then his own conceits would not be concerned in the matter. If Marcion, however, shall be able to lay claim to this inspired character, it will be necessary for it to be shown. There must be no doubt or paltering. [18] For all heresy is thrust out by this wedge of the truth, that Christ is proved to be the revealer of no God else but the Creator. [19]

---

[1] This quotation, however, is from Jer. xxxi. 32.
[2] Jer. iv. 4.
[3] Hos. ii. 11.
[4] Slightly altered from Isa. i. 13, 14.
[5] Nihil præscribit de.
[6] i.e., " the old God," as he has just called Him.
[7] Concessare debebat.
[8] Ps. ii. 3, 1, 2.
[9] Æmulum.

[10] Derogaretur.
[11] Nutabat.
[12] Census.
[13] In Creatore christianizet.
[14] Obduxeris.　For this sense of the word. see *Apol. i. sub init.* " sed obducimur," etc.
[15] Sacramenti.
[16] Definitio.
[17] That is, " inspired."
[18] Nihil retractare oportebat.
[19] [Kaye, p. 274.]

CHAP. XXII.—GOD'S ATTRIBUTE OF GOODNESS CONSIDERED AS NATURAL; THE GOD OF MARCION FOUND WANTING HEREIN. IT CAME NOT TO MAN'S RESCUE WHEN FIRST WANTED.

But how shall (this) Antichrist be fully overthrown unless we relax our defence by mere prescription,[1] and give ourselves scope for rebutting all his other attacks? Let us therefore next take the very person of God Himself, or rather His shadow or phantom,[2] as we have it in Christ, and let Him be examined by that condition which makes Him superior to the Creator. And undoubtedly there will come to hand unmistakeable rules for examining God's goodness. My first point, however, is to discover and apprehend the attribute, and then to draw it out into rules. Now, when I survey the subject in its aspects of time, I nowhere descry it[3] from the beginning of material existences, or at the commencement of those causes, with which it ought to have been found, proceeding thence to do[4] whatever had to be done. For there was death already, and sin the sting of death, and that malignity too of the Creator, against which the goodness of the other god should have been ready to bring relief; falling in with this as the primary rule of the divine goodness (if it were to prove itself a natural *agency*), at once coming as a succour when the cause for it began. For in God all things should be natural and inbred, just like His own condition indeed, in order that they may be eternal, and so not be accounted casual[5] and extraneous, and thereby temporary and wanting in eternity. In God, therefore, goodness is required to be both perpetual and unbroken,[6] such as, being stored up and kept ready in the treasures of His natural properties, might precede its own causes and material developments; and if thus preceding, might *underlie*[7] every first material cause, instead of looking at it from a distance,[8] and standing aloof from it.[9] In short, here too I must inquire, Why his[10] goodness did not operate from the beginning? no less pointedly than when we inquired concerning himself, Why he was not revealed from the very first? Why, then, did it not? since he had to be revealed by his goodness

if he had any existence. That God should at all fail in power must not be thought, much less that He should not discharge all His natural functions; for if these were restrained from running their course, they would cease to be natural. Moreover, the nature of God Himself knows nothing of inactivity. Hence (His goodness) is reckoned as having a beginning,[11] if it acts. It will thus be evident that He had no unwillingness to exercise His goodness at any time on account of His nature. Indeed, it is impossible that He should be unwilling because of His nature, since that so directs itself that it would no longer exist if it ceased to act. In Marcion's god, however, goodness ceased from operation at some time or other. A goodness, therefore, which could thus at any time have ceased its action was not natural, because with natural properties such cessation is incompatible. And if it shall not prove to be natural, it must no longer be believed to be eternal nor competent to Deity; because it cannot be eternal so long as, failing to be natural, it neither provides from the past nor guarantees for the future any means of perpetuating itself. Now as a fact it existed not from the beginning, and, doubtless, will not endure to the end. For it is possible for it to fail in existence some future[12] time or other, as it has failed in some past[13] period. Forasmuch, then, as the goodness of Marcion's god failed in the beginning (for he did not from the first deliver man), this failure must have been the effect of will rather than of infirmity. Now a wilful suppression of goodness will be found to have a malignant end in view. For what malignity is so great as to be unwilling to do good when one can, or to thwart[14] what is useful, or to permit injury? The whole description, therefore, of Marcion's Creator will have to be transferred[15] to his new god, who helped on the ruthless[16] proceedings of the former by the retardation of his own goodness. For whosoever has it in his power to prevent the happening of a thing, is accounted responsible for it if it should occur. Man is condemned to death for tasting the fruit of one poor tree,[17] and thence proceed sins with their penalties; and now all are perishing who yet never saw a single sod of Paradise. And all this your better god either is ignorant of, or else brooks. Is it that[18] he might on this account be deemed the better, and the Creator be re-

---

[1] In his book, *De Præscrip. Hæret.*, [cap. xv.] Tertullian had enjoined that heretics ought not to be argued with, but to be met with the authoritative rule of the faith. He here proposes to forego that course.
[2] Marcion's *Docetic* doctrine of Christ as having only *appeared* in human shape, without an actual incarnation, is indignantly confuted by Tertullian in his *De Carne Christi*, c. v.
[3] That is, the principle in question—the *bonitas Dei*.
[4] Exinde agens.
[5] Obvenientia.
[6] Jugis.
[7] Susciperet.
[8] Despiceret.
[9] Destitueret.
[10] That is, Marcion's god's.

[11] Censetur.
[12] Quandoque.
[13] Aliquando.
[14] Cruciare.
[15] Rescribetur.
[16] Sævitias.
[17] Arbusculæ.
[18] Si ut?

garded as all that the worse? Even if this were his purpose he would be malicious enough, for both wishing to aggravate his rival's obloquy by permitting His (evil) works to be done, and by keeping the world harrassed by the wrong. What would you think of a physician who should encourage a disease by withholding the remedy, and prolong the danger by delaying his· prescription, in order that his cure might be more costly and more renowned? Such must be the sentence to be pronounced against Marcion's god: tolerant of evil, encouraging wrong, wheedling about his grace, prevaricating in his goodness, which he did not exhibit simply on its own account, but which he must mean to exhibit purely, if he is good by nature and not by acquisition,[1] if he is supremely good in attribute[2] and not by discipline, if he is God from eternity and not from Tiberius, nay (to speak more truly), from Cerdon only and Marcion. As the case now stands,[3] however, such a god as we are considering would have been more fit for Tiberius, that the goodness of the Divine Being might be inaugurated in the world under his imperial sway!

CHAP. XXIII.—GOD'S ATTRIBUTE OF GOODNESS CONSIDERED AS RATIONAL. MARCION'S GOD DEFECTIVE HERE ALSO; HIS GOODNESS IRRATIONAL AND MISAPPLIED.

Here is another rule for him. All the properties of God ought to be as rational as they are natural. I require reason in His goodness, because nothing else can properly be accounted good than that which is rationally good; much less can goodness itself be detected in any irrationality. More easily will an evil thing which has something rational belonging to it be accounted good, than that a good thing bereft of all reasonable quality should escape being regarded as evil. Now I deny that the goodness of Marcion's god is rational, on this account first, because it proceeded to the salvation of a human creature which was alien to him. I am aware of the plea which they will adduce, that that is rather[4] a primary and perfect goodness which is shed voluntarily and freely upon strangers without any obligation of friendship,[5] on the principle that we are bidden to love even our enemies, such as are also on that very account strangers to us. Now, inasmuch as from the first he had no regard for man, a stranger to him from the first, he settled beforehand, by this neglect of his, that he had nothing to do with an alien creature. Besides, the rule of loving a stranger or enemy is preceded by the precept of your loving your neighbour as yourself; and this precept, although coming from the Creator's law, even you ought to receive, because, so far from being abrogated by Christ, it has rather been confirmed by Him. For you are bidden to love your enemy and the stranger, in order that you may love your neighbour the better. The requirement of the undue is an augmentation of the due benevolence. But the due precedes the undue, as the principal quality, and more worthy of the other, for its attendant and companion.[6] Since, therefore, the first step in the reasonableness of the divine goodness is that it displays itself on its proper object[7] in righteousness, and only at its second stage on an alien object by a redundant righteousness over and above that of scribes and Pharisees, how comes it to pass that the second is attributed to him who fails in the first, not having man for his proper object, and who makes his goodness on this very account defective? Moreover, how could a defective benevolence, which had no proper object whereon to expend itself, overflow[8] on an alien one? Clear up the first step, and then vindicate the next. Nothing can be claimed as rational without order, much less can reason itself[9] dispense with order in any one. Suppose now *the divine* goodness begin at the second stage of its rational operation, that is to say, on the stranger, this second stage will not be consistent in rationality if it be impaired in any way else.[10] For only then will even the second stage of goodness, that which is displayed towards the stranger, be accounted rational, when it operates without wrong to him who has the first claim.[11] It is righteousness[12] which before everything else makes all goodness rational. It will thus be rational in its principal stage, when manifested on its proper object, if it be righteous. And thus, in like manner, it will· be able to appear rational, when displayed towards the stranger, if it be not unrighteous. But what sort of goodness is that which is manifested in wrong, and *that*

---

[1] Accessione.
[2] Ingenio.
[3] Nunc. [Comp. chapter xv. *supra*, p. 282.]
[4] Atquin.
[5] Familiaritatis.
[6] This is the sense of the passage as read by Oehler: "Antecedit autem debita indebitam, ut principalis, ut dignior ministra et comite sua, id est indebita." Fr. Junius, however, added the word " prior " which begins the next sentence to these words, making the last clause run thus: " ut dignior ministra, et comite sua, id est indebita, prior "—" as being more worthy of an attendant, and as being prior to its companion, that is, the undue benevolence." It is difficult to find any good use of the " prior " in the next sentence, " Prior igitur cum prima bonitatis ratio sit," etc., as Oehler and others point it.
[7] In rem suam.
[8] Redundavit.
[9] Ratio ipsa, i.e., rationality, or the character of reasonableness, which he is now vindicating.
[10] Alio modo destructus.
[11] Cujus est res.
[12] Justitia, *right* as opposed to the *wrong* (injuria) of the preceding sentence.

in behalf of an alien creature? For peradventure a benevolence, even when operating injuriously, might be deemed to some extent rational, if exerted for one of our own house and home.[1] By what rule, however, can an unjust benevolence, displayed on behalf of a stranger, to whom not even an honest one is legitimately due, be defended as a rational one? For what is more unrighteous, more unjust, more dishonest, than so to benefit an alien slave as to take him away from his master, claim him as the property of another, and suborn him against his master's life; and all this, to make the matter more iniquitous still, whilst he is yet living in his master's house, and on his master's garner, and still trembling beneath his stripes? Such a deliverer,[2] I had almost said[3] kidnapper,[4] would even meet with condemnation in the world. Now, no other than this is the character of Marcion's god, swooping upon an alien world, snatching away man from his God,[5] the son from his father, the pupil from his tutor, the servant from his master—to make him impious to his God, undutiful to his father, ungrateful to his tutor, worthless to his master. If, now, the rational benevolence makes man such, what sort of being prithee[6] would the irrational make of him? None I should think more shameless than him who is baptized to his[7] god in water which belongs to another, who stretches out his hands[8] to his god towards a heaven which is another's, who kneels to his god on ground which is another's, offers his thanksgivings to his god over bread which belongs to another,[9] and distributes[10] by way of alms and charity, for the sake of his god, gifts which belong to another God. Who, then, is that so good a god of theirs, that man through him becomes evil; so propitious, too, as to incense against man that other God who is, indeed, his own proper Lord?

But as God is eternal and rational, so, I think, He is perfect in all things. "Be ye perfect, even as your Father which is in heaven is perfect."[11] Prove, then, that the goodness of your god also is a perfect one. That it is indeed *imperfect* has been already sufficiently shown, since it is found to be neither natural nor rational. The same conclusion, however, shall now be made clear[12] by another method; it is not simply[13] imperfect, but actually[14] feeble, weak, and exhausted, failing to embrace the full number[15] of its material objects, and not manifesting itself in them all. For all are not put into a state of salvation[16] by it; but the Creator's subjects, both Jew and Christian, are all excepted.[17] Now, when the greater part thus perish, how can that goodness be defended as a perfect one which is inoperative in most cases, is somewhat only in few, naught in many, succumbs to perdition, and is a partner with destruction?[18] And if so many shall miss salvation, it will not be with goodness, but with malignity, that the greater perfection will lie. For as it is the operation of goodness which brings salvation, so is it malevolence which thwarts it.[19] Since, however, this goodness) saves but few, and so rather leans to the alternative of not saving, it will show itself to greater perfection by not interposing help than by helping. Now, you will not be able to attribute goodness (to your god) in reference to the Creator, (if accompanied with) failure towards all. For whomsoever you call in to judge the question, it is as a dispenser of goodness, if so be such a title can be made out,[20] and not as a squanderer thereof, as you claim your god to be, that you must submit the divine character for determination. So long, then, as you prefer your god to the Creator on the simple ground of his goodness, and since he professes to have this attribute as solely and wholly his own, he ought not to have been wanting in it to any one. However, I do not now wish to prove that Marcion's god is imperfect in goodness because of the perdition of the greater number. I am content to illustrate

---

[1] Pro domestico, opposed to the *pro extraneo*, the alien or stranger of the preceding and succeeding context.
[2] Assertor.
[3] Nedum.
[4] Plagiator.
[5] i.e., the Creator.
[6] Oro te.
[7] Alii Deo. The strength of this phrase is remarkable by the side of the oft-repeated aliena.
[8] Therefore Christians used to lift their hands and arms towards heaven in prayer. Compare *The Apology*, chap. 30, (where the *manibus expansis* betokens the open hand, not merely as the heathen *tendens* ad sidera palmas). See also *De Orat.* c. 13, and other passages from different writers referred to in the "Tertullian" of the Oxford *Library of the Fathers*, p. 70. [See the figures in the Catacombs as represented by Parker, Marriott and others.]
[9] To the same effect Irenæus had said : "How will it be consistent in them to hold that the bread on which thanks are given is the body of their Lord, and that the cup is His blood, if they do not acknowledge that He is the Son of the Creator of the world, that is, the Word of God?" (Rigalt.) [The consecrated bread is still *bread*, in Patristic theology.]
[10] Operatur, a not unfrequent use of the word. Thus Prudentius (*Psychom.* 572) opposes *operatio* to *avaritia*.

[11] Matt. v. 48.
[12] Traducetur.
[13] Nec jam.
[14] Immo.
[15] Minor numero.
[16] Non fiunt salvi. [Kaye, p. 347.]
[17] Pauciores.
[18] Partiaria exitii.
[19] Non facit salvos.
[20] Si forte (*i.e.* εἰ τύχοι εἴπερ ἄρα, with a touch of irony,—a frequent phrase in Tertullian.)

this imperfection by the fact that even those whom he saves are found to possess but an imperfect salvation—that is, they are saved only so far as the soul is concerned,[1] but lost in their body, which, according to him, does not rise again. Now, whence comes this halving of salvation, if not from a failure of goodness? What could have been a better proof of a perfect goodness, than the recovery of the whole man to salvation? Totally damned by the Creator, he should have been totally restored by the most merciful god. I rather think that by Marcion's rule the body is baptized, is deprived of marriage,[2] is cruelly tortured in confession. But although sins are attributed to the body, yet they are preceded by the guilty concupiscence of the soul; nay, the first motion of sin must be ascribed to the soul, to which the flesh acts in the capacity of a servant. By and by, when freed from the soul, the flesh sins no more.[3] So that in this matter goodness is unjust, and likewise imperfect, in that it leaves to destruction the more harmless substance, which sins rather by compliance than in will. Now, although Christ put not on the verity of the flesh, as your heresy is pleased to assume, He still vouchsafed to take upon Him the semblance thereof. Surely, therefore, some regard was due to it from Him, because of this His feigned assumption of it. Besides, what else is man than flesh, since no doubt it was the corporeal rather than the spiritual[4] element from which the Author of man's nature gave him his designation?[5] "And the LORD God made man of the dust of the ground," not of spiritual essence; this afterwards came from the divine afflatus: "and man became a living soul." What, then, is man? Made, no doubt of it, of the dust; and God placed him in paradise, because He moulded him, not breathed him, into being—a fabric of flesh, not of spirit. Now, this being the case, with what face will you contend for the perfect character of that goodness which did not fail in some one particular only of man's deliverance, but in its general capacity? If that is a plenary grace and a substantial mercy which brings salvation to the soul alone, this were the better life which we now enjoy whole and entire; whereas to rise again but in part will be a chastisement, not a liberation. The

proof of the perfect goodness is, that man, after his rescue, should be delivered from the domicile and power of the malignant deity unto the protection of the most good and merciful God. Poor dupe of Marcion, fever[6] is hard upon you; and your painful flesh produces a crop of all sorts of briers and thorns. Nor is it only to the Creator's thunderbolts that you lie exposed, or to wars, and pestilences, and His other heavier strokes, but even to His creeping insects. In what respect do you suppose yourself liberated from His kingdom when His flies are still creeping upon your face? If your deliverance lies in the future, why not also in the present, that it may be perfectly wrought? Far different is our condition in the sight of Him who is the Author, the Judge, the injured[7] Head of our race! You display Him as a merely good God; but you are unable to prove that He is perfectly good, because you are not by Him perfectly delivered.

CHAP. XXV.—GOD IS NOT A BEING OF SIMPLE GOODNESS; OTHER ATTRIBUTES BELONG TO HIM. MARCION SHOWS INCONSISTENCY IN THE PORTRAITURE OF HIS SIMPLY GOOD AND EMOTIONLESS GOD.

As touching this question of goodness, we have in these outlines of our argument shown it to be in no way compatible with Deity,—as being neither natural,[8] nor rational, nor perfect, but wrong,[9] and unjust, and unworthy of the very name of goodness,—because, as far as the congruity of the divine character is concerned, it cannot indeed be fitting that that Being should be regarded as God who is alleged to have *such* a goodness, and that not in a modified way, but simply and solely. For it is, furthermore, at this point quite open to discussion, whether God ought to be regarded as a Being of simple goodness, to the exclusion of all those other attributes,[10] sensations, and affections, which the Marcionites indeed transfer from their god to the Creator, and which we acknowledge to be worthy characteristics of the Creator too, but only because we consider Him to be God. Well, then, on this ground we shall deny him to be God in whom all things are not to be found which befit the Divine Being. If (Marcion) chose[11] to take any one of the school of Epicurus, and entitle him God in the name of Christ, on the ground

---

[1] Anima tenus. Comp. *De Præscr. Hær.* 33, where Marcion, as well as Apelles, Valentinus, and others, are charged with the Sadducean denial of the resurrection of the flesh, which is censured by St. Paul, 1 Cor. xv. 12.
[2] Compare *De Præscr. Hær.* 33, where Marcion and Apelles are brought under St. Paul's reproach in 1 Tim. iv. 3.
[3] Hactenus. [Kaye, p. 260.]
[4] Animalis (from *anima*, the vital principle. "the breath of life") is here opposed to corporalis.
[5] הָאָדָם, *homo*, from הָאֲדָמָה, *humus*, the ground; see the Hebrew of Gen. ii. 7.

[6] Febricitas.
[7] Offensum, probably in respect of the Marcionite treatment of His attributes.
[8] Ingenitam. In chap. xxii. this word seems to be synonymous with *naturalem.* Comp. book ii. 3, where it has this sense in the phrase "Deo ingenita."
[9] Improbam.
[10] Appendicibus.
[11] Affectavit.

that what is happy and incorruptible can bring no trouble either on itself or anything else (for Marcion, while poring over [1] this opinion of the divine indifference, has removed from him all the severity and energy of the judicial [2] character), it was his duty to have developed his conceptions into some imperturbable and listless god (and then what could *he* have had in common with Christ, who occasioned trouble both to the Jews by what He taught, and to Himself by what He felt?), or else to have admitted that he was possessed of the same emotions as others [3] (and in such case what would he have had to do with Epicurus, who was no friend [4] to either him or Christians?). For that a being who in ages past [5] was in a quiescent state, not caring to communicate any knowledge of himself by any work all the while, should come after so long a time to entertain a concern for man's salvation, of course by his own will,—did he not by this very fact become susceptible of the impulse [6] of a new volition, so as palpably to be open to all other emotions? But what volition is unaccompanied with the spur of desire? [7] Who wishes for what he desires not? Moreover, care will be another companion of the will. For who will wish for any object and desire to have it, without also *caring* to obtain it? When, therefore, (Marcion's god) felt both a will and a desire for man's salvation, he certainly occasioned some concern and trouble both to himself and others. This Marcion's theory suggests, though Epicurus demurs. For he [8] raised up an adversary against himself in that very thing against which his will, and desire, and care were directed,—whether it were sin or death,—and more especially in their Tyrant and Lord, the Creator of man. Again, [9] nothing will ever run its course without hostile rivalry, [10] which shall not (itself) be without a hostile aspect. In fact, [11] when willing, desiring, and caring to deliver man, (Marcion's god) already in the very act encounters a rival, both in Him from whom He effects the deliverance (for of course [12] he means the liberation to be an opposition to Him), and also in those things from which the deliverance is wrought (the intended liberation being to the advantage of some other things). For it must needs be, that upon rivalry its own

ancillary passions [13] will be in attendance, against whatever objects its emulation is directed: anger, discord, hatred, disdain, indignation, spleen, loathing, displeasure. Now, since all these emotions are present to rivalry; since, moreover, the rivalry which arises in liberating man excites them; and since, again, this deliverance of man is an operation of goodness, it follows that this goodness avails nothing without its endowments, [14] that is to say, without those sensations and affections whereby it carries out its purpose [15] against the Creator; so that it cannot even in this be ruled [16] to be irrational, as if it were wanting in proper sensations and affections. These points we shall have to insist on [17] much more fully, when we come to plead the cause of the Creator, where they will also incur our condemnation.

CHAP. XXVI.—IN THE ATTRIBUTE OF JUSTICE, MARCION'S GOD IS HOPELESSLY WEAK AND UNGODLIKE. HE DISLIKES EVIL, BUT DOES NOT PUNISH ITS PERPETRATION.

But it is here sufficient that the extreme perversity of their god is proved from the mere exposition of his lonely goodness, in which they refuse to ascribe to him such emotions of mind as they censure in the Creator. Now, if he is susceptible of no feeling of rivalry, or anger, or damage, or injury, as one who refrains from exercising judicial power, I cannot tell how any system of discipline—and that, too, a plenary one—can be consistent in him. For how is it possible that he should issue commands, if he does not mean to execute them; or forbid sins, if he intends not to punish them, but rather to decline the functions of the judge, as being a stranger to all notions of severity and judicial chastisement? For why does he forbid the commission of that which he punishes not when perpetrated? It would have been far more right, if he had not forbidden what he meant not to punish, than that he should punish what he had not forbidden. Nay, it was his duty even to have permitted what he was about to prohibit in so unreasonable a way, as to annex no penalty to the offence. [18] For even now that is tacitly permitted which is forbidden without any infliction of vengeance. Besides, he only forbids the commission of that which he does not like to have done. Most listless, therefore, is he, since he takes no offence at the doing of what he dislikes to be done, although dis-

[1] Ruminans.
[2] Judiciarias vires.
[3] De ceteris motibus.
[4] Nec necessario.
[5] Retro.
[6] Concussibilis.
[7] Concupiscentiæ.
[8] (i.e., Marcion's god.)
[9] Porro.
[10] Æmulatione.
[11] Denique.
[12] Scilicet.

[13] Officiales suæ.
[14] Suis dotibus.
[15] Administratur.
[16] Præscribatur.
[17] Defendemus.
[18] Ut non defensurus. Defendo = vindico. See Oehler's note for other instances.

pleasure ought to be the companion of his violated will. Now, if he is offended, he ought to be angry; if angry, he ought to inflict punishment. For such infliction is the just fruit of anger, and anger is the debt of displeasure, and displeasure (as I have said) is the companion of a violated will. However, he inflicts no punishment; therefore he takes no offence.

He takes no offence, therefore his will is not wronged, although that is done which he was unwilling to have done; and the transgression is now committed with the acquiescence of[1] his will, because whatever offends not the will is not committed against the will. Now, if this is to be the principle of the divine virtue or goodness, to be unwilling indeed that a thing be done and to prohibit it, and yet not be moved by its commission, we then allege that he has been moved already when he declared his unwillingness; and that it is vain for him not to be moved by the accomplishment of a thing after being moved at the possibility thereof, when he willed it not to be done. For he prohibited it by his not willing it. Did he not therefore do a judicial act, when he declared his unwillingness, and consequent prohibition of it? For he judged that it ought not to be done, and he deliberately declared[2] that it should be forbidden. Consequently by this time even he performs the part of a judge. If it is unbecoming for God to discharge a judicial function, or at least only so far becoming that He may merely declare His unwillingness, and pronounce His prohibition, then He may not even punish for an offence when it is committed. Now, nothing is so unworthy of the Divine Being as not to execute retribution on what He has disliked and forbidden. *First*, He owes the infliction of chastisement to whatever sentence or law He promulges, for the vindication of His authority and the maintenance of submission to it; *secondly*, because hostile opposition is inevitable to what He has disliked to be done, and by that dislike forbidden. Moreover, it would be a more unworthy course for God to spare the evil-doer than to punish him, especially in the most good and holy God, who is not otherwise fully good than as the enemy of evil, and *that* to such a degree as to display His love of good by the hatred of evil, and to fulfil His defence of the former by the extirpation of the latter.

CHAP. XXVII.—DANGEROUS EFFECTS TO RELIGION AND MORALITY OF THE DOCTRINE OF SO WEAK A GOD.

Again, he plainly judges evil by not willing it, and condemns it by prohibiting it; while, on the other hand, he acquits it by not avenging it, and lets it go free by not punishing it. What a prevaricator of truth is such a god! What a dissembler with his own decision! Afraid to condemn what he really condemns, afraid to hate what he does not love, permitting that to be done which he does not allow, choosing to indicate what he dislikes rather than deeply examine it! This will turn out an imaginary goodness, a phantom of discipline, perfunctory in duty, careless in sin. Listen, ye sinners; and ye who have not yet come to this, hear, that you may attain to such a pass! A better god has been discovered, who never takes offence, is never angry, never inflicts punishment, who has prepared no fire in hell, no gnashing of teeth in the outer darkness! He is purely and simply good. He indeed forbids all delinquency, but only in word. He is in you, if you are willing to pay him homage,[3] for the sake of appearances, that you may seem to honour God; for your fear he does not want. And so satisfied are the Marcionites with such pretences, that they have no fear of their god at all. They say it is only a bad man who will be feared, a good man will be loved. Foolish man, do you say that he whom you call Lord ought not to be feared, whilst the very title you give him indicates a power which must itself be feared? But how are you going to love, without some fear that you do not love? Surely (such a god) is neither your Father, towards whom your love for duty's sake should be consistent with fear because of His power; nor your proper[4] Lord, whom you should love for His humanity and fear as your teacher.[5] Kidnappers[6] indeed are loved after this fashion, but they are not feared. For power will not be feared, except it be just and regular, although it may possibly be loved even when corrupt: for it is by allurement that it stands, not by authority; by flattery, not by proper influence. And what can be more direct flattery than not to punish sins? Come, then, if you do not fear God as being good, why do you not boil over into every kind of lust, and so realize that which is, I believe, the main enjoyment of life to all who fear not God? Why do you not frequent the customary pleasures of the maddening circus, the bloodthirsty arena, and

---

[1] Secundum.
[2] Pronunciavit.

[3] Obsequium subsignare.
[4] Legitimus.
[5] Propter disciplinam.
[6] Plagiarii. The *Plagiarius* is the ἀνδραποδιστής or the ψυχαγωγός of Alex. Greek. This "man-stealing" profession was often accompanied with agreeable external accomplishments. Nempe ψυχαγωγοί, quia blandis et mellitis verbis servos alienos sollicitant, et ad se alliciunt. Clemens Alex. *Strom.* i. λύκοι ἅρπαγες προβάτων κωδίοις ἐγκεκρυμμένοι, ἀνδραποδισταί τε καὶ ψυχαγωγοὶ εὐγλῶσσοι, κλέπτοντες μὲν ἀφανῶς, κ.τ.λ.—Desid. Herald. *Animad. ad Arnobium*, p. 101.

the lascivious theatre?[1] Why in persecutions also do you not, when the censer is presented, at once redeem your life by the denial of your faith? God forbid, you say with redoubled[2] emphasis. So you do fear sin, and by your fear prove that He is an object of fear Who forbids the sin. This is quite a different matter from that obsequious homage you pay to the god whom you do not fear, which is identical in perversity indeed to is own conduct, in prohibiting a thing without annexing the sanction of punishment. Still more vainly do they act, who when asked, What is to become of every sinner in that great day? reply, that he is to be cast away out of sight. Is not even this a question of judicial determination? He is adjudged to deserve rejection, and that by a sentence of condemnation; unless the sinner is cast away forsooth for his salvation, that even a leniency like this may fall in consistently with the character of your most good and excellent god! And what will it be to be cast away, but to lose that which a man was in the way of obtaining, were it not for his rejection—that is, his salvation? Therefore his being cast away will involve the forfeiture of salvation; and this sentence cannot possibly be passed upon him, except by an angry and offended authority, who is also the punisher of sin—that is, by a judge.

CHAP. XXVIII.—THIS PERVERSE DOCTRINE DEPRIVES BAPTISM OF ALL ITS GRACE. IF MARCION BE RIGHT, THE SACRAMENT WOULD CONFER NO REMISSION OF SINS, NO REGENERATION, NO GIFT OF THE SPIRIT.

And what will happen to him after he is cast away? He will, they say, be thrown into the Creator's fire. Then has no remedial provision been made (by their god) for the purpose of banishing those that sin against him, without resorting to the cruel measure of delivering them over to the Creator? And what will the Creator then do? I suppose He will prepare for them a hell doubly charged with brimstone,[3] as for blasphemers against Himself; except indeed their god in his zeal, as perhaps might happen, should show clemency to his rival's revolted subjects. Oh, what a god is this! everywhere perverse; nowhere rational; in all cases vain; and therefore a nonentity![4]—in whose state, and condition, and nature, and every appointment, I see no coherence and consistency; no, not even in the very sacrament of his faith! For

what end does baptism serve, according to him? If the remission of sins, how will he make it evident that he remits sins, when he affords no evidence that he retains them? Because he would retain them, if he performed the functions of a judge. If deliverance from death, how could he deliver *from* death, who has not delivered *to* death? For he must have delivered the sinner to death, if he had from the beginning condemned sin. If the regeneration of man, how can he regenerate, who has never generated? For the repetition of an act is impossible to him, by whom nothing any time has been ever done. If the bestowal of the Holy Ghost, how will he bestow the Spirit, who did not at first impart the life? For the life is in a sense the supplement[5] of the Spirit. He therefore seals man, who had never been unsealed[6] in respect of him;[7] washes man, who had never been defiled so far as he was concerned;[7] and into this sacrament of salvation wholly plunges that flesh which is beyond the pale of salvation![8] No farmer will irrigate ground that will yield him no fruit in return, except he be as stupid as Marcion's god. Why then impose sanctity upon our most infirm and most unworthy flesh, either as a burden or as a glory? What shall I say, too, of the uselessness of a discipline which sanctifies what is already sanctified? Why burden the infirm, or glorify the unworthy? Why not remunerate with salvation what it burdens or else glorifies? Why keep back from a work its due reward, by not recompensing the flesh with salvation? Why even permit the honour of sanctity in it to die?

CHAP. XXIX.—MARCION FORBIDS MARRIAGE. TERTULLIAN ELOQUENTLY DEFENDS IT AS HOLY, AND CAREFULLY DISCRIMINATES BETWEEN MARCION'S DOCTRINE AND HIS OWN MONTANISM.

The flesh is not, according to Marcion, immersed in the water of the sacrament, unless it be[9] in virginity, widowhood, or celibacy, or has purchased by divorce a title to baptism, as if even generative impotents[10] did not all receive their flesh from nuptial union. Now, such a scheme as this must no doubt involve the proscription of marriage. Let us see, then, whether it be a just one: not as if we

---

[1] Comp. *Apology*, 38.
[2] Absit, inquis, absit. [i.e., the throwing of a grain of incense into the censer, before the Emperor's image or that of a heathen god.]
[3] Sulphuratiorem gehennam.
[4] Ita neminem.

[5] Suffectura. A something whereon the Spirit may operate; so that the Spirit has a *præfectura* over the anima. [Kaye, p. 179.]
[6] Resignatum. Tertullian here yields to his love of antithesis, and makes almost nonsense of *signo* and *resigno*. The latter verb has the meaning *violate* (in opposition to *signo*, in the phrase *virgo signata*, a pure unviolated virgin).
[7] Apud se.
[8] Exsortem salutis.
[9] Free from all matrimonial impurity.
[10] Spadonibus. This word is more general in sense than *eunuch*, embracing such as are impotent both by nature and by castration. White and Riddle's *Lat. Dict. s. v.*

aimed at destroying the happiness of sanctity, as do certain Nicolaitans in their maintenance of lust and luxury, but as those who have come to the knowledge of sanctity, and pursue it and prefer it, without detriment, however, to marriage; not as if we superseded a bad thing by a good, but only a good thing by a better. For we do not reject marriage, but simply refrain from it.[1] Nor do we prescribe sanctity[2] as the rule, but only recommend it, observing it as a good, yea, even the better state, if each man uses it carefully[3] according to his ability; but at the same time earnestly vindicating marriage, whenever hostile attacks are made against it is a polluted thing, to the disparagement of the Creator. For He bestowed His blessing on matrimony also, as on an honourable estate, for the increase of the human race; as He did indeed on the whole of His creation,[4] for wholesome and good uses. Meats and drinks are not on this account to be condemned, because, when served up with too exquisite a daintiness, they conduce to gluttony; nor is raiment to be blamed, because, when too costlily adorned, it becomes inflated with vanity and pride. So, on the same principle, the estate of matrimony is not to be refused, because, when enjoyed without moderation, it is fanned into a voluptuous flame. There is a great difference between a cause and a fault,[5] between a state and its excess. Consequently it is not an institution of this nature that is to be blamed, but the extravagant use of it; according to the judgment of its founder Himself, who not only said, "Be fruitful, and multiply,"[6] but also, "Thou shalt not commit adultery," and, "Thou shalt not covet thy neighbour's wife;"[7] and who threatened with death the unchaste, sacrilegious, and monstrous abomination both of adultery and unnatural sin with man and beast.[8] Now, if any limitation is set to marrying—such as the spiritual rule,[9] which prescribes but one marriage under the Christian obedience,[10] maintained by the authority of the Paraclete,[11]—it will be His prerogative to fix the limit Who had once been diffuse in His permission; His to gather, Who once scattered; His to cut down the tree, Who planted it; His to reap the harvest, Who sowed the seed; His to declare, "It remaineth that they who have wives be as though they had none,"[12] Who once said, "Be fruitful, and multiply;" His the end to Whom belonged the beginning. Nevertheless, the tree is not cut down as if it deserved blame; nor is the corn reaped, as if it were to be condemned,—but simply because their time is come. So likewise the state of matrimony does not require the hook and scythe of sanctity, as if it were evil; but as being ripe for its discharge, and in readiness for that sanctity which will in the long run bring it a plenteous crop by its reaping. For this leads me to remark of Marcion's god, that in reproaching marriage as an evil and unchaste thing, he is really prejudicing the cause of that very sanctity which he seems to serve. For he destroys the material on which it subsists; if there is to be no marriage, there is no sanctity. All proof of abstinence is lost when excess is impossible; for sundry things have thus their evidence in their contraries. Just as "strength is made perfect in weakness,"[13] so likewise is continence made manifest by the permission to marry. Who indeed will be called continent, if that be taken away which gives him the opportunity of pursuing a life of continence? What room for temperance in appetite does famine give? What repudiation of ambitious projects does poverty afford? What bridling of lust can the eunuch merit? To put a complete stop, however, to the sowing of the human race, may, for aught I know, be quite consistent for Marcion's most good and excellent god. For how could he desire the salvation of man, whom he forbids to be born, when he takes away that institution from which his birth arises? How will he find any one on whom to set the mark of his goodness, when he suffers him not to come into existence? How is it possible to love him whose origin he hates? Perhaps he is afraid of a redundant population, lest he should be weary in liberating so many; lest he should have to make many heretics; lest Marcionite parents should produce too many noble disciples of Marcion. The cruelty of Pharaoh, which slew its victims at their birth, will not prove to be more inhuman in comparison.[14] For while he destroyed lives, our heretic's god refuses to give them: the one removes from life, the other admits none to it. There is no difference in either as to their homicide—man is slain by both of them; by the former just after birth, by the latter as yet unborn. Thanks should we owe thee, thou

---

[1] Tertullian's *Montanism* appears here.
[2] i.e., abstinence from marriage.
[3] Secundo. [This, indeed, seems to be a fair statement of Patristic doctrine concerning marriage. As to our author's variations see Kaye, p. 378.]
[4] Universum conditionis.
[5] *Causa* in its proper sense is, "that through which anything takes place;" its just and normal state, therefore. *Culpa* is the derangement of the causa; some flaw in it.
[6] Gen. i. 28.
[7] Ex. xx. 14, 17.
[8] Lev. xx. 10, 13, 15.
[9] Ratio.
[10] In fide. Tertullian uses (*De Pud.* 18) "ante fidem" as synonymous with *ante baptismum*; similarly "post fidem."
[11] [Bad as this is, does it argue the lapse of our author as at this time complete?]

[12] 1 Cor. vii. 29.
[13] 2 Cor. xii. 9.
[14] This is the force of the *erit* instead of the past tense.

god of our heretic, hadst thou only checked[1] the dispensation of the Creator in uniting male and female; for from such a union indeed has thy Marcion been born! Enough, however, of Marcion's god, who is shown to have absolutely no existence at all, both by our definitions[2] of the one only Godhead, and the condition of his attributes.[3] The whole course, however, of this little work aims directly at this conclusion. If, therefore, we seem to anybody to have achieved but little result as yet, let him reserve his expectations, until we examine the very Scripture which Marcion quotes.

---

[1] Isses in, i.e., obstitisses, *check* or *resist*, for then Marcion would, of course, not have been born : the common text has *esses in*.

[2] Tertullian has discussed these "definitions" in chap. ii. vii., and the "conditions" from chap. viii. onward. He will "examine the Scripture" passages in books iv. and v. Fr. Junius.

[3] Statuum.

THE FIVE BOOKS AGAINST MARCION.

BOOK II.[1]

WHEREIN TERTULLIAN SHOWS THAT THE CREATOR, OR DEMIURGE, WHOM MARCION CALUMNIATED, IS THE TRUE AND GOOD GOD.

CHAP. I.—THE METHODS OF MARCION'S ARGU-
MENT INCORRECT AND ABSURD. THE PROPER
COURSE OF THE ARGUMENT.

THE occasion of reproducing this little
work, the fortunes of which we noticed in
the preface of our first book, has furnished us
with the opportunity of distinguishing, in our
treatment of the subject of two Gods in opposition to Marcion, each of them with a description and section of his own, according to the
division of the subject-matter, defining one
of the gods to have no existence at all, and
maintaining of the Other that He is rightly[2]
God; thus far keeping pace with the heretic
of Pontus, who has been pleased to admit
one unto, and exclude the other.[3] For he
could not build up his mendacious scheme
without pulling down the system of truth.
He found it necessary to demolish[4] some
other thing, in order to build up the theory
which he wished. This process, however,
is like constructing a house without preparing
suitable materials.[5] The discussion ought to
have been directed to this point alone, that he
is no god who supersedes the Creator. Then,
when the false god had been excluded by certain rules which prescriptively settle what is
the character of the One only perfect Divinity,
there could have remained no longer any
question as to the true God. The proof of
His existence would have been clear, and
that, too, amid the failure of all evidence in
support of any other god; and still clearer[6]

would have seemed the point as to the honour in which He ought without controversy
to be held: that He ought to be worshipped
rather than judged; served reverentially rather
than handled critically, or even dreaded for
His severity. For what was more fully needed
by man than a careful estimate of[7] the true
God, on whom, so to speak, he had alighted,[8]
because there was no other god?

CHAP. II.—THE TRUE DOCTRINE OF GOD THE
CREATOR. THE HERETICS PRETENDED TO A
KNOWLEDGE OF THE DIVINE BEING, OPPOSED
TO AND SUBVERSIVE OF REVELATION. GOD'S
NATURE AND WAYS PAST HUMAN DISCOVERY.
ADAM'S HERESY.

We have now, then, cleared our way to the
contemplation of the Almighty God, the
Lord and Maker of the universe. His greatness, as I think, is shown in this, that from
the beginning He made Himself known: He
never hid Himself, but always shone out
brightly, even before the time of Romulus,
to say nothing of that of Tiberius; with the
exception indeed that the heretics, and they
alone, know Him not, although they take
such pains about Him. They on this account
suppose that another god must be assumed
to exist, because they are more able to censure than deny Him whose existence is so
evident, deriving all their thoughts about
God from the deductions of sense; just as if
some blind man, or a man of imperfect vision,[9] chose to assume some other sun of milder
and healthier ray, because he sees not that
which is the object of sight.[10] There is, O

---

[1] [Contains no marks of Montanism of a decisive nature. Kaye, p. 54.]
[2] Digne.
[3] From the dignity of the supreme Godhead.
[4] Snbruere.
[5] Propria paratura.
[6] With the *tanto* (answering to the previous *quanto*) should be understood *magis*, a frequent omission in our author.

[7] Cura in.
[8] Inciderat.
[9] Fluitantibus oculis.
[10] Quem videat non videt.

man, but one sun which rules [1] this world; and even when you think otherwise of him, he is best and useful; and although to you he may seem too fierce and baneful, or else, it may be, too sordid and corrupt, he yet is true to the laws of his own existence. Unable as you are to see through those laws, you would be equally impotent to bear the rays of any other sun, were there one, however great and good. Now, you whose sight is defective [2] in respect of the inferior god, what is your view of the sublimer One? Really you are too lenient [3] to your weakness; and set not yourself to the proof [4] of things, holding God to be certainly, undoubtedly, and therefore sufficiently known, the very moment you have discovered Him to exist, though you know Him not except on the side where He has willed His proofs to lie. But you do not even deny God intelligently,[5] you treat of Him ignorantly;[6] nay, you accuse Him with a semblance of intelligence,[7] whom if you did but know Him, you would never accuse, nay, never treat of.[8] You give Him His name indeed, but you deny the essential truth of that name, that is, the greatness which is called God; not acknowledging it to be such as, were it possible for it to have been known to man in every respect,[9] would not be greatness. Isaiah even so early, with the clearness of an apostle, foreseeing the thoughts of heretical hearts, asked, "Who hath known the mind of the Lord? or who hath been His counsellor? With whom took He counsel? . . . or who taught Him knowledge, and showed to Him the way of understanding?"[10] With whom the apostle agreeing exclaims, "Oh the depth of the riches both of the wisdom and knowledge of God! how unsearchable are His judgments, and His ways past finding out!"[11] "His judgments unsearchable," as being those of God the Judge; and "His ways past finding out," as comprising an understanding and knowledge which no man has ever shown to Him, except it may be those critics of the Divine Being, who say, God ought not to have been this,[12] and He ought rather to have been that; as if any one knew what is in God, except the Spirit of God.[13] Moreover, having the

spirit of the world, and "in the wisdom of God by wisdom knowing not God,"[14] they seem to themselves to be wiser [15] than God; because, as the wisdom of the world is foolishness with God, so also the wisdom of God is folly in the world's esteem. We, however, know that "the foolishness of God is wiser than men, and the weakness of God is stronger than men."[16] Accordingly, God is then especially great, when He is small [17] to man; then especially good, when not good in man's judgment; then especially unique, when He seems to man to be two or more. Now, if from the very first "the natural man, not receiving the things of the Spirit of God,"[18] has deemed God's law to be foolishness, and has therefore neglected to observe it; and as a further consequence, by his not having faith, "even that which he seemeth to have hath been taken from him"[19]—such as the grace of paradise and the friendship of God, by means of which he might have known all things of God, if he had continued in his obedience—what wonder is it, if he,[20] reduced to his material nature, and banished to the toil of tilling the ground, has in his very labour, downcast and earth-gravitating as it was, handed on that earth-derived spirit of the world to his entire race, wholly natural [21] and heretical as it is, and not receiving the things which belong to God? Or who will hesitate to declare the great sin of Adam to have been heresy, when he committed it by the choice [22] of his own will rather than of God's? Except that Adam never said to his fig-tree, Why hast thou made me thus? He confessed that he was led astray; and he did not conceal the seducer. He was a very rude heretic. He was disobedient; but yet he did not blaspheme his Creator, nor blame that Author of his being, Whom from the beginning of his life he had found to be so good and excellent, and Whom he had perhaps [23] made his own judge from the very first.

CHAP. III.—GOD KNOWN BY HIS WORKS. HIS GOODNESS SHOWN IN HIS CREATIVE ENERGY; BUT EVERLASTING IN ITS NATURE; INHERENT IN GOD, PREVIOUS TO ALL EXHIBITION OF IT. THE FIRST STAGE OF THIS GOODNESS PRIOR TO MAN.

It will therefore be right for us, as we enter on the examination of the known God, when

---

[1] Temperat.
[2] Cæcutis.
[3] Quin potius parcis.
[4] In periculo extenderis.
[5] Ut sciens.
[6] Ut nesciens.
[7] Quasi sciens.
[8] Retractares.
[9] Omnifariam.
[10] Comp. Isa. xl. 13, 14, with Rom. xi. 34.
[11] Rom. xi. 33.
[12] Sic non debuit Deus. This perhaps may mean, God ought not to have *done* this, etc.
[13] 1 Cor. ii. 11.

[14] Cor. i. 21.
[15] Consultiores.
[16] 1 Cor. i. 25.
[17] Pusillus.
[18] 1 Cor. ii. 14.
[19] Luke viii. 18; comp. Matt. xiii. 12.
[20] That is, the natural man, the ψυχικός.
[21] Animali = ψυχικῷ.
[22] Electionem. By this word our author translates the Greek αἵρεσις. Comp. *De Præscr. Her.* 6, p. 245, *supra.*
[23] Si forte.

the question arises, in what condition He is known to us, to begin with His works, which are prior to man; so that His goodness, being discovered immediately along with Himself, and then constituted and prescriptively settled, may suggest to us some sense whereby we may understand how the subsequent order of things came about. The disciples of Marcion, moreover, may possibly be able, while recognising the goodness of our God, to learn how worthy it is likewise of the Divine Being, on those very grounds whereby we have proved it to be unworthy in the case of their god. Now this very point,[1] which is a material one in their scheme,[2] *Marcion* did not find in any other god, but eliminated it for himself out of his own god. The first goodness, then,[3] was that of the Creator, whereby God was unwilling to remain hidden for ever; in other words, (unwilling) that there should not be a something by which God should become known. For what, indeed, is so good as the knowledge and fruition[4] of God? Now, although it did not transpire[5] that this was good, because as yet there existed nothing to which it could transpire, yet God foreknew what good would eventually transpire, and therefore He set Himself about developing[6] His own perfect goodness, for the accomplishment of the good which was to transpire; not, indeed, a sudden goodness issuing in some accidental boon[7] or in some excited impulse,[8] such as must be dated simply from the moment when it began to operate. For if it did itself produce its own beginning when it began to operate, it had not, in fact, a beginning itself when it acted. When, however, an initial act had been once done by it, the scheme of temporal seasons began, for distinguishing and noting which, the stars and luminaries of heaven were arranged in their order. "Let them be," says God, "for seasons, and for days, and years."[9] Previous, then, to this temporal course, (the goodness) which created time had not time; nor before that beginning which the same goodness originated, had it a beginning. Being therefore without all order of a beginning, and all mode of time, it will be reckoned to possess an age, measureless in extent[10] and endless in duration;[11] nor will it be possible to regard it as a sudden or adventitious or impulsive emotion,

because it has nothing to occasion such an estimate of itself; in other words, no sort of temporal sequence. It must therefore be accounted an eternal attribute, inbred in God,[12] and everlasting,[13] and on this account worthy of the Divine Being, putting to shame for ever[14] the benevolence of Marcion's god, subsequent as he is to (I will not say) all beginnings and times, but to the very malignity of the Creator, if indeed malignity could possibly have been found in goodness.

CHAP. IV.—THE NEXT STAGE OCCURS IN THE CREATION OF MAN BY THE ETERNAL WORD. SPIRITUAL AS WELL AS PHYSICAL GIFTS TO MAN. THE BLESSINGS OF MAN'S FREE-WILL.

The goodness of God having, therefore, provided man for the pursuit of the knowledge of Himself, added this to its original notification,[15] that it first prepared a habitation for him, the vast fabric (of the world) to begin with, and then afterwards[16] the vaster one (of a higher world,[17]) that he might on a great as well as on a smaller stage practise and advance in his probation, and so be promoted from the *good* which God had given him, that is, from his high position, to God's *best;* that is, to some higher abode.[18] In this good work *God* employs a most excellent minister, even His own Word. "My heart" He says, "hath emitted my most excellent Word."[19] Let Marcion take hence his first lesson on the noble fruit of this truly most excellent tree. But, like a most clumsy clown, he has grafted a good branch on a bad stock. The sapling, however, of his blasphemy shall be never strong: it shall wither with its planter, and thus shall be manifested the nature of the good tree. Look at the total result: how fruitful was the Word! God issued His *fiat*, and it was done: God also saw that it was

---

[12] Deo ingenita " Natural to," or " inherent in."
[13] Perpetua. [Truly, a sublime Theodicy.]
[14] Suffundens jam hinc.
[15] Præconio suo.
[16] Postmodum . . . postmodum.
[17] See Bp. Bull on *The State of Man before the Fall. Works,* ii. 73–81.
[18] Habitaculum majus.
[19] " Eructavit cor. meum Sermonem optimum " is Tertullian's reading of Ps. xlv. 1, " My heart is inditing a good matter," A. V., which the Vulgate, Ps. xliv. 1, renders by " Eructavit cor meum verbum bonum," and the Septuagint by Ἐξηρεύξατο ἡ καρδία μου λόγον ἀγαθόν. This is a tolerably literal rendering of the original words, רָחַשׁ לִבִּי דָּבָר טוֹב. In these words the Fathers used to descry an adumbration of the mystery of the Son's eternal generation from the Father, and His coming forth in time to create the world. See Bellarmine, *On the Psalms* (Paris ed. 1861), vol. i. 292. The Psalm is no doubt eminently Messianic, as both Jewish and Christian writers have ever held. See Perowne, *The Psalms,* vol. i. p. 216. Bishop Bull reviews at length the theological opinions of Tertullian, and shows that he held the eternity of the Son of God, whom he calls " Sermo " or " Verbum Dei." See *Defensio Fidei Nicænæ* (translation in the ",Oxford Library of the Fathers," by the translator of this work) vol. ii. 509–545. In the same volume, p. 482, the passage from the Psalm before us is similarly applied by Novatian: " Sic Dei Verbum processit, de quo dictum est, *Eructavit cor meum Verbum bonum.*" [See vol. ii. p. 98, this series: and Kaye, p. 515.]

---

[1] That is, " the goodness " of God.
[2] Agnitionis, their *Gnostic* scheme.
[3] Denique. This particle refers back to the argument previous to its interruption by the allusion to Marcion and his followers.
[4] Fructus, the enjoyment of God's works.
[5] Apparebat. [Was not manifest.]
[6] Commisit in.
[7] Obventiciæ bonitatis.
[8] Provocaticiæ animationis.
[9] Gen. i. 14.
[10] Immensa.
[11] Interminabili.

good;[1] not as if He were ignorant of the good until He saw it; but because it was good, He therefore saw it, and honoured it, and set His seal upon it; and consummated[2] the goodness of His works by His vouchsafing to them that contemplation. Thus God blessed what He made good, in order that He might commend Himself to you as whole and perfect, good both in word and act.[3] As yet the Word knew no malediction, because He was a stranger to malefaction.[4] We shall see what reasons required *this* also of God. Meanwhile the world consisted of all things good, plainly foreshowing how much good was preparing for him for whom all this was provided. Who indeed was so worthy of dwelling amongst the works of God, as he who was His own image and likeness? That image was wrought out by a goodness even more operative than its wont,[5] with no imperious word, but with friendly hand preceded by an almost affable[6] utterance: "Let us make man in our image, after our likeness."[7] Goodness spake the word; Goodness formed man of the dust of the ground into so great a substance of the flesh, built up out of one material with so many qualities; Goodness breathed into him a soul, not dead, but living. Goodness gave him dominion[8] over all things, which he was to enjoy and rule over, and even give names to. In addition to this, Goodness annexed pleasures[9] to man; so that, while master of the whole world,[10] he might tarry among higher delights, being translated into paradise, out of the world into the Church.[11] The self-same Goodness provided also a help meet for him, that there might be nothing in his lot that was not good. For, said He, that the man be alone is not good.[12] He knew full well what a blessing to him would be the sex of Mary,[13] and also of the Church. The law, however, which you find fault with,[14] and wrest into a subject of contention, was imposed on man by Goodness, aiming at his happiness, that he might cleave to God, and so not show himself an abject creature rather than a free one, nor reduce himself to the level of the other animals, his subjects, which were free from God, and exempt from all tedious subjection;[15] but might, as the sole human being, boast that he alone was worthy of receiving laws from God; and as a rational being, capable of intelligence and knowledge, be restrained within the bounds of rational liberty, subject to Him who had subjected all things unto him. To secure the observance of this law, Goodness likewise took counsel by help of this sanction: "In the day that thou eatest thereof, thou shalt surely die."[16] For it was a most benignant act of His thus to point out the issues of transgression, lest ignorance of the danger should encourage a neglect of obedience. Now, since[17] it was given as a reason previous to the imposition of the law, it also amounted to a motive for subsequently observing it, that a penalty was annexed to its transgression; a penalty, indeed, which He who proposed it was still unwilling that it should be incurred. Learn then the goodness of our God amidst these things and up to this point; learn it from His excellent works, from His kindly blessings, from His indulgent bounties, from His gracious providences, from His laws and warnings, so good and merciful.

CHAP. V. — MARCION'S CAVILS CONSIDERED. HIS OBJECTION REFUTED, I.E., MAN'S FALL SHOWED FAILURE IN GOD. THE PERFECTION OF MAN'S BEING LAY IN HIS LIBERTY, WHICH GOD PURPOSELY BESTOWED ON HIM. THE FALL IMPUTABLE TO MAN'S OWN CHOICE.

Now then, ye dogs, whom the apostle puts outside,[18] and who yelp at the God of truth, let us come to your various questions. These are the bones of contention, which you are perpetually gnawing! If God is good, and prescient of the future, and able to avert evil, why did He permit man, the very image and likeness of Himself, and, by the origin of his soul, His own substance too, to be deceived by the devil, and fall from obedience of the law into death? For if He had been good, and so unwilling that such a catastrophe should happen, and prescient, so as not to be ignorant of what was to come to pass, and powerful enough to hinder its occurrence, that issue would never have come about, which should be impossible under these three conditions of the divine greatness. Since, however, it has occurred, the contrary proposition is most certainly true, that God must

---

[1] Gen. i.
[2] Dispungens, i.e., examinans et probans et ita quasi consummans (Oehler).
[3] This twofold virtue is very tersely expressed: "Sic et *benedicebat* quæ *benefaciebat*."
[4] This, the translator fears, is only a clumsy way of representing the terseness of our author's "maledicere" and "malefacere."
[5] Bonitas et quidem operantior.
[6] Blandiente.
[7] Gen. i. 26.
[8] Præfecit.
[9] Delicias.
[10] Totius orbis possidens.
[11] There is a profound thought here; in his tract, *De Pœnit.* 10, he says, "Where *one or two* are, is the church, and the church is Christ." Hence what he here calls Adam's "higher delights," even spiritual blessings in Christ with Eve. [Important note in Kaye, p. 304.]
[12] See Gen. ii. 18.
[13] Sexum Mariæ. For the Virgin Mary gave birth to Christ, the Saviour of men; and the virgin mother the Church, the spouse of Christ, gives birth to Christians (Rigalt.).
[14] Arguis.

[15] Ex fastidio liberis.
[16] Gen. ii. 17.
[17] Porro si.
[18] Rev. xxii. 15.

be deemed neither good, nor prescient, nor powerful. For *as* no such issue could have happened had God been such as He is reputed—good, and prescient, and mighty—*so* has this issue actually happened, because He is not such a God. In reply, we must first vindicate those attributes in the Creator which are called in question—namely, His goodness and foreknowledge, and power. But I shall not linger long over this point[1] for Christ's own definition[2] comes to our aid at once. From works must proofs be obtained. The Creator's works testify at once to His goodness, since they are good, as we have shown, and to His power, since they are mighty, and spring indeed out of nothing. And even if they were made out of some (previous) matter, as some[3] will have it, they are even thus out of nothing, because they *were* not what they *are*. In short, both they are great because they are good; and[4] God is likewise mighty, because all things are His own, whence He is almighty. But what shall I say of His prescience, which has for its witnesses as many prophets as it inspired? After all,[5] what title to prescience do we look for in the Author of the universe, since it was by this very attribute that He foreknew all things when He appointed them their places, and appointed them their places when He foreknew them? There is sin itself. If He had not foreknown this, He would not have proclaimed a caution against it under the penalty of death. Now, if there were in God such attributes as must have rendered it both impossible and improper for any evil to have happened to man,[6] and yet evil did occur, let us consider man's condition also—whether *it* were not, in fact, rather the cause why that came to pass which could not have happened through God. I find, then, that man was by God constituted free, master of his own will and power; indicating the presence of God's image and likeness in him by nothing so well as by this constitution of his nature. For it was not by his face, and by the lineaments of his body, though they were so varied in his human nature, that he expressed his likeness to the form of God; but he showed his stamp[7] in that essence which he derived from God Himself (that is, the spiritual,[8] which answered to the form of God), and in the freedom and power of his will. This his state was confirmed even by the very law which God then imposed upon

him. For a law would not be imposed upon one who had it not in his power to render that obedience which is due to law; nor again, would the penalty of death be threatened against sin, if a contempt of the law were impossible to man in the liberty of his will. So in the Creator's subsequent laws also you will find, when He sets before man good and evil, life and death, that the entire course of discipline is arranged in precepts by God's calling men from sin, and threatening and exhorting them; and this on no other ground than[9] that man is free, with a will either for obedience or resistance.

CHAP. VI.—THIS LIBERTY VINDICATED IN RESPECT OF ITS ORIGINAL CREATION; SUITABLE ALSO FOR EXHIBITING THE GOODNESS AND THE PURPOSE OF GOD. REWARD AND PUNISHMENT IMPOSSIBLE IF MAN WERE GOOD OR EVIL THROUGH NECESSITY AND NOT CHOICE.

But although we shall be understood, from our argument, to be only so affirming man's unshackled power over his will, that what happens to him should be laid to his own charge, and not to God's, yet that you may not object, even now, that he ought not to have been so constituted, since his liberty and power of will might turn out to be injurious, I will first of all maintain that he was rightly so constituted, that I may with the greater confidence commend both his actual constitution, and the additional fact of its being worthy of the Divine Being; the cause which led to man's being created with such a constitution being shown to be the better one. Moreover, man thus constituted will be protected by both the goodness of God and by His purpose,[10] both of which are always found in concert in our God. For His purpose is no purpose without goodness; nor is His goodness goodness without a purpose, except forsooth in the case of Marcion's god, who is purposelessly[11] good, as we have shown.[12] Well, then, it was proper that God should be known; it was no doubt[13] a good and reasonable[14] thing. Proper also was it that there should be something worthy of knowing God. What could be found so worthy as the image and likeness of God? This also was undoubtedly good and reasonable. Therefore it was proper that (he who is) the image and likeness of God should be formed with a free will and a mastery of him-

---

1 Articulo.
2 John x. 25.
3 He refers to Hermogenes · see *Adv. Hermog.* chap. xxxii.
4 Vel . . . vel.
5 Quanquam.
6 As the Marcionites alleged.
7 Signatus est.
8 Animæ.

9 Nec alias nisi.
10 Ratio, or, "His reason." We have used both words, which are equally suitable to the Divine Being, as seemed most convenient.
11 Irrationaliter, or, "irrationally."
12 See above, book i. chap. xxiii. p. 288.
13 Utique.
14 Rationale, or, "consistent with His purpose."

self;[1] so that this very thing—namely, freedom of will and self-command—might be reckoned as the image and likeness of God in him. For this purpose such an essence[2] was adapted[3] to man as suited this character,[4] even the afflatus of the Deity, Himself free and uncontrolled.[5] But if you will take some other view of the case,[6] how came it to pass[7] that man, when in possession of the whole world, did not above all things reign in self-possession[8]—a master over others, a slave to himself? The goodness of God, then, you can learn from His gracious gift[9] to man, and His purpose from His disposal of all things.[10] At present, let God's *goodness* alone occupy our attention, that which gave so large a gift to man, even the liberty of his will. God's *purpose* claims some other opportunity of treatment, offering as it does instruction of like import. Now, God alone is good by nature. For He, who has that which is without beginning, has it not by creation,[11] but by nature. Man, however, who exists entirely by creation, having a beginning, along with that beginning obtained the form in which he exists; and thus he is not by nature disposed to good, but by creation, not having it as his own attribute to be good, because, (as we have said,) it is not by nature, but by creation, that he is disposed to good, according to the appointment of his good Creator, even the Author of all good. In order, therefore, that man might have a goodness of his own,[12] bestowed[13] on him by God, and there might be henceforth in man a property, and in a certain sense a natural attribute of goodness, there was assigned to him in the constitution of his nature, as a formal witness[14] of the goodness which God bestowed upon him, freedom and power of the will, such as should cause good to be performed spontaneously by man, as a property of his own, on the ground that no less than this[15] would be required in the matter of a goodness which was to be voluntarily exercised by him, that is to say, by the liberty of his will, without either favour or servility to the constitution of his nature, so that man

should be good[16] just up to this point,[17] if he should display his goodness in accordance with his natural constitution indeed, but still as the result of his will, as a property of his nature; and, by a similar exercise of volition,[18] should show himself to be too strong[19] in defence against evil also (for even this God, of course, foresaw), being free, and master of himself; because, if he were wanting in this prerogative *of self-mastery*, so as to perform even good by necessity and not will, he would, in the helplessness of his servitude, become subject to the usurpation of evil, a slave as much to evil as to good. Entire freedom of will, therefore, was conferred upon him in both tendencies; so that, as master of himself, he might constantly encounter good by spontaneous observance of it, and evil by its spontaneous avoidance; because, were man even otherwise circumstanced, it was yet his bounden duty, in the judgment of God, to do justice according to the motions[20] of his will, regarded, of course, as free. But the reward neither of good nor of evil could be paid to the man who should be found to have been either good or evil through necessity and not choice. In this really lay[21] the law which did not exclude, but rather prove, *human* liberty by a spontaneous rendering of obedience, or a spontaneous commission of iniquity; so patent was the liberty of man's will for either issue. Since, therefore, both the goodness and purpose of God are[22] discovered in the gift to man of freedom in his will, it is not right, after ignoring the original definition of goodness and purpose which it was necessary to determine previous to any discussion of the subject, on subsequent facts to presume to say that God ought not in such a way to have formed man, because the issue was other than what was assumed to be[23] proper for God. We ought rather,[24] after duly considering that it behoved God so to create *man*, to leave this consideration unimpaired, and to survey the other aspects of the case. It is, no doubt, an easy process for persons who take offence at the fall of man, before they have looked into the facts of his creation, to impute the blame of what happened to the Creator, without any examination of His purpose. To conclude: the goodness of God, then fully considered from the beginning of His works, will be enough to convince us that nothing evil could

---

[1] Suæ potestatis.
[2] Substantia.
[3] Accommodata.
[4] Status.
[5] Suæ potestatis.
[6] Sed et alias.
[7] Quale erat.
[8] Animi sui possessione.
[9] Dignatione.
[10] Ex dispositione. The same as the "universa disponendo" above.
[11] Institutione.
[12] Bonum jam suum, not *bonitatem*.
[13] Emancipatum.
[14] Libripens. The language here is full of legal technicalities, derived from the Roman usage in conveyance of property. "Libripens quasi arbiter mancipationis" (Rigalt.).
[15] Quoniam (with a subj.) et hoc.

[16] Bonus consisteret.
[17] Ita demum.
[18] Proinde.
[19] Fortior.
[20] Meritis.
[21] Constituta est.
[22] Our author's word *invenitur* (in the singular) combines the *bonitas* and *ratio* in one view.
[23] The verb is *subj.*, "deceret.
[24] Sed, with *oportet* understood.

possibly have come forth from God; and the liberty of man will, after a second thought,[1] show us that it alone is chargeable with the fault which itself committed.

CHAP. VII.—IF GOD HAD ANYHOW CHECKED MAN'S LIBERTY, MARCION WOULD HAVE BEEN READY WITH ANOTHER AND OPPOSITE CAVIL. MAN'S FALL FORESEEN BY GOD. PROVISION MADE FOR IT REMEDIALLY AND CONSISTENTLY WITH HIS TRUTH AND GOODNESS.

By such a conclusion all is reserved[2] unimpaired to God; both His natural goodness, and the purposes of His governance and foreknowledge, and the abundance of His power. You ought, however, to deduct from God's attributes both His supreme earnestness of purpose[3] and most excellent truth in His whole creation, if you would cease to inquire whether anything could have happened against the will of God. For, while holding this earnestness and truth of the good God, which are indeed[4] capable of proof from the rational creation, you will not wonder at the fact that God did not interfere to prevent the occurrence of what He wished not to happen, in order that He might keep from harm what He wished. For, since He had once for all allowed (and, as we have shown, worthily allowed) to man freedom of will and mastery of himself, surely He from His very authority in creation permitted *these gifts* to be enjoyed: to be enjoyed, too, so far as lay in Himself, according to His own character as God, that is, for good (for who would permit anything hostile to himself?); and, so far as lay in man, according to the impulses of his liberty (for who does not, when giving anything to any one to enjoy, accompany the gift with a permission to enjoy it with all his heart and will?). The necessary consequence,[5] therefore, was, that God must separate from the liberty which He had once for all bestowed upon man (in other words, keep within Himself), both His foreknowledge and power, through which He might have prevented man's falling into danger when attempting wrongly to enjoy his liberty. Now, if He had interposed, He would have rescinded the liberty of man's will, which He had permitted with set purpose, and in goodness. But, suppose God had interposed; suppose Him to have abrogated man's liberty, by warning him from the tree, and keeping off the subtle serpent from his interview with the woman;

would not Marcion then exclaim, What a frivolous, unstable, and faithless Lord, cancelling the gifts He had bestowed! Why did He allow any liberty of will, if He afterwards withdrew it? Why withdraw it after allowing it? Let Him choose where to brand Himself with error, either in His original constitution of man, or in His subsequent abrogation thereof! If He had checked (man's freedom), would He not then seem to have been rather deceived, through want of foresight into the future? But in giving it full scope, who would not say that He did so in ignorance of the issue of things? God, however, did foreknow that man would make a bad use of his created constitution; and yet what can be so worthy of God as His earnestness of purpose, and the truth of His created works, be they what they may? Man must see, if he failed to make the most of[6] the good gift he had received, how that he was himself guilty in respect of the law which he did not choose to keep, and not that the Lawgiver was committing a fraud against His own law, by not permitting its injunctions to be fulfilled. Whenever you are inclined to indulge in such censure[7] (and it is the most becoming for you) against the Creator, recall gently to your mind in His behalf[8] His earnestness, and endurance, and truth, in having given completeness[9] to His creatures both as rational and good.

CHAP. VIII.—MAN, ENDUED WITH LIBERTY, SUPERIOR TO THE ANGELS. OVERCOMES EVEN THE ANGEL WHICH LURED HIM TO HIS FALL, WHEN REPENTANT AND RESUMING OBEDIENCE TO GOD.

For it was not merely that he might live the natural life that God had produced man, but[10] that he should live virtuously, that is, in relation to God and to His law. Accordingly, God gave him *to live* when he was formed into a living soul; but He charged him *to live virtuously* when he was required to obey a law. So also God shows that man was not constituted for death, by now wishing that he should be restored to life, preferring the sinner's repentance to his death.[11] As, therefore, God designed for man a condition of life, so man brought on himself a state of death; and this, too, neither through infirmity nor through ignorance, so that no blame can be imputed to the Creator. No doubt it was an angel who was the seducer; but then the victim of that seduction was free, and master of himself;

---

[1] Recogitata. [Again, a noble Theodicy.]
[2] Salva.
[3] Gravitatem.
[4] Sed, for scilicet, not unfrequent with our author.
[5] That is, from the Marcionite position referred to in the second sentence of this chapter, in opposition to that of Tertullian which follows.
[6] Si non bene dispunxisset.
[7] Peroraturus.
[8] Tibi insusurra pro Creatore.
[9] Functo.
[10] Ut non, "as if he were not," etc.
[11] Ezek. xviii. 23.

and as being the image and likeness of God, was stronger than any angel; and as being, too, the *afflatus* of the Divine Being, was nobler than that material spirit of which angels were made. *Who maketh*, says he, *His angels spirits, and His ministers a flame of fire.*[1] He would not have made all things subject to man, if he had been too weak for the dominion, and inferior to the angels, to whom He assigned no such subjects; nor would He have put the burden of law upon him, if he had been incapable of sustaining so great a weight; nor, again, would He have threatened with the penalty of death a creature whom He knew to be guiltless on the score of his helplessness: in short, if He had made him infirm, it would not have been by liberty and independence of will, but rather by the withholding from him these endowments. And thus it comes to pass, that even now also, the same human being, the same substance of his soul, the same condition as Adam's, is made conqueror over the same devil by the self-same liberty and power of his will, when it moves in obedience to the laws of God.[2]

CHAP. IX.—ANOTHER CAVIL ANSWERED, I.E., THE FALL IMPUTABLE TO GOD, BECAUSE MAN'S SOUL IS A PORTION OF THE SPIRITUAL ESSENCE OF THE CREATOR. THE DIVINE AFFLATUS NOT IN FAULT IN THE SIN OF MAN, BUT THE HUMAN WILL WHICH WAS ADDITIONAL TO IT.

But, you say, in what way soever the substance of the Creator is found to be susceptible of fault, when the *afflatus* of God, that is to say, the soul,[3] offends in man, it cannot but be that that fault of the portion is referrible to the original whole. Now, to meet this objection, we must explain the nature[4] of the soul. We must at the outset hold fast the meaning of the Greek scripture, which has *afflatus*, not spirit.[5] Some interpreters of the Greek, without reflecting on the difference of the words, and careless about their exact meaning, put spirit for *afflatus*; they thus afford to heretics an opportunity of tarnishing[6] the Spirit of God, that is to say, God Himself, with default. And now comes the question. *Afflatus*, observe then, is less than spirit, although it comes from spirit; it is the spirit's

gentle breeze,[7] but it is not the spirit. Now a breeze is rarer than the wind; and although it proceeds from wind, yet a breeze is not the wind. One may call a breeze the image of the spirit. In the same manner, man is the image of God, that is, of spirit; for God is spirit. *Afflatus* is therefore the image of the spirit. Now the image is not in any case equal to the very thing.[8] It is one thing to be like the reality, and another thing to be the reality itself. So, although the *afflatus* is the image of the spirit, it is yet not possible to compare the image of God in such a way, that, because the reality—that is, the spirit, or in other words, the Divine Being—is faultless, therefore the *afflatus* also, that is to say, the image, ought not by any possibility to have done wrong. In this respect will the image be less than the reality, and the *afflatus* inferior to the spirit, in that,[3] while it possesses beyond doubt the true lineaments of divinity, such as an immortal soul, freedom and its own mastery over itself, foreknowledge in a great degree,[9] reasonableness, capacity of understanding and knowledge, it is even in these respects an image still, and never amounts to the actual power of Deity, nor to absolute exemption from fault,—a property which is only conceded to God, that is, to the reality, and which is simply incompatible with an image. An image, although it may express all the lineaments of the reality, is yet wanting in its intrinsic power; it is destitute of motion. In like manner, the soul, the image of the spirit, is unable to express the simple power thereof, that is to say, its happy exemption from sinning.[10] Were it otherwise,[11] it would not be soul, but spirit; not man, who received a soul, but God. Besides, to take another view of the matter,[12] not everything which pertains to God will be regarded as God, so that you would not maintain that His *afflatus* was God, that is, exempt from fault, because it is the breath of God. And in an act of your own, such as blowing into a flute, you would not thereby make the flute human, although it was your own human breath which you breathed into it, precisely as God breathed of His own Spirit. In fact,[13] the Scripture, by expressly saying[14] that God breathed into man's nostrils the breath of life, and that man became thereby a living soul, not a life-giving spirit, has distinguished that *soul* from the condition of the Creator. The work must

---

[1] Ps. civ. 4.
[2] [On capp. viii. and ix. See Kaye's references in notes p. 178 et seqq.]
[3] Anima, for *animus*. This meaning seems required throughout this passage, where afterwards occurs the phrase *immortalis anima.*
[4] Qualitas.
[5] Πνοήν, not πνεῦμα; so the Vulgate has *spiraculum*, not *spiritum*. [Kaye (p. 247) again refers to Profr. Andrews Norton of Harvard for valuable remarks concerning the use of the word *spiritus* by the ancients. *Evidences*, Vol. III. p. 160, note 7.]
[6] Infuscandi.

[7] Aurulam.
[8] Veritati.
[9] Plerumque.
[10] Non delinquendi felicitatem.
[11] Ceterum.
[12] Et alias autem.
[13] Denique.
[14] Gen. ii. 7.

necessarily be distinct from the workman, and it is inferior to him.   The pitcher will not be the potter, although made by the potter; nor in like manner, will the *afflatus*, because made by the spirit, be on that account the spirit.   The soul has often been called by the same name as the breath.   You should also take care that no descent be made from the breath to a still lower quality.   So you have granted (you say) the infirmity of the soul, which you denied before !   Undoubtedly, when you demand for it an equality with God, that is, a freedom from fault, I contend that it is infirm. But when the comparison is challenged with an angel, I am compelled to maintain that the head over all things is the stronger of the two, to whom the angels are ministers,[1] who is destined to be the judge of angels,[2] if he shall stand fast in the law of God—an obedience which he refused at first.   Now this disobedience[3] it was possible for the *afflatus* of God to commit: it was possible, but it was not proper.   The *possibility* lay in its slenderness of nature, as being the breath and not the spirit; the *impropriety*, however, arose from its power of will, as being free, and not a slave. It was furthermore assisted by the warning against committing sin under the threat of incurring death, which was meant to be a support for its slender nature, and a direction for its liberty of choice.   So that the soul can no longer appear to have sinned, because it has an affinity with God, that is to say, through the *afflatus*, but rather through that which was an addition to its nature, that is, through its free-will, which was indeed given to it by God in accordance with His purpose and reason, but recklessly employed[4] by man according as he chose.   This, then, being the case, the entire course[5] of God's action is purged from all imputation to evil.   For the liberty of the will will not retort its own wrong on Him by whom it was bestowed, but on him by whom it was improperly used.   What is the evil, then, which you want to impute to the Creator ? If it is man's sin, it will not be God's fault, because it is man's doing; nor is that Being to be regarded as the author of the sin, who turns out to be its forbidder, nay, its condemner.   If death is the evil, death will not give the reproach of being its own author to Him who threatened it, but to him who despised it.   For by his contempt he introduced it, which assuredly[6] would not have appeared had man not despised it.

If, however, you choose to transfer the account[7] of evil from man to the devil as the instigator of sin, and in this way, too, throw the blame on the Creator, inasmuch as He created the devil,—for He maketh those spirtual beings, the angels—then it will follow that[8] what was made, that is to say, the angel, will belong to Him who made it; while that which was not made by God, even the devil, or accuser,[9] cannot but have been made by itself; and this by false detraction[10] from God: first, how that God had forbidden them to eat of every tree; then, with the pretence that they should not die if they ate; thirdly, as if God grudged them the property of divinity. Now, whence originated this malice of lying and deceit towards man, and slandering of God ?   Most certainly not from God, who made the angel good after the fashion of His good works.   Indeed, before he became the devil, he stands forth the wisest of creatures; and[11] wisdom is no[11] evil.   If you turn to the prophecy of Ezekiel, you will at once perceive that this angel was both by creation good and by choice corrupt.   For in the person of the prince of Tyre it is said in reference to the devil: "Moreover, the word of the Lord came unto me, saying, Son of man, take up a lamentation upon the king of Tyrus, and say unto him, Thus saith the Lord God: Thou sealest up the sum, full of wisdom, perfect in beauty" (this belongs to him as the highest of the angels, the archangel, the wisest of all); "amidst the delights of the paradise of thy God wast thou born" (for it was there, where God had made the angels in a shape which resembled the figure of animals).   "Every precious stone was thy covering, the sardius, the topaz, and the diamond, the beryl, the onyx, and the jasper, the sapphire, the emerald, and the carbuncle; and with gold hast thou filled thy barns and thy treasuries.   From the day when thou wast created, when I set thee, a cherub, upon the holy mountain of God, thou wast in the midst of stones of fire, thou wast irreproachable in thy days, from the day of thy creation, until thine iniquities were discovered.   By the abundance of thy

---

[1] Heb. i. 14.
[2] 1 Cor. vi. 3.
[3] Hoc ipsum, referring to the *noluit* of the preceding clause.
[4] Agitatum.
[5] Dispositio.
[6] Utique.

[7] Elogium.
[8] Ergo.
[9] Delator.
[10] Deferendo, in reference to the word *delator*, our author's synonyme for διάβολος.
[11] Nisi.

merchandise thou hast filled thy storehouses, and thou' hast sinned," etc.[1] This description, it is manifest, properly belongs to the transgression of the angel, and not to the prince's: for none among human beings was either born in the paradise of God, not even Adam himself, who was rather translated thither; nor placed with a cherub upon God's holy mountain, that is to say, in the heights of heaven, from which the Lord testifies that Satan fell; nor detained amongst the stones of fire, and the flashing rays of burning constellations, whence Satan was cast down like lightning.[2] No, it is none else than the very author of sin who was denoted in the person of a sinful man: he was once irreproachable, at the time of his creation, formed for good by God, as by the good Creator of irreproachable creatures, and adorned with every angelic glory, and associated with God, good with the Good; but afterwards of his own accord removed to evil. *From the day when thine iniquities*,[3] says he, *were discovered*,—attributing to him those injuries wherewith he injured man when he was expelled from his allegiance to God,—even from that time did he sin, when he propagated his sin, and thereby plied "the abundance of his merchandise," that is, of his wickedness, even the tale[4] of his transgressions, because he was himself as a spirit no less (than man) created, with the faculty of free-will. For God would in nothing fail to endow a being who was to be next to Himself with a liberty of this kind. Nevertheless, by precondemning him, God testified that he had departed from the condition[5] of his created nature, through his own lusting after the wickedness which was spontaneously conceived within him; and at the same time, by conceding a permission for the operation of his designs, He acted consistently with the purpose of His own goodness, deferring the devil's destruction for the self-same reason as He postponed the restitution of man. For He afforded room for a conflict, wherein man might crush his enemy with the same freedom of his will as had made him succumb to him (proving that the fault was all his own, not God's), and so worthily recover his salvation by a victory; wherein also the devil might receive a. more bitter punishment, through being vanquished by him whom he had previously injured; and wherein God might be discovered to be so much the more good, as waiting[6] for man to return from his present

life to a more glorious paradise, with a right to pluck of the tree of life.[7]

CHAP. XI.—IF, AFTER MAN'S SIN, GOD EXERCISED HIS ATTRIBUTE OF JUSTICE AND JUDGMENT, THIS WAS COMPATIBLE WITH HIS GOODNESS, AND ENHANCES THE TRUE IDEA OF THE PERFECTION OF GOD'S CHARACTER.

Up to the fall of man, therefore, from the beginning God was simply good; after that He became a judge both severe and, as the Marcionites will have it, cruel. Woman is at once condemned to bring forth in sorrow, and to serve her husband,[8] although before she had heard without pain the increase of her race proclaimed with the blessing, *Increase and multiply*, and although she had been destined to be a help and not a slave to her male partner. Immediately the earth is also cursed,[9] which before was blessed. Immediately spring up briers and thorns, where once had grown grass, and herbs, and fruitful trees. Immediately arise sweat and labour for bread, where previously on every tree was yielded spontaneous food and untilled[10] nourishment. Thenceforth it is "man *to* the ground," and not as before, "*from* the ground; *to death* thenceforth, but before, *to life*; thenceforth with coats of skins, but before, nakedness without a blush. Thus God's prior goodness was from[11] nature, His subsequent severity from[11] a cause. The one was innate, the other accidental; the one His own, the other adapted;[12] the one issuing from Him, the other admitted by Him. But then *nature* could not have rightly permitted His goodness to have gone on inoperative, nor the *cause* have allowed His severity to have escaped in disguise or concealment. God provided the one for Himself, the other for the occasion.[13] You should now set about showing also that the position of a judge is allied with evil, who have been dreaming of another god as a purely good one—solely because you cannot *understand the Deity to be* a judge; although we have proved God to be also a judge. Or if not a judge, at any rate a perverse and useless originator of a discipline which is not to be vindicated—in other words, not to be judged. You do not, however, disprove God's being a judge, who have no proof to show that He is a judge. You will undoubtedly have to accuse justice herself, which provides the judge, or else to reckon her among the species

---

[1] Ezek. xxviii. 11–16 (Sept.).
[2] Luke x. 18.
[3] Læsuræ = " injuries." Ἀδικήματα ἐν σοι—*Iniquitates* in te."—HIERON.
[4] Censum.
[5] Forma.
[6] Sustinens.

[7] [Kaye, p. 313.]
[8] Gen. iii. 16.
[9] Gen. iii. 18.
[10] Secura.
[11] Secundum.
[12] Accommodata.
[13] Rei.

of evil, that is, to add injustice to the titles of goodness. But then justice is an evil, if injustice is a good. And yet you are forced to declare injustice to be one of the worst of things, and by the same rule are constrained to class justice amongst the most excellent. Since there is nothing hostile[1] to evil which is not good, and no enemy of good which is not evil. It follows, then, that as injustice is an evil, so in the same degree is justice a good. Nor should it be regarded as simply a species of goodness, but as the practical observance[2] of it, because goodness (unless justice be so controlled as to be just) will not be goodness, if it be unjust. For nothing is good which is unjust; while everything, on the other hand, which is just is good.

CHAP. XII.—THE ATTRIBUTES OF GOODNESS AND JUSTICE SHOULD NOT BE SEPARATED. THEY ARE COMPATIBLE IN THE TRUE GOD. THE FUNCTION OF JUSTICE IN THE DIVINE BEING DESCRIBED.

Since, therefore, there is this union and agreement between goodness and justice, you cannot prescribe[3] their separation. With what face will you determine the separation of your two Gods, regarding in their separate condition one as distinctively the good God, and the other as distinctively the just God? Where the just is, there also exists the good. In short, from the very first the Creator was both good and also just. And both His attributes advanced together. His goodness created, His justice arranged, the world; and in this process it even then decreed that the world should be formed of good materials, because it took counsel with goodness. The work of justice is apparent, in the separation which was pronounced between light and darkness, between day and night, between heaven and earth, between the water above and the water beneath, between the gathering together of the sea and the mass of the dry land, between the greater lights and the lesser, between the luminaries of the day and those of the night, between male and female, between the tree of knowledge of death and of life, between the world and paradise, between the aqueous and the earth-born animals. As goodness conceived all things, so did justice discriminate them. With the determination of the latter, everything was arranged and set in order. Every site and quality[4] of the elements, their effect, motion, and state, the rise and setting of each, are the judicial determinations of

the Creator. Do not suppose that His function as a judge must be defined as beginning when evil began, and so tarnish His justice with the cause of evil. By such considerations, then, do we show that this attribute advanced in company with goodness, the author[5] of all things,—worthy of being herself, too, deemed innate and natural, and not as accidentally accruing[6] to God, inasmuch as she was found to be in Him, her Lord, the arbiter of His works.

CHAP. XIII.—FURTHER DESCRIPTION OF THE DIVINE JUSTICE; SINCE THE FALL OF MAN IT HAS REGULATED THE DIVINE GOODNESS. GOD'S CLAIMS ON OUR LOVE AND OUR FEAR RECONCILED.

But yet, when evil afterwards broke out, and the goodness of God began now to have an adversary to contend against, God's justice also acquired another function, even that of directing His goodness according to men's application for it.[7] And this is the result: the divine goodness, being interrupted in that free course whereby God was spontaneously good, is now dispensed according to the deserts of every man; it is offered to the worthy, denied to the unworthy, taken away from the unthankful, and also avenged on all its enemies. Thus the entire office of justice in this respect becomes an agency[8] for goodness: whatever it condemns by its judgment, whatever it chastises by its condemnation, whatever (to use your phrase) it ruthlessly pursues,[9] it, in fact, benefits with good instead of injuring. Indeed, the fear of judgment contributes to good, not to evil. For good, now contending with an enemy, was not strong enough to recommend itself[10] by itself alone. At all events, if it could do so much, it could not keep its ground; for it had lost its impregnability through the foe, unless some power of fear supervened, such as might compel the very unwilling to seek after good, and take care of it. But who, when so many incentives to evil were assailing him, would desire that good, which he could despise with impunity? Who, again, would take care of what he could lose without danger? You read how broad is the road to evil,[11] how thronged in comparison with the opposite: would not all glide down that road were there nothing in it to fear? We dread the Creator's tremendous threats, and yet scarcely turn away from

---

[1] Æmulum.
[2] Tutela.
[3] Cavere. This is Oehler's reading, and best suits the sense of the passage and the style of our author.
[4] Habitus.

[5] Auctrice.
[6] Obventiciam.
[7] Secundum adversionem
[8] Procuratio.
[9] Sævit.
[10] Commendari.
[11] Matt. vii. 13.

evil. What, if He threatened not? Will you call this justice an evil, when it is all unfavourable to evil? Will you deny it to be a good, when it has its eye towards[1] good? What sort of being ought you to wish God to be? Would it be right to prefer that He should be such, that sins might flourish under Him, and the devil make mock at Him? Would you suppose Him to be a good God, who should be able to make a man worse by security in sin? Who is the author of good, but He who also requires it? In like manner, who is a stranger to evil, except Him who is its enemy? Who its enemy, besides Him who is its conqueror? Who else its conqueror, than He who is its punisher? Thus God is wholly good, because in all things He is on the side of good. In fact, He is omnipotent, because able both to help and to hurt. Merely to profit is a comparatively small matter, because it can do nothing else than a good turn. From such a conduct[2] with what confidence can I hope for good, if this is its only ability? How can I follow after the reward of innocence, if I have no regard to the requital of wrong-doing? I must needs have my doubts whether he might not fail in recompensing one or other alternative, who was unequal in his resources to meet both. Thus far, then, justice is the very fulness of the Deity Himself, manifesting God as both a perfect father and a perfect master: a father in His mercy, a master in His discipline; a father in the mildness of His power, a master in its severity; a father who must be loved with dutiful affection, a master who must needs be feared; be loved, because He prefers mercy to sacrifice;[3] be feared because He dislikes sin; be loved, because He prefers the sinner's repentance to his death;[4] be feared, because He dislikes the sinners who do not repent. Accordingly, the divine law enjoins duties in respect of both these attributes: *Thou shalt love God*, and, *Thou shalt fear God*. It proposed one for the obedient man, the other for the transgressor.[5]

CHAP. XIV.—EVIL OF TWO KINDS, PENAL AND CRIMINAL. IT IS NOT OF THE LATTER SORT THAT GOD IS THE AUTHOR, BUT ONLY OF THE FORMER, WHICH ARE PENAL, AND INCLUDED IN HIS JUSTICE.

On all occasions does God meet you: it is He who smites, but also heals; who kills, but also makes alive; who humbles, and yet exalts; who " creates[6] evil," but also " makes peace; "[7]—so that from these very (contrasts of His providence) I may get an answer to the heretics. Behold, they say, how He acknowledges Himself to be the creator of evil in the passage, " It is I who create evil." They take a word whose one form reduces to confusion and ambiguity two kinds of evils (because both sins and punishments are called *evils*), and will have Him in every passage to be understood as the creator of all evil things, in order that He may be designated the author of evil. We, on the contrary, distinguish between the two meanings of the word in question, and, by separating evils of sin from penal evils, *mala culpæ* from *mala pœnæ*, confine to each of the two classes its own author,—the devil as the author of the sinful evils (*culpæ*), and God as the creator of penal evils (*pœnæ*); so that the one class shall be accounted as morally bad, and the other be classed as the operations of justice passing penal sentences against the evils of sin. Of the latter class of evils which are compatible with justice, God is therefore avowedly the creator. They are, no doubt, evil to those by whom they are endured, but still on their own account good, as being just and defensive of good and hostile to sin. In this respect they are, moreover, worthy of God. Else prove them to be unjust, in order to show them deserving of a place in the sinful class, that is to say, evils of injustice; because if they turn out to belong to justice, they will be no longer evil things, but good—evil only to the bad, by whom even directly good things are condemned as evil. In this case, you must decide that man, although the wilful contemner of the divine law, unjustly bore the doom which he would like to have escaped; that the wickedness of those days was unjustly smitten by the deluge, afterwards by the fire (of Sodom); that Egypt, although most depraved and superstitious, and, worse still, the harasser of its guest-population,[8] was unjustly stricken with the chastisement of its ten plagues. *God* hardens the heart of Pharaoh. He deserved, however, to be influenced[9] to his destruction, who had already denied God, already in his pride so often rejected His ambassadors, accumulated heavy burdens on His people, and (to sum up all) as an Egyptian, had long been guilty before God of Gentile idolatry, worshipping the ibis and the crocodile in preference to the living God. Even His own people did God visit in their ingratitude.[10] Against young lads, too,

---

[1] Prospicit.
[2] De ejusmodi.
[3] Hos. vi. 6.
[4] Ezek. xxxiii. 11.
[5] Matt. xxii. 37 f.
[6] Condens.

[7] See Isa. xlv. 7.
[8] Hospitis populi conflictatricem.
[9] Subministrari. In *Apol.* ii., the verb *ministrare* is used to indicate Satan's power in influencing men. [The translator here corrects his own word *seduced* and I have substituted his better word *influenced*. The Lord gave him over to Satan's influence.]
[10] Num. xi. and xxi.

did He send forth bears, for their irreverence to the prophet.[1]

CHAP. XV.—THE SEVERITY OF GOD COMPATIBLE WITH REASON AND JUSTICE. WHEN INFLICTED, NOT MEANT TO BE ARBITRARY, BUT REMEDIAL.

Consider well,[2] then, before all things the justice of the Judge; and if its purpose[3] be clear, then the severity thereof, and the operations of the severity in its course, will appear compatible with reason and justice. Now, that we may not linger too long on the point, (I would challenge you to) assert the other reasons also, that you may condemn *the Judge's* sentences; extenuate the delinquencies of the sinner, that you may blame his judicial conviction. Never mind censuring the Judge; rather prove Him to be an unjust one. Well, then, even though[4] He required the sins of the fathers at the hands of the children, the hardness of the people made such remedial measures necessary[5] for them, in order that, having their posterity in view, they might obey the divine law. For who is there that feels not a greater care for his children than for himself? Again, if the blessing of the fathers was destined likewise for their offspring, previous to[6] any merit on the part of these, why might not the guilt of the fathers also redound to their children? As was the grace, so was the offence; so that the grace and the offence equally ran down through the whole race, with the reservation, indeed, of that subsequent ordinance by which it became possible to refrain from saying, that "the fathers had eaten a sour grape, and the children's teeth were set on edge:"[7] in other words, that the father should not bear the iniquity of the son, nor the son the iniquity of the father, but that every man should be chargeable with his own sin; so that the harshness of the law having been reduced[8] after the hardness of the people, justice was no longer to judge *the race*, but individuals. If, however, you accept the gospel of truth, you will discover on whom recoils the sentence of the Judge, when requiting on sons the sins of their fathers, even on those who had been (hardened enough) to imprecate spontaneously on themselves this condemnation: "His blood be on us, and on our children."[9] *This*, therefore, the providence of God has

ordered throughout its course,[10] even as it had heard it.

CHAP. XVI.—TO THE SEVERITY OF GOD THERE BELONG ACCESSORY QUALITIES, COMPATIBLE WITH JUSTICE. IF HUMAN PASSIONS ARE PREDICATED OF GOD, THEY MUST NOT BE MEASURED ON THE SCALE OF HUMAN IMPERFECTION.

Even His severity then is good, because just: when the judge is good, that is just. Other qualities likewise are good, by means of which the good work of a good severity runs out its course, whether wrath, or jealousy,[11] or sternness.[12] For all these are as indispensable[13] to severity as severity is to justice. The shamelessness of an age, which ought to have been reverent, had to be avenged. Accordingly, qualities which pertain to the judge, when they are actually free from blame, as the judge himself is, will never be able to be charged upon him as a fault.[14] What would be said, if, when you thought the doctor necessary, you were to find fault with his instruments, because they cut, or cauterize, or amputate, or tighten; whereas there could be no doctor of any value without his professional tools? Censure, if you please, the practitioner who cuts badly, amputates clumsily, is rash in his cautery; and even blame his implements as rough tools of his art. Your conduct is equally unreasonable,[15] when you allow indeed that God is a judge, but at the same time destroy those operations and dispositions by which He discharges His judicial functions. We are taught[16] God by the prophets, and by Christ, not by the philosophers nor by Epicurus. We who believe that God really lived on earth, and took upon Him the low estate of human form,[17] for the purpose of man's salvation, are very far from thinking as those do who refuse to believe that God cares for[18] anything. Whence has found its way to the heretics an argument of this kind: If God is angry, and jealous, and roused, and grieved, He must therefore be corrupted, and must therefore die. Fortunately, however, it is a part of the creed of Christians even to believe that God did die,[19] and yet that He is alive for evermore. Superlative is their folly, who prejudge divine things from human; so

---

[1] 2 Kings ii. 23, 24. [See notes 4, 5, 9, following.]
[2] Dispice.
[3] Ratio.
[4] Nam et si.
[5] Compulerat.
[6] Sine adhuc.
[7] Jer. xxxi. 29.
[8] Edomita, cf. chap. xix. *sub init.* and xxix.
[9] Matt. xxvii. 25.

[10] Omnis providentia.
[11] Æmulatio.
[12] Sævitia.
[13] Debita.
[14] Exprobrari.
[15] Proinde est enim.
[16] Erudimur.
[17] Habitus.
[18] Curare.
[19] [See Vol. II. p. 71 (this series), for an early example of this *Communicatio idiomatum.*]

that, because in man's corrupt condition there are found passions of this description, therefore there must be deemed to exist in God also sensations[1] of the same kind. Discriminate between the natures, and assign to them their respective senses, which are as diverse as their natures require, although they seem to have a community of designations. We read, indeed, of God's right hand, and eyes, and feet: these must not, however, be compared with those of human beings, because they are associated in one and the same name. Now, as great as shall be the difference between the divine and the human body, although their members pass under identical names, so great will also be the diversity between the divine and the human soul, notwithstanding that their sensations are designated by the same names. These sensations in the human being are rendered just as corrupt by the corruptibility of man's substance, as in God they are rendered incorruptible by the incorruption of the divine essence. Do you really believe the Creator to be God? By all means, is your reply. How then do you suppose that in God there is anything human, and not that all is divine? Him whom you do not deny to be God, you confess to be not human; because, when you confess Him to be God, you have, in fact, already determind that He is undoubtedly diverse from every sort of human conditions. Furthermore, although you allow, with others,[2] that man was inbreathed by God into a living soul, not God by man, it is yet palpably absurd of you to be placing human characteristics in God rather than divine ones in man, and clothing God in the likeness of man, instead of man in the image of God. And this, therefore, is to be deemed the likeness of God in man, that the human soul have the same emotions and sensations as God, although they are not of the same kind; differing as they do both in their conditions and their issues according to their nature. Then, again, with respect to the opposite sensations,—I mean meekness, patience, mercy, and the very parent of them all, goodness,—why do you form your opinion of[3] the divine displays of these (from the human qualities)? For we indeed do not possess them in perfection, because it is God alone who is perfect. So also in regard to those others,—namely, anger and irritation: we are not affected by them in so happy a manner, because God alone is truly happy, by reason of His property of incorruptibility. Angry He will possibly be, but not irritated,

nor dangerously tempted;[4] He will be moved, but not subverted.[5] All appliances He must needs use, because of all contingencies; as many sensations as there are causes: anger because of the wicked, and indignation because of the ungrateful, and jealousy because of the proud, and whatsoever else is a hinderance to the evil. So, again, mercy on account of the erring, and patience on account of the impenitent, and pre-eminent resources[6] on account of the meritorious, and whatsoever is necessary to the good. All these affections He is moved by in that peculiar manner of His own, in which it is profoundly fit[7] that He should be affected; and it is owing to Him that man is also similarly affected in a way which is equally his own.

CHAP. XVII.—TRACE GOD'S GOVERNMENT IN HISTORY AND IN HIS PRECEPTS, AND YOU WILL FIND IT FULL OF HIS GOODNESS.

These considerations show that the entire order of God as Judge is an operative one, and (that I may express myself in worthier words) protective of His Catholic[8] and supreme goodness, which, removed as it is from judiciary emotions, and pure in its own condition, the Marcionites refuse to acknowledge to be in one and the same Deity, "raining on the just and on the unjust, and making His sun to rise on the evil and on the good,"[9]— a bounty which no other god at all exercises. It is true that Marcion has been bold enough to erase from the gospel this testimony of Christ to the Creator; but yet the world itself is inscribed *with the goodness of its Maker*, and the inscription is read by each man's conscience. Nay, this very long-suffering of the Creator will tend to the condemnation of Marcion; that patience, (I mean,) which waits for the sinner's repentance rather than his death, which prefers mercy to sacrifice,[10] averting from the Ninevites the ruin which had been already denounced against them,[11] and vouchsafing to Hezekiah's tears an extension of his life,[12] and restoring his kingly state to the monarch of Babylon after his complete repentance;[13] that mercy, too, which conceded to the devotion of the people the son of Saul when about to die,[14] and gave free forgiveness to David on his confessing his sins against

[4] Periclitabitur.
[5] Evertetur.
[6] Præstantiam, "Qua scilicet præstat præmia vel supplicia" (Rigalt.).
[7] Condecet.
[8] *Catholic*, because diffused throughout creation (Pamelius).
[9] Matt. v. 45. T. predicates this (by the word *pluentem*) strictly of the "*goodness*" of God, the *quam*.
[10] Hos. vi. 6.
[11] Jonah iii. 10.
[12] 2 Kings xx. 1.
[13] Dan. iv. 33.
[14] 1 Sam. xiv. 45.

[1] Status.
[2] Pariter.
[3] Præsumitis. [So of generation, Sonship, etc.]

the house of Uriah;[1] which also restored the house of Israel as often as it condemned it, and addressed to it consolation no less frequently than reproof. Do not therefore look at God simply as Judge, but turn your attention also to examples of His conduct as the Most Good.[2] Noting Him, as you do, when He takes vengeance, consider Him likewise when He shows mercy.[3] In the scale, against His severity place His gentleness. When you shall have discovered both qualities to co-exist in the Creator, you will find in Him that very circumstance which induces you to think there is another God. Lastly, come and examine into His doctrine, discipline, precepts, and counsels. You will perhaps say that there are equally good prescriptions in human laws. But Moses and God existed before all your Lycurguses and Solons. There is not one after-age[4] which does not take from primitive sources. At any rate, my Creator did not learn from your God to issue such commandments as: Thou shalt not kill; thou shalt not commit adultery; thou shalt not steal; thou shalt not bear false witness; thou shalt not covet what is thy neighbour's; honour thy father and thy mother; and, thou shalt love thy neighbour as thyself. To these prime counsels of innocence, chastity, and justice, and piety, are also added prescriptions of humanity, as when every seventh year slaves are released for liberty;[5] when at the same period the land is spared from tillage; a place is also granted to the needy; and from the treading ox's mouth the muzzle is removed, for the enjoyment of the fruit of his labour before him, in order that kindness first shown in the case of animals might be raised from such rudiments[6] to the refreshment[7] of men.

CHAP. XVIII.—SOME OF GOD'S LAWS DEFENDED AS GOOD, WHICH THE MARCIONITES IMPEACHED, SUCH AS THE LEX TALIONIS. USEFUL PURPOSES IN A SOCIAL AND MORAL POINT OF VIEW OF THIS, AND SUNDRY OTHER ENACTMENTS.

But what parts of the law can I defend as good with a greater confidence than those which heresy has shown such a longing for?— as the statute of retaliation, requiring eye for eye, tooth for tooth, and stripe for stripe.[8] Now there is not here any smack of a per-

mission to mutual injury; but rather, on the whole, a provision for restraining violence. To a people which was very obdurate, and wanting in faith towards God, it might seem tedious, and even incredible, to expect from God that vengeance which was subsequently to be declared by the prophet: "Vengeance is mine; I will repay, saith the Lord."[9] Therefore, in the meanwhile, the commission of wrong was to be checked[10] by the fear of a retribution immediately to happen; and so the permission of this retribution was to be the prohibition of provocation, that a stop might thus be put to all hot-blooded[11] injury, whilst by the permission of the second the first is prevented by fear, and by this deterring of the first the second fails to be committed. By the same law another result is also obtained,[12] even the more ready kindling of fear of retaliation by reason of the very savour of passion which is in it. There is no more bitter thing, than to endure the very suffering which you have inflicted upon others. When, again, the law took somewhat away from men's food, by pronouncing unclean certain animals which were once blessed, you should understand this to be a measure for encouraging continence, and recognise in it a bridle imposed on that appetite which, while eating angels' food, craved after the cucumbers and melons of the Egyptians. Recognise also therein a precaution against those companions of the appetite, even lust and luxury, which are usually chilled by the chastening of the appetite.[13] For "the people sat down to eat and to drink, and rose up to play."[14] Furthermore, that an eager wish for money might be restrained, so far as it is caused by the need of food, the desire for costly meat and drink was taken out of their power. Lastly, in order that man might be more readily educated by God for fasting, he was accustomed to such articles of food as were neither plentiful nor sumptuous, and not likely to pamper the appetite of the luxurious. Of course the Creator deserved all the greater blame, because it was from His own people that He took away food, rather than from the more ungrateful Marcionites. As for the burdensome sacrifices also, and the troublesome scrupulousness of their ceremonies[15] and oblations, no one should blame them, as if God specially required them for Himself: for He plainly asks, "To what purpose is the multitude of your sacrifices unto me?" and,

---

[1] 2 Sam. xii. 13.
[2] Optimi.
[3] Indulget.
[4] Posteritas.
[5] Lev. xxv. 4, etc.
[6] Erudiretur.
[7] Refrigeria. [1 Cor. ix. 10.]
[8] Ex. xxi. 24.

[9] Deut. xxxii. 35; Rom. xii. 19.
[10] Repastinaretur.
[11] Æstuata.
[12] Qua et alias.
[13] Ventris.
[14] Ex. xxxii. 6.
[15] Operationes.

" Who hath required them at your hand?"[1] But he should see herein a careful provision[2] on God's part, which showed His wish to bind to His own religion a people who were prone to idolatry and transgression by that kind of services wherein consisted the superstition of that period; that He might call them away therefrom, while requesting it to be performed to Himself, as if He desired that no sin should be committed in making idols.

CHAP. XIX.—THE MINUTE PRESCRIPTIONS OF THE LAW MEANT TO KEEP THE PEOPLE DEPENDENT ON GOD. THE PROPHETS SENT BY GOD IN PURSUANCE OF HIS GOODNESS. MANY BEAUTIFUL PASSAGES FROM THEM QUOTED IN ILLUSTRATION OF THIS ATTRIBUTE.

But even in the common transactions of life, and of human intercourse at home and in public, even to the care of the smallest vessels, He in every possible manner made distinct arrangement; in order that, when they everywhere encountered these legal instructions, they might not be at any moment out of the sight of God. For what could better tend to make a man happy, than having " his delight in the law of the Lord?" " In that law would he meditate day and night.[3] It was not in severity that its Author promulgated this law, but in the interest of the highest benevolence, which rather aimed at subduing[4] the nation's hardness of heart, and by laborious services hewing out a fealty which was (as yet) untried in obedience: for I purposely abstain from touching on the mysterious senses of the law, considered in its spiritual and prophetic relation, and as abounding in types of almost every variety and sort. It is enough at present, that it simply bound a man to God, so that no one ought to find fault with it, except him who does not choose to serve God. To help forward this beneficent, not onerous, purpose of the law, the prophets were also ordained by the self-same goodness of God, teaching precepts worthy of God, how that men should " cease to do evil, learn to do well, seek judgment, judge the fatherless,[5] and plead for the widow:"[6] be fond of the divine expostulations:[7] avoid contact with the wicked:[8] " let the oppressed go free:"[9] dismiss the unjust sentence.[10] " deal their bread to the hungry; bring the outcast into their house; cover the naked, when they see him; nor hide themselves from their own flesh and kin:"[11] " keep their tongue from evil, and their lips from speaking guile: depart from evil, and do good; seek peace, and pursue it:"[12] be angry, and sin not; that is, not persevere in anger, or be enraged:[13] " walk not in the counsel of the ungodly; nor stand in the way of sinners; nor sit in the seat of the scornful."[14] Where then? " Behold, how good and how pleasant it is for brethren to dwell together in unity;"[15] meditating (as they do) day and night in the law of the Lord, because " it is better to trust in the Lord than to put confidence in man; better to hope in the Lord than in man."[16] For what recompense shall man receive from God? " He shall be like a tree planted by the rivers of water, that bringeth forth his fruit in his season; his leaf also shall not wither, and whatsoever he doeth shall prosper."[17] " He that hath clean hands and a pure heart, who hath not taken God's name in vain, nor sworn deceitfully to his neighbour, he shall receive blessing from the Lord, and mercy from the God of his salvation."[18] " For the eyes of the Lord are upon them that fear Him, upon them that hope in His mercy, to deliver their souls from death," even eternal death, " and to nourish them in their hunger," that is, after eternal life.[19] " Many are the afflictions of the righteous, but the Lord delivereth them out of them all."[20] " Precious in the sight of the Lord is the death of His saints."[21] " The Lord keepeth all their bones; not one of them shall be broken."[22] The Lord will redeem the souls of His servants.[23] We have adduced these few quotations from a mass of the Creator's Scriptures; and no more, I suppose, are wanted to prove Him to be a most good God, for they sufficiently indicate both the precepts of His goodness and the first-fruits[24] thereof.

CHAP. XX.—THE MARCIONITES CHARGED GOD WITH HAVING INSTIGATED THE HEBREWS TO SPOIL THE EGYPTIANS. DEFENCE OF THE DIVINE DISPENSATION IN THAT MATTER.

But these " saucy cuttles "[25] (of heretics)

---

[1] Isa. i. 11, 12.
[2] Industriam.
[3] Ps. i. 2.
[4] Edomantis, cf. chap. xv. *sub fin.* and xxix.
[5] Pupillo.
[6] Isa. i. 16, 17.
[7] Quæstiones, alluding to Isa. i. 18: δεῦτε καὶ διαλεχθῶμεν, λέγει Κύριος.
[8] Alluding to Isa. lviii. 6: " Loose the bands of wickedness."
[9] Isa. lviii. 6.
[10] A lax quotation, perhaps, of the next clause in the same verse: " Break every yoke."
[11] Isa. lviii. 7, slightly changed from the second to the third person.
[12] Ps. xxxiv. 13, 14.
[13] Comp. Ps. iv. 4.
[14] Ps. i. 1.
[15] Ps. cxxxiii. 1.
[16] Ps. cxviii. 4.
[17] Ps. i. 3.
[18] Ps. xxiv. 4, 5. He has slightly misquoted the passage.
[19] Ps. xxxiii. 18, 19, slightly altered.
[20] Ps. xxxiv. 19.
[21] Ps. cxvi. 15.
[22] Ps. xxxiv. 20, modified.
[23] Ps. xxxiv. 22.
[24] Præmissa.
[25] *Sepia isti.* Pliny, in his *Nat. Hist.* ix. 29, says: " The males of the cuttles kind are spotted with sundry colours more dark and

under the figure of whom the law about things to be eaten[1] prohibited this very kind of piscatory aliment, as soon as they find themselves confuted, eject the black venom of their blasphemy, and so spread about in all directions the object which (as is now plain) they severally have in view, when they put forth such assertions and protestations as shall obscure and tarnish the rekindled light[2] of the Creator's bounty. We will, however, follow their wicked design, even through these black clouds, and drag to light their tricks of dark calumny, laying to the Creator's charge with especial emphasis the fraud and theft of gold and silver which the Hebrews were commanded by Him to practise against the Egyptians. Come, unhappy heretic, I cite even you as a witness; first look at the case of the two nations, and then you will form a judgment of the Author of the command. The Egyptians put in a claim on the Hebrews for these gold and silver vessels.[3] The Hebrews assert a counter claim, alleging that by the bond[4] of their respective fathers, attested by the written engagement of both parties, there were due to them the arrears of that laborious slavery of theirs, for the bricks they had so painfully made, and the cities and palaces[5] which they had built. What shall be your verdict, you discoverer[6] of the most good God? That the Hebrews must admit the fraud, or the Egyptians the compensation? For they maintain that thus has the question been settled by the advocates on both sides,[7] of the Egyptians demanding their vessels, and the Hebrews claiming the requital of their labours. But for all they say,[8] the Egyptians justly renounced their restitution-claim then and

there; while the Hebrews to this day, in spite of the Marcionites, re-assert their demand for even greater damages,[9] insisting that, however large was their loan of the gold and silver, it would not be compensation enough, even if the labour of six hundred thousand men should be valued at only "a farthing"[10] a day apiece. Which, however, were the more in number—those who claimed the vessel, or those who dwelt in the palaces and cities? Which, too, the greater—the grievance of the Egyptians against the Hebrews, or "the favour"[11] which they displayed towards them? Were free men reduced to servile labour, in order that the Hebrews might simply proceed against the Egyptians by action at law for injuries; or in order that their officers might on their benches sit and exhibit their backs and shoulders shamefully mangled by the fierce application of the scourge? It was not by a few plates and cups—in all cases the property, no doubt, of still fewer rich men—that any one would pronounce that compensation should have been awarded to the Hebrews, but both by all the resources of these and by the contributions of all the people.[12] If, therefore, the case of the Hebrews be a good one, the Creator's case must likewise be a good one; that is to say, his command, when He both made the Egyptians unconsciously grateful, and also gave His own people their discharge in full[13] at the time of their migration by the scanty comfort of a tacit requital *of their long servitude.* It was plainly less than their due which He commanded to be exacted. The Egyptians ought to have given back their men-children[14] also to the Hebrews.

CHAP. XXI.—THE LAW OF THE SABBATH-DAY EXPLAINED. THE EIGHT DAYS' PROCESSION AROUND JERICHO. THE GATHERING OF STICKS A VIOLATION.

Similarly on other points also, you reproach Him with fickleness and instability for contradictions in His commandments, such as that He forbade work to be done on Sabbath-days, and yet at the siege of Jericho ordered the ark to be carried round the walls during eight days; in other words, of course, actually on a Sabbath. You do not, however, consider the law of the Sabbath: they are human works, not divine, which it prohibits.[15] For it says, "Six days shalt thou labour, and do all thy work; but the seventh day is the Sabbath of

---

blackish, yea, and more firme and steady, than the female. If the female be smitten with the trout-speare, they will come to succour her; but she again is not so kind to them: for if the male be stricken, she will not stand to it, but runs away. But both of them, if they perceive that they be taken in such streights that they cannot escape, shed from them a certain black humor like to ink; and when the water therewith is troubled and made duskish, therein they hide themselves, and are no more seen " (Holland's *Translation*, p. 250). Our epithet "*saucy* cuttle" comes from Shakespere, *Henry* IV. 2, 4, where, however, the word seems employed in a different sense.

[1] Deut. xiv.
[2] Relucentem, "rekindled" by the confutation.
[3] *Vasa* = the jewels and the raiment mentioned in Ex. iii. 22.
[4] Nomine. [Here our author exhibits his tact as a jurisconsult.]
[5] Villis.
[6] Elector.
[7] For a discussion of the spoiling of the Egyptians by the Israelites, the reader is referred to Calmet's *Commentary*, on Ex. iii. 22, where he adduces, besides this passage of Tertullian, the opinions of Irenæus, *adv. Hæres.* iv. 49; Augustine, *contra Faust.* ii. 71; Theodoret, *Quæst. in Exod.* xxiii.; Clement of Alex. *Stromat.* i. 1; of Philo, *De Vita Moysis*, i.; Josephus, *Antiqq.* ii. 8, who says that "the Egyptians freely gave all to the Israelites;" of Melchior Canus, *Loc. Theoll.* i. 4. He also refers to the book of Wisdom, x. 17–20. These all substantially agree with our author. See also a full discussion in Selden, *De Jure Nat. et Gentium*, vii. 8, who quotes from the Gemara, *Sanhedrin*, c. ii. f. 91a; and *Bereshith Rabba*, par. 61 f., 68, col. 2, where such a tribunal as Tertullian refers to is mentioned as convened by Alexander the Great, who, after hearing the pleadings, gave his assent to the claims of the advocates of Israel.
[8] Tamen.

[9] Amplius.
[10] Singulis nummis. [Clem. Alex. *Strom.* i. 23. Vol. II., p. 336, *supra.*]
[11] Gratia Hebræorum, either a reference to Ex. iii. 21, or meaning, perhaps, "the unpaid services of the Hebrews."
[12] Popularium omnium.
[13] Expunxit.
[14] Ex. i. 18, 22. [An ingenious and eloquent defence.]
[15] Ex. xx. 9, 10.

the Lord thy God: in it thou shalt not do any work." What work? Of course your own. The conclusion is, that from the Sabbath-day He removes those works which He had before enjoined fòr the six days, that is, your own works; in other words, human works of daily life. Now, the carrying around of the ark is evidently not an ordinary daily duty, nor yet a human one; but a rare and a sacred work, and, as being then ordered by the direct precept of God, a divine one. And I might fully explain what this signified, were it not a tedious process to open out the forms [1] of all the Creator's proofs, which you would, moreover, probably refuse to allow. It is more to the point, if you be confuted on plain matters [2] by the simplicity of truth rather than curious reasoning. Thus, in the present instance, there is a clear distinction respecting the Sabbath's prohibition of human labours, not divine ones. Accordingly, the man who went and gathered sticks on the Sabbath-day was punished with death. For it was his own work which he did; and this [3] the law forbade. They, however, who on the Sabbath carried the ark round Jericho, did it with impunity. For it was not their own work, but God's, which they executed, and that too, from His express commandment.

CHAP. XXII.—THE BRAZEN SERPENT AND THE GOLDEN CHERUBIM WERE NOT VIOLATIONS OF THE SECOND COMMANDMENT. THEIR MEANING.

Likewise, when forbidding the similitude to be made of all things which are in heaven, and in earth, and in the waters, He declared also the reasons, as being prohibitory of all material exhibition [4] of a latent [5] idolatry. For He adds: "Thou shalt not bow down to them, nor serve them." The form, however, of the brazen serpent which the Lord afterwards commanded Moses to make, afforded no pretext [6] for idolatry, but was meant for the cure of those who were plagued with the fiery serpents. [7] I say nothing of what was figured by this cure. [8] Thus, too, the golden Cherubim and Seraphim were purely an ornament in the figured fashion [9] of the ark; adapted to ornamentation for reasons totally remote from all condition of idolatry, on account of which the making a likeness is prohibited; and they are evidently not at variance with [10] this law of prohibition, because they are not found in that form [11] of similitude, in reference to which the prohibition is given. We have spoken [12] of the rational institution of the sacrifices, as calling off their homage from idols to God; and if He afterwards rejected this homage, saying, "To what purpose is the multitude of your sacrifices unto me?" [13]—He meant nothing else than this to be understood, that He had never really required such homage for Himself. For He says, "I will not eat the flesh of bulls;" [14] and in another passage: "The everlasting God shall neither hunger nor thirst." [15] Although He had respect to the offerings of Abel, and smelled a sweet savour from the holocaust of Noah, yet what pleasure could He receive from the flesh of sheep, or the odour of burning victims? And yet the simple and God-fearing mind of those who offered what they were receiving from God, both in the way of food and of a sweet smell, was favourably accepted before God, in the sense of respectful homage [16] to God, who did not so much want what was offered, as that which prompted the offering. Suppose now, that some dependant were to offer to a rich man or a king, who was in want of nothing, some very insignificant gift, will the amount and quality of the gift bring dishonour [17] to the rich man and the king; or will the consideration [18] of the homage give them pleasure? Were, however, the dependant, either of his own accord or even in compliance with a command, to present to him gifts suitably to his rank, and were he to observe the solemnities due to a king, only without faith and purity of heart, and without any readiness for other acts of obedience, will not that king or rich man consequently exclaim: "To what purpose is the multitude of your sacrifices unto me? I am full of your solemnities, your feast-days, and your Sabbaths." [19] By calling them *yours*, as having been performed [20] after the giver's own will, and not according to the religion of God (since he displayed them as his own, and not as God's), *the Almighty in this passage*, demonstrated how suitable to the conditions of the case, and how reasonable, was His rejection of those very offerings which He had commanded to be made to Him.

---

[1] Figuras.
[2] De absolutis.
[3] [He was not punished for gathering sticks, but for setting an example of contempt of the Divine Law.]
[4] Substantiam.
[5] Cæcæ.
[6] Titulum. [See Vol. II. p. 477, this series.]
[7] Num. xxi. 8, 9.
[8] See John iii. 14.
[9] Exemplum.

[10] Refragari.
[11] Statu.
[12] In chap. xviii. towards the end. [p. 311. *supra*.]
[13] Isa., i. 11.
[14] Ps. l. 13.
[15] An inexact quotation of Isa. xl. 28.
[16] Honorem.
[17] Infuscabit.
[18] Titulus.
[19] See Isa. i. 11-14.
[20] *Fecerat* seems the better reading; *q.d.* "which he had performed," etc. Oehler reads *fecerant*.

CHAP. XXIII.—GOD'S PURPOSES IN ELECTION AND REJECTION OF THE SAME MEN, SUCH AS KING SAUL, EXPLAINED, IN ANSWER TO THE MARCIONITE CAVIL.

Now, although you will have it that He is inconstant[1] in respect of persons, sometimes disapproving where approbation is deserved; or else wanting in foresight, bestowing approbation on men who ought rather to be reprobated, as if He either censured[2] His own past judgments, or could not forecast His future ones; yet[3] nothing is so consistent for even a good judge[4] as both to reject and to choose on the merits of the present moment. Saul is chosen,[5] but he is not yet the despiser of the prophet Samuel.[6] Solomon is rejected; but he is now become a prey to foreign women, and a slave to the idols of Moab and Sidon. What must the Creator do, in order to escape the censure of the Marcionites? Must He prematurely condemn men, who are thus far correct in their conduct, because of future delinquencies? But it is not the mark of a good God to condemn beforehand persons who have not yet deserved condemnation. Must He then refuse to eject sinners, on account of their previous good deeds? But it is not the characteristic of a just judge to forgive sins in consideration of former virtues which are no longer practised. Now, who is so faultless among men, that God could always have him in His choice, and never be able to reject him? Or who, on the other hand, is so void of any good work, that God could reject him for ever, and never be able to choose him? Show me, then, the man who is always good, and he will not be rejected; show me, too, him who is always evil, and he will never be chosen. Should, however, the same man, being found on different occasions in the pursuit of both (good and evil) be recompensed[7] in both directions by God, who is both a good and judicial Being, He does not change His judgments through inconstancy or want of foresight, but dispenses reward according to the deserts of each case with a most unwavering and provident decision.[8]

CHAP. XXIV.—INSTANCES OF GOD'S REPENTANCE, AND NOTABLY IN THE CASE OF THE NINEVITES, ACCOUNTED FOR AND VINDICATED.

Furthermore, with respect to the repentance which occurs in His conduct,[9] you interpret it with similar perverseness just as if it were with fickleness and improvidence that He repented, or on the recollection of some wrong-doing; because He actually said, "It repenteth me that I have set up Saul to be king,"[10] "very much as if He meant that His repentance savoured of an acknowledgment of some evil work or error. Well,[11] this is not always implied. For there occurs even in good works a confession of repentance, as a reproach and condemnation of the man who has proved himself unthankful for a benefit. For instance, in this case of Saul, the Creator, who had made no mistake in selecting him for the kingdom, and endowing him with His Holy Spirit, makes a statement respecting the goodliness of his person, how that He had most fitly chosen him as being at that moment the choicest man, so that (as He says) there was not his fellow among the children of Israel.[12] Neither was He ignorant how he would afterwards turn out. For no one would bear you out in imputing lack of foresight to that God whom, since you do not deny Him to be divine, you allow to be also foreseeing; for this proper attribute of divinity exists in Him. However, He did, as I have said, burden[13] the guilt of Saul with the confession of His own repentance; but as there is an absence of all error and wrong in His choice of Saul, it follows that this repentance is to be understood as upbraiding another[14] rather than as self-incriminating.[15] Look here then, say you: I discover a self-incriminating case in the matter of the Ninevites, when the book of Jonah declares, "And God repented of the evil that He had said that He would do unto them; and He did it not."[16] In accordance with which Jonah himself says unto the Lord, "Therefore I fled before unto Tarshish; for I knew that Thou art a gracious God and merciful, slow to anger, and of great kindness, and repentest Thee of the evil."[17] It is well, therefore, that he premised the attribute[18] of the most good God as most patient over the wicked, and most abundant in mercy and kindness over such as acknowledged and bewailed their sins, as the Ninevites were then doing. For if He who has this attribute is the Most Good, you will have first to relinquish that position of yours, that the very contact with[19] evil is incompatible with such a Being, that is, with the most good God. And because

---

[1] Levem.
[2] Damnet.
[3] Atquin.
[4] Or, "for one who is a good man and a judge."
[5] 1 Sam. ix.
[6] 1 Sam. xiii.
[7] Dispungetur.
[8] Censura.
[9] Apud illum.
[10] 1 Sam. xv. 11.
[11] Porro.
[12] 1 Sam. ix. 2.
[13] Onerabat.
[14] Invidiosam.
[15] Criminosam.
[16] Jonah iii. 10.
[17] Jonah iv. 2.
[18] Titulum.
[19] Malitiæ concursum.

Marcion, too, maintains that a good tree ought not to produce bad fruit ; but yet he has mentioned " evil " (in the passage under discussion), which the most good God is incapable of,[1] is there forthcoming any explanation of these " evils," which may render them compatible with even the most Good? There is. We say, in short, that evil in the present case [2] means, not what may be attributed to the Creator's nature as an evil being, but what may be attributed to His power as a judge. In accordance with which He declared, " I create evil,"[3] and, " I frame evil against you;"[4] meaning not to sinful evils, but avenging ones. What sort of stigma [5] pertains to these, congruous as they are with God's judicial character, we have sufficiently explained.[6] Now, although these are called " evils," they are yet not reprehensible in a judge ; nor because of this their name do they show that the judge is evil : so in like manner will this particular evil [7] be understood to be one of this class of judiciary evils, and along with them to be compatible with (God as) a judge. The Greeks also sometimes [8] use the word " evils " for troubles and injuries (not malignant ones), as in this passage of yours [9] is also meant. Therefore, if the Creator repented of such evil as this, as showing that the creature deserve dcondemnation, and ought to be punished for his sin, then, in [10] the present instance no fault of a criminating nature will be imputed to the Creator, for having deservedly and worthily decreed the destruction of a city so full of iniquity. What therefore He had justly decreed, having no evil purpose in His decree, He decreed from the principle of justice,[11] not from malevolence. Yet He gave it the name of " evil," because of the evil and desert involved in the very suffering itself. Then, you will say, if you excuse the evil under name of justice, on the ground that He had justly determined destruction against the people of Nineveh, He must even on this argument be blameworthy, for having repented of an act of justice, which surely should not be repented of. Certainly not,[12] my reply is; God will never repent of an act of justice. And it now remains that we should understand what God's repentance means. For although

man repents most frequently on the recollection of a sin, and occasionally even from the unpleasantness [13] of some good action, this is never the case with God. For, inasmuch as God neither commits sin nor condemns a good action, in so far is there no room in Him for repentance of either a good or an evil deed. Now this point is determined for you even in the scripture which we have quoted. Samuel says to Saul, " The Lord hath rent the kingdom of Israel from thee this day, and hath given it to a neighbour of thine that is better than thou;"[14] and into two parts shall Israel be divided: " for He will not turn Himself, nor repent; for He does not repent as a man does."[15] According, therefore, to this definition, the divine repentance takes in all cases a different form from that of man, in that it is never regarded as the result of improvidence or of fickleness, or of any condemnation of a good or an evil work. What, then, will be the mode of God's repentance? It is already quite clear,[16] if you avoid referring it to human conditions. For it will have no other meaning than a simple change of a prior purpose; and this is admissible without any blame even in a man, much more [17] in God, whose every purpose is faultless. Now in Greek the word for repentance (μετάνοια) is formed, not from the confession of a sin, but from a change of mind, which in God we have shown to be regulated by the occurrence of varying circumstances.

CHAP. XXV.—GOD'S DEALINGS WITH ADAM AT THE FALL, AND WITH CAIN AFTER HIS CRIME, ADMIRABLY EXPLAINED AND DEFENDED.

It is now high time that I should, in order to meet all [18] objections of this kind, proceed to the explanation and clearing up [19] of the other trifles,[20] weak points, and inconsistencies, as you deemed them. God calls out to Adam,[21] Where art thou? as if ignorant where he was; and when he alleged that the shame of his nakedness was the cause (of his hiding himself), He inquired whether he had eaten of the tree, as if He were in doubt. By no means;[22] God was neither uncertain about the commission of the sin, nor ignorant of Adam's whereabouts. It was certainly proper to summon the offender, who was concealing himself from the consciousness of his sin, and to bring him forth into the presence of his Lord, not merely by the calling out of his name, but

---

[1] Non capit.
[2] Nunc.
[3] Isa. xlv. 7.
[4] Jer. xviii. 11.
[5] Infamiam.
[6] See above, chap. xiv. [p. 308, *supra*.]
[7] Malitia, i.e., " the evil " mentioned in the cited Jonah iii. 10.
[8] Thus, according to St. Jerome, in Matt. vi. 34, κακία means κάκωσις. " Sufficient for the day is *the evil* thereof "—the occurrent adversities.
[9] In isto articulo.
[10] Atqui hic.
[11] Or, " in his capacity as Judge," ex justitia.
[12] Immo.

[13] Ingratia.
[14] 1 Sam. xv. 28.
[15] Ver. 29, but inexactly quoted.
[16] Relucet.
[17] Nedum.
[18] Ut omnia expediam.
[19] Purgandas.
[20] Pusillitates.
[21] Gen. iii. 9, 11.
[22] Immo.

with a home-thrust blow[1] at the sin which he had at that moment committed. For the question ought not to be read in a merely interrogative tone, Where art thou, Adam? but with an impressive and earnest voice, and with an air of imputation, Oh, Adam, *where art thou?*—as much as to intimate: thou art no longer here, thou art in perdition—so that the voice is the utterance of One who is at once rebuking and sorrowing.[2] But of course some part of paradise had escaped the eye of Him who holds the universe in His hand as if it were a bird's nest, and to whom heaven is a throne and earth a footstool; so that He could not see, before He summoned him forth, where Adam was, both while lurking and when eating of the forbidden fruit! The wolf or the paltry thief escapes not the notice of the keeper of your vineyard or your garden! And God, I suppose, with His keener vision,[3] from on high was unable to miss the sight of[4] aught which lay beneath Him! Foolish heretic, who treat with scorn[5] so fine an argument of God's greatness and man's instruction! God put the question with an appearance of uncertainty, in order that even here He might prove man to be the subject of a free will in the alternative of either a denial or a confession, and give to him the opportunity of freely acknowledging his transgression, and, so far,[6] of lightening it.[7] In like manner He inquires of Cain where his brother was, just as if He had not yet heard the blood of Abel crying from the ground, in order that he too might have the opportunity from the same power of the will of spontaneously denying, and to this degree aggravating, his crime; and that thus there might be supplied to us examples of confessing sins rather than of denying them: so that even then was initiated the evangelic doctrine, " By thy words[8] thou shalt be justified, and by thy words thou shalt be condemned."[9] Now, although Adam was by reason of his condition under law[10] subject to death, yet was hope preserved to him by the Lord's saying, " Behold, Adam is become as one of us;"[11] that is, in consequence of the future taking of the man into the divine nature. Then what follows? " And now, lest he put forth his hand, and take also of the tree of life, (and eat), and live for ever." Insert-

ing thus the particle of present time, " And now," He shows that He had made for a time, and at present, a prolongation of man's life. Therefore He did not actually[12] curse Adam and Eve, for they were candidates for restoration, and they had been relieved[13] by confession. Cain, however, He not only cursed; but when he wished to atone for his sin by death, He even prohibited his dying, so that he had to bear the load of this prohibition in addition to his crime. This, then, will prove to be the ignorance of our God, which was simulated on this account, that delinquent man should not be unaware of what he ought to do. Coming down to the case of Sodom and Gomorrha, he says: " I will go down now, and see whether they have done altogether according to the cry of it which is come unto me; and if not, I will know."[14] Well, was He in this instance also uncertain through ignorance, and desiring to know? Or was this a necessary tone of utterance, as expressive of a minatory and not a dubious sense, under the colour of an inquiry? If you make merry at God's " going down," as if He could not except by the descent have accomplished His judgment, take care that you do not strike your own God with as hard a blow. For He also came down to accomplish what He wished.

CHAP. XXVI.—THE OATH OF GOD: ITS MEANING. MOSES, WHEN DEPRECATING GOD'S WRATH AGAINST ISRAEL, A TYPE OF CHRIST.

But God also swears. Well, is it, I wonder, by the God of Marcion? No, no, he says; a much vainer oath—by Himself![15] What was He to do, when He knew[16] of no other God; especially when He was swearing to this very point, that besides himself there was absolutely no God? Is it then of swearing falsely that you convict[17] Him, or of swearing a vain oath? But it is not possible for him to appear to have sworn falsely, when he was ignorant, as you say he was, that there was another God. For when he swore by that which he knew, he really committed no perjury. But it was not a vain oath for him to swear that there was no other God. It would indeed be a vain oath, if there had been no persons who believed that there were other Gods, like the worshippers of idols then, and the heretics of the present day. Therefore He swears by Himself, in order that you may believe God, even when He swears that there

---

[1] Sugillatione.
[2] Dolendi.
[3] Oculatiorem.
[4] Præterire.
[5] Naso.
[6] Hoc nomine.
[7] Relevandi.
[8] Ex ore tuo, " out of thine own mouth."
[9] Matt. xii. 37.
[10] Propter statum legis.
[11] Gen. iii. 22. [II. Peter, i. 4.]

[12] Ipsum. [Comp. Heb. ix. 8, and Rev. xxii. 14.]
[13] Relevatos.
[14] Gen. xviii. 21. [Marcion's god also " comes down." p. 284, *supra.*]
[15] See Jer. xxii. 5.
[16] Isa. xliv. 8.
[17] Deprehendis.

is besides Himself no other God at all. But you have yourself, O Marcion, compelled God to do this. For even so early as then were you foreseen. Hence, if He swears both in His promises and His threatenings, and thus extorts [1] faith which at first was difficult, nothing is unworthy of God which causes men to believe in God. But (you say) God was even then mean [2] enough in His very fierceness, when, in His wrath against the people for their consecration of the calf, He makes this request of His servant Moses: "Let me alone, that my wrath may wax hot against them, and that I may consume them; and I will make of thee a great nation." [3] Accordingly, you maintain that Moses is better than his God, as the deprecator, nay the averter, of His anger. "For," said he, "Thou shalt not do this; or else destroy me along with them." [4] Pitiable are ye also, as well as the people, since you know not Christ, prefigured in the person of Moses, as the deprecator of the Father, and the offerer of His own life for the salvation of the people. It is enough, however, that the nation was at the instant really given to Moses. That which he, as a servant, was able to ask of the Lord, the Lord required of Himself. For this purpose did He say to His servant, "Let me alone, that I may consume them," in order that by his entreaty, and by offering himself, he might hinder [5] (the threatened judgment), and that you might by such an instance learn how much privilege is vouchsafed [6] with God to a faithful man and a prophet.

CHAP. XXVII.—OTHER OBJECTIONS CONSIDERED. GOD'S CONDESCENSION IN THE INCARNATION. NOTHING DEROGATORY TO THE DIVINE BEING IN THIS ECONOMY. THE DIVINE MAJESTY WORTHILY SUSTAINED BY THE ALMIGHTY FATHER, NEVER VISIBLE TO MAN. PERVERSENESS OF THE MARCIONITE CAVILS.

And now, that I may briefly pass in review [7] the other points which you have thus far been engaged in collecting, as mean, weak, and unworthy, for demolishing [8] the Creator, I will propound them in a simple and definite statement: [9] that God would have been unable to hold any intercourse with men, if He had not taken on Himself the emotions and affections of man, by means of which He could temper the strength of His majesty, which would no doubt have been incapable of en-

durance to the moderate capacity of man, by such a humiliation as was indeed degrading [10] to Himself, but necessary for man, and such as on this very account became worthy of God, because nothing is so worthy of God as the salvation of man. If I were arguing with heathens, I should dwell more at length on this point; although with heretics too the discussion does not stand on very different grounds. Inasmuch as ye yourselves have now come to the belief that God moved about [11] in the form and all other circumstances of man's nature, [12] you will of course no longer require to be convinced that God conformed Himself to humanity, but feel yourselves bound by your own faith. For if the God (in whom ye believe,) even from His higher condition, prostrated the supreme dignity of His majesty to such a lowliness as to undergo death, even the death of the cross, why can you not suppose that some humiliations [13] are becoming to our God also, only more tolerable than Jewish contumelies, and crosses, [14] and sepulchres? Are these the humiliations which henceforth are to raise a prejudice against Christ (the subject as He is of human passions [15]) being a partaker of that Godhead [16] against which you make the participation in human qualities a reproach? Now we believe that Christ did ever act in the name of God the Father; that He actually [17] from the beginning held intercourse with (men); actually [18] communed with [19] patriarchs and prophets; was the Son of the Creator; was His Word; whom God made His Son [20] by emitting Him from His own self, [21] and thenceforth set Him over every dispensation and (administration of) His will, [22] making Him a little lower than the angels, as is written in David. [23] In which lowering of His condition He received from the Father a dispensation in those very respects which you blame as human; from the very beginning learning, [24] even then, (that state of a) man which He was destined in the end to become. [25] It is He

[1] Extorquens.
[2] Pusillus.
[3] Ex. xxxii. 10.
[4] An allusion to, rather than a quotation of, Ex. xxxii. 32.
[5] Non sineret.
[6] Quantum liceat.
[7] Absolvam.
[8] Ad destructionem.
[9] Ratione.

[10] Indigna.
[11] Diversatum.
[12] Conditionis.
[13] Pusillitates.
[14] Patibulis.
[15] i.e., the sensations of our emotional nature.
[16] Ejus Dei.
[17] Ipsum.
[18] Ipsum.
[19] Congressum.
[20] On this mode of the eternal generation of the Son from the Father, as the Λόγος προφορικός, the reader is referred for much patristic information to Bp. Bull's *Defensio Fid. Nic.* (transl. in *Anglo-Cath. Library* by the translator of this work).
[21] Proferendo ex semet ipso.
[22] Voluntati.
[23] Ps. viii. 6.
[24] Ediscens, "practising" or "rehearsing."
[25] This doctrine of theology is more fully expressed by our author in a fine passage in his *Treatise against Praxeas*, xvi. (Oehler, vol. ii. p. 674), of which the translator gave this version in Bp. Bull's *Def. Nic. Creed*, vol. i. p. 18: "The Son hath executed judgment from the beginning, throwing down the haughty

who descends, He who interrogates, He who demands, He who swears. With regard, however, to the Father, the very gospel which is common to us will testify that He was never visible, according to the word of Christ: " No man knoweth the Father, save the Son."[1] For even in the Old Testament He had declared, " No man shall see me, and live."[2] He means that the Father is invisible, in whose authority and in whose name was He God who appeared as the Son of God. But with us[3] Christ is received in the person of Christ, because even in this manner is He our *God*. Whatever attributes therefore you require as worthy of God, must be found in the Father, who is invisible and unapproachable, and placid, and (so to speak) the God of the philosophers; whereas those qualities which you censure as unworthy must be supposed to be in the Son, who has been seen, and heard, and encountered, the Witness and Servant of the Father, uniting in Himself man and God, God in mighty deeds, in weak ones man, in order that He may give to man as much as He takes from God. What in your esteem is the entire disgrace of my God, is in fact the sacrament of man's salvation. God held converse with man, that man might learn to act as God. God dealt on equal terms[4] with man, that man might be able to deal on equal terms with God. God was found little, that man might become very great. You who disdain such a God, I hardly know whether you *ex fide* believe that God was crucified. How great, then, is your perversity in respect of the two characters of the Creator! You designate Him as *Judge*, and reprobate as cruelty that severity of the Judge which only acts in accord with the merits of cases. You require God to be *very good*, and yet despise as meanness that gentleness of His which accorded with His kindness, (and) held lowly converse in proportion to the mediocrity of man's estate. He pleases you not, whether great or little, neither as your judge nor as your friend! What if the same features should be discovered in your God? That *He* too is a judge, we have already shown in the proper section:[5] that from being a judge He must needs be severe; and from being severe He must also be cruel, if indeed cruel.[6]

CHAP. XXVIII.—THE TABLES TURNED UPON MARCION, BY CONTRASTS, IN FAVOUR OF THE TRUE GOD.

Now, touching the weaknesses and malignities, and the other (alleged), notes (of the Creator), I too shall advance *antitheses* in rivalry to Marcion's. If my God knew not of any other superior to Himself, your god also was utterly unaware that there was any beneath himself. It is just what Heraclitus " the obscure "[7] said; whether it be up or down,[8] it comes to the same thing. If, indeed, he was not ignorant (of his position), it must have occurred to Him from the beginning. Sin and death, and the author of sin too—the devil—and all the evil which my God permitted to be, this also, did your god permit; for he allowed Him to permit it. Our God changed His purposes;[9] in like manner yours did also. For he who cast his look so late in the human race, changed that purpose, which for so long a period had refused to cast that look. Our God repented Him of the evil in a given case; so also did yours. For by the fact that he at last had regard to the salvation of man, he showed such a repentance of his previous disregard[10] as was due for a wrong deed. But neglect of man's salvation will be accounted a wrong deed, simply because it has been remedied[11] by his repentance in the conduct of your god. Our God you say commanded a fraudulent act, but in a matter of gold and silver. Now, inasmuch as man is more precious than gold and silver, in so far is your god more fraudulent still, because he robs man of his Lord and Creator. Eye for eye does our God require; but your god does even a greater injury, (in your ideas,) when he prevents an act of retaliation. For what man will not return a blow, without waiting to be struck a second time.[12] Our

---

tower, and dividing the tongues, punishing the whole world by the violence of waters, raining upon Sodom and Gomorrha fire and brimstone 'the LORD from the LORD.' For He it was who at all times came down to hold converse with men, from Adam on to the patriarchs and the prophets, in vision, in dream, in mirror, in dark saying ; ever from the beginning laying the foundation of the course (of His dispensations), which He meant to follow out unto the end. Thus was He ever learning (practising or rehearsing) ; and the God who conversed with men upon earth could be no other than the Word, which was to be made flesh. But He was thus learning (or rehearsing, *ediscebat*) in order to level for us the way of faith, that we might the more readily believe that the Son of God had come down into the world, if we knew that in times past also something similar had been done." The original thus opens : " Filius itaque est qui ab initio *judicavit*." This the author connects with John iii. 35, Matt. xxviii. 18, John v. 22. The "*judgment*" is dispensational from the first to the last. Every *judicial* function of God's providence from Eden to the judgment day is administered by the Son of God. This office of *judge* has been largely dealt with in its general view by Tertullian, in this book ii. against Marcion (see chap. xi.–xvii.).
[1] Matt. xi. 27.
[2] Ex. xxxiii. 20.
[3] Penes nos. Christians, not Marcionites. [Could our author have regarded himself as formally at war with the church, at this time ?]
[4] Ex æquo agebat.

[5] In the 1st book, 25th and following chapters.
[6] Sævum.
[7] Tenebrosus. Cicero, *De finibus*, ii. says : " Heraclitus qui cognomento Σκοτεινὸς perhibetur, quia de natura nimis obscure memoravit."
[8] Sursum et deorsum. An allusion to Heraclitus' doctrine of constant change, flux and reflux, out of which all things came. Καὶ τὴν μεταβολὴν ὁδὸν ἄνω κάτω, τόν τε κόσμον γίνεσθαι κατὰ ταύτην, κ.τ.λ. " Change is the way *up and down ;* the world comes into being thus," etc. (Diogenes Laertius, ix. 8).
[9] Sententias.
[10] Dissimulationes.
[11] Non nisi emendata.
[12] Non repercussus.

God (you say) knows not whom He ought to choose. Nor does your god, for if he had foreknown the issue, he would not have chosen the traitor Judas. If you allege that the Creator practised deception[1] in any instance, there was a far greater mendacity in your Christ, whose very body was unreal.[2] Many were consumed by the severity of my God. Those also who were not saved by your god are verily disposed by him to ruin. My God ordered a man to be slain. Your god willed himself to be put to death; not less a homicide against himself than in respect of him by whom he meant to be slain. I will moreover prove to Marcion that they were many who were slain by his god; for he made every one a homicide: in other words, he doomed him to perish, except when people failed in no duty towards Christ.[3] But the straightforward virtue of truth is contented with few resources.[4] Many things will be necessary for falsehood.

CHAP. XXIX.—MARCION'S OWN ANTITHESES, IF ONLY THE TITLE AND OBJECT OF THE WORK BE EXCEPTED, AFFORD PROOFS OF THE CONSISTENT ATTRIBUTES OF THE TRUE GOD.

But I would have attacked Marcion's own *Antitheses* in closer and fuller combat, if a more elaborate demolition of them were required in maintaining for the Creator the character of a good God and a Judge, after[5] the examples of both points, which we have shown to be so worthy of God. Since, however, these two attributes of goodness and justice do together make up the proper fulness of the Divine Being as omnipotent, I am able to content myself with having now compendiously refuted his *Antitheses*, which aim at drawing distinctions out of the qualities of the (Creator's) artifices,[6] or of His laws, or of His great works; and thus sundering Christ from the Creator, as the most Good from the Judge, as One who is merciful from Him who is ruthless, and One who brings salvation from Him who causes ruin. The truth is,[7] they[8] rather unite the two Beings whom they arrange in those diversities (of attribute), which yet are compatible in God. For only take away the title of Marcion's book,[9] and the intention and purpose of the work itself, and you could get no better demonstration than that the self-same God was both very good and a Judge, inasmuch as these two characters are only competently found in God. Indeed, the very effort which is made in the selected examples to oppose Christ to the Creator, conduces all the more to their union. For so entirely one and the same was the nature of the Divine Beings, the good and the severe, as shown both by the same examples and in similar proofs, that It willed to display Its goodness to those on whom It had first inflicted Its severity. The difference in time was no matter of surprise, when the same God was afterwards merciful in presence of evils which had been subdued,[10] who had once been so austere whilst they were as yet unsubdued. Thus, by help of the *Antitheses*, the dispensation of the Creator can be more readily shown to have been *reformed* by Christ, rather than *destroyed*;[11] *restored*, rather than *abolished*;[12] especially as you sever your own god from everything like acrimonious conduct,[13] even from all rivalry whatsoever with the Creator. Now, since this is the case, how comes it to pass that the *Antitheses* demonstrate Him to have been the Creator's rival in every disputed cause?[14] Well, even here, too, I will allow that in these causes my God has been a jealous God, who has in His own right taken especial care that all things done by Him should be in their beginning of a robuster growth;[15] and this in the way of a good, because rational[16] emulation, which tends to maturity. In this sense the world itself will acknowledge His "antitheses," from the contrariety of its own elements, although it has been regulated with the very highest reason.[17] Wherefore, most thoughtless Marcion, it was your duty to have shown that one (of the two Gods you teach) was a God of light, and the other a God of darkness; and then you would have found it an easier task to persuade us that one was a God of goodness, the other a God of severity. However, the "antithesis" (or variety of administration) will rightly be His property, to whom it actually belongs in (the government of) the world.

---

[1] Mentitum.
[2] Non verum. An allusion to the Docetism of Marcion.
[3] Nihil deliquit in Christum, that is, Marcion's Christ.
[4] Paucis amat.
[5] Secundum.
[6] Ingeniorum.
[7] Enim.
[8] i.e., Marcion's *Antitheses*.
[9] *Antitheses* so called because Marcion in it had set passages out of the O. T. and the N. T. in opposition to each other, intending his readers to infer from the apparent disagreement that the law and the gospel were not from the same author (Bp. Kaye on Tertullian, p. 468).

[10] Pro rebus edomitis. See chap. xv. and xix., where he refers to *the law* as the subduing instrument.
[11] Repercussus: perhaps "refuted."
[12] Exclusus.
[13] Ab omni motu amariore.
[14] Singulas species, a law term.
[15] Arbustiores. A figurative word, taken from vines more firmly supported on trees instead of on frames. He has used the word *indomitis* above to express his meaning.
[16] Rationali. Compare chap. vi. of this book, where the "*ratio*," or purpose of God, is shown to be consistent with His goodness in providing for its highest development in man's interest.
[17] Ratione: in reference to God's *ratio* or purpose in creation. See chap. vi. note 10. [p. 301, *supra*.]

THE FIVE BOOKS AGAINST MARCION.

Book III.

WHEREIN CHRIST IS SHOWN TO BE THE SON OF GOD, WHO CREATED THE WORLD; TO HAVE BEEN PREDICTED BY THE PROPHETS; TO HAVE TAKEN HUMAN FLESH LIKE OUR OWN, BY A REAL INCARNATION.

CHAP. I.—INTRODUCTORY: A BRIEF STATEMENT OF THE PRECEDING ARGUMENT IN CONNECTION WITH THE SUBJECT OF THIS BOOK.

FOLLOWING the track of my original treatise, the loss of which we are steadily proceeding[1] to restore, we come now, in the order of our subject, to treat of Christ, although this be a work of supererogation,[2] after the proof which we have gone through that there is but one only God. For no doubt it has been already ruled with sufficient clearness, that Christ must be regarded as pertaining to[3] no other God than the Creator, when it has been determined that no other God but the Creator should be the object of our faith. Him did Christ so expressly preach, whilst the apostles one after the other also so clearly affirmed that Christ belonged to[4] no other God than Him whom He Himself preached—that is, the Creator—that no mention of a second God (nor, accordingly, of a second Christ) was ever agitated previous to Marcion's scandal. This is most easily proved by an examination[5] of both the apostolic and the heretical churches,[6] from which we are forced to declare that *there* is undoubtedly a subversion of the rule (of faith), where any opinion is found of later date,[7]—a point which I have inserted in my first book.[8] A discussion of it would unquestionably be of value even now, when we are about to make a separate examination into (the subject of) Christ; because, whilst proving Christ to be the Creator's *Son*, we are effectually shutting out the God of Marcion. Truth should employ all her available resources, and in no limping way.[9] In our compendious rules of faith, however, she has it all her own way.[10] But I have resolved, like an earnest man,[11] to meet my adversary every way and everywhere in the madness of his heresy, which is so great, that he has found it easier to assume that that Christ has come who was never heard of, than He who has always been predicted.

CHAP. II.—WHY CHRIST'S COMING SHOULD BE PREVIOUSLY ANNOUNCED.

Coming then at once to the point,[12] I have to encounter the question, Whether Christ ought to have come so suddenly?[13] (I answer, No.) First, because He was the Son of God His Father. For this was a point of order, that the Father should announce[14] the Son before the Son should testify of the Father, and that the Father should testify of the Son before the Son should testify of the Father. Secondly, because, in addition to the title of Son, He was the Sent. The authority,[15] therefore, of the Sender must needs have first appeared

---

[1] Perseveramus.
[2] Ex abundanti.
[3] i.e., "as the Son of, or sent by, no other God."
[4] i.e., "was the Son of, or sent by, no other God."
[5] Recensu.
[6] [Surely Tertullian, when he wrote this, imagined himself not separated formally from the Apostolic churches. Of which see *De Præscriptione*, (p. 258) *supra*.]
[7] Ubi *posteritas* invenitur. Compare *De Præscript. Hæret.* 34, where Tertullian refers to "that definite rule, before laid down, touching 'the later date' (illo fine supra dicto *posteritatis*), whereby they (i.e., certain novel opinions) would at once be condemned on the ground of their age alone." In 31 of the same work he contrasts "*posteritatem mendacitatis*" with "*principalitatem veritatis*"—"the later date of falsehood" with "the primary date of truth." [pp. 258, 260, *supra*.]

[8] See book i. chap. 1.
[9] Non ut laborantem. "Qui enim laborant non totis sed fractis utuntur viribus." Πανστρατιᾳ πανσυδιη; Anglice, "with all her might."
[10] In præscript. compendiis vincit.
[11] Ut gestientem.
[12] Hinc denique.
[13] As Marcion makes Him.
[14] Profiteretur.
[15] Patrocinium.

in a testimony of the Sent; because none who comes in the authority of another does himself set it forth[1] for himself on his own assertion, but rather looks out for protection from it, for first comes the support[2] of him who gives him his authority. Now (Christ) will neither be acknowledged as Son if the Father never named Him, nor be believed in as the Sent One if no Sender[3] gave Him a commission: the Father, if any, purposely naming Him; and the Sender, if any, purposely commissioning Him. Everything will be open to suspicion which transgresses a rule. Now the primary order of all things will not allow that the Father should come after the Son in recognition, or the Sender after the Sent, or God after Christ. Nothing can take precedence of its own original in being acknowledged, nor in like manner can it in its ordering.[4] Suddenly a Son, suddenly Sent, and suddenly Christ! On the contrary, I should suppose that from God nothing comes suddenly, because there is nothing which is not ordered and arranged by God. And if ordered, why not also foretold, that it may be proved to have been ordered by the prediction, and by the ordering to be divine? And indeed so great a work, which (we may be sure) required preparation,[5] as being for the salvation of man, could not have been on that very account a sudden thing, because it was through faith that it was to be of avail.[6] Inasmuch, then, as it had to be believed in order to be of use, so far did it require, for the securing of this faith, a preparation built upon the foundations of pre-arrangement and fore-announcement. Faith, when informed by such a process, might justly be required[7] of man by God, and by man be reposed in God; it being a duty, after that knowledge[8] has made it a possibility, to believe those things which a man had learned indeed to believe from the fore-announcement.[9]

CHAP. III.—MIRACLES ALONE, WITHOUT PROPHECY, AN INSUFFICIENT EVIDENCE OF CHRIST'S MISSION.

A procedure[10] of this kind, you say, was not necessary, because He was forthwith to prove Himself the Son and the Sent One, and the Christ of God in very deed, by means of the evidence of His wonderful works.[11] On my side, however, I have to deny that evidence simply of this sort was sufficient as a testimony to Him. He Himself afterwards deprived it of its authority,[12] because when He declared that many would come and "show great signs and wonders,"[13] so as to turn aside the very elect, and yet for all that were not to be received, He showed how rash was belief in signs and wonders, which were so very easy of accomplishment by even false christs. Else how happens it, if He meant Himself to be approved and understood, and received on a certain evidence—I mean that of miracles—that He forbade the recognition of those others who had the very same sort of proof to show, and whose coming was to be quite as sudden and unannounced by any authority?[14] If, because He came before them, and was beforehand with them in displaying the signs of His mighty deeds, He therefore seized the first right to men's faith,—just as the first comers do the first place in the baths,—and so forestalled all who came after Him in that right, take care that He, too, be not caught in the condition of the later comers, if He be found to be behindhand with the Creator, who had already been made known, and had already worked miracles like Him,[15] and like Him had forewarned men not to believe in others, even such as should come after Him. If, therefore, to have been the first to come and utter this warning, is to bar and limit faith,[16] He will Himself have to be condemned, because He was later in being acknowledged; and authority to prescribe such a rule about later comers will belong to the Creator alone, who could have been posterior to none. And now, when I am about to prove that the Creator sometimes displayed by His servants of old, and in other cases reserved for His Christ to display, the self-same miracles which you claim as solely due to faith in your Christ, I may fairly even from this maintain that there was so much the greater reason wherefore Christ should not be believed in simply on account of His miracles, inasmuch as these would have shown Him to belong to none other (God) than the Creator, because answering to the mighty deeds of the Creator, both as performed by His servants and reserved for[17] His Christ; although, even if some other proofs should be found in your Christ —new ones, to wit—we should more readily believe that they, too, belong to the same God as do the old ones, rather than to him who

---

[1] Defendit, "insist on it."
[2] Suggestu.
[3] Mandator.
[4] Dispositione, "its being ordered or arranged."
[5] Parabatur.
[6] Per fidem profuturum.
[7] Indiceretur.
[8] Agnitione.
[9] Prædicatione, "prophecy."
[10] Ordo.
[11] Virtutum, "miracles."

[12] Exauctoravit.
[13] Matt. xxiv. 24. [See Kaye, p. 125.]
[14] Auctore.
[15] Proinde.
[16] Cludet, *quasi* claudet.
[17] Repromissis in.

has no other than new[1] proofs, such as are wanting in the evidences of that antiquity which wins the assent of faith,[2] so that even on this ground he ought to have come announced as much by prophecies of his own, building up faith in him, as by miracles, especially in opposition to the Creator's Christ, who was to come fortified by signs and prophets of His own, in order that he might shine forth as the rival of Christ by help of evidence of different kinds. But how was his Christ to be foretold by a god who was himself never predicted? This, therefore, is the unavoidable inference, that neither your god nor your Christ is an object of faith, because God ought not to have been unknown, and Christ ought to have been made known through God.[3]

CHAP. IV.—MARCION'S CHRIST NOT THE SUBJECT OF PROPHECY. THE ABSURD CONSEQUENCES OF THIS THEORY OF THE HERETIC.

He[4] disdained, I suppose, to imitate the order of our God, as one who was displeasing to him, and was by all means to be vanquished. He wished to come, as a new being in a new way—a son previous to his father's announcement, a sent one before the authority of the sender; so that he might in person[5] propagate a most monstrous faith, whereby it should come to be believed that Christ was come before it should be known that He had an existence. It is here convenient to me to treat that other point: Why he came not after Christ? For when I observe that, during so long a period, his lord[6] bore with the greatest patience the very ruthless Creator who was all the while announcing His Christ to men, I say, that whatever reason impelled him to do so, postponing thereby his own revelation and interposition, the self-same reason imposed on him the duty of bearing with the Creator (who had also in *His* Christ dispensations of His own to carry out); so that, after the completion and accomplishment of the entire plan of the rival God and the rival Christ,[7] he might then superinduce his own proper dispensation. But he grew weary of so long an endurance, and so failed to wait till the end of the Creator's course. It was of no use, his enduring that his Christ should be predicted, when he refused to permit him to be manifested.[8]

Either it was without just cause that he interrupted the full course of his rival's time, or without just cause did he so long refrain from interrupting it. What held him back at first? Or what disturbed him at last? As the case now stands, however,[9] he has committed himself in respect of both, having revealed himself so tardily after the Creator, so hurriedly before His Christ; whereas he ought long ago to have encountered the one with a confutation, the other to have forborne encountering·as yet—not to have borne with the one so long in His ruthless hostility, nor to have disquieted the other, who was as yet quiescent! In the case of both, while depriving them of their title to be considered the most good God, he showed himself at least capricious and uncertain; lukewarm (in his resentment) towards the Creator, but fervid against His Christ, and powerless[10] in respect of them both! For he no more restrained the Creator than he resisted His Christ. The Creator still remains such as He really is. His Christ also will come,[11] just as it is written of Him. Why did he[12] come after the Creator, since he was unable to correct Him by punishment?[13] Why did he reveal himself before Christ, whom he could not hinder from appearing?[14] If, on the contrary,[15] he did chastise the Creator, he revealed himself, (I suppose,) after Him in order that things which require correction might come first. On which account also, (of course,) he ought to have waited for Christ to appear first, whom he was going to chastise in like manner; then he would be His punisher coming after Him,[16] just as he had been in the case of the Creator. There is another consideration: since he will at his second advent come after Him, that as he at His first coming took hostile proceedings against the Creator, destroying the law and the prophets, which were His, so he may, to be sure,[17] at his second coming proceed in opposition to Christ, upsetting[18] His kingdom. Then, no doubt, he would terminate his

arrival on the scene first? Of course, M. must be understood to deny that the Christ of the New Testament is the subject of the Old Testament prophecies at all. Hence T.'s anxiety to adduce *prophecy* as the main evidence of our Lord as being really the Creator's Christ.
[9] Atquin.
[10] Vanus.
[11] The reader will remember that Tertullian is here arguing on Marcion's ground, according to whom the Creator's Christ, the Christ predicted through the O. T., was not yet come. Marcion's Christ, however, had proved himself so weak to stem the Creator's course, that he had no means really of checking the Creator's Christ from coming. It had been better, adds Tertullian, if Marcion's Christ had waited for the Creator's Christ to have first appeared.
[12] Marcion's Christ.
[13] Emendare.
[14] Revocare.
[15] Aut si.
[16] Posterior emendator futurus: an instance of Tertullian's style in paradox.
[17] Vero.
[18] Redarguens.

[1] Tantummodo nova.
[2] Egentia experimentis fidei victricis vetustatis.
[3] i.e., through God's announcement by prophecy.
[4] Your God.
[5] Ipse.
[6] Ejus (i.e. Marcionis) Dominum, meaning Marcion's God, who had not yet been revealed.
[7] The Creator and His Christ, as rivals of Marcion's.
[8] He twits Marcion with introducing his Christ on the scene *too soon*. He ought to have waited until the *Creator's* Christ (prophesied of through the Old Testament) had come. Why allow Him to be predicted, and then forbid His actual coming, by his own

course, and then (if ever)[1] be worthy of belief; for else, if his work has been already perfected, it would be in vain for him to come, for there would indeed be nothing that he could further accomplish.

CHAP. V.—SUNDRY FEATURES OF THE PRO-PHETIC STYLE: PRINCIPLES OF ITS INTERPRE-TATION.

These preliminary remarks I have ventured to make[2] at this first step of the discussion, and while the conflict is, as it were, from a distance. But inasmuch as I shall now from this point have to grapple with my opponent on a distinct issue and in close combat, I perceive that I must advance even here some lines, at which the battle will have to be delivered; they are the Scriptures of the Creator. For as I shall have to prove that Christ was from the Creator, according to these (Scriptures), which were afterwards accomplished in the Creator's Christ, I find it necessary to set forth the form and, so to speak, the nature of the Scriptures themselves, that they may not distract the reader's attention by being called into controversy at the moment of their application to subjects of discussion, and by their proof being confounded with the proof of the subjects themselves. Now there are two conditions of prophetic announcement which I adduce, as requiring the assent of our adversaries in the future stages of the discussion. One, that future events are sometimes announced as if they were already passed. For it is[3] consistent with Deity to regard as accomplished facts whatever It has determined on, because there is no difference of time with that Being in whom eternity itself directs a uniform condition of seasons. It is indeed more natural[4] to the prophetic divination to represent as seen and already brought to pass,[5] even while foreseeing it, that which it foresees; in other words, that which is by all means future. As for instance, in Isaiah: "I gave my back to the smiters, and my cheeks (I exposed) to their hands. I hid not my face from shame and spitting."[6] For whether it was Christ even then, as we hold, or the prophet, as the Jews say, who pronounced these words concerning himself, in either case, that which as yet had not happened sounded as if it had been already accomplished. Another characteristic will be, that very many events are figuratively predicted by means of enigmas and allegories and parables, and that they

must be understood in a sense different from the literal description. For we both read of "the mountains dropping down new wine,"[7] but not as if one might expect "*must*" from the stones, or its decoction from the rocks; and also hear of "a land flowing with milk and honey,"[8] but not as if you were to suppose that you would ever gather Samian cakes from the ground; nor does God, forsooth, offer His services as a water-bailiff or a farmer when He says, "I will open rivers in a dry land; I will plant in the wilderness the cedar and the box-tree."[9] In like manner, when, foretelling the conversion of the Gentiles, He says, "The beasts of the field shall honour me, the dragons and the owls," He surely never meant to derive[10] His fortunate omens from the young of birds and foxes, and from the songsters of marvel and fable. But why enlarge on such a subject? When the very apostle whom our heretics adopt,[11] interprets the law which allows an unmuzzled mouth to the oxen that tread out the corn, not of cattle, but of ourselves;[12] and also alleges that the rock which followed (the Israelites) and supplied them with drink was Christ;[13] teaching the Galatians, moreover, that the two narratives of the sons of Abraham had an allegorical meaning in their course;[14] and to the Ephesians giving an intimation that, when it was declared in the beginning that a man should leave his father and mother and become one flesh with his wife, he applied this to Christ and the church.[15]

CHAP. VI.—COMMUNITY IN CERTAIN POINTS OF MARCIONITE AND JEWISH ERROR. PROPHE-CIES OF CHRIST'S REJECTION EXAMINED

Since, therefore, there clearly exist these two characteristics in the Jewish prophetic literature, let the reader remember,[16] whenever we adduce any evidence therefrom, that, by mutual consent,[17] the point of discussion is not the form of the scripture, but the subject it is called in to prove. When, therefore, our heretics in their phrenzy presumed to say that that Christ was come who had never been fore-announced, it followed that, on their assumption, that Christ had not yet appeared who

---

[1] Si forte.
[2] Proluserim.
[3] [An important principle, See Kaye, p. 325.]
[4] Familiare.
[5] Expunctum.
[6] Ch. l. 6, slightly altered.
[7] Joel iii. 18.
[8] Ex. iii. 8, 17; Deut. xxvi. 9, 15.
[9] Isa. xli. 18, 19, inexactly quoted.
[10] Relaturus.
[11] Hæreticorum apostolus. We have already referred to Marcion's acceptance of St. Paul's epistles. It has been suggested that Tertullian in the text uses *hæreticorum apostolus* as synonymous with *ethnicorum apostolus* = "apostle of the Gentiles," in which case the allusion to St. Paul would of course be equally clear. But this interpretation is unnecessary.
[12] 1 Cor. ix. 9.
[13] 1 Cor. x. 4; compare below, book v., chap. vii.
[14] Gal. iv. 22, 24.
[15] Eph. v. 31, 32.
[16] "Remember, O reader."
[17] Constitisse.

had always been predicted; and thus they are obliged to make common cause with[1] Jewish error, and construct their arguments with its assistance, on the pretence that the Jews were themselves quite certain that it was some other who came: so they not only rejected Him as a stranger, but slew Him as an enemy, although they would without doubt have acknowledged Him, and with all religious devotion followed Him, if He had only been one of themselves. Our shipmaster[2] of course got his craft-wisdom not from the Rhodian law,[3] but from the Pontic,[4] which cautioned him against believing that the Jews had no right to sin against their Christ; whereas (even if nothing like their conduct had been predicted against them) human nature alone, liable to error as it is, might well have induced him to suppose that it was quite possible for the Jews to have committed such a sin, considered as men, without assuming any unfair prejudice regarding their feelings, whose sin was antecedently so credible. Since, however, it was actually foretold that they would not acknowledge Christ, and therefore would even put Him to death, it will therefore follow that He was both ignored[5] and slain by them, who were beforehand pointed out as being about to commit such offences against Him. If you require a proof of this, instead of turning out those passages of Scripture which, while they declare Christ to be capable of suffering death, do thereby also affirm the possibility of His being rejected (for if He had not been rejected, He could not really suffer anything), but rather reserving them for the subject of His sufferings, I shall content myself at the present moment with adducing those which simply show that there was a probability of Christ's rejection. This is quickly done, since the passages indicate that the entire power of understanding was by the Creator taken from the people. "I will take away," says He, "the wisdom of their wise men; and the understanding of their prudent men will I hide;"[6] and again: "With your ear ye shall hear, and not understand; and with your eyes ye shall see, but not perceive: for the heart of this people hath growth fat, and with their ears they hear heavily, and their eyes have they shut; lest they hear with their ears, and see with their eyes, and understand with the heart, and be converted, and I heal them."[7] Now this

blunting of their sound senses they had brought on themselves, loving God with their lips, but keeping far away from Him in their heart. Since, then, Christ was announced by the Creator, "who formeth the lightning, and createth the wind, and declareth unto man His Christ," as the prophet Joel says,[8] since the entire hope of the Jews, not to say of the Gentiles too, was fixed on the manifestation of Christ,—it was demonstrated that they, by their being deprived of those powers of knowledge and understanding—wisdom and prudence, would fail to know and understand that which was predicted, even Christ; when the chief of their wise men should be in error respecting Him—that is to say, their scribes and prudent ones, or Pharisees; and when the people, like them, should hear with their ears and not understand Christ while teaching them, and see with their eyes and not perceive Christ, although giving them signs. Similarly it is said elsewhere: "Who is blind, but my servant? or deaf, but he who ruleth over them?"[9] Also when He upbraids them by the same Isaiah: "I have nourished and brought up children, and they have rebelled against me. The ox knoweth his owner, and the ass his master's crib: but Israel doth not know; my people doth not consider."[10] We indeed, who know for certain that Christ always spoke in the prophets, as the Spirit of the Creator (for so says the prophet: "The person of our Spirit, Christ the Lord,"[11] who from the beginning was both heard and seen as the Father's vicegerent in the name of God), are well aware that His words, when actually upbraiding Israel, were the same as those which it was foretold that He should denounce against him: "Ye have forsaken the Lord, and have provoked the Holy One of Israel to anger."[12] If, however, you would rather refer to God Himself, instead of to Christ, the whole imputation of Jewish ignorance from the first, through an unwillingness to allow that even anciently[13] the Creator's word and Spirit—that is to say, His Christ—was despised and not acknowledged by them, you will even in this subterfuge be defeated.

---

[1] Sociari cum.
[2] Marcion.
[3] The model of wise naval legislation, much of which found its way into the Roman pandects.
[4] Symbol of barbarism and ignorance—a heavy joke against the once seafaring heretic.
[5] Ignoratus, "rejected of men."
[6] Isa. xxix. 14.
[7] Isa. vi. 9, 10. Quoted with some verbal differences.

[8] A supposed quotation of Amos iv. 13. See Oehler's marginal reference. If so, the reference to Joel is either a slip of Tertullian or a corruption of his text ; more likely the former, for the best MSS. insert Joel's name. Amos iv. 13, according to the LXX., runs, Ἀπαγγέλλων εἰς ἀνθρώπους τὸν Χριστὸν αὐτοῦ, which exactly suits Tertullian's quotation. Junius supports the reference to Joel, supposing that Tertullian has his ch. ii. 31 in view, as compared with Acts ii. 16-33. This is too harsh an interpretation. It is simpler and better to suppose that Tertullian really meant to quote the LXX. of the passage in Amos, but in mistake named Joel as his prophet.
[9] Isa. xlii. 19, altered.
[10] Isa. i. 2, 3.
[11] This seems to be a translation with a slight alteration of the LXX. version of Lam. iv. 20, πνεῦμα προσώπου ἡμῶν Χριστὸς Κύριος.
[12] Isa. i. 4.
[13] Retro.

For when you do not deny that the Creator's Son and Spirit and Substance is also His Christ, you must needs allow that those who have not acknowledged the Father have failed likewise to acknowledge the Son through the identity of their natural substance;[1] for if in Its fulness It has baffled man's understanding, much more has a portion of It, especially when partaking of the fulness.[2] Now, when these things are carefully considered, it becomes evident how the Jews both rejected Christ and slew Him; not because they regarded Him as a strange Christ, but because they did not acknowledge Him, although their own. For how could they have understood the strange One, concerning whom nothing had ever been announced, when they failed to understand Him about whom there had been a perpetual course of prophecy? That admits of being understood or being not understood, which, by possessing a substantial basis for prophecy,[3] will also have a subject-matter[4] for either knowledge or error; whilst that which lacks such matter admits not the issue of wisdom. So that it was not as if He belonged to another[5] god that they conceived an aversion for Christ, and persecuted Him, but simply as a man whom they regarded as a wonder-working juggler,[6] and an enemy[7] in His doctrines. They brought Him therefore to trial as a mere man, and one of themselves too—that is, a Jew (only a renegade and a destroyer of Judaism)—and punished Him according to their law. If He had been a stranger, indeed, they would not have sat in judgment over Him. So far are they from appearing to have understood Him to be a strange Christ, that they did not even judge Him to be a stranger to their own human nature.[8]

CHAP. VII.—PROPHECY SETS FORTH TWO DIF-
FERENT CONDITIONS OF CHRIST, ONE LOWLY,
THE OTHER MAJESTIC. THIS FACT POINTS TO
TWO ADVENTS OF CHRIST.

Our heretic will now have the fullest opportunity of learning the clue[9] of his errors along with the Jew himself, from whom he has borrowed his guidance in this discussion. Since, however, the blind leads the blind, they fall into the ditch together. We affirm that, as there are two conditions demonstrated by the prophets to belong to Christ, so these presignified the same number of advents; one, and that the first, was to be in lowliness,[10] when He had to be led as a sheep to be slain as a victim, and to be as a lamb dumb before the shearer, not opening His mouth, and not fair to look upon.[11] For, says (the prophet), we have announced concerning Him: "He is like a tender plant,[12] like a root out of a thirsty ground; He hath no form nor comeliness; and we beheld Him, and He was without beauty: His form was disfigured;"[13] "marred more than the sons of men; a man stricken with sorrows, and knowing how to bear our infirmity;"[14] "placed by the Father as a stone of stumbling and a rock of offence;"[15] "made by Him a little lower than the angels;"[16] declaring Himself to be "a worm and not a man, a reproach of men, and despised of the people."[17] Now these signs of degradation quite suit His first coming, just as the tokens of His majesty do His second advent, when He shall no longer remain "a stone of stumbling and a rock of offence," but after His rejection become "the chief corner-stone," accepted and elevated to the top place[18] of the temple, even His church, being that very stone in Daniel, cut out of the mountain, which was to smite and crush the image of the secular kingdom.[19] Of this advent the same prophet says: "Behold, one like the Son of man came with the clouds of heaven, and came to the Ancient of days; and they brought Him before Him, and there was given Him dominion and glory, and a kingdom, that all people, nations, and languages should serve Him. His dominion is an everlasting dominion, which shall not pass away; and His kingdom that which shall not be destroyed."[20] Then indeed He shall have both a glorious form, and an unsullied beauty above the sons of men. "Thou art fairer," says (the Psalmist), "than the children of men; grace is poured into Thy lips; therefore God hath blessed Thee for ever. Gird Thy sword upon Thy thigh, O most mighty, with Thy glory and Thy majesty."[21] For the Father, after making Him a little lower than the angels, "will crown Him with glory and honour, and put all things under His feet."[22] "Then

---

[1] Per ejusdem substantiæ conditionem.
[2] He seems here to allude to such statements of God's being as Col. ii. 9.
[3] Substantiam prædicationis.
[4] Materiam.
[5] Alterius, "the other," i.e., Marcion's rival God.
[6] Planum in signis, cf. the *Magum in potestate* of Apolog. 21.
[7] Æmulum, "a rival," i.e., to Moses.
[8] Nec hominem ejus ut alienum judicaverunt, "His manhood they judged not to be different."
[9] Rationem.
[10] Humilitate.
[11] A reference to, rather than quotation from, Isa. liii. 7.
[12] Sicut puerulus, "like a little boy," or, "a sorry slave."
[13] Isa. liii. 2, 3, according to the Septuagint.
[14] See Isa. lii. 14, liii. 3, 4.
[15] Isa. viii. 14.
[16] Ps. viii. 6.
[17] Ps. xxii. 7.
[18] Consummationem: an allusion to Zech. iv. 7.
[19] See Dan. ii. 34.
[20] Dan. vii. 13, 14.
[21] Ps. xlv. 2, 3.
[22] Ps. viii. 5, 6.

shall they look on Him whom they have pierced, and they shall mourn for Him, tribe after tribe;"[1] because, no doubt, they once refused to acknowledge Him in the lowliness of His human condition. He is even a man, says Jeremiah, and who shall recognise Him? Therefore, asks Isaiah, "who shall declare His generation?"[2] So also in Zechariah, Christ Jesus, the true High Priest of the Father, in the person of Joshua, nay, in the very mystery of His name,[3] is portrayed in a twofold dress with reference to both His advents. At first He is clad in sordid garments, that is to say, in the lowliness of suffering and mortal flesh: then the devil resisted Him, as the instigator of the traitor Judas, not to mention his tempting Him after His baptism: afterwards He was stripped of His first filthy raiment, and adorned with the priestly robe[4] and mitre, and a pure diadem;[5] in other words, with the glory and honour of His second advent.[6] If I may offer, moreover, an interpretation of the two goats which were presented on "the great day of atonement,"[7] do they not also figure the two natures of Christ? They were of like size, and very similar in appearance, owing to the Lord's identity of aspect; because He is not to come in any other form, having to be recognised by those by whom He was also wounded and pierced. One of these goats was bound[8] with scarlet,[9] and driven by the people out of the camp[10] into the wilderness,[11] amid cursing, and spitting, and pulling, and piercing,[12] being thus marked with all the signs of the Lord's own passion; while the other, by being offered up for sins, and given to the priests of the temple for meat, afforded proofs of His second appearance, when (after all sins have been expiated) the priests of the spiritual temple, that is, the church, are to enjoy the flesh, as it were,[13] of the Lord's own grace, whilst the residue go away from salvation without tasting it.[14] Since, therefore, the first advent was prophetically declared both as most obscure in its types, and as deformed with every kind of indignity, but the second as glorious and altogether worthy of God, they would on this very account, while confining their regards to that which they were easily able both to understand and to believe, even the second advent, be not undeservedly deceived respecting the more obscure, and, at any rate, the more lowly first coming. Accordingly, to this day they deny that their Christ has come, because He has not appeared in majesty, while they ignore the fact that He was to come also in lowliness.

CHAP. VIII.—ABSURDITY OF MARCION'S DOCETIC OPINIONS; REALITY OF CHRIST'S INCARNATION.

Our heretic must now cease to borrow poison from the Jew—"the asp," as the adage runs, "from the viper"[15]—and henceforth vomit forth the virulence of his own disposition, as when he alleges Christ to be a phantom. Except, indeed, that this opinion of his will be sure to have others to maintain it in his precocious and somewhat abortive Marcionites, whom the Apostle John designated as antichrists, when they denied that Christ was come in the flesh; not that they did this with the view of establishing the right of the other god (for on this point also they had been branded by the same apostle), but because they had started with assuming the incredibility of an incarnate God. Now, the more firmly the antichrist Marcion had seized this assumption, the more prepared was he, of course, to reject the bodily substance of Christ, since he had introduced his very god to our notice as neither the author nor the restorer of the flesh; and for this very reason, to be sure, as pre-eminently good, and most remote from the deceits and fallacies of the Creator. His Christ, therefore, in order to avoid all such deceits and fallacies, and the imputation, if possible, of belonging to the Creator, was not what he appeared to be, and feigned himself to be what he was not—incarnate without being flesh, human without being man, and likewise a divine Christ without being God! But why should he not have propagated also the phantom of God? Can I believe him on the subject of the internal nature, who was all wrong touching the external substance? How will it be possible to believe him true on a mystery, when he has been found so false on a plain fact? How,

---

[1] Zech. xii. 10, 12.
[2] Isa. liii. 8.
[3] Joshua, i.e., Jesus.
[4] Podere.
[5] Cidari munda.
[6] See Zech. iii.
[7] Jejunio, see Lev. xvi. 5, 7, etc.
[8] Circumdatus.
[9] Perhaps in reference to Heb. ix. 19.
[10] Civitatem, "city."
[11] In perditionem.
[12] This treatment of the scape-goat was partly ceremonial, partly disorderly. The Mischna (*Yoma* vi. 4-6) mentions the scarlet ribbon which was bound round the animal's head between the horns, and the "pulling" (rather plucking out of its hair); but this latter was an indignity practised by scoffers and guarded against by Jews. Tertullian repeats the whole of this passage, *Adv. Jud.* xiv. Similar use is made of the type of the scape-goat by other fathers, as Justin Martyr (*Dial. cum Tryph.*) and Cyril of Alex. (*Epist. ad Acacium*). In his book ix. *Against Julian*, he expressly says: "Christ was described by the two goats,—as dying for us in the flesh, and then (as shown by the scape-goat) overcoming death in His divine nature." See Tertullian's passages illustrated fully in Rabbi Chiga, *Addit. ad Cod. de die Expiat.* (in Ugolini, *Thes.* i. 88).
[13] Quasi visceratione. [See Kaye's important comment, p. 426.]

[14] Jejunantibus.
[15] So Epiphanius, *adv. Hæres.* i. 23. 7, quotes the same proverb, ὡς ἀσπὶς παρ' ἐχίδνης ἰὸν δανιζομένη. [Tom. II. p. 144. Ed. Oehler.]

moreover, when he confounds the truth of the spirit with the error of the flesh,[1] could he combine within himself that communion of light and darkness, or truth and error, which the apostle says cannot co-exist?[2] Since, however, Christ's being flesh is now discovered to be a lie, it follows that all things which were done by the flesh of Christ were done untruly,[3]—every act of intercourse,[4] of contact, of eating or drinking,[5] yea, His very miracles. If with a touch, or by being touched, He freed any one of a disease, whatever was done by any corporeal act cannot be believed to have been truly done in the absence of all reality in His body itself. Nothing substantial can be allowed to have been effected by an unsubstantial thing; nothing full by a vacuity. If the habit were putative, the action was putative; if the worker were imaginary the works were imaginary. On this principle, too, the sufferings of Christ will be found not to warrant faith in Him. For He suffered nothing who did not truly suffer; and a phantom could not truly suffer. God's entire work, therefore, is subverted. Christ's death, wherein lies the whole weight and fruit of the Christian name, is denied, although the apostle asserts[6] it so expressly[7] as undoubtedly real, making it the very foundation of the gospel, of our salvation, and of his own preaching.[8] "I have delivered unto you before all things," says he, "how that Christ died for our sins, and that he was buried, and that He rose again the third day." Besides, if His flesh is denied, how is His death to be asserted; for death is the proper suffering of the flesh, which returns through death back to the earth out of which it was taken, according to the law of its Maker? Now, if His death be denied, because of the denial of His flesh, there will be no certainty of His resurrection. For He rose not, for the very same reason that He died not, even because He possessed not the reality of the flesh, to which as death accrues, so does resurrection likewise. Similarly, if Christ's resurrection be nullified, ours also is destroyed. If Christ's *resurrection* be not realized,[9] neither shall that be for which Christ came. For just as they, who said that there is no resurrection of the dead, are refuted by the apostle from the resurrection of Christ, so, if the resurrection of Christ falls

to the ground, the resurrection of the dead is also swept away.[10] And so our faith is vain, and vain also is the preaching of the apostles. Moreover, they even show themselves to be false witnesses of God, because they testified that He raised up Christ, whom He did not raise. And we remain in our sins still.[11] And those who have slept in Christ have perished; destined, forsooth,[12] to rise again, but peradventure in a phantom state,[13] just like Christ.

CHAP. IX.—REFUTATION OF MARCION'S OBJECTIONS DERIVED FROM THE CASES OF THE ANGELS, AND THE PRE-INCARNATE MANIFESTATIONS OF THE SON OF GOD.

Now, in this discussion of yours,[14] when you suppose that we are to be met with the case of the Creator's angels, as if they held intercourse with Abraham and Lot in a phantom state, that of merely putative flesh,[15] and yet did truly converse, and eat, and work, as they had been commissioned to do, you will not, to begin with, be permitted to use as examples the acts of that God whom you are destroying. For by how much you make your god a better and more perfect being, by just so much will all examples be unsuitable to him of that God from whom he totally differs, and without which difference he would not be at all better or more perfect. But then, secondly, you must know that it will not be conceded to you, that in the angels there was only a putative flesh, but one of a true and solid human substance. For if (on your terms) it was no difficulty to him to manifest true sensations and actions in a putative flesh, it was much more easy for him still to have assigned the true substance of flesh to these true sensations and actions, as the proper maker and former thereof. But your god, perhaps on the ground of his having produced no flesh at all, was quite right in introducing the mere phantom of that of which he had been unable to produce the reality. My God, however, who formed that which He had taken out of the dust of the ground in the true quality of flesh, although not issuing as yet from conjugal seed, was equally able to apply to angels too a flesh of any material whatsoever, who built even the world out of nothing, into so many and so various bodies, and that at a word! And, really, if your god promises to men some time or other the true nature of

---

[1] As in his Docetic views of the body of Christ.
[2] 2 Cor. vi. 14.
[3] Mendacio.
[4] Congressus.
[5] Convictus.
[6] Demandat.
[7] Tam impresse, "so strongly."
[8] 1 Cor. xv. 3, 4, 14, 17, 18.
[9] Valebit.

[10] Aufertur.
[11] 1 Cor. xv. 13–18
[12] Sane.
[13] Phantasmate forsitan.
[14] Ista. [See Kaye, p. 205.]
[15] [Pamelius attributes this doctrine to Appelles a disciple of Marcion, of whom See Kaye, pp. 479, 480.]

angels[1] (for he says, "They shall be like the angels"), why should not my God also have fitted on to angels the true substance of men, from whatever source derived? For not even you will tell me, in reply, whence is obtained that angelic nature on your side; so that it is enough for me to define this as being fit and proper to God, even the verity of that thing which was objective to three senses—sight, touch, and hearing. It is more difficult for God to practise deception[2] than to produce real flesh from any material whatever, even without the means of birth. But for other heretics, also, who maintain that the flesh in the angels ought to have been born of flesh, if it had been really human, we have an answer on a sure principle, to the effect that it was truly *human* flesh, and yet *not born*. It was truly human, because of the truthfulness of God, who can neither lie nor deceive, and because (angelic beings) cannot be dealt with by men in a human way except in human substance: it was withal unborn, because none[3] but Christ could become incarnate by being born of the flesh in order that by His own nativity He might regenerate[4] our birth, and might further by His death also dissolve our death, by rising again in that flesh in which, that He might even die, He was born. Therefore on that occasion He did Himself appear with the angels to Abraham in the verity of the flesh, which had not as yet undergone birth, because it was not yet going to die, although it was even now learning to hold intercourse amongst men. Still greater was the propriety in angels, who never received a dispensation to die for us, not having assumed even a brief experience[5] of flesh by being born, because they were not destined to lay it down again by dying; but from whatever quarter they obtained it, and by what means soever they afterwards entirely divested themselves of it, they yet never pretended it to be unreal flesh. Since the Creator "maketh His angels spirits, and His ministers a flame of fire"—as truly spirits as also fire—so has He truly made them flesh likewise; wherefore we can now recall to our own minds, and remind the heretics also, that He has promised that He will one day form men into angels, who once formed angels into men.

CHAP. X.—THE TRULY INCARNATE STATE MORE WORTHY OF GOD THAN MARCION'S FANTASTIC FLESH.

Therefore, since you are not permitted to resort to any instances of the Creator, as alien from the subject, and possessing special causes of their own, I should like you to state yourself the design of your god, in exhibiting his Christ not in the reality of flesh. If he despised it as earthly, and (as you express it) full of dung,[6] why did he not on that account include the likeness of it also in his contempt? For no honour is to be attributed to the image of anything which is itself unworthy of honour. As the natural state is, so will the likeness be. But how could he hold converse with men except in the image of human substance?[7] Why, then, not rather in the reality thereof, that his intercourse might be real, since he was under the necessity of holding it? And to how much better account would this necessity have been turned by ministering to faith rather than to a fraud![8] The god whom you make is miserable enough, for this very reason that he was unable to display his Christ except in the effigy of an unworthy, and indeed an alien, thing. In some instances, it will be convenient to use even unworthy things, if they be only our own, as it will also be quite improper to use things, be they ever so worthy, if they be not our own.[9] Why, then, did he not come in some other worthier substance, and especially his own, that he might not seem as if he could not have done without an unworthy and an alien one? Now, since my Creator held intercourse with man by means of even a bush and fire, and again afterwards by means of a cloud and column,[10] and in representations of Himself used bodies composed of the elements, these examples of divine power afford sufficient proof that God did not require the instrumentality of false or even of real flesh. But yet, if we look steadily into the subject, there is really no substance which is worthy of becoming a vestment for God. Whatsoever He is pleased to clothe Himself withal, He makes worthy of Himself—only without untruth.[11] Therefore how comes it to pass that he should have thought the verity of the flesh, rather than its unreality, a disgrace? Well, but he honoured it by his fiction of it. How great, then, is that flesh, the very phantasy of which was a necessity to the superior God!

CHAP. XI.—CHRIST WAS TRULY BORN; MARCION'S ABSURD CAVIL IN DEFENCE OF A PUTATIVE NATIVITY.

All these illusions of an imaginary corpo-

---

1 Luke xx. 36.
2 Mentiri.
3 i.e, among the angels.
4 Reformaret.
5 Commeatum.

6 Stercoribus infersam.
7 A Marcionite argument.
8 Stropham, a player's trick; so in *Spectac.* 29.
9 Alienis.
10 Globum.
11 Mendacio.

reity[1] in (his) Christ, Marcion adopted with this view, that his nativity also might not be furnished with any evidence from his human substance, and that thus the Christ of the Creator might be free to have assigned to Him all predictions which treated of Him as one capable of human birth, and therefore fleshly. But most foolishly did our Pontic heresiarch act in this too. As if it would not be more readily believed that flesh in the Divine Being should rather be unborn than untrue, this belief having in fact had the way mainly prepared for it by the Creator's angels when they conversed in flesh which was real, although unborn. For indeed the notorious Philumena[2] persuaded Apelles and the other seceders from Marcion rather to believe that Christ did really carry about a body of flesh; not derived to Him, however, from birth, but one which He borrowed from the elements. Now, as Marcion was apprehensive that a belief of the fleshly body would also involve a belief of birth, undoubtedly He who seemed to be man was believed to be verily and indeed born. For a certain woman had exclaimed, " Blessed is the womb that bare Thee, and the paps which Thou hast sucked ! "[3] And how else could they have said that His mother and His brethren were standing without ?[4] But we shall see more of this in the proper place.[5] Surely, when He also proclaimed Himself as the Son of man, He, without doubt, confessed that He had been born. Now I would rather refer all these points to an examination of the gospel; but still, as I have already stated, if he, who seemed to be man, had by all means to pass as having been born, it was vain for him to suppose that faith in his nativity was to be perfected[6] by the device of an imaginary flesh. For what advantage was there in that being not true which was held to be true, whether it were his flesh or his birth? Or if you should say, let human opinion go for nothing;[7] you are then honouring your god under the shelter of a deception, since he knew himself to be something different from what he had made men to think of him. In that case you might possibly have assigned to him a putative nativity even, and so not have hung the question on this point. For

silly women fancy themselves pregnant sometimes, when they are corpulent[8] either from their natural flux[9] or from some other malady. And, no doubt, it had become his duty, since he had put on the mere mask of his substance, to act out from its earliest scene the play of his phantasy, lest he should have failed in his part at the beginning of the flesh. You have, of course,[10] rejected the sham of a nativity, and have produced true flesh itself. And, no doubt, even the real nativity of a God is a most mean thing.[11] Come then, wind up your cavils[12] against the most sacred and reverend works of nature; inveigh against all that you are; destroy the origin of flesh and life; call the womb a sewer of the illustrious animal— in other words, the manufactory for the production of man; dilate on the impure and shameful tortures of parturition, and then on the filthy, troublesome, contemptible issues of the puerperal labour itself ! But yet, after you have pulled all these things down to infamy, that you may affirm them to be unworthy of God, birth will not be worse for Him than death, infancy than the cross, punishment than nature, condemnation than the flesh. If Christ truly suffered all this, to be born was a less thing for Him. If Christ suffered evasively,[13] as a phantom; evasively, too, might He have been born. Such are Marcion's chief arguments by which he makes out another Christ; and I think that we show plainly enough that they are utterly irrelevant, when we teach how much more truly consistent with God is the reality rather than the falsehood of that condition[14] in which He manifested His Christ. Since He was "the truth," He was flesh; since He was flesh, He was born. For the points which this heresy assaults are confirmed, when the means of the assault are destroyed. Therefore if He is to be considered in the flesh,[15] because He was born; and born, because He is in the flesh, and because He is no phantom,—it follows that He must be acknowledged as Himself the very Christ of the Creator, who was by the Creator's prophets foretold as about to come in the flesh, and by the process of human birth.[16]

CHAP. XII.—ISAIAH'S PROPHECY OF EMMANUEL. CHRIST ENTITLED TO THAT NAME.

And challenge us first, as is your wont, to consider Isaiah's description of Christ, while

---

[1] Corpulentiæ.
[2] This woman is called in *De Præscr. Hæret.* 6, " an angel of deceit," and (in 30) " a virgin, but afterwards a monstrous prostitute." Our author adds : " Induced by her tricks and miracles, Apelles introduced a new heresy." See also Eusebius, *Hist. Eccl.* v. 13 ; Augustin, *De Hæres.* 42 ; Hieronymus, *Epist. adv. Ctesiph.* p. 477, tom. iv. ed. Benedictin.
[3] Luke xi. 27.
[4] Luke viii. 20.
[5] Below, iv. 26 ; also in *De carne Christi*, cap. vii.
[6] Expungendam, " consummated," a frequent use of the word in our author.
[7] Viderit opinio humana.

[8] Inflatæ.
[9] Sanguinis tributo.
[10] Plane, ironically said.
[11] Turpissimum.
[12] Perora.
[13] Mendacio.
[14] Habitus.
[15] Carneus.
[16] Ex nativitate.

you contend that in no point does it suit. For, to begin with, you say that Isaiah's Christ will have to be called Emmanuel;[1] then, that He takes the riches of Damascus and the spoils of Samaria against the king of Assyria.[2] But yet He who is come was neither born under such a name, nor ever engaged in any warlike enterprise. I must, however, remind you that you ought to look into the contexts[3] of the two passages. For there is immediately added the interpretation of Emmanuel, "God with us;" so that you have to consider not merely the name as it is uttered, but also its meaning. The utterance is Hebrew, *Emmanuel*, of the prophet's own nation; but the meaning of the word, *God with us*, is by the interpretation made common property. Inquire, then, whether this name, God-with-us, which is Emmanuel, be not often used for the name of Christ,[4] from the fact that Christ has enlightened the world. And I suppose you will not deny it, inasmuch as you do yourself admit that He is called God-with-us, that is, Emmanuel. Else if you are so foolish, that, because with you He gets the designation God-with-us, not Emmanuel, you therefore are unwilling to grant that He is come whose property it is to be called Emmanuel, as if this were not the same name as God-with-us, you will find among the Hebrew Christians, and amongst Marcionites too, that they name Him Emmanuel when they mean Him to be called God-with-us; just indeed as every nation, by whatever word they would express God-with-us, has called Him Emmanuel, completing the sound in its sense. Now since Emmanuel is God-with-us, and God-with-us is Christ, who is in us (for "as many of you as are baptized into Christ, have put on Christ"[5]), Christ is as properly implied in the meaning of the name, which is God-with-us, as He is in the pronunciation of the name, which is Emmanuel. And thus it is evident that He is now come who was foretold as Emmanuel, because what Emmanuel signifies is come, that is to say, God-with-us.

CHAP. XIII.—ISAIAH'S PROPHECIES CONSIDERED. THE VIRGINITY OF CHRIST'S MOTHER A SIGN. OTHER PROPHECIES ALSO SIGNS. METAPHOR-ICAL SENSE OF PROPER NAMES IN SUNDRY PASSAGES OF THE PROPHETS.

You are equally led away by the sound of names,[6] when you so understand the riches of Damascus, and the spoils of Samaria, and

the king of Assyria, as if they portended that the Creator's Christ was a warrior, not attending to the promise contained in the passage, "For before the Child shall have knowledge to cry, My father and My mother, He shall take away the riches of Damascus and the spoil of Samaria before the king of Assyria."[7] You should first examine the point of age, whether it can be taken to represent Christ as even yet a man,[8] much less a warrior. Although, to be sure, He might be about to call to arms by His cry as an infant; might be about to sound the alarm of war not with a trumpet, but with a little rattle; might be about to seek His foe, not on horseback, or in chariot, or from parapet, but from nurse's neck or nursemaid's back, and so be destined to subjugate Damascus and Samaria from His mother's breasts! It is a different matter, of course, when the babes of your barbarian Pontus spring forth to the fight. They are, I ween, taught to lance before they lacerate;[9] swathed at first in sunshine and ointment,[10] afterwards armed with the satchel,[11] and rationed on bread and butter![12] Now, since nature, certainly, nowhere grants to man to learn warfare before life, to pillage the wealth of a Damascus before he knows his father and mother's name, it follows that the passage in question must be deemed to be a figurative one. Well, but nature, says he, does not permit "a virgin to conceive," and still the prophet is believed. And indeed very properly; for he has paved the way for the incredible thing being believed, by giving a reason for its occurrence, in that it was to be for a sign. "Therefore," says he, "the Lord himself shall give you a *sign;* behold, a virgin shall conceive, and bear a son."[13] Now a sign from God would not have been a sign,[14] unless it had been some novel and prodigious thing. Then, again, Jewish cavillers, in order to disconcert us, boldly pretend that Scripture does not hold[15] that a virgin, but only a young woman,[16] is to conceive and bring

---

[1] Isa. vii. 14.
[2] Isa. viii. 4. Compare *adv. Judæos*, 9.
[3] Cohærentia.
[4] Agitetur in Christo.
[5] Gal. iii. 27.
[6] Compare with this chapter, T.'s *adv. Judæos*, 9.

[7] Isa. viii. 4.
[8] Jam hominem, jam virum in *Adv. Judæos*, "at man's estate.
[9] Lanceare ante quam lancinare. This play on the words points to the very early training of the barbarian boys to war. *Lancinare* perhaps means, "to nibble the nipple with the gum."
[10] He alludes to the suppling of their young joints with oil, and then drying them in the sun.
[11] Pannis.
[12] Butyro.
[13] Isa. vii. 14.
[14] The *tam dignum* of this place is "jam signum" in *adv. Judæos.*
[15] Contineat.
[16] This opinion of Jews and Judaizing heretics is mentioned by Irenæus, *Adv. Hæret.* iii. 21 (Stieren's ed. i. 532) ; Eusebius, *Hist. Eccles.* v. 8 ; Jerome, *Adv. Helvid.* (ed. Benedict), p. 132. Nor has the cavil ceased to be held, as is well known, to the present day. The הָעַלְמָה of Isa. vii. 4 is supposed by the Jewish Fuerst to be *Isaiah's wife,* and he quotes Kimchi's authority ; while the neologian Gesenius interprets the word, *a bride,* and rejects the Catholic notion of an unspotted virgin. To make way, however, for their view, both Fuerst and Gesenius have to reject the LXX. rendering, παρθένος.

forth. They are, however, refuted by this consideration, that nothing of the nature of *a sign* can possibly come out of what is a daily occurrence, the pregnancy and child-bearing of a young woman. A virgin mother is justly deemed to be proposed[1] by God as *a sign*, but a warlike infant has no like claim to the distinction; for even in such a case[2] there does not occur the character of a sign. But after the sign of the strange and novel birth has been asserted, there is immediately afterwards declared as a sign the subsequent course of the Infant,[3] who was to eat butter and honey. Not that this indeed is of the nature of a sign, nor is His "refusing the evil;" for this, too, is only a characteristic of infancy.[4] But His destined capture of the riches of Damascus and the spoil of Samaria before the king of Assyria *is no doubt a wonderful sign*.[5] Keep to the measure of His age, and seek the purport of the prophecy, and give back also to the truth of the gospel what you have taken away from it in the lateness of your heresy,[6] and the prophecy at once becomes intelligible and declares its own accomplishment. Let those eastern magi wait on the new-born Christ, presenting to Him, (although) in His infancy, their gifts of gold and frankincense; and surely an Infant will have received the riches of Damascus without a battle, and unarmed.

For besides the generally known fact, that the riches of the East, that is to say, its strength and resources, usually consist of gold and spices, it is certainly true of the Creator, that He makes gold the riches of the other[7] nations also. Thus He says by Zechariah: "And Judah shall also fight at Jerusalem, and shall gather together all the wealth of the nations round about, gold and silver."[8] Moreover, respecting that gift of gold, David also says: "And there shall be given to Him of the gold of Arabia;"[9] and again: "The kings of Arabia and Saba shall offer to Him gifts."[10] For the East generally regarded the magi as kings; and Damascus was anciently deemed to belong to Arabia, before it was transferred to Syrophœnicia on the division of the Syrias (by Rome).[11] Its riches Christ then received, when He received the tokens thereof in the gold and spices; while the

spoils of Samaria were the magi themselves. These having discovered Him and honoured Him with their gifts, and on bended knee adored Him as their God and King, through the witness of the star which led their way and guided them, became the spoils of Samaria, that is to say, of idolatry, because, as it is easy enough to see,[12] they believed in Christ. He designated idolatry under the name of Samaria, as that city was shameful for its idolatry, through which it had then revolted from God from the days of king Jeroboam. Nor is this an unusual manner for the Creator, (in His Scriptures[13]) figuratively to employ names of places as a metaphor derived from the analogy of their sins. Thus He calls the chief men of the Jews "rulers of Sodom," and the nation itself "people of Gomorrah."[14] And in another passage He also says: "Thy father was an Amorite, and thy mother an Hittite,"[15] by reason of their kindred iniquity;[16] although He had actually called them His sons: "I have nourished and brought up *children*."[17] So likewise by Egypt is sometimes understood, in His sense,[18] the whole world as being marked out by superstition and a curse.[19] By a similar usage Babylon also in our (St.) John is a figure of the city of Rome, as being like (Babylon) great and proud in royal power, and warring down the saints of God. Now it was in accordance with this style that He called the magi by the name of Samaritans, because (as we have said) they had practised idolatry as did the Samaritans. Moreover, by the phrase "before *or against* the king of Assyria," understand "against Herod;" against whom the magi then opposed themselves, when they refrained from carrying him back word concerning Christ, whom he was seeking to destroy.

CHAP. XIV.—FIGURATIVE STYLE OF CERTAIN MESSIANIC PROPHECIES IN THE PSALMS. MILITARY METAPHORS APPLIED TO CHRIST.

This interpretation of ours will derive confirmation, when, on your supposing that Christ is in any passage called a warrior, from the mention of certain arms and expressions of that sort, you weigh well the analogy of their other meanings, and draw your conclusions accordingly. "Gird on Thy sword," says David, "upon Thy thigh."[20] But what do you read about Christ just before? "Thou art fairer

---

[1] Disposita.
[2] Et hic.
[3] Alius ordo jam infantis.
[4] Infantia est. Better in *adv. Judæos*, "est infantiæ."
[5] The italicised words we have added from *adv. Judæos*, "hoc est mirabile signum."
[6] *Posterior. Posteritas* is an attribute of heresy in T.'s view.
[7] Ceterarum, other than the Jews, i.e., Gentiles.
[8] Zech. xiv. 14.
[9] Ps. lxxii. 15.
[10] Ps. lxxii. 10.
[11] See Otto's *Justin Martyr*, ii. 273, n. 23. [See Vol. I. p. 238, *supra*.]

[12] Videlicet.
[13] The *Creatori* here answers to the *Scripturis divinis* of the parallel passage in *adv. Judæos*. Of course there is a special force in this use of the *Creator's* name here against Marcion.
[14] Isa. i. 10.
[15] Ezek. xvi. 3.
[16] To the sins of these nations.
[17] Isa. i. 2.
[18] Apud illum, i.e., Creatorem
[19] Maledictionis.
[20] Ps. xlv. 3.

than the children of men ; grace is poured forth upon Thy lips."[1] It amuses me to imagine that blandishments of fair beauty and graceful lips are ascribed to one who had to gird on His sword for war ! So likewise, when it is added, "Ride on prosperously in Thy majesty,"[2] the reason is subjoined: "Because of truth, and meekness, and righteousness."[3] But who shall produce *these* results with the sword, and not their opposites rather —deceit, and harshness, and injury—which, it must be confessed, are the proper business of battles? Let us see, therefore, whether that is not some other sword, which has so different an action. Now the Apostle John, in the Apocalypse, describes a sword which proceeded from the mouth of God as "a doubly sharp, two-edged one."[4] This may be understood to be the Divine Word, who is doubly edged with the two testaments of the law and the gospel—sharpened with wisdom, hostile to the devil, arming us against the spiritual enemies of all wickedness and concupiscence, and cutting us off from the dearest objects for the sake of God's holy name. If, however, you will not acknowledge John, you have our common master Paul, who "girds our loins about with truth, and puts on us the breastplate of righteousness, and shoes us with the preparation of the gospel of peace, not of war; who bids us take the shield of faith, wherewith we may be able to quench all the fiery darts of the devil, and the helmet of salvation, and the sword of the Spirit, which (he says) is the word of God."[5] This sword the Lord Himself came to send on earth, and not peace.[6] If he is your Christ, then even he is a warrior. If he is not a warrior, and the sword he brandishes is an allegorical one, then the Creator's Christ in the psalm too may have been girded with the figurative sword of the Word, without any martial gear. The above-mentioned "fairness" of His beauty and "grace of His lips" would quite suit such a sword, girt as it even then was upon His thigh in the passage of David, and sent as it would one day be by Him on earth. For this is what He says: "Ride on prosperously in Thy majesty[7]"— *advancing* His word into every land, so as to call all nations: destined to *prosper* in the success of that faith which received Him, and *reigning*, from the fact that[8] He conquered death by His resurrection. "Thy right hand," says He, "shall wonderfully lead Thee forth,"[9] even the might of Thy spiritual grace, whereby the knowledge of Christ is spread. "Thine arrows are sharp;"[10] everywhere Thy precepts fly about, Thy threatenings also, and convictions[11] of heart, pricking and piercing each conscience. "The people shall fall under Thee,"[12] that is, in adoration. Thus is the Creator's Christ mighty in war, and a bearer of arms; thus also does He now take the spoils, not of Samaria alone, but of all nations. Acknowledge, then, that His spoils are figurative, since you have learned that His arms are allegorical. Since, therefore, both the Lord speaks and His apostle writes such things[13] in a figurative style, we are not rash in using His interpretations, the records[14] of which even our adversaries admit; and thus in *so* far will it be Isaiah's Christ who has come, in *as* far as He was not a warrior, because it is not of such a character that He is described by Isaiah.

CHAP. XV.—THE TITLE CHRIST SUITABLE AS A NAME OF THE CREATOR'S SON, BUT UNSUITED TO MARCION'S CHRIST.

Touching then the discussion of His flesh, and (through that) of His nativity, and incidentally[15] of His name Emmanuel, let this suffice. Concerning His other names, however, and especially that of Christ, what has the other side to say in reply? If the name of Christ is as common with you as is the name of God —so that as the Son of both Gods may be fitly called Christ, so each of the Fathers may be called Lord—reason will certainly be opposed to this argument. For the name of God, as being the natural designation of Deity, may be ascribed to all those beings for whom a divine nature is claimed,—as, for instance, even to idols. The apostle says: "For there be that are called gods, whether in heaven or in earth."[16] The name of Christ, however, does not arise from nature, but from dispensation;[17] and so becomes the proper name of Him to whom it accrues in consequence of the dispensation. Nor is it subject to be shared in by any other God, especially a rival, and one that has a dispensation of His own, to whom it will be also necessary that He should possess names apart from all others. For how happens it that, after they have de-

---

[1] Ps. xlv. 2.
[2] Literally, " Advance, and prosper, and reign."
[3] Ps. xlv. 4.
[4] Rev. i. 16.
[5] Eph. vi. 14-17.
[6] Matt. x. 34.
[7] " Advance, and prosper, and reign."
[8] Exinde qua.
[9] Ps. xlv. 4, but changed.
[10] Ps. xlv. 5.
[11] Traductiones.
[12] Ps. xlv. 5.
[13] Ejusmodi.
[14] Exempla.
[15] Interim.
[16] 1 Cor. viii. 5.
[17] Ex dispositione. This word seems to mean what is implied in the phrases, "Christian *dispensation*," "Mosaic *dispensation*," etc.

vised different dispensations for two Gods, they admit into this diversity of dispensation a *community* of names; whereas no proof could be more useful of two Gods being rival ones, than if there should be found coincident with their (diverse) dispensations a diversity also of names? For that is not a state of *diverse* qualities, which is not distinctly indicated[1] in the specific meanings[2] of their designations. Whenever these are wanting, there occurs what the Greeks call the *katachresis*[3] of a term, by its improper application to what does not belong to it.[4] In God, however, there ought, I suppose, to be no defect, no setting up of His dispensations by *katachrestic* abuse of words. Who is this god, that claims for his son names from the Creator? I say not names which do not belong to him, but ancient and well-known names, which even in this view of them would be unsuitable for a novel and unknown god. How is it, again, that he tells us that "a piece of new cloth is not sewed on to an old garment," or that "new wine is not trusted to old bottles,"[5] when he is himself patched and clad in an old suit[6] of names? How is it he has rent off the gospel from the law, when he is wholly invested with the law,—in the name, forsooth, of Christ? What hindered his calling himself by some other name, seeing that he preached another (gospel), came from another source, and refused to take on him a real body, for the very purpose that he might not be supposed to be the Creator's Christ? Vain, however, was his unwillingness to seem to be He whose name he was willing to assume; since, even if he had been truly corporeal, he would more certainly escape being taken for the Christ of the Creator, if he had not taken on him His name. But, as it is, he rejects the substantial verity of Him whose name he has assumed, even though he should give a proof of that verity by his name. For Christ means *anointed*, and to be anointed is certainly an affair[7] of the body. He who had not a body, could not by any possibility have been anointed; he who could not by any possibility have been anointed, could not in any wise have been called Christ. It is a different thing (quite), if he only assumed the phantom of a name too. But how, he asks, was he to insinuate himself into being believed by the Jews, except through a name which was usual and familiar amongst them? Then 'tis a

fickle and tricksty God whom you describe! To promote any plan by deception, is the resource of either distrust or of maliciousness. Much more frank and simple was the conduct of the false prophets against the Creator, when they came in His name as their own God.[8] But I do not find that any good came of this proceeding,[9] since they were more apt to suppose either that Christ was their own, or rather was some deceiver, than that He was the Christ of the other god; and this the gospel will show.

CHAP. XVI.—THE SACRED NAME JESUS MOST SUITED TO THE CHRIST OF THE CREATOR. JOSHUA A TYPE OF HIM.

Now if he caught at the name *Christ*, just as the pickpocket clutches the dole-basket, why did he wish to be called *Jesus* too, by a name which was not so much looked for by the Jews? For although we, who have by God's grace attained to the understanding of His mysteries, acknowledge that *this* name also was destined for Christ, yet, for all that, the fact was not known to the Jews, from whom wisdom was taken away. To this day, in short, it is Christ that they are looking for, not Jesus; and they interpret Elias to be Christ rather than Jesus. He, therefore, who came also in a name in which Christ was not expected, might have come only in that name which was solely anticipated for Him.[10] But since he has mixed up the two,[11] the expected one and the unexpected, his twofold project is defeated. For if he be *Christ* for the very purpose of insinuating himself as the Creator's, then *Jesus* opposes him, because Jesus was not looked for in the Christ of the Creator; or if he be *Jesus*, in order that he might pass as belonging to the other (God), then *Christ* hinders him, because Christ was not expected to belong to any other than the Creator. I know not which one of these names may be able to hold its ground.[12] In the Christ of the Creator, however, both will keep their place, for in *Him* a Jesus too is found. Do you ask, how? Learn it then here, with the Jews also who are partakers of your heresy. When Oshea the son of Nun was destined to be the successor of Moses, is not his old name then changed, and for the first time he is called[13] Joshua? It is true, you say. This, then, we first observe, was a figure of Him who was to come. For inasmuch as Jesus Christ was to introduce a new generation[14] (because we are born in the wilderness of this world) into

[1] Consignatur.
[2] Proprietatibus.
[3] Quintilian, *Inst.* viii. 6, defines this as a figure "which lends a name to things which have it not."
[4] De alieno abutendo.
[5] Matt. ix. 16, 17.
[6] Senio.
[7] Passio.
[8] Adversus Creatorem, in sui Dei nomine venientes.
[9] i.e., to the Marcionite position.
[10] That is, Christ.
[11] Surely it is *Duo*, not *Deo*.
[12] Constare.
[13] Incipit vocari.
[14] Secundum populum.

the promised land which flows with milk and honey, that is, into the possession of eternal life, than which nothing can be sweeter; inasmuch, too, as this was to be brought about not by Moses, that is to say, not by the discipline of the law, but by Joshua, by the grace of the gospel, our circumcision being effected by a knife of stone, that is, (by the circumcision) of Christ, for Christ is a rock (or stone), therefore that great man,[1] who was ordained as a type of this mystery, was actually consecrated with the figure of the Lord's own name, being called Joshua. This name Christ Himself even then testified to be His own, when He talked with Moses. For who was it that talked with him, but the Spirit of the Creator, which is Christ? When He therefore spake this commandment to the people, "Behold, I send my angel before thy face, to keep thee in the way, and to bring thee into the land which I have prepared for thee; attend to him, and obey his voice and do not provoke him; for he has not shunned you,[2] since my name is upon him,"[3] He called him an *angel* indeed, because of the greatness of the powers which he was to exercise, and because of his prophetic office,[4] while announcing the will of God; but *Joshua* also (Jesus), because it was a type[5] of His own future name. Often[6] did He confirm that name of His which He had thus conferred upon (His servant); because it was not the name of *angel*, nor *Oshea*, but *Joshua* (Jesus), which He had commanded him to bear as his usual appellation for the time to come. Since, therefore, both these names are suitable to the Christ of the Creator, they are proportionately unsuitable to the *non-Creator's* Christ; and so indeed is all the rest of (our Christ's) destined course.[7] In short, there must now for the future be made between us that certain and equitable rule, necessary to both sides, which shall determine that there ought to be absolutely nothing at all in common between the Christ of the other god and the Creator's Christ. For you will have as great a necessity to maintain their diversity as we have to resist it, inasmuch as *you* will be as unable to show that the Christ of the other god has come, until you have prvoed him to be a far different being from the Creator's Christ, as *we*, to claim Him (who has come) as the Creator's, until we have shown Him to be such a one as the Creator has appointed. Now respecting their names, such is our conclusion against (Mar-

cion).[8] I claim for myself Christ; I maintain for myself Jesus.

CHAP. XVII.—PROPHECIES IN ISAIAH AND THE PSALMS RESPECTING CHRIST'S HUMILIATION.

Let us compare with Scripture the rest of His dispensation. Whatever that poor despised body[9] may be, because it was an object of touch[10] and sight,[11] it shall be my Christ, be He inglorious, be He ignoble, be He dishonoured; for such was it announced that He should be, both in bodily condition and aspect. Isaiah comes to our help again: "We have announced (His way) before Him," says he; "He is like a servant,[12] like a root in a dry ground; He hath no form nor comeliness; we saw Him, and He had neither form nor beauty; but His form was despised, marred above all men."[13] Similarly the Father addressed the Son just before: "Inasmuch as many will be astonished at Thee, so also will Thy beauty be without glory from men."[14] For although, in David's words, "He is fairer than the children of men,"[15] yet it is in that figurative state of spiritual grace, when He is girded with the sword of the Spirit, which is verily His form, and beauty, and glory. According to the same prophet, however, He is in bodily condition "a very worm, and no man; a reproach of men, and an outcast of the people."[16] But no internal quality of such a kind does He announce as belonging to Him. In Him dwelt the fulness of the Spirit; therefore I acknowledge Him to be "the rod of the stem of Jesse." His blooming flower shall be my Christ, upon whom hath rested, according to Isaiah, "the spirit of wisdom and understanding, the spirit of counsel and might, the spirit of knowledge and of piety, and of the fear of the Lord."[17] Now to no man, except Christ, would the diversity of spiritual proofs suitably apply. He is indeed like a flower for the Spirit's grace, reckoned indeed of the stem of Jesse, but thence to derive His descent through Mary. Now I purposely demand of you, whether you grant to Him the destination[18] of all this humiliation, and suffering, and tranquillity, from which He will be the Christ of Isaiah,—a man of sorrows, and acquainted with grief, who was led as a sheep to the slaughter, and who, like a lamb before the shearer, opened

1 Vir.
2 Non celavit te, "not concealed Himself from you.'
3 Ex. xxiii. 20, 21.
4 Officium prophetæ.
5 Sacramentum.
6 Identidem.
7 Reliquus ordo.
8 Obduximus.
9 Corpusculum illud.
10 Habitum.
11 Conspectum.
12 Puerulus, "little child," perhaps.
13 Sentences out of Isa. lii. 14 and liii. 2, etc.
14 Isa. lii. 14.
15 Ps. xlv. 2.
16 Ps. xxii. 6.
17 Isa. xi. 1, 2.
18 Intentionem.

not His mouth;[1] who did not struggle nor cry, nor was His voice heard in the street; who broke not the bruised reed—that is, the shattered faith of the Jews—nor quenched the smoking flax—that is, the freshly-kindled[2] ardour of the Gentiles. He can be none other than the Man who was foretold. It is right that His conduct[3] be investigated according to the rule of Scripture, distinguishable as it is unless I am mistaken, by the twofold operation of preaching[4] and of miracle. But the treatment of both these topics I shall so arrange as to postpone, to the chapter wherein I have determined to discuss the actual gospel of Marcion, the consideration of His wonderful doctrines and miracles—with a view, however, to our present purpose. Let us here, then, in general terms complete the subject which we had entered upon, by indicating, as we pass on,[5] how Christ was fore-announced by Isaiah as a preacher: "For who is there among you," says he, "that feareth the Lord, that obeyeth the voice of His Son?"[6] And likewise as a healer: "For," says he, "He hath taken away our infirmities, and carried our sorrows."[7]

CHAP. XVIII.[8]—TYPES OF THE DEATH OF CHRIST. ISAAC; JOSEPH; JACOB AGAINST SIMEON AND LEVI; MOSES PRAYING AGAINST AMALEK; THE BRAZEN SERPENT.

On the subject of His death,[9] I suppose, you endeavour to introduce a diversity of opinion, simply because you deny that the suffering of the cross was predicted of the Christ of the Creator, and because you contend, moreover, that it is not to be believed that the Creator would expose His Son to that kind of death on which He had Himself pronounced a curse. "Cursed," says He, "is every one who hangeth on a tree."[10] But what is meant by this curse, worthy as it is of the simple prediction of the cross, of which we are now mainly inquiring, I defer to consider, because in another passage[11] we have given the reason[12] of the thing preceded by proof. First, I shall offer a full explanation[13]

of the types. And no doubt it was proper that this mystery should be prophetically set forth by types, and indeed chiefly by that method: for in proportion to its incredibility would it be a stumbling-block, if it were set forth in bare prophecy; and in proportion too, to its grandeur, was the need of obscuring it in shadow,[14] that the difficulty of understanding it might lead to prayer for the grace of God. First, then, Isaac, when he was given up by his father as an offering, himself carried the wood for his own death. By this act he even then was setting forth the death of Christ, who was destined by His Father as a sacrifice, and carried the cross whereon He suffered. Joseph likewise was a type of Christ, not indeed on this ground (that I may not delay my course[15]), that he suffered persecution for the cause of God from his brethren, as Christ did from His brethren after the flesh, the Jews; but when he is blessed by his father in these words: "His glory is that of a bullock; his horns are the horns of a unicorn; with them shall he push the nations to the very ends of the earth,"[16]—he was not, of course, designated as a mere unicorn with its one horn, or a minotaur with two; but Christ was indicated in him—a bullock in respect of both His characteristics: to some as severe as a Judge, to others gentle as a Saviour, whose horns were the extremities of His cross. For of the antenna, which is a part of a cross, the ends are called *horns*; while the midway stake of the whole frame is the *unicorn*. By this virtue, then, of His cross, and in this manner "horned," He is both now pushing all nations through faith, bearing them away from earth to heaven; and will then push them through judgment, casting them down from heaven to earth. He will also, according to another passage in the same scripture, be a bullock, when He is spiritually interpreted to be Jacob against Simeon and Levi, which means against the scribes and the Pharisees; for it was from them that these last derived their origin.[17] *Like* Simeon and Levi, they consummated their wickedness by their heresy, with which they persecuted Christ. "Into their counsel let not my soul enter; to their assembly let not my heart be united: for in their anger they slew men," that is, the prophets; "and in their self-will they hacked the sinews of a bullock,"[18] that is, of Christ. For against Him did they wreak their fury after they

---

[1] Isa. liii. 3, 7.
[2] Momentaneum.
[3] Actum.
[4] Prædicationis.
[5] Interim.
[6] Isa. l. 10.
[7] Isa. liii. 4.
[8] Compare *adv. Judæos*, chap. 10. [pp. 165, 166, *supra*.]
[9] De exitu.
[10] Compare Deut. xxi. 23 with Gal. iii. 13.
[11] The words "quia *et alias* antecedit rerum probatio rationem," seem to refer to the parallel passage in *adv. Judæos*, where he has described the Jewish law of capital punishment, and argued for the exemption of Christ from its terms. He begins that paragraph with saying, "Sed hujus maledictionis sensum antecedit rerum ratio." [See, p. 164, *supra*.]
[12] Perhaps *rationale* or procedure.
[13] Edocebo.

[14] Magis obumbrandum.
[15] But he may mean, by "*ne demorer cursum*," "that I may not obstruct the course of the type," by taking off attention from its true force. In the parallel place, however, another turn is given to the sense; Joseph is a type, "*even on this ground*—that I may but briefly allude to it—that he suffered," etc.
[16] Deut. xxxiii. 17.
[17] Census.
[18] Gen. xlix. 6. The last clause is, "ceciderunt nervos tauro."

had slain His prophets, even by affixing Him with nails to the cross. Otherwise, it is an idle thing[1] when, after slaying men, he inveighs against them for the torture of a bullock! Again, in the case of Moses, wherefore did he at that moment particularly, when Joshua was fighting Amalek, pray in a sitting posture with outstretched hands, when in such a conflict it would surely have been more seemly to have bent the knee, and smitten the breast, and to have fallen on the face to the ground, and in such prostration to have offered prayer? Wherefore, but because in a battle fought in the name of that Lord who was one day to fight against the devil, the shape was necessary of that very cross through which Jesus was to win the victory? Why, once more, did the same Moses, after prohibiting the likeness of everything, set up the golden serpent on the pole; and as it hung there, propose it as an object to be looked at for a cure?[2] Did he not here also intend to show the power of our Lord's cross, whereby that old serpent the devil was vanquished, —whereby also to every man who was bitten by spiritual serpents, but who yet turned with an eye of faith to it, was proclaimed a cure from the bite of sin, and health for evermore?

CHAP. XIX.—PROPHECIES OF THE DEATH OF CHRIST.

Come now, when you read in the words of David, how that "the Lord reigneth from the tree,"[3] I want to know what you understand by it. Perhaps you think some wooden[4] king of the Jews is meant!—and not Christ, who overcame death by His suffering on the cross, and thence reigned! Now, although death reigned from Adam even to Christ, why may not Christ be said to have reigned from the tree, from His having shut up the kingdom of death by dying upon the tree of His cross? Likewise Isaiah also says: "For unto us a child is born."[5] But what is there unusual in this, unless he speaks of the Son of God? "To us is given He whose government is upon His shoulder."[5] Now, what king is there who bears the ensign of his dominion upon his shoulder, and not rather upon his head as a diadem, or in his hand as a sceptre, or else as a mark in some royal apparel? But the one new King of the new ages, Jesus Christ, carried on His shoulder both the power and the excellence of His new glory, even His cross; so that, according to our former

prophecy, He might thenceforth reign from the tree as Lord. This tree it is which Jeremiah likewise gives you intimation of, when he prophesies to the Jews, who should say, "Come, let us destroy the tree with the fruit, (the bread) thereof,"[6] that is, His body. For so did God in your own gospel even reveal the sense, when He called His body *bread*; so that, for the time to come, you may understand that He has given to His body the figure of bread, whose body the prophet of old figuratively turned into bread, the Lord Himself designing to give by and by an interpretation of the mystery. If you require still further prediction of the Lord's cross, the twenty-first Psalm[7] is sufficiently able to afford it to you, containing as it does the entire passion of Christ, who was even then prophetically declaring[8] His glory. "They pierced," says He, "my hands and my feet,"[9] which is the special cruelty of the cross. And again, when He implores His Father's help, He says, "Save me from the lion's mouth," that is, the jaws of death, "and my humiliation from the horns of the unicorns;" in other words, from the extremities of the cross, as we have shown above. Now, David himself did not suffer this cross, nor did any other king of the Jews; so that you cannot suppose that this is the prophecy of any other's passion than His who alone was so notably crucified by the nation. Now should the heretics, in their obstinacy,[10] reject and despise all these interpretations, I will grant to them that the Creator has given us no signs of the cross of His Christ; but they will not prove from this concession that He who was crucified was another (Christ), unless they could somehow show that this death was predicted as His by their own god, so that from the diversity of predictions there might be maintained to be a diversity of sufferers,[11] and thereby also a diversity of persons. But since there is no prophecy of even Marcion's Christ, much less of his cross, it is enough for my Christ that there is a prophecy merely of death. For, from the fact that the *kind* of death is not declared, it was possible for the death of the cross to have been still intended, which would then have to be assigned to another (Christ), if the prophecy had had reference to another. Besides,[12] if he should be unwilling to allow that the death of my Christ was predicted, his confusion

---

[1] Vanum.
[2] Spectaculum salutare.
[3] Ps. xcvi. 10, with *a ligno* added.
[4] Lignarium aliquem regem.
[5] Isa. ix. 6.

[6] Jer. xi. 19.
[7] The twenty-second Psalm. A.V.
[8] Canentis.
[9] Ps. xxii. 16.
[10] Hæretica duritia.
[11] Passionum, literally *sufferings*, which would hardly give the sense.
[12] Nisi.

must be the greater[1] if he announces that his own Christ indeed died, whom he denies to have had a nativity, whilst denying that my Christ is mortal, though he allows Him to be capable of birth. However, I will show him the death, and burial, and resurrection of my Christ all[2] indicated in a single sentence of Isaiah, who says, "His sepulture was removed from the midst of them." Now there could have been no sepulture without death, and no removal of sepulture except by resurrection. Then, finally, he added: "Therefore He shall have many for his inheritance, and He shall divide the spoil of the many, because He poured out His soul unto death."[3] For there is here set forth the cause of this favour to Him, even that it was to recompense Him for His suffering of death. It was equally shown that He was to obtain this recompense for His death, was certainly to obtain it after His death by means of the resurrection.[4]

CHAP. XX.[5]—THE SUBSEQUENT INFLUENCE OF CHRIST'S DEATH IN THE WORLD PREDICTED. THE SURE MERCIES OF DAVID. WHAT THESE ARE.

It is sufficient for my purpose to have traced thus far the course of Christ's dispensation in these particulars. This has proved Him to be such a one as prophecy announced He should be, so that He ought not to be regarded in any other character than that which prediction assigned to Him; and the result of this agreement between the facts of His course and the Scriptures of the Creator should be the restoration of belief in them from that prejudice which has, by contributing to diversity of opinion, either thrown doubt upon, or led to a denial of, a considerable part of them. And now we go further and build up the superstructure of those kindred events[6] out of the Scriptures of the Creator which were predicted and destined to happen after Christ. For the dispensation would not be found complete, if He had not come after whom it had to run on its course.[7] Look at all nations from the vortex of human error emerging out of it up to the Divine Creator, the Divine Christ, and deny Him to be the object of prophecy, if you dare. At once there will occur to you the Father's promise in the Psalms: "Thou art my Son, this day have I begotten Thee. Ask of me, and I shall give Thee the heathen for Thine inheritance, and the uttermost parts of the earth for Thy pos-

session."[8] You will not be able to put in a claim for some son of David being here meant, rather than Christ; or for the ends of the earth being promised to David, whose kingdom was confined to the Jewish nation simply, rather than to Christ, who now embraces the whole world in the faith of His gospel. So again He says by Isaiah: "I have given Thee for a dispensation of the people, for a light of the Gentiles, to open the eyes of the blind," that is, those that be in error, "to bring out the prisoners from the prison," that is, to free them from sin, "and from the prison-house," that is, of death, "those that sit in darkness"—even that of ignorance.[9] If these things are accomplished through Christ, they would not have been designed in prophecy for any other than Him through whom they have their accomplishment. In another passage He also says: "Behold, I have set Him as a testimony to the nations, a prince and commander to the nations; nations which know Thee not shall invoke Thee, and peoples shall run together unto Thee."[10] You will not interpret these words of David, because He previously said, "I will make an everlasting covenant with you, even the sure mercies of David."[11] Indeed, you will be obliged from these words all the more to understand that Christ is reckoned to spring from David by carnal descent, by reason of His birth[12] of the Virgin Mary. Touching this promise of Him, there is the oath to David in the psalm, "Of the fruit of thy body[13] will I set upon thy throne."[14] What body is meant? David's own? Certainly not. For David was not to give birth to a son.[15] Nor his wife's either. For instead of saying, "Of the fruit of thy body," he would then have rather said, "Of the fruit of thy wife's body." But by mentioning *his*[16] body, it follows that He pointed to some one of his race of whose body the flesh of Christ was to be the fruit, which bloomed forth from[17] Mary's womb. He named the fruit of the body (womb) alone, because it was peculiarly fruit of the womb, of the womb only in fact, and not of the husband also; and he refers the womb (body) to David, as to the chief of the race and father of the family. Because it could not consist with a virgin's condition to consort her with a husband,[18] He therefore attributed the body (womb) to the father.

1 Quo magis erubescat.
2 Et—et—et.
3 Isa. liii. 12.
4 Both His own and His people's.
5 Comp. *adv. Judæos*, 11 and 12.
6 Ea paria.
7 Evenire.
8 Ps. ii. 7.
9 Isa. xlii. 6, 7.
10 Isa. lv. 4, 5.
11 Isa. lv. 3.
12 Censum. [Kaye, p. 149.]
13 Ventris, "womb."
14 Ps. cxxxii. 11.
15 He treats "body" as here meaning *womb*.
16 Ipsius.
17 Floruit ex.
18 Viro deputare.

That new dispensation, then, which is found in Christ now, will prove to be what the Creator then promised under the appellation of "the sure mercies of David," which were Christ's, inasmuch as Christ sprang from David, or rather His very flesh itself was David's "sure mercies," consecrated by religion, and "sure" after its resurrection. Accordingly the prophet Nathan, in the first of Kings,[1] makes a promise to David for his seed, "which shall proceed," says he, "out of thy bowels."[2] Now, if you explain this simply of Solomon, you will send me into a fit of laughter. For David will evidently have brought forth Solomon! But is not Christ here designated the seed of David, as of that womb which was derived from David, that is, Mary's? Now, because Christ rather than any other[3] was to build the temple of God, that is to say, a holy manhood, wherein God's Spirit might dwell as in a better temple, Christ rather than David's son Solomon was to be looked for as[4] the Son of God. Then, again, the throne for ever with the kingdom for ever is more suited to Christ than to Solomon, a mere temporal king. From Christ, too, God's mercy did not depart, whereas on Solomon even God's anger alighted, after his luxury and idolatry. For Satan[5] stirred up an Edomite as an enemy against him. Since, therefore, nothing of these things is compatible with Solomon, but only with Christ, the method of our interpretations will certainly be true; and the very issue of the facts shows that they were clearly predicted of Christ. And so in Him we shall have "the sure mercies of David." *Him*, not David, has God appointed for a testimony to the nations; *Him*, for a prince and commander to the nations, not David, who ruled over Israel alone. It is Christ whom all nations now invoke, which knew Him not; Christ to whom all races now betake themselves, whom they were ignorant of before. It is impossible that that should be said to be future, which you see (daily) coming to pass.

CHAP. XXI.—THE CALL OF THE GENTILES UNDER THE INFLUENCE OF THE GOSPEL FORETOLD.

So you cannot get out of this notion of yours a basis for your difference between the two Christs, as if the Jewish Christ were or-dained by the Creator for the restoration of the people alone[6] from its dispersion, whilst yours was appointed by the supremely good God for the liberation of the whole human race. Because, after all, the earliest Christians are found on the side of the Creator, not of Marcion,[7] all nations being called to His kingdom, from the fact that God set up that kingdom from the tree (of the cross), when no Cerdon was yet born, much less a Marcion. However, when you are refuted on the call of the *nations*, you betake yourself to *proselytes*. You ask, who among the nations can turn to the Creator, when those whom the prophet names are proselytes of individually different and private condition?[8] "Behold," says Isaiah, "the proselytes shall come unto me through Thee," showing that they were even proselytes who were to find their way to God through Christ. But nations (Gentiles) also, like ourselves, had likewise their mention (by the prophet) as trusting in Christ. "And in His name," says he, "shall the Gentiles trust." Besides, the proselytes whom you substitute for the nations in prophecy, are not in the habit of trusting in Christ's name, but in the dispensation of Moses, from whom comes their instruction. But it was in the last days that the choice[9] of the nations had its commencement.[10] In these very words Isaiah says: "And it shall come to pass in the last days, that the mountain of the Lord," that is, God's eminence, "and the house of God," that is, Christ, the Catholic temple of God, in which God is worshipped, "shall be established upon mountains," over all the eminences of virtues and powers; "and all nations shall come unto it; and many people shall go and say, Come ye, and let us go up to the mountain of the Lord, and to the house of the God of Jacob; and He will teach us His way, and we will walk in it: for out of Sion shall go forth the law, and the word of the Lord from Jerusalem."[11] The gospel will be this "way," of the new law and the new word in Christ, no longer in Moses. "And He shall judge among the nations," even concerning their error. "And these shall rebuke a large nation," that of the Jews themselves and their proselytes. "And they shall beat their swords into ploughshares, and their spears[12] into prun-

---

[1] The four books of *the Kings* were sometimes regarded as *two*, "the first" of which contained 1 and 2 *Samuel*, "the second" 1 and 2 *Kings*. The reference in this place is to 2 Samuel vii. 12.
[2] He here again makes *bowels* synonymous with *womb*.
[3] Magis.
[4] Habendus in.
[5] In 1 Kings xi. 14, "the Lord" is said to have done this. Comp. 2 Sam. xxiv. 1 with 1 Chron. xxi. 1.
[6] i.e., the Jews.
[7] Or perhaps, "are found to belong to the Creator's Christ, not to Marcion's."
[8] Marcion denied that there was any prophecy of national or *Gentile* conversion ; it was only the conversion of individual proselytes that he held.
[9] Allectio.
[10] Exorta est.
[11] Isa. ii. 2, 3.
[12] Sibynas, Σιβύνη· ὅπλον δόρατι παραπλήσιον. Hesychius, "*Sibynam* appellant Illyrii telum venabuli simile." Paulus, *ex Festo*, p. 336, Müll. (Oehler.)

ing-hooks;'' in other words, they shall change into pursuits of moderation and peace the dispositions of injurious minds, and hostile tongues, and all kinds of evil, and blasphemy. "Nation shall not lift up sword against nation," shall not stir up discord. "Neither shall they learn war any more,"[1] that is, the provocation of hostilities; so that you here learn that Christ is promised not as powerful in war, but pursuing peace. Now you must deny either that these things were predicted, although they are plainly seen, or that they have been accomplished, although you read of them; else, if you cannot deny either one fact or the other, they must have been accomplished in Him of whom they were predicted. For look at the entire course of His call up to the present time from its beginning, how it is addressed to the nations (Gentiles) who are in these last days approaching to God the Creator, and not to proselytes, whose election[2] was rather an event of the earliest days. Verily the apostles have annulled[3] that belief of yours.

CHAP. XXII.—THE SUCCESS OF THE APOSTLES, AND THEIR SUFFERINGS IN THE CAUSE OF THE GOSPEL, FORETOLD.

You have the work of the apostles also predicted: "How beautiful are the feet of them which preach the gospel of peace, which bring good tidings of good,"[4] not of war nor evil tidings. In response to which is the psalm, "Their sound is gone through all the earth, and their words to the ends of the world;"[5] that is, the words of them who carry round about the law that proceeded from Sion and the Lord's word from Jerusalem, in order that that might come to pass which was written: "They who were far from my righteousness, have come near to my righteousness and truth."[6] When the apostles girded their loins for this business, they renounced the elders and rulers and priests of the Jews. Well, says he, but was it not above all things that they might preach the other god? Rather[7] (that they might preach) that very self-same God, whose scripture they were with all their might fulfilling! "Depart ye, depart ye," exclaims Isaiah; "go ye out from thence, and touch not the unclean thing," that is blasphemy against Christ; "Go ye out of

the midst of her," even of the synagogue "Be ye separate who bear the vessels of the Lord."[8] For already had the Lord, according to the preceding words (of the prophet), revealed His Holy One with His arm, that is to say, Christ by His mighty power, in the eyes of the nations, so that all the[9] nations and the utmost parts of the earth have seen the salvation, which was from God. By thus departing from Judaism itself, when they exchanged the obligations and burdens of the law for the liberty of the gospel, they were fulfilling the psalm, "Let us burst their bonds asunder, and cast away their yoke from us;" and this indeed (they did) after that "the heathen raged, and the people imagined vain devices;" after that "the kings of the earth set themselves, and the rulers took their counsel together against the Lord, and against His Christ."[10] What did the apostles thereupon suffer? You answer: Every sort of iniquitous persecutions, from men that belonged indeed to that Creator who was the adversary of Him whom they were preaching. Then why does the Creator, if an adversary of Christ, not only predict that the apostles should incur this suffering, but even express His displeasure[11] thereat? For He ought neither to predict the course of the other god, whom, as you contend, He knew not, nor to have expressed displeasure at that which He had taken care to bring about. "See how the righteous perisheth, and no man layeth it to heart; and how merciful men are taken away, and no man considereth. For the righteous man has been removed from the evil person."[12] Who is this but Christ? "Come, say they, let us take away the righteous, because He is not for our turn, (and He is clean contrary to our doings)."[13] Premising, therefore, and likewise subjoining the fact that Christ suffered, He foretold that His just ones should suffer equally with Him—both the apostles and all the faithful in succession; and He signed them with that very seal of which Ezekiel spake: "The Lord said unto me, Go through the gate, through the midst of Jerusalem, and set the mark *Tau* upon the foreheads of the men."[14] Now the Greek letter *Tau* and our own letter T is the very form of the cross, which He predicted would be the sign on our

---

[1] Isa. ii. 4.
[2] Allectio.
[3] Junius explains the author's *induxerunt* by deleverunt; i.e., "they annulled your opinion about proselytes being the sole called, by their promulgation of the gospel."
[4] Isa. lii. 7 and Rom. x. 15.
[5] Ps. xix. 5.
[6] Pamelius regards this as a quotation from Isa. xlvi. 12, 13, only put *narratively*, in order to indicate briefly its realization.
[7] Atquin.

[8] Isa. lii. 11.
[9] Universæ.
[10] Comp. Ps. ii. 2, 3, with Acts iv. 25-30.
[11] Exprobrat.
[12] Isa. lvii. 1.
[13] Wisd. of Sol. ii. 12.
[14] Ezek. ix. 4. The MS. which T. used seems to have agreed with the versions of Theodotion and Aquila mentioned thus by Origen (*Selecta in Ezek.*): ὁ δὲ Ἀκύλας καὶ Θεοδοτίων φασί, Σημείωσις τοῦ Θαῦ ἐπὶ τὰ μέτωπα, κ.τ.λ. Origen, in his own remarks, refers to *the sign of the cross*, as indicated by this letter. Ed. Bened. (by Migne), iii. 802.

foreheads in the true Catholic Jerusalem,[1] in which, according to the twenty-first Psalm, the brethren of Christ or children of God would ascribe glory to God the Father, in the person of Christ Himself addressing His Father; "I will declare Thy name unto my brethren; in the midst of the congregation will I sing praise unto Thee." For that which had to come to pass in our day in His name, and by His Spirit, He rightly foretold would be of Him. And a little afterwards He says: "My praise shall be of Thee in the great congregation."[2] In the sixty-seventh Psalm He says again: "In the congregations bless ye the Lord God."[3] So that with this agrees also the prophecy of Malachi: "I have no pleasure in you, saith the Lord; neither will I accept your offerings: for from the rising of the sun, even unto the going down of the same, my name shall be great among the Gentiles; and in every place sacrifice shall be offered unto my name, and a pure offering"[4] —such as the ascription of glory, and blessing, and praise, and hymns. Now, inasmuch as all these things are also found amongst you, and the sign upon the forehead,[5] and the sacraments of the church, and the offerings of the pure sacrifice, you ought now to burst forth, and declare that the Spirit of the Creator prophesied of your Christ.

CHAP. XXIII.—THE DISPERSION OF THE JEWS, AND THEIR DESOLATE CONDITION FOR REJECTING CHRIST, FORETOLD.

Now, since you join the Jews in denying that their Christ has come, recollect also what is that end which they were predicted as about to bring on themselves after the time of Christ, for the impiety wherewith they both rejected and slew Him. For it began to come to pass from that day, when, according to Isaiah, "a man threw away his idols of gold and of silver, which they made into useless and hurtful objects of worship;"[6] in other words, from the time when he threw away his idols after the truth had been made clear by Christ. Consider whether what follows in the prophet has not received its fulfilment: "The Lord of hosts hath taken away from Judah and from Jerusalem, amongst other things, both the prophet and the wise artificer;"[7] that is, His Holy Spirit, who builds the

church, which is indeed the temple, and household and city of God. For thenceforth God's grace failed amongst them; and "the clouds were commanded to rain no rain upon the vineyard" of Sorech; to withhold, that is, the graces of heaven, that they shed no blessing upon "the house of Israel," which had but produced "the thorns" wherewith it had crowned the Lord, and "instead of righteousness, the cry" wherewith it had hurried Him away to the cross.[8] And so in this manner the law and the prophets were until John, but the dews of divine grace were withdrawn from the nation. After his time their madness still continued, and the name of the Lord was blasphemed by them, as saith the Scripture: "Because of you my name is continually blasphemed amongst the nations"[9] (for from them did the blasphemy originate); neither in the interval from Tiberius to Vespasian did they learn repentance.[10] Therefore "has their land become desolate, their cities are burnt with fire, their country strangers are devouring before their own eyes; the daughter of Sion has been deserted like a cottage in a vineyard, or a lodge in a garden of cucumbers,"[11] ever since the time when "Israel acknowledged not the Lord, and the people understood Him not, but forsook Him, and provoked the Holy One of Israel unto anger."[12] So likewise that conditional threat of the sword, "If ye refuse and hear me not, the sword shall devour you,"[13] has proved that it was Christ, for rebellion against whom they have perished. In the fifty-eighth Psalm He demands of the Father their dispersion: "Scatter them in Thy power."[14] By Isaiah He also says, as He finishes a prophecy of their consumption by fire:[15] "Because of me has this happened to you; ye shall lie down in sorrow."[16] But all this would be unmeaning enough, if they suffered this retribution not on account of Him, who had in prophecy assigned their suffering to His own cause, but for the sake of the Christ of the other god. Well, then, although you affirm that it is the Christ of the other god who was driven to the cross by the powers and authorities of the Creator, as it were by hostile beings, still I have to say, See how manifestly He was defended[17] by the Creator: there were given to Him both "the wicked for His burial," even those who had strenuously maintained that

---

1 [Ambiguous, according to Kaye, p. 304, may mean a transition from Paganism to true Christianity.]
2 Ps. xxii. 22, 25.
3 Ps. lxviii. 26.
4 Mal. i. 10, 11.
5 [Kaye remarks that traditions of *practice*, unlike the traditions of doctrine, may be varied according to times and circumstances. See p. 286.]
6 Isa. ii. 20.
7 Architectum, Isa. iii. 1–3, abridged.

8 Isa. v. 6, 7.
9 Isa. lii. 5.
10 Compare *Adv. Judæos*, 13, p. 171, for a like statement.
11 Isa. i. 7, 8.
12 Isa. i. 3, 4.
13 Isa. i. 20.
14 Ps. lix. 11.
15 Exustionem.
16 Isa. l. 11.
17 Defensus, perhaps "claimed."

His corpse had been stolen, " and the rich for His death,"[1] even those who had redeemed Him from the treachery of Judas, as well as from the lying report of the soldiers that His body had been taken away. Therefore these things either did not happen to the Jews on His account, in which case you will be refuted by the sense of the Scriptures tallying with the issue of the facts and the order of the times, or else they did happen on His account, and then the Creator could not have inflicted the vengeance except for His own Christ; nay, He must have rather had a reward for Judas, if it had been his master's enemy whom they put to death. At all events,[2] if the Creator's Christ has not come yet, on whose account the prophecy dooms them to such sufferings, they will have to endure the sufferings when He shall have come. Then where will there be a daughter of Sion to be reduced to desolation, for there is none now to be found? Where will there be cities to be burnt with fire, for they are now in heaps?[3] Where a nation to be dispersed, which is already in banishment? Restore to Judæa its former state, that the Creator's Christ may find it, and then you may contend that another Christ has come. But then, again,[4] how is it that He can have permitted to range through[5] His own heaven one whom He was some day to put to death on His own earth, after the more noble and glorious region of His kingdom had been violated, and His own very palace and sublimest height had been trodden by him? Or was it only in appearance rather than he did this?[6] God is no doubt[7] a jealous God! Yet he gained the victory. You should blush with shame, who put your faith in a vanquished god! What have you to hope for from him, who was not strong enough to protect himself? For it was either through his infirmity that he was crushed by the powers and human agents of the Creator, or else through maliciousness, in order that he might fasten so great a stigma on them by his endurance of their wickedness.

CHAP. XXV.—CHRIST'S MILLENNIAL AND HEAVENLY GLORY IN COMPANY WITH HIS SAINTS.

Yes, certainly,[8] you say, I do hope from Him that which amounts in itself to a proof of the diversity (of Christs), God's kingdom in an everlasting and heavenly possession. Besides, your Christ promises to the Jews

their primitive condition, with the recovery of their country; and after this life's course is over, repose in Hades[9] in Abraham's bosom. Oh, most excellent God, when He restores in amnesty[10] what He took away in wrath! Oh, what a God is yours, who both wounds and heals, creates evil and makes peace! Oh, what a God, that is merciful even down to Hades! I shall have something to say about Abraham's bosom in the proper place.[11] As for the restoration of Judæa, however, which even the Jews themselves, induced by the names of places and countries, hope for just as it is described,[12] it would be tedious to state at length[13] how the figurative[14] interpretation is spiritually applicable to Christ and His church, and to the character and fruits thereof; besides, the subject has been regularly treated[15] in another work, which we entitle De Spe Fidelium.[16] At present, too, it would be superfluous[17] for this reason, that our inquiry relates to what is promised in heaven, not on earth. But we do confess that a kingdom is promised to us upon the earth, although before heaven, only in another state of existence; inasmuch as it will be after the resurrection for a thousand years in the divinely-built city of Jerusalem,[18] "let down from heaven,"[19] which the apostle also calls "our mother from above;"[20] and, while declaring that our πολίτευμα, or citizenship, is in heaven,[21] he predicates of it[22] that it is really a city in heaven. This both Ezekiel had knowledge of[23] and the Apostle John beheld.[24] And the word of the new prophecy which is a part of our belief,[25] attests how it foretold that there would be for a sign a picture of this very city exhibited to view previous to its manifestation. This prophecy, indeed, has been very lately fulfilled in an expedition to the East.[26] For it is evident from the testimony of even heathen witnesses, that in Judæa there was suspended

1 See Isa. liii. 9.
2 Certe.
3 Compare a passage in the Apology, chap. xxi. p. 34, supra.
4 Jam vero.
5 Admiserit per.
6 Hoc affectavit.
7 Plane.
8 Immo.

9 Apud inferos.
10 Placatus.
11 See below, in book iv. chap. iv.
12 Ita ut describitur, i.e., in the literal sense.
13 Persequi.
14 Allegorica.
15 Digestum.
16 On the Hope of the Faithful. This work, which is not extant (although its title appears in one of the oldest MSS. of Tertullian, the Codex Agobardinus), is mentioned by St. Jerome in his Commentary on Ezekiel, chap. xxxvi.; in the preface to his Comment. on Isaiah, chap. xviii.; and in his notice of Papias of Hierapolis (Oehler).
17 Otiosum.
18 [See Kaye's important Comment. p. 345.]
19 Rev. xxi. 2.
20 Gal. iv. 26.
21 Phil. iii. 20, "our conversation," A. V.
22 Deputat.
23 Ezek. xlviii. 30-35.
24 Rev. xxi. 10-23.
25 That is, the Montanist. [Regarded as conclusive: but not conclusive evidence of an accomplished lapse from Catholic Communion.]
26 He means that of Severus against the Parthians. Tertullian is the only author who mentions this prodigy.

in the sky a city early every morning for forty days. As the day advanced, the entire figure of its walls would wane gradually,[1] and sometimes it would vanish instantly.[2] We say that this city has been provided by God for receiving the saints on their resurrection, and refreshing them with the abundance of all really spiritual blessings, as a recompense for those which in the world we have either despised or lost; since it is both just and God-worthy that His servants should have their joy in the place where they have also suffered affliction for His name's sake. Of the heavenly kingdom this is the process.[3] After its thousand years are over, within which period is completed the resurrection of the saints, who rise sooner or later according to their deserts, there will ensue the destruction of the world and the conflagration of all things at the judgment: we shall then be changed in a moment into the substance of angels, even by the investiture of an incorruptible nature, and so be removed to that kingdom in heaven of which we have now been treating, just as if it had not been predicted by the Creator, and as if it were proving Christ to belong to the other god and as if he were the first and sole revealer of it. But now learn that it has been, in fact, predicted by the Creator, and that even without prediction it has a claim upon our faith in respect of[4] the Creator. What appears to be probable to you, when Abraham's seed, after the primal promise of being like the sand of the sea for multitude, is destined likewise to an equality with the stars of heaven—are not these the indications both of an earthly and a heavenly dispensation?[5] When Isaac, in blessing his son Jacob, says, "God give thee of the dew of heaven, and the fatness of the earth,"[6] are there not in his words examples of both kinds of blessing? Indeed, the very form of the blessing is in this instance worthy of notice. For in relation to Jacob, who is the type of the later and more excellent people, that is to say ourselves,[7] first comes the promise of the heavenly dew, and afterwards that about the fatness of the earth. So are we first invited to heavenly blessings when we are separated from the world, and afterwards we thus find ourselves in the way of obtaining also earthly blessings. And your own gospel likewise has it in this wise: "Seek ye first the kingdom of God, and these things shall be added unto

you."[8] But to Esau the blessing promised is an earthly one, which he supplements with a heavenly, after the fatness of the earth, saying, "Thy dwelling shall be also of the dew of heaven."[9] For the dispensation of the Jews (who were in Esau, the prior of the sons in birth, but the later in affection[10]) at first was imbued with earthly blessings through the law, and afterwards brought round to heavenly ones through the gospel by faith. When Jacob sees in his dream the steps of a ladder set upon the earth, and reaching to heaven, with angels ascending and descending thereon, and the Lord standing above, we shall without hesitation venture to suppose,[11] that by this ladder the Lord has in judgment appointed that the way to heaven is shown to men, whereby some may attain to it, and others fall therefrom. For why, as soon as he awoke out of his sleep, and shook through a dread of the spot, does he fall to an interpretation of his dream? He exclaims, "How terrible is this place!" And then adds, "This is none other than the house of God; this is the gate of heaven!"[12] For he had seen Christ the Lord, the temple of God, and also the gate by whom heaven is entered. Now surely he would not have mentioned the gate of heaven, if heaven is not entered in the dispensation of the[13] Creator. But there is now a gate provided by Christ, which admits and conducts *to glory*. Of this Amos says: "He buildeth His ascensions into heaven;"[14] certainly not for Himself alone, but for His people also, who will be with Him. "And Thou shalt bind them about Thee," says he, "like the adornment of a bride."[15] Accordingly the Spirit, admiring such as soar up to the celestial realms by these ascensions, says, "They fly, as if they were kites; they fly as clouds, and as young doves, unto me"[16]—that is, simply like a dove.[17] For we shall, according to the apostle, be caught up into the clouds to meet the Lord (even the Son of man, who shall come in the clouds, according to Daniel[18]), and so shall we ever be with the Lord,[19] so long as He remains both on the earth and in heaven, who, against such as are thankless

---

[1] Evanescente.
[2] Et alias de proximo nullam: or "de proximo" may mean, "on a near approach."
[3] Ratio.
[4] Apud: or, "in the dispensation of the Creator."
[5] Dispositionis.
[6] Gen. xxvii. 28.
[7] Nostri, i.e., Christians. [Not *Montanist*, but Catholic.]

[8] Luke xii. 31.
[9] Gen. xxvii. 39.
[10] Judæorum enim dispositio in Esau priorum natu et posteriorum affectu filiorum. This is the original of a difficult passage, in which Tertullian, who has taken Jacob as a type of the later, the Christian church, seems to make Esau the symbol of the former, the Jewish church, which, although prior in time, was later in allegiance to the full truth of God.
[11] Temere, si forte, interpretabimur.
[12] Gen. xxviii. 12–17.
[13] Apud.
[14] Amos. ix. 6.
[15] Isa. xlix. 18.
[16] Isa. lx. 8.
[17] In allusion to the dove as the symbol of the Spirit, see Matt. iii. 16.
[18] Dan vii. 13.
[19] 1 Thess. iv. 17.

for both one promise and the other, calls the elements themselves to witness: "Hear, O heaven, and give ear, O earth."[1] Now, for my own part indeed, even though Scripture held out no hand of heavenly hope to me (as, in fact, it so often does), I should still possess a sufficient presumption[2] of even this promise, in my present enjoyment of the earthly gift; and I should look out for something also of the heavenly, from Him who is the God of heaven as well as of earth. I should thus believe that the Christ who promises the higher blessings is (the Son) of Him who had also promised the lower ones; who had, moreover, afforded proofs of greater gifts by smaller ones; who had reserved for His Christ alone this revelation[3] of a (perhaps[4]) unheard of kingdom, so that, while the earthly glory was announced by His servants, the heavenly might have God Himself for its messenger. *You*, however, argue for another Christ, from the very circumstance that He proclaims a new kingdom. You ought first to bring forward some example of His beneficence,[5] that I may have no good reason for doubting the credibility of the great promise, which you say ought to be hoped for; nay, it is before all things necessary that you should prove that a heaven belongs to Him, whom you declare to be a promiser of heavenly things. As it is, you invite us to dinner, but do not point out your house; you assert a kingdom, but show us no royal state.[6] Can it be that your Christ promises a kingdom of heaven, without having a heaven; as He displayed Himself man, without having flesh? O what a phantom from first to last![7] O hollow pretence of a mighty promise!

---

[1] Isa. i. 2.
[2] Præjudicium.
[3] Præconium.
[4] Si forte.
[5] Indulgentiæ.
[6] Regiam: perhaps "capital" or "palace."
[7] Omne.

THE FIVE BOOKS AGAINST MARCION.

BOOK IV.[1]

IN WHICH TERTULLIAN PURSUES HIS ARGUMENT. JESUS IS THE CHRIST OF THE CREATOR. HE DERIVES HIS PROOFS FROM ST. LUKE'S GOSPEL; THAT BEING THE ONLY HISTORICAL PORTION OF THE NEW TESTAMENT PARTIALLY ACCEPTED BY MARCION. THIS BOOK MAY ALSO BE REGARDED AS A COMMENTARY ON ST. LUKE. IT GIVES REMARKABLE PROOF OF TERTULLIAN'S GRASP OF SCRIPTURE, AND PROVES THAT "THE OLD TESTAMENT IS NOT CONTRARY TO THE NEW." IT ALSO ABOUNDS IN STRIKING EXPOSITIONS OF SCRIPTURAL PASSAGES, EMBRACING PROFOUND VIEWS OF REVELATION, IN CONNECTION WITH THE NATURE OF MAN.

CHAP. I.—EXAMINATION OF THE ANTITHESES OF MARCION, BRINGING THEM TO THE TEST OF MARCION'S OWN GOSPEL. CERTAIN TRUE ANTITHESES IN THE DISPENSATIONS OF THE OLD AND THE NEW TESTAMENTS. THESE VARIATIONS QUITE COMPATIBLE WITH ONE AND THE SAME GOD, WHO ORDERED THEM.

EVERY opinion and the whole scheme[2] of the impious and sacrilegious Marcion we now bring to the test[3] of that very Gospel which, by his process of interpolation, he has made his own. To encourage a belief *of this Gospel* he has actually[4] devised for it a sort of dower,[5] in a work composed of contrary statements set in opposition, thence entitled *Antitheses*, and compiled with a view to such a severance of the law from the gospel as should divide the Deity into two, nay, diverse, gods —one for each Instrument, or Testament[6] as it is more usual to call it; that by such means he might also patronize[7] belief in "the Gospel according to the Antitheses." These, however, I would have attacked in special combat, hand to hand; that is to say, I would have encountered singly the several devices of the Pontic heretic, if it were not much more convenient to refute them in and with that very gospel to which they contribute their support. Although it is so easy to meet them at once with a peremptory demurrer,[8] yet, in order that I may both make them admissible in argument, and account them valid expressions of opinion, and even contend that they make for our side, that so there may be all the redder shame for the blindness of their author, we have now drawn out some *antitheses* of our own in opposition to Marcion. And indeed[9] I do allow that one order did run its course in the old dispensation under the Creator,[10] and that another is on its way in the new under Christ. I do not deny that there is a difference in the language of their documents, in their precepts of virtue, and in their

---

[1] [The remarks of Bishop Kaye on our author's *Marcion* are simply invaluable, and the student cannot dispense with what is said more particularly of this Book. See Kaye, pp. 450-480.]
[2] Paraturam.
[3] Provocamus ad. [Kaye, p. 469, refers to Schleiermacher's *Critical Essay* on St. Luke and to a learned note of Mr. Andrews Norton of Harvard (vol. iii. Appendix C.) for valuable remarks on Marcion's Gospel.]
[4] Et, emphatic.
[5] Dotem quandam.
[6] [See cap. 2, *infra*.]
[7] Patrocinaretur.
[8] Præscriptive occurrere. This law term (the Greek παραγραφή) seems to refer to the Church's "rule of faith" (præscriptio), which he might at once put in against Marcion's heresy; only he prefers to refute him on his own ground.
[9] Atque adeo.
[10] Apud Creatorem.

teachings of the law; but yet all this diversity is consistent with one and the same God, even Him by whom it was arranged and also foretold. Long ago[1] did Isaiah declare that "out of Sion should go forth the law, and the word of the Lord from Jerusalem"[2]—some other law, that is, and another word. In short, says he, "He shall judge among the nations, and shall rebuke many people;"[3] meaning not those of the Jewish people only, but of the nations which are judged by the new law of the gospel and the new word of the apostles, and are amongst themselves rebuked of their old error as soon as they have believed. And as the result of this, "they beat their swords into ploughshares, and their spears (which are a kind of hunting instruments) into pruning-hooks;"[4] that is to say, minds, which once were fierce and cruel, are changed by them into good dispositions productive of good fruit. And again: "Hearken unto me, hearken unto me, my people, and ye kings, give ear unto me; for a law shall proceed from me, and my judgment for a light to the nations;"[5] wherefore He had determined and decreed that the nations also were to be enlightened by the law and the word of the gospel. This will be that law which (according to David also) is unblameable, because "perfect, converting the soul"[6] from idols unto God. This likewise will be the word concerning which the same Isaiah says, "For the Lord will make a decisive word in the land."[7] Because the New Testament is compendiously short,[8] and freed from the minute and perplexing[9] burdens of the law. But why enlarge, when the Creator by the same prophet foretells the renovation more manifestly and clearly than the light itself? "Remember not the former things, neither consider the things of old" (the old things have passed away, and new things are arising). "Behold, I will do new things, which shall now spring forth."[10] So by Jeremiah: "Break up for yourselves new pastures,[11] and sow not among thorns, and circumcise yourselves in the foreskin of your heart."[12] And in another passage: "Behold, the days come, saith the Lord, that I will make a new covenant with the house of Jacob, and with the house of Judah; not according to the covenant that I made with their fathers in the day when I arrested their dis-

pensation, in order to bring them out of the land of Egypt."[13] He thus shows that the ancient covenant is temporary only, when He indicates its change; also when He promises that it shall be followed by an eternal one. For by Isaiah He says: "Hear me, and ye shall live; and I will make an everlasting covenant with you," adding "the sure mercies of David,"[14] in order that He might show that that covenant was to run its course in Christ. That He was of the family of David, according to the genealogy of Mary,[15] He declared in a figurative way even by the rod which was to proceed out of the stem of Jesse.[16] Forasmuch then as he said, that from the Creator there would come other laws, and other words, and new dispensations of covenants, indicating also that the very sacrifices were to receive higher offices, and that amongst all nations, by Malachi when he says: "I have no pleasure in you, saith the Lord, neither will I accept your sacrifices at your hands. For from the rising of the sun, even unto the going down of the same, my name shall be great among the Gentiles; and in every place a sacrifice is offered unto my name, even a pure offering"[17]—meaning simple prayer from a pure conscience,—it is of necessity that every change which comes as the result of innovation, introduces a diversity in those things of which *the change* is made, from which diversity arises also a contrariety. For as there is nothing, after it has undergone a change, which does not become different, so there is nothing different which is not contrary.[18] Of that very thing, therefore, there will be predicated a contrariety in consequence of its diversity, to which there accrued a change of condition after an innovation. He who brought about the change, the same instituted the diversity also; He who foretold the innovation, the same announced beforehand the contrariety likewise. Why, in your interpretation, do you impute a difference in the state of things to a difference of powers? Why do you wrest to the Creator's prejudice those examples from which you draw your antitheses, when you may recognise them all in His sensations and affections? "I will wound," He says, "and I will heal;" "I will kill," He says again, "and I will make alive"[19]—even

---

[1] Olim.
[2] Isa. ii. 3.
[3] Isa. ii. 4.
[4] Isa. ii. 4.
[5] Isa. li. 4, according to the Sept.
[6] Ps. xix. 7.
[7] T.'s version of Isa. x. 23. "Decisus Sermo" = "determined" of A. V.
[8] Compendiatum.
[9] Laciniosis.
[10] Isa. xliii. 18, 19.
[11] Novate novamen novum. Agricultural words.
[12] Altered version of Jer. iv. 3, 4.

[13] Jer. xxxi. 31, 32, with slight change.
[14] Isa. lv. 3.
[15] Secundum Mariæ censum. See Kitto's *Cyclopædia of Biblical Literature* (third edition), in the article "Genealogy of Jesus Christ," where the translator of this work has largely given reasons for believing that St. Luke in his genealogy, (chap. iii.) has traced the descent of the Virgin MARY. To the authorities there given may be added this passage of Tertullian, and a fuller one, *Adversus Judæos*, ix., towards the end. [p. 164, *supra*.]
[16] Isa. xi. 1.
[17] Mal. i. 10, 11.
[18] To its former self.
[19] Deut. xxxii. 39.

the same "who createth evil and maketh peace;"[1] from which you are used even to censure Him with the imputation of fickleness and inconstancy, as if He forbade what He commanded, and commanded what He forbade. Why, then, have you not reckoned up the *Antitheses* also which occur in the natural works of the Creator, who is for ever contrary to Himself? You have not been able, unless I am misinformed, to recognise the fact,[2] that the world, at all events,[3] even amongst your people of Pontus, is made up of a diversity of elements which are hostile to one another.[4] It was therefore your bounden duty first to have determined that the.god of the light was one being, and the god of darkness was another, in such wise that you might have been able to have distinctly asserted one of them to be the god of the law and the other the god of the gospel. It is, however, the settled conviction already[5] of my mind from manifest proofs, that, as His works and plans[6] exist in the way of *Antitheses*, so also by the same rule exist the mysteries of His religion.[7]

CHAP. II.—ST. LUKE'S GOSPEL, SELECTED BY MARCION AS HIS AUTHORITY, AND MUTILATED BY HIM. THE OTHER GOSPELS EQUALLY AUTHORITATIVE. MARCION'S TERMS OF DISCUSSION, HOWEVER, ACCEPTED, AND GRAPPLED WITH ON THE FOOTING OF ST. LUKE'S GOSPEL ALONE.

You have now our answer to the *Antitheses* compendiously indicated by us.[8] I pass on to give a proof of the Gospel[9]—not, to be sure, of Jewry, but of Pontus—having become meanwhile[10] adulterated; and this shall indicate[11] the order by which we proceed. We lay it down as our first position, that the evangelical Testament[12] has apostles for its authors,[13] to whom was assigned by the Lord Himself this office of publishing the gospel. Since, however, there are apostolic[14] men also,[15] they are yet not alone, but appear with apostles and after apostles; because the

preaching of disciples might be open to the suspicion of an affectation of glory, if there did not accompany it[16] the authority of the masters, which means that of Christ,[17] for it was that which made the apostles their masters. Of the apostles, therefore, John and Matthew first instil[18] faith into us ; whilst of apostolic men, Luke and Mark renew it afterwards.[19] These all start with the same principles of the faith,[20] so far as relates to one only God the Creator and His Christ, how that He was born of the Virgin, and came to fulfil[21] the law and the prophets. Never mind[22] if there does occur some variation in the order of their narratives, provided that there be agreement in the essential matter[23] of the faith, in which there is disagreement with Marcion. Marcion, on the other hand, you must know,[24] ascribes no author to his Gospel, as if it could not be allowed him to affix a title to that from which it was no crime (in his eyes) to subvert[25] the very body. And here I might now make a stand, and contend that a work ought not to be recognised, which holds not its head erect, which exhibits no consistency, which gives no promise of credibility from the fulness of its title and the just profession of its author. But we prefer to join issue[26] on every point; nor shall we leave unnoticed[27] what may fairly be understood to be on our side.[28] Now, of the authors whom we possess, Marcion seems to have singled out Luke[29] for his mutilating process.[30] Luke, however, was not an apostle, but only an apostolic man; not a master, but a disciple, and so inferior to a master— at least as far subsequent to[31] him as the apostle whom he followed (and that, no doubt, was Paul[32]) was subsequent to the others; so that, had Marcion even published his Gospel in the name of St. Paul himself, the single authority of the document,[33] destitute of all support from preceding authorities, would not be a sufficient basis for our faith. There would be still wanted that Gospel which St. Paul found in existence, to which he yielded

---

[1] Isa. xlv. 7.
[2] Recogitare.
[3] Saltim.
[4] Æmularum invicem.
[5] Præjudicatum est.
[6] In the external world.
[7] Sacramenta.
[8] Expeditam a nobis.
[9] [The term εὐαγγέλιον was often employed for a written book, says Kaye (p. 298), who refers to Book i. cap. i. *supra, etc.*]
[10] Interim, perhaps " occasionally.'
[11] Præstructuram.
[12] Instrumentum. [See cap. i, *supra*. And, above, note 9. Also in cap. iii. and the Apology, (cap. xlvii.) he calls the Testaments, *Digests*, or *Sancta Digesta*.]
[13] By this canon of his, that the true Gospels must have for their authors either apostles or companions and disciples of apostles, he shuts out the false Gospels of the heretics, such as the Ebionites, Encratites, Nazarenes, and Marcionites (Le Prieur).
[14] Apostolicos, companions of the apostles associated in the authorship.
[15] He means, of course, St. Mark and St. Luke.

[16] Adsistat illi.
[17] Immo Christi.
[18] Insinuant.
[19] Instaurant.
[20] Isdem regulis.
[21] Supplementum.
[22] Viderit.
[23] De capite.
[24] Scilicet.
[25] Evertere.
[26] Congredi.
[27] Dissimulamus.
[28] Ex nostro.
[29] Compare Irenæus, *Adversus Hæreses* (Harvey), i. 25 and iii. 11 ; also Epiphanius, *Hær.* xlii. See also the editor's notes on the passages in Irenæus, who quotes other authorities also, and shows the particulars of Marcion's mutilations. [Vol. I. 429.]
[30] Quem cæderet.
[31] Posterior.
[32] See Hieronymi, *Catal. Scriptt. Eccles.* 7, and Fabricius' notes.
[33] Instrumenti.

his belief, and with which he so earnestly wished his own to agree, that he actually on that account went up to Jerusalem to know and consult the apostles, "lest he should run, or had been running in vain;"[1] in other words, that the faith which he had learned, and the gospel which he was preaching, might be in accordance with theirs. Then, at last, having conferred with the (primitive) authors, and having agreed with them touching the rule of faith, they joined their hands in fellowship, and divided their labours thenceforth in the office of preaching the gospel, so that they were to go to the Jews, and St. Paul to the Jews and the Gentiles. Inasmuch, therefore, as the enlightener of St. Luke himself desired the authority of his predecessors for both his own faith and preaching, how much more may not I require for Luke's Gospel that which was necessary for the Gospel of his master.[2]

CHAP. III.[3]—MARCION INSINUATED THE UN-
TRUSTWORTHINESS OF CERTAIN APOSTLES
WHOM ST. PAUL REBUKED. THE REBUKE
SHOWS THAT IT CANNOT BE REGARDED AS
DEROGATING FROM THEIR AUTHORITY. THE
APOSTOLIC GOSPELS PERFECTLY AUTHENTIC.

In the scheme of Marcion, on the contrary,[4] the mystery[5] of the Christian religion begins from the discipleship of Luke. Since, however, it was on its course previous to that point, it must have had[6] its own authentic materials,[7] by means of which it found its own way down to St. Luke; and by the assistance of the testimony which it bore, Luke himself becomes admissible. Well, but[8] Marcion, finding the Epistle of Paul to the Galatians (wherein he rebukes even apostles[9]) for "not walking uprightly according to the truth of the gospel,"[10] as well as accuses certain false apostles of perverting the gospel of Christ), labours very hard to destroy the character[11] of those Gospels which are published as genuine[12] and under the name of apostles, in order, forsooth, to secure for his own Gospel the credit which he takes away from them. But then, even if he censures

Peter and John and James, who were thought to be pillars, it is for a manifest reason. They seemed to be changing their company[13] from respect of persons. And yet as Paul himself "became all things to all men,"[14] that he might gain all, it was possible that Peter also might have betaken himself to the same plan of practising somewhat different from what he taught. And, in like manner, if false apostles also crept in, their character too showed itself in their insisting upon circumcision and the Jewish ceremonies. So that it was not on account of their preaching, but of their conversation, that they were marked by St. Paul, who would with equal impartiality have marked them with censure, if they had erred at all with respect to God the Creator or His Christ. Each several case will therefore have to be distinguished. When Marcion complains that apostles are suspected (for their prevarication and dissimulation) of having even depraved the gospel, he thereby accuses Christ, by accusing those whom Christ chose. If, then, the apostles, who are censured simply for inconsistency of walk, composed the Gospel in a pure form,[15] but false apostles interpolated their true record; and if our own copies have been made from these,[16] where will that genuine text[17] of the apostle's writings be found which has not suffered adulteration? Which was it that enlightened Paul, and through him Luke? It is either completely blotted out, as if by some deluge—being obliterated by the inundation of falsifiers—in which case even Marcion does not possess the true Gospel; or else, is that very *edition* which Marcion alone possesses *the* true one, that is, of the apostles? How, then, does that agree with ours, which is said not to be (the work) of apostles, but of Luke? Or else, again, if that which Marcion uses is not to be attributed to Luke simply because it does agree with ours (which, of course,[18] is, also adulterated in its title), then it is the work of apostles. Our Gospel, therefore, which is in agreement with it, is equally the work of apostles, but also adulterated in its title.[19]

CHAP. IV.—EACH SIDE CLAIMS TO POSSESS THE
TRUE GOSPEL. ANTIQUITY THE CRITERION
OF TRUTH IN SUCH A MATTER. MARCION'S
PRETENSIONS AS AN AMENDER OF THE GOSPEL.

We must follow, then, the clue[20] of our discussion, meeting every effort of our opponents

---

[1] Gal. ii. 2.
[2] [Dr. Holmes not uniformly, yet constantly inserts the prefix St. before the name of Paul, and brackets it, greatly disfiguring the page. It is not in our author's text, but I venture to dispense with the ever-recurring brackets.]
[3] This is Oehler's arrangement of the chapter, for the sake of the sense. The former editions begin this third chapter with "Sed enim Marcion nactus."
[4] Aliud est si.
[5] Sacramentum.
[6] Habuit utique.
[7] Paraturam.
[8] Sed enim.
[9] See Gal. ii. 13, 14.
[10] Compare what has been already said in book i. chap. 20, and below in book v. chap. 3. See also Tertullian's treatise, *De Præscript. Hæret.* chap. 23. [Kaye, p. 275.]
[11] Statum.
[12] Propria.

[13] Variare convictum.
[14] 1 Cor. ix. 22.
[15] Integrum.
[16] Inde nostra digesta.
[17] Germanum instrumentum.
[18] That is, according to the Marcionite cavil.
[19] De titulo quoque.
[20] Funis ducendus est.

with reciprocal vigor. I say that *my* Gospel is the true one; Marcion, that *his* is. I affirm that Marcion's Gospel is adulterated; Marcion, that mine is. Now what is to settle the point for us, except it be that principle[1] of *time*, which rules that the authority lies with that which shall be found to be more ancient; and assumes as an elemental truth,[2] that corruption (of doctrine) belongs to the side which shall be convicted of comparative lateness in its origin.[3] For, inasmuch as error[4] is falsification of truth, it must needs be that truth therefore precede error. A thing must exist prior to its suffering any casualty;[5] and an object[6] must precede all rivalry to itself. Else how absurd it would be, that, when we have proved our position to be the older one, and Marcion's the later, ours should yet appear to be the false one, before it had even received from truth its objective existence;[7] and Marcion's should also be supposed to have experienced rivalry at our hands, even before its publication; and, in fine, that that should be thought to be the truer position which is the later one—a century[8] later than the publication of all the many and great facts and records of the Christian religion, which certainly could not have been published *without*, that is to say, *before*, the truth of the gospel. With regard, then, to the pending[9] question, of Luke's Gospel (so far as its being the common property[10] of ourselves and Marcion enables it to be decisive of the truth,[11]) that portion of it which we alone receive[12] is so much older than Marcion, that Marcion, himself once believed it, when in the first warmth of faith he contributed money to the Catholic church, which along with himself was afterwards rejected,[13] when he fell away from our truth into his own heresy. What if the Marcionites have denied that he held the primitive faith amongst ourselves, in the face even of his own letter? What, if they do not acknowledge the letter? They, at any rate, receive his *Antitheses;* and more than that, they make ostentatious use[14] of them. Proof out of these is enough for me. For if the Gospel, said to be Luke's which is current amongst us[15] (we shall see whether it be also

current with Marcion), is the very one which, as Marcion argues in his *Antitheses,* was interpolated by the defenders of Judaism, for the purpose of such a conglomeration with it of the law and the prophets as should enable them out of it to fashion their Christ, surely he could not have so argued about it, unless he had found it (in such a form). No one censures things before they exist,[16] when he knows not whether they will come to pass. Emendation never precedes the fault. To be sure,[17] an amender of that Gospel, which had been all topsy-turvy[18] from the days of Tiberius to those of Antoninus, first presented himself in Marcion alone—so long looked for by Christ, who was all along regretting that he had been in so great a hurry to send out his apostles without the support of Marcion! But for all that,[19] heresy, which is for ever mending the Gospels, and corrupting them in the act, is an affair of man's audacity, not of God's authority; and if Marcion be even a disciple, he is yet not " above his master;"[20] if Marcion be an apostle, still as Paul says, " Whether it be I or they, so we preach;"[21] if Marcion be a prophet, even " the spirits of the prophets will be subject to the prophets,"[22] for they are not the authors of confusion, but of peace; or if Marcion be actually an angel, he must rather be designated " as anathema than as a preacher of the gospel,"[23] because it is a strange gospel which he has preached. So that, whilst he amends, he only confirms both positions: both that our Gospel is the prior one, for he amends that which he has previously fallen in with; and that *that* is the later one, which, by putting it together out of the emendations of ours, he has made his own Gospel, and a novel one too.

CHAP. V.—BY THE RULE OF ANTIQUITY, THE CATHOLIC GOSPELS ARE FOUND TO BE TRUE, INCLUDING THE REAL ST. LUKE'S. MARCION'S ONLY A MUTILATED EDITION. THE HERETIC'S WEAKNESS AND INCONSISTENCY IN IGNORING THE OTHER GOSPELS.[24]

On the whole, then, if that is evidently more true which is earlier, if that is earlier which is from the very beginning, if that is from the beginning which has the apostles for its authors, then it will certainly be quite as evident, that that comes down from the apos-

---

[1] Ratio.
[2] Præjudicans.
[3] Posterius revincetur. See *De Præscriptione Hæret.*, which goes on this principle of time. Compare especially chapters xxix. and xxx. [p. 256, *supra.*]
[4] Falsum.
[5] Passione.
[6] Materia.
[7] De veritate materiam.
[8] Sæculo post.
[9] Interim.
[10] Communio ejus.
[11] De veritate disceptat.
[12] Quod est secundum nos. [A note of T.'s position.]
[13] Projectam. [Catholic = Primitive.]
[14] Præferunt.
[15] Penes nos.

[16] Post futura.
[17] Sane.
[18] Eversi.
[19] Nisi quod.
[20] Matt. x. 24.
[21] 1 Cor. xv. 11.
[22] 1 Cor. xiv. 32.
[23] Gal. i. 8.
[24] [On this whole chapter and subject, consult Kaye, pp. 278-289.]

tles, which has been kept as a sacred deposit [1] in the churches of the apostles. Let us see what milk the Corinthians drank from Paul; to what rule *of faith* the Galatians were brought for correction; what the Philippians, the Thessalonians, the Ephesians read *by it;* what utterance also the Romans give, so very near [2] (to the apostles), to whom Peter and Paul conjointly [3] bequeathed the gospel even sealed with their own blood. We have also *St*. John's foster churches.[4] For although Marcion rejects his Apocalypse, the order [5] of the bishops (thereof), when traced up to their origin, will yet rest on John as their author. In the same manner is recognised the excellent source [6] of the other churches. I say, therefore, that in them (and not simply such of them as were founded by apostles, but in all those which are united with them in the fellowship of the mystery *of the gospel of Christ*[7]) that Gospel of Luke which we are defending with all our might has stood its ground from its very first publication; whereas Marcion's Gospel is not known to most people, and to none whatever is it known without being at the same time [8] condemned. It too, of course,[9] has its churches, but specially its own—as late as they are spurious; and should you want to know their original,[10] you will more easily discover apostasy in it than apostolicity, with Marcion forsooth as their founder, or some one of Marcion's swarm.[11] Even wasps make combs;[12] so also these Marcionites make churches. The same authority of the apostolic churches will afford evidence [13] to the other Gospels also, which we possess equally through their means,[14] and according to their usage—I mean the Gospels of John and Matthew—whilst that which Mark published may be affirmed to be Peter's [15] whose interpreter Mark was. For even Luke's form [16] of the Gospel men unsually ascribe to Paul.[17] And it may well seem [18] that the works which disciples publish belong to their masters. Well, then, Marcion ought to be called to a strict account [19] concerning these (other Gospels) also,

for having omitted them, and insisted in preference [20] on Luke; as if they, too, had not had free course in the churches, as well as Luke's Gospel, from the beginning. Nay, it is even more credible that they [21] existed from the very beginning; for, being the work of apostles, they were prior, and coeval in origin with [22] the churches themselves. But how comes it to pass, if the apostles published nothing, that their disciples were more forward in such a work; for they could not have been disciples, without any instruction from their masters? If, then, it be evident that these (Gospels) also were current in the churches, why did not Marcion touch them—either to amend them if they were adulterated, or to acknowledge them if they were uncorrupt? For it is but natural [23] that they who were perverting the gospel, should be more solicitous about the perversion of those things whose authority they knew to be more generally received. Even the false apostles (were so called) on this very account, because they imitated the apostles by means of their falsification. In *as* far, then, as he might have amended what there was to amend, if found corrupt, in *so* far did he firmly imply [24] that all was free from corruption which he did not think required amendment. In short,[25] he simply amended what he thought was corrupt; though, indeed, not even this justly, because it was not really corrupt. For if the (Gospels) of the apostles [26] have come down to us in their integrity, whilst Luke's, which is received amongst us,[27] so far accords with their rule as to be on a par with them in permanency of reception in the churches, it clearly follows that Luke's Gospel also has come down to us in like integrity until the sacrilegious treatment of Marcion. In short, when Marcion laid hands on it, it then became diverse and hostile to the Gospels of the apostles. I will therefore advise his followers, that they either change these Gospels, however late to do so, into a conformity with their own, whereby they may seem to be in agreement with the apostolic writings (for they are daily retouching their work, as daily they are convicted by us); or else that they blush for their master, who stands self-condemned [28] either way—when once [29] he hands on the truth of the gospel conscience smitten, or again [29] subverts it by shameless tampering.

---

[1] Sacrosanctum. Inviolate. Westcott, *On the Canon*, p. 384. Compare *De Præscript. Hæret.* c. 36, *supra*.
[2] De proximo. Westcott renders this, "who are nearest to us." See *in loco*.
[3] et . . . . et. [N.B. Not Peter's See, then.]
[4] Alumnas ecclesias. He seems to allude to the seven churches of the Apocalypse.
[5] [Not the *Order* of bishops (as we now speak) but of their succession from St. John. Kaye, p. 219.]
[6] Generositas.
[7] De societate sacramenti. [i.e. Catholic Unity.]
[8] Eadem.
[9] Plane.
[10] Censum.
[11] Examine.
[12] Favos. See Pliny, *Nat. Hist.* xi. 21.
[13] Patrocinabitur. [Jones on the Canon, Vol. I. p. 66.]
[14] Proinde per illas.
[15] See Hieronymus, *Catal. Scriptt. Eccles.* c. 8.
[16] Digestum.
[17] See above, chap. 2. p. 347.
[18] Capit videri.   [19] Flagitandus.

[20] Potius institerit.
[21] The Gospels of the apostles John and Matthew, and perhaps Mark's also, as being St. Peter's.
[22] Dedicata cum.
[23] Competit.
[24] Confirmavit.
[25] Denique.
[26] Apostolica, i.e., evangelia.
[27] That is, the canonical Gospel of St. Luke, as distinct from Marcion's corruption of it. [N.B. "Us" = Catholics.]
[28] Traducto.
[29] Nunc—nunc.

Such are the summary arguments which we use, when we take up arms[1] against heretics for the faith[2] of the gospel, maintaining both that order of periods, which rules that a late date is the mark of forgers,[3] and that authority of churches[4] which lends support to the tradition of the apostles; because truth must needs precede the forgery, and proceed straight from those by whom it has been handed on.

CHAP. VI.—MARCION'S OBJECT IN ADULTERATING THE GOSPEL. NO DIFFERENCE BETWEEN THE CHRIST OF THE CREATOR AND THE CHRIST OF THE GOSPEL. NO RIVAL CHRIST ADMISSIBLE. THE CONNECTION OF THE TRUE CHRIST WITH THE DISPENSATION OF THE OLD TESTAMENT ASSERTED.

But we now advance a step further on, and challenge (as we promised to do) the very Gospel of Marcion, with the intention of thus proving that it has been adulterated. For it is certain[5] that the whole aim at which he has strenuously laboured even in the drawing up of his *Antitheses*, centres in this, that he may establish a diversity between the Old and the New Testaments, so that his own Christ may be separate from the Creator, as belonging to this rival god, *and* as alien from the law and the prophets. It is certain, also, that with this view[6] he has erased everything that was contrary to his own opinion and made for the Creator, as if it had been interpolated by His advocates, whilst everything which agreed with his own opinion he has retained. The latter statements we shall strictly examine;[7] and if they shall turn out rather for our side, and shatter the assumption of Marcion, we shall embrace them. It will then become evident, that in retaining them he has shown no less of the defect of blindness, which characterizes heresy, than he displayed when he erased all the former class of subjects. Such, then, is to be[8] the drift and form of my little treatise; subject, of course, to whatever condition may have become requisite on both sides of the question.[9] Marcion has laid down the position, that Christ who in the days of Tiberius was, by a previously unknown god, revealed for the salvation of all nations, is a different being from Him who was ordained by God the Creator for the restoration

of the Jewish state, and who is yet to come. Between these he interposes the separation of[10] a great and absolute difference—as great as lies between what is just and what is good;[11] as great as lies between the law and the gospel; as great, (in short,) as is the difference between Judaism and Christianity. Hence will arise also our rule,[12] by which we determine[13] that there ought to be nothing in common between the Christ of the rival god and the Creator; but that (Christ) must be pronounced to belong to the Creator,[14] if He has administered His dispensations, fulfilled His prophecies, promoted[15] His laws, given reality to[16] His promises, revived His mighty power,[17] remoulded His determinations[18] expressed His attributes, His properties. This law and this rule I earnestly request the reader to have ever in his mind, and so let him begin to investigate whether Christ be Marcion's or the Creator's.

CHAP. VII.—MARCION REJECTED THE PRECEDING PORTION OF ST. LUKE'S GOSPEL. THEREFORE THIS REVIEW OPENS WITH AN EXAMINATION OF THE CASE OF THE EVIL SPIRIT IN THE SYNAGOGUE OF CAPERNAUM. HE WHOM THE DEMON ACKNOWLEDGED WAS THE CREATOR'S CHRIST.

In the fifteenth year of the reign of Tiberius[19] (for such is Marcion's proposition) he "came down to the Galilean city of Capernaum," of course meaning[20] from the heaven of the Creator, to which he had previously descended from his own. What then had been his course,[21] for him to be described as first descending from his own heaven to the Creator's? For why should I abstain from censuring those parts of the statement which do not satisfy the requirement of an ordinary narrative, but always end in a falsehood? To be sure, our censure has been once for all expressed in the question, which we have already[22] suggested: Whether, when descending through the Creator's domain, and indeed in hostility to him, he could possibly have been admitted by him, and by him been transmitted to the earth, which was equally his territory? Now, however, I want also to know the remainder of his course down, as-

---

[1] Expedimur.
[2] Fide, integrity.
[3] Posteritati falsariorum præscribentem.
[4] [Mark the authority of churches. He uses the plural—*quod ab omnibus.*]
[5] Certe, for certo.
[6] Propterea.
[7] Conveniemus.
[8] Sic habebit.
[9] This seems to be the sense of the words, "sub illa utique conditione quæ ex utraque parte condicta sit."

[10] Scindit.
[11] That is, between what is severe and judicial and punitive on one side, that is, the Creator's; and what is mild, merciful, and forgiving, on the other, that is, the Redeemer's side (Rigalt.).
[12] Præscriptio.
[13] Defigimus.
[14] Creatoris pronunciandum.
[15] Adjuverit.
[16] Repræsentaverit.
[17] Restauraverit virtutes ejus.
[18] Sententias reformaverit.
[19] Luke iii. 1 and iv. 31.
[20] Utique.
[21] Ecquid ordinis.
[22] See above, book i. chap. xxiii. [Comp. i. cap. xix.]

suming that he came down. For we must
not be too nice in inquiring[1] whether it is
supposed that he was *seen* in any place. To
come into view[2] indicates[3] a sudden unexpected glance, which for a moment fixed[4] the
eye upon the object that passed before the
view, without staying. But when it happens
that a descent has been effected, it is apparent,
and comes under the notice of the eyes.[5]
Moreover, it takes account of *fact*, and thus
obliges one to examine in what condition,
with what preparation,[6] with how much violence or moderation, and further, at what time
of the day or night, the descent was made;
who, again, saw the descent, who reported it,
who, seriously avouched the fact, which certainly was not easy to be believed, even after
the asseveration. It is, in short, too bad[7]
that Romulus should have had in Proculus an
avoucher of his ascent to heaven, when the
Christ of (this) god could not find any one to
announce his descent from heaven; just as
if the ascent of the one and the descent of
the other were not effected on one and the
same ladder of falsehood! Then, what had
he to do with Galilee, if he did not belong to
the Creator by whom[8] that region was destined (for His Christ) when about to enter on
His ministry?[9] As Isaiah says: "Drink in
this first, and be prompt, O region of Zabulon
and land of Nephthalim, and ye others who
(inhabit) the sea-coast, and that of Jordan,
Galilee of the nations, ye people who sit in
darkness, behold a great light; upon you, who
inhabit (that) land, sitting in the shadow of
death, the light hath arisen."[10] It is, however, well that Marcion's god does claim to be
the enlightener of the nations, that so he
might have the better reason for coming down
from heaven; only, if it must needs be,[11] he
should rather have made Pontus his place of
descent than Galilee. But since both the
place and the work of illumination according

to the prophecy are compatible with Christ,
we begin to discern[12] that He is the subject
of the prophecy, which shows that at the very
outset *of His ministry*, He came not to destroy
the law and the prophets, but rather to fulfil
them;[13] for Marcion has erased the passage
as an interpolation.[14] It will, however, be vain
for him to deny that Christ uttered in word
what He forthwith did partially indeed. For
the prophecy about place He at once fulfilled,
From heaven straight to the synagogue. As
the adage runs: "The business on which we
are come, do at once." Marcion must even
expunge from the Gospel, "I am not sent but
unto the lost sheep of the house of Israel;"[15]
and, "It is not meet to take the children's
bread, and to cast it to dogs,"[16]—in order,
forsooth, that Christ may not appear to be an
Israelite. But facts will satisfy me instead of
words. Withdraw all the sayings of my
Christ, His acts shall speak. Lo, He enters
the synagogue; surely (this is going) to the
lost sheep of the house of Israel. Behold, it is
to Israelites first that He offers the "bread"
of His doctrine; surely it is because they
are "children" that He shows them this priority.[17] Observe, He does not yet impart it
to others; surely He passes them by as
"dogs." For to whom else could He better
have imparted it, than to such as were strangers to the Creator, if He especially belonged
not to the Creator? And yet how could He
have been admitted into the synagogue—one
so abruptly appearing,[18] so unknown; one, of
whom no one had as yet been apprised of His
tribe, His nation, His family, and lastly, His
enrolment in the census of Augustus—that
most faithful witness of the Lord's nativity,
kept in the archives of Rome? They certainly would have remembered, if they did
not know Him to be circumcised, that He
must not be admitted into their most holy
places. And even if He had the general right
of entering[19] the synagogue (like other Jews),
yet the function of giving instruction was allowed only to a man who was extremely well
known, and examined and tried, and for some
time invested with the privilege after experience duly attested elsewhere. But "they
were all astonished at His doctrine." Of
course they were; "for, says (St. Luke),
"His word was with power[20]—not because He
taught in opposition to the law and the proph-

[1] This is here the force of *viderit*, our author's very favourite idiom.
[2] Apparere.
[3] Sapit.
[4] Impegerit.
[5] Descendisse autem, dum fit, videtur et subit oculos. Probably this bit of characteristic Latinity had better be rendered thus: "The accomplishment of a descent, however, is, whilst happening, a visible process, and one that meets the eye." Of the various readings, " dum sit," " dum it," " dum fit," we take the last with Oehler, only understanding the clause as a parenthesis.
[6] Suggestu.
[7] Indignum.
[8] Cui.
[9] Ingressuro prædicationem.
[10] This is the literal rendering of Tertullian's version of the prophet's words, which occur chap. ix. 1, 2. The first clause closely follows the LXX. (ed. Tisch.) : Τοῦτο πρῶτον πίε, ταχὺ ποίει. This curious passage is explained by Grotius (on Matt. iv. 14) as a mistake of ancient copyists ; as if what the Seventy had originally rendered ταχὺ ποίει, from the *hiphil* of קלל, had been faultily written ταχὺ πίε, and the latter had crept into the text with the marginal note πρῶτον, instead of a repetition of ταχὺ. However this be, Tertullian's old Latin Bible had the passage thus : " Hoc primum bibito, cito facito, regio Zabulon," etc.
[11] Si utique.

[12] Agnoscere.
[13] Matt. v. 17.
[14] Additum.
[15] Matt. xv. 24.
[16] Matt. xv. 26.
[17] Præfert.
[18] Tam repentinus.
[19] Etsi passim adiretur.
[20] Luke iv. 32.

ets. No doubt, His divine discourse[1] gave forth both power and grace, building up rather than pulling down the substance of the law and the prophets. Otherwise, instead of "astonishment, they would feel horror. It would not be admiration, but aversion, prompt and sure, which they would bestow on one who was the destroyer of law and prophets, and the especial propounder as a natural consequence of a rival god; for he would have been unable to teach anything to the disparagement of the law and the prophets, and so far of the Creator also, without premising the doctrine of a different and rival divinity. Inasmuch, then, as the Scripture makes no other statement on the matter than that the simple force and power of His word produced astonishment, it more naturally[2] shows that His teaching was in accordance with the Creator, by not denying (that it was so), than that it was in opposition to the Creator, by not asserting (such a fact). And thus He will either have to be acknowledged as belonging to Him,[3] in accordance with whom He taught; or else will have to be adjudged a deceiver, since He taught in accordance with One whom He had come to oppose. In the same passage, "the spirit of an unclean devil" exclaims: "What have we to do with Thee, Thou Jesus? Art Thou come to destroy us? I know Thee who Thou art, the Holy One of God."[4] I do not here raise the question whether this appellation was suitable to one who ought not to be called Christ, unless he were sent by the Creator.[5] Elsewhere[6] there has been already given a full consideration of His titles. My present discussion is, how the evil spirit could have known that He was called by such a name, when there had never at any time been uttered about Him a single prophecy by a god who was unknown, and up to that time silent, of whom it was not possible for Him to be attested as "the Holy One," as (of a god) unknown even to his own Creator. What similar event could he then have published[7] of a new deity, whereby he might be taken for "the holy one" of the rival god? Simply that he went into the synagogue, and did nothing even in word against the Creator? As therefore he could not by any means acknowledge him, whom he was ignorant of, to be Jesus and the Holy One of God; so did he acknowledge Him whom he knew (to be

both). For he remembered how that the prophet had prophesied[8] of "the Holy One" of God, and how that God's name of "Jesus" was in the son of Nun.[9] These facts he had also received[10] from the angel, according to our Gospel: "Wherefore that which shall be born of thee shall be called *the Holy One*, the Son of God;"[11] and, "Thou shalt call his name *Jesus*."[12] Thus he actually had (although only an evil spirit) some idea of the Lord's dispensation, rather than of any strange and heretofore imperfectly understood one. Because he also premised this question: "What have we to do with Thee?"—not as if referring to a strange Jesus, to whom pertain the *evil* spirits of the Creator. Nor did he say, What hast Thou to do with us? but, "What have we to do with Thee?" as if deploring himself, and deprecating his own calamity; at the prospect of which he adds: "Art Thou come to destroy us?" So completely did he acknowledge in Jesus the Son of that God who was judicial and avenging, and (so to speak) severe,[13] and not of him who was simply good,[14] and knew not how to destroy or how to punish! Now for what purpose have we adduced this passage first?[15] In order to show that Jesus was neither acknowledged by the evil spirit, nor affirmed by Himself, to be any other than the Creator's. Well, but Jesus rebuked him, you say. To be sure he did, as being an envious (spirit); and in his very confession only petulant, and evil in adulation—just as if it had been Christ's highest glory to have come for the destruction of demons, and not for the salvation of mankind; whereas His wish really was that His disciples should not glory in the subjection of evil spirits but in the fair beauty of salvation.[16] Why else[17] did He rebuke him? If it was because he was entirely wrong (in his invocation), then He was neither Jesus nor the Holy One of God; if it was because he was partially wrong—for having supposed him to be, rightly enough,[18] Jesus and the Holy One of God, but also as belonging to the Creator—most unjustly would He have rebuked him for thinking what he knew he ought to think (about Him), and for not supposing that of Him which he knew not that he ought to suppose—that he was another Jesus, and the holy one of the other god. If,

---

[1] Eloquium.
[2] Facilius.
[3] That is, the Creator.
[4] Luke iv. 33, 34.
[5] Si non Creatoris.
[6] See above, in book iii. chap. xii., on the name *Emmanuel;* in chap. xv., on the name *Christ;* and in chap. xvi., on the name *Jesus.*
[7] Quid tale ediderit.

[8] Ps. xvi. 10, and probably Dan. ix. 24.
[9] Compare what was said above in book iii., chap. xvi. p. 335.
[10] Exceperat.
[11] Such is our author's reading of Luke i. 35.
[12] Matt. i. 21.
[13] Sævi.
[14] Optimi.
[15] Præmisimus.
[16] De candida salutis: see Luke x. 20.
[17] Aut cur.
[18] Quidem.

28

however, the rebuke has not a more probable meaning[1] than that which we ascribe to it, follows that the evil spirit made no mistake, and was not rebuked for lying; for it was Jesus Himself, besides whom it was impossible for the evil spirit to have acknowledged any other, whilst Jesus affirmed that He was He whom the evil spirit had acknowledged, by not rebuking him for uttering a lie.

CHAP. VIII.—OTHER PROOFS FROM THE SAME CHAPTER, THAT JESUS, WHO PREACHED AT NAZARETH, AND WAS ACKNOWLEDGED BY CERTAIN DEMONS AS CHRIST THE SON OF GOD, WAS THE CREATOR'S CHRIST. AS OCCASION OFFERS, THE DOCETIC ERRORS OF MARCION ARE EXPOSED.

The Christ of the Creator had[2] to be called a *Nazarene* according to prophecy; whence the Jews also designate us, on that very account,[3] *Nazerenes*[4] after Him. For we are they of whom it is written, "Her Nazarites were whiter than snow;"[5] even they who were once defiled with the stains of sin, and darkened with the clouds of ignorance. But to Christ the title Nazarene was destined to become a suitable one, from the hiding-place of His infancy, for which He went down and dwelt at Nazareth,[6] to escape from Archelaus the son of Herod. This fact I have not refrained from mentioning on this account, because it behoved Marcion's Christ to have forborne all connection whatever with the *domestic* localities of the Creator's Christ, when he had so many towns in Judæa which had not been by the prophets thus assigned[7] to the Creator's Christ. But Christ will be (the Christ) of the prophets, wheresoever He is found in accordance with the prophets. And yet even at Nazareth He is not remarked as having preached anything new,[8] whilst in another *verse* He is said to have been rejected[9] by reason of a simple proverb.[10] Here at once, when I observe that they laid their hands on Him, I cannot help drawing a conclusion respecting His bodily substance, which cannot be believed to have been a phantom,[11] since it was capable of being touched and even violently handled, when He was seized and taken and led to the very brink of a precipice. For although He escaped through the midst of them, He had already experienced their rough treatment, and afterwards made His way, no doubt[12] because the crowd (as usually happens) gave way, or was even broken through; but not because it was eluded as by an impalpable disguise,[13] which, if there had been such, would not at all have submitted to any touch.

"Tangere enim et tangi, nisi corpus, nulla potest res,"[14] is even a sentence worthy of a place in the world's wisdom. In short, He did himself touch others, upon whom He laid His hands, which were capable of being felt, and conferred the blessings of healing,[15] which were not less true, not less unimaginary, than were the hands wherewith He bestowed them. He was therefore the very Christ of Isaiah, the healer of our sicknesses.[16] "Surely," says he, "He hath borne our griefs and *carried* our sorrows." Now the Greeks are accustomed to use for *carry* a word which also signifies to *take away*. A general promise is enough for me in passing.[17] Whatever were the cures which Jesus effected, He is mine. We will come, however, to the kinds of cures. To liberate men, then, from evil spirits, is a cure of sickness. Accordingly, wicked spirits (just in the manner of our former example) used to go forth with a testimony, exclaiming, "Thou art the Son of God,"[18]—of what God, is clear enough from the case itself. But they were rebuked, and ordered not to speak; precisely because[19] Christ willed Himself to be proclaimed by *men*, not by unclean spirits, as the Son of God—even that Christ alone to whom this was befitting, because He had sent beforehand men through whom He might become known, and who were assuredly worthier preachers. It was natural to Him[20] to refuse the proclamation of an unclean spirit, at whose command there was an abundance of saints. He, however,[21] who had never been foretold (if, indeed, he wished to be acknowledged; for if he did not wish so much, his coming was in vain), would not have spurned the testimony of an alien or any sort of substance, who did not happen to have a substance of his own,[22] but had descended in an alien one. And now, too, as the destroyer also of the Creator, he would have desired nothing better

---

[1] Verisimiliorem statum.
[2] Habebat.
[3] Ipso nomine, or by His very name.
[4] Nazaræos; or, *Nazarites*. [Christians were still so called by the Jews in the Third Century. Kaye, 446.]
[5] Lam. iv. 7.
[6] Descendit apud, see Luke iv. 16-30.
[7] Emancipata.
[8] Luke iv. 23.
[9] Luke iv. 29.
[10] Luke iv. 24.
[11] A rebuke of Marcion's *Docetic* views of Christ.

[12] Scilicet.
[13] Per caliginem.
[14] "For nothing can touch and be touched but a bodily substance." This line from Lucretius, *De Rerum Natura*, i. 305, is again quoted by Tertullian in his *De Anima*, chap. v. (Oehler).
[15] Luke iv. 40.
[16] See Isa. liii. 4.
[17] Interim.
[18] Luke iv. 41.
[19] Proinde enim.
[20] Illius erat.
[21] Porro.
[22] Propriæ non habebat.

than to be acknowledged by *His* spirits, and to be divulged for the sake of being feared:[1] only that Marcion says[2] that his god is not feared; maintaining that a good being is not an object of fear, but only a judicial being, in whom reside the grounds[3] of fear—anger, severity, judgments, vengeance, condemnation. But it was from fear, undoubtedly, that the evil spirits were cowed.[4] Therefore they confessed that (Christ) was the Son of a God who was to be feared, because they would have an occasion of not submitting if there were none for fearing. Besides, He showed that He was to be feared, because He drave them out, not by persuasion like a good being, but by command and reproof. Or else did he[5] reprove them, because they were making him an object of fear, when all the while he did not want to be feared? And in what manner did he wish them to go forth, when they could not do so except with fear? So that he fell into the dilemma[6] of having to conduct himself contrary to his nature, whereas he might in his simple goodness have at once treated them with leniency. He fell, too, into another false position[7]—of prevarication, when he permitted himself to be feared by the demons as the Son of the Creator, that he might drive them out, not indeed by his own power, but by the authority of the Creator. "He departed, and went into a desert place."[8] This was, indeed, the Creator's customary region. It was proper that the Word[9] should there appear in body, where He had aforetime, wrought in a cloud. To the gospel was suitable that condition of place[10] which had once been determined on for the law.[11] "Let the wilderness and the solitary place, therefore, be glad and rejoice;" so had Isaiah promised.[12] When "stayed" by the crowds, He said, " I must preach the kingdom of God to other cities also."[13] Had He displayed His God anywhere yet? I suppose as yet nowhere. But was He speaking of those who knew of another god also? I do not believe so. If, therefore, neither He had preached, nor they had known, any other God but the Creator, He was announcing the kingdom of that God whom He knew to be the only God known to those who were listening to Him.

CHAP. IX.—OUT OF ST. LUKE'S FIFTH CHAPTER ARE FOUND PROOFS OF CHRIST'S BELONGING TO THE CREATOR, E.G. IN THE CALL OF FISHERMEN TO THE APOSTOLIC OFFICE, AND IN THE CLEANSING OF THE LEPER. CHRIST COMPARED WITH THE PROPHET ELISHA.

Out of so many kinds of occupations, why indeed had He such respect for that of fishermen, as to select from it for apostles Simon and the sons of Zebedee (for it cannot seem to be the mere fact itself for which the narrative was meant to be drawn out[14]), saying to Peter, when he trembled at the very large draught of the fishes, "Fear not; from henceforth thou shalt catch men?"[15] By saying this, He suggested to them the meaning of the fulfilled prophecy, that it was even He who by Jeremiah had foretold, "Behold, I will send many fishers; and they shall fish them,"[16] that is, men. Then at last they left their boats, and followed Him, understanding that it was He who had begun to accomplish what He had declared. It is quite another case, when he affected to choose from the college of shipmasters, intending one day to appoint the shipmaster Marcion his apostle. We have indeed already laid it down, in opposition to his *Antitheses*, that the position of Marcion derives no advantage from the diversity which he supposes to exist between the Law and the Gospel, inasmuch as even this was ordained by the Creator, and indeed predicted in the promise of the new Law, and the new Word, and the new Testament. Since, however, he quotes with especial care,[17] as a proof in his domain,[18] a certain companion in misery (συνταλαίπωρον), and associate in hatred (συμμισούμενον), with himself, for the cure of leprosy,[19] I shall not be sorry to meet him, and before anything else to point out to him the force of the law figuratively interpreted, which, in this example of a leper (who was not to be touched, but was rather to be removed from all intercourse with others), prohibited any communication with a person who was defiled with sins, with whom the apostle also forbids us even to eat food,[20] forasmuch as the taint of sins would be communicated as if contagious, wherever a man should mix himself with the sinner. The Lord, therefore, wishing that the law should be more profoundly understood as signifying spiritual truths by carnal facts[21]—and thus[22] not de-

---

[1] Præ timore.
[2] See above, book i. chap. vii. xxvi. and xxvii.
[3] Materiæ.
[4] Cedebant.
[5] Aut nunquid.
[6] Necessitatem.
[7] In aliam notam.
[8] Luke iv. 42.
[9] Sermonem. [*Nota Bene*, Acts vii. 38.]
[10] Habitus loci.
[11] The law was given in *the wilderness* of Sinai ; see Ex. xix. 1.
[12] Isa. xxxv. 1.
[13] Luke iv. 42, 43.

[14] Argumentum processurum erat.
[15] See Luke v. 1-11.
[16] Jer. xvi. 16.
[17] Attentius argumentatur.
[18] Apud illum, i.e., the Creator.
[19] Luke v. 12-14.
[20] 1 Cor. v. 11.
[21] Per carnalia, by *material* things.
[22] Hoc nomine.

stroying, but rather building up, that *law* which He wanted to have more earnestly acknowledged—touched the leper, by whom (even although as man He might have been defiled) He could not be defiled as God, being of course incorruptible. The prescription, therefore, could not be meant for Him, that He was bound to observe the law and not touch the unclean person, seeing that contact with the unclean would not cause defilement to Him. I thus teach that this (immunity) is consistent in my Christ, the rather when I show that it is not consistent in yours. Now, if it was as an enemy[1] of the law that He touched the leper—disregarding the precept of the law by a contempt of the defilement—how could he be defiled, when he possessed not a body[2] which could be defiled? For a phantom is not susceptible of defilement. He, therefore, who could not be defiled, as being a phantom, will not have an immunity from pollution by any divine power, but owing to his fantastic vacuity; nor can he be regarded as having despised pollution, who had not in fact any material capacity[3] for it; nor, in like manner, as having destroyed the law, who had escaped defilement from the occasion of his phantom nature, not from any display of virtue. If, however, the Creator's prophet Elisha cleansed Naaman the Syrian alone,[4] to the exclusion of[5] so many lepers in Israel,[6] this fact contributes nothing to the distinction of Christ, as if he were in this way the better one for cleansing this Israelite leper, although a stranger to him, whom his own Lord had been unable to cleanse. The cleansing of the Syrian rather[7] was significant throughout the nations of the world[8] of their own cleansing in Christ their light,[9] steeped as they were in the stains of the seven deadly sins:[10] idolatry, blasphemy, murder, adultery, fornication, false-witness, and fraud.[11] Seven times,

therefore, as if once for each,[12] did he wash in Jordan; both in order that he might celebrate the expiation of a perfect hebdomad;[13] and because the virtue and fulness of the one baptism was *thus* solemnly imputed[14] to Christ, alone, who was one day to establish on earth not only a revelation, but also a baptism, endued with compendious efficacy.[15] Even Marcion finds here an antithesis:[16] how that Elisha indeed required a material resource, applied water, and that seven times; whereas Christ, by the employment of a word only, and that but once for all, instantly effected[17] the cure. And surely I might venture[18] to claim[19] the Very Word also as of the Creator's substance. There is nothing of which He who was the primitive Author is not also the more powerful one. Forsooth,[20] it is incredible that that power of the Creator should have, by a word, produced a remedy for a single malady, which once by a word brought into being so vast a fabric as the world! From what can the Christ of the Creator be better discerned, than from the power of His word? But Christ is on this account another (Christ), because He acted differently from Elisha—because, *in fact*, the master is more powerful than his servant! Why, Marcion, do you lay down the rule, that things are done by servants just as they are by their very masters? Are you not afraid that it will turn to your discredit, if you deny that Christ belongs to the Creator, on the ground that He was *once* more powerful than a servant of the Creator—since, in comparison with the weakness of Elisha, He is acknowledged to be the greater, if indeed greater![21] For the cure is the same, although there is a difference in the working of it. What has your Christ performed more than my Elisha? Nay, what great thing has the word of your Christ performed, when it has *simply* done that which a river of the Creator effected? On the same principle occurs all the rest. So far as renouncing all human glory went, He forbade the man to publish abroad *the cure;* but so far as the honour of the law was concerned, He requested that the usual course should be followed: "Go, show thyself to the priest, and

---

[1] Æmulus.
[2] Another allusion to Marcion's *Docetic* doctrine.
[3] Materiam.
[4] Unicum.
[5] Ex., literally, "alone of." So Luke iv. 27.
[6] Compare 2 Kings v. 9-14 with Luke iv. 27.
[7] Facilius—rather than of Israelites.
[8] Per Nationes. [Bishop Andrewes thus classifies the "Sins of the Nations," as Tertullian's idea seems to have suggested: (1) *Pride,* Amorite; (2) *Envy,* Hittite; (3) *Wrath,* Perizzite; (4) *Gluttony* Girgashite; (5) *Lechery,* Hivite; (6) *Covetousness,* Canaanite; (7) *Sloth,* Jebusite.]
[9] Compare, in Simeon's song, Luke ii. 32, the designation, "A light to lighten the Gentiles."
[10] [See Elucidation I.]
[11] Such seems to be the meaning of the obscure passage in the original, "Syro facilius emundato significato per nationes emundationis in Christo lumine earum quæ septem maculis, capitalium delictorum inhorrerent, idolatria," etc. We have treated *significato* as one member of an ablative absolute clause, from *significatum,* a noun occurring in Gloss. Lat. Gr. synonymous with δήλωσις. Rigault, in a note on the passage, imputes the obscurity to Tertullian's arguing on the Marcionite hypothesis. "Marcion," says he, "held that the prophets, like Elisha, belonged to the Creator, and Christ to the good God. To magnify Christ's beneficence, he prominently dwells on the alleged fact, that Christ, although a stranger to the Creator's world, yet vouchsafed to do good in it. This vain conceit Tertullian refutes from the Mar-

cionite hypothesis itself. God the Creator, said they, had found Himself incapable of cleansing this Israelite; but He had more easily cleansed the Syrian. Christ, however, cleansed the Israelite, and so showed himself the superior power. Tertullian denies both positions."
[12] Quasi per singulos titulos.
[13] There was a mystic completeness in the number *seven.*
[14] Dicabatur.
[15] Sicut sermonem compendiatum, ita et lavacrum. In chap. i. of this book, the N.T. is called the *compendiatum.* This illustrates the present phrase.
[16] Et hoc opponit.
[17] Repræsentavit.
[18] Quasi non audeam.
[19] Vindicare in.
[20] Plane. An ironical cavil from the Marcionite view.
[21] Si tamen major.

present the offering which Moses command-ed."[1] For the figurative signs of the law in its types He still would have observed, be-cause of their prophetic import.[2] These types signified that a man, once a sinner, but afterwards purified[3] from the stains thereof by the word of God, was bound to offer unto God in the temple a gift, even prayer and thanksgiving in the church through Christ Jesus, who is the Catholic Priest of the Father.[4] Accordingly He added: "that it may be for a testimony unto you"—one, no doubt, whereby He would testify that He was not destroying the law, but fulfilling it; whereby, too, He would testify that it was He Himself who was foretold as about to undertake[5] their sicknesses and infirmities. This very con-sistent and becoming explanation of "the testimony," that adulator of his own Christ, Marcion seeks to exclude under the cover of mercy and gentleness. For, being both good (such are his words), and knowing, besides, that every man who had been freed from leprosy would be sure to perform the solemni-ties of the law, therefore He gave this pre-cept. Well, what then? Has He continued in his goodness (that is to say, in his permis-sion of the law) or not? For if he has perse-vered in his goodness, he will never become a destroyer of the law; nor will he ever be accounted as belonging to another god, be-cause there would not exist that destruction of the law which would constitute his claim to belong to the other god. If, however, he has not continued good, by a subsequent de-struction of the law, it is a false testimony which he has since imposed upon them in his cure of the leper; because he has forsaken his goodness, in destroying the law. If, there-fore, he was good whilst upholding the law,[6] he has now become evil as a destroyer of the law. However, by the support which he gave to the law, he affirmed that the law was good. For no one permits himself in the support of an evil thing. Therefore he is not only bad if he has permitted obedience to a bad law; but even worse still, if he has appeared[7] as the destroyer of a good law. So that if he commanded the offering of the gift because he knew that every cured leper would be sure to bring one; he possibly abstained from com-manding what he knew would be spontane-ously done. In vain, therefore, was his com-ing down, as if with the intention of destroy-ing the law, when he makes concessions to the keepers of the law. And yet,[8] because he knew their disposition,[9] he ought the more earnestly to have prevented their neglect of the law,[10] since he had come for this purpose. Why then did he not keep silent, that man might of his own simple will obey the law? For then might he have seemed to some ex-tent[11] to have persisted in his patience. But he adds also his own authority increased by the weight of this "testimony." Of what tes-timony, I ask,[12] if not that of the assertion of the law? Surely it matters not in what way he asserted the law—whether as good, or as supererogatory,[13] or as patient, or as incon-stant—provided, Marcion, I drive you from your position.[14] Observe,[15] he commanded that the law should be fulfilled. In whatever way he commanded it, in the same way might he also have first uttered that sentiment:[16] "I came not to destroy the law, but to fulfil it."[17] What business, therefore, had you to erase out of the Gospel that which was quite consistent in it?[18] For you have confessed that, in his goodness, he did in act what you deny that he did in word.[19] We have there-fore good proof that He uttered the word, in the fact that He did the deed; and that you have rather expunged the Lord's word, than that our (evangelists)[20] have inserted it.

CHAP. X.—FURTHER PROOFS OF THE SAME TRUTH IN THE SAME CHAPTER, FROM THE HEALING OF THE PARALYTIC, AND FROM THE DESIGNATION SON OF MAN WHICH JESUS GIVES HIMSELF. TERTULLIAN SUSTAINS HIS ARGU-MENT BY SEVERAL QUOTATIONS FROM THE PROPHETS.

The sick of the palsy is healed,[21] and that in public, in the sight of the people. For, says Isaiah, "they shall see the glory of the Lord, and the excellency of our God."[22] What glory, and what excellency? "Be strong, ye weak hands, and ye feeble knees:"[23] this refers to the palsy. "Be strong; fear not."[24] *Be strong* is not vainly repeated, nor is *fear not* vainly added; because with the

---

[1] Luke v. 14.
[2] Utpote prophetatæ.
[3] Emaculatum.
[4] [i.e., the Great High Priest whose sacrifice is accepted of the Father, for the sins of the whole world.]
[5] Suscepturus: *to carry* or *take away.*
[6] Legis indultor.
[7] Advenit.

[8] Atquin.
[9] Formam.
[10] Ab ea avertendos.
[11] Aliquatenus.
[12] Jam.
[13] Supervacuus.
[14] Gradu.
[15] Ecce.
[16] Sententiam.
[17] Matt. v. 17.
[18] Quod salvum est.
[19] That is, you retain the passage in St. Luke, which relates the *act* of honouring the law; but you reject that in St. Matthew, which contains Christ's profession of honouring the law.
[20] Nostros: or, perhaps, "our people,"—that is, the Catholics.
[21] Luke v. 16–26.
[22] Isa. xxxv. 2.
[23] Isa. xxxv. 3 in an altered form.
[24] Isa. xxxv. 4.

renewal of the limbs there was to be, according to the promise, a restoration also of bodily energies: "Arise, and take up thy couch;" and likewise moral courage[1] not to be afraid of those who should say, "Who can forgive sins, but God alone?" So that you have here not only the fulfilment of the prophecy which promised a particular kind of healing, but also of the symptoms which followed the cure. In like manner, you should also recognise Christ in the same prophet as the forgiver of sins. "For," he says, "He shall remit to many their sins, and shall Himself take away our sins."[2] For in an earlier passage, speaking in the person of the Lord himself, he had said: "Even though your sins be as scarlet, I will make them as white as snow; even though they be like crimson, I will whiten them as wool."[3] In the scarlet colour He indicates the blood of the prophets; in the crimson, that of the Lord, as the brighter. Concerning the forgiveness of sins, Micah also says: "Who is a God like unto Thee? pardoning iniquity, and passing by the transgressions of the remnant of Thine heritage. He retaineth not His anger as a testimony *against them*, because He delighteth in mercy. He will turn again, and will have compassion upon us; He wipeth away our iniquities, and casteth our sins into the depths of the sea."[4] Now, if nothing of this sort had been predicted of Christ, I should find in the Creator examples of such a benignity as would hold out to me the promise of similar affections also in the Son of whom He is the Father. I see how the Ninevites obtained forgiveness of their sins from the Creator[5] —not to say from Christ, even then, because from the beginning He acted in the Father's name. I read, too, how that, when David acknowledged his sin against Uriah, the prophet Nathan said unto him, "The Lord hath cancelled[6] thy sin, and thou shalt not die;"[7] how king Ahab in like manner, the husband of Jezebel, guilty of idolatry and of the blood of Naboth, obtained pardon because of his repentance;[8] and how Jonathan the son of Saul blotted out by his deprecation the guilt of a violated fast.[9] Why should I recount the frequent restoration of the nation itself after the forgiveness of their sins?—by that God, indeed, who will have mercy rather than sacrifice, and a sinner's repentance rather than his

death.[10] You will first have to deny that the Creator ever forgave sins; then you must in reason show[11] that He never ordained any such prerogative for His Christ; and so you will prove how novel is that boasted[12] benevolence of the, of course, novel Christ when you shall have proved that it is neither compatible with[13] the Creator nor predicted by the Creator. But whether to remit sins can appertain to one who is said to be unable to retain them; and whether to absolve can belong to him who is incompetent even to condemn, and whether to forgive is suitable to him against whom no offence can be committed, are questions which we have encountered elsewhere,[14] when we preferred to drop suggestions[15] rather than treat them anew.[16] Concerning the Son of man our rule[17] is a twofold one: that Christ cannot lie, so as to declare Himself the Son of man, if He be not truly so; nor can He be constituted the Son of man, unless He be born of a human parent, either father or mother. And then the discussion will turn on the point, of which human parent He ought to be accounted the son—of the father or the mother? Since He is (begotten) of God the Father, He is not, of course, (the son) of a human father. If He is not of a human father, it follows that He must be (the son) of a human mother. If of a human mother, it is evident that she must be a virgin. For to whom a human father is not ascribed, to his mother a husband will not be reckoned; and then to what mother a husband is not reckoned, the condition of virginity belongs.[18] But if His mother be not a virgin, two fathers will have to be reckoned to Him—a divine and a human one. For she must have a husband, not to be a virgin; and by having a husband, she would cause two fathers—one divine, the other human—to accrue to Him, who would thus be Son both of God and of a man. Such a nativity (if one may call it so)[19] the mythic stories assign to Castor or to Hercules. Now, if this distinction be observed, that is to say, if He be Son of man as born of His mother, because not begotten of a father, and His mother be a virgin, because His father is not human—He will be that Christ whom Isaiah foretold that a virgin should conceive.[20] On what principle you, Marcion, can admit Him Son of man, I

---

[1] Animi vigorem.
[2] This seems to be Isa. liii. 12, last clause.
[3] Isa. i. 18.
[4] Mic. vii. 18, 19.
[5] Jonah iii. 10.
[6] Circumduxit.
[7] 2 Sam. xii. 13.
[8] 1 Kings xxi. 29.
[9] Resignati jejunii. See 1 Sam. xiv. 43–45.

[10] Ezek. xxxiii. 11.
[11] Consequens est ut ostendas.
[12] Istam.
[13] Parem.
[14] See book i. chap. xxvi.–xxviii.
[15] Admonere.
[16] Retractare: give a set treatise about them.
[17] Præscriptio.
[18] To secure *terseness* in the premises, we are obliged to lengthen out the brief terms of the conclusion, *virgo est.*
[19] Si forte.
[20] Isa. vii. 14.

cannot possibly see.   If through a human father, then you deny him to be Son of God; if through a divine one *also*,[1] then you make Christ the Hercules of fable; if through a human mother only, then you concede my point; if not through a human father *also*,[2] then He is not the son of any man,[3] and He must have been guilty of a lie for having declared Himself to be what He was not.   One thing alone can help you in your difficulty: boldness on your part either to surname your God as actually the human father of Christ, as Valentinus did[4] with his Æon; or else to deny that the Virgin was human, which even Valentinus did not do.   What now, if Christ be described[5] in Daniel by this very title of "Son of man?"   Is not this enough to prove that He is the Christ of prophecy?   For if He gives Himself that appellation which was provided in the prophecy for the Christ of the Creator, He undoubtedly offers Himself to be understood as Him to whom (the appellation) was assigned by the prophet.   But perhaps[6] it can be regarded as a simple identity of names;[7] and yet we have maintained[8] that neither Christ nor Jesus ought to have been called by these names, if they possessed any condition of diversity.   But as regards the appellation "Son of man," in *as* far as it occurs by accident,[9] in *so* far there is a difficulty in its occurrence along with[10] a casual identity of names.   For it is of pure[11] accident, especially when the same cause does not appear[12] whereby the identity may be occasioned.   And therefore, if Marcion's Christ be also said to be born of man, then he too would receive an identical appellation, and there would be two Sons of man, as also two Christs and two Jesuses.   Therefore, since the appellation is the sole right of Him in whom it has a suitable reason,[13] if it be claimed for another in whom there is an identity of name, but not of appellation,[14] then the identity of name even looks suspicious in him for whom is claimed without reason the identity of appellation.   And it follows that He must be believed to be One and the Same, who is found to be the more fit to receive both the name and the appellation; while the other is

excluded, who has no right to the appellation, because he has no reason to show for it.   Nor will any other be better entitled to both than He who is the earlier, and has had allotted to Him the name of Christ and the appellation of Son of man, even the Jesus of the Creator.   It was He who was seen by the king of Babylon in the furnace with His martyrs: "the fourth, who was like the Son of man."[15]   He also was revealed to Daniel himself expressly as "the Son of man, coming in the clouds of heaven" as a Judge, as also the Scripture shows.[16]   What I have advanced might have been sufficient concerning the designation in prophecy of the Son of man.   But the Scripture offers me further information, even in the interpretation of the Lord Himself.   For when the Jews, who looked at Him as merely man, and were not yet sure that He was God also, as being likewise the Son of God, rightly enough said that a man could not forgive sins, but God alone, why did He not, following up their point[17] about *man*, answer them, that He[18] had power to remit sins; inasmuch as, when He mentioned the Son of man, He also named a human being? except it were because He wanted, by help of the very designation "Son of man" from the book of Daniel, so to induce them to reflect[19] as to show them that He who remitted sins was God and man—that only Son of man, indeed, in the prophecy of Daniel, who had obtained the power of judging, and thereby, of course, of forgiving sins likewise (for He who judges also absolves); so that, when once that objection of theirs[20] was shattered to pieces by their recollection of Scripture, they might the more easily acknowledge Him to be the Son of man himself by His own actual forgiveness of sins.   I make one more observation,[21] how that He has nowhere as yet professed Himself to be the Son of God—but for the first time in this passage, in which for the first time He has remitted sins; that is, in which for the first time He has used His function of *judgment*, by the absolution.   All that the opposite side has to allege in argument against these things, (I beg you) carefully weigh[22] what it amounts to.   For it must needs strain itself to such a pitch of infatuation as, on the one hand, to maintain that (their Christ) is also Son of man, in order to save Him from the charge of falsehood; and, on the other hand, to deny that He was born of woman, lest they grant

---

1 Si et Dei.
2 Si neque patris.
3 On Marcion's principles, it must be remembered.
4 Compare T.'s treatise, *Adversus Valentinianos*, chap. xii.
5 Censetur.
6 Si forte.
7 Nominum communio simplex.
8 Defendimus.   See above, book iii. chap. xv. xvi.
9 Ex accidenti obvenit.
10 Super.
11 Proprio.
12 Non convenit.
13 Causam.
14 The context explains the difference between *nomen* and *appellatio*.   The former refers to the name *Jesus* or *Christ*, the latter to the designation *Son of man*.

15 Dan. iii. 25.
16 Dan. vii. 13.
17 Secundum intentionem eorum.
18 Eum: that is, *man*.
19 Repercutere.
20 Scandalo isto.
21 Denique.
22 Dispice.

that He was the Virgin's son. Since, however, the divine authority and the nature of the case, and common sense, do not admit this insane position of the heretics, we have here the opportunity of putting in a veto[1] in the briefest possible terms, *on the substance of Christ's body*, against Marcion's phantoms. Since He is born of man, being the Son of man. He is body derived from body.[2] You may, I assure you,[3] more easily find a man born without a heart or without brains, like Marcion himself, than without a body, like Marcion's Christ. And let this be the limit to your examination of the heart, or, at any rate, the brains of the heretic of Pontus.[4]

CHAP. XI.—THE CALL OF LEVI THE PUBLICAN. CHRIST IN RELATION TO THE BAPTIST. CHRIST AS THE BRIDEGROOM. THE PARABLE OF THE OLD WINE AND THE NEW. ARGUMENTS CONNECTING CHRIST WITH THE CREATOR.

The publican who was chosen by the Lord,[5] he adduces for a proof that he was chosen, as a stranger to the law and uninitiated in[6] Judaism, by one who was an adversary to the law. The case of Peter escaped his memory, who, although he was a man of the law, was not only chosen by the Lord, but also obtained the testimony of possessing knowledge which was given to him by the Father.[7] He had nowhere read of Christ's being foretold as the light, and hope, and expectation of the Gentiles! *He*, however, rather spoke of the Jews in a favourable light, when he said, "The whole needed not a physician, but they that are sick."[8] For since by "those that are sick" he meant that the heathens and publicans should be understood, whom he was choosing, he affirmed of the Jews that they were "whole" for whom he said that a physician was not necessary. This being the case, he makes a mistake in coming down[9] to destroy the law, as if for the remedy of a diseased condition, because they who were living under it were "whole," and "not in want of a physician." How, moreover, does it happen that he proposed the similitude of a *physician*, if he did not verify it? For, just as nobody uses a physician for healthy persons, so will no one do so for strangers, in so far as he is one of Marcion's god-made men,[10] having to himself

both a creator and preserver, and a specially good physician, in his Christ. This much the comparison predetermines, that a physician is more usually furnished by him to whom the sick people belong. Whence, too, does John come upon the scene? Christ, suddenly; and just as suddenly, John![11] After this fashion occur all things in Marcion's system. They have their own special and plenary course[12] in the Creator's dispensation. Of John, however, what else I have to say will be found in another passage.[13] To the several points which now come before us an answer must be given. This, then, I will take care to do[14]—demonstrate that, reciprocally, John is suitable to Christ, and Christ to John, the latter, of course, as a prophet of the Creator, just as the former is the Creator's Christ; and so the heretic may blush at frustrating, to his own frustration, the mission of John *the Baptist*. For if there had been no ministry of John at all—"the voice," as Isaiah calls him, "of one crying in the wilderness," and the preparer of the ways of the Lord by denunciation and recommendation of repentance; if, too, he had not baptized (Christ) Himself[15] along with others, nobody could have challenged the disciples of Christ, as they ate and drank, to a comparison with the disciples of John, who were constantly fasting and praying; because, if there existed any diversity[16] between Christ and John, and their followers respectively, no exact comparison would be possible, nor would there be a single point where it could be challenged. For nobody would feel surprise, and nobody would be perplexed, although there should arise rival predictions of a diverse deity, which should also mutually differ about modes of conduct,[17] having a prior difference about the authorities[18] upon which they were based. Therefore Christ belonged to John, and John to Christ; while both belonged to the Creator, and both were of the law and the prophets, preachers and masters. Else Christ would have rejected the discipline of John, as of the rival god, and would also have defended the disciples, as very properly pursuing a different walk, because consecrated to the service of another and contrary deity. But as it is, while modestly[19] giving a reason why "the children of the bridegroom are unable to fast during the

---

[1] Interpellandi.
[2] Corpus ex corpore.
[3] Plane: introducing the sharp irony.
[4] This is perhaps the best sense of T.'s sarcasm: "Atque adeo (*thus far*) inspice cor Pontici aut (*or else*) cerebrum.
[5] He means Levi or St. Matthew; see Luke v. 27–39.
[6] Profanum.
[7] Matt. xvi. 17.
[8] Luke v. 31.
[9] Male descendit.
[10] Homo a deo Marcionis.

[11] See chap. vii. of this book, and chap. ii. of book iii.
[12] Plenum ordinem.
[13] See below, chap. xviii.
[14] Tuebor.
[15] Ipsum.
[16] Marcion's *diversitas* implied an utter incompatibility between John and Christ; for it assigned John to the Creator, from whom it took Christ away.
[17] De disciplinis: or, "about discipleships."
[18] De auctoritatibus; or, "about the authors thereof."
[19] Humiliter.

time the bridegroom is with them," but promising that "they should afterwards fast, when the bridegroom was taken away from them,"[1] He neither defended the disciples, (but rather excused them, as if they had not been blamed without some reason), nor rejected the discipline of John, but rather allowed[2] it, referring it to the time of John, although destining it for His own time. Otherwise His purpose would have been to reject it,[3] and to defend its opponents, if He had not Himself already belonged to it as then in force. I hold also that it is my Christ who is meant by the bridegroom, of whom the psalm says: "He is as a bridegroom coming out of his chamber; His going forth is from the end of the heaven, and His return is back to the end of it again."[4] By the mouth of Isaiah He also says exultingly of the Father: "Let my soul rejoice in the Lord; for He hath clothed me with the garment of salvation and with the tunic of joy, as a bridegroom. He hath put a mitre round about my head, as a bride."[5] To Himself likewise He appropriates[6] the church, concerning which the same[7] Spirit says to Him: "Thou shalt clothe Thee with them all, as with a bridal ornament."[8] This spouse Christ invites home to Himself also by Solomon from the call of the Gentiles, because you read: "Come with me from Lebanon, my spouse."[9] He elegantly makes mention of Lebanon (the mountain, of course) because it stands for the name of frankincense with the Greeks;[10] for it was from idolatry that He betrothed Himself the church. Deny now, Marcion, your utter madness, (if you can)! Behold, you impugn even the law of your god. He unites not in the nuptial bond, nor, when contracted, does he allow it; no one does he baptize but a *cœlebs* or a eunuch; until death or divorce does he reserve baptism.[11] Wherefore, then, do you make his Christ a bridegroom? This is the designation of Him who united man and woman, not of him who separated them. You have erred also in that declaration of Christ, wherein He seems to make a difference between things new and old. You are inflated about the old bottles, and brain-muddled with the new wine;

and therefore to the old (that is to say, to the prior) gospel you have sewed on the patch of your new-fangled heresy. I should like to know in what respect the Creator is inconsistent with Himself.[12] When by Jeremiah He gave this precept, "Break up for yourselves new pastures,"[13] does He not turn away from the old state of things? And when by Isaiah He proclaims how "old things were passed away; and, behold, all things, which I am making, are new,"[14] does He not advert to a new state of things? We have generally been of opinion[15] that the destination of the former state of things was rather promised by the Creator, and exhibited in reality by Christ, only under the authority of one and the same God, to whom appertain both the old things and the new. For new wine is not put into old bottles, except by one who has the old bottles; nor does anybody put a new piece to an old garment, unless the old garment be forthcoming to him. That person only[16] does not do a thing when it is not to be done, who has the materials wherewithal to do it if it were to be done. And therefore, since His object in making the comparison was to show that He was separating the new condition[17] of the gospel from the old state[18] of the law, He proved that that[19] from which He was separating His own[20] ought not to have been branded[21] as a separation[22] of things which were alien to each other; for nobody ever unites his own things with things that are alien to them,[23] in order that he may afterwards be able to separate them from the alien things. A separation is possible by help of the conjunction through which it is made. Accordingly, the things which He separated He also proved to have been once one; as they would have remained, were it not for His separation. But still we make this concession, that there is a separation, by reformation, by amplification,[24] by progress; just as the fruit is separated from the seed, although the fruit comes from the seed. So likewise the gospel is separated from the law, whilst it advances[25] from the law—a different thing[26] from it, but not an alien one; diverse, but not contrary. Nor in Christ do we even find any novel form of discourse. Whether He proposes simili-

[1] Luke v. 34, 35.
[2] Concessit.
[3] Rejecturus alioquin.
[4] Ps. xix. 5, 6.
[5] Isa. lxi. 10.
[6] Deputat.
[7] The same, which spake again by Isaiah.
[8] Isa. xlix. 18.
[9] Song of Sol. iv. 8.
[10] There is also in Hebrew an affinity between לְבֹנָה, "frankincense," and לְבָנוֹן, "Lebanon." [Note this strange but reiterated and emphatic identification of incense with *idolatry*. In the Gentile church it was thoroughly identified with Paganism.]
[11] See also book i. chap. xxix. [On this reservation of Baptism see Elucidation II.]

[12] Alter.
[13] Jer. iv. 3.
[14] His reading of (probably) Isa. xliii. 19; comp. 2 Cor. v. 17
[15] Olim statuimus.
[16] Ille.
[17] Novitas.
[18] Vetustas.
[19] That is, "the oldness of the law."
[20] That is, "the newness of the gospel."
[21] Notandam.
[22] Separatione. The more general reading is *separationem*.
[23] Alienis: i.e., "things not his own."
[24] Amplitudinem.
[25] Provehitur, "is developed."
[26] Aliud.

tudes or refute questions, it comes from the seventy-seventh Psalm. " I will open," says He, " my mouth in a parable " (that is, in a similitude); " I will utter *dark* problems " (that is, I will set forth questions).[1] If you should wish to prove that a man belonged to another race, no doubt you would fetch your proof from the idiom of his language.

CHAP. XII.—CHRIST'S AUTHORITY OVER THE SABBATH. AS ITS LORD HE RECALLED IT FROM PHARISAIC NEGLECT TO THE ORIGINAL PUR-POSE OF ITS INSTITUTION BY THE CREATOR. THE CASE OF THE DISCIPLES WHO PLUCKED THE EARS OF CORN ON THE SABBATH. THE WITHERED HAND HEALED ON THE SABBATH.

Concerning the Sabbath also I have this to premise, that this question could not have arisen, if Christ did not publicly proclaim[2] the Lord of the Sabbath. Nor could there be any discussion about His annulling[3] the Sab-bath, if He had a right[4] to annul it. More-over, He would have the right, if He belonged to the rival god; nor would it cause surprise to any one that He did what it was right for Him to do. Men's astonishment therefore arose from their opinion that it was improper for Him to proclaim the Creator to be God, and yet to impugn His Sabbath. Now, that we may decide these several points first, lest we should be renewing them at every turn to meet each argument of our adversary which rests on some novel institution[5] of Christ, let this stand as a settled point, that discussion concerning the novel character of each insti-tution ensued on this account, because as nothing was as yet advanced *by Christ* touch-ing any new deity, so discussion thereon was inadmissible; nor could it be retorted, that from the very novelty of each several institu-tion another deity was clearly enough demon-strated by Christ, inasmuch as it was plain that novelty was not in itself a characteristic to be wondered at in Christ, because it had been foretold by the Creator. And it would have been, of course, but right that a new[6] god should first be expounded, and his disci-pline be introduced afterwards; because it would be the god that would impart authority to the discipline, and not the discipline to the god; except that (to be sure) it has happened that Marcion acquired his very perverse opinions not from a master, but his master from his opinion ! All other points respecting the Sabbath I thus rule. If Christ interfered

with[7] the Sabbath, He simply acted after the Creator's example; inasmuch as in the siege of the city of Jericho the carrying around the walls of the ark of the covenant for eight days running, and therefore on a Sabbath-day, actually[8] annulled the Sabbath, by the Cre-ator's command—according to the opinion of those who think this of Christ *in this passage of St. Luke,* in their ignorance that neither Christ nor the Creator violated the Sabbath, as we shall by and by show. And yet the Sabbath was actually then broken[9] by Joshua,[10] so that the present charge might be alleged also against Christ. But even if, as being not the Christ of the Jews, He displayed a hatred against the Jews' most solemn day, He was only professedly following[11] the Creator, as being His Christ, in this very hatred of the Sabbath; for He exclaims by the mouth of Isaiah: " Your new moons and your Sabbaths my soul hateth."[12] Now, in whatever sense these words were spoken, we know that an abrupt defence must, in a subject of this sort, be used in answer to an abrupt challenge. I shall now transfer the discussion to the very matter in which the teaching of Christ seemed to annul the Sabbath. The disciples had been hungry; on that *the Sabbath* day they had plucked some ears and rubbed them in their hands; by thus preparing their food, they had violated the holy day. Christ excuses them, and became their accomplice in breaking the Sabbath. The Pharisees bring the charge against Him. Marcion sophistically inter-prets the stages of the controversy (if I may call in the aid of the truth of my Lord to ridi-cule his arts), both in the scriptural record and in *Christ's* purpose.[13] For from the Crea-tor's Scripture, and from the purpose of Christ, there is derived a colourable prece-dent[14]—as from the example of David, when he went into the temple on the Sabbath, and provided food by boldly breaking up the shew-bread.[15] Even he remembered that this privi-lege (I mean the dispensation from fasting) was allowed to the Sabbath from the very beginning, when the Sabbath-day itself was instituted. For although the Creator had forbidden that the manna should be gathered for two days, He yet permitted it on the one occasion only of the day before the Sabbath,

---

[1] See Ps. lxxviii. 2.
[2] Circumferret.
[3] Cur destrueret.
[4] Deberet.
[5] Institutione: or, *teaching*, perhaps.
[6] Alium.

[7] Intervertit.
[8] Operatione.
[9] Concussum est sabbatum.
[10] Per Jesum.
[11] Professus . . . sequebatur.
[12] Isa. i. 14.
[13] This obscure passage runs thus in the original: " Marcion captat status controversiæ (ut aliquid ludam cum mei Domini veritate), scripti et voluntatis." *Status* is a technical word in rhetoric. " Est quæstio quæ ex prima causarum conflictione nas-citur." See Cicero, *Topic.* c. 25, *Part.* c. 29; and Quintilian, *Instit. Rhetor.* iii. 6. (Oehler).
[14] Sumitur color.
[15] Luke vi. 1-4; 1 Sam. xxi. 2-6.

in order that the yesterday's provision of food might free from fasting the feast of the following Sabbath-day. Good reason, therefore, had the Lord for pursuing the same principle in the annulling of the Sabbath (since that is the word which men will use); good reason, too, for expressing the Creator's will,[1] when He bestowed the privilege of not fasting on the Sabbath-day. In short, He would have then and there[2] put an end to the Sabbath, nay, to the Creator Himself, if He had commanded His disciples to fast on the Sabbath-day, contrary to the intention[3] of the Scripture and of the Creator's will. But because He did not directly defend[4] His disciples, but excuses them; because He interposes human want, as if deprecating censure; because He maintains the honour of the Sabbath as a day which is to be free from gloom rather than from work;[5] because he puts David and his companions on a level with His own disciples in their fault and their extenuation; because He is pleased to endorse[6] the Creator's indulgence;[7] because He is Himself good according to *His* example—is He therefore alien from the Creator? Then the Pharisees watch whether He would heal on the Sabbath-day,[8] that they might accuse Him—surely as a violator of the Sabbath, not as the propounder of a new god; for perhaps I might be content with insisting on all occasions on this one point, that another Christ[9] is nowhere proclaimed. The Pharisees, however, were in utter error concerning the law of the Sabbath, not observing that its terms were conditional, when it enjoined rest from labour, making certain distinctions of labour. For when it says of the Sabbath-day, "In it thou shalt not do any work of thine,"[10] by the word *thine*[11] it restricts the prohibition to human work—which every one performs in his own employment or business—and not to divine work. Now the work of healing or preserving is not proper to man, but to God. So again, in the law it says, "Thou shalt not do any manner of work in it,"[12] except what is to be done for any soul,[13] that is to say, in the matter of de-

livering the soul;[14] because what is God's work may be done by human agency for the salvation of the soul. By God, however, would that be done which the man Christ was to do, for He was likewise God.[15] Wishing, therefore, to initiate them into this meaning of the law by the restoration of the withered hand, He inquires, "Is it lawful on the Sabbath-days to do good, or not? to save life, or to destroy it?"[16] In order that He might, whilst allowing that amount of work which He was about to perform for a soul,[17] remind them what works the law of the Sabbath forbade—even human works; and what it enjoined—even divine works, which might be done for the benefit of any soul,[18] He was called "Lord of the Sabbath,"[19] because He maintained[20] the Sabbath as His own institution. Now, even if He had annulled the Sabbath, He would have had the right to do so,[21] as being its Lord, (and) still more as He who instituted it. But He did not utterly destroy it, although its Lord, in order that it might henceforth be plain that the Sabbath was not broken[22] by the Creator, even at the time when the ark was carried around Jericho. For that was really[23] God's work, which He commanded Himself, and which He had ordered for the sake of the lives of His servants when exposed to the perils of war. Now, although He has in a certain place expressed an aversion of Sabbaths, by calling them *your Sabbaths*,[24] reckoning them as men's Sabbaths, not His own, because they were celebrated without the fear of God by a people full of iniquities, and loving God "with the lip, not the heart,"[25] He has yet put His own Sabbaths (those, that is, which were kept according to His prescription) in a different position; for by the same prophet, in a later passage,[26] He declared them to be "true, and delightful, and inviolable." Thus Christ did not at all rescind the Sabbath: He kept the law thereof, and both in the former case did a work which was beneficial to the life of His disciples, for He indulged them with the relief of food when they were hungry, and in the present instance cured the withered hand; in each case in-

---

[1] Affectum.
[2] Tunc demum.
[3] Statum.
[4] Non constanter tuebatur.
[5] Non contristandi quam vacandi.
[6] [This adoption of an *Americanism* is worthy of passing notice.]
[7] Placet illi quia Creator indulsit.
[8] Luke vi. 7.
[9] That is, the Christ of another God.
[10] Ex. xx. 16
[11] It is impossible to say where Tertullian got this reading. Perhaps his LXX. copy might have had (in Ex. xx. 10): Οὐ ποιήσεις ἐν αὐτῇ πᾶν ἔργον σου, instead of σου; every clause ending in σου, which follows in that verse. No critical authority, however, now known warrants such a reading. [It is probably based inferentially on verse 9, "all *thy* work."]
[12] Ex. xii. 16.
[13] The LXX. of the latter clause of Ex. xii. 16 thus runs: πλὴν

ὅσα ποιηθήσεται πάσῃ ψυχῇ. Tertullian probably got this reading from this clause, although the Hebrew is to this effect: "Save that which every man (or, *every soul*) must eat," which the Vulgate renders: "Exceptis his, quæ ad vescendum pertinent."
[14] Liberandæ animæ: perhaps *saving life*.
[15] In salutem animæ: or, for saving life.
[16] Luke vi. 9.
[17] Pro anima : or, for a life.
[18] Animæ omni : or, any life,
[19] Luke vi. 5.
[20] Tuebatur.
[21] Merito.
[22] Destructum. We have, as has been most convenient, rendered this word by *annul, destroy break.*
[23] Et.
[24] Isa. i. 13, 14.
[25] Isa. xxix. 13.
[26] Isa. lviii. 13 and lvi. 2.

timating by facts, " I came not to destroy, the law, but to fulfil it, "[1] although Marcion has gagged [2] His mouth by this word.[3] For even in the case before us He fulfilled the law, while interpreting its condition; *moreover*, He exhibits in a clear light the different kinds of work, while doing what the law excepts from the sacredness of the Sabbath [4] *and* while imparting to the Sabbath-day itself, which from the beginning had been consecrated by the benediction of the Father, an additional sanctity by His own beneficent action. For He furnished to this day divine safeguards,[5]—a course which [6] His adversary would have pursued for some other days, to avoid honouring the Creator's Sabbath, and restoring to the Sabbath the works which were proper for it. Since, in like manner, the prophet Elisha on this day restored to life the dead son of the Shunammite woman,[7] you see, O Pharisee, and you too, O Marcion, how that it was *proper employment* for the Creator's Sabbaths of old [8] to do good, to save life, not to destroy it; how that Christ introduced nothing new, which was not after the example,[9] the gentleness, the mercy, and the prediction also of the Creator. For in this very example He fulfils [10] the prophetic announcement of a specific healing: " The weak hands are strengthened," as were also " the feeble knees " [11] in the sick of the palsy.

CHAP. XIII.—CHRIST'S CONNECTION WITH THE CREATOR SHOWN. MANY QUOTATIONS OUT OF THE OLD TESTAMENT PROPHETICALLY BEAR ON CERTAIN EVENTS OF THE LIFE OF JESUS—SUCH AS HIS ASCENT TO PRAYING ON THE MOUNTAIN; HIS SELECTION OF TWELVE APOSTLES; HIS CHANGING SIMON'S NAME TO PETER, AND GENTILES FROM TYRE AND SIDON RESORTING TO HIM.

Surely to Sion He brings good tidings, and to Jerusalem peace and all blessings; He goes up into a mountain, and there spends a night in prayer,[12] and He is indeed heard by the Father. Accordingly turn over the prophets, and learn therefrom His entire course.[13] " Into the high mountain," says Isaiah, " get Thee up, who bringest good tidings to Sion; lift up Thy voice with strength, who bringest good tidings to Jerusalem." [14] "They were mightily [15] astonished at His doctrine; for He was teaching as one who had power." [16] And again: " Therefore, my people shall know my name in that day." What name *does the prophet mean*, but Christ's? "That I am He that doth speak—even I." [17] For it was He who used to speak in the prophets—the Word, the Creator's Son. " I am present, while it is the hour, upon the mountains, as one that bringeth glad tidings of peace, as one that publisheth good tidings of good." [18] So one of the twelve (minor prophets), Nahum: " For behold upon the mountain the swift feet of Him that bringeth glad tidings of peace." [19] Moreover, concerning the voice of His prayer to the Father by night, the psalm manifestly says: " O my God, I will cry in the day-time, and Thou shalt hear; and in the night season, and it shall not be in vain to me." [20] In another passage touching the same voice and place, the psalm says: " I cried unto the Lord with my voice, and He heard me out of His holy mountain." [21] You have a representation of the name; you have the action of the Evangelizer; you have a mountain for the site; and the night as the time; and the sound of a voice; and the audience of the Father: you have, (in short,) the Christ of the prophets. But why was it that He chose *twelve* apostles,[22] and not some other number? In truth,[23] I might from this very point conclude [24] of my Christ, that He was foretold not only by the words of prophets, but by the indications of facts. For of this number I find figurative hints up and down the Creator's dispensation [25] in the twelve springs of Elim;[26] in the twelve gems of Aaron's priestly vestment;[27] and in the twelve stones appointed by Joshua to be taken out of the Jordan, and set up for the ark of the covenant. Now, the same number of apostles was thus portended, as if they were to be fountains and rivers which should water the Gentile world, which was formerly dry and destitute of knowledge (as He says by Isaiah: " I will put streams in the unwatered ground " [28]); as if they were to be gems to shed lustre upon the church's sacred

[1] Matt. v. 17.
[2] Obstruxit.
[3] " Destroy " . . . It was hardly necessary for Oehler to paraphrase our author's characteristically strong sentence by, " since Marcion *thought that he had* gagged," etc.
[4] In other words, " permits to be done on the Sabbath."
[5] Præsidia.
[6] Quod, not *quæ*, as if in apposition with *præsidia*.
[7] See 2 Kings iv. 23,
[8] Olim.
[9] Forma.
[10] Repræsentat.
[11] Isa. xxxv. 3.
[12] Luke vi. 12.
[13] Ordinem.
[14] Isa. xl. 9.
[15] In vigore. Or this phrase may qualify the noun thus: " They were astonished at His doctrine, *in its might.*"
[16] Luke iv. 32.
[17] Isa. lii. 6.
[18] Our author's reading of Isa. lii. 7.
[19] Nahum i. 15.
[20] Ps. xxii. 2.
[21] Ps. iii. 4.
[22] Luke vi. 13-19.
[23] Næ.
[24] Interpretari.
[25] Apud creatorem.
[26] Num. xxxiii. 9.
[27] Ex. xxviii. 13-21.
[28] Isa. xliii. 20.

robe, which Christ, the High Priest of the Father, puts on; as if, also, they were to be stones massive in their faith, which the true Joshua took out of the laver of the Jordan, and placed in the sanctuary of His covenant. What equally good defence of such a number has Marcion's Christ to show? It is impossible that anything can be shown to have been done by him unconnectedly,[1] which cannot be shown to have been done by my Christ in connection (with preceding types).[2] To him will appertain the event[3] in whom is discovered the preparation for the same.[4] Again, He changes the name of Simon to Peter,[5] inasmuch as the Creator also altered the names of Abram, and Sarai, and Oshea, by calling the latter Joshua, and adding a syllable to each of the former. But why *Peter*? If it was because of the vigour of his faith, there were many solid materials which might lend a name from their strength. Was it because Christ was both a rock and a stone? For we read of His being placed "for a stone of stumbling and for a rock of offence."[6] I omit the rest of the passage.[7] Therefore He would fain[8] impart to the dearest of His disciples a name which was suggested by one of His own especial designations in figure; because it was, I suppose, more peculiarly fit than a name which might have been derived from no figurative description of Himself.[9] There come to Him from Tyre, and from other districts even, a transmarine multitude. This fact the psalm had in view: "And behold tribes of foreign people, and Tyre, and the people of the Ethiopians; they were there. Sion is my mother, shall a man say; and in her was born a man" (forasmuch as the God-man was born), and He built her by the Father's will; that you may know how Gentiles then flocked to Him, because He was born the God-man who was to build the church according to the Father's will—even of other races also.[10] So says Isaiah too: "Behold, these come from far; and these from the north and from the west;"[11] and these from the land of the Persians."[12] Concerning whom He says again: "Lift up thine eyes round about, and behold, all these have gathered themselves together."[13] And yet again:

"Thou seest these unknown and strange ones; and thou wilt say in thine heart, Who hath begotten me these? But who hath brought me up these? And these, where have they been?"[14] Will such a Christ not be (the Christ) of the prophets? And what will be the Christ of the Marcionites? Since perversion of truth is their pleasure, he could not be (the Christ) of the prophets.

CHAP. XIV.—CHRIST'S SERMON ON THE MOUNT. IN MANNER AND CONTENTS IT SO RESEMBLES THE CREATOR'S DISPENSATIONAL WORDS AND DEEDS. IT SUGGESTS THEREFORE THE CONCLUSION THAT JESUS IS THE CREATOR'S CHRIST. THE BEATITUDES.

I now come to those ordinary precepts of His, by means of which He adapts the peculiarity[15] of His doctrine to what I may call His official proclamation as the Christ.[16] "Blessed are the needy" (for no less than this is required for interpreting the word in the Greek,[17] "because theirs is the kingdom of heaven."[18] Now this very fact, that He begins with beatitudes, is characteristic of the Creator, who used no other voice than that of blessing either in the first fiat or the final dedication of the universe: for "my heart," says He, "hath indited a very good word."[19] This will be that "very good word" of blessing which is admitted to be the initiating principle of the New Testament, after the example of the Old. What is there, then, to wonder at, if He entered *on His ministry* with the very attributes[20] of the Creator, who ever in language of the same sort loved, consoled, protected, *and* avenged the beggar, and the poor, and the humble, and the widow, and the orphan? So that you may believe this private bounty as it were of Christ to be a rivulet streaming from the springs of salvation. Indeed, I hardly know which way to turn amidst so vast a wealth of *good* words like these; as if I were in a forest, or a meadow, or an orchard of apples. I must therefore look out for such matter as chance may present to me.[21] In the psalm he exclaims: "Defend the fatherless and the needy; do justice to the humble and the poor; deliver the poor, and rid the needy out of the hand of the wicked."[22]

---

[1] Simpliciter: i.e., *simply*, or without relation to any types or prophecies.
[2] Non simpliciter.
[3] Res.
[4] Rei præparatura.
[5] Luke vi. 14. [Elucidation III.]
[6] Isa. viii. 14 ; Rom. ix. 33 ; 1 Pet. ii. 8.
[7] Cætera.
[8] Affectavit.
[9] De non suis: opposed to the *de figuris suis peculiariter*. [St. Peter was not the *dearest* of the Apostles though he was the *foremost*.]
[10] Ps. lxxxvii. 4, 5, according to the Septuagint.
[11] Mari.
[12] Isa. xlix. 12.
[13] Isa. xlix. 18.

[14] Isa. xlix. 21.
[15] Proprietatem.
[16] The original runs thus : " Venio nunc ad ordinarias sententias ejus, per quas proprietatem doctrinæ suæ inducit ad edictum, ut ita dixerim, Christi." There is here an allusion to the *edict* of the Roman prætor, that is, his *public announcement*, in which he states (when entering on his office) the rules by which he will be guided in the administration of the same (see White and Riddle, *Latin Dict. s. v.* Edictum).
[17] οἱ πτωχοί, not πένητες.
[18] Luke vi. 20.
[19] Ps. xlv. 1. [And see Vol. I. p. 213 *supra*.]
[20] Affectibus.
[21] Prout incidit.
[22] Ps. lxxxii. 3, 4.

Similarly in the seventy-first Psalm: "In righteousness shall He judge the needy amongst the people, and shall save the children of the poor." [1] And in the following words he says of Christ: "All nations shall serve Him." [2] Now David only reigned over the Jewish nation, so that nobody can suppose that this was spoken of David; whereas *He* had taken upon Himself the condition of the poor, and such as were oppressed with want, "Because He should deliver the needy out of the hand of the mighty man; He shall spare the needy and the poor, and shall deliver the souls of the poor. From usury and injustice shall He redeem their souls, and in His sight shall their name be honoured." [3] Again: "The wicked shall be turned into hell, even all the nations that forget God; because the needy shall not alway be forgotten; the endurance of the poor shall not perish for ever." [4] Again: "Who is like unto the Lord our God, who dwelleth on high, and yet looketh on the humble things that are in heaven and on earth!—who raiseth up the needy from off the ground, and out of the dunghill exalteth the poor; that He may set him with the princes of His people," [5] that is, in His own kingdom. And likewise earlier, in the book of Kings, [6] Hannah the mother of Samuel gives glory to God in these words: "He raiseth the poor man from the ground, and the beggar, that He may set him amongst the princes of His people (that is, in His own kingdom), and on thrones of glory" (even royal ones)." [7] And by Isaiah how He inveighs against the oppressors of the needy! "What mean ye that ye set fire to my vineyard, and that the spoil of the poor is in your houses? Wherefore do ye beat my people to pieces, and grind the face of the needy?" [8] And again: "Woe unto them that decree unrighteous decrees; for in their decrees they decree wickedness, turning aside the needy from judgment, and taking away their rights from the poor of my people." [9] These righteous judgments He requires for the fatherless also, and the widows, as well as for consolation [10] to the very needy themselves. "Do justice to the fatherless, and deal justly with the widow; and come, let us be reconciled, [11] saith the Lord." [12] To him, for whom in every stage of lowliness there is provided so much of the Creator's compassionate regard, shall be given that kingdom also which is promised by Christ, to whose merciful compassion belong, and for a great while have belonged, [13] those to whom the promise is made. For even if you suppose that the promises of the Creator were earthly, but that Christ's are heavenly, it is quite clear that heaven has been as yet the property of no other God whatever, than Him who owns the earth also; quite clear that the Creator has given even the lesser promises (of earthly blessing), in order that I may more readily believe Him concerning His greater promises (of heavenly blessings) also, than (Marcion's god), who has never given proof of his liberality by any preceding bestowal of minor blessings. "Blessed are they that hunger, for they shall be filled." [14] I might connect this clause with the former one, because none but the poor and needy suffer hunger, if the Creator had not specially designed that the promise of a similar blessing should serve as a preparation for the gospel, that so men might know it to be His. [15] For thus does He say, by Isaiah, concerning those whom He was about to call from the ends of the earth—that is, the Gentiles: "Behold, they shall come swiftly with speed:" [16] *swiftly*, because hastening towards the fulness of the times; *with speed*, because unclogged by the weights of the ancient law. They shall neither hunger nor thirst. Therefore *they shall be filled*,—a promise which is made to none but those who hunger and thirst. And again He says: "Behold, my servants shall be filled, but ye shall be hungry; behold, my servants shall drink, but ye shall be thirsty." [17] As for these oppositions, we shall see whether they are not premonitors of Christ. [18] Meanwhile the promise of fulness to the hungry is a provision of God the Creator. "Blessed are they that weep, for they shall laugh." [19] Turn again to the passage of Isaiah: "Behold, my servants shall exult with joy, but ye shall be ashamed; behold, my servants shall be glad, but ye shall cry for sorrow of heart." [20] And recognise these oppositions also in the dispensation of Christ. Surely gladness and joyous exultation is promised to those who are in an opposite condition—to the sorrowful, and sad, and anxious. Just as it is said in the 125th Psalm: "They who sow in tears shall reap in joy." [21] Moreover, laughter is as much an

---

[1] Ps. lxxii. 4.
[2] Ps. lxxii. 11.
[3] Ps. lxxii. 12, 13, 14.
[4] Ps. ix. 17, 18.
[5] Ps. cxiii. 5-8.
[6] The books of "Samuel" were also called the books of "Kings."
[7] 1 Sam. ii. 8.
[8] Isa. iii. 14, 15.
[9] Isa. x. 1, 2.
[10] Solatii.
[11] Tertullian seems to have read διαλλαχθῶμεν instead of διαλεχθῶμεν, *let us reason together*, in his LXX.
[12] Isa. i. 17, 18.

[13] Jamdudum pertinent.
[14] Luke vi. 21.
[15] In evangelii scilicet sui præstructionem.
[16] Isa. v. 26.
[17] Isa. lxv. 13.
[18] An Christo præministrentur.
[19] Luke vi. 21.
[20] Isa. lxv. 13, 14.
[21] Ps. cxxvi. 5.

accessory to the exulting and glad, as weeping is to the sorrowful and grieving. Therefore the Creator, in foretelling matters for laughter and tears, was the first who said that those who mourned should laugh. Accordingly, He who began (His course) with consolation for the poor, and the humble, and the hungry, and the weeping, was at once eager[1] to represent Himself as Him whom He had pointed out by the mouth of Isaiah: "The Spirit of the Lord is upon me, because He hath anointed me to preach good tidings unto the poor."[2] "Blessed are the needy, because theirs is the kingdom of heaven."[3] "He hath sent me to bind up the broken-hearted."[4] "Blessed are they that hunger, for they shall be filled."[5] "To comfort all that mourn."[6] "Blessed are they that weep, for they shall laugh."[7] "To give unto them that mourn in Sion, beauty (or glory) for ashes, and the oil of joy for mourning, and the garment of praise for the spirit of heaviness."[8] Now since Christ, as soon as He entered on His course,[9] fulfilled such a ministration as this, He is either, Himself, He who predicted His own coming to do all this; or else if he is not yet come who predicted this, the charge to Marcion's Christ must be a ridiculous one (although I should perhaps add a necessary[10] one), which bade him say, "Blessed shall ye be, when men shall hate you, and shall reproach you, and shall cast out your name as evil, for the Son of man's sake."[11] In this declaration there is, no doubt, an exhortation to patience. Well, what did the Creator say otherwise by Isaiah? "Fear ye not the reproach of men, nor be diminished by their contempt."[12] What reproach? what contempt? That which was to be incurred for the sake of the Son of man. What Son of man? He who (is come) according to the Creator's will. Whence shall we get our proof? From the very cutting off, which was predicted against Him; as when He says by Isaiah to the Jews, who were the instigators of hatred against Him: "Because of you, my name is blasphemed amongst the Gentiles;"[13] and in another passage: "Lay the penalty on[14] Him who surrenders[15] His own life, who is held in contempt by the Gen-

tiles, whether servants or magistrates."[16] Now, since hatred was predicted against that Son of man who has His mission from the Creator, whilst the Gospel testifies that the name of Christians, as derived from Christ, was to be hated for the Son of man's sake, because He is Christ, it determines the point that that was the Son of man in the matter of hatred who came according to the Creator's purpose, and against whom the hatred was predicted. And even if He had not yet come, the hatred of His name which exists at the present day could not in any case have possibly preceded Him who was to bear the name.[17] But He has both suffered the penalty[18] in our presence, and surrendered His life, laying it down for our sakes, and is held in contempt by the Gentiles. And He who was born (into the world) will be that very Son of man on whose account our name also is rejected.

CHAP. XV.—SERMON ON THE MOUNT CONTINUED. ITS WOES IN STRICT AGREEMENT WITH THE CREATOR'S DISPOSITION. MANY QUOTATIONS OUT OF THE OLD TESTAMENT IN PROOF OF THIS.

"In the like manner," says He,[19] "did their fathers unto the prophets." What a turncoat[20] is *Marcion's* Christ! Now the destroyer, now the advocate of the prophets! He destroyed them as their rival, by converting their disciples; he took up their cause as their friend, by stigmatizing[21] their persecutors. But,[22] in *as* far as the defence of the prophets could not be consistent in the Christ of Marcion, who came to destroy them; in *so* far is it becoming to the Creator's Christ that He should stigmatize those who persecuted the prophets, for He in all things accomplished their predictions. Again, it is more characteristic of the Creator to upbraid sons with their fathers' sins, than it is of that god who chastizes no man for even his own misdeeds. But you will say, He cannot be regarded as defending the prophets simply because He wished to affirm the iniquity of the Jews for their impious dealings with their own prophets. Well, then, in this case,[23] no sin ought to have been charged against the Jews: they were rather deserving of praise and approbation when they maltreated[24] those whom

[1] Gestivit.
[2] Isa. lxi. 1.
[3] Luke vi. 20.
[4] Isa. lxi. 1.
[5] Luke vi. 21.
[6] Isa. lxi. 2.
[7] Luke vi. 21.
[8] Isa. lxi. 3.
[9] Statim admissus.
[10] Said in irony, as if Marcion's Christ deserved the rejection.
[11] Luke vi. 22.
[12] His reading of Isa. li. 7.
[13] Isa. lii. 5.
[14] Sancite.
[15] Circumscribit,

[16] Famulis et magistratibus. It is uncertain what passage this quotation represents. It sounds like some of the clauses of Isa. liii.
[17] Personam nominis.
[18] Sancitur.
[19] Luke vi. 26.
[20] Versipellem. An indignant exclamation on Marcion's Christ.
[21] Suggillans.
[22] Porro.
[23] Hic.
[24] Suggillaverunt. This is Oehler's emendation; the common reading is *figuraverunt.*

the absolutely good god *of Marcion*, after so long a time, bestirred himself[1] to destroy. I suppose, however, that by this time he had ceased to be the absolutely good god;[2] he had now sojourned a considerable while even with the Creator, and was no longer (like) the god of Epicurus[3] purely and simply. For see how he condescends[4] to curse, and proves himself capable of taking offence and feeling anger! He actually pronounces a *woe!* But a doubt is raised against us as to the import of this word, as if it carried with it less the sense of a curse than of an admonition. Where, however, is the difference, since even an admonition is not given without the sting of a threat, especially when it is embittered with a *woe?* Moreover, both admonition and threatening will be the resources of him[5] who knows how to feel angry. For no one will forbid the doing of a thing with an admonition or a threat, except him who will inflict punishment for the doing of it. No one would inflict punishment, except him who was susceptible of anger. Others, again, admit that the word implies a curse; but they will have it that Christ pronounced the woe, not as if it were His own genuine feeling, but because the woe is from the Creator, and He wanted to set forth to them the severity of the Creator, in order that He might the more commend His own long-suffering[6] in His beatitudes. Just as if it were not competent to the Creator, in the pre-eminence of both His attributes as the good God and Judge, that, as He had made clemency[7] the preamble of His benediction so He should place severity in the sequel of His curses; thus fully developing His discipline in both directions, both in following out the blessing and in providing against the curse.[8] He had already said of old, "Behold, I have set before you blessing and cursing."[9] Which statement was really a presage of[10] this temper of the gospel. Besides, what sort of being is that who, to insinuate a belief in his own goodness, invidiously contrasted[11] with it the Creator's severity? Of little worth is the recommendation which has for its prop the defamation of another. And yet by thus setting forth the severity of the Creator, he, in fact, affirmed Him to be an object of fear.[12] Now if He be an object of fear, He is of course more worthy of being

obeyed than slighted; and thus Marcion's Christ begins to teach favourably to the Creator's interests.[13] Then, *on the admission above mentioned*, since the woe which has regard to the rich is the Creator's, it follows that it is not Christ, but the Creator, who is angry with the rich; while Christ approves of[14] the incentives of the rich[15]—I mean, their pride, their pomp,[16] their love of the world, and their contempt of God, owing to which they deserve the woe of the Creator. But how happens it that the reprobation of the rich does not proceed from the same *God* who had just before expressed approbation of the poor? There is nobody but reprobates the opposite of that which he has approved. If, therefore, there be imputed to the Creator the woe pronounced against the rich, there must be claimed for Him also the promise of the blessing upon the poor; and thus the entire work of the Creator devolves on Christ.—If to Marcion's god there be ascribed the blessing of the poor, he must also have imputed to him the malediction of the rich; and thus will he become the Creator's equal,[17] both good and judicial; nor will there be left any room for that distinction whereby two gods are made; and when this distinction is removed, there will remain the verity which pronounces the Creator to be the one only God. Since, therefore, "*woe*" is a word indicative of malediction, or of some unusually austere[18] exclamation; and since it is by Christ uttered against the rich, I shall have to show that the Creator is also a despiser[19] of the rich, as I have shown Him to be the defender[20] of the poor, in order that I may prove Christ to be on the Creator's side in this matter, even when He enriched Solomon.[21] But *with respect to this man*, since, when a choice was left to him, he preferred asking for what he knew to be well-pleasing to God—even wisdom—he further merited the attainment of the riches, which he did not prefer. The endowing of a man indeed with riches, is not an incongruity to God, for by the help of riches even rich men are comforted and assisted; moreover, by them many a work of justice and charity is carried out. But yet there are serious faults[22] which accompany riches; and it is because of these that woes are denounced on the rich, even in the Gospel. "Ye have received," says He, "your consolation;"[23] that is, of course, from

[1] Motus est.
[2] Deus optimus.
[3] That is, apathetic, inert, and careless about human affairs.
[4] Demutat.
[5] Ejus erunt.
[6] Sufferentiam.
[7] Benignitatem.
[8] Ad maledictionem præcavendam.
[9] Deut. xxx. 19.
[10] Portendebat in.
[11] Opposuit.
[12] Timendum.
[13] Creatori docere.
[14] Ratas habet.
[15] Divitum causas.
[16] Gloriam.
[17] Erit par creatoris.
[18] Austerioris.
[19] Aspernatorem.
[20] Advocatorem.
[21] 1 Kings iii. 5-13.
[22] Vitia.
[23] Luke vi. 24. [See Southey's *Wesley*, on " Riches," vol. ii. p.310.]

their riches, in the pomps and vanities of the world which these purchase for them. Accordingly, in Deuteronomy, Moses says: "Lest, when thou hast eaten and art full, and hast built goodly houses, and when thy herds and thy flocks multiply, as well as thy silver and thy gold, thine heart be then lifted up, and thou forget the Lord thy God."[1] In similar terms, when king Hezekiah became proud of his treasures, and gloried in them rather than in God before those who had come on an embassy from Babylon,[2] (the Creator) breaks forth[3] against him by the mouth of Isaiah: "Behold, the days come when all that is in thine house, and that which thy fathers have laid up in store, shall be carried to Babylon."[4] So by Jeremiah likewise did He say: "Let not the rich man glory in his riches; but let him that glorieth even glory in the Lord."[5] Similarly against the daughters of Sion does He inveigh by Isaiah, when they were haughty through their pomp and the abundance of their riches,[6] just as in another passage He utters His threats against the proud and noble: "Hell hath enlarged herself, and opened her mouth, and down to it shall descend the illustrious, and the great, and the rich (this shall be Christ's 'woe to the rich'); and man[7] shall be humbled," even he that exalts himself with riches; "and the mighty man[8] shall be dishonoured," even he who is mighty from his wealth.[9] Concerning whom He says again: "Behold, the Lord of hosts shall confound the pompous together with their strength: those that are lifted up shall be hewn down, and such as are lofty shall fall by the sword."[10] And who are these but the rich? Because they have indeed received their consolation, glory, and honour, and a lofty position from their wealth. In Ps. xlviii. He also turns off our care from these, and says: "Be not thou afraid when one is made rich, and when his glory is increased: for when he shall die, he shall carry nothing away; nor shall his glory descend along with him."[11] So also in Ps. lxi.: "Do not desire riches; and if they do yield you their lustre,[12] do not set your heart upon them."[13] Lastly, this very same *woe* is pronounced of old by Amos against the rich, who also abounded in delights. "Woe unto them," says he, "who

sleep upon beds of ivory, and deliciously stretch themselves upon their couches; who eat the kids from the flocks of the goats, and sucking calves from the flocks of the heifers, while they chant to the sound of the viol; as if they thought they should continue long, and were not fleeting; who drink their refined wines, and anoint themselves with the costliest ointments."[14] Therefore, even if I could do nothing else than show that the Creator dissuades men from riches, without at the same time first condemning the rich, in the very same terms in which Christ also did, no one could doubt that, from the same authority, there was added a commination against the rich in that woe of Christ, from whom also had first proceeded the dissuasion against the material sin of these persons, that is, their riches. For such commination is the necessary sequel to such a dissuasive. He inflicts a woe also on "the full, because they shall hunger; on those too which laugh now, because they shall mourn."[15] To these will correspond these opposites which occur, as we have seen above, in the benedictions of the Creator: "Behold, my servants shall be full, but ye shall be hungry"—even because ye have been filled; "behold, my servants shall rejoice, but ye shall be ashamed"[16]—even ye who shall mourn, who now are laughing. For as it is written in the psalm, "They who sow in tears shall reap in joy,"[17] so does it run in the Gospel: They who sow in laughter, that is, in joy, shall reap in tears. These principles did the Creator lay down of old; and Christ has renewed them, by simply bringing them into prominent view,[18] not by making any change in them. "Woe unto you, when all men shall speak well of you! for so did their fathers to the false prophets."[19] With equal stress does the Creator, by His prophet Isaiah, censure those who seek after human flattery and praise: "O my people, they who call you happy mislead you, and disturb the paths of your feet."[20] In another passage He forbids all implicit trust in man, and likewise in the applause of man; as by the prophet Jeremiah: "Cursed be the man that trusteth in man."[21] Whereas in Ps. cxvii. it is said: "It is better to trust in the Lord than to put confidence in man; it is better to trust in the Lord than to place hope in princes."[22] Thus everything which is caught at by men is adjured by the Creator, down to their good

---

[1] Deut. viii. 12–14.
[2] Tertullian says, *ex Perside*.
[3] Insilit.
[4] Isa. xxxix. 6.
[5] Jer. ix. 23, 24.
[6] Isa. iii. 16–24.
[7] Homo: "the mean man," A.V.
[8] Vir.
[9] Isa. v. 14.
[10] Isa. x. 33.
[11] Ps. xlix. 16, 17.
[12] Relucent.
[13] Ps. lxii. 11.

[14] Amos vi. 1–6.
[15] Luke vi. 25.
[16] Isa. lxv. 13.
[17] Ps. cxxvi. 5.
[18] Distinguendo.
[19] Luke vi. 26.
[20] Isa. iii. 12.
[21] Jer. xvii. 5.
[22] Ps. cxviii. 8, 9.

24

words.[1] It is as much His property to condemn the praise and flattering words bestowed on the false prophets by their fathers, as to condemn their vexatious and persecuting treatment of the (true) prophets. As the injuries suffered by the prophets could not be imputed[2] to their own God, so the applause bestowed on the false prophets could not have been displeasing to any other god but the God of the *true* prophets.

CHAP. XVI.—THE PRECEPT OF LOVING ONE'S ENEMIES. IT IS AS MUCH TAUGHT IN THE CREATOR'S SCRIPTURES OF THE OLD TESTAMENT AS IN CHRIST'S SERMON. THE LEX TALIONIS OF MOSES ADMIRABLY EXPLAINED IN CONSISTENCY WITH THE KINDNESS AND LOVE WHICH JESUS CHRIST CAME TO PROCLAIM AND ENFORCE IN BEHALF OF THE CREATOR. SUNDRY PRECEPTS OF CHARITY EXPLAINED.

"But I say unto you which hear" (displaying here that old injunction, of the Creator: "Speak to the ears of those who lend them to you"[3]), "Love your enemies, and bless[4] those which hate you, and pray for them which calumniate you."[5] These commands the Creator included in one precept by His prophet Isaiah: "Say, Ye are our brethren, to those who hate you."[6] For if they who are our enemies, and hate us, and speak evil of us, and calumniate us, are to be called our brethren, surely He did in effect bid us bless them that hate us, and pray for them who calumniate us, when He instructed us to reckon them as brethren. Well, but Christ plainly teaches a new kind of patience,[7] when He actually prohibits the reprisals which the Creator permitted in requiring "an eye for an eye,"[8] and a tooth for a tooth,"[9] and bids us, on the contrary, "to him who smiteth us on the one cheek, to offer the other also, and to give up our coat to him that taketh away our cloak."[10] No doubt these are supplementary additions by Christ, but they are quite in keeping with the teaching of the Creator. And therefore this question must at once be determined,[11] Whether the discipline of patience be enjoined by[12] the Creator? When by Zechariah He commanded, "Let none of you imagine evil against his *brother*,"[13] He did not expressly include his *neighbour;* but then in another passage He says, "Let none of you imagine evil in your hearts against his *neighbour*."[14] He who counselled that an injury should be forgotten, was still more likely to counsel the patient endurance of it. But then, when He said, "Vengeance is mine, and I will repay,"[15] He thereby teaches that patience calmly waits for the infliction of vengeance. Therefore, inasmuch as it is incredible[16] that the same (God) should seem to require "a tooth for a tooth and an eye for an eye," in return for an injury, who forbids not only all reprisals, but even a revengeful thought or recollection of an injury, in so far does it become plain to us in what sense He required "an eye for an eye and a tooth for a tooth,"—not, indeed, for the purpose of permitting the repetition of the injury by retaliating it, which it virtually prohibited when it forbade vengeance; but for the purpose of restraining the injury in the first instance, which it had forbidden on pain of retaliation or reciprocity;[17] so that every man, in view of the permission to inflict a second (or retaliatory) injury, might abstain from the commission of the first (or provocative) wrong. For He knows how much more easy it is to repress violence by the prospect of retaliation, than by the promise of (indefinite) vengeance. Both results, however, it was necessary to provide, in consideration of the nature and the faith of men, that the man who believed in God might expect vengeance from God, while he who had no faith (to restrain him) might fear the laws which prescribed retaliation.[18] This purpose[19] of the law, which it was difficult to understand, Christ, as the Lord of the Sabbath and of the law, and of all the dispensations of the Father, both revealed and made intelligible,[20] when He commanded that "the other cheek should be offered (to the smiter)," in order that He might the more effectually extinguish all reprisals of an injury, which the law had wished to prevent by the method of retaliation, (and) which most certainly revelation[21] had manifestly restricted, both by prohibiting the memory of the wrong, and referring the vengeance thereof to God. Thus, whatever (new

---

[1] Nedum benedictionem.
[2] Non pertinuissent ad.
[3] 2 Esdras xv. 1, and comp. Luke vi. 27, 28.
[4] Benedicite. St. Luke's word, however, is καλῶς ποιεῖτε, "do good."
[5] Calumniantur. St. Luke's word applies to injury of *speech* as well as of *act.*
[6] Isa. lxvi. 5.
[7] "We have here the sense of Marcion's objection. I do not suppose Tertullian quotes his very words."—LE PRIEUR.
[8] Le Prieur refers to a similar passage in Tertullian's *De Patientia*, chap. vi. Oehler quotes an eloquent passage in illustration from Valerianus Episc. *Hom.* xiii.
[9] Ex. xxi. 24.
[10] Luke vi. 29.
[11] Renuntiandum est.

[12] Penes.
[13] Zech. vii. 10.
[14] Zech. viii. 17.
[15] Deut. xxxii. 35; comp. Rom. xii. 19 and Heb. x. 30.
[16] Fidem non capit.
[17] Talione, opposito.
[18] Leges talionis. [Judicial, not personal, reprisals.]
[19] Voluntatem.
[20] Compotem facit. That is, says Oehler, *intellectus sui.*
[21] Prophetia.

provision) Christ introduced, He did it not in opposition to the law, but rather in further-ance of it, without at all impairing the pre-scription[1] of the Creator. If, therefore,[2] one looks carefully[3] into the very grounds for which patience is enjoined (and *that* to such a full and complete extent), one finds that it cannot stand if it is not the precept of the Creator, who promises vengeance, who pre-sents Himself as the judge (in the case). If it were not so,[4]—if so vast a weight of patience —which is to refrain from giving blow for blow; which is to offer the other cheek; which is not only not to return railing for railing, but contrariwise blessing; and which, so far from keeping the coat, is to give up the cloak also —is laid upon me by one who means not to help me,—(then all I can say is,) he has taught me patience to no purpose,[5] because he shows me no reward to his precept—I mean no fruit of such patience. There is re-venge which he ought to have permitted me to take, if he meant not to inflict it himself; if he did not give me that permission, then he should himself have inflicted it;[6] since it is for the interest of discipline itself that an in-jury should be avenged. For by the fear of vengeance all iniquity is curbed. But if li-cence is allowed to it without discrimination,[7] it will get the mastery—it will put out (a man's) both eyes; it will knock out[8] every tooth in the safety of its impunity. This, however, is (the principle) of your good and simply beneficent god—to do a wrong to patience, to open the door to violence, to leave the righteous undefended, and the wicked unre-strained! " Give to every one that asketh of thee "[9]—to the indigent of course, or rather to the indigent more especially, although not to the affluent likewise. But in order that no man may be indigent, you have in Deuterono-my a provision commanded by the Creator to the creditor.[10] " There shall not be in thine hand an indigent man; so that the Lord thy God shall bless thee with blessings," [11]—*thee* meaning the creditor to whom it was owing that the man was not indigent. But more than this. To one who does not ask, He bids a gift to be given. " Let there be, not," He says, " a poor man in thine hand; " in other words, see that there be not, so far as thy will can prevent;[12] by which command, too, He

all the more strongly by inference requires[13] men to give to him that asks, as in the following words also: " If there be among you a poor man of thy brethren, thou shalt not turn away thine heart, nor shut thine hand from thy poor brother. But thou shalt open thine hand wide unto him, and shalt surely lend him as much as he wanteth." [14] Loans are not usually given, except to such as ask for them. On this subject of lending,[15] however, more here-after.[16] Now, should any one wish to argue that the Creator's precepts extended only to a man's brethren, but Christ's to all that ask, so as to make the latter a new and different precept, (I have to reply) that one rule only can be made out of those principles, which show the law of the Creator to be repeated in Christ.[17] For that is not a different thing which Christ enjoined to be done towards all men, from that which the Creator prescribed in favour of a man's brethren. For although that is a greater charity, which is shown to strangers, it is yet not preferable to that[18] which was previously due to one's neighbours. For what man will be able to bestow the love (which proceeds from knowledge of character,[19] upon strangers? Since, however, the second step[20] in charity is towards strangers, while the first is towards one's neighbours, the second step will belong to him to whom the first also belongs, more fitly than the second will belong to him who owned no first.[21] Ac-cordingly, the Creator, when following the course of nature, taught in the first instance kindness to *neighbours*,[22] intending afterwards to enjoin it towards *strangers;* and when fol-lowing the method of His dispensation, He limited charity first to the Jews, but afterwards extended it to the whole race of mankind. So long, therefore, as the mystery *of His govern-ment*[23] was confined to Israel, He properly commanded that pity should be shown only to a man's brethren; but when Christ had given to Him " the Gentiles for His heritage, and the ends of the earth for His possession," then began to be accomplished what was said by Hosea: " Ye are not my people, who were my people; ye have not obtained mercy, who

---

[1] Disciplinas: or, " lessons."
[2] Denique.
[3] Consideram, or, as some of the editions have it, *consideremus.*
[4] Alioquin.
[5] In vacuum.
[6] Præstare, i.e. debuerat præstare.
[7] Passim.
[8] Excitatura.
[9] Luke vi. 30.
[10] Datori.
[11] The author's reading of Deut. xv. 4.
[12] Cura ultro ne sit.

[13] Præjudicat.
[14] Deut. xv. 7, 8.
[15] De fenore.
[16] Below, in the next chapter.
[17] This obscure passage runs thus: " Immo unum erit ex his per quæ lex Creatoris erit in Christo."
[18] Prior ea.
[19] This is the idea, apparently, of Tertullian's question: " Quis enim poterit *diligere* extraneos ? " But a different turn is given to the sense in the older reading of the passage : Quis enim non diligens proximos poterit diligere extraneos ? " For who that loveth not his neighbours will be able to love strangers ? " The inserted words, however, were inserted conjecturally by Fulvius Ursinus without MS. authority.
[20] Gradus.
[21] Cujus non extitit primus
[22] In proximos.
[23] Sacramentum.

once obtained mercy''[1]—that is, the (Jewish) nation. Thenceforth Christ extended to all men the law of His Father's compassion, excepting none from His mercy, as He omitted none in His invitation. So that, whatever was the ampler scope of His teaching, He received it all in His heritage of the nations. "And as ye would that men should do to you, do ye also to them likewise."[2] In this command is no doubt implied its counterpart: "And as ye would *not* that men should do to you, so should ye also *not* do to them likewise." Now, if this were the teaching of the new and previously unknown and not yet fully proclaimed deity, who had favoured me with no instruction beforehand, whereby I might first learn what I ought to choose or to refuse for myself, and to do to others what I would wish done to myself, not doing to them what I should be unwilling to have done to myself, it would certainly be nothing else than the chance-medley of my own sentiments[3] which he would have left to me, binding me to no proper rule of wish or action, in order that I might do to others what I would like for myself, or refrain from doing to others what I should dislike to have done to myself. For he has not, in fact, defined what I ought to wish or not to wish for myself as well as for others, so that I shape my conduct[4] according to the law of my own will, and have it in my power[5] not to render[6] to another what I would like to have rendered to myself—love, obedience, consolation, protection, and such like blessings; and in like manner to do to another what I should be unwilling to have done to myself—violence, wrong, insult, deceit, and evils of like sort. Indeed, the heathen who have not been instructed by God act on this incongruous liberty of the will and the conduct.[7] For although good and evil are severally known by nature, yet life is not thereby spent[8] under the discipline of God, which alone at last teaches men the proper liberty of their will and action in faith, as in the fear of God. The god of Marcion, therefore, although specially revealed, was, in spite of his revelation, unable to publish any summary of the precept in question, which had hitherto been so confined,[9] and obscure, and dark, and admitting of no ready interpretation, except according to my own arbitrary thought,[10] because he had provided no previous discrimina-

tion in the matter of such a precept. This, however, was not the case with my God, for[11] He always and everywhere enjoined that the poor, and the orphan, and the widow should be protected, assisted, refreshed; thus by Isaiah He says: "Deal thy bread to the hungry, and them that are houseless bring into thine house; when thou seest the naked, cover him."[12] By Ezekiel also He thus describes the just man: "His bread will he give to the hungry, and the naked will he cover with a garment."[13] That teaching was even then a sufficient inducement to me to do to others what I would that they should do unto me. Accordingly, when He uttered such denunciations as, "Thou shalt do no murder; thou shalt not commit adultery; thou shalt not steal; thou shalt not bear false witness,"[14]—He taught me to refrain from doing to others what I should be unwilling to have done to myself; and therefore the precept developed in the Gospel will belong to Him alone, who anciently drew it up, and gave it distinctive point, and arranged it after the decision of His own teaching, and has now reduced it, suitably to its importance,[15] to a compendious formula, because (as it was predicted in another passage) the Lord—that is, Christ—"was to make (or utter) a concise word on earth."[16]

CHAP. XVII.—CONCERNING LOANS. PROHIBITION OF USURY AND THE USURIOUS SPIRIT. THE LAW PREPARATORY TO THE GOSPEL IN ITS PROVISIONS; SO IN THE PRESENT INSTANCE. ON REPRISALS. CHRIST'S TEACHING THROUGHOUT PROVES HIM TO BE SENT BY THE CREATOR.

And now, on the subject of a loan, when He asks, "And if ye lend to them of whom ye hope to receive, what thank have ye?"[17] compare with this the following words of Ezekiel, in which He says of the before-mentioned just man, "He hath not given his money upon usury, nor will he take any increase"[18]—meaning the redundance of interest,[19] which is usury. The first step was to eradicate the fruit of the money lent,[20] the more easily to accustom a man to the loss, should it happen, of the money *itself*, the in-

---

[1] The sense rather than the words of Hos. i. 6, 9.
[2] Luke vi. 31.
[3] Passivitatem sententiæ meæ.
[4] Parem factum.
[5] Possim.
[6] Præstare.
[7] Hac inconvenientia voluntatis et facti.　Will and action.
[8] Non agitur.
[9] Strictum.
[10] Pro meo arbitrio.

[11] At enim.　The Greek ἀλλὰ γάρ.
[12] Isa. lviii. 7.
[13] Ezek. xviii. 7.
[14] Ex. xx. 13–16.
[15] Merito.
[16] "Recisum sermonem facturus in terris Dominus." This reading of Isa. x. 23 is very unlike the original, but (as frequently happens in Tertullian) is close upon the Septuagint version: Ὅτι λόγον συντετμημένον Κύριος ποιήσει ἐν τῇ οἰκουμένῃ ὅλῃ. [Rom. ix. 28.]
[17] Luke vi. 34.　[Bossuet, *Traité de l'usure*, Opp. ix. 48.]
[18] Ezek. xviii. 8.　[Huet, *Règne Social*, etc., p. 334. Paris, 1858.]
[19] Literally, what redounds to the loan.
[20] Fructum fenoris: the interest.

terest of which he had learnt to lose. Now this, we affirm, was the function of the law as preparatory to the gospel. It was engaged in forming the faith of such as would learn,[1] by gradual stages, for the perfect light of the Christian discipline, through the best precepts of which it was capable,[2] inculcating a benevolence which as yet expressed itself but falteringly.[3] For *in the passage of Ezekiel* quoted above He says, "And thou shalt restore the pledge of the loan"[4]—to him, certainly, who is incapable of repayment, because, as a matter of course, He would not anyhow prescribe the restoration of a pledge to one who was solvent. Much more clearly is it enjoined in Deuteronomy: "Thou shalt not sleep upon his pledge; thou shalt be sure to return to him his garment about sunset, and he shall sleep in his own garment."[5] Clearer still is a former passage: "Thou shalt remit every debt which thy neighbour oweth thee; and of thy brother thou shalt not require it, because it is called the release of the Lord thy God."[6] Now, when He commands that a debt be remitted to a man who shall be unable to pay it (for it is a still stronger argument when He forbids its being asked for from a man who is even able to repay it), what else does He teach than that we should lend to those of whom we cannot receive again, inasmuch as He has imposed so great a loss on lending? "And ye shall be the children of God."[7] What can be more shameless, than for him to be making us his *children*, who has not permitted us to make children for ourselves by forbidding marriage?[8] How does he propose to invest his followers with a name which he has already erased? I cannot be the son of a eunuch! Especially when I have for my Father the same great Being whom the universe claims for its! For is not the Founder of the universe as much a Father, even of all men, as (Marcion's) castrated deity,[9] who is the maker of no existing thing? Even if the Creator had not united male and female, and if He had not allowed any living creature whatever to have children, I yet had this relation to Him[10] before Paradise, before the fall, before the expulsion, before the two became one.[11]

I became His son a second time,[12] as soon as He fashioned me[13] with His hands, and gave me motion with His inbreathing. Now again He names me His son, not begetting me into natural life, but into spiritual life.[14] "Because," says He, "He is kind unto the unthankful and to the evil."[15] Well done,[16] Marcion! how cleverly have you withdrawn from Him the showers and the sunshine, that He might not seem to be a Creator! But who is this kind being[17] which hitherto has not been even known? How can he be kind who had previously shown no evidences of such a kindness as this, which consists of the loan to us of sunshine and rain?—who is not destined to receive from the human race (the homage due to that) Creator,—who, up to this very moment, in return for His vast liberality in the gift of the elements, bears with men while they offer to idols, more readily than Himself, the due returns of His graciousness. *But God* is truly kind even in spiritual blessings. "The utterances[18] of the Lord are sweeter than honey and honeycombs."[19] He then has taunted[20] men as ungrateful who deserved to have their gratitude—even He, whose sunshine and rain even you, O Marcion, have enjoyed, but without gratitude! Your god, however, had no right to complain of man's ingratitude, because he had used no means to make them grateful. Compassion also does He teach: "Be ye merciful," says He, "as your Father also that had mercy upon you."[21] This injunction will be of a piece with, "Deal thy bread to the hungry; and if he be houseless, bring him into thine house; and if thou seest the naked, cover him;"[22] also with, "Judge the fatherless, plead with the widow."[23] I recognise here that ancient doctrine of Him who "prefers mercy to sacrifice."[24] If, however, it be now some other being which teaches mercy, on the ground of his own mercifulness, how happens it that he has been wanting in mercy to me for so vast an age? "Judge not, and ye shall not be judged; condemn not, and ye shall not be condemned; forgive, and ye. shall be forgiven; give, and it shall be given unto you: good measure, pressed down, and running over, shall men give into your bosom. For with the same measure that ye meas-

---

1 Quorundam tunc fidem.
2 Primis quibusque præceptis.
3 Balbutientis adhuc benignitatis. [Elucidation IV.]
4 Pignus reddes dati (i.e., fenoris) is his reading of a clause in Ezek. xviii. 16.
5 Deut. xxiv. 12, 13.
6 Deut. xv. 2.
7 Luke vi. 35. In the original the phrase is, υἱοὶ τοῦ ὑψίστου.
8 One of the flagrant errors of Marcion's belief of God. See above, chap. xi.
9 Quam spado.
10 Hoc eram ejus.
11 Ante duos unum. Before God made Adam and Eve one flesh, "I was *created* Adam, not became so by birth."—FR. JUNIUS.

12 Denuo.
13 Me enixus est.
14 Non in animam sed in spiritum.
15 Luke vi. 35.
16 Euge.
17 Suavis.
18 Eloquia.
19 Ps. xix. 11.
20 Suggillavit.
21 Reading of Luke vi. 36.
22 Isa. lviii. 7.
23 Isa. i. 17.
24 Hos. vi. 6.

ure withal, it shall be measured to you again.''[1] As it seems to me, this passage announces a retribution proportioned to the merits. But from whom shall come the retribution? If only from men, in that case he teaches a merely human discipline and recompense; and in everything we shall have to obey man: if from the Creator, as the Judge and the Recompenser of merits, then He compels our submission to Him, in whose hands[2] He has placed a retribution which will be acceptable or terrible according as every man shall have judged or condemned, acquitted or dealt with,[3] his neighbour; if from (Marcion's god) himself, he will then exercise a judicial function which Marcion denies. Let the Marcionites therefore make their choice: Will it not be just the same inconsistency to desert the prescription of their master, as to have Christ teaching in the interest of men or of the Creator? But ''a blind man will lead a blind man into the ditch.''[4] Some persons believe Marcion. But ''the disciple is not above his master.''[5] Apelles ought to have remembered this—a corrector of Marcion, although his disciple.[6] The heretic ought to take the beam out of his own eye, and then he may convict[7] the Christian, should he suspect a mote to be in *his* eye. Just as a good tree cannot produce evil fruit, so neither can truth generate heresy; and as a corrupt tree cannot yield good fruit, so heresy will not produce truth. Thus, Marcion brought nothing good out of Cerdon's evil treasure; nor Apelles out of Marcion's.[8] For in applying to these heretics the figurative words which Christ used of men in general, we shall make a much more suitable interpretation of them than if we were to deduce out of them two gods, according to Marcion's grievous exposition.[9] I think that I have the best reason possible for insisting still upon the position which I have all along occupied, that in no passage to be anywhere found has another God been revealed by Christ. I wonder that in this place alone Marcion's hands should have felt benumbed in their adulterating labour.[10] But even robbers have their qualms now and then. There is no wrong-doing without fear, because there is none without a guilty

conscience. So long, then, were the Jews cognisant of no other god but Him, beside whom they knew none else; nor did they call upon any other than Him whom alone they knew. This being the case, who will He clearly be[11] that said, ''Why callest thou me Lord, Lord?''[12] Will it be he who had as yet never been called on, because never yet revealed;[13] or He who was ever regarded as the Lord, because known from the beginning—even the God of the Jews? Who, again, could possibly have added, '' and do not the things which I say?'' Could it have been he who was only then doing his best[14] to teach them? Or He who from the beginning had addressed to them His messages[15] both by the law and the prophets? He could then upbraid them with disobedience, even if He had no ground at any time else for His reproof. The fact is, that He who was then imputing to them their ancient obstinacy was none other than He who, before the coming of Christ, had addressed to them these words, ''This people honoureth me with their lips, but their heart standeth far off from me.''[16] Otherwise, how absurd it were that a new god, a new Christ, the revealer of a new and so grand a religion should denounce as obstinate and disobedient those whom he had never had it in his power to make trial of!

CHAP. XVIII.—CONCERNING THE CENTURION'S FAITH. THE RAISING OF THE WIDOW'S SON. JOHN BAPTIST, AND HIS MESSAGE TO CHRIST; AND THE WOMAN WHO WAS A SINNER. PROOFS EXTRACTED FROM ALL OF THE RELATION OF CHRIST TO THE CREATOR.

Likewise, when extolling the centurion's faith, how incredible a thing it is, that *He* should confess that He had '' found so great a faith not even in Israel,''[17] to whom Israel's faith was in no way interesting![18] But not from the fact (here stated by Christ)[19] could it have been of any interest to Him to approve and compare what was hitherto crude, nay, I might say, hitherto naught. Why, however, might He not have used the example of faith in another[20] god? Because,

---

[1] Luke vi. 37, 38.
[2] Apud quem.
[3] Mensus fuerit.
[4] Luke vi. 39.
[5] Luke vi. 40.
[6] De discipulo.
[7] Revincat.
[8] Luke vi. 41-45. Cerdon is here referred to as Marcion's master, and Apelles as Marcion's pupil.
[9] Scandalum. See above, book i. chap. ii., for Marcion's perverse application of the figure of the good and the corrupt tree.
[10] In hoc solo adulterium Marcionis manus stupuisse miror. He means that this passage has been left uncorrupted by M. (as if his hand failed in the pruning process), foolishly for *him*.

[11] Videbitur.
[12] Luke vi. 46.
[13] Editus.
[14] Temptabat. Perhaps, '' was tampering with them.''
[15] Eloquia.
[16] Isa. xxix. 13.
[17] Luke vii. 1-10.
[18] Comp. Epiphanius, *Hæres.* xlii., *Refut.* 7, for the same argument: Εἰ οὐδὲ ἐν τῷ Ἰσραὴλ τοιαύτην πίστιν εὗρεν, κ.τ.λ. '' If He found not so great faith, even in Israel, as He discovered in this Gentile centurion, He does not therefore condemn the faith of Israel. For if He were alien from Israel's God, and did not pertain to Him, even as His father, He would certainly not have inferentially praised Israel's faith'' (Oehler).
[19] Nec exinde. This points to Christ's words, '' I have not *found* such faith in Israel.''—OEHLER.
[20] Alienæ fidei.

if He had done so, He would have said that no such faith had ever had existence in Israel; but as the case stands,[1] He intimates that He ought to have found so great a faith in Israel, inasmuch as He had indeed come for the purpose of finding it, being in truth the God and Christ of Israel, and had now stigmatized[2] it, only as one who would enforce and uphold it. If, indeed, He had been its antagonist,[3] He would have preferred finding it to be such faith,[4] having come to weaken and destroy it rather than to approve of it. He raised also the widow's son from death.[5] This was not a strange miracle.[6] The Creator's prophets had wrought such; then why not His Son much rather? Now, so evidently had the Lord Christ introduced no other god for the working of so momentous a miracle as this, that all who were present gave glory to the Creator, saying: "A great prophet is risen up among us, and God hath visited His people."[7] What God? He, of course, whose people they were, and from whom had come their prophets. But if they glorified the Creator, and Christ (on hearing them, and knowing their meaning) refrained from correcting them even in their very act of invoking[8] the Creator in that vast manifestation *of His glory* in this raising of the dead, undoubtedly He either announced no other God but Him, whom He thus permitted to be honoured in His own beneficent acts and miracles, or else how happens it that He quietly permitted these persons to remain so long in their error, especially as He came for the very purpose to cure them of their error? But John is offended[9] when he hears of the miracles of Christ, as of an alien god.[10] Well, I on my side[11] will first explain the reason of his offence, that I may the more easily explode the scandal[12] of our heretic. Now, that the very Lord Himself of all might, the Word and Spirit of the Father,[13] was operating and preaching on earth, it was necessary that the portion of the Holy Spirit which, in the form

of the prophetic gift,[14] had been through John preparing the ways of the Lord, should now depart from John,[15] and return back again of course to the Lord, as to its all-embracing original.[16] Therefore John, being now an ordinary person, and only one of the many,[17] was offended indeed as a man, but not because he expected or thought of another Christ as teaching or doing nothing new, for he was not even expecting such a one.[18] Nobody will entertain doubts about any one whom (since he knows him not to exist) he has no expectation or thought of. Now John was quite sure that there was no other God but the Creator, even as a Jew, especially as a prophet.[19] Whatever doubt he felt was evidently rather[20] entertained about Him[21] whom he knew indeed to exist but knew not whether He were the very *Christ.* With this fear, therefore, even John asks the question, "Art thou He that should come, or look we for another?"[22]—simply inquiring whether He was come as He whom he was looking for. "Art thou He that should come?" *i.e.* Art thou the coming One? "or look we for another?" *i.e.* Is He whom we are expecting some other than Thou, if Thou art not He whom we expect to come? For he was supposing,[23] as all men then thought, from the similarity of the miraculous evidences,[24] that a prophet might possibly have been meanwhile sent, from whom the Lord Himself, whose coming was then expected, was different, and to whom He was superior.[25] And there lay John's difficulty.[26] He was in doubt whether He was actually come whom all men were looking for; whom, moreover, they ought to have recognised by His predicted works, even as the Lord sent word to John, that it was by means of these very works that He was to be recognised.[27] Now, inasmuch as these predictions evidently related to the Creator's Christ—as we have proved in the examination of each of them— it was perverse enough, if he gave himself

---

[1] Ceterum.
[2] Suggillasset.
[3] Æmulus.
[4] Eam talem, that is, the faith of Israel.
[5] Luke vii. 11-17.
[6] Documentum.
[7] Luke vii. 16.
[8] Et quidem adhuc orantes.
[9] Comp. Epiphanius, *Hæres.* xlii., *Schol.* 8, cum Refut. ; Tertullian, *De Præscript. Hæret.* 8 ; and *De Bapt.* 10.
[10] Ut ulterius. This is the absurd allegation of Marcion. So Epiphanius (Le Prieur).
[11] Ego.
[12] Scandalum. Playing on the word "*scandalum*" in its application to the Baptist and to Marcion.
[13] " It is most certain that the Son of God, the second Person of the Godhead, is in the writings of the fathers throughout called by the title of *Spirit, Spirit of God,* etc. : with which usage agree the Holy Scriptures. See Mark ii. 8 ; Rom. i. 3, 4 ; 1 Tim. iii. 16 ; Heb. ix. 14 ; 1 Pet. iii. 18-20 ; also John vi. 63, compared with 56." —BP. BULL, *Def. Nic. Creed* (translated by the translator of this work), vol. i. p. 48 and note X. [The whole passage should be consulted.]

[14] Ex forma prophetici moduli.
[15] Tertullian stands alone in the notion that St. John's inquiry was owing to any withdrawal of the Spirit, so soon before his martyrdom, or any diminution of his faith. The contrary is expressed by Origen, *Homil.* xxvii., on Luke vii. ; Chrysostom on Matt. xi. ; Augustine, *Sermon.* 66, *de Verbo ;* Hilary on Matthew ; Jerome on Matthew, and *Epist.* 121, *ad Algas. ;* Ambrose on Luke, book v. § 93. They say mostly that the inquiry was for the sake of his disciples (Oxford *Library of the Fathers,* vol. x. p. 267, note *e*). [Elucidation V.]
[16] Ut in massalem suam summam.
[17] Unus jam de turba.
[18] Eundem.
[19] Etiam prophetes.
[20] Facilius.
[21] Jesus.
[22] Luke vii. 20.
[23] Sperabat.
[24] Documentorum.
[25] Major.
[26] Scandalum.
[27] Luke vii. 21, 22.

out to be *not* the Christ of the Creator, and rested the proof of his statement on those very evidences whereby he was urging his claims to be received as the Creator's Christ. Far greater still is his perverseness when, not being the Christ of John,[1] he yet bestows on John his testimony, affirming him to be a prophet, nay more, his messenger,[2] applying to him the Scripture, "Behold, I send my messenger before thy face, which shall prepare thy way before thee."[3] He graciously[4] adduced the prophecy in the superior sense of the alternative mentioned by the perplexed John, in order that, by affirming that His own precursor was already come in the person of John, He might quench the doubt[5] which lurked in his question: "Art thou He that should come, or look we for another?" Now that the forerunner had fulfilled his mission, and the way of the Lord was prepared, He ought now to be acknowledged as that (Christ) for whom the forerunner had made ready the way. *That forerunner was* indeed "greater than all of women born;"[6] but for all that, He who was least in the kingdom of God[7] was not subject to him;[8] as if the kingdom in which the least person was greater than John belonged to one God, while John, who was greater than all of women born, belonged himself to another God. For whether He speaks of *any* "least person" by reason of his humble position, or of Himself, as being thought to be less than John—since all were running into the wilderness after John rather than after Christ ("What went ye out into the wilderness to see?"[9])—the Creator has equal right[10] to claim as His own both John, greater than any born of women, and Christ, or every "least person *in the kingdom of heaven*," who was destined to be greater than John in that kingdom, although equally pertaining to the Creator, and who would be so much greater than the prophet,[11] because he would not have been offended at Christ, *an infirmity* which then lessened *the greatness of* John. We have already spoken of the forgiveness[12] of sins. The behaviour of "the woman which was a sinner," when she covered the Lord's feet with her kisses, bathed them with her tears, wiped them with the hairs of her head, anointed them with ointment,[13] produced an evidence that what she handled was not an empty phantom,[14] but a really solid body, and that her repentance as a sinner deserved forgiveness according to the mind of the Creator, who is accustomed to prefer mercy to sacrifice.[15] But even if the stimulus of her repentance proceeded from her faith, she heard her justification by faith through her repentance pronounced in the words, "Thy faith hath saved thee," by Him who had declared by Habakkuk, "The just shall live by his faith."[16]

CHAP. XIX.—THE RICH WOMEN OF PIETY WHO FOLLOWED JESUS CHRIST'S TEACHING BY PARABLES. THE MARCIONITE CAVIL DERIVED FROM CHRIST'S REMARK, WHEN TOLD OF HIS MOTHER AND HIS BRETHREN. EXPLANATION OF CHRIST'S APPARENT REJECTION OF THEM.

The fact that certain rich women clave to Christ, "which ministered unto Him of their substance," amongst whom was the wife of the king's steward, is a subject of prophecy. By Isaiah *the Lord* called these wealthy ladies —"Rise up, ye women that are at ease, and hear my voice"[17]—that He might prove[18] them first as disciples, and then as assistants and helpers: "Daughters, hear my words in hope; this day of the year cherish the memory of, in labour with hope." For it was "in labour" that they followed Him, and "with hope" did they minister to Him. On the subject of *parables*, let it suffice that it has been once for all shown that this kind of language[19] was with equal distinctness promised by the Creator. But there is that direct mode of His speaking[20] to the people— "Ye shall hear with the ear, but ye shall not understand"[21]—which now claims notice as

---

[1] That is, not the Creator's Christ—whose prophet John was—therefore a different Christ from Him whom John announced. This is said, of course, on the Marcionite hypothesis (Oehler).

[2] Angelum.

[3] Luke vii. 26, 27, and Mal. iii. 1–3.

[4] Eleganter.

[5] Scrupulum.

[6] Luke vii. 28.

[7] That is, *Christ*, according to Epiphanius. See next note.

[8] Comp. the Refutation of Epiphanius (*Hæres.* xlii. *Refut.* 8): "Whether with reference to John or to the Saviour, He pronounces a blessing on such as should not be offended in Himself or in John. Nor should they devise for themselves whatsoever things they heard not from him. He also has a greater object in view, on account of which the Saviour said this; even that no one should think that John (who was pronounced to be greater than any born of women) was greater than the Saviour Himself, because even He was born of a woman. He guards against this mistake, and says, 'Blessed is he who shall not be offended in me.' He then adds, 'He that is least in the kingdom of heaven is greater than he.' Now, in respect of His birth in the flesh, the Saviour was less than he by the space of six months. But in the kingdom He was greater, being even his God. For the Only-begotten came not to say aught in secret, or to utter a falsehood in His preaching, as He says Himself, 'In secret have I said nothing, but in public,' etc. (Κἀν τε πρὸς Ἰωάννην ἔχοι . . . ἀλλὰ μετὰ παρρησίας)."—Oehler.

[9] Luke vii. 25.

[10] Tantundem competit creatori.

[11] Major tanto propheta.

[12] De remissa.

[13] Luke vii. 36–50.

[14] Comp. Epiphanius, *Hæres.* xlii., *Refut.* 10, 11.

[15] Hos. vi. 6.

[16] Hab. ii. 4.

[17] Isa. xxxii. 9, 10. Quoted as usual, from the LXX. Γυναῖκες πλούσιαι ἀνάστητε, καὶ ἀκούσατε τῆς φωνῆς μου· θυγατέρες ἐν ἐλπίδι εἰσακούσατε λόγους μου. Ἡμέρας ἐνιαυτοῦ μνείαν ποιήσασθε ἐν ὀδύνῃ μετ' ἐλπίδος

[18] Ostenderet.

[19] Eloquii.

[20] Pronunciatio.

[21] Isa. vi. 9.

having furnished to Christ that frequent form of His earnest instruction: "He that hath ears to hear, let him hear."[1] Not as if Christ, actuated with a diverse spirit, permitted a hearing which the Creator had refused; but because the exhortation followed the threatening. First came, "Ye shall hear with the ear, but shall not understand;" then followed, "He that hath ears to hear, let him hear." For they wilfully refused to hear, although they had ears. He, however, was teaching them that it was the ears of the heart which were necessary; and with *these* the Creator had said that they would not hear. Therefore it is that He adds by His Christ, "Take heed how ye hear,"[2] and hear not,—meaning, of course, with the hearing of the heart, not of the ear. If you only attach a proper, sense to the *Creator's* admonition[3] suitable to the meaning of Him who was rousing the people to hear by the words, "Take heed how ye hear," it amounted to a menace to such as would not hear. In fact,[4] that most merciful god of yours, who judges not, neither is angry, is minatory. This is proved even by the sentence which immediately follows: "Whosoever hath, to him shall be given; and whosoever hath not, from him shall be taken even that which he seemeth to have."[5] What shall be given? The increase of faith, or understanding, or even salvation. What shall be taken away? That, of course, which shall be given. By whom shall the gift and the deprivation be made? If by the Creator it be taken away, by Him also shall it be given. If by Marcion's god it be given, by Marcion's god also will it be taken away. Now, for whatever reason He threatens the "deprivation," it will not be the work of a god who knows not how to threaten, because incapable of anger. I am, moreover, astonished when he says that "a candle is not usually hidden,"[6] who had hidden himself—a greater and more needful light—during so long a time; and when he promises that "everything shall be brought out of its secrecy and made manifest,"[7] who hitherto has kept his god in obscurity, waiting (I suppose) until Marcion be born. We now come to the most strenuously-plied argument of all those who call in question the Lord's nativity. They say that He testifies Himself to His not having been born, when He asks, "Who is my mother, and who are my brethren?"[8] In this manner

heretics either wrest plain and simple words to any sense they choose by their conjectures, or else they violently resolve by a literal interpretation words which imply a conditional sense and are incapable of a simple solution,[9] as in this passage. We, for our part, say in reply, first, that it could not possibly have been told Him that His mother and His brethren stood without, desiring to see Him, if He had had no mother and no brethren. They must have been known to him who announced them, either some time previously, or then at that very time, when they desired to see Him, or sent Him their message. To this our first position this answer is usually given by the other side. But suppose they sent Him the message for the purpose of tempting Him? Well, but the Scripture does not say so; and inasmuch as it is usual for it to indicate what is done in the way of temptation ("Behold, a certain lawyer stood up, and tempted Him;"[10] again, when inquiring about tribute, the Pharisees came to Him, tempting Him[11]), so, when it makes no mention of temptation, it does not admit the interpretation of temptation. However, *although I do not allow this sense*, I may as well ask, by way of a superfluous refutation, for the reasons of the alleged temptation, To what purpose could they have tempted Him by naming His mother and His brethren? If it was to ascertain whether He had been born or not—when was a question raised on this point, which they must resolve by tempting Him in this way? Who could doubt His having been born, when they[12] saw Him before them a veritable man?—whom they had heard call Himself "Son of man?"—of whom they doubted whether He were God or Son of God, from seeing Him, as they did, in the perfect garb of human quality?—supposing Him rather to be a prophet, a great one indeed,[13] but still one who had been born as man? Even if it had been necessary that He should thus be tried in the investigation of His birth, surely any other proof would have better answered the trial than that to be obtained from mentioning those relatives which it was quite possible for Him, in spite of His true nativity, not at that moment to have had. For tell me now, does a mother live on contemporaneously[14] with her sons in every case? Have all sons brothers born for them?[15] May a man rather not have fathers and sisters (living),

---

[1] Luke viii. 8.
[2] Luke viii. 18.
[3] Pronuntiationi.
[4] Sane: with a touch of irony.
[5] Luke viii. 18.
[6] Luke viii. 16.
[7] Luke viii. 17
[8] Matt. xii. 48.

[9] Rationales. "Quæ voces adhibita ratione sunt interpretandæ."—OEHLER.
[10] Luke x. 25.
[11] Luke xx. 20.
[12] Singular in the original, but (to avoid confusion) here made plural.
[13] In allusion to Luke vii. 16. See above, chap. xviii.
[14] Advivit
[15] Adgenerantur

or even no relatives at all? But there is historical proof[1] that at this very time[2] a *census* had been taken in Judæa by Sentius Saturninus,[3] which might have satisfied their inquiry respecting the family and descent of Christ. Such a method of testing the point had therefore no consistency whatever in it and they "who were standing without" were really "His mother and His brethren." It remains for us to examine His meaning when He resorts to non-literal[4] words, saying "Who is my mother or my brethren?" It seems as if His language amounted to a denial of His family and His birth; but it arose actually from the absolute nature of the case, and the conditional sense in which His words were to be explained.[5] He was justly indignant, that persons so very near to Him "stood *without*," while strangers were *within* hanging on His words, especially as they wanted to call Him away from the solemn work He had in hand. He did not so much deny as disavow[6] them. And therefore, when to the previous question, "Who is my mother, and who are my brethren?"[7] He added the answer "None but they who hear my words and do them," He transferred the names of blood-relationship to others, whom He judged to be more closely related to Him by reason of their faith. Now no one transfers a thing except from him who possesses that which is transferred. If, therefore, He made them "His mother and His brethren" who were not so, how could He deny them these relationships who really had them? Surely only on the condition of their deserts, and not by any disavowal of His near relatives; teaching them by His own actual example,[8] that "whosoever preferred father or mother or brethren to the Word of God,

was not a disciple worthy of Him."[9] Besides,[10] His admission of His mother and His brethren was the more express, from the fact of His unwillingness to acknowledge them. That He adopted others only confirmed those in their relationship to Him whom He refused because of their offence, and for whom He substituted the others, not as being truer relatives, but worthier ones. Finally, it was no great matter if He did prefer to kindred (that) faith which it[11] did not possess.[12]

CHAP. XX.—COMPARISON OF CHRIST'S POWER OVER WINDS AND WAVES WITH MOSES' COMMAND OF THE WATERS OF THE RED SEA AND THE JORDAN. CHRIST'S POWER OVER UNCLEAN SPIRITS. THE CASE OF THE LEGION. THE CURE OF THE ISSUE OF BLOOD. THE MOSAIC UNCLEANNESS ON THIS POINT EXPLAINED.

But "what manner of man is this? for He commandeth even the winds and water!"[13] Of course He is the new master and proprietor of the elements, now that the Creator is deposed, and excluded from their possession! Nothing of the kind. But the elements own[14] their own Maker, just as they had been accustomed to obey His servants also. Examine well the Exodus, Marcion; look at the rod of Moses, as it waves His command to the Red Sea, ampler than all the lakes of Judæa. How the sea yawns from its very depths, then fixes itself in two solidified masses, and so, out of the interval between them,[15] makes a way for the people to pass dry-shod across; again does the same rod vibrate, the sea returns in its strength, and in the concourse of its waters the chivalry of Egypt is engulphed! To that consummation the very winds subserved! Read, too, how that the Jordan was as a sword, to hinder the emigrant nation in their passage across its stream; how that its waters from above stood still, and its current below wholly ceased to run at the bidding of Joshua,[16] when his priests began to pass over![17]

---

1 Constat. [Jarvis, *Introd.* p.204 and p. 536.]
2 Nunc: i.e., when Christ was told of His mother and brethren.
3 " C. Sentius Saturninus, a consular, held this census of the whole empire as principal augur, because Augustus determined to impart the sanction of religion to his institution. The agent through whom Saturninus carried out the census in Judæa was the governor Cyrenius, according to Luke, chap. ii."—Fr. Junius. Tertullian mentions Sentius Saturninus again in *De Pallio*, i. Tertullian's statement in the text has weighed with Sanclemente and others, who suppose that Saturninus was governor of Judæa at the time of our Lord's birth, which they place in 747 A. U.C. "It is evident, however," says Wieseler, "that this argument is far from decisive ; for the New Testament itself supplies far better aids for determining this question than the discordant ecclesiastical traditions,—different fathers giving different dates, which might be appealed to with equal justice ; while Tertullian is even inconsistent with himself, since in his treatise *Adv. Jud.* viii., he gives 751 A. U. C. as the year of our Lord's birth" (Wieseler's *Chronological Synopsis* by Venables, p. 99, note 2). This Sentius Saturninus filled the office of governor of Syria, 744–748. For the elaborate argument of Aug. W. Zumpt, by which he defends St. Luke's chronology, and goes far to prove that Publius Sulpicius Quirinus (or " Cyrenius ") was actually the governor of Syria at the time of the Lord's birth, the reader may be referred to a careful abridgment by the translator of Wieseler's work, pp. 129–135.
4 Non simpliciter. St. Matthew rather than St. Luke is quoted in this interrogative sentence.
5 Ex condicione rationali. See Oehler's note, just above, on the word "*rationales.*"
6 Abdicavit: Rigalt'thinks this *harsh*, and reminds us that at the cross the Lord had not cast away His mother. [Elucidation VI.]
7 This is literally from St. Matthew's narrative, chap. xii. 48.
8 In semetipso.

9 Matt. x. 37.
10 Ceterum.
11 i.e., the kindred. [N.B. He includes the Mother !]
12 We have translated Oehler's text of this passage : " Denique nihil magnum, si fidem sanguini, *quam* non habebat." For once we venture to differ from that admirable editor (and that although he is supported in his view by Fr. Junius), and prefer the reading of the MSS. and the older editions: " Denique nihil magnum, si fidem sanguini, *quem* non habebat." To which we would give an ironical turn, usual to Tertullian, "After all, it is not to be wondered at if He preferred faith to flesh and blood, which he did not himself possess !"—in allusion to Marcion's *Docetic* opinion of Christ.
13 Luke viii. 25.
14 Agnorant.
15 Et pari utrinque stupore discriminis fixum.
16 Josh. iii. 9–17.
17 This obscure passage is thus read by Oehler, from whom we have translated: " Lege extorri familiæ dirimendæ in transitu ejus Jordanis machæram fuisse, cujus impetum atque decursum plane et Jesus docuerat prophetis transmeantibus stare." The *machæram* ("sword") is a metaphor for the *river*. Rigaltius refers to Virgil's figure, *Æneid*, viii. 62, 64, for a justification of the

What will you say to this? If it be your Christ *that is meant above*, he will not be more potent than the servants of the Creator. But I should have been content with the examples I have adduced without addition,[1] if a prediction of His present passage on the sea had not preceded Christ's coming. As psalm is, in fact, accomplished by this[2] crossing over the lake. "The Lord," says the psalmist, "is upon many waters."[3] When He disperses its waves, Habakkuk's words are fulfilled, where he says, "Scattering the waters in His passage."[4] When at His rebuke the sea is calmed, Nahum is also verified: He rebuketh the sea, and maketh it dry,"[5] including the winds indeed, whereby it was disquieted. With what evidence would you have my Christ vindicated? Shall it come from the examples, or from the prophecies, of the Creator? You suppose that He is predicted as a military and armed warrior,[6] instead of one who in a figurative and allegorical sense was to wage a spiritual warfare against spiritual enemies, in spiritual campaigns, and with spiritual weapons: come now, when in one man alone you discover a multitude of demons calling itself *Legion*,[7] of course comprised of spirits, you should learn that Christ also must be understood to be an exterminator of spiritual foes, who wields spiritual arms and fights in spiritual strife; and that it was none other than He,[8] who now had to contend with even a legion of demons. Therefore it is of such a war as this that the Psalm may evidently have spoken: "The Lord is strong, The Lord is mighty in battle."[9] For with the last enemy death did He fight, and through the trophy of the cross He triumphed. Now of what God did the Legion testify that Jesus was the Son?[10] No doubt, of that God whose torments and abyss they knew and dreaded. It seems impossible for them to have remained up to this time in ignorance of what the power of the recent and unknown god was working in the world, because it is very unlikely that the Creator was ignorant thereof. For if He had been at any time ignorant that there was another god above Himself, He had

by this time at all events discovered that there was one at work[11] below His heaven. Now, what their Lord had discovered had by this time become notorious to His entire family within the same world and the same circuit of heaven, in which the strange deity dwelt and acted.[12] As therefore both the Creator and His creatures[13] must have had knowledge of him, if he had been in existence, so, inasmuch as he had no existence, the demons really knew none other than the Christ of their own God. They do not ask of the strange god, what they recollected they must beg of the Creator—not to be plunged into the Creator's abyss. They at last had their request granted. On what ground? Because they had lied? Because they had proclaimed Him to be the Son of a ruthless God? And what sort of god will that be who helped the lying, and upheld his detractors? However, *no need of this thought*, for,[14] inasmuch as they had not lied, inasmuch as they had acknowledged that the God of the abyss was also their God, so did He actually Himself affirm that He was the same whom these demons acknowledged—Jesus, the Judge and Son of the avenging God. Now, behold an inkling[15] of the Creator's failings[16] and infirmities in Christ; for I on my side[17] mean to impute to Him ignorance. Allow me some indulgence in my effort against the heretic. Jesus is touched by the woman who had an issue of blood,[18] He knew not by whom. "Who touched me?" He asks, when His disciples alleged an excuse. He even persists in His assertion of ignorance: "Somebody hath touched me," He says, and advances some proof: "For I perceive that virtue is gone out of me." What says our heretic? Could *Christ* have known the person? And why did He speak as if He were ignorant? Why? Surely it was to challenge her faith, and to try her fear. Precisely as He had once questioned Adam, as if in ignorance: Adam, where art thou?"[19] Thus you have both the Creator excused in the same way as Christ, and Christ acting similarly to[20] the Creator. But in this case He acted as an adversary of the law; and therefore, as the law forbids contact with a woman with an issue,[21] He desired not only that this woman should touch Him, but that He should heal her.[22] Here,

---

simile. Oehler has altered the reading from the *ex sorte familiæ*," etc., of the MSS. to "*extorri familiæ*," etc. The former reading would mean probably: "Read out *of the story* of the nation how that Jordan was as a sword to hinder their passage across its stream." The *sorte* (or, as yet another variation has it, "*et sortes*," "the accounts") meant the national record, as we have it in the beginning of the book of Joshua. But the passage is almost hopelessly obscure.
[1] Solis.
[2] Istius.
[3] Ps. xxix. 3.
[4] Hab. iii. 10, according to the Septuagint.
[5] Nah. i. 4.
[6] See above, book iii. chap. xiii.
[7] Luke viii. 30.
[8] Atque ita ipsum esse.
[9] Ps. xxiv. 8.
[10] Luke viii. 28.

[11] Agentem.
[12] Conversaretur.
[13] Substantiæ: including these demons.
[14] Sed enim: the ἀλλὰ γὰρ of the Greek.
[15] Aliquid.
[16] Pusillitatibus.
[17] Ego.
[18] Luke viii. 43-46.
[19] See above, book iii. chap. xxv.
[20] Adæquatum : on a par with.
[21] Lev. xv. 19.
[22] A Marcionite hypothesis.

then, is a God who is not merciful by nature, but in hostility! Yet, if we find that such was the merit of this woman's faith, that He said unto her, Thy faith hath saved thee,"[1] what are you, that you should detect an hostility to the law in that act, which the Lord Himself shows us to have been done as a reward of faith? But will you have it that this faith of the woman consisted in the contempt which she had acquired for the law? Who can suppose, that a woman who had been hitherto unconscious of any God, uninitiated as yet in any new law, should violently infringe that law by which she was up to this time bound? On what faith, indeed, was such an infringement hazarded? In what God believing? Whom despising? The Creator? Her touch at least was an act of faith. And if of faith in the Creator, how could she have violated His law,[2] when she was ignorant of any other God? Whatever her infringement of the law amounted to, it proceeded from and was proportionate to her faith in the Creator. But how can these two things be compatible? That she violated the law, and violated it in faith, which ought to have restrained her from such violation? I will tell you how her faith was this above all:[3] it made her believe that her God preferred mercy even to sacrifice; she was certain that her God was working in Christ; she touched Him, therefore, not as a holy man simply, nor as a prophet, whom she knew to be capable of contamination by reason of his human nature, but as very God, whom she assumed to be beyond all possibility of pollution by any uncleanness.[4] She therefore, not without reason,[5] interpreted for herself the law, as meaning that such things as are susceptible of defilement become defiled, but not so God, whom she knew for certain to be in Christ. But she recollected this also, that what came under the prohibition of the law[6] was that ordinary and usual issue of blood which proceeds from natural functions every month, and in childbirth, not that which was the result of disordered health. Her case, however, was one of long abounding[7] ill health, for which she knew that the succour of God's mercy was needed, and not the *natural* relief of time. And thus she may evidently be regarded as having discerned[8] the law, instead of breaking it. This will prove to be the faith which was to confer intelligence likewise. "If ye will not believe,"

says (the prophet), "ye shall not understand."[9] When Christ approved of the faith of this woman, which simply rested in the Creator, He declared by His answer to her,[10] that He was Himself the divine object of the faith of which He approved. Nor can I overlook the fact that His garment, by being touched, demonstrated also the truth of His body; for of course[11] it was a body, and not a phantom, which the garment clothed.[12] This indeed is not our point now; but the remark has a natural bearing on the question we are discussing. For if it were not a veritable body, but only a fantastic one, it could not for certain have received contamination, as being an unsubstantial thing.[13] He therefore, who, by reason of this vacuity of his substance, was incapable of contamination, how could he possibly have desired this touch?[14] As an adversary of the law, his conduct was deceitful, for he was not susceptible of a real pollution.

CHAP. XXI.—CHRIST'S CONNECTION WITH THE CREATOR SHOWN FROM SEVERAL INCIDENTS IN THE OLD TESTAMENT, COMPARED WITH ST. LUKE'S NARRATIVE OF THE MISSION OF THE DISCIPLES. THE FEEDING OF THE MULTITUDE. THE CONFESSION OF ST. PETER. BEING ASHAMED OF CHRIST. THIS SHAME IS ONLY POSSIBLE OF THE TRUE CHRIST. MARCIONITE PRETENSIONS ABSURD.

He sends forth His disciples to preach the kingdom of God.[15] Does He here say of what God? He forbids their taking anything for their journey, by way of either food or raiment. Who would have given such a commandment as this, but He who feeds the ravens and clothes[16] the flowers of the field? Who anciently enjoined for the treading of an unmuzzled mouth,[17] that he might be at liberty to gather his fodder from his labour, on the principle that the worker is worthy of his hire?[18] Marcion may expunge such precepts, but no matter, provided the sense of them survives. But when He charges them to shake off the dust of their feet against such as should refuse to receive them, He also bids that this be done as a *witness*. Now no one bears witness except in a case which is decided by judicial process; and whoever orders inhuman conduct to be submitted to the trial by testi-

---

[1] Luke viii. 48.
[2] Ecquomodo legem ejus irrupit.
[3] Primo.
[4] Spurcitia.
[5] Non temere.
[6] In lege taxari.
[7] Illa autem redundavit.
[8] Distinxisse.

[9] Isa. vii. 9.
[10] Luke viii. 48.
[11] Utique.
[12] Epiphanius, in *Hæres.* xlii. *Refut.* 14, has the same remark.
[13] Qua res vacua.
[14] In allusion to the Marcionite hypothesis mentioned above.
[15] Luke ix. 1–6.
[16] Vestit.
[17] Libertatem oris.
[18] Deut. xxv. 4.

mony,[1] does really threaten as a judge. Again, that it was no new god which recommended[2] by Christ, was clearly attested by the opinion of all men, because some maintained to Herod that Jesus was the Christ; others, that He was John; some, that He was Elias; and others, that He was one of the old prophets.[3] Now, whosoever of all these He might have been, He certainly was not raised up for the purpose of announcing another god after His resurrection. He feeds the multitude in the desert place;[4] this, you must know[5] was after the manner of the Old Testament.[6] Or else,[7] if there was not the same grandeur, it follows that He is now inferior to the Creator. For *He*, not for one day, but during forty years, not on the inferior aliment of bread and fish, but with the manna of heaven, supported the lives[8] of not five thousand, but of six hundred thousand human beings. However, such was the greatness *of His miracle*, that He willed the slender supply of food, not only to be enough, but even to prove superabundant;[9] and herein He followed the ancient precedent. For in like manner, during the famine in Elijah's time, the scanty and final meal of the widow of Sarepta was multiplied[10] by the blessing of the prophet throughout the period of the famine. You have the third book of the Kings.[11] If you also turn to the fourth book, you will discover all this conduct[12] of Christ pursued by that man of God, who ordered ten[13] barley loaves which had been given him to be distributed among the people; and when his servitor, after contrasting the large number of the persons with the small supply of the food, answered, "What, shall I set this before a hundred men?" he said again, "Give them, and they shall eat: for thus saith the Lord, They shall eat, and shall leave thereof, according to the word of the Lord."[14] O Christ, even in Thy novelties Thou art old! Accordingly, when Peter, who had been an eyewitness of the miracle, and had compared it with the ancient precedents, and had discovered in them prophetic intimations of what should one day come to pass, answered (as the mouthpiece of them all) the Lord's inquiry, "Whom say ye that I am?"[15] in the words, "Thou art the Christ," he could not but have perceived that He was that Christ, beside whom he knew of none else in the Scriptures, and whom he was now surveying[16] in His wonderful deeds. This conclusion He even Himself confirms by thus far bearing with it, nay, even enjoining silence respecting it.[17] For if Peter was unable to acknowledge Him to be any other than the Creator's *Christ*, while He commanded them "to tell no man that saying," surely[18] He was unwilling to have the conclusion promulged which Peter had drawn. No doubt of that,[19] you say; but as Peter's conclusion was a wrong one, therefore He was unwilling to have a lie disseminated. It was, however, a different reason which He assigned for the silence, even because "the Son of man must suffer many things, and be rejected of the elders, and scribes, and priests, and be slain, and be raised again the third day."[20] Now, inasmuch as these *sufferings* were actually foretold for the Creator's Christ (as we shall fully show in the proper place[21]), so by this application of them to His own case[22] does He prove that it is He Himself of whom they were predicted. At all events, even if they had not been predicted, the reason which He alleged for imposing silence (on the disciples) was such as made it clear enough that Peter had made no mistake, that reason being the necessity of His undergoing these sufferings. "Whosoever," says He, "will save his life, shall lose it; and whosoever will lose his life for my sake, the same shall save it."[23] Surely[24] it is the Son of man[25] who uttered this sentence. Look carefully, then, along with the king of Babylon, into his burning fiery furnace, and there you will discover one "like the Son of man" (for He was not yet really Son of man, because not yet born of man), even as early as then[26] appointing issues such as these. He saved the lives of the three brethren,[27] who had agreed to lose them for God's sake; but He destroyed those of the Chaldæans, when they had preferred to save them by the means of their idolatry. Where is that novelty, which you pretend,[28] in a doctrine which possesses these ancient proofs? But all the predictions have been fulfilled[29] concerning martyrdoms which were to happen, and were to receive

---

[1] In testationem redigi.
[2] Probatum.
[3] Luke ix. 7, 8.
[4] Luke ix. 10–17.
[5] Scilicet.
[6] De pristino more.
[7] Aut.
[8] Protelavit.
[9] Exuberare.
[10] Redundaverant.
[11] 1 Kings xvii. 7–16.
[12] Ordinem.
[13] I have no doubt that *ten* was the word written by our author; for some Greek copies read δέκα, and Ambrose in his *Hexaëmeron*, book vi. chap. ii., mentions the same number (Fr. Junius).
[14] 2 Kings iv. 42–44.
[15] Luke ix, 20.

[16] Recensebat.
[17] Luke ix. 21.
[18] Utique.
[19] Immo.
[20] Luke ix. 22.
[21] See below, chaps. xl.–xliii.
[22] Sic quoque.
[23] Luke ix. 24.
[24] Certe.
[25] Compare above, chap. x., towards the end.
[26] Jam tunc.
[27] Dan. iii. 25, 26.
[28] Ista.
[29] Decucurrerunt.

the recompenses of their reward from God. "See," says Isaiah, "how the righteous perisheth, and no man layeth it to heart; and just men are taken away, and no man considereth."[1] When does this more frequently happen than in the persecution of His saints? This, indeed, is no ordinary matter,[2] no common casualty of the law of nature; but it is that illustrious devotion, that fighting for the faith, wherein whosoever loses his life for God saves it, so that you may here again recognize the Judge who recompenses the evil gain of life with its destruction, and the good loss thereof with its salvation. It is, however, a jealous God whom He here presents to me; one who returns evil for evil. "For whosoever," says He, "shall be ashamed of me, of him will I also be ashamed."[3] Now to none but my Christ can be assigned the occasion[4] of such a shame as this. His whole course[5] was so exposed to shame as to open a way for even the taunts of heretics, declaiming[6] with all the bitterness in their power against the utter disgrace[7] of His birth and bringing-up, and the unworthiness of His very flesh.[8] But how can that Christ of yours be liable to a shame, which it is impossible for him to experience? Since he was never condensed[9] into human flesh in the womb of a woman, although a virgin; never grew from human seed, although only after the law of corporeal substance, from the fluids[10] of a woman; was never deemed flesh before shaped in the womb; never called *fœtus*[11] after such shaping; was never delivered from a ten months' writhing in the womb;[12] was never shed forth upon the ground, amidst the sudden pains of parturition, with the unclean issue which flows at such a time through the sewerage of the body, forthwith to inaugurate the light[13] of life with tears, and with that primal wound which

severs the child from her who bears him;[14] never received the copious ablution, nor the medication of salt and honey;[15] nor did he initiate a shroud with swaddling clothes;[16] nor afterwards did he ever wallow[17] in his own uncleanness, in his mother's lap; nibbling at her breast; long an infant; gradually[18] a boy; by slow degrees[19] a man.[20] But he was revealed[21] from heaven, full-grown at once, at once complete; immediately Christ; simply spirit, and power, and god. But as withal he was not true, because not visible; therefore he was no object to be ashamed of from the curse of the cross, the real endurance[22] of which he escaped, because wanting in bodily substance. Never, therefore, could he have said, "Whosoever shall be ashamed of me." But as for our Christ, He could do no otherwise than make such a declaration;[23] "made" by the Father "a little lower than the angels,"[24] "a worm and no man, a reproach of men, and despised of the people;"[25] seeing that it was His will that "with His stripes we should be healed,"[26] that by His humiliation our salvation should be established. And justly did He humble Himself[27] for His own creature man, for the image and likeness of Himself, and not of another, in order that man, since he had not felt ashamed when bowing down to a stone or a stock, might with similar courage give satisfaction to God for the shamelessness of his idolatry, by displaying an equal degree of shamelessness in his faith, in not being ashamed of Christ. Now, Marcion, which of these courses is better suited to your Christ, in respect of a meritorious shame?[28] Plainly, you ought yourself to blush with shame for having given him a fictitious existence.[29]

CHAP. XXII.—THE SAME CONCLUSION SUPPORTED BY THE TRANSFIGURATION. MARCION INCONSISTENT IN ASSOCIATING WITH CHRIST IN GLORY TWO SUCH EMINENT SERVANTS OF THE CREATOR AS MOSES AND ELIJAH. ST. PETER'S IGNORANCE ACCOUNTED FOR ON A MONTANIST PRINCIPLE.

You ought to be very much ashamed of

---

[1] Isa. lvii. 1.
[2] We have, by understanding *res*, treated these adjectives as nouns. Rigalt. applies them to the *doctrina* of the sentence just previous. Perhaps, however, "*persecutione*" is the noun.
[3] Luke ix. 26.
[4] Materia conveniat.
[5] Ordo.
[6] Perorantibus.
[7] Fœditatem.
[8] Ipsius etiam carnis indignitatem; because His flesh, being capable of suffering and subject to death, seemed to them unworthy of God. So *Adv. Judæos*, chap. xiv., he says: "Primo sordidis indutus est, id est carnis passibilis et mortalis indignitate." Or His "indignity" may have been εἶδος οὐκ ἄξιον τυραννίδος, His "*unkingly aspect*" (as Origen expresses it, *Contra Celsum*, 6); His "form of a servant," or slave, as St. Paul says. See also Tertullian's *De Patientia*, iii. (Rigalt.)
[9] Coagulatur. [Job x. 10.]
[10] Ex feminæ humore.
[11] Pecus. Julius Firmicus, iii. 1, uses the word in the same way: "*Pecus* intra viscera matris artuatim concisum a medicis proferetur." [Jul. Firmicus Maternus, floruit *circa*, A.D. 340.]
[12] Such is probably the meaning of "non decem mensium cruciatu deliberatus." For such is the situation of the infant in the womb, that it seems to writhe (*cruciari*) all curved and contracted (Rigalt.). Latinius read *delibratus* instead of *deliberatus*, which means, "suspended or poised in the womb as in a scale." This has my approbation. I would compare *De Carne Christi*, chap. iv. (Fr. Junius.) Oehler reads *deliberatus* in the sense of *liberatus*.
[13] Statim lucem lacrimis auspicatus.
[14] Primo retinaculi sui vulnere: the cutting of the umbilical nerve. [Contrast Jer. Taylor, on the *Nativity*, Opp. I. p. 34.]
[15] Nec sale ac melle medicatus. Of this application in the case of a recent childbirth we know nothing; it seems to have been meant for the skin. See Pliny, in his *Hist. Nat.* xxii. 25.
[16] Nec pannis jam sepulturæ involucrum initiatus.
[17] Volutatus per immunditias.
[18] Vix.
[19] Tarde.
[20] Expositus.
[21] i.e., he never passed through stages like these.
[22] Veritate.
[23] Debuit pronuntiasse.
[24] Ps. viii. 6.
[25] Ps. xxii. 6.
[26] Isa. liii. 5.
[27] Se deposuit.
[28] Ad meritum confusionis.
[29] Quod illum finxisti.

yourself on this account too, for permitting him to appear on the retired mountain in the company of Moses and Elias,[1] whom he had come to destroy. This, to be sure,[2] was what he wished to be understood as the meaning of that voice from heaven: "This is my beloved Son, hear Him"[3]—*Him*, that is, not Moses or Elias any longer. The voice alone, therefore, was enough, without the display of Moses and Elias; for, by expressly mentioning whom they were to hear, he must have forbidden all[4] others from being heard. Or else, did he mean that Isaiah and Jeremiah and the others whom he did not exhibit were to be heard, since he prohibited those whom he did display? Now, even if their presence was necessary, they surely should not be represented as conversing together, which is a sign of familiarity; nor as associated in glory with him, for this indicates respect and graciousness; but they should be shown in some slough[5] as a sure token of their ruin, or even in that darkness of the Creator which Christ was sent to disperse, far removed from the glory of Him who was about to sever their words and writings from His gospel. This, then, is the way[6] how he demonstrates them to be aliens,[7] even by keeping them in his own company! This is how he shows they ought to be relinquished: he associates them with himself instead! This is how he destroys them: he irradiates them with his glory! How would their own Christ act? I suppose He would have imitated the frowardness (of heresy),[8] and revealed them just as Marcion's Christ was bound to do, or at least as having with Him any others rather than His own prophets! But what could so well befit the Creator's Christ, as to manifest Him in the company of His own fore-announcers?[9]—to let Him be seen with those to whom He had appeared in revelations?—to let Him be speaking with those who had spoken of Him? —to share His glory with those by whom He used to be called the Lord of glory; even with those chief servants of His, one of whom was once the moulder[10] of His people, the other afterwards the reformer[11] thereof; one the initiator of the Old Testament, the other the consummator[12] of the New? Well therefore does Peter, when recognizing the com-

panions of his Christ in their indissoluble connection with Him, suggest an expedient: "It is good for us to be here" (good: that evidently means to be where Moses and Elias are); "and let us make three tabernacles, one for Thee, and one for Moses, and one for Elias. But he knew not what he said."[13] How knew not? Was his ignorance the result of simple error? Or was it on the principle which we maintain[14] in the cause of the new prophecy,[15] that to grace ecstasy or rapture[16] is incident. For when a man is rapt in the Spirit, especially when he beholds the glory of God, or when God speaks through him, he necessarily loses his sensation,[17] because he is overshadowed with the power of God,—a point concerning which there is a question between us and the carnally-minded.[18] Now, it is no difficult matter to prove the rapture[19] of Peter. For how could he have known Moses and Elias, except (by being) in the Spirit? People could not have had their images, or statues, or likenesses; for that the law forbade. How, if it were not that he had seen them in the Spirit? And therefore, because it was in the Spirit that he had now spoken, and not in his natural senses, he could not know what he had said. But if, on the other hand,[20] he was thus ignorant, because he erroneously supposed that (Jesus) was their Christ, it is then evident that Peter, when previously asked by Christ, "Whom they thought Him to be," meant the Creator's Christ, when he answered, "Thou art the Christ;" because if he had been then aware that He belonged to the rival god, he would not have made a mistake here. But if he was in error here because of his previous erroneous opinion,[21] then you may be sure that up to that very day no new divinity had been revealed by Christ, and that Peter had so far made no mistake, because hitherto Christ had revealed nothing of the kind; and that Christ accordingly was not to be regarded as belonging to any other

[13] Luke ix. 33.
[14] This Tertullian seems to have done in his treatise *De Ecstasi*, which is mentioned by St. Jerome—see his *Catalogus Scriptt. Eccles.* (in Tertulliano) ; and by Nicephorus, *Hist. Eccles.* iv. 22, 34. On this subject of ecstasy, Tertullian has some observations in *De Anima*, chap. xxi. and xlv. (Rigalt. and Oehler.)
[15] [Elucidation VII.]
[16] Amentiam.
[17] Excidat sensu.
[18] He calls those the carnally-minded ("psychicos") who thought that ecstatic raptures and revelations had ceased in the church. The term arises from a perverse application of 1 Cor. ii. 14 : Ψυχικὸς δὲ ἄνθρωπος οὐ δέχεται τὰ τοῦ Πνεύματος τοῦ Θεοῦ. In opposition to the wild fanaticism of Montanus, into which Tertullian strangely fell, the Catholics believed that the true prophets, who were filled with the Spirit of God, discharged their prophetic functions with a quiet and tranquil mind. See the anonymous author, *Contra Cataphrygas*, in Eusebius, *Hist. Eccl.* v. 17; Epiphanius, *Hæres.* 48. See also Routh, *Rell. Sacræ*, i. p. 100; and Bp. Kaye, *On the Writings of Tertullian*, edit. 3, pp. 27–36. (Munter's *Primord. Eccles Afric.* p. 138, quoted by Oehler.)
[19] Amentiam.
[20] Ceterum.
[21] According to the hypothesis.

[1] Luke ix. 28–36.
[2] Scilicet, in ironical allusion to a Marcionite opinion.
[3] Luke ix. 35.
[4] Quoscunque.
[5] In sordibus aliquibus.
[6] Sic.
[7] To belong to another god.
[8] Secundum perversitatem.
[9] Prædicatores.
[10] Informator, Moses, as having organized the nation.
[11] Reformator, Elias, the great prophet.
[12] It was a primitive opinion in the Church that Elijah was to come, with Enoch, at the end of the world. See *De Anima*, chap. xxxv. and l.; also Irenæus, *De Hæres.* v. 5. [Vol. I. 530.]

than the Creator, whose entire dispensation[1] he, in fact, here described. He selects from His disciples three witnesses of the impending vision and voice. And this is just the way of the Creator. "In the mouth of three witnesses," says He, "shall every word be established."[2] He withdraws to a mountain. In the nature of the place I see much meaning. For the Creator had originally formed His ancient people on a mountain both with visible glory and His voice. It was only right that the New Testament should be attested[3] on such an elevated spot[4] as that whereon the Old Testament had been composed;[5] under a like covering of cloud also, which nobody will doubt, was condensed out of the Creator's air. Unless, indeed, he[6] had brought down his own clouds thither, because he had himself forced his way through the Creator's heaven;[7] or else it was only a precarious cloud,[8] as it were, of the Creator which he used. On the present (as also on the former)[9] occasion, therefore, the cloud was not silent; but there was the accustomed voice from heaven, and the Father's testimony to the Son; precisely as in the first Psalm He had said, "Thou art my Son, to-day have I begotten thee."[10] By the mouth of Isaiah also He had asked concerning Him, "Who is there among you that feareth God? Let him hear the voice of His Son."[11] When therefore He here presents Him with the words, "This is my (beloved) Son," this clause is of course understood, "whom I have promised." For if He once promised, and then afterwards says, "This is He," it is suitable conduct for one who accomplishes His purpose[12] that He should utter His voice in proof of the promise which He had formerly made; but unsuitable in one who is amenable to the retort, Can you, indeed, have a right to say, "This is my son," concerning whom you have given us no previous information,[13] any more than you have favoured us with a revelation about your own prior existence? "Hear ye Him," therefore, whom from the beginning (the Creator) had declared entitled to be heard in the name of a prophet, since it was as a prophet that He had to be regarded

by the people. "A prophet," says Moses, "shall the Lord your God raise up unto you, of your sons" (that is, of course, after a carnal descent[14]); "unto Him shall ye hearken, as unto me."[15] "Every one who will not hearken unto Him, his soul[16] shall be cut off from amongst his people."[17] So also Isaiah: "Who is there among you that feareth God? Let him hear the voice of His Son."[18] This voice the Father was going Himself to recommend. For, says he,[19] He establishes the words of His Son, when He says, "This is my beloved Son, hear ye Him." Therefore, even if there be made a transfer of the obedient "hearing" from Moses and Elias to[20] Christ, it is still not from another God, or to another Christ; but from[21] the Creator to His Christ, in consequence of the departure of the old covenant and the supervening of the new. "Not an ambassador, nor an angel, but He Himself," says Isaiah, "shall save them;"[22] for it is He Himself who is now declaring and fulfilling the law and the prophets. The Father gave to the Son new disciples,[23] after that Moses and Elias had been exhibited along with Him in the honour of His glory, and had then been dismissed as having fully discharged their duty and office, for the express purpose of affirming for Marcion's information the fact that Moses and Elias had a share in even the glory of Christ. But we have the entire structure[24] of this same vision in Habakkuk also, where the Spirit in the person of some[25] of the apostles says, "O Lord, I have heard Thy speech, and was afraid." What speech was this, other than the words of the voice from heaven, This is my beloved Son, hear ye, Him? "I considered thy works, and was astonished." When could this have better happened than when Peter, on seeing His glory, knew not what he was saying? "In the midst of the two Thou shalt be known"—even Moses and

---

[14] Censum: Some read *sensum*, "sense."
[15] Deut. xviii. 15.
[16] Anima: life.
[17] Deut. xviii. 19.
[18] Isa. l. 10.
[19] Tertullian, by introducing this statement with an "*inquit*," seems to make a quotation of it; but it is only a comment on the actual quotations. Tertullian's invariable object in this argument is to match some event or word pertaining to the Christ of the New Testament with some declaration of the Old Testament. In this instance the approving words of God upon the mount are in Heb. i. 5 applied to the Son, while in Ps. ii. 7 the Son applies them to Himself. Compare the *Adversus Praxean*, chap. xix. (Fr. Junius and Oehler.) It is, however, more likely that Tertullian really means to quote Isa. xliv. 26, "that confirmeth the word of His servant," which Tertullian reads, "Sistens verba filii sui," the Septuagint being, Καὶ ἱστῶν ῥῆμα παιδὸς αὐτοῦ.
[20] In Christo. *In* with an ablative is often used by our author for *in* with an accusative.
[21] Or perhaps "*by* the Creator."
[22] Isa. lxiii. 9, according to the Septuagint; only he reads *faciet* for aorist ἐσωσεν.
[23] A Marcionite position.
[24] Habitum.
[25] Interdum.

---

[1] Totum ordinem, in the three periods represented by Moses, and Elijah, and Christ.
[2] Compare Deut. xix. 15 with Luke ix. 28.
[3] Consignari.
[4] In eo suggestu.
[5] Conscriptum fuerat.
[6] Marcion's god.
[7] Compare above, book i. chap. 15, and book iv. chap. 7.
[8] Precario. This word is used in book v. chap. xii. to describe the *transitoriness* of the Creator's paradise and world.
[9] Nec nunc.
[10] Ps. ii. 7.
[11] Isa. l. 10, according to the Septuagint.
[12] Ejus est exhibentis.
[13] Non præmisisti. Oehler suggests *promisisti*, "have given us no promise."

Elias.[1] These likewise did Zechariah see under the figure of the two olive trees and olive branches.[2] For these are they of whom he says, "They are the two anointed ones, that stand by the Lord of the whole earth." And again Habakkuk says, "His glory covered the heavens" (that is, with that cloud), "and His splendour shall be like the light— even the light, wherewith His very raiment glistened." And if we would make mention of[3] the promise to Moses, we shall find it accomplished here. For when Moses desired to see the Lord, saying, "If therefore I have found grace in Thy sight, manifest Thyself to me, that I may see Thee distinctly,"[4] the sight which he desired to have was of that condition which he was to assume as man, and which as a prophet he knew was to occur. Respecting the *face* of God, however, he had already heard, "No man shall see me, and live." "This thing," said He, "which thou hast spoken, will I do unto thee." Then Moses said, "Show me Thy glory." And the Lord, with like reference to the future, replied, "I will pass before thee in my glory," etc. Then at the last He says, "And then thou shalt see my back."[5] Not loins, or calves of the legs, did he want to behold, but the glory which was to be revealed in the latter days.[6] He had promised that He would make Himself thus face to face visible to him, when He said to Aaron, "If there shall be a prophet among you, I will make myself known to him by vision, and by vision will I speak with him; but not so is my manner to Moses; with *him* will I speak mouth to mouth, even apparently" (that is to say, in the form of man which He was to assume), "and not in dark speeches."[7] Now, although Marcion has denied[8] that he is here represented as speaking with the Lord, but only as standing, yet, inasmuch as he stood "mouth to mouth," he must also have stood "face to face" *with him*, to use his words,[9] not far from him, in His very glory—not to say,[10] in His presence. And with this glory he went away enlightened from Christ, just as he used to do from the Creator; as *then* to dazzle the eyes of the children of Israel, so *now* to smite those of the blinded Marcion, who has failed to see how this argument also makes against him.

CHAP. XXIII. — IMPOSSIBLE THAT MARCION'S CHRIST SHOULD REPROVE THE FAITHLESS GENERATION. SUCH LOVING CONSIDERATION FOR INFANTS AS THE TRUE CHRIST WAS APT TO SHEW, ALSO IMPOSSIBLE FOR THE OTHER. ON THE THREE DIFFERENT CHARACTERS CONFRONTED AND INSTRUCTED BY CHRIST IN SAMARIA.

I take on myself the character[11] of Israel. Let Marcion's Christ stand forth, and exclaim, "O faithless generation![12] how long shall I be with you? how long shall I suffer you?"[13] He will immediately have to submit to this remonstrance from me: "Whoever you are, O stranger,[14] first tell us who you are, from whom you come, and what right you have over us. Thus far, all you possess[15] belongs to the Creator. Of course, if you come from Him, and are acting for Him, we will bear your reproof. But if you come from some other god, I should wish you to tell us what you have ever committed to us belonging to yourself,[16] which it was our duty to believe, seeing that you are upbraiding us with 'faithlessness,' who have never yet revealed to us your own self. How long ago[17] did you begin to treat with us, that you should be complaining of the delay? On what points have you borne with us, that you should adduce[18] your patience? Like Æsop's ass, you are just come from the well,[19] and are filling every place with your braying." I assume, besides,[20] the person of the disciples, against whom he has inveighed:[21] "O perverse nation! how long shall I be with you? how long shall I suffer you?" This outburst of his I might, of course, retort upon him most justly in such words as these: "Whoever you are, O stranger, first tell us who you are, from whom you come, what right you have over us. Thus far, I suppose, you belong to the Creator, and so we have followed you, recognising in you all things which are His. Now, if you come from Him, we will bear your reproof. If, however, you are acting for another, prythee tell us what you have ever conferred upon us that is simply your own, which it had become our duty to believe, seeing that you reproach us with 'faithlessness,' although up to this moment you show us no credentials. How long since did you begin to plead with us, that you are

---

[1] Hab. iii. 2, according to the Septuagint. St. Augustine similarly applied this passage, *De Civit.* Dei, ii. 32.
[2] Zech. iv. 3, 14.
[3] *Commemoremur*: be reminded, or call to mind.
[4] *Cognoscenter*: γνωστῶς, "so as to know Thee."
[5] See Ex. xxxiii. 13–23.
[6] *Posterioribus temporibus.* [The awful ribaldry of Voltaire upon this glorious revelation is based upon the Vulgate reading of Exod. xxxiii. 23, needlessly transferred to our Version, but corrected by the late Revisers.]
[7] Num. xii. 6–8.
[8] *Noluit.*
[9] It is difficult to see what this *inquit* means.
[10] *Nedum.*

[11] Personam: "I personate Israel."
[12] Genitura.
[13] Luke ix. 41.
[14] ἐπερχόμενε. The true Christ is ὁ ἐρχόμενος.
[15] Totum apud te.
[16] De tuo commisisti.
[17] Quam olim.
[18] Imputes.
[19] This fable is not extant (Oehler).
[20] Adhuc.
[21] Insiliit.

25

charging us with delay? Wherein have you borne with us, that you should even boast of your patience? The ass has only just arrived from Æsop's well, and he is already braying.'' Now who would not thus have rebutted the unfairness of the rebuke, if he had supposed its author to belong to him who had had no right as yet to complain? Except that not even He [1] would have inveighed against them, if He had not dwelt among them of old in the law and by the prophets, and with mighty deeds and many mercies, and had always experienced them to be "faithless." But, behold, Christ takes [2] infants, and teaches how all ought to be like them, if they ever wish to be greater.[3] The Creator, on the contrary,[4] let loose bears against children, in order to avenge His prophet Elisha, who had been mocked by them.[5] This antithesis is impudent enough, since it throws together [6] things so different as infants [7] and children,[8]—an age still innocent, and one already capable of discretion—able to mock, if not to blaspheme. As therefore God is a just God, He spared not impious children, exacting as He does honour for every time of life, and especially, of course, from youth. And as God is good, He so loves infants as to have blessed the midwives in Egypt, when they protected the infants of the Hebrews [9] which were in peril from Pharaoh's command.[10] Christ therefore shares this kindness with the Creator. As indeed for Marcion's god, who is an enemy to marriage, how can he possibly seem to be a lover of little children, which are simply the issue of marriage? He who hates the seed, must needs also detest the fruit. Yea, he ought to be deemed more ruthless than the king of Egypt.[11] For whereas Pharaoh forbade infants to be brought up, *he* will not allow them even to be born, depriving them of their ten months' existence in the womb. And how much more credible it is, that kindness to little children should be attributed to Him who blessed matrimony for the procreation of mankind, and in such benediction included also the promise of connubial fruit itself, the first of which is that of infancy![12] The Creator, at the request of Elias, inflicts the blow [13] of fire from heaven in the case of that false prophet (of Baalzebub).[14] I recognise herein the severity of the Judge. And I, on the contrary, the severe rebuke [15] of Christ on His disciples, when they were for inflicting [16] a like visitation on that obscure village of the Samaritans.[17] The heretic, too, may discover that this gentleness of Christ was promised by the selfsame severest Judge. "He shall not contend," says He, "nor shall His voice be heard in the street; a bruised reed shall He not crush, and smoking flax shall He not quench." [18] Being of such a character, He was of course much the less disposed to burn men. For even at that time the Lord said to Elias,[19] "He was not in the fire, but in the still smalll voice." [20] Well, but why does this most humane and merciful God reject the man who offers himself to Him as an inseparable companion? [21] If it were from pride or from hypocrisy that he had said, "I will follow Thee whithersoever Thou goest, ' then, by judicially reproving an act of either pride or hypocrisy as worthy of rejection, He performed the office of a Judge. And, of course, him whom He rejected He condemned to the loss of not following the Saviour.[22] For as He calls to salvation him whom He does not reject, or him whom He voluntarily invites, so does He consign to perdition him whom He rejects. When, however, He answers the man, who alleged as an excuse his father's burial, "Let the dead bury their dead, but go thou and preach the kingdom of God," [23] He gave a clear confirmation to those two laws of the Creator—that in Leviticus, which concerns the sacerdotal office, and forbids the priests to be present at the funerals even of their parents. "The priest," says He, "shall not enter where there is any dead person; [24] and for his father he shall not be defiled" [25]; as well as that in Numbers, which relates to the (Nazarite) vow of separation; for there he who devotes himself to God, among other things, is bidden "not to come at any dead body," not even of his father, or his mother, or his brother.[26] Now it was, I suppose, for the Nazarite and the priestly office that He intended this man whom

---

[1] Nisi quod nec ille. This *ille*, of course, means the Creator's Christ.
[2] Diligit: or, loves.
[3] Luke ix. 47, 48.
[4] Autem.
[5] 2 Kings ii. 23, 24.
[6] Committit.
[7] Parvulos.
[8] Pueros: [young lads].
[9] Partus Hebræos.
[10] Ex. ii. 15-21.
[11] See a like comparison in book i. chap. xxix. p. 294.
[12] Qui de infantia primus est: i.e., *cujus* qui de infantia, etc. [Elucidation VIII.]
[13] Repræsentat plagam.

[14] 2 Kings i. 9-12.
[15] I translate after Oehler's text, which is supported by the oldest authorities. Pamelius and Rigaltius, however, read "Christi lenitatem increpantis eandem animadversionem," etc. ("On the contrary, I recognize the gentleness of Christ, who rebuked His disciples when they," etc.) This reading is only conjectural, suggested by the "Christi lenitatem" of the context.
[16] Destinantes.
[17] Luke ix. 51-56.
[18] Isa. xlii. 2, 3.
[19] Compare *De Patientia*, chap. xv.
[20] 1 Kings xix. 12.
[21] Luke ix. 57, 58.
[22] Salutem: i.e. "Christ, who is our salvation" (Fr. Junius).
[23] Luke ix. 59, 60.
[24] Animam defunctam.
[25] Lev. xxi. 1, according to our author's reading.
[26] Num. vi. 6, 7[?]

He had been inspiring[1] to preach the kingdom of God. Or else, if it be not so, he must be pronounced impious enough who, without the intervention of any precept of the law, commanded that burials of parents should be neglected by their sons. When, indeed, in the third case before us, (Christ) forbids the man "to look back" who wanted first "to bid his family farewell," He only follows out the rule[2] of the Creator. For this (retrospection) He had been against their making, whom He had rescued out of Sodom.[3]

CHAP. XXIV.—ON THE MISSION OF THE SEVENTY DISCIPLES, AND CHRIST'S CHARGE TO THEM. PRECEDENTS DRAWN FROM THE OLD TESTAMENT. ABSURDITY OF SUPPOSING THAT MARCION'S CHRIST COULD HAVE GIVEN THE POWER OF TREADING ON SERPENTS AND SCORPIONS.

He chose also seventy other missionaries[4] besides the twelve. Now why, if the twelve followed the number of the twelve fountains of Elim,[5] should not the seventy correspond to the like number of the palms of that place?[6] Whatever be the *Antitheses* of the comparison, it is a diversity in the causes, not in the powers, which has mainly produced them. But if one does not keep in view the diversity of the *causes*,[7] he is very apt to infer a difference of *powers*.[8] When the children of Israel went out of Egypt, the Creator brought them forth laden with their spoils of gold and silver vessels, and with loads besides of raiment and unleavened dough;[9] whereas Christ commanded His disciples not to carry even a staff[10] for their journey. The former were thrust forth into a desert, but the latter were sent into cities. Consider the difference presented in the occasions,[11] and you will understand how it was one and the same power which arranged the mission[12] of His people according to their poverty in the one case, and their plenty in the other. He cut down[13] their supplies when they could be replenished through the cities, just as He had accumulated[14] them when exposed to the scantiness of the desert. Even shoes He forbade them to carry. For it was He under whose very protection the people wore not out a shoe,[15] even in the wilderness for the space of so many years. "No one," says He, "shall ye salute by the way."[16] What a destroyer of the prophets, forsooth, is Christ, seeing it is from them that He received his precept also! When Elisha sent on his servant Gehazi before him to raise the Shunammite's son from death, I rather think he gave him these instructions:[17] "Gird up thy loins, and take my staff in thine hand, and go thy way: if thou meet any man, salute him not;[18] and if any salute thee, answer him not again."[19] For what is a wayside blessing but a mutual salutation as men meet? So also the Lord commands: "Into whatsoever house they enter, let them say, Peace be to it."[20] Herein He follows the very same example. For Elisha enjoined upon his servant the same salutation when he met the Shunammite; he was to say to her: "Peace to thine husband, peace to thy child."[21] Such will be rather our *Antitheses;* they compare Christ with, instead of sundering Him from, the Creator. "The labourer is worthy of his hire."[22] Who could better pronounce such a sentence than God the Judge? For to decide that the workman deserves his wages, is in itself a judicial act. There is no award which consists not in a process of judgment. The law of the Creator on this point also presents us with a corroboration, for He judges that labouring oxen are as labourers worthy of their hire: "Thou shalt not muzzle," says He, "the ox when he treadeth out the corn."[23] Now, who is so good to man[24] as He who is also merciful to cattle? Now, when Christ pronounced labourers to be worthy of their hire, He, in fact, exonerated from blame the Creator about depriving the Egyptians of their gold and silver vessels.[25] For they who had built for the Egyptians their houses and cities, were surely workmen worthy of their hire, and were not instructed in a fraudulent act, but only set to claim compensation for their hire, which they were unable in any other way to exact from their masters.[26] That the kingdom of God was neither new nor unheard of, He in this way affirmed, whilst at the same time He bids them announce that it was near at hand.[27] Now it is that which

---

[1] Imbuerat.
[2] Sectam.
[3] Gen. xix. 17.
[4] Apostolos: Luke x. 1.
[5] Compare above, book iv. chap. xiii. p. 364.
[6] Ex. xv. 27 and Num. xxxiii. 9.
[7] Causarum: "occasions" or circumstances.
[8] Potestatum. In Marcionite terms, "The *Gods* of the Old and the New Testaments."
[9] Consparsionum. [Punic Latin.] Ex. xii. 34, 35.
[10] Virgam, Luke x. 4 and Matt. x. 10.
[11] Causarum offerentiam.
[12] Expeditionem, with the sense also of "supplies" in the next clause.
[13] Circumcidens.
[14] Struxerat.
[15] Deut. xxix. 5.
[16] Luke x. 4.
[17] See 2 Kings iv. 29. ·
[18] Literally, "bless him not, i.e., salute him not."
[19] Literally, "answer him not, i.e., return not his salutation."
[20] Luke x. 5.
[21] 2 Kings iv. 26. He reads the optative instead of the indicative.
[22] Luke x. 7.
[23] Deut. xxv. 4.
[24] Compare above, book ii. chap. 17, p. 311.
[25] See this argued at length above, in book ii. chap. 20. p. 313.
[26] Dominatoribus.
[27] Luke x. 9.

was once far off, which can be properly said to have become near. If, however, a thing had never existed previous to its becoming near, it could never have been said to have approached, because it had never existed at a distance. Everything which is new and unknown is also sudden.[1] Everything which is sudden, then, first receives the accident of time[2] when it is announced; for it then first puts on appearance of form.[3] Besides it will be impossible for a thing either to have been tardy[4] all the while it remained unannounced,[5] or to have approached[6] from the time it shall begin to be announced.

He likewise adds, that they should say to such as would not receive them: "Notwithstanding ye be sure of this, that the kingdom of God is come nigh unto you."[7] If He does not enjoin this by way of a commination, the injunction is a most useless one. For what mattered it to them that the kingdom was at hand, unless its approach was accompanied with judgment?—even for the salvation of such as received the announcement thereof. How, if there can be a threat without its accomplishment, can you have in a threatening god, one that executes also, and in both, one that is a judicial being?[8] So, again, He commands that the dust be shaken off against them, as a testimony,—the very particles of their ground which might cleave[9] to the sandal, not to mention[10] any other sort of communication with them.[11] But if their churlishness[12] and inhospitality were to receive no vengeance from Him, for what purpose does He premise a testimony, which surely forbodes some threats? Furthermore, when the Creator also, in the book of Deuteronomy, forbids the reception of the Ammonites and the Moabites into the church,[13] because, when His people came from Egypt, they fraudulently withheld provisions from them with inhumanity and inhospitality,[14] it will be manifest that the prohibition of intercourse descended to Christ from Him. The form of it which He uses—"He that despiseth you, despiseth me"[15]—the Creator had also addressed to Moses: "Not against thee have

they murmured, but against me."[16] Moses, indeed, was as much an apostle as the apostles were prophets. The authority of both offices will have to be equally divided, as it proceeds from one and the same Lord, (the God) of apostles and prophets. Who is He that shall bestow "the power of treading on serpents and scorpions?"[17] Shall it be He who is the Lord of all living creatures or who is not god over a single lizard? Happily the Creator has promised by Isaiah to give this power even to little children, of putting their hand in the cockatrice 'den and on the hole of the young asps without at all receiving hurt.[18] And, indeed, we are aware (without doing violence to the literal sense of the passage, since even these noxious animals have actually been unable to do hurt where there has been faith) that under the figure of scorpions and serpents are portended evil spirits, whose very prince is described[19] by the name of serpent, dragon, and every other most conspicuous beast in the power of the Creator.[20] This power the Creator conferred first of all upon His Christ, even as the ninetieth Psalm says to Him: "Upon the asp and the basilisk shalt Thou tread; the lion and the dragon shalt Thou trample under foot."[21] So also Isaiah: "In that day the Lord God shall draw His sacred, great, and strong sword" (even His Christ) "against that dragon, that great and tortuous serpent; and He shall slay him in that day."[22] But when the same prophet says, "The way shall be called a clean and holy way; over it the unclean thing shall not pass, nor shall be there any unclean way; but the dispersed shall pass over it, and they shall not err therein; no lion shall be there, nor any ravenous beast shall go up thereon; it shall not be found there,"[23] he points out the way of faith, by which we shall reach to God; and then to this way of faith he promises this utter crippling[24] and subjugation of all noxious animals. Lastly, you may discover the suitable times of the promise, if you read what precedes the passage: "Be strong, ye weak hands and ye feeble knees: then the eyes of the blind shall be opened, and the ears of the deaf shall hear; then shall the lame man leap as an hart, and the tongue of the dumb shall be articulate."[25] When, therefore, He proclaimed the benefits of His cures, then also did He put the scorpions and the

---

[1] Subitum.
[2] Accipit tempus,
[3] Inducens speciem.
[4] Tardasse.
[5] The announcement (according to the definition) defining the beginning of its existence in time.
[6] Appropinquasse.
[7] Luke x. 11.
[8] Et judicem in utroque.
[9] Hærentia.
[10] Nedum.
[11] Luke x. 11.
[12] Inhumanitas.
[13] Ecclesiam. There is force in thus using Christian terms for Jewish ordinances, full as he is of the identity of the God of the old with Him of the new covenant.
[14] Deut. xxiii. 3.
[15] Luke x. 16.

[16] Num. xiv. 27.
[17] Luke x. 19.
[18] Isa. xi. 8, 9.
[19] Deputetur.
[20] Penes Creatorem.
[21] Ps. xci. 13.
[22] Isa. xxvii. 1, Sept.
[23] Isa. xxxv. 8, 9, Sept.
[24] Evacuationem.
[25] Isa. xxxv. 3, 5, 6, Sept.

serpents under the feet of His saints—even He who had first received this power from the Father, in order to bestow it upon others, and then manfested it forth conformably to the order of prophecy.[1]

CHAP. XXV.—CHRIST THANKS THE FATHER FOR REVEALING TO BABES WHAT HE HAD CONCEALED FROM THE WISE. THIS CONCEALMENT JUDICIOUSLY EFFECTED BY THE CREATOR. OTHER POINTS IN ST. LUKE'S CHAP. X. SHOWN TO BE ONLY POSSIBLE TO THE CREATOR'S CHRIST.

Who shall be invoked as the Lord of heaven, that does not first show Himself[2] to have been the maker thereof? For He says, "I thank thee, (O Father,) and own Thee, Lord of heaven, because those things which had been hidden from the wise and prudent, Thou has revealed unto babes."[3] What things are these? And whose? And by whom hidden? And by whom revealed? If it was by Marcion's god that they were hidden and revealed, it was an extremely iniquitous proceeding;[4] for nothing at all had he ever produced[5] in which anything could have been hidden—no prophecies, no parables, no visions, no evidences[6] of things, or words, or names, obscured by allegories and figures, or cloudy enigmas, but he had concealed the greatness even of himself, which he was with all his might revealing by his Christ. Now in what respect had the wise and prudent done wrong,[7] that God should be hidden from them, when their wisdom and prudence had been insufficient to come to the knowledge of Him? No way had been provided by himself,[8] by any declaration of his works, or any vestiges whereby they might become[9] wise and prudent. However, if they had even failed in any duty towards a god whom they knew not, suppose him now at last to be known, still they ought not to have found a jealous god in him who is introduced as unlike the Creator. Therefore, since he had neither provided any materials in which he could have hidden anything, nor had any offenders from whom he could have hidden himself; since, again, even if he had had any, he ought not to have hidden himself from them, he will not now be himself the revealer, who was not previously the concealer; so neither will any be the Lord of heaven nor the Father of

Christ but He in whom all these attributes consistently meet.[10] For He conceals by His preparatory apparatus of prophetic obscurity, the understanding of which is open to faith (for "if ye will not believe, ye shall not understand"[11]); and He had offenders in those wise and prudent ones who would not seek after God, although He was to be discovered in His so many and mighty works,[12] or who rashly philosophized about Him, and thereby furnished to heretics their arts;[13] and lastly, He is a jealous God. Accordingly,[14] that which Christ thanks God for doing, He long ago[15] announced by Isaiah: "I will destroy the wisdom of the wise, and the understanding of the prudent will I hide."[16] So in another passage He intimates both that He has concealed, and that He will also reveal: "I will give unto them treasures that have been hidden, and secret ones will I discover to them."[17] And again: "Who else shall scatter the tokens of ventriloquists,[18] and the devices of those who divine out of their own heart; turning wise men backward, and making their counsels foolish?"[19] Now, if He has designated His Christ as an enlightener of the Gentiles, saying, "I have set thee for a light of the Gentiles;"[20] and if we understand these to be meant in the word babes[21]—as having been once dwarfs in knowledge and infants in prudence, and even now also babes in their lowliness of faith—we shall of course more easily understand how He who had once hidden "these things," and promised a revelation of them through Christ, was the same God as He who had now revealed them unto babes. Else, if it was Marcion's god who revealed the things which had been formerly hidden by the Creator, it follows[22] that he did the Creator's work by setting forth His deeds.[23] But he did it, say you, for His destruction, that he might refute them.[24] Therefore he ought to have refuted them to those from whom the Creator had hidden them, even the wise and prudent. For if he had a kind intention in what he did, the gift of knowledge was due to those from whom the Creator had detained it, instead of the babes, to whom the Creator had grudged no gift. But after all, it is, I presume, the edifica-

---

[1] Secundum ordinem prædicationis.
[2] Ostenditur.
[3] Luke x. 21.
[4] Satis inique.
[5] Præmiserat.
[6] Argumenta.
[7] Deliquerant.
[8] On the Marcionite hypothesis.
[9] Deducerentur.

[10] In quem competunt omnia.
[11] Isa. vii. 9.
[12] Rom. i. 20-23.
[13] Ingenia.
[14] Denique.
[15] Olim.
[16] Isa. xxix. 14, Sept.
[17] Isa. xlv. 3, Sept.
[18] Ventriloquorum, Greek ἐγγαστριμύθων.
[19] Isa. xliv. 25, Sept.
[20] Isa. xlii. 6 and xlix. 6.
[21] Luke x. 21.
[22] Ergo.
[23] Res ejus edisserens.
[24] Uti traduceret eas.

tion [1] rather than the demolition [2] of the law and the prophets which we have thus far found effected in Christ. "All things," He says, " are delivered unto me of my Father." [3] You may believe Him, if He is the Christ of the Creator to whom all things belong; because the Creator has not delivered to a Son who is less than Himself all things, which He created by [4] Him, that is to say, by His Word. If, on the contrary, he is the notorious stranger, [5] what are the " all things" which have been delivered to him by the Father? Are they the Creator's? Then the things which the Father delivered to the Son are good, and the Creator is therefore good, since all His "things" are good; whereas he [6] is no longer good who has invaded another's good (domains) to deliver it to his son, thus teaching robbery [7] of another's goods. Surely he must be a most mendacious being, who had no other means of enriching his son than by helping himself to another's property! Or else, [8] if nothing of the Creator's has been delivered to him by the Father, by what right [9] does he claim for himself (authority over) man? Or again, if man has been delivered to him, and man alone, then man is not "all things." But Scripture clearly says that a transfer of all things has been made to the Son. If, however, you should interpret this "all" of the whole human race, that is, all nations, then the delivery of even these to the Son is within the purpose of the Creator: [10] " I will give Thee the heathen for Thine inheritance, and the uttermost parts of the earth for Thy possession." [11] If, indeed, he has some things of his own, the whole of which he might give to his son, along with the man of the Creator, then show some one thing of them all, as a sample, that I may believe; lest I should have as much reason not to believe that all things belong to him, of whom I see nothing, as I have ground for believing that even the things which I see not are His, to whom belongs the universe, which I see. But "no man knoweth who the Father is, but the Son; and who the Son is, but the Father, and he to whom the Son will reveal Him." [12] And so it was an unknown · god that Christ preached! And other heretics, too, prop themselves up by this passage; alleging in opposition to it that the Creator was known to

all, both to Israel by familiar intercourse, and to the Gentiles by nature. Well, how is it He Himself testifies that He was not known to Israel? "But Israel doth not know me, and my people doth not consider me;" [13] nor to the Gentiles: "For, behold," says He, "of the nations I have no man." [14] Therefore He reckoned them "as the drop of a bucket," [15] while "Sion He left as a look-out [16] in a vineyard." [17] See, then, whether there be not here a confirmation of the prophet's word, when he rebukes that ignorance of man toward God which continued to the days of the Son of man. For it was on this account that he inserted the clause that the Father is known by him to whom the Son has revealed Him, because it was even He who was announced as set by the Father to be a light to the Gentiles, who of course required to be enlightened concerning God, as well as to Israel, even by imparting to it a fuller knowledge of God. Arguments, therefore, will be of no use for belief in the rival god which may be suitable [18] for the Creator, because it is only such as are unfit for the Creator which will be able to advance belief in His rival. If you look also into the next words, "Blessed are the eyes which see the things which ye see, for I tell you that prophets have not seen the things which ye see," [19] you will find that they follow from the sense above, that no man indeed had come to the knowledge of God as he ought to have done, [20] since even the prophets had not seen the things which were being seen under Christ. Now if He had not been my Christ, He would not have made any mention of the prophets in this passage. For what was there to wonder at, if they had not seen the things of a god who had been unknown to them, and was only revealed a long time after them? What blessedness, however, could theirs have been, who were then seeing what others were naturally [21] unable to see, since it was of things which they had never predicted that they had not obtained the sight; [22] if it were not because they might justly [23] have seen the things pertaining to their God, which they had even predicted, but which they at the same time [24] had not seen? This, however, will be the blessedness of others, even of such as were seeing the things which

[1] Constructionem.
[2] Destructionem.
[3] Luke x. 22.
[4] Per.
[5] ἐπερχόμενος ille ; on which see above, chap. xxiii. p. 385
[6] Marcion's god.
[7] Alieno abstinere.
[8] Aut si.
[9] Ecquomodo.
[10] Creatoris est.
[11] Ps. ii. 8.
[12] Luke x. 22.

[13] Isa. i. 3.
[14] This passage it is not easy to identify. [See Is. lxiii. 3.] The books point to Isa. lxv. 5, but there is there no trace of it.
[15] Isa. xl. 15. [Compare Is. lxiii. 3. Sept.]
[16] Speculam.
[17] When the vintage was gathered, Isa. i. 8.
[18] Quæ competere possunt.
[19] Luke x. 23, 24.
[20] Ut decuit.
[21] Merito.
[22] Repræsentationem.
[23] Æque.
[24] Tamen.

others had only foretold. We shall by and by show, nay, we have already shown, that in Christ those things were seen which had been foretold, but yet had been hidden from the very prophets who foretold them, in order that they might be hidden also from the wise and the prudent. In the true Gospel, a certain doctor of the law comes to the Lord and asks, "What shall I do to inherit *eternal life?*" In the heretical gospel life only is mentioned, without the attribute *eternal;* so that the lawyer seems to have consulted Christ simply about the life which the Creator in the law promises to prolong,[1] and the Lord to have therefore answered him according to the law, "Thou shalt love the Lord thy God with all thy heart, and with all thy soul, and with all thy strength,"[2] since the question was concerning the conditions of *mere* life. But the lawyer of course knew very well in what way the life which the law meant[3] was to be obtained, so that his question could have had no relation to the life whose rules he was himself in the habit of teaching. But seeing that even the dead were now raised by Christ, and being himself excited to the hope of an eternal life by these examples of a restored[4] one, he would lose no more time in merely looking on (at the wonderful things which had made him) so high in hope.[5] He therefore consulted him about the attainment of eternal life. Accordingly, the Lord, being Himself the same,[6] and introducing no new precept other than that which relates above all others[7] to (man's) entire salvation, even including the present and the future life,[8] places before him[9] the very essence[10] of the law—that he should in every possible way love the Lord his God. If, indeed, it were only about a lengthened life, such as is at the Creator's disposal, that he inquired and Christ answered, and not about the eternal life, which is at the disposal of Marcion's god, how is he to obtain the eternal one? Surely not in the same manner as the prolonged life. For in proportion to the difference of the reward must be supposed to be also the diversity of the services. Therefore your disciple, Marcion,[11] will not obtain his eternal life in consequence of loving your God, in the same way as the man who loves the Creator will secure the lengthened life. But how happens it that, if

He is to be loved who promises the prolonged life, He is not much more to be loved who offers the eternal life? Therefore both one and the other life will be at the disposal of one and the same Lord; because one and the same discipline is to be followed[12] for one and the other life. What the Creator teaches to be loved, that must He necessarily maintain[13] also by Christ,[14] for that rule holds good here, which prescribes that greater things ought to be believed of Him who has first lesser proofs to show, than of him for whom no preceding smaller presumptions have secured a claim to be believed in things of higher import. It matters not[15] then, whether the word *eternal* has been interpolated by us.[16] It is enough for me, that the Christ who invited men to the eternal—not the lengthened—life, when consulted about the temporal life which he was destroying, did not choose to exhort the man rather to that eternal life which he was introducing. Pray, what would the Creator's Christ have done, if He who had made man for loving the Creator did not belong to the Creator? I suppose He would have said that the Creator was not to be loved!

CHAP. XXVI. — FROM ST. LUKE'S ELEVENTH CHAPTER OTHER EVIDENCE THAT CHRIST COMES FROM THE CREATOR. THE LORD'S PRAYER AND OTHER WORDS OF CHRIST. THE DUMB SPIRIT AND CHRIST'S DISCOURSE ON OCCASION OF THE EXPULSION. THE EXCLAMATION OF THE WOMAN IN THE CROWD.

When in a certain place he had been praying to that Father above,[17] looking up with insolent and audacious eyes to the heaven of the Creator, by whom in His rough and cruel nature he might have been crushed with hail and lightning—just as it was by Him contrived that he was (afterwards) attached to a cross[18] at Jerusalem—one of his disciples came to him and said, "Master, teach us to pray, as John also taught his disciples." This he said, forsooth, because he thought that different prayers were required for different gods! Now, he who had advanced such a conjecture as this should first show that another god had been proclaimed by Christ. For nobody would have wanted to know how to pray, before he had learned whom he was to pray to. If, however, he had already learned this, prove it. If you find nowhere any proof, let me tell you[19] that it was to the Creator that he asked

---

[1] Ex. xx. 12 and Deut. vi. 2.
[2] Luke x. 27.
[3] Legalem.
[4] Recidivæ.
[5] This is perhaps the meaning of " ne plus aliquid observationis exigeret sublimior spe."
[6] Nec alius.
[7] Principaliter.
[8] Et utramque vitam.
[9] Ei opponit.
[10] Caput.
[11] Dei tui . . . Marcionites.

[12] Captanda.
[13] Præstet.
[14] i.e., he must needs have it taught and recommended by Christ.
[15] Viderit.
[16] As Marcion pretended.
[17] Luke xi. 1.
[18] Suffigi.
[19] Scito.

for instruction in prayer, to whom John's disciples also used to pray. But, inasmuch as John had introduced some new order of prayer, this disciple had not improperly presumed to think that he ought also to ask of Christ whether they too must not (according to some special rule of their Master) pray, not indeed to another god, but in another manner. Christ accordingly[1] would not have taught His disciple prayer before He had given him the knowledge of God Himself. Therefore what He actually taught was prayer to Him whom the disciple had already known. In short, you may discover in the import[2] of the prayer what God is addressed therein. To whom can I say, " Father ? "[3] To him who had nothing to do with making me, from whom I do not derive my origin? Or to Him, who, by making and fashioning me, became my parent?[4] Of whom can I ask for His Holy Spirit? Of him who gives not even the mundane spirit;[5] or of Him " who maketh His angels spirits," and whose Spirit it was which in the beginning hovered upon the waters.[6] Whose kingdom shall I wish to come—his, of whom I never heard as the king of glory; or His, in whose hand are even the hearts of kings? Who shall give me my daily[7] bread? Shall it be he who produces for me not a grain of millet-seed;[8] or He who even from heaven gave to His people day by day the bread of angels?[9] Who shall forgive me my trespasses?[10] He who, by refusing to judge them, does not retain them; or He who, unless He forgives them, will retain them, even to His judgment? Who shall suffer us not to be led into temptation? He before whom the tempter will never be able to tremble; or He who from the beginning has beforehand condemned[11] the angel tempter? If any one, with such a form,[12] invokes another god and not the Creator, he does not pray; he only blasphemes.[13] In like manner, from whom must I ask that I may receive? Of whom seek, that I may find? To whom knock, that it may be opened to me?[14] Who has to give to him that asks, but He to whom all things belong, and whose am I also that am the asker? What, however, have I lost before that other god, that I should seek of him and find it. If it be wisdom and

prudence, it is the Creator who has hidden them. Shall I resort to him, then, in quest of them? If it be health[15] and life, they are at the disposal of the Creator. Nor must anything be sought and found anywhere else than there, where it is kept in secret that it may come to light. So, again, at no other door will I knock than at that out of which my privilege has reached me.[16] In fine, if to receive, and to find, and to be admitted, is the fruit of labour and earnestness to him who has asked, and sought, and knocked, understand that these duties have been enjoined, and results promised, by the Creator. As for that most excellent god of yours, coming as he professes gratuitously to help man, who was not his (creature),[17] he could not have imposed upon him any labour, or (endowed him with) any earnestness. For he would by this time cease to be the most excellent god, were he not spontaneously to give to every one who does not ask, and permit every one who seeks not to find, and open to every one who does not knock. The Creator, on the contrary,[18] was able to proclaim these duties and rewards by Christ, in order that man, who by sinning had offended his God, might toil on (in his probation), and by his perseverance in asking might receive, and in seeking might find, and in knocking might enter. Accordingly, the preceding similitude[19] represents the man who went at night and begged for the loaves, in the light of a friend and not a stranger, and makes him knock at a friend's house and not at a stranger's. But even if he has offended, man is more of a friend with the Creator than with the god of Marcion. At His door, therefore, does he knock to whom he had the right of access; whose gate he had found; whom he knew to possess bread; in bed now with His children, whom He had willed to be born.[20] Even though the knocking is late in the day, it is yet the Creator's time. To Him belongs the latest hour who owns an entire age[21] and the end thereof. As for the new god, however, no one could have knocked at his door late, for he has hardly yet[22] seen the light of morning. It is the Creator, who once shut the door to the Gentiles, which was then knocked at by the Jews, that both rises and gives, if not now to man as a friend, yet not as a stranger, but, as He says, " because

[1] Proinde.
[2] Sensum.
[3] Luke xi. 2.
[4] Generavit.
[5] Mundialis spiritus : perhaps " the breath of life."
[6] Gen. i. 2.
[7] Luke xi. 3.
[8] Milium.
[9] Ps. lxviii. 25.
[10] Luke xi. 4.
[11] Prædamnavit.
[12] Hoc ordine.
[13] Infamat.
[14] Luke xi. 9.

[15] Salutem : perhaps salvation.
[16] Unde sum functus. This obscure clause may mean " the right of praying," or " the right of access, and boldness to knock."
[17] Ad præstandum non suo homini.
[18] Autem.
[19] See Luke xi. 5–8.
[20] A sarcastic allusion to the ante-nuptial error of Marcion, which he has exposed more than once (see book i. chap. xxix. and book iv. chap. xxiii. p. 386.).
[21] Sæculum.
[22] Tantum quod = vixdum (Oehler).

of his importunity." [1] *Importunate*, however, the recent god could not have permitted any one to be in the short time (since his appearance). [2] Him, therefore, whom you call the Creator recognise also as "Father." It is even He who knows what His children require. For when they asked for bread, He gave them manna from heaven; and when they wanted flesh, He sent them abundance of quails—not a serpent for a fish, nor for an egg a scorpion. [3] It will, however, appertain to Him not to give evil instead of good, who has both one and the other in His power. Marcion's god, on the contrary, not having a scorpion, was unable to refuse to give what he did not possess; only He (could do so), who, having a scorpion, yet gives it not. In like manner, it is He who will give the Holy Spirit, at whose command [4] is also the unholy spirit. When He cast out the "demon which was dumb" [5] (and by a cure of this sort verified Isaiah), [6] and having been charged with casting out demons by Beelzebub, He said, "If I by Beelzebub cast out demons, by whom do your sons cast them out?" [7] By such a question what does He otherwise mean, than that He ejects the spirits by the same power by which their sons also did—that is, by the power of the Creator? For if you suppose the meaning to be, "If I by Beelzebub, etc., by whom your sons?"—as if He would reproach them with having the power of Beelzebub,—you are met at once by the preceding sentence, that "Satan cannot be divided against himself." [8] So that it was not by Beelzebub that even they were casting out demons, but (as we have said) by the power of the Creator; and that He might make this understood, He adds: "But if I with the finger of God cast out demons, is not the kingdom of God come near unto you?" [9] For the magicians who stood before Pharaoh and resisted Moses called the power of the Creator "*the finger of God.*" [10] It was the finger of God, because it was a sign [11] that even a thing of weakness was yet abundant in strength. This Christ also showed, when, recalling to notice (and not obliterating) those ancient wonders which were really His own, [12] He said that the power of God must be understood to be the finger of none other God than Him, under [13] whom it had received this

appellation. *His* kingdom, therefore, was come near to them, whose power was called His "finger." Well, therefore, did He connect [14] with the parable of "the strong man armed," whom "a stronger man still overcame," [15] the prince of the demons, whom He had already called Beelzebub and Satan; signifying that it was he who was overcome by the finger of God, and not that the Creator had been subdued by another god. Besides, [16] how could His kingdom be still standing, with its boundaries, and laws, and functions, whom, even if the whole world were left entire to Him, Marcion's god could possibly seem to have overcome as "the stronger than He," if it were not in consequence of His law that even Marcionites were constantly dying, by returning in their dissolution [17] to the ground, and were so often admonished by even a scorpion, that the Creator had by no means been overcome? [18] "A (certain) mother of the company exclaims, 'Blessed is the womb that bare Thee, and the paps which Thou hast sucked;' but the Lord said, 'Yea, rather, blessed are they that hear the word of God, and keep it.'" [19] Now He had in precisely similar terms rejected His mother or His brethren, whilst preferring those who heard and obeyed God. [20] His mother, however, was not here present with Him. On that former occasion, therefore, He had not denied that He was her son by birth. [21] On hearing this (salutation) the second time, He the second time transferred, as He had done before, [22] the "blessedness" to His disciples from the womb and the paps of His mother, from whom, however, unless He had in her (a real mother) He could not have transferred it.

CHAP. XXVII.—CHRIST'S REPREHENSION OF THE PHARISEES SEEKING A SIGN. HIS CENSURE OF THEIR LOVE OF OUTWARD SHOW RATHER THAN INWARD HOLINESS. SCRIPTURE ABOUNDS WITH ADMONITIONS OF A SIMILAR PURPORT. PROOFS OF HIS MISSION FROM THE CREATOR.

I prefer elsewhere refuting [23] the faults which the Marcionites find in the Creator. It is here enough that they are also found in Christ. [24] Behold how unequal, inconsistent, and capricious he is! Teaching one thing

---

[1] Luke xi. 8.
[2] Tam cito.
[3] Luke xi. 11–13.
[4] Apud quem.
[5] Luke xi. 14.
[6] Isa. xxix. 18.
[7] Luke xi. 19.
[8] Luke xi. 18.
[9] Luke xi. 20.
[10] Ex. viii. 19.
[11] Significaret.
[12] Vetustatum scilicet suarum.
[13] Apud.

[14] Applicuit.
[15] Luke xi. 21, 22.
[16] Ceterum.
[17] Defluendo.
[18] The *scorpion* here represents any class of the lowest animals, especially such as stung. The Marcionites impiously made it a reproach to the Creator, that He had formed such worthless and offensive creatures. Compare book i. chap. 17, note 5. p.283.
[19] Luke xi. 27, 28.
[20] See above, on Luke viii. 21.
[21] Natura.
[22] Proinde.
[23] Purgare.
[24] From the Marcionite point of view.

and doing another, he enjoins "giving to every one that seeks;" and yet he himself refuses to give to those "who seek a sign."[1] For a vast age he hides his own light from men, and yet says that a candle must not be hidden, but affirms that it ought to be set upon a candlestick, that it may give light to all.[2] He forbids cursing *again*, and cursing much more of course; and yet he heaps his *woe* upon the Pharisees and doctors of the law.[3] Who so closely resembles my God as His own Christ? We have often already laid it down for certain,[4] that He could not have been branded[5] as the destroyer of the law if He had promulged another god. Therefore even the Pharisee, who invited Him to dinner in the passage before us,[6] expressed some surprise[7] in His presence that He had not washed before He sat down to meat, in accordance with the law, since it was the God of the law that He was proclaiming.[8] Jesus also interpreted the law to him when He told him that they "made clean the outside of the cup and the platter, whereas their inward part was full of ravening and wickedness." *This He said*, to signify that by the cleansing of vessels was to be understood before God the purification of men, inasmuch as it was about a man, and not about an unwashed vessel, that even this Pharisee had been treating in His presence. He therefore said: "You wash the outside of the cup," that is, the flesh, "but you do not cleanse your inside part,"[9] that is, the soul; adding: "Did not He that made the outside," that is, the flesh, "also make the inward part," that is to say, the soul?—by which assertion He expressly declared that to the same God belongs the cleansing of a man's external and internal nature, both alike being in the power of Him who prefers mercy not only to man's washing,[10] but even to sacrifice.[11] For He subjoins the command: "Give what ye possess as alms, and all things shall be clean unto you."[12] Even if another god could have enjoined mercy, he could not have done so previous to his becoming known. Furthermore, it is in this passage evident that they[13] were not reproved concerning their God, but concerning a point of His instruction to them, when He prescribed to them figuratively the cleansing of

their vessels, but really the works of merciful dispositions. In like manner, He upbraids them for tithing paltry herbs,[14] but at the same time "passing over hospitality[15] and the love of God."[16] The vocation and the love of what God, but Him by whose law of tithes they used to offer their rue and mint? For the whole point of the rebuke lay in this, that they cared about small matters in His service of course, to whom they failed to exhibit their weightier duties when He commanded them: "Thou shalt love with all thine heart, and with all thy soul, and with all thy strength, the Lord thy God, who hath called thee out of Egypt."[17] Besides, time enough had not yet passed to admit of Christ's requiring so premature—nay, as yet so distasteful[18]—a love towards a new and recent, not to say a hardly yet developed,[19] deity. When, again, He upbraids those who caught at the uppermost places and the honour of public salutations, He only follows out the Creator's course,[20] who calls ambitious persons of this character "rulers of Sodom,"[21] who forbids us "to put confidence even in princes,"[22] and pronounces him to be altogether wretched who places his confidence in man. But whoever[23] aims at high position, because he would glory in the officious attentions[24] of other people, (in every such case,) inasmuch as He forbade such attentions (in the shape) of placing hope and confidence in man, He at the same time[25] censured all who were ambitious of high positions. He also inveighs against the doctors of the law themselves, because they were "lading men with burdens grievous to be borne, which they did not venture to touch with even a finger of their own;"[26] but not as if He made a mock of[27] the burdens of the law with any feeling of detestation towards it. For how could He have felt aversion to the law, who used with so much earnestness to upbraid them for passing over its weightier matters, alms-giving, hospitality,[28] and the love of God? Nor, indeed, was it only these great things (which He recognized), but even[29] the tithes of rue and the cleansing of cups. But,

---

[1] Luke xi. 29.
[2] Luke xi. 33.
[3] Luke vi. 28, also xi. 37-52.
[4] Fiximus.
[5] Denotari.
[6] Tunc.
[7] Retractabat.
[8] Circumferret.
[9] Luke xi. 39.
[10] Lavacro.
[11] Matt. ix. 13, xii. 7 ; comp. Hos. viii. 6.
[12] Luke xi. 41.
[13] The Pharisees and lawyers.

[14] Holuscula.
[15] Marcion's gospel had κλῆσιν (vocationem, perhaps a general word for *hospitality*) instead of κρίσιν, *judgment*,—a quality which M. did not allow in his god. See Epiphanius, *Hæres.* xlii., Schol. 26 (Oehler and Fr. Junius).
[16] Luke xi. 42.
[17] Deut. vi. 5.
[18] Amaxam.
[19] Nondum palam facto.
[20] Sectam administrat.
[21] Isa. i. 10.
[22] Ps. cxviii. 9.
[23] Quodsiquis.
[24] Officiis.
[25] Idem.
[26] Luke xi. 46.
[27] Suggillans.
[28] Vocationem: Marcion's κλῆσιν.
[29] Nedum.

in truth, He would rather have deemed them excusable for being unable to carry burdens which could not be borne. What, then, are the burdens which He censures?[1] None but those which they were accumulating of their own accord, when they taught for commandments the doctrines of men; for the sake of private advantage joining house to house, so as to deprive their neighbour of his own; cajoling[2] the people, loving gifts, pursuing rewards, robbing the poor of the rights of judgment, that they might have the widow for a prey and the fatherless for a spoil.[3] Of these Isaiah also says, " Woe unto them that are strong in Jerusalem ! "[4] and again, " They that demand you shall rule over you."[5] And who did this more than the lawyers?[6] Now, if these offended Christ, it was as belonging to Him that they offended Him. He would have aimed no blow at the teachers of an alien law. But why is a " woe " pronounced against them for "building the sepulchres of the prophets whom their fathers had killed?"[7] They rather deserved praise, because by such an act of piety they seemed to show that they did not allow the deeds of their fathers. Was it not because (Christ) was jealous[8] of such a disposition as the Marcionites denounce,[9] visiting the sins of the fathers upon the children unto the fourth generation? What " key," indeed, was it which these lawyers had,[10] but the interpretation of the law? Into the perception of this they neither entered themselves, even because they did not believe (for " unless ye believe, ye shall not understand "); nor did they permit others to enter, because they preferred to teach them for commandments even the doctrines of men. When, therefore, He reproached those who did not themselves enter in, and also shut the door against others, must He be regarded as a disparager of the law, or as a supporter of it? If a disparager, those who were hindering the law ought to have been pleased; if a supporter, He is no longer an enemy of the law.[11] But all these imprecations He uttered in order to tarnish the Creator as a cruel Being,[12] against whom such as offended were destined to have a " woe." And who would not rather have feared to provoke a cruel Being,[13] by withdraw-

ing allegiance[14] from Him? Therefore the more He represented the Creator to be an object of fear, the more earnestly would He teach that He ought to be served. Thus would it behove the Creator's Christ to act.

CHAP. XXVIII.—EXAMPLES FROM THE OLD TESTAMENT, BALAAM, MOSES, AND HEZEKIAH, TO SHOW HOW COMPLETELY THE INSTRUCTION AND CONDUCT OF CHRIST[15] ARE IN KEEPING WITH THE WILL AND PURPOSE OF THE CREATOR.

Justly, therefore, was the hypocrisy of the Pharisees displeasing to Him, loving God as they did with their lips, but not with their heart. " Beware," He says to the disciples, " of the leaven of the Pharisees, which is hypocrisy," not the proclamation of the Creator. The Son hates those who refused obedience[16] to the Father; nor does He wish His disciples to show such a disposition towards Him—not (let it be observed) towards another god, against whom such hypocrisy indeed might have been admissible, as that which He wished to guard His disciples against. It is the example of the Pharisees which He forbids. It was in respect of Him against whom the Pharisees were sinning that (Christ) now forbade His disciples to offend. Since, then, He had censured their hypocrisy, which covered the secrets of the heart, and obscured with superficial offices the mysteries of unbelief, because (while holding the key of knowledge) it would neither enter in itself, nor permit others to enter in, He therefore adds, " There is nothing covered that shall not be revealed; neither hid, which shall not be known,"[17] in order that no one should suppose that He was attempting the revelation and the recognition of an hitherto unknown and hidden god. When He remarks also on their murmurs and taunts, in saying of Him, " This man casteth out devils only through Beelzebub," *He means* that all these imputations would come forth to the light of day, and be in the mouths of men in consequence of the promulgation of the Gospel. He then turns to His disciples with these words, " I say unto you, my friends, Be not afraid of them which can only kill the body, and after that have no more power over you."[18] They will, however, find Isaiah had already said, " See how the just man is taken away, and no man layeth it to heart."[19] " But I will show you whom ye shall fear: fear Him who, after

---

[1] Taxat.
[2] Clamantes.
[3] See Isa. v. 5, 23, and x. 2.
[4] Isa. xxviii. 14.
[5] The books point to Isa. iii. 3, 4 for this ; but there is only a slight similarity in the latter clause, even in the Septuagint.
[6] Legis doctores : the νομικοί of the Gospels.
[7] Luke xi. 47.
[8] Zelotes.
[9] Arguunt.
[10] Luke xi. 52.
[11] As Marcion held Him to be.
[12] A Marcionite position.
[13] Sævum.

[14] Deficiendo.
[15] As narrated by St. Luke xii. 1-21.
[16] Contumaces.
[17] Luke xii. 2.
[18] Luke xii 4.
[19] Isa. lvii. 1.

He hath killed, hath power to cast into hell " (meaning, of course, the Creator); " yea, I say unto you, fear Him." [1] Now, it would here be enough for my purpose that He forbids offence being given to Him whom He orders to be feared; and that He orders Him to be respected [2] whom He forbids to be offended; and that He who gives these commands belongs to that very *God* for whom He procures this fear, this absence of offence, and this respect. But this conclusion I can draw also from the following words: " For I say unto you, Whosoever shall confess me before men, him will I also confess before God." [3] Now they who shall confess Christ will have to be slain [4] before men, but they will have nothing more to suffer after they have been put to death by them. These therefore will be they whom He forewarns above not to be afraid of being only killed; and this forewarning He offers, in order that He might subjoin a clause on the necessity of confessing Him: " Every one that denieth me before men shall be denied before God " [5]—by Him, of course, who would have confessed him, if he had only confessed *God*. Now, He who will confess the confessor is the very same God who will also deny the denier of Himself. Again, if it is the confessor who will have nothing to fear after his violent death, [6] it is the denier to whom everything will become fearful after his natural death. Since, therefore, that which will have to be feared after death, even the punishment of hell, belongs to the Creator, the denier, too, belongs to the Creator. As with the denier, however, so with the confessor: if he should deny God, he will plainly have to suffer from God, although from men he had nothing more to suffer after they had put him to death. And so Christ is the Creator's, because He shows that all those who deny Him ought to fear the Creator's hell. After deterring *His disciples* from denial of Himself, He adds an admonition to fear blasphemy: " Whosoever shall speak against the Son of man, it shall be forgiven him; but whosoever shall speak against the Holy Ghost, it shall not be forgiven him." [7] Now, if both the remission and the retention of sin savour of a judicial God, the Holy Ghost, who is not to be blasphemed, will belong to Him, who will not forgive the blasphemy; just as He who, in the preceding passage, was not to be denied, belonged to Him who would, after He had killed, also cast into hell. Now, since it is Christ who averts blasphemy from the Creator, I am at a loss to know in what manner His adversary [8] could have come. Else, if by these sayings He throws a black cloud of censure [9] over the severity of Him who will not forgive blasphemy and will kill even to hell, it follows that the very spirit of that rival god may be blasphemed with impunity, and his Christ denied; and that there is no difference, in fact, between worshipping and despising him; but that, as there is no punishment for the contempt, so there is no reward for the worship, which men need expect. When " brought before magistrates," and. examined, He forbids them " to take thought how they shall answer;" " for," says He, " the Holy Ghost shall teach you in that very hour what ye ought to say." [10] If such an injunction [11] as this comes from the Creator, the precept will only be His by whom an example was previously given. The prophet Balaam, in Numbers, when sent forth by king Balak to curse Israel, with whom he was commencing war, was at the same moment [12] filled with the Spirit. Instead of the curse which he was come to pronounce, he uttered the blessing which the Spirit at that very hour inspired him with; having previously declared to the king's messengers, and then to the king himself, that he could only speak forth that which God should put into his mouth. [13] The novel doctrines of the new Christ are such as the Creator's servants initiated long before! But see how clear a difference there is between the example of Moses and of Christ. [14] Moses voluntarily interferes with brothers [15] who were quarrelling, and chides the offender: " Wherefore smitest thou thy fellow?" He is, however, rejected by him: " Who made thee a prince or a judge over us?" [16] Christ, on the contrary, when requested by a certain man to compose a strife between him and his brother about dividing an inheritance, refused His assistance, although in so honest a cause. Well, then, my Moses is better than your Christ, aiming as he did at the peace of brethren, *and* obviating their wrong. But *of course the case must be different with Christ*, for he is the Christ of the simply good and non-judicial god. " Who," says he, " made me a judge over you?" [17] No other word of excuse was he able to find,

[1] Luke xii. 5.
[2] Demereri.
[3] Luke xii. 8.
[4] Occidi habebunt.
[5] Luke xii. 9.
[6] Post occisionem.
[7] Luke xii. 10.
[8] So full of blasphemy, as he is, against the Creator
[9] Infuscet.
[10] Luke xii. 11, 12.
[11] Documentum.
[12] Simul.
[13] Num. xxii.-xxiv.
[14] A Marcionite objection.
[15] " Two men of the Hebrews."—A. V.
[16] Ex. ii. 13, 14.
[17] Luke xii. 13, 14.

without using[1] that with which the wicked man and impious brother had rejected[2] the defender of probity and piety! In short, he approved of the excuse, although a bad one, by his use of it; and of the act, although a bad one, by his refusal to make peace between brothers. Or rather, would He not show His resentment[3] at the rejection of Moses with such a word? And therefore did He not wish in a similar case of contentious brothers, to confound them with the recollection of so harsh a word? Clearly so. For He had Himself been present in Moses, who heard such a rejection—even He, the Spirit of the Creator.[4] I think that we have already, in another passage,[5] sufficiently shown that the glory of riches is condemned by our God, "who putteth down the mighty from their throne, and exalts the poor from the dunghill."[6] From Him, therefore, will proceed the parable of the rich man, who flattered himself about the increase of his fields, and to whom God said: "Thou fool, this night shall they require thy soul of thee; then whose shall those things be which thou hast provided?"[7] It was just in the like manner that the king *Hezekiah* heard from Isaiah the sad doom of his kingdom, when he gloried, before the envoys of Babylon,[8] in his treasures and the deposits of his precious things.[9]

CHAP. XXIX.—PARALLELS FROM THE PROPHETS TO ILLUSTRATE CHRIST'S TEACHING IN THE REST OF THIS CHAPTER OF ST. LUKE. THE STERNER ATTRIBUTES OF CHRIST, IN HIS JUDICIAL CAPACITY, SHOW HIM TO HAVE COME FROM THE CREATOR. INCIDENTAL REBUKES OF MARCION'S DOCTRINE OF CELIBACY, AND OF HIS ALTERING OF THE TEXT OF THE GOSPEL.

Who would be unwilling that we should distress ourselves[10] about sustenance for our life, or clothing for our body,[11] but He who has provided these things already for man; and who, therefore, while distributing them to us, prohibits all anxiety respecting them as an outrage[12] against his liberality?—who has adapted the nature of "life" itself to a condition "better than meat," and has fashioned the material of "the body," so as to make it "more than raiment;" whose "ravens, too,

neither sow nor reap, nor gather into storehouses, and are yet fed" by Himself; whose "lilies and grass also toil not, nor spin, and yet are clothed" by Him; whose "Solomon, moreover, was transcendent in glory, and yet was not arrayed like" the humble flower.[13] Besides, nothing can be more abrupt than that one God should be distributing His bounty, while the other should bid us take no thought about (so kindly a) distribution—and that, too, with the intention of derogating (from his liberality). Whether, indeed, it is as depreciating the Creator that he does not wish such trifles to be thought of, concerning which neither the crows nor the lilies labour, because, forsooth, they come spontaneously to hand[14] by reason of their very worthlessness,[15] will appear a little further on. Meanwhile, how is it that He chides them as being "of little faith?"[16] What faith? Does He mean that faith which they were as yet unable to manifest perfectly in a god who has hardly yet revealed,[17] and whom they were in process of learning as well as they could; or that faith which they for this express reason owed to the Creator, because they believed that He was of His own will supplying these wants of the human race, and therefore took no thought about them? Now, when He adds, "For all these things do the nations of the world seek after,"[18] even by their not believing in God as the Creator and Giver of all things, since He was unwilling that they should be like these nations, He therefore upbraided them as being defective of faith in the same God, in whom He remarked that the Gentiles were quite wanting in faith. When He further adds, "But your Father knoweth that ye have need of these things,"[19] I would first ask, what Father Christ would have to be here understood? If He points to their own Creator, He also affirms Him to be good, who knows what His children have need of; but if He refers to that other god, how does he know that food and raiment are necessary to man, seeing that he has made no such provision for him? For if he had known the want, he would have made the provision. If, however, he knows what things man has need of, and yet has failed to supply them, he is in the failure guilty of either malignity or weakness. But when he confessed that these things are necessary to man, he really affirmed that they are *good*. For nothing that is evil is necessary. So that he will not be any longer

---

[1] Ne uteretur.
[2] Excusserat. Oehler interprets the word by *temptaverat*.
[3] Nunquid indigne tulerit.
[4] This is an instance of the title "*Spirit*" being applied to the divine nature of the Son. See Bp. Bull's *Def. Nic. Fid.* (by the translator). [See note 13, p. 375, *supra*.]
[5] Above, chap. xv. of this book, p. 369, *supra*.
[6] Comp. 1 Sam. ii. 8 with Ps. cxiii. 7 and Luke i. 52
[7] Luke xii. 16–20.
[8] Apud Persas.
[9] Isa. xxxix.
[10] Agere curam : take thought.—A. V.
[11] Luke xii. 22–28.
[12] Æmulam.

[13] Flosculo: see Luke xii. 24–27.
[14] Ultro subjectis.
[15] Pro sua vilitate.
[16] Luke xii. 28.
[17] Tantum quod revelato.
[18] Luke xii. 30.
[19] Luke xii. 30.

a depreciator of the works and the indulgences of the Creator, that I may here complete the answer[1] which I deferred giving above. Again, if it is another god who has foreseen man's wants, and is supplying them, how is it that *Marcion's Christ* himself promises them?[2] Is he liberal with another's property?[3] "Seek ye," says he, "the kingdom of God, and *all* these things shall be added unto you"—by himself, of course. But if *by himself*, what sort of being is he, who shall bestow the things of another? If by *the Creator*, whose all things are, then who[4] is he that promises what belongs to another? If these things are "additions" to the kingdom, they must be placed in the second rank;[5] and the second rank belongs to Him to whom the first also does; His are the food and raiment, whose is the kingdom. Thus to the Creator belongs the entire promise, the full reality[6] of its parables, the perfect equalization[7] of its similitudes; for these have respect to none other than Him to whom they have a parity of relation in every point.[8] We are servants because we have a Lord in our God. We ought "to have our loins girded:"[9] in other words, we are to be free from the embarrassments of a perplexed and much occupied life; "to have our lights burning,"[10] that is, our minds kindled by faith, and resplendent with the works of truth. And thus "to wait for our Lord,"[11] that is, Christ. Whence "returning?" If "from the wedding," He is *the Christ* of the Creator, for the wedding is His. If He is not the Creator's, not even Marcion himself would have gone to the wedding, although invited, for in his god he discovers one who hates the nuptial bed. The parable would therefore have failed in the person of the Lord, if He were not a Being to whom a wedding is consistent. In the next parable also he makes a flagrant mistake, when he assigns to the person of the Creator that "thief, whose hour, if the father of the family had only known, he would not have suffered his house to be broken through."[12] How can the Creator wear in any way the aspect of a thief, Lord as He is of all mankind? No one pilfers or plunders his own property, but he[13] rather acts the part of one who swoops down on the things of another, and alienates man from his Lord.[14]

Again, when He indicates to us that the devil is "the thief," whose hour at the very beginning of the world, if man had known, would never have been broken in upon[15] by him, He warns us "to be ready," for this reason, because "we know not the hour when the Son of man shall come"[16]—not as if He were Himself the thief, but rather as being the judge of those who prepared not themselves, and used no precaution against the thief. Since, then, He is the Son of man, I hold Him to be the Judge, and in the Judge I claim[17] the Creator. If then in this passage he displays the Creator's Christ under the title "Son of man," that he may give us some presage[18] of the thief, of the period of whose coming we are ignorant, you still have it ruled above, that no one is the thief of his own property; besides which, there is our principle also unimpaired[19]—that in *as* far as He insists on the Creator as an object of fear, in *so* far does He belong to the Creator, and does the Creator's work. When, therefore, Peter asked whether He had spoken the parable "unto them, or even to all,"[20] He sets forth for them, and for all who should bear rule in the churches, the similitude of stewards.[21] That steward who should treat his fellow-servants well in his lord's absence, would on his return be set as ruler over all his property; but he who should act otherwise should be severed, and have his portion with the unbelievers, when his lord should return on the day when he looked not for him, at the hour when he was not aware[22]—even that Son of man, the Creator's Christ, not a thief, but a Judge. He accordingly, in this passage, either presents to us the Lord as a Judge, and instructs us in His character,[23] or else as the simply good god; if the latter, he now also affirms his judicial attribute, although the heretic refuses to admit it. For an attempt is made to modify this sense when it is applied to his god,—as if it were an act of serenity and mildness simply to sever the man off, and to assign him a portion with the unbelievers, under the idea that he was not summoned (before the judge), but only returned to his own state! As if this very process did not imply a judicial act! What folly! What will be the end of the severed ones? Will it not be the forfeiture of salvation, since their separation will be from those who shall attain salvation? What, again, will be the condition of the un-

---

[1] Expunxerim.
[2] Luke xii. 31.
[3] De alieno bonus
[4] Qualis.
[5] Secundo gradu.
[6] Status.
[7] Peræquatio.
[8] Cui per omnia pariaverint.
[9] Luke xii. 35.
[10] Luke xii. 35.
[11] Luke xii. 36.
[12] Luke xii. 39.
[13] Sed ille potius.
[14] A censure on Marcion's Christ.

[15] Suffossus.
[16] Luke xi. 40.
[17] Defendo.
[18] Portendat.
[19] Salvo.
[20] Luke xii. 41.
[21] Actorum.
[22] Luke xii. 41-46.
[23] Illi catechizat.

believers? Will it not be damnation? Else, if these severed and unfaithful ones shall have nothing to suffer, there will, on the other hand, be nothing for the accepted and the believers to obtain. If, however, the accepted and the believers shall attain salvation, it must needs be that the rejected and the unbelieving should incur the opposite issue, even the loss of salvation. Now here is a judgment, and He who holds it out before us belongs to the Creator. Whom else than the God of retribution can I understand by Him who shall "beat His servants with stripes," either "few or many," and shall exact from them what He had committed to them? Whom is it suitable[1] for me to obey, but Him who remunerates? Your Christ proclaims, "I am come to send fire on the earth."[2] That[3] most lenient being, the lord who has no hell, not long before had restrained his disciples from demanding fire on the churlish village. Whereas He[4] burnt up Sodom and Gomorrah with a tempest of fire. Of Him the psalmist sang, "A fire shall go out before Him, and burn up His enemies round about."[5] By Hosea He uttered the threat, "I will send a fire upon the cities of Judah;"[6] and[7] by Isaiah, "A fire has been kindled in mine anger." He cannot lie. If it is not He who uttered His voice out of even the burning bush, it can be of no importance[8] what fire you insist upon being understood. Even if it be but figurative fire, yet, from the very fact that he takes from my element illustrations for His own sense, He is mine, because He uses what is mine. The similitude of fire must belong to Him who owns the reality thereof. But He will Himself best explain the quality of that fire *which He mentioned*, when He goes on to say, "Suppose ye that I am come to give peace on earth? I tell you, Nay; but rather division."[9] It is written "*a sword*,"[10] but Marcion makes an emendation[11] of the word, just as if a *division* were not the work of the *sword*. He, therefore, who refused to give peace, intended also the fire of destruction. As is the combat, so is the burning. As is

the sword, so is the flame. Neither is suitable for its lord. He says at last, "The father shall be divided against the son, and the son against the father; the mother against the daughter, and the daughter against the mother; the mother-in-law against the daughter-in-law, and the daughter-in-law against the mother-in-law."[12] Since this battle among the relatives[13] was sung by the prophet's trumpet in the very words, I fear that Micah[14] must have predicted it to Marcion's Christ! On this account He pronounced them "hypocrites," because they could "discern the face of the sky and the earth, but could not distinguish this time,"[15] when of course He ought to have been recognised, fulfilling (as he was) all things which had been predicted concerning them, and teaching them so. But then who could know the times of him of whom he had no evidence to prove his existence? Justly also does He upbraid them for "not even of themselves judging what is right."[16] Of old does He command by Zechariah, "Execute the judgment of truth and peace;"[17] by Jeremiah, "Execute judgment and righteousness;"[18] by Isaiah, "Judge the fatherless, plead for the widow,"[19] charging it as a fault upon the vine of Sorech,[20] that when "He looked for righteousness therefrom, there was only a cry"[21] (of oppression). The same God who had taught them to act as He commanded them,[22] was now requiring that they should act of their own accord.[23] He who had sown the precept, was now pressing to an abundant harvest from it. But how absurd, that he should now be commanding them to judge righteously, who was destroying God the righteous Judge! For the Judge, who commits to prison, and allows no release out of it without the payment of "the very last mite,"[24] they treat of in the person of the Creator, with the view of disparaging Him. Which cavil, however, I deem it necessary to meet with the same answer.[25] For as often as the Creator's severity is paraded before us, so often is Christ (shown to be) His, to whom He urges submission by the motive of fear.

---

[1] Decet.
[2] Luke xii. 49.
[3] Ille: Marcion's Christ.
[4] Iste: the Creator.
[5] Ps. xcvii. 3.
[6] Hos. viii. 14.
[7] Vel: or, "if you please;" indicating some uncertainty in the quotation. The passage is more like Jer. xv. 14 than anything in Isaiah (see, however, Isa. xxx. 27, 30).
[8] Viderit.
[9] Luke xii. 51.
[10] Pamelius supposes that Tertullian here refers to St. Matthew's account, where the word is μάχαιραν, on the ground that the MSS. and versions of St. Luke's Gospel invariably read διαμερισμόν. According to Rigaltius, however, Tertullian means that *sword* is written in Marcion's Gospel of Luke, as if the heretic had adulterated the passage. Tertullian no doubt professes to quote all along from the Gospel of Luke, according to Marcion's reading.
[11] St. Luke's word being διαμερισμόν (*division*), not μάχαιραν (*sword*).

[12] Luke xii. 53.
[13] Parentes.
[14] Mic. vii. 6.
[15] Luke xii. 56.
[16] Luke xii. 57.
[17] Zech. viii. 16.
[18] Jer. xxii. 3.
[19] Isa. i. 17.
[20] Tertullian calls by a proper name the vineyard which Isaiah (in his chap. v.) designates "the vineyard of the Lord of hosts," and interprets to be "the house of Israel" (ver. 7). The designation comes from ver. 2, where the original clause וַיִּטָּעֵהוּ שֹׂרֵק is translated in the Septuagint, Καὶ ἐφύτευσα ἄμπελον Σωρήκ. Tertullian is most frequently in close agreement with the LXX.
[21] Isa. v. 7.
[22] Ex praecepto.
[23] Ex arbitrio.
[24] Luke xii. 58, 59.
[25] Eodem gradu.

CHAP. XXX.—PARABLES OF THE MUSTARD-SEED, AND OF THE LEAVEN. TRANSITION TO THE SOLEMN EXCLUSION WHICH WILL ENSUE WHEN THE MASTER OF THE HOUSE HAS SHUT THE DOOR. THIS JUDICIAL EXCLUSION WILL BE ADMINISTERED BY CHRIST, WHO IS SHOWN THEREBY TO POSSESS THE ATTRIBUTE OF THE CREATOR.

When the question was again raised concerning a cure performed on the Sabbath-day, how did He discuss it: "Doth not each of you on the Sabbath loose his ass or his ox from the stall, and lead him away to watering?"[1] When, therefore, He did a work according to the condition prescribed by the law, He affirmed, instead of breaking, the law, which commanded that no work should be done, except what might be done for any living being;[2] and if for any one, then how much more for a human life? In the case of the parables, it is allowed that I[3] everywhere require a congruity. "The kingdom of God," says He, "is like a grain of mustard-seed which a man took and cast into his garden." Who must be understood as meant by the man? Surely Christ, because (although Marcion's) he was called "the Son of man." He received from the Father the seed of the kingdom, that is, the word of the gospel, and sowed it in his garden—in the world, of course[4]—in man at the present day, for instance.[5] Now, whereas it is said, "in his garden," but neither the world nor man is his property, but the Creator's, therefore He who sowed seed in His own ground is shown to be the Creator. Else, if, to evade this snare,[6] they should choose to transfer the person of the man from Christ to any person who receives the seed of the kingdom and sows it in the garden of his own heart, not even this meaning[7] would suit any other than the Creator. For how happens it, if the kingdom belong to the most lenient god, that it is closely followed up by a fervent judgment, the severity of which brings weeping?[8] With regard, indeed, to the following similitude, I have my fears lest it should somehow[9] presage the kingdom of the rival god! For He compared it, not to the unleavened bread which the Creator is more familiar with, but to leaven.[10] Now this is a capital conjecture for men who are begging for arguments. I must, however,

on my side, dispel one fond conceit by another,[11] and contend with even leaven is suitable for the kingdom of the Creator, because after it comes the oven, or, if you please,[12] the furnace of hell. How often has He already displayed Himself as a Judge, and in the Judge the Creator? How often, indeed, has He repelled, and in the repulse condemned? In the present passage, for instance, He says, "When once the master of the house is risen up;"[13] but in what sense except that in which Isaiah said, "When He ariseth to shake terribly the earth?"[14] "And hath shut to the door," thereby shutting out the wicked, of course; and when these knock, He will answer, "I know you not whence ye are;" and when they recount how "they have eaten and drunk in His presence," He will further say to them, "Depart from me, all ye workers of iniquity; there shall be weeping and gnashing of teeth."[15] But where? Outside, no doubt, when they shall have been excluded with the door shut on them by Him. There will therefore be punishment inflicted by Him who excludes for punishment, when they shall behold the righteous entering the kingdom of God, but themselves detained without. By whom detained outside? If by the Creator, who shall be within receiving the righteous into the kingdom? The good God. What, therefore, is the Creator about,[16] that He should detain outside for punishment those whom His adversary shut out, when He ought rather to have kindly received them, if they must come into His hands,[17] for the greater irritation of His rival? But when about to exclude the wicked, he must, of course, either be aware that the Creator would detain them for punishment, or not be aware. Consequently either the wicked will be detained by the Creator against the will of the excluder, in which case he will be inferior to the Creator, submitting to Him unwillingly; or else, if the process is carried out with his will, then he himself has judicially determined its execution; and then he who is the very originator of the Creator's infamy, will not prove to be one whit better than the Creator. Now, if these ideas be incompatible with reason—of one being supposed to punish, and the other to liberate—then to one only power will appertain both the judgment and the kingdom and while they both belong to one, He who executeth judgment can be none else than the Christ of the Creator.

[1] Luke xiii. 15.
[2] Omni animæ.
[3] Recognoscor.
[4] Utique.
[5] Puta.
[6] Laqueum.
[7] Materia.
[8] Lacrimosa austeritate, see Luke xiii. 28.
[9] Forte.
[10] Luke xiii. 20, 21.
[11] Vanitatem vanitate.
[12] Vel.
[13] Luke xiii. 25.
[14] Isa. ii. 19.
[15] Luke xiii. 25–28.
[16] Quid ergo illuc Creatori.
[17] Si itique.

CHAP. XXXI.—CHRIST'S ADVICE TO INVITE THE POOR IN ACCORDANCE WITH ISAIAH. THE PARABLE OF THE GREAT SUPPER A PICTORIAL SKETCH OF THE CREATOR'S OWN DISPENSATIONS OF MERCY AND GRACE. THE REJECTIONS OF THE INVITATION PARALLELED BY QUOTATIONS FROM THE OLD TESTAMENT. MARCION'S CHRIST COULD NOT FULFIL THE CONDITIONS INDICATED IN THIS PARABLE. THE ABSURDITY OF THE MARCIONITE INTERPRETATION.

What kind of persons does He bid should be invited to a dinner or a supper?[1] Precisely such as he had pointed out by Isaiah: "Deal thy bread to the hungry man; and the beggars—even such as have no home—bring in to thine house,"[2] because, no doubt, they are "unable to recompense" your act of humanity. Now, since Christ forbids the recompense to be expected now, but promises it "at the resurrection," this is the very plan[3] of the Creator, who dislikes those who love gifts and follow after reward. Consider also to which deity[4] is better suited the parable of him who issued invitations: "A certain man made a great supper, and bade many."[5] The preparation for the supper is no doubt a figure of the abundant provision[6] of eternal life. I first remark, that strangers, and persons unconnected by ties of relationship, are not usually invited to a supper; but that members of the household and family are more frequently the favoured guests. To the Creator, then, it belonged to give the invitation, to whom also appertained those who were to be invited—whether considered as *men*, through their descent from Adam, or as *Jews*, by reason of their fathers; not to him who possessed no claim to them either by nature or prerogative. My next remark is,[7] if He issues the invitations who has prepared the supper, then, in this sense the supper is the Creator's, who sent to warn the guests. These had been indeed previously invited by the fathers, but were to be admonished by the prophets. *It certainly is not the feast of him* who never sent a messenger to warn—who never did a thing before towards issuing an invitation, but came down himself on a sudden—only then[8] beginning to be known, when already[8] giving his invitation; only then inviting, when already compelling to his banquet; appointing one and the same hour both for the supper and the invitation. But when invited, they excuse themselves.[9] And fairly enough, if the invitation came from the other god, because it was so sudden; if, however, the excuse was not a fair one, then the invitation was not a sudden one. Now, if the invitation was not a sudden one, it must have been given by the Creator—even by Him of old time, whose call they had at last refused. They first refused it when they said to Aaron, "Make us gods, which shall go before us;"[10] and again, afterwards, when "they heard indeed with the ear, but did not understand"[11] their calling of God. In a manner most germane[12] to this parable, He said by Jeremiah: "Obey my voice, and I will be your God, and ye shall be my people; and ye shall walk in all my ways, which I have commanded you."[13] This is the invitation of God. "But," says He, "they hearkened not, nor inclined their ear."[14] This is the refusal of the people. "They departed, and walked every one in the imagination of their evil heart."[15] "I have bought a field—and I have bought some oxen—and I have married a wife."[16] And still He urges them: "I have sent unto you all my servants the prophets, rising early even before day-light."[17] The Holy Spirit is here meant, the admonisher of the guests. "Yet my people hearkened not unto me, nor inclined their ear, but hardened their neck."[18] This was reported to the Master of the family. Then He was moved (He did well to be moved; for, as Marcion denies emotion to his god, He must be therefore my God), and commanded them to invite out of "the streets and lanes of the city."[19] Let us see whether this is not the same in purport as His words by Jeremiah: "Have I been a wilderness to the house of Israel, or a land left uncultivated?"[20] That is to say: "Then have I none whom I may call to me; have I no place whence I may bring them?" "Since my people have said, We will come no more unto thee."[21] Therefore He sent out to call others, but from the same city.[22] My third remark is this,[23] that although the place abounded with people, He yet commanded that they gather men from the highways and the hedges. In other words, we are now gathered out of the

---

[1] Luke xiv. 12–14.
[2] Isa. lviii. 7.
[3] Forma.
[4] Cui parti.
[5] Luke xiv. 16.
[6] Saturitatem.
[7] Dehinc.
[8] Tantum quod . . . jam.

[9] Luke xiv. 18.
[10] Ex. xxxii. 1.
[11] Isa. vi. 10.
[12] Pertinentissime.
[13] Jer. vii. 23.
[14] Jer. vii. 24.
[15] Jer. xi. 8.
[16] Luke xiv. 18–20.
[17] Jer. vii. 25; also xxv. 4, xxvi. 5, xxxv. 15, xliv. 4.
[18] Jer. vii. 26.
[19] Luke xiv. 21.
[20] Jer. ii. 31.
[21] Jer. ii. 31.
[22] Luke xiv. 23.
[23] Dehinc.

Gentile strangers; with that jealous resentment, no doubt, which He expressed in Deuteronomy: "I will hide my face from them, and I will show them what shall happen in the last days [1] (how that others shall possess their place); for they are a froward generation, children in whom is no faith. They have moved me to jealousy by that which is no god, and they have provoked me to anger with their idols; and I will move them to jealousy with those which are not a people: I will provoke them to anger with a foolish nation" [2]—even with us, whose hope the Jews still entertain.[3] But this hope the Lord says they should not realize;[4] "Sion being left as a cottage [5] in a vineyard, as a lodge in a garden of cucumbers," [6] since the nation rejected the latest invitation to Christ. (Now, I ask,) after going through all this course of the Creator's dispensation and prophecies, what there is in it which can possibly be assigned to him who has done all his work at one hasty stroke,[7] and possesses neither the Creator's [8] course nor His dispensation in harmony with the parable? Or, again in what will consist his first invitation,[9] and what his admonition [10] at the second stage? Some at first would surely decline; others afterwards must have accepted.[11] But now he comes to invite both parties promiscuously out of the city,[12] out of the hedges,[13] contrary to the drift [14] of the parable. It is impossible for him now to condemn as scorners of his invitation [15] those whom he has never yet invited, and whom he is approaching with so much earnestness. If, however, he condemns them beforehand as about to reject his call, then beforehand he also predicts [16] the election of the Gentiles in their stead. Certainly [17] he means to come the second time for the very purpose of preaching to the heathen. But even if he does mean to come again, I imagine it will not be with the intention of any longer inviting guests, but of giving to them their places. Meanwhile, you who interpret the call to this supper as an invitation to a heavenly banquet of spiritual satiety and pleasure, must remember that the earthly promises also of wine and oil and corn, and even of the city, are equally employed by the Creator as figures of spiritual things.

CHAP. XXXII.—A SORT OF SORITES, AS THE LOGICIANS CALL IT, TO SHOW THAT THE PARABLES OF THE LOST SHEEP AND THE LOST DRACHMA HAVE NO SUITABLE APPLICATION TO THE CHRIST OF MARCION.

Who sought after the lost sheep and the lost piece of silver? [18] Was it not the loser? But who was the loser? Was it not he who once possessed [19] them? Who, then, was that? Was it not he to whom they belonged? [20] Since, then, *man* is the property of none other than the Creator, He possessed Him who owned him; He lost him who once possessed him; He sought him who lost him; He found him who sought him; He rejoiced who found him. Therefore the purport [21] of neither parable has anything whatever to do with him [22] to whom belongs neither the sheep nor the piece of silver, that is to say, *man*. For he lost him not, because he possessed him not; and he sought him not, because he lost him not; and he found him not, because he sought him not; and he rejoiced not, because he found him not. Therefore, to rejoice over the sinner's repentance—that is, at the recovery of lost man—is the attribute of Him who long ago professed that He would rather that the sinner should repent and not die.

CHAP. XXXIII.—THE MARCIONITE INTERPRETATION OF GOD AND MAMMON REFUTED. THE PROPHETS JUSTIFY CHRIST'S ADMONITION AGAINST COVETOUSNESS AND PRIDE. JOHN BAPTIST THE LINK BETWEEN THE OLD AND THE NEW DISPENSATIONS OF THE CREATOR. SO SAID CHRIST—BUT SO ALSO HAD ISAIAH SAID LONG BEFORE. ONE ONLY GOD, THE CREATOR, BY HIS OWN WILL CHANGED THE DISPENSATIONS. NO NEW GOD HAD A HAND IN THE CHANGE

What the two masters are who, He says, cannot be served,[23] on the ground that while one is pleased [24] the other must needs be displeased,[25] He Himself makes clear, when He mentions God and mammon. Then, if you have no interpreter by you, you may learn

---

[1] ἐπ' ἐσχάτων ἡμερῶν, Septuagint.
[2] Deut. xxxii. 20, 21.
[3] Gerunt: although vainly at present ("jam vana in Judæis"—Oehler); Semler conjectures "*gemunt*, bewail.'
[4] Gustaturos.
[5] Specula, "a look-out;" σκηνή is the word in LXX.
[6] Isa. i. 8.
[7] Semel.
[8] This is probably the meaning of a very involved sentence: "Quid ex hoc ordine secundum dispensationem et prædicationes Creatoris recensendo competit illi, cujus (" *Creatoris*"—Oehler) nec ordinem habet nec dispositionem ad parabolæ conspirationem qui totum opus semel facit?"
[9] "By the fathers." See above.
[10] "By the prophets." See also above.
[11] An obscure sentence, which thus runs in the original: "Ante debent alii excusare, postea alii convenisse."
[12] The Jews.
[13] The Gentiles.
[14] Speculum.
[15] Fastidiosos.
[16] Portendit.
[17] Plane: This is a Marcionite position (Oehler).

[18] Luke xv. 1-10.
[19] Habuit.
[20] Cujus fuit: i.e., each of the things respectively.
[21] Argumentum.
[22] Vacat circa eum.
[23] Luke xvi. 13
[24] Defendi.
[25] Offendi.

again from Himself what He would have understood by *mammon*.[1] For when advising us to provide for ourselves the help of friends in worldly affairs, after the example of that steward who, when removed from his office,[2] relieves his lord's debtors by lessening their debts with a view to their recompensing him with their help, He said, "And I say unto you, Make to yourselves friends of the *mammon* of unrighteousness," that is to say, of money, even as the steward had done. Now we are all of us aware that money is the instigator[3] of unrighteousness, and the lord of the whole world. Therefore, when he saw the covetousness of the Pharisees doing servile worship[4] to it, He hurled[5] this sentence against them, "Ye cannot serve God and mammon."[6] Then the Pharisees, who were covetous of riches, derided Him, when they understood that by mammon He meant money. Let no one think that under the word mammon the Creator was meant, and that Christ called them off from the service of the Creator. What *folly!* Rather learn therefrom that one God was pointed out by Christ. For they were two masters whom He named, God and mammon—the Creator and money. You cannot indeed serve God—Him, of course, whom they seemed to serve—and mammon, to whom they preferred to devote themselves.[7] If, however, he was giving himself out as another *god*, it would not be two masters, but three, that he had pointed out. For the Creator was a master, and much more of a master, to be sure,[8] than mammon, and more to be adored, as being more truly our Master. Now, how was it likely that He who had called mammon a master, and had associated him with God, should say nothing of Him who was really the Master of even these, that is, the Creator? Or else, by this silence respecting Him did He concede that service might be rendered to *Him*, since it was to Himself alone and to mammon that He said service could not be (simultaneously) rendered? When, therefore, He lays down the position that God is one, since He would have been sure to mention[9] the Creator if He were Him-self a rival[10] to Him, He did (virtually) name the Creator, when He refrained from insisting[11] that He was Master alone, without a rival god. Accordingly, this will throw light upon the sense in which it was said, "If ye have not been faithful in the unrighteous mammon, who will commit to your trust the true riches?"[12] "In the unrighteous mammon," that is to say, in unrighteous riches, not in the Creator; for even Marcion allows Him to be righteous: "And if ye have not been faithful in that which is another man's, who will give to you that which is mine?"[13] For whatever is unrighteous ought to be foreign to the servants of God. But in what way was the Creator foreign to the Pharisees, seeing that He was the proper God of the Jewish nation? Forasmuch then as the words, "Who will entrust to you the truer riches?" and, "Who will give you that which is mine?" are only suitable to the Creator and not to mammon, He could not have uttered them as alien to the Creator, and in the interest of the rival god. He could only seem to have spoken them in this sense, if, when remarking[14] their unfaithfulness to the Creator and not to mammon, He had drawn some distinctions between the Creator (in his manner of mentioning Him) and the rival god—how that the latter would not commit his own truth to those who were unfaithful to the Creator. How then can he possibly seem to belong to another god, if He be not set forth, with the express intention of being separated[15] from the very thing which is in question. But when the Pharisees "justified themselves before men,"[16] and placed their hope of reward in man, He censured them in the sense in which the prophet Jeremiah said, "Cursed is the man that trusteth in man."[17] Since the prophet went on to say, "But the Lord knoweth your hearts,"[18] he magnified the power of that God who declared Himself to be as a lamp, "searching the reins and the heart."[19] When He strikes at pride in the words: "That which is highly esteemed among men is abomination in the sight of God,"[20] He recalls Isaiah: "For the day of the Lord of hosts shall be upon every one that is proud and lofty, and upon every one that is arrogant and lifted up, and they shall be brought low."[21] I can now make out

---

[1] What in the Punic language is called *Mammon*, says Rigaltius, the Latins call *lucrum*, "gain or lucre." See Augustine, *Serm.* xxxv. *de Verbo domini.* I would add Jerome, *On the* vi. *of Matthew* where he says: "In the Syriac tongue, *riches* are called *mammon*." And Augustine, in another passage, book ii., *On the Lord's Sermon on the Mount*, says: "*Riches* in Hebrew are said to be called *mammon*. This is evidently a Punic word, for in that language the synonyme for *gain (lucrum)* is *mammon*." Compare the same author on Ps. ciii. (Oehler).
[2] Ab actu.
[3] Auctorem.
[4] Famulatam.
[5] Ammentavit.
[6] Luke xvi. 13.
[7] Magis destinabantur : middle voice.
[8] Utique.
[9] Nominaturus.

[10] Alius.
[11] Quem non posuit.
[12] Luke xvi. 11.
[13] Meum : Luke xvi. 12, where, however, the word is τὸ ὑμέτερον, "that which is your own."
[14] Notando.
[15] Ad hoc ut separetur.
[16] Luke xvi. 15.
[17] Jer. xvii. 5.
[18] Jer. xvii. 10, in sense but not in letter.
[19] Jer. xx. 12.
[20] Luke xvi. 15.
[21] Isa. ii. 12 (Sept).

why Marcion's god was for so long an age concealed. He was, I suppose, waiting until he had learnt all these things from the Creator. He continued his pupillage up to the time of John, and then proceeded forthwith to announce the kingdom of God, saying: "The law and the prophets were until John; since that time the kingdom of God is proclaimed."[1] Just as if we also did not recognise in John a certain limit placed between the old dispensation and the new, at which Judaism ceased and Christianity began—without, however, supposing that it was by the power of another god that there came about a cessation[2] of the law and the prophets and the commencement of that gospel in which is the kingdom of God, Christ Himself. For although, as we have shown, the Creator foretold that the old state of things would pass away and a new state would succeed, yet, inasmuch as John is shown to be both the forerunner and the preparer of the ways of that Lord who was to introduce the gospel and publish the kingdom of God, it follows from the very fact that John has come, that Christ must be that very Being who was to follow His harbinger John. So that, if the old course has ceased and the new has begun, with John intervening between them, there will be nothing wonderful in it, because it happens according to the purpose of the Creator; so that you may get a better proof for the kingdom of God from any quarter, however anomalous,[3] than from the conceit that the law and the prophets ended in John, and a new state of things began after him. "More easily, therefore, may heaven and earth pass away—as also the law and the prophets—than that one tittle of the Lord's words should fail."[4] "For," as says Isaiah: "the word of our God shall stand for ever."[5] Since even *then* by Isaiah it was Christ, the Word and Spirit[6] of the Creator, who prophetically described John as "the voice of one crying in the wilderness to prepare the way of the Lord,"[7] and as about to come for the purpose of terminating thenceforth the course of the law and the prophets; by their fulfilment and not their extinction, and in order that the kingdom of God might be announced by Christ, He therefore purposely added the assurance that the elements would more easily pass away than His words fail; affirming, as He did, the further fact, that what He had said concerning John had not fallen to the ground.

CHAP. XXXIV.—MOSES, ALLOWING DIVORCE, AND CHRIST PROHIBITING IT, EXPLAINED. JOHN BAPTIST AND HEROD. MARCION'S ATTEMPT TO DISCOVER AN ANTITHESIS IN THE PARABLE OF THE RICH MAN AND THE POOR MAN IN HADES CONFUTED. THE CREATOR'S APPOINTMENT MANIFESTED IN BOTH STATES.

But Christ prohibits divorce, saying, "Whosoever putteth away his wife, and marrieth another, committeth adultery; and whosoever marrieth her that is put away from her husband, also committeth adultery."[8] In order to forbid divorce, He makes it unlawful to marry a woman that has been put away. Moses, however, permitted repudiation in Deuteronomy: "When a man hath taken a wife, and hath lived with her, and it come to pass that she find no favour in his eyes, because he hath found unchastity in her; then let him write her a bill of divorcement and give it in her hand, and send her away out of his house."[9] You see, therefore, that there is a difference between the law and the gospel—between Moses and Christ?[10] To be sure there is![11] But then you have rejected that other gospel which witnesses to the same verity and the same Christ.[12] There, while prohibiting divorce, He has given us a solution of this special question respecting it: "Moses," says He, "because of the hardness of your hearts, suffered you to give a bill of divorcement; but from the beginning it was not so"[13]—for this reason, indeed, because He who had "made them male and female" had likewise said, "They twain shall become one flesh; what therefore God hath joined together, let not man put asunder."[14] Now, by this answer of His (to the Pharisees), He both sanctioned the provision of Moses, who was His own (servant), and restored to its primitive purpose[15] the institution of the Creator, whose Christ He was. Since, however, you are to be refuted out of the Scriptures which you have received, I will meet you on your own ground, as if your Christ were mine. When, therefore, He prohibited divorce, and yet at the same time represented[16] the Father, even Him who united male and female, must He not have rather exculpated[17] than abolished the enactment of Moses? But, observe, if this Christ be yours when he teaches contrary to Moses and the Creator, on the same principle must He be mine if I can show that

1 Luke xvi. 16.
2 Sedatio: literally, "a setting to rest," ἠρέμησις.
3 Ut undeunde magis probetur . . . regnum Dei.
4 Luke xvi. 17 and xxi. 23.
5 Isa. xl. 8.
6 See above, note on chap. xxviii., towards the end, on this designation of Christ's divine nature.
7 Isa. xl. 3.

8 Luke xvi. 18.
9 Deut. xxiv. 1.
10 A Marcionite challenge.
11 Plane.
12 St. Matthew's Gospel.
13 Matt. xix. 8.
14 Matt. xix. 4, 6.
15 Direxit.
16 Gestans.
17 Excusaverit.

His teaching is not contrary to them. I maintain, then, that there was a condition in the prohibition which He now made of divorce; the case supposed being, that a man put away his wife for the express purpose of[1] marrying another. His words are: "Whosoever putteth away his wife, and marrieth another, committeth adultery; and whosoever marrieth her that is put away from her husband, also committeth adultery,"[2]—"put away," that is, for the reason wherefore a woman ought not to be dismissed, that another wife may be obtained. For he who marries a woman who is unlawfully put away is as much of an adulterer as the man who marries one who is undivorced. Permanent is the marriage which is not rightly dissolved; to marry,[3] therefore, whilst matrimony is undissolved, is to commit adultery. Since, therefore, His prohibition of divorce was a conditional one, He did not prohibit absolutely; and what He did not absolutely forbid, that He permitted on some occasions,[4] when there is an absence of the cause why He gave His prohibition. In very deed[5] His teaching is not contrary to Moses, whose precept He partially[6] defends, I will not[7] say confirms. If, however, you deny that divorce is in any way permitted by Christ, how is it that you on your side[8] destroy marriage, not uniting man and woman, nor admitting to the sacrament of baptism and of the eucharist those who have been united in marriage anywhere else,[9] unless they should agree together to repudiate the fruit of their marriage, and so the very Creator Himself? Well, then, what is a husband to do in your sect,[10] if his wife commit adultery? Shall he keep her? But your own apostle, you know,[11] does not permit "the members of Christ to be joined to a harlot."[12] Divorce, therefore, when justly deserved,[13] has even in Christ a defender. So that Moses for the future must be considered as being confirmed by Him, since he prohibits divorce in the same sense as Christ does, if any unchastity should occur in the wife. For in the Gospel of Matthew he says, "Whosoever shall put away his wife, saving for the cause of fornication, causeth her to commit adultery."[14] He also is deemed equally guilty of adultery, who marries a woman put away by her husband. The Creator, however, except on account of adultery, does not put asunder what He Himself joined together, the same Moses in another passage enacting that he who had married after violence to a damsel, should thenceforth not have it in his power to put away his wife.[15] Now, if a compulsory marriage contracted after violence shall be permanent, how much rather shall a voluntary one, the result of agreement! This has the sanction of the prophet: "Thou shalt not forsake the wife of thy youth."[16] Thus you have Christ following spontaneously the tracks of the Creator everywhere, both in permitting divorce and in forbidding it. You find Him also protecting marriage, in whatever direction you try to escape. He prohibits divorce when He will have the marriage inviolable; He permits divorce when the marriage is spotted with unfaithfulness. You should blush when you refuse to unite those whom even your Christ has united; and repeat the blush when you disunite them without the good reason why your Christ would have them separated. I have[17] now to show whence the Lord derived this decision[18] of His, and to what end He directed it. It will thus become more fully evident that His object was not the abolition of the Mosaic ordinance[19] by any suddenly devised proposal of divorce; because it was not suddenly proposed, but had its root in the previously mentioned John. For John reproved Herod, because he had illegally married the wife of his deceased brother, who had a daughter by her (a union which the law permitted only on the one occasion of the brother dying childless,[20] when it even prescribed such a marriage, in order that by his own brother, and from his own wife,[21] seed might be reckoned to the deceased husband),[22] and was in consequence cast into prison, and finally, by the same Herod, was even put to death. The Lord having therefore made mention of John, and of course of the occurrence of his death, hurled His censure[23] against Herod in the form of unlawful marriages and of adultery, pronouncing as an adulterer even the man who married a woman that had been put away from her husband. This he said in order the more severely to load Herod with guilt, who had taken his brother's wife, after she had been loosed from her husband not less by death than by divorce; who had been impelled

---

[1] Ideo ut.
[2] Luke xvi. 18.
[3] Nubere. This verb is here used of both sexes, in a general sense.
[4] Alias.
[5] Etiam : first word of the sentence.
[6] Alicubi.
[7] Nondum.
[8] Tu.
[9] Alibi : i.e., than in the Marcionite connection.
[10] Apud te.
[11] Scilicet.
[12] 1 Cor. vi. 15.
[13] Justitia divortii.
[14] Matt. v. 32.

[15] Deut. xxii. 28, 29.
[16] Mal. ii. 15.
[17] Debeo.
[18] Sententiam.
[19] Literally, "Moses."
[20] Illiberis. [N. B. He supposes Philip to have been dead.]
[21] Costa: literally, "rib" or "side."
[22] Deut. xxv. 5, 6
[23] Jaculatus est.

thereto by his lust, not by the prescription of the (Levirate) law—for, as his brother had left a daughter, the marriage with the widow could not be lawful on that very account;[1] and who, when the prophet asserted against him the law, had therefore put him to death. The remarks I have advanced on this case will be also of use to me in illustrating the subsequent parable of the rich man[2] tormented in hell, and the poor man resting in Abraham's bosom.[3] For this passage, so far as its letter goes, comes before us abruptly; but if we regard its sense and purport, it naturally[4] fits in with the mention of John wickedly slain, and of Herod, who had been condemned by him for his impious marriage.[5] It sets forth in bold outline[6] the end of both of them, the "torments" of Herod and the "comfort" of John, that even now Herod might hear that warning: "They have there Moses and the prophets, let them hear them."[7] Marcion, however, violently turns the passage to another end, and decides that both the torment and the comfort are retributions of the Creator, reserved in the next life[8] for those who have obeyed the law and the prophets; whilst he defines the heavenly bosom and harbour to belong to Christ and his own god. Our answer to this is, that the Scripture itself which dazzles[9] his sight expressly distinguishes between Abraham's bosom, where the poor man dwells, and the infernal place of torment. "Hell" (I take it) means one thing, and "Abraham's bosom" another. "A great gulf" is said to separate those regions, and to hinder a passage from one to the other. Besides, the rich man could not have " lifted up his eyes,"[10] and from a distance too, except to a superior height, and from the said distance all up through the vast immensity of height and depth. It must therefore be evident to every man of intelligence who has ever heard of the Elysian fields, that there is some determinate place called Abraham's bosom, and that it is designed for the reception of the souls of Abraham's children, even from among the Gentiles (since he is "the father of many nations," which must be classed amongst his family), and of the same faith as that wherewith he himself believed God, without the yoke of the law and the sign of circumcision. This region, therefore, I call

Abraham's bosom. Although it is not in heaven, it is yet higher than hell,[11] and is appointed to afford an interval of rest to the souls of the righteous, until the consummation of all things shall complete the resurrection of all men with the " full recompense of their reward."[12] This consummation will then be manifested in heavenly promises, which Marcion, however, claims for his own god, just as if the Creator had never announced them. Amos, however, tells us of " those stories towards heaven"[13] which Christ " builds "—of course for His people. There also is that everlasting abode of which Isaiah asks, " Who shall declare unto you *the eternal place*, but He (that is, of course, Christ) who walketh in righteousness, speaketh of the straight path, hateth injustice and iniquity?"[14] Now, although this everlasting abode is promised, and the ascending stories (or steps) to heaven are built by the Creator, who further promises that the seed of Abraham shall be even as the stars of heaven, by virtue certainly of the heavenly promise, why may it not be possible,[15] without any injury to that promise, that by Abraham's bosom is meant some temporary receptacle of faithful souls, wherein is even now delineated an image of the future, and where is given some foresight of the glory[16] of both judgments? If so, you have here, O heretics, during your present lifetime, a warning that Moses and the prophets declare one only God, the Creator, and His only Christ, and how that both awards of everlasting punishment and eternal salvation rest with Him, the one only God, who kills and who makes alive. Well, but the admonition, says *Marcion*, of our God from heaven has commanded us not to hear Moses and the prophets, but Christ; Hear Him *is the command*.[17] This is true enough. For the apostles had by that time sufficiently heard Moses and the prophets, for they had followed Christ, being persuaded by Moses and the prophets. For even Peter would not have been able[18] to say, "Thou art the Christ,"[19] unless he had beforehand heard and believed Moses and the prophets, by whom alone Christ had been hitherto announced. Their faith, indeed, had deserved this confirmation by such a voice from heaven as should bid them *hear*

---

[1] The condition being that the deceased brother should have left " *no child* " see (Deut. xxv. 5).
[2] Ad subsequens argumentum divitis.
[3] Luke xvi. 19–31.
[4] Ipsum.
[5] Suggillati Herodis male maritati.
[6] Deformans.
[7] Luke xvi. 29. [Note the origin of this doctrine.]
[8] Apud inferos.
[9] Revincente : perhaps " reproves his eyesight," in the sense of *refutation*.
[10] Luke xvi. 23.

[11] Sublimiorem inferis. [Elucidation VIII.]
[12] Compare Heb. ii. 2 with x. 35 and xi. 26.
[13] Ascensum in cœlum : Sept. ἀνάβασιν εἰς τὸν οὐρανόν, Amos ix. 6. See on this passage the article HEAVEN in Kitto's *Cyclopædia* (3d edit.), vol. ii. p. 245, where the present writer has discussed the probable meaning of the verse.
[14] Isa. xxxiii. 14–16, according to the Septuagint, which has but slight resemblance to the Hebrew.
[15] Cur non capiat.
[16] Candida quædam prospiciatur : where *candida* is a noun substantive (see above, chap. vii. p. 353).
[17] There seems to be here an allusion to Luke ix. 35.
[18] Nec accepisset.
[19] Luke ix. 20.

Him, whom they had recognized as preaching peace, announcing glad tidings, promising an everlasting abode, building for them steps upwards into heaven.[1] Down in hell, however, it was said concerning them: "They have Moses and the prophets; let them hear them!"—even those who did not believe them or at least did not sincerely[2] believe that after death there were punishments for the arrogance of wealth and the glory of luxury, announced indeed by Moses and the prophets, but decreed by that God, who deposes princes from their thrones, and raiseth up the poor from dunghills.[3] Since, therefore, it is quite consistent in the Creator to pronounce different sentences in the two directions *of reward and punishment,* we shall have to conclude that there is here no diversity of gods,[4] but only a difference in the actual matters[5] before us.

CHAP. XXXV.— THE JUDICIAL SEVERITY OF CHRIST AND THE TENDERNESS OF THE CREATOR, ASSERTED IN CONTRADICTION TO MARCION. THE CURE OF THE TEN LEPERS. OLD TESTAMENT ANALOGIES. THE KINGDOM OF GOD WITHIN YOU; THIS TEACHING SIMILAR TO THAT OF MOSES. CHRIST, THE STONE REJECTED BY THE BUILDERS. INDICATIONS OF SEVERITY IN THE COMING OF CHRIST. PROOFS THAT HE IS NOT THE IMPASSIBLE BEING MARCION IMAGINED.

Then, turning to His disciples, He says: "Woe unto him through whom offences come! It were better for him if he had not been born, or if a millstone were hanged about his neck and he were cast into the sea, than that he should offend one of these little ones,"[6] that is, one of His disciples. Judge, then, what the sort of punishment is which He so severely threatens. For it is no stranger who is to avenge the offence done to His disciples. Recognise also in Him the Judge, and one, too, who expresses Himself on the safety of His followers with the same tenderness as that which the Creator long ago exhibited: "He that toucheth you toucheth the apple of my eye."[7] Such identity of care proceeds from one and the same Being. A trespassing brother He will have rebuked.[8] If one failed in this duty of reproof, he in fact sinned, either because out of hatred he wished his brother to continue in sin, or else spared him from mistaken friendship,[9] although possessing

the injunction in Leviticus: "Thou shalt not hate thy brother in thine heart; thy neighbor thou shalt seriously rebuke, and on his account shalt not contract sin."[10] Nor is it to be wondered at, if *He* thus teaches who forbids your refusing to bring back even your brother's cattle, if you find them astray in the road; much more should you bring back your erring brother to himself. He commands you to forgive your brother, should he trespass against you even "seven times."[11] But that surely, is a small matter; for with the Creator there is a larger *grace,* when He sets no limits to forgiveness, indefinitely charging you "not to bear any malice against your brother,"[12] and to give not merely to him who asks, but even to him who does not ask. For His will is, not that you should forgive[13] an offence, but forget it. The law about lepers had a profound meaning as respects[14] the forms of the disease itself, and of the inspection by the high priest.[15] The interpretation of this sense it will, be our task to ascertain. Marcion's labour, however, is to object to us the strictness[16] of the law, with the view of maintaining that here also Christ is its enemy—forestalling[17] its enactments even in His cure of the ten lepers. These He simply commanded to show themselves to the priest; "and as they went, He cleansed them"[18]—without a touch, and without a word, by His silent power and simple will. Well, but what necessity was there for Christ, who had been once for all announced as the healer of our sicknesses and sins, and had proved Himself such by His acts,[19] to busy Himself with inquiries[20] into the qualities *and details* of cures; or for the Creator to be summoned to the scrutiny of the law in the person of Christ? If any part of this healing was effected by Him in a way different from the law, He *yet* Himself did it to perfection; for surely the Lord may by Himself, or by His Son, produce after one manner, and after another manner by His servants the prophets, those proofs of His power and might especially, which (as excelling in glory and strength, because they are His own acts) rightly enough leave in the distance behind them the works which are done by His servants. But enough

---

[1] See Isa. lii. 7, xxxiii. 14 (Sept.), and Amos ix. 6.
[2] Omnino.
[3] See 1 Sam. ii. 6-8, Ps. cxiii. 7, and Luke i. 52.
[4] Divinitatum ; "divine powers."
[5] Ipsarum materiarum.
[6] Luke xvii. 1, 2.
[7] Zech. ii. 8.
[8] Luke xvii. 3.
[9] Ex acceptione personæ. The Greek προσωποληψία, "respect of persons."

[10] Lev. xix. 17. The last clause in A. V. runs, "And not suffer sin upon him ;" but the Sept. gives this reading, καὶ οὐ λήψῃ δι' αὐτὸν ἁμαρτίαν ; nor need the Hebrew mean other than this. The prenominal particle עָלָיו may be well rendered δι' αὐτόι on his account.
[11] Luke xvii. 4.
[12] Lev. xix. 18.
[13] Dones.
[14] Erga : *i.q.* circa.
[15] See Lev. xiii. and xiv.
[16] Morositatem.
[17] Prævenientem.
[18] Luke xvii. 11-19.
[19] Or, perhaps, "had proved the prophecy true by His accomplishment of it."
[20] Retractari.

has been already said on this point in a former passage.[1] Now, although He said in a preceding chapter,[2] that "there were many lepers in Israel in the days of Eliseus the prophet, and none of them was cleansed saving Naaman the Syrian," yet of course the mere number proves nothing towards a difference in the gods, as tending to the abasement[3] of the Creator in curing only one, and the pre-eminence of Him who healed ten. For who can doubt that many might have been cured by Him who cured one more easily than ten by him who had never healed one before? But His main purpose in this declaration was to strike at the unbelief or the pride of Israel, in that (although there were many lepers amongst them, and a prophet was not wanting to them) not one had been moved even by so conspicuous an example to betake himself to God who was working in His prophets. Forasmuch, then, as He was Himself the veritable[4] High Priest of God the Father, He inspected them according to the hidden purport of the law, which signified that Christ was the true distinguisher and extinguisher of the defilements of mankind. However, what was obviously required by the law He commanded should be done: "Go," said He, "show yourselves to the priests."[5] Yet why this, if He meant to cleanse them first? Was it as a despiser of the law, in order to prove to them that, having been cured already on the road, the law was now nothing to them, nor even the priests? Well, the matter must of course pass as it best may,[6] if anybody supposes that Christ had such views as these![7] But there are certainly better interpretations to be found of the passage, and more deserving of belief: how that they were cleansed on this account, because[8] they were obedient, and went as the law required, when they were commanded to go to the priests; and it is not to be believed that persons who observed the law could have found a cure from a god that was destroying the law. Why, however, did He not give such a command to the leper who first returned?[9] Because Elisha did not in the case of Naaman the Syrian, and yet was not on that account less the Creator's agent? This is a sufficient answer. But the believer knows that there is a profounder reason. Consider, therefore, the

true motives.[10] The miracle was performed in the district of Samaria, to which country also belonged one of the lepers.[11] Samaria, however, had revolted from Israel, carrying with it the disaffected nine tribes,[12] which, having been alienated[13] by the prophet Ahijah,[14] Jeroboam settled in Samaria. Besides, the Samaritans were always pleased with the mountains and the wells of their ancestors. Thus, in the Gospel of John, the woman of Samaria, when conversing with the Lord at the well, says, "No doubt[15] Thou art greater," etc.; and again, "Our fathers worshipped in this mountain; but ye say, that in Jerusalem is the place where men ought to worship."[16] Accordingly, He who said, "Woe unto them that trust in the mountain of Samaria,"[17] vouchsafing now to restore that very region, purposely requests the men "to go and show themselves to the priests," because these were to be found only there where the temple was; submitting[18] the Samaritan to the Jew, inasmuch as "salvation was of the Jews,"[19] whether to the Israelite or the Samaritan. To the tribe of Judah, indeed, wholly appertained the promised Christ,[20] in order that men might know that at Jerusalem were both the priests and the temple; that there also was the womb[21] of religion, and its *living* fountain, not its *mere* "well."[22] Seeing, therefore, that they recognised[23] the truth that at Jerusalem the law was to be fulfilled, He healed them whose salvation was to come[24] of faith[25] without the ceremony of the law. Whence also, astonished that one only out of the ten was thankful for his release to the divine grace, He does not command him to offer a gift according to the law, because he had already paid his tribute of gratitude when "he glorified God;[26] for thus did the Lord will that law's requirement should be interpreted. And yet who was the God to whom the Samaritan gave thanks, because thus far not even had an Israelite heard of another god? Who else but He by whom all had hitherto been

---

[1] See above in chap. ix.
[2] Præfatus est: see Luke iv. 27.
[3] Destructionem.
[4] Authenticus. "He was the *true*, the original Priest, of whom the priests under the Mosaic law were only copies" (Bp. Kaye, *On the Writings of Tertullian*, pp. 293, 294, and note 8).
[5] Luke xvii. 14.
[6] Et utique viderit.
[7] Tam opiniosus.
[8] Qua: "I should prefer *quia*" (Oehler).
[9] Pristino leproso: but doubtful.

[10] Causas.
[11] Luke xvii. 17.
[12] Schisma illud ex *novem* tribubus. There is another reading which substitutes the word *decem*. "It is, however, immaterial; either number will do *roundly*. If 'ten' be the number, it must be understood that the tenth is divided, accurately making nine and a half tribes. If 'nine' be read, the same amount is still made up, for *Simeon* was reckoned with *Judah*, and half of the tribe of Benjamin remained loyal" (Fr. Junius).
[13] Avulsas.
[14] 1 Kings xi. 29-39 and xii. 15.
[15] Næ.
[16] John iv. 12, 20.
[17] Amos vi. 1.
[18] Subiciens: or "subjecting."
[19] John iv. 22.
[20] Tota promissio Christus.
[21] Matricem.
[22] Fontem non puteum salutis.
[23] Agnovisse.
[24] Justificandos.
[25] Luke xvii. 19.
[26] Luke xvii. 15.

healed through Christ? And therefore it was said to him, "Thy faith hath made thee whole,"[1] because he had discovered that it was his duty to render the true oblation to Almighty God—even thanksgiving—in His true temple, and before His true High Priest *Jesus* Christ. But it is impossible either that the Pharisees should seem to have inquired of the Lord about the coming of the kingdom of the rival god, when no other god has ever yet been announced by Christ; or that He should have answered them concerning the kingdom of any other god than Him of whom they were in the habit of asking Him. "The kingdom of God," He says, "cometh not with observation; neither do they say, Lo here! or, lo there! for, behold, the kingdom of God is within you."[2] Now, who will not interpret the words *"within you"* to mean *in your hand, within your power*, if you hear, and do the commandment of God? If, however, the kingdom of God lies in His commandment, set before your mind Moses on the other side, according to our *antitheses*, and you will find the self-same view of the case.[3] "The commandment is not a lofty one,[4] neither is it far off from thee. It is not in heaven, that thou shouldest say, 'Who shall go up for us to heaven, and bring it unto us, that we may hear it, and do it?' nor is it beyond the sea, that thou shouldest say, 'Who shall go over the sea for us, and bring it unto us, that we may hear it, and do it?' But the word is very nigh unto thee, in thy mouth, and in thy heart, and in thy hands, to do it."[5] This means, "Neither in this place nor that place is the kingdom of God; for, behold, it is within you."[6] And if the heretics, in their audacity, should contend that the Lord did not give an answer about His own kingdom, but only about the Creator's kingdom, concerning which they had inquired, then the following words are against them. For He tells them that "the Son of man must suffer many things, and be rejected," before His coming,[7] at which His kingdom will be really[8] revealed. In this statement He shows that it was His own kingdom which His answer to them had contemplated, and which was now awaiting His own sufferings and rejection. But having to be rejected and afterwards to be acknowledged, and taken up[9] and glorified, He borrowed the very word "rejected" from the passage,

where, under the figure of *a stone*, His twofold manifestation was celebrated by David—the first in rejection, the second in honour: "The stone," says He, "which the builders rejected, is become the head-stone of the corner. This is the Lord's doing."[10] Now it would be idle, if we believed that God had predicted the humiliation, or even the glory, of any *Christ* at all, that He could have designed His prophecy for any but Him whom He had foretold under the figure of a *stone*, and a *rock*, and a *mountain*.[11] If, however, He speaks of His own coming, why does He compare it with the days of Noe and of Lot,[12] which were dark and terrible—a mild and gentle God as He is? Why does He bid us "remember Lot's wife,"[13] who despised the Creator's command, and was punished for her contempt, if He does not come with judgment to avenge the infraction of His precepts? If He really does punish, like the Creator,[14] if He is my Judge, He ought not to have adduced examples for the purpose of instructing me from Him whom He yet destroys, that *He*[15] might not seem to be my instructor. But if He does not even here speak of His own coming, but of the coming of the Hebrew Christ,[16] let us still wait in expectation that He will vouchsafe to us some prophecy of His own advent; meanwhile we will continue to believe that He is none other than He whom He reminds us of in every passage.

CHAP. XXXVI.—THE PARABLES OF THE IMPORTUNATE WIDOW, AND OF THE PHARISEE AND THE PUBLICAN. CHRIST'S ANSWER TO THE RICH RULER. THE CURE OF THE BLIND MAN. HIS SALUTATION—SON OF DAVID. ALL PROOFS OF CHRIST'S RELATION TO THE CREATOR. MARCION'S ANTITHESIS BETWEEN DAVID AND CHRIST CONFUTED.

When He recommends perseverance and earnestness in prayer, He sets before us the parable of the judge who was compelled to listen to the widow, owing to the earnestness and importunity of her requests.[17] He show us that it is God the judge whom we must importune with prayer, and not Himself, if He is not Himself the judge. But He added, that "God would avenge His own elect."[18] Since, then, He who judges will also Himself be the avenger, He proved that the Creator

---

[1] Luke xvii. 19.
[2] Luke xvii. 20, 21.
[3] Una sententia.
[4] Excelsum: Sept. ὑπέρογχος.
[5] Deut. xxx. 11–13.
[6] Luke xvii. 21.
[7] Luke xvii. 25.
[8] Substantialiter.
[9] Assumi.
[10] Ps. cxviii. 21.
[11] See Isa. viii. 14 and 1 Cor. x. 4.
[12] Luke xvii. 26–30.
[13] Luke xvii. 32.
[14] Ut ille.
[15] Ille: emphatic.
[16] That is, the *Creator's* Christ from the Marcionite point of view.
[17] Luke xviii. 1–3
[18] Luke xviii. 7, 8.

is on that account the specially good God,[1] whom He represented as the avenger of His own elect, who cry day and night to Him. And yet, when He introduces *to our view* the Creator's temple, and describes two men worshipping therein with diverse feelings—the Pharisee in pride, the publican in humility— and shows us how they accordingly went down to their homes, one rejected,[2] the other justified,[3] He surely, by thus teaching us the proper discipline of prayer, has determined that that God must be prayed to from whom men were to receive this discipline of prayer —whether condemnatory of pride, or justifying in humility.[4] I do not find from Christ any temple, any suppliants, any sentence (of approval or condemnation) belonging to any other god than the Creator. Him does He enjoin us to worship in humility, as the lifter-up of the humble, not in pride, because He brings down[5] the proud. What other god has He manifested to me to receive my supplications? With what formula of worship, with what hope (shall I approach him?) I trow, none. For the prayer which He has taught us suits, as we have proved,[6] none but the Creator. It is, of course, another matter if He does not wish to be prayed to, because He is the supremely and spontaneously good God! But who is this good God? There is, He says, "none but one."[7] It is not as if He had shown us that one of two gods was the supremely good; but He expressly asserts that there is one only good God, who is the only good, because He is the only God. Now, undoubtedly,[8] He is the good God who "sendeth rain on the just and on the unjust, and maketh His sun to rise on the evil and on the good;"[9] sustaining and nourishing and assisting even Marcionites themselves! When afterwards "a certain man asked him, 'Good Master, what shall I do to inherit eternal life?'" (Jesus) inquired whether he *knew* (that is, in other words, whether he *kept*) the commandments of the Creator, in order to testify[10] that it was by the Creator's precepts that eternal life is acquired.[11] Then, when he affirmed that from his youth up he had kept all the principal commandments, (Jesus) said to him: "One thing thou yet lackest: sell all that thou hast, and give to the poor, and thou shalt have treasure in

heaven; and come, follow me."[12] Well now, Marcion, and all ye who are companions in misery, and associates in hatred[13] with that heretic, what will you dare say to this? Did Christ rescind the forementioned commandments: "Do not kill, Do not commit adultery, Do not steal, Do not bear false witness, Honour thy father and thy mother?" Or did He both keep them, and then add[14] what was wanting to them? This very precept, however, about giving to the poor, was very largely[15] diffused through the pages of the law and the prophets. This vainglorious observer of the commandments was therefore convicted[16] of holding money in much higher estimation (than charity). This verity of the gospel then stands unimpaired: "I am not come to destroy the law and the prophets, but rather to fulfil them."[17] He also dissipated other doubts, when He declared that the name of God and of the Good belonged to one and the same being, at whose disposal were also the everlasting life and the treasure in heaven and Himself too—whose commandments He both maintained and augmented with His own supplementary precepts. He may likewise be discovered in the following passage of Micah, saying: "He hath showed thee, O man, what is good; and what doth the Lord require of thee, but to do justly, and to love mercy, and to be ready to follow the Lord thy God?"[18] Now Christ is the man who tells us what is *good*, even the knowledge of the law. "Thou knowest," says He, "the commandments." "To do justly"—"Sell all that thou hast;" "to love mercy"—"Give to the poor:" "and to be ready to walk with God"—"And come," says He, "follow me."[19] The Jewish nation was from its beginning so carefully divided into tribes and clans, and families and houses, that no man could very well have been ignorant of his descent—even from the recent assessments of Augustus, which were still probably extant at this time.[20] But the Jesus of Marcion (although there could be no doubt of a person's having been born, who was seen to be a man), as being unborn, could not, of course, have possessed any public testimonial[21] of his descent, but was to be regarded as one of that obscure class of whom nothing was in any way

---

[1] Meliorem Deum.
[2] Reprobatum.
[3] Luke xviii. 10-14.
[4] Sive reprobatricem superbiæ, sive justificatricem humilitatis.
[5] Destructorem.
[6] See above, chap. xxvi. p. 392.
[7] Luke xviii. 19.
[8] Utique.
[9] Matt. v. 45.
[10] Ad contestandum.
[11] Luke xviii. 18-20.

[12] Luke xviii. 21, 22,
[13] See above, chap. ix., near the beginning.
[14] Adjecit quod deerat.
[15] Ubique.
[16] Traduceretur.
[17] Matt. v. 17.
[18] Mic. vi. 8. The last clause agrees with the Septuagint: καὶ ἕτοιμον εἶναι τοῦ πορεύεσθαι μετὰ Κυρίου Θεοῦ σου.
[19] The clauses of Christ's words, which are here adapted to Micah's, are in every case broken with an *inquit.*
[20] Tunc pendentibus: i.e., at the time mentioned in the story of the blind man.
[21] Notitiam.

known. Why then did the blind man, on hearing that He was passing by, exclaim, "Jesus, Thou Son of David, have mercy on me?"[1] unless he was considered, in no uncertain manner,[2] to be the Son of David (in other words, to belong to David's family) through his mother and his brethren, who at some time or other had been made known to him by public notoriety? "Those, however, who went before rebuked the blind man, that he should hold his peace."[3] And properly enough; because he was very noisy, not because he was wrong about the son of David. Else you must show me, that those who rebuked him were aware that Jesus was not the Son of David, in order that they may be supposed to have had this reason for imposing silence on the blind man. But even if you could show me this, still (the blind man) would more readily have presumed that they were ignorant, than that the Lord could possibly have permitted an untrue exclamation about Himself. But the Lord "stood patient."[4] Yes; but not as confirming the error, for, on the contrary, He rather displayed the Creator. Surely He could not have first removed this man's blindness, in order that he might afterwards cease to regard Him as the Son of David! However,[5] that you may not slander[6] His patience, nor fasten on Him any charge of dissimulation, nor deny Him to be the Son of David, He very pointedly confirmed the exclamation of the blind man—both by the actual gift of healing, and by bearing testimony to his faith: "Thy faith," say Christ, "hath made thee whole."[7] What would you have the blind man's faith to have been? That Jesus was descended from that (alien) god (of Marcion), to subvert the Creator and overthrow the law and the prophets? That He was not the destined offshoot from the root of Jesse, and the fruit of David's loins, the restorer[8] also of the blind? But I apprehend there were at that time no such stone-blind persons as Marcion, that an opinion like this could have constituted the faith of the blind man, and have induced him to confide in the mere *name*,[9] of Jesus, the Son of David. He, who knew all this of Himself,[10] and wished others to know it also, endowed the faith of this man —although it was already gifted with a better sight, and although it was in possession of the

true light—with the external vision likewise, in order that we too might learn the rule of faith, and at the same time find its recompense. Whosoever wishes to see Jesus the Son of David must believe in Him through the Virgin's birth.[11] He who will not believe this will not hear from Him the salutation, "Thy faith hath saved thee." And so he will remain blind, falling into *Antithesis* after *Antithesis*, which mutually destroy each other,[12] just as "the blind man leads the blind down into the ditch."[13] For (here is one of Marcion's *Antitheses*): whereas David in old time, in the capture of Sion, was offended by the blind who opposed his admission (into the stronghold)[14]—in which respect (I should rather say) that they were a type of people equally blind,[15] who in after-times would not admit Christ to be the son of David —so, on the contrary, Christ succoured the blind man, to show by this act that He was not David's son, and how different in disposition He was, kind to the blind, while David ordered them to be slain.[16] If all this were so, why did *Marcion* allege that the blind man's faith was of so worthless[17] a stamp? The fact is,[18] the Son of David so acted,[19] that the *Antithesis* must lose its point by its own absurdity.[20] Those persons who offended David were blind, and the man who now presents himself as a suppliant to David's son is afflicted with the same infirmity.[21] Therefore the Son of David was appeased with some sort of satisfaction by the blind man when He restored him to sight, and added His approval of the faith which had led him to believe the very truth, that he must win to his help[22] the Son of David by earnest entreaty. But, after all, I suspect that it was the audacity (of the old Jebusites) which offended David, and not their malady.

CHAP. XXXVII.—CHRIST AND ZACCHÆUS. THE SALVATION OF THE BODY AS DENIED BY MARCION. THE PARABLE OF THE TEN SERVANTS ENTRUSTED WITH TEN POUNDS. CHRIST A JUDGE, WHO IS TO ADMINISTER THE WILL OF THE AUSTERE MAN, I.E. THE CREATOR.

"Salvation comes to the house" of Zac-

---

[1] Luke xviii. 38.
[2] Non temere.
[3] Luke xviii. 39.
[4] Luke xviii. 40.
[5] Atquin.
[6] Infamaretis.
[7] Luke xviii. 42.
[8] Remunerator.
[9] That is, in the sound only, and phantom of the word; an allusion to the *Docetic* absurdity of Marcion.
[10] That is, that He was "Son of David," etc.

[11] Censum: that is, must believe Him born of her.
[12] This, perhaps, is the meaning in a clause which is itself more antithetical than clear: "Ruens in antithesim, ruentem et ipsam antithesim."
[13] In book iii. chap. vii. (at the beginning), occurs the same proverb of Marcion and the Jews. See p. 327
[14] See 2 Sam. v. 6–8.
[15] The Marcionites.
[16] See 2 Sam. v. 8.
[17] Fidei equidem pravæ: see preceding page, note 3.
[18] Atquin.
[19] Et hoc filius David: i.e., *præstitit*, "showed Himself good," perhaps.
[20] De suo retundendam. Instead of *contrast*, he shows the *similarity* of the cases.
[21] Ejusdem carnis: i.e., *infirmæ* (Oehler).
[22] Exorandum sibi.

chæus even.[1] For what reason? Was it because he also believed that Christ came by Marcion? But the blind man's cry was still sounding in the ears of all: "Jesus, Thou Son of David, have mercy on me." And "all the people gave praise unto God"—not Marcion's, but David's. Now, although Zacchæus was probably a Gentile,[2] he yet from his intercourse with Jews had obtained a smattering[3] of their Scriptures, and, more than this, had, without knowing it, fulfilled the precepts of Isaiah: "Deal thy bread," said the prophet, "to the hungry, and bring the poor that are cast out into thine house."[4] This he did in the best possible way, by receiving the Lord, and entertaining Him in his house. "When thou seest the naked, cover him."[5] This he promised to do, in an equally satisfactory way, when he offered the half of his goods for all works of mercy.[6] So also "he loosened the bands of wickedness, undid the heavy burdens, let the oppressed go free, and broke every yoke,"[7] when he said, "If I have taken anything from any man by false accusation, I restore him fourfold."[8] Therefore the Lord said, "This day is salvation come to this house."[9] Thus did He give His testimony, that the precepts of the Creator spoken by the prophet tended to salvation.[10] But when He adds, "For the Son of man is come to seek and to save that which was lost,"[11] my present contention is not whether *He* was come to save what was lost, *to whom* it had once belonged, and *from whom* what He came to save had fallen away; but I approach a different question. *Man*, there can be no doubt of it, is here the subject of consideration. Now, since he consists of two parts,[12] body and soul, the point to be inquired into is, in which of these two man would seem to have been lost? If in his body, then it is his body, not his soul, which is lost. What, however, is lost, the Son of man saves. The body,[13] therefore, has the salvation. If, (on the other hand,) it is in his soul that man is lost, salvation is designed for the lost soul; and the body which is not

lost is safe. If, (to take the only other supposition,) man is wholly lost, in both his natures, then it necessarily follows that salvation is appointed for the entire man; and then the opinion of the heretics is shivered to pieces,[14] who say that there is no salvation of the flesh. And this affords a confirmation that Christ belongs to the Creator, who followed the Creator in promising the salvation of the whole man. The parable also of the (ten) servants, who received their several recompenses according to the manner in which they had increased their lord's money by trading,[15] proves Him to be a God of judgment—even a God who, in strict account,[16] not only bestows honour, but also takes away what a man seems to have.[17] Else, if it is the Creator whom He has here delineated as the "austere man," who "takes up what he laid not down, and reaps what he did not sow,"[18] my instructor even here is He, (whoever He may be,) to whom belongs the money He teaches me fruitfully to expend.[19]

CHAP. XXXVIII.—CHRIST'S REFUTATIONS OF THE PHARISEES. RENDERING DUES TO CÆSAR AND TO GOD. NEXT OF THE SADDUCEES, RESPECTING MARRIAGE IN THE RESURRECTION. THESE PROVE HIM NOT TO BE MARCION'S BUT THE CREATOR'S CHRIST. MARCION'S TAMPERINGS IN ORDER TO MAKE ROOM FOR HIS SECOND GOD, EXPOSED AND CONFUTED.

Christ knew "the baptism of John, whence it was."[20] Then why did He ask them, as if He knew not? He knew that the Pharisees would not give Him an answer; then why did He ask in vain? Was it that He might judge them out of their own mouth, or their own heart? Suppose you refer these points to an excuse of the Creator, or to *His* comparison with Christ; then consider what would have happened if the Pharisees had replied to His question. Suppose their answer to have been, that John's baptism was "of men," they would have been immediately stoned to death.[21] Some Marcion, in rivalry to Marcion, would have stood up[22] and said: O most excellent God; how different are his ways from the Creator's! Knowing that men would rush down headlong over it, He placed them

---

[1] Luke xix. 9.
[2] The older reading, which we here follow, is: "Enimvero Zacchæus etsi allophylus fortasse," etc. Oehler, however, points the passage thus: "Enimvero Zacchæus etsi allophylus, fortasse," etc., removing the doubt, and making Zacchæus "of another race" than the Jewish, for certain. This is probably more than Tertullian meant to say.
[3] Aliqua notitia afflatus.
[4] Isa. lviii. 7.
[5] In the same passage.
[6] For the history of Zacchæus, see Luke xix. 1-10.
[7] Isa. lviii. 6.
[8] Luke xix. 8
[9] Luke xix. 9.
[10] Salutaria esse.
[11] Luke xix. 10.
[12] Substantiis.
[13] Caro: "the flesh," here a synonym with the *corpus* of the previous clauses.

[14] Elisa est.
[15] Secundum rationem feneratæ.
[16] Ex parte severitatis.
[17] This phrase comes not from the present passage, but from Luke viii. 18, where the words are ὁ δοκεῖ ἔχειν; *here* the expression is ὁ ἔχει only.
[18] Luke xix. 22.
[19] The original of this obscure sentence is as follows: "Aut si et hic Creatorem finxerit austerum . . . . . hic quoque me ille instruit eujus pecuniam ut fenerem edocet.
[20] Luke xx. 4.
[21] Luke xx. 6.
[22] Existeret.

actually[1] on the very precipice. For thus do men treat of the Creator respecting His law of the tree.[2] But John's baptism was "from heaven." "Why, therefore," asks Christ, "did ye not believe him?"[3] He therefore who had wished men to believe John, purposing to censure[4] them because they had not believed him, belonged to Him whose sacrament John was administering. But, at any rate,[5] when He actually met their refusal to say what they thought, with such reprisals as, "Neither tell I you by what authority I do these things,"[6] He returned evil for evil! "Render unto Cæsar the things which be Cæsar's, and unto God the things which be God's."[7] What will be "the things which are God's?" Such things as are like Cæsar's *denarius*—that is to say, His image and similitude. That, therefore, which he commands to be "rendered unto God," the Creator, is *man*, who has been stamped with His image, likeness, name, and substance.[8] Let Marcion's god look after his own mint.[9] Christ bids the *denarius* of man's imprint to be rendered to His Cæsar, (His Cæsar I say,) not the Cæsar of a strange god.[10] The truth, however, must be confessed, this god has not a *denarius* to call his own! In every question the just and proper rule is, that the meaning of the answer ought to be adapted to the proposed inquiry. But it is nothing short of madness to return an answer altogether different from the question submitted to you. God forbid, then, that we should expect from Christ[11] conduct which would be unfit even to an ordinary man! The Sadducees, who said there was no resurrection, in a discussion on that subject, had proposed to the Lord a case of law touching a certain woman, who, in accordance with the legal prescription, had been married to seven brothers who had died one after the other. The question therefore was, to which husband must she be reckoned to belong in the resurrection?[12] This, (observe,) was the gist of the inquiry, this was the sum and substance of the dispute. And to it Christ was obliged to return a direct answer. He had nobody to fear; that it should seem advisable[13] for Him either to evade their questions, or to make

them the occasion of indirectly mooting[14] a subject which He was not in the habit of teaching publicly at any other time. He therefore gave His answer, that "the children of this world marry."[15] You see how pertinent it was to the case in point. Because the question concerned the next world, and He was going to declare that no one marries there, He opens the way by laying down the principle, that here, where there is death, there is also marriage. "But they whom God shall account worthy of the possession of that world and the resurrection from the dead, neither marry nor are given in marriage; forasmuch as they cannot die any more, since they become equal to the angels, being made the children of God and of the resurrection."[16] If, then, the meaning of the answer must not turn on any other point than on the proposed question, and since the question proposed is fully understood from this sense of the answer,[17] then the Lord's reply admits of no other interpretation than that by which the question is clearly understood.[18] You have both the time in which marriage is permitted, and the time in which it is said to be unsuitable, laid before you, not on their own account, but in consequence of an inquiry about the resurrection. You have likewise a confirmation of the resurrection itself, and the whole question which the Sadducees mooted, who asked no question about another god, nor inquired about the proper law of marriage. Now, if you make Christ answer questions which were not submitted to Him, you, in fact, represent Him as having been unable to solve the points on which He was really consulted, and entrapped of course by the cunning of the Sadducees. I shall now proceed, by way of supererogation,[19] and after the rule (I have laid down about questions and answers),[20] to deal with the arguments which have any consistency in them.[21] They procured then a copy of the Scripture, and made short work with its text, by reading it thus:[22] "Those whom *the god of that world* shall account worthy." They

---

[1] Ipse.
[2] "Of knowledge of good and evil." The "*law*" thereof occurs in Gen. iii. 3.
[3] Luke xx. 5.
[4] Increpaturus.
[5] Certe. [The word *sacrament* not technical here.]
[6] Luke xx. 8.
[7] Luke xx. 25.
[8] Materia.
[9] Monetam.
[10] Non alieno.
[11] Quo magis absit a Christo.
[12] Luke xx. 27–33.
[13] Ut videatur.

[14] Subostendisse.
[15] Luke xx. 34.
[16] Luke xx. 35, 36.
[17] Surely Oehler's *responsio* ought to be *responsionis*, as the older books have it.
[18] Absolvitur.
[19] Ex abundanti.
[20] We have translated here, *post præscriptionem*, according to the more frequent sense of the word, *præscriptio*. But there is another meaning of the word, which is not unknown to our author, equivalent to our *objection* or *demurrer*, or (to quote Oehler's definition) "clausula qua reus adversarii intentionem oppugnat—the form by which the defendant rebuts the plaintiff's charge." According to this sense, we read: "I shall now proceed . . . and after putting in a demurrer (or taking exception) against the tactics of my opponent."
[21] Cohærentes.
[22] Decucurrerunt in legendo: or, "they ran through it, by thus reading."

add the phrase "*of that world*" to the word "*god*," whereby they make another god— "the god of that world;" whereas the passage ought to be read thus: "Those whom God shall account worthy of the possession of that world" (removing the distinguishing phrase "*of this world*" to the end of the clause,[1] in other words, "Those whom God shall account worthy of obtaining and rising to that world." For the question submitted to Christ had nothing to do with *the god*, but only with *the state*, of that world. It was: "Whose wife should this woman be in that world after the resurrection?"[2] They thus subvert His answer respecting the essential question of marriage, and apply His words, "The children of this world marry and are given in marriage," as if they referred to the Creator's men, and His permission to them to marry; whilst they themselves whom the god of that world—that is, the rival god—accounted worthy of the resurrection, do not marry even here, because they are not children of this world. But the fact is, that, having been consulted about marriage in *that* world, not in this present one, He had simply declared the non-existence of that to which the question related. They, indeed, who had caught the very force of His voice, and pronunciation, and expression, discovered no other sense than what had reference to the matter of the question. Accordingly, the Scribes exclaimed, "Master, Thou hast well said."[3] For He had affirmed the resurrection, by describing the form[4] thereof in opposition to the opinion of the Sadducees. Now, He did not reject the attestation of those who had assumed His answer to bear this meaning. If, however, the Scribes thought Christ was David's Son, whereas (David) himself calls Him Lord,[5] what relation has this to Christ? David did not literally confute[6] an error of the Scribes, yet David asserted the honour of Christ, when he more prominently affirmed that He was his Lord than his Son, —an attribute which was hardly suitable to the destroyer of the Creator. But how consistent is the interpretation on our side of the question! For He, who had been a little while ago invoked by the blind man as "the Son of David,"[7] then made no remark on the subject, not having the Scribes in His presence; whereas He now purposely moots the point · before them, and *that* of His own accord,[8] in order that He might show Himself whom the blind man, following the doctrine of the Scribes, had simply declared to be the Son of David, to be also his Lord. He thus honoured the blind man's faith which had acknowledged His Sonship to David; but at the same time He struck a blow at the tradition of the Scribes, which prevented them from knowing that He was also (David's) Lord. Whatever had relation to the glory of the Creator's Christ, no other would thus guard and maintain[9] but Himself the Creator's Christ.

CHAP. XXXIX.—CONCERNING THOSE WHO COME IN THE NAME OF CHRIST. THE TERRIBLE SIGNS OF HIS COMING. HE WHOSE COMING IS SO GRANDLY DESCRIBED BOTH IN THE OLD TESTAMENT AND THE NEW TESTAMENT, IS NONE OTHER THAN THE CHRIST OF THE CREATOR. THIS PROOF ENHANCED BY THE PARABLE OF THE FIG-TREE AND ALL THE TREES. PARALLEL PASSAGES OF PROPHECY.

As touching the propriety of His names, it has already been seen[10] that both of them[11] are suitable to Him who was the first both to announce His *Christ* to mankind, and to give Him the further name[12] of *Jesus*. The impudence, therefore, of Marcion's Christ will be evident, when he says that many will come in his name, whereas this name does not at all belong to *him*, since he is not the Christ and Jesus of the Creator, to whom these names do properly appertain; and more especially when he prohibits those to be received whose very equal in imposture he is, inasmuch as he (equally with them[13]) comes in a name which belongs to another—unless it was his business to warn off from a mendaciously assumed name the disciples (of One) who, by reason of His name being properly given to Him, possessed also the verity thereof. But when "they shall by and by come and say, I am Christ,"[14] they will be received by you, who have already received one altogether like them.[15] Christ, however, comes in His own

---

[1] We have *adapted*, rather than translated, Tertullian's words in this parenthesis. His words of course suit the order of the Latin, which differs from the English. The sentence in Latin is, "Quos autem dignatus est Deus illius ævi possessione et resurrectione a mortuis." The phrase in question is *illius ævi*. Where shall it stand? The Marcionites placed it after "*Deus*" in government, but Tertullian (following the undoubted meaning of the sentence) says it depends on "*possessione et resurrectione*," i.e., "worthy of *the possession, etc., of that world*." To effect this construction, he says, "Ut facta hic distinctione post deum ad sequentia pertineat illius ævi;" i.e, he requests that a stop be placed after the word "*deus*," whereby the phrase "*illius ævi*" will belong to the words which follow—"*possessione et resurrectione a mortuis*."
[2] Luke xx. 33.
[3] Luke xx. 39.
[4] Formam : "its condition " or " process.'
[5] Luke xx. 41-44.
[6] Non obtundebat.

[7] Luke xviii. 38.
[8] Luke xx. 41.
[9] Tueretur.
[10] See above : book iii. chap. xv. and xvi. pp. 333, 334.
[11] The *illam* here refers to the *nominum* proprietas, i.e., His title CHRIST and His name JESUS.
[12] Transnominaret.
[13] Proinde.
[14] Luke xxi. 8.
[15] Consimilem : of course Marcion's Christ ; the Marcionite being challenged in the "*you*."

name. What will you do, then, when He Himself comes who is the very Proprietor of these names, the Creator's Christ and Jesus? Will you reject Him? But how iniquitous, how unjust and disrespectful to the good God, that you should not receive Him who comes in His own name, when you have received another in His name! Now, let us see what are the signs which He ascribes to the times. "Wars," I observe, "and kingdom against kingdom, and nation against nation, and pestilence, and famines, and earthquakes, and fearful sights, and great signs from heaven"[1]—all which things are suitable for a severe and terrible God. Now, when He goes on to say that "all these things must needs come to pass,"[2] what does He represent Himself to be? The Destroyer, or the Defender of the Creator? For He affirms that these appointments of His must fully come to pass; but surely as the good God, He would have frustrated rather than advanced events so sad and terrible, if they had not been His own (decrees). "But before all these," He foretells that persecutions and sufferings were to come upon them, which indeed were "to turn for a testimony to them," and for their salvation.[3] Hear what is predicted in Zechariah: "The Lord of hosts[4] shall protect them; and they shall devour them, and subdue them with sling-stones; and they shall drink their blood like wine, and they shall fill the bowls as it were of the altar. And the Lord shall save them in that day, even His people, like sheep; because as sacred stones they roll,"[5] etc. And that you may not suppose that these predictions refer to such sufferings as await them from so many wars with strangers,[6] consider the nature (of the sufferings). In a prophecy of wars which were to be waged with legitimate arms, no one would think of enumerating stones as weapons, which are better known in popular crowds and unarmed tumults. Nobody measures the copious streams of blood which flow in war by bowlfuls, nor limits it to what is shed upon a single altar. No one gives the name of sheep to those who fall in battle with arms in hand, and while repelling force with force, but only to those who are slain, yielding themselves up in their own place of duty and with patience, rather than fighting in self-defence. In short, as he says, "they roll as sacred stones," and not like soldiers fight. Stones are they, even foundation-stones, upon which we are ourselves edified—"built," as St.

Paul says, "upon the foundation of the apostles,"[7] who, like "consecrated stones," were rolled up and down exposed to the attack of all men. And therefore in this passage He forbids men "to meditate before what they answer" when brought before tribunals,[8] even as once He suggested to Balaam the message which he had not thought of,[9] nay, contrary to what he had thought; and promised "a mouth" to Moses, when he pleaded in excuse the slowness of his speech,[10] and that wisdom which, by Isaiah, He showed to be irresistible: "One shall say, I am the Lord's, and shall call himself by the name of Jacob, and another shall subscribe himself by the name of Israel."[11] Now, what plea is wiser and more irresistible than the simple and open[12] confession made in a martyr's cause, who "prevails with God"—which is what "Israel" means?[13] Now, one cannot wonder that He forbade "premeditation," who actually Himself received from the Father the ability of uttering words in season: "The Lord hath given to me the tongue of the learned, that I should know how to speak a word in season (to him that is weary);"[14] except that Marcion introduces to us a Christ who is not subject to the Father. That persecutions from one's nearest friends are predicted, and calumny out of hatred to His name,[15] I need not again refer to. But "by patience,"[16] says He, "ye shall yourselves be saved."[17] Of this very patience the Psalm says, "The patient endurance of the just shall not perish for ever;"[18] because it is said in another Psalm, "Precious (in the sight of the Lord) is the death of the just"—arising, no doubt, out of their patient endurance, so that Zechariah declares: ."A crown shall be to them that endure."[19] But that you may not boldly contend that it was as announcers of another god that the apostles were persecuted by the Jews, remember that even the prophets suffered the same treatment of the Jews, and that they were not the heralds of any other god than the Creator. Then, having shown what was to be the period of the destruction, even "when Jerusalem should

---

1 Luke xxi. 9–11.
2 Compare, in Luke xxi., verses 9, 22, 28, 31–33, 35, and 36.
3 Verses 12, 13.
4 Omnipotens: παντοκράτωρ (Sept.) ; of hosts—A. V.
5 Zech. ix. 15, 16 (Septuagint).
6 Allophylis.

7 Eph. ii. 20.
8 Luke xxi. 12–14.
9 Num. xxii.–xxiv
10 Ex. iv. 10–12.
11 Isa. xliv. 5.
12 Exserta.
13 See Gen. xxxii. 28.
14 Isa. l. 4.
15 Luke xxi. 16, 17.
16 Per tolerantiam : "endurance."
17 Comp. Luke xxi. 19 with Matt. xxiv. 13.
18 Ps. ix. 18.
19 After the Septuagint he makes a plural appellative ("eis qui toleraverint," LXX. τοῖς ὑπομένουσι) of the Hebrew לְחֹלְדָי, which in
A. V. and the Vulgate (and also Gesenius and Fuerst) is the dative of a proper name.

begin to be compassed with armies,"[1] He described the signs of the end of all things: "portents in the sun, and the moon, and the stars, and upon the earth distress of nations in perplexity—like the sea roaring—by reason of their expectation of the evils which are coming on the earth."[2] That "the very powers also of heaven have to be shaken,"[3] you may find in Joel: "And I will show wonders in the heavens and in the earth—blood and fire, and pillars of smoke; the sun shall be turned into darkness, and the moon into blood, before the great and terrible day of the Lord come."[4] In Habakkuk also you have this statement: "With rivers shall the earth be cleaved; the nations shall see thee, and be in pangs. Thou shalt disperse the waters with thy step; the deep uttered its voice; the height of its fear was raised;[5] the sun and the moon stood still in their course; into light shall thy coruscations go; and thy shield shall be (like) the glittering of the lightning's flash; in thine anger thou shalt grind the earth, and shalt thresh the nations in thy wrath."[6] There is thus an agreement, I apprehend, between the sayings of the Lord and of the prophets touching the shaking of the earth, and the elements, and the nations thereof. But what does the Lord say afterwards? "And then shall they see the Son of man coming from the heavens with very great power. And when these things shall come to pass, ye shall look up, and raise your heads; for your redemption hath come near," that is, at the time of the kingdom, of which the parable itself treats.[7] "So likewise ye, when ye shall see these things come to pass, know ye that the kingdom of God is nigh at hand."[8] This will be the great day of the Lord, and of the glorious coming of the Son of man from heaven, of which Daniel wrote: "Behold, one like the Son of man came with the clouds of heaven,"[9] etc. "And there was given unto Him the kingly power,"[10] which (in the parable) "He went away into a far country to receive for Himself," leaving money to His servants wherewithal to trade and get increase[11]—even (that universal kingdom of) all nations, which in the Psalm the Father had promised to give to Him: Ask of me, and I will give Thee the heathen for Thine inheritance."[12] "And all *that* glory shall serve Him; His dominion shall be an everlasting one, which shall not be taken from Him, and His kingdom that which shall not be destroyed,"[13] because in it "men shall not die, neither shall they marry, but be like the angels."[14] It is about the same advent of the Son of man and the benefits thereof that we read in Habakkuk: "Thou wentest forth for the salvation of Thy people, even to save Thine anointed ones,"[15]—in other words, those who shall look up and lift their heads, being redeemed in the time of His kingdom. Since, therefore, these descriptions of the promises, on the one hand, agree together, as do also those of the great catastrophes, on the other—both in the predictions of the prophets and the declarations of the Lord, it will be impossible for you to interpose any distinction between them, as if the catastrophes could be referred to the Creator, as the terrible God, being such as the good god (of Marcion) ought not to permit, much less expect —whilst the promises should be ascribed to the good god, being such as the Creator, in His ignorance of the said god, could not have predicted. If, however, He did predict these promises as His own, since they differ in no respect from the promises of Christ, He will be a match in the freeness of His gifts with the good god himself; and evidently no more will have been promised by your Christ than by my Son of man. (If you examine) the whole passage of this Gospel Scripture, from the inquiry of the disciples[16] down to the parable of the fig-tree[17] you will find the sense in its connnection suit in every point the Son of man, so that it consistently ascribes to Him both the sorrows and the joys, and the catastrophes and the promises; nor can you separate them from Him in either respect. Forasmuch, then, as there is but one Son of man whose advent is placed between the two issues of catastrophe and promise, it must needs follow that to that one Son of man belong both the judgments upon the nations, and the prayers of the saints. He who thus comes in midway so as to be common to both issues, will terminate one of them by inflicting judgment on the nations at His coming; and will at the same time commence the other by fulfilling the prayers of His saints: so that if (on the one hand) you grant that the coming of the Son of man is (the advent) of *my Christ*, then, when you ascribe to Him the infliction of the judgments which precede His appearance, you are compelled also to assign to

---

[1] Luke xxi. 20.
[2] Luke xxi. 25, 26.
[3] Luke xxi. 26.
[4] Joel iii. 30, 31.
[5] Elata: "fear was raised to its very highest."
[6] Hab. iii. 9–12 (Septuagint).
[7] Luke xxi. 27, 28.
[8] Luke xxi. 31.
[9] Dan. vii. 13.
[10] Dan. vii. 14.
[11] Luke xix. 12, 13, etc.
[12] Ps. ii. 8.

[13] Dan. vii. 14.
[14] Luke xx. 35, 36.
[15] Hab. iii. 13.
[16] In Luke xxi. 7.
[17] Luke xxi. 33.

Him the blessings which issue from the same. If (on the other hand) you will have it that it is the coming of *your Christ*, then, when you ascribe to him the blessings which are to be the result of his advent, you are obliged to impute to him likewise the infliction of the evils which precede his appearance. For the evils which precede, and the blessings which immediately follow, the coming of the Son of man, are both alike indissolubly connected with that event. Consider, therefore, which of the two Christs you choose to place in the person of the Son of man, to whom you may refer the execution of the two dispensations. You make either the Creator a most benefi- cent God, or else your own god terrible in his nature! Reflect, in short, on the picture presented in the parable: "Behold the fig- tree, and all the trees; when they produce their fruit, men know that summer is at hand. So likewise ye, when ye see these things come to pass, know ye that the kingdom of God is very near."[1] Now, if the fructification of the common trees[2] be an antecedent sign of the approach of summer, so in like manner do the great conflicts of the world indicate the arrival of that kingdom which they pre- cede. But every sign is His, to whom be- long the thing of which it is the sign; and to everything is appointed its sign by Him to whom the thing belongs. If, therefore, these tribulations are the signs of the kingdom, just as the maturity of the trees is of the sum- mer, it follows that the kingdom is the Cre- ator's to whom are ascribed the tribulations which are the signs of the kingdom. Since the beneficent Deity had premised that these things must needs come to pass, although so terrible and dreadful, as they had been pre- dicted by the law and the prophets, therefore He did not destroy the law and the prophets, when He affirmed that what had been foretold therein must be certainly fulfilled. He fur- ther declares, " that heaven and earth shall not pass away till all things be fulfilled."[3] What things, pray, are these? Are they the things which the Creator made? Then the elements will tractably endure the accomplish- ment of their Maker's dispensation. If, how- ever, they emanate from your excellent god, I much doubt whether[4] the heaven and earth will peaceably allow the completion of things which their Creator's enemy has determined! If the Creator quietly submits to this, then He is no "jealous God." But let heaven and earth pass away, since their Lord has so

determined; only let His word remain for evermore! And so Isaiah predicted that it should.[5] Let the disciples also be warned, " lest their hearts be overcharged with surfeit- ing and drunkenness, and cares of this world; and so that day come upon them unawares, like a snare "[6]—if indeed they should forget God amidst the abundance and occupation of the world. Like this will be found the ad- monition of Moses,—so that He who delivers from " the snare" of that day is none other than He who so long before addressed to men the same admonition.[7] Some places there were in Jerusalem where to teach; other places outside Jerusalem whither to retire[8]— " In the day-time He was teaching in the temple;" just as He had foretold by Hosea: " In my house did they find me, and there did I speak with them."[9] "But at night He went out to the Mount of Olives." For thus had Zechariah pointed out: "And His feet shall stand in that day on the Mount of Olives."[10] Fit hours for an audience there also were. "Early in the morning"[11] must they resort to Him, who (having said by Isa- iah, "The Lord giveth me the tongue of the learned") added, "He hath appointed me the morning, and hath also given me an ear to hear."[12] Now if this is to *destroy* the proph- ets,[13] what will it be to *fulfil* them?

CHAP. XL.—HOW THE STEPS IN THE PASSION OF THE SAVIOUR WERE PREDETERMINED IN PROPHECY. THE PASSOVER. THE TREACHERY OF JUDAS. THE INSTITUTION OF THE LORD'S SUPPER. THE DOCETIC ERROR OF MARCION CONFUTED BY THE BODY AND THE BLOOD OF THE LORD JESUS CHRIST.

In like manner does He also know the very time it behoved Him to suffer, since the law prefigures His passion. Accordingly, of all the festal days of the Jews He chose the pass- over.[14] In this Moses had declared that there was a sacred mystery:[15] "It is the Lord's passover."[16] How earnestly, therefore, does He manifest the bent of His soul: "With de- sire I have desired to eat this passover with you before I suffer."[17] What a destroyer of the law was this, who actually longed to keep

---

[1] Luke xxi. 29–31.
[2] Arbuscularum.
[3] Luke xxi. 33.
[4] Nescio an.

[5] Isa. xl. 8.
[6] Luke xxi. 34, 35. [Here follows a rich selection of parallels to Luke xxi. 34–38.]
[7] Comp. Deut. viii. 12–14.
[8] Luke xxi. 37.
[9] Hosea xii. 4. One reading of the LXX. is, ἐν τῷ οἴκῳ μου εὑρεσάν με.
[10] Zech. xiv. 4.
[11] Luke xxi. 38.
[12] Isa. l. 4.
[13] Literally, "the prophecies."
[14] Luke xxii. 1.
[15] Sacramentum.
[16] Lev. xxiii. 5.
[17] Luke xxii. 15.

its passover! Could it be that He was so fond of Jewish lamb?[1] But was it not because He had to be "led like a lamb to the slaughter; and because, as a sheep before her shearers is dumb, so was He not to open His mouth,"[2] that He so profoundly wished to accomplish the symbol of His own redeeming blood? He might also have been betrayed by any stranger, did I not find that even here too He fulfilled a Psalm: "He who did eat bread with me hath lifted up[3] his heel against me."[4] And without a price might He have been betrayed. For what need of a traitor was there in the case of one who offered Himself to the people openly, and might quite as easily have been captured by force as taken by treachery? This might no doubt have been well enough for another Christ, but would not have been suitable in One who was accomplishing prophecies. For it was written, "The righteous one did they sell for silver."[5] The very amount and the destination[6] of the money, which on Judas' remorse was recalled *from its first purpose of a fee,*[7] and appropriated to the purchase of a potter's field, as narrated in the Gospel of Matthew, were clearly foretold by Jeremiah:[8] "And they took the thirty pieces of silver, the price of Him who was valued,[9] and gave them for the potter's field." When He so earnestly expressed His desire to eat the passover, He considered it *His own* feast; for it would have been unworthy of God to desire to partake of what was not His own. Then, having taken the bread and given it to His disciples, He made it His own body, by saying, "This is my body,"[10] that is, the figure of my body. A figure, however, there could not have been, unless there were first a veritable body.[11] An

empty thing, or phantom, is incapable of a figure. If, however, (as Marcion might say,) He pretended the bread was His body, because He lacked the truth of bodily substance, it follows that He must have given bread for us. It would contribute very well to the support of Marcion's theory of a phantom body,[12] that bread should have been crucified! But why call His body bread, and not rather (some other edible thing, say) a melon,[13] which Marcion must have had in lieu of a heart! He did not understand how ancient was this figure of the body of Christ, who said Himself by Jeremiah: "I was like a lamb or an ox that is brought to the slaughter, and I knew not that[14] they devised a device against me, saying, *Let us cast the tree upon His bread,*"[15] which means, of course, the cross upon His body. And thus, casting light, as He always did, upon the ancient prophecies,[16] He declared plainly enough what He meant by the *bread*, when He called the bread His own body. He likewise, when mentioning the cup and making the *new* testament to be sealed "in His blood,"[17] affirms the reality of His body. For no blood can belong to a body which is not *a body* of flesh. If any sort of body were presented to our view, which is not one of flesh, not being fleshly, it would not possess blood. Thus, from the evidence of the flesh, we get a proof of the body, and a proof of the flesh from the evidence of the blood. In order, however, that you may discover how anciently wine is used as a figure for blood, turn to Isaiah, who asks, "Who is this that cometh from Edom, from Bosor with garments dyed in red, so glorious in His apparel, in the greatness of his might? Why are thy garments red, and thy raiment as his who cometh from the treading of the full winepress?"[18] The prophetic Spirit contemplates the Lord as if He were already on His way to His passion, clad in His fleshly nature; and as He was to suffer therein, He represents the bleeding condition of His flesh under the metaphor of garments dyed in red, as if reddened in the treading and crushing process of the winepress, from which the labourers descend reddened with the wine-juice, like men stained in blood. Much more clearly still does the book of Genesis foretell this, when

---

[1] Vervecina Judaica. In this rough sarcasm we have of course our author's contempt of Marcionism.
[2] Isa. liii. 7.
[3] Levabit : literally, "shall lift up," etc.
[4] Ps. xli. 9.
[5] Amos ii. 6.
[6] Exitum.
[7] Revocati.
[8] This passage more nearly resembles Zech. xi. 12 and 13 than anything in Jeremiah, although the transaction in Jer. xxxii. 7-15 is noted by the commentators, as referred to. Tertullian had good reason for mentioning Jeremiah and not Zechariah, because the apostle whom he refers to (Matt. xxvii. 3-10) had distinctly attributed the prophecy to Jeremiah ("Jeremy the prophet," ver. 9). This is not the place to do more than merely refer to the voluminous controversy which has arisen from the apostle's mention of *Jeremiah* instead of Zechariah. It is enough to remark that Tertullian's argument is unaffected by the discrepancy in the name of the particular prophet. On all hands *the prophecy* is admitted, and this at once satisfies our author's argument. For the MS. evidence in favour of the unquestionably correct reading, τότε ἐπληρώθη τὸ ῥηθὲν διὰ Ἰερεμίου τοῦ προφήτου, κ.τ.λ., the reader is referred to Dr. Tregelles' *Critical Greek Testament, in loc. ;* only to the convincing amount of evidence collected by the very learned editor must now be added the subsequently obtained authority of Tischendorf's *Codex Sinaiticus.*
[9] Appretiati vel honorati. There is nothing in the original or the Septuagint to meet the second word *honorati,* which may refer to the "*honorarium,*" or "fee paid on admission to a post of honour,"—a term of Roman law, and referred to by Tertullian himself.
[10] Luke xxii. 19. [See Jewell's Challenge, p. 266, *supra.*]
[11] Corpus veritatis : meant as a thrust against Marcion's *Docetism.*

[12] Ad vanitatem Marcionis. [Note 9, p. 289.]
[13] Peponem. In his *De Anima,* c. xxxii., he uses this word in strong irony: "Cur non magis et *pepo,* tam insulsus."
[14] [This text, imperfectly quoted in the original, is filled out by Dr. Holmes.]
[15] So the Septuagint in Jer. xi. 19, ξύλον εἰς τὸν ἄρτον αὐτοῦ (A. V. "Let us destroy the tree with the fruit"). See above, book iii. chap. xix. p. 337.
[16] Illuminator antiquitatum. This general phrase includes typical ordinances under the law, as well as the sayings of the prophets.
[17] Luke xxii. 20.
[18] Isa. lxiii. 1 (Sept. slightly altered).

(in the blessing of Judah, out of whose tribe Christ was to come according to the flesh) it even then delineated Christ in the person of that patriarch,[1] saying, "He washed His garments in wine, and His clothes in the blood of grapes"[2]—in His garments and clothes the prophecy pointed out his flesh, and His blood in the wine. Thus did He now consecrate His blood in wine, who then (by the patriarch) used the figure of wine to describe His blood.

CHAP. XLI.—THE WOE PRONOUNCED ON THE TRAITOR A JUDICIAL ACT, WHICH DISPROVES CHRIST TO BE SUCH AS MARCION WOULD HAVE HIM TO BE. CHRIST'S CONDUCT BEFORE THE COUNCIL EXPLAINED. CHRIST EVEN THEN DIRECTS THE MINDS OF HIS JUDGES TO THE PROPHETIC EVIDENCES OF HIS OWN MISSION. THE MORAL RESPONSIBILITY OF THESE MEN ASSERTED.

"Woe," says He, "to that man by whom the Son of man is betrayed!"[3]   Now it is certain that in this *woe* must be understood the imprecation and threat of an angry and incensed Master, unless Judas was to escape with impunity after so vast a sin.   If he were meant to escape with impunity, the "*woe*" was an idle word; if not, he was of course to be punished by Him against whom he had committed the sin of treachery.   Now, if He knowingly permitted the man, whom He[4] deliberately elected to be one of His companions, to plunge into so great a crime, you must no longer use an argument against the Creator in Adam's case, which may now recoil on your own God:[5] either that he was *ignorant*, and had no foresight to hinder the future sinner;[6] or that he was *unable* to hinder him, even if he was ignorant;[7] or else that he was *unwilling*, even if he had the foreknowledge and the ability; and so deserved the stigma of maliciousness, in having permitted the man of his own choice to perish in his sin.   I advise you therefore (willingly) to acknowledge the Creator in that god of yours, rather than against your will to be assimilating your excellent god to Him.   For in the case of Peter,[8] too, he gives you proof that he is a jealous God, when he destined the apostle, after his presumptuous protestations of zeal, to a flat

denial of him, rather than *prevent his fall.*[9] The Christ of the prophets was destined, moreover, to be betrayed with a kiss,[10] for He was the Son indeed of Him who was "honoured *with the lips*" by the people.[11] When led before the council, He is asked whether He is the Christ.[12]   Of what Christ could the Jews have inquired [13] but their own? Why, therefore, did He not, even at that moment, declare to them the rival (Christ)? You reply, In order that He might be able to suffer.   In other words, that this most excellent god might plunge men into crime, whom he was still keeping in ignorance.   But even if he had told them, he would yet have to suffer. For he said, "If I tell you, ye will not believe."[14]   And refusing to believe, they would have continued to insist on his death.   And would he not even more probably still have had to suffer, if had announced himself as sent by the rival god, and as being, therefore, the enemy of the Creator?   It was not, then, in order that He might suffer, that He at that critical moment refrained from proclaiming[15] Himself the other *Christ*, but because they wanted to extort a confession from His mouth, which they did not mean to believe even if He had given it to them, whereas it was their bounden duty to have acknowledged Him in consequence of His works, which were fulfilling their Scriptures.   It was thus plainly His course to keep Himself at that moment unrevealed,[16] because a spontaneous recognition was due to Him.   But yet for all this, He with a solemn gesture[17] says, "Hereafter shall the Son of man sit on the right hand of the power of God."[18]   For it was on the authority of the prophecy of Daniel that He intimated to them that He was "the Son of man,"[19] and of David's Psalm, that He would "sit at the right hand of God."[20]   Accordingly, after He had said this, and so suggested a comparison of the Scripture, a ray of light did seem to show them whom He would have them understand Him to be; for they say: "Art thou then the Son of God?"[21] Of what God, but of Him whom alone they knew?   Of what God but of Him whom they remembered in the Psalm as having said to

---

[1] In Juda.
[2] Gen. xlix. 11.
[3] Luke xxii. 22.
[4] Ipse.
[5] This is an *argumentum ad hominem* against Marcion for his cavil, which was considered above in book ii. chap. v.-viii. p. 300.
[6] Obstitit peccaturo.
[7] Si ignorabat.   One would have expected "si *non* ignorabat," like the "si sciebat" of the next step in the argument.
[8] The original of this not very clear sentence is: "Nam et Petrum præsumptorie aliquid elocutum negationi potius destinando zeloten deum tibi ostendit."

[9] Luke xxii. 34 and 54-62.
[10] Luke xxii. 47-49.
[11] Isa. xxix. 13.
[12] Luke xxii. 66, 67.
[13] Oehler's admirable edition is also carefully *printed* for the most part, but surely his *quæsisset* must here be *quæsissent.*
[14] Luke xxii. 67.
[15] Supersedit ostendere.
[16] i.e., not to answer that question of theirs.   This seems to be the force of the perfect tense, "*occultasse se.*"
[17] He makes Jesus stretch forth His hand, *porrigens manum* inquit.
[18] Luke xxii. 69.
[19] Dan. vii. 13.
[20] Ps. cx. 1.
[21] Luke xxii. 70.

His Son, "Sit Thou on my right hand?" Then He answered, "Ye say that I am;"[1] as if He meant: It is *ye* who say this—not I. But at the same time He allowed Himself to be all that they had said, in this their second question.[2] By what means, however, are you going to prove to us that they pronounced the sentence "*Ergo tu filius Dei es*" interrogatively, and not affirmatively?[3] Just as, (on the one hand,) because He had shown them in an indirect manner,[4] by passages of Scripture, that they ought to regard Him as the Son of God, they therefore meant their own words, "Thou art then the Son of God," to be taken in a like (indirect) sense,[5] as much as to say, "You do not wish to say this of yourself plainly,[6] so, (on the other hand,) He likewise answered them, "Ye say that I am," in a sense equally free from doubt, even affirmatively;[7] and so completely was His statement to this effect, that they insisted on accepting that sense which His statement indicated.[8]

CHAP. XLII.—OTHER INCIDENTS OF THE PASSION MINUTELY COMPARED WITH PROPHECY. PILATE AND HEROD. BARABBAS PREFERRED TO JESUS. DETAILS OF THE CRUCIFIXION. THE EARTHQUAKE AND THE MID-DAY DARKNESS. ALL WONDERFULLY FORETOLD IN THE SCRIPTURES OF THE CREATOR. CHRIST'S GIVING UP THE GHOST NO EVIDENCE OF MARCION'S DOCETIC OPINIONS. IN HIS SEPULTURE THERE IS A REFUTATION THEREOF.

For when He was brought before Pilate, they proceeded to urge Him with the serious charge[9] of declaring Himself to be *Christ the King;*[10] that is, undoubtedly, as the Son of God, who was to sit at God's right hand. They would, however, have burdened Him[11] with some other title, if they had been uncertain whether He had called Himself *the Son of God*— if He had not pronounced the words, "Ye say that I am," so as (to admit) that He was that which they said He was. Likewise, when Pilate asked Him, "Art thou Christ (the King)?" He answered, as He had before (to the Jewish council)[12] "Thou sayest that I am"[13] in order that He might not seem to

have been driven by a fear of his power to give him a fuller answer. "And so the Lord hath stood on His trial."[14] And he placed His people on their trial. The Lord Himself comes to a trial with "the elders and rulers of the people," as Isaiah predicted.[15] And then He fulfilled all that had been written of His passion. At that time "the heathen raged, and the people imagined vain things; the kings of the earth set themselves, and the rulers gathered themselves together against the Lord and against His Christ."[16] The *heathen* were Pilate and the Romans; the *people* were the tribes of Israel; the *kings* were represented in Herod, and the *rulers* in the chief priests. When, indeed, He was sent to Herod gratuitously[17] by Pilate,[18] the words of Hosea were accomplished, for he had prophesied of Christ: "And they shall carry Him bound as a present to the king."[19] Herod was "exceeding glad" when he saw Jesus, but he heard not a word from Him.[20] For, "as a lamb before the shearer is dumb, so He opened not His mouth,"[21] because "the Lord had given to Him a disciplined tongue, that he might know how and when it behoved Him to speak"[22]—even that "tongue which clave to His jaws," as the Psalm[23] said it should, through His not speaking. Then Barabbas, the most abandoned criminal, is released, as if he were the innocent man; while the most righteous Christ is delivered to be put to death, as if he were the murderer.[24] Moreover two malefactors are crucified around Him, in order that He might be reckoned amongst the transgressors.[25] Although His raiment was, without doubt, parted among the soldiers, and partly distributed by lot, yet Marcion has erased it all (from his Gospel),[26] for he had his eye upon the Psalm: "They parted my garments amongst them, and cast lots upon my vesture."[27] You may as well take away the cross itself! But even then the Psalm is not silent concerning it: "They pierced my hands and my feet."[28] Indeed, the details of the whole event are therein read: "Dogs compassed me about;

---

[1] Luke xxii. 70.
[2] Or does he suppose that they repeated this same question *twice?* His words are, "dum rursus interrogant."
[3] Either, "Art thou," or, "Thou art, then, the Son of God."
[4] Oblique.
[5] Ut, quia . . . . sic senserunt.
[6] Aperte.
[7] Æque ita et ille confirmative respondit.
[8] Ut perseveraverint in eo quod pronuntiatio sapiebat . . . . See Luke xxii. 71.
[9] Onerare cœperunt.
[10] "King Messiah;" λέγοντα ἑαυτὸν Χριστὸν βασιλέα εἶναι, Luke xxiii. 1, 2.
[11] Gravassent.
[12] Proinde.
[13] Luke xxiii. 3.

[14] Constitutus est in judicio. The Septuagint has καταστήσεται εἰς κρίσιν, "shall stand on His trial."
[15] Isa. iii. 13, 14 (Septuagint).
[16] Ps. ii. 1, 2.
[17] Velut munus. This is a definition, in fact, of the *xenium* in the verse from Hosea. This ξένιον was the Roman *lautia*, "a state entertainment to distinguished foreigners in the city."
[18] Luke xxiii. 7.
[19] Hos. x. 6 (Sept. ξένια τῷ βασιλεῖ).
[20] Luke xxiii. 8, 9.
[21] Isa. liii. 7.
[22] Isa. l. 4 (Sept.).
[23] Ps. xxii. 15.
[24] Luke xxiii. 25.
[25] Comp. Luke xxiii. 33 with Isa. liii. 12.
[26] This remarkable suppression was made to escape the wonderful minuteness of *the prophetic* evidence to the details of Christ's death.
[27] Ps. xxii. 18.
[28] Ps. xxii. 16.

the assembly of the wicked enclosed me around. All that looked upon me laughed me to scorn; they did shoot out their lips and shake their heads, (saying,) He hoped in God, let Him deliver Him." [1]   Of what use now is (your tampering with) the testimony of His garments? If you take it as a booty for your false Christ, still all the Psalm (compensates) the vesture of Christ.[2]   But, behold, the very elements are shaken. For their Lord was suffering. If, however, it was their enemy to whom all this injury was done, the heaven would have gleamed with light, the sun would have been even more radiant, and the day would have prolonged its course [3]—gladly gazing at Marcion's Christ suspended on his gibbet! These proofs[4] would still have been suitable for me, even if they had not been the subject of prophecy. Isaiah says: "I will clothe the heavens with blackness." [5] This will be the day, concerning which Amos also writes: And it shall come to pass in that day, saith the Lord, that the sun shall go down at noon and the earth shall be dark in the clear day." [6]   (At noon)[7] the veil of the temple was rent" [8] by the escape of the cherubim,[9] which " left the daughter of Sion as a cottage in a vineyard, as a lodge in a garden of cucumbers." [10]   With what constancy has He also, in Psalm xxx., laboured to present to us the very Christ! He calls with a loud voice to the Father, " Into Thine hands I commend my spirit," [11] that even when dying He might expend His last breath in fulfilling the prophets. Having said this, He gave up the ghost." [12]   Who? Did the spirit [13] give itself up; or the flesh the spirit? But the spirit could not have breathed itself out. That which breathes is one thing, that which is breathed is another. If the spirit is breathed it must needs be breathed by another. If, however, there had been nothing there but spirit, it would be said to have *departed* rather than *expired*.[14]   What, however, breathes out spirit but the flesh, which both *breathes* the spirit whilst it has it, and *breathes it out* when it loses it? Indeed, if it was not flesh (upon the cross), but a phantom [15] of flesh (and [16] a phantom is but spirit, and [16] so the spirit breathed its own self out, and departed as it did so), no doubt the phantom departed, when the spirit which was the phantom departed: and so the phantom and the spirit disappeared together, and were nowhere to be seen.[17]   Nothing therefore remained upon the cross, nothing hung there, after " the giving up of the ghost;" [18] there was nothing to beg of Pilate, nothing to take down from the cross, nothing to wrap in the linen, nothing to lay in the new sepulchre.[19] Still it was not *nothing* [20] that was there. What was there, then? If a phantom Christ was yet there. If Christ had departed, He had taken away the phantom also. The only shift left to the impudence of the heretics, is to admit that what remained there was the phantom of a phantom! But what if Joseph knew that it was a body which he treated with so much piety? [21]   That same Joseph "who had not consented " with the Jews in their crime ? [22]   The " happy man who walked not in the counsel of the ungodly, nor stood in the way of sinners, nor sat in the seat of the scornful." [23]

CHAP. XLIII.—CONCLUSIONS. JESUS AS THE CHRIST OF THE CREATOR PROVED FROM THE EVENTS OF THE LAST CHAPTER OF ST. LUKE. THE PIOUS WOMEN AT THE SEPULCHRE. THE ANGELS AT THE RESURRECTION. THE MANIFOLD APPEARANCES OF CHRIST AFTER THE RESURRECTION. HIS MISSION OF THE APOSTLES AMONGST ALL NATIONS. ALL SHOWN TO BE IN ACCORDANCE WITH THE WISDOM OF THE ALMIGHTY FATHER, AS INDICATED IN PROPHECY. THE BODY OF CHRIST AFTER DEATH NO MERE PHANTOM. MARCION'S MANIPULATION · OF THE GOSPEL ON THIS POINT.

It was very meet that the man who buried the Lord should thus be noticed in prophecy, and thenceforth be " blessed;" [24] since prophecy does not omit the (pious) office of the women who resorted before day-break to the sepulchre with the spices which they had pre-

---

[1] Ps. xxii. 16, 7, 8.
[2] We append the original of these obscure sentences: " Quo jam testimonium vestimentorum? Habe falsi tui prædam; totus psalmus vestimenta sunt Christi." The general sense is apparent. If Marcion does suppress the details about Christ's garments at the cross, to escape the inconvenient proof they afford that Christ is the object of the prophecies, yet there are so many other points of agreement between this wonderful Psalm and St. Luke's history of the crucifixion (not expunged, as it would seem, by the heretic), that they quite compensate for the loss of this passage about the garments (Oehler).
[3] Comp. Josh. x. 13.
[4] Argumenta.
[5] Isa. l. 3.
[6] Amos viii. 9.
[7] Here you have the meaning of the sixth hour.
[8] Luke xxiii. 45.
[9] Ezek. xi. 22, 23.
[10] Isa. i. 8.
[11] Comp. Luke xxiii. 46 with Ps. xxxi. 5.
[12] Luke xxiii. 46.
[13] Spiritus: or " breath."
[14] Expirasse : considered *actively*, " breathed out," in reference to the " *expiravit* " of the verse 46 above.

[15] A sharp rebuke of Marcion's *Docetism* here follows.
[16] Autem.
[17] Nusquam comparuit phantasma cum spiritu.
[18] Post expirationem.
[19] See these stages in Luke xxiii. 47-55.
[20] Non nihil : "a something."
[21] This argument is also used by Epiphanius to prove the reality of Christ's body, *Hæres.* xl. *Confut.* 74. The same writer also employs for the same purpose the incident of *the women returning from the sepulchre*, which Tertullian is going to adduce in his next chapter, *Confut.* 75 (Oehler).
[22] Luke xxiii. 51.
[23] Ps. i. 1.
[24] The *first* word of the passage just applied to Joseph.

pared.[1] For of this incident it is said by Hosea: "To seek my face they will watch till day-light, saying unto me, Come, and let us return to the Lord: for He hath taken away, and He will heal us; He hath smitten, and He will bind us up; after two days will He revive us: in the third day He will raise us up."[2] For who can refuse to believe that these words often revolved[3] in the thought of those women between the sorrow of that desertion with which at present they seemed to themselves to have been smitten by the Lord, and the hope of the resurrection itself, by which they rightly supposed that all would be restored to them? But when "they found not the body (of the Lord Jesus),"[4] "His sepulture was removed from the midst of them,"[5] according to the prophecy of Isaiah. "Two angels, however, appeared there."[6] For just so many honorary companions[7] were required by the word of God, which usually prescribes "*two witnesses.*"[8] Moreover, the women, returning from the sepulchre, and from this vision of the angels, were foreseen by Isaiah, when he says, "Come, ye women, who return from the vision;"[9] that is, "come," to report the resurrection of the Lord. It was well, however, that the unbelief of the disciples was so persistent, in order that to the last we might consistently maintain that Jesus revealed Himself to the disciples as none other than the Christ of the prophets. For as two of them were taking a walk, and when the Lord had joined their company, without its appearing that it was He, and whilst He dissembled His knowledge of what had just taken place,[10] they say: "But we trusted that it had been He which should have redeemed Israel,"[11]—meaning their own, that is, the Creator's Christ. So far had He been from declaring Himself to them as another Christ! They could not, however, deem Him to be the Christ of the Creator; nor, if He was so deemed by them, could He have tolerated this opinion concerning Himself, unless He were really He whom He was supposed to be. Otherwise He would actually be the author of error, and the prevaricator of truth, contrary to the character of the good God. But at no time even after His resurrection did He reveal Himself to them as any other than what, on their own showing, they had always thought Him to be. He pointedly[12] reproached them: "O fools, and slow of heart in not believing that which He spake unto you."[13] By saying this, He proves that He does not belong to the rival god, but to the same God. For the same thing was said by the angels to the women: "Remember how He spake unto you when He was yet in Galilee, saying, The Son of man must be delivered up, and be crucified, and on the third day rise again."[14] "*Must* be delivered up; "and why, except that it was so written by God the Creator? He therefore upbraided them, because they were offended solely at His passion, and because they doubted of the truth of the resurrection which had been reported to them by the women, whereby (they showed that) they had not believed Him to have been the very same as they had thought Him to be. Wishing, therefore, to be believed by them in this wise, He declared Himself to be just what they had deemed Him to be—the Creator's Christ, the Redeemer of Israel. But as touching the reality of His body, what can be plainer? When they were doubting whether He were not a phantom—nay, were supposing that He was one—He says to them, "Why are ye troubled, and why do thoughts arise in your hearts? See[15] my hands and my feet, that it is I myself; for a spirit hath not bones, as ye see me have."[16] Now Marcion was unwilling to expunge from his Gospel some statements which even made against him—I suspect, on purpose, to have it in his power from the passages which he did not suppress, when he could have done so, either to deny that he had expunged anything, or else to justify his suppressions, if he made any. But he spares only such passages as he can subvert quite as well by explaining them away as by expunging them from the text. Thus, in the passage before us, he would have the words, "A spirit hath not bones, as ye see me have," so transposed, as to mean, "A spirit, such as ye see me to be, hath not bones;" that is to say, it is not the nature of a spirit to have bones. But what need of so tortuous a construction, when He might have simply said, "A spirit hath not bones, even as you observe that I have not?" Why, moreover, does He offer His hands and His feet for their examination—limbs which consist of bones—if He had no bones? Why, too, does He add, "Know that

---

[1] Luke xxiv. 1.
[2] Hos. v. 15 and vi. 1, 2.
[3] Volutata.
[4] Luke xxiv. 3.
[5] Isa. lvii. 2, according to the Septuagint, ἡ ταφὴ αὐτοῦ ἦρται ἐκ τοῦ μέσου.
[6] Luke xxiv. 4.
[7] Tot fere laterensibus.
[8] Deut. xvii. 6, xix. 15, compared with Matt. xviii. 16 and 2 Cor. xiii. 1.
[9] Isa. xxvii. 11, according to the Septuagint, γυναίκες ἐρχόμεναι ἀπὸ θέας, δεῦτε.
[10] Luke xxiv. 13-19.
[11] Luke xxiv. 21.

[12] Plane.
[13] Luke xxiv. 25.
[14] Luke xxiv. 6, 7.
[15] Videte. The original is much stronger ψηλαφήσατέ με καὶ ἴδετε, "*handle me*, and see." Two sentences thrown into one.
[16] Luke xxiv. 37-39.

it is I myself,"[1] when they had before known Him to be corporeal? Else, if He were altogether a phantom, why did He upbraid them for supposing Him to be a phantom? But whilst they still believed not, He asked them for some meat,[2] for the express purpose of showing them that He had teeth.[3]

And now, as I would venture to believe,[4] we have accomplished our undertaking. We have set forth Jesus Christ as none other than the Christ of the Creator. Our proofs we have drawn from His doctrines, maxims,[5] affections, feelings, miracles, sufferings, and even resurrection—as foretold by the prophets.[6] Even to the last He taught us (the same truth of His mission), when He sent forth His apostles to preach His gospel "among all nations;"[7] for He thus fulfilled the psalm: "Their sound is gone out through all the earth, and their words to the end of the world."[8] Marcion, I pity you; your labour has been in vain. For the Jesus Christ who appears in your Gospel is mine.

[1] Luke xxiv. 39.
[2] Luke xxiv. 41.
[3] An additional proof that He was no phantom.
[4] Ut opinor.
[5] Sententiis.
[6] Prophetarum.
[7] Luke xxiv. 47 and Matt. xxviii. 19.
[8] Ps. xix. 4.

DR. HOLMES' NOTE

Dr. Holmes appends the following as a note to the Fourth Book. (See cap. vi. p 351.)

The following statement, abridged from Dr. Lardner (*The History of Heretics*, chap. x. secs. 35–40), may be useful to the reader, in reference to the subject of the preceding Book:—Marcion received but eleven books of the New Testament, and these strangely curtailed and altered. He divided them into two parts, which he called τὸ Εὐαγγέλιον (*the Gospel*) and τὸ Ἀποστολικόν (*the Apostolicon*).

(1.) The former contained nothing more than a mutilated, and sometimes interpolated, edition of ST. LUKE; the name of that evangelist, however, he expunged from the beginning of his copy. Chaps. i. and ii. he rejected entirely, and began at iii. 1, reading the opening verse thus: "In the xv. year of Tiberius Cæsar, God descended into Capernaum, a city of Galilee."

(2.) According to Irenæus, Epiphanius, and Theodoret, he rejected the genealogy and baptism of Christ; whilst from Tertullian's statement (chap. vii.) it seems likely that he connected what part of chap. iii.—vers. 1, 2—he chose to retain, with chap. iv. 31, at a leap.

(3). He further eliminated the history of the tempation. That part of chap. iv. which narrates Christ's going into the synagogue at Nazareth and reading out of Isaiah he also rejected, and all afterwards to the end of ver. 30.

(4.) Epiphanius mentions sundry slight alterations in capp. v. 14, 24, vi. 5, 17. In chap. viii. 19 he expunged ἡ μήτηρ αὐτοῦ, καὶ ἀδελφοὶ αὐτοῦ. From Tertullian's remarks (chap. xix.), it would seem at first as if Marcion had added to his Gospel that answer of our Saviour which we find related by St. Matthew, chap. xii. 48: "Who is my mother, and who are my brethren?" For he represents Marcion (as in *De carne Christi*, vii., he represents other heretics, who deny the nativity) as making use of these words for his favourite argument. But, after all, Marcion might use these words against those who allowed the authenticity of Matthew's Gospel, without inserting them in his own Gospel; or else Tertullian might quote from memory, and think that to be in Luke which was only in Matthew —as he has done at least in three instances. (Lardner refers two of these instances to passages in chap. vii. of this Book iv., where Tertullian mentions, as erasures from Luke, what really are found in Matthew v. 17 and xv. 24. The third instance referred to by Lardner probably occurs at the end of chap. ix. of this same Book iv., where Tertullian again mistakes Matt. v. 17 for a passage of Luke, and charges Marcion with expunging it; curiously enough, the mistake recurs in chap. xii. of the same Book.) In Luke x. 21 Marcion omitted the first πάτερ and the words καὶ τῆς γῆς, that he might not allow Christ to call His Father the Lord of earth, or of this world. The second πατήρ·in this verse, not open to any inconvenience, he retained. In chap. xi. 29 he omitted the last words concerning the sign of the prophet Jonah; he also omitted all the 30th, 31st, and 32d verses; in ver. 42 he read κλῆσιν, '*calling*,' instead of κρίσιν, '*judgment.*' He rejected verses 49, 50, 51, because the passage related to the prophets. He entirely omitted chap. xii. 6; whilst in ver. 8 he read ἐμπροσθεν τοῦ Θεοῦ instead of ἐμπροσθεν τῶν ἀγγέλων τοῦ Θεοῦ. He seems to have left out all the 28th verse, and expunged ὑμῶν from verses 30 and 32, reading only ὁ πατήρ. In ver. 38, instead of the words ἐν τῇ δευτέρα φυλακῇ, καὶ ἐν τῇ τρίτη φυλακῇ, he read ἐν τῇ ἑσπερινῇ φυλακῇ. In chap. xiii. he omitted the first five verses, whilst in the 28th verse of the same chapter, where we read, "When ye shall see Abraham, and Isaac, and Jacob, and all the prophets in the kingdom of God, and ye yourselves thrust out," he read (by altering, adding, and transposing), "When ye shall see all the just in the kingdom of God, and you yourselves cast out, and bound without, there shall be weeping and gnashing of teeth." He likewise excluded all the remaining verses of this chapter. All chap. xv. after the 10th verse, in which is contained the parable of the prodigal son, he eliminated from his Gospel. In xvii. 10 he left out all the words after λέγετε. He made many alterations in the story of the ten lepers; he left out part of ver. 12, all ver. 13, and altered ver. 14, reading thus: "There met Him ten lepers; and He sent them away, saying, Show yourselves to the priest;" after which he inserted a clause from chap. iv. 27: "There were many lepers in the days of Eliseus the prophet, but none of them were cleansed, but Naaman the Syrian." In chap. xviii. 19 he added the words ὁ πατήρ, and in ver. 20 altered οἶδας, *thou knowest*, into the first person. He entirely omitted verses 31–33, in which our blessed Saviour declares that the things foretold by the prophets concerning His sufferings, and death, and resurrection, should all be fulfilled. He expunged *nineteen* verses out of chap. xix., from the end of ver. 27 to the beginning of ver. 47. In chap. xx. he omitted *ten* verses, from the end of ver. 8 to the end of ver. 18. He rejected also verses 37 and 38, in which there is a reference to Moses. Marcion also erased of chap. xxi. the first eighteen verses, as well as verses 21 and 22, on account of this clause, "that all things which are written may be fulfilled;" xx. 16 was left out by him, so also verses 35–37, 50, and 51 (and, adds Lardner, conjecturally, not herein following his authority Epiphanius, also vers. 38 and 49). In chap. xxiii. 2, after the words "perverting the nation," Marcion added, "and destroying the law and the prophets;" and again, after "forbidding to give tribute unto Cæsar," he added, "and perverting women and children." He also erased ver. 43. In chap. xxiv. he omitted that part of the conference between our Saviour and the two disciples going to Emmaus, which related to the prediction of His sufferings, and which is contained in verses 26 and 27. These two verses he omitted, and changed the words at the end of ver. 25, ἐλάλησαν οἱ προφῆται, into ἐλάλησα ὑμῖν. Such are the alterations, according to Epiphanius, which Marcion made in his Gospel from St. Luke. Tertullian says (in the 4th chapter of the preceding Book) that Marcion erased the passage which gives an account of the parting of the raiment of our Saviour among the soldiers. But the reason he assigns for the erasure—'*respiciens Psalmi prophetiam*'—shows that in this, as well as in the few other instances which we have already named, where Tertullian has charged Marcion with so altering passages, his memory deceived him into mistaking Matthew for Luke, for the reference to the passage in the Psalm is only given by St. Matthew xxvii. 35.

(5.) On an impartial review of these alterations, some seem to be but slight; others might be nothing but various readings; but others, again, are undoubtedly designed perversions. There were, however, passages enough left unaltered and unexpunged by the Marcionites, to establish the reality of the flesh and blood of Christ, and to prove that the God of the Jews was the Father of Christ, and of perfect goodness as well as justice. Tertullian, indeed, observes (chap. xliii.) that "Marcion purposely avoided erasing all the passages which made against him, that he might with the greater confidence deny having erased any at all, or at least that what he had omitted was for very good reasons."

(6.) To show the unauthorized and unwarrantable character of these alterations, omissions, additions, and corruptions, the Catholic Christians asserted that their copies of St. Luke's Gospel were more ancient than Marcion's (so Tertullian in chap. iii. and iv. of this Book iv.); and they maintained also the genuineness and integrity of the unadulterated Gospel, in opposition to that which had been curtailed and altered by him (chap. v.).

ELUCIDATIONS.

I.

(Deadly Sins, cap. IX., p. 356.)

To maintain a modern and wholly uncatholic system of Penitence, the schoolmen invented a technical scheme of sins *mortal* and sins *venial*, which must not be read into the Fathers, who had no such technicalities in mind. By "deadly sins" they meant all such as St. John recognizes (I. John, v. 16, 17,) and none other; that is to say sins of surprise and infirmity, sins having in them no malice or wilful disobedience, such as an impatient word, or a momentary neglect of duty. Should a dying man commit a deliberate sin and then expire, even after a life of love and obedience, who could fail to recognize the fearful nature of such an end? But, should his last word be one of infirmity and weakness, censurable but not involving wilful disobedience, surely we may consider it as provided for by the comfortable words—"there is a sin not unto death." Yet "all unrighteousness is sin," and the Fathers held that all sin should be repented of and confessed before God; because all sin when it *is finished* bringeth forth death."

. In St. Augustine's time, when moral theology became systematized in the West, by his mighty genius and influence, the following were recognized degrees of guilt: (1.) Sins deserving excommunication. (2.) Sins requiring to be confessed to the brother offended in order to God's forgiveness, and (3.) sins covered by God's gracious covenant, when daily confessed in the Lord's Prayer, in public, or in private. And this classification was professedly based on Holy Scripture. Thus: (1.) on the text—"To deliver such an one unto Satan, etc." (I. Cor. v. 4, 5). (2.) On the text—(Matt. xviii. 15), "Confess your sins one to another, brethren" (St. James v. 16), and (3.) on the text—(St. Matt. vi. 12,) "Forgive us our trespasses as we forgive them that trespass against us." This last St. Augustine[1] regards as the "daily medication" of our ordinary life, habitual penitence and faith and the baptismal covenant being presupposed.

The modern Trent theology has vastly amplified the scholastic teachings and refinements, and the elevation of Liguori to the rank of a church-doctor has virtually made the whole system *de fide* with the Latins. The Easterns know nothing of this modern and uncatholic teaching, and it is important that the student of the Ante-Nicene *Patrologia* should be on his guard against the novel meanings which the Trent theology imposes upon orthodox (Nicene) language. The long ages during which Eastern orthodoxy has been obscured by

[1] Opp. Tom. vi. p. 228. Ed. Migne.

the sufferings and consequent ignorance of the Greeks, have indeed tainted their doctrinal and practical system, but it still subsists in amazing contrast with Latin impurity. See, on the "indulgences," of the latter, the "Orthodox Theology of Macarius, Bishop of Vinnitza," Tom. II. p. 541, Paris, 1860.

II.

(Reservation of Baptism, cap. xi., note, p. 361.)

It is important, here, to observe the heretical origin of a sinful superstition which becomes conspicuous in the history of Constantine. If the church tolerated it in his case, it was doubtless in view of this extraordinary instance of one, who was a heathen still, at heart, becoming a guardian and protector of the persecuted Faithful. It is probable that he was regarded as a Cyrus or a Nebuchadnezzar whom God had raised up to protect and to deliver His people; who was to be honoured and obeyed as "God's minister" (Rom. xiii. 4,) in so far, and for this purpose. The church was scrupulous and he was superstitious; it would have been difficult to discipline him and worse not to discipline him. Tacitly, therefore, he was treated as a *catechumen*, but was not formally admitted even to that class. He permitted Heathenism, and while he did so, how could he be received as a Christian? The Christian church never became responsible for his life and character, but strove to reform him and to prepare him for a true confession of Christ at some "convenient season." In this, there seems to have been a great fault somewhere, chargeable perhaps to Eusebius or to some other Christian counsellor; but, when could any one say—"the emperor is sincere and humble and penitent and ought now to be received into the church." It was a *political* conversion, and as such was accepted, and Constantine was a heathen till near his death. As to his final penitence and acceptance—"Forbear to judge." II. Kings, x. 29–31.

Concerning his baptism, see Eusebius, *de Vita Const.* iv. 61, see also, Mosheim's elaborate and candid views of the whole subject: *First Three Centuries*, Vol. II. 460–471.

III.

(Peter, cap. xiii. p. 365.)

The great Gallican, Launoy, doctor of the Sorbonne, has proved that the Fathers understand the Rock to be Christ, while, only rarely, and that *rhetorically*, not dogmatically, St. Peter is called a stone or a rock; a usage to which neither Luther nor Calvin could object. Tertullian himself, when he speaks dogmatically, is in accord with other Fathers, and gives no countenance to the modern doctrine of Rome. See *La Papauté*, of the Abbé Guettée, pp. 42–61. It is important, also, to note that the primacy of St. Peter, more or less, whatever it may have been in the mind of the Fathers, was wholly *personal*, in their view. Of the fables which make it hereditary and a purtenance of Rome they knew nothing.

IV.

(Loans, cap. xvii. p. 372.)

The whole subject of *usury*, in what it consists, *etc.*, deserves to receive more attention than it does in our times, when *nominal* Christians are *steeped* in the sin of money-traffic to the injury of neighbours, on a scale truly gigantic. God's word clearly rebukes this sin. So does the Council of Nice.[1] Now by what is the sin defined? Certainly by the *spirit* of the Gospel; but, is it also, by the letter? A sophistical casuistry which maintains the letter, and then sophisticates and refines so as to explain it all away, is the product of school divinity and of modern Jesuitry; but even the great Bossuet is its apologist. (See his *Traité de l' Usure.* opp. ix. p. 49, etc., ed. Paris, 1846.) But for an exhaustive review of the whole matter, I ask attention to Huet, *Le Règne Social*, etc. (Paris, 1853) pp. 334–345.

---

[1] Calmet. Opp. i. 483 and Tom. x., p. 525.

V.

(The Baptist, cap. xviii. p. 375.)

The interpretation of Tertullian, however, has the all-important merit (which Bacon and Hooker recognize as cardinal) of flowing from the Scripture without squeezing. (1.) Our Lord sent the message to John as a personal and tender assurance to *him*. (2.) The story illustrates the *decrease* of which the Baptist had spoken prophetically (St. John, iii. 30); and (3.) it sustains the great principle that Christ alone is without sin, this being the one fault recorded of the Baptist, otherwise a singular instance of sinlessness. The B. Virgin's fault (gently reproved by the Lord, St. John ii. 4.), seems in like manner introduced on this principle of exhibiting the only sinless One, in His Divine perfections as without spot. So even Joseph and Moses (Ps. *cvi.* 33, and Gen. *xlvii.* 20.) are shewn "to be but men." The policy of Joseph has indeed been extravagantly censured.

VI.

(Harshness, cap. xix., note 6., p. 378. Also, cap. xxvi. p. 393.)

Tertullian seems with reflect the early view of the church as to our Lord's total abnegation of all filial relations with the Virgin, when He gave to her St. John, instead of Himself, on the Cross. For this purpose He had made him the beloved disciple and doubtless charged him with all the duties with which he was to be clothed. Thus He fulfilled the figurative law of His priesthood, as given by Moses, (Deut. *xxxiii.* 9,) and crucified himself, from the beginning, according to his own Law (St. Luke, xiv. 26, 27,) which he identifies with the Cross, here and also in St. Matthew, x. 37, 38. These then are the steps of His own holy example, illustrating His own precept, for doubtless, as "the Son of man," His filial love was superlative and made the sacrifice the sharper: (1.) He taught Joseph that He had no earthly father, when he said—"Wist ye not that I must be in *my Father's house*," (St. Luke iii. 49, Revised); but, having established this fact, he then became "subject" to both his parents, till His public ministry began. (2.) At this time, He seems to have admonished His mother, that He could not recognize her authority any longer, (St. John, ii. 4,) having now entered upon His work as the Son of God. (3.) Accordingly, He refused, thenceforth, to know her save only as one of His redeemed, excepting her in nothing from this common work for all the Human Race, (St. Matt. xii. 48,) in the passage which Tertullian so forcibly expounds. (4.) Finally, when St. Mary draws near to the cross, apparently to claim the final recognition of the previous understanding (St. John, ii. 4,) to which the Lord had referred her at Cana—He fulfils His last duty to her in giving her a son instead of Himself, and thereafter (5) recognizes her no more; not even in His messages after the Resurrection, nor when He met her with other disciples. He rewards her, instead, with the infinite love He bears to all His saints, and with the brightest rewards which are bestowed upon Faith. In this consists her superlative excellence and her conspicuous glory among the Redeemed (St. Luke, i. 47, 48,) in Christ's account.

VII.

(Children, cap. xxiii. p. 386.)

In this beautiful testimony of our author to the sanctity of marriage, and the blessedness of its fruits, I see his austere spirit reflecting the spirit of Christ so tenderly and so faithfully, in the ·love of children, that I am warmly drawn to him. I cannot give him up to Montanism at this period of his life and labours. Surely, he was as yet merely persuaded that the prophetic *charismata* were not extinct, and that they had been received by his

Phrygian friends, although he may still have regarded them as *prophesying* subject to all the infirmities which St. Paul attributes even to persons elevated by spiritual gifts. (I. Cor. *xiv.*) Why not recognize him in all his merits, until his open and senile lapse is complete?

VIII.

(Hades, cap. xxxiv. p. 406.)

Here again our author shews his unsettled view as to *Sheol* or *Hades*, on which see Kaye, pp. 247–250. Here he distinguishes between the *Inferi* and Abraham's bosom; but (in B. iii. cap. 24.) he has already, more aptly, regarded the *Inferi*, or *Hades*, as the common receptacle of departed spirits, where a "great gulf" indeed, separates between the two classes.

A *caricature* may sometimes illustrate characteristic features more powerfully than a true portrait. The French call the highest gallery in theatres, *paradis;* and I have sometimes explained it by the fact that the modern drama originated in the monkish *Mysteries*, revived so profanely in our own day. To reconcile the poor to a bad place they gave it the name of *Paradise*, thus illustrating their Mediæval conceptions; for trickling down from Tertullian his vivid notions seem to have suffused all Western theology on this subject. Thus, then, one vast receptacle receives all the dead. The *pit*, as we very appropriately call it in English, answers to the place of lost spirits, where the rich man was in torments. Above, are ranged the family of Abraham reclining, as it were, in their father's bosom, by turns. Far above, under skylights, (for the old Mysteries were celebrated in the day-time) is *the Paradise*, where the Martyrs see God, and are represented as "under the altar" of heaven itself. Now, abandoning our grotesque illustration, but using it for its *topography*, let us conceive of our own globe, as having a world-wide concavity such as they imagined, from literalizing the *under-world* of Sheol. In its depths is the *Phylace* (I. Pet. iii. 19,) of "spirits in prison." In a higher region repose the blessed spirits in "Abraham's bosom." Yet nearer to the ethereal vaults, are the martyrs in Paradise, looking out into heavenly worlds. The immensity of the scale does not interfere with the vision of spirits, nor with such communications as Abraham holds with his lost son in the history of Dives and Lazarus. Here indeed Science comes to our aid, for if the *telephone* permits such conversations while we are in the flesh, we may at least imagine that the subtile spirit can act in like manner, apart from such contrivances. Now, so far as Tertullian is consistent with himself, I think these explanations may clarify his words and references. The Eastern Theology is less inconsistent and bears the marks alike of Plato and of Origen. But of this hereafter. Of *a place*, such as the Mediæval *Purgatory*, affirmed as *de fide* by the Trent creed, the Fathers knew nothing at all. See Vol. II. p. 490, also 522, this Series.

ADDITIONAL NOTE.

(Passage not easy to identify, p. 390, note 14.)

Easy enough, by the LXX. See Isaiah lxiii. 3. *καὶ τῶν εθνῶν οὐκ ἐστιν ἀνὴρ μετ' εμοῦ.* The first verse, referring to Edom, leads our author to accentuate this point of Gentile ignorance.

THE FIVE BOOKS AGAINST MARCION.

Book V.

WHEREIN TERTULLIAN PROVES, WITH RESPECT TO ST. PAUL'S EPISTLES, WHAT HE HAD PROVED IN THE PRECEDING BOOK WITH RESPECT TO ST. LUKE'S GOSPEL. FAR FROM BEING AT VARIANCE, THEY WERE IN PERFECT UNISON WITH THE WRITINGS OF THE OLD TESTAMENT, AND THEREFORE TESTIFIED THAT THE CREATOR WAS THE ONLY GOD, AND THAT THE LORD JESUS WAS HIS CHRIST. AS IN THE PRECEDING BOOKS, TERTULLIAN SUPPORTS HIS ARGUMENT WITH PROFOUND REASONING, AND MANY HAPPY ILLUSTRATIONS OF HOLY SCRIPTURE.

CHAP. I.—INTRODUCTORY. THE APOSTLE PAUL HIMSELF NOT THE PREACHER OF A NEW GOD. CALLED BY JESUS CHRIST, ALTHOUGH AFTER THE OTHER APOSTLES, HIS MISSION WAS FROM THE CREATOR. STATES HOW. THE ARGUMENT, AS IN THE CASE OF THE GOSPEL, CONFINING PROOFS TO SUCH PORTIONS OF ST. PAUL'S WRITINGS AS MARCION ALLOWED.

THERE is nothing without a beginning but God alone. Now, inasmuch as the beginning occupies the first place in the condition of all things, so it must necessarily take precedence in the treatment of them, if a clear knowledge is to be arrived at concerning their condition; for you could not find the means of examining even the quality of anything, unless you were certain of its existence, and that after discovering its origin.[1] Since therefore I am brought, in the course of my little work, to this point,[2] I require to know of Marcion the origin of his apostle[3] even—I, who am to some degree a new disciple,[4] the follower of no other master; who at the same time[5] can believe nothing, except that nothing ought to be believed hastily[6] (and *that* I may further say is hastily believed, which is believed without any examination[7] of its beginning); in short, I who have the best reason possible for bringing this inquiry to a most careful solution,[8] since a man is affirmed to me to be an apostle whom I do not find mentioned in the Gospel in the catalogue[9] of the apostles. Indeed, when I hear that this man was chosen by the Lord after He had attained His rest in heaven, I feel that a kind of improvidence is imputable to Christ, for not knowing before that this man was necessary to Him; and because He thought that he must be added to the apostolic body in the way of a fortuitous encounter[10] rather than a deliberate selection; by necessity (so to speak), and not voluntary choice, although the members of the apostolate had been duly ordained, and were now dismissed to their several missions. Where-

---

[1] Cum cognoveris unde sit.
[2] Materiam.
[3] We have already more than once referred to Marcion's preference for *St. Paul.* "The reason of the preference thus given to that apostle was his constant and strenuous opposition to the Judaizing Christians, who wished to reimpose the yoke of the Jewish ceremonies on the necks of their brethren. This opposition the Marcionites wished to construe into a direct denial of the authority of the Mosaic law. They contended also from St. Paul's assertion, that he received his appointment to the apostolic office not from man, but from Christ, that he alone delivered the genuine doctrines of the gospel. This deference for St. Paul accounts also for Marcion's accepting *St. Luke's* Gospel as the only authentic one,

as we saw in the last book of this treatise; it was because that evangelist had been the companion of St. Paul" (Bp. Kaye, *On the Writings of Tertullian*, 3d edition, pp. 474, 475).
[4] Novus aliqui discipulus.
[5] Interim.
[6] Temere.
[7] Agnitione.
[8] Ad sollicitudinem.
[9] In albo.
[10] Ex incursu: in allusion to St. Paul's sudden conversion, Acts ix. 3-8. [On St. Paul's Epistles, see p. 324, *supra.*]

fore, O shipmaster of Pontus,[1] if you have never taken on board your small craft[2] any contraband goods or smuggler's cargo, if you have never thrown overboard or tampered with a freight, you are still more careful and conscientious, I doubt not, in divine things; and so I should be glad if you would inform us under what bill of lading[3] you admitted the Apostle Paul on board, who ticketed him,[4] what owner forwarded him,[5] who handed him to you,[6] that so you may land him without any misgiving,[7] lest he should turn out to belong to him,[8] who can substantiate his claim to him by producing all his apostolic writings.[9] He professes himself to be "an apostle"—to use his own, words—"not of men, nor by man, but by Jesus Christ."[10] Of course, any one may make a profession concerning himself; but his profession is only rendered valid by the authority of a second person. One man signs, another countersigns;[11] one man appends his seal, another registers in the public records.[12] No one is at once a proposer and a seconder to himself. Besides, you have read, no doubt, that "many shall come, saying, I am Christ."[13] Now if any one can pretend that he is Christ, how much more might a man profess to be an apostle of Christ! But still, for my own part, I appear[14] in the character of a disciple and an inquirer; that so I may even thus[15] both refute your belief, who have nothing to support it, and confound your shamelessness, who make claims without possessing the means of establishing them. Let there be a Christ, let there be an apostle, although of another god; *but what matter?* since they are only to draw their proofs out of the Testament of the Creator. Because even the book of Genesis so long ago promised me *the Apostle* Paul. For among the types and prophetic blessings which he pronounced over his sons, Jacob, when he turned his attention to Benjamin, exclaimed, "Benjamin shall ravin as a wolf; in the morning He shall devour the prey, and at night he shall impart nourishment."[16] He foresaw

that Paul would arise out of the tribe of Benjamin, a voracious wolf, devouring his prey in the morning: in order words, in the early period of his life he would devastate the Lord's sheep, as a persecutor of the churches; but in the evening he would give them nourishment, which means that in his declining years he would educate the fold of Christ, as the teacher of the Gentiles. Then, again, in Saul's conduct towards David, exhibited first in violent persecution of him, and then in remorse and reparation,[17] on his receiving from him good for evil, we have nothing else than an anticipation[18] of Paul in Saul—belonging, too, as they did, to the same tribe—and of Jesus in David, from whom He descended according to the Virgin's genealogy.[19] Should you, however, disapprove of these types,[20] the Acts of the Apostles,[21] at all events, have handed down to me this career of Paul, which you must not refuse to accept. Thence I demonstrate that from a persecutor he became "an apostle, not of men, neither by man;"[22] thence am I led to believe *the Apostle* himself; thence do I find reason for rejecting your defence of him,[23] and for bearing fearlessly your taunt. "Then you deny the Apostle Paul." I do not calumniate him whom I defend.[24] I deny him, to compel you to the proof of him. I deny him, to convince you that he is mine. If you have regard to our belief you should admit the particulars which comprise it. If you challenge us to your belief, (pray) tell us what things constitute its basis.[25] Either prove the truth of what you believe, or failing in your proof, (tell us) how you believe. Else what conduct is yours,[26] believing in opposition to Him from whom alone comes the proof of that which you believe? Take now from my point of view[27] the apostle, in the same manner as you have received the Christ—the apostle shown to be as much *mine* as the Christ is. And here, too, we will fight within the same lines, and challenge our

[1] Marcion is frequently called "*Ponticus Nauclerus,*" probably less on account of his own connection with a seafaring life, than that of his countrymen, who were great sailors. Comp. book i. 18. (*sub fin.*) and book iii. 6. [pp. 284, 325.]
[2] In acatos tuas.
[3] Quo symbolo.
[4] Quis illum tituli charactere percusserit.
[5] Quis transmiserit tibi.
[6] Quis imposuerit.
[7] Constanter.
[8] Ne *illius* probetur, i.e., to the *Catholic,* for Marcion did not admit all St. Paul's epistles (Semler).
[9] Omnia apostolatus ejus instrumenta.
[10] Gal. i. 1.
[11] Subscribit.
[12] Actis refert.
[13] Luke xxi. 8.
[14] Conversor.
[15] Jam hinc.
[16] Gen. xlix 27, Septuagint, the latter clause being καὶ εἰς τὸ ἑσπέρας δίδωσι τροφήν.

[17] Satisfactio.
[18] Non aliud portendebat quam.
[19] Secundum Virginis censum.
[20] Figurarum sacramenta.
[21] Although *St. Luke* wrote the Acts of the Apostles, Marcion does not seem to have admitted this book into his New Testament. "It is clearly excluded from his catalogue, as given by Epiphanius. The same thing appears from the more ancient authority of Tertullian, who begins his Book v. against Marcion with showing the absurdity of his conduct in rejecting the history and acts of the apostles, and yet receiving St. Paul as the chief of the apostles, whose name is never mentioned in the Gospel with the other apostles, especially since the account given by Paul himself in Gal. i. ii. confirms the account which we have in the Acts. But the reason why he rejected this book is (as Tertullian says) very evident, since from it we can plainly show that the God of the Christians and the God of the Jews, or the Creator, was the same being and that Christ was sent by Him, and by no other" (Lardner Works, *Hist. of Heretics,* chap. x. sec. 41).
[22] Gal. i. 1.
[23] Inde te a defensione ejus expello.
[24] An insinuation that Marcion's defence of Paul was, in fact, a calumny of the apostle.
[25] Præstruant eam.
[26] Qualis es.
[27] Habe nunc de meo.

adversary on the mere ground of a simple rule,[1] that even an apostle who is said not to belong to the Creator—nay, is displayed as in actual hostility to the Creator—can be fairly regarded as teaching[2] nothing, knowing nothing, wishing nothing in favour of the Creator whilst it would be a first principle with him to set forth[3] another god with as much eagerness as he would use in withdrawing us from the law of the Creator. It is not at all likely that he would call men away from Judaism without showing them at the same time what was the god in whom he invited them to believe; because nobody could possibly pass from allegiance to the Creator without knowing to whom he had to cross over. For either Christ had already revealed another god—in which case the apostle's testimony would also follow to the same effect, for fear of his not being else regarded[4] as an apostle of the god whom Christ had revealed, and because of the impropriety of his being concealed by the apostle who had been already revealed by Christ—or Christ had made no such revelation concerning God; *then* there was all the greater need why the apostle should reveal a God who could now be made known by no one else, and who would undoubtedly be left without any belief at all, if he were revealed not even by an apostle. We have laid down this as our first principle, because we wish at once to profess that we shall pursue the same method here in the apostle's case as we adopted before in Christ's case, to prove that he proclaimed no new god;[5] that is, we shall draw our evidence from the epistles of *St*. Paul himself. Now, the garbled form in which we have found the heretic's Gospel will have already prepared us to expect to find[6] the epistles also mutilated by him with like perverseness—and that even as respects their number.[7]

CHAP. II.—ON THE EPISTLE TO THE GALATIANS. THE ABOLITION OF THE ORDINANCES OF THE MOSAIC LAW NO PROOF OF ANOTHER GOD. THE DIVINE LAWGIVER, THE CREATOR HIMSELF, WAS THE ABROGATOR. THE APOSTLE'S DOCTRINE IN THE FIRST CHAPTER SHOWN TO ACCORD WITH THE TEACHING OF THE OLD TESTAMENT. THE ACTS OF THE APOSTLES SHOWN TO BE GENUINE AGAINST MARCION. THIS BOOK AGREES WITH THE PAULINE EPISTLES.

The epistle which we also allow to be the most decisive[8] against Judaism, is that wherein the apostle instructs the Galatians. For the abolition of the ancient law we fully admit, and hold that it actually proceeds from the dispensation of the Creator,—a point which we have already often treated in the course of our discussion, when we showed that the innovation was foretold by the prophets of our God.[9] Now, if the Creator indeed promised that " the ancient things should pass away,"[10] to be superseded by a new course of things which should arise, whilst Christ marks the period of the separation when He says, " The law and the prophets were until John "[11] —thus making the Baptist the limit between the two dispensations of the old things then terminating—and the new things then beginning, the apostle cannot of course do otherwise, (coming as he does) in Christ, who was revealed after John, than invalidate " the old things " and confirm " the new," and yet promote thereby the faith of no other god than the Creator, at whose instance[12] it was foretold that the ancient things should pass away. Therefore both the abrogation of the law and the establishment of the gospel help my argument even in this epistle, wherein they both have reference to the fond assumption of the Galatians, which led them to suppose that faith in Christ (the Creator's Christ, of course) was obligatory, but without annulling the law, because it still appeared to them a thing incredible that the law should be set aside by its own author. Again,[13] if they had at all heard of any other god from the apostle, would they not have concluded at once, of themselves, that they must give up the law of that God whom they had left, in order to follow another? For what man would be long in learning, that he ought to pursue a new discipline, after he had taken up with a new god? Since, however,[14] the same God was declared in the gospel which had always been so well known in the law, the only change being in the dispensation,[15] the sole point of the question to be discussed was, whether the law of the Creator ought by the gospel to be excluded in the Christ of the Creator? Take away this point, and the controversy falls to the ground. Now, since they would all know of themselves,[16] on the withdrawal of this point, that they must of course renounce all submission to the Creator by reason of their

---

[1] In ipso gradu præscriptionis.
[2] Oportere docere . . . sapere . . . velle.
[3] Edicere.
[4] Ne non haberetur.
[5] Nullum alium deum circumlatum.
[6] Præjudicasse debebit.
[7] Marcion only received *ten* of St. Paul's epistles, and these altered by himself.

[8] Principalem.
[9] See above, in book i. chap. xx., also in book iv. chap. i.
[10] Comp. Isa. xliii. 18, 19, and lxv. 17, with 2 Cor. v. 17.
[11] Luke xvi. 16.
[12] Apud quem.
[13] Porro.
[14] Immo quia.
[15] Disciplina.
[16] Ultro.

faith in another god, there could have been no call for the apostle to teach them so earnestly that which their own belief must have spontaneously suggested to them. Therefore the entire purport of this epistle is simply to show us that the supersession[1] of the law comes from the appointment of the Creator—a point, which we shall still have to keep in mind.[2] Since also he makes mention of no other god (and he could have found no other opportunity of doing so, more suitable than when his purpose was to set forth the reason for the abolition of the law—especially as the prescription of a new god would have afforded a singularly good and most sufficient reason), it is clear enough in what sense he writes, "I marvel that ye are so soon removed from Him who hath called you to His grace to *another* gospel"[3]—(He means) "another" as to the conduct it prescribes, not in respect of its worship; "another" as to the discipline it teaches, not in respect of its divinity; because it is the office of[4] Christ's gospel to call men from the law to grace, not from the Creator to another god. For nobody had induced them to apostatize from[5] the Creator, that they should seem to "be removed to another gospel," simply when they return again to the Creator. When he adds, too, the words, "which is not another,"[6] he confirms the fact that the gospel which he maintains is the Creator's. For the Creator Himself promises the gospel, when He says by Isaiah: "Get thee up into the high mountain, thou that bringest to Sion good tidings; lift up thy voice with strength, thou that bringest the gospel to Jerusalem."[7] Also when, with respect to the apostles personally, He says, "How beautiful are the feet of them that preach the gospel of peace, that bring good tidings of good"[8]—even proclaiming the gospel to the Gentiles, because He also says, "In His name shall the Gentiles trust;"[9] that is, in the name of Christ, to whom He says, "I have given thee as a light of the Gentiles."[10] However, you will have it that it is the gospel of a new god which was then set forth by the apostle. So that there are two gospels for[11] two gods; and the apostle made a great mistake when he said that "there is not another" gospel,[12] since there is (on the hypothesis)[13] another; and so he might have made a better defence of his gospel, by rather demonstrating this, than by insisting on its being but one. But perhaps, to avoid this difficulty, you will say that he therefore added just afterwards, "Though an angel from heaven preach any other gospel, let him be accursed,"[14] because he was aware that the Creator was going to introduce a gospel! But you thus entangle yourself still more. For this is now the mesh in which you are caught. To affirm that there are two gospels, is not the part of a man who has already denied that there is another. His meaning, however, is clear, for he has mentioned himself first (in the anathema): "But though *we* or an angel from heaven preach any other gospel."[15] It is by way of an example that he has expressed himself. If even he himself might not preach any other gospel, then neither might an angel. He said "angel'" in this way, that he might show how much more men ought not to be believed, when neither an angel nor an apostle ought to be; not that he meant to apply[16] an angel to the gospel of the Creator. He then cursorily touches on his own conversion from a persecutor to an apostle—confirming thereby the Acts of the Apostles,[17] in which book may be found the very subject[18] of this epistle, how that certain persons interposed, and said that men ought to be circumcised, and that the law of Moses was to be observed; and how the apostles, when consulted, determined, by the authority of the Holy Ghost, that "a yoke should not be put upon men's necks which their fathers even had not been able to bear."[19] Now, since the Acts of the Apostles thus agree with Paul, it becomes apparent why you reject them. It is because they declare no other God than the Creator, and prove Christ to belong to no other God than the Creator; whilst the promise of the Holy Ghost is shown to have been fulfilled in no other document than the Acts of the Apostles. Now, it is not very likely that these[20] should be found in agreement with the apostle, on the one hand, when they described his career in accordance with his own statement; but should, on the other hand, be at variance with him when they announce the (attribute of) divinity in the Creator's Christ—as if Paul

---

[1] Discessionem.
[2] Ut adhuc suggeremus.
[3] Gal. i. 6, 7.
[4] Deberet.
[5] Moverat illos a.
[6] Gal. i. 7.
[7] Isa. xl. 9 (Septuagint).
[8] Isa. lii. 7.
[9] We have here an instance of the high authority of the Septuagint version. It comes from the Seventy: Καὶ ἐπὶ τῷ ὀνόματι αὐτοῦ ἔθνη ἐλπιοῦσιν (Isa. xlii. 4). From this Tertullian, as usual, quoted it. But what is much more important, St. Matthew has adopted it; see chap. xii. ver. 21. This beautiful promise of the Creator does not occur in its well-known form in the Hebrew original.
[10] Isa. xlii. 6.
[11] Apud: "administered by."

[12] Gal. i. 7.
[13] Cum sit.
[14] Gal. i. 8.
[15] Gal. i. 8.
[16] Referret.
[17] A similar remark occurs in *Præscript. Hæretic.* c. xxiii. p. 253.
[18] Ipsa materia.
[19] See Gal. i. 11-24, compared with Acts xv. 5-29.
[20] "The Acts of the Apostles" is always a *plural* phrase in Tertullian.

did not follow[1] the preaching of the apostles when he received from them the prescription[2] of not teaching the Law.[3]

CHAP. III.—ST. PAUL QUITE IN ACCORDANCE WITH ST. PETER AND OTHER APOSTLES OF THE CIRCUMCISION. HIS CENSURE OF ST. PETER EXPLAINED, AND RESCUED FROM MARCION'S MISAPPLICATION. THE STRONG PROTESTS OF THIS EPISTLE AGAINST JUDAIZERS. YET ITS TEACHING IS SHOWN TO BE IN KEEPING WITH THE LAW AND THE PROPHETS. MARCION'S TAMPERING WITH ST. PAUL'S WRITINGS CENSURED.

But with regard to the countenance[4] of Peter and the rest of the apostles, he tells us[5] that "fourteen years after he went up to Jerusalem," in order to confer with them[6] about the rule which he followed in his gospel, lest perchance he should all those years have been running, and be running still, in vain, (which would be the case,) of course, if his preaching of the gospel fell short of their method.[7] So great had been his desire to be approved and supported by those whom you wish on all occasions[8] to be understood as in alliance with Judaism! When indeed he says, that "neither was Titus circumcised,"[9] he for the first time shows us that circumcision was the only question connected with the maintenance[10] of the law, which had been as yet agitated by those whom he therefore calls "false brethren unawares brought in."[11] These persons went no further than to insist on a continuance of the law, retaining unquestionably a sincere belief in the Creator. They perverted the gospel in their teaching, not indeed by such a tampering with the Scripture[12] as should enable them to expunge[13] the Creator's Christ, but by so retaining the ancient *régime* as not to exclude the Creator's law. Therefore he says : "Because of false brethren unawares brought in, who came in privily to spy out our liberty which we have in Christ, that they might bring us into bondage, to whom we gave place by subjection not even for an hour."[14] Let us only attend to the clear[15] sense and to the reason of the thing, and the perversion of the

Scripture will be apparent. When he first says, "Neither Titus, who was with me, being a Greek, was *compelled* to be circumcised," and then adds, "And *that* because of false brethren unawares brought in,"[16] etc., he gives us an insight into his reason[17] for acting in a clean contrary way,[18] showing us wherefore he did that which he would neither have done nor shown to us, if that had not happened which induced him to act as he did. But then[19] I want you to tell us whether they would have yielded to the subjection that was demanded,[20] if these false brethren had not crept in to spy out their liberty? I apprehend not. They therefore gave way (in a partial concession), because there were persons whose weak faith required consideration.[21] For their rudimentary belief, which was still in suspense about the observance of the law, deserved this concessive treatment,[22] when even the apostle himself had some suspicion that he might have run, and be still running, in vain.[23] Accordingly, the false brethren who were the spies of their Christian liberty must be thwarted in their efforts to bring it under the yoke of their own Judaism before that Paul discovered whether his labour had been in vain, before that those who preceded him in the apostolate gave him their right hands of fellowship, before that he entered on the office of preaching to the Gentiles, according to their arrangement with him.[24] He therefore made some concession, as was necessary, for a time; and this was the reason why he had Timothy circumcised,[25] and the Nazarites introduced into the temple,[26] which incidents are described in the Acts. Their truth may be inferred from their agreement with the apostle's own profession, how "to the Jews he became as a Jew, that he might gain the Jews, and to them that were under

---

[1] Ut non secutus sit.
[2] Formam.
[3] Dedocendæ legis; i.e., of Moses.
[4] Ad patrocinium.
[5] *Scribit* often takes the place of *inquit;* naturally enough as referring to the epistles.
[6] Gal. ii. 1, 2.
[7] Formam.
[8] Si quando.
[9] Gal. ii. 3.
[10] Ex defensione.
[11] Gal. ii. 4.
[12] Interpolatione Scripturæ.
[13] Qua effingerent.
[14] Gal. ii. 4, 5.
[15] Ipsi.

[16] Gal. ii. 3, 4.
[17] Incipit reddere rationem.
[18] Contrarii utique facti. [Farrar, *St. Paul*, pp. 232 and 261.]
[19] Denique.
[20] See Conybeare and Howson, *in loc.*
[21] Fuerunt propter quos crederetur.
[22] The following statement will throw light upon the character of *the two classes* of Jewish professors of Christianity referred to by Tertullian: " A pharisaic section was sheltered in its bosom (of the church at Jerusalem), which continually strove to turn Christianity into a sect of Judaism. These men were restless agitators, animated by the bitterest sectarian spirit; and although they were numerically a small party, yet we know the power of a turbulent minority. But besides these Judaizing zealots, there was a large proportion of the Christians at Jerusalem, whose Christianity, though more sincere than that of those just mentioned, was yet very weak and imperfect . . . Many of them still only knew of a Christ after the flesh—a Saviour of Israel—a Jewish Messiah. Their minds were in a state of transition between the law and the gospel ; and it was of great consequence not to shock their prejudices too rudely ; lest they should be tempted to make shipwreck of their faith and renounce their Christianity altogether." These were they whose prejudices required to be wisely consulted in things which did not touch the foundation of the gospel (Conybeare and Howson's *St. Paul*, People's Edition, vol. ii. pp. 259, 260.)
[23] Gal. ii. 2.
[24] Ex censu eorum: see Gal. ii. 9, 10.
[25] Acts xvi. 3.
[26] Acts xxi. 23–26.

the law, as under the law,"—and so here with respect to those who come in secretly,—"and lastly, how he became all things to all men, that he might gain all."[1] Now, inasmuch as the circumstances require such an interpretation as this, no one will refuse to admit that Paul preached that God and that Christ whose law he was excluding all the while, however much he allowed it, owing to the times, but which he would have had summarily to abolish if he had published a new god. Rightly, then, did Peter and James and John give their right hand of fellowship to Paul, and agree on such a division of their work, as that Paul should go to the heathen, and themselves to the circumcision.[2] Their agreement, also, "to remember the poor"[3] was in complete conformity with the law of the Creator, which cherished the poor and needy, as has been shown in our observations on your Gospel.[4] It is thus certain that the question was one which simply regarded the law, while at the same time it is apparent what portion of the law it was convenient to have observed. Paul, however, censures Peter for not walking straightforwardly according to the truth of the gospel. No doubt he blames him; but it was solely because of his inconsistency in the matter of "eating,"[5] which he varied according to the sort of persons (whom he associated with) "fearing them which were of the circumcision,"[6] but not on account of any perverse opinion touching another god. For if such a question had arisen, others also would have been "resisted face to face" by the man who had not even spared Peter on the comparatively small matter of his doubtful conversation. But what do the Marcionites wish to have believed (on the point)? For the rest, the apostle must (be permitted to) go on with his own statement, wherein he says that "a man is not justified by the works of the law, but by faith:"[7] faith, however, in the same God to whom belongs the law also. For of course he would have bestowed no labour on severing faith from the law, when the difference of the god would, if there had only been any, have of itself produced such a severance. Justly, therefore, did he refuse to "build up again (the structure of the law) which he had overthrown."[8] The law, indeed, had to be overthrown, from the moment when John "cried in the wilderness, Prepare ye the ways of the Lord," that valleys[9] and

hills and mountains may be filled up and levelled, and the crooked and the rough ways be made straight and smooth[10]—in other words, that the difficulties of the law might be changed into the facilities of the gospel. For he remembered that the time was come of which the Psalm spake, "Let us break their bands asunder, and cast off their yoke from us;"[11] since the time when "the nations became tumultuous, and the people imagined vain counsels;" when "the kings of the earth stood up, and the rulers were gathered together against the Lord, and against His Christ,"[12] in order that thenceforward man might be justified by the liberty of faith, not by servitude to the law,[13] "because the just shall live by his faith."[14] Now, although the prophet Habakkuk first said this, yet you have the apostle here confirming the prophets, even as Christ did. The object, therefore, of the faith whereby the just man shall live, will be that same God to whom likewise belongs the law, by doing which no man is justified. Since, then, there equally are found the curse in the law and the blessing in faith, you have both conditions set forth by[15] the Creator: "Behold," says He, "I have set before you a blessing and a curse."[16] You cannot establish a diversity of authors because there happens to be one of things; for the diversity is itself proposed by one and the same author. Why, however, "Christ was made a curse for us,"[17] is declared by the apostle himself in a way which quite helps our side, as being the result of the Creator's appointment. But yet it by no means follows, because the Creator said of old, "Cursed is every one that hangeth on a tree,"[18] that Christ belonged to another god, and on that account was accursed even then in the law. And how, indeed, could the Creator have cursed by anticipation one whom He knew not of? Why, however, may it not be more suitable for the Creator to have delivered His own Son to His own curse, than to have submitted Him to the malediction of that god of yours,—in behalf, too, of man, who is an alien to him? Now, if this appointment of the Creator respecting His Son appears to you to be a cruel one, it is equally so in the case of your own god; if, on the contrary, it be in accordance with reason in your god, it is

---

[1] 1 Cor. ix. 20, 22.
[2] Gal. ii. 9.
[3] Gal. ii. 10.
[4] See above, book iv. chap. xiv. p. 365.
[5] Victus: see Gal. ii. 12 ; or, *living*, see ver. 14.
[6] Gal. ii. 12.
[7] Gal. ii. 16.
[8] Gal. ii. 18 (see Conybeare and Howson).
[9] Rivi: the *wadys* of the East.

[10] Luke iii. 4, 5.
[11] Ps. ii. 3.
[12] Ps. ii. 1, 2.
[13] Gal. ii. 16 and iii. 11.
[14] Hab. ii. 4.
[15] Apud.
[16] Deut. xi. 26.
[17] Gal. iii. 13.
[18] The LXX. *version* of Deut. xxi. 23 is quoted by St. Paul in Gal. iii. 13.

equally so—nay, much more so—in mine. For it would be more credible that that God had provided blessing for man, through the curse of Christ, who formerly set both a blessing and a curse before man, than that he had done so, who, according to you,[1] never at any time pronounced either. "We have received, therefore, the promise of the Spirit," as the apostle says, "through faith," even that faith by which the just man lives, in accordance with the Creator's purpose.[2] What I say, then, is this, that that God is the object of faith who prefigured the grace of faith. But when he also adds, "For ye are all the children of faith,"[3] it becomes clear that what the heretic's industry erased was the mention of Abraham's name; for by faith the apostle declares us to be "*children of Abraham*,"[4] and after mentioning him he expressly called us "children of faith" also. But how are we children of faith? and of whose faith, if not Abraham's? For since "Abraham believed God, and it was accounted to him for righteousness;"[5] since, also, he deserved for that reason to be called "the father of many nations," whilst we, who are even more like him[6] in believing in God, are thereby justified as Abraham was, and thereby also obtain life—since the just lives by his faith,—it therefore happens that, as he in the previous passage called us "sons of Abraham," since he is in faith our (common) father,[7] so here also he named us "children of faith," for it was owing to his faith that it was promised that Abraham should be the father of (many) nations. As to the fact itself of his calling off faith from circumcision, did he not seek thereby to constitute us the children of Abraham, who had believed previous to his circumcision in the flesh?[8] In short,[9] faith in one of two gods cannot possibly admit us to the dispensation[10] of the other,[11] so that it should impute righteousness to those who believe in him, and make the just live through him, and declare the Gentiles to be his children through faith. Such a dispensation as this belongs wholly to Him through whose appointment it was already made known by the call of this self-same Abraham, as is conclusively shown[12] by the natural meaning.[13]

[1] Apud te.
[2] According to the promise of a prophet of the Creator. See Hab. ii. 4.
[3] Gal. iii. 26.
[4] Gal. iii. 7, 9, 29.
[5] Gal. iii. 6.
[6] Magis proinde: as sharing in the faith he had, "being yet uncircumcised." See Rom. iv. 11.
[7] Patris fidei.
[8] In integritate carnis.
[9] Denique.
[10] Formam: "plan" or "arrangement."
[11] Alterius dei . . . dei alterius.
[12] Revincatur.
[13] Ipso sensu.

CHAP. IV.—ANOTHER INSTANCE OF MARCION'S TAMPERING WITH ST. PAUL'S TEXT. THE FULNESS OF TIME, ANNOUNCED BY THE APOSTLE, FORETOLD BY THE PROPHETS. MOSAIC RITES ABROGATED BY THE CREATOR HIMSELF. MARCION'S TRICKS ABOUT ABRAHAM'S NAME. THE CREATOR, BY HIS CHRIST, THE FOUNTAIN OF THE GRACE AND THE LIBERTY WHICH ST. PAUL ANNOUNCED. MARCION'S DOCETISM REFUTED.

"But," says he, "I speak after the manner of men: when we were children, we were placed in bondage under the elements of the world."[14] This, however, was not said "after the manner of men." For there is no figure[15] here, but literal truth. For (with respect to the latter clause of this passage), what child (in the sense, that is, in which the Gentiles are children) is not in bondage to the elements of the world, which he looks up to[16] in the light of a god? With regard, however, to the former clause, there was a figure (as the apostle wrote it); because after he had said, "I speak after the manner of men," he adds), "Though it be but a man's covenant, no man disannulleth, or addeth thereto."[17] For by the figure of the permanency of a human covenant he was defending the divine testament. "To Abraham were the promises made, and to his seed. He said not 'to seeds,' as of many; but as of one, 'to thy seed,' which is Christ."[18] Fie on[19] Marcion's sponge! But indeed it is superfluous to dwell on what he has erased, when he may be more effectually confuted from that which he has retained.[20] "But when the fulness of time was come, God sent forth His Son"[21]— the God, of course, who is the Lord of that

[14] This apparent quotation is in fact a patching together of two sentences from Gal. iii. 15 and iv. 3 (Fr. Junius). "If I may be allowed to guess from the manner in which Tertullian expresseth himself, I should imagine that Marcion erased the whole of chap. iii. after the word λέγω in ver. 15, and the beginning of chap. iv., until you come to the word ὅτε in ver. 3. Then the words will be connected thus: 'Brethren, I speak after the manner of men . . . when we were children we were in bondage under the elements of the world; but when the fulness of time was come, God sent forth His Son.' This is precisely what the argument of Tertullian requires, and they are the very words which he connects together" (Lardner, *Hist. of Heretics*, x. 43). Dr. Lardner, touching Marcion's omissions in this chap. iii. of the Epistle to the Galatians, says: "He omitted vers. 6, 7, 8, in order to get rid of the mention of Abraham, and of the gospel having been preached to him." This he said after St. Jerome, and then adds: "He ought also to have omitted part of ver. 9, σὺν τῷ πιστῷ Ἀβραάμ, which seems to have been the case, according to T.'s manner of stating the argument against him" (Works, *History of Heretics*, x. 43).
[15] Exemplum.
[16] Suspicit
[17] Gal. iii. 15. This, of course, is consistent in St. Paul's argument. Marcion, however, by erasing all the intervening verses, and affixing the phrase "*after the manner of men*" to the plain assertion of Gal. iv. 3, reduces the whole statement to an absurdity.
[18] Gal. iii. 16.
[19] Erubescat.
[20] So, instead of pursuing the contents of chap. iii., he proceeds to such of chap. iv. as Marcion reserved.
[21] Gal. iv. 4.

very succession of times which constitutes *an age;* who also ordained, as "*signs*" of time, suns and moons and constellations and stars; who furthermore both predetermined and predicted that the revelation of His Son should be postponed to the end of the times.[1] "It shall come to pass *in the last days*, that the mountain (of the house) of the Lord shall be manifested";[2] "and *in the last days* I will pour out of my Spirit upon all flesh"[3] as Joel says. It was characteristic of Him (only)[4] to wait patiently for the fulness of time, to whom belonged the end of time no less than the beginning. But as for that idle god, who has neither any work nor any prophecy, nor accordingly any time, to show for himself, what has *he* ever done to bring about the fulness of time, or to wait patiently its completion? If nothing, what an impotent state to have to wait for the Creator's time, in servility to the Creator! But for what end did He send His Son? "To redeem them that were under the law,"[5] in other words, to "make the crooked ways straight, and the rough places smooth," as Isaiah says[6]—in order that old things might pass away, and a new course begin, even "the new law out of Zion, and the word of the Lord from Jerusalem,"[7] and "that we might receive the adoption of sons,"[8] that is, the Gentiles, who once were not sons. For He is to be "the light of the Gentiles," and "in His name shall the Gentiles trust."[9] That we may have, therefore, the assurance that we are the children of God, "He hath sent forth His Spirit into our hearts, crying, Abba, Father."[10] For "in the last days," saith He, "I will pour out of my Spirit upon all flesh."[11] Now, from whom comes this grace, but from Him who proclaimed the promise thereof? Who is (our) Father, but He who is also our Maker? Therefore, after such affluence (of grace), they should not have returned "to weak and beggarly elements."[12] By the Romans, however, the rudiments of learning are wont to be called *elements*. He did not therefore seek, by any depreciation of the mundane elements, to turn them away from their god, although, when he said just before, "Howbeit, then, ye serve them which by nature are no gods,"[13] he censured the error of that physical or natural superstition which holds the elements to be god; but at the God of those elements he aimed not in this censure.[14] He tells us himself clearly enough what he means by "*elements*," even the rudiments of the law: "Ye observe days, and months, and times, and years"[15]—the sabbaths, I suppose, and "the preparations,"[16] and the fasts, and the "high days."[17] For the cessation of even these, no less than of circumcision, was appointed by the Creator's decrees, who had said by Isaiah, "Your new moons, and your sabbaths, and your high days I cannot bear; your fasting, and feasts, and ceremonies my soul hateth;"[18] also by Amos, "I hate, I despise your feast-days, and I will not smell in your solemn assemblies;"[19] and again by Hosea, "I will cause to cease all her mirth, and her feast-days, and her sabbaths, and her new moons, and all her solemn assemblies."[20] The institutions which He set up Himself, you ask, did He then destroy? Yes, rather than any other. Or if another destroyed them, he only helped on the purpose of the Creator, by removing what even He had condemned. But this is not the place to discuss the question why the Creator abolished His own laws. It is enough for us to have proved that He intended such an abolition, that so it may be affirmed that the apostle determined nothing to the prejudice of the Creator, since the abolition itself proceeds from the Creator. But as, in the case of thieves, something of the stolen goods is apt to drop by the way, as a clue to their detection; so, as it seems to me, it has happened to Marcion: the last mention of Abraham's name he has left untouched (in the epistle), although no passage required his erasure more than this, even in his partial alteration of the text.[21] "For (it is written) that Abraham had two sons, the one by a bond maid, the other by a free woman; but he who was of the bond maid was born after the flesh, but he of the free woman was by promise: which things are allegorized"[22] (that is to say, they presaged something besides *the literal history*); "for these are the

---

[1] In extremitatem temporum.
[2] Isa. ii. 2 (Sept).
[3] Joel iii. 28, as quoted by St. Peter, Acts ii. 17.
[4] Ipsius.
[5] Gal. iv. 5.
[6] Isa. xl. 4.
[7] Isa. ii. 3.
[8] Gal. iv. 5.
[9] Isa. xlii, 4, 6.
[10] Gal. iv. 6.
[11] Joel iii. 28, as given in Acts ii, 17.
[12] Gal. iv. 9.

[13] Gal. iv. 8.
[14] Nec sic taxans.
[15] Gal. iv. 10.
[16] Cœnas puras: probably the παρασκευαί mentioned in John xix. 31.
[17] See also John xix. 31.
[18] Isa. i. 13, 14.
[19] Amos v. 21.
[20] Hos. ii. 11.
[21] In other words, Marcion has indeed tampered with the passage, omitting some things; but (strange to say) he has left untouched the statement which, from his point of view, most required suppression.
[22] Allegorica: on the importance of rendering ἀλληγορούμενα by this participle rather than by the noun "an allegory," as in A. V., see Bp. Marsh's *Lectures on the Interpretation of the Bible*, pp. 351–354.

two covenants," or the two exhibitions (of the divine plans),[1] as we have found the word interpreted,"the one from the Mount Sinai," in relation to the synagogue of the Jews, according to the law, "which gendereth to bondage"—"the other gendereth" (to liberty, being raised) above all principality, and power, and dominion, and every name that is named, not only in this world, but in that which is to come, "which is the mother of us all," in which we have the promise of (Christ's) holy church; by reason of which he adds in conclusion: " So then, brethren, we are not children of the bond woman, but of the free."[2] In this passage he has undoubtedly shown that Christianity had a noble birth, being sprung, as the mystery of the allegory indicates, from that son of Abraham who was born of the free woman; whereas from the son of the bond maid came the legal bondage of Judaism. Both dispensations, therefore, emanate from that same God by whom,[3] as we have found, they were both sketched out beforehand. When he speaks of "the liberty wherewith Christ hath made us free,"[4] does not the very phrase indicate that He is the Liberator who was once the Master? For Galba himself never liberated slaves which were not his own, even when about to restore free men to their liberty.[5] By Him, therefore, will liberty be bestowed, at whose command lay the enslaving power of the law. And very properly. It was not meet that those who had received liberty should be " entangled again with the yoke of bondage "[6]—that is, of the law; now that the Psalm had its prophecy accomplished: " Let us break their bands asunder, and cast away their cords from us, since the rulers have gathered themselves together against the Lord and against His Christ."[7] All those, therefore, who had been delivered from the yoke of slavery he would earnestly have to obliterate the very mark of slavery—even circumcision, on the authority of the prophet's prediction. He remembered how that Jeremiah had said, " Circumcise the foreskins of your heart;"[8] as Moses likewise had enjoined, " Circumcise your hard hearts"[9]—not

the *literal* flesh. If, now, he were for excluding circumcision, as the messenger of a new god, why does he say that " in Christ neither circumcisoin availeth anything, nor uncircumcision?"[10] For it was his duty to prefer the rival principle of that which he was abolishing, if he had a mission from the god who was the enemy of circumcision. Furthermore, since both circumcision and uncircumcision were attributed to the same Deity, both lost their power[11] in Christ, by reason of the excellency of faith—of that faith concerning which it had been written, " And in His name shall the Gentiles trust ?"[12]—of that faith "which," he says "worketh by love."[13] By this saying he also shows that the Creator is the source of that grace. For whether he speaks of the love which is due to God, or that which is due to one's neighbor—in either case, the Creator's grace is meant: for it is He who enjoins the first in these words, " Thou shalt love God with all thine heart, and with all thy soul, and with all thy strength;"[14] and also the second in another passage: " Thou shalt love thy neighbour as thyself."[15] " But he that troubleth you shall have to bear judgment."[16] From what God? From (Marcion's) most excellent god? But he does not execute judgment. From the Creator? But neither will He condemn the maintainer of circumcision. Now, if none other but the Creator shall be found to execute judgment, it follows that only He, who has determined on the cessation of the law, shall be able to condemn the defenders of the law; and what, if he also affirms the law in that portion of it where it ought (to be permanent)? " For," says he, " all the law is fulfilled in you hy this: ' Thou shalt love thy neighbour as thyself.' "[17] If, indeed, he will have it that by the words " *it is fulfilled*" it is implied that the law no longer has *to be* fulfilled, then of course he does not mean that I should any more love my neighbour as myself, since this precept must have ceased together with the law. But no ! we must evermore continue to observe this commandment. The Creator's law, therefore, has received the approval of the rival god, who has, in fact, bestowed upon it not the sentence of a summary dismissal,[18] but the favour of a compendious acceptance;[19]

[1] Ostensiones : *revelationes* perhaps.
[2] Gal. iv. 21–26, 31.
[3] Apud quem.
[4] Gal. v. 1.
[5] Tertullian, in his terse style, takes the case of the emperor, as the highest potentate, who, if any, might make free with his power. He seizes the moment when Galba was saluted emperor on Nero's death, and was the means of delivering so many out of the hands of the tyrant, in order to sharpen the point of his illustration.
[6] Gal. v. 1.
[7] Ps. ii. 3, 2
[8] Jer. iv. 4.
[9] Deut. x. 16.

[10] Gal. v. 6.
[11] Utraque vacabat.
[12] Isa. xlii. 4.
[13] Gal. v. 6.
[14] Deut. vi. 5.
[15] Lev. xix. 18.
[16] Gal. v. 10.
[17] Gal. v. 14.
[18] Dispendium.
[19] Compendium : the terseness of the original cannot be preserved in the translation.

the gist of it all being concentrated in this one precept! But this condensation of the law is, in fact, only possible to Him who is the Author of it. When, therefore, he says, "Bear ye one another's burdens, and so fulfill the law of Christ,"[1] since this cannot be accomplished except a man love his neighbour as himself, it is evident that the precept, "Thou shalt love thy neighbour as thyself" (which, in fact, underlies the injunction, "Bear ye one another's burdens"), is really "the law of Christ," though literally the law of the Creator. Christ, therefore, is the Creator's Christ, as Christ's law is the Creator's law. "Be not deceived,[2] God is not mocked."[3] But Marcion's god *can* be mocked; for he knows not how to be angry, or how to take vengeance. "For whatsoever a man soweth, that shall he also reap."[4] It is then the God of recompense and judgment who threatens[5] this. "Let us not be weary in well-doing;"[6] and "as we have opportunity, let us do good."[7] Deny now that the Creator has given a commandment to do good, and then a diversity of precept may argue a difference of gods. If, however, He also announces recompense, then from the same God must come the harvest both of death[8] and of life. But "in due time we shall reap;"[9] because in Ecclesiastes it is said, "For everything there will be a time."[10] Moreover, "the world is crucified unto me," who am a servant of the Creator—"the world," (I say,) but not the God who made the world—"and I unto the world,"[11] not unto the God who made the world. *The world*, in the apostle's sense, here means life and conversation according to worldly principles; it is in renouncing these that we and they are mutually crucified and mutually slain. He calls them "persecutors of Christ."[12] But when he adds, that "he bare in his body the *scars*[13] of Christ"—since scars, of course, are accidents of body[14]—he therefore expressed the truth, that the flesh of Christ is not putative, but real and substantial,[15] the scars of which he represents as borne upon his body.

CHAP. V.—THE FIRST EPISTLE TO THE CORINTHIANS. THE PAULINE SALUTATION OF GRACE AND PEACE SHOWN TO BE ANTI-MARCIONITE. THE CROSS OF CHRIST PURPOSED BY THE CREATOR. MARCION ONLY PERPETUATES THE OFFENCE AND FOOLISHNESS OF CHRIST'S CROSS BY HIS IMPIOUS SEVERANCE OF THE GOSPEL FROM THE CREATOR. ANALOGIES BETWEEN THE LAW AND THE GOSPEL IN THE MATTER OF WEAK THINGS, AND FOOLISH THINGS AND BASE THINGS.

My preliminary remarks[16] on the preceding epistle called me away from treating of its superscription,[17] for I was sure that another opportunity would occur for considering the matter, it being of constant recurrence, and in the same form too, in every epistle. The point, then, is, that it is not (the usual) *health* which the apostle prescribes for those to whom he writes, but "grace and peace."[18] I do not ask, indeed, what a destroyer of Judaism has to do with a formula which the Jews still use. For to this day they salute each other[19] with the greeting of "peace," and formerly in their Scriptures they did the same. But I understand him by his practice[20] plainly enough to have corroborated the declaration of the Creator: "How beautiful are the feet of them that bring glad tidings of good, who preach the gospel of *peace!*"[21] For the herald of *good*, that is, of God's "grace" was well aware that along with it "peace" also was to be proclaimed.[22] Now, when he announces these blessings as "from God the Father and the Lord Jesus,"[23] he uses titles that are common to both, which are also adapted to the mystery of our faith;[24] and I suppose it to be impossible accurately to determine what God is declared to be the Father and the Lord Jesus, unless (we consider) which of their accruing attributes are more suited to them severally.[25] First, then, I assert that none other than the Creator and Sustainer of both man and the universe can be acknowledged as Father *and* Lord; next, that to the Father also the title of Lord accrues by reason of His power, and that the Son too receives the same through the Father; then that "grace and peace" are not only His who had them published, but His likewise to whom offence had been given. For neither does *grace* exist, except after offence; nor *peace*, except after war. Now, both the

---

[1] Gal. vi. 2.
[2] Erratis: literally, "ye are deceived."
[3] Gal. vi. 7.
[4] Gal. vi. 7.
[5] Intentat.
[6] Gal. vi. 9.
[7] Gal. vi. 10.
[8] Corruptionis.
[9] Gal. vi. 9.
[10] Eccles. iii. 17.
[11] Gal. vi. 14.
[12] See Gal. vi. 17, κόπους μοι μηδεὶς παρεχέτω, "let no one harass me."
[13] Stigmata : the scars not of circumcision, but of wounds suffered for His sake (Conybeare and Howson).
[14] Corporalia.
[15] Solidam.
[16] Præstructio.

[17] Titulo.
[18] 1 Cor. i. 3.
[19] Appellant.
[20] Officio.
[21] Isa. lii. 7.
[22] Pacem quam præferendam.
[23] 1 Cor. i. 3.
[24] Competentibus nostro quoque sacramento.
[25] Nisi ex accedentibus cui magis competant.

people (of Israel) by their transgression of His laws,[1] and the whole race of mankind by their neglect of natural duty,[2] had both sinned and rebelled against the Creator. Marcion's god, however, could not have been offended, both because he was unknown to everybody, and because he is incapable of being irritated. What *grace*, therefore, can be had of a god who has not been offended? What *peace* from one who has never experienced rebellion? "The cross of Christ," he says, "is to them that perish foolishness; but unto such as shall obtain salvation, it is the power of God and the wisdom of God."[3] And then, that we may known from whence this comes, he adds: "For it is written, 'I will destroy the wisdom of the wise, and will bring to nothing the understanding of the prudent.'"[4] Now, since these are the Creator's words, and since what pertains to the doctrine[5] of the cross he accounts as foolishness, therefore both the cross, and also Christ by reason of the cross, will appertain to the Creator, by whom were predicted the incidents of the cross. But if[6] the Creator, as an enemy, took away their wisdom in order that the cross of Christ, considered as his adversary, should be accounted foolishness, how by any possibility can the Creator have foretold anything about the cross of a Christ who is not His own, and of whom He knew nothing, when He published the prediction? But, again, how happens it, that in the system of a Lord[7] who is so very good, and so profuse in mercy, some carry off salvation, when they believe the cross to be the wisdom and power of God, whilst others incur perdition, to whom the cross of Christ is accounted folly;—(how happens it, I repeat,) unless it is in the Creator's dispensation to have punished both the people *of Israel* and the human race, for some great offence committed against Him, with the loss of wisdom and prudence? What follows will confirm this suggestion, when he asks, "Hath not God infatuated the wisdom of this world?"[8] and when he adds the reason why: "For after that, in the wisdom of God, the world by wisdom knew not God, it pleased God[9] by the foolishness of preaching to save them that believe."[10] But first a word about the expression "*the world;*" because in this passage particularly,[11] the heretics expend a

great deal of their subtlety in showing that by *world* is meant *the lord of the world*. We, however, understand the term to apply to any person that is in the world, by a simple idiom of human language, which often substitutes that which contains for that which is contained. "The circus shouted," "The forum spoke," and "The basilica murmured," are well-known expressions, meaning that the people in these places did so. Since then the man, not the god, of the world[12] in his wisdom knew not God, whom indeed he ought to have known (both the Jew by his knowledge of the Scriptures, and all the human race by their knowledge of God's works), therefore that God, who was not acknowledged in His wisdom, resolved to smite men's knowledge with His foolishness, by saving all those who believe in the folly of the preached cross. "Because the Jews require signs," who ought to have already made up their minds about God, "and the Greeks seek after wisdom,"[13] who rely upon their own wisdom, and not upon God's. If, however, it was a new god that was being preached, what sin had the Jews committed, in seeking after signs to believe; or the Greeks, when they hunted after a wisdom which they would prefer to accept? Thus the very retribution which overtook both Jews and Greeks proves that God is both a jealous God and a Judge, inasmuch as He infatuated the world's wisdom by an angry[14] and a judicial retribution. Since, then, the causes[15] are in the hands of Him who gave us the Scriptures which we use, it follows that the apostle, when treating of the Creator, (as Him whom both Jew and Gentile as yet have) not known, means undoubtedly to teach us, that the God who is to become known (in Christ) is the Creator. The very "stumbling-block" which he declares Christ to be "to the Jews,"[16] points unmistakeably[17] to the Creator's prophecy respecting Him, when by Isaiah He says: "Behold I lay in Sion a stone of stumbling and a rock of offence."[18] This rock or stone is Christ.[19] This stumbling-stone Marcion retains still.[20]

---

[12] That is, "man who lives in the world, not God who made the world."
[13] 1 Cor. i. 22.
[14] Æmula.
[15] Causæ: the *reasons* of His retributive providence.
[16] 1 Cor. i. 23.
[17] Consignat.
[18] Isa. viii. 14.
[19] Isa. xxviii. 16
[20] "Etiam Marcion servat." These words cannot mean, as they have been translated, that "Marcion even retains these words" of prophecy; for whenever Marcion fell in with any traces of this prophecy of Christ, he seems to have expunged them. In Luke ii. 34 holy Simeon referred to it, but Marcion rejected this chapter of the evangelist; and although he admitted much of chap. xx., it is remarkable that he erased the ten verses thereof from the end of the eighth to the end of the eighteenth. Now in vers. 17, 18, Marcion found the prophecy again referred to. See Epiphanius, *Adv. Hæres.* xlii. *Schol.* 55.

---

[1] Disciplinæ.
[2] Per naturæ dissimulationem. This Fr. Junius explains by τὴν φύσεως ἀφοσίωσιν, in the sense of "*original sin*" (ἀφοσιοῦσθαι seems to point to sin requiring *expiation*).
[3] 1 Cor. i. 18.
[4] 1 Cor. i. 19, from Isa. xxix. 14.
[5] Causam.
[6] Aut si: introducing a Marcionite cavil.
[7] Apud dominum.
[8] 1 Cor. i. 20.
[9] Boni duxit Deus, εὐδόκησεν ὁ Θεός.
[10] 1 Cor. i. 21.　　　[11] Hic vel maxime.

Now, what is that "foolishness of God which is wiser than men," but the cross and death of Christ? What is that "weakness of God which is stronger than men,"[1] but the nativity and incarnation[2] of God? If, however, Christ was not born of the Virgin, was not constituted of human flesh, and thereby really suffered neither death nor the cross, there was nothing in Him either of foolishness or weakness; nor is it any longer true, that "God hath chosen the foolish things of the world to confound the wise;" nor, again, hath "God chosen the weak things of the world to confound the mighty;" nor "the base things" and the least things "in the world, and things which are despised, which are even as nothing" (that is, things which really[3] are not), "to bring to nothing things which are" (that is, which really are).[4] For nothing in the dispensation of God is found to be mean, and ignoble, and contemptible. Such only occurs in man's arrangement. The very Old Testament of the Creator[5] itself, it is possible, no doubt, to charge with foolishness, and weakness, and dishonour, and meanness, and contempt. What is more foolish and more weak than God's requirement of bloody sacrifices and of savoury holocausts? What is weaker than the cleansing of vessels and of beds?[6] What more dishonourable than the discoloration of the reddening skin?[7] What so mean as the statute of retaliation? What so contemptible as the exception in meats and drinks? The whole of the Old Testament, the heretic, to the best of my belief, holds in derision. For God has chosen the foolish things of the world to confound its wisdom. Marcion's god has no such discipline, because he does not take after[8] (the Creator) in the process of confusing opposites by their opposites, so that "no flesh shall glory; but, as it is written, He that glorieth, let him glory in the Lord."[9] In what Lord? Surely in Him who gave this precept.[10] Unless, forsooth, the Creator enjoined us to glory in the god of Marcion!

CHAP. VI.—THE DIVINE WAY OF WISDOM, AND GREATNESS, AND MIGHT. GOD'S HIDING OF HIMSELF, AND SUBSEQUENT REVELATION. TO MARCION'S GOD SUCH A CONCEALMENT AND MANIFESTATION IMPOSSIBLE. GOD'S PREDESTINATION. NO SUCH PRIOR SYSTEM OF INTENTION POSSIBLE TO A GOD PREVIOUSLY UNKNOWN AS WAS MARCION'S. THE POWERS OF THE WORLD WHICH CRUCIFIED CHRIST. ST. PAUL, AS A WISE MASTER-BUILDER, ASSOCIATED WITH PROPHECY. SUNDRY INJUNCTIONS OF THE APOSTLE PARALLEL WITH THE TEACHING OF THE OLD TESTAMENT.

By all these statements, therefore, does he show us what God he means, when he says, "We speak the wisdom of God among them that are perfect."[11] It is that God who has confounded the wisdom of the wise, who has brought to nought the understanding of the prudent, who has reduced to folly[12] the world's wisdom, by choosing its foolish things, and disposing them to the attainment of salvation. This wisdom, he says, once lay hidden in things that were foolish, weak, and lacking in honour; once also was latent under figures, allegories, and enigmatical types; but it was afterwards to be revealed in Christ, who was set "as a light to the Gentiles,"[13] by the Creator who promised through the mouth of Isaiah that He would discover "the hidden treasures, which eye had not seen."[14] Now, that that god should have ever hidden anything who had never made a covert wherein to practise concealment, is in itself a wholly incredible idea. If he existed, concealment of himself was out of the question—to say nothing[15] of any of his religious ordinances.[16] The Creator, on the contrary, was as well known in Himself as His ordinances were. These, we know, were publicly instituted[17] in Israel; but they lay overshadowed with latent meanings, in which the wisdom of God was concealed,[18] to be brought to light by and by amongst "the perfect," when the time should come, but "pre-ordained in the counsels of God before the ages."[19] But whose ages, if not the Creator's? For because ages consist of times, and times are made up of days, and months, and years; since also days, and months, and years are measured by suns, and moons, and stars, which He ordained for this purpose (for "they shall be," says He, "for signs of the months and the years"),[20] it clearly follows that the ages belong to the Creator, and that nothing of what was foreordained before the ages can be said to be the property of any other being than Him who claims the ages also as His own. Else let Marcion show that the ages belong to his god. He must then also claim the world itself for

[1] 1 Cor. i. 25.
[2] Caro.
[3] Vere.
[4] 1 Cor. i. 27,
[5] Apud Creatorem etiam vetera: (*vetera*, i.e.) "veteris testamenti institutiones " (Oehler).
[6] Lex. xv. *passim*.
[7] Lev. xiii. 2–6.
[8] Æmulatur.
[9] 1 Cor. i. 29, 31.
[10] By Jeremiah, chap. ix. 23, 24.
[11] 1 Cor. ii. 6, 7.
[12] Infatuavit.
[13] Isa. xlii. 6.
[14] Isa. xlv. 3 (Septuagint)
[15] Nedum.
[16] Sacramenta.
[17] Palam decurrentia.
[18] Delitescebat.
[19] 1 Cor. ii. 7.
[20] Gen. i. 14, inexactly quoted.

him; for it is in it that the ages are reckoned, the vessel as it were [1] of the times, as well as the signs thereof, or their order. But he has no such demonstration to show us. I go back therefore to the point, and ask him this question: Why did (his god) fore-ordain our glory before the ages of the Creator? I could understand his having predetermined it before the ages, if he had revealed it at the commencement of time.[2] But when he does this almost at the very expiration of all the ages [3] of the Creator, his predestination before the ages, and not rather within the ages, was in vain, because he did not mean to make any revelation of his purpose until the ages had almost run out their course. For it is wholly inconsistent in him to be so forward in planning purposes, who is so backward in revealing them. In the Creator, however, the two courses were perfectly compatible—both the predestination before the ages and the revelation at the end thereof, because that which He both fore-ordained and revealed He also in the intermediate space of time announced by the pre-ministration of figures, and symbols, and allegories. But because (the apostle) subjoins, on the subject of our glory, that "none of the princes of this world knew it, for had they known it they would not have crucified the Lord of glory,"[4] the heretic argues that the princes of this world crucified the Lord (that is, the Christ of the rival god) in order that this *blow* might even recoil [5] on the Creator Himself. Any one, however, who has seen from what we have already said how our glory must be regarded as issuing from the Creator, will already have come to the conclusion that, inasmuch as the Creator settled it in His own secret purpose, it properly enough was unknown to all the princes [6] and powers of the Creator, on the principle that servants are not permitted to know their masters' plans, much less the fallen angels and the leader of transgression himself, the devil; for I should contend that *these*, on account of their fall, were greater strangers still to any knowledge of the Creator's dispensations. But it is no longer open to me [7] even to interpret the princes and powers of this world as the Creator's, since the apostle imputes ignorance to *them*, whereas even the devil according to our Gospel recognised Jesus in the temptation,[8] and, according to the record which is common to both (Marcionites and

ourselves) the evil spirit knew that Jesus was the Holy One of God, and that Jesus was His name, and that He was come to destroy them.[9] The parable also of the strong man armed, whom a stronger than he overcame and seized his goods, is admitted by Marcion to have reference to the Creator:[10] therefore the Creator could not have been ignorant any longer of the God of glory, since He is overcome by him;[11] nor could He have crucified him whom He was unable to cope with. The inevitable inference, therefore, as it seems to me, is that we must believe that the princes and powers of the Creator did knowingly crucify the God of glory in His Christ, with that desperation and excessive malice with which the most abandoned slaves do not even hesitate to slay their masters. For it is written in my Gospel [12] that "Satan entered into Judas."[13] According to Marcion, however, the apostle in the passage under consideration [14] does not allow the imputation of ignorance, with respect to the Lord of glory, to the powers of the Creator; because, indeed, he will have it that these are not meant by "the princes of this world." But (the apostle) evidently [15] did not speak of spiritual princes; so that he meant secular ones, those of the princely people, (chief in the divine dispensation, although) not, of course, amongst the nations of the world, and their rulers, and king Herod, and even Pilate, and, as represented by him,[16] that power of Rome which was the greatest in the world, and then presided over by him. Thus the arguments of the other side are pulled down, and our own proofs are thereby built up. But you still maintain that our glory comes from your god, with whom it also lay in secret. Then why does your god employ the self-same Scripture [17] which the apostle also relies on? What has your god to do at all with the sayings of the prophets? "Who hath discovered the mind of the Lord, or who hath been His counsellor?"[18] So says Isaiah. What has he also to do with illustrations from our God? For when (the apostle) calls himself "a wise master-builder,"[19] we find that the Creator by Isaiah designates the teacher who sketches [20] out the divine discipline by the same title, "I will take away from Judah *the cunning artifi-*

---

[1] Quodammodo.
[2] Introductione sæculi.
[3] Pæne jam totis sæculis prodactis.
[4] 1 Cor. ii. 8.
[5] Ut et hoc recidat
[6] Virtutibus.
[7] Sed jam nec mihi competit.
[8] Matt. iv. 1-11.

[9] Luke iv. 34.
[10] In Creatoris accipitur apud Marcionem.
[11] Considered, in the hypothesis, as Marcion's god.
[12] Apud me.
[13] Luke xxii. 3.
[14] 1 Cor. ii. 8.
[15] Videtur.
[16] Et quo.
[17] Instrumento.
[18] Isa. xl. 13.
[19] 1 Cor. iii. 10.
[20] Depalatorem.

cer,"[1] etc. And was it not Paul himself who was there foretold, destined "to be taken away from Judah"—that is, from Judaism—for the erection of Christianity, in order "to lay that only foundation, which is Christ?"[2] Of this work the Creator also by the same prophet says, "Behold, I lay in Sion for a foundation a precious stone and honourable; and he that resteth thereon shall not be confounded."[3] Unless it be, that God professed *Himself* to be the builder up of an earthly work, that so He might not give any sign of His Christ, as destined to be the foundation of such as believe in Him, upon which every man should build at will the superstructure of either sound or worthless doctrine; forasmuch as it is the Creator's function, when a man's work shall be tried by fire, (or) when a reward shall be recompensed to him by fire; because it is by fire that the test is applied to the building which you erect upon the foundation which is laid by Him, that is, the foundation of His Christ.[4] "Know ye not that ye are the temple of God, and that the Spirit of God dwelleth in you?"[5] Now, since man is the property, and the work, and the image and likeness of the Creator, having his flesh formed by Him of the ground, and his soul of His *afflatus*, it follows that Marcion's god wholly dwells in a temple which belongs to another, if so be we are not the Creator's temple. But "if any man defile the temple of God, he shall be himself destroyed"[6]—of course, by the God of the temple.[7] If you threaten an avenger, you threaten us with the Creator. "Ye must become fools, that ye may be wise."[8] Wherefore? "Because the wisdom of this world is foolishness with God."[9] With what God? Even if the ancient Scriptures have contributed nothing in support of our view thus far,[10] an excellent testimony turns up in what (the apostle) here adjoins: "For it is written, He taketh the wise in their own craftiness; and again, The Lord knoweth the thoughts of the wise, that

they are vain."[11] For in general we may conclude for certain that he could not possibly have cited the authority of that God whom he was bound to destroy, since he would not teach for Him.[12] "Therefore," says he, "let no man glory in man;"[13] an injunction which is in accordance with the teaching of the Creator, "wretched is the man that trusteth in man;"[14] again, "It is better to trust in the Lord than to confide in man;"[15] and the same thing is said about glorying (in princes).[16]

CHAP. VII.—ST. PAUL'S PHRASEOLOGY OFTEN SUGGESTED BY THE JEWISH SCRIPTURES. CHRIST OUR PASSOVER—A PHRASE WHICH INTRODUCES US TO THE VERY HEART OF THE ANCIENT DISPENSATION. CHRIST'S TRUE CORPOREITY. MARRIED AND UNMARRIED STATES. MEANING OF THE TIME IS SHORT. IN HIS EXHORTATIONS AND DOCTRINE, THE APOSTLE WHOLLY TEACHES ACCORDING TO THE MIND AND PURPOSES OF THE GOD OF THE OLD TESTAMENT. PROHIBITION OF MEATS AND DRINKS WITHDRAWN BY THE CREATOR.

"And the hidden things of darkness He will Himself bring to light,"[17] even by Christ; for He has promised Christ to be a Light,[18] and Himself He has declared to be a lamp, "searching the hearts and reins."[19] From Him also shall "praise be had by every man,"[20] from whom proceeds, as from a judge, the opposite also of praise. But here, at least, you say he interprets the world to be the God thereof, when he says: "We are made a spectacle unto the world, and to angels, and to men."[21] For if by world he meant the people thereof, he would not have afterwards specially mentioned "*men*." To prevent, however, your using such an argument as this, the Holy Ghost has providentially explained the meaning of the passage thus: "We are made a spectacle to the world," *i.e.* "both to *angels*," who minister therein, "and to *men*," who are the objects of their ministration.[22] Of course,[23] a man of the noble courage of our apostle (to say nothing of the Holy Ghost) was afraid, when writing to the children whom he had begotten in

---

[1] So the A. V. of Isa. iii. 3; but the Septuagint and St. Paul use the self-same term, σοφὸς ἀρχιτέκτων.
[2] 1 Cor. iii. 11.
[3] Isa. xxviii. 16.
[4] We add the original of this sentence: "Nisi si structorem se terreni operis Deus profitebatur, ut non de suo Christo significaret, qui futurus esset fundamentum credentium in eum, super quod prout quisque superstruxerit, dignam scilicet vel indignam doctrinam si opus ejus per ignem probabitur, si merces illi per ignem rependetur, creatoris est, quia per ignem judicatur vestra superædificatio, utique sui fundamenti, id est sui Christi." Tertullian is arguing upon an hypothesis suggested by Marcion's withdrawal of *his* Christ from everything "terrene." Such a process as is described by St. Paul in this passage, 1 Cor. i. 12–15, must be left to the Creator and *His* Christ.
[5] 1 Cor. iii. 16.
[6] The text has *vitiabitur*, "shall be *defiled*."
[7] 1 Cor. iii. 17.
[8] 1 Cor. iii. 18.
[9] 1 Cor. iii. 19.
[10] The older reading, "*adhuc* sensum pristina præjudicaverunt," we have preferred to Oehler's "ad hunc sensum," etc.

[11] 1 Cor. iii. 19, 20; Job v. 13; Ps. xciv. 11.
[12] Si non illi doceret.
[13] 1 Cor. iii. 21.
[14] Jer. xvii. 5.
[15] Ps. cxviii. 8.
[16] Ps. cxviii. 9.
[17] 1 Cor. iv. 5.
[18] Isa. xlii. 6.
[19] Ps. vii. 9.
[20] 1 Cor. iv. 5.
[21] 1 Cor. iv. 9.
[22] Our author's version is no doubt right. The Greek does not admit the co-ordinate, triple conjunction of the A.V.: Θέατρον ἐγενήθημεν τῷ κόσμῳ—καὶ ἀγγέλοις καὶ ἀνθρώποις.
[23] Nimirum: introducing a strong ironical sentence against Marcion's conceit.

the gospel, to speak freely of the God of the world; for against Him he could not possibly seem to have a word to say, except only in a straightforward manner![1] I quite admit, that, according to the Creator's law,[2] the man was an offender "who had his father's wife."[3] He followed, no doubt,[4] the principles of natural and public law. When, however, he condemns the man "to be delivered unto Satan,"[5] he becomes the herald of an avenging God. It does not matter[6] that he also said, "For the destruction of the flesh, that the spirit may be saved in the day of the Lord,"[7] since both in the destruction of the flesh and in the saving of the spirit there is, on His part, judicial process; and when he bade "the wicked person be put away from the midst of them,"[8] he only mentioned what is a very frequently recurring sentence of the Creator. "Purge out the old leaven, that ye may be a new lump, as ye are unleavened."[9] The unleavened bread was therefore, in the Creator's ordinance, a figure of us (Christians). "For even Christ our passover is sacrificed for us."[10] But why is Christ our passover, if the passover be not a type of Christ, in the similitude of the blood which saves, and of the Lamb, which is Christ?[11] Why does (the apostle) clothe us and Christ with symbols of the Creator's solemn rites, unless they had relation to ourselves? When, again, he warns us against fornication, he reveals the resurrection of the flesh. "The body," says he, "is not for fornication, but for the Lord; and the Lord for the body,"[12] just as the temple is for God, and God for the temple. A temple will therefore pass away[13] with its god, and its god with the temple. You see, then, how that "He who raised up the Lord will also raise us up."[14] In the body will He raise us, because the body is for the Lord, and the Lord for the body. And suitably does he add the question: "Know ye not that your bodies are the members of Christ?"[15] What has the heretic to say? That these members of Christ will not rise again, for they are no longer our own? "For," he says, "ye are bought with a price."[16] A price! surely

none at all was paid, since Christ was a phantom, nor had He any corporeal substance which He could pay for our bodies! But, in truth, Christ had wherewithal to redeem us; and since He has redeemed, at a great price, these bodies of ours, against which fornication must not be committed (because they are now members of Christ, and not our own), surely He will secure, on His own account, the safety of those whom He made His own at so much cost! Now, how shall we glorify, how shall we exalt, God in our body,[17] which is doomed to perish? We must now encounter the subject of marriage, which Marcion, more continent[18] than the apostle, prohibits. For the apostle, although preferring the grace of continence,[19] yet permits the contraction of marriage and the enjoyment of it,[20] and advises the continuance therein rather than the dissolution thereof.[21] Christ plainly forbids divorce, Moses unquestionably permits it.[22] Now, when Marcion wholly prohibits all carnal intercourse to the faithful (for we will say nothing[23] about his catechumens), and when he prescribes repudiation of all engagements before marriage, whose teaching does he follow, that of Moses or of Christ? Even Christ,[24] however, when He here commands "the wife not to depart from her husband, or if she depart, to remain unmarried or be reconciled to her husband,"[25] both permitted divorce, which indeed He never absolutely prohibited, and confirmed (the sanctity) of marriage, by first forbidding its dissolution; and, if separation had taken place, by wishing the nuptial bond to be resumed by reconciliation. But what reasons does (the apostle) allege for continence? Because "the time is short."[26] I had almost thought it was because in Christ there was another god! And yet He from whom emanates this shortness of the time, will also send what suits the said brevity. No one makes provision for the time which is another's. You degrade your god, O Marcion, when you make him circumscribed at all by the Creator's time. Assuredly also, when (the apostle) rules that marriage should be "only in the Lord,"[27] that no Christian should intermarry with a

---

[1] Nisi exserte.
[2] Lev. xviii. 8.
[3] 1 Cor. v. 1.
[4] Secutus sit.
[5] 1 Cor. v. 5.
[6] Viderit.
[7] 1 Cor. v. 5.
[8] 1 Cor. v. 13.
[9] 1 Cor. v. 7.
[10] 1 Cor. v. 7.
[11] Ex. xii.
[12] 1 Cor. vi. 13.
[13] Peribit.
[14] 1 Cor. vi. 14.
[15] 1 Cor. vi. 15.
[16] 1 Cor. vi. 20.

[17] 1 Cor. vi. 20.
[18] Constantior: ironically predicated.
[19] 1 Cor. vii. 7, 8.
[20] 1 Cor. vii. 9, 13, 14.
[21] 1 Cor. vii. 27.
[22] One of Marcion's *Antitheses.*
[23] Viderint.
[24] Et Christus: Pamelius and Rigaltius here read "Christi *apostolus.*" Oehler defends the text as the author's phrase suggested (as Fr. Junius says) by the preceding words, "*Moses or Christ.*" To which we may add, that in this particular place St. Paul mentions his injunction as *Christ's especially,* οὐκ ἐγώ, ἀλλ' ὁ Κύριος, 1 Cor. vii. 10.
[25] 1 Cor. vii. 10, 11.
[26] 1 Cor. vii. 29.
[27] 1 Cor. vii. 39.

heathen, he maintains a law of the Creator, who everywhere prohibits marriage with strangers. But when he says, "although there be that are called gods, whether in heaven or in earth,"[1] the meaning of his words is clear—not as if there were gods in reality, but as if there were some who are called gods, without being truly so. He introduces his discussion about meats offered to idols with a statement concerning idols (themselves): "We know that an idol is nothing in the world."[2] Marcion, however, does not say that the Creator is not God; so that the apostle can hardly be thought to have ranked the Creator amongst those who are called gods, without being so; since, even if they had been gods, "to us there is but one God, the Father."[3] Now, from whom do all things come to us, but from Him to whom all things belong? And pray, what things are these? You have them in a preceding part of the epistle: "All things are yours; whether Paul, or Apollos, or Cephas, or the world, or life, or death, or things present, or things to come."[4] He makes the Creator then the God of all things, from whom proceed both the world and life and death, which cannot possibly belong to the other god. From Him, therefore, amongst the "*all things*" comes also Christ.[5] When he teaches that every man ought to live of his own industry,[6] he begins with a copious induction of examples—of soldiers, and shepherds, and husbandmen.[7] But he[8] wanted divine authority. What was the use, however, of adducing the Creator's, which he was destroying? It was vain to do so; for his god had no such authority! (The apostle) says: "Thou shalt not muzzle the ox that treadeth out the corn,"[9] and adds: "Doth God take care of oxen?" Yes, of oxen, for the sake of men! For, says he, "it is written for our sakes."[10] Thus he showed that the law had a symbolic reference to ourselves, and that it gives its sanction in favour of those who live of the gospel. (He showed) also, that those who preach the gospel are on this account sent by no other god but Him to whom belongs the law, which made provision for them, when he says: "For our sakes was this written."[11] Still he declined to use this power which the law gave him, because he preferred

working without any restraint.[12] Of this he boasted, and suffered no man to rob him of such glory[13]—certainly with no view of destroying the law, which he proved that another man might use. For behold Marcion, in his blindness, stumbled at the rock whereof our fathers drank in the wilderness. For since "that rock was Christ,"[14] it was, of course, the Creator's, to whom also belonged the people. But why resort to the figure of a sacred sign given by an extraneous god?[15] Was it to teach the very truth, that ancient things prefigured the Christ who was to be educed[16] out of them? For, being about to take a cursory view of what befell the people (of Israel) he begins with saying: "Now these things happened as examples for us."[17] Now, tell me, were these examples given by the Creator to men belonging to a rival god? Or did one god borrow examples from another, and a hostile one too? He withdraws me to himself in alarm[18] from Him from whom he transfers my allegiance. Will his antagonist make me better disposed to him? Should I now commit the same sins as the people, shall I have to suffer the same penalties, or not?[19] But if not the same, how vainly does he propose to me terrors which I shall not have to endure! From whom, again, shall I have to endure them? If from the Creator, what evils does it appertain to *Him* to inflict? And how will it happen that, jealous God as He is, He shall punish the man who offends His rival, instead of rather encouraging[20] him. If, however, from the other god—but *he* knows not how to punish. So that the whole declaration of the apostle lacks a reasonable basis, if it is not meant to relate to the Creator's discipline. But the fact is, the apostle's conclusion corresponds to the beginning: "Now all these things happened unto them for ensamples; and they are written for our admonition, upon whom the ends of the world are come."[21] What a Creator! how prescient already, and considerate in warning Christians who belong to another god! Whenever cavils occur the like to those which have been already dealt with, I pass them by; certain others I despatch briefly. A great argument for another god is the permission to eat of all kinds of meats, contrary to the law.[22] Just as if we did not ourselves allow that the burdensome

---

[1] 1 Cor. viii. 5.
[2] 1 Cor. viii. 4.
[3] 1 Cor. viii. 6.
[4] 1 Cor. iii. 21, 22.
[5] 1 Cor. iii. 23.
[6] 1 Cor. ix. 13.
[7] 1 Cor. ix. 7.
[8] He turns to Marcion's god.
[9] 1 Cor. ix. 9 and Deut. xxv. 4.
[10] 1 Cor. xi. 10.
[11] Comp. 1 Cor. ix. 13, 14, with Deut. xviii. 1, 2.

[12] Gratis.
[13] 1 Cor. ix. 15.
[14] 1 Cor. x. 4.
[15] Figuram extranei sacramenti.
[16] Recensendum.
[17] 1 Cor. x. 6.
[18] Me terret sibi.
[19] 1 Cor. x. 7-10.
[20] Magis quam foveat.
[21] 1 Cor. x. 11.
[22] 1 Cor. x. 25-27.

ordinances of the law were abrogated—but by Him who imposed them, who also promised the new condition of things.[1] The same, therefore, who prohibited meats, also restored the use of them, just as He had indeed allowed them from the beginning. If, however, some strange god had come to destroy our God, his foremost prohibition would certainly have been, that his own votaries should abstain from supporting their lives on the resources of his adversary.

CHAP. VIII.—MAN THE IMAGE OF THE CREATOR, AND CHRIST THE HEAD OF THE MAN. SPIRITUAL GIFTS. THE SEVENFOLD SPIRIT DESCRIBED BY ISAIAH. THE APOSTLE AND THE PROPHET COMPARED. MARCION CHALLENGED TO PRODUCE ANYTHING LIKE THESE GIFTS OF THE SPIRIT FORETOLD IN PROPHECY IN HIS GOD.

"The head of every man is Christ."[2] What Christ, if He is not the author of man? The *head* he has here put for *authority;* now "authority" will accrue to none else than the "author." Of what man indeed is He the head? Surely of him concerning whom he adds soon afterwards: "The man ought not to cover his head, forasmuch as he is the image of God."[3] Since then he is the image of the Creator (for *He*, when looking on Christ His Word, who was to become man, said, "Let us make man in our own image, after our likeness"[4]), how can I possibly have another head but Him whose image I am? For if I am the image of the Creator, there is no room in me for another head. But wherefore "ought the woman to have power over her head, because of the angels?"[5] If it is because "she was created for the man,"[6] and taken out of the man, according to the Creator's purpose, then in this way too has the apostle maintained the discipline of that God from whose institution he explains the reasons of His discipline. He adds: "Because of the angels."[7] What angels? In other words, whose angels? If he means the fallen angels of the Creator,[8] there is great propriety in his meaning. It is right that that face which was a snare to them should wear some mark of a humble guise and obscured beauty. If, however, the angels of the rival god are referred to, what fear is there for them? for not even Marcion's disciples, (to say nothing of his angels,) have

any desire for women. We have often shown before now, that the apostle classes heresies as evil[9] among "works of the flesh," and that he would have those persons accounted estimable[10] who shun heresies as an evil thing. In like manner, when treating of the gospel,[11] we have proved from the sacrament of the bread and the cup[12] the verity of the Lord's body and blood in opposition to Marcion's phantom; whilst throughout almost the whole of my work it has been contended that all mention of judicial attributes points conclusively to the Creator as to a God who judges. Now, on the subject of "spiritual gifts,"[13] I have to remark that these also were promised by the Creator through Christ; and I think that we may derive from this a very just conclusion that the bestowal of a gift is not the work of a god other than Him who is proved to have given the promise. Here is a prophecy of Isaiah "There shall come forth a rod out of the stem of Jesse, and a flower[14] shall spring up from his root; and upon Him shall rest the Spirit of the Lord." After which he enumerates the special gifts of the same "The spirit of wisdom and understanding, the spirit of counsel and might, the spirit of knowledge and of religion.[15] And with the fear of the Lord[16] shall the Spirit fill Him."[17] In this figure of *a flower* he shows that Christ was to arise out of the rod which sprang from the stem of Jesse; in other words, from the virgin of the race of David, the son of Jesse. In this Christ the whole *substantia* of the Spirit would have to rest, not meaning that it would be as it were some subsequent acquisition accruing to Him who was always, even before His incarnation, the Spirit of God;[18] so that you cannot argue from this that the prophecy has reference to that Christ who (as mere man of the race only of David) was to obtain Spirit of his God. (The prophet says,) on the contrary, that from the time when (the true Christ) should appear in the flesh as *the flower predicted,*[19] rising from the root of Jesse, there would have to rest upon Him the entire operation of the Spirit of grace, which, so far as the Jews were concerned, would cease and come to an end. This result the case itself shows; for after this time the Spirit

---

[1] Novatianem.
[2] 1 Cor. xi. 3.
[3] 1 Cor. xi. 7.
[4] Gen. i. 26.
[5] 1 Cor. xi. 10.
[6] 1 Cor. xi. 9.
[7] 1 Cor. xi. 10.
[8] See more concerning these in chap. xviii. of this book. Comp. Gen. vi. 1-4.
[9] 1 Cor. xi. 18, 19.
[10] Probabiles: "approved."
[11] See above, in book iv. chap. xl.
[12] Luke xxii. 15-20 and 1 Cor. xi. 23-29.
[13] 1 Cor. xii. 1.
[14] Flos: Sept. ἄνθος.
[15] Religionis: Sept. εὐσεβείας.
[16] Timor Dei: Sept. φόβος Θεοῦ.
[17] Isa. xi. 1-3.
[18] We have more than once shown that by Tertullian and other ancient fathers, *the divine nature* of Christ was frequently designated "Spirit."
[19] Floruisset in carne.

of the Creator never breathed amongst *them*. From Judah were taken away "the wise man, and the cunning artificer, and the counsellor, and the prophet;"[1] that so it might prove true that "the law and the prophets were until John."[2] Now hear how he declared that by Christ Himself, when returned to heaven, these spiritual gifts were to be sent: "He ascended up on high," that is, into heaven; "He led captivity captive," meaning death or slavery of man; "He gave gifts to the sons of men,"[3] that is, the gratuities, which we call *charismata*. He says specifically "*sons of men*,"[4] and not men promiscuously; thus exhibiting to us those who were the children of men truly so called, choice men, apostles. "For," says he, "I have begotten you through the gospel;"[5] and "Ye are my children, of whom I travail again in birth."[6] Now was absolutely fulfilled that promise of the Spirit which was given by the word of Joel: "In the last days will I pour out of my Spirit upon all flesh, and their sons and their daughters shall prophesy; and upon my servants and upon my handmaids will I pour out of my Spirit."[7] Since, then, the Creator promised the gift of His Spirit in the latter days; and since Christ has in these last days appeared as the dispenser of spiritual gifts (as the apostle says, "When the fulness of the time was come, God sent forth His Son;"[8] and again, "This I say, brethren, that the time is short'"[9]), it evidently follows in connection with this prediction of the last days, that this gift of the Spirit belongs to Him who is the Christ of the predicters. Now compare the Spirit's specific graces, as they are described by the apostle, and promised by the prophet Isaiah. "To one is given," says he, "by the Spirit the word of wisdom;" this we see at once is what Isaiah declared to be "the spirit of wisdom." "To another, the word of knowledge;" this will be "the (prophet's) spirit of understanding and counsel." "To another, faith by the same Spirit;" this will be "the spirit of religion and the fear of the Lord." "To another, the gifts of healing, and to another the working of miracles;" this will be "the spirit of might." "To another prophecy, to another discerning of spirits, to another divers kinds of tongues, to another the interpretation of tongues;" this will be "the spirit of knowl-edge."[10] See how the apostle agrees with the prophet both in making the distribution of the one Spirit, and in interpreting His special graces. This, too, I may confidently say: he who has likened the unity of our body throughout its manifold and divers members to the compacting together of the various gifts of the Spirit,[11] shows also that there is but one Lord of the human body and of the Holy Spirit. This Spirit, (according to the apostle's showing,)[12] meant not[13] that the service[14] of these gifts should be in the body,[15] nor did He place them in the human body); and on the subject of the superiority of love[16] above all these gifts, He even taught the apostle that it was the chief commandment,[17] just as Christ has shown it to be: "Thou shalt love the Lord with all thine heart and soul,[18] with all thy strength, and with all thy mind, and thy neighbour as thine own self."[19] When he mentions the fact that "*it is written in the law*,"[20] how that the Creator would speak with other tongues and other lips, whilst confirming indeed the gift of tongues by such a mention, he yet cannot be thought to have affirmed that the gift was that of another god by his reference to the Creator's prediction.[21] In precisely the same manner,[22] when enjoining on women silence in the church, that they speak not for the mere sake[23] of learning[24] (although that even they have the right of prophesying, he has already shown[25] when he covers the woman that prophesies with a veil), he goes to the law for his sanction that woman should be under obedience.[26] Now this law, let me say once for all, he ought to have made no other acquaintance with, than to destroy it. But that we may now leave the subject of spiritual gifts, facts themselves will be enough to prove which of us acts rashly in claiming them for his God, and whether it is possible that they are opposed to our side, even if[27] the Creator promised them for His Christ who is not yet revealed, as being destined only for the Jews, to have their operations in His time, in His Christ, and among His people. Let Marcion

1 See Isa. iii. 2, 3.
2 Luke xvi. 16.
3 1 Cor. xii. 4–11 ; Eph. iv. 8, and Ps. lxviii. 18.
4 He argues from his own reading, *filiis hominum*.
5 1. Cor. iv. 15.
6 Gal. iv. 19.
7 Joel ii. 28, 29, applied by St. Peter, Acts ii. 17, 18.
8 Gal. iv. 4.
9 1 Cor. vii. 29. [The verse filled out by the translator.]
10 Comp. 1 Cor. xii. 8–11 and Isa. xi. 1–3.
11 1 Cor. xii. 12–30, compared with Eph. iv. 16.
12 This seems to be the force of the subjunctive verb *noluerit*.
13 Noluerit.
14 Meritum.
15 They are *spiritual* gifts, not endowments of body.
16 De dilectione præferenda.
17 Compare 1 Cor. xii. 31, xiii. 1, 13.
18 Totis præcordiis.
19 Luke x. 27.
20 "Here, as in John x. 34, xii. 34, xv. 25, '*the law*' is used for the Old Testament generally, instead of being, as usual, confined to the Pentateuch. The passage is from Isa. xxviii. 11 " (Dean Stanley, *On the Corinthians, in loc.*).
21 1 Cor. xiv. 21.
22 Æque.
23 Duntaxat gratia.
24 1 Cor. xiv. 34, 35.
25 1 Cor. xi. 5, 6. [See Kaye, p. 228.]
26 1 Cor. xiv. 34, where Gen. iii. 16 is referred to.
27 Et si: These words introduce the Marcionite theory.

then exhibit, as gifts of his god, some prophets, such as have not spoken by human sense, but with the Spirit of God, such as have both predicted things to come, and have made manifest[1] the secrets of the heart;[2] let him produce a psalm, a vision, a prayer[3]—only let it be by the Spirit,[4] in an ecstasy, that is, in a rapture,[5] whenever an interpretation of tongues has occurred to him; let him show to me also, that any woman of boastful tongue[6] in his community has ever prophesied from amongst those specially holy sisters of his. Now all these signs (of spiritual gifts) are forthcoming from my side without any difficulty, and they agree, too, with the rules, and the dispensations, and the instructions of the Creator; therefore without doubt the Christ, and the Spirit, and the apostle, belong severally[7] to my God. Here, then, is my frank avowal for any one who cares to require it.

CHAP. IX.—THE DOCTRINE OF THE RESURRECTION. THE BODY WILL RISE AGAIN. CHRIST'S JUDICIAL CHARACTER. JEWISH PERVERSIONS OF PROPHECY EXPOSED AND CONFUTED. MESSIANIC PSALMS VINDICATED. JEWISH AND RATIONALISTIC INTERPRETATIONS ON THIS POINT SIMILAR. JESUS—NOT HEZEKIAH OR SOLOMON—THE SUBJECT OF THESE PROPHECIES IN THE PSALMS. NONE BUT HE IS THE CHRIST OF THE OLD AND THE NEW TESTAMENTS.

Meanwhile the Marcionite will exhibit nothing of this kind; he is by this time afraid to say which side has the better right to a Christ who is not yet revealed. Just as my Christ is to be expected,[8] who was predicted from the beginning, so his Christ therefore has no existence, as not having been *announced* from the beginning. Ours is a better faith, which believes in a future Christ, than the heretic's, which has none at all to believe in. Touching the resurrection of the dead,[9] let us first inquire how some persons then denied it. No doubt in the same way in which it is even now denied, since the resurrection of the flesh has at all times men to deny it. But many wise men claim for the soul a divine nature, and are confident of its undying destiny, and even the multitude worship the dead[10] in the

presumption which they boldly entertain that their souls survive. As for our bodies, however, it is manifest that they perish either at once by fire or the wild beasts,[11] or even when most carefully kept by length of time. When, therefore, the apostle refutes those who deny the resurrection of the flesh, he indeed defends, in opposition to them, the precise matter of their denial, that is, the resurrection of the body. You have the whole answer wrapped up in this.[12] All the rest is superfluous. Now in this very point, which is called the resurrection of the dead, it is requisite that the proper force of the words should be accurately maintained.[13] The word *dead* expresses simply what has lost the vital principle,[14] by means of which it used to live. Now the body is that which loses life, and as the result of losing it becomes dead. To the *body*, therefore, the term dead is only suitable. Moreover, as resurrection accrues to what is dead, and dead is a term applicable only to a body, therefore the body alone has a resurrection incidental to it. So again the word Resurrection, or (*rising again*), embraces only that which has fallen down. "To rise," indeed, can be predicated of that which has never fallen down, but had already been always lying down. But "to rise *again*" is predicable only of that which has fallen down; because it is by rising *again*, in consequence of its having fallen down, that it is said to have *re*-risen.[15] For the syllable RE always implies iteration (or happening *again*). We say, therefore, that the body falls to the ground by death, as indeed facts themselves show, in accordance with the law of God. For to the body it was said, ("Till thou return to the ground, for out of it wast thou taken; for) dust thou art, and unto dust shalt thou return."[16] That, therefore, which came from the ground shall return to the ground. Now that which falls down returns to the ground; and that rises again which falls down. "Since by man came death, by man came also the resurrection."[17] Here in the word *man*, who consists of bodily substance, as we have often shown already, is presented to me the body of Christ. But if we are all so made alive in Christ, as we die in Adam, it follows of necessity that we are made alive in Christ as a bodily substance, since we died in Adam as a bodily substance. The similarity, indeed, is not complete, unless our revival[18] in Christ concur in identity

---

[1] Traduxerint.
[2] 1 Cor. xiv. 25.
[3] 1 Cor. xiv. 26.
[4] Duntaxat spiritalem: These words refer to the previous ones, "not spoken by human sense, but with the Spirit of God." [Of course here is a touch of his *fanaticism*; but, he bases it on (1 Cor. xiv.) a mere question of fact: had these *charismata* ceased?]
[5] Amentia.
[6] Magnidicam.
[7] Erit.
[8] He here argues, as it will be readily observed, from the Marcionite theory alluded to, near the end of the last chapter.
[9] 1 Cor. xv. 12.
[10] See his treatise, *De Resur. Carnis*, chap. i. (Oehler).
[11] An allusion to the deaths of martyrs.

[12] Compendio.
[13] Defendi.
[14] Animam.
[15] The reader will readily see how the English fails to complete the illustration with the ease of the Latin, "*surgere*," "*iterum surgere*," "*resurgere*."
[16] Gen. iii. 19. ["Was not said unto the Soul —says our own Longfellow, in corresponding words.]
[17] 1 Cor. xv. 21.
[18] Vivificatio.

of substance with our mortality[1] in Adam. But at this point[2] (the apostle) has made a parenthetical statement[3] concerning Christ, which, bearing as it does on our present discussion, must not pass unnoticed. For the resurrection of the body will receive all the better proof, in proportion as I shall succeed in showing that Christ belongs to that God who is believed to have provided this resurrection of the flesh in His dispensation. When he says, "For He must reign, till He hath put all enemies under His feet,"[4] we can see at once[5] from this statement that he speaks of a God of vengeance, and therefore of Him who made the following promise to Christ: "Sit Thou at my right hand, until I make Thine enemies Thy footstool. The rod of Thy strength shall the Lord send forth from Sion, and He shall rule along with Thee in the midst of Thine enemies."[6] It is necessary for me to lay claim to those Scriptures which the Jews endeavour to deprive us of, and to show that they sustain my view. Now they say that this Psalm[7] was a chant in honour of Hezekiah,[8] because "he went up to the house of the Lord,"[9] and God turned back and removed his enemies. Therefore, (as they further hold,) those other words, "Before the morning star did I beget thee from the womb,"[10] are applicable to Hezekiah, and to the birth of Hezekiah. We on our side[11] have published Gospels (to the credibility of which we have to thank[12] them[13]

[1] Mortificatio.
[2] Adhuc.
[3] Interposuit aliquid.
[4] 1 Cor. xv. 25, 27.
[5] Jam quidem.
[6] Ps. cx. 1, 2, and viii. 6.
[7] Ps. cx.
[8] In Ezechiam cecinisse.
[9] 2 Kings xix.14 ; but the words are, " quia is sederit ad dexteram templi," a sentence which occurs neither in the LXX. nor the original.
[10] Tertullian, as usual, argues from the *Septuagint*, which in the latter clause of Ps. cx. 3 has ἐκ γαστρὸς πρὸ ἑωσφόρου ἐγέννησά σε ; and so the *Vulgate* version has it. This Psalm has been variously applied by the Jews. Raschi (or Rabbi Sol. Jarchi) thinks it is most suitable to *Abraham*, and possibly to *David*, in which latter view D. Kimchi agrees with him. Others find in *Solomon* the best application ; but more frequently is *Hezekiah* thought to be the subject of the Psalm, as Tertullian observes. Justin Martyr (in *Dial. cum Tryph.*) also notices this application of the Psalm. But Tertullian in the next sentence appears to recognize the sounder opinion of the *older* Jews, who saw in this Ps. cx. a prediction of MESSIAH. This opinion occurs in the Jerusalem Talmud, in the tract *Berachoth*, 5. Amongst the *more recent* Jews who also hold the sounder view, may be mentioned Rabbi Saadias Gaon, on Dan. vii. 13, and R. Moses Hadarsan (singularly enough quoted by Raschi in another part of his commentary (Gen. xxxv. 8), with others who are mentioned by Wetstein, *On the New Testament*, Matt. xxii. 44. *Modern* Jews, such as Moses Mendelsohn, reject the Messianic sense ; and they are followed by the commentators of the Rationalist school amongst ourselves and in Germany. J. Olshausen, after Hitzig, comes down in his interpretation of the Psalm as late as the Maccabees, and sees a suitable accomplishment of its words in the honours heaped upon *Jonathan* by Alexander son of Antiochus Epiphanes (see 1 Macc. x. 20). For the refutation of so inadequate a commentary, the reader is referred to Delitzsch on Ps. cx. The variations of opinion, however, in this school, are as remarkable as the fluctuations of the Jewish writers. The latest work on the Psalms which has appeared amongst us (*Psalms, chronologically arranged*, by four Friends), after Ewald, places the *accomplishment* of Ps. cx. in what may be allowed to have been its *occasion*—David's victories over the neighboring heathen.   [11] Nos.

for having given some confirmation, indeed, already in so great a subject[14]); and these declare that the Lord was born *at night*, that so it might be "before the morning star," as is evident both from the star especially, and from the testimony of the angel, who at night announced to the shepherds that Christ had at that moment been born,[15] and again from the place of the birth, for it is towards night that persons arrive at the (eastern) "inn." Perhaps, too, there was a mystic purpose in Christ's being born at night, destined, as He was, to be the light of the truth amidst the dark shadows of ignorance. Nor, again, would God have said, "I have begotten Thee," except to His true Son. For although He says of all the people (Israel), "I have begotten[16] children,"[17] yet He added not "from the womb." Now, why should He have added so superfluously this phrase "from the womb" (as if there could be any doubt about any one's having been born from the womb), unless the Holy Ghost had wished the words to be with especial care[18] understood of Christ? "I have begotten Thee from the womb," that is to say, *from a womb only*, without a man's seed, making it a condition of a fleshly body[19] that it should come out of a womb. What is here added (in the Psalm), "Thou art a priest for ever,"[20] relates to (Christ) Himself. Hezekiah was no priest; and even if he had been one, he would not have been a priest *for ever*. "After the order," says He, "of Melchizedek." Now what had Hezekiah to do with Melchizedek, the priest of the most high God, and him uncircumcised too, who blessed the circumcised Abraham, after receiving from him the offering of tithes? To Christ, however, "the order of Melchizedek" will be very suitable; for Christ is the proper and legitimate High Priest of God. He is the Pontiff of the priesthood of the uncircumcision, constituted such, even then, for the Gentiles, by whom He was to be more fully received, although at His last coming He will favour with His acceptance and blessing the circumcision also, even the race of Abraham, which by and by is to acknowledge Him. Well, then, there is also another Psalm, which begins with these words: "Give Thy judgments, O God, to the King," that is, to Christ who was to come as King, "and Thy righteousness unto the King's son,"[21] that is, to Christ's people; for His

[12] Debemus.
[13] Istos: that is, the Jews (Rigalt.).
[14] Utique jam in tanto opere.
[15] Natum esse quum maxime.
[16] Generavi : Sept. ἐγέννησα.
[17] Isa. i. 2.
[18] Curiosius.
[19] Deputans carni ; a note against *Docetism*.
[20] Ps. cx. 4.   [21] Ps. lxxii. 1.

sons are they who are born again in Him. But it will here be said that this Psalm has reference to Solomon. However, will not those portions of the Psalm which apply to Christ alone, be enough to teach us that all the rest, too, relates to Christ, and not to Solomon? "He shall come down," says He, "like rain upon a fleece,[1] and like dropping showers upon the earth,"[2] describing His descent from heaven to the flesh as gentle and unobserved.[3] Solomon, however, if he had indeed any descent at all, came not down like a shower, because he descended not from heaven. But I will set before you more literal points.[4] "He shall have dominion," says the Psalmist, "from sea to sea, and from the river unto the ends of the earth."[5] To Christ alone was this given; whilst Solomon reigned over only the moderately-sized kingdom of Judah. "Yea, all kings shall fall down before Him." Whom, indeed, shall they all thus worship, except Christ? "All nations shall serve Him."[6] To whom shall all thus do homage, but Christ? "His name shall endure for ever." Whose name has this eternity of fame, but Christ's? "Longer than the sun shall His name remain," for longer than the sun shall be the Word of God, even Christ. "And in Him shall all nations be blessed."[7] In Solomon was no nation blessed; in Christ every nation. And what if the Psalm proves Him to be even God? "They shall call Him blessed."[8] (On what ground?) Because "blessed is the Lord God of Israel, who only doeth wonderful things."[9] "Blessed also is His glorious name, and with His glory shall all the earth be filled."[10] On the contrary, Solomon (as I make bold to affirm) lost even the glory which he had from God, seduced by his love of women even into idolatry. And thus, the statement which occurs in about the middle of this Psalm, "His enemies shall lick the dust"[11] (of course, as having been, (to use the apostle's phrase,) "put under His feet"[12]), will bear upon the very object which I had in view, when I both introduced the Psalm, and insisted on my opinion of its sense,—namely, that I might demonstrate both the glory of His kingdom and the subjection of His enemies in pursu-

ance of the Creator's own plans, with the view of laying down[13] this conclusion, that none but He can be believed to be *the Christ* of the Creator.

CHAP. X.—DOCTRINE OF THE RESURRECTION OF THE BODY, CONTINUED. HOW ARE THE DEAD RAISED? AND WITH WHAT BODY DO THEY COME? THESE QUESTIONS ANSWERED IN SUCH A SENSE AS TO MAINTAIN THE TRUTH OF THE RAISED BODY, AGAINST MARCION. CHRIST AS THE SECOND ADAM CONNECTED WITH THE CREATOR OF THE FIRST MAN. LET US BEAR THE IMAGE OF THE HEAVENLY. THE TRIUMPH OVER DEATH IN ACCORDANCE WITH THE PROPHETS. HOSEA AND ST. PAUL COMPARED.

Let us now return to the resurrection, to the defence of which against heretics of all sorts we have given indeed sufficient attention in another work of ours.[14] But we will not be wanting (in some defence of the doctrine) even here, in consideration of such persons as are ignorant of that little treatise. "What," asks he, "shall they do who are baptized for the dead, if the dead rise not?"[15] Now, never mind[16] that practice, (whatever it may have been.) The *Februarian* lustrations[17] will perhaps[18] answer him (quite as well), by praying for the dead.[19] Do not then suppose that the apostle here indicates some new *god* as the author and advocate of this (baptism for the dead. His only aim in alluding to it was) that he might all the more firmly insist upon the resurrection of the body, in proportion as they who were vainly baptized for the dead resorted to the practice from their belief of *such* a resurrection. We have the apostle in another passage defining "but one baptism."[20] To be "baptized for the dead" therefore means, in fact, to be baptized for the body;[21] for, as we have shown, it is the

[1] Super vellus: so Sept. ἐπὶ πόκον.
[2] Ps. lxxii. 6.
[3] Similarly the Rabbis Saadias Gaon and Hadarsan, above mentioned in our note, beautifully applied to *Messiah's* placid birth, "without a human father," the figures of Ps. cx. 3, "womb of the morning," "dew of thy birth."
[4] Simpliciora.
[5] Ps. lxx. 8.
[6] Ps. lxx. 11.
[7] Ps. lxx. 17.
[8] Ps. lxx. 17.
[9] Ps. lxx. 18.
[10] Ps. lxx. 19.
[11] Ps. lxx. 9.
[12] 1 Cor. xv. 25, 27.
29

[13] Consecuturus.
[14] He refers to his *De Resurrect. Carnis.* See chap. xlviii.
[15] 1 Cor. xv. 29.
[16] Viderit.
[17] "Kalendæ Februariæ. The great expiation or lustration, celebrated at Rome in the month which received its name from the festival, is described by Ovid, *Fasti*, book ii., lines 19–28, and 267–452, in which latter passage the same feast is called *Lupercalia.* Of course as the rites were held on the 15th of the month, the word *kalendæ* has here not its more usual meaning (Paley's edition of the *Fasti*, pp. 52–76). Ochler refers also to Macrobius, *Saturn.* i. 13; Cicero, *De Legibus*, ii. 21; Plutarch, *Numa*, p. 132. He well remarks (note *in loc.*), that Tertullian, by intimating that the heathen rites of the *Februa* will afford quite as satisfactory an answer to the apostle's question, as the Christian superstition alluded to, not only means no authorization of the said superstition for himself, but expresses his belief that St. Paul's only object was to gather some evidence for the great doctrine of the resurrection from the faith which underlay the practice alluded to. In this respect, however, the heathen festival would afford a much less pointed illustration; for though it was indeed a lustration for the dead, περὶ νεκρῶν, and had for its object their happiness and welfare, it went no further than a vague notion of an indefinite immortality, and it touched not the recovery of the body. There is therefore force in Tertullian's *si forte.*
[18] Si forte.
[19] τῷ εὔχεσθαι ὑπὲρ τῶν νεκρῶν (Rigalt.).
[20] Eph. iv. 5.
[21] Pro corporibus.

body which becomes *dead*. What, then, shall they do who are baptized for the body,[1] if the body[2] rises not again? We stand, then, on firm ground (when we say) that[3] the next question which the apostle has⋅ discussed equally relates to the body. But "some man will say, 'How are the dead raised up? With what body do they come?'"[4] Having established the doctrine of the resurrection which was denied, it was natural[5] to discuss what would be the sort of body (in the resurrection), of which no one had an idea. On this point we have other opponents with whom to engage. For Marcion does not in any wise admit the resurrection of the flesh, and it is only the salvation of the soul which he promises; consequently the question which he raises is not concerning *the sort* of body, but the very *substance* thereof. Notwithstanding,[6] he is most plainly refuted even from what the apostle advances respecting the quality of the body, in answer to those who ask, "How are the dead raised up? with what body do they come?" For as he treated of the sort of *body*, he of course *ipso facto* proclaimed in the argument that it was a *body* which would rise again. Indeed, since he proposes as his examples "wheat grain, or some other grain, to which God giveth a body, such as it hath pleased Him;"[7] since also he says, that "to every seed is its own body;"[8] that, consequently,[9] "there is one kind of flesh of men, whilst there is another of beasts, and (another) of birds; that there are also celestial bodies and bodies terrestrial; and that there is one glory of the sun, and another glory of the moon, and another glory of the stars"[10]—does he not therefore intimate that there is to be[11] a resurrection of the flesh or body, which he illustrates by fleshly and corporeal samples? Does he not also guarantee that the resurrection shall be accomplished by that God from whom proceed all the (creatures which have served him for) examples? "So also," says he, "is the resurrection of the dead."[12] How? Just as the grain, which is sown a body, springs up a body. This sowing of the body he called the dissolving thereof in the ground, "because it is sown in corruption," (but "is raised) to honour and power."[13] Now, just as in the case of the

grain, so here: to Him will belong the work in the revival of the body, who ordered the process in the dissolution thereof. If, however, you remove the body from the resurrection which you submitted to the dissolution, what becomes of the diversity in the issue? Likewise, "although it is sown a natural body, it is raised a spiritual body."[14] Now, although the natural principle of life[15] and the spirit have each a body proper to itself, so that the "natural body" may fairly be taken[16] to signify the soul,[17] and "the spiritual body" the spirit, yet that is no reason for supposing[18] the apostle to say that the soul is to become spirit in the resurrection, but that *the body* (which, as being born along with the soul, and as retaining its life by means of the soul,[19] admits of being called animal (or *natural*[20]) *will become spiritual*, since it rises through the Spirit to an eternal life. In short, since it is not the soul, but the flesh which is "sown in corruption," when it turns to decay in the ground, it follows that (after such dissolution) the soul is no longer the natural body, but the flesh, which was the natural body, (is the subject of the future change), forasmuch as of a natural body it is made a spiritual body, as he says further down, "That was not first which is spiritual."[21] For to this effect he just before remarked of Christ Himself: "The first man Adam was made a living soul, the last Adam was made a quickening spirit."[22] Our heretic, however, in the excess of his folly, being unwilling that the statement should remain in this shape, altered "last Adam" into "last Lord;"[23] because he feared, of course, that if he allowed the Lord to be the last (or second) Adam, we should contend that Christ, being the second Adam, must needs belong to that God who owned also the first Adam. But the falsification is transparent. For why is there a first Adam, unless it be that there is also a second Adam? For things are not classed together unless they be severally alike, and have an identity of either name, or substance, or origin.[24] Now, although among things which are even individually diverse, one must be first and another last, yet they must have one author. If, however, the author be a different

[1] Eph. iv. 5.
[2] Corpora.
[3] Ut, with the subjunctive verb *induxerit*.
[4] 1 Cor. xv. 35.
[5] Consequens erat.
[6] Porro.
[7] 1 Cor. xv. 37, 38.
[8] 1 Cor. xv. 38.
[9] Ut.
[10] 1 Cor. xv. 39–41
[11] Portendit.
[12] 1 Cor. xv. 42.
[13] 1 Cor. xv. 42, 43.
[14] 1 Cor. xv. 44.
[15] Anima: we will call it *soul* in the context.
[16] Possit videri.
[17] Animam.
[18] Non ideo.
[19] Animam.
[20] Animale. The terseness of his argument, by his use of the same radical terms *Anima* and *Animale*, is lost in the English. [See Cap. 15 *infra*. Also, Kaye p. 180. St. Augustine seems to tolerate our author's views of a corporal spirit in his treatise *de Hæresibus*.]
[21] 1 Cor. xv. 46.
[22] 1 Cor. xv. 45.
[23] ὁ ἔσχατος Ἀδάμ into ὁ ἔσχατος Κύριος.
[24] Vel auctoris.

one, he himself indeed may be called the last. But the thing which he introduces is the first, and that only can be the last, which is like this first in nature.[1] It is, however, not like the first in nature, when it is not the work of the same author. In like manner (the heretic) will be refuted also with the word "man:" "The first man is of the earth, earthy; the second man is the Lord from heaven."[2] Now, since the first was a *man*, how can there be a second, unless he is a *man* also? Or, else, if the second is "Lord," was the first "Lord" also?[3] It is, however, quite enough for me, that in his Gospel he admits the Son of man to be both Christ and Man; so that he will not be able to deny Him (in this passage), in the "Adam" *and* the "man" (of the apostle). What follows will also be too much for him. For when the apostle says, "As is the earthy," that is, *man*, "such also are they that are earthy"— men again, of course; "therefore as is the heavenly," meaning the Man, from heaven, "such are the men also that are heavenly."[4] For he could not possibly have opposed to earthly *men* any heavenly beings that were not *men* also; his object being the more accurately to distinguish their state and expectation by using this name in common for them both. For in respect of their present state and their future expectation he calls men earthly and heavenly, still reserving their parity of name, according as they are reckoned (as to their ultimate condition[5]) in Adam or in Christ. Therefore, when exhorting them to cherish the hope of heaven, he says: "As we have borne the image of the earthy, so let us also bear the image of the heavenly,"[6]—language which relates not to any condition of resurrection life, but to the rule of the present time. He says, *Let us bear*, as a precept; not *We shall bear*, in the sense of a promise—wishing us to walk even as he himself was walking, and to put off the likeness of the earthly, that is, of the old man, in the works of the flesh. For what are this next words? "Now this I say, brethren, that flesh and blood cannot inherit the king-dom of God."[7] He means the works of the flesh and blood, which, in his Epistle to the Galatians, deprive men of the kingdom of God.[8] In other passages also he is accustomed to put the natural condition instead of the works that are done therein, as when he says, that "they who are in the flesh cannot please God."[9] Now, when shall we be able to please God except whilst we are in this flesh? There is, I imagine, no other time wherein a man can work. If, however, whilst we are even naturally living in the flesh, we yet eschew the deeds of the flesh, then we shall not be in the flesh; since, although we are not absent from the substance of the flesh, we are notwithstanding strangers to the sin thereof. Now, since in the word *flesh* we are enjoined to put off, not the substance, but the works of the flesh, therefore in the use of the same word the kingdom of God is denied to the works of the flesh, not to the substance thereof. For not that is condemned in which evil is done, but only the evil which is done in it. To administer poison is a crime, but the cup in which it is given is not guilty. So the body is the vessel of the works of the flesh, whilst the soul which is within it mixes the poison of a wicked act. How then is it, that the soul, which is the real author of works of the flesh, shall attain to[10] the king-dom of God, after the deeds done in the body have been atoned for, whilst the body, which was nothing but (the soul's) ministering agent, must remain in condemnation? Is the cup to be punished, but the poisoner to escape? Not that we indeed claim the kingdom of God for the flesh: all we do is, to assert a resur-rection for the substance thereof, as the gate of the kingdom through which it is entered. But the resurrection is one thing, and the kingdom is another. The resurrection is first, and afterwards the kingdom. We say, there-fore, that the flesh rises again, but that when changed it obtains the kingdom. "For the dead shall be raised incorruptible," even those who had been corruptible when their bodies fell into decay; "and we shall be changed, in a moment, in the twinkling of an eye."[11] For this corruptible"—and as he spake, the apostle seemingly pointed to his own flesh—"must put on incorruption, and this mortal must put on immortality,"[12] in order, indeed, that it may be rendered a fit substance for the kingdom of God. "For we shall be like the angels."[13] This will be the

---

[1] Par.
[2] 1 Cor. xv. 47.
[3] Marcion seems to have changed *man* into *Lord*, or rather to have omitted the ἄνθρωπος of the second clause, letting the verse run thus : ὁ πρῶτος ἄνθρωπος ἐκ γῆς χοϊκός, ὁ δεύτερος Κύριος ἐξ οὐρανοῦ. Anything to cut off all connection with the Creator.
[4] The οἱ ἐπουράνιοι, the "*de cœlo homines*," of this ver. 48 are Christ's risen people ; comp. Phil. iii. 20, 21 (Alford).
[5] Secundum exitum.
[6] 1 Cor. xv. 49. T. argues from the reading φορέσωμεν (instead of φορέσομεν), which indeed was had by many of the fathers, and (what is still more important) is found in the *Codex Sinaiticus.* We add the critical note of Dean Alford on this reading: "ACDFKL rel latt copt goth, Theodotus, Basil, Cæsarius, Cyril, Macarius, Methodius (who prefixes ἵνα), Chrysostom, Epiphanius, Ps. Athan-asius, Damascene, Irenæus (int), Tertullian, Cyprian, Hilary, Jerome." Alford retains the usual φορέσομεν, on the strength chiefly of the *Codex Vaticanus.*

[7] 1 Cor. xv. 50.
[8] Gal. v. 19–21.
[9] Rom. viii. 8.
[10] Merebitur.
[11] 1 Cor. xv. 52.
[12] 1 Cor. xv. 53.
[13] Matt. xxii. 30 and Luke xx. 36.

perfect change of our flesh—only after its resurrection.[1] Now if, on the contrary,[2] there is to be no flesh, how then shall it put on incorruption and immortality? Having then become something else by its change, it will obtain the kingdom of God, no longer the (old) flesh and blood, but the body which God shall have given it. Rightly then does the apostle declare, "Flesh and blood cannot inherit the kingdom of God;"[3] for this (honour) does he ascribe to the changed condition[4] which ensues on the resurrection. Since, therefore, shall then be accomplished the word which was written by the Creator, "O death, where is thy victory"—or thy struggle?[5] "O death, where is thy sting?"[6] —written, I say, by the Creator, for He wrote them by His prophet[7]—to Him will belong the gift, that is, the kingdom, who proclaimed the word which is to be accomplished in the kingdom. And to none other God does he tell us that "thanks" are due, for having enabled us to achieve "the victory" even over death, than to Him from whom he received the very expression[8] of the exulting and triumphant challenge to the mortal foe.

CHAP. XI.—THE SECOND EPISTLE TO THE CORINTHIANS. THE CREATOR THE FATHER OF MERCIES. SHOWN TO BE SUCH IN THE OLD TESTAMENT, AND ALSO IN CHRIST. THE NEWNESS OF THE NEW TESTAMENT. THE VEIL OF OBDURATE BLINDNESS UPON ISRAEL, NOT REPREHENSIBLE ON MARCION'S PRINCIPLES. THE JEWS GUILTY IN REJECTING THE CHRIST OF THE CREATOR. SATAN, THE GOD OF THIS WORLD. THE TREASURE IN EARTHEN VESSELS EXPLAINED AGAINST MARCION. THE CREATOR'S RELATION TO THESE VESSELS, I.E. OUR BODIES.

If, owing to the fault of human error, the word God has become a common name (since in the world there are said and believed to be "gods many"[9]), yet "the blessed God," (who is "the Father) of our Lord Jesus Christ,"[10] will be understood to be no other God than the Creator, who both blessed all things (that He had made), as you find in Genesis,[11] and is Himself "blessed by all things," as Daniel tells us.[12] Now, if the title

of Father may be claimed for (Marcion's) sterile god, how much more for the Creator? To none other than Him is it suitable, who is also "the Father of mercies,"[13] and (in the prophets) has been described as "full of compassion, and gracious, and plenteous in mercy."[14] In Jonah you find the signal act of His mercy, which He showed to the praying Ninevites.[15] How inflexible was He at the tears of Hezekiah![16] How ready to forgive Ahab, the husband of Jezebel, the blood of Naboth, when he deprecated His anger.[17] How prompt in pardoning David on his confession of his sin[18]—preferring, indeed, the sinner's repentance to his death, of course because of His gracious attribute of mercy.[19] Now, if Marcion's god has exhibited or proclaimed any such thing as this, I will allow him to be "the Father of mercies." Since, however, he ascribes to him this title only from the time he has been revealed, as if he were the father of mercies from the time only when he began to liberate the human race, then we on our side, too,[20] adopt the same precise date of his alleged revelation; but it is that we may deny him! It is then not competent to him to ascribe any quality to his god, whom indeed he only promulged by the fact of such an ascription; for only if it were previously evident that his god had an existence, could he be permitted to ascribe an attribute to him. The ascribed attribute is only an accident; but accidents[21] are preceded by the statement of the thing itself of which they are predicated, especially when another claims the attribute which is ascribed to him who has not been previously shown to exist. Our denial of his existence will be all the more peremptory, because of the fact that the attribute which is alleged in proof of it belongs to that God who has been already revealed. Therefore "the New Testament" will appertain to none other than Him who promised it—if not "its letter, yet its spirit;"[22] and herein will lie its newness. Indeed, He who had engraved its letter in stones is the same as He who had said of its spirit, "I will pour out of my Spirit upon all flesh."[23] Even if "the letter killeth, yet the Spirit giveth life;"[24] and both belong to Him who says: "I kill, and I make alive; I wound,

[1] Sed resuscitatæ.
[2] Aut si.
[3] 1 Cor. xv. 50.
[4] Demutatione.
[5] Suggested by the ἰσχυσας of Sept. in Isa. xxv. 8.
[6] 1 Cor. xv. 55.
[7] Isa. xxv. 8 and (especially) Hos. xiii. 14.
[8] The Septuagint version of the passage in Hosea is, ποῦ ἡ δίκη σου, θάνατε; ποῦ τὸ κέντρον σου, ᾅδη, which is very like the form of the apostrophe in 1 Cor. xv. 55.
[9] 1 Cor. viii. 5.
[10] 2 Cor. i. 3.
[11] Gen. i. 22.
[12] Dan. ii. 19, 20, iii. 28, 29, iv. 34, 37.

[13] 2 Cor. i. 3.
[14] Ps. lxxxvi. 15, cxii. 4, cxlv. 8; Jonah iv. 2.
[15] Jonah iii. 8.
[16] 2 Kings xx. 3, 5.
[17] 1 Kings xxi. 27, 29.
[18] 2 Sam. xii. 13.
[19] Ezek. xxxiii. 11.
[20] Atquin et nos.
[21] The Contingent qualities in logic.
[22] 2 Cor. iii. 6.
[23] Joel ii. 28.
[24] 2 Cor. iii. 6.

and I heal."[1] We have already made good the Creator's claim to this twofold character of judgment and goodness[2]—"killing in the letter" through the law, and "quickening in the Spirit" through the Gospel. Now these attributes, however different they be, cannot possibly make two gods; for they have already (in the prevenient dispensation of the Old Testament) been found to meet in One.[3] He alludes to Moses' veil, covered with which "his face could not be stedfastly seen by the children of Israel."[4] Since he did this to maintain the superiority of the glory of the New Testament, which is permanent in its glory, over that of the Old, "which was to be done away,"[5] this fact gives support to my belief which exalts the Gospel above the law; and you must look well to it that it does not even more than this. For only *there* is superiority possible where was previously the thing over which superiority can be affirmed. But then he says, "But their minds were blinded"[6]—of the world; certainly not the Creator's mind, but the minds of the people which are in the world.[7] Of Israel he says, Even unto this day the same veil is upon their heart;"[8] showing that the veil which was on the face of Moses was a figure of the veil which is on the heart of the nation still; because even now Moses is not seen by them in heart, just as he was not then seen by them in eye. But what concern has Paul with the veil which still obscures Moses from their view, if the Christ of the Creator, whom Moses predicted, is not yet come? How are the hearts of the Jews represented as still covered and veiled, if the predictions of Moses relating to Christ, in whom it was their duty to believe through him, are as yet unfulfilled? What had the apostle of a strange Christ to complain of, if the Jews failed in understanding the mysterious announcements of their own God, unless the veil which was upon their hearts had reference to that blindness which concealed from their eyes the Christ of Moses? Then, again, the words which follow, But when it shall turn to the Lord, the evil shall be taken away,"[9] properly refer to the Jew, over whose gaze Moses' veil is spread, to the effect that, when he is turned to the faith of Christ, he will understand how Moses spoke of Christ. But how shall the veil of the Creator be taken away by the

Christ of another god, whose mysteries the Creator could not possibly have veiled—unknown mysteries, as they were of an unknown god? So he says that "we now with open face" (meaning *the candour* of the heart, which in the Jews had been covered with a veil), ".' beholding Christ, are changed into the same image, from that glory" (wherewith Moses was transfigured as by the glory of the Lord) "to another glory."[10] By thus setting forth the glory which illumined the person of Moses from his interview with God, and the veil which concealed the same from the infirmity of the people, and by superinducing thereupon the revelation and the glory of the Spirit in the person of Christ—"even as," to use his words, "by the Spirit of the Lord"[11]—he testifies that the whole Mosaic system[12] was a figure of Christ, of whom the Jews indeed were ignorant, but who is known to us Christians. We are quite aware that some passages are open to ambiguity, from the way in which they are read, or else from their punctuation, when there is room for these two causes of ambiguity. The latter method has been adopted by Marcion, by reading the passage which follows, "in whom the God of this world,"[13] as if it described the Creator as the God of this world, in order that he may, by these words, imply that there is another God for the other world. We, however, say that the passage ought to be punctuated with a comma after God, to this effect: "In whom God hath blinded the eyes of the unbelievers of this world."[14] "In whom" means the Jewish unbelievers, from some of whom the gospel is still hidden under Moses' veil. Now it is these whom God had threatened for "loving Him indeed with the lip, whilst their heart was far from Him,"[15] in these angry words: "Ye shall hear with your ears, and not understand; and see with your eyes, but not perceive;"[16] and, "If ye will nòt believe, ye shall not understand;"[17] and again, "I will take away the wisdom of their wise men,

---

[1] Deut. xxxii. 39.
[2] See above in book ii. [cap. xi. p. 306.]
[3] Apud unum recenseri prævenerunt.
[4] 2 Cor. iii. 7, 13.
[5] 2 Cor. iii. 7, 8.
[6] Obtunsi : "blunted," 2 Cor. iii. 14.
[7] He seems to have read the clause as applying to the *world*, but St. Paul certainly refers only to the obdurate Jews. The text is : "Sed obtunsi sunt sensus mundi.
[8] 2 Cor. iii. 15.
[9] 2 Cor. iii. 16.

[10] 2 Cor. iii. 18.
[11] 2 Cor. iii. 18, but T.'s reading is "tanquam a domino spirituum" ("even as by the Lord of the Spirits," probably the sevenfold Spirit). The original is, καθάπερ ἀπὸ Κυρίου Πνεύματος, "by the Lord the Spirit."
[12] Moysi ordinem totum.
[13] 2 Cor. iv. 4.
[14] He would stop off the phrase τοῦ αἰῶνος τούτου from ὁ Θεὸς, and remove it to the end of the sentence as a qualification of τῶν ἀπίστων. He adds another interpretation just afterwards, which, we need not say, is both more consistent with the sense of the passage and with the *consensus* of Christian writers of all ages, although "it is historically curious" (as Dean Alford has remarked) "that Irenæus (*Hæres.* iv. 48, Origen, Tertullian (v. 11, *contra Marcion*), Chrysostom, Œcumenius, Theodoret, Theophylact, all repudiate, in their zeal against the Marcionites and the Manichæans, the grammatical rendering, and take τῶν ἀπίστων τοῦ αἰῶνος τούτου together" (Greek Testament, *in loc.*). [I have corrected Alford's reference to Tertullian which he makes B. iv. 11.]
[15] Isa. xxix. 13.
[16] Isa. vi. 10 (only adapted).
[17] Isa. vii. 9, Sept.

and bring to nought[1] the understanding of their prudent ones." But these words, of course, He did not pronounce against them for concealing the gospel of the unknown God. At any rate, if there is a God of this world,[2] He blinds the heart of the unbelievers of this world, because they have not of their own accord recognised His Christ, who ought to be understood from His Scriptures.[3] Content with my advantage, I can willingly refrain from noticing to any greater length[4] this point of ambiguous punctuation, so as not to give my adversary any advantage,[5] indeed, I might have wholly omitted the discussion. A simpler answer I shall find ready to hand in interpreting "the god of this world" of the devil, who once said, as the prophet describes him: "I will be like the Most High; I will exalt my throne in the clouds."[6] The whole superstition, indeed, of this world has got into his hands,[7] so that he blinds effectually the hearts of unbelievers, and of none more than the apostate Marcion's. Now he did not observe how much this clause of the sentence made against him: "For God, who commanded the light to shine out of darkness, hath shined in our hearts, to (give) the light of the knowledge (of His glory) in the face of (Jesus) Christ."[8] Now who was it that said, "Let there be light?"[9] And who was it that said to Christ concerning giving light to the world: "I have set Thee as a light to the Gentiles"[10]—to them, that is, "who sit in darkness and in the shadow of death?"[11] (None else, surely, than He), to whom the Spirit in the Psalm answers, in His foresight of the future, saying, "The light of Thy countenance, O Lord, hath been displayed upon us."[12] Now the countenance (or person[13]) of the Lord here is Christ. Wherefore the apostle said above: Christ, who is the image of God."[14] Since Christ, then, is the person of the Creator, who said, "Let there be light," it follows that Christ and the apostles, and the gospel, and the veil, and Moses—nay, the whole of the dispensations—belong to the God who is the Creator of this world, according to the testimony of the clause (above adverted to), and certainly not to him who never said, "Let there be light." I here pass over discussion about another epistle, which we hold to have been written to the Ephesians, but the heretics to the Laodiceans. In it he tells[15] them to remember, that at the time when they were Gentiles they were without Christ, aliens from (the commonwealth of) Israel, without intercourse, without the covenants and any hope of promise, nay, without God, even in his own world,[16] as the Creator thereof. Since therefore he said, that the Gentiles were without God, whilst their god was the devil, not the Creator, it is clear that he must be understood to be the lord of this world, whom the Gentiles received as their god—not the Creator, of whom they were in ignorance. But how does it happen, that "the treasure which we have in these earthen vessels of ours"[17] should not be regarded as belonging to the God who owns the vessels? Now since God's glory is, that so great a treasure is contained in earthen vessels, and since these earthen vessels are of the Creator's make, it follows that the glory is the Creator's; nay, since these vessels of His smack so much of the excellency of the power of God, that power itself must be His also! Indeed, all these things have been consigned to the said "earthen vessels" for the very purpose that His excellence might be manifested forth. Henceforth, then, the rival god will have no claim to the glory, and consequently none to the power. Rather, dishonour and weakness will acrue to him, because the earthen vessels with which he had nothing to do have received all the excellency! Well, then, if it be in these very earthen vessels that he tells us we have to endure so great sufferings,[18] in which we bear about with us the very dying of God,[19] (Marcion's) god is really ungrateful and unjust, if he does not mean to restore this same substance of ours at the resurrection, wherein so much has been endured in loyalty to him, in which Christ's very death is borne about, wherein too the excellency of his power is treasured.[20] For he gives prominence to the statement, "That the life also of Christ may be manifested in our body,"[21] as a contrast to the preceding, that His death is borne about in our body. Now of *what life of Christ* does he here speak? Of that which we are now living? Then how is it, that in the words which follow he exhorts us not to the things

---

[1] Sept. κρύψω, "will hide."
[2] Said concessively, in reference to M.'s position above mentioned.
[3] Marcion's "God of this world" being the God of the Old Testament.
[4] Hactenus : pro *non amplius* (Oehler) tractasse.
[5] "A fuller criticism on this slight matter might give his opponent the advantage, as apparently betraying a penury of weightier and more certain arguments" (Oehler).
[6] Isa. xiv. 14.
[7] Mancipata est illi.
[8] 2 Cor. iv. 6.
[9] Gen. i. 3.
[10] Isa. xlix. 6 (Sept. quoted in Acts xiii. 47).
[11] Isa. ix. 2 and Matt. iv. 16.
[12] Ps. iv. 7 (Sept.).
[13] Persona : the πρόσωπον of the Septuagint.
[14] 2 Cor. iv. 4.

[15] Ait.
[16] Eph. ii. 12.
[17] 2 Cor. iv. 7.
[18] 2 Cor. iv. 8–12.
[19] Oehler, after Fr. Junius, defends the reading "mortificationem *dei*," instead of Domini, in reference to Marcion, who seems to have so corrupted the reading.
[20] 2 Cor. iv. 10.
[21] 2 Cor. iv. 10.

which are seen and are temporal, but to those which are not seen and are eternal[1]—in other words, not to the present, but to the future? But if it be of the future life of Christ that he speaks, intimating that it is to be made manifest in our body,[2] then he has clearly predicted the resurrection of the flesh.[3] He says, too, that "our outward man perishes,"[4] not meaning by an eternal perdition after death, but by labours and sufferings, in reference to which he previously said, "For which cause we will not faint."[5] Now, when he adds of "the inward man" also, that it "is renewed day by day," he demonstrates both issues here—the wasting away of the body by the wear and tear[6] of its trials, and the renewal of the soul[7] by its contemplation of the promises.

CHAP. XII.—THE ETERNAL HOME IN HEAVEN. BEAUTIFUL EXPOSITION BY TERTULLIAN OF THE APOSTLE'S CONSOLATORY TEACHING AGAINST THE FEAR OF DEATH, SO APT TO ARISE UNDER ANTI-CHRISTIAN OPPRESSION. THE JUDGMENT-SEAT OF CHRIST—THE IDEA, ANTI-MARCION-ITE. PARADISE. JUDICIAL CHARACTERISTICS OF CHRIST WHICH ARE INCONSISTENT WITH THE HERETICAL VIEWS ABOUT HIM; THE APOSTLE'S SHARPNESS, OR SEVERITY, SHOWS HIM TO BE A FIT PREACHER OF THE CREATOR'S CHRIST.

As to the house of this our earthly dwelling-place, when he says that "we have an eternal home in heaven, not made with hands,"[8] he by no means would imply that, because it was built by the Creator's hand, it must perish in a perpetual dissolution after death.[9] He treats of this subject in order to offer consolation against the fear of death and the dread of this very dissolution, as is even more manifest from what follows, when he adds, that "in this tabernacle of our earthly body we do groan, earnestly desiring to be clothed upon with the vesture which is from heaven,[10] if so be, that having been unclothed,[11] we shall not be found naked;" in other words, shall regain that of which we have been divested, even our body. And again he says: "We that are in this tabernacle do groan, not as if we were oppressed[12] with an unwillingness to be unclothed, but

(we wish) to be clothed upon."[13] He here says expressly, what he touched but lightly[14] in his first epistle, (where he wrote:) "The dead shall be raised incorruptible" (meaning those who had undergone mortality), "and we shall be changed" (whom God shall find to be yet in the flesh).[15] Both those shall be raised incorruptible, because they shall regain their body—and that a renewed one, from which shall come their incorruptibility; and these also shall, in the crisis of the last moment, and from their instantaneous death, whilst encountering the oppressions of antichrist, undergo a change, obtaining therein not so much a divestiture of body as "a clothing upon" with the vesture which is from heaven.[16] So that whilst these shall put on over their (changed) body this heavenly raiment, the dead also shall for their part[17] recover their body, over which they too have a supervesture to put on, even the incorruption of heaven;[18] because of these it was that he said: "This corruptible must put on incorruption, and this mortal must put on immortality."[19] The one put on this (heavenly) apparel,[20] when they recover their bodies; the others put it on as a supervesture,[21] when they indeed hardly lose them (in the suddenness of their change). It was accordingly not without good reason that he described them as "not wishing indeed to be unclothed," but (rather as wanting) "to be clothed upon;"[22] in other words, as wishing not to undergo death, but to be surprised into life,[23] "that this mortal (body) might be swallowed up of life,"[24] by being rescued from death in the supervesture of its changed state. This is why he shows us how much better it is for us not to be sorry, if we should be surprised by death, and tells us that we even hold of God "the earnest of His Spirit"[25] (pledged as it were thereby to have "the clothing upon," which is the object of our hope), and that "so long as we are in the flesh, we are absent from the Lord;"[26] moreover, that we ought on this account to prefer[27] "rather to be absent from the body and to be present with the Lord,"[28] and so to be ready to meet even death with joy. In this

[1] 2 Cor. iv. 16–18.
[2] 2 Cor. iv. 11.
[3] 2 Cor. iv. 14.
[4] 2 Cor. iv. 16.
[5] 2 Cor. iv. 16.
[6] Vexatione.
[7] Animi.
[8] 2 Cor. v. 1.
[9] As Marcion would have men believe.
[10] 2 Cor. v. 2, 3.
[11] Despoliati.
[12] Gravemur.
[13] 2 Cor. v. 4.
[14] Strinxit.
[15] 1 Cor. xv. 52.
[16] Superinduti magis quod de cœlo quam exuti corpus.
[17] Utique et mortui.
[18] De cœlo.
[19] 1 Cor. xv. 53.
[20] Induunt.
[21] Superinduunt.
[22] 2 Cor. v. 4.
[23] Vita præveniri.
[24] 2 Cor. v. 4; and see his treatise, De Resurrect. Carnis, cap. xlii.
[25] 2 Cor. v. 5.
[26] 2 Cor. v. 6.
[27] Boni ducere.
[28] 2 Cor. v. 8.

view it is that he informs us how "we must all appear before the judgment-seat of Christ, that every one may receive the things done in his body, according as he hath done either good or bad."[1] Since, however, there is then to be a retribution according to men's merits, how will any be able to reckon with[2] God? But by mentioning both the judgment-seat and the distinction between works good and bad, he sets before us a Judge who is to award both sentences,[3] and has thereby affirmed that all will have to be present at the tribunal in their bodies. For it will be impossible to pass sentence except on the body, for what has been done in the body. God would be unjust, if any one were not punished or else rewarded in that very condition,[4] wherein the merit was itself achieved. "If therefore any man be in Christ, he is a new creature; old things are passed away; behold, all things are become new;"[5] and so is accomplished the prophecy of Isaiah.[6] When also he (in a later passage) enjoins us "to cleanse ourselves from all filthiness of flesh and blood"[7] (since this substance enters not the kingdom of God[8]); when, again, he "espouses the church as a chaste virgin to Christ,"[9] a spouse to a spouse in very deed,[10] an image cannot be combined and compared with what is opposed to the real nature of the thing (with which it is compared). So, when he designates "false apostles, deceitful workers transforming themselves" into likenesses of himself,"[11] of course by their hypocrisy, he charges them with the guilt of disorderly conversation, rather than of false doctrine.[12] The contrariety, therefore, was one of conduct, not of gods.[13] If "Satan himself, too, is transformed into an angel of light,"[14] such an assertion must not be used to the prejudice of the Creator. The Creator is not an angel, but God. Into a god of light, and not an angel of light, must Satan then have been said to be transformed, if he did not mean to call him "the angel," which both we and Marcion know him to be. *On Paradise* is the title of a treatise of ours, in which is discussed all that the subject admits of.[15] I shall here simply wonder, in connec-

tion with this matter, whether a god who has no dispensation of any kind on earth could possibly have a paradise to call his own—without perchance availing himself of the paradise of the Creator, to use it as he does His world—much in the character of a mendicant.[16] And yet of the removal of a man from earth to heaven we have an instance afforded us by the Creator in Elijah.[17] But what will excite my surprise still more is the case (next supposed by Marcion), that a God so good and gracious, and so averse to blows and cruelty, should have suborned the angel Satan—not his own either, but the Creator's—"to buffet" the apostle,[18] and then to have refused his request, when thrice entreated to liberate him! It would seem, therefore, that Marcion's god imitates the Creator's conduct, who is an enemy to the proud, even "putting down the mighty from their seats."[19] Is he then the same God as He who gave Satan power over the person of Job that his "strength might be made perfect in weakness?"[20] How is it that the censurer of the Galatians[21] still retains the very formula of the law: "In the mouth of two or three witnesses shall every word be established?"[22] How again is it that he threatens sinners "that he will not spare" them[23]—he, the preacher of a most gentle god? Yea, he even declares that "the Lord hath given to him the power of using sharpness in their presence!"[24] Deny now, O heretic, (at your cost,) that your god is an object to be feared, when his apostle was for making himself so formidable!

CHAP. XIII.—THE EPISTLE TO THE ROMANS. ST. PAUL CANNOT HELP USING PHRASES WHICH BESPEAK THE JUSTICE OF GOD, EVEN WHEN HE IS EULOGIZING THE MERCIES OF THE GOSPEL. MARCION PARTICULARLY HARD IN HIS MUTILATION OF THIS EPISTLE. YET OUR AUTHOR ARGUES ON COMMON GROUND. THE JUDGMENT AT LAST WILL BE IN ACCORDANCE WITH THE GOSPEL. THE JUSTIFIED BY FAITH EXHORTED TO HAVE PEACE WITH GOD. THE ADMINISTRATION OF THE OLD AND THE NEW DISPENSATIONS IN ONE AND THE SAME HAND.

Since my little work is approaching its ter-

[1] 2 Cor. v. 10.
[2] Deputari cum.
[3] 2 Cor. v. 10.
[4] Per id, per quod, i. e., corpus.
[5] 2 Cor. v. 17.
[6] Isa. xliii. 19.
[7] His reading of 2 Cor. vii. 1.
[8] 1 Cor. xv. 50.
[9] 2 Cor. xi. 2.
[10] Utique ut sponsam sponso.
[11] 2 Cor. xi. 13.
[12] Prædicationis adulteratæ.
[13] A reference to Marcion's other god of the New Testament, of which he tortured the epistles (and this passage among them) to produce the evidence.
[14] 2 Cor. xi. 14.

[15] Patitur. The work here referred to is not extant ; it is, however, referred to in the *De Anima*, c. lv.
[16] Precario: "that which one must beg for." See, however, above, book iv. chap. xxii. p. 384, note 8, for a different turn to this word.
[17] 2 Kings ii. 11.
[18] 2 Cor. xii. 7, 8.
[19] 1 Sam ii. 7, 8 ; Ps. cxlvii. 6 ; Luke i. 52.
[20] Job i. 12 and 2 Cor. xii. 9.
[21] Gal. i. 6–9.
[22] 2 Cor. xiii. 1.
[23] 2 Cor. xiii. 2.
[24] 2 Cor. xiii. 10.

mination,[1] I must treat but briefly the points which still occur, whilst those which have so often turned up must be put aside. I regret still to have to contend about the law—after I have so often proved that its replacement (by the gospel)[2] affords no argument for another god, predicted as it was indeed in Christ, and in the Creator's own plans[3] ordained for *His* Christ. (But I must revert to that discussion) so far as (the apostle leads me, for) this very epistle looks very much as if it abrogated[4] the law. We have, however, often shown before now that God is declared by the apostle to be a Judge; and that in the Judge is implied an Avenger; and in the Avenger, the Creator. And so in the passage where he says: "I am not ashamed of the gospel (of Christ): for it is the power of God unto salvation to every one that believeth; to the Jew first, and also to the Greek; for therein is the righteousness of God revealed from faith to faith,"[5] he undoubtedly ascribes both the gospel and salvation to Him whom (in accordance with our heretic's own distinction) I have called the *just* God, not the *good* one. It is He who removes (men) from confidence in the law to faith in the gospel—that is to say,[6] His own law and His own gospel. When, again, he declares that "the wrath (of God) is revealed from heaven against all ungodliness and unrighteousness of men, who hold the truth in unrighteousness,"[7] (I ask) the wrath of what God? Of the Creator certainly. The truth, therefore, will be His, whose is also the wrath, which has to be revealed to avenge the truth. Likewise, when adding, "We are sure that the judgment of God is according to truth,"[8] he both vindicated that wrath from which comes this judgment for the truth, and at the same time afforded another proof that the truth emanates from the same God whose wrath he attested, by witnessing to His judgment. *Marcion's averment* is quite a different matter, that[9] the Creator in anger avenges Himself on the truth of the rival god which had been detained in unrighteousness. But what serious gaps Marcion has made in this epistle especially, by withdrawing whole passages at his will, will be clear from the unmutilated text of our own copy.[10] It is enough for my purpose to accept in evidence of its truth what he has seen fit to leave unerased, strange instances as they

are also of his negligence and blindness. If, then, God will judge the secrets of men—both of those who have sinned in the law, and of those who have sinned without law (inasmuch as they who know not the law yet do by nature the things contained in the law)[11]—surely the God who shall judge is He to whom belong both the law, and that nature which is the rule[12] to them who know not the law. But how will He conduct this judgment? "According to my gospel," says (*the apostle*), "by (*Jesus*) Christ."[13] So that both the gospel and Christ must be His, to whom appertain the law and the nature which are to be vindicated by the gospel and Christ—even at that judgment of God which, as he previously said, was to be according to truth.[14] The wrath, therefore, which is to vindicate truth, can only be revealed from heaven by the God of wrath;[15] so that this sentence, which is quite in accordance with that previous one wherein the judgment is declared to be the Creator's,[16] cannot possibly be ascribed to another god who is not a judge, and is incapable of wrath. It is only consistent in Him amongst whose attributes are found the judgment and the wrath of which I am speaking, and to whom of necessity must also appertain the *media* whereby these attributes are to be carried into effect, even the gospel and Christ. Hence his invective against the transgressors of the law, who teach that men should not steal, and yet practise theft themselves.[17] (This invective he utters) in perfect homage[18] to the law of God, not as if he meant to censure the Creator Himself with having commanded[19] a fraud to be practised against the Egyptians to get their gold and silver at the very time when He was forbidding men to steal,[20]—adopting such methods as they are apt (shamelessly) to charge upon Him in other particulars also. Are we then to suppose[21] that the apostle abstained through fear from openly calumniating God, from whom notwithstanding He did not hesitate to withdraw men? Well, but he had gone so far in his censure of the Jews, as to point against them the denunciation of the prophet, "Through you the name of God is blasphemed (among the Gentiles)."[22] But how absurd, that he should himself blaspheme Him for blaspheming whom he upbraids them

---

[1] Profligatur.
[2] Concessionem.
[3] Apud Creatorem.
[4] Excludere.
[5] Rom. i. 16, 17
[6] Utique.
[7] Rom. i. 18.
[8] Rom. ii. 2.
[9] Aliud est si.
[10] Nostri instrumenti.

[11] Rom. ii. 12-16.
[12] Instar legis: "which is as good as a law to them," etc.
[13] Rom. ii. 16.
[14] Rom. ii. 2.
[15] Rom. i. 18.
[16] See the remarks on verses 16 and 17 above.
[17] Rom. ii. 21.
[18] Ut homo.
[19] Ex. iii. 22.
[20] Ex. xx. 15; see above, book iv. chap. xxiv. p. 387.
[21] Scilicet verebatur.
[22] Rom. ii. 24.

as evil-doers ! He prefers even circumcision of heart to neglect of it in the flesh. Now it is quite within the purpose of the God of the law that circumcision should be that of the heart, not in the flesh; in the spirit, and not in the letter.[1] Since this is the circumcision recommended by Jeremiah: "Circumcise (yourselves to the Lord, and take away) the foreskins of your heart;"[2] and even of Moses: "Circumcise, therefore, the hardness of your heart,"[3]—the *Spirit* which circumcises the heart will proceed from Him who prescribed the *letter* also which clips[4] the flesh; and "the Jew which is one inwardly" will be a subject of the self-same God as he also is who is "a Jew outwardly;"[5] because the apostle would have preferred not to have mentioned a Jew at all, unless he were a servant of the God of the Jews. It was once[6] the law; now it is "the righteousness of God which is by the faith of (Jesus) Christ."[7] What means this distinction? Has your god been subserving the interests of the Creator's dispensation, by affording time to Him and to His law? Is the "*Now*" in the hands of Him to whom belonged the "*Then*"? Surely, then, the law was His, whose is now the righteousness of God. It is a distinction of dispensations, not of gods. He enjoins those who are justified by faith in Christ and not by the law to have peace with God.[8] With what God? Him whose enemies we have never, in any dispensation,[9] been? Or Him against whom we have rebelled, both in relation to His written law and His law of nature? Now, as peace is only possible towards Him with whom there once was war, we shall be both justified by Him, and to Him also will belong the Christ, in whom we are justified by faith, and through whom alone God's[10] enemies can ever be reduced to peace. "Moreover," says he, "the law entered, that

the offence might abound."[11] And wherefore this? "In order," he says, "that (where sin abounded), grace might much more abound."[12] Whose grace, if not of that God from whom also came the law? Unless it be, forsooth, that[13] the Creator intercalated His law for the mere purpose of[14] producing some employment for the grace of a rival god, an enemy to Himself (I had almost said, a god unknown to Him), "that as sin had" in His own dispensation[15] "reigned unto death, even so might grace reign through righteousness unto (eternal) life by Jesus Christ,"[16] His own antagonist! For this (I suppose it was, that) the law of the Creator had "concluded all under sin,"[17] and had brought in "all the world as guilty (before God)," and had "stopped every mouth,[18] so that none could glory through it, in order that grace might be maintained to the glory of the Christ, not of the Creator, but of Marcion! I may here anticipate a remark about the substance of Christ, in the prospect of a question which will now turn up. For he says that "we are dead to the law."[19] It may be contended that Christ's body is indeed a body, but not exactly[20] flesh. Now, whatever may be the substance, since he mentions "the body of Christ,"[21] whom he immediately after states to have been "raised from the dead,"[22] none other body can be understood than that of the flesh,[23] in respect of which the law was called (the law) of death.[24] But, behold, he bears testimony to the law, and excuses it on the ground of sin: "What shall we say, therefore? Is the law sin? God forbid."[25] Fie on you, Marcion. "God forbid!" (See how) the apostle recoils from all impeachment of the law. I, however, have no acquaintance with sin except through the law.[26] But how high an encomium of the law (do we obtain) from

---

[1] Rom. ii. 29.
[2] Jer. iv. 4.
[3] Deut. x. 16 (Sept.).
[4] Metens.
[5] Rom. ii. 28.
[6] Tunc.
[7] Rom. iii. 21, 22.
[8] Tertullian, by the word "*enjoins*" (monet), seems to have read the passage in Rom. v. 1 in the hortatory sense with ἔχωμεν, "*let us have* peace with God." If so, his authority must be added to that exceedingly strong MS. authority which Dean Alford (*Greek Test. in loc.*) regrets to find overpowering the received reading of ἔχομεν, "*we have*," etc. We subjoin Alford's critical note in support of the ἔχωμεν, which (with Lachmann) he yet admits into his more recent text: "AB (originally) CDKLfh (originally) m 17 latt (including F-lat); of the versions the older Syriac (Peschito) and Copt; of the fathers, Chrysostom, Cyril, Theodoret, Damascene, Theophylact, Œcumenius, Rufinus, Pelagius, Orosius, Augustine, Cassiodorus," before whom I would insert Tertullian, and the *Codex Sinaiticus*, in its original state; although, like its great rival in authority, the *Codex Vaticanus*, it afterwards received the reading ἔχομεν. These second readings of these MSS., and the later Syriac (Philoxenian), with Epiphanius, Didymus, and Sedulius, are the almost only authorities quoted for the received text. [Dr. H. over-estimates the "rival" *Codices*.]
[9] Nusquam.
[10] Ejus.

[11] Rom. v. 20.
[12] Rom. v. 20.
[13] Nisi si: an ironical particle.
[14] Ideo ut.
[15] Apud ipsum.
[16] Rom. v. 21.
[17] Gal. iii. 22.
[18] Rom. iii. 19.
[19] Rom. vii. 4, also Gal. ii. 19. This (although a quotation) is here a Marcionite argument; but there is no need to suppose, with Pamelius, that Marcion tampers with Rom. vi. 2. Oehler also supposes that this is the passage quoted. But no doubt it is a correct quotation from the *seventh chapter*, as we have indicated.
[20] Statim (or, perhaps, in respect of the derivation,) "firmly" or "stedfastly."
[21] Ejus.
[22] Rom. vii. 4.
[23] In this argument Tertullian applies with good effect the terms "flesh" and "body," making the first (which he elsewhere calls the "*terrena materia*" of our nature (*ad Uxor.* i. 4)) the proof of the reality of the second, in opposition to Marcion's *Docetic* error. "Σὰρξ is not = σῶμα, but as in John i. 14, the *material* of which man is in the body compounded" (Alford).
[24] Compare the first part of ver. 4 with vers. 5 and 6 and viii. 2, 3.
[25] Rom. vii. 7.
[26] This, which is really the second clause of Rom. vii. 7, seems to be here put as a Marcionite argument of disparagement to the law.

this fact, that by it there comes to light the latent presence of sin![1]   It was not the law, therefore, which led me astray, but "sin, taking occasion by the commandment."[2] Why then do you, (O Marcion,) impute to the God of the law what His apostle dares not impute even to the law itself? Nay, he adds a climax: "The law is holy, and its commandment just and good."[3]   Now if he thus reverences the Creator's law, I am at a loss to know how he can destroy the Creator Himself. Who can draw a distinction, and say that there are two gods, one just and the other good, when He ought to be believed to be both one and the other, whose commandment is both "*just* and *good*?" Then, again, when affirming the law to be "spiritual"[4] he thereby implies that it is prophetic, and that it is figurative. Now from even this circumstance I am bound to conclude that Christ was predicted by the law but figuratively, so that indeed He could not be recognised by all the Jews.

CHAP. XIV.—THE DIVINE POWER SHOWN IN CHRIST'S INCARNATION.   MEANING OF ST. PAUL'S PHRASE.   LIKENESS OF SINFUL FLESH. NO DOCETISM IN IT.   RESURRECTION OF OUR REAL BODIES.   A WIDE CHASM MADE IN THE EPISTLE BY MARCION'S ERASURE.   WHEN THE JEWS ARE UPBRAIDED BY THE APOSTLE FOR THEIR MISCONDUCT TO GOD; INASMUCH AS THAT GOD WAS THE CREATOR, A PROOF IS IN FACT GIVEN THAT ST. PAUL'S GOD WAS THE CREATOR.   THE PRECEPTS AT THE END OF THE EPISTLE, WHICH MARCION ALLOWED, SHOWN TO BE IN EXACT ACCORDANCE WITH THE CREATOR'S SCRIPTURES.

If the Father "sent His Son in the likeness of sinful flesh,"[5] it must not therefore be said that the flesh which He seemed to have was but a phantom.   For he in a previous verse ascribed sin to the flesh, and made it out to be "the law of sin dwelling in his members," and "warring against the law of the mind."[6] On this account, therefore, (does he mean to say that) the Son was sent in the likeness of sinful flesh, that He might redeem this sinful flesh by a like substance, even a fleshly one, which bare a resemblance to sinful flesh, although it was itself free from sin.   Now this will be the very perfection of divine power to effect the salvation (of man) in a nature like his own.[7]   For it would be no great matter if the Spirit of God remedied the flesh; but when

a flesh, which is the very copy[8] of the sinning substance—itself flesh also—only without sin, (effects the remedy, then doubtless it is a great thing).   The *likeness*, therefore, will have reference to the quality[9] of the sinfulness, and not to any falsity[10] of the substance. Because he would not have added the attribute "sinful,"[11] if he meant the "likeness" to be so predicated of the substance as to deny the verity thereof; in that case he would only have used the word "flesh," and omitted the "sinful."   But inasmuch as he has put the two together, and said "sinful flesh," (or "flesh of sin,")[12] he has both affirmed the substance, that is, the flesh and referred the *likeness* to the fault of the substance, that is, to its sin.   But even suppose[13] that the likeness was predicated of the substance, the truth of the said substance will not be thereby denied. Why then *call* the true *substance like?* Because it is indeed true, only not of a seed of like condition[14] with our own; but true still, as being of a nature[15] not really unlike ours.[16] And again, in contrary things there is no likeness.   Thus the likeness of flesh would not be called *spirit*, because flesh is not susceptible of any likeness to spirit; but it would be called *phantom*, if it seemed to be that which it really was not.   It is, however, called *likeness*, since it is what it seems to be.   Now it is (what it seems to be), because it is on a par with the other thing (with which it is compared).[17]   But a phantom, which is merely such and nothing else,[18] is not a likeness. The apostle, however, himself here *comes to our aid; for*, while explaining in what sense he would not have us "live in the flesh,"

---

[1] Per quam liquit delictum latere: a playful paradox, in the manner of our author, between *liquere* and *latere.*
[2] Rom. vii. 8.
[3] Rom. vii. 13.
[4] Rom. vii. 14.
[5] Rom. viii. 3.
[6] Sensus νοός in Rom. vii. 23.
[7] Pari.

[8] Consimilis.
[9] Titulum.
[10] Mendacium.
[11] This vindication of these terms of the apostle from *Docetism* is important.   The word which our A.V. has translated *sinful* is a stronger term in the original.   It is not the adjective ἁμαρτωλοῦ, but the substantive ἁμαρτίας, amounting to "flesh of sin," *i.e.* (as Dean Alford interprets it) "the flesh whose attribute and character is *sin*."   "The words ἐν ὁμοιώματι σαρκὸς ἁμαρτίας, De Wette observes, appear almost to border on Docetism, but in reality contain a perfectly true and consistent sentiment; σὰρξ ἁμαρτίας; is flesh, or human nature, possessed with sin. . . . The likeness, predicated in Rom. viii. 3, must be referred not only to σάρξ, but also to the epithet τῆς ἁμαρτίας" (*Greek Testament, in loc.*).
[12] Carnis peccati.
[13] Puta nunc.
[14] Statu.
[15] Censu: perhaps "birth."   This word, which originally means the *censor's* registration, is by our author often used for *origo* and *natura*, because in the registers were inserted the birthdays and the parents' names (Oehler).
[16] It is better that we should give the original of this sentence. Its structure is characteristically difficult, although the general sense, as Oehler suggests, is clear enough: "Quia vera quidem, sed non ex semine de statu simili (similis, *Latinius* and *Junius* and *Semler*), sed vera de censu non vero dissimili (dissimilis, *the older reading* and *Semler's*)."   We add the note of Fr. Junius: "The meaning is, that Christ's flesh is true indeed, in what they call the identity of its *substance*, although not of its *origin* (ortus) and *qualities*—not of its origin, because not of a (father's) seed, as in the case of ourselves; not of qualities, because these have not in Him the like condition which they have in us."
[17] Dum alterius par est.
[18] Qua hoc tantum est.

although in the flesh—even by not living in the works of the flesh [1]—he shows that when he wrote the words, "Flesh and blood cannot inherit the kingdom of God," [2] it was not with the view of condemning the substance (of the flesh), but the works thereof; and because it is possible for these not to be committed by us whilst we are still in the flesh, they will therefore be properly chargeable, [3] not on the substance of the flesh, but on its conduct. Likewise, if "the body indeed is dead because of sin" (from which statement, we see that not the death of the soul is meant, but that of the body), "but the spirit is life because of righteousness," [4] *it follows that this life* accrues to that which incurred death because of sin, that is, *as we have just seen,* the body. Now *the body* [5] is only restored to him who had lost it; so that the resurrection of the dead implies the resurrection of their bodies. He accordingly subjoins: "He that raised up Christ from the dead, shall also quicken your mortal bodies." [6] In these words he both affirmed the resurrection of the flesh (without which nothing can rightly be called [7] body, nor can anything be properly regarded as mortal), and proved the bodily substance of Christ, inasmuch as our own mortal bodies will be quickened in precisely the same way as He was raised; and that was in no other way than in the body. I have here a very wide gulf of expunged Scripture to leap across; [8] however, I alight on the place where the apostle bears record of Israel "that they have a zeal of God"— their own God, of course—"but not according to knowledge. For," says he, "being ignorant of (the righteousness of) God, and going about to establish their own righteousness, they have not submitted themselves unto the righteousness of God; for Christ is the end of the law for righteousness to every one that believeth." [9] Hereupon we shall be confronted with an argument of the heretic, that the Jews were ignorant of the superior God, [10] since, in opposition to him, they set up their own righteousness—that is, the righteousness of their law—not receiving Christ, the end (or

finisher) of the law. But how then is it that he bears testimony to their zeal for their own God, if it is not in respect of the same God that he upbraids them for their ignorance? They were affected indeed with zeal for God, but it was not an intelligent zeal: they were, in fact, ignorant of Him, because they were ignorant of His dispensations by Christ, who was to bring about the consummation of the law; and in this way did they maintain their own righteousness in opposition to Him. But so does the Creator Himself testify to their ignorance concerning Him: "Israel hath not known me; my people have not understood me;" [11] and as to their preferring the establishment of their own righteousness, (the Creator again describes them as) "teaching for doctrines the commandments of men;" [12] moreover, as "having gathered themselves together against the Lord and against His Christ" [13]—from ignorance of Him, of course. Now nothing can be expounded of another god which is applicable to the Creator; otherwise the apostle would not have been just in reproaching the Jews with ignorance in respect of a god of whom they knew nothing. For where had been their sin, if they only maintained the righteousness of their own God against one of whom they were ignorant? But he exclaims: "O the depth of the riches and the wisdom of God; how unsearchable also are His ways!" [14] Whence this outburst of feeling? Surely from the recollection of the Scriptures, which he had been previously turning over, as well as from his contemplation of the mysteries which he had been setting forth above, in relation to the faith of Christ coming from the law. [15] If Marcion had an object in his erasures, [16] why does his apostle utter such an exclamation, because his god has no riches for him to contemplate? So poor and indigent was he, that he created nothing, predicted nothing—in short, possessed nothing; for it was into the world of another God that he descended. The truth is, the Creator's resources and riches, which once had been hidden, were now disclosed. For so had He promised: "I will give to them treasures which have been hidden, and which men have not seen will I open to them." [17] Hence, then, came the exclama-

---

[1] See Rom. viii. 5-13.
[2] 1 Cor. xv. 50.
[3] Non ad reatum substantiæ sed ad conversationis pertinebunt.
[4] Rom. viii. 10.
[5] Understand "*corpus*" (Oehler).
[6] Rom. viii. 11.
[7] Dici capit: *capit*, like the Greek ἐνδέχεται, means, "is capable or susceptible ; " often so in Tertullian.
[8] We do not know from either Tertullian or Epiphanius what mutilations Marcion made in this epistle. This particular gap did not extend further than from Rom. viii. 11 to x. 2. "However, we are informed by Origen (or rather Rufinus in his edition of Origen's commentary on this epistle, on xiv. 23) that Marcion omitted the last two chapters as spurious, ending this epistle of his *Apostolicon* with the 23d verse of chap. xiv. It is also observable that Tertullian quotes no passage from chaps. xv. xvi. in his confutation of Marcion from this epistle" (Lardner).
[9] Rom. x. 2-4.
[10] The god of the New Testament, according to Marcion.

[11] Isa. i. 3.
[12] Isa. xxix. 13 (Sept.)
[13] Ps. ii. 2.
[14] Rom. xi. 33.
[15] In fidem Christi ex lege venientem. By "the law" he means the Old Testament in general, and probably refers to Rom. x. 17.
[16] Rigaltus (after Fulvius Ursinus) read "*non erasit*," but with insufficient authority ; besides, the context shows that he was referring to the large erasure which he had already mentioned, so that the *non* is inadmissible. Marcion must, of course, be understood to have retained Rom. xi. 33 ; hence the argument in this sentence.
[17] Isa. xlv. 3.

tion, "O the depth of the riches and the wisdom of God!" For His treasures were now opening out. This is the purport of what Isaiah said, and of (the apostle's own) subsequent quotation of the self-same passage, of the prophet: "Who hath known the mind of the Lord? or who hath been His counsellor? Who hath first given to Him, and it shall be recompensed to him again?"[1] Now, (Marcion,) since you have expunged so much from the Scriptures, why did you retain these words, as if they too were not the Creator's words? But come now, let us see without mistake[2] the precepts of your new god: "Abhor that which is evil, and cleave to that which is good."[3] Well, is the precept different in the Creator's teaching? "Take away the evil from you, depart from it, and be doing good."[4] *Then again:* "Be kindly affectioned one to another with brotherly love."[5] Now is not this of the same import as: "Thou shalt love thy neighbour as thy self?"[6] (Again, your apostle says:) "Rejoicing in hope;"[7] that is, of God. *So says the Creator's Psalmist:* "It is better to hope in the Lord, than to hope even in princes."[8] "Patient in tribulation."[9] You have (this in) the Psalm: "The Lord hear thee in the day of tribulation."[10] "Bless, and curse not,"[11] (says your apostle.) But what better teacher of this will you find than Him who created all things, and blessed them? "Mind not high things, but condescend to men of low estate. Be not wise in your own conceits."[12] For against such a disposition Isaiah pronounces a woe.[13] "Recompense to no man evil for evil."[14] (Like unto which is the Creator's precept:) "Thou shalt not remember thy brother's evil against thee."[15] (Again:) "Avenge not yourselves;"[16] *for it is written,* "Vengeance is mine, I will repay, saith the Lord."[17] "Live peaceably with all men."[18] The retaliation of the law, therefore, permitted not retribution for an injury; it rather repressed any attempt thereat by the fear of a recompense. Very properly, then, did he sum up the entire teaching of the Creator in this precept of His: "Thou shalt love thy neighbour as thyself."[19] Now, if this is the recapitulation of the law from the very law itself, I am at a loss to know who is the God of the law. I fear He must be Marcion's god (after all).[20] If also the gospel of Christ is fulfilled in this same precept, but not the Creator's Christ, what is the use of our contending any longer whether Christ did or did not say, "I am not come to destroy the law, but to fulfil it?"[21] In vain has (our man of) Pontus laboured to deny this statement.[22] If the gospel has not fulfilled the law, then all I can say is,[23] the law has fulfilled the gospel. But it is well that in a *later* verse he threatens us with "the judgment-seat of Christ,"—the Judge, of course, and the Avenger, and therefore the Creator's (Christ). This *Creator,* too, however much he may preach up another god, he certainly sets forth for us as a Being to be served,[24] if he holds Him thus up as an object to be feared.

CHAP. XV.—THE FIRST EPISTLE TO THE THESSALONIANS. THE SHORTER EPISTLES PUNGENT IN SENSE AND VERY VALUABLE. ST. PAUL UPBRAIDS THE JEWS FOR THE DEATH FIRST OF THEIR PROPHETS AND THEN OF CHRIST. THIS A PRESUMPTION THAT BOTH CHRIST AND THE PROPHETS PERTAINED TO THE SAME GOD. THE LAW OF NATURE, WHICH IS IN FACT THE CREATOR'S DISCIPLINE, AND THE GOSPEL OF CHRIST BOTH ENJOIN CHASTITY. THE RESURRECTION PROVIDED FOR IN THE OLD TESTAMENT BY CHRIST. MAN'S COMPOUND NATURE.

I shall not be sorry to bestow attention on the shorter epistles also. Even in brief works there is much pungency.[25] The Jews had slain their prophets.[26] I may ask, What has this to do with the apostle of the rival god, one so amiable withal, who could hardly be said to condemn even the failings of his own people; and who, moreover, has himself some hand in making away with the same prophets

---

[1] Isa. xl. 13, quoted (according to the Sept.) by the apostle in Rom. xi. 34, 35.
[2] Plane : ironically.
[3] Rom. xii. 9.
[4] Ps. xxxiv. 14.
[5] Rom. xii. 10.
[6] Lev. xix. 18.
[7] Rom. xii. 12.
[8] Ps. cxviii. 9.
[9] Rom. xii. 12.
[10] Ps. xx. 1.
[11] Rom. xii. 12.
[12] Rom. xii. 16.
[13] Isa. v. 21.
[14] Rom. xii. 17.
[15] Lev. xix. 17, 18.
[16] Rom. xii. 19.
[17] Rom. xiii. 19, quoted from Deut. xxxii. 25.
[18] Rom. xii. 18.

[19] Rom. xiii. 9.
[20] Ironically said. He has been quoting all along from *Marcion's* text of St. Paul, turning its testimony against Marcion.
[21] Matt. v. 17.
[22] For although he rejected St. Matthew's Gospel, which contains the statement, he retained St. Paul's epistle, from which the statement is clearly proved.
[23] Ecce.
[24] Promerendum.
[25] Sapor. We have here a characteristic touch of his diligent and also intrepid spirit. Epiphanius says this short epistle "was so entirely corrupted by Marcion, that he had himself selected nothing from it whereon to found any refutations of him or of his doctrine." Tertullian, however, was of a different mind ; for he has made it evident, that though there were alterations made by Marcion, yet sufficient was left untouched by him to show the absurdity of his opinions. Epiphanius and Tertullian entertained, respectively, similar opinions of Marcion's treatment of the second epistle, which the latter discusses in the next chapter (Lardner).
[26] 1 Thess. ii. 15.

whom he is destroying? What injury did Israel commit against him in slaying those whom he too has reprobated, since he was the first to pass a hostile sentence on them? But *Israel* sinned aginst their own God. He upbraided their iniquity to whom the injured *God* pertains; and certainly he is anything but the adversary of the injured *Deity*. Else he would not have burdened them with the charge of killing even the Lord, in the words, "Who both killed the Lord *Jesus* and their own prophets," although (the pronoun) *their own* be an addition of the heretics.[1] Now, what was there so very acrimonious[2] in their killing Christ the proclaimer of the new god, after they had put to death also the prophets of their own god? The fact, however, of their having slain the Lord and His servants, is put as a case of climax.[3] Now, if it were the Christ of one god and the prophets of another god whom they slew, he would certainly have placed the impious crimes on the same level, instead of mentioning them in the way of a climax; but they did not admit of being put on the same level: the climax, therefore, was only possible[4] by the sin having been in fact committed against one and the same Lord in the two respective circumstances.[5] To one and the same Lord, then, belonged Christ and the prophets. What that "sanctification of ours" is, which he declares to be "the will of God," you may discover from the opposite conduct which he forbids. That we should "abstain from fornication," not from marriage; that every one "should know how to possess his vessel in honour."[6] In what way? "Not in the lust of concupiscence, even as the Gentiles."[7] Concupiscence, however, is not ascribed to marriage even among the Gentiles, but to extravagant, unnatural, and enormous sins.[8] The law of nature[9] is opposed to luxury as well as to grossness and uncleanness;[10] it does not forbid connubial intercourse, but concupiscence; and it takes care of[11] our vessel by the honourable estate of matrimony. This passage (of the apostle) I would treat in such a way as to maintain the superiority of the other and higher sanctity, preferring continence and virginity to marriage, but by no means pro-

hibiting the latter. For my hostility is directed against[12] those who are for destroying the God of marriage, not those who follow after chastity. He says that those who "remain unto the coming of Christ," along with "the dead in Christ, shall rise first," being "caught up in the clouds to meet the Lord in the air."[13] I find it was in their foresight of all this, that the heavenly intelligences gazed with admiration on "the Jerusalem which is above,"[14] and by the mouth of Isaiah said long ago: "Who are these that fly as clouds, and as doves with their young ones, unto me?"[15] Now, as Christ has prepared for us this ascension into heaven, He must be the Christ of whom Amos[16] spoke: "It is He who builds His ascent up to the heavens,"[17] even for Himself and His people. Now, from whom shall I expect (the fulfilment of) all this, except from Him whom I have heard give the promise thereof? What "spirit" does he forbid us to "quench," and what "prophesyings" to "despise?"[18] Not the Creator's spirit, nor the Creator's prophesyings, Marcion of course replies. For *he* has already quenched and despised the thing which he destroys, and is unable to forbid what he has despised.[19] It is then incumbent on Marcion now to display in his church that spirit of his god which must not be quenched, and the prophesyings which must not be despised. And since he has made such a display as he thinks fit, let him know that we shall challenge it whatever it may be to the rule[20] of the grace and power of the Spirit and the prophets—namely, to foretell the future, to reveal the secrets of the heart, and to explain mysteries. And when he shall have failed to produce and give proof of any such criterion, we will then on our side bring out both the Spirit and the prophecies of the Creator, which utter predictions according to His will. Thus it will be clearly seen of what the apostle spoke, even of those things which were to happen in the church of his God; and as long as He endures, so long also does His Spirit work, and so long are His promises repeated.[21] Come now, you who deny the salvation of the flesh, and who, whenever there occurs the specific mention of *body* in a case of this sort,[22] interpret it as meaning

---

[1] All the best MSS., including the *Codices Alex.*, *Vat.*, and *Sinait.*, omit the ἰδίους, as do Tertullian and Origen. Marcion has Chrysostom and the *received text*, followed by our A. V., with him.
[2] Amarum.
[3] Status exaggerationis.
[4] Ergo exaggerari non potuit nisi.
[5] Ex utroque titulo.
[6] 1 Thess. iv. 3, 4.
[7] 1 Thess. iv. 5.
[8] Portentuosis.
[9] The rule of Gentile life.
[10] We have here followed Oehler's reading, which is more intelligible than the four or five others given by him.
[11] Tractet.
[12] Retundo.
[13] 1 Thess. iv. 15-17.
[14] Gal. iv. 26.
[15] Isa. lx. 8.
[16] Oehler and Fr. Junius here read Amos, but all the other readings give *Hosea*; but see above, book iii. chap. xxiv., where Amos was read by all.
[17] Amos ix. 6.
[18] 1 Thess. v. 19, 20.
[19] Nihil fecit. This is precisely St. Paul's ἐξουθενεῖν, "to annihilate" (A.V. "*despise*"), in 1 Thess. v. 20.
[20] Formam.
[21] Celebratur.
[22] Si quando corpus in hujus modi prænominatur.

anything rather than the substance of the flesh, (tell me) how is it that the apostle has given certain distinct names to all (our faculties), and has comprised them all in one prayer for their safety, desiring that our " spirit and soul and body may be preserved blameless unto the coming of our Lord and Saviour (Jesus) Christ?"[1] Now he has here propounded the soul and the body as two several and distinct things.[2] For although the soul has a kind of body of a quality of its own,[3] just as the spirit has, yet as the soul and the body are distinctly named, the soul has its own peculiar appellation, not requiring the common designation of *body*. This is left for "the flesh," which having no proper name (in this passage), necessarily makes use of the common designation. Indeed, I see no other substance in man, after *spirit* and *soul*, to which the term *body* can be applied except "the flesh." This, therefore, I understand to be meant by the word "body"—as often as the latter is not specifically named. Much more do I so understand it in the present passage, where the flesh[4] is expressly called by the name "body."

CHAP. XVI.—THE SECOND EPISTLE TO THE THESSALONIANS. AN ABSURD ERASURE OF MARCION; ITS OBJECT TRANSPARENT. THE FINAL JUDGMENT ON THE HEATHEN AS WELL AS THE JEWS COULD NOT BE ADMINISTERED BY MARCION'S CHRIST. THE MAN OF SIN—WHAT? INCONSISTENCY OF MARCION'S VIEW. THE ANTICHRIST. THE GREAT EVENTS OF THE LAST APOSTASY WITHIN THE PROVIDENCE AND INTENTION OF THE CREATOR, WHOSE ARE ALL THINGS FROM THE BEGINNING. SIMILARITY OF THE PAULINE PRECEPTS WITH THOSE OF THE CREATOR.

We are obliged from time to time to recur to certain topics in order to affirm *truths* which are connected with them. We repeat then here, that as the Lord is by the apostle proclaimed[5] as the awarder of both weal and woe,[6] He must be either the Creator, or (as Marcion would be loth to admit) One like the Creator—"with whom it is a righteous thing to recompense tribulation to them who afflict us, and to ourselves, who are afflicted, rest, when the Lord Jesus shall be revealed as coming from heaven with the angels of His might and in flaming fire."[7] The heretic, however, has erased *the flaming fire*, no doubt that he might extinguish all traces herein of our own God. But the folly of the obliteration is clearly seen. For as the apostle declares that the Lord will come "to take vengeance on them that know not God and that obey not the gospel, who," he says, "shall be punished with everlasting destruction from the presence of the Lord, and from the glory of His power"[8] —it follows that, as He comes to inflict punishment, He must require "the flaming fire." Thus on this consideration too we must, notwithstanding Marcion's opposition, conclude that Christ belongs to a God who kindles the flames[9] (of vengeance), and therefore to the Creator, inasmuch as He takes vengeance on such as know not the Lord, that is, on the heathen. For he has mentioned separately "those who obey not the gospel *of our Lord Jesus Christ*,"[10] whether they be sinners among Christians or among Jews. Now, to inflict punishment on the heathen, who very likely have never heard of the Gospel, is not the function of that God who is naturally unknown, and who is revealed nowhere else than in the Gospel, and therefore cannot be known by all men.[11] The Creator, however, ought to be known even by (the light of) nature, for He may be understood from His works, and may thereby become the object of a more widely spread knowledge. To *Him*, therefore, does it appertain to punish such as know not God, for none ought to be ignorant of Him. In the (apostle's) phrase, "From the presence of the Lord, and from the glory of His power,"[12] he uses the words of Isaiah, who for the express reason makes the self-same Lord "arise to shake terribly the earth."[13] Well, but who is "the man of sin, the son of perdition," who must first be revealed before the Lord comes; "who opposeth and exalteth

---

[1] 1 Thess. v. 23. For a like application of this passage, see also our author's treatise, *De Resurrect. Carnis*, cap. xlvii. [Elucidation I.]
[2] It is remarkable that our author quotes this text of the *three* principles, in defence only of *two* of them. But he was strongly opposed to the idea of any absolute division between the *soul* and the *spirit*. A distinction between these united parts, he might, under limitations, have admitted ; but all idea of an actual separation and *division* he opposed and denied. See his *De Anima*, cap. x. St. Augustine more fully still maintained a similar opinion. See also *his De Anima*, iv. 32. Bp. Ellicott, in his interesting sermon *On the Threefold Nature of Man*, has given these references, and also a sketch of patristic opinion on this subject. The early fathers, Justin Martyr, Clement of Alex., Origen, as well as Didymus of Alex., Gregory Nyssen., and Basil, held distinctly the threefold nature. Our own divines, as is natural, are also divided in view. Bp. Bull, Hammond, and Jackson hold the *trichotomy*, as the triple nature is called ; others, like Bp. Butler, deny the possibility of dividing our immaterial nature into two parts. This variation of opinion seems to have still representatives among our most recent commentators: while Dean Alford holds the triplicity of our nature literally with St. Paul, Archdeacon Wordsworth seems to agree with Bp. Butler in regarding *soul* and *spirit* as component parts of one principle. See also Bp. Ellicott's *Destiny of the Creature*, sermon v. and notes.
[3] On this paradox, that souls are corporeal, see his treatise *De Anima*, v., and following chapters (Oehler). [See also cap. x. *supra*.]
[4] Quæ = caro.

[5] Circumferri.
[6] Utriusque meriti : " of both the eternal sentences."
[7] 2 Thess. i. 6-8.
[8] 2 Thess. i. 8, 9.
[9] Crematoris Dei.
[10] 2 Thess. i. 8.
[11] Non omnibus scibilis.
[12] 2 Thess. i. 9.
[13] Isa. ii. 19. The whole verse is to the point.

himself above all that is called God, or that is worshipped; who is to sit in the temple of God, and boast himself as being God?"[1]　According indeed to our view, he is Antichrist; as it is taught us in both the ancient and the new prophecies,[2] and *especially* by the Apostle John, who says that "already many false prophets are gone out into the world," the fore-runners of Antichrist, who deny that Christ is come in the flesh,[3] and do not acknowledge[4] Jesus (to be the Christ), meaning in God the Creator.　According, however, to Marcion's view, it is really hard to know whether He might not be (after all) the Creator's Christ; because according to him *He* is not yet come.　But whichsoever of the two it is, I want to know why he comes "in all power, and with lying signs and wonders?"[5] "Because," he says, "they received not the love of the truth, that they might be saved; for which cause God shall send them an instinct of delusion[6] (to believe a lie), that they all might be judged who believed not the truth, but had pleasure in unrighteousness."[7] If therefore he be Antichrist, (as we hold), and *comes* according to the Creator's purpose, it must be God the Creator who sends him to fasten in their error those who did not believe the truth, that they might be saved; *His* likewise must be the truth and the salvation, who avenges (the contempt of) them by sending error as their substitute[8]—that is, the Creator, to whom that very wrath is a fitting attribute, which deceives with a lie those who are not captivated with truth.　If, however, he is not Antichrist, as we suppose (him to be) then He is the Christ of the Creator, as Marcion will have it.　In this case how happens it that he[9] can suborn the Creator's Christ to avenge his truth?　But should he after all agree with us, that Antichrist is here meant, I must then likewise ask how it is that he finds Satan, an angel of the Creator, necessary to his purpose?　Why, too, should

Antichrist be slain by Him, whilst commissioned by the Creator to execute the function[10] of inspiring men with their love of untruth?　In short, it is incontestable that the emissary,[11] and the truth, and the salvation belong to Him to whom also appertain the wrath, and the jealousy,[12] and "the sending of the strong delusion,"[13] on those who despise and mock, as well as upon those who are ignorant of Him; and therefore even Marcion will now have to come down a step, and concede to us that his god is "a jealous god."　(This being then an unquestionable position, I ask) which God has the greater right to be angry?　He, as I suppose, who from the beginning of all things has given to man, as primary witnesses for the knowledge of Himself, nature in her (manifold) works, kindly providences, plagues,[14] and indications (of His divinity),[15] but who in spite of all this evidence has not been acknowledged; or he who has been brought out to view[16] once for all in one only copy of the gospel—and even that without any sure authority—which actually makes no secret of proclaiming another god?　Now He who has the right of inflicting the vengeance, has also sole claim to that which occasions[17] the vengeance, I mean the Gospel; (in other words,) both the truth and (its accompanying) salvation.　The charge, that "if any would not work, neither should he eat,"[18] is in strict accordance with the precept of Him who ordered that "the mouth of the ox that treadeth out the corn should not be muzzled."[19]

CHAP. XVII.—THE EPISTLE TO THE LAODICEANS. THE PROPER DESIGNATION IS TO THE EPHESIANS. RECAPITULATION OF ALL THINGS IN CHRIST FROM THE BEGINNING OF THE CREATION. NO ROOM FOR MARCION'S CHRIST HERE. NUMEROUS PARALLELS BETWEEN THIS EPISTLE AND PASSAGES IN THE OLD TESTAMENT. THE PRINCE OF THE POWER OF THE AIR, AND THE GOD OF THIS WORLD—WHO? CREATION AND REGENERATION THE WORK OF ONE GOD. HOW CHRIST HAS MADE THE LAW OBSOLETE. A VAIN ERASURE OF MARCION'S. THE APOSTLES AS WELL AS THE PROPHETS FROM THE CREATOR.

We have it on the true tradition[20] of the Church, that this epistle was sent to the Ephe-

---

[1] 2 Thess. ii. 3, 4.
[2] The prophets of the Old and the New Testament.
[3] 1 John iv. 1-3.
[4] Solventes Jesum. This expression receives some explanation from the Vulgate version of 1 John iv. 3: "Et omnis spiritus qui *solvit* Jesum Christum ex Deo non est." From Irenæus, Vol. I., 443 (Harvey, ii. 89), we learn that the Gnostics *divided* Jesus from Christ: "Alterum quidem Jesum intelligunt, alterum autem Christum,"—an error which was met in that clause of the creed expressing faith in "*One Lord Jesus Christ*." Grabe, after Socrates, *Hist. Eccles.* vii. 32, says that the oldest MSS. of St. John's epistle read πᾶν πνεῦμα ὁ λύει τὸν Ἰησοῦν. If so, Tertullian must be regarded as combining the two readings, viz., that which we find in the received text and this just quoted. Thus Grabe. It would be better to say that T. read ver. 2 as we have it, only omitting Ἰησοῦν; and in ver. 3 read the old lection to which Socrates refers instead of πᾶν πνεῦμα ὁ μὴ ὁμολογεῖ.
[5] 2 Thess. ii. 9.
[6] Instinctum fallaciæ.
[7] 2 Thess. ii. 10-12.
[8] Summissu erroris.
[9] Marcion, or rather *his* Christ, who on the hypothesis absurdly employs the Creator's Christ on the flagrantly inconsistent mission of avenging *his* truth, *i.e.* Marcionism.

[10] Habens fungi . . . Creatori.
[11] Angelum : the Antichrist *sent* by the Creator.
[12] Æmulatio.
[13] 2 Thess. ii. 11.
[14] Plagis: "heavy strokes," in opposition to the previous "*beneficiis.*"
[15] Prædicationibus : see Rom. i. 20.
[16] Productus est.
[17] Materia.
[18] 2 Thess. iii. 10.
[19] Deut. xxv. 4.
[20] Veritati.　.

sians, not to the Laodiceans. Marcion, however, was very desirous of giving it the new title (of Laodicean),[1] as if he were extremely accurate in investigating such a point. But of what consequence are the titles, since in writing to a certain church the apostle did in fact write to all? It is certain that, whoever they were to whom he wrote,[2] he declared Him to be God in Christ with whom all things agree which are predicted.[3] Now, to what god will most suitably belong all those things which relate to "that good pleasure, which *God* hath purposed in the mystery of His will, that in the dispensation of the fulness of times He might *recapitulate*" (if I may so say, according to the exact meaning of the Greek word[4]) " all things in Christ, both which are in heaven and which are on earth,"[5] but to Him whose are all things from their beginning, yea the beginning itself too; from whom issue the times and the dispensation of the fulness of times, according to which all things up to the very first are gathered up in Christ? What *beginning*, however, has the other god; that is to say, how can anything proceed from him, who has no work to show? And if there be no beginning, how can there be *times*? If no times, what *fulness* of times can there be? And if no fulness, what *dispensation*? Indeed, what has he ever done on earth, that any long dispensation of times to be fulfilled can be put to his account, for the accomplishment of all things in Christ, even of things in heaven? Nor can we possibly suppose that any things whatever have been at any time done in heaven by any other God than Him by whom, as all men allow, all things have been done on earth. Now, if it is impossible for all these things from the beginning to be reckoned to any other God than the Creator, who will believe that an alien god has recapitulated them in an alien Christ, instead of their own proper Author in His own Christ? If, again, they belong to the Creator, they must needs be separate from the other god; and if separate, then opposed to him. But then how can opposites be gathered together into him by whom they are in short destroyed? Again, what Christ do the following words announce, when *the apostle* says: " That we should be to the praise of His glory, who first trusted in Christ?"[6] Now who could have first trusted—*i.e.* *previously* trusted[7]—in God, before His advent, except the Jews to whom

Christ was previously announced, from the beginning? He who was thus *foretold*, was also *foretrusted*. Hence the apostle refers the statement to himself, that is, to the Jews, in order that he may draw a distinction with respect to the Gentiles, (when he goes on to say:) " In whom ye also trusted, after that ye heard the word of truth, the gospel (of your salvation); in whom ye believed, and were sealed with His Holy Spirit of promise."[8] Of what promise? That which was made through Joel: " In the last days will I pour out of my Spirit upon all flesh,"[9] that is, on all nations. Therefore the Spirit and the Gospel will be found in the Christ, who was foretrusted, because foretold. Again, " the Father of glory "[10] is He whose Christ, when ascending to heaven, is celebrated as " the King of Glory " in the Psalm: " Who is this King of Glory? the Lord of Hosts, He is the King of Glory."[11] From Him also is besought " the spirit of wisdom,"[12] at whose disposal is enumerated that sevenfold distribution of the spirit of grace by Isaiah.[13] He likewise will grant " the enlightenment of the eyes of the understanding,"[14] who has also enriched our natural eyes with light; to whom, moreover, the blindness of the people is offensive: "And who is blind, but my servants? . . . yea, the servants of God have become blind."[15] In His gift, too, are " the riches (of the glory) of His inheritance in the saints,"[16] who promised such an inheritance in the call of the Gentiles: "Ask of me, and I will give Thee the heathen for Thine inheritance."[17] It was He who " wrought in Christ His mighty power, by raising Him from the dead, and setting Him at His own right hand, and putting all things under His feet "[18]—even the same who said: " Sit Thou on my right hand, until I make Thine enemies Thy footstool."[19] For in another passage the Spirit says to the Father concerning the Son: " Thou hast put all things under His feet."[20] Now, if from all these facts which are found in the Creator there is yet to be deduced[21] another god and another Christ, let us go in quest of the Creator. I suppose, forsooth,[22] we find Him, when he speaks of such as " were dead in trespasses and sins, wherein they had walked

[1] Titulum interpolare gestiit : or, " of corrupting its title."
[2] Certe tamen.
[3] For a discussion on the title of this epistle in a succinct shape, the reader is referred to Dean Alford's *Gr. Test.* vol. iii. *Prolegomena*, chap. ii. sec. 2.
[4] ἀνακεφαλαιώσασθαι, " to sum up into a head."
[5] Eph. i. 9, 10.
[6] Eph. i. 12.
[7] He explains " præsperasse by *ante* sperasse."

[8] Eph. i. 13.
[9] Joel ii. 28.
[10] Eph. ii. 17.
[11] Ps. xxiv. 10.
[12] Eph. i. 17.
[13] Isa. xi. 2.
[14] Eph. i. 18.
[15] Isa. xlii. 19 (Sept.).
[16] Eph. i. 18.
[17] Ps. ii. 8.
[18] Eph. i. 19-22.
[19] Ps. cx. 1.
[20] Ps. viii. 7.
[21] Infertur.
[22] Plane.

according to the course of this world, according to the prince of the power of the air, who worketh in the children of disobedience."[1] But Marcion must not here interpret the world as meaning the God of the world.[2] For a creature bears no resemblance to the Creator; the thing made, none to its Maker; the world, none to God. He, moreover, who is the Prince of the power of the ages must not be thought to be called the prince of the power of the air; for He who is chief over the higher powers derives no title from the lower powers, although these, too, may be ascribed to Him. Nor, again, can He possibly seem to be the instigator[3] of that unbelief which He Himself had rather to endure at the hand of the Jews and the Gentiles alike. We may therefore simply conclude that[4] these designations are unsuited to the Creator. There is another being to whom they are more applicable —and the apostle knew very well who that was. Who then is he? Undoubtedly he who has raised up "children of disobedience" against the Creator Himself ever since he took possession of that "air" of His; even as the prophet makes him say: "I will set my throne *above the stars; . . . I will go up* above the clouds; I will be like the Most High."[5] This must mean the devil, whom in another passage (since such will they there have the apostle's meaning to be) we shall recognize in the appellation *the god of this world.*[6] For he has filled the whole world with the lying pretence of his own divinity. To be sure,[7] if *he* had not existed, we might then possibly have applied these descriptions to the Creator. But the apostle, too, had lived in Judaism; and when he parenthetically observed of the sins (of that period of his life), "in which also we all had our conversation in times past,"[8] he must not be understood to indicate that the Creator was the lord of sinful men, and the prince of this air; but as meaning that in his Judaism he had been one of the children of disobedience, having the devil as his instigator —when he persecuted the church and the Christ of the Creator. Therefore he says: "We also were the children of wrath," but "by nature."[9] Let the heretic, however, not contend that, because the Creator called the Jews *children,* therefore the Creator is the lord of wrath.[10] For when (the apostle) says, "We

were by nature the children of wrath," inasmuch as the Jews were not the Creator's children *by nature,* but by the election of their fathers, he (must have) referred their being children of wrath to nature, and not to the Creator, adding this at last, "even as others,"[11] who, of course, were not children of God. It is manifest that sins, and lusts of the flesh, and unbelief, and anger, are ascribed to the common nature of all mankind, the devil however leading that nature astray,[12] which he has already infected with the implanted germ of sin. "We," says he, "are His workmanship, created in Christ."[13] It is one thing to make (as a workman), another thing to create. But he assigns both to One. Man is the workmanship of the Creator. He therefore who made man (at first), created him also in Christ. As touching the substance of nature, He "made" him; as touching the work of grace, He "created" him. Look also at what follows in connection with these words: "Wherefore remember, that ye being in time past Gentiles in the flesh, who are called uncircumcision by that which has the name of circumcision in the flesh made by the hand—that at that time ye were without Christ, being aliens from the commonwealth of Israel, and strangers from the covenants of promise,[14] having no hope, and without God in the world."[15] Now, without what God and without what Christ were these Gentiles? Surely, without Him to whom commonwealth[16] of Israel belonged, and the covenants and the promise. "But now in Christ," says he, "ye who were sometimes far off are made nigh by His blood."[17] From whom were they far off before? From the (privileges) whereof he speaks above, even from the Christ of the Creator, from the commonwealth of Israel, from the covenants, from the hope of the promise, from God Himself. Since this is the case, the Gentiles are consequently now in Christ made nigh to these (blessings), from which they were once far off. But if we are in Christ brought so very nigh to the commonwealth of Israel, which comprises the religion of the divine Creator, and to the covenants and to the promise, yea to their very God Himself, it is quite ridiculous (to suppose that) the Christ of the other god has brought us to this proximity to the Creator from afar. The apostle had in mind that it had been predicted concerning the call of

---

[1] Eph. ii. 1, 2.
[2] Deo mundi : i.e. the God who made the world.
[3] Operator : in reference to the expression in ver. 2, "who now *worketh*," etc.
[4] Sufficit igitur si.
[5] Isa. xiv. 13, 14. An inexact quotation from the *Septuagint.*
[6] On this and another meaning given to the phrase in 2 Cor. iv. 4, see above, chap. xi.
[7] Plane : an ironical particle here.
[8] Eph. ii. 3.
[9] Eph. ii. 3.

[10] In Marcion's sense.
[11] Eph. ii. 3.
[12] Captante.
[13] Eph. ii. 10.
[14] Literally, "the covenants and their promise."
[15] Eph. ii. 11, 12.
[16] Conversatio : rather, "intercourse with Israel."
[17] Eph. ii. 13.

the Gentiles from their distant alienation in words like these: "They who were far off from me have come to my righteousness."[1] For the Creator's righteousness no less than His peace was announced in Christ, as we have often shown already. Therefore he says: "He is our peace, who hath made both one"[2]—that is, the Jewish nation and the Gentile world. What is near, and what was far off, now that "the middle wall has been broken down" of their "enmity," (are made one) "in His flesh."[3] But Marcion erased the pronoun *His*, that he might make the enmity refer to flesh, as if (the apostle spoke) of a carnal enmity, instead of the enmity which was a rival to Christ.[4] And thus you have (as I have said elsewhere) exhibited the stupidity of Pontus, rather than the adroitness of a Marrucinian,[5] for you here deny him *flesh* to whom in the verse above you allowed *blood!* Since, however, He has made the law obsolete[6] by His own precepts, even by Himself fulfilling the law (for superfluous is, "Thou shalt not commit adultery," when He says, "Thou shalt not look on a woman to lust after her;" superfluous also is, "Thou shalt do no murder," when He says, "Thou shalt not speak evil of thy neighbour,") it is impossible to make an adversary of the law out of one who so completely promotes it.[7] "For to create[8] in Himself of twain," for He who had *made* is also the same who *creates* (just as we have found it stated above: "For we are His workmanship, created in Christ *Jesus*"),[9] "one new man, making peace" (really new, and really man—no phantom—but new, and newly born of a virgin by the Spirit of God), "that He might reconcile both unto God"[10] (even the God whom both races had offended—both Jew and Gentile), "in one body," says he, "having in it slain the enmity by the cross."[11] Thus we find from this passage also, that there was in Christ a fleshly body, such as was able to endure the cross. "When, therefore, He came and preached peace to them that were near and to them which were afar off," we both obtained "access to the Father," being "now no more strangers and foreigners, but fellow-citizens with the saints, and of the household of God" (even of Him from whom, as we have shown above, we were aliens, and placed far off), "built upon the foundation of the apostles"[12]—(the apostle added), "and the prophets;" these words, however, the heretic erased, forgetting that the Lord had set in His Church not only apostles, but prophets also. He feared, no doubt, that our building was to stand in Christ upon the foundation of the ancient prophets,[13] since the apostle himself never fails to build us up everywhere with (the words of) the prophets. For whence did he learn to call Christ "the chief corner-stone,"[14] but from the figure given him in the Psalm: "The stone which the builders rejected is become the head (stone) of the corner?"[15]

CHAP. XVIII.—ANOTHER FOOLISH ERASURE OF MARCION'S EXPOSED. CERTAIN FIGURATIVE EXPRESSIONS OF THE APOSTLE, SUGGESTED BY THE LANGUAGE OF THE OLD TESTAMENT. COLLATION OF MANY PASSAGES OF THIS EPISTLE, WITH PRECEPTS AND STATEMENTS IN THE PENTATEUCH, THE PSALMS, AND THE PROPHETS. ALL ALIKE TEACH US THE WILL AND PURPOSE OF THE CREATOR.

As our heretic is so fond of his pruning-knife, I do not wonder when syllables are expunged by his hand, seeing that entire pages are usually the matter on which he practises his effacing process. The apostle declares that to himself, "less than the least of all saints, was the grace given" of enlightening all men as to "what was the fellowship of the mystery, which during the ages had been hid in God, who created all things."[16] The heretic erased the preposition *in*, and made the clause run thus: ("what is the fellowship of the mystery) which hath for ages been hidden from the God who created all things."[17] The falsification, however, is flagrantly[18] absurd. For the apostle goes on to infer (from his own statement): "in order that unto the principalities and powers in heavenly places might become known through the church the manifold wisdom of God."[19] *Whose* principalities and powers does he mean? If the Creator's,

---

[1] This is rather an allusion to, than a quotation of, Isa. xlvi. 12, 13.
[2] Eph. ii. 14.
[3] Eph. ii. 15.
[4] "The law of commandments contained in ordinances."
[5] He expresses the proverbial adage very tersely, "non Marrucine, sed Pontice."
[6] Vacuam fecit.
[7] Ex adjutore.
[8] Conderet: "create," to keep up the distinction between this and *facere*, "to make."
[9] Eph. ii. 10.
[10] Eph. ii. 15–16.
[11] Eph. ii. 16.

[12] Eph. ii. 17–20.
[13] "Because, if our building as Christians rested in part upon that foundation, our God and the God of the Jews must be the same, which Marcion denied" (Lardner).
[14] Eph. ii. 20.
[15] Ps. cxviii. 22.
[16] Eph. iii. 8, 9.
[17] The passage of St. Paul, as Tertullian expresses it, Quæ dispensatio sacramenti occulti ab ævis in Deo, qui omnia condidit." According to Marcion's alteration, the latter part runs, "*Occulti ab ævis Deo, qui omnia condidit.*" The original is, Τίς ἡ οἰκονομία τοῦ μυστηρίου τοῦ ἀποκεκρυμμένου ἀπὸ τῶν αἰώνων ἐν τῷ Θεῷ (compare Col. iii. 3) τῷ τὰ πάντα κτίσαντι. Marcion's removal of the ἐν has no warrant of MS. authority ; it upsets St. Paul's doctrine, as attested in other passages, and destroys the grammatical structure.
[18] Emicat.
[19] Eph. iii. 10.

how does it come to pass that such a God as He could have meant His wisdom to be displayed to the principalities and powers, but not to Himself? For surely no principalities could possibly have understood anything without their sovereign Lord. Or if (the apostle) did not mention God in this passage, on the ground that He (as their chief) is Himself reckoned among these (principalities), then he would have plainly said that the mystery had been hidden from the principalities and powers of Him who had created all things, including Him amongst them. But if he states that it was hidden from them, he must needs be understood[1] as having meant that it was manifest to Him. *From God*, therefore, the mystery was not hidden; but it was hidden *in God*, the Creator of all things, from His principalities and powers. For "who hath known the mind of the Lord, or who hath been His counsellor?"[2] Caught in this trap, the heretic probably changed the passage, with the view of saying that *his* god wished to make known to his principalities and powers the fellowship of his own mystery, of which God, who created all things, had been ignorant. But what was the use of his obtruding this ignorance of *the Creator*, who was a stranger to the superior god,[3] and far enough removed from him, when even his own servants had known nothing about him? To the Creator, however, the future was well known. Then why was not that also known to Him, which had to be revealed beneath His heaven, and on His earth? From this, therefore, there arises a confirmation of what we have already laid down. For since the Creator was sure to know, some time or other, that hidden mystery of the superior god, even on the supposition that the true reading was (as Marcion has it) —"hidden from the God who created all things"—he ought then to have expressed the conclusion: "in order that the manifold wisdom of God might be made known to Him, and then to the principalities and powers of God, whosoever He might be, with whom the Creator was destined to share their knowledge." So palpable is the erasure in this passage, when thus read, consistently with its own true bearing. I, on my part, now wish to engage with you in a discussion on the allegorical expressions of the apostle. What figures of speech could the novel god have found in the prophets (fit for himself)? "He led captivity captive," says the apostle.[4] With what arms? In what conflicts? From the devas-

tation of what country? From the overthrow of what city? What women, what children, what princes did the Conqueror throw into chains? For when by David Christ is sung as "girded with His sword upon His thigh,"[5] or by Isaiah as "taking away the spoils of Samaria and the power of Damascus,"[6] you make Him out to be[7] really and truly a warrior confest to the eye.[8] Learn then now, that His is a spiritual armour and warfare, since you have already discovered that the captivity is spiritual, in order that you may further learn that *this* also belongs to Him, even because the apostle derived the mention of the captivity from the same prophets as suggested to him his precepts likewise: "Putting away lying," (says he,) "speak every man truth with his neighbour;"[9] and again, using the very words in which the Psalm[10] expresses his meaning, (he says,) "Be ye angry, and sin not;"[11] "Let not the sun go down upon your wrath."[12] "Have no fellowship with the unfruitful works of darkness;"[13] for (in the Psalm it is written,) "With the holy man thou shalt be holy, and with the perverse thou shalt be perverse;"[14] and, "Thou shalt put away evil from among you."[15] Again, "Go ye out from the midst of them; touch not the unclean thing; separate yourselves, ye that bear the vessels of the Lord."[16] (The apostle says further:) "Be not drunk with wine, wherein is excess,"[17]—a precept which is suggested by the passage (of the prophet), where the seducers of the consecrated (Nazarites) to drunkenness are rebuked: "Ye gave wine to my holy ones to drink."[18] This prohibition from drink was given also to the high priest Aaron and his sons, "when they went into the holy place."[19] The command, to "sing to the Lord with psalms and hymns,"[20] comes suitably from him who knew that those who "drank wine with drums and psalteries" were blamed by God.[21] Now, when I find to what God belong these precepts, whether in their germ or their development, I have no difficulty in knowing to whom the apostle also belongs. But he declares that "wives ought to be in subjection to their

---

[1] Debebat.
[2] Isa. xl. 13.
[3] Marcion's god, of course.
[4] Eph. iv. 8 and Ps. lxviii. 19.

[5] Ps. xlv. 3.
[6] Isa. viii. 4.
[7] Extundis.
[8] See above, book iii. chap. xiii. and xiv. p. 332.
[9] Eph. iv. 25.
[10] Ps. iv. 4.
[11] Eph. iv. 26.
[12] Eph. iv. 26.
[13] Eph. v. 11.
[14] Ps. xviii. 26.
[15] Deut. xxi. 21, quoted also in 1 Cor. v. 13.
[16] Isa. lii. 11, quoted in 2 Cor. vi. 17.
[17] Eph. v. 18.
[18] Amos ii. 12.
[19] Lev. x. 9,
[20] Eph. v. 19.
[21] Isa. v. 11, 12.

husbands:"[1] what reason does he give for this? "Because," says he, "the husband is the head of the wife."[2] Pray tell me, Marcion, does your god build up the authority of his law on the work of the Creator? This, however, is a comparative trifle; for he actually derives from the same source the condition of his Christ and his Church; for he says: "even as Christ is the head of the Church;"[3] and again, in like manner: "He who loveth his wife, loveth his own flesh, even as Christ loved the Church."[4] You see how your Christ and your Church are put in comparison with the work of the Creator. How much honour is given to the flesh in the name of the church! "No man," says the apostle, "ever yet hated his own flesh" (except, of course, Marcion alone), "but nourisheth and cherisheth it, even as the Lord doth the Church."[5] But you are the only man that hates his flesh, for you rob it of its resurrection. It will be only right that you should hate the Church also, because it is loved by Christ on the same principle.[6] Yea, Christ loved the flesh even as the Church. For no man will love the picture of his wife without taking care of it, and honouring it and crowning it. The likeness partakes with the reality in the privileged honour. I shall now endeavour, from my point of view,[7] to prove that the same God is (the God) of the man[8] and of Christ, of the woman and of the Church, of the flesh and the spirit, by the apostle's help who applies the Creator's injunction, and adds even a comment on it: "For this cause shall a man leave his father and his mother, (and shall be joined unto his wife), and they two shall be one flesh. This is a great mystery."[9] In passing,[10] (I would say that) it is enough for me that the works of the Creator are great mysteries[11] in the estimation of the apostle, although they are so vilely esteemed by the heretics. "But I am speaking," says he, "of Christ and the Church."[12] This he says in explanation of the mystery, not for its disruption. He shows us that the mystery was prefigured by Him who is also the author of the mystery. Now what is Marcion's opinion? The Creator could not possibly have furnished figures to an unknown god, or, if a known one, an adversary to Himself. The superior god, in fact, ought to

have borrowed nothing from the inferior; he was bound rather to annihilate Him. "Children should obey their parents."[13] Now, although Marcion has erased (the next clause), "which is the first commandment with promise,"[14] still the law says plainly, "Honour thy father and thy mother."[15] Again, (the apostle writes:) "Parents, bring up your children in the fear and admonition of the Lord."[16] For you have heard how it was said to them of old time: "Ye shall relate these things to your children; and your children in like manner to their children."[17] Of what use are two gods to me, when the discipline is but one? If there must be two, I mean to follow Him who was the first to teach the lesson. But as our struggle lies against "the rulers of this world,"[18] what a host of Creator Gods there must be![19] For why should I not insist upon this point here, that he ought to have mentioned but *one* "ruler of this world," if he meant only the Creator to be the being to whom belonged all the powers which he previously mentioned? Again, when in the preceding verse he bids us "put on the whole armour of God, that we may be able to stand against the wiles of the devil,"[20] does he not show that all the things which he mentions after the devil's name really belong to the devil—"the principalities and the powers, and the rulers of the darkness of this world,"[21] which we also ascribe to the devil's authority? Else, if "the devil" means the Creator, who will be the devil in the Creator's dispensation?[22] As there are two gods, must there also be two devils, and a plurality of powers and rulers of this world? But how is the Creator both a devil and a god at the same time, when the devil is not at once both god and devil? For either they are both of them gods, if both of them are devils; or else He who is God is not also devil, as neither is he god who is the devil. I want to know indeed by what perversion[23] the word *devil* is at all applicable to the Creator. Perhaps he perverted some purpose of the superior god—conduct such as He experienced Himself from the archangel, who lied indeed for the purpose. For He did not forbid (our first parents) a taste of the miserable tree,[24] from any apprehension that they would become gods;

---

[1] Eph. v. 22, 24.
[2] Eph. v. 23.
[3] Eph. v. 23.
[4] Eph. v. 25, 28.
[5] Eph. v. 29.
[6] Proinde.
[7] Ego.
[8] Masculi.
[9] Eph. v. 31, 32.
[10] Inter ista.
[11] Magna sacramenta.
[12] Eph. v. 32.

[13] Eph. vi. 1.
[14] Eph. vi. 2. "He did this (says Lardner) in order that the Mosaic law might not be thought to be thus established."
[15] Ex. xx. 12.
[16] Eph. vi. 4.
[17] Ex. x. 2.
[18] Eph. vi. 12.
[19] An ironical allusion to Marcion's interpretation, which he has considered in a former chapter, of the title *God of this world*.
[20] Eph. vi. 11.
[21] Eph. vi. 12.
[22] Apud Creatorem.
[23] Ex qua delatura.
[24] Illius arbusculæ.

His prohibition was meant to prevent their dying after the transgression. But "the spiritual wickedness"[1] did not signify the Creator, because of the apostle's additional description, "in heavenly places;"[2] for the apostle was quite aware that "spiritual wickedness" had been at work in heavenly places, when angels were entrapped into sin by the daughters of men.[3] But how happened it that (the apostle) resorted to ambiguous descriptions, and I know not what obscure enigmas, for the purpose of disparaging[4] the Creator, when he displayed to the Church such constancy and plainness of speech in "making known the mystery of the gospel for which he was an ambassador in bonds," owing to his liberty in preaching—and actually requested (the Ephesians) to pray to God that this "open-mouthed utterance" might be continued to him?[5]

CHAP. XIX.—THE EPISTLE TO THE COLOSSIANS. TIME THE CRITERION OF TRUTH AND HERESY. APPLICATION OF THE CANON. THE IMAGE OF THE INVISIBLE GOD EXPLAINED. PRE-EXISTENCE OF OUR CHRIST IN THE CREATOR'S ANCIENT DISPENSATIONS. WHAT IS INCLUDED IN THE FULNESS OF CHRIST. THE EPICUREAN CHARACTER OF MARCION'S GOD. THE CATHOLIC TRUTH IN OPPOSITION THERETO. THE LAW IS TO CHRIST WHAT THE SHADOW IS TO THE SUBSTANCE.

I am accustomed in my prescription against all heresies, to fix my compendious criterion[6] (of truth) in the testimony of *time;* claiming *priority* therein as our rule, and alleging *lateness* to be the characteristic of every heresy. This shall now be proved even by the apostle, when he says: "For the hope which is laid up for you in heaven, whereof ye heard before in the word of the truth of the gospel; which is come unto you, as it is unto all the world."[7] For if, even at that time, the tradition of the gospel had spread everywhere, how much more now! Now, if it is our gospel which has spread everywhere, rather than any heretical gospel, much less Marcion's, which only dates from the reign of Antoninus,[8] then ours will be the gospel of the apostles. But should Marcion's gospel succeed in filling the whole world, it would not even in that case be entitled

to the character of apostolic. For this quality, it will be evident, can only belong to that gospel which was the first to fill the world; in other words, to the gospel of that God who of old declared this of its promulgation: "Their sound is gone out through all the earth, and their words to the end of the world."[9] He calls Christ "the image of the invisible God."[10] We in like manner say that the Father of Christ is invisible, for we know that it was the Son who was seen in ancient times (whenever any appearance was vouchsafed to men in the name of God) as the image of (the Father) Himself. He must not be regarded, however, as making any difference between a visible and an invisible God; because long before he wrote this we find a description of our God to this effect: "No man can see the Lord, and live."[11] If Christ is not "the first-begotten before every creature,"[12] as 'that "Word of God by whom all things were made, and without whom nothing was made;"[13] if "all things were" not "in Him created, whether in heaven or on earth, visible and invisible, whether they be thrones or dominions, or principalities, or powers;" if "all things were" not "created by Him and for Him" (for these truths Marcion ought not to allow concerning Him), then the apostle could not have so positively laid it down, that "He is before all."[14] For how is He before all, if He is not before *all things?*[15] How, again, is He before all things, if He is not "the first-born of every creature"—if He is not the Word of the Creator?[16] Now how will he be* proved to have been before all things, who appeared after all things? Who can tell whether he had a prior existence, when he has found no proof that he had any existence at all? In what way also could it have "pleased (the Father) that in Him should all fulness dwell?"[17] For, to begin with, what fulness is that which is not comprised of the constituents which Marcion has removed from it,— even those that were "created in Christ, whether in heaven or on earth," whether angels or men? which is not made of the things that are visible and invisible? which consists not of thrones and dominions and principalities and powers? If, on the other hand,[18] our false apostles and Judaizing gospellers[19] have in-

---

[1] Spiritalia nequitiæ: "wicked spirits."
[2] Eph vi. 12.
[3] Gen. vi. 1-4. See also Tertullian, *De Idol.* 9; *De Habit. Mul.* 2; *De cultu Femin.* 10; *De Vel. Virg.* 7; *Apolog.* 22. See also Augustin, *De Civit. Dei.* xv. 23.
[4] Ut taxaret. Of course he alludes to Marcion's absurd exposition of the 12th verse, in applying St. Paul's description of wicked spirits to the Creator.
[5] Eph. vi. 19, 20.
[6] Compendium figere.
[7] Col. i. 5, 6.
[8] Antoniniani Marcionis: see above in book i. chap. xix.

[9] Ps. xix. 4.
[10] Col. i. 15.
[11] Ex. xxxiii. 20.
[12] Col. i. 15. Our author's "primogenitus conditionis" is St. Paul's πρωτότοκος πάσης κτίσεως, for the meaning of which see Bp. Ellicott, *in loc.*
[13] John i. 3.
[14] Ante omnes.
[15] Ante amina.
[16] *Creatoris* is our author's word.
[17] Col. i. 19.
[18] Aut si.
[19] Evangelizatores.

troduced all these things out of their own stores, and Marcion has applied them to constitute the fulness of his own god, (this hypothesis, absurd though it be, alone would justify him;) for how, on any other supposition,[1] could the rival and the destroyer of the Creator have been willing that His fulness should dwell in his Christ? To whom, again, does He "reconcile all things by Himself, making peace by the blood of His cross,"[2] but to Him whom those very things had altogether[3] offended, against whom they had rebelled by transgression, (but) to whom they had at last returned?[4] *Conciliated* they might have been to a strange god; but *reconciled* they could not possibly have been to any other than their own God. Accordingly, ourselves "who were sometime alienated and enemies in our mind by wicked works"[5] does He reconcile to the Creator, against whom we had committed offence—worshipping the creature to the prejudice of the Creator. · As, however, he says elsewhere,[6] that the Church is the body of Christ, so here also (the apostle) declares that he "fills up that which is behind of the afflictions of Christ in his flesh for His body's sake, which is the Church."[7] But you must not on this account suppose that on every mention of His body the term is only a metaphor, instead of meaning real flesh. For he says above that we are "reconciled in His body through death;"[8] meaning, of course, that He died in that body wherein death was possible through the flesh: (therefore he adds,) not *through the Church*[9] (*per ecclesiam*), but expressly *for the sake of the Church* (*propter ecclesiam*),exchanging body for body—one of flesh for a spiritual one. When, again, he warns them to "beware of subtle words and philosophy," as being "a vain deceit," such as is "after the rudiments of the world" (not understanding thereby the mundane fabric of sky and earth, but worldly learning, and "the tradition of men," subtle in their speech and their philosophy),[10] it would be tedious, and the proper subject of a separate work, to show how in this sentence (of the apostle's) all heresies are condemned, on the ground of their consisting of the resources of subtle speech and the rules of philosophy. But (once for all) let Marcion know that the principle term of his creed comes from the school of Epicurus, implying that the Lord is stupid and indifferent;[11] wherefore he refuses to say that He is an object to be feared. Moreover, from the porch of the Stoics he brings out *matter*, and places it on a par with the Divine Creator.[12] He also denies the resurrection of the flesh,—a truth which none of the schools of philosophy agreed together to hold.[13] But how remote is our (Catholic) verity from the artifices of this heretic, when it dreads to arouse the anger of God, and firmly believes that He produced all things out of nothing, and promises to us a restoration from the grave of the same flesh (that died) and holds without a blush that Christ was born of the virgin's womb! At this, philosophers, and heretics, and the very heathen, laugh and jeer. For "God hath chosen the foolish things of the world to confound the wise"[14]—that God, no doubt, who in reference to this very dispensation of His threatened long before that He would "destroy the wisdom of the wise."[15] Thanks to this simplicity of truth, so opposed to the subtlety and vain deceit of philosophy, we cannot possibly have any relish for such perverse opinions. Then, if God "quickens us together with Christ, forgiving us our trespasses,"[16] we cannot suppose that sins are forgiven by Him against whom, as having been all along unknown, they could not have been committed. Now tell me, Marcion, what is your opinion of the apostle's language, when he says, "Let no man judge you in meat, or in drink, or in respect of a holy day, or of the new moon, or of the sabbath, which is a shadow of things to come, but the body is of Christ?"[17] We do not now treat of the law, further than (to remark) that the apostle here teaches clearly how it has been abolished, even by passing from shadow to substance—that is, from figurative types to the reality, which is Christ. The shadow, therefore, is His to whom belongs the body also; in other words, the law is His, and so is Christ. If you separate the law and Christ, assigning one to one god and the other to another, it is the same as if you were to at-

---

[1] Ceterum quale.
[2] Col. i. 20.
[3] "Una ipsa" is Oehler's reading instead of *universa*.
[4] Cujus novissime fuerant.
[5] Col. i. 21.
[6] Eph. i. 23.
[7] Col. i. 24.
[8] Col. i. 22.
[9] As if only in a *metaphorical* body, in which sense the Church is "His body."
[10] Col. ii. 8.

[11] "Dominum inferens *hebetem ;*" with which may be compared Cicero (*De Divin.* ii. 50, 103) : "Videsne Epicurum quem hebetem et rudem dicere solent Stoici. . . . qui negat, quidquam deos nec alieni curare, nec sui." The *otiose* and *inert* character of the god of Epicurus is referred to by Tertullian not unfrequently ; see above, in book iv. chap. xv. ; *Apolog.* 47, and *Ad Nationes*, ii. 2 ; whilst in *De Anima*, 3, he characterizes the philosophy of Epicurus by a similar term : " Prout aut Platonis honor, aut Zenonis vigor, aut Aristotelis tenor, aut *Epicuri stupor* aut Heracliti mæror, aut Empedoclis furor persuaserunt."
[12] The Stoical dogma of *the eternity* of matter and its *equality* with God was also held by Hermogenes ; see his *Adv. Hermogenem*, c. 4, "Materiam parem Deo infert."
[13] Pliny, *Nat. Hist.* vii. 55, refers to the peculiar opinion of Democritus on this subject (Fr. Junius).
[14] 1 Cor. i. 27.
[15] Isa. xxix. 14, quoted 1 Cor. i. *19* ; comp. Jer. viii. 9 and Job v. 12, 13.
[16] Col. ii. 13.
[17] Col. ii. 16, 17.

tempt to separate the shadow from the body of which it is the shadow. Manifestly Christ has relation to the law, if the body has to its shadow. But when he blames those who alleged visions of angels as their authority for saying that men must abstain from meats— " you must not touch, you must not taste "— in a voluntary humility, (at the same time) " vainly puffed up in the fleshly mind, and not holding the Head, " [1] (the apostle) does not in these terms attack the law or Moses, as if it was at the suggestion of superstitious angels that he had enacted his prohibition of sundry aliments. For Moses had evidently received the law from God. When, therefore, he speaks of their " following the commandments and doctrines of men, " [2] he refers to the conduct of those persons who " held not the Head," even Him in whom all things are gathered together; [3] for they are all recalled to Christ, and concentrated in Him as their initiating principle [4]—even the meats and drinks which were indifferent in their nature. All the rest of his precepts, [5] as we have shown sufficiently, when treating of them as they occurred in another epistle, [6] emanated from the Creator, who, while predicting that " old things were to pass away, " and that He would " make all things new," [7] commanded men " to break up fresh ground for themselves," [8] and thereby taught them even then to put off the old man and put on the new.

CHAP. XX.—THE EPISTLE TO THE PHILIPPIANS. THE VARIANCES AMONGST THE PREACHERS OF CHRIST NO ARGUMENT THAT THERE WAS MORE THAN ONE ONLY CHRIST. ST. PAUL'S PHRASES—FORM OF A SERVANT, LIKENESS, AND FASHION OF A MAN—NO SANCTION OF DOCETISM. NO ANTITHESIS (SUCH AS MARCION ALLEGED) IN THE GOD OF JUDAISM AND THE GOD OF THE GOSPEL DEDUCIBLE FROM CERTAIN CONTRASTS MENTIONED IN THIS EPISTLE. A PARALLEL WITH A PASSAGE IN GENESIS. THE RESURRECTION OF THE BODY, AND THE CHANGE THEREOF.

When (the apostle) mentions the several motives of those who were preaching the gospel, how that some, " waxing confident by his bonds, " were more fearless in speaking the word," while others " preached Christ even out of envy and strife, and again others out of

good-will " many also " out of love," and certain " out of contention," and some " in rivalry to himself, " [9] he had a favourable opportunity, no doubt, [10] of taxing what they preached with a diversity of doctrine, as if it were no less than this which caused so great a variance in their tempers. But while he exposes these tempers as the sole cause of the diversity, he avoids inculpating the regular mysteries of the faith, [11] and affirms that there is, notwithstanding, but one Christ and His one God, whatever motives men had in preaching Him. Therefore, says he, it matters not to me " whether it be in pretence or in truth that Christ is preached," [12] because one Christ alone was announced, whether in their " pretentious " or their " truthful " faith. For it was to the faithfulness of their preaching that he applied the word *truth*, not to the rightness of the rule itself, because there was indeed but one rule; whereas the conduct of the preachers varied: in some of them it was true, *i. e.* single-minded, while in others it was sophisticated with over-much learning. This being the case, it is manifest that that Christ was the subject of their preaching who was always the theme of the prophets. Now, if it were a completely different Christ that was being introduced by the apostle, the novelty of the thing would have produced a diversity (in belief). For there would not have been wanting, in spite of the novel teaching, [13] men to interpret the preached gospel of the Creator's Christ, since the majority of persons everywhere now-a-days are of our way of thinking, rather than on the heretical side. So that the apostle would not in such a passage as the present one have refrained from remarking and censuring the diversity. Since, however, there is no blame of a diversity, there is no proof of a novelty. Of course [14] the Marcionites suppose that they have the apostle on their side in the following passage in the matter of Christ's substance—that in Him there was nothing but a phantom of flesh. For he says of Christ, that, " being in the form of God, He thought it not robbery to be equal with God; [15] but emptied [16] Himself, and took upon Him the *form* of a servant," *not the reality*, " and was made in the *likeness* of man," *not a man*, " and was found in *fashion* as a man," [17] *not in his substance*, that is to say, his flesh; just as if to a sub-

[1] Col. ii. 18, 19, 21.
[2] Col. ii. 22.
[3] Recensentur : Eph. i. 10.
[4] Initium.
[5] Contained in Vol. iii. and iv.
[6] In the Epistle to the Laodiceans or Ephesians ; see his remarks in the preceding chapter of this book v.
[7] Isa. xliii. 18, 19, and lxv. 17 ; 2 Cor. v. 17.
[8] Jer. iv. 3. This and the passage of Isaiah just quoted are also cited together above, book iv. chap. i. and ii. p. 345.

[9] Phil. i. 14-17.
[10] Utique.
[11] Regulas sacramentorum.
[12] Phil. i. 18.
[13] Nihilominus.
[14] Plane.
[15] Compare the treatise, *De Resur. Carnis*, c. vi. (Oehler).
[16] Exhausit ἐκένωσε.
[17] Phil. ii. 6, 7.

stance there did not accrue both *form* and *likeness* and *fashion*. It is well for us that in another passage (the apostle) calls Christ "the image of the invisible God."[1] For will it not follow with equal force from that passage, that Christ is not truly God, because the apostle places Him in *the image* of God, if, (as Marcion contends,) He is not truly man because of His having taken on Him *the form* or *image* of a man? For in both cases the true substance will have to be excluded, if *image* (or "fashion") and *likeness* and *form* shall be claimed for a phantom. But since he is truly God, as the Son of the Father, in His fashion and image, He has been already by the force of this conclusion determined to be truly man, as the Son of man, "found in the fashion" and image "of a man." For when he propounded[2] Him as thus "*found*" in the manner[3] of a man, he *in fact* affirmed Him to be most certainly human. For what is *found*, manifestly possesses existence. Therefore, as He was found to be God by His mighty power, so was He found to be man by reason of His flesh, because the apostle could not have pronounced Him to have "become obedient unto death,"[4] if He had not been constituted of a mortal substance. Still more plainly does this appear from the apostle's additional words, "even the death of the cross."[5] For he could hardly mean this to be a climax[6] to the human suffering, to extol the virtue[7] of His obedience, if he had known it all to be the imaginary process of a phantom, which rather eluded the cross than experienced it, and which displayed no virtue[8] in the suffering, but only illusion. But "those things which he had once accounted gain," and which he enumerates in the preceding verse—"trust in the flesh," the sign of "circumcision," his origin as "an Hebrew of the Hebrews," his descent from "the tribe of Benjamin," his dignity in the honours of the Pharisee[9]—he now reckons to be only "loss" to himself;[10] (in other words,) it was not the God of the Jews, but their stupid obduracy, which he repudiates. These are also the things "which he counts but dung for the excellency of the knowledge of Christ"[11] (but by no means for the rejection of God the Creator); "whilst he has not his own righteousness, which is of the law, but that which

is through Him," *i.e.* Christ, "the righteousness which is of God."[12] Then, say you, according to this distinction the law did not proceed from the God of Christ. Subtle enough! But here is something still more subtle for you. For when (the apostle) says, "Not (the righteousness) which is of the law, but that which is through Him," he would not have used the phrase *through Him* of any other than Him to whom the law belonged. "Our conversation," says he, "is in heaven."[13] I here recognise the Creator's ancient promise to Abraham: "I will multiply thy seed as the stars of heaven."[14] Therefore "one star differeth from another star in glory."[15] If, again, Christ in His advent from heaven "shall change the body of our humiliation, that it may be fashioned like unto His glorious body,"[16] it follows that this body of ours shall rise again, which is now in a state of humiliation in its sufferings and according to the law of mortality drops into the ground. But how shall it be changed, if it shall have no real existence? If, however, this is only said of those who shall be found in the flesh[17] at the advent of God, and who shall have to be changed,[18] what shall they do who will rise first? They will have no substance from which to undergo a change. But he says (elsewhere), "We shall be caught up together with them in the clouds, to meet the Lord (in the air)."[19] Then, if we are to be caught up alone with them, surely we shall likewise be changed together with them.

CHAP. XXI.—THE EPISTLE TO PHILEMON. THIS EPISTLE NOT MUTILATED. MARCION'S INCONSISTENCY IN ACCEPTING THIS, AND REJECTING THREE OTHER EPISTLES ADDRESSED TO INDIVIDUALS. CONCLUSIONS. TERTULLIAN VINDICATES THE SYMMETRY AND DELIBERATE PURPOSE OF HIS WORK AGAINST MARCION.

To this epistle alone did its brevity avail to protect it against the falsifying hands of Marcion. I wonder, however, when he received (into his *Apostolicon*) this letter which was written but to one man, that he rejected the two epistles to Timothy and the one to Titus, which all treat of ecclesiastical discipline. His aim, was, I suppose, to carry out his interpolating process even to the number of (St.

---

[1] Col. i. 15.
[2] Posuit.
[3] Inventum ratione.
[4] Phil. ii. 8.
[5] Phil. ii. 8.
[6] Non enim exaggeraret.
[7] Virtutem: perhaps the *power*.
[8] See the preceding note.
[9] Candidæ pharisaeæ : see Phil. iii. 4–6.
[10] Phil. iii. 7.
[11] Phil. iii. 8.

[12] Phil. iii. 9.
[13] Phil. iii. 20.
[14] Gen. xxii. 17.
[15] 1 Cor. xv. 41.
[16] Phil. iii. 21. [I have adhered to the original Greek, by a trifling verbal change, because Tertullian's argument requires it.]
[17] 1 Cor. xv. 51, 52.
[18] *Deputari*, which is an old reading, should certainly be *demutari*, and so say the best authorities. Oehler reads the former, but contends for the latter.
[19] 1 Thess. iv. 16, 17.

Paul's) epistles. And now, reader,[1] I beg you to remember that we have here adduced proofs out of the apostle, in support of the subjects which we previously[2] had to handle, and that we have now brought to a close[3] the topics which we deferred to this (portion of our) work. (This favour I request of you,) that you may not think that any repetition here has been superfluous, for we have only fulfilled our former engagement to you; nor look with suspicion on any postponement there, where we merely set forth the essential points (of the argument).[4] If you carefully examine the entire work, you will acquit us of either having been redundant here, or diffident there, in your own honest judgment.[5]

---

[1] Inspector: perhaps *critic*.
[2] Retro: in the former portions of this treatise.
[3] Expunxerimus.

[4] Qua eruimus ipsa ista.
[5] [Elucidation II.]

ELUCIDATIONS.

I

(Soul and Spirit, cap. xv. and notes 1 and 2, p. 463.)

Dr. Holmes, in the learned note which follows, affords me a valuable addition to my scanty remarks on this subject in former volumes. See (Vol. I. pp. 387, 532,) references to the great work of Professor Delitzsch, in notes on Irenæus. In Vol. II. p. 102, I have also mentioned M. Heard's work, on the *Tripartite Nature of Man*. With reference to the disagreement of the learned on this great matter, let me ask is it not less real than apparent? The *dichotomy* to which Tertullian objected, and the *trichotomy* which Dr. Holmes makes a name of "*the triple nature*," are terms which rather suggest a process of "dividing asunder of soul and spirit," and which involve an ambiguity that confuses the inquiry. Now, while the gravest objections may be imagined, or even demonstrated, against a process which seems to destroy the unity and individuality of a Man, does not every theologian accept the analytical formula of the apostle and recognize the *bodily*, the *animal* and the *spiritual* in the life of man? If so is there not fundamental agreement as to I. Thess. v. 23, and difference only, relatively, as to functions and processes, or as to the way in which truth on these three points ought to be stated? On this subject there are good remarks in the *Speaker's Commentary* on the text aforesaid, but the exhaustive work of Delitzsch deserves study.

Man's whole nature in Christ, seems to be sanctified by the Holy Spirit's suffusion of man's *spirit;* this rules and governs the *psychic* nature and through it the *body*.

II.

(The entire work, cap. xxi. p. 474.)

He who has followed Tertullian through the mazes in which Marcion, in spite of shifts and turnings innumerable, has been hunted down, and defeated, must recognize the great work performed by this author in behalf of Christian Orthodoxy. It seems to have been the plan of Christ's watchful care over His Church, that, in the earliest stages of its existence the enemy should be allowed to display his utmost malice and to bring out all his forces against Truth. Thus, before the meeting of Church-councils the language of faith had grown up, and clear views and precise statements of doctrine had been committed to the idioms of human thought. But, the labours of Tertullian are not confined to these diverse purposes. With all the faults of his acute and forensic mind, how powerfully he illuminates the Scriptures and glorifies them as containing the whole system of the Faith. How rich are his quotations, and how penetrating his conceptions of their uses. Besides all this, what an introduction he gives us to the modes of thought which were becoming familiar in the West,

and which were converting the Latin tongue to new uses, and making it capable of expressing Augustine's mind and so of creating new domains of Learning among the nations of
Europe.

If I have treated tenderly the reputation of this great Master, in my notes upon his Marcion, it is with a twofold purpose. (1.) It seems to me due to truth that his name should
be less associated with his deplorable lapse than with his long and faithful services to the
Church, and (2.) that the student should thus follow his career with a pleasure and with a
confidence the lack of which perpetually annoys us when we give the first place to the Montanist and not to the Catholic. Let this be our spirit in accompanying him into his fresh
campaigns against "the grievous wolves" foreseen by St. Paul with tears. Acts *xx.* 29, 30.

But as our Author invokes a careful examination of his "entire work," let the student
recur to Irenæus (Vol. I. p. 352, etc.) and observe how formidable, from the beginning, was
the irreligion of Marcion. His doctrines did truly "eat like a canker," assailing the Scriptures by mutilations and corruptions of the text itself. No marvel that Tertullian shows
him no quarter, though we must often regret the forensic violence of his retort. As to the
Dualism which, through Marcion, thus threatened the first article of the Creed, consult the
valuable remarks of the *Encyc. Britannica*, ("Mithras"). Mithras became known to the
Romans *circa* B.C. 70, and his worship flourished under Trajan and his successors. An able
writer remarks that it was natural "Dualism should develop itself out of primitive Zoro-
astrianism. The human mind has ever been struck with a certain antagonism of which it
has sought to discover the cause. Evil seems most easily accounted for by the supposition
of an evil Person; and the continuance of an equal struggle, without advantage to either
side, seems to imply the equality of that evil Person with the author of all good. Thus
Dualism had its birth. Many came to believe in the existence of two co-eternal and co-
equal Persons, one good and the other evil, between whom there has been from all eternity
a perpetual conflict, and between whom the same conflict must continue to rage through all
coming time."

AGAINST HERMOGENES.

CONTAINING AN ARGUMENT AGAINST HIS OPINION THAT MATTER IS ETERNAL.

[TRANSLATED BY DR. HOLMES.]

CHAP. I.—THE OPINIONS OF HERMOGENES, BY THE PRESCRIPTIVE RULE OF ANTIQUITY, SHOWN TO BE HERETICAL. NOT DERIVED FROM CHRISTIANITY, BUT FROM HEATHEN PHILOSOPHY. SOME OF THE TENETS MENTIONED.

WE are accustomed, for the purpose of shortening argument,[1] to lay down the rule against heretics of the *lateness* of their date.[2] For in *as* far as by our rule, priority is given to the truth, which also foretold that there would be heresies, in *so* far must all later opinions be prejudged as heresies, being such as were, by the more ancient rule of truth, predicted as (one day) to happen. Now, the doctrine of Hermogenes has this[3] taint of novelty. He is, in short,[4] a man *living* in the world at the present time; by his very nature a heretic, and turbulent withal, who mistakes loquacity for eloquence, and supposes impudence to be firmness, and judges it to be the duty of a good conscience to speak ill of individuals.[5] Moreover, despises God's law in his painting,[6] maintaining repeated marriages,[7] alleges the law of God in defence of lust,[8] *and yet* despises it in respect of his art.[9] He falsifies by a two-fold process—with his cautery and his pen.[10]

He is a thorough adulterer, both doctrinally and carnally, since he is rank indeed with the contagion of your marriage-hacks,[11] and has also failed in cleaving to the rule of faith as much as the apostle's own Hermogenes.[12] However, never mind the man, when it is his doctrine which I question. He does not appear to acknowledge any other Christ as Lord,[13] though he holds Him in a different way; but by this difference in his faith he really makes Him another being,—nay, he takes from Him everything which is God, since he will not have it that He made all things of nothing. For, turning away from Christians to the philosophers, from the Church to the Academy and the Porch, he learned there from the Stoics how to place Matter (on the same level) with the Lord, just as if it too had existed ever both unborn and unmade, having no beginning at all nor end, out of which, according to him,[14] the Lord afterwards created all things.

CHAP. II.—HERMOGENES, AFTER A PERVERSE INDUCTION FROM MERE HERETICAL ASSUMPTIONS, CONCLUDES THAT GOD CREATED ALL THINGS OUT OF PRE-EXISTING MATTER.

Our very bad painter has coloured this his primary shade absolutely without any light, with such arguments as these: He begins with laying down the premiss,[15] that the Lord made all things either out of Himself, or out of nothing, or out of something; in order that, after he has shown that it was impossible for Him to have made them either out of Himself or out of nothing, he might thence affirm the residuary proposition that He made them out of something, and therefore that that something was Matter. He could not have made all things, he says, of Himself; because whatever

---

[1] Compendii gratia. [The reference here to the *De Præscript.* forbids us to date this tract earlier than 207 A.D. Of this Hermogenes, we only know that he was probably a Carthaginian, a painter, and of a versatile and clever mind.]
[2] This is the criterion prescribed in the *Præscript. Hæret.* xxxi. xxxiv., and often applied by Tertullian. See our *Anti-Marcion*, pp. 272, 345, 470 and *passim*.
[3] The *tam novella* is a relative phrase, referring to the fore-mentioned *rule*.
[4] Denique.
[5] Maledicere singulis.
[6] Probably by painting idols (Rigalt.; and so Neander).
[7] It is uncertain whether Tertullian means to charge Hermogenes with defending *polygamy*, or only *second marriages*, in the phrase *nubit assidue*. Probably the latter, which was offensive to the rigorous Tertullian; and so Neander puts it.
[8] Quoting Gen. i. 28, "Be fruitful and multiply" (Rigalt.).
[9] Disregarding the law when it forbids the representation of idols. (Rigalt.)
[10] Et cauterio et stilo. The former instrument was used by the encaustic painters for *burning in* the wax colours into the ground of their pictures (Westropp's *Handbook of Archæology*, p. 219). Tertulliau charges Hermogenes with using his encaustic art to the injury of the Scriptures, by practically violating their precepts in his artistic works; and with usinghis pen (stilus) in corrupting the doctrine thereof by his heresy.

[11] By the *nubentium contagium*, Tertullian, in his Montanist rigour, censures those who married more than once.
[12] 2 Tim. i. 15.
[13] Thus differing from Marcion.
[14] The force of the subjunctive, ex qua *fecerit*.
[15] Præstruens.

things the Lord made of Himself would have been parts of Himself; but [1] He is not dissoluble into parts,[2] because, being the Lord, He is indivisible,and unchangeable,and always the same. Besides, if He had made anything out of Himself, it would have been something of Himself. Everything, however, both which was made and which He made must be accounted imperfect, because it was made of a part, and He made it of a part; or if, again, it was a whole which He made, who is a whole Himself, He must in that case have been at once both a whole, and yet not a whole; because it behoved Him to be a whole, that He might produce Himself,[3] and yet not a whole, that He might be produced out of Himself.[4] But this is a most difficult position. For if He were in existence, He could not be made, for He was in existence already; if, however, he were not in existence, He could not make, because He was a nonentity. *He maintains*, moreover, that He who always exists, does not *come into* existence,[5] but exists for ever and ever. He accordingly concludes that He made nothing out of Himself, since He never passed into such a condition [6] as made it possible for Him to make anything out of Himself. In like manner, he contends that He could not have made all things out of nothing—thus: He defines the Lord as a being who is good, nay, very good, who must will to make things as good and excellent as He is Himself; indeed it were impossible for Him either to will or to make anything which was not good, nay, very good itself. Therefore all things ought to have been made good and excellent by Him, after His own condition. Experience shows,[7] however, that things which are even evil were made by Him: not, of course, of His own will and pleasure; because, if it had been of His own will and pleasure, He would be sure to have made nothing unfitting or unworthy of Himself. That, therefore, which He made not of His own will must be understood to have been made from the fault of something, and that is from Matter, without a doubt.

CHAP. III.—AN ARGUMENT OF HERMOGENES. THE ANSWER: WHILE GOD IS A TITLE ETERNALLY APPLICABLE TO THE DIVINE BEING, LORD AND FATHER ARE ONLY RELATIVE APPELLATIONS, NOT ETERNALLY APPLICABLE. AN INCONSISTENCY IN THE ARGUMENT OF HERMOGENES POINTED OUT

He adds also another point: that as God was always God, there was never a time when God was not also Lord. But [8] it was in no way possible for Him to be regarded as always Lord, in the same manner as He had been always God, if there had not been always, in the previous eternity,[9] a something of which He could be regarded as evermore the Lord. So he concludes [10] that God always had Matter co-existent with Himself as the Lord thereof. Now, this tissue [11] of his I shall at once hasten to pull abroad. I have been willing to set it out in form to this length, for the information of those who are unacquainted with the subject, that they may know that his other arguments likewise need only be [12] understood to be refuted. We affirm, then, that the name of *God* always existed with Himself and in Himself—but not eternally so the *Lord*. Because the condition of the one is not the same as that of the other. God is the designation of the substance itself, that is, of the Divinity; but Lord is (the name) not of substance, but of power. I *maintain* that the substance existed always with its own name, which is God; *the title* Lord was afterwards added, as the indication indeed [13] of something accruing. For from the moment when those things began to exist, over which the power of a Lord was to act, *God*, by the accession of that power, both became Lord and received the name thereof. Because God is in like manner a Father, and He is also a Judge; but He has not always been Father and Judge, merely on the ground of His having always been God. For He could not have been the Father previous to the Son, nor a Judge previous to sin. There was, however, a time when neither sin existed with Him, nor the Son; the former of which was to constitute the Lord a Judge, and the latter a Father. In this way He was not Lord previous to those things of which He was to be the Lord. But He was only to become Lord at some future time: just as He became the Father by the Son, and a Judge by sin, so also did He become Lord by means of those things which He had made, in order that they might serve Him. Do I seem to you to be weaving arguments,[14] Hermogenes? How neatly does Scripture lend us its aid,[15] when it applies the two titles to Him with a distinction, and reveals them each at its proper time! For (the title) *God*, indeed, which

---

[1] Porro.
[2] In partes non devenire.
[3] Ut faceret semetipsum.
[4] Ut fieret de semetipso.
[5] Non fieri.

[6] Non ejus fieret conditionis.
[7] Inveniri.
[8] Porro.
[9] Retro.
[10] Itaque.
[11] Conjecturam.
[12] Tam. . . quam.
[13] Scilicet.
[14] Argumentari : in the sense of *argutari*.
[15] Naviter nobis patrocinatur.

always belonged to Him, it names at the very first: "In the beginning God created the heaven and the earth;"[1] and as long as He continued making, one after the other, those things of which He was to be the Lord, it merely mentions God. "And *God* said," "and *God* made," "and *God* saw;"[2] but nowhere do we yet find the *Lord*. But when He completed the whole creation, and especially man himself, who was destined to understand His sovereignty in a way of special propriety, He then is designated[3] Lord. Then also *the Scripture* added the name *Lord*: "And the Lord God, *Deus Dominus*, took the man, whom He had formed;"[4] "And the Lord God commanded Adam."[5] Thenceforth He, who was previously God only, is the *Lord*, from the time of His having something of which He might be the Lord. For to Himself He was always God, but to all things was He only then God, when He became also Lord. Therefore, in *as* far as (Hermogenes) shall suppose that Matter was eternal, on the ground that the Lord was eternal, in *so* far will it be evident that nothing existed, because it is plain that the Lord *as such* did not always exist. Now I mean also, on my own part,[6] to add a remark for the sake of ignorant persons, of whom Hermogenes is an extreme instance,[7] and actually to retort against him his own arguments.[8] For when he denies that Matter was born or made, I find that, even on these terms, the title *Lord* is unsuitable to God in respect of Matter, because it must have been free,[9] when by not having a beginning it had not an author. The fact of its past existence it owed to no one, so that it could be a subject to no one. Therefore ever since God exercised His power over it, by creating (all things) out of Matter, although it had all along experienced God as its Lord, yet Matter does, after all, demonstrate that God did not exist in the relation of Lord to it,[10] although all the while He was really so.[11]

CHAP. IV.—HERMOGENES GIVES DIVINE ATTRIBUTES TO MATTER, AND SO MAKES TWO GODS.

At this point, then, I shall begin to treat of Matter, how that, (according to Hermog-

enes,)[12] God compares it with Himself as equally unborn, equally unmade, equally eternal, set forth as being without a beginning, without an end. For what other estimate[13] of God is there than eternity? What other condition has eternity than to have ever existed, and to exist yet for evermore by virtue of its privilege of having neither beginning nor end? Now, since this is the property of God, it will belong to God alone, whose property it is—of course[14] on this ground, that if it can be ascribed to any other being, it will no longer be the property of God, but will belong, along with Him, to that being also to which it is ascribed. For "although there be that are called gods" in name, "whether in heaven or in earth, yet to us there is but one God the Father, of whom are all things;"[15] whence the greater reason why, in our view,[16] that which is the property[17] of God ought to be regarded as pertaining to God alone, and why (as I have already said) that should cease to be such a property, when it is shared by another being. Now, since He is God, it must necessarily be a unique mark of this quality,[18] that it be confined to One. Else, what will be unique and singular, if that is not which has nothing equal to it? What will be principal, if that is not which is above all things, before all things, and from which all things proceed? By possessing these He is God alone, and by His sole possession of them He is One. If another also shared in the possession, there would then be as many gods as there were possessors of these attributes of God. Hermogenes, therefore, introduces two gods: he introduces Matter as God's equal. God, however, must be One, because that is God which is supreme; but nothing else can be supreme than that which is unique; and that cannot possibly be unique which has anything equal to it; and Matter will be equal with God when it is held to be[19] eternal.

CHAP. V.—HERMOGENES COQUETS WITH HIS OWN ARGUMENT, AS IF RATHER AFRAID OF IT. AFTER INVESTING MATTER WITH DIVINE QUALITIES, HE TRIES TO MAKE IT SOMEHOW INFERIOR TO GOD.

But God is God, and Matter is Matter. As if a mere difference in their names prevented equality,[20] when an identity of condition is claimed for them! Grant that their nature is

[1] Gen. i. 1.
[2] Gen. i. 3, etc.
[3] Cognominatur: as if by way of *surname*, Deus Domi...us.
[4] Gen. ii. 15.
[5] Gen. ii. 16.
[6] Et ego.
[7] Extrema linea. Rhenanus sees in this phrase a slur against Hermogenes, who was an artist. Tertullian, I suppose, meant that Hermogenes was extremely ignorant.
[8] Experimenta.
[9] Libera: and so not a possible *subject* for the Lordship of God.
[10] Matter having, by the hypothesis, been *independent of God*, and so incapable of giving Him any title to Lordship.
[11] Fuit hoc utique. In Hermogenes' own opinion, which is thus shown to have been contradictory to itself, and so absurd.
[12] Quod, with the subjunctive comparet.
[13] Census.
[14] Scilicet.
[15] 1 Cor. viii. 5.
[16] Apud nos.
[17] The property of being eternal.
[18] Unicum sit necesse est.
[19] Censetur.
[20] Comparationi.

different; assume, too, that their form is not identical,—what matters it so long as their absolute state have but one mode?[1] God is unborn; is not Matter also unborn? God ever exists; is not Matter, too, ever existent? Both are without beginning; both are without end; both are the authors of the universe— both He who created it, and the Matter of which He made it. For it is impossible that Matter should not be regarded as the author[2] of all things, when the universe is composed of it. What answer will he give? Will he say that Matter is not then comparable with God as soon as[3] it has something belonging to God; since, by not having total (divinity), it cannot correspond to the whole extent of the comparison? But what more has he reserved for God, that he should not seem to have accorded to Matter the full amount of the Deity?[4] He says in reply, that even though this is the prerogative of Matter, both the authority and the substance of God must remain intact, by virtue of which He is regarded as the sole and prime Author, as well as the Lord of all things. Truth, however, maintains the unity of God in such a way as to insist that whatever belongs to God Himself belongs to Him alone. For so will it belong to Himself if it belong to Him alone; and therefore it will be impossible that another god should be admitted, when it is permitted to no other being to possess anything of God. Well, then, you say, we ourselves at that rate possess nothing of God. But indeed we do, and shall continue to do—only it is from Him that we receive it, and not from ourselves. For we shall be even gods, if we shall deserve to be among those of whom He declared, "I have said, Ye are gods,"[5] and, "God standeth in the congregation of the gods."[6] But this comes of His own grace, not from any property in us, because it is He alone who can make gods. The property of Matter, however, he[7] makes to be that which it has in common with God. Otherwise, if it received from God the property which belongs to God,—I mean its attribute[8] of eternity,— one might then even suppose that it both possesses an attribute in common with God, and yet at the same time is not God. But what inconsistency is it for him[9] to allow that there is a conjoint possession of an attribute with God, and also to wish that what he does not refuse to Matter should be, after all, the exclusive privilege of God!

CHAP. VI.—THE SHIFTS TO WHICH HERMOGENES IS REDUCED, WHO DEIFIES MATTER, AND YET IS UNWILLING TO HOLD HIM EQUAL WITH THE DIVINE CREATOR.

He declares that God's attribute is still safe to Him, of being the only God, and the First, and the Author of all things, and the Lord of all things, and being incomparable to any—qualities which he straightway ascribes to Matter also. He is God, to be sure. God shall also attest the same; but He has also sworn sometimes by Himself, that there is no other God like Him.[10] Hermogenes, however, will make Him a liar. For Matter will be such a God as He—being unmade, unborn, without beginning, and without end. God will say, "I am the first!"[11] Yet how is He the first, when Matter is co-eternal with Him? Between co-eternals and contemporaries there is no sequence of rank.[12] Is then, Matter also the first? "I," says the Lord, "have stretched out the heavens alone."[13] But indeed He was not alone, when that likewise stretched them out, of which He made the expanse. When he asserts the position that Matter was *eternal*, without any encroachment on the condition of God, let him see to it that we do not in ridicule turn the tables on him, that God similarly was eternal without any encroachment on the condition of Matter—the condition of Both being still common to Them. The position, therefore, remains unimpugned[14] both in the case of Matter, that it did itself exist, only along with God; and that God existed alone, but with Matter. It also was first with God, as God, too, was first with it; it, however, is not comparable with God, as God, too, is not to be compared with it; with God also it was the Author (of all things), and with God their Sovereign. In this way *he proposes that God* has something, and yet not the whole, of Matter. For Him, accordingly, Hermogenes has reserved nothing which he had not equally conferred on Matter, so that it is not Matter which is compared with God, but rather God who is compared with Matter. Now, inasmuch as those qualities which we claim as peculiar to God—to have always existed, without a beginning, without an end, and to have been the First, and Alone, and the Author of all things—are also compatible to Matter, I want to know what property Matter possesses

[1] Ratio.
[2] Auctrix.
[3] Statim si.
[4] Totum Dei.
[5] Ps. lxxxii. 6.
[6] Ver. 1.
[7] Hermogenes.
[8] Ordinem: or course.
[9] Quale autem est: "how comes it to pass that."
[10] Isa. xlv. 23.
[11] Isa. xli. 4, xliv. 6, xlviii. 12.
[12] Ordo.
[13] Isa. xliv. 24
[14] Salvum ergo erit.

different and alien from God, and hereby special to itself, by reason of which it is incapable of being compared with God? That Being, in which occur[1] all the properties of God, is sufficiently predetermined without any further comparison.

CHAP. VII.—HERMOGENES HELD TO HIS THEORY IN ORDER THAT ITS ABSURDITY MAY BE EXPOSED ON HIS OWN PRINCIPLES.

When he contends that matter is less than God, and inferior to Him, and therefore diverse from Him, and for the same reason not a fit subject of comparison with Him, who is a greater and superior Being, I meet him with this prescription, that what is eternal and unborn is incapable of any diminution and inferiority, because it is simply this which makes even God to be as great as He is, inferior and subject to none—nay, greater and higher than all. For, just as all things which are born, or which come to an end, and are therefore not eternal, do, by reason of their exposure at once to an end and a beginning, admit of qualities which are repugnant to God—I mean diminution and inferiority, because they are born and made—so likewise God, for this very reason, is unsusceptible of these accidents, because He is absolutely unborn,[2] and also unmade. And yet such also is the condition of Matter.[3] Therefore, of the two Beings which are eternal, as being unborn and unmade—God and Matter—by reason of the identical mode of their common condition (both of them equally possessing that which admits neither of diminution nor subjection —that is, the attribute of eternity), we affirm that neither of them is less or greater than the other, neither of them is inferior or superior to the other; but that they both stand on a par in greatness, on a par in sublimity, *and* on the same level of that complete and perfect felicity of which eternity is reckoned to consist. Now we must not resemble the heathen in our opinions; for they, when constrained to acknowledge God, insist on having other deities below Him. The Divinity, however, has no degrees, because it is unique; and if it shall be found in Matter—as being equally unborn and unmade and eternal—it must be resident in both alike,[4] because in no case can it be inferior to itself. In what way, then, will Hermogenes have the courage to draw distinctions; aud thus to subject matter to God, an eternal to the Eternal, an unborn to the Unborn, an author to the Author?

seeing that it dares to say, I also am the first; I too am before all things; and I am that from which all things proceed; equal we have been, together we have been—both alike without beginning, without end; both alike without an Author, without a God.[5] What God, then, is He who subjects me to a contemporaneous, co-eternal power? If it be He who is called God, then I myself, too, have my own (divine) name. Either I am God, or He is Matter, because we both are that which neither of us is. Do you suppose, therefore, that he[6] has not made Matter equal with God, although, forsooth, he pretends it to be inferior to Him?

CHAP. VIII.—ON HIS OWN PRINCIPLES, HERMOGENES MAKES MATTER, ON THE WHOLE, SUPERIOR TO GOD.

Nay more,[7] he even prefers Matter to God, and rather subjects God to it, when he will have it that God made all things out of Matter. For if He drew His resources from it[8] for the creation of the world, Matter is already found to be the superior, inasmuch as it furnished Him with the means of effecting His works; and God is thereby clearly subjected to Matter, of which the substance was indispensable to Him. For there is no one but requires that which he makes use of;[9] no one but is subject to the thing which he requires, for the very purpose of being able to make use of it. So, again, there is no one who, from using what belongs to another, is not inferior to him of whose property he makes use; and there is no one who imparts[10] of his own for another's use, who is not in this respect superior to him to whose use he lends his property. On this principle,[11] Matter itself, no doubt,[12] was not in want of God, but rather lent itself to God, who was in want of it—rich and abundant and liberal as it was —to one who was, I suppose, too small, and too weak, and too unskilful, to form what He willed out of nothing. A grand service, verily,[13] did it confer on God in giving Him means at the present time whereby He might be known to be God, and be called Almighty —only that He is no longer Almighty, since He is not powerful enough for this, to produce all things out of nothing. To be sure,[14] Matter bestowed somewhat on itself also— even to get its own self acknowledged with God as God's co-equal, nay more, as His

---

[1] Recensentur.
[2] Nec natus omnino.
[3] Of course, according to Hermogenes, whom Tertullian refutes with an *argumentum ad hominem*.
[4] Aderit utrobique.

[5] That is, having no God superior to themselves.
[6] Hermogenes.
[7] Atquin etiam.
[8] Ex illa usus est.
[9] De cujus utitur.
[10] Præstat.
[11] Itaque.
[12] Quidem.
[13] Revera.
[14] Sane.

helper; only there is this drawback, that Hermogenes is the only man that has found out this fact, besides the philosophers—those patriarchs of all heresy.[1] For the prophets knew nothing about it, nor the apostles thus far, nor, I suppose, even Christ.

CHAP. IX.—SUNDRY INEVITABLE BUT INTOLERABLE CONCLUSIONS FROM THE PRINCIPLES OF HERMOGENES.

He cannot say that it was as its Lord that God employed Matter for His creative works, for He could not have been the Lord of a substance which was co-equal with Himself. Well, but perhaps it was a title derived from the will of another,[2] which he enjoyed—a precarious holding, and not a lordship,[3] and *that* to such a degree, that[4] although Matter was evil, He yet endured to make use of an evil substance, owing, of course, to the restraint of His own limited power,[5] which made Him impotent to create out of nothing, not in consequence of His power; for if, as God, He had at all possessed power over Matter, which He knew to be evil, He would first have converted it into good—as its Lord and the good God—that so He might have a good thing to make use of, instead of a bad one. But being undoubtedly good, only not the Lord withal, He, by using such power[6] as He possessed, showed the necessity He was under of yielding to the condition of Matter, which He would have amended if He had been its Lord. Now this is the answer which must be given to Hermogenes when he maintains that it was by virtue of His Lordship that God used Matter—even of His non-possession of any right to it, on the ground, of course, of His not having Himself made it. Evil then, on your terms,[7] must proceed from *God* Himself, since He is—I will not say the Author of evil, because He did not form it, but—the permitter thereof, as having dominion over it.[8] If indeed Matter shall prove not even to belong to God at all, as being evil, it follows,[9] that when He made use of what belonged to another, He used it either on a precarious title[10] because He was in need of it, or else by violent possession because He was stronger than it. For by three methods is the property of others obtained,—by right,

by permission, by violence; in other words, by lordship, by a title derived from the will of another,[11] by force. Now, as lordship is out of the question, Hermogenes must choose which (of the other methods) is suitable to God. Did He, then, make all things out of Matter, by permission, or by force? But, in truth, would not God have more wisely determined that nothing at all should be created, than that it should be created by the mere sufferance of another, or by violence, and that, too, with[12] a substance which was evil?

CHAP. X.—TO WHAT STRAITS HERMOGENES ABSURDLY REDUCES THE DIVINE BEING. HE DOES NOTHING SHORT OF MAKING HIM THE AUTHOR OF EVIL.

Even if Matter had been the perfection of good,[13] would it not have been equally indecorous in Him to have thought of the property of another, however good, (to effect His purpose by the help of it)? It was, therefore, absurd enough for Him, in the interest of His own glory, to have created the world in such a way as to betray His own obligation to a substance which belonged to another—and that even not good. Was He then, asks (Hermogenes), to make all things out of nothing, that so evil things themselves might be attributed to His will? Great, in all conscience,[14] must be the blindness of our heretics which leaves them to argue in such a way that they either insist on the belief of another God supremely good, on the ground of their thinking the Creator to be the author of evil, or else they set up Matter with the Creator, in order that they may derive evil from Matter, not from the Creator. And yet there is absolutely no god at all that is free from such a doubtful plight, so as to be able to avoid the appearance even of being the author of evil, whosoever he is that—I will not say, indeed, has made, but still—has permitted evil to be made by some author or other, and from some source or other. Hermogenes, therefore, ought to be told[15] at once, although we postpone to another place our distinction concerning the mode of evil,[16] that even he has effected no result by this device of his.[17] For observe how God is found to be, if not the Author of, yet at any rate the conniver at,[18] evil, inasmuch as He, with all His extreme goodness, endured evil in Matter be-

[1] They are so deemed in the *de Præscript. Hæret.* c. vii.
[2] We have rather paraphrased the word "precario"—"obtained by prayer." [See p. 456.]
[3] Domino: opposed to "precario."
[4] Ideo. . . ut.
[5] Mediocritatis.
[6] Tali: i. e. potestate.
[7] Jam ergo: introducing an *argumentum ad hominem* against Hermogenes.
[8] Quia dominator.
[9] Ergo.
[10] Aut precario: "as having begged for it."

[11] Precario: See above, note 2, p. 482.
[12] *De* is often in Tertullian the sign of an instrumental noun.
[13] Optima.
[14] Bona fide.
[15] Audiat.
[16] De mali ratione.
[17] Hac sua injectione. See our *Anti-Marcion*, iv. i., for this word, p. 345.
[18] Assentator. Fr. Junius suggests "adsectator" of the stronger meaning "promoter;" nor does Oehler object.

fore He created the world, although, as being good, and the enemy of evil, He ought to have corrected it. For He either was able to correct it, but was unwilling; or else was willing, but being a weak God, was not able. If He was able and yet unwilling, He was Himself evil, as having favoured evil; and thus He now opens Himself to the charge of evil, because even if He did not create it, yet still, since it would not be existing if He had been against its existence, He must Himself have then caused it to exist, when He refused to will its non-existence. And what is more shameful than this? When He willed that to be which He was Himself unwilling to create, He acted in fact against His very self,[1] inasmuch as He was both willing that that should exist which He was unwilling to make, and unwilling to make that which He was willing should exist. As if what He willed was good, and at the same time what he refused to be the Maker of was evil. What He judged to be evil by not creating it, He also proclaimed to be good by permitting it to exist. By bearing with evil as a good instead of rather extirpating it, He proved Himself to be the promoter thereof; criminally,[2] if through His own will—disgracefully, if through necessity. God must either be the servant of evil or the friend thereof, since He held converse with evil in Matter—nay more, effected His works out of the evil thereof.

CHAP. XI.—HERMOGENES MAKES GREAT EFFORTS TO REMOVE EVIL FROM GOD TO MATTER. HOW HE FAILS TO DO THIS CONSISTENTLY WITH HIS OWN ARGUMENT.

But, after all,[3] by what proofs does Hermogenes persuade us that Matter is evil? For it will be impossible for him not to call that evil to which he imputes evil. Now we lay down this principle,[4] that what is eternal cannot possibly admit of diminution and subjection, so as to be considered inferior to another co-eternal Being. So that we now affirm that evil is not even compatible with it,[5] since it is incapable of subjection, from the fact that it cannot in any wise be subject to any, because it is eternal. But inasmuch as, on other grounds,[6] it is evident what is eternal as God is the highest good, whereby also He alone is good—as being eternal, and therefore good—as being God, how can evil be inherent in Matter, which (since it is eternal)

must needs be believed to be the highest good? Else if that which is eternal prove to be also capable of evil, this (evil) will be able to be also believed of God to His prejudice;[7] so that it is without adequate reason that he has been so anxious[8] to remove evil from God; since evil must be compatible with an eternal Being, even by being made compatible with Matter, as Hermogenes makes it. But, as the argument now stands,[9] since what is eternal can be deemed evil, the evil must prove to be invincible and insuperable, as being eternal; and in that case[10] it will be in vain that we labour "to put away evil from the midst of us;"[11] in that case, moreover, God vainly gives us such a command and precept; nay more, in vain has God appointed any judgment at all, when He means, indeed,[12] to inflict punishment with injustice. But if, on the other hand, there is to be an end of evil, when the chief thereof, the devil, shall "go away into the fire which God hath prepared for him and his angels"[13] —having been first "cast into the bottomless pit;"[14] when likewise "the manifestation of the children of God"[15] shall have "delivered the creature"[16] from evil, which had been "made subject to vanity;"[17] when the cattle restored in the innocence and integrity of their nature[18] shall be at peace[19] with the beasts of the field, when also little children shall play with serpents;[20] when the Father shall have put beneath the feet of His Son His enemies,[21] as being the workers of evil, —if in this way an *end* is compatible with evil, it must follow of necessity that a *beginning* is also compatible with it; and Matter will turn out to have a beginning, by virtue of its having also an end. For whatever things are set to the account of evil,[22] have a compatibility with the condition of evil.

CHAP. XII.—THE MODE OF CONTROVERSY CHANGED. THE PREMISSES OF HERMOGENES ACCEPTED, IN ORDER TO SHOW INTO WHAT CONFUSION THEY LEAD HIM.

Come now, let us suppose Matter to be evil, nay, very evil, by *nature* of course, just as

[1] Adversum semetipsum.
[2] Male: in reference to His alleged complicity with *evil*.
[3] Et tamen.
[4] Definimus.
[5] Competere illi.
[6] Alias.
[7] Et in Deum credi.
[8] Gestivit.
[9] Jam vero.
[10] Tum.
[11] 1 Cor. v. 13.
[12] Utique: with a touch of irony, in the *argumentum ad hominem*.
[13] Matt. xxv. 41.
[14] Rev. xx. 3.
[15] Rom. viii. 19.
[16] Rom. viii. 21.
[17] Rom. viii. 20.
[18] Conditionis: "creation."
[19] Condixerint.
[20] Isa. xi. 6.
[21] Ps. cx. 1.
[22] Male deputantur.

we believe God to be good, even very good, in like manner by *nature*. Now nature must be regarded as sure and fixed, just as persistently fixed in evil in the case of Matter, as immoveable and unchangeable in good in the case of God. Because, as is evident,[1] if nature admits of change from evil to good in Matter, it can be changed from good to evil in God. Here some man will say, Then will "children not be raised up to Abraham from the stones?"[2] Will "generations of vipers not bring forth the fruit of repentance?"[3] And "children of wrath" fail to become sons of peace, if nature be unchangeable? Your reference to such examples as these, my friend,[4] is a thoughtless[5] one. For things which owe their existence to birth—such as stones and vipers and human beings—are not apposite to the case of Matter, which is unborn; since their nature, by possessing a beginning, may have also a termination. But bear in mind[6] that Matter has once for all been determined to be eternal, as being unmade, unborn, and therefore supposably of an unchangeable and incorruptible nature; and this from the very opinion of Hermogenes himself, which he alleges against us when he denies that God was able to make (anything) of Himself, on the ground that what is eternal is incapable of change, because it would lose—so the opinion runs[7]—what it once was, in becoming by the change that which it was not, if it were not eternal. But as for the Lord, who is also eternal, (he maintained) that He could not be anything else than what He always is. Well, then, I will adopt this definite opinion of his, and by means thereof refute him. I blame Matter with a like censure, because out of it, evil though it be—nay, very evil—good things have been created, ay, "very good" ones: "And God saw that they were good, and God blessed them"[8]—because, of course, of their very great goodness; certainly not because they were evil, or very evil. Change is therefore admissible in Matter; and this being the case, it has lost its condition of eternity; in short,[9] its beauty is decayed in death.[10] Eternity, however, cannot be lost, because it cannot be eternity, except by reason of its immunity from loss. For the same reason also it is incapable of change, inasmuch as, since it is eternity, it can by no means be changed.

CHAP. XIII.—ANOTHER GROUND OF HERMOGENES THAT MATTER HAS SOME GOOD IN IT. ITS ABSURDITY.

Here the question will arise How creatures were made good out of it,[11] which were formed without any change at all?[12] How occurs the seed of what is good, ay, very good, in that which is evil, nay, very evil? Surely a good tree does not produce evil fruit,[13] since there is no God who is not good; nor does an evil tree yield good fruit, since there is not Matter except what is very evil. Or if we were to grant him that there is some germ of good *in it*, then there will be no longer a uniform nature (pervading it), that is to say, one which is evil throughout; but instead thereof (we now encounter) a double nature, partly good and partly evil; and again the question will arise, whether, in a subject which is good and evil, there could possibly have been found a harmony for light and darkness, for sweet and bitter? So again, if qualities so utterly diverse as good and evil have been able to unite together,[14] and have imparted to Matter a double nature, productive of both kinds of fruit, then no longer will absolutely[15] good things be imputable to God, just as evil things are not ascribed to Him, but both qualities will appertain to Matter, since they are derived from the property of Matter. At this rate, we shall owe to God neither gratitude for good things, nor grudge[16] for evil ones, because He has produced no work of His own proper character.[17] From which circumstance will arise the clear proof that He has been subservient to Matter.

CHAP. XIV.—TERTULLIAN PUSHES HIS OPPONENT INTO A DILEMMA.

Now, if it be also argued, that although Matter may have afforded Him the opportunity, it was still His own will which led Him to the creation of good creatures, as having detected[18] what was good in matter—although this, too, be a discreditable supposition[19]—yet, at any rate, when He produces evil likewise out of the same (Matter), He is a servant to Matter, since, of course,[20] it is not of His own accord that He produces this too, having nothing else that He can do than to effect creation out of an evil *stock*[21]—unwillingly, no

---

[1] Scilicet.
[2] Mat. iii. 9.
[3] Verses 7, 8.
[4] O homo.
[5] Temere.
[6] Tene.
[7] Scilicet.
[8] Gen. i. 21, 22.
[9] Denique.
[10] That is, of course, by its own natural law.

[11] Matter.
[12] i. e. in their nature, Matter being evil, and they good, on the hypothesis.
[13] Matt. vii. 18.
[14] Concurrisse.
[15] Ipsa.
[16] Invidiam.
[17] Ingenio.
[18] Nactus.
[19] Turpe.
[20] Utique.
[21] Ex malo.

doubt, as being good; of necessity, too, as being unwilling; and as an act of servitude, because from necessity. Which, then, is the worthier thought, that He created evil things of necessity, or of His own accord? Because it was indeed of necessity that He created them, if out of Matter; of His own accord, if out of nothing. For you are now labouring in vain when you try to avoid making God the Author of evil things; because, since He made all things of Matter, they will have to be ascribed to Himself, who made them, just because[1] He made them. Plainly the interest of the question, whence He made all things, identifies itself with (the question), whether He made all things out of nothing; and it matters not whence He made all things, so that He made all things thence, whence most glory accrued to Him.[2] Now, more glory accrued to Him from a creation of His own will than from one of necessity; in other words, from a creation out of nothing, than from one out of Matter. It is more worthy to believe that God is free, even as the Author of evil, than that He is a slave. Power, whatever it be, is more suited to Him than infirmity.[3] If we thus even admit that matter had nothing good in it, but that the Lord produced whatever good He did produce of His own power, then some other questions will with equal reason arise. First, since there was no good at all in Matter, *it is clear* that good was not made of Matter, on the express ground indeed that Matter did not possess it. Next, if *good was* not *made* of Matter, it must then have been made of God; if not of God, then it must have been made of nothing.—For this is the alternative, on Hermogenes' own showing.[4]

CHAP. XV.—THE TRUTH, THAT GOD MADE ALL THINGS FROM NOTHING, RESCUED FROM THE OPPONENT'S FLOUNDERINGS.

Now, if good was neither produced out of matter, since it was not in it, evil as it was, nor out of God, since, according to the position of Hermogenes, nothing could have been produced out of god, it will be found that good was created out of nothing, inasmuch as it was formed of none—neither of Matter nor of God. And if good was formed out of nothing, why not evil too? Nay, if anything was formed out of nothing, why not all things? Unless indeed it be that the divine might was insufficient for the production of *all* things, though it produced a something out of noth-

ing. Or else if good proceeded from evil matter, since it issued neither from nothing nor from God, it will follow that it must have proceeded from the conversion of Matter contrary to that unchangeable attribute which has been claimed for *it, as* an eternal being.[5] Thus, in regard to the source whence good derived its existence, Hermogenes will now have to deny the possibility of such. But still it is necessary that (good) should proceed from some one of those sources from which he has denied the very possibility of its having been derived. Now if evil be denied to be of nothing for the purpose of denying it to be the work of God, from whose will there would be too much appearance of its being derived, and be alleged to proceed from Matter, that it may be the property of that very thing of whose substance it is assumed to be made, even here also, as I have said, God will have to be regarded as the Author of evil; because, whereas it had been His duty[6] to produce all good things out of Matter, or rather good things simply, by His identical attribute of power and will, He did yet *not only* not produce all good things, but even (some) evil things—of course, either willing that the evil should exist if He was able to cause their non-existence, or not being strong enough to effect that all things should be good, if being desirous of that result, He failed in the accomplishment thereof; since there can be no difference whether it were by weakness or by will, that the Lord proved to be the Author of evil. Else what was the reason that, after creating good things, as if Himself good, He should have also produced evil things, as if He failed in His goodness, since He did not confine Himself to the production of things which were simply consistent with Himself? What necessity was there, after the production of His proper work, for His troubling Himself about Matter also by producing evil likewise, in order to secure His being alone acknowledged as good from His good, and at the same time[7] to prevent Matter being regarded as evil from (created) evil? Good would have flourished much better if evil had not blown upon it. For Hermogenes himself explodes the arguments of sundry persons who contend that evil things were necessary to impart lustre to the good, which must be understood from their contrasts. This, therefore, was not the ground for the production

---

[1] Proinde quatenus.

[2] We subjoin the original of this sentence: " Plane sic interest unde fecerit ac si de nihilo fecisset, nec interest unde fecerit, ut inde fecerit unde eum magis decuit.

[3] Pusillitas.

[4] Secundum Hermogenis dispositionem.

[5] Contra denegatam æterni conversationem. Literally, " Contrary to that convertibility of an eternal nature which has been denied (by Hermogenes) to be possible." It will be obvious why we have, in connection with the preceding clause preferred the equivalent rendering of our text. For the denial of Hermogenes, which Tertullian refers to, see above, chap. xii. p. 484.

[6] Debuisset protulisse.

[7] This clumsy expedient to save the character of both God and Matter was one of the weaknesses of Hermogenes' system.

of evil; but if some other reason must be sought for the introduction thereof, why could it not have been introduced even from nothing,[1] since the very same reason would exculpate the Lord from the reproach of being thought the author of evil, which now excuses *the existence of* evil things, when He produces them out of Matter? And if there is this excuse, then the question is completely[2] shut up in a corner, where they are unwilling to find it, who, without examining into the reason itself of evil, or distinguishing how they should either attribute it to God or separate it from God, do in fact expose God to many most unworthy calumnies.[3]

CHAP. XVI.—A SERIES OF DILEMMAS. THEY SHOW THAT HERMOGENES CANNOT ESCAPE FROM THE ORTHODOX CONCLUSION.

On the very threshold,[4] then, of this doctrine,[5] which I shall probably have to treat of elsewhere, I distinctly lay it down as my position, that both good and evil must be ascribed either to God, who made them out of Matter; or to Matter itself, out of which He made them; or both one and the other to both of them together,[6] because they are bound together—both He who created, and that out of which He created; or (lastly) one to One, and the other to the Other,[7] because after Matter and God there is not a third. Now if both should prove to belong *to God*, God evidently will be the author of evil; but God, as being good, cannot be the author of evil. Again, if both are ascribed *to Matter*, Matter will evidently be the very mother of good,[8] but inasmuch as Matter is wholly evil, it cannot be the mother of good. But if both one and the other should be thought to belong to Both together, then in this case also Matter will be comparable with God; and both will be equal, being on equal terms allied to evil as well as to good. Matter, however, ought not to be compared with God, in order that it may not make two gods. If, (lastly,) one be ascribed to One, and the other to the Other— that is to say, let the good be God's, and the evil belong to Matter—then, on the one hand, evil must not be ascribed to God, nor, on the other hand, good to Matter. And God, moreover, by making both good things and evil things out of Matter, creates *them* along with

it. This being the case, I cannot tell how Hermogenes[9] is to escape from my conclusion; for he supposes that God cannot be the author of evil, in what way soever He created evil out of Matter, whether it was of His own will, or of necessity, or from the reason (of the case). If, however, He is the author of evil, who was the actual Creator, Matter being simply associated *with Him* by reason of its furnishing Him with substance,[10] you now do away with the cause[11] of *your* introducing Matter. For it is not the less *true*, that it is by means of Matter that God shows Himself the author of evil, although Matter has been assumed *by you* expressly to prevent God's seeming to be the author of evil. Matter being therefore excluded, since the cause of it is excluded, it remains that God, without doubt, must have made all things out of nothing. Whether evil things were amongst them we shall see, when it shall be made clear what are evil things, and whether those things are evil which you at present deem to be so. For it is more worthy of God that He produced even these of His own will, by producing them out of nothing, than from the predetermination of another,[12] (which must have been the case) if He had produced them out of Matter. It is liberty, not necessity, which suits the character of God. I would much rather that He should have even willed to create evil of Himself, than that He should have lacked ability to hinder its creation.

CHAP. XVII.—THE TRUTH OF GOD'S WORK IN CREATION. YOU CANNOT DEPART IN THE LEAST FROM IT, WITHOUT LANDING YOURSELF IN AN ABSURDITY.

This rule is required by the nature of the One-only God,[13] who is One-only in no other way than as the sole God; and in no other way sole, than as having nothing else (co-existent) with Him. So also He will be first, because all things are after Him; and all things are after Him, because all things are by Him; and all things are by Him, because they are of nothing: so that reason coincides with the Scripture, which says: "Who hath known the mind of the Lord? or who hath been His counsellor? or with whom took He counsel? or who hath shown to Him the way of wisdom and knowledge? Who hath first given to

---

[1] Cur non et ex nihilo potuerit induci?
[2] Ubique et undique.
[3] Destructionibus. "Ruin of character" is the true idea of this strong term.
[4] Præstructione. The notion is of the *foundation* of an edifice: here = "preliminary remarks" (see our *Anti-Marcion*, v. 5, p. 438).
[5] Articuli.
[6] Utrumque utrique.
[7] Alterum alteri.
[8] Boni matrix.
[9] The usual reading is "Hermogenes." Rigaltius, however, reads "Hermogenis," of which Oehler approves; so as to make Tertullian say, "I cannot tell how I can avoid the opinion of Hermogenes, who," etc. etc.
[10] Per substantiæ suggestum.
[11] Excusas jam causam. Hermogenes held that Matter was eternal, to exclude God from the authorship of evil. This *causa* of Matter he was now illogically evading. Excusare = ex, causa, "to cancel the cause."
[12] De præjudicio alieno.
[13] Unici Dei.

Him, and it shall be recompensed to him again?"[1] Surely none! Because there was present with Him no power, no material, no nature which belonged to any other than Himself. But if it was with some (portion of Matter)[2] that He effected His creation, He must have received from that (Matter) itself both the design and the treatment of its order, as being "the way of wisdom and knowledge." For He had to operate conformably with the quality of the thing, and according to the nature of Matter, not according to His own will; in consequence of which He must have made[3] even evil things suitably to the nature not of Himself, but of Matter.

CHAP. XVIII.—AN EULOGY ON THE WISDOM AND WORD OF GOD, BY WHICH GOD MADE ALL THINGS OF NOTHING.

If any material was necessary to God in the creation of the world, as Hermogenes supposed, God had a far nobler and more suitable one in His own wisdom[4]—one which was not to be gauged by the writings of[5] philosophers, but to be learnt from the words of[5] prophets. This alone, indeed, knew the mind of the Lord. For "who knoweth the things of God, and the things in God, but the Spirit, which is in Him?"[6] Now His wisdom is that Spirit. This was His counsellor, the very way of His wisdom and knowledge.[7] Of this He made all things, making them through It, and making them with It. "When He prepared the heavens," so says (the Scripture[8]), "I was present with Him; and when He strengthened above the winds the lofty clouds, and when He secured the fountains[9] which are under the heaven, I was present, compacting these things[10] along with Him. I was He[11] in whom He took delight; moreover, I daily rejoiced in His presence: for He rejoiced when He had finished the world, and amongst the sons of men did He show forth His pleasure."[12] Now, who would not rather approve of[13] this as the fountain and origin of all things—of this as, in very deed, the Matter of all Matter, not liable to any end,[14] not diverse in condition, not restless in

motion, not ungraceful in form, but natural, and proper, and duly proportioned, and beautiful, such truly as even God might well have required, who requires His own and not another's? Indeed, as soon as He perceived It to be necessary for His creation of the world, He immediately creates It, and generates It in Himself. "The Lord," says the Scripture, "possessed[15] me, the beginning of His ways for the creation of His works. Before the worlds He founded me; before He made the earth, before the mountains were settled in their places; moreover, before the hills He generated me, and prior to the depths was I begotten."[16] Let Hermogenes then confess that the very Wisdom of God is declared to be born and created, for the especial reason that we should not suppose that there is any other being than God alone who is unbegotten and uncreated. For if that, which from its being inherent in the Lord[17] was of Him and in Him, was yet not without a beginning,—I mean[18] His wisdom, which was then born and created, when in the thought of God It began to assume motion[19] for the arrangement of His creative works,—how much more impossible[20] is it that anything should have been without a beginning which was extrinsic to the Lord![21] But if this same Wisdom is the Word of God, in the capacity[22] of Wisdom, and (as being He) without whom nothing was made, just as also (nothing) was set in order without Wisdom, how can it be that anything, except the Father, should be older, and on this account indeed nobler, than the Son of God, the only-begotten and first-begotten Word? Not to say that[23] what is unbegotten is stronger than that which is born, and what is not made more powerful than that which is made. Because that which did not require a Maker to give it existence, will be much more elevated in rank than that which had an author to bring it into being. On this principle, then,[24] if evil is indeed unbegotten, whilst the Son of God is begotten ("for," says God, "my heart hath emitted my most excellent Word"[25]), I am not quite sure that evil may not be introduced by good, the stronger by the weak, in the same way as the unbegotten is by the begotten. Therefore on this ground Hermogenes puts Matter even before God, by putting it before the Son. Because the

[1] Rom. xi. 34, 35 ; comp. Isa. xl. 14.
[2] De aliquo.
[3] Adeo ut fecerit.
[4] Sophiam suam scilicet.
[5] Apud.
[6] 1 Cor. ii. 11.
[7] Isa. xl. 14.
[8] Or the "inquit" may indicate the very words of "Wisdom."
[9] Fontes. Although Oehler prefers Junius' reading "montes," he yet retains "fontes," because Tertullian (in ch. xxxii. below) has the unmistakable reading "fontes" in a like connection.
[10] Compingens.
[11] Ad quem: the expression is masculine.
[12] Prov. viii. 27-31.
[13] Commendet.
[14] "Non fini subditam" is Oehler's better reading than the old "sibi subditam."

[15] Condidit : created.
[16] See Prov. viii.
[17] Intra Dominum.
[18] Scilicet.
[19] Cœpti agitari.
[20] Multo magis non capit.
[21] Extra Dominum.
[22] Sensu.
[23] Nedum.
[24] Proinde.
[25] On this version of Ps. xlv. 1., and its application by Tertullian, see our *Anti-Marcion* (p. 299, note 5).

Son is the Word, and "the Word is God," [1] and "I and my Father are one." [2] But after all, perhaps, [3] the Son will patiently enough submit to having that preferred before Him, which (by Hermogenes), is made equal to the Father!

CHAP. XIX.—AN APPEAL TO THE HISTORY OF CREATION. TRUE MEANING OF THE TERM BEGINNING, WHICH THE HERETIC CURIOUSLY WRESTS TO AN ABSURD SENSE.

But I shall appeal to the original document [4] of Moses, by help of which they on the other side vainly endeavour to prop up their conjectures, with the view, of course, of appearing to have the support of that authority which is indispensable in such an inquiry. They have found their opportunity, as is usual with heretics, in wresting the plain meaning of certain words. For instance the very *beginning*, [5] when God made the heaven and the earth, they will construe as if it meant something substantial and embodied, [6] to be regarded as Matter. We, however, insist on the proper signification of every word, *and say* that *principium* means beginning,—being a term which is suitable to represent things which begin to exist. For nothing which has come into being is without a beginning, nor can this its commencement be at any other moment than when it begins to have existence. Thus *principium* or beginning, is simply a term of inception, not the name of a substance. Now, inasmuch as the heaven and the earth are the principal works of God, and since, by His making them first, He constituted them in an especial manner the beginning of His creation, before all things else, with good reason does the Scripture preface (its record of creation) with the words, " In the beginning God made the heaven and the earth;" [7] just as it would have said, "At last God made the heaven and the earth," if God had created these after all the rest. Now, if the beginning is a substance, the end must also be material. No doubt, a substantial thing [8] may be the beginning of some other thing which may be formed out of it; thus the clay is the beginning of the vessel, and the seed is the beginning of the plant. But when we employ the word beginning in this sense of *origin*, and not in that of *order*, we do not omit to mention also the name of

that particular thing which we regard as the origin of the other. On the other hand, [9] if we were to make such a statement as this, for example, " In the beginning the potter made a basin or a water-jug," the word beginning will not here indicate a material substance (for I have not mentioned the clay, which is the beginning *in this sense*, but only the *order* of the work, meaning that the potter made the basin and the jug first, before anything else—intending afterwards to make the rest. It is, then, to the order of the works that the word beginning has reference, not to the origin of their substances. I might also explain this word *beginning* in another way, which would not, however, be inapposite. [10] The Greek term for beginning, which is ἀρχή, admits the sense not only of priority of order, but of power as well; whence princes and magistrates are called ἄρχοντες. Therefore in this sense too, *beginning* may be taken for princely authority and power. It was, indeed, in His transcendent authority and power, that God made the heaven and the earth.

CHAP. XX.—MEANING OF THE PHRASE—IN THE BEGINNING. TERTULLIAN CONNECTS IT WITH THE WISDOM OF GOD, AND ELICITS FROM IT THE TRUTH THAT THE CREATION WAS NOT OUT OF PRE-EXISTENT MATTER.

But in proof that the Greek word means nothing else than beginning, and that *beginning* admits of no other sense than the *initial* one, we have that (Being) [11] even acknowledging such a beginning, who says: " The Lord possessed [12] me, the beginning of His ways for the creation of His works." [13] For since all things were made by the Wisdom of God, it follows that, when God made both the heaven and the earth *in principio*—that is to say, in the beginning—He made them in His Wisdom. If, indeed, beginning had a *material* signification, the Scripture would not have informed us that God made so and so *in principio*, at the beginning, but rather *ex principio*, of the beginning; for He would not have created *in*, but *of*, matter. When Wisdom, however, was referred to, it was quite right to say, in the beginning. For it was in Wisdom that He made all things at first, because by meditating and arranging His plans therein, [14] He had in fact already done (the work of creation); and if He had even intended to create out of matter, He would yet have effected His creation when He previously medi-

---

[1] John i. 1.
[2] John x. 30.
[3] Nisi quod.
[4] Originale instrumentum : which may mean " the document which treats of the origin of all things."
[5] Principium.
[6] Corpulentum.
[7] Gen. i. 1.
[8] Substantivum aliquid.

[9] De cetero.
[10] Non ab re tamen.
[11] Illam . . . quæ.
[12] Condidit : " created."
[13] Prov. viii. 22.
[14] In qua : in Wisdom.

tated on it and arranged it in His Wisdom, since It[1] was in fact the beginning of His ways: this meditation and arrangement being the primal operation of Wisdom, opening as it does the way to the works by the act of meditation and thought.[2] This authority of Scripture I claim for myself even from this circumstance, that whilst it shows me the God who created, and the works He created, it does not in like manner reveal to me the source from which He created. For since in every operation there are three principal things, He who makes, and that which is made, and that of which it is made, there must be three names mentioned in a correct narrative of the operation—the person of the maker, the sort of thing which is made,[3] *and* the material of which it is formed. If the material is not mentioned, while the work and the maker of the work are both mentioned, it is manifest that He made the work out of nothing. For if He had had anything to operate upon, it would have been mentioned as well as (the other two particulars).[4] In conclusion, I will apply the Gospel as a supplementary testimony to the Old Testament. Now in this there is all the greater reason why there should be shown the material (if there were any) out of which God made all things, inasmuch as it is therein plainly revealed by whom He made all things. " In the beginning was the Word "[5]—that is, the same beginning, of course, in which God made the heaven and the earth,[6]—" and the Word was with God, and the Word was God. All things were made by Him, and without Him nothing was made."[7] Now, since we have here clearly told us who the Maker was, that is, God, and what He made, even all things, and through whom He made them, even His Word, would not the order of the narrative have required that the source out of which all things were made by God through the Word should like-wise be declared, if they had been in fact made out of anything? What, therefore, did not exist, the Scripture was unable to mention; and by not mentioning it, it has given us a clear proof that there was no such thing: for if there had been, the Scripture would have mentioned it.

CHAP. XXI.—A RETORT OF HERESY ANSWERED. THAT SCRIPTURE SHOULD IN SO MANY WORDS TELL US THAT THE WORLD WAS MADE OF NOTHING IS SUPERFLUOUS.

But, you will say to me, if you determine

that all things were made of nothing, on the ground that it is not told us that anything was made out of pre-existent Matter, take care that it be not contended on the opposite side, that on the same ground all things were made out of Matter, because it is not likewise expressly said that anything was made out of nothing. Some arguments may, of course,[8] be thus retorted easily enough; but it does not follow that they are on that account fairly admissible, where there is a diversity in the cause. For I maintain that, even if the Scripture has not expressly declared that all things were made out of nothing—just as it abstains (from saying that they were formed) out of Matter—there was no such pressing need for expressly indicating the creation of all things out of nothing, as there was of their creation out of Matter, if that had been their origin. Because, in the case of what is made out of nothing, the very fact of its not being indicated that it was made of any particular thing shows that it was made of nothing; and there is no danger of its being supposed that it was made of anything, when there is no indication at all of what it was made of. In the case, however, of that which is made out of something, unless the very fact be plainly declared, that it was made out of something, there will be danger, until[9] it is shown of what it was made, first of its appearing to be made of nothing, because it is not said of what it was made; and then, should it be of such a nature[10] as to have the appearance of having certainly been made of something, there will be a similar risk of its seeming to have been made of a far different material from the proper one, so long as there is an absence of statement of what it was made of. Then, if God had been unable to make all things of nothing, the Scripture could not possibly have added that He had made all things of nothing: (there could have been no room for such a statement,) but it must by all means have informed us that He had made all things out of Matter, since Matter must have been the source; because the one case was quite to be understood,[11] if it were not actually stated, whereas the other case would be left in doubt unless it were stated.

CHAP. XXII.—THIS CONCLUSION CONFIRMED BY THE USAGE OF HOLY SCRIPTURE IN ITS HISTORY OF THE CREATION. HERMOGENES IN DANGER OF THE WOE PRONOUNCED AGAINST ADDING TO SCRIPTURE.

And to such a degree has the Holy Ghost

---

[1] Wisdom.
[2] De cogitatu.
[3] Species facti.
[4] Proinde.
[5] John i. 1.
[6] Gen. i. 1.

[7] John i. 1-3.
[8] Plane.
[9] Dum ostenditur; which Oehler and Rigalt. construe as "donec ostendatur." One reading has " dum *non* ostenditur," "so long as it is not shown."
[10] Ea conditione.
[11] In totum habebat intelligi.

made this the rule of His Scripture, that
whenever anything is made out of anything,
He mentions both the thing that is made and
the thing of which it is made. " Let the earth,"
says He, " bring forth grass, the herb yielding seed, and the fruit-tree yielding fruit after
its kind, whose seed is in itself, after its kind.
And it was so. And the earth brought forth
grass, and herb yielding seed after its kind,
and the tree yielding fruit, whose seed was in
itself, after its kind."¹ And again: "And
God said, Let the waters bring forth abundantly the moving creatures that have life,
and fowl that may fly above the earth through
the firmament of heaven. And it was so.
And God created great whales, and every living creature that moveth, which the waters
brought forth abundantly, after their kind."²
Again afterwards: "And God said, Let the
earth bring forth the living creature after his
kind, cattle, and creeping thing, and beasts
of the earth after their kind."³ If therefore
God, when producing other things out of
things which had been already made, indicates
them by the prophet, and tells us what He
has produced from such and such a source⁴
(although we might ourselves suppose them
to be derived from some source or other,
short of nothing;⁵ since there had already
been created certain things, from which they
might easily seem to have been made); if the
Holy Ghost took upon Himself so great a concern for our instruction, that we might know
from what everything was produced,⁶ would
He not in like manner have kept us well informed about both the heaven and the earth,
by indicating to us what it was that He made
them of, if their original consisted of any
material substance, so that the more He
seemed to have made them of nothing, the
less in fact was there as yet made, from which
He could appear to have made them? Therefore, just as He shows us the original out of
which He drew such things as were derived
from a given source, so also with regard to
those things of which He does not point out
whence He produced them, He confirms (by
that silence our assertion) that they were produced out of nothing. "In the beginning,"
then, "God made the heaven and the
earth."⁷ I revere⁸ the fulness of His Scripture, in which He manifests to me both the
Creator and the creation. In the gospel,

moreover, I discover a Minister and Witness
of the Creator, even His Word.⁹ But whether
all things were made out of any underlying
Matter, I have as yet failed anywhere to
find. Where such a statement is written, Hermogenes' shop¹⁰ must tell us. If it is nowhere written, then let it fear the *woe* which
impends on all who add to or take away from
*the written word.*¹¹

CHAP. XXIII.—HERMOGENES PURSUED TO AN-
OTHER PASSAGE OF SCRIPTURE. THE ABSURD-
ITY OF HIS INTERPRETATION EXPOSED.

But he draws an argument from the following words, where it is written: "And the earth
was without form, and void."¹² For he re-
solves¹³ the word *earth* into Matter, because
that which is made out of it is the earth.
And to the word *was* he gives the same direction, as if it pointed to what had always
existed unbegotten and unmade. It was
without form, moreover, *and* void, because
he will have Matter to have existed shapeless
and confused, and without the finish of a
maker's hand.¹⁴ Now these opinions of his I
will refute singly; but first I wish to say to
him, by way of general answer: We are of
opinion that Matter is pointed at in these
terms. But yet does the Scripture intimate
that, because Matter was in existence before
all, anything of *like* condition¹⁵ was even
formed out of it? Nothing of the kind. Matter might have had existence, if it so pleased
—or rather if Hermogenes so pleased. It
might, I say, have existed, and yet God might
not have made anything out of it, either as
it was unsuitable to Him to have required the
aid of anything, or at least because He is not
shown to have made anything out of Matter.
Its existence must therefore be without a cause,
you will say. Oh, no! certainly¹⁶ not without cause. For even if the world were not
made out of it, yet a heresy has been hatched
therefrom; and a specially impudent one too,
because it is not Matter which has produced
the heresy, but the heresy has rather made
Matter itself.

CHAP. XXIV.—EARTH DOES NOT MEAN MATTER
AS HERMOGENES WOULD HAVE IT.

I now return to the several points¹⁷ by
means of which he thought that Matter was
signified. And first I will inquire about the

¹ Gen. i. 11, 12.
² Gen. i. 20, 21.
³ Ver. 24.
⁴ Quid unde protulerit: properly a double question = " what
was produced, and whence?"
⁵ Unde unde . . . dumne.
⁶ Quid unde processerit: properly a double question = " what
was produced, and whence?"
⁷ Gen. i. 1.
⁸ Adoro: reverently admire.
⁹ John i. 3.
¹⁰ Officina.
¹¹ Rev. xxii. 18, 19.
¹² Gen. i. 2.
¹³ Redigit in.
¹⁴ Inconditam: we have combined the two senses of the word.
¹⁵ Tale aliquid.
¹⁶ Plane: ironical.
¹⁷ Articulos.

terms. For we read only of one of them, *Earth;* the other, namely *Matter,* we do not meet with. I ask, then, since Matter is not mentioned in Scripture, how the term earth can be applied to it, which marks a substance of another kind? There is all the greater need why mention should also have been made of Matter, if this has acquired the further sense of Earth, in order that I may be sure that Earth is one and the same name as Matter, and so not claim the designation for merely one substance, as the proper name thereof, and by which it is better known; or else be unable (if I should feel the inclination) to apply it to some particular species of Matter, instead, indeed,[1] of making it the common term[2] of all Matter. For when a proper name does not exist for that thing to which a common term is ascribed, the less apparent[3] is the object to which it may be ascribed, *the more* capable will it be of being applied to any other object whatever. Therefore, even supposing that Hermogenes could show us the *name*[4] Matter, he is bound to prove to us further, that the same object has the *surname*[5] Earth, in order that he may claim for it both designations alike.

CHAP. XXV.—THE ASSUMPTION THAT THERE ARE TWO EARTHS MENTIONED IN THE HISTORY OF THE CREATION, REFUTED.

He accordingly maintains that there are two earths set before us in the passage in question: one, which God made in the beginning; the other being the Matter of which God made the world, and concerning which it is said, "And the earth was without form, and void."[6] Of course, if I were to ask, to which of the two earths the name *earth* is best suited,[7] I shall be told that the earth which was made derived the appellation from that of which it was made, on the ground that it is more likely that the offspring should get its name from the original, than the original from the offspring. This being the case, another question presents itself to us, whether it is right and proper that this earth which God made should have derived its name from that out of which He made it? For I find from Hermogenes and the rest of the *Materialist* heretics,[8] that while the one earth

was indeed "without form, and void," this one of ours obtained from God in an equal degree[9] both form, and beauty, and symmetry; and therefore that the earth which was created was a different thing from that out of which it was created. Now, having become a different thing, it could not possibly have shared with the other in its name, after it had declined from its condition. If *earth* was the proper name of the (original) Matter, this world of ours, which is not Matter, because it has become another thing, is unfit to bear the name of earth, seeing that that name belongs to something else, and is a stranger to its nature. But (you will tell me) Matter which has undergone creation, that is, our earth, had with its original a community of name no less than of kind. By no means. For although the pitcher is formed out of the clay, I shall no longer call it clay, but a pitcher; so likewise, although *electrum*[10] is compounded of gold and silver, I shall yet not call it either gold or silver, but *electrum*. When there is a departure from the nature of any thing, there is likewise a relinquishment of its name —with a propriety which is alike demanded by the designation and the condition. How great a change indeed from the condition of that earth, which is Matter, has come over this earth of ours, is plain even from the fact that the latter has received this testimony to its goodness in Genesis, "And God saw that it was good;"[11] while the former, according to Hermogenes, is regarded as the origin and cause of all evils. Lastly, if the one is Earth because the other is, why also is the one not Matter as the other is? Indeed, by this rule both the heaven and all creatures ought to have had the names of *Earth* and *Matter,* since they all consist of Matter. I have said enough touching the designation Earth, by which he will have it that Matter is understood. This, as everybody knows, is the name of one of the elements; for so we are taught by nature first, and afterwards by Scripture, except it be that credence must be given to that Silenus who talked so confidently in the presence of king Midas of another world, according to the account of Theopompus. But the same author informs us that there are also several gods.

CHAP. XXVI.—THE METHOD OBSERVED IN THE HISTORY OF THE CREATION, IN REPLY TO THE PERVERSE INTERPRETATION OF HERMOGENES.

We, however, have but one God, and but

---

[1] Nec utique.
[2] Communicare.
[3] We have construed Oehler's reading : "Quanto non comparet" (*i.e.*, by a frequent ellipse of Tertullian, "quanto *magis* non comparet"). Fr. Junius, however, suspects that instead of "quanto" we should read "quando :" this would produce the sense, "since it is not apparent to what object it may be ascribed," etc.
[4] Nominatam.
[5] Cognominatam.
[6] Gen. i. 2.
[7] Quæ cui nomen terræ accommodare debeat. This is literally a double question, asking about the fitness of the name, and to which earth it is best adapted.

[8] He means those who have gone wrong on the eternity of *matter.*
[9] Proinde.
[10] A mixed metal, of the colour of *amber.*
[11] Gen. i. 31.

one earth too, which in the beginning God made.[1] The Scripture, which at its very outset proposes to run through the order thereof, tells us as its first information that it was created; it next proceeds to set forth what sort of earth it was.[2] In like manner with respect to the heaven, it informs us first of its creation—"In the beginning God made the heaven:"[3] it then goes on to introduce its arrangement; how that God both separated "the water which was below the firmament from that which was above the firmament,"[4] and called the firmament heaven,[5]—the very thing He had created in the beginning. Similarly it (afterwards) treats of man: "And God created man, in the image of God made He him."[6] It next reveals how He made him: "And (the Lord) God formed man of the dust of the ground, and breathed into his nostrils the breath of life; and man became a living soul."[7] Now this is undoubtedly[8] the correct and fitting mode for the narrative. First comes a prefatory statement, then follow the details in full;[9] first the subject is named, then it is described.[10] How absurd is the other view of the account,[11] when even before he[12] had premised any mention of his subject, i.e. Matter, without even giving us its name, he all on a sudden promulged its form and condition, describing to us its quality before mentioning its existence,—pointing out the figure of the thing formed, but concealing its name ! But how much more credible is our opinion, which holds that Scripture has only subjoined the arrangement of the subject after it has first duly described its formation and mentioned its name ! Indeed, how full and complete[13] is the meaning of these words: " In the beginning God created the heaven and the earth; but[14] the earth was without form, and void,"[15]—the very same earth, no doubt, which God made, and of which the Scripture had been speaking at that very moment.[16] For that very "but"[17] is inserted into the narrative like a clasp,[18] (in its function) of a conjunctive particle, to

connect *the two sentences indissolubly together:* " *But* the earth." This word carries back the mind to that earth of which mention had just been made, and binds the sense thereunto.[19] Take away this " but," and the tie is loosened; so much so that the passage, " But the earth was without form, and void," may then seem to have been meant for any other earth.

CHAP. XXVII.—SOME HAIR-SPLITTING USE OF WORDS IN WHICH HIS OPPONENT HAD INDULGED.

But you next praise your eyebrows, and toss back your head, and beckon with your finger, in characteristic disdain,[20] and say: There is the *was*, looking as if it pointed to an eternal existence,—making its subject, of course, unbegotten and unmade, and on that account worthy of being supposed to be Matter. Well now, for my own part, I shall resort to no affected protestation,[21] but simply reply that " *was* " may be predicated of everything—even of a thing which has been created, which was born, which once was not, and which is not *your* Matter. For of everything which has being, from whatever source it has it, whether it has it by a beginning or without a beginning, the word " *was* " will be predicated from the very fact that it exists. To whatever thing the first tense[22] of the verb is applicable for *definition*, to the same will be suitable the later form[23] of the verb, when it has to descend to *relation.* " Est " (it is) forms the essential part[24] of a definition, " erat " (it was) of a relation. Such are the trifles and subtleties of heretics, who wrest and bring into question the simple meaning of the commonest words. A grand question it is, to be sure,[25] whether " the earth *was*," which was made ! The real point of discussion is, whether " being without form, and void," is a state which is more suitable to that which was created, or to that of which it was created, so that the predicate (*was*) may appertain to the same thing to which the subject (*that which was*) also belongs.[26]

CHAP. XXVIII.—A CURIOUS INCONSISTENCY IN HERMOGENES EXPOSED. CERTAIN EXPRESSIONS IN THE HISTORY OF CREATION VINDICATED IN THE TRUE SENSE.

But we shall show not only that this condition[27] agreed with this earth of ours, but that

---

[1] Gen. i. 1.
[2] Qualitatem ejus: unless this means " *how* He made it," like the " qualiter fecerit " below.
[3] Gen. i. 1.
[4] Gen. i. 7.
[5] Ver. 8.
[6] Gen. i. 27.
[7] Gen. ii. 7.
[8] Utique.
[9] Prosequi.
[10] Primo præfari, postea prosequi; nominare, deinde describere. This properly is an *abstract* statement, given with Tertullian's usual terseness: " First you should ('decet') give your preface, then follow up with details : first name your subject, then describe it."
[11] Alioquin.
[12] Hermogenes, whose view of the narrative is criticised.
[13] Integer.
[14] Autem.
[15] Gen. i. 1, 2.
[16] Cum maxime edixerat.
[17] The " autem " of the note just before this.   Fibula.

[19] Alligat sensum.
[20] Implied in the emphatic *tu.*
[21] Sine u.lo lenocinio pronunciationis.
[22] Prima positio : the first inflection perhaps, i. e. *the present tense.*
[23] Declinatio : the past tense.
[24] Caput.
[25] Scilicet.
[26] This seems to be the meaning of the obscure passage, " Ut ejusdem sit *Erat* cujus et quod erat.
[27] Habitum.

it did not agree with that other (insisted on by Hermogenes). For, inasmuch as pure Matter was thus subsistent with God,[1] without the interposition indeed of any element at all (because as yet there existed nothing but itself and God), it could not of course have been invisible. Because, although *Hermogenes* contends that darkness was inherent in the substance of Matter, a position which we shall have to meet in its proper place,[2] yet darkness is visible even to a human being (for the very fact that there is the darkness is an evident one), much more is it so to God. If indeed it[3] had been invisible, its quality would not have been by any means discoverable. How, then, did Hermogenes find out[4] that that substance was "without form," and confused and disordered, which, as being invisible, was not palpable to his senses? If this mystery was revealed to him by God, he ought to give us his proof. I want to know also, whether (the substance in question) could have been described as "void." That certainly is "void" which is imperfect. Equally certain is it, that nothing can be imperfect but that which is made; it is imperfect when it is not fully made.[5] Certainly, you admit. Matter, therefore, which was not made at all, could not have been imperfect; and what was not imperfect was not "void." Having no beginning, because it was not made, it was also unsusceptible of any void-condition.[6] For this void-condition is an accident of beginning. The earth, on the contrary, which was made, was deservedly called "void." For as soon as it was made, it had the condition of being imperfect, previous to its completion.

CHAP. XXIX.—THE GRADUAL DEVELOPMENT OF COSMICAL ORDER OUT OF CHAOS IN THE CREATION, BEAUTIFULLY STATED.

God, indeed, consummated all His works in a due order; at first He paled them out,[7] as it were, in their unformed elements, and then He arranged them[8] in their finished beauty. For He did not all at once inundate light with the splendour of the sun, nor all at once temper darkness with the moon's assuaging ray.[9] The heaven He did not all at once bedeck[10] with constellations and stars, nor did He at once fill the seas with their teem-

ing monsters.[11] The earth itself He did not endow with its varied fruitfulness all at once; but at first He bestowed upon it being, and then He filled it, that it might not be made in vain.[12] For thus says Isaiah: "He created it not in vain; He formed it to be inhabited."[13] Therefore after it was made, and while awaiting its perfect state,[14] it was "without form, and void:" "void" indeed, from the very fact that it was without form (as being not yet perfect to the sight, and at the same time unfurnished as yet with its other qualities);[15] and "without form," because it was still covered with waters, as if with the rampart of its fecundating moisture,[16] by which is produced our flesh, in a form allied with its own. For to this purport does David say:[17] "The earth is the Lord's, and the fulness thereof; the world, and all that dwell therein: He hath founded it upon the seas, and on the streams hath He established it."[18] It was when the waters were withdrawn into their hollow abysses that the dry land became conspicuous,[19] which was hitherto covered with its watery envelope. Then it forthwith becomes "visible,"[20] God saying, "Let the water be gathered together into one mass,[21] and let the dry land appear."[22] "*Appear*," says He, not "*be made*." It had been already made, only in its invisible condition it was then waiting[23] to appear. "Dry," because it was about to become such by its severance from the moisture, but yet "land." "And God called the dry land *Earth*,"[24] not Matter. And so, when it afterwards attains its perfection, it ceases to be accounted void, when God declares, "Let the earth bring forth grass, the herb yielding seed after its kind, and according to its likeness, and the fruit-tree yielding fruit, whose seed is in itself, after its kind."[25] Again: "Let the earth bring forth the living creature after his kind, cattle, and creeping things, and beasts of the earth, after their kind."[26] Thus the divine Scripture accomplished its full order. For to that, which it had at first described as "without form (invisible) and void," it gave both visibility and completion. Now no other Matter was "without form (invisible) and void."

---

[1] Deo subjacebat.
[2] See below, ch. xxx. p. 494.
[3] Matter.
[4] "Compertus est" is here a deponent verb.
[5] Minus factum.
[6] Rudimento. Tertullian uses the word "rudis" (unformed) for the scriptural term ("void"); of this word "rudimentum" is the abstract.
[7] Depalans.
[8] Dedicans : "disposed" them.
[9] Solatio lunæ : a beautiful expression !
[10] Significavit.

[11] Belluis.
[12] In vacuum : void.
[13] Isa. xlv. 18.
[14] Futura etiam perfecta.
[15] De reliquo nondum instructa.
[16] Genitalis humoris.
[17] Canit : "sing," as the Psalmist.
[18] Ps. xxiv. 1.
[19] Emicantior.
[20] "Visibilis" is here the opposite of the term "invisibilis," which Tertullian uses for the Scripture phrase "without form."
[21] In congregatione una.
[22] Gen. i. 9.
[23] Sustinebat : i. e. expectabat (Oehler).
[24] Gen. i. 10.
[25] Ver. 11.
[26] Ver. 24.

Henceforth, then, Matter will have to be visible and complete. So that I must[1] see Matter, since it has become visible. I must likewise recognize it as a completed thing, so as to be able to gather from it the herb bearing seed, and the tree yielding fruit, and that living creatures, made out of it, may minister to my need. Matter, however, is nowhere,[2] but the Earth is here, confessed to my view. I see it, I enjoy it, ever since it ceased to be "without form (invisible), and void." Concerning it most certainly did Isaiah speak when he said, "Thus saith the Lord that created the heavens, He was the God that formed the earth, and made it."[3] The same earth for certain did He form, which He also made. Now how did He form[4] it? Of course by saying, "Let the dry land appear."[5] Why does He command it to appear, if it were not previously invisible? *His purpose was* also, that He might thus prevent His having made it in vain, by rendering it visible, and so fit for use. And thus, throughout, proofs arise to us that this earth which we inhabit is the very same which was both created and formed[6] by God, and that none other was "without form, and void," than that which had been created and formed. It therefore follows that the sentence, "Now the earth was without form, and void," applies to that same earth which God mentioned separately along with the heaven.[7]

CHAP. XXX.—ANOTHER PASSAGE IN THE SACRED HISTORY OF THE CREATION, RELEASED FROM THE MISHANDLING OF HERMOGENES.

The following words will in like manner apparently corroborate the conjecture of Hermogenes, "And darkness was upon the face of the deep, and the Spirit of God moved upon the face of the water;"[8] as if these blended[9] substances, presented us with arguments for his massive pile *of Matter*.[10] Now, so discriminating an enumeration of certain and distinct elements (as we have in this passage), which severally designates "darkness," "the deep" "the Spirit of God," "the waters," forbids the inference that anything confused or (from such confusion) uncertain is meant. Still more, when He ascribed to them their own places,[11] "darkness *on the face of* the deep," "the Spirit *upon the face of* the waters," He repudiated all confusion in the substances; and by demonstrating their separate position,[12] He demonstrated also their distinction. Most absurd, indeed, would it be that Matter, which is introduced to our view as "without form," should have its "formless" condition maintained by so many words indicative of form,[13] without any intimation of what that confused body[14] is, which must of course be supposed to be unique,[15] since it is without form.[16] For that which is without form is uniform; but even[17] that which is without form, when it is blended together[18] from various component parts,[19] must necessarily have one outward appearance;[20] and it has not any appearance, until it has the one appearance (which comes) from many parts combined.[21] Now Matter either had those specific parts[22] within itself, from the words indicative of which it had to be understood—I mean "darkness," and "the deep," and "the Spirit," and "the waters"—or it had them not. If it had them, how is it introduced as being "without form?"[23] If it had them not, how does it become known?[24]

CHAP. XXXI.—A FURTHER VINDICATION OF THE SCRIPTURE NARRATIVE OF THE CREATION, AGAINST A FUTILE VIEW OF HERMOGENES.

But this circumstance, too, will be caught at, that Scripture meant to indicate of the heaven only, and this earth of yours,[25] that God made it in the beginning, while nothing of the kind *is said* of the above-mentioned specific parts;[26] and therefore that these, which are not described as having been made, appertain to unformed Matter. To this point[27] also we must give an answer. Holy Scripture would be sufficiently explicit, if it had declared that the heaven and the earth, as the very highest works of creation, were made by God, possessing of course their own special appurtenances,[28] which might be understood to be implied in these highest works themselves. Now the appurtenances of the heaven and the earth, made then in the beginning, were the darkness and the deep, and the spirit, and the waters. For the depth and the darkness underlay the earth. Since

---

[1] Volo.
[2] He means, of course, the theoretic "Matter" of Hermogenes.
[3] Isa. xlv. 18.
[4] Demonstravit: "make it visible." Tertullian here all along makes *form* and *visibility* synonymous.
[5] Gen. i. 9.
[6] Ostensam: "manifested" (see note 10, p. 96).
[7] Cum cælo separavit: Gen. i. 1.
[8] Gen. i. 2.
[9] Confusæ.
[10] Massalis illius molis.
[11] Situs.

[12] Dispositionem.
[13] Tot formarum vocabulis.
[14] Corpus confusionis.
[15] Unicum.
[16] Informe.
[17] Autem.
[18] Confusum.
[19] Ex varietate.
[20] Unam speciem.
[21] Unam ex multis speciem.
[22] Istas species.
[23] Non habens formas.
[24] Agnoscitur.
[25] Ista: the earth, which has been the subject of contention.
[26] Speciebus.
[27] Scrupulo: doubt or difficulty.
[28] Suggestus: "Hoc est, apparatus, ornatus" (Oehler).

the deep was under the earth, and the darkness was over the deep, undoubtedly both the darkness and the deep were under the earth. Below the heaven, too, lay the spirit [1] and the waters. For since the waters were over the earth, which they covered, whilst the spirit was over the waters, both the spirit and the waters were alike over the earth. Now that which is over the earth, is of course under the heaven. And even as the earth brooded over the deep and the darkness, so also did the heaven brood over the spirit and the waters, and embrace them. Nor, indeed, is there any novelty in mentioning only that which contains, as pertaining to the whole,[2] and understanding that which is contained as included in it, in its character of a portion.[3] Suppose now I should say the city built a theatre and a circus, but the stage[4] was of such and such a kind, and the statues were on the canal, and the obelisk was reared above them all, would it follow that, because I did not distinctly state that these specific things[5] were made by the city, they were therefore not made by it along with the circus and the theatre? Did I not, indeed, refrain from specially mentioning the formation of these particular things because they were implied in the things which I had already said were made, and might be understood to be inherent in the things in which they were contained? But this example may be an idle one as being derived from a human circumstance; I will take another, which has the authority of Scripture itself. It says that "God made man of the dust of the ground and breathed into his nostrils the breath of life, and man became a living soul." [6] Now, although it here mentions the nostrils,[7] it does not say that they were made by God; so again it speaks of skin[8] and bones, and flesh and eyes, and sweat and blood, in subsequent passages,[9] and yet it never intimated that they had been created by God. What will Hermogenes have to answer? That the human limbs must belong to Matter, because they are not specially mentioned as objects of creation? Or are they included in the formation of man? In like manner, the deep and the darkness, and the spirit and the waters, were *as* members of the heaven and the earth. For in the bodies the limbs were made, in the

bodies the limbs too were mentioned. No element but what is a member of that element in which it is contained. But all elements are contained in the heaven and the earth.

CHAP. XXXII.—THE ACCOUNT OF THE CREATION IN GENESIS A GENERAL ONE. CORROBORATED, HOWEVER, BY MANY OTHER PASSAGES OF THE OLD TESTAMENT, WHICH GIVE ACCOUNT OF SPECIFIC CREATIONS. FURTHER CAVILLINGS CONFUTED.

This is the answer I should give in defence of the Scripture before us, for seeming here to set forth [10] the formation of the heaven and the earth, as if (they were) the sole bodies *made*. It could not but know that there were those who would at once in the bodies understand their several members also, and therefore it employed this concise mode of speech. But, at the same time, it foresaw that there would be stupid and crafty men, who, after paltering with the virtual meaning,[11] would require for the several members a word descriptive of their formation too. It is therefore because of such persons, that *Scripture* in other passages teaches us of the creation of the individual parts. You have Wisdom saying, "But before the depths was I brought forth," [12] in order that you may believe that the depths were also "brought forth"—that is, created—just as we create sons also, though we "bring them forth." It matters not whether the depth was made or born, so that a beginning be accorded to it, which *however* would not be, if it were subjoined [13] to matter. Of darkness, indeed, the Lord Himself by Isaiah says, "I formed the light, and I created darkness." [14] Of the wind [15] also Amos says, "He that strengtheneth the thunder,[16] and createth the wind, and declareth His Christ [16] unto men;" [17] thus showing that that wind was created which was reckoned with the formation of the earth, which was wafted over the waters, balancing and refreshing and animating all things: not (as some suppose) meaning God Himself by *the spirit*,[18] on the ground that "God is a Spirit," [19] because the waters would not be able to bear up their Lord; but He speaks of that spirit of which the winds consist, as He says by Isaiah, "Because my spirit went forth from me, and I made every blast." [20] In like manner the

[1] It will be observed that Tertullian applies the *spiritus* to the *wind* as a creature.
[2] Qua summale.
[3] Qua portionale.
[4] Scena.
[5] Has species.
[6] Gen. ii. 7.
[7] Both in the quotation and here, Tertullian read "faciem" where we read "nostrils."
[8] Cutem: another reading has "costam," rib.
[9] See Gen. ii. 21, 23, iii. 5, 19, iv. 10.

[10] Quatenus hic commendare videtur.
[11] Dissimulato tacito intellectu.
[12] Prov. viii. 24.
[13] Subjecta.
[14] Isa. xlv. 7.
[15] De spiritu. This shows that Tertullian took *the spirit* of Gen. i. 2 in the inferior sense.
[16] So also the Septuagint.
[17] Amos iv. 13.
[18] The "wind."
[19] John iv. 24.
[20] Flatum: "breath;" so LXX. of Isa. lvii. 16.

same Wisdom says of the waters, "Also when He made the fountains strong, things which[1] are under the sky, I was fashioning[2] them along with Him."[3] Now, when we prove that these particular things were created by God, although they are only mentioned in Genesis, without any intimation of their having been made, we shall perhaps receive from the other side the reply, that these were made, it is true,[4] but out of Matter, since the very statement of Moses, "And darkness was on the face of the deep, and the spirit of God moved on the face of the waters,"[5] refers to Matter, as indeed do all those other Scriptures here and there,[6] which demonstrate that the separate parts were made out of Matter. It must follow, then,[7] that as earth consisted of earth, so also depth consisted of depth, and darkness of darkness, and the wind and waters of wind and waters. And, as we said above,[8] Matter could not have been without form, since it had specific parts, which were formed out of it—although as separate things[9]—unless, indeed, they were not separate, but were the very same with those out of which they came. For it is really impossible that those specific things, which are set forth under the same names, should have been diverse; because in that case[10] the operation of God might seem to be useless,[11] if it made things which existed already; since that alone would be a creation,[12] when things came into being, which had not been (previously) made. Therefore, to conclude, either Moses then pointed to Matter when he wrote *the words:* "And darkness was on the face of the deep, and the spirit of God moved on the face of the waters;" or else, inasmuch as these specific parts *of creation* are afterwards shown in other passages to have been made by God, they ought to have been with equal explicitness[13] shown to have been made out of the Matter which, *according to you,* Moses had previously mentioned;[14] or else, *finally,* if Moses pointed to those specific parts, and not to Matter, I want to know where Matter has been pointed out *at all.*

---

[1] Fontes, quæ.
[2] Modulans.
[3] Prov. viii. 28.
[4] Plane.
[5] Gen. i. 2.
[6] In disperso.
[7] Ergo: Tertullian's answer.
[8] Ch. xxx., towards the end.
[9] Ut et aliæ.
[10] Jam.
[11] Otiosa.
[12] Generatio: creation in the highest sense of matter issuing from the maker. Another reading has "generosiora essent," for our "generatio sola esset," meaning that "those things would be nobler which had not been made," which is obviously quite opposed to Tertullian's argument.
[13] Æque.
[14] Præmiserat.

CHAP. XXXIII.—STATEMENT OF THE TRUE DOCTRINE CONCERNING MATTER. ITS RELATION TO GOD'S CREATION OF THE WORLD.

But although Hermogenes finds it amongst his own colourable pretences[15] (for it was not in his power to discover it in the Scriptures of God), it is enough for us, both that it is certain that all things were made by God, and that there is no certainty whatever that they were made out of Matter. And even if Matter had *previously* existed, we must have believed that it had been really made by God, since we maintained (no less) when we held the rule of faith to be,[16] that nothing except God was uncreated.[17] Up to this point there is room for controversy, until Matter is brought to the test of the Scriptures, and fails to make good its case.[18] The conclusion of the whole is this: I find that there was nothing made, except out of nothing; because that which I find was made, I know did not *once* exist. Whatever[19] was made out of something, has its origin in something made: for instance, out of the ground was made the grass, and the fruit, and the cattle, and the form of man himself; so from the waters were produced the animals which swim and fly. The original fabrics[20] out of which such creatures were produced I may call their *materials,*[21] but then even these were created by God.

CHAP. XXXIV.—A PRESUMPTION THAT ALL THINGS WERE CREATED BY GOD OUT OF NOTHING AFFORDED BY THE ULTIMATE REDUCTION OF ALL THINGS TO NOTHING. SCRIPTURES PROVING THIS REDUCTION VINDICATED FROM HERMOGENES' CHARGE OF BEING MERELY FIGURATIVE.

Besides,[22] the belief that everything was made from nothing will be impressed upon us by that ultimate dispensation of God which will bring back all things to nothing. For "the very heaven shall be rolled together as a scroll;"[23] nay, it shall come to nothing along with the earth itself, with which it was made in the beginning. "Heaven and earth shall pass away," [24] says He. "The first heaven and the first earth passed away,"[25] "and there was found no place for them,"[26] because, of course, that which comes to an

---

[15] Colores. See our "Anti-Marcion," p. 217, *Edin.,* where the word *pretension* should stand instead of *precedent.*
[16] Præscribentes.
[17] Innatum: see above, note 12.
[18] Donec ad Scripturas provocata deficiat exhibitio materiæ.
[19] Etiamsi quid.
[20] Origines.
[21] Materias. There is point in this use of the plural of the controverted term *materia.*
[22] Ceterum.
[23] Isa. xxxiv. 4; Matt. xxiv. 29; 2 Pet. iii. 10; Rev. vi. 14.
[24] Matt. xxiv. 35.
[25] Rev. xxi. 1.
[26] Rev. xx. 11.

end loses locality. In like manner David says, "The heavens, the works of Thine hands, shall themselves perish. For even as a vesture shall He change them, and they shall be changed."[1] Now to be changed is to fall from that primitive state which they lose whilst undergoing the change. "And the stars too shall fall from heaven, even as a fig-tree casteth her green figs[2] when she is shaken of a mighty wind."[3] "The mountains shall melt like wax at the presence of the Lord;"[4] that is, "when He riseth to shake terribly the earth."[5] "But I will dry up the pools;"[6] and "they shall seek water, and they shall find none."[7] Even "the sea shall be no more."[8] Now if any person should go so far as to suppose that all these passages ought to be spiritually interpreted, he will yet be unable to deprive them of the true accomplishment of those issues which must come to pass just as they have been written. For all figures of speech necessarily arise out of real things, not out of chimerical ones; because nothing is capable of imparting anything of its own for a similitude, except it actually be that very thing which it imparts in the similitude. I return therefore to the principle[9] which defines that all things which have come from nothing shall return at last to nothing. For God would not have made any perishable thing out of what was eternal, that is to say, out of Matter; neither out of greater things would He have created inferior ones, to whose character it would be more agreeable to produce greater things out of inferior ones, —in other words, what is eternal out of what is perishable. This is the promise He makes even to our flesh, and it has been His will to deposit within us this pledge of His own virtue and power, in order that we may believe that He has actually[10] awakened the universe out of nothing, as if it had been steeped in death,[11] in the sense, of course, of its previous non-existence for the purpose of its coming into existence.[12]

CHAP. XXXV.—CONTRADICTORY PROPOSITIONS ADVANCED BY HERMOGENES RESPECTING MATTER AND ITS QUALITIES.

As regards all other points touching Matter,

although there is no necessity why we should treat of them (for our first point was the manifest proof of its existence), we must for all that pursue our discussion just as if it did exist, in order that its non-existence may be the more apparent, when these other points concerning it prove inconsistent with each other, and in order at the same time that Hermogenes may acknowledge his own contradictory positions. Matter, says he, at first sight seems to us to be incorporeal; but when examined by *the light of* right reason, it is found to be neither corporeal nor incorporeal. What is this right reason of yours,[13] which declares nothing right, that is, nothing certain ? For, if I mistake not, everything must of necessity be either corporeal or incorporeal (although I may for the moment[14] allow that there is a certain incorporeality in even substantial things,[15] although their very substance is the body of particular things); at all events, after the corporeal and the incorporeal there is no third *state*. But if it be contended[16] that there is a third state discovered by this right reason of Hermogenes, which makes Matter neither corporeal nor incorporeal, (I ask,) Where is it? what sort of thing is it? what is it called? what is its description? what is it understood to be? This only has his reason declared, that Matter is neither corporeal nor incorporeal.

CHAP. XXXVI.—OTHER ABSURD THEORIES RESPECTING MATTER AND ITS INCIDENTS EXPOSED IN AN IRONICAL STRAIN. MOTION IN MATTER. HERMOGENES' CONCEITS RESPECTING IT.

But see what a contradiction he next advances[17] (or perhaps some *other* reason[18] occurs to him), when he declares that Matter is partly corporeal and partly incorporeal. Then must Matter be considered (to embrace) both conditions, in order that it may not have either? For it will be corporeal, and incorporeal in spite of[19] the declaration of that antithesis,[20] which is plainly above giving any

---

[1] Ps. cii. 25, 26.
[2] Acerba sua " grossos suos " (Rigalt.). So our marginal reading.
[3] Rev. vi. 13.
[4] Ps. xcvii. 5.
[5] Isa. ii. 19.
[6] Isa. xlii. 15.
[7] Isa. xli. 17.
[8] Etiam mare hactenus, Rev. xxi. 1.
[9] Causam.
[10] Etiam.
[11] Emortuam.
[12] In hoc, ut esset. Contrasted with the " non erat " of the previous sentence, this must be the meaning, as if it were " ut fieret."

[13] Ista.
[14] Interim.
[15] De substantiis duntaxat.
[16] Age nunc sit : " But grant that there is this third state."
[17] Subicit.
[18] Other than " *the right reason* " above named.
[19] Adversus.
[20] The original, "Adversus renuntiationem reciprocationis illius," is an obscure expression. Oehler, who gives this reading in his edition, after the *editio princeps*, renders the term " reciprocationis" by the phrase " negative conversion" of the proposition that Matter is corporeal and incorporeal (q. d. " Matter is neither corporeal nor incorporeal"). Instead, however, of the reading " reciprocationis," Oehler would gladly read " rectæ rationis," after most of the editions. He thinks that this allusion to " the right reason," of which Hermogenes boasted, and of which the absurd conclusion is exposed in the context, very well suits the sarcastic style of Tertullian. If this, the general reading, be adopted, we must render the whole clause thus : " For it will be corporeal and incorporeal, in spite of the declaration of that *right reason* (of Hermogenes), which is plainly enough above giving any reason," etc. etc.

reason for its opinion, just as that "other reason" also was. Now, by the corporeal part of Matter, he means that of which bodies are created; but by the incorporeal part *of Matter*, he means its uncreated [1] motion. If, says he, *Matter* were simply a body, there would appear to be in it nothing incorporeal, that is, (no) motion; if, on the other hand, it had been wholly incorporeal, no body could be formed out of it. What a peculiarly right [2] reason have we here ! Only if you make your sketches as right as you make your reason, Hermogenes, no painter would be more stupid [3] than yourself. For who is going to allow you to reckon *motion* as a moiety of *Matter*, seeing that it is not a substantial thing, because it is not corporeal, but an accident (if indeed it be even that) of a substance and a body? Just as action [4] is, and impulsion, just as a slip is, or a fall, so is motion. When anything moves even of itself, its motion is the result of impulse; [5] but certainly it is no part of its substance in your sense, [6] when you make motion the incorporeal part of matter. All things, indeed, [7] have motion—either of themselves as animals, or of others as inanimate things; but yet we should not say that either a man or a stone was both corporeal and incorporeal because they had both a body and motion: *we should say* rather that all things have one form of simple [8] corporeality, which is the essential quality [9] of substance. If any incorporeal *incidents* accrue to them, as actions, or passions, or functions, [10] or desires, we do not reckon these parts as of the things. How then does he contrive to assign an *integral* portion of Matter to *motion*, which does not pertain to substance, but to a certain condition [11] of substance? Is not this incontrovertible? [12] Suppose you had taken it into your head [13] to represent matter as immoveable, would then the immobility seem to you to be a moiety of its form? *Certainly not.* Neither, in like manner, could motion. But I shall be at liberty to speak of motion elsewhere. [14]

CHAP. XXXVII.—IRONICAL DILEMMAS RESPECTING MATTER, AND SUNDRY MORAL QUALITIES FANCIFULLY ATTRIBUTED TO IT.

I see now that you are coming back again to that reason, which has been in the habit of declaring to you nothing in the way of certainty. For just as you introduce to our notice Matter as being neither corporeal nor incorporeal, so you allege of it that it is neither good nor evil; and you say, whilst arguing further on it in the same strain: "If it were good; seeing that it had ever been so, it would not require the arrangement of itself by God; [15] if it were naturally evil, it would not have admitted of a change [16] for the better, nor would God have ever applied to such a nature any attempt at arrangement of it, for His labour would have been in vain." Such are your words, which it would have been well if you had remembered in other passages also, so as to have avoided any contradiction of them. As, however, we have already treated to some extent of this ambiguity of good and evil touching Matter, I will now reply to the only proposition and argument of yours which we have before us. I shall not stop to repeat my opinion, that it was your bounden duty to have said for certain that Matter was either good or bad, or in some third condition; but (I must observe) that you have not here even kept to the statement which you chose to make before. Indeed, you retract what you declared—that Matter is neither good nor evil; because you imply that it is evil when you say, "If it were good, it would not require to be set in order by God;" so again, when you add, "If it were naturally evil, it would not admit of any change for the better," you seem to intimate [17] that it is good. And so you attribute to it a close relation [18] to good and evil, although you declared it neither good nor evil. With a view, however, to refute the argument whereby you thought you were going to clinch your proposition, I here contend: If Matter had always been good, why should it not have *still* wanted a change for the better? Does that which is good never desire, never wish, never feel able to advance, so as to change its good for a better? And in like manner, if *Matter* had been by nature evil, why might it not have been changed by God as the more powerful Being, as able to convert the nature of stones into children of Abraham? [19] Surely by such means you not only compare the Lord with Matter, but you even put Him below [20] it, since you affirm that [21] the nature of Matter could not

---

[1] Inconditum. See above ch. xviii., in the middle. Notwithstanding the absurdity of Hermogenes' idea, it is impossible to translate this word *irregular*, as it has been proposed to do by Genoude.
[2] Rectior.
[3] Bardior.
[4] Actus : being driven.
[5] Actus ejus est motus.
[6] Sicut tu.
[7] Denique.
[8] Solius.
[9] Res.
[10] Officia.

[11] Habitum.
[12] Quid enim ?
[13] Si placuisset tibi.
[14] See below, ch. xli., p. 500.
[15] Compositionem Dei.
[16] Non accepisset translationem.
[17] Subostendis.
[18] Affinem.
[19] Matt. iii. 9.
[20] Subicis.
[21] This is the force of the subjunctive verb.

possibly be brought under control by Him, and trained to something better. But although you are here disinclined to allow that Matter is by nature evil, yet in another passage you will deny having made such an admission.[1]

CHAP. XXXVIII.—OTHER SPECULATIONS OF HERMOGENES, ABOUT MATTER AND SOME OF ITS ADJUNCTS, SHOWN TO BE ABSURD. FOR INSTANCE, ITS ALLEGED INFINITY.

My observations touching the *site*[2] of Matter, as also concerning its *mode*,[3] have one and the same object in view—to meet and refute your perverse positions. You put Matter below God, and thus, of course, you assign a place to it below God. Therefore Matter is local.[4] Now, if it is local, it is within locality; if within locality, it is bounded[5] by the place within which it is; if it is bounded, it has an outline,[6] which (painter as you are in your special vocation) you know is the boundary to every object susceptible of outline. Matter, therefore, cannot be infinite, which, since it is in space, is bounded by space; and being thus determinable by space, it is susceptible of an outline. You, however, make it infinite, when you say: "It is on this account infinite, because it is always existent." And if any of your disciples should choose to meet us by declaring your meaning to be that Matter is infinite in time, not in its corporeal mass,[7] still what follows will show that (you mean) corporeal infinity *to be an attribute of Matter*, that it is in respect of bulk immense and uncircumscribed. "Wherefore," say you, "it is not fabricated as a whole, but *in* its parts."[8] In bulk, therefore, is it infinite, not in time. And you contradict yourself[9] when you make *Matter* infinite in bulk, and at the same time ascribe place to it, including it within space and local outline. But yet at the same time I cannot tell why God should not have entirely formed it,[10] unless it be because He was either impotent or envious. I want therefore to know the moiety of that which was not wholly formed (by God), in order that I may understand what kind of thing the entirety was. It was only right that God should have made it

known as a model of antiquity,[11] to set off the glory of His work.

CHAP. XXXIX.—THESE LATTER SPECULATIONS SHOWN TO BE CONTRADICTORY TO THE FIRST PRINCIPLES RESPECTING MATTER, FORMERLY LAID DOWN BY HERMOGENES.

Well, now, since it seems to you to be the correcter thing,[12] let Matter be circumscribed[13] by means of changes and displacements; let it also be capable of comprehension, since (as you say) it is used as material by God,[14] on the ground of its being convertible, mutable, and separable. For its changes, you say, show it to be inseparable. And here you have swerved from your own lines[15] which you prescribed respecting the person of God when you laid down the rule that God made it not out of His own self, because it was not possible for Him to become divided[16] seeing that He is eternal and abiding for ever, and therefore unchangeable and indivisible. Since Matter too is estimated by the same eternity, having neither beginning nor end, it will be unsusceptible of division, of change, for the same reason that God also is. Since it is associated with Him in the joint possession of eternity, it must needs share with Him also the powers, the laws, and the conditions of eternity. In like manner, when you say, "All things simultaneously throughout the universe[17] possess portions of it,[18] that so the whole may be ascertained from[19] its parts," you of course mean to indicate those parts which were produced out of it, and which are now visible to us. How then is this possession (of Matter) by all things throughout the universe effected—that is, of course, from the very beginning[20]—when the things which are now visible to us are different in their condition[21] from what they were in the beginning?

CHAP. XL.—SHAPELESS MATTER AN INCONGRUOUS ORIGIN FOR GOD'S BEAUTIFUL COSMOS. HERMOGENES DOES NOT MEND HIS ARGUMENT BY SUPPOSING THAT ONLY A PORTION OF MATTER WAS USED IN THE CREATION.

You say that Matter was reformed for the better[22]—from a worse condition, of course; and *thus* you would make the better a copy of

---

[1] Te confessum.
[2] De situ.
[3] Oehler here restores the reading "quod et de *modo*," instead of "de *motu*," for which Pamelius contends. Oehler has the MSS. on his side, and Fr. Junius, who interprets "*modo*" here to mean "mass or quantity." Pamelius wishes to suit the passage to the preceding context (see ch. xxxvi.) ; Junius thinks it is meant rather to refer to what follows, by which it is confirmed.
[4] In loco.
[5] Determinatur.
[6] Lineam extremam.
[7] Modo corporis : or "bulk."
[8] Nec tota fabricatur, sed partes ejus. This perhaps means : "It is not its entirety, but its parts, which are used in creation."
[9] Obduceris : here a verb of the middle voice.
[10] In reference to the opinion above mentioned, "Matter is not fabricated as a whole, but in parts."

[11] Ut exemplarium antiquitatis.
[12] Rectius.
[13] Definitiva.
[14] Ut quæ fabricatur, inquis, a Deo.
[15] Lineis. Tertullian often refers to Hermogenes' profession of painting.
[16] In partes venire.
[17] Omnia ex omnibus.
[18] i. e. of Matter.
[19] Dinoscatur ex.
[20] Utique ex pristinis.
[21] Aliter habeant.
[22] In melius reformatam.

the worse. Everything was in confusion, but now it is reduced to order; and would you also say, that out of order, disorder is produced? No one thing is the exact mirror[1] of another thing; that is to say, it is not its co-equal. Nobody ever found himself in a barber's looking-glass look like an ass[2] instead of a man; unless it be he who supposes that unformed and shapeless Matter answers to Matter which is now arranged and beautified in the fabric of the world. What is there now that is without form in the world, what was there once that was formed[3] in Matter, that the world is the mirror of Matter? Since the world is known among the Greeks by a term denoting *ornament*,[4] how can it present the image of unadorned[5] Matter, in such a way that you can say the whole is known by its parts? To that whole will certainly belong even the *portion* which has not yet become formed; and you have already declared that the whole *of Matter* was not used as material *in the creation*.[6] It follows, then, that this rude, and confused, and unarranged portion cannot be recognized in the polished, and distinct and well-arranged *parts of creation*, which indeed can hardly with propriety be called parts of Matter, since they have quitted[7] its condition, by being separated from it in the transformation they have undergone.

CHAP. XLI.—SUNDRY QUOTATIONS FROM HER-
    MOGENES. HOW UNCERTAIN AND VAGUE ARE
    HIS SPECULATIONS RESPECTING MOTION IN
    MATTER, AND THE MATERIAL QUALITIES OF
    GOOD AND EVIL.

I come back to the point of *motion*,[8] that I may show how slippery you are at every step. Motion in Matter was disordered, and confused, and turbulent. This is why you apply to it the comparison of a boiler of hot water surging over. Now how is it, that in another passage another sort of motion is affirmed by you? For when you want to represent Matter as neither good nor evil, you say: "Matter, which is the substratum (of creation)[9] possessing as it does motion in an equable impulse,[10] tends in no very great degree either to good or to evil." Now if it had this equable impulse, it could not be turbulent, nor be like the boiling water of the caldron; it would rather be even and regular, oscillating

indeed of its own accord between good and evil, but yet not prone or tending to either side. It would swing, as the phrase is, in a just and exact balance. Now this is not unrest; this is not turbulence or inconstancy;[11] but rather the regularity, and evenness, and exactitude of a motion, inclining to neither side. If it oscillated this way and that way, and inclined rather to one particular side, it would plainly in that case merit the reproach of unevenness, and inequality, and turbulence. Moreover, although the motion *of Matter* was not prone either to good or to evil, it would still, of course, oscillate between good and evil; so that from this circumstance too it is obvious that Matter is contained within certain limits,[12] because its motion, while prone to neither good nor evil, since it had no natural bent either way, oscillated from either between both, and therefore was contained within the limits of the two. But you, in fact, place both good and evil in a local habitation,[13] when you assert that motion in Matter inclined to neither of them. For Matter which was local,[14] when inclining neither hither nor thither, inclined not to the places in which good and evil were. But when you assign locality to good and evil, you make them corporeal by making them local, since those things which have local space must needs first have bodily substance. In fact,[15] incorporeal things could not have any locality of their own except in a body, when they have access to a body.[16] But when Matter inclined not to good and evil, it was as corporeal or local *essences* that it did not incline' to them. You err, therefore, when you will have it that good and evil are substances. For you make substances of the things to which you assign locality;[17] but you assign locality when you keep motion in Matter poised equally distant from both sides.[18]

CHAP. XLII.—FURTHER EXPOSURE OF INCON-
    SISTENCIES IN THE OPINIONS OF HERMOGENES
    RESPECTING THE DIVINE QUALITIES OF MAT-
    TER.

You have thrown out all your views loosely and at random,[19] in order that it might not be apparent, by too close a proximity, how contrary they are to one another. I, however, mean to gather them together and compare them. You allege that motion in Matter is

---

[1] Speculum.
[2] Mulus.
[3] Speciatum: εἰδοποιηθέν, "arranged in specific forms."
[4] Κόσμος.
[5] Inornatæ: *unfurnished* with forms of beauty.
[6] Non totam eam fabricatam.
[7] Recesserunt a forma ejus.
[8] From which he has digressed since ch. xxxvi., p. 497.
[9] Subjacens materia.
[10] Æqualis momenti motum.

[11] Passivitas.
[12] Determinabilem.
[13] In loco facis: "you localise."
[14] In loco.
[15] Denique.
[16] Cum corpori accedunt: or, "when they are added to a body."
[17] Loca: "places;" one to each.
[18] Cum ab utraque regione suspendis: equally far from good and evil.
[19] Dispersisti omnia.

without regularity,[1] and you go on to say that Matter aims at a shapeless condition, and then, in another passage, that it desires to be set in order by God. Does that, then, which affects to be without form, want to be put into shape? Or does that which wants to be put into shape, affect to be without form? You are unwilling that God should seem to be equal to Matter; and then again you say that it has a common condition[2] with God. "For it is impossible," you say, "if it has nothing in common with God, that it can be set in order by Him." But if it had anything in common with God, it did not want to be set in order,[3] being, forsooth, a part of the Deity through a community of condition; or else even God was susceptible of being set in order[3] by Matter, by His having Himself something in common with it. And now you herein subject God to necessity, since there was in Matter something on account of which He gave it form. You make it, however, a common attribute of both of them, that they set themselves in motion by themselves, and that they are ever in motion. What less do you ascribe to Matter than to God? There will be found all through a fellowship of divinity in this freedom and perpetuity of motion. Only in God motion is regular,[4] in Matter irregular.[5] In both, however, there is equally the attribute of Deity—both alike having free and eternal motion. At the same time, you assign more to Matter, to which belonged the privilege of thus moving itself in a way not allowed to God.

CHAP. XLIII.—OTHER DISCREPANCIES EXPOSED AND REFUTED RESPECTING THE EVIL IN MATTER BEING CHANGED TO GOOD.

On the subject of motion I would make this further remark. Following the *simile* of the boiling caldron, you say that motion in Matter, before it was regulated, was confused,[6] restless, incomprehensible by reason of excess in the commotion.[7] Then again you go on to say, "But it waited for the regulation[8] of God, and kept its irregular motion incomprehensible, owing to the tardiness of its irregular motion." Just before you ascribe commotion, ɯere tardiness, to motion. Now observe how many slips you make respecting the nature of Matter. In a former passage[9] you say, "If Matter were

naturally evil, it would not have admitted of a change for the better; nor would God have ever applied to it any attempt at arrangement, for His labour would have been in vain." You therefore concluded your two opinions, that Matter was not by nature evil, and that its nature was incapable of being changed by God; and then, forgetting them, you afterwards drew this inference: "But when it received adjustment from God, it relinquished its nature." Now, inasmuch as it was transformed to good, it was of course transformed from evil; and if by God's setting it in order it relinquished[11] the nature of evil, it follows that its nature came to an end;[12] now its nature was evil before the adjustment, but after the transformation it might have relinquished that nature.

CHAP. XLIV.—CURIOUS VIEWS RESPECTING GOD'S METHOD OF WORKING WITH MATTER EXPOSED. DISCREPANCIES IN THE HERETIC'S OPINION ABOUT GOD'S LOCAL RELATION TO MATTER.

But it remains that I should show also how you make God work. You are plainly enough at variance with the philosophers; but neither are you in accord with the prophets. The Stoics maintain that God pervaded Matter, just as honey the honeycomb. You, however, affirm that it is not by pervading Matter that God makes the world, but simply by appearing, and approaching it, just as beauty affects[13] a thing by simply appearing, and a loadstone by approaching it. Now what similarity is there in God forming the world, and beauty wounding a soul, or a magnet attracting iron? For even if God appeared to Matter, He yet did not wound it, as beauty does the soul; if, again, He approached it, He yet did not cohere to it, as the magnet does to the iron. Suppose, however, that your examples are suitable ones. Then, of course,[14] it was by appearing and approaching to Matter that God made the world, and He made it when He appeared and when He approached to it. Therefore, since He had not made it before then,[15] He had neither appeared nor approached to it. Now, by whom can it be believed that God had not appeared to Matter—of the same nature as it even was owing to its eternity? Or that He had been at a distance from it—even He whom we believe to be existent everywhere, and everywhere apparent; whose praises all things chant, even inanimate things and things incorporeal, ac-

[1] Inconditum.
[2] "Communionem."
[3] Ornari : "to be adorned."
[4] Composite.
[5] Incondite.
[6] Concretus.
[7] Certaminis.
[8] Compositionem : "arrangement."
[9] See above, ch. xxxvii. p. 498.

[10] Ornata.
[11] Cessavit a.
[12] Cessavit.
[13] Facit quid decor.
[14] Certe.
[15] Retro.

cording to (the prophet) Daniel?[1] How immense the place, where God kept Himself so far aloof from Matter as to have neither appeared nor approached to it before the creation of the world! I suppose He journeyed to it from a long distance, as soon as He wished to appear and approach to it.

CHAP. XLV.—CONCLUSION. CONTRAST BETWEEN THE STATEMENTS OF HERMOGENES AND THE TESTIMONY OF HOLY SCRIPTURE RESPECTING THE CREATION. CREATION OUT OF NOTHING, NOT OUT OF MATTER.

But it is not thus that the prophets and the apostles have told us that the world was made by God merely appearing and approaching Matter. They did not even mention any Matter, but (said) that Wisdom was first set up, the beginning of His ways, for His works.[2] Then that the Word was produced, "through whom all things were made, and without whom nothing was made."[3] Indeed, "by the Word of the Lord were the heavens made, and all their hosts by the breath of His mouth."[4] He is the Lord's right hand,[5] indeed His two hands, by which He worked and constructed *the universe.* "For," says He, "the heavens are the works of Thine hands,"[6] wherewith "He hath meted out the heaven, and the earth with a span."[7] Do not be willing so to cover God with flattery, as to contend that He produced by His mere appearance and simple approach so many vast substances, instead of rather forming them by His own energies. For this is proved by Jeremiah when he says, "God hath made the earth by His power, He hath established the world by His wisdom, and hath stretched out the heaven by His understanding."[8] These are the energies by the stress of which He made this universe.[9] His glory is greater if He laboured. At length on the seventh day He rested from His works. Both one and the other were after His manner. If, on the contrary,[10] He made this world simply by appearing and approaching it, did He, on the completion of His work, cease to appear and approach it any more. Nay rather,[11] God began to appear more conspicuously and to be everywhere accessible[12] from the time when the world was made. You see, therefore, how all things consist by the operation of that God who "made the earth by His power, who established the world by His wisdom, and stretched out the heaven by His understanding;" not appearing merely, nor approaching; but applying the almighty efforts of His mind, His wisdom, His power, His understanding, His word, His Spirit, His might. Now these things were not necessary to Him, if He had been perfect by simply appearing and approaching. They are, however, His "invisible things," which, according to the apostle, "are from the creation of the world clearly seen by the things that are made;[13] *they are no parts* of a nondescript[14] Matter, but they are the sensible[15] evidences of Himself. "For who hath known the mind of the Lord,"[16] of which (the apostle) exclaims: "O the depth of the riches both of His wisdom and knowledge! how unsearchable are His judgments, and His ways past finding out!"[17] Now what clearer truth do these words indicate, than that all things were made out of nothing? They are incapable of being found out or investigated, except by God alone. Otherwise, if they were traceable or discoverable in Matter, they would be capable of investigation. Therefore, in *as far as* it has become evident that Matter had no prior existence (even from this circumstance, that it is impossible[18] for it to have had such an existence as is assigned to it), in *so* far is it proved that all things were made by God out of nothing. It must be admitted, however,[19] that Hermogenes, by describing for Matter a condition like his own—irregular, confused, turbulent, of a doubtful and precipate and fervid impulse—has displayed a specimen of his own art, and painted his own portrait.

[1] Dan. iii. 21.
[2] Prov. viii. 22, 23.
[3] John i. 3.
[4] Spiritu Ipsius: "by His Spirit." See Ps. xxxiii. 6.
[5] Isa. xlviii. 13.
[6] Ps. cii. 25.
[7] Isa. xl. 12 and xlviii. 13.
[8] Jer. li. 15.
[9] Ps. lxiv. 7.
[10] Aut si.

[11] Atquin
[12] Ubique conveniri.
[13] Rom. i. 20.
[14] Nescio quæ.
[15] Sensualia.
[16] Rom. xi. 34.
[17] Ver. 33.
[18] Nec competat.
[19] Nisi quod.

AGAINST THE VALENTINIANS.

IN WHICH THE AUTHOR GIVES A CONCISE ACCOUNT OF, TOGETHER WITH SUNDRY CAUSTIC ANIMADVERSIONS ON, THE VERY FANTASTIC THEOLOGY OF THE SECT. THIS TREATISE IS PROFESSEDLY TAKEN FROM THE WRITINGS OF JUSTIN, MILTIADES, IRENÆUS, AND PROCULUS.

[TRANSLATED BY DR. ROBERTS.]

CHAP. I.—INTRODUCTORY. TERTULLIAN COMPARES THE HERESY TO THE OLD ELEUSINIAN MYSTERIES. BOTH SYSTEMS ALIKE IN PREFERRING CONCEALMENT OF ERROR AND SIN TO PROCLAMATION OF TRUTH AND VIRTUE.

THE Valentinians, who are no doubt a very large body of heretics—comprising as they do so many apostates from the truth, who have a propensity for fables, and no discipline to deter them (therefrom) care for nothing so much as to obscure[1] what they preach, if indeed they (can be said to) preach who obscure *their doctrine.* The officiousness with which they guard their doctrine is an officiousness which betrays their guilt.[2] Their disgrace is proclaimed in the very earnestness with which they maintain their religious system. Now, in the case of those Eleusinian mysteries, which are the very heresy of Athenian superstition, it is their secrecy that is their disgrace. Accordingly, they previously beset all access to their body with tormenting conditions;[3] *and* they require a long initiation before they enrol (their members),[4] even instruction during five years for their perfect disciples,[5] in order that they may mould[6] their opinions by this suspension of full knowledge, and apparently raise the dignity of their mysteries in proportion to the craving for them which they have previously created. Then follows the duty of silence. Carefully is that guarded, which is so long in finding. All the divinity, however, lies in their secret recesses:[7] there are revealed *at last* all the aspirations of the fully initiated,[8] the entire mystery of the sealed tongue, the symbol of virility. But this allegorical representation,[9] under the pretext of nature's reverend name, obscures a real sacrilege by help of an arbitrary symbol,[10] and by *empty* images obviates[11] the reproach of falsehood![12] In like manner, the heretics who are now the object of our remarks,[13] the Valentinians, have formed Eleusinian dissipations[14] of their own, consecrated by a profound silence, having nothing of the heavenly in them but their mystery.[15] By the help of the sacred names and titles and arguments of true religion, they have fabricated the vainest and foulest figment for men's pliant liking,[16] out of the affluent suggestions of Holy Scripture, since from its many springs many *errors* may well emanate. If you propose to them inquiries sincere and honest, they answer you with stern[17] look and contracted brow, and say, "The subject is profound." If you try them with subtle questions, with the ambiguities of their double tongue, they affirm a community of faith (with yourself). If you intimate to

---

[1] Occultant. [This tract may be assigned to any date not earlier than A. D. 207. Of this Valentinus, see cap. iv. *infra*, and *de Præscript.* capp. 29, 30, *supra.*]
[2] We are far from certain whether we have caught the sense of the original, which we add, that the reader may judge for himself, and at the same time observe the terseness of our author: "Custodiæ officium conscientiæ officium est, confusio prædicatur, dum religio asseveratur."
[3] Et aditum prius cruciant.
[4] Antequam consignant.
[5] Epoptas: see Suidas, *s.v.* 'Επόπται.
[6] Ædificent.
[7] Adytis.
[8] Epoptarum.
[9] Dispositio.
[10] Patrocinio coactæ figuræ.
[11] Excusat.
[12] "Quid enim aliud est simulachrum nisi falsum?" (Rigalt.)
[13] Quos nunc destinamus.
[14] Lenocinia.
[15] Taciturnitate.
[16] Facili caritati. Oehler, after Fr. Junius, gives, however, this phrase a subjective turn thus: "by affecting a charity which is easy to them, costing nothing."
[17] Concreto.

them that you understand *their opinions*, they insist on knowing nothing themselves. If you come to a close engagement with them, they destroy your own fond hope of a victory over them by a self-immolation.[1] Not even to their own disciples do they commit a secret before they have made sure of them. They have the knack of persuading men before instructing them; although truth persuades by teaching, but does not teach by first persuading.

CHAP. II.—THESE HERETICS BRAND THE CHRISTIANS AS SIMPLE PERSONS. THE CHARGE ACCEPTED, AND SIMPLICITY EULOGIZED OUT OF THE SCRIPTURES.

For this reason we are branded[2] by them as simple, and as being merely so, without being wise also; as if indeed wisdom were compelled to be wanting in simplicity, whereas the Lord unites them both: "Be ye therefore wise as serpents, and simple as doves."[3] Now if we, on our parts, be accounted foolish because we are simple, does it then follow that they are not simple because they are wise? Most perverse, however, are they who are not simple, even as they are most foolish who are not wise. And yet, (if I must choose) I should prefer taking[4] the *latter* condition for the lesser fault; since it is perhaps better to have a wisdom which falls short in quantity, than that which is bad in quality[5]—better to be in error than to mislead. Besides, the face of the Lord[6] is patiently waited for by those who "seek Him in simplicity of heart," as says the very Wisdom—not of Valentinus, but—of Solomon.[7] Then, again, infants have borne[8] by their blood a testimony to Christ. (Would you say) that it was children who shouted "Crucify Him"?[9] They were neither children nor infants; in other words, they were not simple. The apostle, too, bids us to "become children again" towards God,[10] "to be as children in malice" by our simplicity, yet as being also "wise in our practical faculties."[11] At the same time, with respect to the order of development in Wisdom, I have admitted[12] that it flows from simplicity. In brief, "the dove" has usually

served to figure Christ; "the serpent," to tempt Him. The one even from the first has been the harbinger of divine peace; the other from the beginning has been the despoiler of the divine image. Accordingly, simplicity alone[13] will be more easily able to know and to declare God, *whereas* wisdom alone will rather do Him violence,[14] and betray Him.

CHAP. III.—THE FOLLY OF THIS HERESY. IT DISSECTS AND MUTILATES THE DEITY. CONTRASTED WITH THE SIMPLE WISDOM OF TRUE RELIGION. TO EXPOSE THE ABSURDITIES OF THE VALENTINIAN SYSTEM IS TO DESTROY IT.

Let, then, the serpent hide himself as much as he is able, and let him wrest[15] all his wisdom in the labyrinths of his obscurities; let him dwell deep down in the ground; let him worm himself into secret holes; let him unroll his length through his sinuous joints;[16] let him tortuously crawl, though not all at once,[17] beast as he is that skulks the light. Of our dove, however, how simple is the very home! —always in high and open places, and facing the light! As the symbol of the Holy Spirit, it loves the (radiant) East, that figure of Christ.[18] Nothing causes truth a blush, except only being hidden, because no man will be ashamed to give ear thereto. *No man will be ashamed* to recognise Him as God whom nature has already commended to him, whom he already perceives in all His works,[19] —Him indeed who is simply, for this reason, imperfectly known; because man has not thought of Him as only one, because he has named Him in a plurality (of gods), and adored Him in other *forms*. Yet,[20] to induce oneself to turn from this multitude of deities to another crowd,[21] to remove from a familiar authority to an unknown one, to wrench oneself from what is manifest to what is hidden, is to offend faith on the very threshold. Now, even suppose that you are initiated into the entire fable, will it not occur to you that you have heard something very like it from your fond nurse[22] when you were a baby, amongst

---

[1] Sua cæde.
[2] Notamur.
[3] Matt. x. 16.
[4] In the original the phrase is put *passively:* "malim eam partem meliori sumi vitio."
[5] How terse is the original! minus sapere quam pejus.
[6] Facies Dei.
[7] Wisd. of Sol. i. 1.
[8] Litaverunt: "consecrated."
[9] Tertullian's words are rather suggestive of sense than of syntax: "Pueros vocem qui crucem clamant?"
[10] Secundum Deum: "according to God's will."
[11] 1 Cor. xiv. 20, where Tertullian renders the ταῖς φρεσί (A. V. "understanding") by "sensibus."
[12] Dedi.

[13] i.e., without wisdom.
[14] Concutere.
[15] Torqueat.
[16] Per anfractus.
[17] Nec semel totus.
[18] By this remark it would seem that Tertullian read sundry passages in his Latin Bible similarly to the subsequent Vulgate version. For instance, in Zech. vi. 12, the prophet's words הִנֵּה־אִישׁ צֶמַח שְׁמוֹ ("Behold the Man, whose name is the BRANCH"), are rendered in the Vulgate, "Ecce Vir *Oriens* nomen ejus." Similarly in Zech. iii. 8, "Servum meum adducam ORIENTEM." (Compare Luke i. 78, where the Ἀνατολὴ ἐξ ὕψους ("the day-spring from on high") is in the same version "*Oriens ex alto.*")
[19] Or, perhaps, "whom it (nature) feels in all its works."
[20] Alioquin.
[21] Alloquin a turba eorum et aliam frequentiam suadere: which perhaps is best rendered, "But from one rabble of gods to frame and teach men to believe in another set," etc.
[22] A nutricula.

the lullabies she sang to you[1] about the towers of Lamia, and the horns of the sun?[2] Let, however, any man approach the subject from a knowledge of the faith which he has otherwise learned, as soon as he finds so many names of Æons, so many marriages, so many offsprings, so many exits, so many issues, felicities *and* infelicities of a dispersed and mutilated Deity, will all that man hesitate at once to pronounce that these are " the fables and endless genealogies " which the inspired apostle[3] by anticipation condemned, whilst these seeds of heresy were even then shooting forth? Deservedly, therefore, must they be regarded as wanting in simplicity, and as merely prudent, who produce such fables not without difficulty, and defend them only indirectly, who at the same time do not thoroughly instruct those whom they teach. This, of course, shows their astuteness, if their lessons are disgraceful; their unkindness, if they are honourable. As for us, however, who are the simple folk, we know all about it. In short, this is the very first weapon with which we are armed for our encounter; it unmasks[4] and brings to view[5] the whole of their depraved system.[6] And in this we have the first augury of our victory; because even merely to point out that which is concealed with so great an outlay of artifice,[7] is to destroy it.

CHAP. IV.—THE HERESY TRACEABLE TO VALENTINUS, AN ABLE BUT RESTLESS MAN. MANY SCHISMATICAL LEADERS OF THE SCHOOL MENTIONED. ONLY ONE OF THEM SHOWS RESPECT TO THE MAN WHOSE NAME DESIGNATES THE ENTIRE SCHOOL.

We know, I say, most fully their actual origin, and we are quite aware why we call them Valentinians, although they affect to disavow their name. They have departed, it is true,[8] from their founder, yet is their origin by no means destroyed; and even if it chance to be changed, the very change bears testimony to the fact. Valentinus had expected to become a bishop, because he was an able man both in genius and eloquence. Being indignant, however, that another obtained the dignity by reason of a claim which confessorship[9] had given him, he broke with the church of the true faith. Just like those (restless) spirits which, when roused by ambition, are usually inflamed with the desire of revenge, he applied himself with all his might[10] to exterminate the truth; and finding the clue[11] of a certain old opinion, he marked out a path for himself with the subtlety of a serpent. Ptolemæus afterwards entered on the same path, by distinguishing the names and the numbers of the Ænons into personal substances, which, however, he kept apart from God. Valentinus had included these in the very essence of the Deity, as senses and affections of motion. Sundry bypaths were then struck off therefrom, by Heraclean and Secundus and the magician Marcus. Theotimus worked hard about " the images of the law." Valentinus, however, was as yet nowhere, and still the Valentinians derive their name from Valentinus. Axionicus at Antioch is the only man who at the present time does honour[12] to the memory of Valentinus, by keeping his rules[13] to the full. But this heresy is permitted to fashion itself into as many various shapes as a courtezan, who usually changes and adjusts her dress every day. And why not? When they review that spiritual seed of theirs in every man after this fashion, whenever they have hit upon any novelty, they forthwith call their presumption a revelation, their own perverse ingenuity a spiritual gift; but (they deny all) unity, *admitting only* diversity.[14] And thus we clearly see that, setting aside their customary dissimulation, most of them are in a divided state, being ready to say (and that sincerely) of certain points of their belief, " This is not so;" and, " I take this in a different sense;" and, " I do not admit that." By this variety, indeed, innovation is stamped on the very face of their rules; besides which, it wears all the colourable features of ignorant conceits.[15]

CHAP. V.—MANY EMINENT CHRISTIAN WRITERS HAVE CAREFULLY AND FULLY REFUTED THE HERESY. THESE THE AUTHOR MAKES HIS OWN GUIDES.

My own path, however, lies along the original tenets[16] of their chief teachers, not with the self-appointed leaders of their promiscuous[17] followers. Nor shall we hear it said of us from any quarter, that we have of our own mind fashioned our own materials, since these have been already produced, both in respect of the opinions and their refutations, in carefully written volumes, by so many eminently

---

[1] Inter somni difficultates.
[2] These were child's stories at Carthage in Tertullian's days.
[3] Apostoli spiritus: see 1 Tim. i. 4.
[4] Detectorem.
[5] Designatorem.
[6] Totius conscientiæ illorum.
[7] Tanto impendio.
[8] Enim.
[9] Martyrii.
[10] Conversus.
[11] Semitam.
[12] Consolatur.
[13] Regularum: the particulars of his system. [Here comes in the word, borrowed from heresy, which shaped Monasticism in after times and created the *regular* orders.]
[14] Nec unitatem, sed diversitatem: sctl. appellant.
[15] Colores ignorantiarum.
[16] Archetypis.
[17] Passivorum.

holy and excellent men, not only those who have lived before us, but those also who were contemporary with the heresiarchs themselves: for instance Justin, philosopher and martyr;[1] Miltiades, the sophist[2] of the churches; Irenæus, that very exact inquirer into all doctrines;[3] our own Proculus, the model[4] of chaste old age and Christian eloquence. All these it would be my desire closely to follow in every work of faith, even as in this particular one. Now if there are no heresies at all, but what those who refute them are supposed to have fabricated, then the apostle who predicted them[5] must have been guilty of falsehood. If, however, there are heresies, they can be no other than those which are the subject of discussion. No writer can be supposed to have so much time on his hands[6] as to fabricate materials which are already in his possession.

CHAP. VI.—ALTHOUGH WRITING IN LATIN HE PROPOSES TO RETAIN THE GREEK NAMES OF THE VALENTINIAN EMANATIONS OF DEITY. NOT TO DISCUSS THE HERESY BUT ONLY TO EXPOSE IT. THIS WITH THE RAILLERY WHICH ITS ABSURDITY MERITS.

In order then, that no one may be blinded by so many outlandish[7] names, collected together, and adjusted at pleasure,[8] and of doubtful import, I mean in this little work, wherein we merely undertake to propound this (heretical) mystery, to explain in what manner we are to use them. Now the rendering of some of these *names* from the Greek to as to produce an equally obvious sense of the word, is by no means an easy process: in the case of some others, the genders are not suitable; while others, again, are more familiarly known in their Greek form. For the most part, therefore, we shall use the Greek names; their meanings will be seen on the margins of the pages. Nor will the Greek be unaccompanied with the Latin *equivalents;* only these will be marked in lines above, for the purpose of explaining[9] the personal names, rendered necessary by the ambiguities of such of them as admit some different meaning. But although I must postpone all discussion, and be content at present with the mere exposition (of the heresy), still, wherever any scandalous feature

shall seem to require a castigation, it must be attacked[10] by all means, if only with a passing thrust.[11] Let the reader regard it as the skirmish before the battle. It will be my drift to show how to wound[12] rather than to inflict deep gashes. If in any instance mirth be excited, this will be quite as much as the subject deserves. There are many things which deserve refutation in such a way as to have no gravity expended on them. Vain and silly topics are met with especial fitness by laughter. Even the truth may indulge in ridicule, because it is jubilant; it may play with its enemies, because it is fearless.[13] Only we must take care that its laughter be not unseemly, and so itself be laughed at; but wherever its mirth is decent, there it is a duty *to indulge it.* And so at last I enter on my task.

CHAP. VII.—THE FIRST EIGHT EMANATIONS, OR ÆONS, CALLED THE OGDOAD, ARE THE FOUNTAIN OF ALL THE OTHERS. THEIR NAMES AND DESCENT RECORDED.

Beginning with Ennius,[14] the Roman poet, he simply spoke of "the spacious saloons[15] of heaven,"—either on account of their elevated site, or because in Homer he had read about Jupiter banqueting therein. As for *our* heretics, however, it is marvellous what storeys upon storeys[16] and what heights upon heights, they have hung up, raised *and* spread out as a dwelling for each several god of theirs. Even our Creator has had arranged for Him the saloons of Ennius in the fashion of private rooms,[17] with chamber piled upon chamber, and assigned to each god by just as many staircases as there were heresies. The universe, *in fact*, has been turned into "rooms to let."[18] Such storeys of the heavens you would imagine to be detached tenements in some happy isle of the blessed,[19] I know not where. There the god even of the Valentinians has his dwelling in the attics. They call him indeed, as to his essence, Αἰὼν τέλειος (*Perfect Æon*), but in respect of his personality, Προαρχή (*Before the Beginning*), Ἡ Ἀρχή (*The Beginning*), and sometimes Bythos (Depth),[20] a name

---

[1] [See Vol. I. pp. 171, 182, this series].
[2] In a good sense, from the elegance of his style.
[3] [See Vol. I. p. 326, of this series. Tertullian appropriates the work of Irenæus, (B. i.) against the Gnostics without further ceremony: translation excepted.]
[4] Dignitas. [Of this Proculus see Kaye, p. 55.]
[5] 1 Cor. xi. 19.
[6] Otiosus.
[7] Tam peregrinis.
[8] Compactis.
[9] Ut signum hoc sit.

[10] Or *stormed* perhaps; *expugnatio* is the word.
[11] Delibatione transfunctoria.
[12] Ostendam vulnera.
[13] Secura.
[14] Primus omnium.
[15] Cœnacula: dining halls.
[16] Supernitates supernitatum.
[17] Ædicularum.
[18] Meritorium.
[19] This is perhaps a fair rendering ·of "Insulam Feliculam credas tanta tabulata cœlorum, nescio ubi." "Insula" is sometimes "a detached house." It is difficult to say what "Felicula" is; it seems to be a diminutive of Felix. It occurs in Arrian's *Epictetica* as the name of a slave.
[20] We follow Tertullian's mode of designation all through. He, for the most part, gives the Greek names in Roman letters, but not quite always.

which is most unfit for one who dwells in the heights above! They describe him as unbegotten, immense, infinite, invisible, and eternal; as if, when they described him to be such as we know that he ought to be, they straightway prove him to be a being who may be said to have had such an existence even before all things else. I indeed insist upon[1] it that he is such a being; and there is nothing which I detect in beings of this sort more obvious, than that they who are said to have been before all things—things, too, not their own—are found to be behind all things. Let it, however, be granted that this Bythos of theirs existed in the infinite ages of the past in the greatest and profoundest repose, in the extreme rest of a placid and, if I may use the expression, stupid divinity, such as Epicurus has enjoined upon us. And yet, although they would have him be alone, they assign to him a second person in himself and with himself, Ennoea (*Thought*), which they also call both Charis (*Grace*) and Sige (*Silence*). Other things, as it happened, conduced in this most agreeable repose to remind him of the need of by and by producing out of himself the beginning of all things. This he deposits in lieu of seed in the genital region, as it were, of the womb of his Sige. Instantaneous conception is the result: Sige becomes pregnant, and is delivered, of course in silence; and her offspring is Nus (Mind), very like his father and his equal in every respect. In short, he alone is capable of comprehending the measureless and incomprensible greatness of his father. Accordingly he is even called the Father himself, and the Beginning of all things, and, with great propriety, Monogenes (*The Only-begotten*). And yet not with absolute propriety, since he is not born alone. For along with him a female also proceeded, whose name was Veritas[2] (*Truth*). But how much more suitably might Monogenes be called Protogenes (*First begotten*), since he was begotten first! Thus Bythos and Sige, Nus and Veritas, are alleged to be the first fourfold team[3] of the Valentinian set (of gods)[4] the parent stock and origin of them all. For immediately when[5] Nus received the function of a procreation of his own, he too produces out of himself Sermo (*the Word*) and Vita (*the Life*). If this latter existed not previously, of course she existed not in Bythos. And a pretty absurdity would it be, if Life existed not in God! However, this off-spring also produces fruit, having for its mission the initiation of the universe and the formation of the entire Pleroma: it procreates Homo (*Man*) and Ecclesia (*the Church*). Thus you have an Ogdoad, a double Tetra, out of the conjunctions of males and females —the cells[6] (so to speak) of the primordial Æons, the fraternal nuptials of the Valentinian gods, the simple originals[7] of heretical sanctity and majesty, a rabble[8]—shall I say of criminals[9] or of deities?[10]—at any rate, the fountain of all ulterior fecundity.

CHAP. VIII.—THE NAMES AND DESCENT OF OTHER ÆONS; FIRST HALF A SCORE, THEN TWO MORE, AND ULTIMATELY A DOZEN BESIDES. THESE THIRTY CONSTITUTE THE PLEROMA. BUT WHY BE SO CAPRICIOUS AS TO STOP AT THIRTY?

For, behold, when the second Tetrad—Sermo and Vita, Homo and Ecclesia[11]—had borne fruit to the Father's glory, having an intense desire of themselves to present to the Father something similar of their own, they bring other issue into being[12]—conjugal of course, as the others were[13]—by the union of the twofold nature. On the one hand, Sermo and Vita pour out at a birth a half-score of Æons; on the other hand, Homo and Ecclesia produce a couple more, so furnishing an equipoise to their parents, since this pair with the other ten make up just as many as they did themselves procreate. I now give the names of the half-score whom I have mentioned: Bythios (*Profound*) and Mixis (*Mixture*), Ageratos (*Never old*) and Henosis (*Union*), Autophyes (*Essential nature*) and Hedone (*Pleasure*), Acinetos (*Immoveable*) and Syncrasis (*Commixture,*) Monogenes (*Only-begotten*) and Macaria (*Happiness*). On the other hand, these will make up the number twelve (to which I have also referred): Paracletus (*Comforter*) and Pistis (*Faith*), Patricas (*Paternal*) and Elpis (*Hope*), Metricos (*Maternal*) and Agape (*Love*), Ainos (*Praise*)[14] and Synesis (*Intelligence*), Ecclesiasticus (*Son of Ecclesia*) and Macariotes (*Blessedness*), Theletus[15] (*Perfect*) and Sophia (*Wisdom*). I cannot help[16] here quoting from a like example what may serve to show the import of

---

[1] Expostulo: "I postulate as a first principle."
[2] Tertullian is responsible for this *Latin* word amongst the Greek names. The strange mixture occurs often.
[3] Quadriga.
[4] Factionis.
[5] Ibidem simul.

[6] Cellas.
[7] Census.
[8] Turbam.
[9] Criminum.
[10] Numinum.
[11] We everywhere give Tertullian's own names, whether of Greek form or Latin. On their first occurrence we also give their English sense.
[12] Ebulliunt.
[13] Proinde conjugales.
[14] Of this name there are two forms—Αἶνος (*Praise*) and Ἀεινοῦς (*Eternal Mind*).
[15] Or Τελετός (Teletus). Another form of this Æon's name is Φιλητός (*Philetus = Beloved*). Oehler always reads Theletus.
[16] Cogor.

these names. In the schools of Carthage there was once a certain Latin rhetorician, an excessively cool fellow,[1] whose name was Phosphorus. He was personating a man of valour, and wound up[2] with saying, " I come to you, excellent citizens, from battle, with victory for myself, with happiness for you, full of honour, covered with glory, the favourite of fortune, the greatest of men, decked with triumph." And forthwith his scholars begin to shout for the school of Phosphorus, φεῦ[3] (ah !) Are you a believer in[4] Fortunata, and Hedone, and Acinetus, and Theletus? Then shout out your φεῦ for the school of Ptolemy.[5] This must be that mystery of the Pleroma, the fulness of the thirty-fold divinity. Let us see what special attributes[6] belong to these numbers—four, and eight, and twelve. Meanwhile with the number thirty all fecundity ceases. The generating force and power and desire of the Æons is spent.[7] As if there were not still left some strong rennet for curdling numbers.[8] As if no other names were to be got out of the page's hall![9] For why are there not sets of fifty and of a hundred procreated? Why, too, are there no comrades and boon companions[10] named *for them*?

CHAP. IX.—OTHER CAPRICIOUS FEATURES IN THE SYSTEM. THE ÆONS UNEQUAL IN ATTRIBUTES. THE SUPERIORITY OF NUS; THE VAGARIES OF SOPHIA RESTRAINED BY HOROS. GRAND TITLES BORNE BY THIS LAST POWER.

But, further, there is an " acceptance[11] of persons," inasmuch as Nus alone among them all enjoys the knowledge of the immeasurable Father, joyous and exulting, while they of course pine in sorrow. To be sure, Nus, so far as in him lay, both wished and tried to impart to the others also all that he had learnt about the greatness and incomprehensibility of the Father; but his mother, Sige, interposed—she who (you must know) imposes silence even on her own beloved heretics;[12] although they affirm that this is done at the will of the Father, who will have all to be inflamed

with a longing after himself. Thus, while they are tormenting themselves with these internal desires, while they are burning with the secret longing to know the Father, the crime is almost accomplished. For of the twelve Æons which Homo and Ecclesia had produced, the youngest by birth (never mind the solecism, since Sophia (Wisdom) is her name), unable to restrain herself, breaks away without the society of her husband Theletus, in quest of the Father and contracts that kind of sin which had indeed arisen amongst the others who were conversant with Nus but had flowed on to this *Æon*,[13] that is, to Sophia; as is usual with maladies which, after arising in one part of the body, spread abroad their infection to some other limb. The fact is,[14] under a pretence of love to the Father, she was overcome with a desire to rival Nus, who alone rejoiced in the knowledge of the Father.[15] But when Sophia, straining after impossible aims, was disappointed of her hope, she is both overcome with difficulty, and racked with affection. *Thus* she was all but swallowed up by reason of the charm and toil (of her research),[16] and dissolved into the remnant of *his* substance;[17] nor would there have been any other alternative for her than perdition, if she had not by good luck fallen in with Horos (*Limit*). He too had considerable power. He is the foundation of the great[18] universe, and, externally, the guardian thereof. To him they give the additional names of Crux (*Cross*), and Lytrotes (*Redeemer*,) and Carpistes (*Emancipator*).[19] When Sophia was thus rescued from danger, and tardily persuaded, she relinquished further research after the Father, found repose, and laid aside all her excitement,[20] *or* Enthymesis (*Desire*,) along with the passion which had come over her.

CHAP. X.—ANOTHER ACCOUNT OF THE STRANGE ABERRATIONS OF SOPHIA, AND THE RESTRAINING SERVICES OF HOROS. SOPHIA WAS NOT HERSELF, AFTER ALL, EJECTED FROM THE PLEROMA, BUT ONLY HER ENTHYMESIS.

But some dreamers have given another account of the aberration[21] and recovery of

---

[1] Frigidissimus.
[2] Cum virum fortem peroraret . . . inquit.
[3] Tertullian's joke lies in the equivocal sense of this cry, which may mean either admiration and joy, or grief and rage.
[4] Audisti : interrogatively.
[5] See above, chap. iv. p. 505.
[6] Privilegia.
[7] Castrata.
[8] Tanta numerorum coagula.
[9] The *pædagogium* was either the place where boys were trained as pages (often for lewd purposes), or else the boy himself of such a character.
[10] Oehler reads, " hetæri (ἑταῖροι) et syntrophi." Another reading, supported by Rigaltius, is " sterceiæ," instead of the former word, which gives a very contemptuous sense, suitable to Tertullian's irony.
[11] Exceptio.
[12] Tertullian has, above, remarked on the silent and secret practices of the Valentinians : see chap. i. p. 503.

[13] In hunc derivaret.
[14] Sed enim.
[15] De Patre.
[16] Præ vi dulcedinis et laboris.
[17] It is not easy to say what is the meaning of the words, " Et in reliquam substantiam dissolvi." Rigaltius renders them : " So that whatever substance was left to her was being dissolved." This seems to be forcing the sentence unnaturally. Irenæus (according to the Latin translator) says : " Resolutum in universam substantiam," " Resolved into his (the Father's) general substance," i. 2, 2. [Vol. I. p. 317.]
[18] Illius.
[19] So Grabe ; but *Reaper*, according to Neander.
[20] Animationem.
[21] Exitum.

Sophia. After her vain endeavours, and the disappointment of her hope, she was, I suppose, disfigured with paleness and emaciation, and that neglect of her beauty which was natural to one who[1] was deploring the denial of the Father,—an affliction which was no less painful than his loss. Then, in the midst of all this sorrow, she by herself alone, without any conjugal help, conceived and bare a female offspring. Does this excite your surprise? Well, even the hen has the power of being able to bring forth by her own energy.[2] They say, too, that among vultures there are only females, which become parents alone. At any rate, she was another without aid from a male, and she began at last to be afraid that her end was even at hand. She was all in doubt about the treatment[3] of her case, and took pains at self-concealment. Remedies *could* nowhere *be found*. For where, then, should we have tragedies and comedies, from which to borrow the process of exposing what has been born without connubial modesty? While the thing is in this evil plight, she raises her eyes, and turns them to the Father. Having, however, striven in vain, as her strength was failing her, she'falls to praying. Her entire kindred also supplicates in her behalf, and especially Nus. Why not? What was the cause of so vast an evil? Yet not a single casualty[4] befell Sophia without its effect. All her sorrows operate. Inasmuch as all that conflict of hers contributes to the origin of Matter. *Her* ignorance, *her* fear, *her* distress, become substances. Hereupon the Father by and by, being moved, produces in his own image, with a view to these *circumstances*[5] the Horos whom we have mentioned above; (and this he does) by means of Monogenes Nus, a male-female (Æon), because there is this variation of statement about the Father's[6] sex. They also go on to tell us that Horos is likewise called Metagogius, that is, "a conductor about," as well as Horothetes (*Setter of Limits*). By his assistance they declare that Sophia was checked in her illicit courses, and purified from all evils, and henceforth strengthened (in virtue), and restored to the conjugal state: (they add) that she indeed remained within the bounds[7] of the Pleroma, but that her Enthymesis, with the accruing[8] Passion, was banished by Horos, and crucified and cast out from the Pleroma,—even as they say, *Malum foras!*

(Evil, avaunt!) Still, that was a spiritual essence, as being the natural impulse of an Æon, although without form or shape, inasmuch as it had apprehended nothing, and therefore was pronounced to be an infirm and feminine fruit.[9]

CHAP. XI.—THE PROFANE ACCOUNT GIVEN OF THE ORIGIN OF CHRIST AND THE HOLY GHOST STERNLY REBUKED. AN ABSURDITY RESPECTING THE ATTAINMENT OF THE KNOWLEDGE OF GOD ABLY EXPOSED.

Accordingly, after the banishment of the Enthymesis, and the return of her mother Sophia to her husband, the (illustrious) Monogenes, the Nus,[10] released indeed from all care and concern of the Father, in order that he might consolidate all things, and defend and at last fix the Pleroma, and so prevent any concussion of the kind again, once more[11] emits a new couple[12] (blasphemously named). I should suppose the coupling of two males to be a very shameful thing, or else the one[13] must be a female, and so the male is discredited[14] by the female. One divinity is assigned in the case of all these, to procure a complete adjustment among the Æons. Even from this fellowship in a common duty two schools actually arise, two chairs,[15] and, to some extent,[16] the inauguration of a division in the doctrine of Valentinus. It was the function of Christ to instruct the Æons in the nature of their conjugal relations[17] (you see what the whole thing was, of course!), and how to form some guess about the unbegotten,[18] and to give them the capacity of generating within themselves the knowledge of the Father; it being impossible to catch the idea of him, or comprehend him, or, in short, even to enjoy any perception of him, either by the eye or the ear, except through Monogenes (the Only-begotten). Well, I will even grant them what they allege about knowing the Father, so that they do not refuse us (the attainment of) the same. I would rather point out what is perverse in their doctrine, how they were taught that the incomprehensible part of the Father was the cause of their own perpetuity,[19] whilst that which might be com-

---

[1] Uti quæ.
[2] Comp. Aristotle, *Hist. Anim.* vi. 2; Pliny, *H. N.* x. 58, 60.
[3] Ratione.
[4] Exitus.
[5] In hæc : in relation to the case of Sophia.
[6] Above, in chap. viii. we were told that Nus, who was so much like the Father, was himself called "Father."
[7] In censu.
[8] Appendicem.

[9] Literally, "infirm fruit and a female," *i.e.* "had not shared in any male influence, but was a purely female production." See our *Irenæus*, i. 4. [Vol. I. p. 321.]
[10] Ille nus.
[11] Iterum : above.
[12] Copulationem : The profane reference is to Christ and the Spirit.
[13] [A shocking reference to the Spirit which I modify to *one* of the Divine Persons.]
[14] Vulneratur.
[15] Cathedræ.
[16] Quædam.
[17] Conjugiorum.
[18] Innati conjectationem.
[19] Perpetuitatis : *i.e.* "what was unchangeable in their condition and nature."

prehended of him was the reason[1] of their generation and formation. Now by these several positions[2] the tenet, I suppose, is insinuated, that it is expedient for God not to be apprehended, on the very ground that the incomprehensibility of His character is the cause of perpetuity; whereas what in Him is comprehensible is productive, not of perpetuity, but rather of conditions which lack perpetuity—namely, nativity and formation. The Son, indeed, they made capable of comprehending the Father. The manner in which He is comprehended, the recently produced Christ fully taught them. To the Holy Spirit, however, belonged the special gifts, whereby they, having been all set on a complete par in respect of their earnestness to learn, should be enabled to offer up their thanksgiving, and be introduced to a true tranquillity.

CHAP. XII.—THE STRANGE JUMBLE OF THE PLEROMA. THE FRANTIC DELIGHT OF THE MEMBERS THEREOF. THEIR JOINT CONTRIBUTION OF PARTS SET FORTH WITH HUMOROUS IRONY.

Thus they are all on the self-same footing in respect of form and knowledge, all of them having become what each of them severally is; none being a different being, because they are all what the others are.[3] They are all turned into[4] Nuses, into Homos, into Theletuses;[5] and so in the case of the females, into Siges, into Zoes, into Ecclesias, into Forunatas, so that Ovid would have blotted out his own Metamorphoses if he had only known our larger one in the present day. Straightway they were reformed and thoroughly established, and being composed to rest from the truth, they celebrate the Father in a chorus[6] of praise in the exuberance of their joy. *The Father* himself also revelled[7] in the glad feeling; of course, because his children and grandchildren sang so well. And why should he not revel in absolute delight? Was not the Pleroma freed (from all danger)? What ship's captain[8] fails to rejoice even with indecent frolic? Every day we observe the uproarious ebullitions of sailors' joys.[9] Therefore, as sailors always exult over the reckoning they pay in common, so do these Æons enjoy a similar pleasure, one as they

now all are in form, and, as I may add,[10] in feeling too. With the concurrence of even their new brethren and masters,[11] they contribute into one common stock the best and most beautiful thing with which they are severally adorned. Vainly, as I suppose. For if they were all one by reason by the abovementioned thorough equalization, there was no room for the process of a common reckoning,[12] which for the most part consists of a pleasing variety. They all contributed the one good thing, which they all were. There would be, in all probability, a formal procedure[13] in the mode or in the form of the very equalization in question. Accordingly, out of the donation which they contributed[14] to the honour and glory of the Father, they jointly fashion[15] the most beautiful constellation of the Pleroma, and its perfect fruit, Jesus. Him they also surname[16] Soter (*Saviour*) and Christ, and Sermo (*Word*) after his ancestors;[17] and lastly Omnia (*All Things*), as formed from a universally culled nosegay,[18] *like* the jay of Æsop, the Pandora of Hesiod, the bowl[19] of Accius, the honeycake of Nestor, the miscellany of Ptolemy. How much nearer the mark, if these idle title-mongers had called him Pancarpian, after certain Athenian customs.[20] By way of adding external honour also to their wonderful puppet, they produce for him a body-guard of angels of like nature. If this be their mutual condition, it may be all right; if, however, they are consubstantial with Soter (for I have discovered how doubtfully the case is stated), where will be his eminence when surrounded by attendants who are co-equal with himself?

CHAP. XIII.—FIRST PART OF THE SUBJECT, TOUCHING THE CONSTITUTION OF THE PLEROMA, BRIEFLY RECAPITULATED. TRANSITION TO THE OTHER PART, WHICH IS LIKE A PLAY OUTSIDE THE CURTAIN.

In this series, then, is contained the first emanation of Æons, who are alike born, and are married, and produce offspring: there are the most dangerous fortunes of Sophia in her ardent longing for the Father, the most seasonable help of Horos, the expiation of her

---

[1] Rationem ; perhaps "the means."
[2] Hac dispositione.
[3] Nemo aliud quia alteri omnes.
[4] Refunduntur.
[5] The reader will, of course, see that we give a familiar English plural to these names, as better expressing Tertullian's irony.
[6] Concinunt.
[7] Diffundebatur.
[8] Nauclerus: "pilot."
[9] Tertullian lived in a seaport at Carthage.

[10] Nedum.
[11] Christ and the Holy Spirit, [i.e. blasphemously.]
[12] Symbolæ ratio.
[13] Ratio.
[14] Ex ære collaticio. In reference to the common *symbola*, Tertullian adds the proverbial formula, "quod aiunt" (as they say).
[15] Compingunt.
[16] Cognominant.
[17] De patritis. Irenæus' word here is πατρωνυμικῶς ("*patronymice*").
[18] Ex omnium defloratione.
[19] Patina.
[20] Alluding to the olive-branch, ornamented with all sorts of fruits (compare our "Christmas tree"), which was carried about by boys in Athens on a certain festival (White and Riddle).

Enthymesis and accruing Passion, the instruction of Christ and the Holy Spirit, their tutelar reform of the Æons, the piebald ornamentation of Soter, the consubstantial retinue[1] of the angels. All that remains, according to you, is the fall of the curtain and the clapping of hands.[2] What remains, in my opinion, however, is, that you should hear and take heed. At all events, these things are said to have been played out within the company of the Pleroma, the first scene of the tragedy. The rest of the play, however, is beyond the curtain—I mean outside of the Pleroma. And yet if it be such within the bosom of the Father, within the embrace of the guardian Horos, what must it be outside, in free space,[3] where God did not exist?

CHAP. XIV.—THE ADVENTURES OF ACHAMOTH OUTSIDE THE PLEROMA. THE MISSION OF CHRIST IN PURSUIT OF HER. HER LONGING FOR CHRIST. HOROS' HOSTILITY TO HER. HER CONTINUED SUFFERING.

For Enthymesis, or rather Achamoth—because by this inexplicable[4] name alone must she be henceforth designated—when in company with the vicious Passion, her inseparable companion, she was expelled to places devoid of that light which is the substance of the Pleroma, even to the void and empty region of Epicurus, she becomes wretched also because of the place of her banishment. She is indeed without either form or feature, even an untimely and abortive production. Whilst she is in this plight,[5] Christ descends from[6] the heights, conducted by Horos, in order to impart form to the abortion, out of his own energies, the form of substance only, but not of knowledge also. Still she is left with some property. She has restored to her the odour of immortality, in order that she might, under its influence, be overcome with the desire of better things than belonged to her present plight.[7] Having accomplished His merciful mission, not without the assistance of the Holy Spirit, Christ returns to the Pleroma. It is usual out of an abundance of things[8] for names to be also forthcoming. Enthymesis came from action;[9] whence Achamoth came is still a question; Sophia emanates from the Father, the Holy Spirit from an angel. She entertains a regret for Christ immediately after she had discovered her desertion by him. Therefore she hurried forth herself, in quest of the light of Him Whom she did not at all discover, as He operated in an invisible manner; for how else would she make search for His light, which was as unknown to her as He was Himself? Try, however, she did, and perhaps would have found Him, had not the self-same Horos, who had met her mother so opportunely, fallen in with the daughter quite as unseasonably, so as to exclaim at her IAO! just as we hear the cry "Porro Quirites" ("Out of the way, Romans!"), or else "Fidem Cæsaris!" ("By the faith of Cæsar!"), whence (as they will have it) the name IAO comes to be found is the Scriptures.[10] Being thus hindered from proceeding further, and being unable to surmount[11] the Cross, that is to say, Horos, because she had not yet practised herself in the part of Catullus' *Laureolus*,[12] *and* given over, as it were, to that passion of hers in a manifold and complicated mesh, she began to be afflicted with every impulse thereof, with sorrow,—because she had not accomplished her enterprise, with fear,—lest she should lose her life, even as she had lost the light, with consternation, *and* then with ignorance. But not as her mother (did she suffer this), for *she* was an Æon. Hers, however, was a worse suffering, considering her condition; for another tide of emotion still overwhelmed her, even of conversion to the Christ, by Whom she had been restored to life, and had been directed[13] to this very conversion.

CHAP. XV.—STRANGE ACCOUNT OF THE ORIGIN OF MATTER, FROM THE VARIOUS AFFECTIONS OF ACHAMOTH. THE WATERS FROM HER TEARS; LIGHT FROM HER SMILE.

Well, now, the Pythagoreans may learn, the Stoics may know, Plato himself (may discover), whence Matter, which they will have to be unborn, derived both its origin and substance for all this pile of the world—(a mystery) which not even the renowned[14] Mercurius Trismegistus, master (as he was) of all

---

[1] Comparaticium antistatum. The latter word Oehler explains, "ante ipsum stantes;" the former, "quia genus eorum comparari poterat substantiæ Soteris" (so Rigaltus).
[2] The reader will see how obviously this is meant in Tertullian's "Quod superest, inquis, vos valete et plaudite." This is the well-known allusion to the end of the play in the old Roman theatre. See Quintilian, vi. 1, 52; comp. Horace, *A.P.* 155. Tertullian's own parody to this formula, immediately after, is: "Immo quod superest, inquam, vos audite et proficite."
[3] In libero: which may be, however, "beyond the control of Horos."
[4] Ininterpretabili.
[5] Tertullian's "Dum ita rerum habet" is a copy of the Greek οὕτω τῶν πραγμάτων ἐχουσο.
[6] Deflectitur a.
[7] Casus sui.
[8] Rerum ex liberalitatibus.
[9] De actia fuit. [See Vol. I. pp. 320, 321.]
[10] It is not necessary, with Rigaltius, to make a difficulty about this, when we remember that Tertullian only refers to a silly conceit of the Valentinians touching the origin of the sacred name.
[11] Or does " nec habens *supervolare* crucem " mean " being unable to *elude* the cross?" As if Tertullian meant, in his raillery, to say, that Achamoth had not the skill of the player who played the part of Laureolus. Although so often suspended on the gibbet, he had of course as often escaped the real penalty.
[12] A notorious robber, the hero of a play by Lutatius Catullus, who is said to have been crucified.
[13] Temperata.
[14] Ille.

physical philosophy, thought out.[1] You have just heard of "Conversion," one element in the "Passion" (we have so often mentioned). Out of this the whole life of the world,[2] and even that of the Demiurge himself, our God, is said to have had its being. Again, you have heard of "sorrow" and "fear." From these all other created things[3] took their beginning. For from her[4] tears flowed the entire mass of waters. From this circumstance one may form an idea of the calamity[5] which she encountered, so vast were the kinds of the tears wherewith she overflowed. She had salt tear-drops, she had bitter, and sweet, and warm, and cold, and bituminous, and ferruginous, and sulphurous, and even[6] poisonous, so that the Nonacris exuded therefrom which killed Alexander; and the river of the Lyncestæ[7] flowed from the same source, which produces drunkenness; and the Salmacis[8] was derived from the same source, which renders men effeminate. The rains of heaven Achamoth whimpered forth,[9] and we on our part are anxiously employed in saving up in our cisterns the very wails and tears of another. In like manner, from the "consternation" and "alarm" (of which we have also heard), bodily elements were derived. And yet amidst so many circumstances of solitude, in this vast prospect of destitution, she occasionally smiled at the recollection of the sight of Christ, and from this smile of joy light flashed forth. How great was this beneficence of Providence, which induced her to smile, and all that we might not linger for ever in the dark! Nor need you feel astonished how[10] from her joy so splendid an element[11] could have beamed upon the world, when from her sadness even so necessary a provision[12] flowed forth for man. O illuminating smile! O irrigating tear! And yet it might now have acted as some alleviation amidst the horror of her situation; for she might have shaken off all the obscurity thereof as often as she had a mind to smile, even not to be obliged to turn suppliant to those who had deserted her.[13]

CHAP. XVI.—ACHAMOTH PURIFIED FROM ALL IMPURITIES OF HER PASSION BY THE PARACLETE, ACTING THROUGH SOTER, WHO OUT OF THE ABOVE-MENTIONED IMPURITIES ARRANGES MATTER, SEPARATING ITS EVIL FROM THE BETTER QUALITIES.

She, too, resorts to prayers, after the manner of her mother. But Christ, Who now felt a dislike to quit the Pleroma, appoints the Paraclete as his deputy. To her, therefore, he despatches Soter,[14] (who must be the same as Jesus, to whom the Father imparted the supreme power over the whole body of the Æons, by subjecting them all to him, so that "by him," as the apostle says, "all things were created"[15]), with a retinue and cortege of contemporary angels, and (as one may suppose) with the dozen fasces. Hereupon Achamoth, being quite struck with the pomp of his approach, immediately covered herself with a veil, moved at first with a dutiful feeling of veneration and modesty; but afterwards she surveys him calmly, and his prolific equipage.[16] With such energies as she had derived from the contemplation, she meets him with the salutation, Κύριε, χαῖρε ("Hail, Lord")! Upon this, I suppose, he receives her, confirms and conforms her in knowledge, as well as cleanses[17] her from all the outrages of Passion, without, however, utterly severing them, with an indiscriminateness like that which had happened in the casualties which befell her mother. For such vices as had become inveterate and confirmed by practice he throws together; and when he had consolidated them in one mass, he fixes them in a separate body, so as to compose the corporeal condition of Matter, extracting out of her inherent, incorporeal passion such an aptitude of nature[18] as might qualify it to attain to a reciprocity of bodily substances,[19] which should emulate one another, so that a twofold condition of the substances might be arranged; one full of evil through its faults, the other susceptible of passion from conversion. This will prove to be Matter, which has set us in battle array against Hermogenes, and all others who presume to teach that God made all things out of Matter, not out of nothing.

CHAP. XVII.—ACHAMOTH IN LOVE WITH THE ANGELS. A PROTEST AGAINST THE LASCIVIOUS FEATURES OF VALENTINIANISM. ACHAMOTH BECOMES THE MOTHER OF THREE NATURES.

Then Achamoth, delivered at length from all her evils, wonderful to tell[20] goes on and

---

[1] Recogitavit.
[2] "Omnis anima hujus mundi" may, however, mean "every living soul." So Bp. Kaye, *On Tertullian*, p. 487.
[3] Cetera.
[4] Achamoth's.
[5] Exitum.
[6] Utique.
[7] These two rivers, with their peculiar qualities, are mentioned by Pliny, *H.N.* ii. 103; [and the latter by Milton against Salmasius.]
[8] Ovid. *Metam.* iv. 286.
[9] Pipiavit.
[10] Qui.
[11] As light.
[12] Instrumentum: water is meant.
[13] Christ and the Holy Spirit. Oehler.
[14] Saviour: another title of their Paraclete.
[15] Col i. 16.
[16] Fructiferumque suggestum.
[17] Expumicat.
[18] Habilitatem atque naturam. We have treated this as a hendiadys.
[19] Æquiparantias corpulentiarum.
[20] Ecce.

bears fruit with greater results. For warmed with the joy of so great an escape from her unhappy condition, and at the same time heated with the actual contemplation of the angelic luminaries (one is ashamed) *to use such language,* but there is no other way of expressing one's meaning), she during the emotion somehow became personally inflamed with desire[1] towards them, and at once grew pregnant with a spiritual conception, at the very image of which the violence of her joyous transport, and the delight of her prurient excitement, had imbibed and impressed upon her. She at length gave birth to an offspring, and then there arose a leash of natures,[2] from a triad of causes,—one material, arising from her passion; another animal, arising from her conversion; the third spiritual, which had its origin in her imagination.

CHAP. XVIII.—BLASPHEMOUS OPINION CONCERNING THE ORIGIN OF THE DEMIURGE, SUPPOSED TO BE THE CREATOR OF THE UNIVERSE.

Having become a better proficient[3] in practical conduct by the authority which, we may well suppose,[4] accrued to her from her three children, she determined to impart form to each of the natures. The spiritual one, however, she was unable to touch, inasmuch as she was herself spiritual. For a participation in the same nature has, to a very great extent,[5] disqualified like and consubstantial beings from having superior power over one another. Therefore[6] she applies herself solely to the animal nature, adducing the instructions of Soter[7] (for her guidance). And first of all (she does) what cannot be described and read, and heard of, without an intense horror at the blasphemy thereof: she produces this God of ours, the God of all except of the heretics, the Father and Creator[8] and King of all things, which are inferior to him. For from him do they proceed. If, however, they proceed from him, and not rather from Achamoth, or if only secretly from her, without his perceiving her, he was impelled to all that he did, even like a puppet[9] which is moved from the outside. In fact, it was owing to this very ambiguity about the personal agency in the works which were done, that they coined for him the mixed name of (*Motherly Father*),[10] whilst his other appella-

tions were distinctly assigned according to the conditions and positions of his works: so that they call him *Father* in relation to the animal substances to which they give the place of honour[11] on his right hand; whereas, in respect of the material substances which they banish[12] to his left hand, they name him *Demiurgus;* whilst *his title King* designates his authority over both classes, *nay* over the universe.[13]

CHAP. XIX.—PALPABLE ABSURDITIES AND CONTRADICTIONS IN THE SYSTEM RESPECTING ACHAMOTH AND THE DEMIURGE.

And yet there is not any agreement between the propriety of the names and that of the works, from which all the names are suggested; since all of them ought to have borne the name of her by whom the things were done, unless after all[14] it turn out that they were not made by her. For, although they say that Achamoth devised these forms in honour of the Æons, they yet[15] transfer this *work* to Soter as its author, when they say that he[16] operated through her, so far as to give her the very image of the invisible and unknown Father—that is, the image which was unknown and invisible to the Demiurge; whilst he[17] formed this same Demiurge in imitation[18] of Nus the son *of Propator;*[19] and whilst the archangels, who were the work of the Demiurge, resembled the other Æons. Now, when I hear of such images of the three, I ask, do you not wish me to laugh at these pictures of their most extravagant painter? At the female Achamoth, a picture of the Father? At the Demiurge, ignorant of his mother, much more so of his father? At the picture of Nus, ignorant of his father too, and the ministering angels, facsimiles of their lords? This is painting a mule from an ass, and sketching Ptolemy from Valentinus.

CHAP. XX—THE DEMIURGE WORKS AWAY AT CREATION, AS THE DRUDGE OF HIS MOTHER ACHAMOTH, IN IGNORANCE ALL THE WHILE OF THE NATURE OF HIS OCCUPATION.

The Demiurge therefore, placed as he was without the limits of the Pleroma in the ignominious solitude of his eternal exile, founded a new empire—this world (of ours)—by clear-

---

[1] Subavit et ipsa.
[2] Trinitas generum.
[3] Exercitior.
[4] Scilicet.
[5] Fere.
[6] Eo animo.
[7] See above, chap. xvi. p. 512.
[8] Demiurgum.
[9] Et velut sigillario. "*Sigillarium* est νευρόσπαστον," Oehler.
[10] The Father acting through and proceeding from his Mother.

[11] Commendant.
[12] Delegant.
[13] Communiter in universitatem.
[14] Jam.
[15] Rursus.
[16] This is the force of the "qui" with the subjunctive verb.
[17] Soter.
[18] Effingeret.
[19] There seems to be a relative gradation meant among these *extra-Pleroma* beings, as there was among the Æons of the Pleroma ; and, further, a relation between the two sets of beings —Achamoth bearing a relation to Propator, the Demiurge to Nus, etc.

ing away the confusion and distinguishing the difference between the two substances which severally constituted it,[1] the animal and the material. Out of incorporeal (elements) he constructs bodies, heavy, light, erect[2] and stooping, celestial and terrene. He then completes the sevenfold stages of heaven itself, with his own throne above all. Whence he had the additional name of Sabbatum from the hebdomadal nature of his abode; his mother Achamoth, too, had the title Ogdoada, after the precedent of the primeval Ogdoad.[3] These heavens, however, they consider to be intelligent,[4] and sometimes they make angels of them, as indeed they do of the Demiurge himself; as also (they call) Paradise the fourth archangel, because they fix it above the third heaven, of the power of which Adam partook, when he sojourned there amidst its fleecy clouds[5] and shrubs.[6] Ptolemy remembered perfectly well the prattle of his boyhood,[7] that apples grew in the sea, and fishes on the tree; after the same fashion, he assumed that nut-trees flourished in the skies. The Demiurge does his work in ignorance, and therefore perhaps he is unaware that trees ought to be planted only on the ground. His mother, of course, knew all about it: how is it, then, that she did not suggest the fact, since she was actually executing her own operation? But whilst building up so vast an edifice for her son by means of those works, which proclaim him at once to be father, god and, king before the conceits of the Valentinians, why she refused to let them be known to even him,[8] is a question which I shall ask afterwards.

CHAP. XXI.—THE VANITY AS WELL AS IGNORANCE OF THE DEMIURGE. ABSURD RESULTS FROM SO IMPERFECT A CONDITION.

Meanwhile you must believe[9] that Sophia has the surnames of earth and of Mother—"Mother-Earth," of course—and (what may excite your laughter still more heartily) even Holy Spirit. In this way they have conferred all honour on that female, I suppose even a beard, not to say other things. Besides,[10] the Demiurge had so little mastery over things,[11] on the score,[12] you must know,[13] of

his inability to approach spiritual essences, (constituted as he was) of animal elements, that, imagining himself to be the only being, he uttered this soliloquy: "I am God, and beside me there is none else."[14] But for all that, he at least was aware that he had not himself existed before. He understood, therefore, that he had been created, and that there must be a creator of a creature of some sort or other. How happens it, then, that he seemed to himself to be the only being, notwithstanding his uncertainty, and although he had, at any rate, some suspicion of the existence of some creator?

CHAP. XXII.—ORIGIN OF THE DEVIL, IN THE CRIMINAL EXCESS OF THE SORROW OF ACHAMOTH. THE DEVIL, CALLED ALSO MUNDITENENS, ACTUALLY WISER THAN THE DEMIURGE, ALTHOUGH HIS WORK.

The odium felt amongst them[15] against the devil is the more excusable,[16] even because the peculiarly sordid character of his origin justifies it.[17] For he is supposed by them to have had his origin in that criminal excess[18] of her[19] sorrow, from which they also derive the birth of the angels, and demons, and all the wicked spirits. Yet they affirm that the devil is the work of the Demiurge, and they call him Munditenens[20] (*Ruler of the World*), and maintain that, as he is of a spiritual nature, he has a better knowledge of the things above than the Demiurge, an animal being. He deserves from them the pre-eminence which all heresies provide him with.

CHAP. XXIII.—THE RELATIVE POSITIONS OF THE PLEROMA. THE REGION OF ACHAMOTH, AND THE CREATION OF THE DEMIURGE. THE ADDITION OF FIRE TO THE VARIOUS ELEMENTS AND BODIES OF NATURE.

Their most eminent powers, moreover, they confine within the following limits, as in a citadel. In the most elevated of all summits presides the tricenary Pleroma,[21] Horos marking off its boundary line. Beneath it, Achamoth occupies the intermediate space for her abode,[22] treading down her son. For under her comes the Demiurge in his own Hebdomad, or rather the Devil, *sojourning* in this world in common with ourselves, formed, as has been said above, of the same elements

---

[1] Duplicis substantiæ illius disclusæ.
[2] Sublimantia.
[3] Ogdoadis primogenitalis: what Irenæus calls "the first-begotten and primary Ogdoad of the Pleroma" (See our *Irenæus*, Vol. I. ; also above, chap. vii. p, 506.)
[4] Noëros.
[5] Nubeculas.
[6] Arbusculas.
[7] Puerilium dicibulorum.
[8] *Sibi* here must refer to the secondary agent of the sentence.
[9] Tenendum.
[10] Alioquin.
[11] Adeo rerum non erat compos.
[12] Censu.
[13] Scilicet.

[14] Isa. xlv. 5, xlvi. 9.
[15] Infamia apud illos
[16] Tolerabilior.
[17] Capit : "capax est," nimirum "infamiæ" (Fr. Junius).
[18] Ex nequitia.
[19] Achamoth's.
[20] Irenæus' word is Κοσμοκράτωρ ; see also Eph. vi. 12.
[21] Above, in chap. viii., he has mentioned the Pleroma as "the fulness of the thirtyfold divinity."
[22] Metatur.

and the same body, out of the most profitable calamities of Sophia; inasmuch as, (if it had not been for these,) our spirit would have had no space for inhaling and ejecting[1] air—that delicate vest of all corporeal creatures, that revealer of all colours, that instrument of the seasons—if the sadness of Sophia had not filtered it, just as her fear did the animal existence, and her conversion the Demiurge himself. Into all these elements and bodies fire was fanned. Now, since they have not as yet explained to us the original sensation of this[2] in Sophia, I will on my own responsibility[3] conjecture that its spark was struck out of the delicate emotions[4] of her (feverish grief). For you may be quite sure that, amidst all her vexations, she must have had a good deal of fever.[5]

CHAP. XXIV.—THE FORMATION OF MAN BY THE DEMIURGE. HUMAN FLESH NOT MADE OF THE GROUND, BUT OF A NONDESCRIPT PHILOSOPHIC SUBSTANCE.

Such being their conceits respecting God, or, if you like,[6] the gods, of what sort are their figments concerning man? For, after he had made the world, the Demiurge turns his hands to man, and chooses for him as his substance not any portion of "the dry land," as they say, of which alone we have any knowledge (although it was, at that time, not yet dried by the waters becoming separated from the earthy residuum, and only afterwards became dry), but of the invisible substance of that matter, which philosophy indeed dreams of, from its fluid and fusible composition, the origin of which I am unable to imagine, because it exists nowhere. Now, since fluidity and fusibility are qualities of liquid matter, and since everything liquid flowed from Sophia's tears, we must, as a necessary conclusion, believe that muddy earth is constituted of Sophia's eye-rheums and viscid discharges,[7] which are just as much the dregs of tears as mud is the sediment of waters. Thus does the Demiurge mould man as a potter does his clay, and animates him with his own breath. Made after his image and likeness, he will therefore be both material and animal. A fourfold being! For in respect of his "image," he must be deemed clayey,[8] that is to say, material, although the Demiurge is not composed of matter; but as to his "likeness," he is animal, for such,

too, is the Demiurge. You have two (of his constituent elements). Moreover, a coating of flesh was, as they allege, afterwards placed over the clayey substratum, and it is this tunic of skin which is susceptible of sensation.

CHAP. XXV.—AN EXTRAVAGANT WAY OF ACCOUNTING FOR THE COMMUNICATION OF THE SPIRITUAL NATURE TO MAN. IT WAS FURTIVELY MANAGED BY ACHAMOTH, THROUGH THE UNCONSCIOUS AGENCY OF HER SON.

In Achamoth, moreover, there was inherent a certain property of a spiritual germ, of her mother Sophia's substance; and Achamoth herself had carefully severed off (the same quality), and implanted it in her son the Demiurge, although he was actually unconscious of it. It is for you to imagine[9] the industry of this clandestine arrangement. For to this end had she deposited and concealed (this germ), that, whenever the Demiurge came to impart life to Adam by his inbreathing, he might at the same time draw off from the vital principle[10] the spiritual seed, and, as by a pipe, inject it into the clayey nature; in order that, being then fecundated in the material body as in a womb, and having fully grown there, it might be found fit for one day receiving the perfect Word.[11] When, therefore, the Demiurge commits to Adam the transmission of his own vital principle,[12] the spiritual man lay hid, *although* inserted by his breath, and at the same time introduced into the body, because the Demiurge knew no more about his mother's seed than about herself. To this seed they give the name of Ecclesia (*the Church*), the mirror of the church above, and the perfection[13] of man; tracing this *perfection* from Achamoth, just as they do the animal nature from the Demiurge, the clayey material of the body (they derive) from the primordial substance,[14] the flesh from Matter. So that you have a new Geryon here, only a fourfold (rather than a threefold) monster.

CHAP. XXVI.—THE THREE SEVERAL NATURES— THE MATERIAL, THE ANIMAL, AND THE SPIRITUAL, AND THEIR SEVERAL DESTINATIONS. THE STRANGE VALENTINIAN OPINION ABOUT THE STRUCTURE OF SOTER'S NATURE.

In like manner they assign to each of them a separate end.[15] To the material, that is to say the carnal (nature), which they also call "the left-handed," they assign undoubted

---

[1] Reciprocandi.
[2] Fire.
[3] Ego.
[4] Motiunculis.
[5] Febricitasse.
[6] Vel.
[7] Ex pituitis et gramis
[8] Choïcus.

[9] Accipe
[10] Anima derivaret.
[11] Sermoni perfecto.
[12] Traducem animæ suæ
[13] Censum.
[14] Or, the substance of Ἀρχή.
[15] Exitum.

destruction; to the animal (nature), which they also call " the right-handed," a doubtful issue, inasmuch as it oscillates between the material and the spiritual, and is sure to fall at last on the side to which it has mainly gravitated. As regards the spiritual, however, (they say) that it enters into the formation of the animal, in order that it may be educated in company with it and be disciplined by repeated intercourse with it. For the animal (nature) was in want of training even by the senses: for this purpose, accordingly, was the whole structure of the world provided; for this purpose also did Soter (*the Saviour*) present Himself in the world—even for the salvation of the animal (nature). By yet another arrangement they will have it that He, in some prodigious way,[1] clothed Himself with the primary portions[2] of those substances, the whole of which He was going to restore to salvation; in such wise that He assumed the spiritual nature from Achamoth, whilst He derived the animal (being), Christ, afterwards from the Demiurge; His corporal substance, however, which was constructed of an animal nature (only with wonderful and indescribable skill), He wore for a dispensational purpose, in order that He might, in spite of His own unwillingness,[3] be capable of meeting persons, and of being seen and touched by them, and even of dying. But there was nothing material assumed by Him, inasmuch as *that* was incapable of salvation. As if He could possibly have been more required by any others than by those who were in want of salvation ! And all this, in order that by severing the condition of our flesh from Christ they may also deprive it of the hope of salvation !

CHAP. XXVII.—THE CHRIST OF THE DEMIURGE, SENT INTO THE WORLD BY THE VIRGIN. NOT OF HER. HE FOUND IN HER, NOT A MOTHER, BUT ONLY A PASSAGE OR CHANNEL. JESUS DESCENDED UPON CHRIST, AT HIS BAPTISM, LIKE A DOVE ; BUT, BEING INCAPABLE OF SUFFERING, HE LEFT CHRIST TO DIE ON THE CROSS ALONE.

I now adduce[4] (what they say) concerning Christ, upon whom some of them engraft Jesus with so much licence, that they foist into Him a spiritual seed together with an animal *inflatus*. Indeed, I will not undertake to describe[5] these incongruous crammings,[6] which they have contrived in relation both to their men and their gods. Even the Demiurge has a Christ of His own—His natural Son. An animal, in short, produced by Himself, proclaimed by the prophets—His position being one which must be decided by prepositions; in other words, He was produced *by means of* a virgin, rather than *of* a virgin ! On the ground that, having descended into the virgin rather in the manner of a passage through her than of a birth by her, He came into existence *through* her, not *of* her—not experiencing a mother in her, but nothing more than a way. Upon this same Christ, therefore (so they say), Jesus descended in the sacrament of baptism, in the likeness of a dove. Moreover, there was even in Christ accruing from Achamoth the condiment of a spiritual seed, in order of course to prevent the corruption of all the other stuffing.[7] For after the precedent of the principal Tetrad, they guard him with four substances—the spiritual one of Achamoth, the animal one of the Demiurge, the corporeal one, which cannot be described, and that of Soter, or, in other phrase, the columbine.[8] As for Soter (*Jesus*), he remained in Christ to the last, impassible, incapable of injury, incapable of apprehension. By and by, when it came to a question of capture, he departed from him during the examination before Pilate. In like manner, his mother's seed did not admit of being injured, being equally exempt from all manner of outrage,[9] and being undiscovered even by the Demiurge himself. The animal and carnal Christ, however, does suffer after the fashion[10] of the superior Christ, who, for the purpose of producing Achamoth, had been stretched upon the cross, that is, Horos, in a substantial though not a cognizable[11] form. In this manner do they reduce all things to mere images—Christians themselves being indeed nothing but imaginary beings !

CHAP. XXVIII.—THE DEMIURGE CURED OF HIS IGNORANCE BY THE SAVIOUR'S ADVENT, FROM WHOM HE HEARS OF THE GREAT FUTURE IN STORE FOR HIMSELF.

Meanwhile the Demiurge, being still ignorant of everything, although he will actually have to make some announcement himself by the prophets, but is quite incapable of even this part of his duty (because they divide authority over the prophets[12] between Achamoth, the Seed, and the Demiurge), no sooner

---

[1] Monstruosum illum.
[2] Prosicias induisse.   Irenæus says, " Assumed the first-fruits," τὰς ἀπαρχάς.
[3] Ingratis.
[4] Reddo.
[5] Nescio quæ.
[6] Fartilia.

[7] Farsura.
[8] That which descended like a dove.
[9] Æque insubditivam.
[10] In delineationem.
[11] Agnitionali.
[12] Prophetiale patrocinium.

heard of the advent of Soter (*Saviour*) than he runs to him with haste and joy, with all his might, like the centurion in the Gospel.[1] And being enlightened by him on all points, he learns from him also of his own prospect how that he is to succeed to his mother's place. Being thenceforth free from all care, he carries on the administration of this world, mainly under the plea of protecting the church, for as long a time as may be necessary and proper.

CHAP. XXIX.—THE THREE NATURES AGAIN ADVERTED TO. THEY ARE ALL EXEMPLIFIED AMONGST MEN. FOR INSTANCE, BY CAIN, AND ABEL, AND SETH.

I will now collect from different sources, by way of conclusion, what they affirm concerning the dispensation[2] of the whole human race. Having at first stated their views as to *man's* threefold nature—which was, however, united in one[3] in the case of Adam—they then proceed after him to divide it (into three) with their especial characteristics, finding opportunity for such distinction in the posterity of Adam himself, in which occurs a threefold division as to moral differences. Cain, and Abel, and Seth, who were in a certain sense the sources of the human race, become the fountain-heads of just as many qualities[4] of nature and essential character.[5] The material nature,[6] which had become reprobate for salvation, they assign to Cain; the animal nature, which was poised between divergent hopes, they find[7] in Abel; the spiritual, preordained for certain salvation, they store up[7] in Seth. In this way also they make a twofold distinction among souls, as to their property of good and evil—according to the material condition derived from Cain, or the animal from Abel. Men's spiritual state they derive over and above the other conditions,[8] from Seth adventitiously,[9] not in the way of nature, but of grace,[10] in such wise that Achamoth infuses it[11] among superior beings like rain[12] into good souls, that is, those who are enrolled in the animal class. Whereas the material class—in other words, those which are bad souls—they say, never receive the

blessings of salvation;[13] for that nature they have pronounced to be incapable of any change or reform in its natural condition.[14] This grain, then, of spiritual seed is modest and very small when cast from her hand, but under her instruction[15] increases and advances into full conviction, as we have already said;[16] and the souls, on this very account, so much excelled all others, that the Demiurge, even then in his ignorance, held them in great esteem. For it was from their list that he had been accustomed to select men for kings and for priests; and these even now, if they have once attained to a full and complete knowledge of these foolish conceits of theirs,[17] since they are already naturalized in the fraternal bond of the spiritual state, will obtain a sure salvation, nay, one which is on all accounts their due.

CHAP. XXX.—THE LAX AND DANGEROUS VIEWS OF THIS SECT RESPECTING GOOD WORKS. THAT THESE ARE UNNECESSARY TO THE SPIRITUAL MAN.

For this reason it is that they neither regard works[18] as necessary for themselves, nor do they observe any of the calls of duty, eluding even the necessity of martyrdom on any pretence which may suit their pleasure. For this rule, (they say), is enjoined upon the animal seed, in order that the salvation, which we do not possess by any privilege of our state,[19] we may work out by right[20] of our conduct. Upon us, who are of an imperfect nature,[21] is imprinted the mark of this (animal) seed, because we are reckoned *as sprung* from the loves of Theletus,[22] and consequently as an abortion, just as their mother was. But *woe* to us indeed, should we in any point transgress the yoke of discipline, should we grow dull in the works of holiness and justice, should we desire to make our confession anywhere else, I know not where, and not before the powers of this world at the tribunals of the chief magistrates![23] As for them, however, they may prove their nobility by the dissoluteness[24] of their life and their diligence[25] in sin, since Achamoth fawns on them as her own; for she, too, found sin no unprofitable pursuit. Now it is held amongst them, that, for the purpose of honouring the celestial

---

[1] Matt. viii. 5, 6.
[2] De dispositione.
[3] Inunitam.
[4] Argumenta.
[5] Essentiæ.
[6] Choicum : "the clayey." Having the doubtful issues, which arise from freedom of the will (Oehler).
[7] Recondunt : or, " discover."
[8] Superducunt.
[9] De obvenientia
[10] Indulgentiam.
[11] The " quos" here relates to "spiritalem statum," but expressing the *sense* rather than the grammatical propriety, refers to the plural idea of " good souls" (Oehler).
[12] Depluat.
[13] Salutaria.

[14] We have tried to retain the emphatic repetition, " inreformabilem naturæ naturam."
[15] Eruditu hujus.
[16] Above, in ch. xxv. p. 515.
[17] Istarum næniarum.
[18] Operationes : the doing of (good) works."
[19] As, forsooth, we should in the *spiritual* state.
[20] Suffragio.
[21] Being animal, not spiritual.
[22] See above. ch. ix. x. p. 508.
[23] See *Scorpiace*, ch. x. *infra*.
[24] Passivitate.
[25] " Diligentia" may mean " proclivity " (Rigalt.).

marriages,[1] it is necessary to contemplate and celebrate the mystery always by cleaving to a companion, that, is to a woman; otherwise (they account any man) degenerate, and a bastard[2] to the truth, who spends his life in the world without loving a woman or uniting himself to her. Then what is to become of the eunuchs whom we see amongst them?

CHAP. XXXI. — AT THE LAST DAY GREAT CHANGES TAKE PLACE AMONGST THE ÆONS AS WELL AS AMONG MEN. HOW ACHAMOTH AND THE DEMIURGE ARE AFFECTED THEN. IRONY ON THE SUBJECT.

It remains that we say something about the end of the world,[3] and the dispensing of reward. As soon as Achamoth has completed the full harvest of her seed, and has then proceeded to gather it into her garner, or, after it has been taken to the mill and ground to flour, has hidden it in the kneading-trough with yeast until the whole be leavened, then shall the end speedily come.[4] Then, to begin with, Achamoth herself removes from the middle region,[5] from the second stage to the highest, since she is restored to the Pleroma: she is immediately received by that paragon of perfection[6] Soter, as her spouse of course, and they two afterwards consummate[7] new nuptials. This must be the spouse of the Scripture,[8] the Pleroma of espousals (for you might suppose that the Julian laws[9] were interposing, since there are these migrations from place to place). In like manner, the Demiurge, too, will then change the scene of his abode from the celestial Hebdomad[10] to the higher regions, to his mother's now vacant saloon[11]—by this time knowing her, without however seeing her. (A happy coincidence !) For if he had caught a glance of her, he would have preferred never to have known her.

CHAP. XXXII.—INDIGNANT IRONY EXPOSING THE VALENTINIAN FABLE ABOUT THE JUDICIAL TREATMENT OF MANKIND AT THE LAST JUDGMENT. THE IMMORALITY OF THE DOCTRINE.

As for the human race, its end will be to the following effect:—To all which bear the earthy[12] and material mark there accrues an entire destruction, because "all flesh is grass,"[13] and amongst these is the soul of mortal man, except when it has found salvation by faith. The souls of just men, that is to say, our souls, will be conveyed to the Demiurge in the abodes of the middle region. We are duly thankful; we shall be content to be classed with our god, in whom lies our own origin.[14] Into the palace of the Pleroma nothing of the animal nature is admitted—nothing but the spiritual swarm of Valentinus. There, then, the first process is the despoiling of men themselves, that is, men within the Pleroma.[15] Now this despoiling consists of the putting off of the souls in which they appear to be clothed, which they will give back to their Demiurge as they had obtained[16] them from him. They will then become wholly intellectual spirits—impalpable,[17] invisible[18] —and in this state will be readmitted invisibly to the Pleroma—stealthily, if the case admits of the idea.[19] What then? They will be dispersed amongst the angels, the attendants on Soter. As sons, do you suppose? Not at all. As servants, then? No, not even so. Well, as phantoms? Would that it were nothing more ! Then in what capacity, if you are ashamed to tell us? In the capacity of brides. Then will they end[20] their Sabine rapes with the sanction of wedlock. This will be the guerdon of the spiritual, this the recompense of their faith ! Such fables have their use. Although but a Marcus or a Gaius,[21] full-grown in this flesh of ours, with a beard and such like proofs (of virility,) it may be a stern husband, a father, a grandfather, a great-grandfather (never mind what, in fact, if only a male), you may perhaps in the bridal-chamber of the Pleroma—I have already said so tacitly[22]—even become the parent by an angel of some Æon of high numerical rank.[23] For the right celebration of these nuptials, instead of the torch and veil, I suppose that secret fire is then to burst forth, which, after devastating the whole existence of things, will itself also be reduced to nothing at last, after everything has been reduced to ashes; and so their fable too will be ended.[24] But I, too,

---

[1] Of the Æons.
[2] Nec legitimum : "not a lawful son."
[3] De consummatione.
[4] Urgebit.
[5] See above, ch. xxiii. p. 514.
[6] Compacticius ille.
[7] Fient.
[8] Query, the Holy Scriptures, or the writings of the Valentintians ?
[9] Very severe against adultery, and even against celibacy.
[10] In ch. xx. this "scenam de Hebdomade cælesti" is called "cælorum septemplicem scenam"="the sevenfold stage of heaven."
[11] Cœnaculum. See above, ch. vii. p. 506.
[12] Choicæ : "clayey."

[13] Isa. xl. 6.
[14] See above, in ch. xxiv. p. 515.
[15] Interiores.
[16] Averterant.
[17] Neque detentui obnoxii.
[18] Neque conspectui obnoxii.
[19] Si ita est: or, "since such is the fact."
[20] Claudent.
[21] But slaves, in fact.
[22] This parenthetic clause, "tacendo jam dixi," perhaps means, "I say this with shame," "I would rather not have to say it."
[23] The common reading is, "Onesimum Æonem," an Æon called Onesimus, in supposed allusion to Philemon's Onesimus. But this is too far-fetched. Oehler discovers in "Onesimum" the corruption of some higher number ending in "esimum."
[24] This is Oehler's idea of "et nulla jam fabula." Rigaltius, however, gives a good sense to this clause : "All will come true at last ; there will be no fable."

am no doubt a rash man, in having exposed so great a mystery in so derisive a way: I ought to be afraid that Achamoth, who did not choose to make herself known even to her own son, would turn mad, that Theletus would be enraged, that Fortune[1] would be irritated. But I am yet a liege-man of the Demiurge. I have to return after death to the place where there is no more giving in marriage, where I have to be clothed upon rather than to be despoiled,—where, even if I am despoiled of my sex, I am classed with angels—not a male angel, nor a female one. There will be no one to do aught against me, nor will they then find any male energy in me.

CHAP. XXXIII.—THESE REMAINING CHAPTERS AN APPENDIX TO THE MAIN WORK. IN THIS CHAPTER TERTULLIAN NOTICES A DIFFERENCE AMONG SUNDRY FOLLOWERS OF PTOLEMY, A DISCIPLE OF VALENTINUS.

I shall now at last produce, by way of *finale*,[2] after so long a story, those points which, not to interrupt the course of it, and by the interruption distract the reader's attention, I have preferred reserving to this place. They have been variously advanced by those who have improved on[3] the doctrines of Ptolemy. For there have been in his school "disciples above their master," who have attributed to their Bythus two wives —Cogitatio (*Thought*) and Voluntas (*Will*). For Cogitatio alone was not sufficient wherewith to produce any offspring, although from the two wives procreation was most easy to him. The former bore him Monogenes (*Only-Begotten*) and Veritas (*Truth*). Veritas was a female after the likeness of Cogitatio; Monogenes a male, bearing a resemblance to Voluntas. For it is the strength of Voluntas which procures the masculine nature,[4] inasmuch as she affords efficiency to Cogitatio.

CHAP. XXXIV.—OTHER VARYING OPINIONS AMONG THE VALENTINIANS RESPECTING THE DEITY. CHARACTERISTIC RAILLERY.

Others of purer mind, mindful of the honour of the Deity, have, for the purpose of freeing him from the discredit of even single wedlock, preferred assigning no sex whatever to Bythus; and therefore very likely they talk of "this deity " in the neuter gender rather than "this god." Others again, on the other hand, speak of him as both masculine and feminine, so that the worthy chronicler Fenestella must not suppose that an hermaphrodite

was only to be found among the good people of Luna.

CHAP. XXXV.—YET MORE DISCREPANCIES. JUST NOW THE SEX OF BYTHUS WAS AN OBJECT OF DISPUTE ; NOW HIS RANK COMES IN QUESTION. ABSURD SUBSTITUTES FOR BYTHUS CRITICISED BY TERTULLIAN.

There are some who do not claim the first place for Bythus, but only a lower one. They put their Ogdoad in the foremost rank; itself, however, derived from a Tetrad, but under different names. For they put Pro-arche (*Before the Beginning*) first, Anennœtos (*Inconceivable*) second, Arrhetos (*Indescribable*) third, Aoratos (*Invisible*) fourth. Then after Pro-arche they say Arche (*Beginning*) came forth and occupied the first and the fifth place; from Anennœtos came Acataleptos (*Incomprehensible*) in the second and the sixth place; from Arrhetos came Anonomastos (*Nameless*) in the third and the seventh place; from Aoratos[5] came Agennetos (*Unbegotten*) in the fourth and the eight place. Now by what method he arranges this, that each of these Æons should be born in two places, and that, too, at such intervals, I prefer to be ignorant of than to be informed. For what can be right in a system which is propounded with such absurd particulars?

CHAP. XXXVI.—LESS REPREHENSIBLE THEORIES IN THE HERESY. BAD IS THE BEST OF VALENTINIANISM.

How much more sensible are they who, rejecting all this tiresome nonsense, have refused to believe that any one Æon has descended from another by steps like these, which are really neither more nor less Gemonian;[6] but that on a given signal[7] the eightfold emanation, of which we have heard,[8] issued all at once from the Father and His Ennœa (*Thought*),[9]—that it is, in fact, from His mere motion that they gain their designations. When, as they say, He thought of producing offspring, He on that account gained the name of FATHER. After producing, because the issue which He produced was true, He received the name of *Truth*. When He wanted Himself to be manifested, He on that account was announced as *Man*. Those, moreover, whom He preconceived in His thought when He produced them, were then designated *the Church*. As man, He uttered

---

[1] The same as *Macariotes*, in ch. viii. above, p. 507.
[2] Velut epicitharisma.
[3] Emendatoribus.
[4] Censum.

[5] Tertullian, however, here gives the Latin synonyme, *Invisibilis*.
[6] The "Gemonian steps" on the Aventine led to the Tiber, to which the bodies of executed criminals were dragged by hooks, to be cast into the river.
[7] Mappa, quod aiunt, missa : a proverbial expression.
[8] Istam.
[9] See above, ch. vii, p. 506.

His *Word;* and so this *Word* is His first-be-gotten Son, and to the Word was added *Life.* And by this process the first Ogdoad was completed. However, the whole of this tiresome story is utterly poor and weak.

CHAP. XXXVII.—OTHER TURGID AND RIDICULOUS THEORIES ABOUT THE ORIGIN OF THE ÆONS AND CREATION, STATED AND CONDEMNED.

Now listen to some other buffooneries[1] of a master who is a great swell among them,[2] and who has pronounced his *dicta* with an even priestly authority. They run thus: There comes, says he, before all things Pro-arche, the inconceivable, and indescribable, and nameless, which I for my own part call Monotes (*Solitude*). With this was associated another power, to which also I give the name of Henotes (*Unity*). Now, inasmuch as Monotes and Henotes—that is to say, Solitude and Union—were only one being, they produced, and yet not in the way of production,[3] the intellectual, innascible, invisible beginning of all things, which human language[4] has called Monad (*Solitude*).[5] This has inherent in itself a consubstantial force, which it calls Unity.[6] These powers, accordingly, Solitude or Solitariness, *and* Unity, or Union, propagated all the other emanations of Æons.[7] Wonderful distinction, to be sure! Whatever change Union and Unity may undergo, Solitariness and Solitude is profoundly supreme. Whatever designation you give the power, it is one and the same.

CHAP. XXXVIII.—DIVERSITY IN THE OPINIONS OF SECUNDUS, AS COMPARED WITH THE GENERAL DOCTRINE OF VALENTINUS.

Secundus is a trifle more human, as he is briefer: he divides the Ogdoad into a pair of Tetrads, a right hand one and a left hand one, *one* light and *the other* darkness. Only he is unwilling to derive the power which apostatized and fell away[8] from any one of the Æons, but from the fruits which issued from their substance.

CHAP. XXXIX.—THEIR DIVERSITY OF SENTIMENT AFFECTS THE VERY CENTRAL DOCTRINE OF CHRISTIANITY, EVEN THE PERSON AND CHARACTER OF THE LORD JESUS. THIS DIVERSITY VITIATES EVERY GNOSTIC SCHOOL.

Now, concerning even the Lord Jesus, into how great a diversity of opinion are they divided! One party form Him of the blossoms of all the Æons.[9] Another party will have it that He is made up only of those ten whom *the Word* and *the Life*[10] produced;[11] from which circumstance the titles of the Word and the Life were suitably transferred to Him. Others, again, that He rather sprang from the twelve, the offspring of *Man* and *the Church;*[12] and therefore, they say, He was designated "Son of man." Others, moreover, maintain that He was formed by *Christ* and *the Holy Spirit,* who have to provide for the establishment of the universe,[13] and that He inherits by right His Father's appellation. Some there are who have imagined that another origin must be found for the title "Son of man;" for they have had the presumption to call the Father Himself *Man,* by reason of the profound mystery of this title: so that what can you hope for more ample concerning faith in that God, with whom you are now yourself on a par? Such conceits are constantly cropping out[14] amongst them, from the redundance of their mother's seed.[15] And so it happens that the doctrines which have grown up amongst the Valentinians have already extended their rank growth to the woods of the Gnostics.

---

[1] Oehler gives good reasons for the reading "ingenia circulatoria," instead of the various readings of other editors.
[2] Insignioris apud eos magistri.
[3] Non proferentes. Another reading is "non proserentes" (not generating).
[4] Sermo.
[5] Or, solitariness.
[6] Or, Union.
[7] Compare our Irenæus, I. 2, 3. [Vol. I. p. 316.]

[8] Achamoth.
[9] See above, ch. xii. p. 510.
[10] The Æons *Sermo* and *Vita.*
[11] See above, ch. vii. p. 506.
[12] See above, ch. viii. p. 507.
[13] See above, ch. xiv. p. 511.
[14] Superfruticant.
[15] Archamoth is referred to.

V.

ON THE FLESH OF CHRIST.[1]

THIS WAS WRITTEN BY OUR AUTHOR IN CONFUTATION OF CERTAIN
HERETICS WHO DENIED THE REALITY OF CHRIST'S FLESH, OR AT
LEAST ITS IDENTITY WITH HUMAN FLESH—FEARING THAT, IF THEY
ADMITTED THE REALITY OF CHRIST'S FLESH, THEY MUST ALSO
ADMIT HIS RESURRECTION IN THE FLESH; AND, CONSEQUENTLY,
THE RESURRECTION OF THE HUMAN BODY AFTER DEATH.

[TRANSLATED BY DR. HOLMES.]

CHAP. I.—THE GENERAL PURPORT OF THIS WORK. THE HERETICS, MARCION, APELLES, AND VALENTINUS, WISHING TO IMPUGN THE DOCTRINE OF THE RESURRECTION, DEPRIVE CHRIST OF ALL CAPACITY FOR SUCH A CHANGE BY DENYING HIS FLESH.

THEY who are so anxious to shake that belief in the resurrection which was firmly settled[2] before the appearance of our modern Sadducees,[3] as even to deny that the expectation thereof has any relation whatever to the flesh, have great cause for besetting the flesh of Christ also with doubtful questions, as if it either had no existence at all, or possessed a nature altogether different from human flesh. *For they cannot but be apprehensive* that, if it be once determined that *Christ's flesh* was human, a presumption would immediately arise in opposition to them, that that flesh must by all means rise again, which has already risen in Christ. Therefore we shall have to guard our belief in the resurrection[4] from the same armoury, whence they get their weapons of destruction. Let us examine our Lord's bodily substance, for about His spiritual nature all are agreed.[5] It is

His flesh that is in question. Its verity and quality are the points in dispute. Did it ever exist? whence was it derived? and of what kind was it? If we succeed in demonstrating it, we shall lay down a law for our own resurrection. Marcion, in order that he might deny the flesh of Christ, denied also His nativity, or else he denied His flesh in order that he might deny His nativity; because, of course, he was afraid that His nativity and His flesh bore mutual testimony to each other's reality, since there is no nativity without flesh, and no flesh without nativity. As if indeed, under the prompting of that licence which is ever the same in all heresy, he too might not very well have either denied the nativity, although admitting the flesh,—like Apelles, who was first a disciple of his, and afterwards an apostate, —or, while admitting both the flesh and the nativity, have interpreted them in a different sense, as did Valentinus, who resembled Apelles both in his discipleship and desertion *of Marcion*. At all events, he who represented the flesh of Christ to be imaginary was equally able to pass off His nativity as a phantom; so that the virgin's conception, and pregnancy, and child-bearing, and then the whole course[6] of her infant too, would have to be regarded as putative.[7] *These facts pertaining to the nativity of Christ* would escape the notice of the same eyes and the same senses as failed to grasp the full idea[8] of His flesh.

---

[1] In his work *On the Resurrection of the Flesh* (chap. ii.), Tertullian refers to this tract, and calls it "De Carne Domini adversus quatuor hæreses:" the four heresies being those of Marcion, Apelles, Basilides, and Valentinus. Pamelius, indeed, designates the tract by this fuller title instead of the usual one, "De Carne Christi." [This tract contains references to works written while our author was Montanistic, but it contains no positive Montanism. It should not be dated earlier than A.D. 207.]
[2] Moratam.
[3] The allusion is to Matt. xxii. 23; comp. *de Præscr. Hæret.* 33 (Fr. Junius).
[4] Tertullian's phrase is "carnis vota"—the future prospects of the flesh.
[5] Certum est.

[6] Ordo.
[7] Τῷ δοκεῖν haberentur. This term gave name to the *Docetic* errors.
[8] Opinio.

CHAP. II.—MARCION, WHO WOULD BLOT OUT THE RECORD OF CHRIST'S NATIVITY, IS REBUKED FOR SO STARTLING A HERESY.

Clearly enough is the nativity announced by Gabriel.[1] But what has he to do with the Creator's angel?[2] The conception in the virgin's womb is also set plainly before us. But what concern has he with the Creator's prophet, Isaiah?[3] He[4] will not brook delay, since *suddenly* (without any prophetic announcement) did he bring down Christ from heaven.[5] "Away," says he, "with that eternal plaguey taxing of Cæsar, and the scanty inn, and the squalid swaddling-clothes, and the hard stable.[6] We do not care a jot for[7] that multitude of the heavenly host which praised their Lord at night.[8] Let the shepherds take better care of their flock,[9] and let the wise men spare their legs so long a journey;[10] let them keep their gold to themselves.[11] Let Herod, too, mend his manners, so that Jeremy may not glory over him.[12] Spare also the babe from circumcision, that he may escape the pain thereof; nor let him be brought into the temple, lest he burden his parents with the expense of the offering;[13] nor let him be handed to Simeon, lest the old man be saddened at the point of death.[14] Let that old woman also hold her tongue, lest she should bewitch the child."[15] After such a fashion as this, I suppose you have had, O Marcion, the hardihood of blotting out the original records (of the history) of Christ, that His flesh may lose the proofs of its reality. But, prithee, on what grounds (do you do this)? Show me your authority. If you are a prophet, foretell us a thing; if you are an apostle, open your message in public; if a follower of apostles,[16] side with apostles in thought; if you are only a (private) Christian, believe what has been handed down to us: if, however, you are nothing of all this, then (as I have the best reason to say) cease to live.[17] For indeed you are already dead, since you are no Christian, because you do not believe that which by being believed makes men Christian,—nay, you are the more dead, the more you are not a Christian; having fallen

away, after you had been one, by rejecting[18] what you formerly believed, even as you yourself acknowledge in a certain letter of yours, and as your followers do not deny, whilst our (brethren) can prove it.[19] Rejecting, therefore, what you *once* believed, you have completed the act of rejection, by now no longer believing: the fact, however, of your having ceased to believe has not made your rejection of the faith right and proper; nay, rather,[20] by your act of rejection you prove that what you believed previous to the said act was of a different character.[21] What you believed to be of a different character, had been handed down just as *you believed it.* Now[22] that which had been handed down was true, inasmuch as it had been transmitted by those whose duty it was to hand it down. Therefore, when rejecting that which had been handed down, you rejected that which was true. You had no authority for what you did. However, we have already in another treatise availed ourselves more fully of these prescriptive rules against all heresies. Our repetition of them here after that large (treatise) is superfluous,[23] when we ask the reason why you have formed the opinion that Christ was not born.

CHAP. III.—CHRIST'S NATIVITY BOTH POSSIBLE AND BECOMING. THE HERETICAL OPINION OF CHRIST'S APPARENT FLESH DECEPTIVE AND DISHONOURABLE TO GOD, EVEN ON MARCION'S PRINCIPLES.

Since[24] you think that this lay within the competency of your own arbitrary choice, you must needs have supposed that being born[25] was either impossible for God, or unbecoming to Him. With God, however, nothing is impossible but what He does not will. Let us consider, then, whether He willed to be born (for if He had the will, He also had the power, and was born). I put the argument very briefly. If God had willed not to be born, it matters not why, He would not have presented Himself in the likeness of man. Now who, when he sees a man, would deny that he had been born? What *God* therefore willed not to be, He would in no wise have willed the seeming to be. When a thing is distasteful, the very notion[26] of it is scouted; because it makes no difference whether a thing exist or

---

[1] Luke i. 26–38.
[2] This is said in opposition to Marcion, who held the Creator's angel, and everything else pertaining to him, to be evil.
[3] A reference to Isa. vii. 14.
[4] Marcion.
[5] See also our *Anti-Marcion*, iv. 7.
[6] Luke ii. 1–7.
[7] Viderit.
[8] Luke ii. 13.
[9] Luke ii. 8.
[10] Matt. ii. 1.
[11] Matt. ii. 11.
[12] Matt. ii. 16–18, and Jer. xxxi. 15.
[13] Luke ii. 22–24.
[14] Luke ii. 25–35.
[15] Luke ii. 36–38.
[16] Apostolicus.
[17] Morere.

[18] Rescindendo.
[19] Compare our *Anti Marcion*, i. 1, iv. 4 and *de Præscr. Hær.* c. xxx.
[20] Atquin.
[21] Aliter fuisse.
[22] Porro.
[23] Ex abundanti. [Dr. Holmes, in this sentence actually uses the word *lengthy*, for which I have said *large*.]
[24] Quatenus.
[25] Nativitatem.
[26] Opinio.

do not exist, if, when it does not exist, it is yet assumed to exist. It is of course of the greatest importance that there should be nothing false (or pretended) attributed to that which really does not exist.[1] But, say you, His own consciousness (of the truth of His nature) was enough for Him. If any supposed that He had been born, because they saw Him as a man, that was their concern.[2] Yet with how much more dignity and consistency would He have sustained the human character on the supposition that He was truly born; for if He were not born, He could not have undertaken the said character without injury to that consciousness of His which you on your side attribute to His confidence of being able to sustain, although not born, the character of having been born even against His own consciousness![3] Why, I want to know,[4] was it of so much importance, that Christ should, when perfectly aware what He really was, exhibit Himself as being that which He was not? You cannot express any apprehension that,[5] if He had been born and truly clothed Himself with man's nature, He would have ceased to be God, losing what He was, while becoming what He was not. For God is in no danger of losing His own state and condition. But, say you, I deny that God was truly changed to man in such wise as to be born and endued with a body of flesh, on this ground, that a being who is without end is also of necessity incapable of change. For being changed into something else puts an end to the former state. Change, therefore, is not possible to a Being who cannot come to an end. Without doubt, the nature of things which are subject to change is regulated by this law, that they have no permanence in the state which is undergoing change in them, and that they come to an end from thus wanting permanence, whilst they lose that in the process of change which they previously were. But nothing is equal with God; His nature is different[6] from the condition of all things. If, then, the things which differ from God, and from which God differs, lose what existence they had whilst they are undergoing change, wherein will consist the difference of the Divine Being from all other

things except in His possessing the contrary faculty of theirs,—in other words, that God can be changed into all conditions, and yet continue just as He is? On any other supposition, He would be on the same level with those things which, when changed, lose the existence they had before; whose equal, of course, He is not in any other respect, as He certainly is not in the changeful issues[7] of their nature. You have sometimes read and believed that the Creator's angels have been changed into human form, and have even borne about so veritable a body, that Abraham even washed their feet,[8] and Lot was rescued from the Sodomites by their hands;[9] an angel, moreover, wrestled with a man so strenuously with his body, that the latter desired to be let loose, so tightly was he held.[10] Has it, then, been permitted to angels, which are inferior to God, after they have been changed into human bodily form,[11] nevertheless to remain angels? and will you deprive God, their superior, of this faculty, as if Christ could not continue to be God, after His real assumption of the nature of man? Or else, did those angels appear as phantoms of flesh? You will not, however, have the courage to say this; for if it be so held in your belief, that the Creator's angels are in the same condition as Christ, then Christ will belong to the same God as those angels do, who are like Christ in their condition. If you had not purposely rejected in some instances, and corrupted in others, the Scriptures which are opposed to your opinion, you would have been confuted in this matter by the Gospel of John, when it declares that the Spirit descended in the body[12] of a dove, and sat upon the Lord.[13] When the said Spirit was in this condition, He was as truly a dove as He was also a spirit; nor did He destroy His own proper substance by the assumption of an extraneous substance. But you ask what becomes of the dove's body, after the return of the Spirit back to heaven, and similarly in the case of the angels. Their withdrawal was effected in the same manner as their appearance had been. If you had seen how their production out of nothing had been effected, you would have known also the process of their return to nothing. If the initial step was out of sight, so was also the final one. Still there was solidity in their bodily substance, whatever may have been the force by which the body became visible. What is written cannot but have been.

---

[1] If Christ's flesh was not real, the pretence of it was wholly wrong.

[2] Viderint homines.

[3] It did not much matter (according to the view which Tertullian attributes to Marcion) if God did practise deception in affecting the assumption of a humanity which He knew to be unreal. Men took it to be real, and that answered every purpose. God knew better: and He was moreover, strong enough to obviate all inconveniences of the deception by His unfaltering fortitude, etc. All this, however, seemed to Tertullian to be simply damaging and perilous to the character of God, even from Marcion's own point of view.

[4] Edoce.

[5] Non potes dicere ne, etc.

[6] Distat.

[7] In exitu conversionis.

[8] Gen. xviii.

[9] Gen. xix.

[10] Gen. xxxii.

[11] See below in chap. vi. and in the Anti-Marcion, iii. 9.

[12] Corpore.

[13] Matt. iii. 16.

CHAP. IV.—GOD'S HONOUR IN THE INCARNATION OF HIS SON VINDICATED.   MARCION'S DISPARAGEMENT OF HUMAN FLESH INCONSISTENT AS WELL AS IMPIOUS.   CHRIST HAS CLEANSED THE FLESH.   THE FOOLISHNESS OF GOD IS MOST WISE.

Since, therefore, you do not reject the assumption of a body[1] as impossible or as hazardous to the character of God, it remains for you to repudiate and censure it as unworthy of Him. Come now, beginning from the nativity itself, declaim[2] against the uncleanness of the generative elements within the womb, the filthy concretion of fluid and blood, of the growth of the flesh for nine months long out of that very mire. Describe the womb as it enlarges[3] from day to day,—heavy, troublesome, restless even in sleep, changeful in its feelings of dislike and desire. Inveigh now likewise against the shame itself of a woman in travail,[4] which, however, ought rather to be honoured in consideration of that peril, or to be held sacred[5] in respect of (the mystery of) nature. Of course you are horrified also at the infant, which is shed into life with the embarrassments which accompany it from the womb;[6] you likewise, of course, loathe it even after it is washed, when it is dressed out in its swaddling-clothes, graced with repeated anointing,[7] smiled on with nurse's fawns. This reverend course of nature,[8] you, O Marcion, (are pleased to) spit upon; and yet, in what way were you born? You detest a human being at his birth; then after what fashion do you love anybody? Yourself, of course, you had no love of, when you departed from the Church and the faith of Christ. But never mind,[9] if you are not on good terms with yourself, or even if you were born in a way different from other people. Christ, at any rate, has loved even that man who was condensed in his mother's womb amidst all its uncleannesses, even that man who was brought into life out of the said womb, even that man who was nursed amidst the nurse's simpers.[10] For his sake He came down (from heaven), for his sake He preached, for his sake "He humbled Himself even unto

death—the death of the cross."[11] He loved, of course, the being whom He redeemed at so great a cost. If Christ is the Creator's *Son*, it was with justice that He loved His own (creature); if He comes from another god, His love was excessive, since He redeemed a being who belonged to another. Well, then, loving man He loved his nativity also, and his flesh as well. Nothing can be loved apart from that through which whatever exists has its existence. Either take away nativity, and then show us *your* man; or else withdraw the flesh, and then present to our view the being whom God has redeemed—since it is these very conditions[12] which constitute the man whom God has redeemed. And are *you* for turning these conditions into occasions of blushing to the very creature whom He has redeemed, (censuring them), too, us unworthy of Him who certainly would not have redeemed them had He not loved them? Our birth He reforms from death by a second birth from heaven;[13] our flesh He restores from every harassing malady; when leprous, He cleanses it of the stain; when blind, He re-kindles its light; when palsied, He renews its strength; when possessed with devils, He exorcises it; when dead, He reanimates it,—then shall *we* blush to own it? If, to be sure,[14] He had chosen to be born of a mere animal, and were to preach the kingdom of heaven invested with the body of a beast either wild or tame, your censure (I imagine) would have instantly met Him with this demurrer: "This is disgraceful for God, and this is unworthy of the Son of God, and simply foolish." For no other reason than because one thus judges. It *is* of course foolish, if we are to judge God by our own conceptions. But, Marcion, consider well this Scripture, if indeed you have not erased it: "God hath chosen the foolish things of the world, to confound the wise."[15] Now what are those foolish things? Are they the conversion of men to the worship of the true God, the rejection of error, the whole training in righteousness, chastity, mercy, patience, and innocence? These things certainly are not "foolish." Inquire again, then, of what things he spoke, and when you imagine that you have discovered what they are will you find anything to be so "foolish" as believing in a God that has been born, and that of a virgin, and of a fleshly nature too, who wallowed in all the before-mentioned humiliations of nature? But some one may say,

---

[1] Corporationem.
[2] Compare similar passages in the *Anti-Marcion*, iii. 1 and iv. 21.
[3] Insolescentem.
[4] Enitentis.
[5] Religiosum.
[6] Cum suis impedimentis profusum.
[7] Unctionibus formatur.
[8] Hanc venerationem naturæ. Compare Tertullian's phrase, "Illa sanctissima et reverenda opera naturæ," in the *Anti-Marcion*, iii. 11.
[9] Videris.
[10] Per ludibria nutritum. Compare the phrase just before, "smiled on with nurse's fawns"—"blanditiis deridetur." Oehler, however, compares the phrase with Tertullian's expression ("puerperii spurcos, anxios, *ludicros exitus*,") in the *Anti-Marcion*, iv. 21.

[11] Phil. ii. 8.
[12] Hæc: i. e. man's *nativity* and his *flesh*.
[13] Literally, "by a heavenly regeneration."
[14] Revera. [I cannot let the words which follow, stand in the text; they are sufficiently rendered.]
[15] 1 Cor. i. 27.

"These are not the foolish things; they must be other things which God has chosen to confound the wisdom of the world." And yet, acording to the world's wisdom, it is more easy to believe that Jupiter became a bull or a swan, if we listen to Marcion, than that Christ really became a man.

CHAP. V.—CHRIST TRULY LIVED AND DIED IN HUMAN FLESH. INCIDENTS OF HIS HUMAN LIFE ON EARTH, AND REFUTATION OF MARCION'S DOCETIC PARODY OF THE SAME.

There are, to be sure, other things also quite as foolish (as the birth of Christ), which have reference to the humiliations and sufferings of God. Or else, let them call a crucified God "wisdom." But Marcion will apply the knife[1] to this *doctrine* also, and even with greater reason. For which is more unworthy of God, which is more likely to raise a blush of shame, that *God* should be born, or that He should die? that He should bear the flesh, or the cross? be circumcised, or be crucified? be cradled, or be coffined?[2] be laid in a manger, or in a tomb? *Talk of "wisdom!"* You will show more of *that* if you refuse to believe this also. But, after all, you will not be "wise" unless you become a "fool" to the world, by believing "the foolish things of God." Have you, then, cut away[3] all sufferings from Christ, on the ground that, as a mere phantom, He was incapable of experiencing them? We have said above that He might possibly have undergone the unreal mockeries[4] of an imaginary birth and infancy. But answer me at once, you that murder truth: Was not God really crucified? And, having been really crucified, did He not really die? And, having indeed really died, did He not really rise again? Falsely did Paul[5] "determine to know nothing amongst us but Jesus and Him crucified;"[6] falsely has he impressed upon us that He was buried; falsely inculcated that He rose again. False, therefore, is our faith also. And all that we hope for from Christ will be a phantom. O thou most infamous of men, who acquittest of all guilt[7] the murderers of God! For nothing did Christ suffer from them, if He really suffered nothing at all. Spare the whole world's one only hope, thou who art destroying the indispensable dishonour of our faith.[8] Whatsoever is unworthy of God, is

of gain to me. I am safe, if I am not ashamed of my Lord. "Whosoever," says He, "shall be ashamed of me, of him will I also be ashamed."[9] Other matters for shame find I none which can prove me to be shameless in a good sense, and foolish in a happy one, by my own contempt of shame. The Son of God was crucified; I am not ashamed because men must needs be ashamed *of it*. And the Son of God died; it is by all means to be believed, because it is absurd.[10] And He was buried, and rose again; the fact is certain, because it is impossible. But how will all this be true in Him, if He was not Himself true —if He really had not in Himself that which might be crucified, might die, might be buried, and might rise again? *I mean* this flesh suffused with blood, built up with bones, interwoven with nerves, entwined with veins, *a flesh* which knew how to be born, and how to die, human without doubt, as born of a human being. It will therefore be mortal in Christ, because Christ is man and the Son of man. Else why is Christ man and the Son of man, if he has nothing of man, and nothing from man? Unless it be either that man is anything else than flesh, or man's flesh comes from any other source than man, or Mary is anything else than a human being, or Marcion's man is *as* Marcion's god.[11] Otherwise Christ could not be described as being man without flesh, nor the Son of man without any human parent; just as He is not God without the Spirit of God, nor the Son of God without having God for His father. Thus the nature[12] of the two substances displayed Him as man and God, —in one respect born, in the other unborn; in one respect fleshly, in the other spiritual; in one sense weak, in the other exceeding strong; in on sense dying, in the other living. This property of the two states—the divine and the human—is distinctly asserted[13] with equal truth of both natures alike, with the same belief both in respect of the Spirit[14] and of the flesh. The powers of the Spirit,[14] proved Him to be God, His sufferings attested the flesh of man. If His powers were not without the Spirit[14] in like manner, were not His sufferings without the flesh. If His flesh with its sufferings was fictitious, for the same reason was the Spirit false with all its powers. Wherefore halve[15] Christ with a lie? He was wholly the truth. Believe me, He chose

---

[1] Aufer, Marcion. Literally, "Destroy this also, O Marcion."
[2] Educari an sepeliri.
[3] Recidisti.
[4] Vacua ludibria.
[5] Paul was of great authority in Marcion's school.
[6] 1 Cor. ii. 2.
[7] Excusas.
[8] The humiliation which God endured, so indispensable a part of the Christian faith.

[9] Matt. x. 33, Mark. viii. 38, and Luke ix. 26.
[10] Ineptum.
[11] That is, imaginary and unreal.
[12] Census : "the origin."
[13] Dispuncta est.
[14] This term is almost a technical designation of the *divine nature* of Christ in Tertullian. (See our translation of the *Anti-Marcion*, p. 247, note 7, Edin.)
[15] Dimidias.

rather to be born, than in any part to pretend —and that indeed to His own detriment—that He was bearing about a flesh hardened without bones, solid without muscles, bloody without blood, clothed without the tunic *of skin*,[1] hungry without appetite, eating without teeth, speaking without a tongue, so that His word was a phantom to the ears through an imaginary voice. A phantom, too, it was of course after the resurrection, when, showing His hands and His feet for the disciples to examine, He said, "Behold and see that it is I myself, for a spirit hath not flesh and bones, as ye see me have;"[2] without doubt, hands, and feet, and bones are not what a spirit possesses, but *only* the flesh. How do you interpret this statement, Marcion, you who tell us that Jesus comes only from the most excellent God, who is both simple and good? See how He *rather* cheats, and deceives, and juggles the eyes of all, and the senses of all, as well as their access to and contact with Him! You ought rather to have brought Christ down, not from heaven, but from some troop of mountebanks, not as God besides man, but simply as a man, a magician; not as the High Priest of our salvation, but as the conjurer in a show; not as the raiser of the dead, but as the misleader[3] of the living,—except that, if He were a magician, He must have had a nativity !

CHAP. VI.—THE DOCTRINE OF APELLES REFUTED, THAT CHRIST'S BODY WAS OF SIDEREAL SUBSTANCE, NOT BORN. NATIVITY AND MORTALITY ARE CORRELATIVE CIRCUMSTANCES, AND IN CHRIST'S CASE HIS DEATH PROVES HIS BIRTH.

But certain disciples[4] of the heretic of Pontus, compelled to be wiser than their teacher, concede to Christ real flesh, without effect, however, on[5] their denial of His nativity. He might have had, they say, a flesh which was not at all born. So we have found our way "out of a frying-pan," as the proverb runs, "into the fire,"[6]—from Marcion to Apelles. This man having first fallen from the principles of Marcion into (intercourse with) a woman, in the flesh, and afterwards shipwrecked himself, in the spirit, on the virgin Philumene,[7] proceeded from that *time*[8] to preach that the body of Christ was of solid flesh, but without having been born. To this angel, indeed, of Philumene, the apostle will reply in tones like those in which he even then predicted him, saying, "Although an angel from heaven preach any other gospel unto you than that which we have preached unto you, let him be accursed."[9] To the arguments, however, which have been indicated just above, we have now to show our resistance. They allow that Christ really had a body. Whence was the material of it, if not from the same sort of thing as [10] that in which He appeared? Whence came His body, if His body were not flesh? Whence came His flesh, if it were not born? Inasmuch as that which is born must undergo its nativity in order to become flesh. He borrowed, they say, His flesh from the stars, and from the substances of the higher world. And they assert it for a certain principle, that a body without nativity is nothing to be astonished at, because it has been submitted to angels to appear even amongst ourselves in the flesh without the intervention of the womb. We admit, of course, that such facts have been related. But then, how comes it to pass that a faith which holds to a different rule borrows materials for its own arguments from the faith which it impugns? What has it to do with Moses, who has rejected the God of Moses? Since the God is a different one, everything belonging to him must be different also. But let the heretics always use the Scriptures of that God whose world they also enjoy. The fact will certainly recoil on them as a witness to judge them, that they maintain their own blasphemies from examples derived from *Him*.[11] But it is an easy task for the truth to prevail without raising any such demurrer against them. When, therefore, they set forth the flesh of Christ after the pattern of the angels, declaring it to be not born, and yet flesh for all that, I should wish them to compare the causes, both in Christ's case and that of the angels, wherefore they came in the flesh. Never did any angel descend for the purpose of being crucified, of tasting death, *and* of rising again from the dead. Now, since there never was such a reason for angels becoming embodied, you have the cause why they assumed flesh without undergoing birth. They had not come to die, therefore they also (came not) to be born. Christ, however, having been sent to die, had necessarily to be also born, that He might be capable of death; for nothing is in the habit of dying but that

---

[1] See his *Adv. Valentin*, chap. 25.
[2] Luke xxiv. 39.
[3] Avocatorem.
[4] He has Appelles mainly in view.
[5] Sine præjudicio tamen. "Without prejudice to their denial, etc."
[6] The Roman version of the proverb is "out of the lime-kiln into the coal-furnace."
[7] See Tertullian, *de Præscr. Hæret.* c. xxx.
[8] Ab eo: or, "from that *event* of the carnal contact." A good reading, found in most of the old books, is *ab ea*, that is, Philumene.

[9] Gal. i. 8.
[10] Ex ea qualitate in qua.
[11] Ipsius: the Creator.

which is born. Between nativity and mortality there is a mutual contrast. The law[1] which makes us die is the cause of our being born. Now, since Christ died owing to the condition which undergoes death, but that undergoes death which is also born, the consequence was—nay, it was an antecedent necessity—that He must have been born also,[2] by reason of the condition which undergoes birth; because He had to die in obedience to that very condition which, because it begins with birth, ends in death.[3] It was not fitting for Him not to be born under the pretence[4] that it was fitting for Him to die. But the Lord Himself at that very time appeared to Abraham amongst those angels without being born, and yet in the flesh without doubt, in virtue of the before-mentioned diversity of cause. You, however, cannot admit this, since you do not receive that Christ, who was even then rehearsing[5] how to converse with, and liberate, and judge the human race, in the habit of a flesh which as yet was not born, because it did not yet mean to die until both its nativity and mortality were previously (by prophecy) announced. Let them, then, prove to us that those angels derived their flesh from the stars. If they do not prove it because it is not written, neither will the flesh of Christ get its origin therefrom, for which they borrowed the precedent of the angels. It is plain that the angels bore a flesh which was not naturally their own; their nature being of a spiritual substance, although in some sense peculiar to themselves, corporeal; and yet they could be transfigured into human shape, and for the time be able to appear and have intercourse with men. Since, therefore, it has not been told us whence they obtained their flesh, it remains for us not to doubt in our minds that a property of angelic power is this, to assume to themselves bodily shape out of no material substance. How much more, you say, is it (within their competence to take a body) out of some material substance? That is true enough. But there is no evidence of this, because Scripture says nothing. Then, again,[6] how should they who are able to form themselves into that which by nature they are not, be unable to do this out of no material substance? If they become that which they are not, why cannot they so become out of that which is not? But that which has not existence when it comes into existence, is made out of nothing. This is why it is unnecessary

either to inquire or to demonstrate what has subsequently become of their[7] bodies. What came out of nothing, came to nothing. They, who were able to convert *themselves* into flesh have it in their power to convert *nothing itself* into flesh. It is a greater thing to change a nature than to make matter. But even if it were necessary *to suppose* that angels derived their flesh from some material substance, it is surely more credible that it was from some earthly matter than from any kind of celestial substances, since it was composed of so palpably terrene a quality that it fed on earthly aliments. Suppose that even now a celestial *flesh*[8] had fed on earthly aliments, although it was not itself earthly, in the same way that earthly flesh actually fed on celestial aliments, although it had nothing of the celestial nature (for we read of manna having been food for the people: "Man," says *the Psalmist*, "did eat angels' bread,"[9]) yet this does not once infringe the separate condition of the Lord's flesh, because of His different destination. For One who was to be truly a man, even unto death, it was necessary that He should be clothed with that flesh to which death belongs. Now that flesh to which death belongs is preceded by birth.

CHAP. VII.— EXPLANATION OF THE LORD'S QUESTION ABOUT HIS MOTHER AND HIS BRETHREN. ANSWER TO THE CAVILS OF APELLES AND MARCION, WHO SUPPORT THEIR DENIAL OF CHRIST'S NATIVITY BY IT.

But whenever a dispute arises about the nativity, all who reject it as creating a presumption in favour of the reality of Christ's flesh, wilfully deny that God Himself was born, on the ground that He asked, "Who is my mother, and who are my brethren?"[10] Let, therefore, Apelles hear what was our answer to Marcion in that little work, in which we challenged his own (favourite) gospel to the proof, even that the material circumstances of that remark (of the Lord's) should be considered.[11] First of all, nobody would have told Him that His mother and brethren were standing outside, if he were not certain both that He had a mother and brethren, and that they were the very persons whom he was then announcing,—who had either been known to him before, or were then and there discovered by him; although heretics[12] have removed this passage from the gospel, because those who were admiring His doctrine said that His

---

[1] Forma.
[2] Aeque.
[3] Quod, quia nascitur, moritur.
[4] Pro.
[5] Ediscebat. Compare a fine passage of Tertullian on this subject in our *Anti-Marcion*, note 10, p. 112, Edin.
[6] Ceterum.

[7] The angels'.
[8] Sidera. Drawn, as they thought, from the stars.
[9] Ps. lxxviii. 24.
[10] Matt. xii. 48; Luke viii. 20, 21.
[11] See our *Anti-Marcion*, iv. 19.
[12] Literally, "heresies."

supposed father, Joseph the carpenter, and His mother Mary, and His brethren, and His sisters, were very well known to them. But it was with the view of tempting Him, that they had mentioned to Him a mother and brethren which He did not possess. The Scripture says nothing of this, although it is not in other instances silent when anything was done against Him by way of temptation. "Behold," it says, "a certain lawyer stood up, and tempted Him.''[1] And in another passage: "The Pharisees also came unto Him, tempting Him." Who[2] was to prevent its being in this place also indicated that this was done with the view of tempting Him? I do not admit what you advance of your own apart from Scripture. Then there ought to be suggested[3] some occasion[4] for the temptation. What could they have thought to be in Him which required temptation? The question, to be sure, whether He had been born or not? For if this point were denied in His answer, it might come out on the announcement of a temptation. And yet no temptation, when aiming at the discovery of the point which prompts the temptation by its doubtfulness, falls upon one so abruptly, as not to be preceded by the question which compels the temptation whilst raising the doubt. Now, since the nativity of Christ had never come into question, how can you contend that they meant by their temptation to inquire about a point on which they had never raised a doubt? Besides,[5] if He had to be tempted about His birth, this of course was not the proper way of doing it,—by announcing those persons who, even on the supposition of His birth, might possibly not have been in existence. We have all been born, and yet all of us have not either brothers or mother. He might with more probability have had even a father than a mother, and uncles more likely than brothers. Thus is the temptation about His birth unsuitable, for it might have been contrived without any mention of either His mother or His brethren. It is clearly more credible that, being certain that He had both a mother and brothers, they tested His divinity rather than His nativity, whether, when within, He knew what was without; being tried by the untrue announcement of the presence of persons who were not present. But the artifice of a temptation might have been thwarted thus: it might have happened that He knew that those whom they were announcing to be "standing without,"

were in fact absent by the stress either of sickness, or of business, or a journey which He was at the time aware of. No one tempts (another) in a way in which he knows that he may have himself to bear the shame of the temptation. There being, then, no suitable occasion for a temptation, the announcement that His mother and His brethren had actually turned up[6] recovers its naturalness. But there is some ground for thinking that *Christ's* answer denies His mother and brethren for the present, as even Apelles might learn. "The Lord's brethren had not yet believed in Him."[7] So is it contained in the Gospel which was published before Marcion's time; whilst there is at the same time a want of evidence of His mother's adherence to Him, although the Marthas and the other Marys were in constant attendance on Him. In this very passage indeed, their unbelief is evident. Jesus was teaching the way of life, preaching the kingdom of God *and* actively engaged in healing infirmities of body and soul; but all the while, whilst strangers were intent on Him, His very nearest relatives were absent. By and by they turn up, and keep outside; but they do not go in, because, forsooth, they set small store[8] on that which was doing within; nor do they even wait,[9] as if they had something which they could contribute more necessary than that which He was so earnestly doing; but they prefer to interrupt Him, and wish to call Him away from His great work. Now, I ask you, Apelles, or will you Marcion, please (to tell me), if you happened to be at a stage play, or had laid a wager[10] on a foot race or a chariot race, and were called away by such a message, would you not have exclaimed, "What are mother and brothers to me?"[11] And did not Christ, whilst preaching and manifesting God, fulfilling the law and the prophets, *and* scattering the darkness of the long preceding age, justly employ this same form of words, in order to strike the unbelief of those who stood outside, or to shake off the importunity of those who would call Him away from His work? If, however, He had meant to deny His own nativity, He would have found place, time, and means for expressing Himself very differently,[12] and not in words which might be uttered by one who had both a mother and brothers. When denying one's parents in indignation, one does not deny *their existence*,

[1] Luke x. 25.
[2] Literally, "nobody prevented its being, etc."
[3] Subesse.
[4] Materia.
[5] Eo adicimus etiam.

[6] Supervenissent.
[7] John vii. 5.
[8] Non computantes scilicet.
[9] Nec sustinent saltem.
[10] Contendens: "videlicet sponsionibus" (Oehler).
[11] Literally, "Who is my mother, and who are my brethren?"— Christ's own words.
[12] The *alius* is a genitive, and must be taken with *sermonis*.

but censures *their faults*. Besides, He gave others the preference; and since He shows their title to this favour—even because they listened to the word (of God)—He points out in what sense He denied His mother and His brethren. For in whatever sense He adopted as His own those who adhered to Him, in that did He deny as His[1] those who kept aloof from Him. Christ also is wont to do to the utmost that which He enjoins on others. How strange, then, would it certainly[2] have been, if, while he was teaching others not to esteem mother, or father, or brothers, as highly as the word of God, He were Himself to leave the word of God as soon as His mother and brethren were announced to Him! He denied His parents, then, in the sense in which He has taught us to deny ours—for God's work. But there is also another view of the case: in the abjured mother there is a figure of the synagogue, as well as of the Jews in the unbelieving brethren. In their person Israel remained outside, whilst the new disciples who kept close to Christ within, hearing and believing, represented the Church, which He called mother in a preferable sense and a worthier brotherhood, with the repudiation of the carnal relationship. It was in just the same sense, indeed, that He also replied to that exclamation (of a certain woman), not denying His mother's "womb and paps," but designating those as more "blessed who hear the word of God."[3]

CHAP. VIII.—APELLES AND HIS FOLLOWERS, DIS-
PLEASED WITH OUR EARTHLY BODIES, ATTRIB-
UTED TO CHRIST A BODY OF A PURER SORT.
HOW CHRIST WAS HEAVENLY EVEN IN HIS
EARTHLY FLESH.

These passages alone, in which Apelles and Marcion seem to place their chief reliance when interpreted according to the truth of the entire uncorrupted gospel, ought to have been sufficient for proving the human flesh of Christ by a defence of His birth. But since Apelles' precious set[4] lay a very great stress on the shameful condition[5] of the flesh, which they will have to have been furnished with souls tampered with by the fiery author of evil,[6] and so unworthy of Christ; and because they on that account suppose that a sidereal substance is suitable for Him, I am bound to refute them on their own ground. They mention a certain angel of great renown as having created this world of ours, and as having, after

the creation, repented of his work. This indeed we have treated of in a passage by itself; for we have written a little work in opposition to them, *on the question* whether one who had the spirit, and will, and power of Christ for such operations, could have done anything which required repentance, since they describe the *said* angel by the figure of "the lost sheep." The world, then, must be a wrong thing,[7] according to the evidence of its Creator's repentance; for all repentance is the admission of fault, nor has it indeed any existence except through fault. Now, if the world[8] is a fault, as is the body, such must be its parts—faulty too; so in like manner must be the heaven and its celestial (contents), and everything which is conceived and produced out of it. And "a corrupt tree must needs bring forth evil fruit."[9] The flesh of Christ, therefore, if composed of celestial elements, consists of faulty materials, sinful by reason of its sinful origin;[10] so that it must be a part of that substance which they disdain to clothe Christ with, because of its sinfulness, —in other words, our own. Then, as there is no difference in the point of ignominy, let them either devise for Christ some substance of a purer stamp, since they are displeased with our own, or else let them recognise this too, than which even a heavenly substance could not have been better. We read in so many words:[11] "The first man is of the earth, earthy; the second man is the Lord from heaven."[12] This passage, however, has nothing to do with any difference of substance; it only contrasts with the once[13] "earthy" substance of the flesh of the first man, Adam, the "heavenly" substance of the spirit of the second man, Christ. And so entirely does the passage refer the celestial man to the spirit and not to the flesh, that those whom it compares to Him evidently become celestial—by the Spirit, of course—even in this "earthy flesh." Now, since Christ is heavenly even in regard to the flesh, they could not be compared to Him, who are not heavenly in reference to their flesh.[14] If, then, they who become heavenly, as Christ also was, carry about an "earthy" substance of flesh, the conclusion which is affirmed by this fact is, that Christ Himself also was heavenly, but in an "earthy" flesh, even as they are who are put on a level with Him.[15]

---

[1] Abnegavit : "repudiated."
[2] Force of the indicative *quale erat.*
[3] Luke xi. 27, 28. See also our *Anti-Marcion*, p. 292, Edin.
[4] Isti Apelleiaci.
[5] Ignominiam.
[6] Ab igneo illo præside mali : see Tertullian's *de Anima.* xxiii.; *de Resur. Carn.* v. ; *Adv. Omnes Hæres.* vi.

[7] Peccatum.
[8] *Mundus* is here the universe or entire creation.
[9] Matt. vii. 17.
[10] Censu.
[11] Plane.
[12] 1 Cor. xv. 47
[13] Retro.
[14] Secundum carnem.
[15] Ei adæquantur.

CHAP. IX.—CHRIST'S FLESH PERFECTLY NAT-
URAL, LIKE OUR OWN. NONE OF THE SUPER-
NATURAL FEATURES WHICH THE HERETICS
ASCRIBED TO IT DISCOVERABLE, ON A CARE-
FUL VIEW.

We have thus far gone on the principle, that
nothing which is derived from some other
thing, however different it may be from that
from which it is derived, is so different as not to
suggest the source from which it comes. No
material substance is without the witness of
its own original, however great a change into
new properties it may have undergone. There
is this very body of ours, the formation of
which out of the dust of the ground is a truth
which has found its way into Gentile fables;
it certainly testifies its own origin from the two
elements of earth and water,—from the former
by its flesh, from the latter by its blood.
Now, although there is a difference in the appearance of qualities (in other words,that which
proceeds from something else is in development[1] different), yet, after all, what is blood
but red fluid? what is flesh but earth in an
especial[2] form? Consider the respective
qualities,—of the muscles as clods; of the
bones as stones; the mamillary glands as a
kind of pebbles. Look upon the close junc-
tions of the nerves as propagations of roots,
and the branching courses of the veins as
winding rivulets, and the down (which covers
us) as moss, and the hair as grass, and the
very treasures of marrow within our bones as
ores[3] of flesh. All these marks of the earthy
origin were in Christ; and it is they which obscured Him as the Son of God, for He was
looked on as man, for no other reason whatever than because He existed in the corporeal
substance of a man. Or else, show us some
celestial substance in Him purloined from the
Bear, and the Pleiades, and the Hyades.
Well, then, *the characteristics* which we have
enumerated are so many proofs that His was
an earthy flesh, as ours is; but anything new
or anything strange I do not discover. Indeed it was from His words and actions only,
from His teaching and miracles solely, that
men, though amazed, owned Christ to be
man.[4] But if there had been in Him any
new kind of flesh miraculously obtained (from
the stars), it would have been certainly well
known.[5] As the case stood, however, it was
actually the ordinary[6] condition of His terrene flesh which made all things else about
Him wonderful, as when they said, " Whence

hath this man this wisdom and these mighty
works?"[7] Thus spake even they who despised His outward form. His body did not
reach even to human beauty, to say nothing
of heavenly glory.[8] Had the prophets given
us no information whatever concerning His
ignoble appearance, His very sufferings and
the very contumely He endured bespeak it all.
The sufferings attested His human flesh, the
contumely proved its abject condition. Would
any man have dared to touch even with his
little finger, the body *of Christ*, if it had been
of an unusual nature;[9] or to smear His face
with spitting, if it had not invited it[10] (by its
abjectness)? Why talk of a heavenly flesh,
when you have no grounds to offer us for your
celestial theory?[11] Why deny it to be earthy,
when you have the best of reasons for knowing it to be earthy? He hungered under the
devil's *temptation;* He thirsted with the
woman of Samaria; He wept over Lazarus;
He trembles at death (for " the flesh," as He
says, " is weak "[12]); at last, He pours out His
blood. These, I suppose, are celestial marks?
But how, I ask, could He have incurred contempt and suffering in the way I have described, if there had beamed forth in that
flesh of His aught of celestial excellence?
From this, therefore, we have a convincing
proof that in it there was nothing of heaven,
because it must be capable of contempt and
suffering.

CHAP. X.—ANOTHER CLASS OF HERETICS RE-
FUTED. THEY ALLEGED THAT CHRIST'S FLESH
WAS OF A FINER TEXTURE, ANIMALIS, COM-
POSED OF SOUL.

I now turn to another class, who are equally
wise in their own conceit. They affirm that
the flesh of Christ is composed of soul,[13] that
His soul became flesh, so that His flesh is
soul; and as His flesh is of soul, so is His
soul of flesh. But here, again, I must have
some reasons. If, in order to save the soul,
Christ took a soul within Himself, because it
could not be saved except by Him having it
within Himself, I see no reason why, in clothing Himself with flesh, He should have made
that flesh one of soul,[14] as if He could not
have saved the soul in any other way than by
making flesh of it. For while He saves *our*
souls, which are not only not of flesh,[15] but are

---

1 Fit.
2 Sua.
3 Metalla.
4 Christum hominem obstupescebant.
5 Notaretur.
6 Non mira.

7 Matt. xiii. 54.
8 Compare Isa. liii. 2. See also our *Anti-Marcion*, p. 153, Edin.
9 Novum: made of the stars.
10 Merentem.
11 Literally, " why do you suppose it to be celestial."
12 Matt. xxvi. 41.
13 Animalem: " etherialized ; of a finer form, differing from
gross, earthy matter" (Neander).
14 Animalem.
15 Non carneas.

even distinct from flesh, how much more able was He to secure salvation to that soul which He took Himself, when it was also not of flesh? Again, since they assume it as a main tenet,[1] that Christ came forth not to deliver the flesh, but only our soul, how absurd it is, in the first place, that, meaning to save only the soul, He yet made it into just that sort of bodily substance which He had no intention of saving! And, secondly, if He had undertaken to deliver our souls by means of that which He carried, He ought, in that soul which He carried to have carried our *soul*, one (that is) of the same condition as ours; and whatever is the condition of our soul in its secret nature, it is certainly not one of flesh. However, it was not our soul which He saved, if His own was of flesh; for ours is not of flesh. Now, if He did not save our soul on the ground that it was a soul of flesh which He saved, He is nothing to us, because He has not saved our soul. Nor indeed did it need salvation, for it was not our soul really, since it was, on the supposition,[2] a soul of flesh. But yet it is evident that it has been saved. Of flesh, therefore, it was not composed, and it was ours; for it was our *soul* that was saved, since that was in peril *of damnation*. We therefore now conclude that as in Christ the soul was not of flesh, so neither could His flesh have possibly been composed of soul.

CHAP. XI.—THE OPPOSITE EXTRAVAGANCE EXPOSED. THAT IS CHRIST WITH A SOUL COMPOSED OF FLESH—CORPOREAL, THOUGH INVISIBLE. CHRIST'S SOUL, LIKE OURS, DISTINCT FROM FLESH, THOUGH CLOTHED IN IT.

But we meet another argument of theirs, when we raise the question why Christ, in assuming a flesh composed of soul, should seem to have had a soul that was made of flesh? For God, they say, desired to make the soul visible to men, by enduing it with a bodily nature, although it was before invisible; of its own nature, indeed, it was incapable of seeing anything, even its own self, by reason of the obstacle of this flesh, so that it was even a matter of doubt whether it was born or not. The soul, therefore (they further say), was made corporeal in Christ, in order that we might see it when undergoing birth, and death, and (what is more) resurrection. But yet, how was this possible, that by means of the flesh the soul should demonstrate itself[3] to itself or to us, when it could not possibly be ascertained that it would offer this mode of exhibiting itself by the flesh, until the thing came

into existence to which it was unknown,[4] that is to say, the flesh? It received darkness, forsooth, in order to be able to shine! Now,[5] let us first turn our attention to this point, whether it was requisite that the soul should exhibit itself in the manner contended for;[6] and next *consider* whether their previous position be[7] that the soul is wholly invisible—(inquiring further) whether this invisibility is the result of its incorporeality, or whether it actually possesses some sort of body peculiar to itself. And yet, although they say that it is invisible, they determine it to be corporeal, but having somewhat that is invisible. For if it has nothing invisible how can it be said to be invisible? But even its existence is an impossibility, unless it has that which is instrumental to its existence.[8] Since, however, it exists, it must needs have a something through which it exists. If it has this something, *it* must be its body. Everything which exists is a bodily existence *sui generis*. Nothing lacks bodily existence but that which is non-existent. If, then, the soul has an invisible body, He who had proposed to make it[9] visible would certainly have done His work better[10] if He had made that part of it which was accounted invisible, visible; because then there would have been no untruth or weakness in the case, and neither of these flaws is suitable to God. (But as the case stands in the hypothesis) there is *untruth*, since He has set forth the soul as being a different thing from what it really is; and there is *weakness*, since He was unable to make it appear[11] to be that which it is. No one who wishes to exhibit a man covers him with a veil[12] or a mask. This, however, is precisely what has been done to the soul, if it has been clothed with a covering belonging to something else, by being converted into flesh. But even if the soul is, on their hypothesis, supposed[13] to be incorporeal, so that the soul, whatever it is, should by some *mysterious* force of the reason[14] be quite unknown, only not be a body, then in that case it were not beyond the power of God— indeed it would be more consistent with His plan—if He displayed[15] the soul in some new sort of body, different from that which we all have in common, one of which we should have quite a different notion,[16] (being spared

---

[1] Præsumant.
[2] Scilicet.
[3] Demonstraretur: or, "should become apparent."

[4] Cui latebat.
[5] Denique.
[6] Isto modo.
[7] An retro allegent.
[8] Per quod sit.
[9] Eam: the soul.
[10] Dignius: i.e., "in a manner more worthy of Himself."
[11] Demonstrare.
[12] Cassidem.
[13] Deputetur.
[14] Aliqua vi rationis: or, "by some power of its own condition."
[15] Demonstrare.
[16] Notitiæ.

the idea that)[1] He had set His mind on[2] making, without an adequate cause, a visible soul instead of[3] an invisible one—a fit incentive, no doubt, for such questions as they start,[4] by their maintenance of a human flesh for it.[5]   Christ, however, could not have appeared among men except as a man.   Restore, therefore, to Christ His faith; *believe* that He who willed to walk the earth as a man exhibited even a soul of a thoroughly human condition, not making it of flesh, but clothing it with flesh.

CHAP. XII.—THE TRUE FUNCTIONS OF THE SOUL. CHRIST ASSUMED IT IN HIS PERFECT HUMAN NATURE, NOT TO REVEAL AND EXPLAIN IT, BUT TO SAVE IT.   ITS RESURRECTION WITH THE BODY ASSURED BY CHRIST.

Well, now, let it be granted that the soul is made apparent by the flesh,[6] on the assumption that it was evidently necessary[7] that it should be made apparent in some way or other, that is, as being incognizable to itself and to us: there is still an absurd distinction in this *hypothesis*, which implies that we are ourselves separate from our soul, when all that we are is soul.   Indeed,[8] without the soul we are nothing; there is not even the name of a human being, only that of a carcase.   If, then, we are ignorant of the soul, it is in fact the soul that is ignorant of itself.   Thus the only remaining question left for us to look into is, whether the soul was in this matter so ignorant of itself that it became known in any way it could.[9]   The soul, in my opinion,[10] is sensual.[11]   Nothing, therefore, pertaining to the soul is unconnected with sense,[12] nothing pertaining to sense is unconnected with the soul.[13]   And if I may use the expression for the sake of emphasis, I would say, "*Animæ anima sensus est*"—"Sense is the soul's very soul."   Now, since it is the soul that imparts the faculty of perception[14] to all (that have sense), and since it is itself that perceives the very senses, not to say properties, of them all, how is it likely that it did not itself receive sense as its own natural constitution?   Whence is it to know what is necessary for itself under given circumstances, from the very necessity of natural causes, if it knows not its own prop-

erty, and what is necessary for it?   To recognise this indeed is within the competence of every soul; it has, I mean, a practical knowledge of itself, without which knowledge of itself no soul could possibly have exercised its own functions.[15]   I suppose, too, that it is especially suitable that man, the only rational animal, should have been furnished with such a soul as would make him the rational animal, itself being pre-eminently rational.   Now, how can that soul which makes man a rational animal be itself rational if it be itself ignorant of its rationality, being ignorant of its own very self?   So far, however, is it from being ignorant, that it knows its own Author, its own Master, and its own condition.   Before it learns anything about God, it names the name of God.   Before it acquires any knowledge of His judgment, it professes to commend itself to God.   There is nothing one oftener hears of than that there is no hope after death; and yet what imprecations or deprecations does not the soul use according as the man dies after a well or ill spent life!   These reflections are more fully pursued in a short treatise which we have written, "*On the Testimony of the Soul*."[16]   Besides, if the soul was ignorant of itself from the beginning, there is nothing it could[17] have learnt of Christ except its own quality.[18]   It was not its own form that it learnt of Christ, but its salvation.   For this cause did the Son of God descend and take on Him a soul, not that the soul might discover itself in Christ, but Christ in itself.   For its salvation is endangered, not by its being ignorant of itself, but of the word of God.   "The life," says He, "was manifested,"[19] not the soul.   And again, "I am come to save the soul."   He did not say, "to explain"[20] it.   We could not know, of course,[21] that the soul, although an invisible essence, is born and dies, unless it were exhibited corporeally.   We certainly were ignorant that it was to rise again with the flesh.   This is the truth which it will be found was manifested by Christ.   But even this He did not manifest in Himself in a different way than in some Lazarus, whose flesh was no more composed of soul[22] than his soul was of flesh.[23]   What further knowledge, therefore, have we received of the structure[24] of the soul which we were ignorant of before?   What invisible part was there belonging to it which wanted to be made visible by the flesh?

---

[1] Ne.
[2] Gestisset.
[3] Ex.
[4] Istis.
[5] In illam: perhaps "*in it*," as if an ablative case, not an unusual construction in Tertullian.
[6] Ostensa sit.
[7] Si constiterit.
[8] Denique.
[9] Quoquo modo.
[10] Opinor.
[11] Sensualis: endowed with sense.
[12] Nihil animale sine sensu.
[13] Nihil sensuale sine anima.
[14] We should have been glad of a shorter phrase for *sentire* ("to use sense"), had the whole course of the passage permitted it.

[15] Se ministrare.
[16] See especially chap. iv. *supra*.
[17] Debuerat.
[18] Nisi qualis esset.
[19] 1 John i. 2.
[20] Ostendere ; see Luke ix. 56.
[21] Nimirum.
[22] Animalis.
[23] Carnalis.
[24] Dispositione.

CHAP. XIII.—CHRIST'S HUMAN NATURE. THE FLESH AND THE SOUL BOTH FULLY AND UNCONFUSEDLY CONTAINED IN IT.

The soul became flesh that the soul might become visible.[1] Well, then, did the flesh likewise become soul that the flesh might be manifested?[2] If the soul is flesh, it is no longer soul, but flesh. If the flesh is soul, it is no longer flesh, but soul. Where, then, there is flesh, and where there is soul, it has become both one and the other.[3] Now, if they are neither in particular, although they become both one and the other, it is, to say the least, very absurd, that we should understand the soul when we name the flesh, and when we indicate the soul, explain ourselves as meaning the flesh. All things will be in danger of being taken in a sense different from their own proper sense, and, whilst taken in that different sense, of losing their proper one, if they are called by a name which differs from their natural designation. Fidelity in names secures the safe appreciation of properties. When these properties undergo a change, they are considered to possess such qualities as their names indicate. Baked clay, for instance, receives the name of brick.[4] It retains not the name which designated its former state,[5] because it has no longer a share in that state. Therefore, also, the soul of Christ having become flesh,[6] cannot be anything else than that which it has become; nor can it be any longer that which it once was, having become indeed[7] something else. And since we have just had recourse to an illustration, we will put it to further use. Our pitcher, then, which was formed of the clay, is one body, and has one name indicative, of course, of that one body; nor can the pitcher be also called clay, because what it once was, it is no longer. Now that which is no longer (what it was) is also not an inseparable property.[8] And the soul is not an inseparable property. Since, therefore, it has become flesh, the soul is a uniform solid body; it is also a wholly incomplex being,[9] and an indivisible substance. But in Christ we find the soul and the flesh expressed in simple unfigurative[10] terms; that is to say, the soul is called soul, and the flesh, flesh; nowhere is the soul termed flesh, or the flesh, soul; and yet they ought to have been thus (confusedly) named if such had been their condition. *The fact, however, is* that even by *Christ* Himself each substance has been separately mentioned by itself, conformably of course, to the distinction which exists between the properties of both, the soul by itself, and the flesh by itself." "*My soul,*" says He, "*is exceeding sorrowful, even unto death;*"[11] and "*the bread that I will give is my flesh, (which I will give) for the life*[12] *of the world.*"[13] Now, if the soul had been flesh, there would have only been in Christ the soul composed of flesh, or else the flesh composed of soul.[14] Since, however, He keeps the species distinct, the flesh and the soul, He shows them to be two. If two, then they are no longer one; if not one, then the soul is not composed of flesh, nor the flesh of soul. For the soul-flesh, or the flesh-soul, is but one; unless indeed He even had some other soul apart from that which was flesh, and bare about another flesh besides that which was soul. But since He had but one flesh and one soul,—that "soul which was sorrowful, even unto death," and that *flesh which was the* "bread given for the life of the world,"—the number is unimpaired[15] of two substances distinct in kind, thus excludng the unique species of the flesh-comprised soul.

CHAP. XIV.—CHRIST TOOK NOT ON HIM AN ANGELIC NATURE, BUT THE HUMAN. IT WAS MEN, NOT ANGELS, WHOM HE CAME TO SAVE.

But Christ, they say, bare[16] (the nature of) an angel. For what reason? The same which induced Him to become man? Christ, then, was actuated by the motive which led Him to take human nature. Man's salvation was the motive, the restoration of that which had perished. Man had perished; his recovery had become necessary. No such cause, however, existed for Christ's taking on Him the nature of angels. For although there is assigned to angels also perdition in "the fire prepared for the devil and his angels,"[17] yet a restoration is never promised to them. No charge about the salvation of angels did Christ ever receive from the Father; and that which the Father neither promised nor commanded, Christ could not have undertaken. For what object, therefore, did He bear the angelic nature, if it were not (that He might have it) as a powerful helper[18] wherewithal to execute the salvation of man?

---

[1] Ostenderetur: or, "that it might prove itself soul."
[2] Or, "that it might show itself flesh."
[3] Alterutrum: "no matter which."
[4] Testæ: a pitcher, perhaps.
[5] Generis.
[6] Tertullian quotes his opponent's opinion here.
[7] Silicet: in reference to the *alleged* doctrine.
[8] Non adhæret.
[9] Singularitas tota.
[10] Nudis.
[11] Matt. xxvi. 38. Tertullian's quotation is put interrogatively.
[12] "The salvation" (salute) is Tertullian's word.
[13] John vi. 51.
[14] Above, beginning of chap. x.
[15] Salvus.
[16] Gestavit.
[17] Matt. xxv. 41.
[18] Satellitem.

The Son of God, in sooth, was not competent alone to deliver man, whom a solitary and single serpent had overthrown! There is, then, no longer but one God, but one Saviour, if there be two to contrive salvation, and one of them in need of the other. But was it His object indeed to deliver man by an angel? Why, then, come down to do that which He was about to expedite with an angel's help? If by an angel's aid, why *come* Himself also? If He meant to do all by Himself, why have an angel too? He has been, it is true, called "the Angel of great counsel," that is, a messenger, by a term expressive of official function, not of nature. For He had to announce to the world the mighty purpose of the Father, even that which ordained the restoration of man. But He is not on this account to be regarded as an angel, as a Gabriel or a Michael. For the Lord of the vineyard sends even His Son to the labourers to require fruit, as well as His servants. Yet the Son will not therefore be counted as one of the servants because He undertook the office of a servant. I may, then, more easily say, if such an expression is to be hazarded,[1] that the Son is actually an angel, that is, a messenger, from the Father, than that there is an angel in the Son. Forasmuch, however, as it has been declared concerning the Son Himself, Thou hast made Him a little lower than the angels"[2] how will it appear that He put on the nature of angels if He was made lower than the angels, having become man, with flesh and soul as the Son of man? As "the Spirit[3] of God," however, and "the Power of the Highest,"[4] can He be regarded as lower than the angels,—He who is verily God, and the Son of God? Well, but as bearing human nature, He is so far made inferior to the angels; but as bearing angelic nature, He to the same degree loses that inferiority. This opinion will be very suitable for Ebion,[5] who holds Jesus to be a mere man, and nothing more than a descendant of David, and not also the Son of God; although He is, to be sure,[6] in one respect more glorious than the prophets, inasmuch as he declares that there was an angel in Him, just as there was in Zechariah. Only it was never said by Christ, "And the angel, which spake within me, said unto me."[7] Neither, indeed, was ever used by Christ that familiar phrase of all the prophets, "Thus saith the Lord." For He was

Himself the Lord, who openly spake by His own authority, prefacing His words with the formula, "Verily, verily, *I* say unto you." What need is there of further argument? Hear what Isaiah says in emphatic words, "It was no angel, nor deputy, but the Lord Himself who saved them."[8]

CHAP. XV.—THE VALENTINIAN FIGMENT OF CHRIST'S FLESH BEING OF A SPIRITUAL NATURE, EXAMINED AND REFUTED OUT OF SCRIPTURE.

Valentinus, indeed, on the strength of his heretical system, might consistently devise a spiritual flesh for Christ. Any one who refused to believe that that flesh was human might pretend it to be anything he liked, forasmuch as (and this remark is applicable to all *heretics*), if it was not human, and was not born of man, I do not see of what substance Christ Himself spoke when He called Himself man and the Son of man, *saying:* "But now ye seek to kill me, a man that hath told you the truth;"[9] and "The Son of man is Lord of the Sabbath-day."[10] For it is of Him that Isaiah writes: "A man of suffering, and acquainted with the bearing of weakness;"[11] and Jeremiah: "He is a man, and who hath known Him?"[12] and Daniel: "Upon the clouds (He came) as the Son of man."[13] The Apostle Paul likewise says: "The man Christ Jesus is the one Mediator between God and man."[14] Also Peter, in the Acts of the Apostles, speaks of Him as verily human (when he says), "Jesus Christ was a man approved of God among you."[15] These passages alone ought to suffice as a prescriptive[16] testimony in proof that Christ had human flesh derived from man, and not spiritual, and that His flesh was not composed of soul,[17] nor of stellar substance, and that it was not an imaginary flesh; (and no doubt they would be sufficient) if heretics could only divest themselves of all their contentious warmth and artifice. For, as I have read in some writer of Valentinus' wretched faction,[18] they refuse at the outset to believe that a human and earthly substance was created[19] for Christ, lest the Lord should be regarded as inferior to the angels, who are not formed of earthly flesh; whence, too, it would be

---

[1] Si forte.
[2] Ps. viii. 5.
[3] For this designation of the *divine* nature in Christ, see our *Anti-Marcion*, p. 247, note 7, Edin.
[4] Luke i. 35.
[5] Hebioni.
[6] Plane.
[7] Zech. i. 14.

[8] Isa. lxiii. 9.
[9] John viii. 40.
[10] Matt. xii. 8.
[11] Isa. liii. 3, Sept.
[12] Jer. xvii. 9, Sept.
[13] Dan. vii. 13.
[14] 1 Tim. ii. 5.
[15] Acts ii. 22.
[16] Vice præscriptionis.
[17] Animalis.
[18] Factiuncula.
[19] Informatam.

necessary that, if His flesh were like ours, it should be similarly born, not of the Spirit, nor of God, but of the will of man. Why, moreover, should it be born, not of corruptible [seed], but of incorruptible? Why, again, since His flesh has both risen and returned to heaven, is not ours, being like His, also taken up at once? Or else, why does not His flesh, since it is like ours, return in like manner to the ground, and suffer dissolution? Such objections even the heathen used constantly to bandy about.[1] Was the Son of God reduced to such a depth of degradation? Again, if He rose again as a precedent for our hope, how is it that nothing like it has been thought desirable (to happen) to ourselves?[2] Such views are not improper for heathens; and they are fit and natural for the heretics too. For, indeed, what difference is there between them, except it be that the heathen, in not believing, do believe; while the heretics, in believing, do not believe? Then, again, they read: "Thou madest Him a little less than angels;"[3] and they deny the lower nature of that Christ who declares Himself to be, "not a man, but a worm;"[4] who also had "no form nor comeliness, but His form was ignoble, despised more than all men, a man in suffering, and acquainted with the bearing of weakness."[5] Here they discover a human being mingled with a divine one, and so they deny the manhood. They believe that He died, and maintain that a being which has died was born of an incorruptible substance;[6] as if, forsooth, corruptibility[7] were something else than death! But our flesh, too, ought immediately to have risen again. Wait a while. Christ has not yet subdued His enemies, so, as to be able to triumph over them in company with His friends.

CHAP. XVI.—CHRIST'S FLESH IN NATURE, THE SAME AS OURS, ONLY SINLESS. THE DIFFERENCE BETWEEN CARNEM PECCATI AND PECCATUM CARNIS: IT IS THE LATTER WHICH CHRIST ABOLISHED. THE FLESH OF THE FIRST ADAM, NO LESS THAN THAT OF THE SECOND ADAM, NOT RECEIVED FROM HUMAN SEED, ALTHOUGH AS ENTIRELY HUMAN AS OUR OWN, WHICH IS DERIVED FROM IT.

The famous Alexander,[8] too, instigated by his love of disputation in the true fashion of heretical temper, has made himself conspicuous against us; he will have us say that Christ put on flesh of an earthly origin,[9] in order that He might in His own person abolish sinful flesh.[10] Now, even if we did assert this as our opinion, we should be able to defend it in such a way as completely to avoid the extravagant folly which he ascribes to us in making us suppose that the very flesh of Christ was in Himself abolished as being sinful; because we mention our belief (in public),[11] that it is sitting at the right hand of the Father in heaven; and we further declare that it will come again from thence in all the pomp[12] of the Father's glory: it is therefore just as impossible for us to say that it is abolished, as it is for us to maintain that it is sinful, and so made void, since in it there has been no fault. We maintain, moreover, that what has been abolished in Christ is not *carnem peccati*, "sinful flesh," but *peccatum carnis*, "sin in the flesh,"—not the material thing, but its condition;[13] not the substance, but its flaw;[14] and (this we aver) on the authority of the apostle, who says, "He abolished sin in the flesh."[15] Now in another sentence he says that Christ was "in the likeness of sinful flesh,"[16] not, however, as if He had taken on Him "the likeness of the flesh," in the sense of a semblance of body instead of its reality; but he means us to understand likeness to the flesh which sinned,[17] because the flesh of Christ, which committed no sin itself, resembled that which had sinned,—resembled it in its nature, but not in the corruption it received from Adam; whence we also affirm that there was in Christ the same flesh as that whose nature in man is sinful. In the flesh, therefore, *we say* that sin has been abolished, because in Christ that same flesh is maintained without sin, which in man was not maintained without sin. Now, it would not contribute to the purpose of Christ's abolishing sin in the flesh, if He did not abolish it in that flesh in which was the nature of sin, nor (would it conduce) to His glory. For

---

[1] Volutabant: see Lactantius, iv. 22.
[2] De nobis probatum est: or, perhaps, "has been proved to have happened in our own case."
[3] Ps. viii. 6, Sept.
[4] Ps. xxii. 6.
[5] Isa. liii. 3, Sept.
[6] Ex incorruptela.
[7] Corruptela.
[8] Although Tertullian dignifies him with an *ille*, we have no particulars of this man. [It may be that this is an *epithet*, rather than a name, given to some enemy of truth like Alexander the "Coppersmith" (2 Tim. iv. 14) or like that (1 Tim. i. 20), blasphemer, whose character suits the case.]

[9] Census.
[10] So Bp. Kaye renders "*carnem* peccati." [See his valuable note, p. 253.]
[11] We take the *meminerimus* to refer "to the Creed."
[12] Suggestu.
[13] Naturam.
[14] Culpam.
[15] "Tertullian, referring to St. Paul, says of Christ: 'Evacuavit peccatum in carne;' alluding, as I suppose, to Romans viii. 3. But the corresponding Greek in the printed editions is κατέκρινε τὴν ἁμαρτίαν ἐν τῇ σαρκί ('He condemned sin in the flesh'). Had Tertullian a different reading in his Greek MSS., or did he confound Romans viii. 3 with Romans vi. 6, ἵνα καταργηθῇ τὸ σῶμα τῆς ἁμαρτίας ('that the body of sin might be destroyed')? Jerome translates the Greek καταργέω by 'evacuo,' c. xvi. See *Adv. Marcionem*, ver. 14. Dr. Neander has pointed out two passages in which Tertullian has 'damnavit or *damnaverit* delinquentiam in carne.' See *de Res. Carnis.* 46; *de Pudicitiâ.* 17."—Bp. Kaye.
[16] Also in Rom. viii. 3.
[17] Peccatricis carnis.

surely it would have been no strange thing if He had removed the stain of sin in some better flesh, and one which should possess a different, even a sinless, nature! Then, you say, if He took our flesh, Christ's was a sinful one. Do not, however, fetter with mystery a sense which is quite intelligible. For in putting on our flesh, He made it His own; in making it His own, He made it sinless. A word of caution, however, must be addressed to all who refuse to believe that our flesh was in Christ on the ground that it came not of the seed of a human father,[1] let them remember that Adam himself received this flesh of ours without the seed of a human father. As earth was converted into this flesh of ours without the seed of a human father, so also was it quite possible for the Son of God to take to Himself[2] the substance of the self-same flesh, without a human father's agency.[3]

CHAP. XVII.—THE SIMILARITY OF CIRCUMSTAN-CES BETWEEN THE FIRST AND THE SECOND ADAM, AS TO THE DERIVATION OF THEIR FLESH. AN ANALOGY ALSO PLEASANTLY TRACED BETWEEN EVE AND THE VIRGIN MARY.

But, leaving Alexander with his syllogisms, which he so perversely applies in his discussions, as well as with the hymns of Valentinus, which, with consummate assurance, he interpolates as the production of some respectable[4] author, let us confine our inquiry to a single point—Whether Christ received flesh from the virgin?—that we may thus arrive at a certain proof that His flesh was human, if He derived its substance from His mother's womb, although we are at once furnished with clear evidences of the human character of His flesh, from its name and description as that of a man, and from the nature of its constitution, and from the system of its sensations, and from its suffering of death. Now, it will first by necessary to show what previous reason there was for the Son of God's being born of a virgin. He who was going to consecrate a new order of birth, must Himself be born after a novel fashion, concerning which Isaiah foretold how that the Lord Himself would give the sign. What, then, is the sign? " Behold a virgin shall conceive and bear a son."[5] Accordingly, a virgin did conceive and bear " Emmanuel, God with us."[6] This is the new nativity; a man is born in God.

And in this man God was born, taking the flesh of an ancient race, without the help, however, of the ancient seed, in order that He might reform it with a new seed, that is, in a spiritual manner, and cleanse it by the removal of all its ancient stains. But the whole of this new birth was prefigured, as was the case in all other instances, in ancient type, the Lord being born as man by a dispensation in which a virgin was the medium. The earth was still in a virgin state, reduced as yet by no human labour, with no seed as yet cast into its furrows, when, as we are told, God made man out of it into a living soul.[7] As, then, the first Adam is thus introduced to us, it is a just inference that the second Adam likewise, as the apostle has told us, was formed by God into a quickening spirit out of the ground,—in other words, out of a flesh which was unstained as yet by any human generation. But that I may lose no opportunity of supporting my argument from the name of Adam, why is Christ called Adam by the apostle, unless it be that, as man, He was of that earthly origin? And even reason here maintains the same conclusion, because it was by just the contrary[8] operation that God recovered His own image and likeness, of which He had been robbed by the devil. For it was while Eve was yet a virgin, that the ensnaring word had crept into her ear which was to build the edifice of death. Into a virgin's soul, in like manner, must be introduced that Word of God which was to raise the fabric of life; so that what had been reduced to ruin by this sex, might by the selfsame sex be recovered to salvation. As Eve had believed the serpent, so Mary believed the angel.[9] The delinquency which the one occasioned by believing, the other by believing effaced. But (it will be said) Eve did not at the devil's word conceive in her womb. Well, she at all events conceived; for the devil's word afterwards became as seed to her that she should conceive as an outcast, and bring forth in sorrow. Indeed she gave birth to a fratricidal devil; whilst Mary, on the contrary, bare one who was one day to secure salvation to Israel, His own brother after the flesh, and the murderer of Himself. God therefore sent down into the virgin's womb His Word, as the good Brother, who should blot out the memory of the evil brother. Hence it was necessary that Christ should come forth for the salvation of man, in that condition *of flesh* into which man had entered ever since his condemnation.

---

[1] Viri.
[2] Transire in: " to pass into."
[3] Sine coagulo.
[4] Idonei.
[5] Isa. vii. 14.
[6] Matt. i. 23.

[7] Gen. ii. 7.
[8] Æmula.
[9] Literally, " Gabriel."

CHAP. XVIII.—THE MYSTERY OF THE ASSUMP-
TION OF OUR PERFECT HUMAN NATURE BY
THE SECOND PERSON OF THE BLESSED TRINITY.
HE IS HERE CALLED, AS OFTEN ELSEWHERE,
THE SPIRIT.

Now, that we may give a simpler answer, it
was not fit that the Son of God should be
born of a human father's seed, lest, if He were
wholly the Son of a man, He should fail to
be also the Son of God, and have nothing
more than "a Solomon" or "a Jonas,"[1]—as
Ebion[2] thought we ought to believe concerning
Him. In order, therefore, that He who was already the Son of God—of God the Father's
seed, that is to say, the Spirit—might also be the
Son of man, He only wanted to assume flesh,
of the flesh of man[3] without the seed of a
man ;[4] for the seed of a man was unnecessary[5]
for One who had the seed of God. As, then,
before His birth of the virgin, He was able
to have God for His Father without a human
mother, so likewise, after He was born of the
virgin, He was able to have a woman for His
mother without a human father. He is thus
man with God, in short, since He is man's flesh
with God's Spirit[6]—flesh (I say) without seed
from man, Spirit with seed from God. For
as much, then, as the dispensation of God's
purpose[7] concerning His Son required that
He should be born[8] of a virgin, why should
He not have received of the virgin the body
which He bore from the virgin? Because,
(forsooth) it is something else which He took
from God, for "the Word," say they, "was
made flesh."[9] Now this very statement
plainly shows what it was that was made flesh;
nor can it possibly be that[10] anything else than
the Word was made flesh. Now, whether it
was of the flesh that the Word was made flesh,
or whether it was so made of the (divine) seed
itself, the Scripture must tell us. As, however, the Scripture is silent about everything
except what it was that was made (flesh), and
says nothing of that from which it was so
made, it must be held to suggest that from
something else, and not from itself, was the
Word made flesh. And if not from itself, but
from something else, from what can we more
suitably suppose that the Word became flesh
than from that flesh in which it submitted to
the dispensation?[11] And (we have a proof of

the same conclusion in the fact) that the Lord
Himself sententiously and distinctly pronounced, "that which is born of the flesh is
flesh,"[12] even because it is born of the flesh.
But if He here spoke of a human being simply,
and not of Himself, (as you maintain) then
you must deny absolutely that Christ is man,
and must maintain that human nature was not
suitable to Him. And then He adds, "That
which is born of the Spirit is spirit,"[13] because
God is a Spirit, and He was born of God.
Now this description is certainly even more
applicable to Him than it is to those who believe in Him. But if this passage indeed apply to Him, then why does not the preceding
one also? For you cannot divide their relation, and adapt this to Him, and the previous
clause to all other men, especially as you do
not deny that Christ possesses the two substances, both of the flesh and of the Spirit.
Besides, as He was in possession both of flesh
and of Spirit, He cannot possibly, when speaking of the condition of the two substances
which He Himself bears, be supposed to
have determined that the Spirit indeed was
His own, but that the flesh was not His own.
Forasmuch, therefore, as He is of the Spirit
He is God the Spirit, and is born of God;
just as He is also born of the flesh of man,
being generated in the flesh as man.[14]

CHAP. XIX.—CHRIST, AS TO HIS DIVINE NATURE,
AS THE WORD OF GOD, BECAME FLESH, NOT
BY CARNAL CONCEPTION, NOR BY THE WILL
OF THE FLESH AND OF MAN, BUT BY THE
WILL OF GOD. CHRIST'S DIVINE NATURE, OF
ITS OWN ACCORD, DESCENDED INTO THE VIR-
GIN'S WOMB.

What, then, is the meaning of this passage,
"Born[15] not of blood, nor of the will of the
flesh, nor of the will of man, but of God?"[16]
I shall make more use of this passage after
I have confuted those who have tampered
with it. They maintain that it was written
thus (in the plural)[17] "Who were born, not of
blood, nor of the will of the flesh, nor of the
will of man, but of God," as if designating
those who were before mentioned as "believing in His name," in order to point out the
existence of that mysterious seed of the elect
and spiritual which they appropriate to themselves.[18] But how can this be, when all who

[1] Matt. xii. 41, 42.
[2] De Hebionis opinione.
[3] Hominis.
[4] Viri.
[5] Vacabat.
[6] As we have often observed, the term Spiritus is used by Tertullian to express the Divine Nature in Christ. Anti-Marcion,
p. 375, note 13.
[7] Dispositio rationis.
[8] Proferendum.
[9] John i. 14.
[10] Nec periclitatus quasi.
[11] Literally, "in which it became flesh."

[12] John iii. 6.
[13] John iii. 6.
[14] [A very perspicuous statement of the Incarnation is set forth
in this chapter.]
[15] Tertullian reads this in the singular number, "natus est."
[16] John i. 13.
[17] We need not say that the mass of critical authority is against
Tertullian, and with his opponents, in their reading of this passage.
[18] He refers to the Valentinians. See our translation of this
tract against them, chap. xxv., etc., p. 515, supra.

believe in the name of the Lord are, by reason of the common principle of the human race, born of blood, and of the will of the flesh, and of man, as indeed is Valentinus himself? The expression is in the singular number, as referring to the Lord, "He was born of God." And very properly, because Christ is the Word of God, and with the Word the Spirit of God, and by the Spirit the Power of God, and whatsoever else appertains to God. As flesh, however, He is not of blood, nor of the will of the flesh, nor of man, because it was by the will of God that the Word was made flesh. To the flesh, indeed, and not to the Word, accrues the denial of the nativity which is natural to us all as men,[1] because it was as flesh that He had thus to be born, and not as the Word. Now, whilst the passage actually denies that He was born of the will of the flesh, how is it that it did not also deny (that He was born) of the substance of the flesh? For it did not disavow the substance of the flesh when it denied His being "born of blood," but only the matter of the seed, which, as all know, is the warm blood as converted by ebullition[2] into the *coagulum* of the woman's blood. In the cheese, it is from the coagulation that the milky substance acquires that consistency,[3] which is condensed by infusing the rennet.[4] We thus understand that what is denied is the Lord's birth after sexual intercourse (as is suggested by the phrase, "the will of man and of the flesh"), not *His nativity* from a woman's womb. Why, too, is it insisted on with such an accumulation of emphasis that He was not born of blood, nor of the will of the flesh, nor (of the will) of man, if it were not that His flesh was such that no man could have any doubt on the point of its being born from sexual intercourse? Again, although denying His birth from such cohabitation, the passage did not deny that He was born of *real* flesh; it rather affirmed this, by the very fact that it did not deny His birth in the flesh in the same way that it denied His birth from sexual intercourse. Pray, tell me, why the Spirit of God[5] descended into a woman's womb at all, if He did not do so for the purpose of partaking of flesh from the womb. For He could have become *spiritual* flesh[6] without such a process,—much more simply, indeed, without the womb than in it. He had no reason for enclosing Himself within one, if He was to bear forth nothing from it. Not without reason, however, did He descend into a womb. Therefore He received (flesh) therefrom; else, if He received nothing therefrom, His descent into it would have been without a reason, especially if He meant to become flesh of that sort which was not derived from a womb, that is to say, a spiritual one.[7]

CHAP. XX.—CHRIST BORN OF A VIRGIN, OF HER SUBSTANCE. THE PHYSIOLOGICAL FACTS OF HIS REAL AND EXACT BIRTH OF A HUMAN MOTHER, AS SUGGESTED BY CERTAIN PASSAGES OF SCRIPTURE.

But to what shifts you resort, in your attempt to rob the syllable *ex* (*of*)[8] of its proper force as a preposition, and to substitute another for it in a sense not found throughout the Holy Scriptures! You say that He was born *through*[9] a virgin, not *of*[10] a virgin, and *in* a womb, not *of* a womb, because the angel in the dream said to Joseph, "That which is born in her" (not of her) "is of the Holy Ghost."[11] But the fact is, if he had meant "of her," he must have said "in her;" for that which was of her, was also in her. The angel's expression, therefore, "in her," has precisely the same meaning as the phrase "of her." It is, however, a fortunate circumstance that Matthew also, when tracing down the Lord's descent from Abraham to Mary, says, "Jacob begat Joseph the husband of Mary, *of whom* was born Christ."[12] But Paul, too, silences these critics[13] when he says, "God sent forth His Son, made of a woman."[14] Does he mean *through* a woman, or *in* a woman? Nay more, for the sake of greater emphasis, he uses the word "*made*" rather than *born*, although the use of the latter expression would have been simpler. But by saying "*made*," he not only confirmed the statement, "The Word was made flesh,"[15] but he also asserted the reality of the flesh which was made of a virgin We shall have also the support of the Psalms on this point,— not the "Psalms" indeed of Valentinus the apostate, and heretic, and Platonist, but the Psalms of David, the most illustrious saint and well-known prophet. He sings to us of Christ, and through his voice Christ indeed also sang concerning Himself. Hear, then, Christ the Lord speaking to God the Father: "Thou art He that didst draw[16] me out of my

---

[1] Formalis nostræ nativitatis.
[2] Despumatione.
[3] Vis.
[4] Medicando. [This is based on Job x. 10, a favourite passage with the Fathers in expounding the generative process.]
[5] i. e. The Son of God.
[6] Which is all that the heretics assign to Him.

[7] Such as Valentinus ascribed to Him. See above, c. xv. p. 511.
[8] Indicating the *material* or *ingredient*, "out of."
[9] Per.
[10] Ex.
[11] Matt. i. 20.
[12] Matt. i. 16.
[13] Grammaticis.
[14] Gal. iv. 4.
[15] John i. 14.
[16] Avulsisti.

mother's womb."[1] Here is the first point. "Thou art my hope from my mother's breasts; upon Thee have I been cast from the womb."[2] Here is another point. "Thou art my God from my mother's belly."[3] Here is a third point. Now let us carefully attend to the sense of these passages. "Thou didst draw me," He says, "out of the womb." Now what is it which is *drawn*, if it be not that which adheres, that which is firmly fastened to anything from which it is drawn in order to be sundered? If He clave not to the womb, how could He have been drawn from it? If He who clave thereto was drawn from it, how could He have adhered to it, if it were not that, all the while He was in the womb, He was tied to it, as to His origin,[4] by the umbilical cord, which communicated growth to Him from the matrix? Even when one strange matter amalgamates with another, it becomes so entirely incorporated[5] with that with which it amalgamates, that when it is drawn off from it, it carries with it some part of the body from which it is torn, as if in consequence of the severance of the union and growth which the constituent pieces had communicated to each other. But what were His "mother's breasts" which He mentions? No doubt they were those which He sucked. Midwives, and doctors, and naturalists, can tell us, from the nature of women's breasts, whether they usually flow at any other time than when the womb is affected with pregnancy, when the veins convey therefrom the blood of the lower parts[6] to the *mamilla*, and in the act of transference convert the secretion into the nutritious[7] substance of milk. Whence it comes to pass that during the period of lactation the monthly issues are suspended. But if the Word was made flesh of Himself without any communication with a womb, no mother's womb operating upon Him with its usual function and support, how could the lacteal fountain have been conveyed (from the womb) to the breasts, since (the womb) can only effect the change by actual possession *of the proper substance?* But it could not possibly have had blood for transformation into milk, unless it possessed the causes of blood also, that is to say, the severance (by birth)[8] of its own flesh *from the mother's womb.* Now it is easy to see what was the novelty of Christ's being born of a virgin. It was simply this, that (He was born) of a virgin in the real manner which we have indicated, in order that our regeneration might have virginal purity,—spiritually cleansed from all pollutions through Christ, who was Himself a virgin, even in the flesh, in that He was *born* of a virgin's flesh.

CHAP. XXI.—THE WORD OF GOD DID NOT BECOME FLESH EXCEPT IN THE VIRGIN'S WOMB AND OF HER SUBSTANCE. THROUGH HIS MOTHER HE IS DESCENDED FROM HER GREAT ANCESTOR DAVID. HE IS DESCRIBED BOTH IN THE OLD AND IN THE NEW TESTAMENT AS "THE FRUIT OF DAVID'S LOINS."

Whereas, then, they contend that the novelty (of Christ's birth) consisted in this, that as the Word of God became flesh without the seed of a human father, so there should be no flesh of the virgin mother (assisting in the transaction), why should not the novelty rather be confined to this, that His flesh, although not born of seed, should yet have proceeded from flesh? I should like to go more closely into this discussion. "Behold," says he, "a virgin shall conceive in the womb."[9] *Conceive* what? I ask. The Word of God, of course, and not the seed of man, and in order, certainly, to bring forth a son. "For," says he, "she shall bring forth a son."[10] Therefore, as the act of conception was her own,[11] so also what she brought forth was her own, also, although the cause of conception[12] was not. If, on the other hand, the Word became flesh of Himself, then He both conceived and brought forth Himself, and the prophecy is stultified. For in that case a virgin did *not* conceive, and did *not* bring forth; since whatever she brought forth from the conception of the Word, is not her own flesh. But is this the only statement of prophecy which will be frustrated?[13] Will not the angel's announcement also be subverted, that the virgin should "conceive in her womb and bring forth a son?"[14] And will not in fact every scripture which declares that Christ had a mother? For how could she have been His mother, unless He had been in her womb? But then He received nothing from her womb which could make her a mother in whose womb He had been.[15] Such a name as this[16] a strange flesh ought not *to assume.* No flesh can speak of a mother's womb but that which is itself the offspring of that womb; nor can any be the offspring of the said womb if it owe its

1 Ps. xxii. 9.
2 Vers. 9, 10.
3 Ver. 10.
4 i. e. of His flesh.
5 Concarnatus et convisceratus: "united in flesh and internal structure."
6 Sentinam illam inferni sanguinis.
7 Lactiorem.
8 Avulsionem.

9 Isa. vii. 14 ; Matt. i. 23.
10 See the same passages.
11 Ipsius.
12 Quod concepit : or, "what she conceived."
13 Evacuabitur.
14 Luke i. 31.
15 An objection.
16 The rejoinder.

birth solely to itself. Therefore even Elisabeth must be silent although she is carrying in her womb the prophetic babe, which was already conscious of his Lord, and is, moreover, filled with the Holy Ghost.[1] For without reason does she say, "and whence is this to me that the mother of my Lord should come to me?"[2] If it was not as her son, but only as a stranger that Mary carried Jesus in her womb, how is it she says, "Blessed is the fruit of thy womb?[3] What is this fruit of the womb, which received not its germ from the womb, which had not its root in the womb, which belongs not to her whose is the womb, and which is no doubt the real fruit of the womb—even Christ? Now, since He is the blossom of the stem which sprouts from the root of Jesse; since, moreover, the root of Jesse is the family of David, and the stem of the root is Mary descended from David, and the blossom of the stem is Mary's son, who is called Jesus Christ, will not He also be the fruit? For the blossom is the fruit, because through the blossom and from the blossom every product advances from its rudimental condition[4] to perfect fruit. What then? *They* deny to the fruit its blossom, and to the blossom its stem, and to the stem its root; so that the root fails to secure[5] for itself, by means of the stem, that special product which comes from the stem, even the blossom and the fruit; for every step indeed in a genealogy is traced from the latest up to the first, so that it is now a well-known fact that the flesh of Christ is inseparable,[6] not merely from Mary, but also from David through Mary, and from Jesse through David. "This fruit," therefore, "of David's loins," that is to say, of his posterity in the flesh, God swears to him that "He will raise up to sit upon his throne."[7] If "of David's loins," how much rather is He of Mary's loins, by virtue of whom He is in "the loins of David?"

CHAP. XXII.—HOLY SCRIPTURE IN THE NEW TESTAMENT, EVEN IN ITS VERY FIRST VERSE, TESTIFIES TO CHRIST'S TRUE FLESH. IN VIRTUE OF WHICH HE IS INCORPORATED IN THE HUMAN STOCK OF DAVID, AND ABRAHAM, AND ADAM.

They may, then, obliterate the testimony of the devils which proclaimed Jesus the son of David; but whatever unworthiness there be in this testimony, that of the apostles they will never be able to efface. There is, first of all, Matthew, that most faithful chronicler[8] of the Gospel, because the companion of the Lord; for no other reason in the world than to show us clearly the fleshly original[9] of Christ, he thus begins *his Gospel:* "The book of the generation of Jesus Christ, the son of David, the son of Abraham."[10] With a nature issuing from such fountal sources, and an order gradually descending to the birth of Christ, what else have we here described than the very flesh of Abraham and of David conveying itself down, step after step, to the very virgin, and at last introducing Christ,—nay, producing Christ Himself of the virgin? Then, again, there is Paul, who was at once both a disciple, and a master, and a witness of the selfsame Gospel; as an apostle of the same Christ, also, he affirms that Christ "was made of the seed of David, according to the flesh,"[11]—which, therefore, was His own likewise. Christ's flesh, then, is of David's seed. Since He is of the seed of David in consequence of Mary's flesh, He is therefore of Mary's flesh because of the seed of David. In what way so ever you torture the statement, He is either of the flesh of Mary because of the seed of David, or He is of the seed of David because of the flesh of Mary. The whole discussion is terminated by the same apostle, when he declares Christ to be "the seed of Abraham." And if of Abraham, how much more, to be sure, of David, as a more recent *progenitor!* For, unfolding the promised blessing upon all nations in the person[12] of Abraham, "And in thy seed shall all nations of the earth be blessed," he adds, "He saith not, And to seeds, as of many; but as of one, And to thy seed, which is Christ."[13] When we read and believe these things, what sort of flesh ought we, and can we, acknowledge in Christ? Surely none other than Abraham's, since Christ is "the seed of Abraham;" none other than Jesse's, since Christ is the blossom of "the stem of Jesse;" none other than David's, since Christ is "the fruit of David's loins;" none other than Mary's, since Christ came from Mary's womb; and, higher still, none other than Adam's, since Christ is "the second Adam." The consequence, therefore, is that they must either maintain, that those (ancestors) had a spiritual flesh, that so there might be derived to Christ the same condition of substance, or else allow that the flesh of Christ was not a spiritual one, since it is not traced from the origin[14] of a spiritual stock.

---

[1] Luke i. 41.
[2] Ver. 43.
[3] Ver. 42.
[4] Eruditur.
[5] Quominus vindicet.
[6] Adhærere.
[7] Ps. cxxxii. 11 ; also Acts ii. 30.

[8] Commentator.
[9] Originis carnalis : i. e. "origin of the flesh of."
[10] Matt. i. 1.
[11] Rom. i. 3 ; 2 Tim. ii. 8.
[12] In nomine : or, "for the sake of."
[13] Gal. iii. 8, 16.
[14] Censetur.

We acknowledge, however, that the prophetic declaration of Simeon is fulfilled, which he spoke over the recently-born Saviour:[1] "Behold, this *child* is set for the fall and rising again of many in Israel, and for a sign that shall be spoken against."[2] The sign (here meant) is that of the birth of Christ, according to Isaiah: "Therefore the Lord Himself shall give you *a sign:* behold, a virgin shall conceive and bear a son."[3] We discover, then, what the sign is which is to be spoken against—the conception and the parturition of the Virgin Mary, concerning which these sophists[4] say: "She a virgin and yet not a virgin bare, and yet did not bear;" just as if such language, if indeed it must be uttered, would not be more suitable even for ourselves to use! For "she bare," because she produced offspring of her own flesh and "yet she did not bear," since she produced Him not from a husband's seed; she was "a virgin," so far as (abstinence) from a husband went, and "yet not a virgin," as regards her bearing a child. *There is not, however, that parity of reasoning which the heretics affect: in other words* it does not follow that for the reason "she did not bear,"[5] she who was "not a virgin" was "yet a virgin," even because she became a mother without any fruit of her own womb. But with us there is no equivocation, nothing twisted into a double sense.[6] Light is light; and darkness, darkness; yea is yea; and nay, nay; "whatsoever is more than these cometh of evil."[7] She who bare (really) bare; and although she was a virgin when she conceived, she was a wife[8] when she brought forth *her son.* Now, as a wife, she was under the very law of "opening the womb,"[9] wherein it was quite immaterial whether the birth of the male was by virtue of a husband's co-operation or not;[10] it was the same sex[11] that opened her womb. Indeed, hers is the womb on account of which it is written of others also: "Every male that openeth the womb shall be called holy to the Lord."[12] For who is really holy but the Son

of God? Who properly opened the womb but He who opened *a closed one?*[13] But it is marriage which opens the womb in all cases. *The virgin's womb,* therefore, was especially[14] opened, because it was especially closed. Indeed[15] she ought rather to be called not a virgin than a virgin, becoming a mother at a leap, as it were, before she was a wife. And what must be said more on this point? Since it was in this sense that the apostle declared that the Son of God was born not of a virgin, but "of a woman," he in that statement recognised the condition of the "opened womb" which ensues in marriage.[16] We read in Ezekiel of "a heifer[17] which brought forth, and still did not bring forth." Now, see whether it was not in view of your own future contentions about the womb of Mary, that even then the Holy Ghost set His mark upon you in this passage; otherwise[18] He would not, contrary to His usual simplicity of style (in this prophet), have uttered a sentence of such doubtful import, *especially* when Isaiah says, "She shall conceive and bear a son."[19]

CHAP. XXIV.—DIVINE STRICTURES ON VARIOUS
HERETICS DESCRIED IN VARIOUS PASSAGES OF
PROPHETICAL SCRIPTURE. THOSE WHO ASSAIL
THE TRUE DOCTRINE OF THE ONE LORD JESUS
CHRIST, BOTH GOD AND MAN, THUS CON-
DEMNED.

For when Isaiah hurls denunciation against our very heretics, especially in his "Woe to them that call evil good, and put darkness for light,"[20] he of course sets his mark upon those amongst you[21] who preserve not in the words they employ the light of their true significance, (by taking care) that the *soul* should mean only that which is so called, and the *flesh* simply that which is confest to our view and *God* none other than the One who is preached.[22] Having thus Marcion in his prophetic view, he says, "I am God, and there is none else; there is no God beside me."[23] And when in another passage he says, in like manner, "Before me there was no God,"[24] he strikes at those inexplicable genealogies of the Valentinian Æons. Again, there is an answer to Ebion in the Scripture: "Born,[25] not of blood, nor

---

[1] Literally, "Lord."
[2] Luke ii. 34.
[3] Isa. vii. 14.
[4] Academici isti: "this school of theirs."
[5] i. e. "Because she produced not her son from her husband's seed."
[6] Defensionem.
[7] Matt. v. 37.
[8] Nupsit.
[9] Nupsit ipsa patefacti corporis lege.
[10] De vi masculi admissi an emissi.
[11] i. e. "The male."
[12] Ex. xiii. 2 ; Luke ii. 23.

[13] Clausam : i.e. a virgin's.
[14] Magis.
[15] Utique.
[16] Nuptialem passionem.
[17] Epiphanius (*Hær.* xxx. 30) quotes from the apocryphal Ezekiel this passage : Τέξεται ἡ δάμαλις, καὶ ἐροῦσιν—οὐ τέτοκεν. So Clem. Alex. *Stromata*, vii. Oehler.
[18] Ceterum.
[19] Isa. vii. 14.
[20] Isa. v. 20.
[21] Istos.
[22] Prædicatur.
[23] Isa. xlv. 5.
[24] Isa. xlvi. 9.
[25] John i. 13. Tertullian's quotation is, as usual, in the singular, "*natus.*"

of the will of the flesh, nor of the will of man, but of God." In like manner, in the passage, "If even an angel of heaven preach unto you any other gospel than *that which* we *have* preached unto you, let him be anathema," [1] he calls attention to the artful influence of Philumene,[2] the virgin friend of Apelles. Surely he is antichrist who denies that Christ has come in the flesh.[3] By declaring that His flesh is simply and absolutely true, and taken in the plain sense of its own nature, *the Scripture* aims a blow at all who make distinctions in it.[4] In the same way, also, when it defines the very Christ to be but one, it shakes the fancies of those who exhibit a multiform Christ, who make Christ to be one being and Jesus another,—representing one as escaping out of the midst of the crowds, and the other as detained by them; one as appearing on a solitary mountain to three companions, clothed with glory in a cloud, the other as an ordinary man holding intercourse with all,[5] one as magnanimous, but the other as timid; lastly, one as suffering death, the other as risen again, by means of which event they maintain a resurrection of their own also, only in another flesh. Happily, however, He who suffered "will come again from heaven,"[6] and by all shall He be seen, who rose again from the dead. They too who crucified Him shall see and acknowledge Him; that is to say, His very flesh, against which they spent their fury, and without which it would be impossible for Himself either to exist or to be seen; so

that they must blush with shame who affirm that His flesh sits in heaven void of sensation, like a sheath only, Christ being withdrawn from it; as well as those who (maintain) that His flesh and soul are just the same thing,[7] or else that His soul is all that exists,[8] but that His flesh no longer lives.

CHAP. XXV.—CONCLUSION. THIS TREATISE FORMS A PREFACE TO THE OTHER WORK, "ON THE RESURRECTION OF THE FLESH," PROVING THE REALITY OF THE FLESH WHICH WAS TRULY BORN, AND DIED, AND ROSE AGAIN.

Bnt let this suffice on our present subject; for I think that by this time proof enough has been adduced of the flesh in Christ having both been born of the virgin, and being human in its nature. And this discussion alone might have been sufficient, without encountering the isolated opinions which have been raised from different quarters. We have, however, challenged these opinions to the test, both of the arguments which sustain them, and of the Scriptures which are appealed to,—and this we have done *ex abundanti;* so that we have, by showing what the flesh of Christ was, and whence it was derived, also predetermined the question, against all objectors, of what that flesh was not. The resurrection, however, of our own flesh will have to be maintained in another little treatise, and so bring to a close this present one, which serves as a general preface, and which will pave the way *for the approaching subject* now that it is plain what kind of body that was which rose again in Christ.

[1] Gal. i. 8.
[2] Comp. *de Præscr. Hæret.* c. xxx. p. 257, *supra.*
[3] 1 John iv. 3.
[4] Disceptatores ejus.
[5] Ceteris passivum.
[6] Acts i. 11.

[7] Tantundem.
[8] Tantummodo.

ELUCIDATIONS.

I.

(In the body of a dove, cap. iii. p. 523.)

The learned John Scott, in his invaluable work *The Christian Life,*[1] identifies the glory shed upon the Saviour at his baptism, with that mentioned by Ezekiel (Cap. xliii. 2) and adds: "In this same glorious splendor was Christ arrayed first at his Baptism and afterward at his Transfiguration. . . . By the Holy Ghost's descending *like a Dove*, it is not necessary we should understand his descending in the shape or form of a Dove, but that in some glorious form, or appearance, he descended in the same manner as a Dove descends . . . . Came down from above just as a dove with his wings spread forth is observed to do,

[1] I quote the Ed. London, 1739, Vol. V., p. 249.

and lighted upon our Saviour's head.'' I quote this as the opinion of one of the most learned and orthodox of divines, but not as my own, for I cannot reconcile it, as he strives to do, with St. Luke iii. 22. Compare Justin Martyr, vol. i. p. 243, and note 6, this series. Grotius observes, says Dr. Scott, that in the apocryphal *Gospel of the Nazarenes*, it is said that at the Baptism of our Lord "a great light shone round about the place.''

II.

(His mother and His brethren, cap. vii. p. 527.)

It is not possible that the author of this chapter had ever conceived of the Blessed Virgin otherwise than as " Blessed among women,'' indeed, but enjoying no especial prerogative as the mother of our Lord. He speaks of " denying her '' and "putting her away '' after He began His Ministry, as He requires His ministers to do, after His example. How extraordinary this language— " the repudiation of carnal relationship. '' According to our author, never charged with heresy on this point, the high rewards of the holy Mary, in the world to come will be those due to her faith, not to the blessing of " her breasts and of her womb.'' Christ designates those as " more blessed,'' who hear His word and keep it. This the Blessed Virgin did pre-eminently, and herein was her own greater blessedness; that is, (our author shews) her crown of glory depends chiefly, like that of other saints, on her faith and works, not on her mere Maternity.

ON THE RESURRECTION OF THE FLESH.

THE HERETICS AGAINST WHOM THIS WORK IS DIRECTED, WERE THE SAME WHO MAINTAINED THAT THE DEMIURGE, OR THE GOD WHO CREATED THIS WORLD AND GAVE THE MOSAIC DISPENSATION, WAS OPPOSED TO THE SUPREME GOD. HENCE THEY ATTACHED AN IDEA OF INHERENT CORRUPTION AND WORTHLESSNESS TO ALL HIS WORKS —AMONGST THE REST, TO THE FLESH OR BODY OF MAN; AFFIRM-ING THAT IT COULD NOT RISE AGAIN, AND THAT THE SOUL ALONE WAS CAPABLE OF INHERITING IMMORTALITY.[1]

[TRANSLATED BY DR. HOLMES.]

CHAP. I.—THE DOCTRINE OF THE RESURREC-TION OF THE BODY BROUGHT TO LIGHT BY THE GOSPEL. THE FAINTEST GLIMPSES OF SOMETHING LIKE IT OCCASIONALLY MET WITH IN HEATHENISM. INCONSISTENCIES OF PAGAN TEACHING.

THE resurrection of the dead is the Chris-tian's trust.[2] By it we are believers. To the belief of this (article of the faith) truth compels us—that truth which God reveals, but the crowd derides, which supposes that nothing will survive after death. And yet they do honour[3] to their dead, and that too in the most expensive way according to their be-quest, and with the daintiest banquets which the seasons can produce,[4] on the presumption that those whom they declare to be incapable of all perception still retain an appetite.[5] But (let the crowd deride): I on my side must de-ride it still more, especially when it burns up its dead with harshest inhumanity, only to pamper them immediately afterwards with gluttonous satiety, using the selfsame fires to honour them and to insult them. What piety is that which mocks *its victims* with cruelty? Is it sacrifice or insult (which the crowd offers), when it burns its offerings to those it has already burnt?[6] But the wise, too, join with the vulgar crowd in their opinion sometimes. There is nothing after death, according to the school of Epicurus. After death all things come to an end, even death itself, says Seneca to like effect. It is satis-factory, however, that the no less important philosophy of Pythagoras and Empedocles, and the Plantonists, take the contrary view, and declare the soul to be immortal; affirming, morever, in a way which most nearly ap-proaches (to our own doctrine),[7] that the soul actually returns into bodies, although not the same bodies, and not even those of human beings inavariably: thus Euphorbus is sup-posed to have passed into Phythagoras, and Homer into a peacock. They firmly pro-nounced the soul's renewal[8] to be in a body,[9] (deeming it) more tolerable to change the quality (of the corporeal state) than to deny it wholly: they at least knocked at the door of truth, although they entered not. Thus the world, with all its errors, does not ignore the resurrection of the dead.

---

[1] See Bp. Kaye, *On Tertullian*, p. 256. A full examination of the tenets of these Gnostic heretics occurs in our author's *Treatise against Marcion*. An able review of Tertullian's line of thought in this work on the resurrection occurs in Neander's *Antignostikus*, Bohn's translation, ii. 478–486. [There is a decisive ebullition of Montanistic fanaticism in cap. xi., and in the second chapter there is a reference to the *De Carne Christi*. Date this treatise *circa* A.D. 208.]
[2] Fiducia.
[3] Parentant.
[4] Pro temporibus esculentorum.
[5] Etiam desiderar-

[6] Cum crematis cremat.
[7] Adhuc proxime: "Christianæ scilicet doctrinæ." Oehler.
[8] Recidivatum.
[9] Corporalem.

CHAP. II.—THE JEWISH SADDUCEES A LINK BE-
TWEEN THE PAGAN PHILOSOPHERS AND THE
HERETICS ON THIS DOCTRINE. ITS FUNDA-
MENTAL IMPORTANCE ASSERTED. THE SOUL
FARES BETTER THAN THE BODY, IN HERETI-
CAL ESTIMATION, AS TO ITS FUTURE STATE.
ITS EXTINCTION, HOWEVER, WAS HELD BY ONE
LUCAN.

Since there is even within the confines of
God's *Church*[1] a sect which is more nearly
allied to the Epicureans than to the prophets,
an opportunity is afforded us of knowing[2]
what estimate Christ forms of the (said sect,
even the) Sadducees. For to Christ was it
reserved to lay bare everything which before was concealed: to impart certainty to
doubtful points; to accomplish those of which
men had had but a foretaste; to give present
reality to the objects of prophecy; *and* to furnish not only by Himself, but actually in Himself, certain proofs of the resurrection of the
dead. It is, however, against other Sadducees
that we have now to prepare ourselves, but
still partakers of their doctrine. For instance,
they allow a moiety of the resurrection; that
is, simply of the soul, despising the flesh, just
as they also do the Lord of the flesh Himself.
No other persons, indeed, refuse to concede
to the substance of the body its recovery from
death,[3] than the heretical inventors of a second
deity. Driven then, as they are, to give a
different dispensation to Christ, so that He
may not be accounted as belonging to the
Creator, they have achieved their first error
in *the article of* His very flesh; contending
with Marcion and Basilides that it possessed
no reality; or else holding, after the heretical
tenets of Valentinus, and according to Apelles, that it had qualities peculiar to itself.
And so it follows that they shut out from all
recovery from death that substance of which
they say that Christ did not partake, confidently assuming that it furnishes the strongest presumption against the resurrection, since
the flesh is already risen in Christ. Hence it
is that we have ourselves previously issued
our volume *On the flesh of Christ;* in which we
both furnish proofs of its reality,[4] in opposition to the idea of its being a vain phantom;
and claim for it a human nature without any
peculiarity of condition—such a nature as has
marked out Christ to be both man and the
Son of man. For when we prove Him to be
invested with the flesh and in a bodily condition, we at the same time refute heresy, by
establishing the rule that no other being than

the Creator must be believed to be God, since
we show that Christ, in whom God is plainly
discerned, is precisely of such a nature as the
Creator promised that He should be. Being
thus refuted touching God as the Creator, and
Christ as the Redeemer of the flesh, they will
at once be defeated also on the resurrection of
the flesh. No procedure, indeed, can be more
reasonable. And we affirm that controversy
with heretics should in most cases be conducted in this way. For due method requires
that conclusions should always be drawn from
the most important premises, in order that
there be a prior agreement on the essential
point, by means of which the particular question under review may be said to have been
determined. Hence it is that the heretics,
from their conscious weakness, never conduct
discussion in an orderly manner. They are
well aware how hard is their task in insinuating
the existence of a second god, to the disparagement of the Creator of the world, who is
known to all men naturally by the testimony
of His works, who is before all others in the
mysteries[5] *of His being*, and is especially
manifested in the prophets;[6] then, under the
pretence of considering a more urgent inquiry,
namely man's own salvation—a question which
transcends all others in its importance—they
begin with doubts about the resurrection; for
there is greater difficulty in believing the resurrection of the flesh than the oneness of the
Deity. In this way, after they have deprived
the discussion of the advantages of its logical
order, and have embarrassed it with doubtful
insinuations[7] in disparagement of the flesh,
they gradually draw their argument to the reception of a second god after destroying and
changing the very ground of our hopes. For
when once a man is fallen or removed from
the sure hope which he had placed in the
Creator, he is easily led away to the object of
a different hope, whom however of his own
accord he can hardly help suspecting. Now
it is by a discrepancy in the promises that a
difference of gods is insinuated. How many
do we thus see drawn into the net, vanquished
on the resurrection of the flesh, before they
could carry their point on the oneness of the
Deity! In respect, then, of the heretics, we
have shown with what weapons we ought to
meet them. And indeed we have already encountered them in treatises severally directed
against them: on the one only God and His
Christ, in our work against Marcion,[8] on the
Lord's flesh, in our book against the four

---

[1] Apud Deum.
[2] Sciemus.
[3] Salutem.
[4] Eam solidam.

[5] In sacramentis.
[6] In prædicationibus : "in the declarations of the prophets."
[7] Scrupulis.
[8] See books ii. and iii. of our *Anti-Marcion*.

heresies,[1] for the special purpose of opening the way to the present inquiry: so that we have now only to discuss the resurrection of the flesh, (treating it) just as if it were uncertain in regard to ourselves also, that is, in the system of the Creator.[2] Because many persons are uneducated; still more are of faltering faith, and several are weak-minded: these will have to be instructed, directed, strengthened, inasmuch as the very oneness of the Godhead will be defended along with the maintenance of our doctrine.[3] For if the resurrection of the flesh be denied, *that prime article of the faith* is shaken; if it be asserted, that is established. There is no need, I suppose, to treat of the soul's safety; for nearly all the heretics, in whatever way they conceive of it, certainly refrain from denying *that*. We may ignore a certain Lucan,[4] who does not spare even this part of our nature, which he follows Aristotle in reducing to dissolution, and substitutes some other thing in lieu of it. Some third nature it is which, according to him, is to rise again, neither soul nor flesh; in other words, not man, but a bear perhaps—for instance, Lucan himself.[5] Even he[6] has received from us a copious notice in our book on the entire condition of the soul,[7] the especial immortality of which we there maintain, whilst we also both acknowledge the dissolution of the flesh alone, and emphatically assert its restitution. Into the body of that work were collected whatever points we elsewhere had to reserve from the pressure of incidental causes. For as it is my custom to touch some questions but lightly on their first occurrence, so I am obliged also to postpone the consideration of them, until the outline can be filled in with complete detail, and the deferred points be taken up on their own merits.

CHAP. III.—SOME TRUTHS HELD EVEN BY THE HEATHEN. THEY WERE, HOWEVER, MORE OFTEN WRONG BOTH IN RELIGIOUS OPINIONS AND IN MORAL PRACTICE. THE HEATHEN NOT TO BE FOLLOWED IN THEIR IGNORANCE OF THE CHRISTIAN MYSTERY. THE HERETICS PERVERSELY PRONE TO FOLLOW THEM.

One may no doubt be wise in the things of God, even from one's natural powers, but only in witness to the truth, not in maintenance of error; (only) when one acts in accordance with, not in opposition to, the divine dispensation. For some things are known even by nature: the immortality of the soul, for instance, is held by many; the knowledge of our God is possessed by all. I may use, therefore, the opinion of a Plato, when he declares, "Every soul is immortal." I may use also the conscience of a nation, when it attests the God of gods. I may, in like manner, use all the other intelligences of our common nature, when they pronounce God to be a judge. "God sees," (say they); and, "I commend you to God."[8] But when they say, "What has undergone death is dead," and, "Enjoy life whilst you live," and, "After death all things come to an end, even death itself;" then I must remember both that "the heart of man is ashes,"[9] according to the estimate of God, and that the very "wisdom of the world is foolishness," (as the inspired word) pronounces it to be.[10] Then, if even the heretic seek refuge in the depraved thoughts of the vulgar, or the imaginations of the world, I must say to him: Part company with the heathen, O heretic! for although you are all agreed in imagining a God, yet while you do so in the name of Christ, so long as you deem yourself a Christian, you are a different man from a heathen: give him back his own views of things, since he does not himself learn from yours. Why lean upon a blind guide, if you have eyes of your own? Why be clothed by one who is naked, if you have put on Christ? Why use the shield of another, when the apostle gives you armour of your own? It would be better for him to learn from you to acknowledge the resurrection of the flesh, than for you from him to deny it; because if Christians must needs deny it, it would be sufficient if they did so from their own knowledge, without any instruction from the ignorant multitude. He, therefore, will not be a Christian who shall deny this doctrine which is confessed by Christians; denying it, moreover, on grounds which are adopted by a man who is not a Christian. Take away, indeed, from the heretics the wisdom which they share with the heathen, and let them support their inquiries from the Scriptures alone: they will then be unable to keep their ground. For that which commends men's common sense is its very simplicity, and its participation in the same feelings, and its community of opinions; and it is deemed to be all the more trustworthy, inasmuch as its definitive statements are naked and open, and known to all. Divine reason, on the contrary, lies in the very pith and mar-

[1] He means the *De Carne Christi*.
[2] Tanquam penes nos quoque incerta, id est penes Creatorem. This obscure clause is very variously read. One reading, approved by Fr. Junius, has: "Tanquam penes nos incertum, dum sit quoque certum penes Creatorem," *q. d.*, "As a subject full of uncertainty as respects ourselves, although of an opposite character in relation to the Creator;" whatever that may mean.
[3] Hoc latere.
[4] Compare *Adv. Omnes Hæreses*, c. vi.
[5] Varro's words help us to understand this rough joke: "*Ursi Lucana origo*," etc. (*De Ling. Lat.* v. 100.)
[6] Iste: rather his *subject* than his person.
[7] i.e. the *De Anima*.
[8] Compare the *De Test. Anim.* ii., and *De Anim.* xlii.
[9] Isa. xliv. 20.
[10] 1 Cor. i. 20, iii. 19.

row of things, not on the surface, and very often is at variance with appearances.

CHAP. IV.—HEATHENS AND HERETICS ALIKE IN THEIR VILIFICATION OF THE FLESH AND ITS FUNCTIONS. THE ORDINARY CAVILS AGAINST THE FINAL RESTITUTION OF SO WEAK AND IGNOBLE A SUBSTANCE.

Hence it is that heretics start at once from this point,[1] from which they sketch the first draft of their dogmas, and afterwards add the details, being well aware how easily men's minds are caught by its influence, (and actuated) by that community of human sentiment which is so favourable to their designs. Is there anything else that you can hear of from the heretic, as *also* from the heathen, earlier in time or greater in extent? Is not (their burden) from the beginning and everywhere an invective against the flesh—against its origin, against its substance, against the casualties and the invariable end which await it; unclean from its first formation of the dregs of the ground, uncleaner afterwards from the mire of its own seminal transmission; worthless,[2] weak, covered with guilt, laden with misery, full of trouble; and after all this record of its degradation, dropping into its original earth and the appellation of a corpse, and destined to dwindle away even from this[3] loathsome name into none henceforth at all—into the very death of all designation? Now you are a shrewd man, no doubt: will you then persuade *yourself*, that after this flesh has been withdrawn from sight, and touch, and memory, it can never be rehabilitated from corruption to integrity, from a shattered to a solid state, from an empty to a full condition, from nothing at all to something—the devouring fires, and the waters of the sea, and the maws of beasts, and the crops of birds and the stomachs of fishes, and time's own great paunch[4] itself, of course yielding it all up again? Shall the same flesh which has fallen to decay be so expected to recover, as that the lame, and the one-eyed, and the blind, and the leper, and the palsied shall come back again, although there can be no pleasure in returning to their old condition? Or shall they be whole, and so have to fear exposure to such sufferings? What, in that case, (must we say) of the consequences of *resuming* the flesh? Will it again be subject to all its present wants, especially meats and drinks? Shall we have with our lungs to float (in air or water),[5] and

suffer pain in our bowels, and with organs of shame to feel no shame, and with all our limbs to toil and labour? Must there again be ulcers, and wounds, and fever, and gout, and once more the wishing to die? Of course these will be the longings incident on the recovery of the flesh, only the repetition of desires to escape out of it. Well now, we have (stated) all this in very subdued and delicate phrases, as suited to the character of our style; but (would you know) how great a licence of unseemly language these men actually use, you must test them in their conferences, whether they be heathens or heretics.

CHAP. V.—SOME CONSIDERATIONS IN REPLY EULOGISTIC OF THE FLESH. IT WAS CREATED BY GOD. THE BODY OF MAN WAS, IN FACT, PREVIOUS TO HIS SOUL.

Inasmuch as all uneducated men, therefore, still form their opinions after these common-sense views, and as the falterers and the weak-minded have a renewal of their perplexities occasioned by the selfsame views; and as the first battering-ram which is directed against ourselves is that which shatters the condition of the flesh, we must on our side necessarily so manage our defences, as to guard, first of all, the condition of the flesh, their disparagement of it being repulsed by our own eulogy. The heretics, therefore, challenged us to use our rhetoric no less than our philosophy. Respecting, then, this frail and poor, worthless body, which they do not indeed hesitate to call evil, even if it had been the work of angels, as Menander and Marcus are pleased to think, or the formation of some fiery being, equally an angel, as Apelles teaches, it would be quite enough for securing respect for the body, that it had the support and protection of even a secondary deity. The angels, we know, rank next to God. Now, whatever be the supreme God of each heretic, I should not unfairly derive the dignity of the flesh likewise from Him to whom was present the will for its production. For, of course, if He had not willed its production, He would have prohibited it, when He knew it was in progress. It follows, then, that even on their principle the flesh is equally the work of God. There is no work but belongs to Him who has permitted it to exist. It is indeed a happy circumstance, that most of their doctrines, including even the harshest, accord to our God the entire formation of man. How mighty He is, you know full well who believe that He is the only God. Let, then, the flesh begin to give you pleasure, since the Creator thereof is so great. But, you say, even the world is the work of God, and yet "the fashion of this

---

[1] Of the resurrection of the body.
[2] Frivolæ.
[3] Isto.
[4] Gula.
[5] Natandum pulmonibus.

world passeth away,"[1] as the apostle himself testifies; nor must it be predetermined that the world will be restored, simply because it is the work of God. And surely if the universe, after its ruin, is not to be formed again, why should a portion of it be? You are right, if a portion is on an equality with the whole. But we maintain that there is a difference. In the first place, because all things were made by the Word of God, and without Him was nothing made.[2] Now the flesh, too, had its existence from the Word of God, because of the principle,[3] that here should be nothing without that Word. "Let us make man,"[4] said He, before He created him, and added, "with our hand," for the sake of his pre-eminence, that so he might not be compared with the rest of creation.[5] And "God," says (the Scripture), "formed man."[6] There is undoubtedly a great difference in the procedure, springing of course from the nature of the case. For the creatures which were made were inferior to him for whom they were made; and they were made for man, to whom they were aferwards made subject by God. Rightly, therefore, had the creatures which were thus intended for subjection, come forth into being at the bidding and command and sole power of the *divine* voice; whilst man, on the contrary, destined to be their lord, was formed by God Himself, to the intent that he might be able to exercise his mastery, being created by the Master *the Lord Himself*. Remember, too, that man is properly called *flesh*, which had a prior occupation in man's designation: "And God formed man the clay of the ground."[7] He now became man, who was hitherto clay. "And He breathed upon his face the breath of life, and man (that is, the clay) became a living soul; and God placed the man whom He had formed in the garden."[8] So that man was clay at first, and only afterwards *man* entire. I wish to impress this on your attention, with a view to your knowing, that whatever God has at all purposed or promised to man, is due not to the soul simply, but to the flesh also; if not arising out of any community in their origin, yet at all events by the privilege *possessed by the latter* in its name.[9]

CHAP. VI.—NOT THE LOWLINESS OF THE MATERIAL, BUT THE DIGNITY AND SKILL OF THE MAKER, MUST BE REMEMBERED, IN GAUGING THE EXCELLENCE OF THE FLESH. CHRIST PARTOOK OF OUR FLESH.

Let me therefore pursue the subject before me—if I can but succeed in vindicating for the flesh as much as was conferred on it by Him who made it, glorying as it even then was, because that poor paltry material, clay, found its way into the hands of God, whatever these were, happy enough at merely being touched by them. But why *this glorying?* Was it that,[10] without any further labour, the clay had instantly assumed its form at the touch of God? The truth is,[11] a great matter was in progress, out of which the creature under consideration[12] was being fashioned. So often then does it receive honour, as often as it experiences the hands of God, when it is touched by them, and pulled, and drawn out, and moulded into shape. Imagine God wholly employed and absorbed in it—in His hand, His eye, His labour, His purpose, His wisdom, His providence, and above all, in His love, which was dictating the lineaments (of this creature). For, whatever was the form and expression which was then given to the clay (by the Creator) Christ was in His thoughts as one day to become man, because the Word, too, was to be both clay and flesh, even as the earth was then. For so did the Father previously say to the Son: "Let us make man in our own image, after our likeness."[13] And God made man, that is to say, the creature which He moulded and fashioned; after the image of God (in other words, of Christ) did He make him And the Word was God also, who being[14] in the image of God, "thought it not robbery to be equal to God."[15] Thus, that clay which was even then putting on the image of Christ, who was to come in the flesh, was not only the work, but also the pledge and surety, of God. To what purpose is it to bandy about the name *earth*, as that of a sordid and grovelling element, with the view of tarnishing the origin of the flesh, when, even if any other material had been available for forming man, it would be requisite that the dignity of the Maker should be taken into consideration, who even by His selection of His material deemed it, and by His management made it, worthy? The hand of Phidias forms the Olympian Jupiter of ivory; worship is given *to the statue*, and it is no longer regarded as a god *formed* out of a most silly animal, but as the world's supreme Deity—

---

[1] 1 Cor. vii. 31.
[2] John i. 3.
[3] Formam.
[4] Gen. i. 26.
[5] Universitati.
[6] Gen. i. 27.
[7] Limum de terra: Gen. ii. 7.
[8] Gen. ii. 7, 8.
[9] It having just been said that *flesh* was man's prior designation.
[10] Quid enim si.
[11] Adeo.
[1] Ista.
[13] Gen. i. 26.

[14] Constitutus.
[15] Phil. ii. 6.

not because of the bulk of the elephant, but on account of the renown of Phidias. Could not therefore the living God, the true God, purge away by His own operation whatever vileness might have accrued to His material, and heal it of all infirmity? Or must this remain *to show* how much more nobly man could fabricate a god, than God could form a man? Now, although the clay is offensive (for its poorness), it is now something else. What I possess is flesh, not earth, even although of the flesh it is said: "Dust thou art, and unto dust shalt thou return."[1] In these words there is the mention of the origin, not a recalling of the substance. The privilege has been granted *to the flesh* to be nobler than its origin, and to have its happiness aggrandized by the change wrought in it. Now, even gold is earth, because of the earth; but it remains earth no longer after it becomes gold, but is a far different substance, more splendid and more noble, though coming from a source which is comparatively faded and obscure. In like manner, it was quite allowable for God that He should clear the gold of our flesh from all the taints, as you deem them, of its *native* clay, by purging the original substance of its dross.

CHAP. VII.—THE EARTHY MATERIAL OF WHICH FLESH IS CREATED WONDERFULLY IMPROVED BY GOD'S MANIPULATION. BY THE ADDITION OF THE SOUL IN MAN'S CONSTITUTION IT BECAME THE CHIEF WORK IN THE CREATION.

But perhaps the dignity of the flesh may seem to be diminished, because it has not been actually manipulated by the hand of God, as the clay was *at first.* Now, when God handled the clay for the express purpose of the growth of flesh out of it afterwards, it was for the flesh that He took all the trouble. But I want you, moreover, to know at what time and in what manner the flesh flourished into beauty out of *its* clay. For it cannot be, as some will have it, that those "coats of skins"[2] which Adam and Eve put on when they were stripped of paradise, were really themselves the forming of the flesh out of clay,[3] because long before that Adam had already recognised the flesh which was in the woman as the propagation of his own substance ("This is now bone of my bone, and flesh of my flesh"[4]), and the very taking of the woman out of the man was supplemented with flesh; but it ought, I should suppose, to have been made good with clay, if Adam was still clay. The clay, therefore,

was obliterated and absorbed into flesh. When *did this happen?* At the time that man became a living soul by the inbreathing of God—by the breath indeed which was capable of hardening clay into another substance, as into some earthenware, so now into flesh. In the same way the potter, too, has it in his power, by tempering the blast of his fire, to modify his clayey material into a stiffer one, and to mould one form after another more beautiful than the original substance, and now possessing both a kind and name of its own. For although the Scripture says, "Shall the clay say to the potter?"[5] that is, Shall man *contend* with God? although the apostle speaks of "earthen vessels"[6] he refers to man, who was originally clay. And the vessel is the flesh, because *this was made* of clay by the breath of the divine *afflatus;* and it was afterwards clothed with "the coats of skins," that is, with the cutaneous covering which was placed over it. So truly is this the fact, that if you withdraw the skin, you lay bare the flesh. Thus, that which becomes a spoil when stripped off, was a vestment as long as it remained laid over. Hence the apostle, when he call circumcision "'a putting off (or spoliation) of the flesh,'"[7] affirmed the skin to be a coat or tunic. Now this being the case, you have both the clay made glorious by the hand of God, and the flesh more glorious still by His breathing upon it, by virtue of which the flesh not only laid aside its clayey rudiments, but also took on itself the ornaments of the soul. You surely are not more careful about God, that *you* indeed should refuse to mount the gems of Scythia and India and the pearls of the Red Sea in lead, or brass, or iron, or even in silver, but should set them in the most precious and most highly-wrought gold; or, again, that you should provide for your finest wines and most costly unguents the most fitting vessels; or, on the same principle, should find for your swords of finished temper scabbards of equal worth; whilst *God* must consign to some vilest sheath the shadow of His own soul, the breath of His own Spirit, the operation of His own mouth, and by so ignominious a consignment secure, of course, its condemnation. Well, then, has He placed, or rather inserted and commingled, it with the flesh? Yes; and so intimate is the union, that it may be deemed to be uncertain whether the flesh bears about the soul, or the soul the flesh; or whether the flesh acts as *apparitor* to the soul, or the soul to the flesh. It is, however, more credible that the soul has service rendered to

---

[1] Gen. iii. 19. ["*Earth* thou art, *etc.*" in text.]
[2] Gen. iii. 31.
[3] A Valentinian notion.
[4] Gen. ii. 23.

[5] Rom. ix. 20.
[6] 2 Cor. vi. 7.
[7] Col. ii. 11.

it,[1] and has the mastery,[2] as being more proximate in character to God.[3] This circumstance even redounds to the glory of the flesh, inasmuch as it both contains an essence nearest to God's, and renders itself a partaker of (the soul's) actual sovereignty. For what enjoyment of nature is there, what produce of the world, what relish of the elements, which is not imparted to the soul by means of the body? How can it be otherwise? Is it not by its means that *the soul* is supported by the entire apparatus of the senses—the sight, the hearing, the taste, the smell, the touch? Is it not by its means that it has a sprinkling of the divine power, there being nothing which it does not effect by its faculty of speech, even when it is only tacitly indicated? And speech is the result of a fleshly organ. The arts come through the flesh; through the flesh also effect is given to the mind's pursuits and powers; all work, too, and business and offices of life, are accomplished by the flesh; and so utterly are the living acts of the soul the work of the flesh, that for the soul to cease to do living acts, would be nothing else than sundering itself from the flesh. So also the very act of dying is a function of the flesh, even as the process of life is. Now, if all things are subject to the soul through the flesh, their subjection is equally due to the flesh. That which is the means and agent of your enjoyment, must needs be also the partaker and sharer of your enjoyment. So that the flesh, which is accounted the minister and servant of the soul, turns out to be also its associate and co-heir. And if all this in temporal things, why not also in things eternal?

CHAP. VIII.—CHRISTIANITY, BY ITS PROVISION FOR THE FLESH, HAS PUT ON IT THE GREATEST HONOUR. THE PRIVILEGES OF OUR RELIGION IN CLOSEST CONNECTION WITH OUR FLESH. WHICH ALSO BEARS A LARGE SHARE IN THE DUTIES AND SACRIFICES OF RELIGION.

Now such remarks have I wished to advance in defence of the flesh, from a general view of the condition of our human nature. Let us now consider its special relation to Christianity, and see how vast a privilege before God has been conferred on this poor and worthless substance. It would suffice to say, indeed, that there is not a soul that can at all procure salvation, except it believe whilst it is in the flesh, so true is it that the flesh is the very condition on which salvation hinges. And since the soul is, in consequence of its salvation, chosen to the service of God, it is

the flesh which actually renders it capable of such service. The flesh, indeed, is washed, in order that the soul may be cleansed; the flesh is anointed, that the soul may be consecrated; the flesh is signed (with the cross), that the soul too may be fortified; the flesh is shadowed with the imposition of hands, that the soul also may be illuminated by the Spirit; the flesh feeds on the body and blood of Christ, that the soul likewise may fatten on *its* God. They cannot then be separated in their recompense, when they are united in their service. Those sacrifices, moreover, which are acceptable to God—I mean conflicts of the soul, fastings, and abstinences, and the humiliations which are annexed to such duty—it is the flesh which performs again and again[4] to its own especial suffering. Virginity, likewise, and widowhood, and the modest restraint in secret on the marriage-bed, and the one only adoption[5] of it, are fragrant offerings to God paid out of the good services of the flesh. Come, tell me what is your opinion of the flesh, when it has to contend for the name of Christ, dragged out to public view, and exposed to the hatred of all men; when it pines in prisons under the cruellest privation of light, in banishment from the world, amidst squalor, filth, and noisome food, without freedom even in sleep, for it is bound on its very pallet and mangled in its bed of straw; when at length before the public view it is racked by every kind of torture that can be devised, and when finally it is spent beneath its agonies, struggling to render its last turn for Christ by dying for Him—upon His own cross many times, not to say by still more atrocious devices of torment. Most blessed, truly, and most glorious, must be the flesh which can repay its Master Christ so vast a debt, and so completely, that the only obligation remaining due to Him is, that it should cease *by death* to owe Him more—all the more bound *even then in gratitude*, because (for ever) set free.

CHAP. IX.—GOD'S LOVE FOR THE FLESH OF MAN, AS DEVELOPED IN THE GRACE OF CHRIST TOWARDS IT. THE FLESH THE BEST MEANS OF DISPLAYING THE BOUNTY AND POWER OF GOD.

To recapitulate, then: Shall that very flesh, which the Divine Creator formed with His own hands in the image of God; which He animated with His own *afflatus*, after the likeness of His own vital vigour; which He set over all the works of His hand, to dwell amongst, to enjoy, and to rule them; which He clothed with His sacraments and His instructions; whose purity He loves, whose mor-

---

[1] Invehi.
[2] Dominari.
[3] John iv. 24.

[4] Instaurat.
[5] Una notitia ejus = monogamia.

tifications He approves; whose sufferings for Himself He deems precious;—(shall that flesh, I say), so often brought near to God, not rise again? God forbid, God forbid, (I repeat), that He should abandon to everlasting destruction the labour of His own hands, the care of His own thoughts, the receptacle of His own Spirit,[1] the queen of His creation, the inheritor of His own liberality, the priestess of His religion, the champion of His testimony, the sister of His Christ! We know by experience the goodness of God; from His Christ we learn that He is the only God, and the very good. Now, as He requires from us love to our neighbour after love to Himself,[2] so He will Himself do that which He has commanded. He will love the flesh which is, so very closely and in so many ways, His neighbour—(He will love it), although infirm, since His strength is made perfect in weakness;[3] although disordered, since "they that are whole need not the physician, but they that are sick;"[4] although not honourable, since "we bestow more abundant honour upon the less honourable members;"[5] although ruined, since He says, "I am come to save that which was lost;"[6] although sinful, since He says, "I desire rather the salvation of the sinner than his death;"[7] although condemned, for says He, "I shall wound, and also heal."[8] Why reproach the flesh with those conditions which wait for God, which hope in God, which receive honour from God, which He succours? I venture to declare, that if such casualties as these had never befallen the flesh, the bounty, the grace, the mercy, (and indeed) all the beneficent power of God, would have had no opportunity to work.[9]

CHAP. X.—HOLY SCRIPTURE MAGNIFIES THE FLESH, AS TO ITS NATURE AND ITS PROSPECTS.

You hold to the scriptures in which the flesh is disparaged; receive also those in which it is ennobled. You read whatever passage abases it; direct your eyes also to that which elevates it. "All flesh is grass."[10] Well, but Isaiah was not content to say only this; but he also declared, "All flesh shall see the salvation of God."[11] They notice God when He says in Genesis, "My Spirit shall not remain among these men, because they are flesh;"[12] but then

He is also heard saying by Joel, "I will pour out of my Spirit upon all flesh."[13] Even the apostle ought not to be known for any one statement in which he is wont to reproach the flesh. For although he says that "in his flesh dwelleth no good thing;"[14] although he affirms that "they who are in the flesh cannot please God,"[15] because "the flesh lusteth against the Spirit;"[16] yet in these and similar assertions which he makes, it is not the *substance* of the flesh, but its *actions*, which are censured. Moreover, we shall elsewhere[17] take occasion to remark, that no reproaches can fairly be cast upon the flesh, without tending also to the castigation of the soul, which compels the flesh to do its bidding. However, let me meanwhile add that in the same passage Paul "carries about in his body the marks of the Lord Jesus;"[18] he also forbids our body to be profaned, as being "the temple of God;"[19] he makes our bodies "the members of Christ;"[20] and he exhorts us to exalt and "glorify God in our body."[21] If, therefore, the humiliations of the flesh thrust off its resurrection, why shall not its high prerogatives rather avail to bring it about?—since it better suits the character of God to restore to salvation what for a while He rejected, than to surrender to perdition what He once approved.

CHAP. XI.—THE POWER OF GOD FULLY COMPETENT TO EFFECT THE RESURRECTION OF THE FLESH.

Thus far touching my eulogy of the flesh, in opposition to its enemies, who are, notwithstanding, its greatest friends also; for there is nobody who lives so much in accordance with the flesh as they who deny the resurrection of the flesh, inasmuch as they despise all its discipline, while they disbelieve its punishment. It is a shrewd saying which the Paraclete utters concerning these persons by the mouth of the prophetess Prisca: "They are carnal,[22] and yet they hate the flesh." Since, then, the flesh has the best guarantee that could possibly accrue for securing to it the recompense of salvation, ought we not also to consider well the power, and might, and competency[23] of God Himself, whether He be so great as to be able to rebuild and restore the edifice of the flesh, which had become dilapidated and

1 Afflatus.
2 Matt. xxii. 37-40.
3 2 Cor. xii. 9.
4 Luke v. 31.
5 1 Cor. xii. 23.
6 Luke xix. 10.
7 Ezek. xviii. 23.
8 Deut. xxxii. 39.
9 Vacuisset.
10 Isa. xl. 7.
11 Isa. xl. 5.
12 Gen. vi. 3, Sept.

13 Joel iii. 1.
14 Rom. viii. 18.
15 Rom. viii. 8.
16 Gal. v. 17.
17 Below, in ch. xvi.
18 Gal. vi. 17.
19 1 Cor. iii. 16.
20 1 Cor. vi. 15.
21 Ver. 20.
22 Carnes. [To explain the state of mind in which this sentence is written, let the reader kindly turn back to Vol. II. p. 4, the paragraph, "As Eusebius informs us, *etc.*"]
23 Licentiam.

blocked up,[1] and in every possible way dislocated?—whether He has promulgated in the public domains of nature any analogies to convince us of His power in this respect, lest any should happen to be still thirsting for the knowledge of God, when faith in Him must rest on no other basis than the belief that He is able to do all things? You have, no doubt, amongst your philosophers men who maintain that this world is without a beginning or a maker. It is, however, much more true, that nearly all the heresies allow it an origin and a maker, and ascribe its creation to our God. Firmly believe, therefore, that He produced it wholly out of nothing, and then you have found the knowledge of God, by believing that He possesses such mighty power. But some persons are too weak to believe all this at first, owing to their views about Matter. They will rather have it, after the philosophers, that the universe was in the beginning made by God out of underlying matter. Now, even if this opinion could be held in truth, since He must be acknowledged to have produced in His reformation of matter far different substances and far different forms from those which Matter itself possessed, I should maintain, with no less persistence, that He produced these things out of nothing, since they absolutely had no existence at all previous to His production of them. Now, where is the difference between a thing's being produced out of nothing or out of something, if so be that what existed not comes into being, when even to have had no existence is tantamount to having been nothing? The contrary is likewise true; for having once existed amounts to having been something. If, however, there *is* a difference, both alternatives support my position. For if God produced all things whatever out of nothing, He will be able to draw forth from nothing even the flesh which had fallen into nothing; or if He moulded other things out of matter, He will be able to call forth the flesh too from somewhere else, into whatever *abyss* it may have been engulphed. And surely He is most competent to re-create who created, inasmuch as it is a far greater work to have produced than to have reproduced, to have imparted a beginning, than to have maintained a continuance. On this principle, you may be quite sure that the restoration of the flesh is easier than its first formation.

CHAP. XII.—SOME ANALOGIES IN NATURE WHICH CORROBORATE THE RESURRECTION OF THE FLESH.

Consider now those very analogies of the

divine power (to which we have just alluded). Day dies into night, and is buried everywhere in darkness. The glory of the world is obscured in the shadow of death; its entire substance is tarnished with blackness; all things become sordid, silent, stupid; everywhere business ceases, and occupations rest. And so over the loss of the light there is mourning. But yet it again revives, with its own beauty, its own dowry, is own sun, same as ever, whole and entire, over all the world, slaying its own death, night—opening its own sepulchre, the darkness—coming forth the heir to itself, until the night also revives—it, too, accompanied with a retinue of its own. For the stellar rays are rekindled, which had been quenched in the morning glow; the distant groups of the constellations are again brought back to view, which the *day's* temporary interval had removed out of sight. Readorned also are the mirrors of the moon, which her monthly course had worn away. Winters and summers return, as do the springtide and autumn, with their resources, their routines, their fruits. Forasmuch as earth receives its instruction from heaven to clothe the trees which had been stripped, to colour the flowers afresh, to spread the grass again, to reproduce the seed which had been consumed, and not to reproduce them until consumed. Wondrous method! from a defrauder to be a preserver, in order to restore, it takes away; in order to guard, it destroys; that it may make whole, it injures; and that it may enlarge, it first lessens. (This process) indeed, renders back to us richer and fuller blessings than it deprived us of—by a destruction which is profit, by an injury which is advantage, and by a loss which is gain. In a word, I would say, all creation is instinct with renewal. Whatever you may chance upon, has already existed; whatever you have lost, returns again without fail. All things return to their former state, after having gone out of sight; all things begin after they have ended; they come to an end for the very purpose of coming into existence again. Nothing perishes but with a view to salvation. The whole, therefore, of this revolving order of things bears witness to the resurrection of the dead. In His works did God write it, before He wrote it in the Scriptures; He proclaimed it in His mighty deeds earlier than in His inspired words. He first sent Nature to you as a teacher, meaning to send Prophecy also as a supplemental instructor, that, being Nature's disciple, you may more easily believe Prophecy, and without hesitation accept (its testimony) when you come to hear what you have seen already on every side; nor doubt that

[1] Oehler explains "devoratum" by "interceptum."

God, whom you have discovered to be the restorer of all things, is likewise the reviver of the flesh. And surely, as all things rise again for man, for whose use they have been provided—but not for man except for his flesh also—how happens it that (the flesh) itself can perish utterly, because of which and for the service of which nothing comes to nought?

CHAP. XIII.—FROM OUR AUTHOR'S VIEW OF A VERSE IN THE NINETY-SECOND PSALM, THE PHŒNIX IS MADE A SYMBOL OF THE RESURRECTION OF OUR BODIES.

If, however, all nature but faintly figures our resurrection; if creation affords no sign precisely like it, inasmuch as its several phenomena can hardly be said to die so much as to come to an end, nor again be deemed to be reanimated, but only re-formed; then take a most complete and unassailable symbol of our hope, for it shall be an animated being, and subject alike to life and death. I refer to the bird which is peculiar to the East, famous for its singularity, marvellous from its posthumous life, which renews its life in a voluntary death; its dying day is its birthday, for on it it departs and returns; once more a phœnix where just now there was none; once more himself, but just now out of existence; another, yet the same. What can be more express and more significant for our subject; or to what other thing can such a phenomenon bear witness? God even in His own Scripture says: "*The righteous* shall flourish like the phœnix;"[1] that is, shall flourish or revive, from death, from the grave—to teach you to believe that a bodily substance may be recovered even from the fire. Our Lord has declared that we are "better than many sparrows:"[2] well, if not better than many a phœnix too, it were no great thing. But must men die once for all, while birds in Arabia are sure of a resurrection?

CHAP. XIV.—A SUFFICIENT CAUSE FOR THE RESURRECTION OF THE FLESH OCCURS IN THE FUTURE JUDGMENT OF MAN. IT WILL TAKE COGNISANCE OF THE WORKS OF THE BODY NO LESS THAN OF THE SOUL.

Such, then, being the outlines of the divine energies which God has displayed as much in the parables *of nature* as in His spoken word, let us now approach His very edicts and decrees, since this is the division which we mainly adopt in our subject-matter. We began with the dignity of the flesh, whether it were of such a nature that when once destroyed it was capable of being restored. Then we pursued an inquiry touching the power of God, whether it was sufficiently great to be habitually able to confer this restoration on a thing which had been destroyed. Now, if we have proved these two points, I should like you to inquire into the (*question of*) cause, whether it be one of sufficient weight to claim the resurrection of the flesh as necessary and as conformable in every way to reason; because there underlies this demurrer: the flesh may be quite capable of being restored, and the Deity be perfectly able to effect the restoration, but a cause for such recovery must needs pre-exist. Admit then a sufficient one, you who learn of a God who is both supremely good as well as just[3]— supremely good from His own (character), just in consequence of ours. For if man had never sinned, he would simply and solely have known God in His superlative goodness, from the attribute of His nature. But now he experiences Him to be a just God also, from the necessity of a cause; still, however, retaining under this very circumstance His excellent goodness, at the same time that He is also just. For, by both succouring the good and punishing the evil, He displays His justice, and at the same time makes both processes contribute proofs of His goodness, whilst on the one hand He deals vengeance, and on the other dispenses reward. But with Marcion[4] you will have the opportunity of more fully learning whether this be the whole character of God. Meanwhile, so perfect is our (God), that He is rightly Judge, because He is the Lord; rightly the Lord, because the Creator; rightly the Creator, because He is God. Whence it happens that that heretic, whose name I know not, holds that He properly is not a Judge, since He is not Lord; properly not Lord, since He is not the Creator. And so I am at a loss to know how He is God, who is neither the Creator, which God is; nor the Lord, which the Creator is. Inasmuch, then, as it is most suitable for *the great Being who is* God, and Lord, and Creator to summon man to a judgment on this very question, whether he has taken care or not to acknowledge and honour his Lord and Creator, this is just such a judgment as the resurrection shall achieve. The entire cause, then, or rather necessity of the resurrection, will be this, namely, that arrangement of the final judgment which shall be most suitable to God. Now, in effecting this arrangement, you must consider·whether the divine censure superintends a judicial ex-

---

[1] Δίκαιος ὡς φοίνιξ ἀνθήσει, Sept. Ps. xcii. 12,—"like a palm tree" (A. V.). We have here a characteristic way of Tertullian's quoting a scripture which has even the least bearing on his subject. [See Vol. I. (this series) p. 12, and same volume, p. viii.]
[2] Matt. x. 33.

[3] He here refers to Marcion.
[4] He here refers his reader to what he has written against Marcion, especially in his books i. and ii.

amination of the two natures of man—both his soul and his flesh. For that which is a suitable object to be judged, is also a competent one to be raised. Our position is, that the judgment of God must be believed first of all to be plenary, and then absolute, so as to be final, and therefore irrevocable; to be also righteous, not bearing less heavily on any particular part; to be moreover worthy of God, being complete and definite, in keeping with His great patience. Thus it follows that the fulness and perfection of the judgment consists simply in representing the interests of the entire human being. Now, since the entire man consists of the union of the two natures, he must therefore appear in both, as it is right that he should be judged in his entirety; nor, of course, did he pass through life except in his entire state. As therefore he lived, so also must he be judged, because he has to be judged concerning the way in which he lived. For life is the cause of judgment, and it must undergo investigation in as many natures as it possessed when it discharged its vital functions.

CHAP. XV.—AS THE FLESH IS A PARTAKER WITH THE SOUL IN ALL HUMAN CONDUCT, SO WILL IT BE IN THE RECOMPENSE OF ETERNITY.

Come now, let our opponents sever the connection of the flesh with the soul in the affairs of life, that they may be emboldened to sunder it also in the recompense of life. Let them deny their association in acts, that they may be fairly able to deny also their participation in rewards. The flesh ought not to have any share in the sentence, if it had none in the cause of it. Let the soul alone be called back, if it alone went away. But (nothing of the kind ever happened); for the soul alone no more departed from life, than it ran through alone the course from which it departed—I mean this present life. Indeed, the soul alone is so far from conducting (the affairs of) life, that we do not withdraw from community with the flesh even our thoughts, however isolated they be, however unprecipitated into act by means of the flesh; since whatever is done in man's heart is done by the soul in the flesh, and with the flesh, and through the flesh. The Lord Himself, in short, when rebuking our thoughts, includes in His censures this aspect of the flesh, (man's heart), the citadel of the soul: "Why think ye evil in your hearts?"[1] and again: "Whosoever looketh on a woman, to lust after her, hath already committed adultery with her in his heart."[2] So that even the thought, without operation and without effect, is an act of the flesh. But if you allow that the faculty which rules the senses, and which they call *Hegemonikon*,[3] has its sanctuary in the brain, or in the interval between the eyebrows, or wheresoever the philosophers are pleased to locate it, the flesh will still be the thinking place of the soul. The soul is never without the flesh, as long as it is in the flesh. There is nothing which the flesh does not transact in company with the soul, when without it it does not exist. Consider carefully, too, whether the thoughts are not administered by the flesh, since it is through the flesh that they are distinguished and known externally. Let the soul only meditate some design, the face gives the indication—the face being the mirror of all our intentions. They may deny all combination in acts, but they cannot gainsay their co-operation in thoughts. Still they enumerate *the sins* of the flesh; surely, then, for its sinful conduct it must be consigned to punishment. But we, moreover, allege against them *the virtues* of the flesh; surely also for its virtuous conduct it deserves a future reward. Again, as it is the soul which acts and impels us in all we do, so it is the function of the flesh to render obedience. Now we are not permitted to suppose that God is either unjust or idle. Unjust, (however He would be,) were He to exclude from reward *the flesh* which is associated in good works; and idle, were He to exempt it from punishment, when it has been an accomplice in evil deeds: whereas human judgment is deemed to be the more perfect, when it discovers the agents in every deed, and neither spares *the guilty* nor grudges *the virtuous* their full share of either punishment or praise with the principals who employed their services.

CHAP. XVI.—THE HERETICS CALLED THE FLESH "THE VESSEL OF THE SOUL," IN ORDER TO DESTROY THE RESPONSIBILITY OF THE BODY. THEIR CAVIL TURNS UPON THEMSELVES AND SHOWS THE FLESH TO BE A SHARER IN HUMAN ACTIONS.

When, however, we attribute to the soul authority, and to the flesh submission, we must see to it that (our opponents) do not turn our position by another argument, by insisting on so placing the flesh in the service of the soul, that it be not (considered as) its servant, lest they should be compelled, if it were so regarded, to admit its companionship (to the soul). For they would argue that servants and companions possess a discretion in discharging the functions of their respective

---

[1] Matt. ix. 4.
[2] Matt. v. 28.

[3] The leading power.

offices, and a power over their will in both relations: in short, (they would claim to be)
men themselves, and therefore (would expect)
to share the credit with their principals, to
whom they voluntarily yielded their assistance;
whereas the flesh had no discretion, no sentiment in itself, but possessing no power of its
own of willing or refusing, it, in fact, appears
to stand to the soul in the stead of a vessel,
as an instrument rather than a servant. The
soul alone, therefore, will have to be judged
(at the last day) pre-eminently as to how it
has employed the vessel of the flesh; the vessel itself, of course, not being amenable to a
judicial award: for who condemns the cup if
any man has mixed poison in it? or who sentences the sword to the beasts, if a man has
perpetrated with it the atrocities of a brigand?
Well, now, we will grant that the flesh is innocent, in so far as bad actions will not be
charged upon it: what, then, is there to hinder
its being saved on the score of its innocence?
For although it is free from all imputation of
good works, as it is of evil ones, yet it is more
consistent with the divine goodness to deliver
the innocent. A beneficent man, indeed, is
bound to do so: it suits then the character of
the Most Bountiful to bestow even gratuitously
such a favour. And yet, as to the cup, I will
not take the poisoned one, into which some
certain death is injected, but one which has
been infected with the breath of a lascivious
woman,[1] or of Cybele's priest, or of a gladiator, or of a hangman: then I want to know
whether you would pass a milder condemnation on it than on the kisses of such persons?
One indeed which is soiled with our own filth,
or one which is not mingled to our own mind,
we are apt to dash to pieces, and then to increase our anger with our servant. As for the
sword, which is drunk with the blood of the
brigand's victims, who would not banish it
entirely from his house, much more from his
bed-room, or from his pillow, from the presumption that he would be sure to dream of
nothing but the apparitions of the souls which
were pursuing and disquieting him for lying
down with *the blade which shed* their own
blood? Take, however, the cup which has no
reproach on it, and which deserves the credit
of a faithful ministration, it will be adorned
by its drinking-master with chaplets, or be
honoured with a handful of flowers. The
sword also which has received honourable
stains in war, and has been thus engaged in
a better manslaughter, will secure its own
praise by consecration. It is quite possible,
then, to pass decisive sentences even on vessels and on instruments, that so they too may

participate in the merits of their proprietors
and employers. *Thus much do I say* from a
desire to meet even this argument, although
there is a failure in the example, owing to the
diversity in the nature of the objects. For
every vessel or every instrument becomes useful from without, consisting as it does of material perfectly extraneous to the substance
of the human *owner or employer;* whereas the
flesh, being conceived, formed, and generated
along with the soul from its earliest existence
in the womb, is mixed up with it likewise in
all its operations. For although it is called
"a vessel" by the apostle, such as he enjoins
to be treated "with honour,"[2] it is yet designated by the same apostle as "the outward
man,"[3]—that clay, of course, which at the
first was inscribed with the title of. . . a
man, not of a cup or a sword, or any paltry
vessel. Now it is called a "*vessel*" in consideration of its capacity, whereby it receives
and contains the soul; but "*man*," from its
community of nature, which renders it in all
operations a servant and not an instrument.
Accordingly, in the judgment it will be held
to be a servant (even though it may have no
independent discretion of its own), on the
ground of its being an integral portion of that
which possesses such discretion, and is not a
mere chattel. And although the apostle is
well aware that the flesh does nothing of itself
which is not also imputed to the soul, he yet
deems the flesh to be "*sinful;*"[4] lest it
should be supposed to be free from all responsibility by the mere fact of its seeming
to be impelled by the soul. So, again, when
he is ascribing certain praiseworthy actions to
the flesh, he says, "*Therefore* glorify and
exalt God in your body,"[5]—being certain
that such efforts are actuated by the soul; but
still he ascribes them to the flesh, because it
is to it that he also promises the recompense.
Besides, neither rebuke, (on the one hand),
would have been suitable to it, if free from
blame; nor, (on the other hand), would exhortation, if it were incapable of glory. Indeed, both rebuke and exhortation would be
alike idle towards the flesh, if it were an
improper object for that recompence which is
certainly received in the resurrection.

CHAP. XVII.—THE FLESH WILL BE ASSOCIATED
WITH THE SOUL IN ENDURING THE PENAL
SENTENCES OF THE FINAL JUDGMENT.

"Every uneducated[6] person who agrees
with our opinion will be apt to suppose that

---

[1] "Frictricis" is Oehler's reading.

[2] 1 Thess. iv. 4.
[3] 2 Cor. iv. 16.
[4] Rom. viii. 3.
[5] 1 Cor. vi. 20.
[6] Simplicior.

the flesh will have to be present at the *final* judgment even on this account, because otherwise the soul would be incapable of suffering pain or pleasure, as being incorporeal; for this is the common opinion. We on our part, however, do here maintain, and in a special treatise on the subject prove, that the soul is corporeal, possessing a peculiar kind of solidity in its nature, such as enables it both to perceive and suffer. That souls are even now susceptible of torment and of blessing in Hades, though they are disembodied, and notwithstanding their banishment from the flesh, is proved by the case of Lazarus. I have no doubt given to my opponent room to say: Since, then, the soul has a bodily substance of its own, it will be sufficiently endowed with the faculty of suffering and sense, so as not to require the presence of the flesh. No, no, (is my reply): it will still need the flesh; not as being unable to feel anything without the help of the flesh, but because it is necessary that it should possess such a faculty along with the flesh. For in *as* far as it has a sufficiency of its own for action, in *so* far has it likewise a capacity for suffering. But the truth is, in respect of action, it labours under some amount of incapacity; for in its own nature it has simply the ability to think, to will, to desire, to dispose: for fully carrying out the purpose, it looks for the assistance of the flesh. In like manner, it also requires the conjunction of the flesh to endure suffering, in order that by its aid it may be as fully able to suffer, as without its assistance it was not fully able to act. In respect, indeed, of those sins, such as concupiscence, and thought, and wish, which it has a competency of its own to commit, it at once [1] pays the penalty of them. Now, no doubt, if these were alone sufficient to constitute absolute desert without requiring the addition of *acts*, the soul would suffice in itself to encounter the full responsibility of the judgment, being to be judged for those things in the doing of which it alone had possessed a sufficiency. Since, however, acts too are indissolubly attached to deserts; since also acts are ministerially effected by the flesh, it is no longer enough that the soul apart from the flesh be requited with pleasure or pain for what are actually works of the flesh, although it has a body (of its own), although it has members (of its own), which in like manner are insufficient for its full perception, just as they are also for its perfect action. Therefore as it has acted in each several instance, so proportionably does it suffer in Hades, being the first to taste of judgment as it was the first to

induce to the commission of sin; but still it is waiting for the flesh in order that it may through the flesh also compensate for its deeds, inasmuch as it laid upon the flesh the execution of its own thoughts. This, in short, will be the process of that judgment which is postponed to the last great day, in order that by the exhibition of the flesh the entire course of the divine vengeance may be accomplished. Besides, (it is obvious to remark) there would be no delaying to the end of that doom which souls are already tasting in Hades, if it was destined for souls alone.

CHAP. XVIII.—SCRIPTURE PHRASES AND PASSAGES CLEARLY ASSERT "THE RESURRECTION OF THE DEAD." THE FORCE OF THIS VERY PHRASE EXPLAINED AS INDICATING THE PROMINENT PLACE OF THE FLESH IN THE GENERAL RESURRECTION.

Thus far it has been my object by prefatory remarks to lay a foundation for the defence of all the Scriptures which promise a resurrection of the flesh. Now, inasmuch as *this verity* is supported by so many just and reasonable considerations—I mean the dignity of the flesh itself,[2] the power and might of God,[3] the analogous cases in which these are displayed,[4] as well as the good reasons for the judgment, and the need thereof[5]—it will of course be only right and proper that the Scriptures should be understood in the sense suggested by such authoritative considerations, and not after the conceits of the heretics, which arise from infidelity solely, because it is deemed incredible that the flesh should be recovered from death and restored to life; not because (such a restoration) is either unattainable by the flesh itself, or impossible for God to effect, or unsuitable to the *final* judgment. Incredible, no doubt, it might be, if it had not been revealed in the word of God;[6] except that, even if it had not been thus first announced by God, it might have been fairly enough assumed, that the revelation of it had been withheld, simply because so many strong presumptions in its favour had been already furnished. Since, however, (the great fact) is proclaimed in so many inspired passages, that is so far a dissuasive against understanding it in a sense different from that which is attested by such arguments as persuade us to its reception, even irrespective of the testimonies of revelation. Let us see, then, first of all in what title this hope of ours is held out to our view.[7]

---

[1] Interim.

[2] As stated in ch. v.-ix.
[3] See ch. xi.
[4] As stated in ch. xii. and xiii.
[5] See ch. xiv.-xvii.
[6] Divinitus.
[7] Proscripta.

There is, I imagine, one divine edict which is exposed to the gaze of all men: it is "The Resurrection of the Dead."[1] These words are prompt, decisive, clear. I mean to take these very terms, discuss them, and discover to what substance they apply. As to the word *resurrectio*, whenever I hear of its impending over a human being, I am forced to inquire what part of him has been destined to *fall*, since nothing can be expected to rise again, unless it has first been prostrated. It is only the man who is ignorant of the fact that the flesh falls by death, that can fail to discover that it stands erect by means of life. Nature pronounces God's sentence: "Dust thou art, and unto dust shall thou return."[2] Even the man who has not heard the sentence, sees the fact. No death but is the ruin of our limbs. This destiny of the body the Lord also described, when, clothed as He was in its very substance, He said, "Destroy this temple, and in three days I will raise it up again."[3] For He showed to what belongs (the incidents of) being destroyed, thrown down, and kept down —even to that to which it also appertains to be lifted and raised up again; although He was at the same time bearing about with Him " a soul that was trembling even unto death,"[4] but which did not fall through death, because even the Scripture informs us that "He spoke of His body."[5] So that it is the flesh which falls by death; and accordingly it derives its name, *cadaver*, from *cadendo*.[6] The soul, however, has no trace of a *fall* in its designation, as indeed there is no mortality in its condition. Nay it is the soul which communicates its ruin to the body when it is breathed out of it, just as it is also destined to raise it up again from the earth when it shall re-enter it. That cannot fall which by its entrance raises; nor can that droop which by its departure causes ruin. I will go further, and say that the soul does not even fall into sleep along with the body, nor does it with its companion even lie down in repose. For it is agitated in dreams, and disturbed: it might, however, rest, if it lay down; and lie down it certainly would, if it fell. Thus that which does not fall even into the likeness of death, does not succumb to the reality thereof. Passing now to the *other* word *mortuorum*, I wish you to look carefully, and see to what substance it is applicable. Were we to allow, under this head, as is sometimes held by the heretics, that the soul is mortal, so that being mortal it shall at-

tain to a resurrection; this would afford a presumption that the flesh also, being no less mortal, would share in the *same* resurrection. But our present point is to derive from the proper signification of this word an idea of the destiny which it indicates. Now, just as the term *resurrection* is predicated of that which falls—that is, the flesh—so will there be the same application of the word *dead*, because what is called "the resurrection of the dead" indicates the rising again of that which is fallen down. We learn this from the case of Abraham, the father of the faithful, a man who enjoyed close intercourse with God. For when he requested of the sons of Heth a spot to bury Sarah in, he said to them, "Give me the possession of a burying place with you, that I may bury my dead,"[7]—meaning, of course, her flesh; for he could not have desired a place to bury her soul in, even if the soul is to be deemed mortal, and even if it could bear to be described by the word "*dead*." Since, then, this word indicates the body, it follows that when "the resurrection of the dead" is spoken of, it is the rising again of *men's* bodies that is meant.

CHAP. XIX.—THE SOPHISTICAL SENSE PUT BY HERETICS ON THE PHRASE "RESURRECTION OF THE DEAD," AS IF IT MEANT THE MORAL CHANGE OF A NEW LIFE.

Now this consideration of the phrase in question, and its signification—besides maintaining, of course, the true meaning of the important words—must needs contribute to this further result, that whatever obscurity our adversaries throw over the subject under the pretence of figurative and allegorical language, the truth will stand out in clearer light, and out of uncertainties certain and definite rules will be prescribed. For some, when they have alighted on a very usual form of prophetic statement, generally expressed in figure and allegory, though not always, distort into some imaginary sense even the most clearly described doctrine of the resurrection of the dead, alleging that even death itself must be understood in a spiritual sense. They say that that which is commonly supposed to be death is not really so,—namely, the separation of body and soul: it is rather the ignorance of God, by reason of which man is dead to God, and is not less buried in error than he would be in the grave. Wherefore that also must be held to be the resurrection, when a man is reanimated by access to the truth, and having dispersed the death of ignorance, and being endowed with new life

---

[1] Resurrectio Mortuorum.
[2] Gen. iii. 19.
[3] John ii. 19.
[4] Matt. xxvi. 38.
[5] John ii. 21.
[6] "*Corpse from falling.*" This, of course, does not show the connection of the words, like the Latin. [Elucidation I.]

[7] Gen. xxiii. 4.

by God, has burst forth from the sepulchre of the old man, even as the Lord likened the scribes and Pharisees to "whited sepulchres."[1] Whence it follows that they who have by faith attained to the resurrection, are with the Lord after they have once put Him on in their baptism. By such subtlety, then, even in conversation have they often been in the habit of misleading our brethren, as if they held a resurrection of the dead *as well as we*. Woe, say they, to him who has not risen in the present body; for they fear that they might alarm their hearers if they at once denied the resurrection. Secretly, however, in their minds they think this: Woe betide the simpleton who during his present life fails to discover the mysteries of heresy; since this, in their view, is the resurrection. There are, however, a great many also, who, claiming to hold a resurrection after the soul's departure, maintain that going out of the sepulchre means escaping out of the world, since in their view the world is the habitation of the dead—that is, of those who know not God; or they will go so far as to say that it actually means escaping out of the body itself, since they imagine that the body detains the soul, when it is shut up in the death of a worldly life, as in a grave.

CHAP. XX.—FIGURATIVE SENSES HAVE THEIR FOUNDATION IN LITERAL FACT. BESIDES, THE ALLEGORICAL STYLE IS BY NO MEANS THE ONLY ONE FOUND IN THE PROPHETIC SCRIPTURES, AS ALLEGED BY THE HERETICS.

Now, to upset all conceits of this sort, let me dispel at once the preliminary idea on which they rest—their assertion that the prophets make all their announcements in figures of speech. Now, if this were the case, the figures themselves could not possibly have been distinguished, inasmuch as the verities would not have been declared, out of which the figurative language is stretched. And, indeed, if all are figures, where will be that of which they are the figures? How can you hold up a mirror for your face, if the face nowhere exists? But, in truth, all are not figures, but there are also literal statements; nor are all shadows, but there are bodies too: so that we have prophecies about the Lord Himself even, which are clearer than the day. For it was not figuratively that the Virgin conceived in her womb; nor in a trope did she bear Emmanuel, that is, Jesus, God with us.[2] Even granting that He was figuratively to take the power of Damascus and the spoils

of Samaria,[3] still it was literally that He was to "enter into judgment with the elders and princes of the people."[4] For in the person of Pilate "the heathen raged," and in the person of Israel "the people imagined vain things;" "the kings of the earth" in Herod, and the rulers in Annas and Caiaphas, were gathered together against the Lord, and against His anointed."[5] He, again, was "led as a sheep to the slaughter, and as a sheep before the shearer," that is, Herod, "is dumb, so He opened not His mouth."[6] "He gave His back to scourges, and His cheeks to blows, not turning His face even from the shame of spitting."[7] "He was numbered with the transgressors;"[8] "He was pierced in His hands and His feet;"[9] "they cast lots for his raiment"[10] "they gave Him gall, and made Him drink vinegar;"[11] "they shook their heads, and mocked Him;"[12] "He was appraised by the traitor in thirty pieces of silver."[13] What figures of speech does Isaiah here give us? What tropes does David? What allegories does Jeremiah? Not even of His mighty works have they used parabolic language. Or else, were not the eyes of the blind opened? did not the tongue of the dumb recover speech?[14] did not the relaxed hands and palsied knees become strong,[15] and the lame leap as an hart?[16] No doubt we are accustomed also to give a spiritual significance to these statements of prophecy, according to the analogy of the physical diseases which were healed by the Lord; but still they were all fulfilled literally: thus showing that the prophets foretold both senses, except that very many of their words can only be taken in a pure and simple signification, and free from all allegorical obscurity; as when we hear of the downfall of nations and cities, of Tyre and Egypt, and Babylon and Edom, and the navy of Carthage; also when they foretell Israel's own chastisements and pardons, its captivities, restorations, and at last its final dispersion. Who would prefer affixing a metaphorical interpretation to all these events, instead of accepting their literal truth? The realities are involved in the words, just as the words are read in the realities. Thus, then, (we find that) the allegorical style is not used in all

---

[1] Matt. xxiii. 27.
[2] Isa. vii. 14; Matt. i. 23.

[3] Isa. viii. 4.
[4] Isa. iii. 13.
[5] Ps. ii. 1, 2.
[6] Isa. liii. 7.
[7] Isa. l. 6, Sept
[8] Isa. liii. 12.
[9] Ps. xxii. 17.
[10] Ver. 18.
[11] Ps. lxix. 22. Tertullian only briefly gives the sense in two words: et potus amaros.
[12] Ps. xxii. 8.
[13] Zech. xi. 12.
[14] Isa. xxxv. 5.
[15] Ver. 3.
[16] Ver. 6.

parts of the prophetic record, although it occasionally occurs in certain portions of it.

CHAP. XXI.—NO MERE METAPHOR IN THE PHRASE RESURRECTION OF THE DEAD. IN PROPORTION TO THE IMPORTANCE OF ETERNAL TRUTHS, IS THE CLEARNESS OF THEIR SCRIPTURAL ENUNCIATION.

Well, if it occurs occasionally in certain portions of it, you will say, then why not in that phrase,[1] where the resurrection might be spiritually understood? There are several reasons why not. First, what must be the meaning of so many important passages of Holy Scripture, which so obviously attest the resurrection of the body, as to admit not even the appearance of a figurative signification? And, indeed, (since some passages are more obscure than others), it cannot but be right— as we have shown above[2]—that uncertain statements should be determined by certain ones, and obscure ones by such as are clear and plain; else there is fear that, in the conflict of certainties and uncertainties, of explicitness and obscurity, faith may be shattered, truth endangered, and the Divine Being Himself be branded as inconstant. Then arises the improbability that the very mystery on which our trust wholly rests, on which also our instruction entirely depends, should have the appearance of being ambiguously announced and obscurely propounded, inasmuch as the hope of the resurrection, unless it be clearly set forth on the sides both of punishment and reward, would fail to persuade any to embrace a religion like ours, exposed as it is to public detestation and the imputation of hostility to others. There is no certain work where the remuneration is uncertain. There is no real apprehension when the peril is only doubtful. But both the recompense of reward, and the danger of losing it, depend on the issues of the resurrection. Now, if even those purposes of God against cities, and nations, and kings, which are merely temporal, local, and personal in their character, have been proclaimed so clearly in prophecy, how is it to be supposed that those dispensations of His which are eternal, and of universal concern to the human race, should be void of all real light in themselves? The grander they are, the clearer should be their announcement, in order that their superior greatness might be believed. And I apprehend that God cannot possibly have ascribed to Him either envy, or guile, or inconsistency, or artifice, by help of which evil qualities it is

that all schemes of unusual grandeur are litigiously promulgated.

CHAP. XXII.—THE SCRIPTURES FORBID OUR SUPPOSING EITHER THAT THE RESURRECTION IS ALREADY PAST, OR THAT IT TAKES PLACE IMMEDIATELY AT DEATH. OUR HOPES AND PRAYERS POINT TO THE LAST GREAT DAY AS THE PERIOD OF ITS ACCOMPLISHMENT.

We must after all this turn our attention to those scriptures also which forbid our belief in such a resurrection as is held by your *Animalists* (for I will not call them *Spiritualists*),[3] that it is either to be assumed *as taking place* now, as soon as men come to the knowledge of the truth, or else that it is accomplished immediately after their departure from this life. Now, forasmuch as the seasons of our entire hope have been fixed in the Holy Scripture, and since we are not permitted to place the accomplishment thereof, as I apprehend, previous to Christ's coming, our prayers are directed towards[4] the end of this world, to the passing away thereof at the great day of the Lord—of His wrath and vengeance—the last day, which is hidden (from all), and known to none but the Father, although announced beforehand by signs and wonders, and the dissolution of the elements, and the conflicts of nations. I would turn out the words of the prophets, if the Lord Himself had said nothing (except that prophecies were the Lord's own word); but it is more to my purpose that He by His own mouth confirms *their statement*. Being questioned by His disciples when those things were to come to pass which He had just been uttering about the destruction of the temple, He discourses to them first of the order of Jewish events until the overthrow of Jerusalem, and then of such as concerned all nations up to the very end of the world. For after He had declared that "Jerusalem was to be trodden down of the Gentiles, until the times of the Gentiles should be fulfilled,"[5]—meaning, of course, those which were to be chosen of God, and gathered in with the remnant of Israel—He then goes on to proclaim, against this world and dispensation (even as Joel had done, and Daniel, and all the prophets with one consent[6]), that "there should be signs in the sun, and in the moon, and in the stars, distress of nations with perplexity, the sea and the waves roaring, men's hearts failing them for fear, and for looking after those things which are coming on the

---

[1] *Resurrectio Mortuorum*, of which we have been speaking.
[2] See ch. xix.

[3] For the opinions of those Valentinians who held that Christ's flesh was composed of soul or of spirit—a refined, ethereal substance—see Tertullian's *De Carne Christi*, cc. x.–xv.
[4] Suspirant in.
[5] Luke xxi. 24.
[6] Joel iii. 9–15 ; Dan. vii. 13, 14.

earth."[1]　"For," says He, "the powers of heaven shall be shaken; and then shall they see the Son of man coming in the clouds, with power and great glory. And when these things begin to come to pass, then look up, and lift up your heads, for your redemption draweth nigh."[2]　He spake of its "drawing nigh," not of its being present already; and of "those things beginning to come to pass," not of their having happened: because when they have come to pass, then our redemption shall be at hand, which is said to be approaching up to that time, raising and exciting our minds to what is then the proximate harvest of our hope. He immediately annexes a parable of this in "the trees which are tenderly sprouting into a flower-stalk, and then developing the flower, which is the precursor of the fruit."[3]　"So likewise ye," (He adds), "when ye shall see all these things come to pass, know ye that the kingdom of heaven is nigh at hand."[4]　"Watch ye, therefore, *and pray* always, that ye may be accounted worthy to escape all those things, and to stand before the Son of man;"[5] that is, no doubt, at the resurrection, after all these things have been previously transacted. Therefore, although there is a sprouting in the acknowledgment of all this mystery, yet it is only in the actual presence of the Lord that the flower is developed and the fruit borne. Who is it then, that has aroused the Lord, now at God's right hand, so unseasonably and with such severity to "shake terribly" (as Isaiah[6] expresses it ("that earth," which, I suppose, is as yet unshattered? Who has thus early put "Christ's enemies beneath His feet" (to use the language of David?), making Him more hurried than the Father, whilst every crowd in our popular assemblies is still with shouts consigning "the Christians to the lions?"[8] Who has yet beheld Jesus descending from heaven in like manner as the apostles saw Him ascend, according to the appointment of the *two* angels?[9]　Up to the present moment they have not, tribe by tribe, smitten their breasts, looking on Him whom they pierced.[10]　No one has as yet fallen in with Elias;[11] no one has as yet escaped from Antichrist;[12] no one has as yet had to bewail the downfall of Babylon.[13]

And is there now anybody who has risen again, except the heretic? *He*, of course, has already quitted the grave of his own corpse—although he is even now liable to fevers and ulcers; he, too, has already trodden down his enemies—although he has even now to struggle with the powers of the world. And as a matter of course, he is already a king—although he even now owes to Cæsar the things which are Cæsar's.[14]

CHAP. XXIII.—SUNDRY PASSAGES OF ST. PAUL, WHICH SPEAK OF A SPIRITUAL RESURRECTION, COMPATIBLE WITH THE FUTURE RESURRECTION OF THE BODY, WHICH IS EVEN ASSUMED IN THEM.

The apostle indeed teaches, in his Epistle to the Colossians, that we were once dead, alienated, and enemies to the Lord in our minds, whilst we were living in wicked works;[15] that we were then buried with Christ in baptism, and also raised again with Him through the faith of the operation of God, who hath raised Him from the dead.[16]　"And you, (adds he), when ye were dead in sins and the uncircumcision of your flesh, hath He quickened together with Him, having forgiven you all trespasses."[17]　And again: "If ye are dead with Christ from the elements of the world, why, as though living in the world, are ye subject to ordinances?"[18]　Now, since he makes us spiritually dead—in such a way, however, as to allow that we shall one day have to undergo a bodily death,—so, considering indeed that we have been also raised in a like spiritual sense, he equally allows that we shall further have to undergo a bodily resurrection. In so many words[19] he says: "Since ye are risen with Christ, seek those things which are above, where Christ sitteth at the right hand of God. Set your affection on things above, not on things on the earth."[20] Accordingly, it is in our mind that he shows that we rise (with Christ), since it is by this alone that we are as yet able to reach to heavenly objects. These we should not "seek," nor "set our affection on," if we had them already in our possession. He also adds: "For ye are dead"—to your sins, he means, not to yourselves—"and your life is hid with Christ in God."[21]　Now that life is not yet apprehended which is hidden. In like manner John says: "And it doth not yet ap-

---

[1] Luke xxi. 25, 26.
[2] Vers. 26–28.
[3] Luke xxi. 29, 30; Matt. xxiv. 32.
[4] Luke xxi. 31; Matt. xxiv. 33.
[5] Luke xxi. 36.
[6] Isa. ii. 19.
[7] Ps. cx. 1.
[8] Compare *The Apology*, xl.; *De Spect.* xxvii.; *De Exhort. Cast.* xii.
[9] Acts i. 11.
[10] Zech. xii. 10; comp. John xix. 37.
[11] Mal. iv. 5.
[12] 1 John iv. 3.
[13] Rev. xviii. 2.

[14] Matt. xxii. 21.
[15] Col. i. 21.
[16] Col. ii. 12.
[17] Ver. 13.
[18] Ver. 20. The last clause in Tertullian is, "Quomodo sententiam fertis?"
[19] Denique.
[20] Col. iii. 1, 2.
[21] Ver. 3.

pear what we shall be: we know, however, that when He shall be manifest, we shall be like Him."[1] We are far indeed from being already what we know not of; we should, of course, be sure to know it if we were already (like Him). It is therefore the contemplation of our blessed hope even in this life by faith (that he speaks of)—not its presence nor its possession, but only its expectation. Concerning this expectation and hope Paul writes to the Galatians: "For we through the Spirit wait for the hope of righteousness by faith."[2] He says "we wait for it," not we are in possession of it. By the righteousness of God, he means that judgment which we shall have to undergo as the recompense *of our deeds*. It is in expectation of this for himself that the apostle writes to the Philippians: "If by any means," says he, "I might attain to the resurrection of the dead. Not as though I had already attained, or were already perfect."[3] And yet he had believed, and had known all mysteries, as an elect vessel and the *great* teacher of the Gentiles; but for all that he goes on to say: "I, however, follow on, if so be I may apprehend that for which I also am apprehended of Christ."[4] Nay, more: "Brethren,"(he adds), "I count not myself to have apprehended: but this one thing (I do), forgetting those things which are behind, and reaching forth unto those things which are before, I press toward the mark for the prize of blamelessness,[5] whereby I may attain it;" meaning the resurrection from the dead in its proper time. Even as he says to the Galatians: "Let us not be weary in well-doing: for *in due season* we shall reap."[6] Similarly, concerning Onesiphorus, does he also write to Timothy: "The Lord grant unto him that he may find mercy in that day;"[7] unto which day and time he charges Timothy himself "to keep what had been committed to his care, without spot, unrebukable, until the appearing of the Lord Jesus Christ: which in His times He shall show, who is the blessed and only Potentate, the King of kings and Lord of lords,"[8] speaking of (Him as) God It is to these same times that Peter in the Acts refers, when he says: "Repent ye therefore, and be converted, that your sins may be blotted out, when the times of refreshing shall come from the presence of the Lord; and He shall send Jesus Christ, which before was preached

unto you: whom the heaven must receive until the times of restitution of all things, which God hath spoken by the mouth of His holy prophets."[9]

CHAP. XXIV.—OTHER PASSAGES QUOTED FROM ST. PAUL, WHICH CATEGORICALLY ASSERT THE RESURRECTION OF THE FLESH AT THE FINAL JUDGMENT.

The character of these times learn, along with the Thessalonians. For we read: "How ye turned from idols to serve the living and true God, and to wait for His Son from heaven, whom He raised from the dead, even Jesus."[10] And again: "For what is our hope, or joy, or crown of rejoicing? Are not even ye in the presence of our Lord God, Jesus Christ, at His coming?"[11] Likewise: "Before God, even our Father, at the coming of the Lord Jesus Christ, with the whole company of His saints."[12] He teaches them that they must "not sorrow concerning them that are asleep," and at the same time explains to them the times of the resurrection, saying, "For if we believe that Jesus died and rose again, even so them also which sleep in Jesus shall God bring with Him. For this we say unto you by the word of the Lord, that we which are alive and remain unto the coming of our Lord, shall not prevent them that are asleep. For the Lord Himself shall descend from heaven with a shout, with the voice of the archangel, and with the trump of God; and the dead in Christ shall rise first: then we which are alive and remain shall be caught up together with them in the clouds, to meet the Lord in the air; and so shall we be ever with the Lord."[13] What archangel's voice, (I wonder), what trump of God is now heard, except it be, forsooth, in the entertainments of the heretics? For, allowing that the word of the gospel may be called "the trump of God," since it was still calling men, yet they must at that time either be dead as to the body, that they may be able to rise again; and then how are they alive? Or else caught up into the clouds; and how then are they here? "Most miserable," no doubt, as the apostle declared them, are they "who in this life only" shall be found to have hope:[14] they will have to be excluded while they are with premature haste seizing that which is promised after this life; erring concerning the truth, no less than Phygellus and Hermogenes.[15] Hence it is that the Holy Ghost, in His greatness, foresee-

[1] 1 John iii. 2.
[2] Gal. v. 5.
[3] Phil. iii. 11, 12.
[4] Ver. 12.
[5] Vers. 13, 14. In the last clause Tertullian reads τῆς ἀνεγκλήσεως = blamelessness, or purity, instead of τῆς ἄνω κλήσεως ="our high calling."
[6] Gal. vi. 9.
[7] 2 Tim i. 18.
[8] 1 Tim. vi. 14, 15, 20.

[9] Acts iii. 19-21.
[10] 1 Thess. i. 9, 10.
[11] 1 Thess. ii. 19. Some MSS. omit "God."
[12] 1 Thess. iii. 13.
[13] 1 Thess. iv. 13-17.
[14] 1 Cor. xv. 19.
[15] 2 Tim. i. 15.

ing clearly all such interpretations as these, suggests (to the apostle), in this very epistle of his to the Thessalonians, *as follows:* "But of the times and the seasons, brethren, there is no necessity for my writing unto you. For ye yourselves know perfectly, that the day of the Lord cometh as a thief in the night. For when they shall say, 'Peace,' and 'All things are safe,' then sudden destruction shall come upon them."[1] Again, in the second *epistle* he addresses them with even greater earnestness: "Now I beseech you, brethren, by the coming of our Lord Jesus Christ, and by our gathering together unto Him, that ye be not soon shaken in mind, nor be troubled, either by spirit, or by word," that is, *the word* of false prophets, "or by letter," that is, *the letter* of false apostles, "as if from us, as that the day of the Lord is at hand. Let no man deceive you by any means. *For that day shall not come,* unless indeed there first come a falling away," he means indeed of this present empire, "and that man of sin be revealed," that is to say, Antichrist, "the son of perdition, who opposeth and exalteth himself above all that is called God or religion; so that he sitteth in the temple of God, affirming that he is God. Remember ye not, that when I was with you, I used to tell you these things? And now ye know what detaineth, that he might be revealed in his time. For the mystery of iniquity doth already work; only he who now hinders must hinder, until he be taken out of the way."[2] What obstacle is there but the Roman state, the falling away of which, by being scattered into ten kingdoms, shall introduce Antichrist upon (its own ruins)? "And then shall be revealed the wicked one, whom the Lord shall consume with the spirit of His mouth, and shall destroy with the brightness of His coming: *even him* whose coming is after the working of Satan, with all power, and signs, and lying wonders, and with all deceivableness of unrighteousness in them that perish."[3]

CHAP. XXV.—ST. JOHN, IN THE APOCALYPSE, EQUALLY EXPLICIT IN ASSERTING THE SAME GREAT DOCTRINE.

In the Revelation of John, again, the order of these times is spread out to view, which "the souls of the martyrs" are taught to wait for beneath the altar, whilst they earnestly pray to be avenged and judged:[4] (taught, I say, to wait), in order that the world may first drink to the dregs the plagues that await it out of the vials of the angels,[5] and that the city of fornication may receive from the ten kings its deserved doom,[6] and that the beast Antichrist with his false prophet may wage war on the Church of God; and that, after the casting of the devil into the bottomless pit for a while,[7] the blessed prerogative of the first resurrection may be ordained from the thrones;[8] and then again, after the consignment of him to the fire, that the judgment of the final and universal resurrection may be determined out of the books.[9] Since, then, the Scriptures both indicate the stages of the last times, and concentrate the harvest of the Christian hope in the very end of the world, it is evident, either that all which God promises to us receives its accomplishment then, and thus what the heretics pretend about a resurrection here falls to the ground; or else, even allowing that a confession of the mystery (of divine truth) is a resurrection, that there is, without any detriment to this view, room for believing in that which is announced for the end. It moreover follows, that the very maintenance of this spiritual resurrection amounts to a presumption in favour of the other bodily resurrection; for if none were announced for that time, there would be fair ground for asserting only this purely spiritual resurrection. Inasmuch, however, as (a resurrection) is proclaimed for the last time, it is proved to be a bodily one, because there is no spiritual one also then announced. For why make a second announcement of a resurrection of only one character, that is, the spiritual one, since this ought to be undergoing accomplishment either now, without any regard to different times, or else then, at the very conclusion of all the periods? It is therefore more competent for us even to maintain a spiritual resurrection a the commencement of *a life of* faith, who acknowledge the full completion thereof at the end of the world

CHAP. XXVI.—EVEN THE METAPHORICAL DESCRIPTIONS OF THIS SUBJECT IN THE SCRIPTURES POINT TO THE BODILY RESURRECTION, THE ONLY SENSE WHICH SECURES THEIR CONSISTENCY AND DIGNITY.

To a preceding objection, that the Scriptures are allegorical, I have still one answer to make —that it is open to us also to defend the bodily character of the resurrection by means of the language of the prophets, which is equally figurative. For consider that primeval sentence which God spake when He called man *earth;* saying, "Earth thou art, and to earth shalt thou return."[10] In respect, of course,

---

[1] 1 Thess. v. 1-3.
[2] 2 Thess. ii. 1-7.
[3] 2 Thess. ii. 8-10.
[4] Rev. vi. 9, 10.
[5] Rev. xvi.

[6] Rev. xviii.
[7] Rev. xx. 2.
[8] Vers. 4-6.
[9] Vers. 12-14.
[10] Gen. iii. 19.

to his fleshly substance, which had been taken out of the ground, and which was the first to receive the name of man, as we have already shown,[1] does not this passage give one instruction to interpret in relation to the *flesh* also whatever of wrath or of grace God has determined for the earth, because, strictly speaking, the earth is not exposed to His judgment, since it has never done any good or evil? "Cursed," no doubt, it was, for it drank the blood *of man;*[2] but even this was as a figure of homicidal flesh. For if the earth has to suffer either joy or injury, it is simply on man's account, that *he* may suffer the joy or the sorrow through the events which happen to his dwelling-place, whereby he will rather have to pay the penalty which, simply on his account, even the earth must suffer. When, therefore, God even threatens the earth, I would prefer saying that He threatens the flesh: so likewise, when He makes a promise to the earth, I would rather understand Him as promising the flesh; as in that passage of David: "The Lord is King, let the earth be glad,"[3]—meaning the flesh of the saints, to which appertains the enjoyment of the kingdom of God. Then he afterwards says: "The earth saw and trembled; the mountains melted like wax at the presence of the Lord,"—meaning, no doubt the flesh of the wicked; and (in a similar sense) it is written: "For they shall look on Him whom they pierced."[4] If indeed it will be thought that both these passages were pronounced simply of the element earth, how can it be consistent that it should shake and melt at the presence of the Lord, at whose royal dignity it before exulted? So again in Isaiah, "Ye shall eat the good of the land,"[5] the expression means the blessings which await the flesh when in the kingdom of God it shall be renewed, and made like the angels, and waiting to obtain the things "which neither eye hath seen, nor ear heard, and which have not entered into the heart of man."[6] Otherwise, how vain that God should invite men to obedience by the fruits of the field and the elements of this life, when He dispenses these to even irreligious men and blasphemers; on a general condition once for all made to man, "sending rain on the good and on the evil, and making His sun to shine on the just and on the unjust!"[7] Happy, no doubt, is faith, if it is to obtain gifts which the enemies of God and Christ not only use, but even abuse,

"worshipping the creature itself in opposition to the Creator!"[8] You will reckon, (I suppose) onions and truffles among earth's bounties, since the Lord declares that "man shall not live on bread alone!"[9] In this way the Jews lose heavenly blessings, by confining their hopes to earthly ones, being ignorant of the promise of heavenly bread, and of the oil of God's unction, and the wine of the Spirit, and of that water of life which has its vigour from the vine of Christ. On exactly the same principle, they consider the special soil of Judæa to be that very holy land, which ought rather to be interpreted of the Lord's flesh, which, in all those who put on Christ, is thenceforward the holy land; holy indeed by the indwelling of the Holy Ghost, truly flowing with milk and honey by the sweetness of His assurance, truly Judæan by reason of the friendship of God. For "he is not a Jew which is one outwardly, but he who is one inwardly."[10] In the same way it is that both God's temple and Jerusalem (must be understood) when it is said by Isaiah: "Awake, awake, O Jerusalem! put on the strength of thine arm; awake, as in thine earliest time,"[11] that is to say, in that innocence which preceded the fall into sin. For how can words of this kind of exhortation and invitation be suitable for that Jerusalem which killed the prophets, and stoned those that were sent to them, and at last crucified its very Lord? Neither indeed is salvation promised to any one land at all, which must needs pass away with the fashion of the whole world. Even if anybody should venture strongly to contend that paradise is the holy land, which it may be possible to designate as the land of our first parents Adam and Eve, it will even then follow that the restoration of paradise will seem to be promised to the flesh, whose lot it was to inhabit and keep it, in order that man may be recalled thereto just such as he was driven from it.

CHAP. XXVII.—CERTAIN METAPHORICAL TERMS EXPLAINED OF THE RESURRECTION OF THE FLESH.

We have also in the Scriptures *robes* mentioned as allegorizing the hope of the flesh. Thus in the Revelation of John it is said: "These are they which have not defiled their clothes with women,"[12]—indicating, of course, virgins, and such as have become "eunuchs for the kingdom of heaven's sake."[13] Therefore they shall be "clothed in white rai-

---

[1] See above, ch. v.
[2] Gen. iv. 11.
[3] Ps. xcvii. 1.
[4] Zech. xii. 10.
[5] Isa. i. 19.
[6] 1 Cor. ii. 9.
[7] Matt. v. 45.

[8] Rom. i. 25.
[9] Matt. iv. 4.
[10] Rom. ii. 28, 29.
[11] Isa. li. 9, Sept.
[12] Rev. iii. 4 and xiv. 4.
[13] Matt. xix. 12.

ment," [1] that is, in the bright beauty of the unwedded flesh. In the gospel even, "the wedding garment" may be regarded as the sanctity of the flesh. [2] And so, when Isaiah tells us what sort of "fast the Lord hath chosen," and subjoins a statement about the reward of good works, he says: "Then shall thy light break forth as the morning, and thy garments, [3] shall speedily arise;" [4] where he has no thought of cloaks or stuff gowns, but means the rising of the flesh, which he declared the resurrection of, after its fall in death. Thus we are furnished even with an allegorical defence of the resurrection of the body. When, then, we read, "Go, my people, enter into your closets for a little season, until my anger pass away," [5] we have in the closets graves, in which they will have to rest for a little while, who shall have at the end of the world departed this life in the last furious onset of the power of Antichrist. Why else did He use the expression *closets*, in preference to some other receptacle, if it were not that the flesh is kept in these closets or cellars salted and reserved for use, to be drawn out thence on a suitable occasion? It is on a like principle that embalmed corpses are set aside for burial in mausoleums and sepulchres, in order that they may be removed therefrom when the Master shall order it. Since, therefore, there is consistency in thus understanding the passage (for what refuge of little closets could possibly shelter us from the wrath of God?), *it appears that* by the very phrase which he uses, "Until His anger pass away," [5] which shall extinguish Antichrist, he in fact shows that after that indignation the flesh will come forth from the sepulchre, in which it had been deposited previous to the *bursting out of the* anger. Now out of the closets nothing else is brought than that which had been put into them, and after the extirpation of Antichrist shall be busily transacted *the great process of* the resurrection.

CHAP. XXVIII.—PROPHETIC THINGS AND ACTIONS, AS WELL AS WORDS, ATTEST THIS GREAT DOCTRINE.

But we know that prophecy expressed itself by things no less than by words. By words, and also by deeds, is the resurrection foretold. When Moses puts his hand into his bosom, and then draws it out again dead, and again puts his hand into his bosom, and plucks it out living, [6] does not this apply as a presage to all mankind?—inasmuch as those three signs [7] denoted the threefold power of God: when it shall, first, in the appointed order, subdue to man the old serpent, the devil, [8] however formidable; then, secondly, draw forth the flesh from the bosom of death; [9] and then, at last, shall pursue all blood (shed) in judgment. [10] On this subject we read in the writings of the same prophet, (how that) God says: "For your blood of your lives will I require of all wild beasts; and I will require it of the hand of man, and of his brother's hand." [11] Now nothing is required except that which is demanded back again, and nothing is thus demanded except that which is to be given up; and that will of course be given up, which shall be demanded and required on the ground of vengeance. But indeed there cannot possibly be punishment of that which never had any existence. Existence, however, it will have, when it is restored in order to be punished. To the flesh, therefore, applies everything which is declared respecting the blood, for without the flesh there cannot be blood. The flesh will be raised up in order that the blood may be punished. There are, again, some statements (of Scripture) so plainly made as to be free from all obscurity of allegory, and yet they strongly require [12] their very simplicity to be interpreted. There is, for instance, that passage in Isaiah: "I will kill, and I will make alive." [13] Certainly His making alive is to take place after He has killed. As, therefore, it is by death that He kills, it is by the resurrection that He will make alive. Now it is the flesh which is killed by death; the flesh, therefore, will be revived by the resurrection. Surely if killing means taking away life from the flesh, and its opposite, reviving, amounts to restoring life to the flesh, it must needs be that the flesh rise again, to which the life, which has been taken away by killing, has to be restored by vivification.

CHAP. XXIX.—EZEKIEL'S VISION OF THE DRY BONES QUOTED.

Inasmuch, then, as even the figurative portions of Scripture, and the arguments of facts, and some plain statements *of Holy Writ*, throw light upon the resurrection of the flesh (although without specially naming the very substance), how much more effectual for de-

---

[1] Rev. iii. 5
[2] Matt. xxii. 11, 12.
[3] There is a curious change of the word here made by Tertullian, who reads ἱμάτια instead of ἰάματα, " thy health," or " healings," which is the word in the Sept.
[4] Isa. lviii. 8.
[5] Isa. xxvi. 20.

[6] Ex. iv. 6, 7.
[7] Ex. iv. 2-9.
[8] Comp. vers. 3, 4.
[9] Comp. vers. 6, 7.
[10] Comp. ver. 9.
[11] Gen. ix. 5.
[12] Sitiant.
[13] Isa. xxxvii. 12, 13, 16. The very words, however, occur not in Isaiah, but in 1 Sam. ii. 6, Deut. xxxii. 39.

termining the question will not those passages be which indicate the actual substance of the body by expressly mentioning it! Take Ezekiel: "And the hand of the Lord," says he, "was upon me; and the Lord brought me forth in the Spirit, and set me in the midst of a plain which was full of bones; and He led me round about them in a circuit: and, behold, there were many on the face of the plain; and, lo, they were very dry. And He said unto me, Son of man, will these bones live? And I said, O Lord God, Thou knowest. And He said unto me, Prophesy upon these bones; and thou shalt say, Ye dry bones, hear the word of the Lord. · Thus saith the Lord God to these bones, Behold, I bring upon you the breath *of life*, and ye shall live: and I will give unto you the spirit, and I will place muscles over you, and I will spread skin upon you; and ye shall live, and shall know that I am the Lord. And I prophesied as the Lord commanded me: and while I prophesy, behold there is a voice, behold also a movement, and bones approached bones. And I saw, and behold sinews and flesh came up over them, and muscles were placed around them; but there was no breath in them. And He said unto me, Prophesy to the wind, son of man, prophesy and say, Thus saith the Lord God, Come from the four winds, O breath, and breathe in these dead men, and let them live. So I prophesied to the wind, as He commanded me, and the spirit entered into the bones, and they lived, and stood upon their feet, strong and exceeding many. And *the Lord* said unto me, Son of man, these bones are the whole house of Israel. They say themselves, Our bones are become dry, and our hope is perished, and we in them have been violently destroyed. Therefore prophesy unto them, (and say), Behold, even I will open your sepulchres, and will bring you out of your sepulchres, O my people, and will bring you into the land of Israel: and ye shall know how that I the Lord opened your sepulchres, and brought you, O my people, out of your sepulchres; and I will give my Spirit unto you, and ye shall live, and shall rest in your own land: and ye shall know how that I the Lord have spoken and done these things, saith the Lord." [1]

CHAP. XXX.—THIS VISION INTERPRETED BY TERTULLIAN OF THE RESURRECTION OF THE BODIES OF THE DEAD. A CHRONOLOGICAL ERROR OF OUR AUTHOR, WHO SUPPOSES THAT EZEKIEL IN HIS CH. XXXI. PROPHESIED BEFORE THE CAPTIVITY.

I am well aware how they torture even this

prophecy into a proof of the allegorical sense, on the ground that by saying, "These bones are the whole house of Israel," He made them a figure of Israel, and removed them from their proper literal condition; and therefore (they contend) that there is here a figurative, not a true prediction of the resurrection, for (they say) the state of the Jews is one of humiliation, in a certain sense dead, and very dry, and dispersed over the plain of the world. Therefore the image of a resurrection is allegorically applied to their state, since it has to be gathered together, and recompacted bone to bone (in other words, tribe to tribe, and people to people), and to be reincorporated by the sinews of power and the nerves of royalty, and to be brought out as it were from sepulchres, that is tó say, from the most miserable and degraded abodes of captivity, and to breathe afresh in the way of a restoration, and to live thenceforward in their own land of Judæa. And what is to happen after all this? They will die, no doubt. And what will there be after death? No resurrection from the dead, of course, since there is nothing of the sort here revealed to Ezekiel. Well, but the resurrection is elsewhere foretold: so that there will be one even in this case, and they are rash in applying this *passage* to the state of Jewish affairs; or even if it do indicate a different recovery from the resurrection which we are maintaining, what matters it to me, provided there be also a resurrection of the body, just as there is a restoration of the Jewish state? In fact, by the very circumstance that the recovery of the Jewish state is prefigured by the reincorporation and reunion of bones, proof is offered that this event will also happen to the bones *themselves;* for the metaphor could not have been formed from bones, if the same thing exactly were not to be realized in them also. Now, although there is a sketch of the true thing in its image, the image itself still possesses a truth of its own: it must needs be, therefore, that that must have a prior existence for itself, which is used figuratively to express some other thing. Vacuity is not a consistent basis for a similitude, nor does nonentity form a suitable foundation for a parable. It will therefore be right to believe that the bones are destined to have a rehabiliment of flesh and breath, such as it is *here* said they will have, by reason indeed of which their renewed state could alone express the reformed condition of Jewish affairs, which is pretended to be the meaning of this passage. It is, however, more characteristic of a religious spirit to maintain the truth on the authority of a literal interpretation, such as is required

[1] Ezek. xxxvii. 1-14.

by the sense of the inspired passage. Now, if this vision had reference to the condition of the Jews, as soon as He had revealed to him the position of the bones, He would at once have added, "These bones are the whole house of Israel," and so forth. But immediately on showing the bones, He interrupts the scene by saying somewhat of the prospect which is most suited to bones; without yet naming Israel, He tries the prophet's own faith: "Son of man, can these bones ever live?" so that he makes answer: "O Lord, Thou knowest." Now God would not, you may be sure, have tried the prophet's faith on a point which was never to be a real one, of which Israel should never hear, *and* in which it was not proper to repose belief. Since, however, the resurrection of the dead was indeed foretold, but Israel, in the distrust of his great unbelief, was offended at it; and, whilst gazing on the condition of the crumbling grave, despaired of a resurrection; or rather, did not direct his mind mainly to it, but to his own harassing circumstances,— therefore God first instructed the prophet (since he, too, was not free from doubt), by revealing to him the process of the resurrection, with a view to his earnest setting forth of the same. He then charged the people to believe what He had revealed to the prophet, telling them that they were themselves, though refusing to believe their resurrection, the very bones which were destined to rise again. Then in the concluding sentence He says, "And ye shall know how that I the Lord have spoken and done these things," intending of course to do that of which He had spoken; but certainly not meaning to do that which He had spoken of, if His design had been to do something different from what He had said.

CHAP. XXXI.—OTHER PASSAGES OUT OF THE PROPHETS APPLIED TO THE RESURRECTION OF THE FLESH.

Unquestionably, if the people were indulging in *figurative* murmurs that their bones were become dry, and that their hope had perished—plaintive at the consequences of their dispersion—then God might fairly enough seem to have consoled their *figurative* despair with a *figurative* promise. Since, however, no injury had as yet alighted on the people from their dispersion, although the hope of the resurrection had very frequently failed amongst them, it is manifest that it was owing to the perishing condition of their bodies that their faith in the resurrection was shaken. God, therefore, was rebuilding the faith which the people were pulling down. But even if it were true that Israel was then depressed at some shock in their existing circumstances, we must not on that account suppose that the purpose of revelation could have rested in a parable: its aim must have been to testify a resurrection, in order to raise the nation's hope to even an eternal salvation and an indispensable restoration, and thereby turn off their minds from brooding over their present affairs. This indeed is the aim of other prophets likewise. "Ye shall go forth," (says Malachi), "from your sepulchres, as young calves let loose from their bonds, and ye shall tread down your enemies."[1] And again, (Isaiah says): "Your heart shall rejoice, and your bones shall spring up like the grass,"[2] because the grass also is renewed by the dissolution and corruption of the seed. In a word, if it is contended that the figure of the rising bones refers properly to the state of Israel, why is the same hope announced to all nations, instead of being limited to Israel only, of reinvesting those osseous remains with bodily substance and vital breath, and of raising up their dead out of the grave? For the language is universal: "The dead shall arise, and come forth from their graves; for the dew which cometh from Thee is medicine to their bones."[3] In another passage *it is written:* "All flesh shall come to worship before me, saith the Lord."[4] When? When the fashion of this world shall begin to pass away. For He said before: "As the new heaven and the new earth, which I make, remain before me, saith the Lord, so shall your seed remain."[5] Then also shall be fulfilled what is written afterwards: "And they shall go forth" (namely, from their graves), "and shall see the carcases of those who have transgressed: for their worm shall never die, nor shall their fire be quenched; and they shall be a spectacle to all flesh"[6] even to that which, being raised again from the dead and brought out from the grave, shall adore the Lord for this great grace.

CHAP. XXXII.—EVEN UNBURIED BODIES WILL BE RAISED AGAIN. WHATEVER BEFALLS THEM GOD WILL RESTORE THEM AGAIN. JONAH'S CASE QUOTED IN ILLUSTRATION OF GOD'S POWER.

But, that you may not suppose that it is merely those bodies which are consigned to tombs whose resurrection is foretold, you have it declared in Scripture: "And I will com-

---

[1] Mal. iv. 2, 3.
[2] Isa. lxvi. 14.
[3] Isa. xxvi. 19.
[4] Isa. lxvi. 23.
[5] Ver. 22.
[6] Isa. lxvi. 24.

mand the fishes of the sea, and they shall cast up the bones which they have devoured; and I will bring joint to joint, and bone to bone." You will ask, Will then the fishes and other animals and carnivorous birds be raised again, in order that they may vomit up what they have consumed, on the ground of your reading in the law of Moses, that blood is required of even all the beasts? Certainly not. But the beasts and the fishes are mentioned in relation to the restoration of flesh and blood, in order the more emphatically to express the resurrection of such bodies as have even been devoured, when redress is said to be demanded of their very devourers. Now I apprehend that in the case of Jonah we have a fair proof of this divine power, when he comes forth from the fish's belly uninjured in both his natures—his flesh and his soul. No doubt the bowels of the whale would have had abundant time during three days for consuming and digesting *Jonah's* flesh, quite as effectually as a coffin, or a tomb, or the gradual decay of some quiet and concealed grave; only that he wanted to prefigure even those beasts (*which symbolize*) especially the men who are wildly opposed to the *Christian* name, or the angels of iniquity, of whom blood will be required by the full exaction of an avenging judgment. Where, then, is the man who, being more disposed to learn than to assume, more careful to believe than to dispute, and more scrupulous of the wisdom of God than wantonly bent on his own, when he hears of a divine purpose respecting sinews and skin, and nerves and bones, will forthwith devise some different application of these words, as if all that is said of the substances in question were not naturally intended for man? For either there is here no reference to the destiny of man—in the gracious provision of the kingdom (of heaven), in the severity of the judgment-day, in all the incidents of the resurrection; or else, if there is any reference to his destiny, the destination must necessarily be made in reference to those substances of which the man is composed, for whom the destiny is reserved. Another question I have also to ask of these very adroit transformers of bones and sinews, and nerves and sepulchres: Why, when anything is declared of the soul, do they not interpret *the soul* to be something else, and transfer it to another signification?—since, whenever any distinct statement is made of a *bodily* substance, they will obstinately prefer taking any other sense whatever, rather than that which the name indicates. If things which pertain to the body are figurative, why are not those which pertain to the soul figurative also? Since, however, things which belong to the soul have nothing allegorical in them, neither therefore have those which belong to the body. For man is as much body as he is soul; so that it is impossible for one of these natures to admit a figurative sense, and the other to exclude it.

CHAP. XXXIII.—SO MUCH FOR THE PROPHETIC SCRIPTURES. IN THE GOSPELS, CHRIST'S PARABLES, AS EXPLAINED BY HIMSELF, HAVE A CLEAR REFERENCE TO THE RESURRECTION OF THE FLESH.

This is evidence enough from the prophetic Scriptures. I now appeal to the Gospels. But here also I must first meet the same sophistry as advanced by those who contend that the Lord, like (the prophets), said everything in the way of allegory, because it is written: "All these things spake Jesus in parables, and without a parable spake He not unto them,"[1] that is, to the Jews. Now the disciples also asked Him, "Why speakest Thou in parables?"[2] And the Lord gave them this answer: "Therefore I speak unto them in parables: because they seeing, see not; and hearing, they hear not, according to the prophecy of Esaias."[3] But since it was to the Jews that He spoke in parables, it was not then to all men; and if not to all, it follows that it was not always and in all things parables with Him, but only in certain things, and when addressing a particular class. But He addressed a particular class when He spoke to the Jews. It is true that He spoke sometimes even to the disciples in parables. But observe how the Scripture relates such a fact: "And He spake a parable unto them."[4] It follows, then, that He did not usually address them in parables; because if He always did so, special mention would not be made of His resorting to this mode of address. Besides, there is not a parable which you will not find to be either explained by the Lord Himself, as that of the sower, (which He interprets) of the management of the word of God;[5] or else cleared by a preface from the writer of the Gospel, as in the parable of the arrogant judge and the importunate widow, *which is expressly applied* to earnestness in prayer;[6] or capable of being spontaneously understood,[7] as in the parable of the fig-tree, which was spared a while in hopes of improvement—an emblem of Jewish sterility. Now,

---

[1] Matt. xiii. 34.
[2] Ver. 10.
[3] Matt. xiii. 13; comp. Isa. vi. 9.
[4] See Luke vi. 39; comp. with ver. 20, and other places, especially in this Gospel.
[5] See Luke viii. 11.
[6] See Luke xviii. 1.
[7] Such cases of obvious meaning, which required no explanation, are referred to in Matt. xxi. 45 and Luke xx. 19.

if even parables obscure not the light of the gospel, how unlikely it is that plain sentences and declarations, which have an unmistakeable meaning, should signify any other thing than their literal sense! But it is by such declarations and sentences that the Lord sets forth either the last judgment, or the kingdom, or the resurrection: "It shall be more tolerable," He says, "for Tyre and Sidon in the day of judgment *than for you*."[1] And, "Tell them that the kingdom of God is at hand."[2] And again, "It shall be recompensed to you at the resurrection of the just."[3] Now, if the mention of these events (I mean the judgment-day, and the kingdom of God, and the resurrection) has a plain and absolute sense, so that nothing about them can be pressed into an allegory, neither should those statements be forced into parables which describe the arrangement, and the process, and the experience of the kingdom *of God*, and of the judgment, and of the resurrection. On the contrary, things which are destined for the body should be carefully understood in a bodily sense,—not in a spiritual sense, as having nothing figurative in their nature. This is the reason why we have laid it down as a preliminary consideration, that the bodily substance both of the soul and of the flesh is liable to the recompense, which will have to be awarded in return for the co-operation of the two natures, that so the corporeality of the soul may not exclude the bodily nature of the flesh by suggesting a recourse to figurative descriptions, since both of them must needs be regarded as destined to take part in the kingdom, and the judgment, and the resurrection. And now we proceed to the special proof of this proposition, that the bodily character of the flesh is indicated by our Lord whenever He mentions the resurrection, at the same time without disparagement to the corporeal nature of the soul,—a point which has been actually admitted but by a few.

CHAP. XXXIV.—CHRIST PLAINLY TESTIFIES TO THE RESURRECTION OF THE ENTIRE MAN. NOT IN HIS SOUL ONLY, WITHOUT THE BODY.

To begin with the passage where He says that He is come to "*to seek and* to save that which is lost."[4] What do you suppose that to be which is lost? Man, undoubtedly. The entire man, or only a part of him? The whole man, of course. In fact, since the trangression which caused man's ruin was committed quite as much by the instigation of the soul from concupiscence as by the action of the flesh from actual fruition, it has marked the entire man with the sentence of transgression, and has therefore made him deservedly amenable to perdition. So that he will be wholly saved, since he has by sinning been wholly lost. Unless it be true that the sheep (of the parable) is a "lost" one, irrespective of its body; then its recovery may be effected without the body. Since, however, it is the bodily substance as well as the soul, making up the entire animal, which was carried on the shoulders of the Good Shepherd, we have here unquestionably an example how man is restored in both his natures. Else how unworthy it were of God to bring only a moiety of man to salvation—and almost less than that; whereas the munificence of princes of this world always claims for itself the merit of a plenary grace! Then must the devil be understood to be stronger for injuring man, ruining him wholly? and must God have the character of comparative weakness, since He does not relieve and help man in his entire state? The apostle, however, suggests that "where sin abounded, there was grace much more abounded."[5] How, in fact, can he be regarded as saved, who can at the same time be said to be lost—lost, that is, in the flesh, but saved as to his soul? Unless, indeed, *their argument* now makes it necessary that the soul should be placed in a "lost" condition, that it may be susceptible of salvation, on the ground that that is properly saved which has been lost. We, however, so understand the soul's immortality as to believe it "lost," not in the sense of destruction, but of punishment, that is, in hell. And if this is the case, then it is not the soul which salvation will affect, since it is "safe" already in its own nature by reason of its immortality, but rather the flesh, which, as all readily allow, is subject to destruction. Else, if the soul is also perishable (in this sense), in other words, not immortal—the condition of the flesh—then this same condition ought in all fairness to benefit the flesh also, as being similarly mortal and perishable, since that which perishes the Lord purposes to save. I do not care now to follow the clue of our discussion, so far as to consider whether it is in one of his natures or in the other that perdition puts in its claim on man, provided that salvation is equally distributed over the two substances, and makes him its aim in respect of them both. For observe, in which substance soever you assume man to have perished, in the other he does not perish. He will therefore be saved in the substance in which

---

[1] Matt. xi. 22.
[2] Matt. x. 7.
[3] Luke xiv. 14.
[4] Luke xix. 10.

[5] Rom. v. 20.

he does not perish, and yet obtain salvation in that in which he does perish. You have (then) the restoration of the entire man, inasmuch as the Lord purposes to save that part of him which perishes, whilst he will not of course lose that portion which cannot be lost. Who will any longer doubt of the safety of both natures, when one of them is to obtain salvation, and the other is not to lose it? And, still further, the Lord explains to us the meaning of the thing when He says: "I came not to do my own will, but the Father's, who hath sent me."[1] What, I ask, is that will? "That of all which He hath given me I should lose nothing, but should raise it up again at the last day."[2] Now, what had Christ received of the Father but that which He had Himself put on? Man, of course, in his texture of flesh and soul. Neither, therefore, of those parts which He has received will He allow to perish; nay, no considerable portion—nay, not the least fraction, of either. If the flesh be, *as our opponents slightingly think,* but a poor fraction, then the flesh is safe, because not a fraction *of man is to perish;* and no larger portion is in danger, because every portion of man is in equally safe keeping with Him. If, however, He will not raise the flesh also up at the last day, then He will permit not only a fraction of man to perish, but (as I will venture to say, in consideration of so important a part) almost the whole of him. But when He repeats His words with increased emphasis, "And this is the Father's will, that every one which seeth the Son, and believeth on Him, may have eternal life: and I will raise him up at the last day,"[3]—He asserts the full extent of the resurrection. For He assigns to each several nature that reward which is suited to its services: both to the flesh, for by it the Son was "seen;" and to the soul, for by it He was "believed on." Then, you will say, to them was this promise given by whom Christ was "seen." Well, be it so; only let the same hope flow on from them to us! For if to them who saw, and therefore believed, such fruit then accrued to the operations of the flesh and the soul, how much more to us! For more "blessed," says Christ, "are they who have not seen, and yet have believed;"[4] since, even if the resurrection of the flesh must be denied to *them,* it must at any rate be a fitting boon to *us, who are* the more blessed. For how could we be blessed, if we were to perish in any part of us?

CHAP. XXXV.—EXPLANATION OF WHAT IS MEANT BY THE BODY, WHICH IS TO BE RAISED AGAIN. NOT THE CORPOREALITY OF THE SOUL.

But He also teaches us, that "He is rather to be feared, who is able to destroy both body and soul in hell," that is, the Lord alone; "not those which kill the body, but are not able to hurt the soul,"[5] that is to say, all human powers. Here, then, we have a recognition of the natural immortality of the soul, which cannot be killed by men; and of the mortality of the body, which may be killed: *whence we learn* that the resurrection of the dead is a resurrection of the flesh; for unless it were raised again, it would be impossible for the flesh to be "killed in hell." But as a question may be here captiously raised about the meaning of "the body" (or "the flesh"), I will at once state that I understand by the human body nothing else than that fabric of the flesh which, whatever be the kind of material of which it is constructed and modified, is seen and handled, and sometimes indeed killed, by men. In like manner, I should not admit that anything but cement and stones and bricks form the *body* of a wall. If any one imports into our argument some body of a subtle, secret nature, he must show, disclose, and prove to me that identical body is the very one which was slain by human violence, and then (I will grant) that it is of such a body that (our scripture) speaks. If, again, the body *or corporeal nature* of the soul[6] is cast in my teeth, it will only be an idle subterfuge! For since both substances are set before us (in this passage, which affirms) that "body and soul" are destroyed in hell, a distinction is obviously made between the two; and we are left to understand the body to be that which is tangible to us, that is, the flesh, which, as it will be destroyed in hell—since it did not "rather fear" being destroyed by God—so also will it be restored to life eternal, since it preferred to be killed by human hands. If, therefore, any one shall violently suppose that the destruction of the soul and the flesh in hell amounts to a final annihilation of the two substances, and not to their penal treatment (as if they were to be consumed, not punished), let him recollect that the fire of hell is eternal—expressly announced as an everlasting penalty; and let him then admit that it is from this circumstance that this never-ending "killing" is more formidable than a merely human murder, which is only temporal. He will then

[1] John vi. 38.
[2] Ver. 39.
[3] Ver. 40.
[4] John xx. 29.

[5] Matt. x. 28.
[6] Tertullian supposed that even the soul was in a certain sense of a corporeal essence. [Compare the speculations of Crusius in Auberlen, *Divine Revelation,* (Translation of A. B. Paton, Edinburgh, Clarks, 1867).]

come to the conclusion that substances must be eternal, when their penal "killing" is an eternal one. Since, then, the body after the resurrection has to be killed by God in hell along with the soul, we surely have sufficient information in this fact respecting both the issues *which await it*, namely the resurrection of the flesh, and its eternal "killing." Else it would be most absurd if the flesh should be raised up and destined to "the killing in hell," in order to be put an end to, when it might suffer such an annihilation (more directly) if not raised again at all. A pretty paradox,[1] to be sure, that an essence must be refitted with life, in order that it may receive that annihilation which has already in fact accrued to it! *But Christ*, whilst confirming us in the self-same hope, adds the example of "the sparrows"—how that "not one of them falls to the ground without the will of God."[2] *He says this*, that you may believe that the flesh which has been consigned to the ground, is able in like manner to rise again by the will of the same God. For although this is not allowed to the sparrows, yet "we are of more value than many sparrows,"[3] for the very reason that, when fallen, we rise again. He affirms, lastly, that "the very hairs of our head are all numbered,"[4] and ir the affirmation He of course includes the promise of their safety; for if they were to be lost, where would be the use of having taken such a numerical care of them? Surely the only use lies (in this truth): "That of all which the Father hath given to me, I should lose none,"[5] —not even a hair, as also not an eye nor a tooth. And yet whence shall come that "weeping and gnashing of teeth,"[6] if not from *eyes and teeth?*—even at that time when the body shall be slain in hell, and thrust out into that outer darkness which shall be the suitable torment of the eyes. He also who shall not be clothed at the marriage feast in the raiment of good works, will have to be "bound hand and foot," —as being, of course, raised in his body. So, again, the very reclining at the feast in the kingdom of God, and sitting on Christ's thrones, and standing at last on His right hand and His left, and eating of the tree of life: what are all these but most certain proofs of a bodily appointment and destination?

CHAP. XXXVI.—CHRIST'S REFUTATION OF THE SADDUCEES, AND AFFIRMATION OF CATHOLIC DOCTRINE.

Let us now see whether (the Lord) has not imparted greater strength to our doctrine in breaking down the subtle cavil of the Sadducees. Their great object, I take it, was to do away altogether with the resurrection, for the Sadducees in fact did not admit any salvation either for the soul or the flesh;[7] and therefore, taking the strongest case they could for impairing the credibility of the resurrection, they adapted an argument from it in support of the question which they started. Their specious inquiry concerned the flesh, whether or not it would be subject to marriage after the resurrection; and they assumed the case of a woman who had married seven brothers, so that it was a doubtful point to which of them she should be restored.[8] Now, let the purport both of the question and the answer be kept steadily in view, and the discussion is settled at once. For since the Sadducees indeed denied the resurrection, whilst the Lord affirmed it; since, too, (in affirming it,) He reproached them as being both ignorant of the Scriptures—those, of course which had declared the resurrection—as well as incredulous of the power of God, though, of course, effectual to raise the dead, and lastly, since He immediately added the words, "Now, that the dead are raised,"[9] (speaking) without misgiving, and affirming the very thing which was being denied, even the resurrection of the dead before Him who is "the God of the living,"—(it clearly follows) that He affirmed this verity in the precise sense in which they were denying it; that it was, in fact, the resurrection of the two natures of man. Nor does it follow, (as they would have it,) that because Christ denied that men would marry, He therefore proved that they would not rise again. On the contrary, He called them "the children of the resurrection,"[10] in a certain sense having by the resurrection to undergo a birth; and after that they marry no more, but in their risen life are "equal unto the angels,"[11] inasmuch as they are not to marry, because they are not to die, but are destined to pass into the angelic state by putting on the raiment of incorruption, although with a change in the substance which is restored to life. Besides, no question could be raised whether we are to marry or die again or not, without involving in doubt the restoration most especially of that substance which has a particular relation both to death and marriage—that is, the flesh. Thus, then, you have the Lord affirming against the Jewish heretics what is now en-

---

[1] Scilicet.
[2] Matt. x. 29.
[3] Ver. 31.
[4] Matt. x. 30.
[5] John vi. 39.
[6] Matt. viii. 12, xiii. 42, xxii. 13, xxv. 30.
[7] Compare Tertullian's *De Præscript. Hæret.* c. xxxiii.
[8] Matt. xxii. 23-32 ; Mark xii. 18-27 ; Luke xx. 27-38.
[9] Luke xx. 37.
[10] Ver. 36.
[11] Ver. 36.

countering the denial of the Christian Sadducees—the resurrection of the entire man.

CHAP. XXXVII.—CHRIST'S ASSERTION ABOUT THE UNPROFITABLENESS OF THE FLESH EXPLAINED CONSISTENTLY WITH OUR DOCTRINE.

He says, it is true, that "the flesh profiteth nothing;"[1] but then, as in the former case, the meaning must be regulated by the subject which is spoken of. Now, because they thought His discourse was harsh and intolerable, supposing that He had really and literally enjoined on them to eat his flesh, He, with the view of ordering the state of salvation as a spiritual thing, set out with the principle, "It is the spirit that quickeneth;" and then added, "The flesh profiteth nothing,"—meaning, of course, to the giving of life. He also goes on to explain what He would have us to understand by *spirit:* "The words that I speak unto you, they are spirit, and they are life." In a like sense He had previously said: "He that heareth my words, and believeth on Him that sent me, hath everlasting life, and shall not come into condemnation, but shall pass from death unto life."[2] Constituting, therefore, His word as the life-giving principle, because that word is spirit and life, He likewise called His flesh by the same appelation; because, too, the Word had become flesh,[3] we ought therefore to desire Him in order that we may have life, and to devour Him with the ear, and to ruminate on Him with the understanding, and to digest Him by faith. Now, just before (the passage in hand), He had declared His flesh to be "the bread which cometh down from heaven,"[4] impressing on (His hearers) constantly under the figure of necessary food the memory of their forefathers, who had preferred the bread and flesh of Egypt to their divine calling.[5] Then, turning His subject to their reflections, because He perceived that they were going to be scattered from Him, He says: "The flesh profiteth nothing." Now what is there to destroy the resurrection of the flesh? As if there might not reasonably enough be something which, although it "profiteth nothing" itself, might yet be capable of being profited by something else. The spirit "profiteth," for it imparts life. The flesh profiteth nothing, for it is subject to death. Therefore He has rather put the two propositions in a way which favours our belief: for by showing what "profits," and what "does not profit," He has likewise thrown

light on the object which receives as well as the subject which gives the "profit." Thus, *in the present instance, we have* the Spirit giving life to the flesh which has been subdued by death; for "the hour," says He, "is coming, when the dead shall hear the voice of the Son of God, and they that hear shall live."[6] Now, what is "the dead" but the flesh? and what is "the voice of God" but the Word? and what is the Word but the Spirit,[7] who shall justly raise the flesh which He had once Himself become, and *that* too from death, which He Himself suffered, and from the grave, which He Himself once entered? Then again, when He says, "Marvel not at this: for the hour is coming, in which all that are in the graves shall hear the voice of the Son of God, and shall come forth; they that have done good, to the resurrection of life; and they that have done evil, unto the resurrection of damnation,"[8]—none will after such words be able to interpret the dead "that are in the graves" as any other than the bodies of the flesh, because the graves themselves are nothing but the resting-place of corpses: for it is incontestable that even those who partake of "the old man," that is to say, sinful men —in other words, those who are dead through their ignorance of God (whom our heretics, forsooth, foolishly insist on understanding by the word "graves"[9])—are plainly here spoken of as having to come from their graves for judgment. But how are graves to come forth from graves?

CHAP. XXXVIII.—CHRIST, BY RAISING THE DEAD, ATTESTED IN A PRACTICAL WAY THE DOCTRINE OF THE RESURRECTION OF THE FLESH.

After the Lord's *words*, what are we to think of the purport of His *actions*, when He raises dead persons from their biers *and* their graves? To what end did He do so? If it was only for the mere exhibition of His power, or to afford the temporary favour of restoration to life, it was really no great matter for Him to raise men to die over again. If, however, as was the truth, it was rather to put in secure keeping men's belief in a future resurrection, then it must follow from the particular form of His own examples, that the said resurrection will be a bodily one. I can never allow it to be said that the resurrection of the future, being destined for the soul only, did then receive these preliminary illustrations of a raising of the flesh, simply because it would have been impossible to have shown the

---

[1] John vi. 63.
[2] John v. 24.
[3] John i. 14.
[4] John vi. 51.
[5] John vi. 31, 49, 58.

[6] John v. 25.
[7] The divine nature of the Son. See our *Anti-Marcion*, pp. 129, 247, note 7, Edin.
[8] John v. 28, 29.
[9] Compare c. xix. above.

resurrection of an invisible soul except by the resuscitation of a visible substance. They have but a poor knowledge of God, who suppose Him to be only capable of doing what comes within the compass of their own thoughts; and after all, they cannot but know full well what His capability has ever been, if they only make acquaintance with the writings of John. For unquestionably he, who has exhibited to our sight the martyrs' hitherto disembodied souls resting under the altar,[1] was quite able to display them before our eyes rising without a body of flesh. I, however, for my part prefer (believing) that it is impossible for God to practise deception (weak as He only could be in respect of artifice), from any fear of seeming to have given preliminary proofs of a thing in a way which is inconsistent with His actual disposal of the thing; nay more, from a fear that, since He was not powerful enough to show us a sample of the resurrection without the flesh, He might with still greater infirmity be unable to display (by and by) the full accomplishment of the sample in the self-same substance *of the flesh*. No example, indeed, is greater than the thing of which it is a sample. Greater, however, it is, if souls with their body are to be raised as the evidence of their resurrection without the body, so as that the entire salvation of man *in soul and body* should become a guarantee for only the half, *the soul;* whereas the condition in all examples is, that that which would be deemed the less—I mean the resurrection of the soul only—should be the foretaste, as it were, of the rising of the flesh also at its appointed time. And therefore, according to our estimate of the truth, those examples of dead persons who were raised by the Lord were indeed a proof of the resurrection both of the flesh and of the soul,—a proof, in fact, that this gift was to be denied to neither substance. Considered, however, as examples only, they expressed all the less significance — *less, indeed,* than Christ will express at last —for they were not raised up for glory and immortality, but only for another death.

CHAP. XXXIX.—ADDITIONAL EVIDENCE AFFORDED TO US IN THE ACTS OF THE APOSTLES.

The Acts of the Apostles, too, attest[2] the resurrection. Now the apostles had nothing else to do, at least among the Jews, than to explain[3] the Old Testament and confirm[4] the New, and above all, to preach God in Christ. Consequently they introduced nothing new concerning the resurrection, besides

announcing it to the glory of Christ: in every other respect it had been already received in simple and intelligent faith, without any question as to what sort of resurrection it was to be, and without encountering any other opponents than the Sadducees. So much easier was it to deny the resurrection altogether, than to understand it in an alien sense. You find Paul confessing his faith before the chief priests, under the shelter of the chief captain,[5] among the Sadducees and the Pharisees: "Men and brethren," he says, "I am a Pharisee, the son of a Pharisee; of the hope and resurrection of the dead I am now called in question by you,"[6]—referring, of course, to the nation's hope; in order to avoid, in his present condition, as an apparent transgressor of the law, being thought to approach to the Sadducees in opinion on the most important article of the faith—even the resurrection. That belief, therefore, in the resurrection which he would not appear to impair, he really confirmed in the opinion of the Pharisees, since he rejected the views of the Sadducees, who denied it. In like manner, before Agrippa also, he says that he was advancing "none other things than those which the prophets had announced."[7] He was therefore maintaining just such a resurrection as the prophets had foretold. He mentions also what is written by "Moses", touching the resurrection of the dead; (and in so doing) he must have known that it would be a rising in the body, since requisition will have to be made therein of the blood of man.[8] He declared it then to be of such a character as the Pharisees had admitted it, and such as the Lord had Himself maintained it, and such too as the Sadducees refused to believe it—such refusal leading them indeed to an absolute rejection of the whole verity. Nor had the Athenians previously understood Paul to announce any other resurrection.[9] They had, in fact, derided his announcement; but they would have indulged no such derision if they had heard from him nothing but the restoration of the soul, for they would have received *that* as the very common anticipation of their own native philosophy. But when the preaching of the resurrection, of which they had previously not heard, by its absolute novelty excited the heathen, and a not unnatural incredulity in so wonderful a matter began to harass the simple faith with many discussions, then the apostle took care in almost every one of his writings to strengthen men's belief of

---

[1] Rev. vi. 9–11.
[2] Tertullian always refers to this book by a *plural* phrase.
[3] Resignandi.
[4] Consignandi.

[5] Sub tribuno.
[6] Acts xxiii. 6.
[7] Acts xxvi. 22.
[8] Gen. ix. 5, 6.
[9] Acts xvii. 32.

this *Christian* hope, pointing out that there was such a hope, and that it had not as yet been realized, and that it would be in the body,—a point which was the especial object of inquiry, and, what was besides a doubtful question, not in a body of a different kind from ours.

CHAP. XL.—SUNDRY PASSAGES OF ST. PAUL WHICH ATTEST OUR DOCTRINE RESCUED FROM THE PERVERSIONS OF HERESY.

Now it is no matter of surprise if arguments are captiously taken from the writings of (the apostle) himself, inasmuch as there "must needs be heresies;"[1] but these could not be, if the Scriptures were not capable of a false interpretation. Well, then, heresies finding that the apostle had mentioned two "men"— "the inner man," that is, the soul, and "the outward man," that is, the flesh—awarded salvation to the soul or inward man, and destruction to the flesh or outward man, because it is written (in the Epistle) to the Corinthians: "Though our outward man decayeth, yet the inward man is renewed day by day."[2] Now, neither the soul by itself alone is "man" (it was subsequently implanted in the clayey mould to which the name *man* had been already given), nor is the flesh without the soul "man": for after the exile of the soul from it, it has the title of corpse. Thus the designation *man* is, in a certain sense, the bond between the two closely united substances, under which designation they cannot but be coherent natures. As for the inward man, indeed, the apostle prefers its being regarded as the mind and heart[3] rather than the soul;[4] in other words, not so much the substance itself as the savour of the substance. Thus when, writing to the Ephesians, he spoke of "Christ dwelling in their inner man," he meant, no doubt, that the Lord ought to be admitted into their senses.[5] He then added, "in your hearts by faith, *rooted and grounded* in love,"—making "faith" and "love" not substantial parts, but only conceptions of the soul. But when he used the phrase "in your hearts," seeing that these are substantial parts of the flesh, he at once assigned to the flesh the actual "inward man," which he placed in the heart. Consider now in what sense he alleged that "the outward man decayeth, while the inward man is renewed day by day." You certainly would not maintain that he could mean that corruption of the flesh which it undergoes from the mo-

ment of death, in its appointed state of perpetual decay; but *the wear and tear* which for the name of Christ it experiences during its course of life before and until death, in harassing cares and tribulations as well as in tortures and persecutions. Now the inward man will have, of course, to be renewed by the suggestion of the Spirit, advancing by faith and holiness day after day, *here* in this life, not *there* after the resurrection, were our renewal is not a gradual process from day to day, but a consummation once for all complete. You may learn this, too, from the following passage, where *the apostle* says: "For our light affliction, which is but for a moment, worketh for us a far more exceeding and eternal weight of glory; while we look not at the things which are seen," that is, our sufferings, "but at the things which are not seen," that is, our rewards: "for the things which are seen are temporal, but the things which are not seen are eternal."[6] For the afflictions and injuries wherewith the outward man is worn away, he affirms to be only worthy of being despised by us, as being light and temporary; preferring those eternal recompenses which are also invisible, and that "weight of glory" which will be a counterpoise for the labours in the endurance of which the flesh here suffers decay. So that the subject in this passage is not that corruption which *they* ascribe to the outward man in the utter destruction of the flesh, with the view of nullifying the resurrection. So also he says elsewhere: "If so be that we suffer with Him, that we may be also glorified together; for I reckon that the sufferings of the present time are not worthy to be compared with the glory that shall be revealed in us."[7] Here again he shows us that our sufferings are less than their rewards. Now, since it is through the flesh that we suffer with *Christ*— for it is the property of the flesh to be worn by sufferings—to the same flesh belongs the recompense which is promised for suffering with Christ. Accordingly, when he is going to assign afflictions to the flesh as its especial liability—according to the statement he had already made—he says, "When we were come into Macedonia, our flesh had no rest;"[8] then, in order to make the soul a fellow-sufferer with the body, he adds, "We were troubled on every side; without were fightings," which of course warred down the flesh, "within were fears," which afflicted the soul.[9] Although, therefore, the outward man decays —not in the sense of missing the resurrection, but of enduring tribulation—it will be under-

[1] 1 Cor. xi. 19.
[2] 2 Cor. iv. 16.
[3] Animum.
[4] Animam.
[5] Eph. iii. 17.

[6] 2 Cor. iv. 17, 18.
[7] Rom. viii. 17, 18.
[8] 2 Cor. vii. 5.
[9] Same verse.

stood from this *scripture* that it is not exposed to its suffering without the inward man. Both, therefore, will be glorified together, even as they have suffered together. Parallel with their participation in troubles, must necessarily run their association also in rewards.

CHAP. XLI.—THE DISSOLUTION OF OUR TABERNACLE CONSISTENT WITH THE RESURRECTION OF OUR BODIES.

It is still the same sentiment which he follows up in the passage in which he puts the recompense above the sufferings: "for we know," he says, "that if our earthly house of this tabernacle were dissolved, we have a house not made with hands, eternal in the heavens;"[1] in other words, owing to the fact that our flesh is undergoing dissolution through its sufferings, we shall be provided with a home—in heaven. He remembered the award (which the Lord assigns) in the Gospel: "Blessed are they who are persecuted for righteousness' sake, for theirs is the kingdom of heaven."[2] Yet, when he thus contrasted the recompense of the reward, he did not deny the flesh's restoration; since the recompense is due to the same substance to which the dissolution is attributed,—that is, of course, the flesh. Because, however, he had called the flesh *a house*, he wished elegantly to use the same term in his comparison of the ultimate reward; promising to the very house, which undergoes dissolution through suffering, a better house through the resurrection. Just as the Lord also promises us many mansions as of a house in His Father's home;[3] although this may possibly be understood of the domicile of this world, on the dissolution of whose fabric an eternal abode is promised in heaven, inasmuch as the following context, having a manifest reference to the flesh, seems to show that these preceding words have no such reference. For the apostle makes a distinction, when he goes on to say, "For in this we groan, earnestly desiring to be clothed upon with our house which is from heaven, if so be that being clothed we shall not be found naked;"[4] which means, before we put off the garment of the flesh, we wish to be clothed with the celestial glory of immortality. Now the privilege of this favour awaits those who shall at the coming of the Lord be found in the flesh, and who shall, owing to the oppressions of the time of Antichrist, deserve by an instantaneous death,[5] which is accomplished by a sudden change, to become qualified to join the rising saints; as he writes to the Thessalonians: "For this we say unto you by the word of the Lord, that we which are alive and remain unto the coming of the Lord shall not prevent them which are asleep. For the Lord Himself shall descend from heaven with a shout, with the voice of the archangel, and with the trump of God: and the dead in Christ shall rise first: then we too shall ourselves be caught up together with them in the clouds, to meet the Lord in the air: and so shall we ever be with the Lord."[6]

CHAP. XLII.—DEATH CHANGES, WITHOUT DESTROYING, OUR MORTAL BODIES. REMAINS OF THE GIANTS.

It is the transformation these shall undergo which he explains to the Corinthians, when he writes: "We shall all indeed rise again (though we shall not all undergo the transformation) in a moment, in the twinkling of an eye, at the last trump"—for none shall experience this change but those only who shall be found in the flesh. "And the dead," he says, "shall be raised, *and* we shall be changed." Now, after a careful consideration of this appointed order, you will be able to adjust what follows to the preceding sense. For when he adds, "This corruptible must put on incorruption, and this mortal must put on immortality,"[7] this will assuredly be that house from heaven, with which we so earnestly desire to be clothed upon, whilst groaning in this our present body,—meaning, of course, over this flesh in which we shall be surprised at last; because he says that we are burdened whilst in this tabernacle, which we do not wish indeed to be stripped of, but rather to be *in it* clothed over, in such a way that mortality may be swallowed up of life, that is, by putting on over us whilst we are transformed that vestiture which is from heaven. For who is there that will not desire, while he is in the flesh, to put on immortality, and to continue his life by a happy escape from death, through the transformation which must be experienced instead of it, without encountering too that *Hades* which will exact the very last farthing?[8] Nothwithstanding, he who has already traversed *Hades* is destined also to obtain the change after the resurrection. For from this circumstance it is that we definitively declare that the flesh will *by all means* rise again, and, from the change that is to come over it, will assume the condition of angels. Now, if it were merely in the case of those who shall be found in the flesh that the

[1] 2 Cor. v. 1.
[2] Matt. v. 10.
[3] John xiv. 2.
[4] 2 Cor. v. 2, 3.
[5] Compendio mortis. Compare our *Anti-Marcion* for the same thoughts and words, v. 12. [p. 455, *supra*.]

[6] 1 Thess. iv. 15-17.
[7] 1 Cor. xv. 51-53.
[8] Comp. Matt. v. 26, and see Tertullian's *De Anima*, xxxv. [and see cap. xliii., *infra*, p. 576.]

change must be undergone, in order that mortality may be swallowed up of life—in other words, that the flesh (be covered) with the heavenly and eternal raiment—it would either follow that those who shall be found in death would not obtain life, deprived as they would then be of the material and so to say the aliment of life, that is, the flesh; or else, these also must needs undergo the change, that in them too mortality may be swallowed up of life, since it is appointed that they too should obtain life. But, you say, in the case of the dead, mortality is already swallowed up of life. No, not in all cases, certainly. For how many will most probably be found of men who had just died—so recently put into their graves, that nothing in them would seem to be decayed? For you do not of course deem a thing to be decayed unless it be cut off, abolished, and withdrawn from our perception, as having in every possible way ceased to be apparent. There are the carcases of the giants of old time; it will be obvious enough that they are not absolutely decayed, for their bony frames are still extant. We have already spoken of this elsewhere.[1] For instance,[2] even lately in this very city,[3] when they were sacrilegiously laying the foundations of the Odeum on a good many ancient graves, people were horror-stricken to discover, after some five hundred years, bones, which still retained their moisture, and hair which had not lost its perfume. It is certain not only that bones remain indurated, but also that teeth continue undecayed for ages—both of them the lasting germs of that body which is to sprout into life again in the resurrection. Lastly, even if everything that is mortal in all the dead shall then be found decayed—at any rate consumed by death, by time, and through age,—is there nothing which will be " swallowed up of life,"[4] nor by being covered over and arrayed in the vesture of immortality? Now, he who says that mortality is going to be swallowed up of life has already admitted that what is dead *is not destroyed* by those other *before-mentioned devourers.* And verily it will be extremely fit that all shall be consummated and brought about by the operations of God, *and* not by the laws of nature. Therefore, inasmuch as what is mortal has to be swallowed up of life, it must needs be brought out to view in order to be so swallowed up; (needful) also to be swallowed up, in order to undergo the ultimate transformation. If you were to say that a fire is to be lighted, you could not possibly alllege that what is to kindle it is sometimes necessary *and* sometimes not. In like manner, when he inserts the words " If so be that being unclothed[5] we be not found naked."[6]—refering, of course, to those who shall not be found in the day of the Lord alive and in the flesh—he did not say that they whom he had just described as unclothed or stripped, were naked in any other sense than meaning that they should be understood to be reinvested with the very same substance they had been divested of. For although they shall be found naked when their flesh has been laid aside, or to some extent sundered or worn away (and this condition may well be called *nakedness,*) they shall afterwards recover it again, in order that, being reinvested with the flesh, they may be able also to have put over that the supervestment of immortality; for it will be impossible for the outside garment to fit except over one who is already dressed.

CHAP. XLIII.—NO DISPARAGEMENT OF OUR DOCTRINE IN ST. PAUL'S PHRASE, WHICH CALLS OUR RESIDENCE IN THE FLESH ABSENCE FROM THE LORD.

In the same way, when he says, " Therefore we are always confident, and fully aware, that while we are at home in the body we are absent from the Lord; for we walk by faith, not be sight,"[7] it is manifest that in this statement there is no design of disparaging the flesh, as if it separated us from the Lord. For there is here pointedly addressed to us an exhortation to disregard this present life, since we are absent from the Lord as long as we are passing through it—walking by faith, not by sight; in other words, in hope, not in reality. Accordingly he adds: " We are indeed confident and deem it good rather to be absent from the body, and present with the Lord;"[8] in order, that is, that we may walk by sight rather than by faith, in realization rather than in hope. Observe how he here also ascribes to the excellence of martyrdom a contempt for the body. For no one, on becoming absent from the body, is at once a dweller in the presence of the Lord, except by the prerogative of martyrdom,[9] he gains a lodging in Paradise, not in the lower regions. Now, had the apostle been at a loss for words to describe the departure from the body? Or does he purposely use a novel phraseology? For, wanting to express our temporary absence

---

[1] *De Anim.* c. li
[2] Sed : for " scilicet.'
[3] Carthage.
[4] 2 Cor. v. 4. [Against Marcion, p. 455, note 24.]

[5] Exuti. He must have read ἐκδυσάμενοι, instead of the reading of nearly all the MS. authorities, ἐνδυσάμενοι.
[6] 2 Cor. v. 3.
[7] 2 Cor. v. 6, 7.
[8] Ver. 8.
[9] Comp. his *De Anima,* c. lv. [Elucidation III.]

from the body, he says that we are strangers, absent from it, because a man who goes abroad returns after a while to his home. Then he says even to all: "We therefore earnestly desire to be acceptable unto God, whether absent or present; for we must all appear before the judgment-seat of Christ Jesus."[1] If all of us, then all of us wholly; if wholly, then our inward man and outward too—that is, our bodies no less than our souls. "That every one," as he goes on to say, "may receive the things done in his body, according to that he hath done, whether it be good or bad."[2] Now I ask, how do you read this passage? Do you take it to be confusedly constructed, with a transposition[3] of ideas? Is the question about what things will have to be received by the body, or the things which have been already done in the body? Well, if the things which are to be borne by the body are meant, then undoubtedly a resurrection of the body is implied; and if the things which have been already done in the body are referred to, (the same conclusion follows): for of course the retribution will have to be paid by the body, since it was by the body that the actions were performed. Thus the apostle's whole argument from the beginning is unravelled in this concluding clause, wherein the resurrection of the flesh is set forth; and it ought to be understood in a sense which is strictly in accordance with this conclusion.

CHAP. XLIV.—SUNDRY OTHER PASSAGES OF ST. PAUL EXPLAINED IN A SENTENCE CONFIRMATORY OF OUR DOCTRINE.

Now, if you will examine the words which precede the passage where mention is made of the outward and the inward man, will you not discover the whole truth, both of the dignity and the hope of the flesh? For, when he speaks of the "light which God hath commanded to shine in our hearts, to give the light of the knowledge of the glory of the Lord in the person of Jesus Christ,"[4] and says that "we have this treasure in earthen vessels,"[5] meaning of course the flesh, which is meant—that the flesh shall be destroyed, because it is "an earthen vessel," deriving its origin from clay; or that it is to be glorified, as being the receptacle of a divine treasure? Now if that true light, which is in the person of Christ, contains in itself life, and that life with its light is committed to the flesh, is that destined to perish which has life entrusted to it? Then, of course, the treasure will perish also; for perishable things are entrusted to things which are themselves perishable, which is like putting new wine into old bottles. When also he adds, "Always bearing about in our body the dying of the Lord Jesus Christ"[6] what sort of substance is that which, after (being called) the temple of God, can now be also designated the tomb of Christ? But why do we bear about in the body the dying of the Lord? In order, as he says, "that His life also may be manifested."[7] Where? "In the body." In what body? "In our mortal body."[8] Therefore in the flesh, which is mortal indeed through sin, but living through grace—how great a grace you may see when the purpose is, "that the life of Christ may be manifested in it." Is it then in a thing which is a stranger to salvation, in a substance which is perpetually dissolved, that the life of Christ will be manifested, which is eternal, continuous, incorruptible, and already the life of God? Else to what epoch belongs that life of the Lord which is to be manifested in our body? It surely is the life which He lived up to His passion, which was not only openly shown among the Jews, but has now been displayed even to all nations. Therefore that life is meant which "has broken the adamantine gates of death and the brazen bars of the lower world,"[9]—a life which thenceforth has been and will be ours. Lastly, it is to be manifested in the body. When? After death. How? By rising in our body, as Christ also *rose in His*. But lest any one should here object, that the life of Jesus has even now to be manifested in our body by the discipline of holiness, and patience, and righteousness, and wisdom, in which the Lord's life abounded, the most provident wisdom of the apostle inserts this purpose: "For we which live are alway delivered unto death for Jesus' sake, that His life may be manifested in our mortal body."[10] In us, therefore, even when dead, does he say that this is to take place in us. And if so, how is this possible except in our body after its resurrection? Therefore he adds in the concluding sentence: "Knowing that He which raised up *the Lord* Jesus, shall raise up us also with Him,"[11] risen as He is already from the dead. But perhaps "*with* Him" means "*like* Him:" well then, if it be *like* Him, it is not of course without the flesh.

---

[1] 2 Cor. v. 9, 10.
[2] 2 Cor. v. 10.
[3] Per hyperbaton.
[4] 2 Cor. iv. 6.
[5] Ver. 7.

[6] 2 Cor. iv. 10.
[7] Ver. 10.
[8] Ver. 10.
[9] Ps. cvii. 16.
[10] 2 Cor. iv. 11.
[11] Ver. 14.

CHAP. XLV.—THE OLD MAN AND THE NEW MAN
OF ST. PAUL EXPLAINED.

But in their blindness they again impale themselves on the point of the old and the new man. When the apostle enjoins us " to put off the old man, which is corrupt according to the deceitful lusts; and to be renewed in the spirit of our mind; and to put on the new man, which after God is created in righteousness and true holiness," [1] (they maintain) that by here also making a distinction between the two substances, *and applying* the old one to the flesh and the new one to the spirit, he ascribes to the old man—that is to say, the flesh—a permanent corruption. Now, if you follow the order of the substances, the soul cannot be the new man because it comes the later of the two; nor can the flesh be the old man because it is the former. For what fraction of time was it that intervened between the *creative* hand of God and His *afflatus?* I will venture to say, that even if the soul was a good deal prior to the flesh, by the very circumstance that the soul had to wait to be itself completed, it made the other [2] really the former. For everything which gives the finishing stroke and perfection to a work, although it is subsequent in its mere order, yet has the priority in its effect. Much more is that prior, without which preceding things could have no existence. If the flesh be the old man, when did it become so? From the beginning? But Adam was wholly a new man, and of that new man there could be no part an old man. And from that time, ever since the blessing which was pronounced upon man's generation, [3] the flesh and the soul have had a simultaneous birth, without any calculable difference in time; so that the two have been even generated together in the womb, as we have shown in our *Treatise on the Soul.* [4] Contemporaneous in the womb, they are also temporally identical in their birth. The two are no doubt produced by human parents [5] of two substances, but not at two different periods; rather they are so entirely one, that neither is before the other *in point of time.* It is more correct (to say), that we are either entirely the old man or entirely the new, for we cannot tell how we can possibly be anything else. But the apostle mentions a very clear mark of the old man. For " put off," says he, " concerning the former conversation, the old man;" [6] (he does) not *say* concerning the seniority of either substance. It is not indeed the flesh which he bids us to put off, but the works which he in another passage shows to be " works of the flesh." [7] He brings no accusation against men's bodies, of which he even writes as follows: " Putting away lying, speak every man truth with his neighbor: for we are members one of another. Be ye angry, and sin not: let not the sun go down upon your wrath: neither give place to the devil. Let him that stole steal no more: but rather let him labour, working with his hands (the thing which is good), that he may have to give to him that needeth. Let no corrupt communication proceed out of your mouth, but that which is good for the edification of faith, that it may minister grace unto the hearers. And grieve not the Holy Spirit of God, whereby ye are sealed unto the day of redemption. Let all bitterness, and wrath, and anger, and clamour, and evil-speaking, be put away from you, with all malice: but be ye kind one to another, tender-hearted, forgiving one another, even as God in Christ hath forgiven you." [8] Why, therefore, do not those who suppose the flesh to be the old man, hasten their own death, in order that by laying aside the old man they may satisfy the apostle's precepts? As for ourselves, we believe that the whole of faith is to be administered *in* the flesh, nay more, *by* the flesh, which has both a mouth for the utterance of all holy words, and a tongue to refrain from blasphemy, and a heart to avoid all irritation, and hands to labour and to give; while we also maintain that as well the old man as the new has relation to the difference of moral conduct, and not to any discrepancy of nature. And just as we acknowledge that that which according to its former conversation was " the old man " was also corrupt, and received its very name in accordance with " its deceitful lusts," so also (do we hold) that it is " the old man in reference to its former conversation," [9] and not in respect of the flesh through any permanent dissolution. Moreover, it is still unimpaired in the flesh, and identical in that nature, even when it has become " the new man;" since it is of its sinful course of life, and not of its corporeal substance, that it has been divested.

CHAP. XLVI.—IT IS THE WORKS OF THE FLESH,
NOT THE SUBSTANCE OF THE FLESH, WHICH
ST. PAUL ALWAYS CONDEMNS.

You may notice that the apostle everywhere condemns the works of the flesh in such a

---

[1] Eph. iv. 22-24.
[2] The flesh.
[3] Gen. i. 28.
[4] See ch. xxvii.
[5] We treat " homines" as a nominative, after Oehler.
[6] Eph. iv. 22.
[7] Gal. v. 19.
[8] Eph. iv. 25-32.
[9] Eph. iv. 22.

way as to appear to condemn the flesh; but no one can suppose him to have any such view as this, since he goes on to suggest another sense, even though somewhat resembling it. For when he actually declares that " they who are in the flesh cannot please God," he immediately recalls the statement from an heretical sense to a sound one, by adding, " But ye are not in the flesh, but in the Spirit."[1] Now, by denying them to be in the flesh who yet obviously were in the flesh, he showed that they were not living amidst the works of the flesh, and therefore that they who could not please God were not those who were in the flesh, but only those who were living after the flesh; whereas they pleased God, who, although existing in the flesh, were yet walking after the Spirit. And, again, he says that " the body is dead;" but it is " because of sin," even as " the Spirit is life because of righteousness."[2] When, however, he thus sets life in opposition to the death which is constituted in the flesh, he unquestionably promises the life of righteousness to the same state for which he determined the death of sin. But unmeaning is this opposition which he makes between the " life " and the " death," if the life is not there where that very thing is to which he opposes it—even the death which is to be extirpated of course from the body. Now, if life thus extirpates death from the body, it can accomplish this only by penetrating thither where that is which it is excluding. But why am I resorting to knotty arguments,[3] when the apostle treats the subject with perfect plainness? " For if," says he, " the Spirit of Him that raised up Jesus from the dead dwell in you, He that raised up Jesus from the dead shall also quicken your mortal bodies, because of His Spirit that dwelleth in you;"[4] so that even if a person were to assume that the soul is " the mortal body," he would (since he cannot possibly deny that the flesh is this also) be constrained to acknowledge a restoration even of the flesh, in consequence of its participation in the selfsame state. From the following words, moreover, you may learn that it is the works of the flesh which are condemned, and not the flesh itself: " Therefore, brethren, we are debtors, not *to the flesh*, to live after the flesh: for if ye live after the flesh ye shall die; but if ye, through the Spirit, do mortify the deeds of the body, ye shall live."[5] Now (that I may answer each point separately), since salvation is promised to those who are living in the flesh, but walking after the Spirit, it is no longer the flesh which is an adversary to salvation, but the working of the flesh. When, however, this operativeness of the flesh is done away with, which is the cause of death, the flesh is shown to be safe, since it is freed from the cause of death. " For the law," says he, " of the Spirit of life in Christ Jesus hath made me free from the law of sin and death,"[6]—that, surely, which he previously mentioned as dwelling in our members.[7] Our members, therefore, will no longer be subject to the law of death, because they cease to serve that of sin, from *both* which they have been set free. " For what the law could not do, in that it was weak through the flesh, God sending His own Son in the likeness of sinful flesh, and through[8] sin condemned sin in the flesh "[9]— not the flesh in sin, for the house is not to be condemned with its inhabitant. He said, indeed, that " sin dwelleth in our body."[10] But the condemnation of sin is the acquittal of the flesh, just as its non-condemnation subjugates it to the law of sin and death. In like manner, he called " the carnal mind " first " death,"[11] and afterwards " enmity against God;"[12] but he never predicated this of the flesh itself. But to what then, you will say, must the carnal mind be ascribed, if it be not to the *carnal* substance itself? I will allow your objection, if you will prove to me that the flesh has any discernment of its own. If, however, it has no conception of anything without the soul, you must understand that the carnal mind must be referred to the soul, although ascribed sometimes to the flesh, on the ground that it is ministered to for the flesh and through the flesh. And therefore (the apostle) says that " sin dwelleth in the flesh," because the soul by which sin is provoked has its temporary lodging in the flesh, which is doomed indeed to death, not however on its own account, but on account of sin. For he says in another passage also: " How is it that you conduct yourselves as if you were even now living in the world?"[13] where he is not writing to dead persons, but to those who ought to have ceased to live after the ways of the world

CHAP. XLVII.—ST. PAUL, ALL THROUGH, PROMISES ETERNAL LIFE TO THE BODY.

For that must be living after the world,

---

[1] Rom. viii. 8, 9.
[2] Ver. 10.
[3] Nodosius.
[4] Rom. viii. 11.
[5] Vers. 12, 13.

[6] Ver. 2.
[7] Rom. vii. 17, 20, 23.
[8] Per delinquentiam: see the *De Carne Christi*, xvi.
[9] Rom. viii. 3.
[10] Rom. vii. 20.
[11] Rom. viii. 6.
[12] Ver. 7.
[13] Col. ii. 20.

which, as the old man, he declares to be "crucified with Christ,"[1] not as a bodily structure, but as moral behaviour. Besides, if we do not understand it in this sense, it is not our bodily frame which has been transfixed (at all events), nor has our flesh endured the cross of Christ; but the sense is that which he has subjoined, "that the body of sin might be made void,"[2] by an amendment of life, not by a destruction of the substance, as he goes on to say, "that henceforth we should not serve sin;"[3] and that we should believe ourselves to be "dead with Christ," in such a manner as that "we shall also live with Him."[4] On the same principle he says: "Likewise reckon ye also yourselves to be dead indeed."[5] To what? To the flesh? No, but "unto sin."[6] Accordingly as to the flesh they will be saved—"alive unto God in Christ Jesus,"[7] through the flesh of course, to which they will not be dead; since it is "unto sin," and not to the flesh, that they are dead. For he pursues the point still further: "Let not sin therefore reign in your mortal body, that ye should obey it, and that ye should yield your members as instruments of unrighteousness unto sin: but yield ye yourselves unto God, as those that are alive from the dead"—not simply alive, but as alive from the dead—"and your members as instruments of righteousness."[8] And again: "As ye have yielded your members servants of uncleanness, and of iniquity unto iniquity, even so now yield your members servants of righteousness unto holiness; for whilst ye were the servants of sin, ye were free from righteousness. What fruit had ye then in those things of which ye are now ashamed? For the end of those things is death. But now, being made free from sin, and become servants to God, ye have your fruit unto holiness, and the end everlasting life. For the wages of sin is death, but the gift of God is eternal life through Jesus Christ our Lord."[9] Thus throughout this series of passages, whilst withdrawing our members from unrighteousness and sin, and applying them to righteousness and holiness, and transferring the same from the wages of death to the donative of eternal life, he undoubtedly promises to the flesh the recompense of salvation. Now it would not at all have been consistent that any rule of holiness and right-

eousness should be especially enjoined for the flesh, if the reward of such a discipline were not also within its reach; nor could even baptism be properly ordered for the flesh, if by its regeneration a course were not inaugurated tending to its restitution; the apostle himself suggesting this idea: "Know ye not, that so many of us as are baptized into Jesus Christ, are baptized into His death? We are therefore buried with Him by baptism into death, that just as Christ was raised up from the dead, even so we also should walk in newness of life."[10] And that you may not suppose that this is said merely of that life which we have to walk in the newness of, through baptism, by faith, the apostle with superlative forethought adds: "For if we have been planted together in the likeness of Christ's death, we shall be also in the likeness of His resurrection."[11] By a figure we die in our baptism, but in a reality we rise again in the flesh, even as Christ did, "that, as sin has reigned in death, so also grace might reign through righteousness unto life eternal, through Jesus Christ our Lord."[12] But how so, unless equally in the flesh? For where the death is, there too must be the life after the death, because also the life was first there, where death subsequently was. Now, if the dominion of death operates only in the dissolution of the flesh, in like manner death's contrary, life, ought to produce the contrary effect, even the restoration of the flesh; so that, just as death had swallowed it up in its strength, it also, after this mortal was swallowed up of immortality, may hear the challenge pronounced against it: "O death, where is thy sting? O grave, where is thy victory?"[13] For in this way "grace shall there much more abound, where sin once abounded."[14] In this way also "shall strength be made perfect in weakness,"[15]—saving what is lost, reviving what is dead, healing what is stricken, curing what is faint, redeeming what is lost, freeing what is enslaved, recalling what has strayed, raising what is fallen; and this from earth to heaven, where, as the apostle teaches the Philippians, "we have our citizenship,[16] from whence also we look for our Saviour Jesus Christ, who shall change our body of humiliation, that it may be fashioned like unto His glorious body"[17]—of course after the resurrection, because Christ Himself was not glorified before He suffered. These must be "the bodies" which he "beseeches" the Romans

[1] Rom. vi. 6.
[2] Evacuetur: καταργηθῇ. A. V. *destroyed*, i.e. deprived of all activity, Rom. vi. 6.
[3] Rom. vi. 6. Tertullian's reading literally is, "that thus far (and no further) we should be servants of sin."
[4] Ver. 8.
[5] Ver. 11.
[6] Ver. 11.
[7] Ver. 11.
[8] Vers. 12, 13.
[9] Vers. 19-23.

[10] Rom. vi. 3, 4.
[11] Ver. 5.
[12] Rom. v. 21.
[13] 1 Cor. xv. 55.
[14] Rom. v. 20.
[15] 2 Cor. xii. 9.
[16] Municipatum.
[17] Phil. iii. 20, 21.

to "present" as "a living sacrifice, holy, acceptable unto God."[1] But how a *living* sacrifice, if these bodies are to perish? How a *holy* one, if they are profanely soiled? How *acceptable to God*, if they are condemned? Come, now, tell me how that passage (in the Epistle) to the Thessalonians—which, because of its clearness, I should suppose to have been written with a sunbeam—is understood by our heretics, who shun the light of Scripture: "And the very God of peace sanctify you wholly." And as if this were not plain enough, it goes on to say: "And may your whole body, and soul, and spirit be preserved blameless unto the coming of the Lord."[2] Here you have the entire substance of man destined to salvation, and *that* at no other time than at the coming of the Lord, which is the key of the resurrection.[3]

CHAP. XLVIII.—SUNDRY PASSAGES IN THE GREAT CHAPTER OF THE RESURRECTION OF THE DEAD EXPLAINED IN DEFENCE OF OUR DOCTRINE.

But "flesh and blood," you say, "cannot inherit the kingdom of God."[4] We are quite aware that this too is written; but although our opponents place it in the front of the battle, we have intentionally reserved the objection until now, in order that we may in our last assault overthrow it, after we have removed out of the way all the questions which are auxiliary to it. However, they must contrive to recall to their mind even now our preceding *arguments*, in order that the occasion which originally suggested this passage may assist our judgment in arriving at its meaning. The apostle, as I take it, having set forth for the Corinthians the details of their church discipline, had summed up the substance of his own gospel, and of their belief in an exposition of the Lord's death and resurrection, for the purpose of deducing therefrom the rule of our hope, and the groundwork thereof. Accordingly he subjoins this statement: "Now if Christ be preached that He rose from the dead, how say some among you that there is no resurrection of the dead? If there be no *resurrection of the dead*, then Christ is not risen: and if Christ be not risen, then is our preaching vain, and your faith is also vain. Yea, and we are found false witnesses of God; because we have testified of God that He raised up Christ, whom He raised not up, *if so be that the dead rise not*. For if the dead rise not, then is not Christ raised: and if Christ be not

raised, your faith is vain, because ye are yet in your sins, and they which have fallen asleep in Christ are perished."[5] Now, what is the point which he evidently labours hard to make us believe throughout this passage? The resurrection of the dead, you say, which was denied: he certainly wished it to be believed on the strength of the example which he adduced—the Lord's resurrection. Certainly, you say. Well now, is an example borrowed from different circumstances, or from like ones? From like ones, by all means, is your answer. How then did Christ rise again? In the flesh, or not? No doubt, since you are told that He "died according to the Scriptures,"[6] and "that He was buried *according to the Scriptures*,"[7] no otherwise than in the flesh, you will also allow that it was in the flesh that He was raised from the dead. For the very same body which fell in death, and which lay in the sepulchre, did also rise again; (and it was) not so much Christ in the flesh, as the flesh in Christ. If, therefore, we are to rise again after the example of Christ, who rose in the flesh, we shall certainly not rise according to that example, unless we also shall ourselves rise again in the flesh. "For," he says, "since by man came death, by man came also the resurrection of the dead."[8] (This he says) in order, on the one hand, to distinguish the two authors—Adam of death, Christ of resurrection; and, on the other hand, to make the resurrection operate on the same substance as the death, by comparing the authors themselves under the designation *man*. For if "as in Adam all die, even so in Christ shall all be made alive,"[9] their vivification in Christ must be in the flesh, since it is in the flesh that arises their death in Adam. "But every man in his own order,"[10] because of course *it will be* also *every man* in his own body. For the *order* will be arranged severally, on account of the individual merits. Now, as the merits must be ascribed to the body, it must needs follow that the order also should be arranged in respect of the bodies, that it may be in relation to their merits. But inasmuch as "some are also baptized for the dead,"[11] we will see whether there be a good reason for this. Now it is certain that they adopted this (practice) with such a presumption as made them suppose that the vicarious baptism (in question) would be beneficial to the flesh of another in anticipation of the resurrection; for unless it were a bodily *resur-*

---

[1] Rom. xii. 1.
[2] 1 Thess. v. 23.
[3] [Note Tertullian's summary of the text, in harmony with the *Tripartite* philosophy of humanity.]
[4] 1 Cor. xv. 50.

[5] 1 Cor. xv. 12–18.
[6] Ver. 3.
[7] Ver. 4.
[8] Ver. 21.
[9] 1 Cor. xv. 22.
[10] Ver. 23.
[11] Ver. 29.

rection, there would be no pledge secured by this process of a corporeal baptism. "Why are they then baptized for the dead,"[1] he asks, unless the bodies rise again which are thus baptized? For it is not the soul which is sanctified by the baptismal bath:[2] its sanctification comes from the "answer."[3] "And why," he inquires, "stand we in jeopardy every hour?"[4]—meaning, of course, through the flesh. "I die daily,"[5] (says he); that is, undoubtedly, in the perils of the body, in which "he even fought with beasts at Ephesus,"[6]—even with those beasts which caused him such peril and trouble in Asia, to which he alludes in his second epistle to the same church *of Corinth:* "For we would not, brethren, have you ignorant of our trouble which came to us in Asia, that we were pressed above measure, above strength, insomuch that we despaired even of life."[7] Now, if I mistake not, he enumerates all these particulars in order that in his unwillingness to have his conflicts in the flesh supposed to be useless, he may induce an unfaltering belief in the resurrection of the flesh. For useless must that conflict be deemed (which is sustained in a body) for which no resurrection is in prospect. "But some man will say, How are the dead to be raised? And with what body will they come?"[8] Now here he discusses the qualities of bodies, whether it be the very same, or different ones, which men are to resume. Since, however, such a question as this must be regarded as a subsequent one, it will in passing be enough for us that the resurrection is determined to be a bodily one even from this, that it is about the quality of *bodies* that the inquiry arises.

CHAP. XLIX.—THE SAME SUBJECT CONTINUED. WHAT DOES THE APOSTLE EXCLUDE FROM THE DEAD? CERTAINLY NOT THE SUBSTANCE OF THE FLESH.

We come now to the very gist[9] of the whole question: What are the substances, and of what nature are they, which the apostle has disinherited of the kingdom of God? The preceding statements give us a clue to this point also. He says: "The first man is of the earth, earthy"—that is, made of dust, that is, Adam; "the second man is from heaven"[10]—that is, the Word of God, which is Christ, in no other way, however, *man* (al-

though "from heaven"), than as being Himself flesh and soul, just as a human being is, just as Adam was. Indeed, in a previous passage He is called "the second Adam,"[11] deriving the identity of His name from His participation in the substance, because not even Adam was flesh of human seed, in which Christ is also like Him.[12] "As is the earthy, such are they also that are earthy; and as is the heavenly, such are they also that are heavenly."[13] *Such* (does he mean), in substance; or first of all in training, and afterwards in the dignity and worth which that training aimed at acquiring? Not in substance, however, by any means will the earthy and the heavenly be separated, designated as they have been by the apostle once for all, as *men.* For even if Christ were the only true "heavenly," nay, super-celestial Being, He is still man, as composed of body and soul; and in no respect is He separated from the quality of "earthiness," owing to that condition of His which makes Him a partaker of both substances. In like manner, those also who after Him are heavenly, are understood to have this celestial quality predicated of them not from their present nature, but from their future glory; because in a preceding sentence, which originated this distinction respecting difference of dignity, there was shown to be "one glory in celestial bodies, and another in terrestrial ones,"[14]—"one glory of the sun, and another glory of the moon, and another glory of the stars: for even one star differeth from another star in glory,"[15] although not in substance. Then, after having thus premised the difference in that worth or dignity which is even now to be aimed at, and then at last to be enjoyed, the apostle adds an exhortation, that we should both here in our training follow the example of Christ, and there attain His eminence in glory: "As we have borne the image of the earthy, let us also bear the image of the heavenly."[16] We have indeed borne the image of the earthy, by our sharing in his trangression, by our participation in his death, by our banishment from Paradise. Now, although the image of Adam is here borne by is in the flesh, yet we are not exhorted to put off the flesh; but if not the flesh, it is the conversation, in order that we may then bear the image of the heavenly in ourselves,—no longer indeed *the image* of God, and no longer *the image* of a Being whose state is in heaven; but after the lineaments of Christ, by our walking here in holiness, righteousness, and

---

[1] Ver. 29.
[2] Lavatione.
[3] Comp. 1 Pet. iii. 21.
[4] 1 Cor. xv. 30.
[5] Ver. 31.
[6] Ver. 32.
[7] 2 Cor. i. 8.
[8] 1 Cor. xv. 35.
[9] Ad carnem et sanguinem revera.
[10] 1 Cor. xv. 47.

[11] Ver. 45.
[12] See *De Carne Christi.* ch. xvi.
[13] 1 Cor. xv. 48.
[14] 1 Cor. xv. 40.
[15] Ver. 41.
[16] Ver. 49.

truth. And so wholly intent on the inculcation of moral conduct is he throughout this passage, that he tells us we ought to bear the image of Christ in this flesh of ours, and in this period of instruction and discipline. For when he says "*let us bear*" in the imperative mood, he suits his words to the present life, in which man exists in no other substance than as flesh and soul; or if it is another, even the heavenly, substance to which this faith (of ours) looks forward, yet the promise is made to that *substance* to which the injunction is given to labour earnestly to merit its reward. Since, therefore, he makes the image both of the earthy and the heavenly consist of moral conduct—the one to be abjured, and the other to be pursued—and then consistently adds, " For this I say" (on account, that is, of what I have already said, because the conjunction "*for*" connects what follows with the preceding words) " that flesh and blood cannot inherit the kingdom of God,"[1]—he means the flesh and blood to be understood in no other sense than the before-mentioned " image of the earthy;" and since this is reckoned to consist in "the old conversation,"[2] which old conversation receives not the kingdom of God, therefore flesh and blood, by not receiving the kingdom of God, are reduced to the *life of the* old conversation. Of course, as the apostle has never put the substance for the works *of man*, he cannot use such a construction here. Since, however, he has declared of men which are yet alive in the flesh, that they " are not in the flesh,"[3] meaning that they are not living in the works of the flesh, you ought not to subvert its form nor its substance, but only the works done in the substance (of the flesh), alienating us from the kingdom of God. It is after displaying to the Galatians these pernicious works that he professes to warn them beforehand, even as he had " told them in time past, that they which do such things should not inherit the kingdom of God,"[4] even because they bore not the image of the heavenly, as they had borne the image of the earthy; and so, in consequence of their old conversation, they were to be regarded as nothing else than flesh and blood. But even if the apostle had abruptly thrown out the sentence that flesh and blood must be excluded from the kingdom of God, without any previous intimation of his meaning, would it not have been equally our duty to interpret these two substances as the old man abandoned to mere flesh and blood—in other words, to eating and drink-

ing, one feature of which would be to speak against the faith of the resurrection: " Let us eat and drink, for to-morrow we die."[5] Now, when the apostle parenthetically inserted this, he censured flesh and blood because of their enjoyment in eating and drinking.

CHAP. L.—IN WHAT SENSE FLESH AND BLOOD ARE EXCLUDED FROM THE KINGDOM OF GOD.

Putting aside, however, all interpretations of this sort, which criminate the works of the flesh and blood, it may be permitted me to claim for the resurrection these very substances, understood in none other than their natural sense. For it is not the resurrection that is directly denied to flesh and blood, but the kingdom of God, which is incidental to[6] the resurrection (for there is a resurrection of judgment[7] also); and there is even a confirmation of the general resurrection of the flesh, whenever a special one is excepted. Now, when it is clearly stated what the condition is to which the resurrection does not lead, it is understood what that is to which it does lead; and, therefore, whilst it is in consideration of *men's* merits that a difference is made in their resurrection by their conduct in the flesh, and not by the substance thereof, it is evident even from this, that flesh and blood are excluded from the kingdom of God in respect of their sin, not of their substance; and although in respect of their natural condition[8] they will rise again for the judgment, because they rise not for the kingdom. Again, I will say, " Flesh and blood cannot inherit the kingdom of God;"[9] and justly (does the apostle declare this of them, considered) alone and in themselves, in order to show that the Spirit is still needed (to qualify them) for the kingdom.[10] For it is " the Spirit that quickeneth" *us* for the kingdom of God; " the flesh profiteth nothing."[11] There is, however, something else which can be profitable thereunto, that is, the Spirit; and through the Spirit, the works also of the Spirit. Flesh and blood, therefore, must in every case rise again, equally, in their proper quality. But they to whom it is granted to enter the kingdom of God, will have to put on the power of an incorruptible and immortal life; for without this, *or* before they are able to obtain it, they cannot enter into the kingdom of God. With good reason, then, flesh and blood, as we have already said, by themselves fail to

---

[1] 1 Cor. xv. 50.
[2] See Eph. iv. 22.
[3] Rom. viii. 9.
[4] Gal. v. 21.

[5] 1 Cor. xv. 32.
[6] Obvenit.
[7] A. V. *damnation*, John v. 29.
[8] Forma.
[9] 1 Cor. xv. 50.
[10] This must be the meaning of the dative *illi*.
[11] John vi. 63.

obtain the kingdom of God. But inasmuch as " this corruptible (that is, the flesh) must put on incorruption, and this mortal (that is, the blood) must put on immortality,"[1] by the change which is to follow the resurrection, it will, for the best of reasons, happen that flesh and blood, after that change and investiture,[2] will become able to inherit the kingdom of God—but not without the resurrection. Some will have it, that by the phrase " flesh and blood," because of its rite of circumcision, Judaism is meant, which is itself too alienated from the kingdom of God, as being accounted " the old or former conversation," and as being designated by this title in another passage of the apostle also, who, " when it pleased God to reveal to him His Son, to preach Him amongst the heathen, immediately conferred not with flesh and blood," as he writes to the Galatians,[3] (meaning by the phrase) the circumcision, that is to say, Judaism.

CHAP. LI.—THE SESSION OF JESUS IN HIS INCARNATE NATURE AT THE RIGHT HAND OF GOD A GUARANTEE OF THE RESURRECTION OF OUR FLESH.

That, however, which we have reserved for a concluding argument, will now stand as a plea for all, and for the apostle himself, who in very deed would have to be charged with extreme indiscretion, if he had so abruptly, as some will have it, and as they say, blindfold, and so indiscriminately, and so unconditionally, excluded from the kingdom of God, and indeed from the court of heaven itself, all flesh and blood whatsoever; since Jesus is still sitting there at the right hand of the Father,[4] man, yet God—the last Adam,[5] yet the primary Word—flesh and blood, yet purer than ours—who " shall descend in like manner as He ascended *into heaven*"[6] the same both in substance and form, as the angels affirmed,[7] so as even to be recognised by those who pierced Him.[8] Designated, as He is, " the Mediator[9] between God and man," He keeps in His own self the deposit of the flesh which has been committed to Him by both parties—the pledge and security of its entire perfection. For as " He has given to us the earnest of the Spirit,"[10] so has He received from us the earnest of the flesh, and has carried it with Him into heaven as a pledge of that complete entirety which is one day to be restored to it. Be not disquieted, O flesh and blood, with any care; in Christ you have acquired both heaven and the kingdom of God. Otherwise, if they say that you are not in Christ, let them also say that Christ is not in heaven, since they have denied you heaven. Likewise " neither shall corruption," says he, " inherit incorruption."[11] *This he says*, not that you may take flesh and blood to be corruption, for they are themselves rather the subjects of corruption, —I mean through death, since death does not so much corrupt, as actually consume, our flesh and blood. But inasmuch as he had plainly said that the works of the flesh and blood could not obtain the kingdom of God, with the view of stating this with accumulated stress, he deprived corruption itself—that is, death, which profits so largely by the works of the flesh and blood—from all inheritance of incorruption. For a little afterwards, he has described what is, as it were, the death of death itself: " Death," says he, " is swallowed up in victory. O death, where is thy sting? O grave, where is thy victory? The sting of death is sin "—here is the *corruption;* " and the strength of sin is the law"[12]—that other law, no doubt, which he has described " in his members as warring against the law of his mind,"[13]—meaning, of course, the actual power of sinning against his will. Now he says in a previous passage (of our Epistle to the Corinthians), that " the last enemy to be destroyed is death."[14] In this way, then, it is that corruption shall not inherit incorruption; in other words, death shall not continue. When and how shall it cease? In that " moment, that twinkling of an eye, at the last trump, when the dead shall rise incorruptible."[15] But what are these, if not they who were corruptible before—that is, our bodies; in other words, our flesh and blood? And we undergo the change. But in what condition, if not in that wherein we shall be found? " For this corruptible must put on incorruption, and this mortal must put on immortality."[16] What mortal is this but the flesh? what corruptible but the blood? Moreover, that you may not suppose the apostle to have any other meaning, in his care to teach you, and that you may understand him seriously to apply his statement to the flesh, when he says " *this* corruptible " and " *this* mortal," he utters the words

---

[1] 1 Cor. xv. 53.
[2] We have kept this word to suit the last Scripture quotation; but Tertullian's word, both here and in the quotation, is " devorata," swallowed up.
[3] See i. 15, 16.
[4] Mark xvi. 19.
[5] 1 Cor. xv. 45.
[6] Acts i. 9.
[7] Ver. 10.
[8] Zech. xii. 10 ; John xix. 37 ; Rev. i. 7.
[9] 1 Tim. ii. 5. Tertullian's word is " sequester," the guardian of a deposit.
[10] 2 Cor. v. 5.

[11] 1 Cor. xv. 50.
[12] 1 Cor. xv. 54-56.
[13] Rom. vii. 23.
[14] 1 Cor. xv. 26.
[15] Ver. 52.
[16] Ver. 53.

while touching the surface of his own body.[1] He certainly could not have pronounced these phrases except in reference to an object which was palpable and apparent. The expression indicates a bodily exhibition. Moreover, a corruptible body is one thing, and corruption is another; so a mortal body is one thing, and mortality is another. For that which suffers is one thing, and that which causes it to suffer is another. Consequently, those things which are subject to corruption and mortality, even the flesh and blood, must needs also be susceptible of incorruption and immortality.

CHAP. LII.—FROM ST. PAUL'S ANALOGY OF THE SEED WE LEARN THAT THE BODY WHICH DIED WILL RISE AGAIN, GARNISHED WITH THE APPLIANCES OF ETERNAL LIFE.

Let us now see in what body he asserts that the dead will come. And with a felicitous sally he proceeds at once to illustrate the point, as if an objector had plied him with some such question. "Thou fool," says he, "that which thou sowest is not quickened, except it die."[2] From this example of the *seed* it is then evident that no other flesh is quickened than that which shall have undergone death, and therefore all the rest of the question will become clear enough. For nothing which is incompatible with the idea suggested by the example can possibly be understood; nor from the clause which follows, "That which thou sowest, thou sowest not the body which shall be,"[3] are you permitted to suppose that in the resurrection a different body is to arise from that which is sown in death. Otherwise you have run away from the example. For if wheat be sown and dissolved in the ground, barley does not spring up. Still it is not[4] the very same grain in kind; nor is its nature the same, or its quality and form. Then whence *comes it*, if it is not the very same? For even the decay is *a proof of* the thing itself, since it is *the decay* of the actual *grain*. Well, but does not the apostle himself suggest in what sense it is that "the body which shall be" is not the body which is sown, even when he says, "But bare grain, it may chance of wheat, or of some other grain; but God giveth it a body as it pleaseth Him?"[5] *Gives it* of course to the grain which he says is sown bare. No doubt, you say. Then the grain is safe enough, to which God has to assign a body. But how safe, if it is

nowhere in existence, if it does not rise again if it rises not again its actual self? If it rises not again, it is not safe; *and* if it is not even safe, it cannot receive a body from God. But there is every possible proof that it is safe. For what purpose, therefore, will God give it "a body, as it pleases Him," even when it already has its own "bare" body, unless it be that in its resurrection it may be no longer bare? That therefore will be additional matter which is placed over the *bare* body; nor is that at all destroyed on which the superimposed matter is put,—nay, it is increased. That, however, is safe which receives augmentation. The truth is, it is sown the barest grain, without a husk to cover it, without a spike even in germ, without the protection of a bearded top, without the glory of a stalk. It rises, however, out of the furrow enriched with a copious crop, built up in a compact fabric, constructed in a *beautiful* order, fortified by cultivation, and clothed around on every side. These are the circumstances which make it another body from God, to which it is changed not by abolition, but by amplification. And to every seed *God* has assigned its own body[6]—not, indeed, its own in the sense of its primitive body—in order that what it acquires from God extrinsically may also at last be accounted its own. Cleave firmly then to the example, and keep it well in view, as a mirror of what happens to the flesh: believe that the very same *flesh* which was once sown *in death* will bear fruit *in resurrection-life*—the same in essence, only more full and perfect; not another, although reappearing in another form. For it shall receive in itself the grace and ornament which God shall please to spread over it, according to its merits. Unquestionably it is in this sense that he says, "All flesh is not the same flesh;"[7] meaning not to deny a community of substance, but a parity of prerogative,—reducing the body to a difference of honour, not of nature. With this view he adds, in a figurative sense, certain examples of animals and heavenly bodies: "There is one flesh of man" (that is, servants of God, but really human), "another flesh of beasts" (that is, the heathen, of whom the prophet actually says, "Man is like the senseless cattle"[8]), "another flesh of birds" (that is, the martyrs which essay to mount up to heaven), "another of fishes" (that is, those whom the water of baptism has submerged).[9] In like manner does he take examples from the heavenly

---

[1] Cutem ipsam. Rufinus says that in the church of Aquileia they touched their bodies when they recited the clause of the creed which they rendered "the resurrection of *this* body."
[2] 1 Cor. xv. 36.
[3] Ver. 37.
[4] An objection of the opponent.
[5] Vers. 37, 38.

[6] 1 Cor. xv. 38.
[7] Ver. 39.
[8] Ps. xlix. 20, Sept.
[9] 1 Cor. xv. 39.

bodies: "There is one glory of the sun" (that is, of Christ), "and another glory of the moon" (that is, of the Church), "and another glory of the stars" (in other words, of the seed of Abraham). "For one star differeth from another star in glory: so there are bodies terrestrial as well as celestial" (Jews, that is, as well as Christians).[1] Now, if this language is not to be construed figuratively, it was absurd enough for him to make a contrast between the flesh of mules and kites, as well as the heavenly bodies and human bodies; for they admit of no comparison as to their condition, nor in respect of their attainment of a resurrection. Then at last, having conclusively shown by his examples that the difference was one of glory, not of substance, he adds: "So also is the resurrection of the dead."[2] How so? In no other way than as differing in glory only. For again, predicating the resurrection of the same substance, and returning once more to (his comparison of) the grain, he says: "It is sown in corruption, it is raised in incorruption; it is sown in dishonour, it is raised in glory; it is sown in weakness, it is raised in power; it is sown a natural body, it is raised a spiritual body."[3] Now, certainly nothing else is raised than that which is sown; and nothing else is sown than that which decays in the ground; and it is nothing else than the flesh which is decayed in the ground. For this was the substance which God's decree demolished, "Earth thou art, and to earth shalt thou return;"[4] because it was taken out of the earth. And it was from this circumstance that the apostle borrowed his phrase of the flesh being "sown," since it returns to the ground, and the ground is the grand depository for seeds which are meant to be deposited in it, and again sought out of it. And therefore he confirms the passage afresh, by putting on it the impress (of his own inspired authority), saying, "For so it is written;"[5] that you may not suppose that the "being sown" means anything else than "thou shalt return to the ground, out of which thou wast taken;" nor that the phrase "for so it is written" refers to any other thing that the flesh.

CHAP. LIII.—NOT THE SOUL, BUT THE NATURAL BODY WHICH DIED, IS THAT WHICH IS TO RISE AGAIN. THE RESURRECTION OF LAZARUS COMMENTED ON. CHRIST'S RESURRECTION, AS THE SECOND ADAM, GUARANTEES OUR OWN.

Some, however, contend that the *soul* is "the natural (or animate) body,"[6] with the view of withdrawing the *flesh* from all connection with the risen body. Now, since it is a clear and fixed point that the body which is to rise again is that which was sown *in death*, they must be challenged to an examination of the very fact itself. Else let them show that the soul was sown after death; in a word, that it underwent death,—that is, was demolished, dismembered, dissolved in the ground, nothing of which was ever decreed against it by God: let them display to our view its corruptibility and dishonour (as well as) its weakness, that it may also accrue to it to rise again in incorruption, and in glory, and in power.[7] Now in the case of Lazarus, (which we may take as) the palmary instance of a resurrection, the flesh lay prostrate in weakness, the flesh was almost putrid in the dishonour *of its decay*, the flesh stank in corruption, and yet it was as *flesh* that Lazarus rose again—with his soul, no doubt. But that soul was incorrupt; nobody had wrapped it in its linen swathes; nobody had deposited it in a grave; nobody had yet perceived it "stink;" nobody for four days had seen it "sown." Well, now, this entire condition, this whole end of Lazarus, the flesh indeed of all men is still experiencing, but the soul of no one. That substance, therefore, to which the apostle's whole description manifestly refers, of which he clearly speaks, must be both the natural (or animate) body when it is sown, and the spiritual body when it is raised again. For in order that you may understand it in this sense, he points to this same conclusion, when in like manner, on the authority of the same passage of Scripture, he displays to us "the first man Adam as made a living soul."[8] Now since Adam was the first man, since also the flesh was man prior to the soul,[9] it undoubtedly follows that it was the flesh that became the living soul. Moreover, since it was a bodily substance that assumed this condition, it was of course the natural (or animate) body that became the living soul. By what designation would they have it called, except that which it became through the soul, except that which it was not previous to the soul, except that which it can never be after the soul, but through its resurrection? For after it has recovered the soul, it once more becomes natural (or animate) body, in order that it may become a spiritual body. For it only resumes in the resurrection the condition which it once

---

[1] 1 Cor. xv. 41.
[2] Ver. 42.
[3] Vers. 42–44.
[4] Gen. iii. 19.
[5] 1 Cor. xv. 45.
[6] What in our version is rendered "*a natural body*," is St Paul's σῶμα ψυχικόν, which the heretics held to be merely a periphrasis for ψυχή. We have rendered Tertullian's phrase *corpus animale* by "animate body," the better to suit the argument.
[7] 1 Cor. xv. 42, 43.
[8] Compare ver. 45 with Gen. ii. 7.
[9] See this put more fully above, c. v., near the end.

had. There is therefore by no means the same good reason why the *soul* should be called the natural (or animate) body, which the *flesh* has for bearing that designation. The flesh, in fact, was a body before it was an animate body. When the flesh was joined by the soul,[1] it then became the natural (or animate) body. Now, although the soul is a corporeal substance,[2] yet, as it is not an animated body, but rather an animating one, it cannot be called the animate (or natural) body, nor can it become that thing which it produces. It is indeed when the soul accrues to something else that it makes that thing animate; but unless it so accrues, how will it ever produce animation? As therefore the flesh was at first an animate (or natural) body on receiving the soul, so at last will it become a spiritual body when invested with the spirit. Now the apostle, by severally adducing this order in Adam and in Christ, fairly distinguishes between the two states, in the very essentials of their difference. And when he calls Christ " the last Adam,"[3] you may from this circumstance discover how strenuously he labours to establish throughout his teaching the resurrection of the flesh, not of the soul. Thus, then, the first man Adam was flesh, not soul, and only afterwards became a living soul; and the last Adam, Christ, was Adam only because He was man, and only man as being flesh, not as being soul. Accordingly the apostle goes on to say: " Howbeit that was not first which is spiritual, but that which is natural, and afterward that which is spiritual,"[4] as in the case of the two Adams. Now, do you not suppose that he is distinguishing between the natural body and the spiritual body in the same flesh, after having already drawn the distinction therein in the two Adams, that is, in the first man and in the last? For from which substance is it that Christ and Adam have a parity with each other? No doubt it is from their flesh, although it may be from their soul also. It is, however, in respect of the flesh that they are both man; for the flesh was man prior *to the soul.* It was actually from it that they were able to take rank, so as to be deemed—one the first, and the other the last man, or Adam. Besides, things which are different in character are only incapable of being arranged in the same order when their diversity is one of substance; for when it is a diversity either in respect of place, or of time, or of condition, they probably do admit of classifi-

cation together. Here, however, they are called first and last, from the substance of their (common) flesh, just as afterwards again the first man (is said to be) of the earth, and the second of heaven;[5] but although He is " of heaven" in respect of the spirit, He is yet according to the flesh. Now since it is the flesh, and not the soul, that makes an order (or classification together) in the two Adams compatible, so that the distinction is drawn between them of " the first man becoming a living soul, and the last a quickening spirit,"[6] so in like manner this distinction between them has already suggested the conclusion that the distinction is due to the flesh; so that it is of the flesh that these words speak: " Howbeit that was not first which is spiritual, but that which is natural, and afterward that which is spiritual."[7] And thus, too, the same *flesh* must be understood in a preceding passage: " That which is sown is the natural body, and that which rises again is the spiritual body; because that is not first which is spiritual, but that which is natural: since the first Adam was made a living soul, the last Adam a quickening spirit."[8] It is all about man, *and* all about the flesh because about man.

What shall we say then? Has not the flesh even now (in this life) the spirit by faith? so that the question still remains to be asked, how it is that the animate (or natural) body can be said to be sown? Surely the flesh has received even here the spirit—but *only its* " earnest;"[9] whereas of the soul (it has received) not the earnest, but the full possession. Therefore it has the name of *animate* (or natural) body, expressly because of the higher substance of the soul (or *anima*,) in which it is sown, destined hereafter to become, through the full possession of the spirit which it shall obtain, the spiritual body, in which it is raised again. What wonder, then, if it is more commonly called after the substance with which it is fully furnished, than after that of which it has yet but a sprinkling?

CHAP. LIV.—DEATH SWALLOWED UP OF LIFE. MEANING OF THIS PHRASE IN RELATION TO THE RESURRECTION OF THE BODY.

Then, again, questions very often are suggested by occasional and isolated terms, just as much as they are by connected sentences. Thus, because of the apostle's expression, " that mortality may be swallowed up of life"[10]—in reference to the flesh—they wrest

---

[1] Animata.
[2] See the *De Anima,* v.-lx., for a full statement of Tertullian's view of the soul's corporeality.
[3] 1 Cor. xv. 45.
[4] 1 Cor. xv. 46.
[5] Ver. 47.
[6] Ver. 45.
[7] Ver. 46.
[8] 1 Cor. xv. 44, 45.
[9] 2 Cor. i. 22, v. 5, and Eph. i. 14.
[10] 2 Cor. v. 4.

the word *swallowed up* into the sense of the actual destruction of the flesh; as if we might not speak of ourselves as swallowing bile, or swallowing grief, meaning that we conceal and hide it, and keep it within ourselves. The truth is, when it is written, " This mortal must put on immortality,"[1] it is explained in what sense it is that " mortality is swallowed up of life "—even whilst, clothed with immortality, it is hidden and concealed, and contained within it, not as consumed, and destroyed, and lost. But death, you will say in reply to me, at this rate, must be safe, even when it has been swallowed up. Well, then, I ask you to distinguish words which are similar in form according to their proper meanings. Death is one thing, and mortality is another. It is one thing for death to be swallowed up, and another thing for mortality to be swallowed up. Death is incapable of immortality, but not so mortality. Besides, as it is written that " this mortal must put on immortality,"[2] how is this possible when it is swallowed up of life? But how is it swallowed up of life, (in the sense of destroyed by it) when it is actually received, and restored, and included in it? For the rest, it is only just and right that death should be swallowed up in utter destruction, since it does itself devour with this same intent. Death, says the apostle, has devoured by exercising its strength, and therefore has been itself devoured in the struggle " *swallowed up in victory.*"[3]   " O death, where is thy sting? O death, where is thy victory?"[4] Therefore life, too, as the great antagonist of death, will in the struggle swallow up for salvation what death, in its struggle, had swallowed up for destruction.

CHAP. LV.—THE CHANGE OF A THING'S CONDITION IS NOT THE DESTRUCTION OF ITS SUBSTANCE.   THE APPLICATION OF THIS PRINCIPLE TO OUR SUBJECT.

Now although, in proving that the flesh shall rise again we *ipso facto* prove that no other *flesh* will partake of that resurrection than that which is in question, yet insulated questions and their occasions do require even discussions of their own, even if they have been already sufficiently met. We will therefore give a fuller explanation of the force and the reason of a change which (is so great, that it) almost suggests the presumption that it is a different flesh which is to rise again; as if, indeed, so great a change amounted to utter cessation, and a complete destruction of the former self.   A distinction, however, must be made between a *change*, however great, and everything which has the character of *distruction*.   For undergoing change is one thing, but being destroyed is another thing.   Now this distinction would no longer exist, if the flesh were to suffer such a change as amounts to destruction.   Destroyed, however, it must be by the change, unless it shall itself persistently remain throughout the altered condition which shall be exhibited in the resurrection.   For precisely as it perishes, if it does not rise again, so also does it equally perish even if it does rise again, on the supposition that it is lost[5] in the change.   It will as much fail of a future existence, as if it did not rise again at all.   And how absurd is it to rise again for the purpose of not having a being, when it had it in its power not to rise again, and so lose its being—because it had already begun its non-existence!   Now, things which are absolutely different, as mutation and destruction are, will not admit of mixture and confusion; in their operations, too, they differ.   One destroys, the other changes.   Therefore, as that which is destroyed is not changed, so that which is changed is not destroyed.   To perish is altogether to cease to be what a thing once was, whereas to be changed is to exist in another condition.   Now, if a thing exists in another condition, it can still be the same thing itself; for since it does not perish, it has its existence still.   A change, indeed, it has experienced, but not a destruction.   A thing may undergo a complete change, and yet remain still the same thing.   In like manner, a man also may be quite himself in substance even in the present life, and for all that undergo various changes—in habit, in bodily bulk, in health, in condition, in dignity, and in age—in taste, business, means, houses, laws and customs—and still lose nothing of his human nature, nor so to be made another man as to cease to be the same; indeed, I ought hardly to say another man, but another thing. This form of change even the Holy Scriptures give us instances of.   The hand of Moses is changed, and it becomes like a dead one, bloodless, colourless, and stiff with cold; but on the recovery of heat, and on the restoration of its natural colour, it is again the same flesh and blood.[6]   Afterwards the face of the same Moses is changed,[7] with a brightness which eye could not bear.   But he was Moses still, even when he was not visible.   So also Stephen had already put on the appearance of an angel,[8] although they were none other

[1] 1 Cor. xv. 53.
[2] 1 Cor. xv. 53.
[3] Ver. 54.
[4] Ver. 55.

[5] Subducitur.
[6] Ex. iv. 6, 7.
[7] Ex. xxxiv. 29, 35.
[8] Acts vi. 15.

than his human knees[1] which bent beneath the stoning. The Lord, again, in the retirement of the mount, had changed His raiment for a robe of light; but He still retained features which Peter could recognise.[2] In that same scene Moses also and Elias gave proof that the same condition of bodily existence may continue even in glory—the one in the likeness of a flesh which he had not yet recovered, the other in the reality of one which he had not yet put off.[3] It was as full of this splendid example that Paul said: "Who shall change our vile body, that it may be fashioned like unto His glorious body."[4] But if you maintain that a transfiguration and a conversion amounts to the annihilation of any substance, then it follows that "Saul, when changed into another man,"[5] passed away from his own bodily substance; and that Satan himself, when "transformed into an angel of light,"[6] loses his own proper character. Such is not my opinion. So likewise changes, conversions, and reformations will necessarily take place to bring about the resurrection, but the substance *of the flesh* will still be preserved safe.

CHAP. LVI.—THE PROCEDURE OF THE LAST JUDGMENT, AND ITS AWARDS, ONLY POSSIBLE ON THE IDENTITY OF THE RISEN BODY WITH OUR PRESENT FLESH.

For how absurd, and in truth how unjust, and in both respects how unworthy of God, for one substance to do the work, and another to reap the reward: that this flesh of ours should be torn by martyrdom, and another wear the crown; or, on the other hand, that this flesh of ours should wallow in uncleanness, and another receive the condemnation! Is it not better to renounce all faith at once in the hope of the resurrection,[7] than to trifle with the wisdom and justice of God?[8] Better that Marcion should rise again than Valentinus. For it cannot be believed that the mind, or the memory, or the conscience of existing man is abolished by putting on that change of raiment which immortality and incorruption supplies; for in that case all the gain and fruit of the resurrection, and the permanent effect[9] of God's judgment both on soul and body,[10] would certainly fall to the ground. If I remember not that it is I who have served Him, how shall I ascribe glory to God? How sing to Him "the new song,"[11] if I am ignorant that it is I who owe Him thanks? But why is exception taken only against the change of the flesh, and not of the soul also, which in all things is superior to the flesh? How happens it, that the self-same soul which in our present flesh has gone through all life's course, which has learnt the knowledge of God, and put on Christ, and sown the hope of salvation in this flesh, must reap its harvest in another flesh of which we know nothing? Verily that must be a most highly favoured flesh, which shall have the enjoyment of life at so gratuitous a rate! But if the soul is not to be changed also, then there is no resurrection of the soul; nor will it be believed to have itself risen, unless it has risen some different thing.

CHAP. LVII.—OUR BODIES, HOWEVER MUTILATED BEFORE OR AFTER DEATH, SHALL RECOVER THEIR PERFECT INTEGRITY IN THE RESURRECTION. ILLUSTRATION OF THE ENFRANCHISED SLAVE.

We now come to the most usual cavil of unbelief. If, they say, it be actually the self-same substance which is recalled *to life* with all its form, and lineaments, and quality, then why not with all its other characteristics? Then the blind, and the lame, and the palsied, and whoever else may have passed away with any conspicuous mark, will return again with the same. What now is the fact, although you in the greatness of your conceit[12] thus disdain to accept from God so vast a grace? Does it not happen that, when you now admit the salvation of only the soul, you ascribe it to men at the cost of half their nature? What is the good of believing in the resurrection, unless your faith embraces the whole of it? If the flesh is to be repaired after its dissolution, much more will it be restored after some violent injury. Greater cases prescribe rules for lesser ones. Is not the amputation or the crushing of a limb the death of that limb? Now, if the death of the whole person is rescinded by its resurrection, what must we say of the death of a part of him? If we are changed for glory, how much more for integrity![13] Any loss sustained by our bodies is an accident to them, but their entirety is their natural property. In this condition we are born. Even if we become injured in the womb, this loss suffered by what is already a human being. Natural condition[14] is prior to injury. As life is bestowed by God, so is

---

[1] Acts vii. 59, 60.
[2] Matt. xvii. 2–4.
[3] Ver. 3.
[4] Phil. iii. 21.
[5] 1 Sam. x. 6.
[6] 2 Cor. xi. 14.
[7] With Marcion.
[8] With Valentinus.
[9] Statu.
[10] Utrobique.
[11] Rev. v. 9, xiv. 3.
[12] Qualiscunque.
[13] Or the recovery of our entire person.
[14] Genus.

it restored by Him. As we are when we receive it, so are we when we recover it. To nature, not to injury, are we restored; to our state by birth, not to our condition by accident, do we rise again. If God raises not men entire, He raises not the dead. For what dead man is entire, although he dies entire? Who is without hurt, that is without life? What body is uninjured, when it is dead, when it is cold, when it is ghastly, when it is stiff, when it is a corpse? When is a man more infirm, than when he is entirely infirm? When more palsied, than when quite motionless? Thus, for a dead man to be raised again, amounts to nothing short of his being restored to his entire condition,—lest he, forsooth, be still dead in that part in which he has not risen again. God is quite able to remake what He once made. This power and this unstinted grace of His He has already sufficiently guaranteed in Christ; and has displayed Himself to us (in Him) not only as the restorer of the flesh, but as the repairer of its breaches. And so the apostle says: "The dead shall be raised incorruptible" (or unimpaired).[1] But how so, unless they become entire, who have wasted away either in the loss of their health, or in the long decrepitude of the grave? For when he propounds the two clauses, that "this corruptible must put on incorruption, and this mortal must put on immortality,"[2] he does not repeat the same statement, but sets forth a distinction. For, by assigning *immortality* to the repeating of death, and *incorruption* to the repairing of the wasted body, he has fitted one to the raising and the other to the retrieval *of the body.* I suppose, moreover, that he promises to the Thessalonians the integrity of the whole substance of man.[3] So that for the great future there need be no fear of blemished or defective bodies. Integrity, whether the result of preservation or restoration, will be able to lose nothing more, after the time that it has given back to it whatever it had lost. Now, when you contend that the flesh will still have to undergo the same sufferings, if the same flesh be said to have to rise again, you rashly set up nature against her Lord, and impiously contrast *her* law against *His* grace; as if it were not permitted the Lord God both to change nature, and to preserve her, without subjection to a law. How is it, then, that we read, "With men these things are impossible, but with God all things are possible;"[4] and again, "God hath chosen the foolish things of the world to confound the wise?"[5] Let

me ask you, if you were to manumit your slave (seeing that the same flesh and soul will remain to him, which once were exposed to the whip, and the fetter, and the stripes), will it therefore be fit for him to undergo the same old sufferings? I trow not. He is instead thereof honoured with the grace of the white robe, and the favour of the gold ring, and the name and tribe as well as table of his patron. Give, then, the same prerogative to God, by virtue of such a change, of reforming our condition, not our nature, by taking away from it all sufferings, and surrounding it with safeguards of protection. Thus our flesh shall remain even after the resurrection—so far indeed susceptible of suffering, as it is the flesh, and the same flesh too; but at the same time impassible, inasmuch as it has been liberated by the Lord for the very end and purpose of being no longer capable of enduring suffering.

CHAP. LVIII.—FROM THIS PERFECTION OF OUR RESTORED BODIES WILL FLOW THE CONSCIOUSNESS OF UNDISTURBED JOY AND PEACE.

"Everlasting joy," says Isaiah, "shall be upon their heads."[6] Well, there is nothing eternal until after the resurrection. "And sorrow and sighing," continues he, "shall flee away."[7] The angel echoes the same to John: "And God shall wipe away all tears from their eyes;"[8] from the same eyes indeed which had formerly wept, and which might weep again, if the loving-kindness of God did not dry up every fountain of tears. And again: "God shall wipe away all tears from their eyes; and there shall be no more death,"[9] and therefore no more corruption, it being chased away by incorruption, even as death is by immortality. If sorrow, and mourning, and sighing, and death itself, assail us from the afflictions both of soul and body, how shall they be removed, except by the cessation of their causes, that is to say, the afflictions of flesh and soul? where will you find adversities in the presence of God? where, incursions of an enemy in the bosom of Christ? where, attacks of the devil in the face of the Holy Spirit?—now that the devil himself and his angels are "cast into the lake of fire."[10] Where now is necessity, and what they call fortune or fate? What plague awaits the redeemed from death, after their eternal pardon? What wrath is there for the reconciled, after grace? What weakness, after their

---

[1] 1 Cor. xv. 52.
[2] 1 Cor. xv. 53.
[3] 1 Thess. iv. 13–17 and v. 23.
[4] Matt. xix. 26.
[5] 1 Cor. i. 27.
[6] Isa. xxxv. 10.
[7] Ver. 10.
[8] Rev. vii. 17.
[9] Rev. xxi. 4.
[10] Rev. xx. 10, 13–15

renewed strength? What risk and danger, after their salvation? That the raiment and shoes of the children of Israel remained unworn and fresh for the space of forty years;[1] that in their very persons the exact point[2] of convenience and propriety checked the rank growth of their nails and hair, so that any excess herein might not be attributed to indecency; that the fires of Babylon injured not either the mitres or the trousers of the three brethren, however foreign such dress might be to the Jews;[3] that Jonah was swallowed by the monster of the deep, in whose belly whole ships were devoured, and after three days was vomited out again safe and sound;[4] that Enoch and Elias, who even now, without experiencing a resurrection (because they have not even encountered death), are learning to the full what it is for the flesh to be exempted from all humiliation, and all loss, and all injury, and all disgrace—translated as they have been from this world, and from this very cause already candidates for everlasting life;[5] —to what faith do these notable facts bear witness, if not to that which ought to inspire in us the belief that they are proofs and documents of our own future integrity *and perfect resurrection?* For, to borrow the apostle's phrase, these were "figures of ourselves;"[6] and they are written that we may believe both that the Lord is more powerful than all natural laws about the body, and that He shows Himself the preserver of the flesh the more emphatically, in that He has preserved for it its very clothes and shoes.

CHAP. LIX.—OUR FLESH IN THE RESURRECTION CAPABLE, WITHOUT LOSING ITS ESSENTIAL IDENTITY, OF BEARING THE CHANGED CONDITIONS OF ETERNAL LIFE, OR OF DEATH ETERNAL.

But, you object, the world to come bears the character of a different dispensation, even an eternal one; and therefore, you maintain, that the non-eternal substance of this life is incapable of possessing a state of such different features. This would be true enough, if man were made for the future dispensation, and not the dispensation for man. The apostle, however, in his epistle says, "Whether it be the world, or life, or death, or things present, or things to come; all are yours:"[7] and he here constitutes us heirs even of the future world. Isaiah gives you no help when he says, "All flesh is grass;"[8] and in another passage, "All flesh shall see the salvation of God."[9] It is the issues of men, not their substances, which he distinguishes. But who does not hold that the judgment of God consists in the twofold sentence, of salvation and of punishment? Therefore it is that "all flesh is grass," which is destined to the fire; and "all flesh shall see the salvation of God," which is ordained to eternal life. For myself, I am quite sure that it is in no other flesh than my own that I have committed adultery, nor in any other flesh am I striving after continence. If there be any one who bears about in his person two instruments of lasciviousness, he has it in his power, to be sure, to mow down[10] "the grass" of the unclean flesh, and to reserve for himself only that which shall see the salvation of God. But when the same prophet represents to us even nations sometimes estimated as "the small dust of the balance,"[11] and as "less than nothing, and vanity,"[12] and sometimes as about to hope and "trust in the name"[13] and arm of the Lord, are we at all misled respecting the Gentile nations *by the diversity of statement?* Are some of them to turn believers, and are others accounted dust, from any difference of nature? Nay, rather Christ has shone as the true light on the nations within the ocean's limits, and from the heaven which is over us all.[14] Why, it is even on this earth that the Valentinians have gone to school for their errors; and there will be no difference of condition, as respects their body and soul, between the nations which believe and those which do not believe. Precisely, then, as He has put a distinction of state, not of nature, amongst the same nations, so also has He discriminated their flesh, which is one and the same substance in those nations, not according to their material structure, but according to the recompense of their merit.

CHAP. LX.—ALL THE CHARACTERISTICS OF OUR BODIES—SEX, VARIOUS LIMBS, ETC.—WILL BE RETAINED, WHATEVER CHANGE OF FUNCTIONS THESE MAY HAVE, OF WHICH POINT, HOWEVER, WE ARE NO JUDGES. ANALOGY OF THE REPAIRED SHIP.

But behold how presistently they still accumulate their cavils against the flesh, especially against its identity, deriving their argu-

---

[1] Deut. xxix. 5.
[2] Justitia.
[3] Dan. iii. 27.
[4] Jonah i. 17, ii. 10.
[5] Gen. v. 24 ; 2 Kings ii. 11.
[6] 1 Cor. x. 6.

[7] 1 Cor. iii. 22.
[8] Isa. xl. 7.
[9] Ver. 5.
[10] Demetere.
[11] Isa. xl. 15.
[12] Ver. 17. The word is *spittle*, which the LXX. uses in the fifteenth verse for the "dust" of the Hebrew Bible.
[13] Isa. xlii. 4, Sept. ; quoted from the LXX. by Christ in Matt. xii. 21, and by St. Paul in Rom. xv. 12.
[14] An allusion to some conceits of the Valentinians, who put men of truest nature and fit for Christ's grace outside of the ocean-bounded earth, etc.

ments even from the functions of our limbs; on the one hand saying that these ought to continue permanently pursuing their labours and enjoyments, as appendages to the same corporeal frame; and on the other hand contending that, inasmuch as the functions of the limbs shall one day come to an end, the bodily frame itself must be destroyed, its permanence without its limbs being deemed to be as inconceivable, as that of the limbs themselves without their functions! What, they ask, will then be the use of the cavity of our mouth, and its rows of teeth, and the passage of the throat, and the branch-way of the stomach, and the gulf of the belly, and the entangled tissue of the bowels, when there shall no longer be room for eating and drinking? What more will there be for these members to take in, masticate, swallow, secrete, digest, eject? Of what avail will be our very hands, and feet, and all our labouring limbs, when even all care about food shall cease? What purpose can be served by loins, conscious of seminal secretions, and all the other organs of generation, in the two sexes, and the laboratories of embryos, and the fountains of the breast, when concubinage, and pregnancy, and infant nurture shall cease? In short, what will be the use of the entire body, when the entire body shall become useless? In reply to all this, we have then already settled the principle that the dispensation of the future state ought not to be compared with that of the present world, and that in the interval between them a change will take place; and we now add the remark, that these functions of our bodily limbs will continue to supply the needs of this life up to the moment when life itself shall pass away from time to eternity, as the natural body gives place to the spiritual, until "this mortal puts on immortality, and this corruptible puts on incorruption:"[1] so that when life shall itself become freed from all wants, our limbs shall then be freed also from their services, and therefore will be no longer wanted. Still, although liberated from their offices, they will be yet preserved for judgment, "that every one may receive the things done in his body."[2] For the judgment-seat of God requires that man be kept entire. Entire, however, he cannot be without his limbs, of the substance of which, not the functions, he consists; unless, forsooth, you will be bold enough to maintain that a ship is perfect without her keel, or her bow, or her stern, and without the solidity of her entire frame. And yet how often have we seen the same ship, after being shattered with the storm

and broken by decay, with all her timbers repaired and restored, gallantly riding on the wave in all the beauty of a renewed fabric! Do we then disquiet ourselves with doubt about God's skill, and will, and rights? Besides, if a wealthy shipowner, who does not grudge money merely for his amusement or show, thoroughly repairs his ship, and then chooses that she should make no further voyages, will you contend that the old form and finish is still not necessary to the vessel, although she is no longer meant for actual service, when the mere safety of a ship requires such completeness irrespective of service? The sole question, therefore, which is enough for us to consider here, is whether the Lord, when He ordains salvation for man, intends it for his flesh; whether it is His will that the selfsame flesh shall be renewed. If so, it will be improper for you to rule, from the inutility of its limbs in the future state, that the flesh will be incapable of renovation. For a thing may be renewed, and yet be useless *from having nothing to do;* but it cannot be said to be useless if it has no existence. If, indeed, it has existence, it will be quite possible for it also not to be useless; *it may possibly have something to do;* for in the presence of God there will be no idleness.

CHAP. LXI.—THE DETAILS OF OUR BODILY SEX, AND OF THE FUNCTIONS OF OUR VARIOUS MEMBERS. APOLOGY FOR THE NECESSITY WHICH HERESY IMPOSES OF HUNTING UP ALL ITS UNBLUSHING CAVILS.

Now you have received your mouth, O man, for the purpose of devouring your food and imbibing your drink: why not, however, for the higher purpose of uttering speech, so as to distinguish yourself from all other animals? Why not rather for preaching *the gospel of God,* that so you may become even His priest and advocate before men? Adam indeed gave their several names to the animals, before he plucked the fruit of the tree; before he ate, he prophesied. Then, again, you received your teeth for the consumption of your meal: why not rather for wreathing your mouth with suitable defence on every opening thereof, small or wide? Why not, too, for moderating the impulses of your tongue, and guarding your articulate speech from failure and violence? Let me tell you, (if you do not know), that there are toothless persons in the world. Look at them, and ask whether even a cage of teeth be not an honour to the mouth. There are apertures in the lower regions of man and woman, by means of which they gratify no doubt their animal passions; but why are they not rather regarded as outlets for the cleanly

[1] 1 Cor. xv. 53.
[2] 2 Cor. v. 10.

discharge of natural fluids? Women, moreover, have within them receptacles where human seed may collect; but are they not designed for the secretion of those sanguineous issues, which their tardier and weaker sex is inadequate to disperse? For even details like these require to be mentioned, seeing that *heretics* single out what parts of our bodies may suit them, handle them without delicacy, and, as their whim suggests, pour torrents of scorn and contempt upon the natural functions of our members, for the purpose of upsetting the resurrection, and making us blush over their cavils; not reflecting that before the functions cease, the very causes of them will have passed away. There will be no more meat, because no more hunger; no more drink, because no more thirst; no more concubinage, because no more child-bearing; no more eating and drinking, because no more labour and toil. Death, too, will cease; so there will be no more need of the nutriment of food for the defence of life, nor will *mothers'* limbs any longer have to be laden for the replenishment of our race. But even in the present life there may be cessations of their office for our stomachs and our generative organs. For forty days Moses[1] and Elias[2] fasted, and lived upon God alone. For even so early was the principle consecrated: " Man shall not live by bread alone, but by every word that proceedeth out of the mouth of God." [3] See here faint outlines of our future strength! We even, as we may be able, excuse our mouths from food, and withdraw our sexes from union. How many voluntary eunuchs are there! How many virgins espoused to Christ! How many, both of men and women, whom nature has made sterile, with a structure which cannot procreate! Now, if even here on earth both the functions and the pleasures of our members may be suspended, with an intermission which, like the dispensation itself, can only be a temporary one, and yet man's safety is nevertheless unimpaired, how much more, when his salvation is secure, and especially in an eternal dispensation, shall we not cease to desire those things, for which, even here below, we are not unaccustomed to check our longings!

CHAP. LXII.—OUR DESTINED LIKENESS TO THE ANGELS IN THE GLORIOUS LIFE OF THE RESURRECTION.

To this discussion, however, our Lord's declaration puts an effectual end: " They shall be," says He, " equal unto the angels." [4]

As by not marrying, because of not dying, so, of course, by not having to yield to any like necessity of our bodily state; even as the angels, too, sometimes were " equal unto " men, by eating and drinking, and submitting their feet to the washing of the bath—having clothed themselves in human guise, without the loss of their own intrinsic nature. If therefore angels, when they became as men, submitted in their own unaltered substance of spirit to be treated as if they were flesh, why shall not men in like manner, when they become " equal unto the angels," undergo in their unchanged substance of flesh the treatment of spiritual beings, no more exposed to the usual solicitations of the flesh in their angelic garb, than were the angels once to those of the spirit when encompassed in human form? We shall not therefore cease to continue in the flesh, because we cease to be importuned by the usual wants of the flesh; just as the angels ceased not therefore to remain in their spiritual substance, because of the suspension of their spiritual incidents. Lastly, Christ said not, " They shall be angels," in order not to repeal their existence as men; but He said, " They shall be equal unto the angels,[5] that He might preserve their humanity unimpaired. When He ascribed an angelic likeness to the flesh,[6] He took not from it its proper substance.

CHAP. LXIII.—CONCLUSION. THE RESURRECTION OF THE FLESH IN ITS ABSOLUTE IDENTITY AND PERFECTION. BELIEF OF THIS HAD BECOME WEAK. HOPES FOR ITS REFRESHING RESTORATION UNDER THE INFLUENCES OF THE PARACLETE.

And so the flesh shall rise again, wholly in every man, in its own identity, in its absolute integrity. Wherever it may be, it is in safe keeping in God's presence, through that most faithful " Mediator between God and man, (the man) Jesus Christ," [7] who shall reconcile both God to man, and man to God; the spirit to the flesh, and the flesh to the spirit. Both natures has He already united in His own self; He has fitted them together as bride and bridegroom in the reciprocal bond of wedded life. Now, if any should insist on making the soul the bride, then the flesh will follow the soul as her dowry. The soul shall never be an outcast, to be had home by the bridegroom bare and naked. She has her dower, her outfit, her fortune in the flesh, which shall accompany her with the love and fidelity of a foster-sister. But suppose the flesh to be the

---

[1] Ex. xxiv. 8.
[2] 1 Kings xix. 8.
[3] Deut. viii. 3; Matt. iv. 4.
[4] Luke xx. 36; Matt. xxii. 30.

[5] ἰσάγγελοι.
[6] Cui.
[7] 1 Tim. ii. 5.

bride, then in Christ Jesus she has in the contract of His blood received His Spirit as her spouse. Now, what you take to be her extinction, you may be sure is only her temporary retirement. It is not the soul only which withdraws from view. The flesh, too, has her departures for a while—in waters, in fires, in birds, in beasts; she may seem to be dissolved into these, but she is only poured into them, as into vessels. And should the vessels themselves afterwards fail to hold her, escaping from even these, and returning to her mother earth, she is absorbed once more, as it were, by its secret embraces, ultimately to stand forth to view, like Adam when summoned to hear from his Lord and Creator the words, "Behold, the man is become as one of us!"[1]—thoroughly "knowing" by that time "the evil" which she had escaped, "and the good" which she has acquired. Why, then, O soul, should you envy the flesh? There is none, after the Lord, whom you should love so dearly; none more like a brother to you, which is even born along with yourself in God. You ought rather to have been by your prayers obtaining resurrection for her: her sins, whatever they were, were owing to you. However, it is no wonder if you hate her; for you have repudiated her Creator.[2] You have accustomed yourself either to deny or change her existence even in Christ[3]—corrupting the very Word of God Himself, who became flesh, either by mutilating or misinterpreting the Scripture,[4] and introducing, above all, apocryphal mysteries *and* blasphemous fables.[5] But yet

Almighty God, in His most gracious providence, by "pouring out of His Spirit in these last days, upon all flesh, upon His servants and on His handmaidens,"[6] has checked these impostures of unbelief and perverseness, reanimated men's faltering faith in the resurrection of the flesh, and cleared from all obscurity and equivocation the ancient Scriptures (of both God's Testaments[7]) by the clear light of their (sacred) words and meanings. Now, since it was "needful that there should be heresies, in order that they which are approved might be made manifest;"[8] since, however, these heresies would be unable to put on a bold front without some countenance from the Scriptures, it therefore is plain enough that the ancient Holy Writ has furnished them with sundry materials for their evil doctrine, which very materials indeed (so distorted) are refutable from the same Scriptures. It was fit and proper, therefore, that the Holy Ghost should no longer withhold the effusions of His gracious light upon these inspired writings, in order that they might be able to disseminate the seeds *of truth* with no admixture of heretical subtleties, and pluck out from it their tares. He has accordingly now dispersed all the perplexities of the past, and their self-chosen allegories and parables, by the open and perspicuous explanation of the entire mystery, through the new prophecy, which descends in copious streams from the Paraclete. If you will only draw water from His fountains, you will never thrist for other doctrine: no feverish craving after subtle questions will again consume you; *but* by drinking in evermore the resurrection of the flesh, you will be satisfied with the refreshing draughts.

---

[1] Gen. iii. 22.
[2] In this apostrophe to the soul, he censures Marcion's heresy.
[3] Compare the *De Carne Christi.*
[4] See the *De Præscript. Hæret.* ch. xxxviii. *supra*, for instances of these diverse methods of heresy. Marcion is mentioned as the *mutilator* of Scripture, by cutting away from it whatever opposed his views ; Valentinus as the *corrupter* thereof, by his manifold and fantastic interpretations.
[5] See the *Adv. Valentinianos, supra.*

[6] Joel ii. 28, 29 ; Acts ii. 17, 18. [See last sentence. He improves upon St. Peter's interpretation of this text (as see below) by attributing his own clear views to the *charismata*, which he regards as still vouchsafed to the more spiritual.]
[7] We follow Oehler's view here, by all means.
[8] 1 Cor. xi. 19.

ELUCIDATIONS.

I.

(Cadaver, cap. xviii. p. 558.)

The Schoolmen and middle-age jurists improved on Tertullian's etymology. He says,—"a cadendo—*cadaver*." But they form the word thus:

*Ca*ro *da*ta *ver*mibus = *Ca-da-ver.*

On this subject see a most interesting discourse of the (paradoxical and sophistical, nay the whimsical) Count Joseph de Maistre, in his *Soirées de St. Pétersbourg.*[1] He

---

[1] Œuvres, Tom. v. p. 111.

remarks on the happy formation of many Latin words, in this manner: *e. g.*, *Cæcus ut ire* = *Cæcutire*, "to grope like a blind man." The French, he says, are not without such examples, and he instances the word *ancêtre* = ancestor, as composed out of *ancien* and *être*, i.e., one of a former existence. *Courage*, he says, is formed from *cœur* and *rage*, this use of rage being the Greek θυμός. He supposes that the English use the word rage in this sense, but I recall only the instance:

> " Chill penury repressed their noble rage,"

from Gray's Elegy. The *Diversions of Purley*, of Horne-Tooke, supply amusing examples of the like in the formation of English words.

II.

(His flesh, the Bread, cap. xxxvii. p. 572.)

Note our author's exposition. He censures those who understood our Lord's words after the letter, as if they were to eat the carnal body. He expounds the *spiritual thing* which gives life as to be understood by the text: "the words that I speak unto you, they are spirit and they are life." His word is the life-giving principle and therefore he called his flesh by the same name: and we are to "devour Him with the ear and to ruminate on Him with the understanding, and to digest Him by faith." The flesh profits nothing, the spirit imparts life. Now, was Tertullian ever censured for this exposition? On the contrary, this was the faith of the Catholic Church, from the beginning. Our Saxon forefathers taught the same, as appears from the *Homily of Ælfric*,[1] A.D. 980, and from the exposition of Ratramn, A.D. 840. The heresy of Transubstantiation was not dogmatic even among Latins, until the Thirteenth century, and it prevailed in England less than three hundred years, when the Catholic doctrine was restored, through the influence of Ratramn's treatise first upon the mind of Ridley and then by Ridley's arguments with Cranmer. Thus were their understandings opened to the Scriptures and to the acknowledging of the Truth, for which they suffered martyrdom. To the reformation we owe the rescue of Ante-Nicene doctrine from the perversions of the Schoolmen and the gradual corruptions of doctrine after the Ninth Century.

III.

(Paradise, cap. xliii. p. 576.)

This sentence reads, in the translation I am editing, as follows: "No one, on becoming absent from the body, is at once a dweller in the presence of the Lord, except by the prerogative of martyrdom, whereby (the saint) gets at once a lodging in Paradise, not in *Hades*." But the original does not say precisely this, nor does the author use the Greek word *Hades*. His words are: "Nemo enim peregrinatus a corpore statim immoratur penes Dominum nisi ex martyrii prœrogativa Paradiso silicet non Inferis diversurus." The passage therefore, is not necessarily as inconsistent with the author's topography of the invisible world, as might seem. "Not in the regions beneath Paradise but in Paradise itself," seems to be the idea; Paradise being included in the world of *Hades*, indeed, but in a lofty region, far enough removed from the *Inferi*, and refreshed by light from the third Heaven and the throne itself, (as this planet is by the light of the Sun,) immensely distant though it be from the final abode of the Redeemed.

---

[1] See Soames' Anglo Saxon Church, cap. xii. p. 465, and cap. xi. pp. 423-430. See also the valuable annotations of Dr. Routh's *Opuscula*, Vol. II. pp. 167-186.

VII.

AGAINST PRAXEAS;[1]

IN WHICH HE DEFENDS, IN ALL ESSENTIAL POINTS, THE DOCTRINE OF THE HOLY TRINITY.[2]

[TRANSLATED BY DR. HOLMES.]

CHAP. I.—SATAN'S WILES AGAINST THE TRUTH. HOW THEY TAKE THE FORM OF THE PRAXEAN HERESY. ACCOUNT OF THE PUBLICATION OF THIS HERESY.

IN various ways has the devil rivalled and resisted the truth. Sometimes his aim has been to destroy the truth by defending it. He maintains that there is one only Lord, the Almighty Creator of the world, in order that out of this *doctrine of the* unity he may fabricate a heresy. He says that the Father Himself came down into the Virgin, was Himself born of her, Himself suffered, indeed was Himself Jesus Christ. Here the *old* serpent has fallen out with himself, since, when he tempted Christ after John's baptism, he approached Him as "the Son of God;" surely intimating that God had a Son, even on the testimony of the very Scriptures, out of which he was at the moment forging his temptation: "If thou be the Son of God, command that these stones be made bread."[3] Again: "If thou be the Son of God, cast thyself down from hence;[4] for it is written, He shall give His angels charge concerning thee"—referring no doubt, to the Father—"and in their hands they shall bear thee up, that thou hurt not thy foot against a stone."[5] Or perhaps, after all, he was only reproaching the Gospels with a lie, saying in fact: "Away with Matthew; away with Luke! *Why heed their words?* In spite of them, *I declare* that it was God Himself that

I approached; it was the Almighty Himself that I tempted face to face; and it was for no other purpose than to tempt Him that I approached Him. If, on the contrary, it had been *only* the Son of God, most likely I should never have condescended to deal with Him." However, he is himself a liar from the beginning,[6] and whatever man he instigates in his own way; as, for instance, Praxeas. For *he* was the first to import into Rome from Asia this kind of heretical pravity, a man in other respects of restless disposition, and above all inflated with the pride of confessorship simply and solely because he had to bear for a short time the annoyance of a prison; on which occasion, even "if he had given his body to be burned, it would have profited him nothing," not having the love of God,[7] whose very gifts he has resisted and destroyed. For after the Bishop of Rome[8] had acknowledged the prophetic gifts of Montanus, Prisca, and Maximilla, and, in consequence of the acknowledgment, had bestowed his peace[9] on the churches of Asia and Phrygia, *he*, by importunately urging false accusations against the prophets themselves and their churches, and insisting on the authority of the bishop's predecessors in the see, compelled him to recall the pacific letter which he had issued, as well as to desist from his purpose of acknowledging the *said* gifts. By this Praxeas did a twofold service for the devil at Rome: he drove away prophecy, and he brought in heresy; he put to flight the Paraclete, and he crucified the Father. Praxeas' tares had been moreover sown, and had produced their fruit here also,[10] while many

---

[1] The error of Praxeas appears to have originated in anxiety to maintain the unity of God; which, he thought, could only be done by saying that the Father, Son, and Holy Ghost were one and the same. He contended, therefore, according to Tertullian, that the Father himself descended into the Virgin, was born of her, suffered, and was in a word Jesus Christ. From the most startling of the deductions from Praxeas' general theory, his opponents gave him and his followers the name of *Patripassians;* from another point in his teaching they were called *Monarchians.* [Probable date not earlier than A.D. 208].
[2] [Elucidation I.]
[3] Matt. iv. 3.
[4] Ver. 6.
[5] Ps. xci. 11.

[6] John viii. 44.
[7] 1 Cor. xiii. 3.
[8] Probably Victor. [Elucidation II.]
[9] Had admitted then to communion.
[10] "The connection renders it very probable that the *hic quoque* of this sentence forms an antithesis to Rome, mentioned before, and that Tertullian expresses himself as if he had written from the very spot where these things had transpired. Hence we are led to conclude that it was *Carthage*."—NEANDER, *Antignostikus*, ii. 519, note 2, Bohn.

were asleep in their simplicity of doctrine; but these tares actually seemed to have been plucked up, having been discovered and exposed by him whose agency God was pleased to employ. Indeed, *Praxeas* had deliberately resumed his old (true) faith, teaching it after his renunciation of error; and there is his own handwriting in evidence remaining among the carnally-minded,[1] in whose society the transaction then took place; afterwards nothing was heard of him. We indeed, on our part, subsequently withdrew from the carnally-minded on our acknowledgment and maintenance of the Paraclete.[2] But the tares *of Praxeas* had then everywhere shaken out their seed, which having lain hid for some while, with its vitality concealed under a mask, has now broken out with fresh life. But again shall it be rooted up, if the Lord will, even now; but if not now, in the day when all bundles of tares shall be gathered together, and along with every other stumbling-block shall be burnt up with unquenchable fire.[3]

CHAP. II.—THE CATHOLIC DOCTRINE OF THE TRINITY AND UNITY. SOMETIMES CALLED THE DIVINE ECONOMY, OR DISPENSATION OF THE PERSONAL RELATIONS OF THE GODHEAD.

In the course of time, then, the Father forsooth was born, and the Father suffered,— God Himself, the Lord Almighty, whom in their preaching they declare to be Jesus Christ. We, however, as we indeed always have done (and more especially since we have been better instructed by the Paraclete, who leads men indeed into all truth), believe that there is one only God, but under the following dispensation, or οἰκονομία, as it is called, that this one only God has also a Son, His Word, who proceeded[4] from Himself, by whom all things were made, and without whom nothing was made. Him *we believe* to have been sent by the Father into the Virgin, and to have been born of her—being both Man and God, the Son of Man and the Son of God, and to have been called by the name of Jesus Christ; *we believe* Him to have suffered, died, and been buried, according to the Scriptures, and, after He had been raised again by the Father and taken back to heaven, to be sitting at the right hand of the Father, *and* that He will come to judge

the quick and the dead; who sent also from heaven from the Father, according to His own promise, the Holy Ghost, the Paraclete,[5] the sanctifier of the faith of those who believe in the Father, and in the Son, and in the Holy Ghost. That this rule of faith has come down to us from the beginning of the gospel, even before any of the older heretics, much more before Praxeas, *a pretender* of yesterday, will be apparent both from the lateness of date[6] which marks all heresies, and also from the absolutely novel character of our new-fangled Praxeas. In this principle also we must henceforth find a presumption of equal force against all heresies whatsoever—that whatever is first is true, whereas that is spurious which is later in date.[7] But keeping this prescriptive rule inviolate, still some opportunity must be given for reviewing (the statements of heretics), with a view to the instruction and protection of divers persons; were it only that it may not seem that each perversion *of the truth* is condemned without examination, and simply prejudged;[8] especially in the case of this heresy, which supposes itself to possess the pure truth, in thinking that one cannot believe in One Only God in any other way than by saying that the Father, the Son, and the Holy Ghost are the very selfsame Person. As if in this way also one were not All, in that All are of One, by unity (that is) of substance; while the mystery of the dispensation[9] is still guarded, which distributes the Unity into a Trinity, placing in their order[10] the three *Persons*— the Father, the Son, and the Holy Ghost: three, however, not in condition,[11] but in degree;[12] not in substance, but in form; not in power, but in aspect;[13] yet of one substance, and of one condition, and of one power, inasmuch as He is one God, from whom these degrees and forms and aspects are reckoned, under the name of the Father, and of the Son, and of the Holy Ghost.[14] How they are susceptible of number without division, will be shown as our treatise proceeds.

CHAP. III.—SUNDRY POPULAR FEARS AND PREJUDICES. THE DOCTRINE OF THE TRINITY IN UNITY RESCUED FROM THESE MISAPPREHENSIONS.

The simple, indeed, (I will not call them unwise and unlearned,) who always constitute

---

[1] On the designation *Psychici*, see our *Anti-Marcion*, p. 263, note 5. Edin.

[2] [This statement may only denote a withdrawal from the communion of the Bishop of Rome, like that of Cyprian afterwards. That prelate had stultified himself and broken faith with Tertullian; but, it does not, necessarily, as Bp. Bull too easily concludes, define his ultimate separation from his own bishop and the North-African church.]

[3] Matt. xiii. 30.

[4] The Church afterwards applied this term exclusively to the Holy Ghost. [That is, the Nicene Creed made it *technically* applicable to the Spirit, making the distinction marked between the *generation* of the Word and the *procession* of the Holy Ghost.]

[5] The "Comforter."

[6] See our *Anti-Marcion*, p. 119, n. 1. Edin.

[7] See his *De Præscript.* xxix.

[8] Tertullian uses similar precaution in his argument elsewhere. See our *Anti-Marcion*, pp. 3 and 119. Edin.

[9] οἰκονομία.

[10] Dirigens.

[11] Statu.

[12] See *The Apology*, ch. xxi.

[13] Specie.

[14] See Bull's *Def. Fid. Nic.*, and the translation (by the translator of this work), in the Oxford Series, p. 202.

the majority of believers, are startled at the dispensation[1] (of the Three in One), on the ground that their very rule of faith withdraws them from the world's plurality of gods to the one only true God; not understanding that, although He is the one only God, He must yet be believed in with His own οἰκονομία. The numerical order and distribution of the Trinity they assume to be a division of the Unity; whereas the Unity which derives the Trinity out of its own self is so far from being destroyed, that it is actually supported by it. They are constantly throwing out against us that we are preachers of two gods and three gods, while they take to themselves pre-eminently the credit of being worshippers of the One God; just as if the Unity itself with irrational deductions did not produce heresy, and the Trinity rationally considered constitute the truth. We, say they, maintain the *Monarchy* (or, *sole government* of God).[2] And so, as far as the sound goes, do even Latins (and ignorant ones too) pronounce the word in such a way that you would suppose their understanding of the μοναρχία (or *Monarchy*) was as complete as their pronunciation of the term. Well, then Latins take pains to pronounce the μοναρχία (or *Monarchy*), while Greeks actually refuse to understand the οἰκονομία, or *Dispensation* (*of the Three in One*). As for myself, however, if I have gleaned any knowledge of either language, I am sure that μοναρχία (or *Monarchy*) has no other meaning than single and individual[3] rule; but for all that, this monarchy does not, because it is the government of one, preclude him whose government it is, either from having a son, or from having made himself actually a son to himself,[4] or from ministering his own monarchy by whatever agents he will. Nay more, I contend that no dominion so belongs to one only, as his own, or is in such a sense singular, or is in such a sense a monarchy, as not also to be administered through other persons most closely connected with it, and whom it has itself provided as officials to itself. If, moreover, there be a son belonging to him whose monarchy it is, it does not forthwith become divided and cease to be a monarchy, if the son also be taken as a sharer in it; but it is as to its origin equally his, by whom it is communicated to the son; and being his, it is quite as much a monarchy (or *sole empire*), since it is held together by two who are so inseparable.[5] Therefore, inasmuch as the Divine Monarchy also is administered by so many

legions and hosts of angels, according as it is written, "Thousand thousands ministered unto Him, and ten thousand times ten thousand stood before Him;"[6] and since it has not from this circumstance ceased to be the rule of one (so as no longer to be a monarchy), because it is administered by so many thousands of powers; how comes it to pass that God should be thought to suffer division and severance in the Son and in the Holy Ghost, who have the second and the third places assigned to them, and who are so closely joined with the Father in His substance, when He suffers no such (division and severance) in the multitude of so many angels? Do you really suppose that Those, who are naturally members of the Father's own substance, pledges of His love,[7] instruments of His might, nay, His power itself and the entire system of His monarchy, are the overthrow and destruction thereof? You are not right in so thinking. I prefer your exercising yourself on the meaning of the thing rather than on the sound of the word. Now you must understand the overthrow of a monarchy to be *this*, when another dominion, which has a framework and a state peculiar to itself (and is therefore a rival), is brought in over and above it: when, *e.g.*, some other god is introduced in opposition to the Creator, as in the opinions of Marcion; or when many gods are introduced, according to your Valentinuses and your Prodicuses. Then it amounts to an overthrow of the Monarchy, since it involves the destruction of the Creator.[8]

CHAP. IV.—THE UNITY OF THE GODHEAD AND THE SUPREMACY AND SOLE GOVERNMENT OF THE DIVINE BEING. THE MONARCHY NOT AT ALL IMPAIRED BY THE CATHOLIC DOCTRINE.

But as for me, who derive the Son from no other source but from the substance of the Father, and (represent Him) as doing nothing without the Father's will, and as having received all power from the Father, how can I be possibly destroying the Monarchy from the faith, when I preserve it in the Son just as it was committed to Him by the Father? The same remark (I wish also to be formally) made by me with respect to the third degree *in the Godhead*, because I believe the Spirit *to proceed* from no other source than from the Father through the Son.[9] Look to it then, that it be not *you* rather who are destroying the Monarchy, when you overthrow the arrangement and dispensa-

---

[1] οἰκονομία
[2] So Bp. Kaye, *On Tertullian*, p. 499.
[3] Unicum.
[4] This was a notion of Praxeas. See ch. x.
[5] Tam unicis.

[6] Dan. vii. 10.
[7] "Pignora" is often used of *children* and *dearest relations*.
[8] [The first sentence of this chapter is famous for a controversy between Priestly and Bp. Horsley, the latter having tra . . . *idiotæ* by the word idiots. See Kaye, p. 498.]
[9] [Compare Cap. viii. *infra*]

tion of it, which has been constituted in just as many names as it has pleased God *to employ*. But it remains so firm and stable in its own state, notwithstanding the introduction into it of the Trinity, that the Son actually has to restore it entire to the Father; even as the apostle says in his epistle, concerning the very end of all: "When He shall have delivered up the kingdom to God, even the Father; for He must reign till He hath put all enemies under His feet;"[1] following of course the words of the Psalm: "Sit Thou on my right hand, until I make Thine enemies Thy footstool."[2] "When, however, all things shall be subdued to Him, (with the exception of Him who did put all things under Him,) then shall the Son also Himself be subject unto Him who put all things under Him, that God may be all in all."[3] We thus see that the Son is no obstacle to the Monarchy, although it is now administered by[4] the Son; because with the Son it is still in its own state, and with its own state will be restored to the Father by the Son. No one, therefore, will impair it, on account of admitting the Son (to it), since it is certain that it has been committed to Him by the Father, and by and by has to be again delivered up by Him to the Father. Now, from this one passage of the epistle of the *inspired* apostle, we have been already able to show that the Father and the Son are two *separate Persons*, not only by the mention of their separate names as Father and the Son, but also by the fact that He who delivered up the kingdom, and He to whom it is delivered up—and in like manner, He who subjected (all things), and He to whom they were subjected—must necessarily be two different Beings.

CHAP. V.—THE EVOLUTION OF THE SON OR WORD OF GOD FROM THE FATHER BY A DIVINE PROCESSION. ILLUSTRATED BY THE OPERATION OF THE HUMAN THOUGHT AND CONSCIOUSNESS.

But since they will have the Two to be but One, so that the Father shall be deemed to be the same as the Son, it is only right that the whole question respecting the Son should be examined, as to whether He exists, and who He is and the mode of His existence. Thus shall the truth itself[5] secure its own sanction[6] from the Scriptures, and the interpretations which guard[7] them. There are

some who allege that even Genesis opens thus in Hebrew: "In the beginning God made for Himself a Son."[8] As there is no ground for this, I am led to other arguments derived from God's own dispensation,[9] in which He existed before the creation of the world, up to the generation of the Son. For before all things God was alone—being in Himself and for Himself universe, and space, and all things. Moreover, He was alone, because there was nothing external to Him but Himself. Yet even not then was He alone; for He had with Him that which He possessed in Himself, that is to say, His own Reason. For God is rational, and Reason was first in Him; and so all things were from Himself. This Reason is His own Thought (or Consciousness)[10] which the Greeks call λόγος, by which term we also designate Word *or Discourse*[11] and therefore it is now usual with our people, owing to the mere simple interpretation of the term, to say that the Word[12] was in the beginning with God; although it would be more suitable to regard Reason as the more ancient; because God had not Word[13] from the beginning, but He had Reason[14] even before the beginning; because also Word itself consists of Reason, which it thus proves to have been the prior existence as being its own substance.[15] Not that this distinction is of any practical moment. For although God had not yet sent *out* His Word,[16] He still had Him within Himself, both in company with and included within His very Reason, as He silently planned and arranged within Himself everything which He was afterwards about to utter[17] through His Word. Now, whilst He was thus planning and arranging with His own Reason, He was actually causing that to become Word which He was dealing with in the way of Word *or Discourse*.[18] And that you may the more readily understand this, consider first of all, from your own self, who are made "in the image and likeness of God,"[19] for what purpose it is that you also possess reason in yourself, who are a rational creature, as being not only made by a rational Artificer, but actually animated out of His substance. Observe, then, that when you are silently con-

---

[1] 1 Cor. xv. 24, 25.
[2] Ps. cx. 1.
[3] 1 Cor. xv. 27, 28.
[4] Apud.
[5] Res ipsa.
[6] Formam, or shape.
[7] Patrocinantibus.

[8] See St. Jerome's *Quæstt. Hebr.* in Genesim, ii. 507.
[9] "Dispositio" means "mutual relations in the Godhead." See Bp. Bull's *Def. Fid. Nicen.*, Oxford translation, p. 516.
[10] Sensus ipsius.
[11] Sermonem. [He always calls the Logos not *Verbum*, but *Sermo*, in this treatise. A masculine word was better to exhibit our author's thought. So Erasmus translates Logos in his N. Testament, on which see Kaye, p. 516.]
[12] Sermonen.
[13] Sermonalis.
[14] Rationalis.
[15] *i.e.*, "Reason is manifestly prior to the Word, which it dictates" (Bp. Kaye, p. 501).
[16] Sermonem.
[17] Dicturus. Another reading is "daturus," about to give.
[18] Sermone.
[19] Gen. i. 26.

versing with yourself, this very process is carried on within you by your reason, which meets you with a word at every movement of your thought, at every impulse of your conception. Whatever you think, there is a word; whatever you conceive, there is reason. You must needs speak it in your mind; and while you are speaking, you admit speech as an interlocutor with you, involved in which there is this very reason, whereby, while in thought you are holding converse with your word, you are (by reciprocal action) producing thought by means of that converse with your word. Thus, in a certain sense, the word is a second *person* within you, through which in thinking you utter speech, and through which also, (by reciprocity of process,) in uttering speech you generate thought. The word is itself a different thing from yourself. Now how much more fully is all this transacted in God, whose image and likeness even you are regarded as being, inasmuch as He has reason within Himself even while He is silent, and involved in that Reason His Word! I may therefore without rashness first lay this down (as a fixed principle) that even then before the creation of the universe God was not alone, since He had within Himself both Reason, and, inherent in Reason, His Word, which He made second to Himself by agitating it within Himself.

CHAP. VI.—THE WORD OF GOD IS ALSO THE WISDOM OF GOD. THE GOING FORTH OF WISDOM TO CREATE THE UNIVERSE, ACCORDING TO THE DIVINE PLAN.

This power and disposition[1] of the Divine Intelligence[2] is set forth also in the Scriptures under the name of Σοφία, Wisdom; for what can be better entitled to the name of Wisdom[3] than the Reason or the Word of God? Listen therefore to Wisdom herself, constituted in the character of a Second Person: "At the first the Lord created me as the beginning of His ways, with a view to His own works, before He made the earth, before the mountains were settled; moreover, before all the hills did He beget me;"[4] that is to say, He created and generated me in His own intelligence. Then, again, observe the distinction between them implied in the companionship of Wisdom with the Lord. "When He prepared the heaven," says *Wisdom*, "I was present with Him; and when He made His strong places upon the winds, which are the clouds above; and when He secured the fountains, (and all things) which are beneath

the sky, I was by, arranging all things with Him; I was by, in whom He delighted; and daily, too, did I rejoice in His presence."[5] Now, as soon as it pleased God to put forth into their respective substances and forms the things which He had planned and ordered within Himself, in conjunction with His Wisdom's Reason and Word, He first put forth the Word Himself, having within Him His own inseparable Reason and Wisdom, in order that all things might be made through Him through whom they had been planned and disposed, yea, and already made, so far forth as (they were) in the mind and intelligence of God. This, however, was still wanting to them, that they should also be openly known, and kept permanently in their proper forms and substances

CHAP. VII.—THE SON BY BEING DESIGNATED WORD AND WISDOM, (ACCORDING TO THE IMPERFECTION OF HUMAN THOUGHT AND LANGUAGE) LIABLE TO BE DEEMED A MERE ATTRIBUTE. HE IS SHOWN TO BE A PERSONAL BEING.

Then, therefore, does the Word also Himself assume His own form and glorious garb,[6] *His own* sound and vocal utterance, when God says, "Let there be light."[7] This is the perfect nativity of the Word, when He proceeds forth from God—*formed*[8] by Him first to devise and think out *all things* under the name of Wisdom—"The Lord created *or formed*[9] me as the beginning of His ways;"[10] then afterward *begotten*, to carry all into effect—"When He prepared the heaven, I was present with Him."[11] Thus does He make Him equal to Him: for by proceeding from Himself He became His first-begotten Son, because begotten before all things;[12] and His only-begotten also, because alone begotten of God, in a way peculiar to Himself, from the womb of His own heart—even as the Father Himself testifies: "My heart," says He, "hath emitted my most excellent Word."[13] *The Father* took pleasure evermore in Him, who equally rejoiced with a reciprocal gladness in the Father's presence: "Thou art my Son, to-day have I begotten Thee;"[14] even before the morning star did I

---

1 " Mutual relations in the Godhead."
2 Sensus.
3 Sapientius.
4 Prov. viii. 22–25.

5 Prov. viii. 27–30.
6 Ornatum.
7 Gen. i. 3.
8 Conditus. [See Theophilus *To Autolycus*, cap. x. note 1, p. 98, Vol. II. of this series. Also *Ibid.* p. 103, note 5. On the whole subject, Bp. Bull, *Defensio Fid. Nicænæ.* Vol. V. pp. 585–592.]
9 Condidit.
10 Prov. viii. 22.
11 Ver. 27.
12 Col. i. 15.
13 Ps. xlv. 1. See this reading, and its application, fully discussed in our note 5, p. 66, of the *Anti-Marcion*. Edin.
14 Ps. ii. 7.

beget Thee. The Son likewise acknowledges the Father, speaking in His own person, under the name of Wisdom: "The Lord formed Me as the beginning of His ways, with a view to His own works; before all the hills did He beget Me."[1] For if indeed Wisdom in this passage seems to say that She was created by the Lord with a view to His works, and to accomplish His ways, yet proof is given in another Scripture that "all things were made by the Word, and without Him was there nothing made;"[2] as, again, in another place (it is said), "By His word were the heavens established, and all the powers thereof by His Spirit"[3]—that is to say, by the Spirit (or Divine Nature) which was in the Word: *thus* is it evident that it is one and the same power which is in one place described under the name of Wisdom, and in another passage under the appellation of the Word, which was initiated for the works of God,[4] which "strengthened the heavens;"[5] "by which all things were made,"[6] "and without which nothing was made."[7] Nor need we dwell any longer on this point, as if it were not the very Word Himself, who is spoken of under the name both of Wisdom and of Reason, and of the entire Divine Soul and Spirit. He became also the Son of God, and was begotten when He proceeded forth from Him. Do you then, (you ask,) grant that the Word is a certain substance, constructed by the Spirit and the communication of Wisdom? Certainly I do. But you will not allow Him to be really a substantive being, by having a substance of His own; in such a way that He may be regarded as an objective thing and a person, and so be able (as being constituted second to God *the Father*,) to make two, the Father and the Son, God and the Word. For you will say, what is a word, but a voice and sound of the mouth, and (as the grammarians teach) air when struck against,[8] intelligible to the ear, but for the rest a sort of void, empty, and incorporeal thing. I, on the contrary, contend that nothing empty and void could have come forth from God, seeing that it is not put forth from that which is empty and void; nor could that possibly be devoid of substance which has proceeded from so great a substance, and has produced such mighty substances: for all things which were made through Him, He Himself (personally) made. How could it be, that He Himself is

nothing, without whom nothing was made? How could He who is empty have made things which are solid, and He who is void have made things which are full, and He who is incorporeal have made things which have body? For although a thing may sometimes be made different from him by whom it is made, yet nothing can be made by that which is a void and empty thing. Is that Word of God, then, a void and empty thing, which is called the Son, who Himself is designated God? "The Word was with God, and the Word was God."[9] It is written, "Thou shalt not take God's name in vain."[10] This for certain is He "who, being in the form of God, thought it not robbery to be equal with God."[11] In what form of God? Of course he means in some form, not in none. For who will deny that God is a body, although "God is a Spirit?"[12] For Spirit has a bodily substance of its own kind, in its own form.[13] Now, even if invisible things, whatsoever they be, have both their substance and their form in God, whereby they are visible to God alone, how much more shall that which has been sent forth from His substance not be without substance! Whatever, therefore, was the substance of the Word that I designate a Person, I claim for it the name of *Son;* and while I recognize the Son, I assert His distinction as second to the Father.[14]

CHAP. VIII.—THOUGH THE SON OR WORD OF GOD EMANATES FROM THE FATHER, HE IS NOT, LIKE THE EMANATIONS OF VALENTINUS, SEPARABLE FROM THE FATHER. NOR IS THE HOLY GHOST SEPARABLE FROM EITHER. ILLUSTRATIONS FROM NATURE.

If any man from this shall think that I am introducing some προβολή—that is to say, some prolation[15] of one thing out of another, as Valentinus does when he sets forth Æon from Æon, one after another—then this is my first reply to you: Truth must not therefore refrain from the use of such a term, and its reality and meaning, because heresy also employs it. The fact is, heresy has rather taken it from Truth, in order to mould it into its own coun-

---

[1] Prov. viii. 22, 25.
[2] John i. 3.
[3] Ps. xxxiii. 6.
[4] Prov. viii. 22.
[5] Ver. 28.
[6] John i. 3.
[7] John i. 3.
[8] Offensus.

[9] John i. 1.
[10] Ex. xx. 7.
[11] Phil. ii. 6.
[12] John iv. 24.
[13] This doctrine of the soul's corporeality in a certain sense is treated by Tertullian in his *De Resurr. Carn.* xvii., and *De Anima* v. By Tertullian, *spirit* and *soul* were considered identical. See our *Anti-Marcion*, p. 451, note 4, Edin.
[14] [On Tertullian's orthodoxy, here, see Kaye, p. 502.]
[15] " The word προβολή properly means anything which proceeds or is sent forth from the substance of another, as the fruit of a tree or the rays of the sun. In Latin it is translated by *prolatio*, *emissio*, or *editio*, or what we now express by the word *development*. In Tertullian's time, Valentinus had given the term a material signification. Tertullian, therefore, has to apologize for using it, when writing against Praxeas, the forerunner of the Sabellians" (Newman's *Arians*, ii. 4 ; reprint, p. 101).

terfeit. Was the Word of God put forth or not? Here take your stand with me, and flinch not. If He was put forth, then acknowledge that the true doctrine has a prolation;[1] and never mind heresy, when in any point it mimics the truth. The question now is, in what sense each side uses a given thing and the word which expresses it. Valentinus divides and separates his prolations from their Author, and places them at so great a distance from Him, that the Æon does not know the Father: he longs, indeed, to know Him, but cannot; nay, he is almost swallowed up and dissolved into the rest of matter.[2] With us, however, the Son alone knows the Father,[3] and has Himself unfolded "the Father's bosom."[4] He has also heard and seen all things with the Father; and what He has been commanded by the Father, that also does He speak.[5] And it is not His own will, but the Father's, which He has accomplished,[6] which He had known most intimately, even from the beginning. "For what man knoweth the things which be in God, but the Spirit which is in Him?"[7] But the Word was formed by the Spirit, and (if I may so express myself) the Spirit is the body of the Word. The Word, therefore, is both always in the Father, as He says, "I am in the Father;"[8] and is always with God, according to what is written, "And the Word was with God;"[9] and never separate from the Father, or other than the Father, since "I and the Father are one."[10] This will be the prolation, taught by the truth,[11] the guardian of the Unity, wherein we declare that the Son is a prolation from the Father, without being separated from Him. For God sent forth the Word, as the Paraclete also declares, just as the root puts forth the tree, and the fountain the river, and the sun the ray.[12] For these are προβολαί, or *emanations*, of the substances from which they proceed. I should not hesitate, indeed, to call the tree the son or offspring of the root, and the river of the fountain, and the ray of the sun; because every original source is a parent, and everything which issues from the origin is an offspring. Much more is (this true of) the Word of God, who has actually received as His own peculiar designation the name of *Son*. But still the tree is not severed from the root, nor the river from the fountain, nor the ray

from the sun; nor, indeed, is the Word separated from God. Following, therefore, the form of these analogies, I confess that I call God and His Word—the Father and His Son —*two*. For the root and the tree are distinctly two things, but correlatively joined; the fountain and the river are also two forms, but indivisible; so likewise the sun and the ray are two forms, but coherent ones. Everything which proceeds from something else must needs be second to that from which it proceeds, without being on that account separated. Where, however, there is a second, there must be two; and where there is a third, there must be three. Now the Spirit indeed is third from God and the Son; just as the fruit of the tree is third from the root, or as the stream out of the river is third from the fountain, or as the apex of the ray is third from the sun. Nothing, however, is alien from that original source whence it derives its own properties. In like manner the Trinity, flowing down from the Father through intertwined and connected steps, does not at all disturb the *Monarchy*,[13] whilst it at the same time guards the state of the *Economy*.[14]

CHAP. IX.—THE CATHOLIC RULE OF FAITH EXPOUNDED IN SOME OF ITS POINTS. ESPECIALLY IN THE UNCONFUSED DISTINCTION OF THE SEVERAL PERSONS OF THE BLESSED TRINITY.

Bear always in mind that this is the rule of faith which I profess; by it I testify that the Father, and the Son, and the Spirit are inseparable from each other, and so will you know in what sense this is said. Now, observe, my assertion is that the Father is one, and the Son one, and the Spirit one, and that They are distinct from Each Other. This statement is taken in a wrong sense by every uneducated as well as every perversely disposed person, as if it predicated a diversity, in such a sense as to imply a separation among the Father, and the Son, and the Spirit. I am, moreover, obliged to say this, when (extolling the *Monarchy* at the expense of the *Economy*) they contend for the identity of the Father and Son and Spirit, that it is not by way of diversity that the Son differs from the Father, but by distribution: it is not by division that He is different, but by distinction; because the Father is not the same as the Son, since they differ one from the other in the mode of their being.[15] For the Father is the entire substance, but the Son is a derivation

---

[1] προβολή.
[2] See *Adv. Valentin.* cc. xiv. xv.
[3] Matt. xi. 27.
[4] John i. 18.
[5] John viii. 26.
[6] John vi. 38.
[7] 1 Cor. ii. 11.
[8] John xiv. 11.
[9] John i. 1.
[10] John x. 30.
[11] Literally, the προβολή, " of the truth."
[12] [Compare cap. iv. *supra*.]

[13] Or oneness of the divine empire.
[14] Or dispensation of the divine tripersonality. See above ch. ii.
[15] "Modulo," in the sense of dispensation or economy. See Oehler and Rigault. on *The Apology*, c. xxi.

and portion of the whole,[1] as He Himself acknowledges: "My Father is greater than I."[2] In the Psalm His inferiority is described as being "a little lower than the angels."[3] Thus the Father is distinct from the Son, being greater than the Son, inasmuch as He who begets is one, and He who is begotten is another; He, too, who sends is one, and He who is sent is another; and He, again, who makes is one, and He through whom the thing is made is another. Happily the Lord Himself employs this expression of the person of the Paraclete, so as to signify not a division or severance, but a disposition (of mutual relations in the Godhead); for He says, "I will pray the Father, and He shall send you another Comforter. . . . even the Spirit of truth,"[4] thus making the Paraclete distinct from Himself, even as we say that the Son is also distinct from the Father; so that He showed a third degree in the Paraclete, as we believe the second degree is in the Son, by reason of the order observed in the *Economy*. Besides, does not the very fact that they have the distinct names of *Father* and *Son* amount to a declaration that they are distinct in personality?[5] For, of course, all things will be what their names represent them to be; and what they are and ever will be, that will they be called; and the distinction indicated by the names does not at all admit of any confusion, because there is none in the things which they designate. "Yes is yes, and no is no; for what is more than these, cometh of evil."[6]

CHAP. X.—THE VERY NAMES OF FATHER AND SON PROVE THE PERSONAL DISTINCTION OF THE TWO. THEY CANNOT POSSIBLY BE IDENTICAL, NOR IS THEIR IDENTITY NECESSARY TO PRESERVE THE DIVINE MONARCHY.

So it is either the Father or the Son, and the day is not the same as the night; nor is the Father the same as the Son, in such a way that Both of them should be One, and One or the Other should be Both,—an opinion which the most conceited "Monarchians" maintain. He Himself, they say, made Himself a Son to Himself.[7] Now a Father makes a Son, and a Son makes a Father;[8] and they who thus become reciprocally related out of each other to each other cannot in any way by themselves simply become so related to themselves, that the Father can make Himself a Son to Himself, and the Son render Himself a Father to Himself. And the relations which God establishes, them does He also guard. A father must needs have a son, in order to be a father; so likewise a son, to be a son, must have a father. It is, however, one thing to have, and another thing to be. For instance, in order to be a husband, I must have a wife; I can never myself be my own wife. In like manner, in order to be a father, I have a son, for I never can be a son to myself; and in order to be a son, I have a father, it being impossible for me ever to be my own father. And it is these relations which make me (what I am), when I come to possess them: I shall then be a father, when I have a son; and a son, when I have a father. Now, if I am to be to myself any one of these relations, I no longer have what I am myself to be: neither a father, because I am to be my own father; nor a son, because I shall be my own son. Moreover, inasmuch as I ought to *have* one of these relations in order to *be* the other; so, if I am to be both together, I shall fail to be one while I possess not the other. For if I must be myself my son, who am also a father, I now cease to have a son, since I am my own son. But by reason of not having a son, since I am my own son, how can I be a father? For I ought to *have* a son, in order to be a father. Therefore I am not a son, because I have not a father, who makes a son. In like manner, if I am myself my father, who am also a son, I no longer have a father, but am myself my father. By not having a father, however, since I am my own father, how can I be a son? For I ought to have a father, in order to be a son. I cannot therefore be a father, because I have not a son, who makes a father. Now all this must be the device of the devil—this excluding and severing one from the other—since by including both together in one under pretence of the *Monarchy*, he causes neither to be held and acknowledged, so that He is not the Father, since indeed He has not the Son; neither is He the Son, since in like manner He has not the Father: for while He is the Father, He will not be the Son. In this way they hold the *Monarchy*, but they hold neither the Father nor the Son. Well, but "with God nothing is impossible."[9] *True enough;* who can be

[1] "In his representation of the distinction (of the Persons of the Blessed Trinity), Tertullian sometimes uses expressions which in aftertimes, when controversy had introduced greater precision of language, were studiously avoided by the orthodox. Thus he calls the Father the whole substance, the Son a derivation from or portion of the whole." (Bp. Kaye, *On Tertullian*, p. 505). After Arius the language of theology received greater precision; but as it is, there is no doubt of the orthodoxy of Tertullian's doctrine, since he so firmly and ably teaches the Son's *consubstantiality* with the Father—equal to Him and inseparable from him. [In other words, Tertullian could not employ a technical phraseology afterwards adopted to give precision to the same orthodox ideas.]
[2] John xiv. 28.
[3] Ps. viii. 5.
[4] John xiv. 16.
[5] Aliud ab alio.
[6] Matt. v. 37.

[7] [Kaye, p. 507, note 3.]
[8] As correlatives, one implying the existence of the other.
[9] Matt. xix. 26.

ignorant of it? W.io also can be unaware that "the things which are impossible with men are possible with God?"[1] "The foolish things also of the world hath God chosen to confound the things which are wise."[2] We have read it all. Therefore, they argue, it was not difficult for God to make Himself both a Father and a Son, contrary to the condition of things among men. For a barren woman to have a child against nature was no difficulty with God; nor was it for a virgin to conceive. Of course nothing is "too hard for the Lord."[3] But if we choose to apply this principle so extravagantly and harshly in our capricious imaginations, we may then make out God to have done anything we please, on the ground that it was not impossible for Him to do it. We must not, however, because He is able to do all things suppose that He has actually done what He has not done. But we must inquire *whether He has really done it.* God could, if He had liked, have furnished man with wings to fly with, just as He gave wings to kites. We must not, however, run to the conclusion that He did this because He was able to do it. He might also have extinguished Praxeas and all other heretics at once; it does not follow, however, that He did, simply because He was able. For it was necessary that there should be both kites and heretics; it was necessary also that the Father should be crucified.[4] In one sense there will be something difficult even for God—namely, that which He has not done—not because He could not, but because He would not, do it. For with God, to be willing is to be able, and to be unwilling is to be unable; all that He has willed, however, He has both been able to accomplish, and has displayed His ability. Since, therefore, if God had wished to make Himself a Son to Himself, He had it in His power to do so; and since, if He had it in His power, He effected *His purpose*, you will then make good your proof of His power and His will (to do even this) when you shall have proved to us that He actually did it.

CHAP. XI.—THE IDENTITY OF THE FATHER AND THE SON, AS PRAXEAS HELD IT, SHOWN TO BE FULL OF PERPLEXITY AND ABSURDITY. MANY SCRIPTURES QUOTED IN PROOF OF THE DISTINCTION OF THE DIVINE PERSONS OF THE TRINITY.

It will be your duty, however, to adduce your proofs out of the Scriptures as plainly as we do, when we prove that He made His Word a Son to Himself. For if He calls Him Son, and if the Son is none other than He who has proceeded from *the Father* Himself, and if the Word has proceeded from *the Father* Himself, He will then be the Son, and not Himself from whom He proceeded. For *the Father* Himself did not proceed from Himself. Now, you who say that the Father is the same as the Son, do really make the same Person both to have sent forth from Himself (and at the same time to have gone out from Himself as) that Being which is God. If it was possible for Him to have done this, He at all events did not do it. You must bring forth the proof which I require of you—one like my own; that is, (you must prove to me) that the Scriptures show the Son and the Father to be the same, just as on our side the Father and the Son are demonstrated to be distinct; I say *distinct*, but not *separate:*[5] for as on my part I produce the words of God Himself, "My heart hath emitted my most excellent Word,"[6] so you in like manner ought to adduce in opposition to me some text where God has said, "My heart hath emitted Myself as my own most excellent Word," in such a sense that He is Himself both the Emitter and the Emitted, both He who sent forth and He who was sent forth, since He is both the Word and God. I bid you also observe,[7] that on my side I advance the passage where the Father said to the Son, "Thou art my Son, this day have I begotten Thee."[8] If you want me to believe Him to be both the Father and the Son, show me some other passage where it is declared, "The Lord said unto Himself, I am my own Son, to-day have I begotten myself;" or again, "Before the morning did I beget myself;"[9] and likewise, "I the Lord possessed Myself the beginning of my ways for my own works; before all the hills, too, did I beget myself;"[10] and whatever other passages are to the same effect. Why, moreover, could God the Lord of all things, have hesitated to speak thus of Himself, if the fact had been so? Was He afraid of not being believed, if He had in so many words declared Himself to be both the Father and the Son? Of one thing He was at any rate afraid—of lying. Of Himself, too, and of His own truth, was He afraid. Believing Him, therefore, to be the true God, I am sure that He declared nothing to exist in any other way than according to His own dispensation and arrangement, and that He had arranged nothing in any other way than ac-

---

[1] Luke xviii. 27.
[2] 1 Cor. i. 27.
[3] Gen. xviii. 14.
[4] An ironical reference to a great paradox in the Praxean heresy.
[5] Distincte, non divise.
[6] For this version of Ps. xlv. 1, see our *Anti-Marcion*, p. 66, note 5, Edin.
[7] Ecce.
[8] Ps. ii. 7.
[9] In allusion to Ps. cx. 3 (Sept.)
[10] In allusion to Prov. viii. 22.

cording to His own declaration. On your side, however, you must make Him out to be a liar, and an impostor, and a tamperer with His word, if, when He was Himself a Son to Himself, He assigned the part of His Son to be played by another, when all the Scriptures attest the clear existence of, and distinction in, (the Persons of) the Trinity, and indeed furnish us with our Rule *of faith*, that He who speaks, and He of whom He speaks, and to whom He speaks, cannot possibly seem to be One and the Same. So absurd and misleading a statement would be unworthy of God, that, when it was Himself to whom He was speaking, He speaks rather to another, and not to His very self. Hear, then, other utterances also of the Father concerning the Son by the mouth of Isaiah: "Behold my Son, whom I have chosen; my beloved, in whom I am well pleased: I will put my Spirit upon Him, and He shall bring forth judgment to the Gentiles."[1] Hear also what He says to the Son: "Is it a great thing for Thee, that Thou shouldest be called my Son to raise up the tribes of Jacob, and to restore the dispersed of Israel? I have given Thee for a light to the Gentiles, that Thou mayest be their salvation to the end of the earth."[2] Hear now also the Son's utterances respecting the Father: "The Spirit of the Lord is upon me, because He hath anointed me to preach the gospel unto men."[3] He speaks of Himself likewise to the Father in the Psalm: "Forsake me not, until I have declared the might of Thine arm to all the generation that is to come."[4] Also to the same purport in another Psalm: "O Lord, how are they increased that trouble me!"[5] But almost all the Psalms which prophesy of[6] the person of Christ, represent the Son as conversing with the Father—that is, *represent* Christ (as speaking) to God. Observe also the Spirit speaking of the Father and the Son, in the character of[7] a third Person: "The Lord said unto my Lord, Sit Thou on my right hand, until I make Thine enemies Thy footstool."[8] Likewise in the words of Isaiah: "Thus saith the Lord to the Lord[9] mine Anointed."[10] Likewise, in the same prophet, He says to the Father respecting the Son: "Lord, who hath believed our report, and to whom is the arm of the Lord revealed? We brought a report concerning Him, as if He were a little child, as

if He were a root in a dry ground, who had no form nor comeliness."[11] These are a few testimonies out of many; for we do not pretend to bring up all the passages of Scripture, because we have a tolerably large accumulation of them in the various heads of our subject, as we in our several chapters call them in as our witnesses in the fulness of their dignity and authority.[12] Still, in these few quotations the distinction of *Persons in* the Trinity is clearly set forth. For there is the Spirit Himself who speaks, and the Father to whom He speaks, and the Son of whom He speaks.[13] In the same manner, the other passages also establish each one of several Persons in His special character—addressed as they in some cases are to the Father or to the Son respecting the Son, in other cases to the Son or to the Father concerning the Father, and again in other instances to the (Holy) Spirit.

CHAP. XII.—OTHER QUOTATIONS FROM HOLY SCRIPTURE ADDUCED IN PROOF OF THE PLURALITY OF PERSONS IN THE GODHEAD.

If the number of the Trinity also offends you, as if it were not connected in the simple Unity, I ask you how it is possible for a Being who is merely and absolutely One and Singular, to speak in plural phrase, saying, "Let us make man in our own image, and after our own likeness;"[14] whereas He ought to have said, "Let me make man in my own image, and after my own likeness," as being a unique and singular Being? In the following passage, however, "Behold the man is become as one of us,"[15] He is either deceiving or amusing us in speaking plurally, if He is One only and singular. Or was it to the angels that He spoke, as the Jews interpret the passage, because these also acknowledge not the Son? Or was it because He was at once the Father, the Son, and the Spirit, that He spoke to Himself in plural terms, making Himself plural on that very account? Nay, it was because He had already His Son close at His side, as a second Person, His own Word, and a third Person also, the Spirit in the Word, that He purposely adopted the plural phrase, "Let *us* make;" and, "in *our* image;" and, "become as one *of us*." For with whom did He make man? and to whom did He make him like? (The answer must be), the Son on

---

1 Isa. xlii. 1.
2 Isa. xlix. 6.
3 Isa. lxi. 1 and Luke iv. 18.
4 Ps. lxxi. 18.
5 Ps. iii. 1.
6 Sustinent.
7 Ex.
8 Ps. cx. 1.
9 Tertullian read Κυρίῳ instead of Κύρῳ, "Cyrus."
10 Isa. xlv. 1.

11 Isa. liii. 1, 2.
12 [See Elucidation III., and also cap. xxv. *infra*.]
13 [See *De Baptismo*, cap. v. p. 344, Ed. Oehler, and note how often our author cites an important text, *by half quotation*, leaving the residue to the reader's memory, owing to the impetuosity of his genius and his style: "Monte decurrens velut amnis, imbres quem super notas aluere ripas fervet, etc."]
14 Gen. i. 26.
15 Gen. iii. 22.

the one hand, who was one day to put on human nature; and the Spirit on the other, who was to sanctify man. With these did He then speak, in the Unity of the Trinity, as with His ministers and witnesses In the following text also He distinguishes among the Persons: "So God created man in His own image; in the image of God created He him."[1] Why say "image of God?" Why not "His own image" merely, if He was only one who was the Maker, and if there was not also One in whose image He made man? But there was One in whose image God was making man, that is to say, Christ's image, who, being one day about to become Man (more surely and more truly so), had already caused the man to be called His image, who was then going to be formed of clay—the image and similitude of the true and perfect Man. But in respect of the previous works of the world what says the Scripture? Its first statement indeed is made, when the Son has not yet appeared: "And God said, Let there be light, and there was light."[2] Immediately there appears the Word, "that true light, which lighteth man on his coming into the world,"[3] and through Him also came light upon the world.[4] From that moment God willed creation to be effected in the Word, Christ being present and ministering unto Him: and so God created. And God said, "Let there be a firmament, . . . and God made the firmament;"[5] and God also said, "Let there be lights (in the firmament); and so God made a greater and a lesser light."[6] But all the rest of the created things did He in like manner make, who made the former ones—I mean the Word of God, "through whom all things were made, and without whom nothing was made."[7] Now if He too is God, according to John, (who says,) "The Word was God,"[8] then you have two Beings —One that commands that the thing be made, and the Other that *executes the order and* creates. In what sense, however, you ought to understand Him to be another, I have already explained, on the ground of Personality, not of Substance—in the way of distinction, not of division.[9] But although I must everywhere hold one only substance in three coherent and inseparable (Persons), yet I am bound to acknowledge, from the necessity of the case, that He who issues a command is different from Him who

executes it. For, indeed, He would not be issuing a command if He were all the while doing the work Himself, while ordering it to be done by the second.[10] But still He did issue the command, although He would not have intended to command Himself if He were only one; or else He must have worked without any command, because He would not have waited to command Himself.

CHAP. XIII.—THE FORCE OF SUNDRY PASSAGES OF SCRIPTURE ILLUSTRATED IN RELATION TO THE PLURALITY OF PERSONS AND UNITY OF SUBSTANCE. THERE IS NO POLYTHEISM HERE, SINCE THE UNITY IS INSISTED ON AS A REMEDY AGAINST POLYTHEISM.

Well then, you reply, if He was God who spoke, and He was also God who created, at this rate, one God spoke and another created; (and thus) two Gods are declared. If you are so venturesome and harsh, reflect a while; and that you may think the better and more deliberately, listen to the psalm in which Two are described as God: "Thy throne, O God, is for ever and ever; the sceptre of Thy kingdom *is a sceptre of righteousness*. Thou hast loved righteousness, and hated iniquity: therefore God, even Thy God, hath anointed Thee *or made Thee His Christ*."[11] Now, since He here speaks to God, and affirms that God is anointed by God, He must have affirmed that Two are God, by reason of the sceptre's royal power. Accordingly, Isaiah also says to the Person of Christ: "The Sabæans, men of stature, shall pass over to Thee; and they shall follow after Thee, bound in fetters; and they shall worship Thee, because God is in Thee: for Thou art our God, yet we knew it not; Thou art the God of Israel."[12] For here too, by saying, "God is in Thee, and "Thou art God," he sets forth Two who were God: (in the former expression *in Thee*, he means) in Christ, and (in the other he means) the Holy Ghost. That is a still grander statement which you will find expressly made in the Gospel: "In the beginning was the Word, and the Word was with God, and the Word was God."[13] There was One "who was," and there was another "with whom" He was. But I find in Scripture the name Lord also applied to them Both: "The Lord said unto my Lord, Sit Thou on my right hand."[14] And Isaiah says this: "Lord, who hath believed our report, and to whom is the arm of the Lord revealed?"[15] Now he would

---

[1] Gen. i. 27.
[2] Gen. i. 3.
[3] John i. 9.
[4] Mundialis lux.
[5] Gen. i. 6, 7.
[6] Gen. i. 14, 16.
[7] John i. 3.
[8] John i. 1.
[9] [Kaye thinks the Athanasian hymn (so called) was composed by some one who had this treatise always in mind. See p. 526.]

[10] Per eum.
[11] Ps. xlv. 6, 7.
[12] Isa. xlv. 14, 15 (Sept.)
[13] John i. 1.
[14] Ps. cx. 1.
[15] Isa. liii. 1.

most certainly have said *Thine Arm*, if he had not wished us to understand that the Father is Lord, and the Son also is Lord. A much more ancient testimony we have also in Genesis: "Then the Lord rained upon Sodom and upon Gomorrah brimstone and fire from the Lord out of heaven."[1] Now, either deny that this is Scripture; or else (let me ask) what sort of man you are, that you do not think words ought to be taken and understood in the sense in which they are written, especially when they are not expressed in allegories and parables, but in determinate and simple declarations? If, indeed, you follow those who did not at the time endure the Lord when showing Himself to be the Son of God, because they would not believe Him to be the Lord, then (I ask you) call to mind along with them the passage where it is written, "I have said, Ye are gods, and ye are children of the Most High;"[2] and again, "God standeth in the congregation of gods;"[3] in order that, if the Scripture has not been afraid to designate as gods human beings, who have become sons of God by faith, you may be sure that the same Scripture has with greater propriety conferred the name of the Lord on the true and one-only Son of God. Very well! you say, I shall challenge you to preach from this day forth (and that, too, on the authority of these same Scriptures) two Gods and two Lords, consistently with your views. God forbid, (is my reply.) For we, who by the grace of God possess an insight into both the times and the occasions of the Sacred Writings, especially we who are followers of the Paraclete, not of human *teachers*, do indeed definitively declare that *Two* Beings are God, the Father and the Son, and, with the addition of the Holy Spirit, even *Three*, according to the principle of the *divine* economy, which introduces *number*, in order that the Father may not, as you perversely infer, be Himself believed to have been born and to have suffered, which it is not lawful to believe, forasmuch as it has not been so handed down. That there are, however, two Gods or two Lords, is a statement which at no time proceeds out of our mouth: not as if it were untrue that the Father is God, and the Son is God, and the Holy Ghost is God, and each is God; but because in earlier times Two were actually spoken of as God, and two as Lord, that when Christ should come He might be both acknowledged as God and designated as Lord, being the Son of Him who is both God and Lord. Now, if there were found in the Scriptures but one Person-

ality of Him who is God and Lord, Christ would justly enough be inadmissible to the title of God and Lord: for (in the Scriptures) there was declared to be none other than One God and One Lord, and it must have followed that the Father should Himself seem to have come down (to earth), inasmuch as only One God and One Lord was ever read of (in the Scriptures), and His entire *Economy* would be involved in obscurity, which has been planned and arranged with so clear a foresight *in His providential dispensation* as matter for our faith. As soon, however, as Christ came, and was recognised by us as the very Being who had from the beginning[4] caused plurality[5] (in the Divine Economy), being the *second* from the Father, and with the Spirit the *third*, and Himself declaring and manifesting the Father more fully (than He had ever been before), the title of Him who is God and Lord was at once restored to the Unity (of the Divine Nature), even because the Gentiles would have to pass from the multitude of their idols to the One Only God, in order that a difference might be distinctly settled between the worshippers of One God and the votaries of polytheism. For it was only right that Christians should shine in the world as "children of light," adoring and invoking Him who is the One God and Lord as "the light of the world." Besides, if, from that perfect knowledge[6] which assures us that the title of God and Lord is suitable both to the Father, and to the Son, and to the Holy Ghost, we were to invoke *a plurality of* gods and lords, we should quench our torches, and we should become less courageous to endure the martyr's sufferings, from which an easy escape would everywhere lie open to us, as soon as we swore by *a plurality of* gods and lords, as sundry heretics do, who hold more gods than One. I will therefore not speak of gods at all, nor of lords, but I shall follow the apostle; so that if the Father and the Son, are alike to be invoked, I shall call the Father "*God*," and invoke Jesus Christ as "*Lord*."[7] But when Christ alone (is mentioned), I shall be able to call Him "*God*," as the same apostle says: "Of whom is Christ, who is over all, God blessed for ever."[8] For I should give the name of "*sun*" even to a sunbeam, considered in itself; but if I were mentioning the sun from which the ray emanates, I certainly should at once withdraw the name of sun from the mere beam. For although I make not two suns, still I shall reckon both the sun and

---

[1] Gen. xix. 24.
[2] Ps. lxxxii. 6.
[3] Ver. 1.

[4] Retro.
[5] Numerum.
[6] Conscientia.
[7] Rom. i. 7.
[8] Rom. ix. 5.

its ray to be as much two things and two forms[1] of one undivided substance, as God and His Word, as the Father and the Son.

CHAP. XIV.—THE NATURAL INVISIBILITY OF THE FATHER, AND THE VISIBILITY OF THE SON WITNESSED IN MANY PASSAGES OF THE OLD TESTAMENT. ARGUMENTS OF THEIR DISTINCTNESS, THUS SUPPLIED.

Moreover, there comes to our aid, when we insist upon the Father and the Son as being *Two*, that regulating principle which has determined God to be invisible. When Moses in Egypt desired to see the face of the Lord, saying, " If therefore I have found grace in Thy sight, manifest Thyself unto me, that I may see Thee and know Thee," [2] *God* said, " Thou canst not see my face; for there shall no man see me, and live:" [3] in other words, he who sees me shall die. Now we find that God has been seen by many persons, and yet that no one who saw Him died (at the sight). *The truth is*, they saw God according to the faculties of men, but not in accordance with the full glory of the Godhead. For the patriarchs are said to have seen God (as Abraham and Jacob), and the prophets (as, for instance Isaiah and Ezekiel), and yet they did not die. Either, then, they ought to have died, since they had seen Him—for (the sentence runs), " No man shall see God, and live;" or else, if they saw God, and yet did not die, the Scripture is false in stating that God said, " If a man see my face, he shall not live." Either way, the Scripture misleads us, when it makes God invisible, and when it produces Him to our sight. Now, then, He must be a different Being who was seen, because of one who was seen it could not be predicated that He is invisible. It will therefore follow, that by Him who is invisible we must understand the Father in the fulness of His majesty, while we recognise the Son as visible by reason of the dispensation of His derived existence;[4] even as it is not permitted us to contemplate the sun, in the full amount of his substance which is in the heavens, but we can only endure with our eyes a ray, by reason of the tempered condition of this portion which is projected from him to the earth. Here some one on the other side may be disposed to contend that the Son is also invisible as being the Word, *and* as being also the Spirit;[5] and, while claiming one nature for the Father and the Son, to affirm that the Father is rather One and the Same *Person* with the Son. But

the Scripture, as we have said, maintains their difference by the distinction it makes between the Visible and the Invisible. They then go on to argue to this effect, that if it was the Son who then spake to Moses, He must mean it of Himself that His face was visible to no one, because He was Himself indeed the invisible Father in the name of the Son. And by this means they will have it that the Visible and the Invisible are one and the same, just as the Father and the Son are the same; (and this they maintain) because in a preceding passage, before He had refused (the sight of) His face to Moses, the Scripture informs us that " the Lord spake face to face with Moses, even as a man speaketh unto his friend;"[6] just as Jacob also says, " I have seen God face to face." [7] Therefore the Visible and the Invisible are one and the same; and both being thus the same, it follows that He is invisible as the Father, and visible as the Son. As if the Scripture, according to our exposition of it, were inapplicable to the Son, when the Father is set aside in His own invisibility. We declare, however, that the Son also, considered in Himself (as the Son), is invisible, in that He is God, and the Word and Spirit of God; but that He was visible before *the days of* His flesh, in the way that He says to Aaron and Miriam, " And if there shall be a prophet amongst you, I will make myself known to him in a vision, and will speak to him in a dream; not as with Moses, with whom I shall speak mouth to mouth, even *apparently*, that is to say, in truth, and not *enigmatically*" that is to say, in image;[8] as the apostle also expresses it, " Now we see through a glass, darkly (or enigmatically), but then face to face." [9] Since, therefore, He reserves to some future time His presence and speech face to face with Moses —a promise which was afterwards fulfilled in the retirement of the mount (of transfiguration), when as we read in the Gospel, " Moses appeared talking with Jesus " [10]—it is evident that in early times it was always in a glass, (as it were,) and an enigma, in vision and dream, that God, I mean the Son of God, appeared—to the prophets and the patriarchs, as also to Moses indeed himself. And even if the Lord did possibly [11] speak with him face to face, yet it was not as man that he could behold His face, unless indeed it was in a glass, (as it were,) and by enigma. Besides, if the Lord so spake with Moses, that Moses actually discerned His face, eye to eye,[12] how

[1] Species.
[2] Ex. xxxiii. 13.
[3] Ver. 20.
[4] Pro modulo derivationis.
[5] *Spiritus* here is the divine nature of Christ.

[6] Ex. xxxiii. 11.
[7] Gen. xxxii. 30.
[8] Num. xii. 6-8.
[9] 1 Cor. xiii. 12.
[10] Mark ix. 4 ; Matt. xvii. 3.
[11] Si forte.
[12] Cominus sciret.

comes it to pass that immediately afterwards, on the same occasion, he desires to see His face,[1] which he ought not to have desired, because he had already seen it? And how, in like manner, does the Lord also say that His face cannot be seen, because He had shown it, if indeed He really had, (as our opponents suppose.) Or what is that face of God, the sight of which is refused, if there was one which was visible to man? "I have seen God," says Jacob, "face to face, and my life is preserved."[2] There ought to be some other face which kills if it be only seen. Well, then, was the Son visible? (Certainly not,[3]) although He was the face of God, except only in vision and dream, and in a glass and enigma, because the Word and Spirit (of God) cannot be seen except in an imaginary form. But, (they say,) He calls the invisible Father His face. For who is the Father? Must He not be the face of the Son, by reason of that authority which He obtains as the begotten of the Father? For is there not a natural propriety in saying of some personage greater (than yourself), That man is my face; he gives me his countenance? "My Father," says Christ, "is greater than I."[4] Therefore the Father must be the face of the Son. For what does the Scripture say? "The Spirit of His person is Christ the Lord."[5] As therefore Christ is the Spirit of the Father's person, there is good reason why, in virtue indeed of the unity, the Spirit of Him to whose person He belonged—that is to say, the Father—pronounced Him to be His "face." Now this, to be sure, is an astonishing thing, that the Father can be taken to be the face of the Son, when He is His head; for "the head of Christ is God."[6]

CHAP. XV.—NEW TESTAMENT PASSAGES QUOTED. THEY ATTEST THE SAME TRUTH OF THE SON'S VISIBILITY CONTRASTED WITH THE FATHER'S INVISIBILITY.

If I fail in resolving this article (of our faith) by passages which may admit of dispute[7] out of the Old Testament, I will take out of the New Testament a confirmation of our view, that you may not straightway attribute to the Father every possible (relation and condition) which I ascribe to the Son. Behold, then, I find both in the Gospels and in the (writings of the) apostles a visible and an invisible God (revealed to us), under a manifest and personal distinction in the condition of both. There is a certain emphatic saying by John: "No man hath seen God at any time;"[8] meaning, of course, at any previous time. But he has indeed taken away all question of time, by saying that God had never been seen. The apostle confirms this statement; for, speaking of God, he says, "Whom no man hath seen, nor can see;"[9] because the man indeed would die who should see Him.[10] But the very same apostles testify that they had both seen and "handled" Christ.[11] Now, if Christ is Himself both the Father and the Son, how can He be both the Visible and the Invisible? In order, however, to reconcile this diversity between the Visible and the Invisible, will not some one on the other side argue that the two statements are quite correct: that He was visible indeed in the flesh, but was invisible before *His appearance in* the flesh; so that He who as the Father was invisible before the flesh, is the same as the Son who was visible in the flesh? If, however, He is the same who was invisible before the incarnation, how comes it that He was actually seen in ancient times before (coming in) the flesh? And by parity of reasoning, if He is the same who was visible after (coming in) the flesh, how happens it that He is now declared to be invisible by the apostles? *How, I repeat, can all this be*, unless it be that He is one, who anciently was visible only in mystery and enigma, and became more clearly visible by His incarnation, even the Word who was also made flesh; whilst *He* is another whom no man has seen at any time, *being* none else than the Father, even Him to whom the Word belongs? Let us, in short, examine who it is whom the apostles saw. "That," says John, "which we have seen with our eyes, which we have looked upon, and our hands have handled, of the Word of life."[12] Now the Word of life became flesh, and was heard, and was seen, and was handled, because He was flesh who, before *He came in* the flesh, was the "Word in the beginning with God" the Father,[13] and not the Father with the Word. For although the Word was God, yet was He with God, because He is God of God; and being joined to the Father, is with the Father.[14] "And we have seen His glory, the glory as of the only begotten of the Father;"[15] that is, of course,

---

[1] Comp. ver. 13 with ver. 11 of Ex. xxxiii.
[2] Gen. xxii. 30.
[3] Involved in the *nunquid.*
[4] John xiv. 28.
[5] Lam. iv. 20. Tertullian reads, "Spiritus personæ *ejus* Christus Dominus." This varies only in the pronoun from the Septuagint, which runs, Πνεῦμα προσώπου ἡμῶν Χριστὸς Κύριος. According to our A. V., "the breath of our nostrils, the anointed of the Lord" (or, "our anointed Lord"), allusion is made, in the destruction of Jerusalem by the Babylonians, to the capture of the king—the last of David's line, "as an anointed prince." Comp. Jer. lii. 9.
[6] 1 Cor. xi. 3.
[7] Quæstionibus.

[8] John i. 18.
[9] 1 Tim. vi. 16.
[10] Ex. xxxiii. 20; Deut. v. 26; Judg. xiii. 22.
[11] 1 John i. 1.
[12] 1 John i. 1.
[13] John i. 1, 2.
[14] Quia cum Patre apud Patrem.
[15] John i. 14.

(the glory) of the Son, even Him who was visible, and was glorified by the invisible Father. And therefore, inasmuch as he had said that the Word of God was God, in order that he might give no help to the presumption of the adversary, (which pretended) that he had seen the Father Himself *and* in order to draw a distinction between the invisible Father and the visible Son, he makes the additional assertion, *ex abundanti* as it were: "No man hath seen God at any time."[1] What God does he mean? The Word? But he has already said: "*Him* we have seen and heard, and our hands have handled the Word of life." Well, (I must again ask,) what God does he mean? It is of course the Father, with whom was the Word, the only begotten Son, who is in the bosom of the Father, and has Himself declared Him.[2] He was both heard and seen, and, that He might not be supposed to be a phantom, was actually handled. Him, too, did Paul behold; but yet he saw not the Father. "Have I not," he says, "seen Jesus *Christ our Lord?*"[3] Moreover, he expressly called Christ God, saying: "Of whom are the fathers, and of whom as concerning the flesh Christ came, who is over all, God blessed for ever."[4] He shows us also that the Son of God, which is the Word of God, is visible, because He who became flesh was called Christ. Of the Father, however, he says to Timothy: "Whom none among men hath seen, nor indeed can see;" and he accumulates the description in still ampler terms: "Who only hath immortality, and dwelleth in the light which no man can approach unto."[5] It was of Him, too, that he had said in a previous passage: "Now unto the King eternal, immortal, invisible, to the only God;"[6] so that we might apply even the contrary qualities to the Son Himself—mortality, accessibility —of whom *the apostle* testifies that "He died according to the Scriptures,"[7] and that "He was seen by himself last of all,"[8]—by means, of course, of the light which was accessible, although it was not without imperilling his sight that he experienced that light.[9] *A like danger to which also befell* Peter, and John, and James, (who confronted not the same light) without risking the loss of their reason and mind; and if they, who were unable to endure the glory of the Son,[10] had only seen the Father, they must have died then and there: "For no man shall see God, and live."[11] This being the case, it is evident that He was always seen from the beginning, who became visible in the end; and that He, (on the contrary,) was not seen in the end who had never been visible from the beginning; and that accordingly there are two—the Visible and the Invisible. It was the Son, therefore, who was always seen, and the Son who always conversed with men, and the Son who has always worked by the authority and will of the Father; because "the Son can do nothing of Himself, but what He seeth Father do"[12]—"do" that is, in His mind and thought.[13] For the Father acts by mind and thought; whilst the Son, who is in the Father's mind and thought,[14] gives effect and form to what He sees. Thus all things were made by the Son, and without Him was not anything made.[15]

CHAP. XVI.—EARLY MANIFESTATIONS OF THE SON OF GOD, AS RECORDED IN THE OLD TESTAMENT; REHEARSALS OF HIS SUBSEQUENT INCARNATION.

But you must not suppose that only the works which relate to the (creation of the) world were made by the Son, but also whatsoever since that time has been done by God. For "the Father who loveth the Son, and hath given all things into His hand,"[16] loves Him indeed from the beginning, and from the very first has handed all things over to Him. Whence it is written, "From the beginning the Word was with God, and the Word was God;"[17] to whom "is given by the Father all power in heaven and on earth."[18] "The Father judgeth no man, but hath committed all judgment to the Son"[19]—from the very beginning even. For when He speaks of all power and all judgment, and says that all things were made by Him, and all things have been delivered into His Hand, He allows no exception (in respect) of time, because they would not be *all things* unless they were *the things of all time.* It is the Son, therefore, who has been from the beginning administering judgment, throwing down the haughty tower, and dividing the tongues, punishing the whole world by the violence of waters, raining upon Sodom and Gomorrah fire and brimstone, as the LORD from the LORD. For

---

[1] 1 John iv. 12.
[2] John i. 18.
[3] 1 Cor. ix. 1.
[4] Rom. ix. 5.
[5] 1 Tim. vi. 16.
[6] 1 Tim. i. 17.
[7] 1 Cor. xv. 3.
[8] Ver. 8.
[9] Acts xxii. 11.
[10] Matt. xvii. 6; Mark ix. 6.

[11] Ex. xxxiii. 20.
[12] John v. 19.
[13] In sensu.
[14] The reading is, "in Patris sensu;" another reading substitutes "sinu" for "sensu;" *q.d.* "the Father's bosom."
[15] John i. 3.
[16] John iii. 35. Tertullian reads the last clause (according to Oehler), "in sinu ejus," *q. d.* "to Him who is in His bosom."
[17] John i. 1.
[18] Matt. xxviii. 18.
[19] John v. 22.

He it was who at all times came down to hold converse with men, from Adam on to the patriarchs and the prophets, in vision, in dream, in mirror, in dark saying; ever from the beginning laying the foundation of the course *of His dispensations*, which He meant to follow out to the very last. Thus was He ever learning even as God to converse with men upon earth, being no other than the Word which was to be made flesh. But He was thus learning (or rehearsing), in order to level for us the way of faith, that we might the more readily believe that the Son of God had come down into the world, if we knew that in times past also something similar had been done.[1] For as it was on our account *and for our learning* that these events are described in the Scriptures, so for our sakes also were they done—(even *ours*, I say), "upon whom the ends of the world are come."[2] In this way it was that even then He knew full well what human feelings and affections were, intending as He always did to take upon Him man's actual component substances, body and soul, making inquiry of Adam (as if He were ignorant),[3] "Where art thou, Adam?"[4]—repenting that He had made man, as if He had lacked foresight;[5] tempting Abraham, as if ignorant of what was in man; offended with persons, and then reconciled to them; and whatever other (weaknesses and imperfections) the heretics lay hold of (in their assumptions) as unworthy of God, in order to discredit the Creator, not considering that these *circumstances* are suitable enough for the Son, who was one day to experience even human sufferings—hunger and thirst, and tears, and actual birth and real death, and in respect of such a dispensation "made by the Father a little less than the angels."[6] But the heretics, you may be sure, will not allow that those things are suitable even to the Son of God, which you are imputing to the very Father Himself, when you pretend[7] that He made Himself less (than the angels) on our account; whereas the Scripture informs us that He who was made less was so affected by another, and not Himself by Himself. What, again, if He was *One* who was "crowned with glory and honour," and He *Another* by whom He was so crowned,[8]—the Son, in fact, by the Father? Moreover, how comes it to pass, that the Almighty Invisible God, "whom no man hath seen nor can see; He who dwelleth in light unapproachable;"[9] "He who dwelleth not

in *temples* made with hands;"[10] "from before whose sight the earth trembles, and the mountains melt like wax;"[11] who holdeth the whole world in His hand "like a nest;"[12] "whose throne is heaven, and earth His footstool;"[13] in whom is every place, but Himself is in no place; who is the utmost bound of the universe;—how happens it, I say, that He (who, though) the Most High, should yet have walked in paradise towards the *cool of the* evening, in quest of Adam; and should have shut up the ark after Noah had entered it; and at Abraham's tent should have refreshed Himself under an oak; and have called to Moses out of the burning bush; and have appeared as "the fourth" in the furnace of the Babylonian monarch (although He is there called the Son of man),—unless all these events had happened as an image, as a mirror, as an enigma (of the future incarnation)? Surely even these things could not have been believed even of the Son of God, unless they had been given us in the Scriptures; possibly also they could not have been believed of the Father, even if they had been given in the Scriptures, since these men bring *Him* down into Mary's womb, and set Him before Pilate's judgment-seat, and bury Him in the sepulchre of Joseph. Hence, therefore, their error becomes manifest; for, being ignorant that the entire order of the divine administration has from the very first had its course through the agency of the Son, they believe that the Father Himself was actually seen, and held converse with men, and worked, and was athirst, and suffered hunger (in spite of the prophet who says: "The everlasting God, *the Lord, the Creator of the ends of the earth*, shall never thirst at all, nor be hungry;"[14] much more, shall neither die at any time, nor be buried!), and therefore that it was uniformly one God, even the Father, who at all times did Himself the things which were really done *by Him* through the agency of the Son.

CHAP. XVII.—SUNDRY AUGUST TITLES, DESCRIPTIVE OF DEITY, APPLIED TO THE SON, NOT, AS PRAXEAS WOULD HAVE IT, ONLY TO THE FATHER.

They more readily supposed that the Father acted in the Son's name, than that the Son acted in the Father's; although the Lord says Himself, "I am come in my Father's name;"[15] and even to the Father He declares, "I have manifested Thy name unto these

---

[1] See our *Anti-Marcion*, p. 112, note 10. Edin.
[2] Comp. 1 Cor. x. 11.
[3] See the treatise, *Against Marcion*. ii. 25, *supra*.
[4] Gen. iii. 9.
[5] Gen. vi. 6.
[6] Ps. viii. 6.
[7] Quasi.
[8] Ps. viii. 6.

[9] 1 Tim. vi. 16.
[10] Acts xvii. 24.
[11] Joel ii. 10; Ps. xcvii. 5.
[12] Isa. x. 14.
[13] Isa. lxvi. 1.
[14] Isa. xl. 28.
[15] John v. 43.

men;"[1] whilst the Scripture likewise says, "Blessed is He that cometh in the name of the Lord,"[2] that is to say, the Son in the Father's name. And as for the Father's names, God Almighty, the Most High, the Lord of hosts, the King of Israel, the "One that is," we say (for so much do the Scriptures teach us) that they belonged suitably to the Son also, and that the Son came under these designations, and has always acted in them, and has thus manifested them in Himself to men. "All things," says He, "which the Father hath are mine."[3] Then why not His names also? When, therefore, you read of Almighty God, and the Most High, and the God of hosts, and the King of Israel the "One that is," consider whether the Son also be not indicated by these designations, who in His own right is God Almighty, in that He is the Word of Almighty God, and has received power over all; is the Most High, in that He is "exalted at the right hand of God," as Peter declares in the Acts;[4] is the Lord of hosts, because all things are by the Father made subject to Him; is the King of Israel, because to Him has especially been committed the destiny of that nation; and is likewise "the One that is," because there are many who are called Sons, but *are not.* As to the point maintained by them, that the name of Christ belongs also to the Father, they shall hear (what I have to say) in the proper place. Meanwhile, let this be my immediate answer to the argument which they adduce from the Revelation of John: "I am the Lord which is, and which was, and which is to come, the Almighty;"[5] and from all other passages which in their opinion make the designation of Almighty God unsuitable to the Son. As if, indeed, *He which is to come* were not almighty; whereas even the Son of the Almighty is as much almighty as the Son of God is God.

CHAP. XVIII.—THE DESIGNATION OF THE ONE GOD IN THE PROPHETIC SCRIPTURES. INTENDED AS A PROTEST AGAINST HEATHEN IDOLATRY, IT DOES NOT PRECLUDE THE CORRELATIVE IDEA OF THE SON OF GOD. THE SON IS IN THE FATHER.

But what hinders them from readily perceiving this community of the Father's titles in the Son, is the statement of Scripture, whenever it determines God to be but One; as if the selfsame Scripture had not also set forth Two both as God and Lord, as we have shown above.[6] Their argument is: Since we find Two and One, therefore Both are One and the Same, both Father and Son. Now the Scripture is not in danger of requiring the aid of any one's argument, lest it should seem to be self-contradictory. It has a method of its own, both when it sets forth one only God, and also when it shows that there are Two, Father and Son; and is consistent with itself. It is clear that the Son is mentioned by it. For, without any detriment to the Son, it is quite possible for it to have rightly determined that God is only One, to whom the Son belongs; since He who has a Son ceases not on that account to exist,—Himself being One only, that is, on His own account, whenever He is named without the Son. And He is named without the Son whensoever He is defined as the principle (of Deity)in the character of "its first Person," which had to be mentioned before the name of the Son; because it is the Father who is acknowledged in the first place, and after the Father the Son is named. Therefore "there is one God," the Father, "and without Him there is none else."[7] And when He Himself makes this declaration, He denies not the Son, but says that there is no other God; and the Son is not different from the Father. Indeed, if you only look carefully at the contexts which follow such statements as this, you will find that they nearly always have distinct reference to the makers of idols and the worshippers thereof, with a view to the multitude of false gods being expelled by the unity of the Godhead, which nevertheless has a Son; and inasmuch as this Son is undivided and inseparable from the Father, so is He to be reckoned as being in the Father, even when He is not named. The fact is, if He had named Him expressly, He would have separated Him, saying in so many words: "Beside me there is none else, *except my Son.*" In short He would have made His Son actually another, after excepting Him from others. Suppose the sun to say, "I am the Sun, and there is none other besides me, except my ray," would you not have remarked how useless was such a statement, as if the ray were not itself reckoned in the sun? He says, then, that there is no God besides Himself in respect of the idolatry both of the Gentiles as well as of Israel; nay, even on account of our heretics also, who fabricate idols with their words, just as the heathen do with their hands; that is to say, they make another God and another Christ. When, therefore, He attested His own unity, the Father took care of the Son's interests, that Christ should not be sup-

---

[1] John xvii. 6.
[2] Ps. cxviii. 26.
[3] John xvi. 15.
[4] Acts ii. 22.
[5] Rev. i. 8.

[6] See above ch. xiii. p. 607.
[7] Isa. xlv. 5.

posed to have come from another God, but from Him who had already said, "I am God, and there is none other beside me,"[1] who shows us that He is the only God, but in company with His Son, with whom "He stretcheth out the heavens alone."[2]

CHAP. XIX.—THE SON IN UNION WITH THE FATHER IN THE CREATION OF ALL THINGS. THIS UNION OF THE TWO IN CO-OPERATION IS NOT OPPOSED TO THE TRUE UNITY OF GOD. IT IS OPPOSED ONLY TO PRAXEAS' IDENTIFICATION THEORY.

But this very declaration of His they will hastily pervert into an argument of His *singleness*. "I have," says He, "stretched out the heaven alone." Undoubtedly *alone* as regards all other powers; and He thus gives a premonitory evidence against the conjectures of the heretics, who maintain that the world was constructed by various angels and powers, who also make the Creator Himself to have been either an angel or some subordinate agent sent to form external things, such as the constituent parts of the world, but who was at the same time ignorant *of the divine purpose*. If, now, it is in this sense that He stretches out the heavens alone, how is it that these heretics assume their position so perversely, as to render inadmissible the singleness of that Wisdom which says, "When He prepared the heaven, I was present with Him?"[3]— even though the apostle asks, "Who hath known the mind of the Lord, or who hath been His counsellor?"[4] meaning, of course, to except that wisdom which was present with Him.[5] In Him, at any rate, and with Him, did (Wisdom) construct the universe, He not being ignorant of what she was making. "Except Wisdom," however, is a phrase of the same sense exactly as "except the Son," who is Christ, "the Wisdom and Power of God,"[6] according to the apostle, who only knows the mind of the Father. "For who knoweth the things that be in God, except the Spirit which is in Him?"[7] Not, observe, *without* Him. There was therefore One who caused God to be not alone, except "alone" from all other *gods*. But (if we are to follow the heretics), the Gospel itself will have to be rejected, because it tells us that all things were made by God through the Word, without whom nothing was made.[8] And if I am not mistaken, there is also another passage in

which it is written: "By the Word of the Lord were the heavens made, and all the hosts of them by His Spirit."[9] Now this Word, the Power of God and the Wisdom of God, must be the very Son of God. So that, if (He did) all things by the Son, He must have stretched out the heavens by the Son, and so not have stretched them out alone, except in the sense in which He is "alone" (and apart) from all other gods. Accordingly He says, concerning the Son, immediately afterwards: "Who else is it that frustrateth the tokens of the liars, and maketh diviners mad, turning wise men backward, and making their knowledge foolish, and confirming the words[10] of His Son?"[11]—as, for instance, when He said, "This is my beloved Son, in whom I am well pleased; hear ye Him."[12] By thus attaching the Son to Himself, He becomes His own interpreter in what sense He stretched out the heavens alone, meaning *alone with His Son*, even as He is one with His Son. The utterance, therefore, will be in like manner the Son's, "I have stretched out the heavens alone,"[13] because *by the Word* were the heavens established.[14] Inasmuch, then, as the heaven was prepared when Wisdom was present in the Word, and since all things were made by the Word, it is quite correct to say that even the Son stretched out the heaven alone, because He alone ministered to the Father's work. It must also be He who says, "I am the First, and to all futurity I AM."[15] The Word, no doubt, was before all things. "In the beginning was the Word;"[16] and in that beginning He was sent forth[17] by the Father. The Father, however, has no beginning, as proceeding from none; nor can He be seen, since He was not begotten. He who has always been alone could never have had order or rank. Therefore, if they have determined that the Father and the Son must be regarded as one and the same, for the express purpose of vindicating the unity of God, that unity of His is preserved intact; for He is one, and yet He has a Son, who is equally with Himself comprehended in the same Scriptures. Since they are unwilling to allow that the Son is *a distinct Person*, second from the Father, lest, being thus second, He should cause two Gods to be spoken of, we have shown above[18] that Two are actually described in Scripture as God and Lord. And to pre-

---

1 Isa. xlv. 5, 18, xliv. 6.
2 Isa. xliv. 24.
3 Prov. viii. 27.
4 Rom. xi. 34.
5 Prov. viii. 30.
6 1 Cor. i. 24.
7 1 Cor. ii. 11.
8 John i. 3.

9 Ps. xxxiii. 6.
10 Isa. xliv. 25.
11 On this reading, see our *Anti-Marcion*, p. 207, note 9. Edin.
12 Matt. iii. 17.
13 Isa. xliv. 24.
14 Ps. xxxiii. 6.
15 Isa. xli. 4 (Sept.)
16 John i. 1.
17 Prolatus.
18 See ch. xiii. p. 107.

vent their being offended at this fact, we give a reason why they are not said to be two Gods and two Lords, but that they are two as Father and Son; and this not by severance of their substance, but from the dispensation wherein we declare the Son to be undivided and inseparable from the Father,—distinct in degree, not in state. And although, when named apart, He is called God, He does not thereby constitute two Gods, but one; and that from the very circumstance that He is entitled to be called God, from His union with the Father.

CHAP. XX.—THE SCRIPTURES RELIED ON BY PRAXEAS TO SUPPORT HIS HERESY BUT FEW. THEY ARE MENTIONED BY TERTULLIAN.

But I must take some further pains to rebut their arguments, when they make selections from the Scriptures in support of their opinion, and refuse to consider the other points, which obviously maintain the rule of faith without any infraction of the unity of the Godhead, and with the full admission[1] of the Monarchy. For as in the Old Testament Scriptures they lay hold of nothing else than, "I am God, and beside me there is no God;"[2] so in the Gospel they simply keep in view the Lord's answer to Philip, "I and my Father are one;"[3] and, "He that hath seen me hath seen the Father; and I am in the Father, and the Father in me."[4] They would have the entire revelation of both Testaments yield to these three passages, whereas the only proper course is to understand the few statements in the light of the many. But in their contention they only act on the principle of all heretics. For, inasmuch as only a few testimonies are to be found (making for them) in the general mass, they pertinaciously set off the few against the many, and assume the later against the earlier. The rule, however, which has been from the beginning established for every case, gives its prescription against the later *assumptions*, as indeed it also does against the fewer.

CHAP. XXI.—IN THIS AND THE FOUR FOLLOWING CHAPTERS IT IS SHEWN, BY A MINUTE ANALYSIS OF ST. JOHN'S GOSPEL, THAT THE FATHER AND SON ARE CONSTANTLY SPOKEN OF AS DISTINCT PERSONS.

Consider, therefore, how many passages present their prescriptive authority to you in this very Gospel before this inquiry of Philip, and previous to any discussion on your part.

And first of all there comes at once to hand the preamble of John to his Gospel, which shows us what He previously was who had to become flesh. "In the beginning was the Word, and the Word was with God, and the Word was God. He was in the beginning with God: all things were made by Him, and without Him was nothing made."[5] Now, since these words may not be taken otherwise than as they are written, there is without doubt shown to be One who was from the beginning, and also One with whom He always was: one the Word of God, the other God (although the Word is also God, but *God* regarded as the Son of God, not as the Father); One through whom were all things, Another by whom were all things. But in what sense we call Him *Another* we have already often described. In that we called Him Another, we must needs imply that He is not identical —not identical indeed, yet not as if separate; *Other* by dispensation, not by division. He, therefore, *who* became flesh was not the very same as He from whom the Word came. "His glory was beheld—the glory as of the only-begotten of the Father;"[6] not, (observe,) as of the Father. He "declared" (what was in) "the bosom of the Father alone;"[7] the Father did not *divulge the secrets of* His own bosom. For this is preceded by another statement: "No man hath seen God at any time."[8] Then, again, when He is designated by John (the Baptist) as "the Lamb of God,"[9] He is not *described as Himself the same with Him* of whom He is the beloved *Son*. He is, no doubt, ever the Son of God, but yet not He Himself of whom He is the Son. This (divine relationship) Nathanael at once recognised in Him,[10] even as Peter did on another occasion: "Thou art the Son of God."[11] And He affirmed Himself that they were quite right in their convictions; for He answered Nathanael: "Because I said, I saw thee under the fig-tree, therefore dost thou believe?"[12] And in the same manner He pronounced Peter to be "blessed," inasmuch as "flesh and blood had not revealed it to him"—that he had perceived the Father— "but the Father which is in heaven."[13] By asserting all this, He determined the distinction which is between the two Persons: that is, the Son then on earth, whom Peter had confessed to be the Son of God; and the

---

[1] Sonitu.
[2] Isa. xlv. 5.
[3] John x. 30.
[4] John xiv. 9, 10.

[5] John i. 1-3.
[6] John i. 14.
[7] Unius sinum Patris. Another reading makes: "He alone (unus) declared," etc. See John i. 18.
[8] John i. 18, first clause.
[9] John i. 29.
[10] John i. 49.
[11] Matt. xvi. 16.
[12] John i. 50.
[13] Matt. xvi. 17.

Father in heaven, who had revealed to Peter the discovery which he had made, that Christ was the Son of God. When He entered the temple, He called it "His Father's house,"[1] *speaking* as the Son. In His address to Nicodemus He says: "So God loved the world, that He gave His only-begotten Son, that whosoever believeth in Him should not perish, but have everlasting life."[2] And again: "For God sent not His Son into the world to condemn the world, but that the world through Him might be saved. He that believeth on Him is not condemned; but he that believeth not is condemned already, because he hath not believed in the name of the only-begotten Son of God."[3] Moreover, when John (the Baptist) was asked what he happened *to know* of Jesus, he said: "The Father loveth the Son, and hath given all things into His hand. He that believeth on the Son hath everlasting life; and he that believeth not the Son shall not see life, but the wrath of God abideth on him."[4] Whom, indeed, did He reveal to the woman of Samaria? Was it not "the Messias which is called Christ?"[5] And so He showed, of course, that He was not the Father, but the Son; and elsewhere He is expressly called "the Christ, the Son of God,"[6] and not the Father. He says, therefore, "My meat is to do the will of Him that sent me, and to finish His work;"[7] whilst to the Jews He remarks respecting the cure of the impotent man, "My Father worketh hitherto, and I work."[8] "My Father and I"—these are the Son's words. And it was on this very account that "the Jews sought the more intently to kill Him, not only because He broke the Sabbath, but also because He said that God was His Father, thus making Himself equal with God. Then indeed did He answer and say unto them, The Son can do nothing of Himself, but what He seeth the Father do; for what things soever He doeth these also doeth the Son likewise. For the Father loveth the Son, and showeth Him all things that He Himself doeth; and He will also show Him greater works than these, that ye may marvel. For as *the Father* raiseth up the dead and quickeneth them, even so the Son also quickeneth whom He will. For the Father judgeth no man, but hath committed all judgment unto the Son, that all men should honour the Son, even as they honour the Father. He that honoureth not the Son, honoureth not the

Father, who hath sent the Son. Verily, verily, I say unto you, He that heareth my words, and believeth on Him that sent me, hath everlasting life, and shall not come into condemnation, but is passed from death unto life. Verily I say unto you, that the hour is coming, when the dead shall hear the voice of the Son of God; and when they have heard it, they shall live. For as the Father hath eternal life in Himself, so also hath He given to the Son to have eternal life in Himself; and He hath given Him authority to execute judgment also, because He is the Son of man"[9]—that is, according to the flesh, even as He is also the Son of God through His Spirit.[10] Afterwards He goes on to say: "But I have greater witness than that of John; for the works which the Father hath given me to finish—those very works bear witness of me that the Father hath sent me. And the Father Himself, which hath sent me, hath also borne witness of me."[11] But He at once adds, "Ye have neither heard His voice at any time, nor seen His shape;"[12] thus affirming that in former times it was not the Father, but the Son, who used to be seen and heard. Then He says at last: "I am come in my Father's name, and ye have not received me."[13] It was therefore always the Son (of whom we read) under the designation of the Almighty and Most High God, and King, and Lord. To those also who inquired "what they should do *to work the works of God*,"[14] He answered, "*This is the work of God*, that ye believe on Him whom He hath sent."[15] He also declares Himself to be "the bread which the Father sent from heaven;"[16] and adds, that "all that the Father gave Him should come to Him, and that He Himself would not reject them,[17] because He had come down from heaven not to do His own will, but the will of the Father; and that the will of the Father was that every one who saw the Son, and believed on Him, should obtain the life (everlasting,) and the resurrection *at the last day*. No man indeed was able to come to Him, except the Father attracted him; whereas every one who had heard and learnt of the Father came to Him."[18] He goes on then expressly to say, "Not that any man hath seen the Father;"[19] thus showing us that it was through the Word of the Father that

[1] John ii. 16.
[2] John iii. 16.
[3] John iii. 17, 18.
[4] John iii. 35, 36.
[5] John iv. 25.
[6] John xx. 31.
[7] John iv. 34.
[8] John v. 17.

[9] John v. 19-27.
[10] i. e. His divine nature.
[11] John v. 36, 37.
[12] Ver. 37.
[13] Ver. 43.
[14] John vi. 29.
[15] Ver. 30.
[16] Ver. 32.
[17] The expression is in the neuter collective form in the original.
[18] John vi. 37-45.
[19] Ver. 46.

men were instructed and taught. Then, when many departed from Him,[1] and He turned to the apostles with the inquiry whether "they also would go away,"[2] what was Simon Peter's answer? "To whom shall we go? Thou hast the words of *eternal* life, and we believe that Thou art the Christ."[3] (Tell me now, did they believe) Him to be the Father, or the Christ of the Father?

CHAP. XXII.—SUNDRY PASSAGES OF ST. JOHN QUOTED, TO SHOW THE DISTINCTION BETWEEN THE FATHER AND THE SON. EVEN PRAXEAS' CLASSIC TEXT—I AND MY FATHER ARE ONE—SHOWN TO BE AGAINST HIM.

Again, whose doctrine does He announce, at which all were astonished?[4] Was it His own or the Father's? So, when they were in doubt among themselves whether He were the Christ (not as being the Father, of course, but as the Son), He says to them "You are not ignorant whence I am; and I am not come of myself, but He that sent me is true, whom ye know not; but I know Him, because I am from Him."[5] He did not say, Because I myself am He; and, I have sent mine own self: but His words are, "He hath sent me." When, likewise, the Pharisees sent men to apprehend Him, He says: "Yet a little while am I with you, and (then) I go unto Him that sent me."[6] When, however, He declares that He is not alone, and uses these words, "but I and the Father that sent me,"[7] does He not show that there are Two—Two, and yet inseparable? Indeed, this was the sum and substance of what He was teaching them, that they were inseparably Two; since, after citing the law when it affirms the truth of two men's testimony,[8] He adds at once: "I am one who am bearing witness of myself; and the Father (is another,) who hath sent me, and beareth witness of me."[9] Now, if He were one—being at once both the Son and the Father—He certainly would not have quoted the sanction of the law, which requires not the testimony of one, but of two. Likewise, when they asked Him where His Father was,[10] He answered them, that they had known neither Himself nor the Father; and in this answer He plainly told them of *Two*, whom they were ignorant of. Granted that "if they had known Him, they would have known the Father also,"[11] this certainly does not imply that He was Himself both Father and Son; but that, by reason of the inseparability of the Two, it was impossible for one of them to be either acknowledged or unknown without the other. "He that sent me," says He, "is true; and I am telling the world those things which I have heard of Him."[12] And the Scripture narrative goes on to explain in an exoteric manner, that "they understood not that He spake to them concerning the Father,"[13] although they ought certainly to have known that the Father's words were *uttered* in the Son, because they read in Jeremiah, "And the Lord said to me, Behold, I have put my words in thy mouth;"[14] and again in Isaiah, "The Lord hath given to me the tongue of learning that I should understand when to speak a word in season."[15] In accordance with which, *Christ* Himself says: "Then shall ye know that I am He and that I am saying nothing of my own self; but that, as my Father hath taught me, so I speak, because He that sent me is with me."[16] This also amounts to a proof that they were Two, (although) undivided. Likewise, when upbraiding the Jews in His discussion with them, because they wished to kill Him, He said, "I speak that which I have seen with my Father, and ye do that which ye have seen with your father;"[17] "but now ye seek to kill me, a man that hath told you the truth which I have heard of God;"[18] and again, "If God were your Father, ye would love me, for I proceeded forth and came from God"[19] (still they are not hereby separated, although He declares that He proceeded forth *from the Father.* Some persons indeed seize the opportunity afforded them in these words *to propound their heresy of His separation;* but His coming out from God is like the ray's procession from the sun, and the river's from the fountain, and the tree's from the seed); "I have not a devil, but I honour my Father;"[20] again, "If I honour myself, my honour is nothing: it is my Father that honoureth me, of whom ye say, that He is your God: yet ye have not known Him, but I know Him; and if I should say, I know Him not, I shall be a liar like unto you; but I know Him, and keep His saying."[21] But when He goes on to say, "*Your father* Abraham rejoiced to see my

---

[1] Ver. 66.
[2] Ver. 67.
[3] Ver. 68.
[4] See John vii. *passim.*
[5] Ver. 28, 29.
[6] Ver. 33.
[7] John viii. 16.
[8] Ver. 17.
[9] Ver. 18.
[10] Ver. 19.

[11] Ver. 19.
[12] John viii. 26.
[13] Ver. 27.
[14] Jer. i. 9.
[15] Isa. l. 4.
[16] John viii. 28, 29.
[17] Ver. 38.
[18] Ver. 40.
[19] Ver. 42.
[20] Ver. 49.
[21] John viii. 54, 55.

day; and he saw it, and was glad,"[1] He certainly proves that it was not the Father that appeared to Abraham, but the Son. In like manner He declares, in the case of the man *born* blind, "that He must do the works of the Father *which had sent Him;*"[2] and after He had given the man sight, He said to him, "Dost thou believe in the Son of God?" Then, upon the man's inquiring who *He* was, He proceeded to reveal Himself to him as that Son *of God* whom He had announced to him as the right object of his faith.[3] In a later passage He declares that He is known by the Father, and the Father by Him;[4] adding that He was so wholly loved by the Father, that He was laying down His life, because He had received this commandment from the Father.[5] When He was asked by the Jews if He were the very Christ[6] (meaning, of course, the Christ of God; for to this day the Jews expect not the Father Himself, but the Christ of God, it being nowhere said that the Father will come as the Christ), He said to them, "I am telling you, and yet ye do not believe: the works which I am doing, in my Father's name, they actually bear witness of me."[7] Witness of what? Of that very thing, to be sure, of which they were making inquiry—whether He were the Christ of God. Then, again, concerning His sheep, and (the assurance) that no man should pluck them out of His hand,[8] He says, "My Father, which gave them to me, is greater than all;"[9] adding immediately, "I and my Father are one."[10] Here, then, they take their stand, too infatuated, nay, too blind, to see in the first place that there is in this passage an intimation of Two Beings—"*I and my Father;*" then that there is a plural predicate, "*are,*" inapplicable to one person only; and lastly, that (the predicate terminates in an abstract, not a personal noun)—"we are one *thing*" *Unum,* not "one person" *Unus.* For if He had said "one Person," He might have rendered some assistance to their opinion. *Unus,* no doubt, indicates the singular number; but (here we have a case where) "Two" are still the subject in the masculine gender. He accordingly says *Unum,* a neuter term, which does not imply singularity of number, but unity of essence, likeness, conjunction, affection on the Father's part, who loves the Son, and submission on the Son's, who obeys the Father's will. When He says, "I and my Father are one" *in essence—Unum—*He shows that there are Two, whom He puts on an equality and unites in one. He therefore adds to this very statement, that He "had showed them many works from the Father," for none of which did He deserve to be stoned.[11] And to prevent their thinking Him deserving of this fate, as if He had claimed to be considered as God Himself, that is, the Father, by having said, "I and my Father are One," representing Himself as the Father's divine Son, and not as God Himself, He says, "If it is written in your law, I said, Ye are gods; and if the Scripture cannot be broken, say ye of Him whom the Father hath sanctified and sent into the world, that He blasphemeth, because He said, I am the Son of God? If I do not the works of my Father, believe me not; but if I do, even if ye will not believe me, still believe the works; and know that I am in the Father, and the Father in me."[12] It must therefore be by the works that the Father is in the Son, and the Son in the Father; and so it is by the works that we understand that the Father is one *with the Son.* All along did He therefore strenuously aim at this conclusion, that while they were of one power and essence, they should still be believed to be Two; for otherwise, unless they were believed to be Two, the Son could not possibly be believed to have any existence at all.

CHAP. XXIII.—MORE PASSAGES FROM THE SAME GOSPEL IN PROOF OF THE SAME PORTION OF THE CATHOLIC FAITH. PRAXEAS' TAUNT OF WORSHIPPING TWO GODS REPUDIATED.

Again, when Martha in a later passage acknowledged Him to be the Son of God,[13] she no more made a mistake than Peter[14] and Nathanael[15] had; and yet, even if she had made a mistake, she would at once have learnt the truth: for, behold, when about to raise her brother from the dead, the Lord looked up to heaven, and, addressing the Father, said—as the Son, of course: "Father, I thank Thee that Thou always hearest me; it is because of these crowds that are standing by that I have spoken *to Thee,* that they may believe that Thou hast sent me."[16] But in the trouble of His soul, (on a later occasion,) He said: "What shall I say? Father, save me from this hour: but for this cause is it that I am come to this hour; only, O Father, do Thou glorify Thy name"[17]—in which He

[1] Ver. 56.
[2] John ix. 4.
[3] Vers. 35–38.
[4] John x. 15.
[5] Vers. 15, 17, 18.
[6] Ver. 24.
[7] Ver. 25.
[8] Vers. 26–28.
[9] Ver. 29.
[10] Ver. 30.

[11] John x. 32.
[12] Vers. 34–38.
[13] John xi. 27.
[14] Matt. xvi. 16.
[15] John i. 49.
[16] John xi. 41, 42.
[17] John xii. 27, 28.

spake as the Son. (At another time) He said: "I am come in my Father's name."[1] Accordingly, the Son's voice was indeed alone sufficient, (when addressed) to the Father. But, behold, with an abundance (of evidence)[2] the Father from heaven replies, for the purpose of testifying to the Son: "This is my beloved Son, in whom I am well pleased; hear ye Him."[3] So, again, in that *asseveration*, "I have both glorified, and will glorify again,"[4] how many Persons do you discover, obstinate Praxeas? Are there not as many as there are voices? You have the Son on earth, you have the Father in heaven. Now this is not a separation; it is nothing but the divine dispensation. We know, however, that God is in the bottomless depths, and exists everywhere; but then it is by power and authority. We are also sure that the Son, being indivisible from Him, is everywhere with Him. Nevertheless, in the Economy or *Dispensation* itself, the Father willed that the Son should be regarded[5] as on earth, and Himself in heaven; whither the Son also Himself looked up, and prayed, and made supplication of the Father; whither also He taught us to raise ourselves, and pray, "Our Father, which art in heaven," etc.,[6]—although, indeed, He is everywhere present. This *heaven* the Father willed to be His own throne; while He made the Son to be "a little lower than the angels,"[7] by sending Him down to the earth, but meaning at the same time to "crown Him with glory and honour,"[8] even by taking Him back to heaven. This He now made good to Him when He said: "I have both glorified *Thee*, and will glorify *Thee again*." The Son offers His request from earth, the Father gives His promise from heaven. Why, then, do you make liars of both the Father and the Son? If either the Father spake from heaven to the Son when He Himself was the Son on earth, or the Son prayed to the Father when He was Himself the Son in heaven, how happens it that the Son made a request of His own very self, by asking it of the Father, since the Son was the Father? Or, on the other hand, how is it that the Father made a promise to Himself, by making it to the Son, since the Father was the Son? Were we even to maintain that they are two separate gods, as you are so fond of throwing out against us, it would be a more tolerable assertion than the maintenance of so versa-

tile and changeful a God as yours! Therefore it was that in the passage before us the Lord declared to the people present: "Not on my own account has this voice addressed me, but for your sakes,"[9] that these likewise may believe both in the Father and in the Son, severally, in their own names and persons and positions. "Then again, Jesus exclaims, and says, He that believeth on me, believeth not on me, but on Him that sent me;"[10] because it is through the Son that men believe in the Father, while the Father also is the authority whence springs belief in the Son. "And he that seeth me, seeth Him that sent me."[11] How so? Even because, (as He afterwards declares,) "I have not spoken from myself, but the Father which sent me: He hath given me a commandment what I should say, and what I should speak."[12] For "the Lord God hath given me the tongue of the learned, that I should know when I ought to speak"[13] the word which I actually speak. "Even as the Father hath said unto me, so do I speak."[14] Now, in what way these things were said to Him, the evangelist and beloved disciple John knew better than Praxeas; and therefore he adds concerning his own meaning: "Now before the feast of the passover, Jesus knew that the Father had given all things into His hands, and that He had come from God, and was going to God."[15] Praxeas, however, would have it that it was the Father who proceeded forth from Himself, and had returned to Himself; so that what the devil put into the heart of Judas was the betrayal, not of the Son, but of the Father Himself. But for the matter of that, things have not turned out well either for the devil or the heretic; because, even in the Son's case, the treason which the devil wrought against Him contributed nothing to his advantage. It was, then, the Son of God, who was in the Son of man, that was betrayed, as the Scripture says afterwards: "Now is the Son of man glorified, and God is glorified in Him."[16] Who is here meant by "God?" Certainly not the Father, but the Word of the Father, who was in the Son of man—that is in the flesh, in which Jesus had been already glorified by *the divine* power and word. "And God," says He, "shall also glorify Him in Himself;"[17] that is to say, the Father shall glorify the Son, because He has Him within Himself; and even though prostrated to the

---

[1] John v. 43.
[2] Or, "by way of excess."
[3] Matt. xvii. 5.
[4] John xii. 28.
[5] Or, *held* (haberi).
[6] Matt. vi. 9.
[7] Ps. viii. 5.
[8] Same ver.

[9] John xii. 30.
[10] John xii. 44.
[11] Ver. 45.
[12] John xii. 49.
[13] Isa. l. 4.
[14] John xii. 50.
[15] John xiii. 1, 3.
[16] Ver. 31.
[17] Ver. 32.

earth, and put to death, He would soon glorify Him by His resurrection, and making Him conqueror over death.

CHAP. XXIV.—ON ST. PHILIP'S CONVERSATION WITH CHRIST. HE THAT HATH SEEN ME, HATH SEEN THE FATHER. THIS TEXT EXPLAINED IN AN ANTI-PRAXEAN SENSE.

But there were some who even then did not understand. For Thomas, who was so long incredulous, said: "Lord, we know not whither Thou goest; and how can we know the way? Jesus saith unto him, I am the way, the truth, and the life: no man cometh unto the Father, but by me. If ye had known me, ye would have known the Father also: but henceforth ye know Him, and have seen Him." [1] And now we come to Philip, who, roused with the expectation of seeing the Father, and not understanding in what sense he was to take "seeing the Father," says: "Show us the Father, and it sufficeth us." [2] Then the Lord answered him: "Have I been so long time with you, and yet hast thou not known me, Philip?" [3] Now whom does He say that they ought to have known?—for this is the sole point of discussion. Was it as the Father that they ought to have known Him, or as the Son? If it was as the Father, Praxeas must tell us how Christ, who had been so long time with them, could have possibly ever been (I will not say understood, but even) supposed to have been the Father. He is clearly defined to us in all Scriptures—in the Old Testament as the Christ of God, in the New Testament as the Son of God. In this character was He anciently predicted, in this was He also declared even by Christ Himself; nay, by the very Father also, who openly confesses Him from heaven as His Son, and as His Son glorifies Him. "This is my beloved Son;" "I have glorified Him, and I will glorify Him." In this character, too, was He believed on by His disciples, and rejected by the Jews. It was, moreover, in this character that He wished to be accepted by them whenever He named the Father, and gave preference to the Father, and honoured the Father. This, then, being the case, it was not the Father whom, after His lengthened intercourse with them, they were ignorant of, but it was the Son; and accordingly the Lord, while upbraiding *Philip* for not knowing Himself who was the object of their ignorance, wished Himself to be acknowledged indeed as that *Being* whom He had reproached them for being ignorant of after so long a time—in a word, as the Son. And now it may be seen

in what sense it was said, "He that hath seen me hath seen the Father," [4]—even in the same in which it was said in a previous passage, "I and my Father are one." [5] Wherefore? Because "I came forth from the Father, and am come *into the world*" [6] and, "I am the way: no man cometh unto the Father, but by me;" [7] and, "No man can come to me, except the Father draw him;" [8] and, "All things are delivered unto me by the Father;" [9] and, "As the Father quickeneth (the dead), so also doth the Son;" [10] and again, "If ye had known me, ye would have known the Father also." [11] For in all these passages He had shown Himself to be the Father's Commissioner, [12] through whose agency even the Father could be seen in His works, and heard in His words, and recognised in the Son's administration of the Father's words and deeds. The Father indeed was invisible, as Philip had learnt in the law, and ought at the moment to have remembered: "No man shall see God, and live." [13] So he is reproved for desiring to see the Father, as if He were a visible Being, and is taught that He only becomes visible in the Son from His mighty works, and not in the manifestation of His person. If, indeed, He meant the Father to be understood as the same with the Son, by saying, "He who seeth me seeth the Father," how is it that He adds immediately afterwards, "Believest thou not that I am in the Father, and the Father in me?" [14] He ought rather to have said: "Believest thou not that I am the Father?" With what view else did He so emphatically dwell on this point, if it were not to clear up that which He wished men to understand—namely, that He was the Son? And then, again, by saying, "Believest thou not that I am in the Father, and the Father in me," [15] He laid the greater stress on His question on this very account, that He should not, because He had said, "He that hath seen me, hath seen the Father," be supposed to be the Father; because He had never wished Himself to be so regarded, having always professed Himself to be the Son, and to have come from the Father. And then He also set the conjunction of the two Persons in the clearest light, in order that no wish might be entertained of seeing the Father as if He were separately visible, and

---

[1] John xiv. 5–7.
[2] Ver. 8.
[3] Ver. 9.

[4] John xiv. 9.
[5] John x. 30.
[6] John xvi. 28.
[7] John xiv. 6.
[8] John vi. 44.
[9] Matt. xi. 27.
[10] John v. 21.
[11] John xiv. 7.
[12] Vicarium.
[13] Ex. xxxiii. 20.
[14] John xiv. 10.
[15] John xiv. 11.

that the Son might be regarded as the representative of the Father. And yet He omitted not to explain how the Father was in the Son, and the Son in the Father. "The words," says He, "which I speak unto you, are not mine,"[1] because indeed they were the Father's words; "but the Father that dwelleth in me, He doeth the works."[2] It is therefore by His mighty works, and by the words of His doctrine, that the Father who dwells in the Son makes Himself visible— even by those *words and works* whereby He abides in Him, and also by Him in whom He abides; the special properties of Both the Persons being apparent from this very circumstance, that He says, "I am in the Father, and the Father is in me."[3] Accordingly He adds: "Believe—" What? That I am the Father? I do not find that it is so written, but rather, "that I am *in* the Father, and the Father in me; or else believe me for my works' sake;"[4] meaning those works by which the Father manifested Himself to be in the Son, not indeed to the sight of man, but to his intelligence.

CHAP. XXV.—THE PARACLETE, OR HOLY GHOST. HE IS DISTINCT FROM THE FATHER AND THE SON AS TO THEIR PERSONAL EXISTENCE. ONE AND INSEPARABLE FROM THEM AS TO THEIR DIVINE NATURE. OTHER QUOTATIONS OUT OF ST. JOHN'S GOSPEL.

What follows Philip's question, and *the Lord's* whole treatment of it, to the end of *John's* Gospel, continues to furnish us with statements of the same kind, distinguishing the Father and the Son, with the properties of each. Then there is the Paraclete *or Comforter*, also, which He promises to pray for to the Father, and to send from heaven after He had ascended to the Father. *He is called* "another Comforter," indeed;[5] but in what way He is *another* we have already shown.[6] "He shall receive of mine," says Christ,[7] just as *Christ* Himself received of the Father's. Thus the connection of the Father in the Son, and of the Son in the Paraclete, produces three coherent Persons, *who are yet distinct* One from Another. These Three are one[8] *essence*, not one *Person*,[9] as it is said, "I and my Father are One,"[10] in respect of unity of substance, not singularity of number. Run through the whole *Gospel*, and you will find that He whom you believe to be the

Father (described as acting for the Father, although you, for your part, forsooth, suppose that "the Father, being the husbandman,"[11] must surely have been on earth) is once more recognised by the Son as in heaven, when, "lifting up His eyes thereto,"[12] He commended His disciples to the safe-keeping of the Father.[13] We have, moreover, in that other Gospel a clear revelation, i.e. *of the Son's distinction from the Father,* "My God, why hast Thou forsaken me?"[14] and again, (in the third Gospel,) "Father, into Thy hands I commend my spirit."[15] But even if (we had not these passages, we meet with satisfactory evidence) after His resurrection and glorious victory over death. Now that all the restraint of His humiliation is taken away, He might, if possible, have shown Himself as the Father to so faithful a woman (as Mary Magdalene) when she approached to touch Him, out of love, not from curiosity, nor with Thomas' incredulity. *But not so;* Jesus saith unto her, "Touch me not, for I am not yet ascended to my Father; but go to my brethren" (and even in this He proves Himself to be the Son; for if He had been the Father, He would have called them His *children*, (instead of His *brethren*), "and say unto them, I ascend unto my Father and your Father, and to my God and your God."[16] *Now, does this mean, I ascend* as the Father to the Father, and as God to God? Or as the Son to the Father, and as the Word to God? Wherefore also does this Gospel, at its very termination, intimate that these things were ever written, if it be not, to use its own words, "that ye might believe that Jesus Christ is the Son of God?"[17] Whenever, therefore, you take any of the statements of this Gospel, and apply them to demonstrate the identity of the Father and the Son, supposing that they serve your views therein, you are contending against the definite purpose of the Gospel. For these things certainly are not written that you may believe that Jesus Christ is the Father, but the Son.[18]

CHAP. XXVI.—A BRIEF REFERENCE TO THE GOSPELS OF ST. MATTHEW AND ST. LUKE. THEIR AGREEMENT WITH ST. JOHN, IN RESPECT TO THE DISTINCT PERSONALITY OF THE FATHER AND THE SON.

In addition to Philip's conversation, and

---

[1] John xiv. 10.
[2] Same ver.
[3] Same ver.
[4] Ver. 11.
[5] John xiv. 16.
[6] See above ch. xiii.
[7] John xvi. 14.
[8] Unum. [On this famous passage see Elucidation III.]
[9] Unus.
[10] John x. 30.

[11] John xv. 1.
[12] John xvii. 1.
[13] John xvii. 11.
[14] Matt. xxvii. 46.
[15] Luke xxiii. 46.
[16] John xx. 17.
[17] John xx. 31.
[18] [A curious anecdote is given by Carlyle in his *Life of Frederick* (Book xx. cap. 6), touching the text of "the Three Witnesses." Gottsched satisfied the king that it was not in the Vienna MS. save in an interpolation of the margin "*in Melanchthon's hand.*" Luther's Version lacks this text.]

the Lord's reply to it, the reader will observe that we have run through John's Gospel *to show* that many other passages of a clear purport, both before and after that chapter, are only in strict accord with that single and prominent statement, which must be interpreted agreeably to all other places, rather than in opposition to them, and indeed to its own inherent and natural sense. I will not here largely use the support of the other Gospels, which confirm our belief by the Lord's *nativity:* it is sufficient to remark that He who had to be born of a virgin is announced in express terms by the angel himself as the Son of God: "The Spirit of God shall come upon thee, and the power of the Highest shall overshadow thee; therefore also the Holy Thing that shall be born of thee shall be called *the Son of God*." [1] On this passage even they will wish to raise a cavil; but truth will prevail. Of course, they say, the Son of God is God, and the power of the highest is the Most High. And they do not hesitate to insinuate [2] what, if it had been true, would have been written. Whom was he [3] so afraid of as not plainly to declare, "God shall come upon thee, and the Highest shall overshadow thee?" Now, by saying "the Spirit of God" (although the Spirit of God *is God*,) and by not directly naming God, he wished that portion [4] of the whole *Godhead* to be understood, which was about to retire into the designation of "the Son." The Spirit of God in this passage must be the same *as the* Word. For just as, when John says, "The Word was made flesh," [5] we understand the Spirit also in the mention of the Word: so here, too, we acknowledge the Word likewise in the name of the Spirit. For both the Spirit is the substance of the Word, and the Word is the operation of the Spirit, and the Two are One (and the same). [6] Now John must mean *One* when he speaks of Him as "having been made flesh," and the angel *Another* when he announces Him as "about to be born," if the Spirit is not the Word, and the Word the Spirit. For just as the Word of God is not actually He whose *Word* He is, so also the Spirit (although He is called God) is not actually He whose *Spirit* He is said to be. Nothing which belongs to something else

is actually the very same thing as that to which it belongs. Clearly, when anything proceeds from a personal subject, [7] and so belongs to him, since it comes from him, it may possibly be such in quality exactly as the personal subject himself is from whom it proceeds, and to whom it belongs. And thus the Spirit is God, and the Word is God, because proceeding from God, but yet is not actually the very same as He from whom He proceeds. Now that which is God of God, although He is an actually existing thing, [8] yet He cannot be God Himself [9] (exclusively), but so far God as He is of the same substance as God Himself, and as being an actually existing thing, and as a portion of the Whole. Much more will "the power of the Highest" not be the Highest Himself, because It is not an actually existing thing, as being Spirit—in the same way as the *wisdom* (of God) and the *providence* (of God) is not God: these *attributes* are not substances, but the accidents of the particular substance. Power is incidental to the Spirit, but cannot itself be the Spirit. These things, therefore, whatsoever they are—(I mean) the Spirit of God, and the Word and the Power—having been conferred on the Virgin, that which is born of her is the Son of God. This He Himself, in those other Gospels also, testifies Himself to have been from His very boyhood: "Wist ye not," says He, "that I must be about *my Father's* business?" [10] Satan likewise knew Him to be this in his temptations: "Since Thou art *the Son of God*." [11] This, accordingly, the devils also acknowledge Him to be: "we know Thee, who Thou art, the *Holy Son of God*." [12] His "*Father*" He Himself adores. [13] When acknowledged by Peter as the "Christ (the Son) of God," [14] He does not deny *the relation*. He exults in spirit when He says to the Father, "I thank Thee, *O Father*, because Thou hast hid these things from the wise and prudent." [15] He, moreover, affirms also that to no man is the Father known, but to *His Son;* [16] and promises that, as *the Son of the Father*, He will confess those who confess Him, and deny those who deny Him, before His Father. [17] He also introduces a parable of the mission to the vineyard of the Son (not the Father), who was sent after so many servants, [18] and slain by the husbandmen, and

---

[1] Luke i. 35.
[2] Inicere.
[3] i.e., the angel of the Annunciation.
[4] On this not strictly defensible term of Tertullian, see Bp. Bull's *Defence of the Nicene Creed*, book ii. ch. vii. sec. 5, Translation, pp. 199, 200.
[5] John i. 14.
[6] "The selfsame Person is understood under the appellation both of *Spirit* and *Word*, with this difference only, that He is called 'the Spirit of God,' so far as He is a Divine Person, . . . and 'the Word,' so far as He is the Spirit in operation, proceeding with sound and vocal utterance from God to set the universe in order."—Bp. BULL, *Def. Nic. Creed*, p. 535, Translation.

[7] Ex ipso.
[8] Substantiva res.
[9] Ipse Deus: i.e., God so wholly as to exclude by identity every other person.
[10] Luke ii. 49.
[11] Matt. iv. 3, 6.
[12] Mark i. 24; Matt. viii. 29.
[13] Matt. xi. 25, 26; Luke x. 21; John xi. 41.
[14] Matt. xvi. 17.
[15] Matt. xi. 25.
[16] Matt. xi. 27; Luke x. 22.
[17] Matt. x. 32, 33.
[18] Matt. xxi. 33-41.

avenged by the Father. He is also ignorant of the last day and hour, which is known to the Father only.[1] He awards the kingdom to His disciples, as He says it had been appointed to Himself by the Father.[2] He has power to ask, if He will, legions of angels from the Father for His help.[3] He exclaims that God had forsaken Him.[4] He commends His spirit into the hands of the Father.[5] After His resurrection He promises in a pledge to His disciples that He will send them the promise of His Father;[6] and lastly, He commands them to baptize into the Father and the Son and the Holy Ghost, not into a unipersonal God.[7] And indeed it is not once only, but three times, that we are immersed into the Three Persons, at each several mention of Their names.

CHAP. XXVII.—THE DISTINCTION OF THE FATHER AND THE SON, THUS ESTABLISHED, HE NOW PROVES THE DISTINCTION OF THE TWO NATURES, WHICH WERE, WITHOUT CONFUSION, UNITED IN THE PERSON OF THE SON. THE SUBTERFUGES OF PRAXEAS THUS EXPOSED.

But why should I linger over matters which are so evident, when I ought to be attacking points on which they seek to obscure the plainest proof? For, confuted on all sides on the distinction between the Father and the Son, which we maintain without destroying their inseparable union—as (by the examples) of the sun and the ray, and the fountain and the river—yet, by help of (their conceit) an indivisible number, (with issues) of two and three, they endeavour to interpret this *distinction* in a way which shall nevertheless tally with their own opinions: so that, all in one Person, they distinguish two, Father and Son, understanding the Son to be flesh, that is man, that is Jesus; and the Father to be spirit, that is God, that is Christ. Thus they, while contending that the Father and the Son are one and the same, do in fact begin by dividing them rather than uniting them. For if Jesus is one, and Christ is another, then the Son will be different from the Father, because the Son is Jesus, and the Father is Christ. Such a *monarchy* as this they learnt, I suppose, in the school of Valentinus, making two—Jesus and Christ. But this conception of theirs has been, in fact, already confuted in what we have previously advanced, because the Word of God or the Spirit of God is also

called the power of the Highest, whom they make the Father; whereas these relations[8] are not themselves the same as He whose relations they are said to be, but they proceed from Him and appertain to Him. However, another refutation awaits them on this point of their heresy. See, say they, it was announced by the angel: "Therefore that Holy Thing which shall be born of thee shall be called the Son of God."[9] Therefore, (they argue,) as it was the flesh that was born, it must be the flesh that is the Son of God. Nay, (I answer,) this is spoken concerning the Spirit of God. For it was certainly of the Holy Spirit that the virgin conceived; and that which He conceived, she brought forth. That, therefore, had to be born which was conceived and was to be brought forth; that is to say, the Spirit, whose "name should be called Emmanuel which, being interpreted, is, God with us."[10] Besides, the flesh is not God, so that it could not have been said concerning it, "That Holy Thing shall be called the Son of God," but only that Divine Being who was born in the flesh, of whom the psalm also says, "Since God became man in the midst of it, and established it by the will of the Father."[11] Now what Divine Person was born in it? The Word, and the Spirit which became incarnate with the Word by the will of the Father. The Word, therefore, is incarnate; and this must be the point of our inquiry: How the Word became flesh,—whether it was by having been transfigured, as it were, in the flesh, or by having really clothed Himself in flesh. Certainly it was by a real clothing of Himself in flesh. For the rest, we must needs believe God to be unchangeable, and incapable of form, as being eternal. But transfiguration is the destruction of that which previously existed. For whatsoever is transfigured into some other thing ceases to be that which it had been, and begins to be that which it previously was not. God, however, neither ceases to be what He was, nor can He be any other thing than what He is. The Word is God, and "the Word of the Lord remaineth for ever,"—even by holding on unchangeably in His own proper form. Now, if He admits not of being transfigured, it must follow that He be understood in this sense to have become flesh, when He comes to be in the flesh, and is manifested, and is seen, and is handled by means of the flesh; since all the other points likewise require to be thus understood. For if the Word became flesh by a transfiguration and change of substance, it follows at

---

[1] Matt. xxiv. 36.
[2] Luke xxii. 29.
[3] Matt. xxvi. 53.
[4] Matt. xxvii. 46.
[5] Luke xxiii. 46.
[6] Luke xxiv. 49.
[7] Non in unum.

[8] Ipsæ.
[9] Luke i. 35.
[10] Matt. i. 23.
[11] His version of Ps. lxxxvii. 5.

once that Jesus must be a substance compounded of [1] two substances—of flesh and spirit,—a kind of mixture, like *electrum*, composed of gold and silver; and it begins to be neither gold (that is to say, spirit) nor silver (that is to say, flesh),—the one being changed by the other, and a third substance produced. Jesus, therefore, cannot at this rate be God, for He has ceased to be the Word, which was made flesh; nor can He be Man incarnate, for He is not properly flesh, and it was flesh which the Word became. Being compounded, therefore, of both, He actually is neither; He is rather some third substance, very different from either. But the truth is, we find that He is expressly set forth as both God and Man; the very psalm which we have quoted intimating (of the flesh), that "God became Man in the midst of it, He therefore established it by the will of the Father,"—certainly in all respects as the Son of God and the Son of Man, being God and Man, differing no doubt according to each substance in its own especial property, inasmuch as the Word is nothing else but God, and the flesh nothing else but Man. Thus does the apostle also teach respecting His two substances, saying, "who was made of the seed of David;"[2] in which words He will be Man and Son of Man. "Who was declared to be the Son of God, according to the Spirit;"[3] in which words He will be God, and the Word—the Son of God. We see plainly the twofold state, which is not confounded, but conjoined in One Person—Jesus, God and Man. Concerning Christ, indeed, I defer what I have to say.[4] (I remark here), that the property of each nature is so wholly preserved, that the Spirit[5] on the one hand did all things in Jesus suitable to Itself, such as miracles, and mighty deeds, and wonders; and the Flesh, on the other hand, exhibited the affections which belong to it. It was hungry under the devil's temptation, thirsty with the Samaritan woman, wept over Lazarus, was troubled even unto death, and at last actually died. If, however, it was only a *tertium quid*, some composite essence formed out of the Two substances, like the *electrum* (which we have mentioned), there would be no distinct proofs apparent of either nature. But by a transfer of functions, the Spirit would have done things to be done by the Flesh, and the Flesh such as are effected by the Spirit; or else such things as are suited neither to the Flesh nor to the Spirit, but confusedly of some third character. Nay

more, on this supposition, either the Word underwent death, or the flesh did not die, if so be the Word was converted into flesh; because either the flesh was immortal, or the Word was mortal. Forasmuch, however, as the two substances acted distinctly, each in its own character, there necessarily accrued to them severally their own operations, and their own issues. Learn then, together with Nicodemus, that "that which is born in the flesh is flesh, and that which is born of the Spirit is Spirit."[6] Neither the flesh becomes Spirit, nor the Spirit flesh. In one *Person* they no doubt are well able to be co-existent. Of them Jesus consists—Man, of the flesh; of the Spirit, God—and the angel designated Him as "the Son of God,"[7] in respect of that nature, in which He was Spirit, reserving for the flesh the appellation "Son of Man." In like manner, again, the apostle calls Him "the Mediator between God and Men,"[8] and so affirmed His participation of both substances. Now, to end the matter, will you, who interpret the Son of God to be flesh, be so good as as to show us what the Son of Man is? Will He then, I want to know, be the Spirit? But you insist upon it that the Father Himself is the Spirit, on the ground that "God is a Spirit," just as if we did not read also that there is "the Spirit of God;" in the same manner as we find that as "the Word was God," so also there is "the Word of God."

CHAP. XXVIII.—CHRIST NOT THE FATHER, AS PRAXEAS SAID. THE INCONSISTENCY OF THIS OPINION, NO LESS THAN ITS ABSURDITY, EXPOSED. THE TRUE DOCTRINE OF JESUS CHRIST ACCORDING TO ST. PAUL, WHO AGREES WITH OTHER SACRED WRITERS.

And so, most foolish heretic, you make *Christ* to be the Father, without once considering the actual force of this name, if indeed Christ is a name, and not rather a surname, or designation; for it signifies "Anointed." But Anointed is no more a proper name than Clothed or Shod; it is only an accessory to a name. Suppose now that by some means Jesus were also called Vestitus (*Clothed*), as He is actually called Christ from the mystery of His anointing, would you in like manner say that Jesus was the Son of God, and at the same time suppose that *Vestitus* was the Father? Now then, concerning Christ, if Christ is the Father, the Father is an Anointed One, and receives the unction of course from another. Else if it is from Himself that He re-

---

[1] Ex.
[2] Rom. i. 3.
[3] Ver. 4.
[4] See next chapter.
[5] i.e., Christ's divine nature.

[6] John iii. 6.
[7] Luke i. 35.
[8] 1 Tim. ii. 5.

ceives it, then you must prove it to us. But we learn no such fact from the Acts of the Apostles in that ejaculation of the Church to God, "Of a truth, Lord, against Thy Holy Child Jesus, whom Thou hast anointed, both Herod and Pontius Pilate with the Gentiles *and the people of Israel* were gathered together."[1] These then testified both that Jesus was the Son of God, and that being the Son, He was anointed by the Father. Christ therefore must be the same as Jesus who was anointed by the Father, and not the Father, who anointed the Son. To the same effect are the words of Peter: "Let all the house of Israel know assuredly that God hath made that same Jesus, whom ye have crucified, both Lord and Christ," that is, *Anointed.*[2] John, moreover, brands that man as "a liar" who "denieth that Jesus is the Christ;" whilst on the other hand he declares that "every one is born of God who believeth that Jesus is the Christ."[3] Wherefore he also exhorts us to believe in the name of His (*the Father's*,) Son Jesus Christ, that "our fellowship may be with the Father, and with His Son Jesus Christ."[4] Paul, in like manner, everywhere speaks of "God the Father, and our Lord Jesus Christ." When writing to the Romans, he gives thanks to God through our Lord Jesus Christ.[5] To the Galatians he declares himself to be "an apostle not of men, neither by man, but through Jesus Christ and God the Father."[6] You possess indeed all his writings, which testify plainly to the same effect, and set forth Two—God the Father, and our Lord Jesus Christ, the Son of the Father. (They also testify) that Jesus is Himself the Christ, and under one or the other designation the Son of God. For precisely by the same right as both names belong to the same Person, even the Son of God, does either name alone without the other belong to the same Person. Consequently, whether it be the name Jesus which occurs alone, Christ is also understood, because Jesus is the Anointed One; or if the name Christ is the only one given, then Jesus is identified with Him, because the Anointed One is Jesus. Now, of these two names *Jesus Christ*, the former is the proper one, which was given to Him by the angel; and the latter is only an adjunct, predicable of Him from His anointing,—thus suggesting the proviso that Christ must be the Son, not the Father. How blind, to be sure, is the man who fails to perceive

that by the name of Christ some other God is implied, if he ascribes to the Father this name of Christ! For if Christ is God the Father, when He says, "I ascend unto my Father and your Father, and to my God and your God,"[7] He of course shows plainly enough that there is above Himself another Father and another God. If, again, the Father is Christ, *He* must be some other Being who "strengtheneth the thunder, and createth the wind, and declareth unto men His Christ."[8] And if "the kings of the earth stood up, and the rulers were gathered together against *the Lord and against* His Christ,"[9] that Lord must be another Being, against whose Christ were gathered together the kings and the rulers. And if, to quote another passage, "Thus saith the Lord to my Lord Christ,"[10] the Lord who speaks to the Father of Christ must be a distinct Being. Moreover, when the apostle in his epistle prays, "That the God of our Lord Jesus Christ may give unto you the spirit of wisdom and of knowledge,"[11] He must be other (than Christ), who is the God of Jesus Christ, the bestower of spiritual gifts. And once for all, that we may not wander through every passage, He "who raised up Christ from the dead, and is also to raise up our mortal bodies,"[12] must certainly be, as the quickener, different from the dead Father,[13] or even from the quickened Father, if Christ who died is the Father.

CHAP. XXIX.—IT WAS CHRIST THAT DIED. THE FATHER IS INCAPABLE OF SUFFERING EITHER SOLELY OR WITH ANOTHER. BLASPHEMOUS CONCLUSIONS SPRING FROM PRAXEAS' PREMISES.

Silence! Silence on such blasphemy. Let us be content with saying that Christ died, the Son of the Father; and *let this suffice*, because the Scriptures have told us so much. For even the apostle, to his declaration—which he makes not without feeling the weight of it —that "Christ died," immediately adds, "according to the Scriptures,"[14] in order that he may alleviate the harshness of the statement by the authority of the Scriptures, and so remove offence from the reader. Now, although when two substances are alleged to be in Christ—namely, the divine and the human—

[1] Acts iv. 27.
[2] Acts ii. 36.
[3] See 1 John ii. 22, iv. 2, 3, and v. 1.
[4] 1 John i. 3.
[5] Rom. i. 8.
[6] Gal. i. 1.
[7] John xx. 17.
[8] Amos iv. 13, Sep.
[9] Ps. ii. 2.
[10] Here Tertullian reads τῷ Χριστῷ μου Κυρίῳ, instead of Κύρῳ, "to Cyrus," in Isa. xlv. 1.
[11] Eph. i. 17.
[12] Rom. viii. 11.
[13] From this deduction of the doctrine of Praxeas, that the *Father must have suffered* on the cross, his opponents called him and his followers *Patripassians.*
[14] 1 Cor. xv. 3.

40

it plainly follows that the divine nature is immortal, and that which is human is mortal, it is manifest in what sense he declares " Christ died "—even in the sense in which He was flesh and Man and the Son of Man, not as being the Spirit and the Word and the Son of God. In short, since he says that it was *Christ* (that is, the Anointed One) that died, he shows us that that which died was the nature which was anointed; in a word, the flesh. Very well, say you; since we on our side affirm our doctrine in precisely the same terms which you use on your side respecting the Son, we are not guilty of blasphemy against the Lord God, for we do not maintain that He died after the divine nature, but only after the human. Nay, but you do blaspheme; because you allege not only that the Father died, but that He died the death of the cross. For " cursed are they which are hanged on a tree,"[1]—a curse which, after the law, is compatible to the Son (inasmuch as " Christ has been made a curse for us,"[2] but certainly not the Father); since, however, you convert Christ into the Father, you are chargeable with blasphemy against the Father. But when we assert that Christ was crucified, we do not malign Him with a curse; we only re-affirm[3] the curse pronounced by the law:[4] nor indeed did the apostle utter blasphemy when he said the same thing as we.[5] Besides, as there is no blasphemy in predicating of the subject that which is fairly applicable to it; so, on the other hand, it is blasphemy when that is alleged concerning the subject which is unsuitable to it. On this principle, too, the Father was not associated in suffering with the Son. *The heretics*, indeed, fearing to incur direct blasphemy against the Father, hope to diminish it by this expedient: they grant us so far that the Father and the Son are Two; adding that, since it is the Son indeed who suffers, the Father is only His fellow-sufferer.[6] But how absurd are they even in this conceit! For what is the meaning of " fellow-suffering," but the endurance of suffering along with another? Now if the Father is incapable of suffering, He is incapable of suffering in company with another; otherwise, if He can suffer with another, He is of course capable of suffering. You, in fact, yield Him nothing by this subterfuge of your fears. You are afraid to say that He is capable of suffering whom you make to be capable of fellow-suffering. Then, again, the

Father is as incapable of fellow-suffering as the Son even is of suffering under the conditions of His existence as God. Well, but how could the Son suffer, if the Father did not suffer with Him ? *My answer is*, The Father is separate from the Son, though not from *Him as* God. For even if a river be soiled with mire and mud, alhough it flows from the fountain identical in nature with it, and is not separated from the fountain, yet the injury which affects the stream reaches not to the fountain; and although it is the water of the fountain which suffers down the stream, still, since it is not affected at the fountain, but only in the river, the fountain suffers nothing, but only the river which issues from the fountain. So likewise the Spirit of God,[7] whatever suffering it might be capable of in the Son, yet, inasmuch as it could not suffer in the Father, *the fountain of the Godhead*, but only in the Son, it evidently could not have suffered,[8] as the Father. But it is enough for me that the Spirit of God suffered nothing as the Spirit of God,[9] since all that It suffered It suffered in the Son. It was quite another matter for the Father to suffer with *the Son in the flesh*. This likewise has been treated by us. Nor will any one deny this, since even we are ourselves unable to suffer for God, unless the Spirit of God be in us, who also utters by our instrumentality[10] whatever pertains to our own conduct and suffering; not, however, that He Himself suffers in our suffering, only He bestows on us the power and capacity of suffering.

CHAP. XXX.—HOW THE SON WAS FORSAKEN BY THE FATHER UPON THE CROSS. THE TRUE MEANING THEREOF FATAL TO PRAXEAS. SO TOO, THE RESURRECTION OF CHRIST, HIS ASCENSION, SESSION AT THE FATHER'S RIGHT HAND, AND MISSION OF THE HOLY GHOST.

However, if you persist in pushing your views further, I shall find means of answering you with greater stringency, and of meeting you with the exclamation of the Lord Himself, so as to challenge you with the question, What is your inquiry and reasoning about *that*? You have Him exclaiming in the midst of His passion: " My God, my God, why hast Thou forsaken me ? "[11] Either, then, the Son suffered, being " forsaken " by the Father, and the Father consequently suffered nothing, inasmuch as He forsook the Son; or else, if it was the Father who suffered, then to what

---

[1] Gal. iii. 13.
[2] Same ver.
[3] Referimus : or, " recite and record."
[4] Deut. xxi. 23.
[5] Gal. iii. 13.
[6] [This passage convinces Lardner that Praxeas was not a Patripassian. *Credib.* Vol. VIII. p. 607.]

[7] That is, the divine nature in general in this place.
[8] That which was open to it to suffer in the Son.
[9] Suo nomine.
[10] De nobis.
[11] Matt. xxvii. 46.

God was it that He addressed His cry? But this was the voice of flesh and soul, that is to say, of man—not of the Word and Spirit, that is to say, not of God; and it was uttered so as to prove the impassibility of God, who "forsook" His Son, so far as He handed over His human substance to the suffering of death. This verity the apostle also perceived, when he writes to this effect: "If the Father spared not His own Son."[1] This did Isaiah before him likewise perceive, when he declared: "And the Lord hath delivered Him up for our offences."[2] In this manner He "forsook" Him, in *not sparing* Him; "forsook" Him, in *delivering Him up*. In all other respects the Father did not forsake the Son, for it was into His Father's hands that the Son commended His spirit.[3] Indeed, after so commending it, He instantly died; and as the Spirit[4] remained with the flesh, the flesh cannot undergo the full extent of death, *i.e.*, *in corruption and decay*. For the Son, therefore, to die, amounted to His being forsaken by the Father. The Son, then, both dies and rises again, according to the Scriptures.[5] It is the Son, too, who ascends to the heights of heaven,[6] and also descends to the inner parts of the earth.[7] "He sitteth at the Father's right hand"[8]—not the Father at His own. He is seen by Stephen, at his martyrdom by stoning, still sitting at the right hand of God,[9] where He will continue to sit, until the Father shall make His enemies His footstool.[10] He will come again on the clouds of heaven, just as He appeared when He ascended into heaven.[11] Meanwhile He has received from the Father the promised gift, and has shed it forth, even the Holy Spirit—the Third Name in the Godhead, and the Third Degree of the Divine Majesty; the Declarer of the One *Monarchy of God*, but at the same time the Interpreter of the *Economy*, to every one who hears and receives the words of the new prophecy;[12] and "the Leader into all truth,"[13] such as is in the Father, and the Son, and the Holy Ghost, according to the mystery of the doctrine of Christ.

CHAP. XXXI.—RETROGRADE CHARACTER OF THE HERESY OF PRAXEAS. THE DOCTRINE OF THE BLESSED TRINITY CONSTITUTES THE GREAT DIFFERENCE BETWEEN JUDAISM AND CHRISTIANITY.

But, (this doctrine of yours bears a likeness) to the Jewish faith, of which this is the substance—so to believe in One God as to refuse to reckon the Son besides Him, and after the Son the Spirit. Now, what difference would there be between us and them, if there were not this distinction *which you are for breaking down?* What need would there be of the gospel, which is the substance of the New Covenant, laying down (as it does) that the Law and the Prophets lasted until John *the Baptist*, if thenceforward the Father, the Son, and the Spirit are not both believed in as Three, and as making One Only God? God was pleased to renew His covenant with man in such a way as that His Unity might be believed in, after a new manner, through the Son and the Spirit, in order that God might now be known openly,[14] in His proper Names and Persons, who in ancient times was not plainly understood, though declared through the Son and the Spirit. Away, then, with[15] those "Antichrists who deny the Father and the Son." For they deny the Father, when they say that He is the same as the Son; and they deny the Son, when they suppose Him to be the same as the Father, by assigning to Them things which are not *Theirs*, and taking away from Them things which are *Theirs*. But "whosoever shall confess that (Jesus) Christ is the Son of God" (not the Father), "God dwelleth in him, and he in God."[16] We believe not the testimony of God in which He testifies to us of His Son. "He that hath not the Son, hath not life."[17] And that man has not the Son, who believes Him to be any other than the Son.

[1] Rom. viii. 32.
[2] This is the sense rather than the words of Isa. liii. 5, 6.
[3] Luke xxiii. 46.
[4] i.e., the divine nature.
[5] 1 Cor. xv. 3, 4.
[6] John iii. 13.
[7] Eph. iv. 9.
[8] Mark xvi. 19; Rev. iii. 21.
[9] Acts vii. 55.
[10] Ps. cx. 1.
[11] Acts i. 11; Luke xxi. 27.
[12] Tertullian was now a [pronounced] Montanist.
[13] John xvi. 13.
[14] Coram.
[15] Viderint.
[16] 1 John iv. 15.
[17] 1 John v. 12.

POSTSCRIPT.

The learned Dr. Holmes, the translator of the Second volume of the Edinburgh series, to which our arrangement has given another position, furnished it with a *Preface* as follows:

"This volume contains all Tertullian's *polemical* works (placed in his second volume by

Oehler, whose text we have followed), with the exception of the long treatise *Against Marcion*, which has already formed a volume of this series, and the *Adversus Judæos*, which, not to increase the bulk of the present volume, appears among the Miscellaneous Tracts.

" For the scanty facts connected with our author's life, and for some general remarks on the importance and style of his writings, the reader is referred to the Introduction of my translation of the *Five Books against Marcion*.

" The treatises which comprise this volume will be found replete with the vigorous thought and terse expression which always characterize Tertullian.

"Brief synopses are prefixed to the several treatises, and headings are supplied to the chapters: these, with occasional notes on difficult passages and obscure allusions, will, it is hoped, afford sufficient aid for an intelligent perusal of these ancient writings, which cannot fail to be interesting alike to the theologian and the general reader,—full as they are of reverence for revealed truth, and at the same time of independence of judgment, adorned with admirable variety and fulness of knowledge, genial humour, and cultivated imagination."

Dr. Holmes further adorned this same volume with a dedication to a valued friend, in the following words:

"*The Right Rev. Father in God*, W. I. TROWER, D.D., *late Lord Bishop of Gibraltar, and formerly Bishop of Glasgow and Galway:*

MY DEAR LORD, In one of our conversations last summer, you were kind enough to express an interest in this publication, and to favour me with some valuable hints on my own share in it. It gives me therefore great pleasure to inscribe your honoured name on the first page of this volume.

I avail myself of this public opportunity of endorsing, on my own account, the high opinion which has long been entertained of your excellent volumes on *The Epistles* and *The Gospels*.

Recalling to mind, as I often do, our pleasant days at Pennycross and Mannamead, I remain, my dear Lord, very faithfully yours, PETER HOLMES."

MANNAMEAD, *March* 10, 1870.

ELUCIDATIONS.

I.

(Sundry doctrinal statements of Tertullian. See p. 601 (*et seqq.*), *supra.*)

I am glad for many reasons that Dr. Holmes appends the following from Bishop Kaye's Account of the Writings of Tertullian:

" On the doctrine of the blessed Trinity, in order to explain his meaning Tertullian borrows illustrations from natural objects. The three Persons of the Trinity stand to each other in the relation of the root, the shrub, and the fruit; of the fountain, the river, and the cut from the river; of the sun, the ray, and the terminating point of the ray. For these illustrations he professes himself indebted to the Revelations of the Paraclete. In later times, divines have occasionally resorted to similar illustrations for the purpose of familiarizing the doctrine of the Trinity to the mind; nor can any danger arise from the proceeding, so long as we recollect that they are illustrations, not arguments—that we must not draw conclusions from them, or think that whatever may be truly predicated of the illustrations, may be predicated with equal truth of that which it was designed to illustrate."

" ' Notwithstanding, however, the intimate union which subsists between the Father, Son, and Holy Ghost, we must be careful,' says Tertullian, ' to distinguish between their Persons.' In his representations of this distinction he sometimes uses expressions which in after times, when controversy had introduced greater precision of language, were studiously avoided by the orthodox. Thus he calls the Father the whole substance—the Son a derivation from or portion of the whole." [1]

"After showing that Tertullian's opinions were generally coincident with the orthodox belief of the Christian Church on the great subject of the Trinity in Unity, Bp. Kaye goes on to say: ' We are far from meaning to assert that expressions may not occasionally be found which are capable of a different interpretation, and which were carefully avoided by the orthodox writers of later times, when the controversies respecting the Trinity had introduced greater precision of language. Pamelius thought it necessary to put the reader on his guard against certain of these expressions; and Semler has noticed, with a sort of ill-natured industry (we call it *ill-natured industry*, because the true mode of ascertaining a writer's opinions is, not to fix upon particular expressions, but to take the general tenor of his language), every passage in the Tract against Praxeas in which there is any appearance of contradiction, or which will bear a construction favourable to the Arian tenets. Bp. Bull also, who conceives the language of Tertullian to be explicit and correct on the subject of the pre-existence and the consubstantiality, admits that he occasionally uses expressions at variance with the co-eternity of Christ. For instance, in the Tract against Hermogenes,[2] we find a passage in which it is expressly asserted that there was a time when the Son was not. Perhaps, however, a reference to the peculiar tenets of Hermogenes will enable us to account for this assertion. That heretic affirmed that matter was eternal, and argued thus: ' God was always God, and always Lord; but the word Lord implies the existence of something over which He was Lord. Unless, therefore, we suppose the eternity of something distinct from God, it is not true that He was always Lord.' Tertullian boldly answered, that God was not always Lord; and that in Scripture we do not find Him called Lord until the work of creation was completed. In like manner, he contended that the titles of *Judge* and *Father* imply the existence of *sin*, and of a *Son*. As, therefore, there was a time when neither sin nor the Son existed, the titles of Judge and Father were not at that time applicable to God. Tertullian could scarcely mean to affirm (in direct opposition to his own statements in the Tract against Praxeas) that there was ever a time when the λόγος, or *Ratio*, or *Sermo Internus* did not exist. But with respect to *Wisdom* and *the Son* (*Sophia* and *Filius*) the case is different. Tertullian assigns to both a beginning of existence: Sophia was created or formed in order to devise the plan of the universe; and the Son was begotten in order to carry that plan into effect. Bp. Bull appears to have given an accurate representation of the matter, when he says that, according to our author, the Reason and Spirit of God, being the substance of the Word and Son, were co-eternal with God; but that the *titles* of Word and Son were not strictly applicable until the former had been emitted to arrange, and the latter begotten to execute, the work of creation. Without, therefore, attempting to explain, much less to defend, all Tertullian's expressions and reasonings, we are disposed to acquiesce in the statement given by Bp. Bull of his opinions (*Defence of the Nicene Creed*, sec. iii. ch. x. (p. 545 of the Oxford translation)): ' From all this it is clear how rashly, as usual, Petavius has pronounced that, "*so far as relates to the eternity*

---

[1] Kaye, pp. 504–596.
[2] Ch. iii. compared with ch. xviii.

of the Word, it is manifest that Tertullian did not by any means acknowledge it." ' To myself, indeed, and as I suppose to my reader also, after the many clear testimonies which I have adduced, the very opposite is manifest, unless indeed Petavius played on the term, *the Word*, which I will not suppose. For Tertullian does indeed teach that the Son of God was made and was called the Word (*Verbum* or *Sermo*) from some definite beginning, *i.e.* at the time when He went out from God the Father with the voice, 'Let there be light' in order to arrange the universe. But, for all that, that he really believed that the very hypostasis which is called the Word and Son of God is eternal, I have, I think, abundantly demonstrated." (The whole of Bp. Bull's remark is worth considering; it occurs in the translation just referred to, pp. 508–545.)—(Pp. 521–525.)

"In speaking also of the Holy Ghost, Tertullian occasionally uses terms of a very ambiguous and equivocal character. He says, for instance (*Adversus Praxean*, c. xii.), that in Gen. i. 26, God addressed the Son, His Word (the Second Person in the Trinity), and *the Spirit in the Word* (the Third Person of the Trinity). Here the distinct personality of the Spirit is expressly asserted; although it is difficult to reconcile Tertullian's words, 'Spiritus in Sermone,' with the assertion. It is, however, certain both from the general tenor of the Tract against Praxeas, and from many passages in his other writings (for instance, *Ad Martyres*, iii.), that the distinct personality of the Holy Ghost formed an article of Tertullian's creed. The occasional ambiguity of his language respecting the Holy Ghost is perhaps in part to be traced to the variety of senses in which the term '*Spiritus*' is used. It is applied generally to God, for 'God is a Spirit' (*Adv. Marcionem*, ii. 9); and for the same reason to the Son, who is frequently called 'the Spirit of God,' and 'the Spirit of the Creator' (*De Oratione*, i. ; *Adv. Praxean*, xiv., xxvi.; *Adv. Marcionem*, v. 8; *Apolog.* xxiii. ; *Adv. Marcionem*, iii. 6, iv. 33). Bp. Bull likewise (*Defence of the Nicene Creed*, i. 2), following Grotius, has shown that the word '*Spiritus*' is employed by the fathers to express the divine nature in Christ."—(Pp. 525, 526.)

II.

(The bishop of Rome, cap. i. p. 597.)

Probably Victor (A.D. 190), who is elsewhere called Victor*inus*, as Oehler conjectures, by a blunderer who tacked the *inus* to his name, because he was thinking of Zephyr*inus*, his immediate successor. This Victor "acknowledged the prophetic gifts of Montanus," and kept up communion with the Phrygian churches that adopted them: but worse than that, he now seems to have patronized the Patri-passion heresy, under the compulsion of Praxeas. So Tertullian says, who certainly had no idea that the Bishop of Rome was the infallible judge of controversies, when he recorded the facts of this strange history. Thus, we find the very founder of "Latin Christianity," accusing a contemporary Bishop of Rome of heresy and the patronage of heresy, in two particulars. Our earliest acquaintance with that See presents us with Polycarp's superior authority, at Rome itself, in maintaining apostolic doctrine and suppressing heresy. "He it was, who coming to Rome," says Irenæus,[1] "in the time of Anicetus, caused many to turn away from the aforesaid heretics (viz. Valentinus and Marcion) to the Church of God, proclaiming that *he had received* this one and sole truth *from the Apostles.*" Anicetus was a pious prelate who never dreamed of asserting a superior claim as the chief depositary of Apostolic orthodoxy, and whose beautiful example in the Easter-questions discussed between Polycarp and himself, is another illustration of the independence of the sister churches, at that period.[2] Nor is it unworthy to be noted, that the next event, in Western history, establishes a like principle against that other and less worthy occupant of the Roman See, of whom we have spoken. Irenæus rebukes Victor for his dogmatism about Easter, and reproaches him with departing from the example of his predecessors in the same See.[1] With Eleutherus he had previously remonstrated, though mildly, for his toleration of heresy and his patronage of the raising schism of Montanus.[2]

III.

(These three are one, cap. xxv. p. 621. Also p. 606.)

Porson having spoken Pontifically upon the matter of the text of "the Three Witnesses," *cadit quæstio, locutus est Augur Apollo.* It is of more importance that Bishop Kaye in his calm wisdom, remarks as follows:[3] "In my opinion, the passage in Tertullian, far from containing an allusion to I. John v. 7, furnishes most decisive proof that he knew nothing of the verse." After this, and the acquiescence of scholars generally, it would be presumption to say a word on the question of quoting it as Scripture. In Textual Criticism it seems to be an established canon that it has no place in the Greek Testament. I submit, however, that, something remains to be said for it, on the ground of the old African Version used and quoted by Tertullian and Cyprian; and I dare to say, that, while there would be no ground whatever for *inserting it* in our English Version, the question of *striking it out* is a widely different one. It would be sacrilege, in my humble opinion, for reasons which will appear, in the following remarks, upon our author.

It appears to me very clear that Tertullian is quoting I. John v. 7. in the passage now under consideration: "*Qui tres unum sunt,* non unus, quomodo dictum est, Ego et Pater unum sumus, *etc.*" Let me refer to a work containing a sufficient answer to Porson, on this point of Tertullian's quotation, which it is easier to pass *sub-silentio,* than to refute. I mean Forster's *New Plea,* of which the full title is placed in the margin.[4] The whole work is worth thoughtful study, but, I name it with reference to this important passage of our author, exclusively. In connection with other considerations on which I have no right to enlarge in this place, it satisfies me as to the primitive origin of the text in the Vulgate, and hence of its right to stand in our English Vulgate until it can be shewn that the Septuagint Version, quoted and honoured by our Lord, is free from similar readings, and divergences from the Hebrew MSS.

Stated as a mere question as to the early African Church,[5] the various versions known as the *Itala,* and the right of the Latin and English Vulgates to remain as they are, the whole question is a fresh one. Let me be pardoned for saying: (1) that I am not pleading for it as a proof-text of the Trinity, having never once quoted it as such in a long ministry, during which I have preached nearly a hundred Trinity-Sunday Sermons; (2) that I consider it as practically Apocryphal, and hence as coming under St. Jerome's law, and being useless to establish doctrine; and (3) that I feel no need of it, owing to the wealth of Scripture on the same subject. Tertullian, himself says that he cites "only a few out of many texts—not pretending to bring up all the passages of Scripture. . . . having produced an accumulation of witnesses in the fulness of their dignity and authority."

To those interested in the question let me commend the learned dissertation of Grabe on the textual case, as it stood in his day.[6] I value it chiefly because it proves that the Greek Testament, elsewhere says, *disjointedly,* what is collected into I. John v. 7. It is, therefore, Holy Scripture in substance, if not in the letter. What seems to me important, how-

---

[1] Eusebius, B. V. cap. 24. Refer also to preceding note, and to Vol. I. p. 310, this Series.

[2] Vol. II. pp. 3 and 4, this Series, also, Eusebius, B. V. Cap. iii.　　　　　　　　　　　　　　　　[3] p. 516.

[4] " A New Plea for the Authenticity of the text of the *Three Heavenly Witnesses :* or, Porson's Letters to Travis eclectically examined, etc. etc. By the Rev. Charles Forster, etc." Cambridge, Deighton, Bell & Co., and London, Bell & Daldy, 1867.

[5] See Milman, *Hist. Lat. Christ.,* 1. p. 29.　　　　　　　　　　[6] See Bull's Works, Vol. V., p. 381.

ever, is the balance it gives to the whole context, and the defective character of the grammar and logic, if it be stricken out. In the Septuagint and the Latin Vulgate of the Old Testament we have a precisely similar case. Refer to Psalm xiii., alike in the Latin and the Greek, as compared with our English Version.[1] Between the third and fourth verses, three whole verses are interpolated: Shall we strike them out? Of course, if certain critics are to prevail over St. Paul, for he quotes them (Rom. iii. 10) with the formula: "As it is written." Now, then, till we expurgate the English Version of the Epistle to the Romans,—or rather the original of St. Paul himself, I employ Grabe's argument only to prove my point, which ·is this, viz., that I. John v. 7 being Scripture, ought to be left untouched in the Versions where it stands, although it be no part of the Greek Testament.

---

[1] Where it is Psalm XIV.

VIII

SCORPIACE.

ANTIDOTE FOR THE SCORPION'S STING.[1]

[TRANSLATED BY REV. S. THELWALL.]

CHAP. I.

THE earth brings forth, as if by suppuration, great evil from the diminutive scorpion. The poisons are as many as are the kinds of it, the disasters as many as are also the species of it, the pains as many as are also the colours of it. Nicander writes *on the subject of scorpions*, and depicts them. And yet to smite with the tail—which tail will be whatever is prolonged from the hindmost part of the body, and scourges—is the one movement which they all use when making an assault. Wherefore that succession of knots in the scorpion, which in the inside is a thin poisoned veinlet, rising up with a bow-like bound, draws tight a barbed sting at the end, after the manner of an engine for shooting missiles. From which circumstance they also call after the scorpion, the warlike implement which, by its being drawn back, gives an impetus to the arrows. The point in their case is also a duct of extreme minuteness, to inflict the wound; and where it penetrates, it pours out poison. The usual time of danger is the summer season: fierceness hoists the sail when the wind is from the south and the south-west. Among cures, *certain* substances supplied by nature have very great efficacy; magic also puts on some bandage; the art of healing counteracts with lancet and cup. For some, making haste, take also beforehand a protecting draught; but sexual intercourse drains it off, and they are dry again. We have faith for a defence, if we are not smitten with distrust itself also, in immediately making the sign[2] and adjuring,[3] and besmearing the heel with the beast. Finally, we often aid in this way even the heathen, seeing we have been endowed by God with that power which the apostle first used when he despised the viper's bite.[4] What, then, does this pen of yours offer, if faith is safe by what it has of its own? That it may be safe by what it has of its own also at other times, when it is subjected to scorpions of its own. These, too, have a troublesome littleness, and are of different sorts, and are armed in one manner, and are stirred up at a definite time, and that not another than one of burning heat. This among Christians is a *season of* persecution. When, therefore, faith is greatly agitated, and the Church burning, as represented by the bush,[5] then the Gnostics break out, then the Valentinians creep forth, then all the opponents of martyrdom bubble up, being themselves also hot to strike, penetrate, kill. For, because they know that many are artless and also inexperienced, and weak moreover, that a very great number in truth are Christians who veer about with the wind and conform to its moods, they perceive that they are never to be approached more than when fear has opened the entrances to the soul, especially when some *display of* ferocity has already arrayed with a crown the faith of martyrs. Therefore, drawing along the tail hitherto, they first of all apply it to the feelings, or whip with it as if on empty space. Innocent persons undergo such suffering. So that you may suppose *the speaker* to be a brother or a heathen of the better sort.

---

[1] [Written about A.D. 205.]
[2] Of the cross over the wounded part. [This translation is frequently weakened by useless interpolations; some of these destroying the author's style, for nothing, I have put into footnotes or dropped.]
[3] *I.e.* adjuring the part, in the name of Jesus, and besmearing the poisoned heel with the gore of the beast, when it has been crushed to death. [So the translator; but the terse rhetoric of the original is not so circumstantial, and refers, undoubtedly, to the lingering influence of miracles, according to St. Mark, xvi. 18.]
[4] Acts xxviii. 3.
[5] Ex. iii. 2.

A sect troublesome to nobody so dealt with! Then they pierce. Men are perishing without a reason. For that they are perishing, and without a reason, is the first insertion. Then they now strike mortally. But the unsophisticated souls[1] know not what is written, and what meaning it bears, where and when and before whom we must confess, *or ought*, save that this, to die for God, is, since He preserves me, not even artlessness, but folly, nay madness. If He kills me, how will it be His duty to preserve me? Once for all Christ died for us, once for all He was slain that we might not be slain. If He demands the like from me in return, does He also look for salvation from my death by violence? Or does God importune for the blood of men, especially if He refuses that of bulls and he-goats?[2] Assuredly He had rather have the repentance than the death of the sinner.[3] And how is He eager for the death of those who are not sinners? Whom will not these, and perhaps other subtle devices containing heretical poisons, pierce either for doubt if not for destruction, or for irritation if not for death? As for you, therefore, do you, if faith is on the alert, smite on the spot the scorpion with a curse, so far as you can, with your sandal, and leave it dying in its own stupefaction? But if it gluts the wound, it drives the poison inwards, and makes it hasten into the bowels; forthwith all the former senses become dull, the blood of the mind freezes, the flesh of the spirit pines away, loathing for the Christian name is accompanied by a sense of sourness. Already the understanding also seeks for itself a place where it may throw up; and thus, once for all, the weakness with which it has been smitten breathes out wounded faith either in heresy or in heathenism. And now the present state of matters is *such, that we are in* the midst of an intense heat, the very dog-star of persecution,—a state originating doubtless with the dog-headed one himself.[4] Of some Christians the fire, of others the sword, of others the beasts, have made trial; others are hungering in prison for the martyrdoms of which they have had a taste in the meantime by being subjected to clubs and claws[5] besides. We ourselves, having been appointed for pursuit, are like hares being hemmed in from a distance; and heretics go about according to their wont. Therefore the state of the times has prompted me to prepare by my pen, in opposition to the little beasts which trouble our sect, our antidote against poison, that I may thereby effect cures. You who read will at the same time drink. Nor is the draught bitter. If the utterances of the Lord are sweeter than honey and the honeycombs,[6] the juices are from that source. If the promise of God flows with milk and honey,[7] the ingredients which go to make that draught have the smack of this. "But woe to them who turn sweet into bitter, and light into darkness."[8] For, in like manner, they also who oppose martyrdoms, representing salvation to be destruction, transmute sweet into bitter, as well as light into darkness; and thus, by preferring this very wretched life to that most blessed one, they put bitter for sweet, as well as darkness for light.

CHAP. II.

But not yet about the good to be got from martyrdom must we learn, without our having first *heard* about the duty of suffering it; nor must we *learn* the usefulness of it, before we have *heard* about the necessity for it. The (question of the) divine warrant goes first— whether God has willed and also commanded ought of the kind, so that they who assert that it is not good are not plied with arguments for thinking it profitable save when they have been subdued.[9] It is proper that heretics be driven[10] to duty, not enticed. Obstinacy must be conquered, not coaxed. And, certainly, that will be pronounced beforehand quite good enough, which will be shown to have been instituted and also enjoined by God. Let the Gospels wait a little, while I set forth their root the Law, while I ascertain the will of God from those writings from which I recall to mind Himself also: "*I am*," says He, "God, thy God, who have brought thee out of the land of Egypt. Thou shalt have no other gods besides me. Thou shalt not make unto thee a likeness of those things which are in heaven, and which are in the earth beneath, and which are in the sea under the earth. Thou shalt not worship them, nor serve them. For I am the Lord thy God."[11] Likewise in the same *book of* Exodus: "Ye yourselves have seen that I have talked with you from heaven. Ye shall not make unto you gods of silver, neither shall ye make unto you gods of gold."[12] To the following effect also, in Deuteromy: "Hear, O Israel; The Lord thy God is one: and thou shalt love the

---

[1] The opponents of martyrdoms are meant.--TR.
[2] Ps. l. 13.
[3] Ezek. xxxiii. 11.
[4] i.e. the devil.—TR.
[5] An instrument of torture, so called.—TR.

[6] Ps. xix. 10.
[7] Ex. iii. 17.
[8] Isa. v. 20.
[9] By those in favour of its having been divinely enjoined.
[10] By argument, of course.—TR.
[11] Ex. xx. 2.
[12] Ex. xx. 22, 23.

Lord thy God with all thy heart and all thy might, and with all thy soul."[1] And again: "Neither do thou forget the Lord thy God, who brought thee forth from the land of Egypt, out of the house of bondage. Thou shalt fear the Lord thy God, and serve Him only, and cleave to Him, and swear by His name. Ye shall not go after strange gods, and the gods of the nations which are round about you, because the Lord thy God is also a jealous God among you, and lest His anger should be kindled against thee, and destroy thee from off the face of the earth."[2] But setting before them blessings and curses, He also says: "Blessings shall be yours, if ye obey the commandments of the Lord your God, whatsoever I command you this day, and do not wander from the way which I have commanded you, to go and serve other gods whom ye know not."[3] And as to rooting them out in every way: "Ye shall utterly destroy all the places wherein the nations, which ye shall possess by inheritance, served their gods, upon mountains and hills, and under shady trees. Ye shall overthrow all their altars, ye shall overturn and break in pieces their pillars, and cut down their groves, and burn with fire the graven images of the gods themselves, and destroy the names of them out of that place."[4] He further urges, when they (the Israelites) had entered the land of promise, and driven out its nations: "Take heed to thy self, that thou do not follow them after they be driven out from before thee, that thou do not inquire after their gods, saying, As the nations serve their gods, so let me do likewise."[5] But also says He: "If there arise among you a prophet himself, or a dreamer of dreams, and giveth thee a sign or a wonder, and it come to pass, and he say, Let us go and serve other gods, whom ye know not, do not hearken to the words of that prophet or dreamer, for the Lord your God proveth you, to know whether ye fear God with all your heart and with all your soul. After the Lord your God ye shall go, and fear Him, and keep His commandments, and obey His voice, and serve Him, and cleave unto Him. But that prophet or dreamer shall die; for he has spoken to turn thee away from the Lord thy God."[6] But also in another section.[7] "If, however, thy brother, the son of thy father or of thy mother, or thy son, or thy daughter, or the wife of thy bosom, or thy friend who is as thine own soul, solicit thee, saying secretly, Let us go and serve other gods, which thou knowest not, nor did thy fathers, of the gods of the nations which are round about thee, very nigh unto thee or far off from thee, do not consent to go with him, and do not hearken to him. Thine eye shall not spare him, neither shalt thou pity, neither shalt thou preserve him; thou shall certainly inform upon him. Thine hand shall be first upon him to kill him, and afterwards the hand of thy people; and ye shall stone him, and he shall die, seeing he has sought to turn thee away from the Lord thy God."[8] He adds likewise concerning cities, that if it appeared that one of these had, through the advice of unrighteous men, passed over to other gods, all its inhabitants should be slain, and everything belonging to it become accursed, and all the spoil of it be gathered together into all its places of egress, and be, even with all the people, burned with fire in all its streets in the sight of the Lord God; and, says He, "it shall not be for dwelling in for ever: it shall not be built again any more, and there shall cleave to thy hands nought of its accursed plunder, that the Lord may turn from the fierceness of His anger."[9] He has, from His abhorrence of idols, framed a series of curses too: "Cursed be the man who maketh a graven or a molten image, an abomination, the work of the hands of the craftsman, and putteth it in a secret place."[10] But in Leviticus He says: "Go not ye after idols, nor make to yourselves molten gods: I am the Lord your God."[11] And in other passages: "The children of Israel are my household servants; these are they whom I led forth from the land of Egypt:[12] I am the Lord your God. Ye shall not make you idols fashioned by the hand, neither rear you up a graven image. Nor shall ye set up a remarkable stone in your land (to worship it): I am the Lord your God."[13] These words indeed were first spoken by the Lord by the lips of Moses, being applicable certainly to whomsoever the Lord God of Israel may lead forth in like manner from the Egypt of a most superstitious world, and from the abode of human slavery. But from the mouth of every prophet in succession, sound forth also utterances of the same God, augmenting the same law of His by a renewal of the same commands, and in the first place announcing no other duty in so special a manner as the being on guard against all making and worshipping of idols; as when

---

[1] Deut. vi. 4.
[2] Deut. vi. 12.
[3] Deut. xi. 27.
[4] Deut. xii. 2, 3.
[5] Deut. xii. 30.
[6] Deut. xiii. 1.
[7] Of course our division of the Scripture by chapter and verse did not exist in the days of Tertullian.—Tr.

[8] Deut. xiii. 6.
[9] Deut. xiii. 16.
[10] Deut. xxvii. 15.
[11] Rev. xix. 4.
[12] The words in the Septuagint are: ὅτι ἐμοὶ οἱ υἱοὶτ Ἰσραὴλ οἰκέται εἰσίν, παῖδές μου οὗτοί εἰσιν οὓς ἐξήγαγον ἐκ γῆς Αἰγύπτου.
[13] Lev. xxv. 55, xxvi. 1.

by the mouth of David He says: "The gods of the nations are silver and gold: they have eyes, and see not; they have ears, and hear not; they have a nose, and smell not; a mouth, and they speak not; hands, and they handle not; feet and they walk not.   Like to them shall be they who make them, and trust in them."[1]

CHAP. III.

Nor should I think it needful to discuss whether God pursues a worthy course in forbidding His own name and honour to be given over to a lie, or does so in not consenting that such as He has plucked*from the maze of false religion should return again to Egypt, or does so in not suffering to depart from Him them whom He has chosen for Himself. Thus that, too, will not require to be treated by us, whether He has wished to be kept the rule which He has chosen to appoint, and whether He justly avenges the abandonment of the rule which He has wished to be kept; since He would have appointed it to no purpose if He had not wished it kept, and would have to no purpose wished it kept if He had been unwilling to uphold it.   My next step, indeed, is to put to the test these appointments of God in opposition to false religions, the completely vanquished as well as also the punished, since on these will depend the entire argument for martyrdoms.   Moses was apart with God on the mountain, when the people, not brooking his absence, which was so needful, seek to make gods for themselves, which, for his own part, he will prefer to destroy.[2] Aaron is importuned, and commands that the earrings of their women be brought together, that they may be thrown into the fire.   For the people were about to lose, as a judgment upon themselves, the true ornaments for the ears, the words of God.   The wise fire makes for them the molten likeness of a calf, reproaching them with having the heart where they have their treasure also,—in Egypt, to wit, which clothed with sacredness, among the other animals, a certain ox likewise.   Therefore the slaughter of three thousand by their nearest relatives, because they had displeased their so very near relative God, solemnly marked both the commencement and the deserts of the trespass.   Israel having, as we are told in Numbers,[3] turned aside at Sethim, the people go to the daughters of Moab to gratify their lust: they are allured to the idols, so that they committed whoredom with the spirit also: finally, they eat of their defiled *sacrifices;*

then they both worship the gods of the nation, and are admitted to the rites of Beelphegor. For this lapse, too, into idolatry, sister to adultery, it took the slaughter of twenty-three thousand by the swords of their countrymen to appease the divine anger.   After the death of Joshua the son of Nave they forsake the God of their fathers, and serve idols, Baalim and Ashtaroth;[4] and the Lord in anger delivered them up to the hands of spoilers, and they continued to be spoiled by them, and to be sold to their adversaries, and could not at all stand before their enemies.   Whithersoever they went forth, His hand was upon them for evil, and they were greatly distressed. And after this God sets judges (*critas*), the same as our censors, over them.   But not even these did they continue steadfastly to obey.   So soon as one of the judges died, they proceeded to transgress more than their fathers had done by going after the gods of others, and serving and worshipping them. Therefore the Lord was angry.   "Since, indeed," He says, "this nation have transgressed my covenant which I established with their fathers, and have not hearkened to my voice, I also will give no heed to remove from before them a man of the nations which Joshua left at his death."[5]   And thus, throughout almost all the annals of the judges and of the kings who succeeded them, while the strength of the surrounding nations was preserved, He meted wrath out to Israel by war and captivity and a foreign yoke, as often as they turned aside from Him, especially to idolatry.

CHAP. IV.

If, therefore, it is evident that from the beginning this kind of worship has both been forbidden—witness the commands so numerous and weighty—and that it has never been engaged in without punishment following, as examples so numerous and impressive show, and that no offence is counted by God so presumptuous as a trespass of this sort, we ought further to perceive the purport of both the divine threatenings and their fulfilments, which was even then commended not only by the not calling in question, but also by the enduring of martyrdoms, for which certainly He had given occasion by forbidding idolatry.   For otherwise martyrdoms would not take place.   And certainly He had supplied, as a warrant for these, His own authority, willing those events to come to pass for the occurrence of which He had given occasion. At present (it is important), for we are getting severely stung concerning the will of God,

[1] Ps. cxxxv. 15, cxv. 4.
[2] Ex. xxxii.
[3] Num. xxv. 1.

[4] Judg. ii. 8-13.
[5] Judg. ii. 20, 21.

and the scorpion repeats the prick, denying the existence of this will, finding fault witn it, so that he either insinuates that there is another god, such that this is not his will, or none the less overthrows ours, seeing such is his will, or altogether denies *this* will of God, if he cannot deny Himself. But, for our part, contending elsewhere about God, and about all the rest of the body of heretical teaching, we now draw before us definite lines[1] for one form of encounter, maintaining that this will, such as to have given occasion for martyrdoms, is that of not another god than the God of Israel, on the ground of the commandments relating to an always forbidden, as well as of the judgments upon a punished, idolatry. For if the keeping of a command involves the suffering of violence, this will be, so to speak, a command about keeping the command, requiring me to suffer that through which I shall be able to keep the command, violence namely, whatever of it threatens me when on my guard against idolatry. And certainly (in the case supposed) the Author of the command extorts compliance with it. He could not, therefore, have been unwilling that those events should come to pass by means of which the compliance will be manifest. The injunction is given me not to make mention of any other god, not even by speaking,—as little by the tongue as by the hand,—to fashion a god, and not to worship or in any way show reverence to another than Him only who thus commands me, whom I am both bid fear that I may not be forsaken by Him, and love with my whole being, that I may die for Him. Serving as a soldier under this oath, I am challenged by the enemy. If I surrender to them, I am as they are. In maintaining this oath, I fight furiously in battle, am wounded, hewn in pieces, slain. Who wished this fatal issue to his soldier, but he who sealed him by such an oath?

CHAP. V.

You have therefore the will of my God. We have cured this prick. Let us give good heed to another thrust touching the character of His will. It would be tedious to show that my God is good,—a truth with which the Marcionites have now been made acquainted by us. Meanwhile it is enough that He is called God for its being necessary that He should be believed to be good. For if any one make the supposition that God is evil, he will not be able to take his stand on both the constituents thereof: he will be bound either to affirm that he whom he has thought to be evil is not God,

or that he whom he has proclaimed to be God is good. Good, therefore, will be the will also of him who, unless he is good, will not be God. The goodness of the thing itself also which God has willed—of martyrdom, I mean —will show this, because only one who is good has willed what is good. I stoutly maintain that martyrdom is good, as required by the God by whom likewise idolatry is forbidden and punished. For martyrdom strives against and opposes idolatry. But to strive against and oppose evil cannot be ought but good. Not as if I denied that there is a rivalry in evil things with one another, as well as in good also; but this ground for it requires a different state of matters. For martyrdom contends with idolatry, not from some malice which they share, but from its own kindness; for it delivers from idolatry. Who will not proclaim that to be good which delivers from idolatry? What else is the opposition between idolatry and martyrdom, than that between life and death? Life will be counted to be martyrdom as much as idolatry to be death. He who will call life an evil, has death to speak of as a good. This frowardness also appertains to men,—to discard what is wholesome, to accept what is baleful, to avoid all dangerous cures, or, in short, to be eager to die rather than to be healed. For they are many who flee from the aid of physic also, many in folly, many from fear and false modesty. And the healing art has manifestly an apparent cruelty, by reason of the lancet, and of the burning iron, and of the great heat of the mustard; yet to be cut and burned, and pulled and bitten, is not on that account an evil, for it occasions helpful pains; nor will it be refused merely because it afflicts, but because it afflicts inevitably will it be applied. The good accruing is the apology for the frightfulness of the work. In short, that man who is howling and groaning and bellowing in the hands of a physician will presently load the same hands with a fee, and proclaim that they are the best operators, and no longer affirm that they are cruel. Thus martyrdoms also rage furiously, but for salvation. God also will be at liberty to heal for everlasting life by means of fires and swords, and all that is painful. But you will admire the physician at least even in that respect, that for the most part he employs like properties in the cures to counteract the properties of the diseases, when he aids, as it were, the wrong way, succouring by means of those things to which the affliction is owing. For he both checks heat by heat, by laying on a greater load; and subdues inflammation by leaving thirst unappeased, by tormenting rather; and contracts the superabundance of

[1] An allusion to what occurred in the games, there being lines to mark the space within which the contests were to be waged.—TR.

bile by every bitter little draught, and stops hemorrhage by opening a veinlet in addition. But you will think that God must be found fault with, and that for being jealous, if He has chosen to contend with a disease and to do good by imitating the malady, to destroy death by death, to dissipate killing by killing, to dispel tortures by tortures, to disperse[1] punishments by punishments, to bestow life by withdrawing it, to aid the flesh by injuring it, to preserve the soul by snatching it away. The wrongheadedness, as you deem it to be, is reasonableness; what you count cruelty is kindness. Thus, seeing God by brief (sufferings) effects cures for eternity, extol your God for your prosperity; you have fallen into His hands, but have happily fallen. He also fell into your sicknesses. Man always first provides employment for the physician; in short, he has brought upon himself the danger of death. He had received from his own Lord, as from a physician, the salutary enough rule to live according to the law, that he should eat of all indeed (that the garden produced) *and* should refrain from only one little tree which in the meantime the Physician Himself knew as a perilous one. He gave ear to him whom he preferred, and broke through self-restraint. He ate what was forbidden, and, surfeited by the trespass, suffered indigestion tending to death; he certainly richly deserving to lose his life altogether who wished to do so. But the inflamed tumour due to the trespass having been endured until in due time the medicine might be mixed, the Lord gradually prepared the means of healing—all the rules of faith, they also bearing a resemblance to (the causes of) the ailment, seeing they annul the word of death by the word of life, and diminish the trespass-listening by a listening of allegiance. Thus, even when that Physician commands one to die, He drives out the lethargy of death. Why does man show reluctance to suffer now from a cure, what he was not reluctant then to suffer from a disorder? Does he dislike being killed for salvation, who did not dislike being killed for destruction?—Will he feel squeamish with reference to the counter poison, who gaped for the poison?

CHAP. VI.

But if, for the contest's sake, God had appointed martyrdoms for us, that thereby we might make trial with our opponent, in order that He may now keep bruising him by whom man chose to be bruised, here too generosity rather than harshness in God holds sway. For He wished to make man, now plucked

from the devil's throat by faith, trample upon him likewise by courage, that he might not merely have escaped from, but also completely vanquished, his enemy. He who had called to salvation has been pleased to summon to glory also, that they who were rejoicing in consequence of their deliverance may be in transports when they are crowned likewise. With what good-will the world celebrates those games, the combative festivals and superstitious contests of the Greeks, involving forms both of worship and of pleasure, has now become clear in Africa also. As yet cities, by sending their congratulations severally, annoy Carthage, which was presented with the Pythian game after the racecourse had attained to an old age. Thus, by the world[2] it has been believed to be a most proper mode of testing proficiency in studies, to put in competition the forms of skill, to elicit the existing condition of bodies and of voices, the reward being the informer, the public exhibition the judge, and pleasure the decision. Where there are mere contests, there are some wounds: fists make reel, heels kick like butting rams, boxing-gloves mangle, whips leave gashes. Yet there will be no one reproaching the superintendent of the contest for exposing men to outrage. Suits for injuries lie outside the racecourse. But to the extent that those persons deal in discoloration, and gore, and swellings, he will design for them crowns, doubtless, and glory, and a present, political privileges, contributions by the citizens, images, statues, and—of such sort as the world can give—an eternity of fame, a resurrection by being kept in remembrance. The pugilist himself does not complain of feeling pain, for he wishes it; the crown closes the wounds, the palm hides the blood: he is excited more by victory than by injury. Will you count this man hurt whom you see happy? But not even the vanquished himself will reproach the superintendent of the contest for his misfortune. Shall it be unbecoming in God to bring forth kinds of skill and rules of His own into public view, into this open ground of the world, to be seen by men, and angels, and all powers?—to test flesh and spirit as to stedfastness and endurance?—to give to this one the palm, to this one distinction, to that one the privilege of citizenship, to that one pay?—to reject some also, and after punishing to remove them with disgrace? You dictate to God, forsooth, the times, or the ways, or the places in which to institute a trial concerning His own troop (of competitors) as if it were not proper for the Judge to pronounce

---

[1] Literally, "disperse in vapour."—Tr.

[2] Literally, "age."—Tr.

the preliminary decision also. Well now, if He had put forth faith to suffer martyrdoms not for the contest's sake, but for its own benefit, ought it not to have had some store of hope, for the increase of which it might restrain desire of its own, and check its wish, in order that it might strive to mount up, seeing they also who discharge earthly functions are eager for promotion? Or how will there be many mansions in our Father's house, if not to accord with a diversity of deserts? How will one star also differ from another star in glory, unless in virtue of disparity in their rays?[1] But further, if, on that account, some increase of brightness also was appropriate to loftiness of faith, that gain ought to have been of some such sort as would cost great effort, poignant suffering, torture, death. But consider the requital, when flesh and life are paid away—than which in man there is nought more precious, the one from the hand of God, the other from His breath—that the very things are paid away in obtaining the benefit of which the benefit consists; that the very things are expended which may be acquired; that the same things are the price which are also the commodities. God had foreseen also other weaknesses incident to the condition of man,—the stratagems of the enemy, the deceptive aspects of the creatures, the snares of the world; that faith, even after baptism, would be endangered; that the most, after attaining unto salvation, would be lost again, through soiling the wedding-dress, through failing to provide oil for their torchlets—would be such as would have to be sought for over mountains and woodlands, and carried back upon the shoulders. He therefore appointed as second supplies of comfort, and the last means of succour, the fight of martyrdom and the baptism—thereafter free from danger—of blood. And concerning the happiness of the man who has partaken of these, David says: "Blessed are they whose iniquities are forgiven, and whose sins are covered. Blessed is the man to whom the Lord will not impute sin."[2] For, strictly speaking, there cannot any longer be reckoned ought against the martyrs, by whom in the baptism (of blood) life itself is laid down. Thus, "love covers the multitude of sins;"[3] and loving God, to wit, with all its strength (by which in the endurance of martyrdom it maintains the fight), with all its life[4] (which it lays down for God), it makes of man a martyr. Shall you call these cures, counsels, methods of judging, spectacles,

(illustrations of) even the barbarity of God? Does God covet man's blood? And yet I might venture to affirm that He does, if man also covets the kingdom of heaven, if man covets a sure salvation, if man also covets a second new birth. The exchange is displeasing to no one, which can plead, in justification of itself, that either benefit or injury is shared by the parties making it.

CHAP. VII.

If the scorpion, swinging his tail in the air, still reproach us with having a murderer for our God, I shall shudder at the altogether foul breath of blasphemy which comes stinking from his heretical mouth; but I will embrace even such a God, with assurance derived from reason, by which reason even He Himself has, in the person of His own Wisdom, by the lips of Solomon, proclaimed Himself to be more than a murderer: Wisdom (*Sophia*), says He has slain her own children.[5] *Sophia* is Wisdom. She has certainly slain them wisely if only into life, and reasonably if only into glory. Of murder by a parent, oh the clever form! Oh the dexterity of crime! Oh the proof of cruelty, which has slain for this reason, that he whom it may have slain may not die! And therefore what follows? Wisdom is praised in hymns, in the places of egress; for the death of martyrs also is praised in song. Wisdom behaves with firmness in the streets, for with good results does she murder her own sons.[6] Nay, on the top of the walls she speaks with assurance, when indeed, according to Esaias, this one calls out, "I am God's;" and this one shouts, "In the name of Jacob;" and another writes, "In the name of Israel."[7] O good mother! I myself also wish to be put among the number of her sons, that I may be slain by her; I wish to be slain, that I may become a son. But does she merely murder her sons, or also torture them? For I hear God also, in another passage, say, "I will burn them as gold is burned, and will try them as silver is tried."[8] Certainly by the means of torture which fires and punishments supply, by the testing martyrdoms of faith. The apostle also knows what kind of God he has ascribed to us, when he writes: "If God spared not His own Son, but gave Him up for us, how did He not with Him also give us all things?"[9] You see how divine Wisdom has murdered even her own proper,

---

[1] 1 Cor. xv. 41.
[2] Ps. xxxii. 1 ; Rom. iv. 7, etc.
[3] 1 Pet. iv. 8.
[4] Matt. xxii. 37.

[5] Prov. i. 2 : "She hath killed her beasts." The corresponding words in the Septuagint are ἔσφαξε τα εαυτῆς θύματα. Augustine, in his *De Civ. Dei*, xvi. 20, explains the victims (θύματα) to be *Martyrum victimas.*—TR.
[6] Prov. i. 20, 21 ; see the Septuagint version.
[7] Isa. xliv. 5.
[8] Zech. xiii. 9.
[9] Rom. viii. 32.

first-born and only Son, who is certainly about to live, nay, to bring back the others also into life. I can say with the Wisdom of God; It is Christ who gave Himself up for our offences.[1] Already has Wisdom butchered herself also. The character of words depends not on the sound only, but on the meaning also, and they must be heard not merely by ears, but also by minds. He who does not understand, believes God to be cruel; although for him also who does not understand, an announcement has been made to restrain his harshness in understanding otherwise *than aright*. "For who," says *the apostle,* "has known the mind of the Lord? or who has been His counsellor, to teach Him? or who has pointed out to Him the way of understanding?"[2] But, indeed, the world has held it lawful for Diana of the Scythians, or Mercury of the Gauls, or Saturn of the Africans, to be appeased by human sacrifices; and in Latium to this day Jupiter has human blood given him to taste in the midst of the city; and no one makes it a matter of discussion, or imagines that it does not occur for some reason, or that it occurs by the will of his God, without having value. If our God, too, to have a sacrifice of His own, had required martyrdoms for Himself, who would have reproached Him for the deadly religion, and the mournful ceremonies, and the altar-pyre, and the undertaker-priest, and not rather have counted happy the man whom God should have devoured?

CHAP. VIII.

We keep therefore the one position, and, in respect of this question only, summon to an encounter, whether martyrdoms have been commanded by God, that you may believe that they have been commanded by reason, if you know that they have been commanded by Him, because God will not command ought without reason. Since the death of His own saints is precious is His sight, as David sings,[3] it is not, I think, that one which falls to the lot of men generally, and is a debt due by all (rather is that one even disgraceful on account of the trespass, and the desert of condemnation *to which it is to be traced*), but that *other* which is met in this very work—in bearing witness for religion, and maintaining the fight of confession in behalf of righteousness and the sacrament. As saith Esaias, "See how the righteous man perisheth, and no one layeth it to heart; and righteous men are taken away, and no one considereth it: for from before the face of unrighteousness the

righteous man perisheth, and he shall have honour at his burial."[4] Here, too, you have both an announcement of martyrdoms, and *of* the recompense they bring. From the beginning, indeed, righteousness suffers violence. Forthwith, as soon as God has begun to be worshipped, religion has got ill-will for her portion. He who had pleased God is slain, and that by his brother. Beginning with kindred blood, in order that it might the more easily go in quest of that of strangers, ungodliness made the object of its pursuit, finally, that not only of righteous persons, but even of prophets also. David is persecuted; Elias put to flight; Jeremias stoned; Esaias cut asunder; Zacharias butchered between the altar and the temple, imparting to the hard stones lasting marks of his blood.[5] That person himself, at the close of the law and the prophets, and called not a prophet, but a messenger, is, suffering an ignominious death, beheaded to reward a dancing-girl. And certainly they who were wont to be led by the Spirit of God used to be guided by Himself to martyrdoms; so that they had even already to endure what they had also proclaimed as requiring to be borne. Wherefore the brotherhood of the three also, when the dedication of the royal image was the occasion of the citizens being pressed to offer worship, knew well what faith, which alone in them had not been taken captive, required,—namely, that they must resist idolatry to the death.[6] For they remembered also the words of Jeremias writing to those over whom that captivity was impending: "And now ye shall see borne upon (men's) shoulders the gods of the Babylonians, of gold and silver and wood, causing fear to the Gentiles. Beware, therefore, that *ye* also do not be altogether like the foreigners, and be seized with fear while ye behold crowds worshipping those gods before and behind, but say in your mind, Our duty is to worship Thee, O Lord."[7] Therefore, having got confidence from God, they said, when with strength of mind they set at defiance the king's threats against the disobedient: "There is no necessity for our making answer to this command of yours. For our God whom we worship is able to deliver us from the furnace of fire and from your hands; and then it will be made plain to you that we shall neither serve your idol, nor worship your golden image which you have set up."[8] O martyrdom even without suffering perfect! Enough did they suffer! enough were they burned,

---

[1] Rom. iv. 25.
[2] Rom. xi. 34.
[3] Ps. cxvi. 15.

[4] Isa. lvii. 1.
[5] Matt. xiv. 3.
[6] Dan. iii. 12.
[7] Baruch vi. 3.
[8] Dan. iii. 16.

whom on this account God shielded, that it might not seem that they had given a false representation of His power. For forthwith, certainly, would the lions, with their pent-up and wonted savageness, have devoured Daniel also, a worshipper of none but God, and therefore accused and demanded by the Chaldeans, if it had been right that the worthy anticipation of Darius concerning God should have proved delusive. For the rest, every preacher of God, and every worshipper also, such as, having been summoned to the service of idolatry, had refused compliance, ought to have suffered, agreeably to the tenor of that argument too, by which the truth ought to have been recommended both to those who were then living and to those following in succession,—(namely), that the suffering of its defenders themselves bespeak trust for it, because nobody would have been willing to be slain but one possessing the truth. Such commands as well as instances, remounting to earliest times, show that believers are under obligation to suffer martyrdom.

CHAP. IX.

It remains for us, lest ancient times may perhaps have had the sacrament[1] (exclusively) their own, to review the modern Christian system, as though, being also from God, it might be different *from what preceded*, and besides, therefore, opposed thereto in its code of rules likewise, so that its Wisdom knows not to murder her own sons! Evidently, in the case of Christ both the divine nature and the will and the sect are different *from any previously known!* He will have commanded either no martyrdoms at all, or those which must be understood in a sense different from the ordinary, being such a person as to urge no one to a risk of this kind, as to promise no reward to them who suffer for Him, because He does not wish them to suffer; and therefore does He say, when setting forth His chief commands, "Blessed are they who are persecuted for righteousness' sake, for theirs is the kingdom of heaven."[2] The following statement, indeed, applies *first* to all without restriction, then specially to the apostles themselves: "Blessed shall ye be when men shall revile you, and persecute you, and shall say all manner of evil against you, for my sake. Rejoice and be exceeding glad, since very great is your reward in heaven; for so used their fathers to do even to the prophets." So that He likewise foretold their having to be themselves also slain, after the example of the prophets. Though, even if He had appointed all this persecution in case He were obeyed for those only who were then apostles, assuredly through them along witu the entire sacrament, with the shoot of the name, with the layer of the Holy Spirit, the rule about enduring persecution also would have had respect to us too, as to disciples by inheritance, and, (as it were,) bushes from the apostolic seed. For even thus again does He address words of guidance to the apostles: "Behold, I send you forth as sheep in the midst of wolves;" and, "Beware of men, for they will deliver you up to the councils, and they will scourge you in their synagogues; and ye shall be brought before governors and kings for my sake, for a testimony against them and the Gentiles," etc.[3] Now when He adds, "But the brother will deliver up the brother to death, and the father the child; and the children shall rise up against their parents, and cause them to be put to death," He has clearly announced with reference to the others, (that they would be subjected to) this form of unrighteous conduct, which we do not find *exemplified* in the case of the apostles. For none of them had experience of a father or a brother as a betrayer, which very many of us have. Then He returns to the apostles: "And ye shall be hated of all men for my name's sake." How much more shall we, for whom there exists the necessity of being delivered up by parents too! Thus, by allotting this very betrayal, now to the apostles, now to all, He pours out the same destruction upon all the possessors of the name, on whom the name, along with the condition that it be an object of hatred, will rest. But he who will endure on to the end—this man will be saved. By enduring what but persecution,—betrayal,—death? For to endure to the end is nought else than to suffer the end. And therefore there immediately follow, "The disciple is not above his master, nor the servant above his own lord;" because, seeing the Master and Lord Himself was stedfast in suffering persecution, betrayal and death, much more will it be the duty of His servants and disciples to bear the same, that they may not seem as if superior to Him, or to have got an immunity from the assaults of unrighteousness, since this itself should be glory enough for them, to be conformed to the sufferings of their Lord and Master; and, preparing them for the endurance of these, He reminds them that they must not fear such persons as kill the body only, but are not able to destroy the soul, but that they must dedicate fear to Him rather

---

[1] Tertullian means martyrdom.—Tr.
[2] Matt. v. 10; Luke vi. 23.
[3] Matt. x. 16.

who has such power that He can kill both body and soul, and destroy them in hell. Who, pray, are these slayers of the body only, but the governors and kings aforesaid—men, I ween? Who is the ruler of the soul also, but God only? Who is this but the threatener of fires *hereafter*, He without whose will not even one of two sparrows falls to the ground; that is, not even one of the two substances of man, flesh or spirit, because the number of our hairs also has been recorded before Him? Fear ye not, therefore. When He adds, "Ye are of more value than many sparrows," He makes promise that we shall not in vain— that is, not without profit—fall to the ground if we choose to be killed by men rather than by God. "Whosoever therefore will confess in me before men, in him will I confess also before my Father who is in heaven;[1] and whosoever shall deny me before men, him will I deny also before my Father who is in heaven." Clear, as I think, are the terms used in announcing, and the way to explain, the confession as well as the denial, although the mode of putting them is different. He who confesses himself a Christian, beareth witness that he is Christ's; he who is Christ's must be in Christ. If he is in Christ, he certainly confesses in Christ, when he confesses himself a Christian. For he cannot be this without being in Christ. Besides, by confessing in Christ he confesses Christ too: since, by virtue of being a Christian, he is in Christ, while *Christ* Himself also is in him. For if you have made mention of day, you have also held out to view the element of light which gives us day, although you may not have made mention of light. Thus, albeit He has not expressly said, "He who will confess me," (yet) the conduct involved in daily confession is not different from what is meant in our Lord's declaration. For he who confesses himself to be what he is, that is, a Christian, confesses that likewise by which he is it, that is, Christ. Therefore he who has denied that he is a Christian, has denied in Christ, by denying that he is in Christ while he denies that he is a Christian; and, on the other hand, by denying that Christ is in him, while He denies that he is in Christ, he will deny Christ too. Thus both he who will deny in Christ, will deny Christ, and he who will confess in Christ will confess Christ. It would have been enough, therefore, though our Lord had made an announcement about confessing merely. For, from His mode of presenting confession, it might be decided beforehand with reference to its opposite too—denial, that is—that denial is repaid by the Lord with denial, just as confession is with confession. And therefore, since in the mould in which the confession has been cast the state of (the case with reference to) denial also may be perceived, it is evident that to another manner of denial belongs what the Lord has announced concerning it, in terms different from those in which He speaks of confession, when He says, "Who will deny me," not "Who will confess in me." For He had foreseen that this form of violence also would, for the most part, immediately follow when any one had been forced to renounce the Christian name,—that he who had denied that he was a Christian would be compelled to deny Christ Himself too by blaspheming Him. As not long ago, alas, we shuddered at the struggle waged in this way by some with their entire faith, which had had favourable omens. Therefore it will be to no purpose to say, "Though I shall deny that I am a Christian, I shall not be denied by Christ, for I have not denied Himself." For even so much will be inferred from that denial, by which, seeing he denies Christ in him by denying that he is a Christian, he has denied *Christ* Himself also. But there is more, because He threatens likewise shame with shame (in return): "Whosoever shall be ashamed of me before men, of him will I also be ashamed before my Father who is in heaven." For He was aware that denial is produced even most of all by shame, that the state of the mind appears in the forehead, and that the wound of shame precedes that in the body.

CHAP. X.

But as to those who think that not here, that is, not within this environment of earth, nor during this period of existence, nor before men possessing this nature shared by us all, has confession been appointed to be made, what a supposition is theirs, being at variance with the whole order of things of which we have experience in these lands, and in this life, and under human authorities! Doubtless, when the souls have departed from their bodies, and begun to be put upon trial in the several stories of the heavens, with reference to the engagement (under which they have come to Jesus), and to be questioned about those hidden mysteries of the heretics, they must then confess before the real powers and the real men,—the Teleti,[2] to wit, and the Abascanti,[3] and the Acineti[4] of Valentinus!

---

[1] The words in the Greek, though correctly rendered in our authorized version, are, when translated literally, what Tertullian represents them to be.—TR.

[2] The perfect.
[3] The spell-resisting.
[4] The steadfast.

For, say *they*, even the Demiurge himself did not uniformly approve of the men of our world, whom he counted as a drop of a bucket,[1] and the dust of the threshing-floor, and spittle and locusts, *and* put on a level even with brute beasts. Clearly, it is so written. Yet not therefore must we understand that there is, besides us, another kind of man, which—for it is evidently *thus* (in the case proposed)—has been able to assume without invalidating a comparison *between the two kinds*, both the characteristics of the race and a unique property. For even if the life was tainted, so that condemned to contempt it might be likened to objects held in contempt, the nature was not forthwith taken away, so that there might be supposed to be another under its name. Rather is the nature preserved, though the life blushes; nor does Christ know other men than those with reference to whom He says, " Whom do men say that I am ? "[2] And, " As ye would that men should do to you, do ye likewise so to them."[3] Consider whether He may not have preserved a race such that He is looking for a testimony to Himself from them, as well as consisting of those on whom He enjoins the interchange of righteous dealing. But if I should urgently demand that those heavenly men be described to me, Aratus will sketch more easily Perseus and Cepheus, and Erigone, and Ariadne, among the constellations. But who prevented the Lord from clearly prescribing that confession by men likewise has to be made where He plainly announced that His own would be; so that the statement might have run thus: " Whosoever shall confess in me before men in heaven, I also will confess in him before my Father who is in heaven ? " He ought to have saved me from this mistake about confession on earth, which He would not have wished me to take part in, if He had commanded one in heaven; for I knew no other men but the inhabitants of the earth, man himself even not having up to that time been observed in heaven. Besides, what is the credibility of the things (alleged), that, being after death raised to heavenly places, I should be put to the test there, whither I would not be translated without being already tested, that I should there be tried in reference to a command where I could not come, but to find admittance ? Heaven lies open to the Christian before the way to it does; because there is no way to heaven, but to him to whom heaven lies open; and he who reaches it will enter. What powers, keeping guard at the gate, do I hear you affirm to exist in accordance with Roman superstition, with a certain Carnus, Forculus, and Limentinus? What powers do you set in order at the railings ? If you have ever read in David, " Lift up your gates, ye princes, and let the everlasting gates be lifted up; and the King of glory shall enter in;"[4] if you have also heard from Amos, " Who buildeth up to the heavens his way of ascent, and is such as to pour forth his abundance (of waters) over the earth;"[5] know that both that way of ascent was thereafter levelled with the ground, by the footsteps of the Lord, and an entrance thereafter opened up by the might of Christ, and that no delay or inquest will meet Christians on the threshold, since they have there to be not discriminated from one another, but owned, and not put to the question, but received in. For though you think heaven still shut, remember that the Lord left here to Peter and through him to the Church, the keys of it, which every one who has been here put to the question, and also made confession, will carry with him. But the devil stoutly affirms that we must confess there, to persuade us that we must deny here. I shall send before me fine documents, to be sure,[6] I shall carry with me excellent keys, the fear of them who kill the body only, but do nought against the soul: I shall be graced by the neglect of this command: I shall stand with credit in heavenly places, who could not stand in earthly: I shall hold out against the greater powers, who yielded to the lesser: I shall deserve to be at length let in, though now shut out. It readily occurs to one to remark further, " If it is in heaven that men must confess, it is here too that they must deny." For where the one is, there both are. For contraries always go together. There will need to be carried on in heaven persecution even, which is the occasion of confession or denial. Why, then, do you refrain, O most presumptuous heretic, from transporting to the world above the whole series of means proper to the intimidation of Christians, and especially to put there the very hatred for the name, where Christ rules at the right hand of the Father? Will you plant there both synagogues of the Jews—fountains of persecution—before which the apostles endured the scourge, and heathen assemblages with their own circus, forsooth, where they readily join in the cry, Death to the third race ?[7] But ye are bound to pro-

[1] Isa. xl. 15.
[2] Matt. xvi. 13.
[3] Matt. vii. 12 and Luke vi. 31.
[4] Ps. xxiv. 7.
[5] Amos ix. 6.
[6] In support of my cause.
[7] More literally, " How long shall we suffer the third race ! " The Christians are meant ; the first race being the heathen, and the second the Jews.—Tr.

duce in the same place both our brothers, fathers, children, mothers-in-law, daughters-in-law and those of our household, through whose agency the betrayal has been appointed; likewise kings, governors, and armed authorities, before whom the matter at issue must be contested. Assuredly there will be in heaven a prison also, destitute of the sun's rays or full of light unthankfully, and fetters of the zones perhaps, and, for a rack-horse, the axis itself which whirls *the heavens round*. Then, if a Christian is to be stoned, hail-storms will be near; if burned, thunderbolts are at hand; if butchered, the armed Orion will exercise his function; if put an end to by beasts, the north will send forth the bears, the Zodiac the bulls and the lions. He who will endure these assaults to the end, the same shall be saved. Will there be then, in heaven, both an end, and suffering, a killing, and the first confession? And where will be the flesh requisite for all this? Where the body which alone has to be killed by men? Unerring reason has commanded us to set forth these things in even a playful manner; nor will any one thrust out the bar consisting in this objection (we have offered), so as not to be compelled to transfer the whole array of means proper to persecution, all the powerful instrumentality which has been provided for dealing with this matter, to the place where he has put the court before which confession should be made. Since confession is elicited by persecution, and persecution ended in confession, there cannot but be at the same time, in attendance upon these, the instrumentality which determines both the entrance and the exit, that is, the beginning and the end. But both hatred for the name will be here, persecution breaks out here, betrayal brings men forth here, examination uses force here, torture rages here, and confession or denial completes this whole course of procedure on the earth. Therefore, if the other things are here, confession also is not elsewhere; if confession is elsewhere, the other things also are not here. Certainly the other things are not elsewhere; therefore neither is confession in heaven. Or, if they will have it that the manner in which the heavenly examination and confession take place is different, it will certainly be also incumbent on them to devise a mode of procedure of their own of a very different kind, and opposed to that method which is indicated in the Scriptures. And we may be able to say, Let them consider (whether what they imagine to exist does so), if so be that this course of procedure, proper to examination and confession on earth—a course which has persecution as the source in which it originates, and which pleads dissension in the state—is preserved to its own faith, if so be that we must believe just as is also written, and understand just as is spoken. Here I endure the entire course (in question), the Lord Himself not appointing a different quarter of the world *for my doing so*. For what does He add after finishing with confession and denial? "Think not that I am come to send peace on earth, but a sword,"— undoubtedly on the earth. "For I am come to set a man at variance against his father, and the daughter against her mother, and the mother-in-law against her daughter-in-law. And a man's foes shall be they of his own household."[1] For so is it brought to pass, that the brother delivers up the brother to death, and the father the son: and the children rise up against the parents, and cause them to die. And he who endureth to the end let that man be saved.[2] So that this whole course of procedure characteristic of the Lord's sword, which has been sent not to heaven, but to earth, makes confession also to be there, which by enduring to the end is to issue in the suffering of death.

CHAP. XI.

In the same manner, therefore, we maintain that the other announcements too refer to the condition of martyrdom. "He," says Jesus, "who will value his own life also more than me, is not worthy of me,"[3]—that is, he who will rather live by denying, than die by confessing, me; and "he who findeth his life shall lose it; but he who loseth it for my sake shall find it."[4] Therefore indeed he finds it, who, in winning life, denies; but he who thinks that he wins it by denying, will lose it in hell. On the other hand, he who, through confessing, is killed, will lose it for the present, but is also about to find it unto everlasting life. In fine, governors themselves, when they urge men to deny, say, "Save your life;" and, "Do not lose your life." How would Christ speak, but in accordance with the treatment to which the Christian would be subjected? But when He forbids thinking about what answer to make at a judgment-seat,[5] He is preparing His own servants *for what awaited them*, He gives the assurance that the Holy Spirit will answer *by them;* and when He wishes a brother to be visited in prison,[6] He is commanding that those about to confess be the object of solicitude; and He is soothing their

---

[1] Matt. x. 34.
[2] Matt. x. 21.
[3] Luke xiv. 26
[4] Matt. x. 39.
[5] Matt. x. 19.
[6] Matt. xxv. 36.

sufferings when He asserts that God will avenge His own elect.[1] In the parable also of the withering of the word[2] after the green blade had sprung up, He is drawing a picture with reference to the burning heat of persecutions. If these announcements are not understood as they are made, without doubt they signify something else than the sound indicates; and there will be one thing in the words, another in their meanings, as is the case with allegories, with parables, with riddles. Whatever wind of reasoning, therefore, these scorpions may catch (in their sails), with whatever subtlety they may attack, there is now one line of defence:[3] an appeal will be made to the facts themselves, whether they occur as the Scriptures represent that they would; since another thing will then be meant in the Scriptures if that very one (which seems to be so) is not found in actual facts. For what is written, must needs come to pass. Besides, what is written will then come to pass, if something different does not. But, lo! we are both regarded as persons to be hated by all men for the sake of the name, as it is written; and are delivered up by our nearest of kin also, as it is written; and are brought before magistrates, and examined, and tortured, and make confession, and are ruthlessly killed, as it is written. So the Lord ordained. If He ordained these events otherwise, why do they not come to pass otherwise than He ordained them, that is, as He ordained them? And yet they do not come to pass otherwise than He ordained. Therefore, as they come to pass, so He ordained; and as He ordained, so they come to pass. For neither would they have been permitted to occur otherwise than He ordained, nor for His part would He have ordained otherwise than He would wish them to occur. Thus these passages of Scripture will not mean ought else than we recognise in actual facts; or if those events are not yet taking place which are announced, how are those taking place which have not been announced? For these events which are taking place have not been announced, if those which are announced are different, and not these which are taking place. Well now, seeing the very occurrences are met with in actual life which are believed to have been expressed with a different meaning in words, what would happen if they were found to have come to pass in a different manner *than had been revealed?* But this will be the waywardness of faith, not to believe what has been demonstrated, to assume the truth of what has not been demonstrated. And to this waywardness I will offer the following objection also, that if these events, which occur as is written, will not be the very ones which are announced, those too (which are meant) ought not to occur as is written, that they themselves also may not, after the example of these *others*, be in danger of exclusion, since there is one thing in the words and another in the facts; and there remains that even the events which have been announced are not seen when they occur, if they are announced otherwise than they have to occur. And how will those be believed (to have come to pass), which will not have been announced as they come to pass? Thus heretics, by not believing what is announced as it has been shown to have taken place, believe what has not been even announced.

CHAP. XII.

Who, now, should know better the marrow of the Scriptures than the school of Christ itself?—the persons whom the Lord both chose for Himself as scholars, certainly to be fully instructed in all points, and appointed to us for masters to instruct us in all points. To whom would He have rather made known the veiled import of His own language, than to him to whom He disclosed the likeness of His own glory—to Peter, John, and James, and afterwards to Paul, to whom He granted participation in (the joys of) paradise too, prior to his martyrdom? Or do they also write differently from what they think—teachers using deceit, not truth? Addressing the Christians of Pontus, Peter, at all events, says, "How great indeed is the glory, if ye suffer patiently, without being punished as evildoers! For this is a lovely feature, *and* even hereunto were ye called, since Christ also suffered for us, leaving you Himself as an example, that ye should follow His own steps."[4] And again: "Beloved, be not alarmed by the fiery trial which is taking place among you, as though some strange thing happened unto you. For, inasmuch as ye are partakers of Christ's sufferings, do ye rejoice; that, when His glory shall be revealed, ye may be glad also with exceeding joy. If ye are reproached for the name of Christ, happy are ye; because glory and the Spirit of God rest upon you: if only none of you suffer as a murderer, or as a thief, or as an evil-doer, or as a busybody in other men's matters; yet (if any man suffer) as a Christian, let him not be ashamed, but let him glorify God on this behalf."[5] John,

---

[1] Luke xviii. 7.
[2] Matt. xiii. 3.
[3] See note 1, cap. iv. p. 637, *supra*.

[4] 1 Pet. ii. 20.
[5] 1 Pet. iv. 12.

in fact, exhorts us to lay down our lives even for our brethren,[1] affirming that there is no fear in love: "For perfect love casteth out fear, since fear has punishment; and he who fears is not perfect in love."[2] What fear would it be better to understand (as here meant), than that which gives rise to denial? What love does he assert to be perfect, but that which puts fear to flight, and gives courage to confess? What penalty will he appoint as the punishment of fear, but that which he who denies is about to pay, who has to be slain, body and soul, in hell? And if he teaches that we must die for the brethren, how much more for the Lord,—he being sufficiently prepared, by his own Revelation too, for giving such advice! For indeed the Spirit had sent the injunction to the angel of the church in Smyrna: "Behold, the devil shall cast some of you into prison, that ye may be tried ten days. Be thou faithful unto death, and I will give thee a crown of life."[3] Also to the angel of the church in Pergamus (mention was made) of Antipas,[4] the very faithful martyr, who was slain where Satan dwelleth. Also to the angel of the church in Philadelphia[5] (it was signified) that he who had not denied the name of the Lord was delivered from the last trial. Then to every conqueror the Spirit promises now the tree of life, and exemption from the second death; now the hidden manna, with the stone of glistening whiteness, and the name unknown (to every man save him that receiveth it); now power to rule with a rod of iron, and the brightness of the morning star; now the being clothed in white raiment, and not having the name blotted out of the book of life, and being made in the temple of God a pillar with the inscription on it of the name of God and of the Lord, and of the heavenly Jerusalem; now a sitting with the Lord on His throne,—which once was persistently refused to the sons of Zebedee.[6] Who, pray, are these so blessed conquerors, but martyrs in the strict sense of the word? For indeed theirs are the victories whose also are the fights; theirs, however, are the fights whose also is the blood. But the souls of the martyrs both peacefully rest in the meantime under the altar,[7] and support their patience by the assured hope of revenge; and, clothed in their robes, wear the dazzling halo of brightness, until others also may fully share in their glory. For yet again a countless throng are revealed, clothed in white and distinguished by palms

of victory, celebrating their triumph doubtless over Antichrist, since one of the elders says, "These are they who come out of that great tribulation, and have washed their robes, and made them white in the blood of the Lamb."[8] For the flesh is the clothing of the soul. The uncleanness, indeed, is washed away by baptism, but the stains are changed into dazzling whiteness by martyrdom. For Esaias also promises, that out of red and scarlet there will come forth the whiteness of snow and wool.[9] When great Babylon likewise is represented as drunk with the blood of the saints,[10] doubtless the supplies needful for her drunkenness are furnished by the cups of martyrdoms; and what suffering the fear of martyrdoms will entail, is in like manner shown. For among all the castaways, nay, taking precedence of them all, are the fearful. "But the fearful," says John—and then come the others—"will have their part in the lake of fire and brimstone."[11] Thus fear, which, as stated in his epistle, love drives out, has punishment.

CHAP. XIII.

But how Paul, an apostle, from being a persecutor, who first of all shed the blood of the church, though afterwards he exchanged the sword for the pen, and turned the dagger into a plough, being *first* a ravening wolf of Benjamin, then himself supplying food as did Jacob,[12]— how he, (I say,) speaks in favour of martyrdoms, now to be chosen by himself also, when, rejoicing over the Thessalonians, he says, "So that we glory in you in the churches of God, for your patience and faith in all your persecutions and tribulations, in which ye endure a manifestation of the righteous judgment of God, that ye may be accounted worthy of His kingdom, for which ye also suffer!"[13] As also in his Epistle to the Romans: "And not only so, but we glory in tribulations also, being sure that tribulation worketh patience, and patience experience, and experience hope; and hope maketh not ashamed."[14] And again: "And if children, then heirs, heirs indeed of God, and joint-heirs with Christ: if so be that we suffer with Him, that we may be also glorified together. For I reckon that the sufferings of this time are not worthy to be compared with the glory which shall be revealed in us."[15] And therefore he afterward says: "Who shall separate us from the love of God? Shall

---

[1] 1 John iii. 16.
[2] 1 John iv. 18.
[3] Rev. ii. 10.
[4] Rev. ii. 13.
[5] Rev. iii. 10.
[6] Matt. xx. 20–23.
[7] Rev. vi. 9.

[8] Rev. vii. 14.
[9] Isa. i. 18.
[10] Rev. xvii. 6.
[11] Rev. xxi. 8.
[12] Gen. xxv. 34, xxvii. 25.
[13] 2 Thess. i. 4.
[14] Rom. v. 3.
[15] Rom. viii. 17.

tribulation, or distress, or famine, or nakedness, or peril, or sword? (As it is written:
For Thy sake we are killed all the day long;
we have been counted as sheep for the slaughter.) Nay, in all these things we are more
than conquerors, through Him who loved us.
For we are persuaded, that neither death, nor
life, nor power, nor height, nor depth, nor any
other creature, shall be able to separate us
from the love of God, which is in Christ Jesus
our Lord." [1] But further, in recounting his
own sufferings to the Corinthians, he certainly
decided that suffering must be borne: " In
labours, (he says,) more abundant, in prisons
very frequent, in deaths oft. Of the Jews
five times received I forty stripes, save one;
thrice was I beaten with rods; once was I
stoned," [2] and the rest. And if these severities will seem to be more grievous than martyrdoms, yet once more he says: " Therefore
I take pleasure in infirmities, in reproaches,
in necessities, in persecutions, in distresses
for Christ's sake." [3] He also says, in verses
occurring in a previous part of the epistle:
" Our condition is such, that we are troubled
on every side, yet not distressed; and are in
need, but not in utter want; since we are harassed by persecutions, but not forsaken; it
is such that we are cast down, but not destroyed; always bearing about in our body the
dying of Christ." [4] " But though," says he,
" our outward man perisheth"—the flesh
doubtless, by the violence of persecutions—
" yet the inward man is renewed day by day"
—the soul, doubtless, by hope in the promises.
" For our light affliction, which is but for a
moment, worketh for us a far more exceeding
and eternal weight of glory; while we look not
at the things which are seen, but at the things
which are not seen. For the things which are
seen are temporal"—he is speaking of troubles; " but the things which are not seen are
eternal"—he is promising rewards. But
writing in bonds to the Thessalonians, [5] he
certainly affirmed that they were blessed,
since to them it had been given not only to
believe on Christ, but also to suffer for His
sake. " Having," says he, " the same conflict which ye both saw in me, and now hear
to be in me." [6] " For though I am offered
upon the sacrifice, I joy and rejoice with you
all; in like manner do ye also joy and rejoice
with me." You see what he decides the bliss
of martyrdom to be, in honour of which he is
providing a festival of mutual joy. When at
length he had come to be very near the at-

tainment of his desire, greatly rejoicing in
what he saw before him, he writes in these
terms to Timothy: " For I am already being
offered, and the time of my departure is at
hand. I have fought the good fight, I have
finished my course, I have kept the faith;
there is laid up for me the crown which the
Lord will give me on that day" [7]—doubtless
of his suffering. Admonition enough did he
for his part also give in preceding passages:
" It is a faithful saying: For if we are dead
with Christ, we shall also live with Him; if
we suffer, we shall also reign with Him; if we
deny Him, He also will deny us; if we believe
not, yet He is faithful: He cannot deny Himself." [8]   " Be not thou, therefore, ashamed
of the testimony of our Lord, nor of me His
prisoner;" [9] for he had said before: " For
God hath not given us the spirit of fear, but
of power, and of love, and of a sound mind." [10]
For we suffer with power from love toward
God, and with a sound mind, when we suffer
for our blamelessness. But further, if He
anywhere enjoins endurance, for what more
than for sufferings is He providing it? If anywhere He tears men away from idolatry, what
more than martyrdoms takes the lead, in
tearing them away to its injury?

<h2 style="text-align:center">CHAP. XIV.</h2>

No doubt the apostle admonishes the Romans [11] to be subject to all power, because
there is no power but of God, and because
(the ruler) does not carry the sword without
reason, and is the servant of God, nay also,
says he, a revenger to execute wrath upon
him that doeth evil. For he had also previously spoken thus: " For rulers are not a
terror to a good work, but to an evil. Wilt
thou then not be afraid of the power? Do
that which is good, and thou shalt have praise
of it. Therefore he is a minister of God to
thee for good. But if thou do that which is
evil, be afraid." Thus he bids you be subject to the powers, not on an opportunity occurring for his avoiding martyrdom, but when
he is making an appeal in behalf of a good
life, under the view also of their being as it
were assistants bestowed upon righteousness,
as it were handmaids of the divine court of
justice, which even here pronounces sentence
beforehand upon the guilty. Then he goes
on also to show how he wishes you to be subject to the powers, bidding you pay " tribute
to whom tribute is due, custom to whom custom," [12] that is, the things which are Cæsar's

[1] Rom. viii. 35.
[2] 2 Cor. xi. 23.
[3] 2 Cor. xii. 10.
[4] 2 Cor. iv. 8.
[5] Should be Philippians: i.e. Phil. i. 29, 30.
[6] Phil. ii. 17.
[7] 2 Tim. iv. 6.
[8] 2 Tim ii. 11.
[9] 2 Tim. i. 8.
[10] 2 Tim. i. 7.
[11] Rom. xiii. 1.
[12] Rom. xiii. 6.

to Cæsar, and the things which are God's to God;[1] but man is the property of God alone. Peter,[2] no doubt, had likewise said that the king indeed must be honoured, yet so that the king be honoured *only* when he keeps to his own sphere, when he is far from assuming divine honours; because both father and mother will be loved along with God, not put on an equality with Him. Besides, one will not be permitted to love even life more than God.

CHAP. XV.

Now, then, the epistles of the apostles also are well known. And do *we*, (you say), in all respects guileless souls and doves merely, love to go astray? I should think from eagerness to live. But let it be so, that meaning departs from their epistles. And yet, that the apostles endured such sufferings, we know: the teaching is clear. This only I perceive in running through the Acts. I am not at all on the search. The prisons there, and the bonds, and the scourges, and the big stones, and the swords, and the onsets by the Jews, and the assemblies of the heathen, and the indictments by tribunes, and the hearing of causes by kings, and the judgment-seats of pro-consuls and the name of Cæsar, do not need an interpreter. That Peter is struck,[3] that Stephen is overwhelmed *by stones*,[4] that James is slain[5] as is a victim at the altar, that Paul is beheaded has been written in their own blood. And if a heretic wishes his confidence to rest upon a public record, the archives of the empire will speak, as would the stones of Jerusalem. We read the lives of the Cæsars: At Rome Nero was the first who stained with blood the rising faith. Then is Peter girt by another,[6] when he is made fast to the cross. Then does Paul obtain a birth suited to Roman citizenship, when in Rome

he springs to life again ennobled by martyrdom. Wherever I read of these occurrences so soon as I do so, I learn to suffer; nor does it signify to me which I follow as teachers of martyrdom, whether the declarations or the deaths of the apostles, save that in their deaths I recall their declarations also. For they would not have suffered ought of a kind they had not previously known they had to suffer. When Agabus, making use of corresponding action too, had foretold that bonds awaited Paul, the disciples, weeping and entreating that he would not venture upon going to Jerusalem, entreated in vain.[7] As for him, having a mind to illustrate what he had always taught, he says, "Why weep ye, and grieve my heart? But for my part, I could wish not only to suffer bonds, but also to die at Jerusalem, for the name of my Lord Jesus Christ." And so they yielded by saying, "Let the will of the Lord be done;" feeling sure, doubtless, that sufferings are included in the will of God. For they had tried to keep him back with the intention not of dissuading, but to show love for him; as yearning for (the preservation of) the apostle, not as counselling against martyrdom. And if even then a Prodicus or Valentinus stood by, suggesting that one must not confess on the earth before men, and must do so the less in truth, that God may not (seem to) thirst for blood, and Christ for a repayment of suffering, as though He besought it with the view of obtaining salvation by it for Himself also, he would have immediately heard from the servant of God what the devil had from the Lord: "Get thee behind me, Satan; thou art an offence unto me. It is written, Thou shalt worship the Lord thy God, and Him only shalt thou serve."[8] But even now it will be right that he hear it, seeing that, long after, he has poured forth these poisons, which not even thus are to injure readily any of the weak ones, if any one in faith will drink, before being hurt, or even immediately after, this draught of ours.

[1] Matt. xxii. 21.
[2] 1 Pet. ii. 13.
[3] It has been thought that the allusion is to the breaking of the legs of the crucified to hasten their death, not to the beating to which the apostles were subjected by the Jewish council: Acts v. 40.—TR.
[4] Acts vii. 59.
[5] James the brother of our Lord, not the James mentioned Acts xii. 2.
[6] John xxi. 18.
[7] Acts xxi. 11.
[8] Matt. xvi. 23 and iv. 10,—a mixing up of two passages of Scripture.

IX

APPENDIX.

AGAINST ALL · HERESIES.[1]

[TRANSLATED·BY THE REV. S. THELWALL.]

CHAP. I.—EARLIEST HERETICS:[2] SIMON MAGUS, MENANDER, SATURNINUS, BASILIDES, NICO-LAUS. [THE WORK BEGINS AS A FRAGMENT.]

OF which heretics I will (to pass by a good deal) summarize some few particulars. For of Judaism's heretics I am silent—Dositheus the Samaritan, I mean, who was the first who had the hardihood to repudiate the prophets, on the ground that they had not spoken under inspiration of the Holy Spirit. Of the Sadducees I am silent, who, springing from the root of this error, had the hardihood to adjoin to this heresy the denial likewise of the resurrection of the flesh.[3] The Pharisees I pretermit, who were "divided" from the Jews by their superimposing of certain additaments to the law, which fact likewise made them worthy of receiving this very name;[4] and, together with them, the Herodians likewise, who said that Herod was Christ. To those I betake myself who have chosen to make the gospel the starting-point of their heresies.

Of these the first of all is Simon Magus, who in the Acts of the Apostles earned a condign and just sentence from the Apostle Peter.[5] He had the hardihood to call himself the Supreme Virtue,[6] that is, the Supreme God; and moreover, (to assert) that the universe[7] had been originated by his angels; that he had descended in quest of an erring dæmon,[8] which was Wisdom; that, in a phantasmal semblance of God, he had *not* suffered among the Jews, but was *as if he had suffered.*[9]

After him Menander, his disciple (likewise a magician[10]), saying the same as Simon. Whatever Simon had affirmed himself to be, this did Menander equally affirm himself to be, asserting that none could possibly have salvation without being baptized in his name.

Afterwards, again, followed Saturninus: he, too, affirming that the innascible[11] Virtue, that is God, abides in the highest regions, and that those regions are infinite, and in the regions immediately above us; but that angels far removed from Him made the lower world;[12] and that, because light from above had flashed refulgently in the lower regions, the angels had carefully tried to form man after the similitude of that light; that man lay crawling on the surface of the earth; that this light and this higher virtue was, thanks to mercy, the salvable spark in man, while all the rest of him perishes;[13] that Christ had not existed in a bodily substance, and had endured a *quasi*-passion in a phantasmal shape merely; that a resurrection of the flesh there will by no means be.

Afterwards broke out the heretic Basilides. He affirms that there is a supreme Deity, by name Abraxas,[14] by whom was created Mind, which in Greek he calls Νοῦς; that thence sprang the Word; that of Him issued Providence, Virtue,[15] and Wisdom; that out of

---

[1] [On p. 14, this volume, see nearly all that need be said, of this spurious treatise. I add a few references to Routh, *Opuscula*, Vol. I. p. 160 etc.. His honouring it with a place in his work must be my apology for not relegating it to the collection of spurious *Tertulliana, sub fine.*]

[2] [Routh says he inadvertently changed his title to read *Advs. Hæreticos*, but that it is better after all, in view of the opening sentence.]

[3] See Acts xxiii. 8, and the references there.

[4] Pharisees = Separatists.

[5] See Acts viii. 9-24.

[6] I use Virtue in this and similar cases in its Miltonic sense.

[7] Mundum.

[8] Or, "intelligence."

[9] Or, "but had undergone *a quasi-passion.*"

[10] Magus.

[11] Innascibilem;" but Fr. Junius' conjecture, "innoscibilem," is agreeable to the Greek "ἄγνωστος."

[12] Mundum.

[13] The text here is partially conjectural, and if correct, clumsy. For the sense, see *de Anima*, c. xxiii. *ad init.*

[14] Or, Abraxes, or Abrasax.

[15] Or, Power.

these subsequently were made Principalities, Powers,[1] and Angels; that there ensued infinite issues and processions of angels; that by these angels 365 heavens were formed, and the world,[2] in honour of Abraxas, whose name, if computed, has in itself this number. Now, among the last of the angels, those who made this world,[2] he places the God of the Jews latest, that is, the God of the Law and of the Prophets, whom he denies to be a God, but affirms to be an angel. To him, he says, was allotted the seed of Abraham, and accordingly he it was who transferred the sons of Israel from the land of Egypt into the land of Canaan; affirming him to be turbulent above the other angels, and accordingly given to the frequent arousing of seditions and wars, yes, and the shedding of human blood. Christ, moreover, he affirms to have been sent, not by this maker of the world,[3] but by the above-named Abraxas; and to have come in a phantasm, and been destitute of the substance of flesh: that it was not He who suffered among the Jews, but that Simon[4] was crucified in His stead: whence, again, there must be no believing on him who was crucified, lest one confess to having believed on Simon. Martyrdoms, he says, are not to be endured. The resurrection of the flesh he strenuously impugns, affirming that salvation has not been promised to *bodies*.

A brother heretic[5] emerged in Nicolaus. He was one of the seven deacons who were appointed in the Acts of the Apostles.[6] He affirms that Darkness was seized with a concupiscence—and, indeed, a foul and obscene one—after Light: out of this permixture it is a shame to say what fetid and unclean (combinations arose). The rest (of his tenets), too, are obscene. For he tells of certain Æons, sons of turpitude, and of conjunctions of execrable and obscene embraces and permixtures,[7] and certain yet baser outcomes of these. He teaches that there were born, moreover, dæmons, and gods, and spirits seven, and other things sufficiently sacrilegious alike and foul, which we blush to recount, and at once pass them by. Enough it is for us that this heresy of the Nicolaitans has been condemned by the Apocalypse of the Lord with the weightiest authority attaching to a sentence, in saying "Because this thou holdest, thou hatest the doctrine of the Nicolaitans, which I too hate."[8]

CHAP. II.—OPHITES, CAINITES, SETHITES.

To these are added those heretics likewise who are called *Ophites:*[9] for they magnify the serpent to such a degree, that they prefer him even to Christ Himself; for it was he, they say, who gave us the origin of the knowledge of good and of evil.[10] His power and majesty (they say) Moses perceiving, set up the brazen serpent; and whoever gazed upon him obtained health.[11] Christ Himself (they say further) in His gospel imitates Moses' serpent's sacred power, in saying: "And as Moses upreared the serpent in the desert, so it behoveth the Son of man to be upreared."[12] Him they introduce to bless their eucharistic (elements).[13] Now the whole parade and doctrine of this error flowed from the following source. They say that from the supreme primary Æon *whom men speak of*[14] there emanated several other inferior Æons. To all these, however, there opposed himself an Æon who name is *Ialdabaoth.*[15] He had been conceived by the permixture of a second Æon with inferior Æons; and afterwards, when he[16] had been desirous of forcing his way into the higher regions, had been disabled by the permixture of the gravity of matter with himself to arrive at the higher regions; had been left in the midst, and had extended himself to his full dimensions, and thus had made the sky.[17] *Ialdabaoth*, however, had descended lower, and had made him seven sons, and had shut from their view the upper regions by self-distension, in order that, since (these) angels could not know what was above,[18] they might think him the sole God. These inferior Virtues and angels, therefore, had made *man;* and, because he had been originated by weaker and mediocre powers, he lay crawling, worm-like. That Æon, however, out of which *Ialdaboath* had proceeded, moved to the heart with envy, had injected into man as he lay a certain spark; excited whereby, he was through prudence to grow wise, and be able to understand the things above. So, again, the *Ialdaboath* aforesaid, turning indignant, had emitted out of himself the Virtue and similitude of *the serpent;* and this had been

---

1 Potestates.
2 Mundum.
3 Mundum.
4 i.e. probably "Simon the Cyrenian." See Matt. xxvii. 32; Mark xv. 21; Luke xxiii. 26.
5 Alter hæreticus. But Fr. Junius suggests "aliter."
6 See Acts vi. 1-6. [But the identity is doubtful.]
7 So Oehler gives in his text. But his suggestion, given in a
note, is perhaps preferable: "and of execrable embraces and permixtures, and obscene conjunctions."
8 See Rev. ii. 6.
9 Or, "Serpentarians," from ὄφις, a serpent.
10 See Gen. iii. 1-7.
11 See Num. xxi. 4-9.
12 John iii. 14.
13 Eucharistia (neut. pl.) = εὐχαριστεῖα (Fr. Junius in Oehler): perhaps "*the place in which* they celebrate the eucharist."
14 These words are intended to give the force of the "illo" of the original.
15 Roberston (*Ch. Hist.* i. p. 39, note 2, ed. 2. 1858) seems to take this word to mean "Son of Darkness or Chaos."
16 "Seque" Oehler reads here, which appears bad enough Latin, unless his "se" after "extendisse" is an error.
17 Or, "heaven."
18 Or, "what the upper regions were."

the Virtue in paradise—that is, this had been the *serpent*—whom Eve had believed as if he had been God the Son.[1] He[2] plucked, say they, from the fruit of the tree, and thus conferred on mankind the knowledge of things good and evil.[3] Christ, moreover, existed not in substance of flesh: salvation of the flesh is not to be hoped for at all.

Moreover, also, there has broken out another heresy also, which is called that of the *Cainites*.[4] And the reason is, that they magnify *Cain* as if he had been conceived of some potent Virtue which operated in him; for Abel had been procreated after being conceived of an inferior Virtue, and accordingly had been found inferior. They who assert this likewise defend the traitor Judas, telling us that he is admirable and great, because of the advantages he is vaunted to have conferred on mankind; for some of them think that thanksgiving is to be rendered to Judas on this account: viz., Judas, they say, observing that Christ wished to subvert the truth, betrayed Him, in order that there might be no possibility of truth's being subverted. And others thus dispute against them, and say: Because the powers of this world[5] were unwilling that Christ should suffer, lest through His death salvation should be prepared for mankind, he, consulting for the salvation of mankind, betrayed Christ, in order that there might be no possibility at all of the salvation being impeded, which *was* being impeded through the Virtues which were opposing Christ's passion; and thus, through the passion of Christ, there might be no possibility of the salvation of mankind being retarded.

But, again, the heresy has started forth which is called that of the *Sethites*.[6] The doctrine of this perversity is as follows. Two human beings were formed by the angels—Cain and Abel. On their account arose great contentions and discords among the angels; for this reason, that Virtue which was above all the Virtues—which they style the Mother—when they said[7] that Abel had been slain, willed this Seth of theirs to be conceived and born in place of Abel, in order that those angels might be escheated who had created those two former human beings, while this pure seed rises and is born. For they say that there had been iniquitous permixtures of two angels and human beings; for which reason that Virtue which (as we have said) they style

the Mother brought on the deluge even, for the purpose of vengeance, in order that that seed of permixture might be swept away, and this only seed which was pure be kept entire. But (in vain): for they who had originated those of the former seed sent into the ark (secretly and stealthily, and unknown to that Mother-Virtue), together with those "eight souls,"[8] the seed likewise of Ham, in order that the seed of evil should not perish, but should, together with the rest, be preserved, and after the deluge be restored to the earth, and, by example of the rest, should grow up and diffuse itself, and fill and occupy the whole orb.[9] Of Christ, moreover, their sentiments are such that they call Him merely Seth, and say that He was instead of the actual Seth.

CHAP. III.—CARPOCRATES, CERINTHUS, EBION.

Carpocrates, futhermore, introduced the following sect. He affirms that there is one Virtue, the chief among the upper (regions): that out of this were produced angels and Virtues, which, being far distant from the upper Virtues, created this world[10] in the lower regions: that Christ was not born of *the Virgin* Mary, but was generated—a mere human being—of the seed of Joseph, superior (they admit) above all others in the practice of righteousness and in integrity of life; that He suffered among the Jews; and that His *soul* alone was received in heaven as having been more firm and hardy than all others: whence he would infer, retaining only the salvation of souls, that there are no resurrections of the body.

After him brake out the heretic Cerinthus, teaching similarly. For he, too, says that the world[10] was originated by those *angels;*[11] and sets forth Christ as born of the seed of Joseph, contending that He was merely human, without divinity; affirming also that the Law was given by angels;[12] representing the God of the Jews as not the Lord, but an angel.

His successor was Ebion,[13] not agreeing with Cerinthus in every point; in that he affirms the world[13] to have been made by God, not by angels; and because it s written, "No disciple above *his* master, nor servant above *his* lord,"[14] sets forth likewise the law

---

[1] Filio Deo.
[2] Or, "she;" but perhaps the text is preferable.
[3] See Gen. iii. 1-7.
[4] See *de Bapt.* c. i.
[5] Mundi.
[6] Or, Sethoites.
[7] "Dicerent;" but Routh (I think) has conjectured "disceret" "when *she learned*," etc., which is very simple and apt.

[8] See 1 Pet. iii. 20.
[9] Cf. Gen. ix. 1, 2, 7, 19.
[10] Mundum.
[11] "Ab illis" is perhaps an error for "ab angelis," by absorption of the first syllable. So Routh had conjectured before me.
[12] "*Ab* angelis:" an erroneous notion, which professed probably to derive support from John i. 17, Acts vii. 53, Gal. iii. 19, where, however, the Greek prepositions should be carefully noted, and ought in no case to be rendered by "ab."
[13] *Al.* Hebion.
[14] See Matt. x. 24; Luke vi. 40; John xiii. 16.

as binding,[1] of course for the purpose of excluding the gospel and vindicating Judaism.

CHAP. IV.—VALENTINUS, PTOLEMY AND SECUNDUS, HERACLEON.

Valentinus the heretic, moreover, introduced many fables. These I will retrench and briefly summarize. For he introduces the Pleroma and the thirty Æons. These Æons, moreover, he explains in the way of syzygies, that is, conjugal unions[2] of some kind. For among the first,[3] he says, were Depth[4] and Silence; of these proceeded Mind and Truth; out of whom burst the Word and Life; from whom, again, were created Man[5] and the Church. But (these are not all); for of these last also proceeded twelve Æons; from Speech,[6] moreover, and Life *proceeded* other ten Æons: such is the Triacontad of Æons, which is made up in the Pleroma of an ogdoad, a decad, and a duodecad. The thirtieth Æon, moreover, willed to see the great Bythus; and, to see him, had the hardihood to ascend into the upper regions; and not being capable of seeing his magnitude, desponded,[7] and almost suffered dissolution, had not some one,—he whom he calls Horos, to wit,—sent to invigorate him, strengthened him by pronouncing the word "Iao."[8] This Æon, moreover, which was thus *reduced* to despondency, he calls Achamoth, (and says) that he was seized with certain regretful passions, and out of his passions gave birth to material essences.[9] For

he was panic-stricken, he says, and terror-stricken, and overcome with sadness; and of these passions he conceived and bare. Hence he made the heaven, and the earth, and the sea, and whatever is in them: for which cause all things made by him are infirm, and frail, and capable of falling, and mortal, inasmuch as he himself was conceived and produced from despondency. He, however, originated this world[10] out of those material essences which Achamoth, by his panic, or terror, or sadness, or sweat, had supplied. For of his panic, he says, was made darkness; of his fear and ignorance, the spirits of wickedness and malignity; of his sadness and tears, the humidities of founts, the material essence of floods and sea. Christ, moreover, was sent by that First-Father who is Bythus. He, moreover, was not in the substance of our flesh; but, bringing down from heaven some spiritual body or other, passed through the Virgin Mary as water through a pipe, neither receiving nor borrowing aught thence. The resurrection of our present flesh he denies, but (maintains that) of some sister-flesh.[11] Of the Law and the prophets some parts he approves, some he disapproves; that is, he disapproves all in reprobating some. A Gospel of his own he likewise has, beside these of ours.

After him arose the heretics Ptolemy and Secundus, who agree throughout with Valentinus, differing only in the following point: viz., whereas Valentinus had feigned but thirty Æons, they have added several more; for they first added four, and subsequently four more. And Valentine's assertion, that it was the thirtieth Æon which strayed out from the Pleroma, (as *falling* into despondency,) they deny; for the one which desponded on account of disappointed yearning to see the First-Father was not of the original triacontad, they say.

There arose, besides, Heracleon, a brother[12]-heretic, whose sentiments pair with Valentine's; but, by some novelty of terminology, he is desirous of seeming to differ in sentiment. For he introduces the notion that there existed first what he terms (a Monad);[13] and then out of that Monad (arose) two, and then the

---

[1] i.e., as Rig.'s quotation from Jerome's *Indiculus* (in Oehler) shows, "because in so far as, Christ observed it."
[2] Conjugations. Cowper uses our word "conjugation" in this sense in one of his humorous pieces. ["Pairing-time."] The "syzygies" consisted of one male and one female Æon each.
[3] Oehler separates "in primis;" but perhaps they ought to be united—"inprimis," or "imprimis"—and taken as = "primo ab initio."
[4] Bythus.
[5] Hominem.
[6] "Sermone:" he said "Verbum" before.
[7] In defectione fuisse.
[8] Cf. *adv. Valent.* cc. x. xiv. [Routh says that this IAO (see note 8) is wanting in the older editions. It was borrowed from the *Adv. Valentin.* to eke out a defect.]
[9] Such appears to be the meaning of this sentence as Oehler gives it. But the text is here corrupt; and it seems plain there must either be something lost relating to this "Achamoth," or else some capital error in the reading, or, thirdly, some gross and unaccountable confusion in the writer: for the sentence as it stands is wholly irreconcilable with what follows. It evidently makes "Achamoth" identical with "the thirtieth Æon" above-named; and yet, without introducing any fresh subject, the writer goes on to state that this despondent Œon, who "conceived and bare," was itself the offspring of despondency, and made an infirm world out of the infirm materials which "Achamoth" supplied it with. Now it is apparent from other sources—as, for instance, from *Tert. adv. Valent.* above referred to—that the "thirtieth Æon" was supposed to be *female, Sophia* (Wisdom) by name, and that she was said to be *the parent* of "Achamoth," or "Enthymesis" (see *adv. Valentin.* cc. ix. x. xi. xiv. xxv.), while "Achamoth" herself appears by some accounts to be also called κάτω Σοφία. The name "Achamoth" itself, which Tertullian (*adv. Valentin.* c. xiv. *ad init.*) calls an "uninterpretable name," is believed to be a representation of a Hebrew word meaning "wisdom;" and hence, possibly, some of the confusion may have arisen,—from a promiscuous use, namely, of the titles "Achamoth" and "Sophia." Moreover, it would appear that some words lower down as to the production by "Achamoth" of "Demiurgus," must have dropped out. Unless these two omissions be supplied, the passage is

wholly unintelligible. Can the fact that the Hebrew word which "Achamoth" represents is a *fem. pl.* in any way explain this confused medley, or help to reconcile conflicting accounts? The ἄνω and κάτω Σοφία seem to point in some degree to some such solution of some of the existing difficulties. "Iao," again, is a word which has caused much perplexity. Can it possibly be connected with ἰάομαι, "to heal?" [See note 8.]
[10] Mundum.
[11] Oehler's suggestion is to vary the pointing so as to give this sense: "The resurrection of this flesh he denies. But of a sister-Law and prophets," etc. But this seems even more harsh than the other.
[12] "Alter," i.e., perhaps another *of the same class.*
[13] It seems almost necessary to supply some word here; and as "Monade" follows, it seemed simple to supply "Monada."

rest of the Æons. Then he introduces the whole *system of* Valentine.

CHAP. V.—MARCUS AND COLARBASUS.

After these there were not wanting a Marcus and a Colarbasus, composing a novel heresy out of the Greek alphabet. For they affirm that without those letters truth cannot be found; nay more, that in those letters the whole plenitude and perfection of truth is comprised; for this was why Christ said, " I am the Alpha and the Omega."[1] In fact, they say that Jesus Christ descended,[2] that is, that *the dove* came down on Jesus;[3] and, since the dove is styled by the Greek name περιστερά —(*peristera*), it has in itself this number DCCCI.[4] These men run through their Ω, Ψ, X, Φ, Υ, T—through the whole alphabet, indeed, up to *A* and *B*—and compute ogdoads and decads. So we may grant it useless and idle to recount all their trifles. What, however, must be allowed not merely vain, but likewise dangerous, is this: they feign a second God, beside the Creator; they affirm that Christ was not in the substance of flesh; they say there is to be no resurrection of the flesh.

CHAP. VI.—CERDO, MARCION, LUCAN, APELLES.

To this is added one Cerdo. He introduces two first causes,[5] that is, two Gods—one good, the other cruel:[6] the good being the superior; the latter, the cruel one, being the creator of the world.[7] He repudiates the prophecies and the Law; renounces God the Creator; maintains that Christ who came was the Son of the superior God; affirms that He was not in the substance of flesh; states Him to have been only in a phantasmal shape, to have not really suffered, but undergone a quasi-passion, and not to have been born of a virgin, *nay*, really not to have been born at all. A resurrection of the soul merely does he ap-

prove, denying that of the body. The Gospel of Luke alone, and that not entire, does he receive. Of the Apostle Paul he takes neither all the epistles, nor in their integrity. The Acts of the Apostles and the Apocalypse he rejects as false.

After him emerged a disciple of his, one Marcion by name, a native of Pontus,[8] son of a bishop, excommunicated because of a rape committed on a certain virgin.[9] He, starting from the fact that it is said, " Every good tree beareth good fruit, but an evil evil,"[10] attempted to approve the heresy of Cerdo; so that his assertions are identical with those of the former heretic before him.

After him arose one Lucan by name, a follower and disciple of Marcion. He, too, wading through the same kinds of blasphemy, teaches the same as Marcion and Cerdo had taught.

Close on their heels follows Apelles, a disciple of Marcion, who after lapsing, into his own carnality,[11] was severed from Marcion. He introduces one God in the infinite upper regions, and states that He made many powers and angels; beside Him, withal, another Virtue, which he affirms to be called Lord, but represents as an angel. By him he will have it appear that the world[12] was originated in imitation of a superior world.[13] With this *lower* world he mingled throughout (a principle of) repentance, because he had not made it so perfectly as that superior world had been originated. The Law and the prophets he repudiates. Christ he neither, like Marcion, affirms to have been in a phantasmal shape, nor yet in substance of a true body, as the Gospel teaches; but says, because He descended from the upper regions, that in the course of His descent He wove together for Himself a starry and airy[14] flesh; and, in His resurrection, restored, in the course of His ascent, to the several individual elements whatever had been borrowed in His descent: and thus—the several parts of His body dispersed—He reinstated in heaven His spirit only. This man denies the resurrection of the flesh. He uses, too, one only apostle; but that is Marcion's, that is, a mutilated one. He teaches the salvation of souls alone.

---

[1] See Rev. i. 7, xxi. 6, xxii. 13.

[2] Denique Jesum Christum descendisse. So Oehler, who does not notice any conjectural emendation, or various reading, of the words. If correct, his reading would refer to the views of a twofold Jesus Christ—a real and a phantasmal one—held by docetic Gnostics, or to such views as Valentine's, in whose system, so far as it is ascertainable from the confused and discrepant accounts of it, there would appear to have been one Æon called Christ, another called Jesus, and a human person called Jesus and Christ, with whom the true Jesus associated Himself. Some such jumble of ideas the two heretics now under review would seem to have held, if Oehler's be the true reading. But the difficulties are somewhat lessened if we accept the very simple emendation which naturally suggests itself, and which, I see, Semler has proposed and Routh inclines to receive, " *in* Jesum Christum descendisse," i. e. " that Christ descended *on* Jesus."

[3] See Matt. iii. 13-17; Mark i. 9-11; Luke iii. 21-22; John i. 29 -34.

[4] Habere *secum* numerum DCCCI. So Oehler, after Jos. Scaliger, who, however, seems to have read " *secum hunc* numerum," for the ordinary reading, " habere *secundum* numerum," which would mean, " represents, *in the way of* numerical value, CCCI."

[5] Initia duo.

[6] Sævum.

[7] Mundi.

[8] " Ponticus genere," lit. " a Pontic *by race*," which of course may not necessarily, like our *native*, imply actual *birth* in Pontus. [Note—" son of a bishop :" an index of early date, though not necessarily Ante-Nicene. A mere forgery of later origin would have omitted it.]

[9] Rig., with whom Oehler agrees, reminds us that neither in the *de Præscr.* nor in the *adv. Marc.*, nor, apparently, in Irenæus, is any such statement brought forward.

[10] See Matt. vii. 17,

[11] See de *Præscr.* c. xxx., and comp. with it what is said of Marcion above.

[12] Mundum.

[13] Mundi.

[14] " Aëream," i.e., composed of the air, the *lower* air, or atmosphere ; not " æthercam," of the *upper* air, or ether.

He has, besides, private but extraordinary lections of his own, which he calls "Manifestations,"[1] of one Philumene,[2] a girl whom he follows as a prophetess. He has, besides, his own books, which he has entitled *books* of Syllogisms, in which he seeks to prove that whatever Moses has written about God is not true, but is false.

CHAP. VII.—TATIAN, CATAPHRYGIANS, CATAPROCLANS, CATÆSCHINETANS.

To all these heretics is added one Tatian, a brother-heretic. This man was Justin Martyr's disciple. After Justin's death he began to cherish different opinions from his. For he wholly savours of Valentinus; adding this, that Adam cannot even attain salvation: as if, when the branches become salvable,[3] the root were not!

Other heretics swell the list who are called Cataphrygians, but their teaching is not uniform. For there are (of them) *some* who are called Cataproclans;[4] there are others who are termed Catæschinetans.[5] These have a blasphemy common, and a blasphemy not common, but peculiar and special. The common blasphemy lies in their saying that the Holy Spirit was in the apostles indeed, the Paraclete was not; and in their saying that the Paraclete has spoken in Montanus more things than Christ brought forward into (the compass of) the Gospel, and not merely more, but likewise better and greater. But the particular one they who follow Æschines have; this, namely, whereby they add this, that they affirm Christ to be Himself Son and Father.

CHAP. VIII.—BLASTUS, TWO THEODOTI, PRAXEAS.

In addition to all these, there is likewise Blastus, who would latently introduce Judaism. For he says the passover is not to be kept otherwise than according to the law of Moses, on the fourteenth of the month. But who would fail to see that evangelical grace is escheated if he recalls Christ to the Law?

Add to these Theodotus the Byzantine, who, after being apprehended for Christ's Name, and apostatizing,[6] ceased not to blaspheme against Christ. For he introduced a doctrine by which to affirm that Christ was merely a human being, but deny His deity; teaching that He was born of the Holy Spirit indeed of a virgin, but was a solitary and bare human being,[7] with no pre-eminence above the rest (of mankind), but only that of righteousness.

After him brake out a second heretical Theodotus, who again himself introduced a sister-sect, and says that the human being Christ Himself[8] was merely conceived alike, and born, of the Holy Spirit and the Virgin Mary, but that He was inferior to Melchizedek; because it is said of Christ, "Thou art a priest unto eternity, after the order of Melchizedek."[9] For that Melchizedek, he says, was a heavenly Virtue of pre-eminent grace; in that Christ acts for human beings, being made their Deprecator and Advocate: Melchizedek does so[10] for heavenly angels and Virtues. For to such a degree, he says, is he better than Christ, that he is ἀπάτωρ (fatherless), ἀμήτωρ (motherless), ἀγενεαλόγητος (without genealogy), of whom neither the beginning nor the end has been comprehended, nor can be comprehended.[11]

But after all these, again, one Praxeas introduced a heresy which Victorinus[12] was careful to corroborate. He asserts that Jesus Christ is God the Father Almighty. Him he contends to have been crucified, and suffered, and died; beside which, with a profane and sacrilegious temerity, he maintains the proposition that He is Himself sitting at His own right hand.[13]

---

[1] Phaneroseis. Oehler refers to *de Præscr.* c. xxx. *q. v.*
[2] φιλουμένη, "loved one."
[3] Salvi. Perhaps if it be questionable whether this word may be so rendered in a correct Latinist, it may be lawful to render it so in so incorrect a one as our present author.
[4] i.e. followers of Proclus.
[5] i.e. followers of Æschines. So this writer takes "Cataphryges" to mean followers of the Phrygians."

[6] Negavit. See *de Idol.* c. xxiii. note 1.
[7] Hominem solitarium atque nudum. The words seem to mean, destitute of anything *super*human.
[8] Et ips*um* hominem Christum tantummodo. I rather incline to read, as in the preceding sentence, "et *ipse:*" "and himself affirms Christ to have been merely human, conceived alike," etc.
[9] See Ps. cx. 4, and the references there.
[10] The Latin here is very careless, unless, with Routh, we suggest "et" for "eo," and render: "and that what Christ does," etc., "Melchizedek does," etc.
[11] See Heb. vii. 1–3.
[12] Who he is, no one knows. Oehler (following the lead of Fabricius on Philaster, cap. 49, p. 102) believes the name to be a mistake for Victor, a bishop of Rome, who (see *Adv. Prax.* c. i.) had held the episcopate when Praxeas was there. His successor was Zephyrinus ; and it is an ingenious conjecture of Oehler, that these two names, the one written as a correction of the other, may have been confused : thus, Victor / Zephyrinus } ; and thus of the two may have made Victorinus.
[13] The form and order of the words here used are certainly remarkably similar to the expressions and order of the "Apostles' Creed."

TERTULLIAN.

PART THIRD.

I.

ON REPENTANCE.[1]

[TRANSLATED BY THE REV. S. THELWALL.]

CHAP. I.—OF HEATHEN REPENTANCE.

REPENTANCE, men understand, so far as nature is able, to be an emotion of the mind arising from disgust[2] at some *previously cherished* worse sentiment: that kind of men *I mean* which even we ourselves were in days gone by—blind, without the Lord's light. From the *reason* of repentance, however, they are just as far as they are from the Author of reason Himself. *Reason*, in fact, is a thing of GOD, inasmuch as there is nothing which God the Maker of all has not provided, disposed, ordained *by reason*—nothing which He has not willed should be handled and understood *by reason.* All, therefore, who are ignorant of God, must necessarily be ignorant also of a thing which is His, because no treasure-house[3] at all is accessible to strangers. And thus, voyaging all the universal course of life without the rudder of reason, they know not how to shun the hurricane which is impending over the world.[4] Moreover, how irrationally they behave in the practice of repentance, it will be enough briefly to show just by this one fact, that they exercise it even in the case of their *good* deeds. They repent of good faith, of love, of simple-heartedness, of patience, of mercy, just in proportion as any deed *prompted by these feelings* has fallen on thankless soil. They execrate their own selves for having done good; and that species chiefly of repentance which is applied to the best works they fix in their heart, making it their care to remember never again to do a good turn. On repentance for *evil* deeds, on the contrary, they lay lighter stress. In short, they make this same (virtue) a means of *sinning* more readily than a means of *right-doing.*

CHAP. II.—TRUE REPENTANCE A THING DIVINE, ORIGINATED BY GOD, AND SUBJECT TO HIS LAWS.

But if they acted as men who had any part in God, and thereby in reason also, they would first weigh well the importance of repentance, and would never apply it in such a way as to make it a ground for *convicting themselves of* perverse self-amendment. In short, they would regulate the limit of their repentance, because they would reach (a limit) in sinning too—by fearing God, I mean. But where there is no fear, in like manner there is no amendment; where there is no amendment, repentance is of necessity vain, for it lacks the fruit for which God sowed it; that is, man's salvation. For God—after so many and so great sins of human temerity, begun by the first of the race, Adam, after the condemnation of man, together with the dowry of the world,[5] after his ejection from paradise and subjection to death—when He had hasted back to His own mercy, did from that time onward inaugurate repentance in His own self, by rescinding the sentence of His first wrath, engaging to grant pardon to His own work and image.[6] And so He gathered together a people for Himself, and fostered them with many liberal distributions of His bounty, and, after so often finding them most ungrateful, ever exhorted them to repentance and sent out the voices of the universal company of the prophets to prophesy. By and by, promising freely the grace which in the last times He was intending to pour as a flood of light on the universal world[7] through His

---

[1] [We pass from the polemical class of our author's writings to those of a practical and ethical character. This treatise on Penitence is the product of our author's best days, and may be dated A. D. 192.]
[2] "Offensa sententiæ pejoris;" or possibly, "the *miscarriage* of some," etc.
[3] Thesaurus.
[4] Sæculo. [Erasmus doubted the genuineness of this treatise, partly because of the comparative purity of its style. See Kaye, p. 42.]

[5] Sæculi dote. With which he had been endowed. Comp. Gen i. 28, Ps. viii. 4-8.
[6] i.e., man.
[7] Orbi.

Spirit, He bade the baptism of repentance lead the way, with the view of first preparing,[1] by means of the sign and seal of repentance, them whom He was calling, through grace, to (inherit) the promise surely made to Abraham. John holds not his peace, saying, " Enter upon repentance, for now shall salvation approach the nations "[2]—the Lord, that is, bringing salvation according to God's promise. To Him John, as His harbinger, directed the repentance (which he preached), whose province was the purging of men's minds, that whatever defilement inveterate error had imparted, whatever contamination in the heart of man ignorance had engendered, *that* repentance should sweep and scrape away, and cast out of doors, and thus prepare the home of the heart, by making it clean, for the Holy Spirit, who was about to supervene, that He might with pleasure introduce Himself thereinto, together with His celestial blessings. Of these blessings the title is *briefly* one—the salvation of man—the abolition of former sins being the preliminary step. This[3] is the (final) cause of repentance, this her work, in taking in hand the business of divine mercy. What is profitable to man does service to God. The *rule* of repentance, however, which we learn when we know the Lord, retains a definite form,—*viz.*, that no violent hands so to speak, be ever laid on *good* deeds or thoughts.[4] For God, never giving His sanction to the reprobation of good *deeds*, inasmuch as they are His own (of which, being the author, He must necessarily be the defender too), is in like manner the acceptor of them, and if the acceptor, likewise the rewarder. Let, then, the ingratitude of men see to it,[5] if it attaches repentance even to good works; let their gratitude see to it too, if the desire of earning it be the incentive to well-doing: earthly and mortal are they each. For how small is your gain if you do good to a grateful man! or your loss if to an ungrateful! A *good* deed has GOD as its debtor, just as an *evil* has too; for a judge is a rewarder of every cause. Well, since, God as Judge presides over the exacting and maintaining[6] of justice, which to Him is most dear; and since it is with an eye to justice that He appoints all the sum of His discipline, is there room for doubting that, just as in all our acts universally, so also in the case of repentance, justice must be rendered to God?—which duty can indeed only be fulfilled on the con-

dition that repentance be brought to bear *only* on *sins*. Further, no deed but an *evil* one deserves to be called *sin*, nor does any one err by well-doing. But if he does not err, why does he invade (the province of) repentance, the private ground of such as do err? Why does he impose on his goodness a duty proper to wickedness? Thus it comes to pass that, when a thing is called into play where it ought not, there, where it ought, it is neglected.

CHAP. III.—SINS MAY BE DIVIDED INTO CORPO-
REAL AND SPIRITUAL. BOTH EQUALLY SUB-
JECT, IF NOT TO HUMAN, YET TO DIVINE IN-
VESTIGATION AND PUNISHMENT.[7]

What things, then, they be for which repentance seems just and due—that is, what things are to be set down under the head of *sin*— the occasion indeed demands that I should note down ; but (to do so) may seem to be unnecessary. For when the Lord is known, our spirit, having been " looked back upon "[8] by its own Author, emerges unbidden into the knowledge of the truth; and being admitted to (an acquaintance with) the divine precepts, is by them forthwith instructed that " that from which God bids us abstain is to be accounted *sin:*" inasmuch as, since it is generally agreed that God is some great *essence* of good, of course nothing but evil would be displeasing to good; in that, between things mutually contrary, friendship there is none. Still it will not be irksome briefly to touch upon the fact[9] that, of sins, some are carnal, that is, corporeal; some spiritual. For since man is composed of this combination of a two-fold substance, the sources of his sins are no other than the sources of his composition. But it is not the fact that body and spirit are two things that constitute the sins mutually different—otherwise they are on this account rather *equal*, because the *two* make up *one*— lest any make the distinction between their *sins* proportionate to the difference between their *substances*, so as to esteem the one lighter, or else heavier, than the other: if it be true, (as it is,) that both flesh and spirit are creatures of God; one wrought by His hand, one consummated by His *afflatus*. Since, then, they equally pertain to the Lord, whichever of them *sins* equally *offends* the Lord. Is it for you to distinguish the acts of the flesh and the spirit, whose communion and conjunction in life, in death, and in resurrection, are

---

[1] Componeret.
[2] Comp. Matt. iii. 1. 2 ; Mark i. 4 ; Luke iii. 4-6.
[3] i.e., man's salvation.
[4] See the latter part of c. i.
[5] Viderit.
[6] Or, " defending."

[7] [Without reference to Luther's theory of justification, we must all adopt this as the test of " a standing or falling church," viz. " How does it deal with sin and the sinner."]
[8] Luke xxii. 61.
[9] Or, " briefly to lay down the rule."

so intimate, that "at that time"[1] they are equally raised up either for life or else for judgment; because, to wit, they have equally either sinned or lived innocently? This we would (once for all) premise, in order that we may understand that no less necessity for repentance is incumbent on *either* part of man, if in anything it have sinned, than on *both*. The *guilt* of both is common; common, too, is the *Judge*—God to wit; common, therefore, is withal the healing medicine of repentance. The source whence sins are named "spiritual" and "corporeal" is the fact that every sin is matter either of *act* or else of *thought:* so that what is in *deed* is "corporeal," because a *deed*, like a *body*, is capable of being *seen* and *touched;* what is in the *mind* is "spiritual," because *spirit* is neither *seen* nor *handled:* by which consideration is shown that sins not of *deed* only, but of *will* too, are to be shunned, and by repentance purged. For if human finitude[2] judges only sins of *deed*, because it is not equal to (piercing) the lurking-places of the *will*, let us not on that account make-light of crimes of the will in God's sight. God is all-sufficient. Nothing from whence any sin whatsoever proceeds is remote from His sight; because He is neither ignorant, nor does He omit to decree it to judgment. He is no dissembler of, nor double-dealer with,[3] His own clear-sightedness. What (shall we say of the fact) that *will* is the *origin* of *deed?* For if any sins are imputed to chance, or to necessity, or to ignorance, let them see to themselves: if these be excepted, there is no sinning save by *will*. Since, then, will is the origin of deed, is it not so much the rather amenable to penalty as it is first in guilt? Nor, if some difficulty interferes with its full accomplishment, is it even in that case exonerated; for it is itself imputed to itself: nor, having done the work which lay in its own power, will it be excusable by reason of that miscarriage of its accomplishment. In fact, how does the Lord demonstrate Himself as adding a superstructure to the Law, except by interdicting sins of the *will* as well (as other sins); while He defines not only the man who had actually invaded another's wedlock to be an adulterer, but likewise him who had contaminated (a woman) by the concupiscence of his gaze?[4] Accordingly it is dangerous enough for the mind to set before itself what it is forbidden to perform, and rashly through the will to perfect its execution. And since the power of this will is such that, even with-

out fully sating its self-gratification, it stands for a deed; as a deed, therefore, it shall be punished. It is utterly vain to say, "I *willed*, but yet I *did* not." Rather you *ought* to carry the thing through, *because* you will; or else not to will, because you do not carry it through. But, by the confession of your consciousness, you pronounce your own condemnation. For if you eagerly desired a *good* thing, you would have been anxious to carry it through; in like manner, as you do not carry an *evil* thing through, you ought not to have eagerly desired it. Wherever you take your stand, you are fast bound by guilt; because you have either *willed* evil, or else have not *fulfilled* good.

CHAP. IV.—REPENTANCE APPLICABLE TO ALL THE KINDS OF SIN. TO BE PRACTISED NOT ONLY, NOR CHIEFLY, FOR THE GOOD IT BRINGS, BUT BECAUSE GOD COMMANDS IT.

To all sins, then, committed whether by flesh or spirit, whether by deed or will, the same *God* who has destined penalty by means of judgment, has withal engaged to grant pardon by means of repentance, saying to the people, "Repent thee, and I will save thee;"[5] and again, "I live, saith the Lord, and I will (have) repentance rather than death."[6] Repentance, then, is "life," since it is preferred to "death." That repentance, O sinner, like myself (nay, rather, less than myself, for pre-eminence in sins I acknowledge to be mine[7]), do you so hasten to, so embrace, as a shipwrecked man the protection[8] of some plank. This will draw you forth when sunk in the waves of sins, and will bear you forward into the port of the divine clemency. Seize the opportunity of unexpected felicity: that you, who sometime were in God's sight nothing but "a drop of a bucket,"[9] and "dust of the threshing-floor,"[10] and "a potter's vessel,"[11] may thenceforward become that "tree which is sown beside[12] the waters, is perennial in leaves, bears fruit at its own time,"[13] and shall not see fire,"[14] nor "axe."[15] Having found "the truth,"[16] repent of errors; repent of having loved what God loves not: even we ourselves do not permit our slave-lads not to hate the things which

---

[1] i.e., in the judgment-day. Compare the phrase "that day and that hour" in Scripture.
[2] Mediocritas.
[3] Prævaricatorem: comp. *ad Ux.* b. ii. c. ii. *ad init.*
[4] Matt. v. 27, 28; comp. *de Idol.* ii.

[5] Comp. Ezek. xviii. 30, 32.
[6] The substance of this is found in Ezek. xxxiii. 11.
[7] Compare 1 Tim. i. 16.
[8] Comp. c. xii. *sub fin.* [Ut naufragus alicuius tabulæ fidem; this expression soon passed into Theological technology, and as "the plank after shipwreck" is universally known.]
[9] Isa. xl. 15.
[10] Dan. ii. 35; Matt. iii. 12.
[11] Ps. ii. 9; Rev. ii. 27.
[12] Penes.
[13] Ps. i. 3; Jer. xvii. 8. Compare Luke xxiii. 31.
[14] Jer. xvii. 8; Matt. iii. 10.
[15] Matt. iii. 10.
[16] John xiv. 6.

are offensive to us; for the principle of voluntary obedience[1] consists in similarity of minds.

To reckon up the good of repentance, the subject-matter is copious, and therefore should be committed to great eloquence. Let us, however, in proportion to our narrow abilities, inculcate one point,— that what God enjoins is good and best. I hold it audacity to dispute about the "good" of a divine precept; for, indeed, it is not the fact that it is good which binds us to obey, but the fact that God has enjoined it. To exact the rendering of obedience the majesty of divine power has the prior[2] right; the authority of Him who commands is prior to the utility of him who serves. "Is it good to repent, or no?" Why do you ponder? God enjoins; nay, He not merely enjoins, but likewise exhorts. He invites by (offering) reward—salvation, to wit; even by an oath, saying "I live,"[3] He desires that credence may be given Him. Oh blessed we, for whose sake God swears! Oh most miserable, if we believe not the Lord even when He swears! What, therefore, God so highly commends, what He even (after human fashion) attests on oath, we are bound of course to approach, and to guard with the utmost seriousness; that, abiding permanently in (the faith of) the solemn pledge[4] of divine grace, we may be able also to persevere in like manner in its fruit[5] and its benefit.

CHAP. V.—SIN NEVER TO BE RETURNED TO AFTER REPENTANCE.[6]

For what I say is this, that the repentance which, being shown us and commanded us through God's grace, recalls us to grace[7] with the Lord, when once learned and undertaken by us ought never afterward to be cancelled by repetition of sin. No pretext of ignorance now remains to plead on your behalf; in that, after acknowledging the Lord, and accepting His precepts[8]—in short, after engaging in repentance of (past) sins—you again betake yourself to sins. Thus, in as far as you are removed from ignorance, in so far are you cemented[9] to contumacy. For if the ground on which you had repented of having sinned was

---

[1] Obsequii.
[2] Or, "paramount."
[3] See ref. 1 on the preceding page. The phrase is "As I live" in the English version.
[4] "Asseveratione:" apparently a play on the word, as compared with "perseverare," which follows.
[5] Or, "enjoyment."
[6] [The formidable doctrine of 1. John iii. 9, v. 18, etc. must excuse our author for his severe adherence to this principle of purifying the heart from habitual sin. But, the church refused to press it against St. Matt. xviii. 22. In our own self-indulgent day, we are more prone, I fear, to presumption than to over strictness. The Roman casuists make *attrition* suffice, and so turn absolution into a mere sponge, and an encouragement to perpetual sinning and formal confession.]
[7] i.e., favour.
[8] Which is solemnly done in baptism.   [9] Adglutinaris.

that you had begun to fear the Lord, why have you preferred to rescind what you did for fear's sake, except because you have ceased to fear? For there is no other thing but contumacy which subverts fear. Since there is no exception which defends from liability to penalty even such as are ignorant of the Lord—because ignorance of God, openly as He is set before men, and comprehensible as He is even on the score of His heavenly benefits, is not possible[10]—how perilous is it for Him to be despised when known? Now, that man does despise Him, who, after attaining by His help to an understanding of things good and evil, offers an affront to his own understanding—that is, to God's gift—by resuming what he understands ought to be shunned, and what he has already shunned: he rejects the Giver in abandoning the gift; he denies the Benefactor in not honouring the benefit. How can he be pleasing to Him, whose gift is displeasing to himself? Thus he is shown to be not only contumacious toward the Lord, but likewise ungrateful. Besides, that man commits no light sin against the Lord, who, after he had by repentance renounced His rival the devil, and had under this appellation subjected him to the Lord, again upraises him by his own return (to the enemy), and makes himself a ground of exultation to him; so that the Evil One, with his prey recovered, rejoices anew against the Lord. Does he not—what is perilous even to say, but must be put forward with a view to edification—place the devil before the Lord? For he seems to have made the comparison who has known each; and to have judicially pronounced him to be the better whose (servant) he has preferred again to be. Thus he who, through repentance for sins, had begun to make satisfaction to the Lord, will, through another repentance of his repentance, make satisfaction to the devil, and will be the more hateful to God in proportion as he will be the more acceptable to His rival. But some say that "God is satisfied if He be looked up to with the heart and the mind, even if this be not done in *outward* act, and that thus they sin without damage to their fear and their faith:" that is, that they violate wedlock without damage to their chastity; they mingle poison for their parent without damage to their filial duty! Thus, then, they will themselves withal be thrust down into hell without damage to their pardon, while they sin without damage to their fear! Here is a primary example of perversity: they sin, because they fear![11] I suppose, if they feared

---

[10] Acts xiv. 15-17: "licet" here may = "lawful," "permissible," "excusable."
[11] "Timent," not "metuunt." "Metus" is the word Tertullian has been using above for religious, reverential fear.

not, they would not sin! Let him, therefore, who would not have God offended not revere Him at all, if fear[1] is the plea for offending! But these dispositions have been wont to sprout from the seed of hypocrites, whose friendship with the devil is indivisible, whose repentance never faithful.

CHAP. VI.—BAPTISM NOT TO BE PRESUMPTUOUSLY RECEIVED. IT REQUIRES PRECEDING REPENTANCE, MANIFESTED BY AMENDMENT OF LIFE.

Whatever, then, our poor ability has attempted to suggest with reference to laying hold of repentance once for all, and perpetually retaining it, does indeed bear upon *all* who are given up to the Lord, as being all competitors for salvation in earning the favour of God; but is chiefly urgent in the case of those young novices who are only just beginning to bedew[2] their ears with divine discourses, and who, as whelps in yet early infancy, and with eyes not yet perfect, creep about uncertainly, and say indeed that they renounce their former deed, and assume (the profession of) repentance, but neglect to complete it.[3] For the very end of desiring importunes them to desire somewhat of their former *deeds;* just as fruits, when they are already beginning to turn into the sourness or bitterness of age, do yet still in some part flatter[4] their own loveliness. Moreover, a presumptuous confidence in baptism introduces all kind of vicious delay and tergiversation with regard to repentance; for, feeling sure of undoubted pardon of their sins, *men* meanwhile steal the intervening time, and make it for themselves into a holiday-time[5] for sinning, rather than a time for learning not to sin. Further, how inconsistent is it to expect pardon of sins (to be granted) to a repentance which they have not fulfilled! This is to hold out your hand for merchandise, but not produce the price. For repentance is the price at which the Lord has determined to award pardon: He proposes the redemption[6] of release from penalty at this compensating exchange of repentance. If, then, sellers first examine the coin with which they make their bargains, to see whether it be cut, or scraped, or adulterated,[7] we believe likewise that the Lord, when about to make us the grant of so costly merchandise, even of eternal life, first institutes a probation of our repentance. "But meanwhile let us defer

the reality of our repentance: it will then, I suppose, be clear that we are amended when we are absolved."[8] By no means; (but our amendment should be manifested) while, pardon being in abeyance, there is still a prospect of penalty; while *the penitent* does not yet merit—so far as merit we can—his liberation; while God is threatening, not while He is forgiving. For what slave, after his position has been changed by reception of freedom, charges himself with his (past) thefts and desertions? What soldier, after his discharge, makes satisfaction for his (former) brands? A sinner is bound to bemoan himself *before* receiving pardon, because the time of repentance is coincident with that of peril and of fear. Not that I deny that the divine benefit—the putting away of sins, I mean—is in every way sure to such as are on the point of entering the (baptismal) water; but what we have to labour for is, that it may be granted us to attain that blessing. For who will grant to you, a man of so faithless repentance, one single sprinkling of any water whatever? To approach it by stealth, indeed, and to get the minister appointed over this business misled by your asseverations, is easy; but God takes foresight for His own treasure, and suffers not the unworthy to steal a march upon it. What, in fact, does He say? "Nothing hid which shall not be revealed."[9] Draw whatever (veil of) darkness you please over your deeds, "God is light."[10] But some think as if God were under a *necessity* of bestowing even on the unworthy, what He has engaged (to give); and they turn His liberality into slavery. But if it is of *necessity* that God grants us the symbol of death,[11] then He does so *unwillingly*. But who permits a gift to be permanently retained which he has granted unwillingly? For do not many afterward fall out of (grace)? is not this gift taken away from many? These, no doubt, are they who do steal a march upon (the treasure), who, after approaching to the faith of repentance, set up on the sands a house doomed to ruin. Let no one, then, flatter himself on the ground of being assigned to the "recruit-classes" of learners, as if on that account he have a licence even now to sin. As soon as you "know the Lord,"[12] you should fear Him; as soon as you have gazed on Him, you should reverence Him. But what difference does *your* "knowing" Him make, while you rest in the same practises as in days bygone, when you knew Him *not?* What, moreover, is it

---

[1] Timor.
[2] Deut. xxxii. 2.
[3] i.e., by baptism.
[4] Adulantur.
[5] "Commeatus," a military word = "furlough," hence "holiday-time."
[6] i.e., repurchase.
[7] Adulter; see *de Idol.* c. i.

[8] i.e., in baptism
[9] Luke viii. 17.
[10] 1 John i. 5.
[11] Symbolum mortis indulget. Comp. Rom. vi. 3, 4, 8; Col. ii. 12, 20.
[12] Jer. xxxi. (LXX. xxxviii.) 34; Heb. viii. 11.

which distinguishes you from a perfected[1] servant of God? Is there one Christ for the baptized, another for the learners? Have they some different hope or reward? some different dread of judgment? some different necessity for repentance? That *baptismal* washing is a sealing of faith, which faith is begun and is commended by the faith of repentance. We are not washed *in order that* we *may* cease sinning, but *because we have* ceased, since in *heart* we have *been* bathed[2] already. For the *first* baptism of a learner is *this*, a perfect fear;[3] thenceforward, in so far as you have understanding of the Lord, faith *is* sound, the conscience having once for all embraced repentance. Otherwise, if it is (only) after the *baptismal* waters that we cease sinning, it is of *necessity*, not of *free-will*, that we put on innocence. Who, then, is preeminent in goodness? he who is not *allowed*, or he whom *it displeases*, to be evil? he who is *bidden*, or he whose *pleasure it is*, to be free from crime? Let us, then, neither keep our hands from theft unless the hardness of bars withstand us, nor refrain our eyes from the concupiscence of fornication unless we be withdrawn by guardians of our persons, if no one who has surrendered himself to the Lord is to cease sinning unless he be bound thereto by baptism. But if any entertain this sentiment, I know not whether he, after baptism, do not feel more sadness to think that he has *ceased* from sinning, than gladness that he hath *escaped* from it. And so it is becoming that learners *desire* baptism, but do not hastily *receive* it: for he who desires it, honours it; he who hastily receives it, disdains it: in the one appears modesty, in the other arrogance; the former satisfies, the latter neglects it; the former covets to merit it, but the latter promises it to himself as a due return; the former takes, the latter usurps it. Whom would you judge worthier, except one who is more amended? whom more amended, except one who is more timid, and on that account has fulfilled the duty of true repentance? for he has feared to continue still in sin, lest he should not merit the reception *of baptism*. But the hasty receiver, inasmuch as he promised it himself (as his due), being forsooth secure (of obtaining it), *could* not fear: thus he fulfilled not repentance either, because he lacked the instrumental agent of repentance, that is, fear.[4] Hasty reception is the portion of irreverence; it inflates the seeker, it despises the Giver. And thus it sometimes deceives,[5] for it promises

to itself *the gift* before it be due; whereby He who is to furnish *the gift* is ever offended.

CHAP. VII.—OF REPENTANCE, IN THE CASE OF SUCH AS HAVE LAPSED AFTER BAPTISM.

So long, Lord Christ, may the blessing of learning or hearing concerning the discipline of repentance be granted to Thy servants, as is likewise behoves them, while *learners*,[6] not to sin; in other words, may they thereafter know nothing of repentance, *and* require nothing of it. It is irksome to append mention of a *second*—nay, in that case, the *last*—hope;[7] lest, by treating of a remedial repenting yet in reserve, we seem to be pointing to a yet further space for sinning. Far be it that any one so interpret our meaning, as if, because there is an opening for repenting, there were even now, on that account, an opening for sinning; and *as if* the redundance of celestial clemency constituted a licence for human temerity. Let no one be less good because God is more so, by repeating his sin as often as he is forgiven. Otherwise be sure he will find an end of *escaping*, when he shall not find one of *sinning*. We have escaped *once*: thus far *and no farther* let us commit ourselves to perils, even if we seem likely to escape a second time.[8] Men in general, after escaping shipwreck, thenceforward declare divorce with ship and sea; and by *cherishing* the memory of the danger, honour the benefit conferred by God,—their deliverance, namely. I praise their fear, I love their reverence; they are unwilling a second time to be a burden to the divine mercy; they fear to seem to trample on *the benefit* which they have attained; they shun, with a solicitude which at all events is good, to make trial a second time of that which they have once learned to fear. Thus the limit of their temerity is the evidence of their fear. Moreover, man's fear[9] is an honour to God. But however, that most stubborn foe (of ours) never gives his malice leisure; indeed, he is then most savage when he fully feels that a man is freed *from his clutches;* he then flames fiercest while he is fast becoming extinguished. Grieve and groan he must of necessity over the fact that, by the grant of pardon, so many works of death[10] in man have been overthrown, so many marks of the condemnation which for-

---

[1] i.e., in baptism.
[2] See John xiii. 10 and Matt. xxiii. 26.
[3] Metus integer.
[4] Metus.
[5] Or, "disappoints," i.e., the hasty recipient himself.
[6] i.e., *before* baptism.
[7] [Elucidation I. See *infra*, this chapter, *sub fine*.]
[8] [When our author wrote to the Martyrs, (see cap. 1.) he was less disposed to such remorseless discipline : and perhaps we have here an element of his subsequent system, one which led him to accept the discipline of Montanism. On this general subject, we shall find enough when we come to Cyprian and Novatian.]
[9] Timor.
[10] "Mortis opera," or "deadly works:" cf. *de Idol.* c. iv. (mid.), "perdition of blood," and the note there.

merly was his own erased. He grieves that that sinner, (now) Christ's servant, is destined to judge him and his angels.[1] And so he observes, assaults, besieges him, in the hope that he may be able in some way either to strike his eyes with carnal concupiscence, or else to entangle his mind with worldly enticements, or else to subvert his faith by fear of earthly power, or else to wrest him from the sure way by perverse traditions: he is never deficient in stumbling-blocks nor in temptations. These poisons of his, therefore, God foreseeing, although the gate of forgiveness has been shut and fastened up with the bar of baptism, has permitted it still to stand somewhat open.[2] In the vestibule He has stationed the second repentance for opening to such as knock: but now once for all, because now for the second time;[3] but never more because the last time it had been in vain. For is not even this once enough? You have what you now deserved not, for you had lost what you had received. If the Lord's indulgence grants you the means of restoring what you had lost, be thankful for the benefit renewed, not to say amplified; for restoring is a greater thing than giving, inasmuch as having lost is more miserable than never having received at all. However, if any do incur the debt of a second repentance, his spirit is not to be forthwith cut down and undermined by despair. Let it by all means be irksome to sin again, but let not to repent again be irksome: irksome to imperil one's self again, but not to be again set free. Let none be ashamed. Repeated sickness must have repeated medicine. You will show your gratitude to the Lord by not refusing what the Lord offers you. You have offended, but can still be reconciled. You have One whom you may satisfy, and Him willing.[4]

CHAP. VIII.—EXAMPLES FROM SCRIPTURE TO PROVE THE LORD'S WILLINGNESS TO PARDON.

This if you doubt, unravel[5] the meaning of "what the Spirit saith to the churches."[6] He imputes to the Ephesians "forsaken love;"[7] reproaches the Thyatirenes with "fornication," and "eating of things sacrificed to idols;"[8] accuses the Sardians of "works not full;"[9] censures the Pergamenes for teaching perverse things;[10] upbraids the Laodiceans for trusting to their riches;[11] and

yet gives them all general monitions to repentance—under comminations, it is true; but He would not utter comminations to one unrepentant if He did not forgive the repentant. The matter were doubtful if He had not withal elsewhere demonstrated this profusion of His clemency. Saith He not,[12] "He who hath fallen shall rise again, and he who hath been averted shall be converted?" He it is, indeed, who "would have mercy rather than sacrifices."[13] The heavens, and the angels who are there, are glad at a man's repentance.[14] Ho! you sinner, be of good cheer! you see where it is that there is joy at your return. What meaning for us have those themes of the Lord's parables? Is not the fact that a woman has lost a drachma, and seeks it and finds it, and invites her female friends to share her joy, an example of a restored sinner?[15] There strays, withal, one little ewe of the shepherd's; but the flock was not more dear than the one: that one is earnestly sought; the one is longed for instead of all; and at length she is found, and is borne back on the shoulders of the shepherd himself; for much had she toiled[16] in straying.[17] That most gentle father, likewise, I will not pass over in silence, who calls his prodigal son home, and willingly receives him repentant after his indigence, slays his best fatted calf, and graces his joy with a banquet.[18] Why not? He had found the son whom he had lost; he had felt him to be all the dearer of whom he had made a gain. Who is that father to be understood by us to be? God, surely: no one is so truly a Father; no one so rich in paternal love. He, then, will receive you, His own son,[20] back, even if you have squandered what you had received from Him, even if you return naked—just because you have returned; and will joy more over your return than over the sobriety of the other;[21] but only if you heartily repent—if you compare your own hunger with the plenty of your Father's "hired servants"—if you leave behind you the swine, that unclean herd—if you again seek your Father, offended though He be, saying, "I have sinned, nor am worthy any longer to be called Thine." Confession of sins lightens, as much as dissimulation aggravates them; for confession is counselled by

---

[1] 1 Cor. vi. 3.
[2] Or, "has permitted somewhat still to stand open."
[3] [See cap. vii. supra.]
[4] To accept the satisfaction.
[5] Evolve: perhaps simply = "read."
[6] Rev. ii. 7, 11, 17, 29, iii. 6, 13, 21.
[7] Rev. ii. 4.
[8] Rev. ii. 20.
[9] Rev. iii. 2.
[10] Rev. ii. 14, 15.
[11] Rev. iii. 17.

[12] Jer. viii. 4 (in LXX.) appears to be the passage meant. The Eng. Ver. is very different.
[13] Hos. vi. 6; Matt. ix. 13. The words in Hosea in the LXX. are, διότι ἔλεος θέλω ἤ θυσίαν (al. καὶ οὐ θυσίαν).
[14] Luke xv. 7, 10.
[15] Luke xv. 8–10.
[16] Or, "suffered."
[17] Luke xv. 3–7.
[18] Luke xv. 11–32.
[19] Cf. Matt. xxiii. 9; and Eph. iii. 14, 15, in the Greek.
[20] Publicly enrolled as such in baptism; for Tertullian here is speaking solely of the "second repentance."
[21] See Luke xv. 29–32.

(a desire to make) satisfaction, dissimulation by contumacy.

The narrower, then, the sphere of action of this second and only (remaining) repentance, the more laborious is its probation; in order that it may not be exhibited in the conscience alone, but may likewise be carried out in some (external) act. This act, which is more usually expressed and commonly spoken of under a Greek name, is ἐξομολόγησις,[1] whereby we confess our sins to the Lord, not indeed as if He were ignorant of them, but inasmuch as by confession satisfaction is settled,[2] of confession repentance is born; by repentance God is appeased. And thus *exomologesis* is a discipline for man's prostration and humiliation, enjoining a demeanor calculated to move mercy. With regard also to the very dress and food, it commands (the penitent) to lie in sackcloth and ashes, to cover his body in mourning,[3] to lay his spirit low in sorrows, to exchange for severe treatment the sins which he has committed; moreover, to know no food and drink but such as is plain,—not for the stomach's sake, to wit, but the soul's; for the most part, however, to feed prayers on fastings, to groan, to weep and make outcries[4] unto the Lord your[5] God; to bow before the feet of the presbyters, and kneel to God's dear ones; to enjoin on all the brethren to be ambassadors to bear his[6] deprecatory supplication (before God). All this *exomologesis* (does), that it may enhance repentance; may honour God by its fear of the (incurred) danger; may, by itself pronouncing against the sinner, stand in the stead of God's indignation, and by temporal mortification (I will not say frustrate, but) expunge eternal punishments. Therefore, while it abases the man, it raises him; while it covers him with squalor, it renders him more clean; while it *ac*cuses, it *ex*cuses; while it condemns, it absolves. The less quarter you give yourself, the more (believe me) will God give you.

Yet most men either shun this work, as being a public exposure[7] of themselves, or else defer it from day to day. I presume (as being) more mindful of modesty than of salvation; just like men who, having contracted some malady in the more private parts of the body, avoid the privity of physicians, and so perish with their own bashfulness. It is intolerable, forsooth, to modesty to make satisfaction to the offended Lord! to be restored to its forfeited[8] salvation! Truly you are honourable in your modesty; bearing an open forehead for sinning, but an abashed one for deprecating! I give no place to bashfulness when I am a gainer by its loss; when itself in some sort exhorts the man, saying, "Respect not me; it is better that I perish through[9] you, *i. e. than you through me.*" At all events, the time when (if ever) its danger is serious, is when it is a butt for jeering speech in the presence of insulters, where one man raises himself on his neighbour's ruin, where there is upward clambering over the prostrate. But among brethren and fellow-servants, where there is common hope, fear,[10] joy, grief, suffering, because there is a common Spirit from a common Lord and Father, why do you think these *brothers* to be anything other than yourself? Why flee from the partners of your own mischances, as from such as will derisively cheer them? The body cannot feel gladness at the trouble of any one member,[11] it must necessarily join with one consent in the grief, and in labouring for the remedy. In a company of two[12] is the church;[13] but the church is Christ.[14] When, then, you cast yourself at the brethren's knees, you are handling *Christ*, you are entreating *Christ*. In like manner, when they shed tears over you, it is *Christ* who suffers, *Christ* who prays the Father for mercy. What a son[15] asks is ever easily obtained. Grand indeed is the reward of modesty, which the concealment of our fault promises us! to wit, if we do hide somewhat from the knowledge of man, shall we equally conceal it from God? Are the judgment of men and the knowledge of God so put upon a par? Is it better to be damned in secret than absolved in public? *But you say*, "It is a miserable thing thus to come to *exomologesis:*" yes, for evil does bring to misery; but where repentance is to be made, the misery ceases, because it is turned into something

---

[1] Utter confession.
[2] For the meaning of "satisfaction," see Hooker *Eccl. Pol.* vi. 5, where several references to the present treatise occur. [Elucidation II.]
[3] Sordibus.
[4] Cf. Ps. xxii. 1 (in LXX. xxii. 3), xxxviii. 8 (in the LXX. xxxvii. 9). Cf. Heb. v. 7.
[5] Tertullian changes here to the second person, unless Oehler's "tuum" be a misprint for "suum."

[6] "Suæ," which looks as if the "tuum" above should be "suum." [St. James, v. 16.]
[7] [Elucidation III.]
[8] Prodactæ.
[9] Per. But "per," according to Oehler, is used by Tertullian as = "propter"—on your account, for your sake.
[10] Metus.
[11] 1 Cor. xii. 26.
[12] In uno et altero.
[13] See Matt. xviii. 20.
[14] i.e. as being His body.
[15] Or, "the Son." Comp. John xi. 41, 42.

salutary. Miserable it is to be cut, and cauterized, and racked with the pungency of some (medicinal) powder: still, the things which heal by unpleasant means do, by the benefit of the cure, excuse their own offensiveness, and make present injury bearable for the sake[1] of the advantage to supervene.

CHAP. XI.—FURTHER STRICTURES ON THE SAME SUBJECT.

What if, besides the shame which they make the most account of, *men* dread likewise the bodily inconveniences; in that, unwashen, sordidly attired, estranged from gladness, they must spend their time in the roughness of sackcloth, and the horridness of ashes, and the sunkenness of face caused by fasting? Is it then becoming for us to supplicate for our sins in scarlet and purple? Hasten hither with the pin for parting the hair, and the powder for polishing the teeth, and some forked implement of steel or brass for cleaning the nails. Whatever of false brilliance, whatever of feigned redness, *is to be had*, let him diligently apply it to his lips or cheeks. Let him furthermore seek out baths of more genial temperature in some gardened or seaside retreat; let him enlarge his expenses; let him carefully seek the rarest delicacy of fatted fowls; let him refine his old wine: and when any shall ask him, "On whom are you lavishing all this?" let him say, "I have sinned against God, and am in peril of eternally perishing: and so now I am drooping, and wasting and torturing myself, that I may reconcile God to myself, whom by sinning I have offended." Why, they who go about canvassing for the obtaining of civil office, feel it neither degrading nor irksome to struggle, in behalf of such their desires, with annoyances to soul and body; and not annoyances merely, but likewise contumelies of all kinds. What meannesses of dress do they not affect? what houses do they not beset with early and late visits?—bowing whenever they meet any high personage, frequenting no banquets, associating in no entertainments, but voluntarily exiled from the felicity of freedom and festivity: and all that for the sake of the fleeting joy of a single year! Do *we* hesitate, when eternity is at stake, to endure what the competitor for consulship or prætorship puts up with?[2] and shall we be tardy in offering to the offended Lord a self-chastisement in food and raiment, which[3] Gentiles lay upon themselves when they have offended no one at all? Such are they of whom Scripture

makes mention: "Woe to them who bind their own sins as it were with a long rope."[4]

CHAP. XII.—FINAL CONSIDERATIONS TO INDUCE TO EXOMOLOGESIS.

If you shrink back from *exomologesis*, consider in your heart the hell,[5] which *exomologesis* will extinguish for you; and imagine first the magnitude of the penalty, that you may not hesitate about the adoption of the remedy. What do we esteem that treasure-house of eternal fire to be, when small vent-holes[6] of it rouse such blasts of flames that neighbouring cities either are already no more, or are in daily expectation of the same fate? The haughtiest[7] mountains start asunder in the birth-throes of their inly-gendered fire; and—which proves to us the *perpetuity* of the judgment—though they start asunder, though they be devoured, yet come they never to an end. Who will not account these occasional punishments inflicted on the mountains as examples of the judgment which menaces the impenitent? Who will not agree that such sparks are but some few missiles and sportive darts of some inestimably vast centre of fire? Therefore, since you know that after the first bulwarks of the Lord's baptism[8] there still remains for you, in *exomologesis* a second reserve of aid against hell, why do you desert your own salvation? Why are you tardy to approach what you know heals you? Even dumb irrational animals recognise in their time of need the medicines which have been divinely assigned them. The stag, transfixed by the arrow, knows that, to force out the steel, and its inextricable lingerings, he must heal himself with dittany. The swallow, if she blinds her young, knows how to give them eyes again by means of her own swallowwort.[9] Shall the sinner, knowing that *exomologesis* has been instituted by the Lord for his restoration, pass that by which restored the Babylonian king[10] to his realms? Long time had he offered to the Lord his repentance, working out his *exomologesis* by a seven years' squalor, with his nails wildly growing after the eagle's fashion, and his unkempt hair wearing the shagginess of a lion. Hard handling! Him whom men were shuddering at, God was receiving back. But, on the other hand, the Egyptian emperor—who, after pur-

---

[1] Or, "by the grace."
[2] Quod securium virgarumque petitio sustinet.
[3] "Quae," neut. pl.

[4] Isa. v. 18 (comp. the LXX.).
[5] Gehennam. Comp. *ad Ux.* ii. c. vi. *ad fin.*
[6] Fumariola, i. e. the craters of volcanoes.
[7] Superbissimi: perhaps a play on the word, which is connected with "super" and "superus," as "haughty" with "high."
[8] For Tertullian's distinction between "the Lord's baptism" and "John's" see *de Bapt.* x.
[9] Or "celandine," which is perhaps only another form of "chelidonia" ("*Chelidonia major*," Linn.).
[10] Dan. iv. 25 sqq. See *de Pa.* xiii.

suing the once afflicted people of God, long denied to their Lord, rushed into the battle[1] —did, after so many warning plagues, perish in the parted sea, (which was permitted to be passable to " the People " alone,) by the backward roll of the waves:[2] for repentance and her handmaid[3] *exomologesis* he had cast away.

Why should I add more touching these two planks[4] (as it were) of human salvation, caring more for the business of the pen[5] than the duty of my conscience? For, sinner as I am of every dye,[6] and born for nothing save repentance, I cannot easily be silent about that concerning which also the very head and fount of the human race, and of human offence, Adam, restored by *exomologesis* to his own paradise,[7] is not silent.

---

[1] Proelium.
[2] Ex. xiv. 15-31.
[3] " Ministerium," the abstract for the concrete : so " servitia " = slaves.
[4] See c. iv. [*Tabula* was the word in cap. iv. but here it becomes *planca*, and *planca post naufragium* is the theological formula, ever since, among Western theologians.]

[5] See *de Bapt.* xii. *sub init.*
[6] Lit. " of all *brands*." Comp. c. vi.: " Does the soldier . . . make satisfaction for his *brands*."
[7] Cf. Gen. iii. 24 with Luke xxiii. 43, 2 Cor. xii. 4, aud Rev. ii. 7. [Elucidation IV.]

ELUCIDATIONS.

I.

(Such as have lapsed, cap. vii., p. 660.)

The pentitential system of the Primitive days, referred to in our author, began to be changed when less public confessions were authorized, on account of the scandals which publicity generated. Changes were as follows:

1. A grave presbyter was appointed to receive and examine voluntary penitents as the Penitentiary of a diocese, and to suspend or reconcile them with due solemnities—*circa* A.D. 250.

2. This plan also became encumbered with difficulties and was abolished in the East, *circa* A. D. 400.

3. A discipline similar to that of the Anglican Church (which is but loosely maintained therein) succeeded, under St. Chrysostom; who frequently maintains the sufficiency of confession according to St. Matt. vi. 6. A Gallican author[1] says—" this is the period regarded by historians as the most brilliant in Church history. At the close of the fourth century, in the great churches of the Orient, *sixty thousand Christians* received the Eucharistic communion, in one day, *in both kinds*, with no other than their private confessions to Almighty God. The scandalous evil-liver alone was repelled from the Eucharistic Table." This continued till *circa* A.D. 700.

4. Particular, but voluntary confessions were now made in the East and West, but with widely various acceptance under local systems of discipline. The absolutions were *precatory:* "may God absolve Thee." This lasted, even in the West, till the compulsory system of the Lateran Council, A.D. 1215.

5. Since this date, so far as the West is concerned, the whole system of corrupt casuistry and enforced confession adopted in the West has utterly destroyed the Primitive doctrine and discipline as to sin and its remedy wherever it prevails. In the East, private confession exists in a system wholly different and one which maintains the Primitive Theology and the Scriptural principle. (1) It is voluntary; (2) it is free from the corrupt system of the casuists; (3) it distinguishes between Ecclesiastical Absolution and that of Him who alone "seeth in secret;" (4) it admits no compromise with *attrition*, but exacts the contrite heart

---

[1] Le Confesseur, par L'Abbé * * * p. 15, Brussels 1866.

and the firm resolve to go and sin no more, and (5) finally, it employs a most guarded and Evangelical formula of remission, of which see Elucidation IV.

II.

(The last hope, cap. vii. p. 662.)

How absolutely the Lateran Council has overthrown the Primitive discipline is here made manifest. The spirit of the latter is expressed by our author in language which almost prompts to despair. It makes sin "exceeding sinful" and even Ecclesiastical forgiveness the reverse of easy. The Lateran System of enforced Confession makes sin easy and restoration to a sinless state equally so: a perpetual resort to the confessor being the only condition for evil living, and a chronic state of pardon and peace. But, let the Greek Church be heard in this matter, rather than an Anglican Catholic. I refer to Macarius, Bishop of Vinnitza and Rector of the Theological Academy of St. Petersburg, as follows: [1] "It is requisite (for the effective reception of Absolution) at least according to the teaching of the Orthodox Church of the Orient, that the following conditions be observed: (1) Contrition for sins, is in the very nature of Penitence, indispensable; (2), consequently, there must be a firm resolution to reform the life; (3) also, faith in Christ and hope in his mercy, with (4) auricular confession before the priest." He allows that this latter condition was not *primitive*, but was a *maternal concession* to penitents of later date: this, however, is voluntary, and of a widely different form from that of the Latin, as will appear below in Elucidation IV.

Now, he contrasts with this the system of Rome, and condemns it, on overwhelming considerations. 1. It makes penances compensations [2] or "satisfaction," offered for sins to divine Justice, this (he says) "is in contradiction with the Christian doctrine of justification, the Scripture teaching one full and entire satisfaction for the sins of the whole human race, once for all presented by our Lord Jesus Christ. This doctrine is equally in conflict with the entire teaching of the Primitive Church."

2. It introduces a false system of *indulgences*, as the consequence of its false premisses.

3. He demonstrates the insufficiency of *attrition*, which respects the fear of punishment, and not sin itself. But the Council of Trent affirms the sufficiency of *attrition*, and permits the confessor to absolve the attrite. Needless to say, the masses accept this wide gate and broad way to salvation rather than the strait gate and narrow way of hating sin and reforming the life, in obedience to the Gospel.

III.

(Among brethren, cap. x., p. 662.)

A controversial writer has lately complained that Bp. Kaye speaks of the *public confession* treated of by our author in this work, and adds—"Tertullian nowhere used the word *public*." The answer is that he speaks of the discipline of *Exomologesis*, which was, in its own nature, as public as preaching. A Gallican writer, less inclined to Jesuitism in the use of words, says frankly: "When one studies this question, with the documents before his eyes, it is impossible not to confess that the Primitive discipline of the Church exhibits not a vestige of the auricular confession afterwards introduced." See Irenæus, *Adv. Hæres.* Vol. I. p. 335, this Series. The Lii. of the canons called Apostolical, reflects a very simple view of the matter, in these words: "If any Bishop or Presbyter will not receive one who *turns from* his sins, but casts him out, let him be deposed: for he grieves Christ, who said, There shall be joy in heaven over one sinner that repenteth." The ascetic spirit of our author seems at war with that of this Canon.

---

[1] *Theol. Dogmat. Orthodoxe*, pp. 529–541, etc.   [2] *Conc. Trident.* Sess. xiv. cap. 8.

IV.

(Exomologesis, cap. xii., p. 663.)

To this day, in the Oriental Churches, the examination of the presbyter who hears the voluntary confession of penitents, is often very primitive in its forms and confined to general inquiries under the Decalogue. The Casuistry of (Dens and Liguori) the Western *Schemata Practica* has not defiled our Eastern brethren to any great extent.

In the office [1] ('Ακολουθία τῶν ἐξομολουγουμένων) we have a simple and beautiful form of prayer and supplication in which the following is the formula of Absolution: " My Spiritual child, who hast confessed to my humility, I, unworthy and a sinner, *have not the power to forgive sins on Earth;* God only can: and through that Divine voice which came to the Apostles, after the Resurrection of our Lord Jesus Christ, saying—' Whosesoever sins, etc.,' we, therein confiding, say—Whatsoever thou hast confessed to my extreme humility, and whatsoever thou hast *omitted to say,* either through ignorance or forgetfulness, *God forgive thee* in this present world and in that which is to come."

The plural (*We* therein confiding) is significant and a token of Primitive doctrine: *i.e.* of confession before the whole Church, (II. Cor. ii. 10.): and note the precatory form—"God forgive thee." The perilous form *Ego te absolvo* is not Catholic: it dates from the thirteenth century and is used in the West only. It is not wholly dropped from the Anglican Office, but has been omitted from the American Prayer-Book.

---

[1] The Great Euchologion, p. 220, Venice, 1851.

II.

ON BAPTISM.

[TRANSLATED BY THE REV. S. THELWALL.]

CHAP. I.—INTRODUCTION.   ORIGIN OF THE TREATISE.

HAPPY is our[1] sacrament of water, in that, by washing away the sins of our early blindness, we are set free *and admitted* into eternal life! A treatise on this matter will not be superfluous; instructing not only such as are just becoming formed (in the faith), but them who, content with having simply believed, without full examination of the grounds[2] of the traditions, carry (in mind), through ignorance, an untried *though* probable faith. The consequence is, that a viper of the Cainite heresy, lately conversant in this quarter, has carried away a great number with her most venomous doctrine, making it her first aim to destroy baptism. Which is quite in accordance with nature; for vipers and asps and basilisks themselves generally do affect arid and waterless places. But we, little fishes, after the example of our ΙΧΘΥΣ[3] Jesus Christ, are born in water, nor have we safety in any other way than by permanently abiding in water; so that most monstrous creature, who had no right to teach even sound doctrine,[4] knew full well how to kill the little fishes, by taking them away from the water!

CHAP. II.—THE VERY SIMPLICITY OF GOD'S MEANS OF WORKING, A STUMBLING-BLOCK TO THE CARNAL MIND.

Well, but how great is the force of perversity for *so* shaking the faith or entirely preventing its reception, that it impugns it on the very principles of which *the faith* consists! There is absolutely nothing which makes men's minds more obdurate than the simplicity of the divine works which are visible in the *act*, when compared with the grandeur which is promised thereto in the *effect;* so that from the very fact, that with so great simplicity, without pomp, without any considerable novelty of preparation, finally, without expense, a man is dipped in water, and amid the utterance of some few words, is sprinkled, and then rises again, not much (or not at all) the cleaner, the consequent attainment of eternity[5] is esteemed the more incredible. I am a deceiver if, on the contrary, it is not from their circumstance, and preparation, and expense, that *idols'* solemnities or mysteries get their credit and authority built up. Oh, miserable incredulity, which quite deniest to God His own properties, simplicity and power! What then? Is it not wonderful, too, that death should be washed away by bathing? But it is the more to be believed if the wonderfulness be the reason why it is *not* believed. For what does it behove divine works to be in their quality, except that they be above all wonder?[6] We also ourselves wonder, but it is *because* we believe. Incredulity, on the other hand, wonders, but does *not* believe: for the simple *acts* it wonders at, as if they were vain; the grand *results*, as if they were impossible. And grant that it be just as you think,[7] sufficient to meet each point is the divine declaration which has forerun: "The foolish things of the world God elected to confound its wisdom;"[8] and, "The things very difficult with men are easy with God."[9] For if God is wise and powerful (which even they who pass Him by do not deny), it is with good reason that He lays the material causes of His own operation in the

---

[1] i. e. Christian (Oehler).
[2] Rationibus.
[3] This curious allusion it is impossible, perhaps, to render in our language. The word ΙΧΘΥΣ (*ikhthus*) in Greek means "a fish;" and it was used as a name for our Lord Jesus, because the initials of the words Ἰησοῦς Χριστὸς Θεοῦ Υἱὸς Σωτήρ (i.e. Jesus Christ the Son of God, the Saviour), make up that word. OEHLER with these remarks, gives abundant references on the point. [Dr. Allix suspects Montanism here, but see Kaye, p. 43, and Lardner, *Credib.* II. p. 335. We may date it *circa* A. D. 193.]
[4] As being a woman. See 1 Tim. ii. 11, 12.

[5] Consecutio æternitatis.
[6] Admirationem.
[7] i.e. that the simple be vain, and the grand impossible.
[8] 1 Cor. i. 27, not quite exactly quoted.
[9] Luke xviii. 27, again inexact.

contraries of wisdom and of power, that is, in foolishness and impossibility; since every virtue receives its cause from those things by which it is called forth.

CHAP. III.—WATER CHOSEN AS A VEHICLE OF DIVINE OPERATION AND WHEREFORE. ITS PROMINENCE FIRST OF ALL IN CREATION.

Mindful of this declaration as of a conclusive prescript, we nevertheless *proceed to* treat *the question,* " How *foolish* and *impossible* it is to be formed anew by water. In what respect, pray, has this material substance merited an office of so high dignity?" The authority, I suppose, of the liquid element has to be examined.[1] This,[2] however, is found in abundance, and that from the very beginning. For *water* is one of those things which, before all the furnishing of the world, were quiescent with God in a yet unshapen[3] state. " In the first beginning," saith *Scripture,* " God made the heaven and the earth. But the earth was invisible, and unorganized,[4] and darkness was over the abyss; and the Spirit of the Lord was hovering[5] over the waters." [6] The first thing, O man, which you have to venerate, is the *age* of the, waters in that their substance is ancient; the second, their *dignity,* in that they were the seat of the Divine Spirit, more pleasing *to Him,* no doubt, than all the other then existing elements. For the darkness was total thus far, shapeless, without the ornament of stars; and the abyss gloomy; and the earth unfurnished; and the heaven unwrought: water[7] alone—always a perfect, gladsome, simple material substance, pure in itself—supplied a worthy vehicle to God. What *of the fact* that waters were in some way the regulating powers by which the disposition of the world thenceforward was constituted by God? For the suspension of the celestial firmament in the midst He caused by "dividing the waters;"[8] the suspension of "the dry land" He accomplished by "separating the waters." After the world had been hereupon set in order through *its* elements, when inhabitants were given it, "the waters" were the first to receive the precept "to bring forth living creatures." [9] Water was the first to produce that which had life, that it might be no wonder in baptism if waters know how to give life.[10] For was not the work of fashioning man himself also

achieved with the aid of waters? Suitable material is found in the *earth,* yet not apt for the purpose unless it be moist and juicy; which (earth) "the waters," separated the fourth day before into their own place, temper with their remaining moisture to a clayey consistency. If, from that time onward, I go forward in recounting universally, or at more length, the evidences of the "authority" of this element which I can adduce to show how great is its power or its grace; how many ingenious devices, how many functions, how useful an instrumentality, it affords the world, I fear I may seem to have collected rather the praises of water than the reasons of baptism; although I should *thereby* teach all the more fully, that it is not to be doubted that God has made the material substance which He has disposed throughout all His products[11] and works, obey Him also in His own peculiar sacraments; that the *material substance* which governs terrestrial life acts as agent likewise in the celestial.

CHAP. IV.—THE PRIMEVAL HOVERING OF THE SPIRIT OF GOD OVER THE WATERS TYPICAL OF BAPTISM. THE UNIVERSAL ELEMENT OF WATER THUS MADE A CHANNEL OF SANCTIFICATION. RESEMBLANCE BETWEEN THE OUTWARD SIGN AND THE INWARD GRACE.

But it will suffice to have *thus* called at the outset those points in which withal is recognised that primary principle of baptism,— which was even then fore-noted by the very attitude *assumed* for a type of baptism,—that the Spirit of God, who hovered over (the waters) from the beginning, would continue to linger over the waters of the baptized.[12] But a holy thing, of course, hovered over a holy; or else, from that which hovered over that which *was* hovered over borrowed a holiness, since it is necessary that in every case an underlying material substance should catch the quality of that which overhangs it, most of all a corporeal of a spiritual, adapted (as the spiritual is) through the subtleness of its substance, both for penetrating and insinuating. Thus the nature of the waters, sanctified by the Holy One, itself conceived withal the power of sanctifying. Let no one say, "Why then, are we, pray, baptized with the very waters which then existed in the first beginning?" Not with those waters, of course, except in so far as the *genus* indeed is one, but the *species* very many. But what is an attribute to the *genus* reappears[13] likewise in the *species.* And accordingly it makes no

---

[1] Compare the Jews' question, Matt. xxi. 23.
[2] Its authority.
[3] Impolita.
[4] Incomposita.
[5] Ferebatur.
[6] Gen. i. 1, 2, and comp. the LXX.
[7] Liquor.
[8] Gen. i. 6, 7, 8.
[9] Animas.
[10] Animare.

[11] Rebus.
[12] Intinctorum.
[13] Redundat.

difference whether a man be washed in a sea or a pool, a stream or a fount, a lake or a trough;[1] nor is there any distinction between those whom John baptized in the Jordan and those whom Peter baptized in the Tiber, unless withal the eunuch whom Philip baptized in the midst of his journeys with chance water, derived (therefrom) more or less of salvation *than others*.[2] All waters, therefore, in virtue of the pristine privilege of their origin, do, after invocation of God, attain the sacramental power of sanctification; for the Spirit immediately supervenes from the heavens, and rests over the waters, sanctifying them from Himself; and being thus sanctified, they imbibe at the same time the power of sanctifying. Albeit the similitude may be admitted to be suitable to the simple act; that, since we are defiled by sins, as it were by dirt, we should be washed from those stains in waters. But as sins do not show themselves in our *flesh* (inasmuch as no one carries on his skin the spot of idolatry, or fornication, or fraud), so persons of that kind are foul in the *spirit*, which is the author of the sin; for the spirit is lord, the flesh servant. Yet they each mutually share the guilt: the spirit, on the ground of command; the flesh, of subservience. Therefore, after the waters have been in a manner endued with medicinal virtue[3] through the intervention of the angel,[4] the spirit is corporeally washed in the waters, and the flesh is in the same spiritually cleansed.

CHAP. V.—USE MADE OF WATER BY THE HEATHEN. TYPE OF THE ANGEL AT THE POOL OF BETHSAIDA.[5]

"Well, but the nations, who are strangers to all understanding of spiritual powers, ascribe to their idols the imbuing of waters with the self-same efficacy." (So they do) but they cheat themselves with waters which are widowed.[6] For washing is the channel through which they are initiated into some sacred rites—of some notorious Isis or Mithras. The gods themselves likewise they honour by washings. Moreover, by carrying water around, and sprinkling it, they everywhere expiate[7] country-seats, houses, temples, and whole cities: at all events, at the Apollinarian and Eleusinian games they are baptized; and they presume that the effect of their doing that is their regeneration and

the remission of the penalties due to their perjuries. Among the ancients, again, whoever had defiled himself with murder, was wont to go in quest of purifying waters. Therefore, if the mere nature of water, in that it is the appropriate material for washing away, leads men to flatter themselves with a belief in omens of purification, how much more truly will waters render that service through the authority of God, by whom all their nature has been constituted! If men think that water is endued with a medicinal virtue by religion, what religion is more effectual than that of the living God? Which fact being acknowledged, we recognise here also the zeal of the devil rivalling the things of God,[8] while we find him, too, practising baptism in his *subjects*. What similarity is there? The unclean cleanses! the ruiner sets free! the damned absolves! He will, forsooth, destroy his own work, by washing away the sins which himself inspires! These (remarks) have been set down by way of testimony against such as reject the faith; if they put no trust in the things of God, the spurious imitations of which, in the case of God's rival, they do trust in. Are there not other cases too, in which, without any sacrament, unclean spirits brood on waters, in spurious imitation of that brooding[9] of the Divine Spirit in the very beginning? Witness all shady founts, and all unfrequented brooks, and the ponds in the baths, and the conduits[10] in *private* houses, or the cisterns and wells which are said to have the property of "spiriting away,"[11] through the power, that is, of a hurtful spirit. Men whom waters have drowned[12] or affected with madness or with fear, they call nymph-caught,[13] or "lymphatic," or "hydrophobic." Why have we adduced these instances? Lest any think it too hard *for belief* that a holy angel of God should grant his presence to waters, to temper them to man's salvation; while the evil angel holds frequent profane commerce with the selfsame element to man's ruin. If it seems a novelty for an angel to be present in waters, an example of what was to come to pass has forerun. An angel, by his intervention, was wont to stir the pool at Bethsaida.[14] They who were complaining of ill-health used to watch for him; for whoever had been the first to descend into them, after his washing, ceased to complain. This figure of corporeal healing sang of a

---

[1] Alveo.
[2] Acts viii. 26–40.
[3] Medicatis.
[4] See c. vi. *ad init.*, and c. v. *ad fin.*
[5] Bethesda, Eng. Ver.
[6] i. e., as Oehler rightly explains, "lacking the Holy Spirit's presence and virtue."
[7] Or, " purify."

[8] [Diabolus Dei Simius.]
[9] Gestationem.
[10] Euripi.
[11] Rapere.
[12] Necaverunt.
[13] "Nympholeptos," restored by Oehler, = νυμφοληπτους.
[14] So Tertullian reads, and some copies, but not the best, of the New Testament in the place referred to, John v. 1–9. [And note Tertullian's textual testimony as to this Scripture.]

spiritual healing, according to the rule by which things carnal are always antecedent [1] as figurative of things spiritual. And thus, when the grace of God advanced to higher degrees among men,[2] an accession *of efficacy* was granted to the waters and to the angel. They who [3] were wont to remedy bodily defects,[4] now heal the spirit; they who used to work temporal salvation,[5] now renew eternal; they who did set free but once in the year, now save peoples in a body [6] daily, death being done away through ablution of sins. The guilt being removed, of course the penalty is removed too. Thus man will be restored for God to His "likeness," who in days bygone had been *conformed* to "the image" of God; (the "image" is counted (to be) in his *form:* the "likeness" in his *eternity:*) for he receives again that Spirit of God which he had then first received from His *afflatus*, but had afterward lost through sin.

CHAP. VI.—THE ANGEL THE FORERUNNER OF THE HOLY SPIRIT. MEANING CONTAINED IN THE BAPTISMAL FORMULA.

Not that *in* [7] the waters we obtain the Holy Spirit; but in the water, under (the witness of) the angel, we are cleansed, and prepared *for* the Holy Spirit. In this case also a type has preceded; for thus was John beforehand the Lord's forerunner, "preparing His ways." [8] Thus, too, does the angel, the witness [9] of baptism, "make the paths straight" [10] for the Holy Spirit, who is about to come upon us, by the washing away of sins, which faith, sealed in (the name of) the Father, and the Son, and the Holy Spirit, obtains. For if "in *the mouth of* three witnesses every word shall stand:" [11]—while, through the benediction, we have the same (three) as witnesses of our faith whom we have as sureties [12] of our salvation too—how much more does the number of the divine names suffice for the assurance of our hope likewise ! Moreover, after the pledging both of the attestation of faith and the promise [13] of salvation under "three witnesses," there is added, of necessity, mention of the Church; [14] inasmuch as, wherever there are three, (that is, the Father,

the Son, and the Holy Spirit,) there is the Church, which is a body of three.[15]

CHAP. VII.—OF THE UNCTION.

After this, when we have issued from the font, [16] we are thoroughly anointed with a blessed unction,—(a practice derived) from the old discipline, wherein on entering the priesthood, *men* were wont to be anointed with oil from a horn, ever since Aaron was anointed by Moses.[17] Whence Aaron is called "Christ," [18] from the "chrism," which is "the unction;" which, when made spiritual, furnished an appropriate name to the Lord, because He was "anointed" with the Spirit by God the Father; as *written* in the Acts: "For truly they were gathered together in this city [19] against Thy Holy Son whom Thou hast anointed." [20] Thus, too, in *our* case, the unction runs carnally, (*i.e.* on the body,) but profits spiritually; in the same way as the *aet* of baptism itself too is carnal, in that we are plunged in water, *but* the *effect* spiritual, in that we are freed from sins.

CHAP. VIII.—OF THE IMPOSITION OF HANDS. TYPES OF THE DELUGE AND THE DOVE.

In the next place the hand is laid on us, invoking and inviting the Holy Spirit through benediction.[21] Shall it be granted possible for human ingenuity to summon a spirit into water, and, by the application of hands from above, to animate their union into one body [22] with another spirit of so clear sound; [23] and shall it not be possible for God, in the case of His own organ,[24] to produce, by means of "holy hands," [25] a sublime spiritual modulation? But this, as well as the former, is derived from the old sacramental rite in which Jacob blessed his grandsons, born of Joseph, Ephrem [26] and Manasses; with his hands laid on them and interchanged, and indeed so transversely slanted one over the other, that, by delineating Christ, they even portended the future benediction into Christ.[27] Then,

---

[1] Compare 1 Cor. xv. 46.
[2] John i. 16, 17.
[3] Qui: i. e. probably "angeli qui."
[4] Vitia.
[5] Or, "health"—salutem.
[6] Conservant populos.
[7] Compare c. viii., where Tertullian appears to regard the Holy Spirit as given *after* the baptized had come up out of the waters and received the "unction."
[8] Luke i. 76.
[9] Arbiter. [Eccles. v. 6, and Acts xii. 15.]
[10] Isa. xl. 3 ; Matt. iii. 3.
[11] Deut. xix. 15: Matt. xviii. 16; 2 Cor. xiii. 1.
[12] Sponsores.
[13] Sponsio.
[14] Compare *de Orat.* c. ii. *sub fin.*

[15] Compare the *de Orat.* quoted above, and *de Patien.* xxi. ; and see Matt. xviii. 20.
[16] Lavacro.
[17] See Ex. xxix. 7 ; Lev. viii. 12 ; Ps. cxxxiii. 2.
[18] i.e. "Anointed." Aaron, or at least the priest, is actually so called in the LXX., in Lev. iv. 5, 16, ὁ ἱερεὺς ὁ Χριστός: as in the Hebrew it is the word whence *Messiah* is derived which is used.
[19] Civitate.
[20] Acts iv. 27. "In this city" (ἐν τῇ πόλει ταύτῃ) is omitted in the English version; and the name Ἰησοῦν, "Jesus," is omitted by Tertullian. Compare Acts x. 38 and Lev. iv. 18 with Isa. lxi. 1 in the LXX.
[21] [See Bunsen, *Hippol.* Vol. III. Sec xiii. p. 22.]
[22] Concorporationem.
[23] The reference is to certain hydraulic organs, which the editors tell us are described by Vitruvius, ix. 9 and x. 13, and Pliny, *H. N.* vii. 37.
[24] i.e. Man. There may be an allusion to Eph. ii. 10, "We are His workmanship," and to Ps. cl. 4.
[25] Compare 1 Tim. ii. 8.
[26] i.e. Ephraim.
[27] In Christum.

over our cleansed and blessed bodies willingly descends from the Father that Holiest Spirit. Over the waters of baptism, recognising as it were His primeval seat,[1] He reposes: (He who) glided down on the Lord " in the shape of a dove,"[2] in order that the nature of the Holy Spirit might be declared by means of the creature (the emblem) of simplicity and innocence, because even in her bodily structure the dove is without literal[3] gall. And accordingly He says, " Be ye simple as doves."[4] Even this is not without the supporting evidence[5] of a preceding figure. For just as, after the waters of the deluge, by which the old iniquity was purged—after the baptism, so to say, of the world—a *dove* was the herald which announced to the earth the assuagement[6] of celestial wrath, when she had been sent her way out of the ark, and had returned with the olive-branch, a sign which even among the nations is the fore-token of *peace;*[7] so by the self-same law[8] of heavenly effect, to earth—that is, to our flesh[9]—as it emerges from the font,[10] after its old sins, flies the *dove* of the Holy Spirit, bringing us the peace of God, sent out from the heavens, where is the Church, the typified ark.[11] But the world returned unto sin; in which point baptism would ill be compared to the deluge. And so it is destined to fire; just as the man too is, who after baptism renews his sins:[12] so that this also ought to be accepted as a sign for our admonition.

CHAP. IX.—TYPES OF THE RED SEA, AND THE WATER FROM THE ROCK.

How many, therefore, are the pleas[13] of nature, how many the privileges of grace, how many the solemnities of discipline, the figures, the preparations, the prayers, which have ordained the sanctity of water? First, indeed, when the people, set unconditionally free,[14] escaped the violence of the Egyptian king by crossing over *through water*, it was *water* that extinguished[15] the king himself, with his entire forces.[16] What figure more manifestly

fulfilled in the sacrament of baptism? The nations are set free from the world[17] by means of *water*, to wit: and the devil, their old tyrant, they leave quite behind, overwhelmed in the *water*. Again, *water* is restored from its defect of " bitterness " to its native grace of " sweetness " by the tree[18] of Moses. That tree was Christ,[19] restoring, to wit, of Himself, the *veins* of sometime envenomed and bitter nature into the all-salutary *waters* of baptism. This is the *water* which flowed continously down for the people from the " accompanying rock;" for if Christ is " the Rock," without doubt we see baptism blest by the *water* in Christ. How mighty is the grace of *water*, in the sight of God and His Christ, for the confirmation of baptism! Never is Christ without *water:* if, that is, He is Himself baptized in *water;*[20] inaugurates in *water* the first rudimentary displays of His power, when invited to the nuptials;[21] invites the thirsty, when He makes a discourse, to His own sempiternal *water;*[22] approves,when teaching concerning love,[23] among works of charity,[24] the cup of *water* offered to a poor (child);[25] recruits His strength at a *well;*[26] walks over the *water;*[27] willingly crosses the *sea;*[28] ministers *water* to His disciples.[29] Onward even to the passion does the witness of baptism last: while He is being surrendered to the cross, *water* intervenes; witness Pilate's hands:[30] when He is wounded, forth from His side bursts *water;* witness the soldier's lance ![31]

CHAP. X.—OF JOHN'S BAPTISM.

We have spoken, so far as our moderate ability permitted, of the *generals* which form the groundwork of the sanctity[32] of baptism. I will now, equally to the best of my power, proceed to the rest of its character, touching certain minor questions.

The baptism announced by John formed the subject, even at that time, of a question, proposed by the Lord Himself indeed to the Pharisees, whether that baptism were heavenly, or truly earthly:[33] about which they were unable to give a consistent[34] answer,

---

[1] See. c. iv. p. 668.
[2] Matt. iii. 16 ; Luke iii. 22.
[3] Ipso. The ancients held this.
[4] Matt. x. 16. Tertullian has rendered ἀκέραιοι (*unmixed*) by " simplices," i.e. without fold.
[5] Argumento.
[6] Pacem.
[7] Paci.
[8] Dispositione.
[9] See *de Orat.* iv. *ad init.*
[10] Lavacro.
[11] Compare *de Idol.* xxiv. *ad fin.*
[12] [II. Pet. i. 9. Heb. x. 26, 27, 29. These awful texts are too little felt by modern Christians. They are too often explained away.]
[13] Patrocinia—" pleas *in defence.*"
[14] " Libere expeditus,' set free, and that without any conditions, such as Pharaoh had from time to time tried to impose. See Ex. viii. 25, 28, x. 10, 11, 24.
[15] " Extinxit," as it does *fire.*
[16] Ex. xiv. 27-30.

[17] Sæculo.
[18] See Ex. xv. 24, 25.
[19] " The Tree of Life," " the True Vine," etc.
[20] Matt. iii. 13-17.
[21] John ii. 1-11.
[22] John vii. 37, 38.
[23] Agape. See *de Orat.* c. 28, *ad fin.*
[24] Dilectionis. See *de Patien.* c. xii.
[25] Matt. x. 42.
[26] John iv. 6.
[27] Matt. xiv. 25.
[28] Mark iv. 36.
[29] John xiii. 1-12.
[30] Matt. xxvii. 24. Comp. *de Orat.* c. xiii.
[31] John xix. 34. See c. xviii. *sub fin.*
[32] Religionem.
[33] Matt. xxi. 25 ; Mark xi. 30 ; Luke xx. 4.
[34] Constanter.

inasmuch as they understood not, because they believed not. But *we*, with but as poor a measure of understanding as of faith, *are* able to determine that that baptism was *divine* indeed, (yet in respect of the command, not in respect of efficacy[1] too, in that we read that John was *sent by the Lord* to perform this duty,)[2] but *human* in its nature: for it conveyed nothing celestial, but it fore-ministered to things celestial; being, to wit, appointed over *repentance*, which is in man's power.[3] In fact, the doctors of the law and the Pharisees, who were unwilling to "believe," did not "repent" either.[4] But if repentance is a thing human, its baptism must necessarily be of the same nature: else, if it had been celestial, it would have given both the Holy Spirit and remission of sins. But none either pardons sins or freely grants the Spirit save God only.[5] Even the Lord Himself said that the Spirit would not descend on any other condition, but that He should first ascend to the Father.[6] What the Lord was not yet conferring, of course the servant could not furnish. Accordingly, in the Acts of the Apostles, we find that men who had "John's baptism" had not received the Holy Spirit, whom they knew not even by hearing.[7] That, then, was no celestial thing which furnished no celestial (endowments): whereas the very thing which *was* celestial in John— the Spirit of prophecy—so completely failed, after the transfer of the whole Spirit to the Lord, that he presently sent to inquire whether He whom he had himself preached,[8] whom he had pointed out when coming to him, were "HE."[9] And so "the baptism of repentance"[10] was dealt with[11] as if it were a candidate for the remission and sanctification shortly about to follow in Christ: for in that John used to preach "baptism *for* the remission of sins,"[12] the declaration was made with reference to a *future* remission; if it be true, (as it is,) that repentance is antecedent, remission subsequent; and this is "preparing the way."[13] But he who "prepares" does not himself "perfect," but procures for another to perfect. John himself professes that the celestial things are not his, but Christ's, by saying, "He who is from the earth speaketh concerning the earth; He who comes from

the *realms* above is above all;"[14] and again, by saying that he "baptized in repentance only, but that One would shortly come who would baptize in the Spirit and fire;"[15]—of course because true and stable faith is baptized with *water*, unto salvation; pretended and weak faith is baptized with *fire*, unto judgment.

CHAP. XI.—ANSWER TO THE OBJECTION THAT "THE LORD DID NOT BAPTIZE."

"But behold," say some, "the Lord came, and baptized not; for we read, 'And yet He used not to baptize, but His disciples!'"[16] As if, in truth, John had preached that He would baptize with His own hands! Of course, his words are not so to be understood, but as simply spoken after an ordinary manner; just as, for instance, we say, "The emperor set forth an edict," or, "The prefect cudgelled him." Pray does the emperor in person set forth, or the prefect in person cudgel? One whose ministers do a thing is always said to do it.[17] So "He will baptize you" will have to be understood as standing for, "Through Him," or "Into Him," "you will be baptized." But let not (the fact) that "He Himself baptized not" trouble any. For into whom should He baptize? Into repentance? Of what use, then, do you make His forerunner? Into remission of sins, which He used to give by a word? Into Himself, whom by humility He was concealing? Into the Holy Spirit, who had not yet descended from the Father? Into the Church, which His apostles had not yet founded? And thus it was with the selfsame "baptism of John" that His disciples used to baptize, as ministers, with which John before had baptized as forerunner. Let none think it was with some other, because no other exists, except that of Christ subsequently; which at that time, of course, could not be given by His disciples, inasmuch as the glory of the Lord had not yet been fully attained,[18] nor the efficacy of the font[19] established through the passion and the resurrection; because neither can our death see dissolution except by the Lord's passion, nor our life be restored without His resurrection.

CHAP. XII.—OF THE NECESSITY OF BAPTISM TO SALVATION.

When, however, the prescript is laid down that "without baptism, salvation is attainable

---

[1] Potestate.
[2] See John i. 33.
[3] It is difficult to see how this statement is to be reconciled with Acts v. 31. [i.e. under the universal illumination, John i. 9.]
[4] Matt. iii. 7-12, xxi. 23, 31, 32.
[5] Mark ii. 8; 1 Thess. iv. 8; 2 Cor. i. 21, 22, v. 5.
[6] John xvi. 6, 7.
[7] Acts xix. 1-7, [John vii. 39.]
[8] Matt. iii. 11, 12; John i. 6-36.
[9] Matt. xi. 2-6; Luke vii. 18-23. [He repeats this view.]
[10] Acts xix. 4.
[11] Agebatur.
[12] Mark i. 4.
[13] Luke i. 76.

[14] John iii. 30, 31, briefly quoted.
[15] Matt. iii. 11, not quite exactly given.
[16] John iv. 2.
[17] For instances of this, compare Matt. viii. 5 with Luke vii. 3, 7; and Mark x. 35 with Matt. xx. 20.
[18] Cf. 1 Pet. i. 11, *ad fin.*
[19] Lavacri.

by none " (chiefly on the ground of that declaration of the Lord, who says, " Unless one be born of water, he hath not life " [1]), there arise immediately scrupulous, nay rather audacious, doubts on the part of some, " how, in acordance with that prescript, salvation is attainable by the apostles, whom—Paul excepted—we do not find baptized in the Lord? Nay, since Paul is the only one of them who has put on *the garment of* Christ's baptism, [2] either the peril of all the others who lack the water of Christ is prejudged, that the prescript may be maintained, or else the prescript is rescinded if salvation has been ordained even for the unbaptized." I have heard—the Lord is my witness—doubts of that kind: that none may imagine me so abandoned as to excogitate, unprovoked, in the licence of my pen, ideas which would inspire others with scruple.

And now, as far as I shall be able, I will reply to them who affirm " that the apostles were unbaptized." For if they had undergone the human baptism of John, and were longing for that of the Lord, *then* since the Lord Himself had defined baptism to be *one;*[3] (saying to Peter, who was desirous[4] of being thoroughly bathed, " He who hath once bathed hath no necessity *to wash* a second time;"[5] which, of course, He would not have said at all to one *not* baptized;) even here we have a conspicuous[6] proof against those who, in order to destroy the sacrament of water, deprive the apostles even of John's baptism. Can it seem credible that " the way of the Lord," that is, the baptism of John, had not then been " prepared " in those persons who were being destined to *open* the way of the Lord throughout the whole world? The Lord Himself, though no " repentance " was due from *Him*, was baptized: was baptism not necessary for *sinners?* As for the fact, then, that " others were not baptized "—they, however, were not companions of Christ, but enemies of the faith, doctors of the law and Pharisees. From which fact is gathered an additional suggestion, that, since the *opposers* of the Lord *refused* to be baptized, they who *followed* the Lord *were* baptized, and were not like-minded with their own rivals: especially when, if there were any one to whom they clave, the Lord had exalted John above him (by the testimony) saying, " Among them who are born of women *there is* none greater than John the Baptist." [7]

Others make the suggestion (forced enough, clearly) " that the apostles then served the turn of baptism when, in their little ship, they were sprinkled and covered with the waves: that Peter himself also was immersed enough when he walked on the sea." [8] It is, however, as I think, one thing to be sprinkled or intercepted by the violence of the sea; another thing to be baptized in obedience to the discipline of religion. But that little ship did present a figure of the Church, in that she is disquieted " in the sea," that is, in the world,[9] " by the waves," that is, by persecutions and temptations; the Lord, through patience, sleeping as it were, until, roused in their last extremities by the prayers of the saints, He checks the world,[10] and restores tranquillity to His own.

Now, whether they were baptized in any manner whatever, or whether they continued unbathed[11] to the end—so that even that saying of the Lord touching the " one bath "[1] does, under the person of Peter, merely regard *us*—still, to determine concerning the salvation of the apostles is audacious enough, because on *them* the prerogative even of first choice,[13] and thereafter of undivided intimacy, might be able to confer the compendious grace of baptism, seeing they (I think) followed Him who was wont to promise salvation to every believer. " Thy faith," He would say, " hath saved thee;"[14] and, " Thy sins shall be remitted thee,"[15] on thy believing, of course, albeit thou be not *yet* baptized. If that[16] was wanting to the apostles, I know not in the faith of what things it was, that, roused by one word of the Lord, *one* left the tollbooth behind for ever;[17] *another* deserted father and ship, and the craft by which he gained his living;[18] *a third*, who disdained his father's obsequies,[19] fulfilled, before he heard it, that highest precept of the Lord, " He who prefers father or mother to me, is not worthy of me." [20]

CHAP. XIII.—ANOTHER OBJECTION : ABRAHAM
PLEASED GOD WITHOUT BEING BAPTIZED.
ANSWER THERETO. OLD THINGS MUST GIVE
PLACE TO NEW, AND BAPTISM IS NOW A LAW.

Here, then, those miscreants[21] provoke

---

[1] John iii. 5, not fully given.
[2] See Gal. iii. 27.
[3] See Eph. iv. 5.
[4] " Volenti," which Oehler notes as a suggestion of Fr. Junius, is adopted here in preference to Oehler's " nolenti."
[5] John xiii. 9, 10.
[6] Exerta. Comp. c. xviii. *sub init.; ad Ux.* ii. c. i. *sub fin.*
[7] Matt. xi. 11, ἐγήγερται omitted.

[8] Matt. viii. 24, xiv. 28, 29. [Our author seems to allow that sprinkling is baptism, but not Christian baptism: a very curious passage. Compare the foot-washing, John xiii. 8.]
[9] Sæculo.
[10] Sæculum.
[11] Illoti.
[12] Lavacrum. [John xiii. 9, 10, as above.]
[13] i.e. of being the first to be chosen.
[14] Luke xviii. 42 ; Mark x. 52.
[15] " Remittentur " is Oehler's reading ; " remittuntur " others read : but the Greek is in the perfect tense. See Mark ii. 5.
[16] i. e. faith, or perhaps the " compendious grace of baptism."
[17] Matt. ix. 9.
[18] Matt. iv. 21, 22.
[19] Luke ix. 59, 60 ; but it is not said there that the man *did* it.
[20] Matt. x. 37.   [21] i.e. probably the Cainites. See c. i.

questions. And so they say, "Baptism is not necessary for them to whom faith is sufficient; for withal, Abraham pleased God by a sacrament of no water, but of faith." But in all cases it is the *later* things which have a conclusive force, and the *subsequent* which prevail over the antecedent. Grant that, in days gone by, there was salvation by means of bare faith, before the passion and resurrection of the Lord. But now that faith has been enlarged, and is become a faith which believes in His nativity, passion, and resurrection, there has been an amplification added to the sacrament,[1] viz., the sealing act of baptism; the clothing, in some sense, of the faith which before was bare, and which cannot exist now without its proper law. For the *law* of baptizing has been *imposed*, and the formula prescribed: "Go," *He* saith, "teach the nations, baptizing them into the name of the Father, and of the Son, and of the Holy Spirit."[2] The comparison with this law of that definition, "Unless a man have been reborn of water and Spirit, he shall not enter into the kingdom of the heavens,"[3] has tied faith to the necessity of baptism. Accordingly, all thereafter[4] *who became* believers used to be baptized. *Then* it was, too,[5] that Paul, when he believed, was baptized; and this is the meaning of the precept which the Lord had given him when smitten with the plague of loss *of sight*, saying, "Arise, and enter Damascus; there shall be demonstrated to thee what thou oughtest to do," to wit,— be baptized, which was the only thing lacking to him. That point excepted, he had sufficiently *learnt and believed* "the Nazarene" to be "the Lord, the Son of God."[6]

CHAP. XIV.—OF PAUL'S ASSERTION, THAT HE HAD NOT BEEN SENT TO BAPTIZE.

But they roll back an *objection* from *that* apostle himself, in that he said, "For Christ sent me not to baptize;"[7] as if by this argument baptism were done away! For *if so*, why did he baptize Gaius, and Crispus, and the house of Stephanas?[8] However, even if Christ had not sent *him* to baptize, yet He had given *other* apostles the precept to baptize. But these words were written to the Corinthians in regard of the circumstances of that particular time; seeing that schisms and dissensions were agitated among them, while one attributes *everything* to Paul, another to Apollos.[9] For which reason the "peacemaking"[10] apostle, for fear he should seem to claim all *gifts* for himself, says that he had been sent "not to baptize, but to preach." For preaching is the prior thing, baptizing the posterior. Therefore the preaching came *first:* but I think baptizing withal was *lawful* to him to whom preaching was.

CHAP. XV.—UNITY OF BAPTISM. REMARKS ON HERETICAL AND JEWISH BAPTISM.

I know not whether any further point is mooted to bring baptism into controversy. Permit me to call to mind what I have omitted above, lest I seem to break off the train of impending thoughts in the middle. There is to us one, and but one, baptism; as well according to the Lord's gospel[11] as according to the apostle's letters,[12] inasmuch as *he says*, "One God, and one baptism, and one church in the heavens."[13] But it must be admitted that the question, "What rules are to be observed with regard to heretics?" is worthy of being treated. For it is to *us*[14] that that assertion[15] refers. Heretics, however, have no fellowship in our discipline, whom the mere fact of their excommunication[16] testifies to be outsiders. I am not bound to recognize in *them* a thing which is enjoined on *me*, because they and we have not the same God, nor one—that is, *the same*—Christ. And therefore their baptism is not one *with ours* either, because it is not *the same; a baptism* which, since they have it not duly, doubtless they have *not at all;* nor is that capable of being *counted* which is not *had.*[17] Thus they cannot *receive* it either, because they *have it not.* But this point has already received a fuller discussion from us in Greek. We enter, then, the font[18] *once: once* are sins washed away, because they ought never to be repeated. But the Jewish Israel bathes daily,[19] because he is daily being defiled: and, for fear that *defilement* should be practised among *us* also, therefore was the definition touching the one bathing[20] made. Happy water, which *once* washes away; which does not mock sinners (with vain hopes); which does not, by

---

[1] i.e. the sacrament, or obligation of faith. See beginning of chapter.
[2] Matt. xxviii. 19: "all" omitted.
[3] John ii.. 5: "shall not" for "cannot;" "kingdom of the heavens"—an expression only occurring in Matthew—for "kingdom of God."
[4] i. e. from the time when the Lord gave the "law."
[5] i. e. not till *after* the "law" had been made.
[6] See Acts ix. 1–31.
[7] 1 Cor. i. 17.
[8] 1 Cor. i. 14, 16.

[9] 1 Cor. i. 11, 12, iii. 3, 4.
[10] Matt. v. 9 ; referred to in *de Patien.* c. ii.
[11] Oehler refers us to c. xii. above, "He who hath once bathed."
[12] i. e. the Epistle to the Ephesians especially.
[13] Eph. iv. 4, 5, 6, but very inexactly quoted.
[14] i. e. us Christians ; or, "Catholics," as Oehler explains it.
[15] i. e. touching the "one baptism."
[16] Ademptio communicationis. [See Bunsen, *Hippol.* III. p. 114, Canon 46.]
[17] Comp. Eccles. i. 15.
[18] Lavacrum.
[19] Compare *de Ora!.* c. xiv.
[20] In John xiii. 10, and Eph. iv. 5.

being infected with the repetition of impurities, again defile them whom it has washed!

CHAP. XVI.—OF THE SECOND BAPTISM—WITH BLOOD.

We *have* indeed, likewise, a *second* font,[1] (itself withal *one with the former*,) of *blood*, to wit; concerning which the Lord said, "I have to be baptized with a baptism,"[2] when He had been baptized already. For He had come "by means of water and blood,"[3] just as John has written; that He might be baptized by the water, glorified by the blood; to make *us*, in like manner, *called* by *water*, *chosen*[4] by *blood*. These two baptisms He sent out from the wound in His pierced side,[5] in order that they who believed in His blood might be bathed with the water; they who had been bathed in the water might likewise drink the blood.[6] This is the baptism which both stands in lieu of the fontal bathing[7] when that has not been received, and restores it when lost.

CHAP. XVII.—OF THE POWER OF CONFERRING BAPTISM.

For concluding our brief subject,[8] it remains to put you in mind also of the due observance of giving and receiving baptism. Of giving it, the chief priest[9] (who is the bishop) has the right: in the next place, the presbyters and deacons, yet not without the bishop's authority, on account of the honour of the Church, which being preserved, peace is preserved. Beside these, even laymen have the right; for what is equally received can be equally given. Unless bishops, or priests, or deacons, be on the spot, *other* disciples are called *i.e. to the work*. The word of the Lord ought not to be hidden by any: in like manner, too, baptism, which is equally God's property,[10] can be administered by all. But how much more is the rule[11] of reverence and modesty incumbent on laymen—seeing that these *powers*[12] belong to their superiors—lest they assume to themselves the *specific*[13] function of the bishop! Emulation of the episcopal office is the mother of schisms. The most holy apostle has said, that "all things

are *lawful*, but not all *expedient*."[14] Let it suffice assuredly, in cases of *necessity*, to avail yourself (of that rule[15]), if at any time circumstance either of place, or of time, or of person compels you (so to do); for *then* the stedfast courage of the succourer, when the situation of the endangered one is urgent, is exceptionally admissible; inasmuch as he will be guilty of a human creature's loss if he shall refrain from bestowing what he had free liberty to bestow. But the woman of pertness,[16] who has usurped the power to teach, will of course not give birth for herself likewise to a right of baptizing, unless some new beast shall arise[17] like the former; so that, just as the one abolished baptism,[18] so some other should in her own right confer it! But if the writings which wrongly go under Paul's name, claim Thecla's example as a licence for women's teaching and baptizing, let them know that, in Asia, the presbyter who composed that writing,[19] as if he were augmenting Paul's fame from his own store, after being convicted, and confessing that he had done it from love of Paul, was removed[20] from his office. For how credible would it seem, that he who has not permitted a *woman*[21] even to *learn* with overboldness, should give a *female*[22] the power of *teaching* and of *baptizing!* "Let them be silent," he says, "and at home consult their own husbands."[23]

CHAP. XVIII.—OF THE PERSONS TO WHOM, AND THE TIME WHEN, BAPTISM IS TO BE ADMINISTERED.

But they whose office it is, know that baptism is not rashly to be administered. "Give to every one who beggeth thee,"[24] has a reference of its own, appertaining especially to almsgiving. On the contrary, this *precept* is rather to be looked at carefully: "Give not the holy thing to the dogs, nor cast your pearls before swine;"[25] and, "Lay not hands easily on *any;* share not other men's sins."[26] If Philip so "easily" baptized the chamberlain, let us reflect that a manifest and conspicuous[27] evidence that the Lord deemed him worthy

---

1 Lavacrum. [See Aquinas, *Quæst.* lxvi. 11.]
2 Luke xii. 50, not given in full.
3 1 John v. 6.
4 Matt. xx. 16 ; Rev. xvii. 14.
5 John xix. 34. See c. ix. *ad fin.*
6 See John vi. 53, etc.
7 Lavacrum. [The three baptisms: *fluminis, flaminis, sanguinis.*]
8 Materiolam.
9 Summus sacerdos. Compare *de Orat.* xxviii., "nos . . . veri sacerdotes," etc. : and *de Ex. Cast.* c. vii., "nonne et laici sacerdotes sumus?"
10 Census.
11 Disciplina.
12 i. e. the powers of administering baptism and "sowing the word." [i.e. "The Keys." *Scorpiace;* p. 643.]
13 Dicatum.

14 1 Cor. x. 23, where μοι in the received text seems interpolated.
15 Or, as Oehler explains it, of your power of baptizing, etc.
16 Quintilla. See c. i.
17 Evenerit. Perhaps Tertullian means literally—though that sense of the word is very rare—"shall issue out of her," alluding to his "pariet" above.
18 See c. i. *ad fin.*
19 The allusion is to a spurious work entitled *Acta Pauli et Theclæ.* [Of which afterwards. But see Jones, *on the Canon,* II. p. 353, and Lardner, *Credibility,* II. p. 305.]
20 Decessisse.
21 Mulieri.
22 Fœminæ.
23 1 Cor. xiv. 34, 35,
24 Luke vi. 30. [See note 4, p. 676.]
25 Matt. vii. 6.
26 1 Tim. v. 22; μηδενὶ omitted, ταχέως rendered by "facile," and μηδὲ by "ne."
27 "Exertam," as in c. xii. : "probatio exerta," "a conspicuous proof."

had been interposed.[1] The Spirit had en-joined Philip to proceed to that road: the eunuch himself, too, was not found idle, nor as one who was suddenly seized with an eager desire to be baptized; but, after going up to the temple for prayer's sake, being intently engaged on the divine Scripture, was thus suitably discovered—to whom God had, unasked, sent an apostle, which one, again, the Spirit bade adjoin himself to the chamberlain's chariot. The Scripture which *he was reading*[2] falls in opportunely with his faith: *Philip*, being requested, is taken to sit beside him; the Lord is pointed out; faith lingers not; water needs no waiting for; the work is completed, and the apostle snatched away. "But Paul too was, in fact, 'speedily' baptized:" for Simon,[3] his host, speedily recognized him to be "an appointed vessel of election." God's approbation sends sure premonitory tokens before it; every "petition"[4] may both deceive and be deceived. And so, according to the circumstances and disposition, and even age, of each individual, the delay of baptism is preferable; principally, however, in the case of little children. For why is it necessary—if (baptism itself) is not so necessary[5]—that the sponsors likewise should be thrust into danger? Who both themselves, by reason of mortality, may fail to fulfil their promises, and may be disappointed by the development of an evil disposition, *in those for whom they stood?* The Lord does indeed say, "Forbid them not to come unto me."[6] Let them "come," then, while they are growing up; let them "come" while they are learning, while they are learning whither to come;[7] let them become Christians[8] when they have become able to know Christ. Why does the innocent period of life hasten to the "remission of sins?" More caution will be exercised in worldly[9] matters: so that one who is *not* trusted with earthly substance *is* trusted with divine! Let them know how to "ask" for salvation, that you may seem (at least) to have given "to him that asketh."[10] For no less cause must the

unwedded also be deferred—in whom *the ground of* temptation is prepared, alike in such as *never were* wedded[11] by means of their maturity, and in the *widowed* by means of their freedom—until they either marry, or else be more fully strengthened for continence. If any understand the weighty import of baptism, they will fear its reception more than its delay: sound faith is secure of salvation.

CHAP. XIX.—OF THE TIMES MOST SUITABLE FOR BAPTISM.

The Passover affords a more *than usually* solemn day for baptism; when, withal, the Lord's passion, in which we are baptized, was completed. Nor will it be incongruous to interpret figuratively *the fact* that, when the Lord was about to celebrate the last Passover, He said to the disciples who were sent to make preparation, "Ye will meet a man bearing water."[12] He points out the place for celebrating the Passover by the sign of *water*. After that, Pentecost is a most joyous space[13] for conferring baptisms;[14] wherein, too, the resurrection of the Lord was repeatedly proved[15] among the disciples, and the hope of the advent of the Lord indirectly pointed to, in that, at that time, when He had been received back into the heavens, the angels[16] told the apostles that "He would so come, as He had withal ascended into the heavens;"[17] at Pentecost, of course. But, moreover, when Jeremiah says, "And I will gather them together from the extremities of the land in the feast-day," he signifies the day of the Passover and of Pentecost, which is properly a "feast-day."[18] However, *every* day is the Lord's; every hour, every time, is apt for baptism: if there is a difference in the *solemnity*, distinction there is none in the *grace*.

CHAP. XX.—OF PREPARATION FOR, AND CONDUCT AFTER, THE RECEPTION OF BAPTISM.

They who are about to enter baptism ought to pray with repeated prayers, fasts, and bendings of the knee, and vigils all the night through, and with the confession of all by-

---

[1] Comp. Acts viii. 26-40.
[2] Acts viii. 28, 30, 32, 33, and Isa. liii. 7, 8, especially in LXX. The quotation, as given in Acts, agrees nearly *verbatim* with the Cod. Alex. there.
[3] Tertullian seems to have confused the "Judas" with whom Saul stayed (Acts ix. 11) with the "Simon" with whom St. Peter stayed (Acts ix. 43); and it was Ananias, not Judas, to whom he was pointed out as "an appointed vessel," and by whom he was baptized. [So above, he seems to have confounded Philip, the deacon, with Philip the apostle.]
[4] See note 24, [where Luke vi. 30 is shown to be abused].
[5] Tertullian has already allowed (in c. xvi) that baptism is not *indispensably* necessary to salvation.
[6] Matt. xix. 14; Mark x. 14; Luke xviii. 16.
[7] Or, "whither they are coming."
[8] i.e. in baptism.
[9] Sæcularibus.
[10] See beginning of chapter, [where Luke vi. 30, is shown to be abused].

[11] Virginibus; but he is speaking about men as well as women. Comp. *de Orat.* c. xxii. [I need not point out the bearings of the above chapter, nor do I desire to interpose any comments. The Editor's interpolations, where purely gratuitous, I have even stricken out, though I agree with them. See that work of genius, *the Liberty of Prophesying*, by Jer. Taylor, sect. xviii. and its candid admissions.]
[12] Mark xiv. 13, Luke xxii. 10, "a small earthen pitcher of water."
[13] [He means the whole fifty days from the Paschal Feast till Pentecost, including the latter. Bunsen *Hippol.* III. 18.]
[14] Lavacris.
[15] Frequentata, i.e. by His frequent appearance. See Acts i. 3, δι' ἡμερῶν τεσσαράκοντα ὀπτανόμενος αὐτοῖς.
[16] Comp. Acts i. 10 and Luke ix. 30: in each place St. Luke says, ἄνδρες δύο: as also in xxiv. 4 of his Gospel.
[17] Acts i. 10, 11; but it is οὐρανόν throughout in the Greek.
[18] Jer. xxxi. 8, xxxviii. 8 in LXX., where ἐν ἑορτῇ φασέκ is found, which is not in the English version.

---

gone sins, that they may express *the meaning* even of the baptism of John: "They were baptized," saith (the Scripture), "confessing their own sins."[1] To us it is matter for thankfulness if we do *now* publicly confess our iniquities or our turpitudes:[2] for we do at the same time both make satisfaction[3] for our former sins, by mortification of our flesh and spirit, and lay beforehand the foundation of defences against the temptations which will closely follow. "Watch and pray," saith (the Lord), "lest ye fall into temptation."[4] And the reason, I believe, why they *were* tempted was, that they fell asleep; so that they deserted the Lord when apprehended, and he who continued to stand by Him, and used the sword, even denied Him thrice: for withal the word had gone before, that "no one *un*tempted should attain the celestial kingdoms."[5] The Lord Himself forthwith after *baptism*[6] temptations surrounded, when in forty days He had kept fast. "Then," some one will say, "it becomes *us*, too, rather to fast *after* baptism."[7] Well, and who forbids you, unless it be the necessity for joy, and the thanksgiving for salvation? But so far as I, with my poor powers, understand, the Lord figuratively retorted upon Israel the reproach *they had cast on the Lord.*[8] For the people,

after crossing the sea, and being carried about in the desert during forty years, although they were there nourished with divine supplies, nevertheless were more mindful of their belly and their gullet than of God. Thereupon the Lord, driven apart into desert places after baptism,[9] showed, by maintaining a fast of forty days, that the man of God lives "not by bread alone," but "by the word of God;"[10] and that temptations incident to fulness or immoderation of appetite are shattered by abstinence. Therefore, blessed *ones*, whom the grace of God awaits, when you ascend from that most sacred font[11] of your new birth, and spread your hands[12] for the first time in the house of your mother,[13] together with your brethren, ask from the Father, ask from the Lord, that His own specialties of grace *and* distributions of gifts[14] may be supplied you. "Ask," saith He, "and ye shall receive."[15] Well, you *have* asked, and have received; you *have* knocked, and it has been opened to you. Only, I pray that, when you are asking, you be mindful likewise of Tertullian the sinner.[16]

---

[1] Matt. iii. 6. [See the collection of Dr. Bunsen for the whole primitive discipline to which Tertullian has reference, *Hippol.* Vol. III. pp. 5–23, and 29.]
[2] Perhaps Tertullian is referring to Prov. xxviii. 13. If we confess *now*, we shall be forgiven, and not put to shame at the judgment day.
[3] See *de Orat.* c. xxiii. *ad fin.*, and the note there.
[4] Matt. xxvi. 41.
[5] What passage is referred to is doubtful. The editors point us to Luke xxii. 28, 29; but the reference is unsatisfactory.
[6] Lavacrum.
[7] Lavacro. Compare the beginning of the chapter.

[8] Viz. by their murmuring for bread (see Ex. xvi. 3, 7); and again—nearly forty years after—in another place. See Num. xxi. 5.
[9] Aquam: just as St. Paul says the Israelites had been "*baptized*" (or "*baptized themselves*") "into Moses in the cloud and *in the sea.*" 1 Cor. x. 2.
[10] Matt. iv. 1–4.
[11] Lavacro.
[12] In prayer: comp. *de Orat.* c. xiv.
[13] i.e. the Church: comp. *de Orat.* c. 2.
[14] 1 Cor. xii. 4–12.
[15] Matt. vii. 7; Luke xi. 9: αἰτεῖτε, καὶ δοθήσεται, ὑμῖν in both places.
[16] [The translator, though so learned and helpful, too often encumbers the text with superfluous interpolations. As many of these, while making the reading difficult, add nothing to the sense yet destroy the terse, crabbed force of the original, I have occasionally restored the spirit of a sentence, by removing them.]

ELUCIDATION.

The argument (p. 673, note 6,) is conclusive, but not clear. The disciples of John must have been baptized by him, (Luke vii. 29, 30,) and "all the people," must have included those whom Jesus called. But, this was not Christ's baptism: See Acts xix. 2, 5. Compare note 8, p. 673. And see the American Editor's "Apollos."

ON PRAYER.

(BY THE REV. S. THELWALL.)

CHAP. I.—GENERAL INTRODUCTION.[1]

THE Spirit of God, and the Word of God, and the Reason of God—Word of Reason, and Reason and Spirit of Word—Jesus Christ our Lord, namely, who is both the one and the other,[2]—has determined for us, the disciples of the New Testament, a new form of prayer; for in this particular also it was needful that new wine should be laid up in new skins, and a new breadth be sewn to a new garment.[3] Besides, whatever had been in bygone days, has either been quite changed, as circumcision; or else supplemented, as the rest of the Law; or else fulfilled, as Prophecy; or else perfected, as faith itself. For the new grace of God has renewed all things from carnal unto spiritual, by superinducing the Gospel, the obliterator of the whole ancient bygone system; in which our Lord Jesus Christ has been approved as the Spirit of God, and the Word of God, and the Reason of God: the Spirit, by which He was mighty; the Word, by which He taught; the Reason, by which He came.[4] So the prayer composed by Christ has been composed of three parts. In speech,[5] by which *prayer* is enunciated, in spirit, by which alone it prevails, even John had taught his disciples to pray,[6]

but all John's doings were laid as groundwork for Christ, until, when "He had increased"—just as the same John used to fore-announce "that it was needful" that "He should increase and himself decrease"[7] —the whole work of the forerunner passed over, together with his spirit itself, unto the Lord. Therefore, after what form of words John taught to pray is not extant, because earthly things have given place to heavenly. "He who is from the earth," says John, "speaketh earthly things; and He who is here from the heavens speaketh those things which He hath seen."[8] And what is the Lord Christ's—as this method of praying is— *that* is *not* heavenly? And so, blessed *brethren*, let us consider His heavenly wisdom: first, touching the precept of praying secretly, whereby He exacted man's faith, that he should be confident that the sight and hearing of Almighty God are present beneath roofs, and extend even into the secret place; and required modesty in faith, that it should offer its religious homage to Him alone, whom it believed to see and to hear everywhere. Further, since wisdom succeeded in the following precept, let it in like manner appertain unto faith, and the modesty of faith, that we think not that the Lord must be approached with a train of words, who, we are certain, takes unsolicited foresight for His own. And yet that very brevity—and let this make for the third grade of wisdom—is supported on the substance of a great and blessed interpretation, and is as diffuse in meaning as it is compressed in words. For it has embraced not only the special duties of prayer, be it veneration of God or petition for man, but almost every discourse of the Lord, every record of *His* Discipline; so that, in fact, in the Prayer is comprised an epitome of the whole Gospel.

---

[1] [After the discipline of Repentance and of Baptism the Laws of Christian Living come into view. Hence this is the logical place for this treatise. See the *Prolegomena* of Muratori and learned annotations, in Routh, *Opuscula* I. p. 173, *et sqq.* We may date it *circa* A. D. 192. For much of the Primitive Discipline, concerning Prayer, see Bunsen, *Hippol.* III. pp. 88–91, etc.]

[2] Oehler's punctuation is followed here. The sentence is difficult, and has perplexed editors and commentators considerably.

[3] Matt. ix. 16, 17; Mark ii. 21, 22; Luke v. 36, 37.

[4] Routh suggests, "fortasse *quâ sensit*," referring to the *Adv. Praxeam*, c. 5.

[5] Sermone.

[6] This is Oehler's punctuation. The edition of Pamelius reads: "So the prayer composed by Christ was composed of three parts: of the speech, by which it is enunciated; of the spirit, by which alone it prevails; of the reason, by which it is taught." Rigaltius and subsequent editors read, "of the reason, by which it is conceived;" but this last clause is lacking in the MSS., and Oehler's reading appears, as he says, to "have healed the words." [Oehler's punctuation must stand; but, the preceding sentence justifies the interpolation of Rigaltius and *heals* more effectually.]

[7] John iii. 30.

[8] John iii. 31, 32.

CHAP. II.—THE FIRST CLAUSE.

The prayer begins with a testimony to God, and with the reward of faith, when we say, " Our Father who art in the heavens; " for (in so saying), we at once pray to God, and commend faith, whose reward this appellation is. It is written, " To them who believed on Him He gave power to be called sons of God." [1] However, our Lord very frequently proclaimed God as a Father to us; nay, even gave a precept " that we call no one on earth father, but the Father whom we have in the heavens: [2] and so, in thus praying, we are likewise obeying the precept. Happy they who recognize their Father ! This is the reproach that is brought against Israel, to which the Spirit attests heaven and earth, saying, " I have begotten sons, and they have not recognized me." [3] Moreover, in saying " Father," we also call Him " God." That appellation is one both of filial duty and of power. Again, in the Father the Son is invoked; " for I," saith He, " and the Father are One." [4] Nor is even our mother the Church passed by, if, that is, in the Father and the Son is recognized the mother, from whom arises the name both of Father and of Son. In one general term, then, or word, we both honour God, together with His own,[5] and are mindful of the precept, and set a mark on such as have forgotten their Father.

CHAP. III.—THE SECOND CLAUSE.

The name of " God the Father " had been published to none. Even Moses, who had interrogated Him on that very point, had heard a different name.[6] To us it has been revealed in the Son, for the Son is now the Father's new name. " I am come," saith He, " in the Father's name;" [7] and again, " Father, glorify Thy name;" [8] and more openly, " I have manifested Thy name to men." [9] That *name*, therefore, we pray may " be hallowed." Not that it is becoming for men to *wish* God *well*, as if there were any other [10] by whom He may be wished well, or as if He would suffer unless we do so wish. Plainly, it is universally becoming for God to be *blessed* [11] in every place and time, on account of the memory of His benefits ever due from every man. But this petition also serves the turn of a blessing. Otherwise, when is the name of God not " holy," and " hallowed " through Himself, seeing that of Himself He sanctifies all others—He to whom that surrounding circle of angels cease not to say, " Holy, holy, holy ? " [12] In like wise, therefore, we too, candidates for angelhood, if we succeed in deserving it, begin even here on earth to learn by heart that strain hereafter to be raised unto God, and the function of future glory. So far, for the glory of God. On the other hand, for our own petition, when we say, " Hallowed be Thy name," we pray this; that it may be hallowed *in us* who are in Him, as well in all others for whom the grace of God is still waiting; [13] that we may obey this precept, too, in " praying for all," [14] even for our personal enemies.[15] And therefore with suspended utterance, not saying, "Hallowed be it *in us*," we say,—" *in all*."

CHAP. IV.—THE THIRD CLAUSE.

According to this model,[16] we subjoin, " Thy will be done in the heavens and on the earth;" [17] not that there is some power withstanding [18] to prevent God's will being done, and we pray for Him the successful achievement of His will; but we pray for His will to be done *in all*. For, by figurative interpretation of *flesh* and *spirit, we* are " heaven " and " earth;" albeit, even if it is to be understood simply, still the sense of the petition is the same, that *in us* God's will be done on earth, to make it possible, namely, for it to be done also in the heavens. What, moreover, *does* God will, but that we should walk according to His Discipline ? We make petition, then, that He supply us with the substance of His will, and the capacity to do it, that we may be saved both in the heavens and on earth; because the sum of His will is the salvation of them whom He has adopted. There is, too, that will of God which the Lord accomplished in preaching, in working, in enduring: for if He Himself proclaimed that He did not His own, but the Father's will, without doubt those things which He used to do *were* the Father's will; [19] unto which things, as unto exemplars, we are now provoked; [20] to preach, to work, to endure even

---

[1] John i. 12.
[2] Matt. xxiii. 9.
[3] Isa. i. 2.
[4] John x. 30.
[5] " i.e., together with the son and the Holy Spirit" (Oehler) ; " His Son and His church " (Dodgson).
[6] Ex. iii. 13–16.
[7] John v. 43.
[8] John xii. 28.
[9] John xvii. 6.
[10] i.e., " any other *god*."
[11] Ps. ciii. 22.
[12] Isa. vi. 3 ; Rev. iv. 8.
[13] Isa. xxx. 18.
[14] 1 Tim. ii. 1.
[15] Matt. v. 44.
[16] Mr. Dodgson renders, " next to this clause ;" but the " *forma* " referred to seems, by what Tertullian proceeds to add, to be what he had said above, " not that it becomes us to wish God well," etc.
[17] We learn from this and other places, that the comparative adverb was wanting in some ancient *formulæ* of the Lord's Prayer. [See Routh, *Opuscula* I. p. 178.]
[18] See note 3.
[19] John vi 38.
[20] For this use of the word " provoke," see Heb. x. 24, Eng. **ver.**

unto death. And we *need* the will of God, that we may be able to fulfil these duties. Again, in saying, "Thy will be done," we are even wishing well to ourselves, in so far that there is nothing of *evil* in the will of God; even if, proportionably to each one's deserts, somewhat other[1] is imposed on us. So by this expression we premonish our own selves unto patience. The Lord also, when He had wished to demonstrate to us, even in His own flesh, the flesh's infirmity, by the reality of suffering, said, "Father, remove this Thy cup;" and remembering Himself, *added*, "save that not my will, but Thine be done."[2] Himself *was* the Will and the Power of the Father: and yet, for the demonstration of the patience which was due, He gave Himself up *to* the Father's Will.

CHAP. V.—THE FOURTH CLAUSE.

"Thy kingdom come" has also reference to that whereto "Thy will be done" refers—*in us*, that is. For when does God not reign, in whose hand is the heart of all kings?[3] But whatever we wish for ourselves we augur for Him, and *to* Him we attribute what *from* Him we expect. And so, if the *manifestation* of the Lord's kingdom pertains unto the will of God and unto our anxious expectation, how do some pray for some protraction of the age,[4] when the kingdom of God, which we pray may arrive, tends unto the consummation of the age?[5] Our wish is, that our reign be hastened, not our servitude protracted. Even if it had not been prescribed in the Prayer that we should ask for the advent of the kingdom, we should, unbidden, have sent forth that cry, hastening toward the realization of our hope. The souls of the martyrs beneath the altar[6] cry in jealousy unto the Lord "How long, Lord, dost Thou not avenge our blood on the inhabitants of the earth?"[7] for, of course, their avenging is regulated by[8] the end of the age. Nay, Lord, Thy kingdom come with all speed,— the prayer of Christians the confusion of the heathen,[9] the exultation of angels, for the sake of which we suffer, nay, rather, for the sake of which we pray!

CHAP. VI.—THE FIFTH CLAUSE.

But how gracefully has the Divine Wisdom arranged the order of the prayer; so that *after* things heavenly—that is, after the "Name" of God, the "Will" of God, and the "Kingdom" of God—it should give earthly necessities also room for a petition! For the Lord had[10] withal issued His edict, "Seek ye first the kingdom, and then even these shall be added:"[11] albeit we may rather understand, "Give us this day our daily bread," *spiritually*. For *Christ* is our Bread; because Christ is Life, and bread is life. "I am," saith He, "the Bread of Life;"[12] and, a little above, "The Bread is the Word of the living God, who came down from the heavens."[13] Then *we find*, too, that His body is reckoned in bread: "This is my body."[14] And so, in petitioning for "daily bread," we ask for perpetuity in Christ, and indivisibility from His body. But, because that word is admissible in a carnal sense too, it cannot be so used without the religious remembrance withal of spiritual Discipline; for (the Lord) commands that *bread* be prayed for, which is the only *food* necessary for believers; for "all other things the nations seek after."[15] The like lesson He both inculcates by examples, and repeatedly handles in parables, when He says, "Doth a father take away *bread* from his children, and hand it to dogs?"[16] and again, "Doth a father give his son a stone when he asks for *bread?*"[17] For He *thus* shows what it is that sons expect from their father. Nay, even that nocturnal knocker knocked for "*bread*."[18] Moreover, He justly added, "Give us *this day*,' seeing He had previously said, "Take no careful thought about the morrow, what ye are to eat."[19] To which subject He also adapted the parable of the man who pondered on an enlargement of his barns for his forthcoming fruits, and on seasons of prolonged security; but that very night he dies.[20]

CHAP. VII.—THE SIXTH CLAUSE.

It was suitable that, after contemplating the liberality of God,[21] we should likewise address His clemency. For what will aliments[22]

---

[1] [Something we might think *other* than good.]
[2] Luke xxii. 42.
[3] Prov. xxi. 1.
[4] Or, "world," *sæculo*.
[5] Or, "world," *sæculi*. See Matt. xxiv. 3, especially in the Greek. By "praying for some protraction in the age," Tertullian appears to refer to some who used to pray that the end might be deferred (Rigalt.).
[6] *altari*.
[7] Rev. vi. 10.
[8] So Dodgson aptly renders "*dirigitur a*.
[9] [See *Ad Nationes*, p. 128, *supra*.]
[10] This is a slight mistake of Tertullian. The words referred to, "Seek ye first," etc., do not occur till the *end* of the chapter in which the prayer is found, so that his pluperfect is out of place.

[He must have been aware of this: he only gives logical order to the thought which existed in the divine mind. See note 10, p. 682.]
[11] Matt. vi. 33.
[12] John vi. 35.
[13] John vi. 33.
[14] Matt. xxvi. 26.
[15] Matt. vi. 32.
[16] Tertullian seems to refer to Matt. xv. 26, Mark vii. 27.
[17] Matt. vii. 9; Luke xi. 11.
[18] Luke xi. 5–9.
[19] Matt. vi. 34 and Luke xii. 29 seem to be referred to; but the same remark applies as in note 10 on the preceding page.
[20] Luke xii. 16–20.
[21] In the former petition, "Give us this day our daily bread."
[22] Such as " " daily bread."

profit us, if we are really *consigned* to them, as it were a bull destined for a victim?[1] The Lord knew Himself to be the only guiltless One, and so He teaches that we beg "to have our debts remitted us." A petition for pardon is a full confession; because he who begs for pardon fully admits his guilt. Thus, too, penitence is demonstrated acceptable to God, who desires it rather than the death of the sinner.[2] Moreover, *debt* is, in the Scriptures, a figure of *guilt;* because it is equally due to the sentence of judgment, and is exacted by it: nor does it evade the justice of exaction, unless the exaction be remitted, just as the lord remitted to that slave *in the parable* his debt;[3] for hither does the scope of the whole parable tend. For the fact withal, that the same servant, after liberated by his lord, does not equally spare his own debtor; and, being on that account impeached before his lord, is made over to the tormentor to pay the uttermost farthing—that is, every guilt, however small: corresponds with our profession that "we also remit to our debtors;" indeed elsewhere, too, in conformity with this Form of Prayer, He saith, "Remit, and it shall be remitted you."[4] And when Peter had put the question whether remission were to be granted to a brother seven times, "Nay," saith He, "seventy-seven times;"[5] in order to remould the Law for the better; because in Genesis *vengeance* was assigned "seven times" in the case of Cain, but in that of Lamech "seventy-seven times."[6]

CHAP. VIII.—THE SEVENTH OR FINAL CLAUSE.

For the completeness of so brief a prayer He added—in order that we should supplicate not touching the remitting merely, but touching the entire averting, of acts of guilt— "Lead us not into temptation:" that is, suffer us not to be led into it, by him (of course) who tempts; but far be the thought that the Lord should seem to tempt,[7] as if He either were ignorant of the faith of any, or else were eager to overthrow it. Infirmity[8] and malice[9] are characteristics of the devil. For *God* had commanded even Abraham to make a sacrifice of his son, for the sake not of tempting, but proving, his faith; in order through him to make an example for that precept of His, whereby He was, by and by, to enjoin that

he should hold no pledges of affection dearer than God.[10] He Himself, when tempted by the devil, demonstrated who it is that presides over and is the originator of temptation.[11] This passage He confirms by subsequent ones, saying, "Pray that ye be not tempted;"[12] yet they *were* tempted, (as they showed) by deserting their Lord, because they had given way rather to sleep than prayer.[13] The final clause, therefore, is consonant, and interprets the sense of "Lead us not into temptation;" for this *sense* is, "But convey us away from the Evil One."

CHAP. IX.—RECAPITULATION.[14]

In summaries of so few words, how many utterances of the prophets, the Gospels, the apostles—how many discourses, examples, parables of the Lord, are touched on! How many duties are simultaneously discharged! The honour of God in the "Father;" the testimony of faith in the "Name;" the offering of obedience in the "Will;" the commemoration of hope in the "Kingdom;" the petition for life in the "Bread;" the full acknowledgment of debts in the prayer for their "Forgiveness;" the anxious dread of temptation in the request for "Protection." What wonder? God alone could teach how he wished Himself prayed to. The religious rite of prayer therefore, ordained by Himself, and animated, even at the moment when it was issuing out of the Divine mouth, by His own Spirit, ascends, by its own prerogative, into heaven, commending to the Father what the Son has taught.

CHAP. X.—WE MAY SUPERADD PRAYERS OF OUR OWN TO THE LORD'S PRAYER.

Since, however, the Lord, the Foreseer of human necessities,[15] said separately, after delivering His Rule of Prayer, "Ask, and ye shall receive;"[16] and *since* there are petitions which are made according to the circumstances of each individual; our additional wants have the right—after beginning with the legitimate and customary prayers as a foundation, as it were—of rearing an outer superstructure of petitions, yet with remembrance of *the Master's* precepts.

---

[1] That is, if we are just to be fed and fattened by them in *body*, as a bull which is destined for sacrifice is, and then, like him, *slain* —handed over to *death?*
[2] Ex. xviii. 23, 32, xxxiii. 11.
[3] Matt. xviii. 21-35.
  Luke vi. 37.
[5] Matt. xviii. 21-22.
[6] Gen. iv. 15, 24.
[7] See Jas. i. 13.
[8] Implied in the one hypothesis—ignorance.
[9] Implied in the other—wishing to overthrow faith.

[10] i e. no children even. The reference is apparently to Matt. x. 37 and Luke xiv. 26, with which may be compared Deut. xiii. 6-10 and xxxiii. 9. If Oehler's reading, which I have followed, be correct, the precept, which is not verbally given till ages after Abraham, is made to have a retrospective force on him.
[11] See Matt. iv. 10; Luke iv. 8.
[12] Luke xxii. 40; Matt. xxvi. 41; Mark xiv. 31.
[13] Routh refers us to *De Bapt.* c. 20, where Tertullian refers to the same event. [Note also his reference to *De Fuga,* cap. ii.]
[14] Here comes in the Codex Ambrosianus, with the title, "Here begins a treatise of Tertullian of divers necessary things;" and from it are taken the headings of the remaining chapters. (See Oehler and Routh.)
[15] See Matt. vi. 8.   [16] Matt. vii. 7; Luke xi. 9.

CHAP. XI.—WHEN PRAYING THE FATHER, YOU ARE NOT TO BE ANGRY WITH A BROTHER.

That we may not be as far from the ears of God as we are from His precepts,[1] the memory of His precepts paves for our prayers a way unto heaven; of which *precepts* the chief is, that we go not up unto God's altar[2] before we compose whatever of discord or offence we have contracted with our brethren.[3] For what sort of deed is it to approach the peace of God[4] without peace? the remission of debts[5] while you retain them? How will he appease his *Father* who is angry with his *brother*, when from the beginning "all anger" is forbidden us?[6] For even Joseph, when dismissing his brethren for the purpose of fetching their father, said, "And be not angry in the way."[7] He warned *us*, to be sure, at that time (for elsewhere our Discipline is called "the Way"[8]), that when, set in "the way" of prayer, we go not unto "the Father" with anger. After that, the Lord, "amplifying the Law,"[9] openly adds *the prohibition of* anger against a brother to *that of* murder.[10] Not even by an evil word does He permit it to be vented.[11] Ever if we *must* be angry, our anger must not be maintained beyond sunset, as the apostle admonishes.[12] But how rash is it either to pass a day without prayer, while you refuse to make satisfaction to your brother; or else, by perseverance in anger, to lose your prayer?

CHAP. XII.—WE MUST BE FREE LIKEWISE FROM ALL MENTAL PERTURBATION.

Nor merely from anger, but altogether from *all* perturbation of mind, ought the exercise of prayer to be free, uttered from a spirit such as the Spirit unto whom it is sent. For a defiled spirit cannot be acknowledged by a holy Spirit,[13] nor a sad by a joyful,[14] nor a fettered by a free.[15] No one grants reception to his adversary: no one grants admittance except to his compeer.

CHAP. XIII.—OF WASHING THE HANDS.

But what reason is there in going to prayer with hands indeed washed, but the spirit foul? —inasmuch as to our hands themselves spiritual purities are necessary, that they may be "lifted up pure"[16] from falsehood, from murder, from cruelty, from poisonings,[17] from idolatry, and all the other blemishes which, conceived by the spirit, are effected by the operation of the hands. These are the true purities;[18] not those which most are superstitiously careful about, taking water at every prayer, even when they are coming from a bath of the whole body. When I was scrupulously making a thorough investigation of this practice, and searching into the reason of it, I ascertained it to be a commemorative act, bearing on the surrender[19] of our Lord. We, *however, pray* to the Lord: we do not *surrender* Him; nay, we ought even to set ourselves in opposition to the example of His surrenderer, and not, on that account, wash our hands. Unless any defilement contracted in human intercourse be a conscientious cause *for washing them*, they are otherwise clean enough, which together with our whole body we once washed in Christ.[20]

CHAP. XIV.—APOSTROPHE.

Albeit Israel washed daily all his limbs over, yet is he never clean. His *hands*, at all events, are ever unclean, eternally dyed with the blood of the prophets, and of the Lord Himself; and on that account, as being hereditary culprits from their privity to their fathers' crimes,[21] they do not dare even to raise them unto the Lord,[22] for fear some Isaiah should cry out,[23] for fear Christ should utterly shudder. We, however, not only raise, but even expand them; and, taking our model from the Lord's passion,[24] even in prayer we confess[25] to Christ.

CHAP. XV.—OF PUTTING OFF CLOAKS.

But since we have touched on one special point of empty observance,[26] it will not be irksome to set our brand likewise on the other points against which the reproach of vanity may deservedly be laid; if, that is, they are observed without the authority of any precept

---

[1] Oehler divides these two chapters as above. The generally adopted division unites this sentence to the preceding chapter, and begins the new chapter with, "The memory of His precepts;" and perhaps this is the preferable division.
[2] *altare.* [Heb. xiii. 10.]
[3] Matt. v. 22, 23.
[4] Perhaps there may be an allusion to Phil iv. 6, 7.
[5] See chap. vii. above, and compare Matt. vi. 14, 15.
[6] "Ab initio" probably refers to the book of Genesis, the *initium*, or beginning of Scripture, to which he is about to refer. But see likewise Eph. iv. 31, Matt. v. 21, 22. [Gen. iv. 6, 7.]
[7] Gen. xlv. 24 : so the LXX.
[8] See Acts ix. 2, xix, 9, 23, in the Greek.
[9] See Matt. v. 17.
[10] Matt. v. 21, 22.
[11] Matt. v. 21, 22 ; 1 Pet. iii. 9, etc.
[12] Eph. iv. 26.
[13] Eph. iv. 30.
[14] John xvii. 14 ; Rom. xiv. 17.
[15] Ps. li. 12.
[16] 1 Tim. ii. 8.
[17] Or, "sorceries."
[18] See Matt. xv. 10, 11, 17-20, xxiii. 25, 26.
[19] By Pilate. See Matt. xxvii. 24. [N. B. *quoad Ritualia.*]
[20] i.e. in baptism.
[21] See Matt. xxiii. 31 ; Luke xi. 48.
[22] I do not know Tertullian's authority for this statement. Certainly Solomon *did* raise *his* hands (1 Kings viii. 54), and David apparently his (see Ps. cxliii. 6, xxviii. 2, lxii. 4, etc.). Compare, too, Ex. xvii. 11, 12. But probably he is speaking only of the Israel of his own day. [Evidently.]
[23] Isa. i. 15.
[24] i.e. from the expansion of the hands on the cross.
[25] Or, "give praise."
[26] i.e. the hand-washing.

either of the Lord, or else of the apostles. For matters of this kind belong not to religion, but to superstition, being studied, and forced, and of curious rather than rational ceremony;[1] deserving of restraint, at all events, even on this ground, that they put us on a level with Gentiles.[2] As, *e.g.*, it is the custom of some to make prayer with cloaks doffed, for so do the nations approach their idols; which practice, of course, were its observance becoming, the apostles, who teach concerning the garb of prayer,[3] would have comprehended *in their instructions*, unless any think that is was in prayer that Paul had left his cloak with Carpus![4] God, forsooth, would not hear cloaked suppliants, who plainly heard the three saints in the Babylonian king's furnace praying in their trousers and turbans.[5]

CHAP. XVI.—OF SITTING AFTER PRAYER.

Again, for the custom which some have of sitting when prayer is ended, I perceive no reason, except that which children give.[6] For what if that Hermas,[7] whose writing is generally inscribed with the title *The Shepherd*, had, after finishing his prayer, not sat down on his bed, but done some other thing: should we maintain that also as a matter for observance? Of course not. Why, even as it is, the sentence, "When I had prayed, and had sat down on my bed," is simply put with a view to the order of the narration, not as a model of discipline. Else we shall have to pray nowhere except where there is a bed! Nay, whoever sits in a *chair* or on a *bench*, will act contrary to that writing. Further: inasmuch as the nations do the like, in sitting down after adoring their petty images; even on this account the practice deserves to be censured in us, because it is observed in the worship of idols. To this is further added the charge of *irreverence*,—intelligible even to the nations themselves, if they had any sense. If, on the one hand, it is irreverent to sit under the eye, and over against the eye, of him whom you most of all revere and venerate; how much more, on the other hand, is that deed *most* irreligious under the eye of the living God, while the angel of prayer is still *standing by*,[8] unless we are upbraiding God that prayer has wearied us!

CHAP. XVII.—OF ELEVATED HANDS.

But we more commend our prayers to God when we pray with modesty and humility, with not even our hands too loftily elevated, but elevated temperately and becomingly; and not even our countenance over-boldly uplifted. For that publican who prayed with humility and dejection not merely in his supplication, but in his countenance too, went his way "more justified" than the shameless Pharisee.[9] The sounds of our voice, likewise, should be subdued; else, if we are to be heard for our noise, how large windpipes should we need! But God is the hearer not of the *voice*, but of the *heart*, just as He is its inspector. The demon of the Pythian oracle says:

"And I do understand the mute, and plainly hear the speechless one."[10]

Do the ears of God wait for sound? How, then, could Jonah's prayer find way out unto heaven from the depth of the whale's belly, through the entrails of so huge a beast; from the very abysses, through so huge a mass of sea? What superior advantage will they who pray too loudly gain, except that they annoy their neighbours? Nay, by making their petitions audible, what less error do they commit than if they were to pray in public?[11]

CHAP. XVIII.—OF THE KISS OF PEACE.

Another custom has now become prevalent. Such are fasting withhold the kiss of peace, which is the seal of prayer, after prayer made with brethren. But when is peace more to be concluded with brethren than when, at the time of some religious observance,[12] our prayer ascends with more acceptability; that they may themselves participate in our observance, and thereby be mollified for transacting with their brother touching their own peace? What prayer is complete if divorced from the "holy kiss?"[13] Whom does peace impede when rendering service to his Lord? What kind of sacrifice is that from which men depart without peace? Whatever our prayer be, it will not be better than the observance of the precept by which we are bidden to conceal our fasts;[14] for *now*, by abstinence from the kiss, we are known to be fasting. But even if there be some reason *for this practice*, still, lest you offend against this precept, you may perhaps defer your "peace" *at home*, where it is not possible for your fast to be en-

---

[1] Or, "reasonable service." See Rom. xii. 1.
[2] Or, "Gentile practices."
[3] See 1 Cor. xi. 3–16.
[4] 2 Tim. iv. 13.
[5] Dan. iii. 21, etc.
[6] i.e. that they have seen it done; for children imitate anything and everything (Oehler).
[7] [Vol. II. p. 18 (Vision V.), this Series. Also, *Ib.* p. 57, note 2. See Routh's quotation from Cotelerius, p. 180, in Volume before noted.]
[8] Routh and Oehler (after Rigaltius) refer us to Tob. xii. 12. They also, with Dodgson, refer to Luke i. 11. Perhaps there may be a reference to Rev. viii. 3, 4.

[9] Luke xviii. 9–14.
[10] Herod. i. 47.
[11] Which is forbidden, Matt. vi. 5, 6.
[12] Such as fasting.
[13] See Rom. xvi. 16; 1 Cor. xvi. 20; 2 Cor. xiii. 12: 1 Thess. v. 26; 1 Pet. v. 14. [The sexes apart.]
[14] Matt. vi. 16–18.

tirely kept secret. But wherever else you can conceal your observance, you ought to remember the precept: thus you may satisfy the requirements of Discipline abroad and of custom at home. So, too, on the day of the passover,[1] when the religious observance of a fast is general, and as it were public, we justly forego the kiss, caring nothing to conceal anything which we do in common with all.

CHAP. XIX.—OF STATIONS.

Similarly, too, touching the days of Stations,[2] most think that they must not be present at the sacrificial prayers, on the ground that the Station must be dissolved by reception of the Lord's Body. Does, then, the Eucharist cancel a service devoted to God, or bind it more to God? Will not your *Station* be more solemn if you have withal *stood* at God's *altar?*[3] When the Lord's Body has been received and reserved,[4] each point is secured, both the participation of the sacrifice and the discharge of duty. If the "Station" has received its name from the example of military life—for we withal are God's military[5]—of course no gladness or sadness chancing to the camp abolishes the "stations" of the soldiers: for gladness will carry out discipline more willingly, sadness more carefully.

CHAP. XX.—OF WOMEN'S DRESS.

So far, however, as regards the dress of women, the variety of observance compels us —men of no consideration whatever—to treat, presumptuously indeed, after the most holy apostle,[6] except in so far as it will not be presumptuously if we treat the subject in accordance with the apostle. Touching modesty of dress and ornamentation, indeed, the prescription of Peter[7] likewise is plain, checking as he does with the same mouth, because with the same Spirit, as Paul, the glory of garments, and the pride of gold, and the meretricious elaboration of the hair.

CHAP. XXI.—OF VIRGINS.

But that point which is promiscuously observed throughout the churches, whether virgins ought to be veiled or no, must be treated of. For they who allow to virgins immunity from head-covering, appear to rest on this;

that the apostle has not defined "virgins" by name, but "women,"[8] as "to be veiled;" nor the sex generally, so as to say "females," but a *class* of the sex, by saying "women:" for if he had named the sex by saying "females," he would have made his limit absolute for *every* woman; but while he names one class of the sex, he separates another class by being silent. For, they say, he might either have named "virgins" specially; or generally, by a compendious term, "females."

CHAP. XXII.—ANSWER TO THE FOREGOING ARGUMENTS.

They who make this concession[9] ought to reflect on the nature of the word itself—what is the meaning of "woman" from the very first records of the sacred writings. Here they find it to be *the name of the sex,* not a *class of the sex:* if, that is, God gave to Eve, when she had not yet known a man, the surname "woman" and "female"[10]—("female," whereby the sex generally; "woman," whereby a class of the sex, is marked).[11] So, since at that time the as yet unwedded Eve was called by the word "woman," that word has been made common even to a virgin.[12] Nor is it wonderful that the apostle—guided, of course, by the same Spirit by whom, as all the divine Scripture, so that book Genesis, was drawn up—has used the selfsame word in writing "women," which, by the example of Eve unwedded, is applicable too to a "virgin." In fact, all the other passages are in consonance herewith. For even by this very fact, that he has not *named* "virgins" (as he does in another place[13] where he is teaching touching marrying), he sufficiently predicates that his remark is made touching *every* woman, and touching *the whole* sex; and that there is no distinction made between a "virgin" *and any other,* while he does not name her at all. For he who elsewhere—namely, where the difference requires—remembers to make the distinction, (moreover, he makes it by designating each species by their appropriate names,) wishes, where he makes *no* distinction (while he does not name each), *no* difference to be understood. What of the fact that in the Greek speech, in which the apostle wrote his letters, it is usual to say, "women" rather than "females;" that is, γυναῖκας

---

[1] i.e. "Good Friday," as it is now generally called.
[2] The word *Statio* seems to have been used in more than one sense in the ancient Church. A passage in the *Shepherd of Hermas*, referred to above (B. iii. Sim. 5), appears to make it ="fast."
[3] "Ara," not "altare."
[4] For receiving at home apparently, when your *station* is over.
[5] See 2 Tim. ii. 1, etc. [See Hermas, Vol. I., p. 33.]
[6] See 1 Cor. xi. 1–16; 1 Tim. ii. 9, 10.
[7] 1 Pet. iii. 1–6.

[8] 1 Cor. xi. 5.
[9] As to the distinction between "women" and "virgins."
[10] Gen. ii. 23. In the LXX. and in the Eng. ver. there is but the one word "woman."
[11] These words are regarded by Dr. Routh as spurious, and not without reason. Mr. Dodgson likewise omits them, and refers to *de Virg. Vel.* cc. 4 and 5.
[12] In *de Virg. Vel.* 5, Tertullian speaks even more strongly: "And so you have the name, I say not now *common*, but *proper* to a virgin ; a name which from the beginning a *virgin* received."
[13] 1 Cor. vii. 34 et seq.

(*gunaikas*) rather than θηλείας (*theleias*)? Therefore if that word,[1] which by interpretation represents what "female" (*femina*) represents,[2] is frequently used *instead* of the name of the sex,[3] he has named the *sex* in saying γυναῖκα; but in the *sex* even the *virgin* is embraced. But, withal, the declaration is plain: "*Every* woman," saith he, " praying and prophesying with head uncovered,[4] dishonoureth her own head."[5] What is "*every* woman, but *woman* of every age, of every rank, of every condition? By saying "every" he excepts nought of womanhood, just as he excepts nought of manhood either from *not* being covered; for just so he says, "*Every man.*"[6] As, then, in the masculine sex, under the name of " man " even the " youth " is *forbidden* to be veiled; so, too, in the feminine, under the name of " woman," even the " virgin " is *bidden* to be veiled. Equally in each sex let the younger age follow the discipline of the elder; or else let the male "virgins,"[7] too, be *veiled*, if the female virgins withal are *not* veiled, because *they* are not mentioned by *name*. Let " man " and " youth" be different, if " woman " and " virgin " are different. For indeed it is " on account of the angels"[8] that he saith women must be veiled, because on account of " the daughters of men " angels revolted from God.[9] Who, then, would contend that "*women*" alone— that is,[10] such as were already wedded and had lost their virginity—were the objects of angelic concupiscence, unless " virgins " are incapable of excelling in beauty and finding lovers? Nay, let us see whether it were not *virgins alone* whom they lusted after; since Scriptures saith " *the daughters* of men; "[11] inasmuch as it might have named "*wives* of men," or " females," indifferently.[12] Likewise, in that it saith, "And they took them to themselves for wives,"[13] it does so on this ground, that, of course, such are " received *for wives*" as are devoid of that title. But it would have expressed itself differently concerning such as were *not* thus devoid. And so (they who are named) are devoid as much of *widowhood* as of *virginity*. So completely has *Paul* by naming the sex generally, mingled " daughters " and species together in the genus. Again, while he says that " nature herself,"[14] which has assigned hair as a tegument and ornament to women, " teaches that veiling is the duty of females, " has not the same tegument and the same honour of the head been assigned also to virgins? If " it is shameful " for a woman to be shorn it is similarly so to a virgin too. From them, then, to whom is assigned one and the same *law* of the head,[15] one and the same *discipline*[16] of the head is exacted, —(which extends) even unto those virgins whom their childhood defends,[17] for from the first[18] *a virgin* was named " female." This custom,[19] in short, even Israel observes; but if *Israel* did *not* observe it, *our* Law,[20] amplified and supplemented, would vindicate the addition for itself; let it be excused for imposing the veil on virgins also. Under *our* dispensation, let that age which is ignorant of its sex[21] retain the privilege of simplicity. For both Eve and Adam, when it befell them to be " wise,"[22] forthwith veiled what they had learnt to know.[23] At all events, with regard to those in whom girlhood has changed (into maturity), their age ought to remember its duties as to nature, so also, to discipline; for they are being transferred to the rank of " women " both in their persons and in their functions. No one is a " virgin " from the time when she is capable of marriage; seeing that, in her, age has by that time been wedded to its own husband, that is, to time.[24] " But some particular *virgin* has devoted herself to God. From that very moment she both changes the fashion of her hair, and converts all her garb into that of a ' woman.' " Let her, then, maintain the character wholly, and perform the whole function of a " virgin: " what she conceals[25] for the sake of God, let her cover quite over.[26] It is our business to entrust to the knowledge of God alone that which the grace of God effects in us, lest we receive from man the reward we hope for from God.[27] Why do you denude before God[28] what you cover

---

[1] γυνή.
[2] Mr. Dodgson appears to think that there is some transposition here ; and at first sight it may appear so. But when we look more closely, perhaps there is no need to make any difficulty : the stress is rather on the words " by *interpretation*," which, of course, is a different thing from " *usage ;*" and by *interpretation* γυνή appears to come *nearer* to " femina " than to " mulier."
[3] θηλεία.
[4] Or, " unveiled."
[5] 1 Cor. xi. 5.
[6] 1 Cor. xi. 4.
[7] For a similar use of the word " virgin," see Rev. xiv. 4.
[8] 1 Cor. xi. 10.
[9] See Gen. vi. 2 in the LXX., with the *v. l.* ed. Tisch. 1860; and compare Tertullian, *de Idol.* c. 9, and the note there Mr. Dodgson refers, too, to *de Virg. Vel.* c. 7, where this curious subject is more fully entered into.
[10] i.e. according to *their* definition, whom Tertullian is refuting.
[11] Gen. vi. 2.
[12] i.e. If *married women* had been meant, either word, " uxores " or " feminæ," could have been used indifferently.
[13] Gen. vi. 2.
[14] 1 Cor. xi. 14.

[15] i.e. long hair
[16] i.e. veiling.
[17] i.e. " exempts."
[18] i.e. from her creation.
[19] Of the universal veiling of women."
[20] i.e. as above, the Sermon on the Mount.
[21] i.e. mere infancy.
[22] Gen. iii. 6.
[23] Gen. ii. 27 (or in the LXX. iii. 1), and iii. 7, 10, 11.
[24] Routh refers us to *de Virg. Vel.* c. 11.
[25] i.e. the redundance of her hair.
[26] i.e. by a veil.
[27] i.e. says Oehler, " lest we postpone the eternal favour of God, which we hope for, to the temporal veneration of men ; a risk which those virgins seemed likely to run, who, when devoted to God, used to go veiled in public, but bareheaded in the church."
[28] i.e. in church.

before men?[1] Will you be more modest in public than in the church? If *your self-devotion* is a grace of God, and you have received it, "why do you boast," saith he, "as if you have not received it?"[2] Why, by your ostentation of yourself, do you judge others? Is it that, by your boasting, you invite others unto good? Nay, but even you yourself run the risk of losing, if you boast; and you drive others unto the same perils! What is assumed from love of boasting is easily destroyed. Be veiled, virgin, if virgin you are; for you ought to blush. If you are a virgin, shrink from (the gaze of) many eyes. Let no one wonder at your face; let no one perceive your falsehood.[3] You do well in falsely assuming the married character, if you veil your head; nay, you do not seem to assume it *falsely,* for you *are* wedded to Christ: to Him you have surrendered your body; act as becomes your Husband's discipline. If He bids the brides of others to be veiled, His own, of course, much more. "But each individual man[4] is not to think that the institution of his predecessor is to be overturned." Many yield up their own judgment, and its consistency, to the custom of others. Granted that *virgins* be not *compelled* to be veiled, at all events such as *voluntarily are* so should not be prohibited; who, likewise, cannot deny themselves to be virgins,[5] content, in the security of a good conscience before God, to damage their own fame.[6] Touching such, however, as are betrothed, I can with constancy "above my small measure"[7] pronounce and attest that they are to be veiled from that day forth on which they shuddered at the first bodily touch of a man by kiss and hand. For in them everything has been forewedded: their age, through maturity; their flesh, through age; their spirit, through consciousness; their modesty, through the experience of the kiss; their hope, through expectation; their mind, through volition. And Rebecca is example enough for us, who, when her betrothed had been pointed out, veiled herself for marriage merely on recognition of him.[8]

CHAP. XXIII.—OF KNEELING.

In the mattter of *kneeling* also prayer is subject to diversity of observance, through the act of some few who abstain from kneeling on the Sabbath; and since this dissension is particularly on its trial before the churches, the Lord will give His grace that the dissentients may either yield, or else indulge their opinion without offence to others. We, however (just as we have received), only on the day of the Lord's Resurrection ought to guard not only against kneeling, but every posture and office of solicitude; deferring even our businesses lest we give any place to the devil.[9] Similarly, too, in the period of Pentecost; which period we distinguish by the same solemnity of exultation.[10] But who would hesitate *every* day to prostrate himself before God, at least in the first prayer with which we enter on the daylight? At fasts, moreover, and Stations, no prayer should be made without kneeling, and the remaining customary marks of humility; for (then)[11] we are not only *praying,* but *deprecating,* and making satisfaction to God our Lord.[12] Touching *times* of prayer nothing at all has been prescribed, except clearly "to pray at every time and every place."[13]

CHAP. XXIV.—OF PLACE FOR PRAYER.

But how "in every place," since we are prohibited[14] (from praying) in public? In every place, he means, which opportunity or even necessity, may have rendered suitable: for that which was done by the apostles[15] (who, in gaol, in the audience of the prisoners, "began praying and singing to God") is not considered to have been done contrary to the precept; nor yet that which was done by Paul,[16] who in the ship, in presence of all, "made thanksgiving to God."[17]

CHAP. XXV.—OF TIME FOR PRAYER.

Touching the *time,* however, the extrinsic[18] observance of certain hours will not be unprofitable—those common hours, I mean, which mark the intervals of the day—the third, the sixth, the ninth—which we

---

[1] i.e. in public; see note 27, *supra.*
[2] 1 Cor. iv. 7.
[3] i.e. as Muratori, quoted by Oehler, says, your "pious" (?) fraud in pretending to be married when you are a virgin; because "devoted" virgins used to dress and wear veils like married women, as being regarded as "wedded to Christ."
[4] i.e. each president of a church, or bishop.
[5] i.e. "are known to be such through the chastity of their manner and life" (Oehler).
[6] "By appearing in public as married women, while in heart they are virgins" (Oehler).
[7] Does Tertullian refer to 2 Cor. x. 13? or does "modulus" mean, as Oehler thinks, "my rule?" [It seems to me a very plain reference to the text before mentioned, and to the Apostolic Canon of not exceeding one's Mission.]
[8] Gen. xxiv. 64, 65.
[9] Eph. iv. 27.
[10] i.e. abstaining from kneeling: *kneeling* being more "a posture of solicitude" and of humility; *standing,* of "exultation."

[11] i.e. at fasts and Stations. [Sabbath=Saturday, *supra.*]
[12] For the meaning of "satisfaction" as used by the Fathers, see Hooker, *Eccl. Pol.* vi. 5.
[13] Eph. vi. 18; 1 Thess. v. 17; 1 Tim. ii. 8.
[14] Matt. vi. 5, 6, which forbids praying in public.
[15] Paul and Silas (Acts xvi. 25).
[16] I have followed Muratori's reading here.
[17] Mr. Dodgson renders "celebrated the Eucharist;" but that rendering appears very doubtful. See Acts xxvii. 35.
[18] Mr. Dodgson supposes this word to mean "outward, as contrasted with the inward, 'praying always.'" Oehler interprets, "ex vita communi." But perhaps what Tertullian says lower down in the chapter, "albeit they stand *simply without any precept enjoining their observance,*" may give us the true clue to his meaning; so that "extrinsecus" would = "extrinsic to any direct injunction of our Lord or His apostles."

may find in the Scriptures to have been more solemn than the rest. The first infusion of the Holy Spirit into the congregated disciples took place at "the third hour."[1] Peter, on the day on which he experienced the vision of Universal Community,[2] (exhibited) in that small vessel,[3] had ascended into the more lofty parts *of the house*, for prayer's sake "at the sixth hour."[4] The same (apostle) was going into the temple, with John, "at the ninth *hour*,"[5] when he restored the paralytic to his health. Albeit these *practices* stand simply without any *precept* for their observance, still it may be granted a good thing to establish some definite presumption, which may both add stringency to the admonition to pray, and may, as it were by a law, tear us out from our businesses unto such a duty; so that—what we read to have been observed by Daniel also,[6] in accordance (of course) with Israel's discipline—we pray at least not less than thrice in the day, debtors as we are to Three—Father, Son, and Holy Spirit: of course, in addition to our regular prayers which are due, without any admonition, on the entrance of light and of night. But, withal, it becomes believers not to take food, and not to go to the bath, before interposing a prayer; for the refreshments and nourishments of the spirit are to be held prior to those of the flesh, and things heavenly prior to things earthly.

CHAP. XXVI.—OF THE PARTING OF BRETHREN.

You will not dismiss a brother who has entered your house without prayer.—"Have you seen," says *Scripture*, "a brother? you have seen your Lord;"[7]—especially "a stranger," lest perhaps he be "an angel." But again, when received yourself by brethren, you will not make[8] earthly refreshments prior to heavenly, for your faith will forthwith be judged. Or else how will you—according to the precept[9]—say, "Peace to this *house*," unless you exchange mutual peace with them who are *in* the house?

CHAP. XXVII.—OF SUBJOINING A PSALM.

The more diligent in prayer are wont to subjoin in their prayers the "Hallelujah,"[10] and such kind of psalms, in the closes of which the company respond. And, of course, every institution is excellent which, for the extolling and honouring of God, aims unitedly to bring Him enriched prayer as a choice victim.[11]

CHAP. XXVIII.—OF THE SPIRITUAL VICTIM, WHICH PRAYER IS.

For this is the spiritual victim[12] which has abolished the pristine sacrifices. "To what purpose," saith He, "(bring ye) me the multitude of your sacrifices? I am full of holocausts of rams, and I desire not the fat of rams, and the blood of bulls and of goats. For who hath required these from your hands?"[13] What, then, God *has* required the Gospel teaches. "An hour will come," saith He, "when the true adorers shall adore the Father in spirit and truth. For God is a Spirit, and accordingly requires His adorers to be such."[14] We are the true adorers and the true priests,[15] who, praying in spirit,[16] sacrifice, in spirit, prayer,—a victim proper and acceptable to God, which assuredly He has required, which He has looked forward to[17] for Himself! This *victim*, devoted from the whole heart, fed on faith, tended by truth, entire in innocence, pure in chastity, garlanded with love,[18] we ought to escort with the pomp[19] of good works, amid psalms and hymns, unto God's altar,[20] to obtain for us all things from God.

CHAP. XXIX.—OF THE POWER OF PRAYER.

For what has God, who exacts it *ever* denied[21] to prayer coming from "spirit and truth?" How mighty specimens of its efficacy do we read, and hear, and believe! *Old-world* prayer, indeed, used to free from fires,[22] and from beasts,[23] and from famine;[24] and yet it had not (then) received its form from Christ. But how far more amply operative is *Christian* prayer! It does not station the angel of dew

---

[1] Acts ii. 1–4, 14, 15.
[2] Communitatis omnis (Oehler). Mr. Dodgson renders, "of every sort of common thing." Perhaps, as Routh suggests, we should read "omnium."
[3] Vasculo. But in Acts it is, σκεῦός τι ὡς ὀθόνην μεγάλην [*Small* is here comparatively used, with reference to *Universality* of which it was the symbol.]
[4] Acts x. 9.
[5] Acts iii. 1: but the man is not said to have been "paralytic," but "lame from his mother's womb."
[6] Dan. vi. 10 ; comp. Ps. lv. 17 (in the LXX. it is liv. 18).
[7] I have ventured to turn the first part of the sentence into a question. What "scripture" this may be, no one knows. [It seems to me a clear reference to Matt. xxv. 38, amplified by the 45th verse, in a way not unusual with our author.] Perhaps, in addition to the passages in Gen. xviii. and Heb. xiii. 2, to which the editors naturally refer, Tertullian may allude to such passages as Mark ix 37, Matt. xxv. 40, 45. [Christo in pauperibus.]
[8] I have followed Routh's conjecture, "feceris" for "fecerit," which Oehler does not even notice.
[9] Luke x. 5.

[10] Perhaps "the great Hallelujah," i.e. the last five psalms.
[11] [The author seems to have in mind (Hos. xiv. 2) "the calves of our lips."]
[12] 1 Pet. ii. 5.
[13] Isa. i. 11. See the LXX.
[14] John iv. 23, 24.
[15] Sacerdotes ; comp. *de Ex. Cast.* c. 7.
[16] 1 Cor. xiv. 15 ; Eph. vi. 18.
[17] Or, "provided."
[18] "Agape," perhaps "the love-feast."
[19] Or, "procession."
[20] Altare.
[21] Routh would read, "What *will* God *deny*?"
[22] Dan. iii.
[23] Dan. vi.
[24] 1 Kings xviii. ; Jas. v. 17, 18.

in mid-fires,[1] nor muzzle lions, nor transfer to the hungry the rustics' bread;[2] it has no delegated grace to avert any sense of suffering;[3] but it supplies the suffering, and the feeling, and the grieving, with endurance: it amplifies grace by virtue, that faith may know what she obtains from the Lord, understanding what—for God's name's sake—she suffers. But in days gone by, withal prayer used to call down[4] plagues, scatter the armies of foes, withhold the wholesome influences of the showers. Now, however, the prayer of righteousness averts all God's anger, keeps bivouac on behalf of personal enemies, makes supplication on behalf of persecutors. Is it wonder if *it* knows how to extort the *rains* of heaven[5] —(prayer) which was *once* able to procure its *fires?*[6]   Prayer is alone that which vanquishes[7] God.   But Christ has willed that it be operative for no evil: He had conferred on it all its virtue in the cause of good.   And so it knows nothing save how to recall the souls of the departed from the very path of death, to transform the weak, to restore the sick, to purge the possessed, to open prison-bars, to loose the bonds of the innocent.   Likewise it washes away faults, repels temptations, extinguishes persecutions, consoles the faint-spirited, cheers the high-spirited, escorts travellers, appeases waves, makes robbers stand aghast, nourishes the poor, governs the rich, upraises the fallen, arrests the falling, confirms the standing.   Prayer is the wall of faith: her arms and missiles[8] against the foe who keeps watch over us on all sides.   And, so never walk we unarmed.   By day, be we mindful of Station; by night, of vigil.   Under the arms of prayer guard we the standard of our General; await we in prayer the angel's trump.[9]   The angels, likewise, all pray; every creature prays; cattle and wild beasts pray and bend their knees; and when they issue from their layers and lairs,[10] they look up heavenward with no idle mouth, making their breath vibrate[11] after their own manner. Nay, the birds too, rising out of the nest, upraise themselves heavenward, and, instead of hands, expand the cross of their wings, and say somewhat to seem like prayer.[12]   What more then, touching the office of prayer? Even the Lord Himself prayed; to whom be honour and virtue unto the ages of the ages!

---

[1] i.e. " the angel who preserved in the furnace the three youths besprinkled, as it were, with dewy shower " (Muratori, quoted by Oehler). [Apocrypha, *The Song, etc.*, verses 26, 27.]

[2] 2 Kings. iv. 42-44.

[3] i.e. in brief, its *miraculous* operations, as they are called, are suspended in these ways.

[4] Or, " inflict."

[5] See *Apolog.* c. 5 (Oehler).

[6] See 2 Kings i.

[7] [A reference to Jacob's wrestling. Also, probably, to Matt. xi. 12.]

[8] Or, " her armour defensive and offensive."

[9] 1 Cor. xv. 52 ; 1 Thess. iv. 16.

[10] Or, " pens and dens."

[11] As if in prayer.

[12] [This beautiful passage should be supplemented by a similar one from St. Bernard : " Nonne et aviculas levat, non onerat pennarum numerositas ipsa? Tolle eas, et reliquum corpus pondere suo fertur ad ima. Sic disciplinam Christi, sic suave jugum, sic onus leve, quo deponimus, eo deprimimur ipsi : quia portat potius quam portatur." Epistola, ccclxxxv. Bernardi Opp. Tom. i. p. 691. Ed. (Mabillon.) Gaume, Paris, 1839. Bearing the cross up-lifts the Christian.]

IV.

AD MARTYRAS.[1]

(TRANSLATED BY THE REV. S. THELWALL.)

CHAP. I.

BLESSED Martyrs Designate,—Along with the provision which our lady mother the Church from her bountiful breasts, and each brother out of his private means, makes for your bodily wants in the prison, accept also from me some contribution to your spiritual sustenance; for it is not good that the flesh be feasted and the spirit starve: nay, if that which is weak be carefully looked to, it is but right that that which is still weaker should not be neglected. Not that I am specially entitled to exhort you; yet not only the trainers and overseers, but even the unskilled, nay, all who choose, without the slightest need for it, are wont to animate from afar by their cries the most accomplished gladiators, and from the mere throng of onlookers useful suggestions have sometimes come; first, then, O blessed, grieve not the Holy Spirit,[2] who has entered the prison with you; for if He had not gone with you there, you would not have been there this day. Do you give all endeavour, therefore, to retain Him; so let Him lead you thence to your Lord. The prison, indeed, is the devil's house as well, wherein he keeps his family. But you have come within its walls for the very purpose of trampling the wicked one under foot in his chosen abode. You had already in pitched battle outside utterly overcome him; let him have no reason, then, to say to himself, "They are now in my domain; with vile hatreds I shall tempt them, with defections or dissensions among themselves." Let him fly from your presence, and skulk away into his own abysses, shrunken and torpid, as though he were an outcharmed or smoked-out snake. Give him not the suc-cess in his own kingdom of setting you at variance with each other, but let him find you armed and fortified with concord; for peace among you is battle with him. Some, not able to find this peace in the Church, have been used to seek it from the imprisoned martyrs.[3] And so you ought to have it dwelling with you, and to cherish it, and to guard it, that you may be able perhaps to bestow it upon others.

CHAP. II.

Other things, hindrances equally of the soul, may have accompanied you as far as the prison gate, to which also your relatives may have attended you. There and thenceforth you were severed from the world; how much more from the ordinary course of worldly life and all its affairs ! Nor let this separation from the world alarm you; for if we reflect that the world is more really the prison, we shall see that you have gone out of a prison rather than into one. The world has the greater darkness, blinding men's hearts. The world imposes the more grievous fetters, binding men's very souls. The world breathes out the worst impurities—human lusts. The world contains the larger number of criminals, even the whole human race. Then, last of all, it awaits the judgment, not of the proconsul, but of God. Wherefore, O blessed, you may regard yourselves as having been translated from a prison to, we may say, a place of safety. It is full of darkness, but ye yourselves are light; it has bonds, but God has made you free. Unpleasant exhalations are there, but ye are an odour of sweetness. The

---

[1] Written in his early ministry, and strict orthodoxy. [It may be dated *circa* A.D. 197, as external evidence will shew.]

[2] Eph. iv. 30. [Some differences had risen between these holy sufferers, as to the personal merits of offenders who had appealed to them for their interest in restoring them to communion.]

[3] [He favours this resource as sanctioned by custom, and gently persuades them, by agreeing as to its propriety, to bestow peace upon others. But, the foresight of those who objected was afterwards justified, for in Cyprian's day this practice led to greater evils, and he was obliged to discourage it (ep. xi.) in an epistle to confessors.]

judge is daily looked for, but ye shall judge the judges themselves. Sadness may be there for him who sighs for the world's enjoyments. The Christian outside the prison has renounced the world, but in the prison he has renounced a prison too. It is of no consequence where you are in the world—you who are not of it. And if you have lost some of life's sweets, it is the way of business to suffer present loss, that after gains may be the larger. Thus far I say nothing of the rewards to which God invites the martyrs. Meanwhile let us compare the life of the world and of the prison, and see if the spirit does not gain more in the prison than the flesh loses. Nay, by the care of the Church and the love of the brethren,[1] even the flesh does not lose there what is for its good, while the spirit obtains besides important advantages. You have no occasion to look on strange gods, you do not run against their images; you have no part in heathen holidays, even by mere bodily mingling in them; you are not annoyed by the foul fumes of idolatrous solemnities; you are not pained by the noise of the public shows, nor by the atrocity or madness or immodesty of their celebrants; your eyes do not fall on stews and brothels; you are free from causes of offence, from temptations, from unholy reminiscences; you are free now from persecution too. The prison does the same service for the Christian which the desert did for the prophet. Our Lord Himself spent much of His time in seclusion, that He might have greater liberty to pray, that He might be quit of the world. It was in a mountain solitude, too, He showed His glory to the disciples. Let us drop the name of prison; let us call it a place of retirement. Though the body is shut in, though the flesh is confined, all things are open to the spirit. In spirit, then, roam abroad; in spirit walk about, not setting before you shady paths or long colonnades, but the way which leads to God. As often as in spirit your footsteps are there, so often you will not be in bonds. The leg does not feel the chain when the mind is in the heavens. The mind compasses the whole man about, and whither it wills it carries him. But where thy heart shall be, there shall be thy treasure.[2] Be there our heart, then, where we would have our treasure.

CHAP. III.

Grant now, O blessed, that even to Christians the prison is unpleasant; yet we were called to the warfare of the living God in our very response to the sacramental words. Well, no soldier comes out to the campaign laden with luxuries, nor does he go to action from his comfortable chamber, but from the light and narrow tent, where every kind of hardness, roughness and unpleasantness must be put up with. Even in peace soldiers inure themselves to war by toils and inconveniences—marching in arms, running over the plain, working at the ditch, making the *testudo*, engaging in many arduous labours. The sweat of the brow is on everything, that bodies and minds may not shrink at having to pass from shade to sunshine, from sunshine to icy cold, from the robe of peace to the coat of mail, from silence to clamour, from quiet to tumult. In like manner, O blessed ones, count whatever is hard in this lot of yours as a discipline of your powers of mind and body. You are about to pass through a noble struggle, in which the living God acts the part of superintendent, in which the Holy Ghost is your trainer, in which the prize is an eternal crown of angelic essence, citizenship in the heavens, glory everlasting. Therefore your Master, Jesus Christ, who has anointed you with His Spirit, and led you forth to the arena, has seen it good, before the day of conflict, to take you from a condition more pleasant in itself, and has imposed on you a harder treatment, that your strength might be the greater. For the athletes, too, are set apart to a more stringent discipline, that they may have their physical powers built up. They are kept from luxury, from daintier meats, from more pleasant drinks; they are pressed, racked, worn out; the harder their labours in the preparatory training, the stronger is the hope of victory. "And they," says the apostle, "that they may obtain a corruptible crown."[3] We, with the crown eternal in our eye, look upon the prison as our training-ground, that at the goal of final judgment we may be brought forth well disciplined by many a trial; since virtue is built up by hardships, as by voluptuous indulgence it is overthrown.

CHAP. IV.

From the saying of our Lord we know that the flesh is weak, the spirit willing.[4] Let us not, withal, take delusive comfort from the Lord's acknowledgment of the weakness of the flesh. For precisely on this account He first declared the spirit willing, that He might show which of the two ought to be subject to the other—that the flesh might yield obedience to the spirit—the weaker to the stronger; the

1 [Who ministered to their fellow-Christians in prison, for the testimony of Jesus. What follows is a sad picture of social life among heathens.]
2 Matt. vi. 21.
3 1 Cor. ix. 25.
4 Matt. xxvi. 41.

former thus from the latter getting strength. Let the spirit hold converse with the flesh about the common salvation, thinking no longer of the troubles of the prison, but of the wrestle and conflict for which they are the preparation. The flesh, perhaps, will dread the merciless sword, and the lofty cross, and the rage of the wild beasts, and that punishment of the flames, of all most terrible, and all the skill of the executioner in torture. But, on the other side, let the spirit set clearly before both itself and the flesh, how these things, though exceeding painful, have yet been calmly endured by many,—and, have even been eagerly desired for the sake of fame and glory; and this not only in the case of men, but of women too, that you, O holy women, may be worthy of your sex. It would take me too long to enumerate one by one the men who at their own self-impulse have put an end to themselves. As to women, there is a famous case at hand: the violated Lucretia, in the presence of her kinsfolk, plunged the knife into herself, that she might have glory for her chastity. Mucius burned his right hand on an altar, that this deed of his might dwell in fame. The philosophers have been out-stripped,—for instance Heraclitus, who, smeared with cowdung, burned himself; and Empedocles, who leapt down into the fires of Ætna; and Peregrinus,[1] who not long ago threw himself on the funeral pile. For women even have despised the flames. Dido did so, lest, after the death of a husband very dear to her, she should be compelled to marry again; and so did the wife of Hasdrubal, who, Carthage being on fire, that she might not behold her husband suppliant as Scipio's feet, rushed with her children into the conflagration, in which her native city was destroyed. Regulus, a Roman general, who had been taken prisoner by the Carthaginians, declined to be exchanged for a large number of Carthaginian captives, choosing rather to be given back to the enemy. He was crammed into a sort of chest; and, everywhere pierced by nails driven from the outside, he endured so many crucifixions. Woman has voluntarily sought the wild beasts, and even asps, those serpents worse than bear or bull, which Cleopatra applied to herself, that she might not fall into the hands of her enemy. But the fear of death is not so great as the fear of torture. And so the Athenian courtezan succumbed to the executioner, when, subjected to torture by the tyrant for having taken part in a conspiracy, still making no betrayal of her confederates, she at last bit off her tongue and spat it in the tyrant's face, that he might be

convinced of the uselessness of his torments, however long they should be continued. Everybody knows what to this day is the great Lacedæmonian solemnity—the διαμαστίγωσις, or scourging; in which sacred rite the Spartan youths are beaten with scourges before the altar, their parents and kinsmen standing by and exhorting them to stand it bravely out. For it will be always counted more honourable and glorious that the soul rather than the body has given itself to stripes. But if so high a value is put on the earthly glory, won by mental and bodily vigour, that men, for the praise of their fellows, I may say, despise the sword, the fire, the cross, the wild beasts, the torture; these surely are but trifling sufferings to obtain a celestial glory and a divine reward. If the bit of glass is so precious, what must the true pearl be worth? Are we not called on, then, most joyfully to lay out as much for the true as others do for the false?

CHAP. V.

I leave out of account now the motive of glory. All these same cruel and painful conflicts, a mere vanity you find among men—in fact, a sort of mental disease—as trampled under foot. How many ease-lovers does the conceit of arms give to the sword? They actually go down to meet the very wild beasts in vain ambition; and they fancy themselves more winsome from the bites and scars of the contest. Some have sold themselves to fires, to run a certain distance in a burning tunic. Others, with most enduring shoulders, have walked about under the hunters' whips. The Lord has given these things a place in the world, O blessed, not without some reason: for what reason, but *now* to animate us, and on that day to confound us if we have feared to suffer for the truth, that we might be saved, what others out of vanity have eagerly sought for to their ruin?

CHAP. VI.

Passing, too, from examples of enduring constancy having such an origin as this, let us turn to a simple contemplation of man's estate in its ordinary conditions, that mayhap from things which happen to us whether we will or no, and which we must set our minds to bear, we may get instruction. How often, then, have fires consumed the living! How often have wild beasts torn men in pieces, it may be in their own forests, or it may be in the heart of cities, when they have chanced to escape from their dens! How many have fallen by the robber's sword! How many have suffered at the hands of enemies the death of the cross, after having been tortured first, yes,

---

[1] [He is said to have perished *circa* A.D. 170.]

and treated with every sort of contumely! One may even suffer in the cause of a man what he hesitates to suffer in the cause of God. In reference to this indeed, let the present time [1] bear testimony, when so many persons of rank have met with death in a mere human being's cause, and that though from their birth and dignities and bodily condition and age such a fate seemed most unlikely; either suffering at his hands if they have taken part against him, or from his enemies if they have been his partisans.

[1] [After the defeat and suicide of Albinus, at Lyons, many persons, some of Senatorial rank, were cruelly put to death.]

V.

APPENDIX.

THE MARTYRDOM OF PERPETUA AND FELICITAS.

(TRANSLATED BY THE REV. R. E. WALLIS, PH.D.)

NOBODY will blame me for placing here the touching' history of these Martyrs. It illustrates the period of history we are now considering, and sheds light on the preceding treatise. I can hardly read it without tears, and it ought to make us love "the noble army of martyrs." I think Tertullian was the *editor* of the story, not its author.[1] Felicitas is mentioned by name in the *De Anima:* and the closing paragraph of this memoir is quite in his style. To these words I need only add that Dr. Routh, who unfortunately decided not to re-edit it, ascribes the first edition to Lucas Holstenius. He was Librarian of the Vatican and died in 1661. The rest may be learned from this INTRODUCTORY NOTICE of the Translator:

Perpetua and Felicitas suffered martyrdom in the reign of Septimius Severus, about the year 202 A.D. Tertullian mentions Perpetua,[2] and a further clue to the date is given in the allusion to the birth-day of "Geta the Cæsar," the son of Septimius Severus. There is therefore, good reason for rejecting the opinion held by some, that they suffered under Valerian and Gallienus. Some think that they suffered at Tuburbium in Mauritania; but the more general opinion is, that Carthage was the scene of their martyrdom.

The "Acta," detailing the sufferings of Perpetua and Felicitas, has been held by all critics to be a genuine document of antiquity. But much difference exists as to who was the compiler. In the writing itself, Perpetua and Saturus are mentioned as having written certain portions of it; and there is no reason to doubt the statement. Who the writer of the remaining portion was, is not known. Some have assigned the work to Tertullian; some have maintained that, whoever the writer was, he was a Montanist, and some have tried to show that both martyrs and narrator were Montanists.[3] The narrator must have been a contemporary; according to many critics, he was an eye-witness of the sufferings of the martyrs. And he must have written the narrative shortly after the events.

Dean Milman says, "There appear strong indications that the acts of these African martyrs are translated from the Greek; at least it is difficult otherwise to account for the frequent untranslated Greek words and idioms in the text.[4]

The Passion of Perpetua and Felicitas was edited by Petrus Possinus, Rome, 1663; by Henr. Valesius, Paris, 1664; and the Bollandists. The best and latest edition is by Ruissart, whose text is adopted in Gallandi's and Migne's collections of the Fathers.

---

[1] Cap. lv. He calls her *fortissima martyr*, and she is one of only two or three contemporary sufferers whom he mentions by name.   [2] [In the *De Anima*, cap. lv. as see above.]

[3] [Yet see the sermons of St. Augustine (if indeed his) on the Passion of these Saints. Sermon 281 and 282, opp. Tom. v. pp. 1284–5.]   [4] *Hist. of Christianity*, vol. i. ch. viii.

THE PASSION OF THE HOLY MARTYRS PERPETUA AND FELICITAS.

PREFACE.[1]

IF ancient illustrations of faith which both testify to God's grace and tend to man's edification are collected in writing, so that by the perusal of them, as if by the reproduction of the facts, as well God may be honoured, as man may be strengthened; why should not new instances be also collected, that shall be equally suitable for both purposes,—if only on the ground that these modern examples will one day become ancient and available for posterity, although in their present time they are esteemed of less authority, by reason of the presumed veneration for antiquity? But let men look to it, if they judge the power of the Holy Spirit to be one, according to the times and seasons; since some things of later date must be esteemed of more account as being nearer to the very last times, in accordance with the exuberance of grace manifested to the final periods determined for the world. For "in the last days, saith the Lord, I will pour out of my Spirit upon all flesh; and their sons and their daughters shall prophesy. And upon my servants and my handmaidens will I pour out of my Spirit; and your young men shall see visions, and your old men shall dream dreams."[2] And thus we—who both acknowledge and reverence, even as we do the prophecies, modern visions as equally promised to us, and consider the other powers of the Holy Spirit as an agency of the Church for which also He was sent, administering all gifts in all, even as the Lord distributed to every one[3] as well needfully collect them in writing, as commemorate them in reading to God's glory; that so no weakness or despondency of faith may suppose that the divine grace abode only among the ancients, whether in respect of the condescension that raised

up martyrs, or that gave revelations; since God always carries into effect what He has promised, for a testimony to unbelievers, to believers for a benefit. And we therefore, what we have heard and handled, declare also to you, brethren and little children, that as well you who were concerned in these matters may be reminded of them again to the glory of the Lord, as that you who know them by report may have communion with the blessed martyrs, and through them with the Lord Jesus Christ, to whom be glory and honour, for ever and ever.[4] Amen.

CHAP. I.—ARGUMENT.—WHEN THE SAINTS WERE APPREHENDED, ST. PERPETUA SUCCESSFULLY RESISTED HER FATHER'S PLEADING, WAS BAPTIZED WITH THE OTHERS, WAS THRUST INTO A FILTHY DUNGEON. ANXIOUS ABOUT HER INFANT, BY A VISION GRANTED TO HER, SHE UNDERSTOOD THAT HER MARTYRDOM WOULD TAKE PLACE VERY SHORTLY.

1. The young catechumens, Revocatus and his fellow-servant Felicitas, Saturninus and Secundulus, were apprehended. And among them also was Vivia Perpetua, respectably born, liberally educated, a married matron, having a father and mother and two brothers, one of whom, like herself, was a catechumen, and a son an infant at the breast. She herself was about twenty-two years of age. From this point onward she shall herself narrate the whole course of her martyrdom, as she left it described by her own hand and with her own mind.

2. "While," says she, "we were still with the persecutors, and my father, for the sake of his affection for me, was persisting in seeking to turn me away, and to cast me down from the faith,—'Father,' said I, 'do you see, let us say, this vessel lying here to be a little pitcher, or something else?' And he said, 'I see it to be so.' And I replied to him, 'Can it be called by any other name than what it

[1] [Both Perpetua and Felicitas were evidently Montanistic in character and impressions, but, the fact that they have never been reputed other than Catholic, goes far to explain Tertullian's position for years after he had withdrawn from communion with the vacillating Victor.]
[2] Joel ii. 28, 29. [The quotation here is a note of Montanistic prepossessions in the writer.]
[3] [Routh notes this as undoubted evidence of a Montanistic author. *Reliquiæ*, Vol. I. p. 455.]
[4] [St. Augustine takes pains to remind us that these *Acta* are not canonical. *De Anima*, cap. 2, opp. Tom. x. p. 481.]

is?' And he said, 'No.' 'Neither can I call myself anything else than what I am, a Christian.' Then my father, provoked at this saying, threw himself upon me, as if he would tear my eyes out. But he only distressed me, and went away overcome by the devil's arguments. Then, in a few days after I had been without my father, I gave thanks to the Lord; and his absence became a source of consolation [1] to me. In that same interval of a few days we were baptized, and to me the Spirit prescribed that in the water of *baptism* nothing else was to be sought for than bodily endurance. [2] After a few days we are taken into the dungeon, and I was very much afraid, because I had never felt such darkness. O terrible day! O the fierce heat of the shock of the soldiery, because of the crowds! I was very unusually distressed by my anxiety for my infant. There were present there Tertius and Pomponius, the blessed deacons who ministered to us, and had arranged by means of a gratuity that we might be refreshed by being sent out for a few hours into a pleasanter part of the prison. Then going out of the dungeon, all attended to their own wants. [3] I suckled my child, which was now enfeebled with hunger. In my anxiety for it, I addressed my mother and comforted my brother, and commended to their care my son. I was languishing because I had seen them languishing on my account. Such solicitude I suffered for many days, and I obtained leave for my infant to remain in the dungeon with me; and forthwith I grew strong and was relieved from distress and anxiety about my infant; and the dungeon became to me as it were a palace, so that I preferred being there to being elsewhere.

•3. "Then my brother said to me, 'My dear sister, you are already in a position of great dignity, and are such that you may ask for a vision, and that it may be made known to you whether this is to result in a passion or an escape.' [4] And I, who knew that I was privileged to converse with the Lord, whose kindnesses I had found to be so great, boldly promised him, and said, 'To-morrow I will tell you.' And I asked, and this was what was shown me. I saw a golden ladder of marvellous height, reaching up even to heaven, and very narrow, so that persons could only ascend it one by one; and on the sides of the ladder was fixed every kind of iron weapon. There were there swords, lances, hooks, daggers; so that if any one went up carelessly, or not looking upwards, he would be torn to pieces, and his flesh would cleave to the iron weapons. And under the ladder itself was crouching a dragon of wonderful size, who lay in wait for those who ascended, and frightened them from the ascent. And Saturus went up first, who had subsequently delivered himself up freely on our account, not having been present at the time that we were taken prisoners. And he attained the top of the ladder, and turned towards me, and said to me, 'Perpetua, I am waiting for [5] you; but be careful that the dragon do not bite you.' And I said, 'In the name of the Lord Jesus Christ, he shall not hurt me.' And from under the ladder itself, as if in fear of me, he slowly lifted up his head; and as I trod upon the first step, I trod upon his head. And I went up, and I saw an immense extent of garden, and in the midst of the garden a white-haired man sitting in the dress of a shepherd, [6] of a large stature, milking sheep; and standing around were many thousand white-robed ones. And he raised his head, and looked upon me, and said to me, 'Thou art welcome, daughter.' And he called me, and from the cheese as he was milking he gave me as it were a little cake, and I received it with folded hands; and I ate it, and all who stood around said Amen. And at the sound of their voices I was awakened, still tasting a sweetness which I cannot describe. And I immediately related this to my brother, and we understood that it was to be a passion, and we ceased henceforth to have any hope in this world.

CHAP. II.—ARGUMENT. PERPETUA, WHEN BESIEGED BY HER FATHER, COMFORTS HIM. WHEN LED WITH OTHERS TO THE TRIBUNAL, SHE AVOWS HERSELF A CHRISTIAN, AND IS CONDEMNED WITH THE REST TO THE WILD BEASTS. SHE PRAYS FOR HER BROTHER DINOCRATES, WHO WAS DEAD.

1. "After a few days there prevailed a report that we should be heard. And then my father came to me from the city, worn out with anxiety. He came up to me, that he might cast me down, saying, 'Have pity my daughter, on my grey hairs. Have pity on your father, if I am worthy to be called a father by you. If with these hands I have brought you up to this flower of your age, if I have preferred you to all your brothers, do not deliver me up to the scorn of men. Have regard to your brothers, have regard to your mother and your aunt, have regard to your son, who will not be able to live after you.

---

[1] "Refrigeravit," Græce ἀνέπαυσεν, *scil.* "requiem dedit."
[2] i. e. the grace of martyrdom.
[3] Sibi vacabant.
[4] Commeatus.

[5] "Sustineo," Græce ὑπομένω, *scil.* "exspecto."
[6] This was an ordinary mode of picturing our Lord in the oratories and on the sacred vessels of those days. [This passage will recall the allegory of Hermas, with which the martyr was doubtless familiar.]

Lay aside your courage, and do not bring us all to destruction; for none of us will speak in freedom if you should suffer anything.' These things said my father in his affection, kissing my hands, and throwing himself at my feet; and with tears he called me not Daughter, but Lady. And I grieved over the grey hairs of my father, that he alone of all my family would not rejoice over my passion. And I comforted him, saying, 'On that scaffold[1] whatever God wills shall happen. For know that we are not placed in our own power, but in that of God.' And he departed from me in sorrow.

2. "Another day, while we were at dinner, we were suddenly taken away to be heard, and we arrived at the town-hall. At once the rumour spread through the neighbourhood of the public place, and an immense number of people were gathered together. We mount the platform. The rest were interrogated, and confessed. Then they came to me, and my father immediately appeared with my boy, and withdrew me from the step, and said in a supplicating tone, 'Have pity on your babe.' And Hilarianus the procurator, who had just received the power of life and death in the place of the proconsul Minucius Timinianus, who was deceased, said, 'Spare the grey hairs of your father, spare the infancy of your boy, offer sacrifice for the well-being of the emperors.' And I replied, 'I will not do so.' Hilarianus said, 'Are you a Christian?' And I replied, 'I am a Christian.' And as my father stood there to cast me down *from the faith*, he was ordered by Hilarianus to be thrown down, and was beaten with rods. And my father's misfortune grieved me as if I myself had been beaten, I so grieved for his wretched old age.[2] The procurator then delivers judgment on all of us, and condemns us to the wild beasts, and we went down cheerfully to the dungeon. Then, because my child had been used to receive suck from me, and to stay with me in the prison, I send Pomponius the deacon to my father to ask for the infant, but my father would not give it him. And even as God willed it, the child no long desired the breast, nor did my breast cause me uneasiness, lest I should be tormented by care for my babe and by the pain of my breasts at once.

3. "After a few days, whilst we were all praying, on a sudden, in the middle of our prayer, there came to me a word, and I named Dinocrates; and I was amazed that that name had never come into my mind until then, and I was grieved as I remembered his misfortune.

And I felt myself immediately to be worthy, and to be called on to ask on his behalf.[3] And for him I began earnestly to make supplication, and to cry with groaning to the Lord. Without delay, on that very night, this was shown to me in a vision.[4] I saw Dinocrates going out from a gloomy place, where also there were several others, and he was parched and very thirsty, with a filthy countenance and pallid colour, and the wound on his face which he had when he died. This Dinocrates had been my brother after the flesh, seven years of age,[5] who died miserably with disease—his face being so eaten out with cancer, that his death caused repugnance to all men. For him I had made my prayer, and between him and me there was a large interval,[6] so that neither of us could approach to the other. And moreover, in the same place where Dinocrates was, there was a pool full of water, having its brink higher than was the stature of the boy; and Dinocrates raised himself up as if to drink. And I was grieved that, although that pool held water, still, on account of the height to its brink, he could not drink. And I was aroused, and knew that my brother was in suffering. But I trusted that my prayer would bring help to his suffering; and I prayed for him every day until we passed over into the prison of the camp, for we were to fight in the camp-show. Then was the birth-day of Geta Cæsar, and I made my prayer for my brother day and night, groaning and weeping that he might be granted to me.

4. "Then, on the day on which we remained in fetters,[7] this was shown to me. I saw that that place which I had formerly observed to be in gloom was now bright; and Dinocrates, with a clean body well clad, was finding refreshment. And where there had been a

---

[2] [St. August. opp. iv. 541.]
[3] [The story in 2 Maccab. xii. 40–45, is there narrated as a thought suggested to the soldiers under Judas, and not discouraged by him, though it concerned men guilty of idolatry and dying in mortal sin, by the vengeance of God. It may have occurred to some Christians that their heathen kindred might, therefore, not be beyond the visitations of the Divine compassion. But, obviously, even were it not an Apocryphal text, it can have no bearing whatever on the case of Christians. The doctrine of Purgatory is that nobody dying in mortal sin can have the benefit of its discipline, or any share in the prayers and oblations of the Faithful, whatever.]
[4] "Oromate." [This vision, it must be observed, has nothing to do with prayers for the *Christian* dead, for this brother of Perpetua was a heathen child whom she supposed to be in the *Inferi*. It illustrates the anxieties Christians felt for those of their kindred who had not died in the Lord; even for children of seven years of age. Could the gulf be bridged and they received into Abraham's bosom? This dream of Perpetua comforted her with a trust that so it should be. Of course this story has been used fraudulently, to help a system of which these times knew nothing. Cyprian says expressly: "Apud Inferos confessio non est, nec exomologesis illic fieri potest." *Epistola lii.* p. 98. Opp. ·Paris, 1574. In the Edinburgh series (translations) this epistle is numbered 51, and elsewhere 54.]
[5] [There is not the slightest reason to suppose that this child had been baptized: the father a heathen and Perpetua herself a recent catechumen. Elucidation.]
[6] "Diadema," or rather "diastema." [Borrowed from Luke xvi. 26. But that gulf could not be passed according to the evangelist.]
[7] "Nervo."

---

[1] "Catasta," a raised platform on which the martyrs were placed either for trial or torture.

wound, I saw a scar; and that pool which I had before seen, *I saw now* with its margin lowered even to the boy's navel. And one drew water from the pool incessantly, and upon its brink was a goblet filled with water; and Dinocrates drew near and began to drink from it, and the goblet did not fail. And when he was satisfied, he went away from the water to play joyously, after the manner of children, and I awoke. Then I understood that he was translated from the place of punishment.

CHAP. III.—ARGUMENT. PERPETUA IS AGAIN TEMPTED BY HER FATHER. HER THIRD VISION, WHEREIN SHE IS LED AWAY TO STRUGGLE AGAINST AN EGYPTIAN. SHE FIGHTS, CONQUERS, AND RECEIVES THE REWARD.

1. "Again, after a few days, Pudens, a sol--dier, an assistant overseer[1] of the prison, who began to regard us in great esteem, perceiving that the great power of God was in us, admitted many brethren to see us, that both we and they might be mutually refreshed. And when the day of the exhibition drew near, my father, worn with suffering, came in to me, and began to tear out his beard, and to throw himself on the earth, and to cast himself down on his face, and to reproach his years, and to utter such words as might move all creation. I grieved for his unhappy old age.[2]

2. "The day before that on which we were to fight, I saw in a vision that Pomponius the deacon came hither to the gate of the prison, and knocked vehemently. I went out to him, and opened the gate for him; and he was clothed in a richly ornamented white robe, and he had on manifold calliculæ.[3] And he said to me, 'Perpetua, we are waiting for you; come!' And he held his hand to me, and we began to go through rough and winding places. Scarcely at length had we arrived breathless at the amphitheatre, when he led me into the middle of the arena, and said to me, 'Do not fear, I am here with you, and I am labouring with you;' and he departed. And I gazed upon an immense assembly in astonishment. And because I knew that I was given to the wild beasts, I marvelled that the wild beasts were not let loose upon me. Then there came forth against me a certain Egyptian, horrible in appearance, with his backers, to fight with me. And there came

to me, as my helpers and encouragers, handsome youths; and I was stripped, and became a man.[4] Then my helpers began to rub me with oil, as is the custom for contest; and I beheld that Egyptian on the other hand rolling in the dust.[5] And a certain man came forth, of wondrous height, so that he even overtopped the top of the amphitheatre; and he wore a loose tunic and a purple robe between two bands over the middle of the breast; and he had on *calliculæ* of varied form, made of gold and silver; and he carried a rod, as if he were a trainer of gladiators, and a green branch upon which were apples of gold. And he called for silence, and said, 'This Egyptian, if he should overcome this woman, shall kill her with the sword; and if she shall conquer him, she shall receive this branch.' Then he departed. And we drew near to one another, and began to deal·out blows. He sought to lay hold of my feet, while I struck at his face with my heels; and I was lifted up in the air, and began thus to thrust at him as if spurning the earth. But when I saw that there was some delay I joined my hands so as to twine my fingers with one another; and I took hold upon his head, and he fell on his face, and I trod upon his head.[6] And the people began to shout, and my backers to exult. And I drew near to the trainer and took the branch; and he kissed me, and said to me, 'Daughter, peace be with you:' and I began to go gloriously to the Sanavivarian gate.[7] Then I awoke, and perceived that I was not to fight with beasts, but against the devil. Still I knew that the victory was awaiting me. This, so far, I have completed several days before the exhibition; but what passed at the exhibition itself let who will write."

CHAP. IV.—ARGUMENT. SATURUS, IN A VISION, AND PERPETUA BEING CARRIED BY ANGELS INTO THE GREAT LIGHT, BEHOLD THE MARTYRS. BEING BROUGHT TO THE THRONE OF GOD, ARE RECEIVED WITH A KISS. THEY RECONCILE OPTATUS THE BISHOP AND ASPASIUS THE PRESBYTER.

1. Moreover, also, the blessed Saturus related this his vision, which he himself committed to writing:—"We had suffered," says he, "and we were gone forth from the flesh, and we were beginning to be borne by four angels into the east; and their hands touched

---

[1] Optio.
[2] [St. Aug. Opp. Tom. v. p. 1284.]
[3] It seems uncertain what may be the meaning of this word. It is variously supposed to signify little round ornaments either of cloth or metal attached to the soldier's dress, or the small bells on the priestly robe. Some also read the word *galliculæ*, small sandals.

[4] [Concerning these visions, see Augustine, *De Anima*, cap. xviii. *et seq.*]
[5] "Afa" is the Greek word ἀφή, *a grip;* hence used of the yellow sand sprinkled over wrestlers, to enable them to grasp one another.
[6] [Ps. xliv. 5. Also lx. 12. xci. 13, cviii. 13.]
[7] This was the way by which the victims spared by the popular clemency escaped from the amphitheatre.

us not. And we floated not supine, looking upwards, but as if ascending a gentle slope. And being set free, we at length saw the first boundless light; and I said, 'Perpetua' (for she was at my side), 'this is what the Lord promised to us; we have received the promise.' And while we are borne by those same four angels, there appears to us a vast space which was like a pleasure-garden, having rose-trees and every kind of flower. And the height of the trees was after the measure of a cypress, and their leaves were falling[1] incessantly. Moreover, there in the pleasure-garden four other angels appeared, brighter than the previous ones, who, when they saw us, gave us honour, and said to the rest of the angels, 'Here they are! Here they are!' with admiration. And those four angels who bore us, being greatly afraid, put us down; and we passed over on foot the space of a furlong in a broad path. There we found Jocundus and Saturninus and Artaxius, who having suffered the same persecution were burnt alive; and Quintus, who also himself a martyr had departed in the prison. And we asked of them where the rest were. And the angels said to us, 'Come first, enter and greet your Lord.'

2. "And we came near to a place, the walls of which were such as if they were built of light; and before the gate of that place stood four angels, who clothed those who entered with white robes. And being clothed, we entered and saw the boundless light, and heard the united voice of some who said without ceasing, 'Holy! Holy! Holy!'[2] And in the midst of that place we saw as it were a hoary man sitting, having snow-white hair, and with a youthful countenance; and his feet we saw not. And on his right hand and on his left were four-and-twenty elders, and behind them a great many others were standing. We entered with great wonder, and stood before the throne; and the four angels raised us up, and we kissed Him, and He passed His hand over our face. And the rest of the elders said to us, 'Let us stand;' and we stood and made peace. And the elders said to us, 'Go and enjoy.' And I said, 'Perpetua, you have what you wish.' And she said to me, 'Thanks be to God, that joyous as I was in the flesh, I am now more joyous here.'

3. "And we went forth, and saw before the entrance Optatus the bishop at the right hand, and Aspasius the presbyter, a teacher,[3]

at the left hand, separate and sad; and they cast themselves at our feet, and said to us, 'Restore peace between us, because you have gone forth and have left us thus.' And we said to them, 'Art not thou our father, and thou our presbyter, that you should cast yourselves at our feet?'' And we prostrated ourselves, and we embraced them; and Perpetua began to speak with them, and we drew them apart in the pleasure-garden under a rose-tree. And while we were speaking with them, the angels said unto them, 'Let them alone, that they may refresh themselves;[4] and if you have any dissensions between you, forgive one another.' And they drove them away. And they said to Optatus, 'Rebuke thy people, because they assemble to you as if returning from the circus, and contending about factious matters.' And then it seemed to us as if they would shut the doors. And in that place we began to recognise many brethren, and moreover martyrs. We were all nourished with an indescribable odour, which satisfied us. Then, I joyously awoke.''

CHAP. V.—ARGUMENT. SECUNDULUS DIES IN THE PRISON. FELICITAS IS PREGNANT, BUT WITH MANY PRAYERS SHE BRINGS FORTH IN THE EIGHTH MONTH WITHOUT SUFFERING. THE COURAGE OF PERPETUA AND OF SATURUS UNBROKEN.

1. The above were the more eminent visions of the blessed martyrs Saturus and Perpetua themselves, which they themselves committed to writing.[5] But God called Secundulus, while he has yet in the prison, by an earlier exit from the world, not without favour, so as to give a respite to the beasts. Nevertheless, even if his soul did not acknowledge cause for thankfulness, assuredly his flesh did.

2. But respecting Felicitas (for to her also the Lord's favour approached in the same way), when she had already gone eight months with child (for she had been pregnant when she was apprehended), as the day of the exhibition was drawing near, she was in great grief lest on account of her pregnancy she should be delayed,—because pregnant women are not allowed to be publicly punished,—and lest she should shed her sacred and guiltless blood among some who had been wicked subsequently. Moreover, also, her fellow-martyrs were painfully saddened lest they should leave so excellent a friend, and as it were companion, alone in the path of the same hope. Therefore, joining together their

---

[1] "Cadebant;" but "ardebant"—"were burning"—seems a more probable reading. [The imitations of *the Shepherd* of Hermas, in this memoir hardly need pointing out.]
[2] Agios.
[3] A presbyter, that is, whose office was to teach, as distinct from other presbyters. See Cyprian, *Epistles*, vol. i. Ep. xxiii. p. 68, note 1, transl. [One of those referred to by St. James iii. 1, and by St. Paul, I. Tim. v. 17.]

[4] More probably, "rest and refresh yourselves." ["Go and enjoy," or, "play," or "take pleasure," in the section preceding.]
[5] [To be regarded, like *the Shepherd* of Hermas, merely as visions, or allegorical romances.]

united cry, they poured forth their prayer to the Lord three days before the exhibition. Immediately after their prayer her pains came upon her, and when, with the difficulty natural to an eight months' delivery, in the labour of bringing forth she was sorrowing, some one of the servants of the *Cataractarii*[1] said to her, "You who are in such suffering now, what will you do when you are thrown to the beasts, which you despised when you refused to sacrifice?" And she replied, "Now it is I that suffer what I suffer; but then there will be another in me, who will suffer for me, because I also am about to suffer for Him." Thus she brought forth a little girl, which a certain sister brought up as her daughter.

3. Since then the Holy Spirit permitted, and by permitting willed, that the proceedings of that exhibition should be committed to writing, although we are unworthy to complete the description of so great a glory; yet we obey as it were the command of the most blessed Perpetua, nay her sacred trust, and add one more testimony concerning her constancy and her loftiness of mind. While they were treated with more severity by the tribune, because, from the intimations of certain deceitful men, he feared lest thay should be withdrawn from the prison by some sort of magic incantations, Perpetua answered to his face, and said, "Why do you not at least permit us to be refreshed, being as we are objectionable to the most noble Cæsar, and having to fight on his birth-day?[2] Or is it not your glory if we are brought forward fatter on that occasion?" The tribune shuddered and blushed, and commanded that they should be kept with more humanity, so that permission was given to their brethren and others to go in and be refreshed with them; even the keeper of the prison trusting them now himself.

4. Moreover, on the day before, when in that last meal, which they call the free meal, they were partaking as far as they could, not of a free supper, but of an *agape;* with the same firmness they were uttering such words as these to the people, denouncing *against them* the judgment of the Lord, bearing witness to the felicity of their passion, laughing at the curiosity of the people who came together; while Saturus said, "To-morrow is not enough for you, for you to behold with pleasure that which you hate. Friends to-day, enemies to-morrow. Yet note our faces diligently, that you may recognise them on that day of judgment." Thus all departed

thence astonished, and from these things many believed.

CHAP. VI.—ARGUMENT. FROM THE PRISON THEY ARE LED FORTH WITH JOY INTO THE AMPHITHEATRE, ESPECIALLY PERPETUA AND FELICITAS. ALL REFUSE TO PUT ON PROFANE GARMENTS. THEY ARE SCOURGED, THEY ARE THROWN TO THE WILD BEASTS. SATURUS TWICE IS UNHURT. PERPETUA AND FELICITAS ARE THROWN DOWN ; THEY ARE CALLED BACK TO THE SANAVIVARIAN GATE. SATURUS WOUNDED BY A LEOPARD, EXHORTS THE SOLDIER. THEY KISS ONE ANOTHER, AND ARE SLAIN WITH THE SWORD.

1. The day of their victory shone forth, and they proceeded from the prison into the amphitheatre, as if to an assembly, joyous and of brilliant countenances; if prechance shrinking, it was with joy, and not with fear. Perpetua followed with placid look, and with step and gait as a matron of Christ, beloved of God; casting down the luster of her eyes from the gaze of all. Moreover, Felicitas, rejoicing that she had safely brought forth, so that she might fight with the wild beasts; from the blood and from the midwife to the gladiator, to wash after childbirth with a second baptism. And when they were brought to the gate, and were constrained to put on the clothing—the men, that of the priests of Saturn, and the women, that of those who were consecrated to Ceres—that noble-minded woman resisted even to the end with constancy. For she said, "We have come thus far of our own accord, for this reason, that our liberty might not be restrained. For this reason we have yielded our minds, that we might not do any such thing as this: we have agreed on this with you." Injustice acknowledged the justice; the tribune yielded to their being brought as simply as they were. Perpetua sang psalms, already treading under foot the head of the Egyptian; Revocatus, and Saturninus, and Saturus uttered threatenings against the gazing people about this martyrdom. When they came within sight of Hilarianus, by gesture and nod, they began to say to Hilarianus, "Thou judgest us," say they, "but God will judge thee." At this the people, exasperated, demanded that they should be tormented with scourges as they passed along the rank of the *venatores*.[3] And they indeed rejoiced that they should have incurred any one of their Lord's passions.

2. But He who had said, "Ask, and ye

---

[1] "The gaolers," so called from the "cataracta," or prison-gate, which they guarded.
[2] [A gentle banter, like that of St. Lawrence on the gridiron.]

[3] A row of men drawn up to scourge them as they passed along, a punishment probably similar to what is called " running the gauntlet."

shall receive,"[1] gave to them when they asked, that death which each one had wished for. For when at any time they had been discoursing among themselves about their wish in respect of their martyrdom, Saturninus indeed had professed that he wished that he might be thrown to all the beasts; doubtless that he might wear a more glorious crown. Therefore in the beginning of the exhibition, he and Revocatus made trial of the leopard, and moreover upon the scaffold they were harassed by the bear. Saturus, however, held nothing in greater abomination than a bear; but he imagined that he would be put an end to with one bite of a leopard. Therefore, when a wild boar was supplied, it was the huntsman rather who had supplied that boar who was gored by that same beast, and died the day after the shows. Saturus only was drawn out; and when he had been bound on the floor near to a bear, the bear would not come forth from his den. And so Saturus for the second time is recalled unhurt.

3. Moreover, for the young women the devil prepared a very fierce cow, provided especially for that purpose contrary to custom, rivalling their sex also in that of the beasts. And so, stripped and clothed with nets, they were led forth. The populace shuddered as they saw one young woman of delicate frame, and another with breasts still dropping from her recent childbirth. So, being recalled, they are unbound.[2] Perpetua is first led in. She was tossed, and fell on her loins; and when she saw her tunic torn from her side, she drew it over her as a veil for her middle, rather mindful of her modesty than her suffering. Then she was called for again, and bound up her dishevelled hair; for it was not becoming for a martyr to suffer with dishevelled hair, lest she should appear to be mourning in her glory. So she rose up; and when she saw Felicitas crushed, she approached and gave her her hand, and lifted her up. And both of them stood together; and the brutality of the populace being appeased, they were recalled to the Sanavivarian gate. Then Perpetua was received by a certain one who was still a catechumen, Rusticus by name, who kept close to her; and she, as if aroused from sleep, so deeply had she been in the Spirit and in an ecstasy, began to look round her, and to say to the amazement of all, "I cannot tell when we are to be led out to that cow." And when she had heard what had already happened, she did not believe it[3]

until she had perceived certain signs of injury in her body and in her dress, and had recognised the catechumen. Afterwards causing that catechumen and the brother to approach, she addressed them, saying, "Stand fast in the faith, and love one another, all of you, and be not offended at my sufferings."

4. The same Saturus at the other entrance exhorted the soldier Pudens, saying, "Assuredly here I am, as I have promised and foretold, for up to this moment I have felt no beast. And now believe with your whole heart. Lo, I am going forth to that beast, and I shall be destroyed with one bite of the leopard." And immediately at the conclusion of the exhibition he was thrown to the leopard; and with one bite of his he was bathed with such a quantity of blood, that the people shouted out to him as he was returning, testimony of his second baptism, "Saved and washed, saved and washed."[4] Manifestly he was assuredly saved who had been glorified in such a spectacle. Then to the soldier Pudens he said, "Farewell, and be mindful of my faith; and let not these things disturb, but confirm you." And at the same time he asked for a little ring from his finger, and returned it to him bathed in his wound, leaving to him an inherited token and the memory of his blood. And then lifeless he is cast down with the rest, to be slaughtered in the usual place. And when the populace called for them into the midst, that as the sword penetrated into their body they might make their eyes partners in the murder, they rose up of their own accord, and transferred themselves whither the people wished; but they first kissed one another, that they might consummate their martyrdom with the kiss of peace. The rest indeed, immoveable and in silence, received the sword-thrust; much more Saturus, who also had first ascended the ladder, and first gave up his spirit, for he also was waiting for Perpetua. But Perpetua, that she might taste some pain, being pierced between the ribs, cried out loudly, and she herself placed the wavering right hand of the youthful gladiator to her throat.[5] Possibly such a woman could not have been slain unless she herself had willed it, because she was feared by the impure spirit.

O most brave and blessed martyrs! O truly called and chosen unto the glory of our Lord Jesus Christ! whom whoever magnifies, and honours, and adores, assuredly ought to read these examples for the edification of the Church, not less than the ancient ones, so that

---

[1] John xvi. 24.
[2] Ita revocatæ discinguntur. Dean Milman prefers reading this, "Thus recalled, they are clad in loose robes."
[3] [Routh, *Reliq.* Vol. I. p. 360.]

[4] A cry in mockery of what was known as the effect of Christian baptism.
[5] [Routh, Reliquiæ, Vol. I. p. 358.]

new virtues also may testify that one and the same Holy Spirit is always operating even until now, and God the Father Omnipotent, and His Son Jesus Christ our Lord, whose is the glory and infinite power for ever and ever. Amen.

ELUCIDATION.

(Dinocrates, cap. ii, p. 701.)

The avidity with which the Latin controversial writers seize upon this fanciful passage, (which, in fact, is subversive of their whole doctrine about Purgatory, as is the text from the *Maccabees*,) makes emphatic the utter absence from the early Fathers of any reference to such a dogma; which, had it existed, must have appeared in every reference to the State of the Dead, and in every account of the discipline of penitents. Arbp. Usher[1] ingeniously turns the tables upon these errorists, by quoting the Prayers for the Dead, which were used in the Early Church, but which, such as they were, not only make no mention of a Purgatory, but refute the dogma, by their uniform limitation of such prayers to the blessed dead, and to their consummation of bliss at the Last day and not before. Such a prayer *seems* to occur in II. Tim. i. 18. The context (vers. 16–18, and iv. 19) strongly supports this view; Onesiphorus is spoken of as if deceased, apparently. But, as Chrysostom understands it, he was only absent (in Rome) from his household. From i. 17 we should infer that he had left Rome.[2]

---

[1] Republished, Oxford, 1838.

[2] See Opp. Tom. xi. p. 657. Ed. Migne.

VI.

OF PATIENCE.[1]

(TRANSLATED BY THE REV. S. THELWALL.)

CHAP. I.—OF PATIENCE GENERALLY ; AND TERTULLIAN'S OWN UNWORTHINESS TO TREAT OF IT.

I Fully confess unto the Lord God that it has been rash enough, if not even impudent, in *me* to have dared compose a treatise on Patience, for *practising* which I am all unfit, being a man of no goodness;[2] whereas it were becoming that such as have addressed themselves to the demonstration and commendation of some particular thing, should themselves first be conspicuous in the practice of that thing, and should regulate the constancy of their commonishing by the authority of their personal conduct, for fear their words blush at the deficiency of their deeds. And would that this "blushing" would bring a remedy, so that shame for *not* exhibiting that which we go to suggest to others should prove a tutorship into exhibiting it; except that the magnitude of some good things—just as of some ills too—is insupportable, so that only the grace of divine inspiration is effectual for attaining and practising them. For what is *most* good rests *most* with God; nor does any other than He who possesses it dispense it, as He deems meet to each. And so to discuss about that which it is not given one to enjoy, will be, as it were, a solace; after the manner of invalids, who since they are without health, know not how to be silent about its blessings. So I, most miserable, ever sick with the heats of *im*patience, must of necessity sigh after, and invoke, and persistently plead for, that health of patience which I possess not; while I recall to mind, and, in the contemplation of my own weakness, digest, *the truth*, that the good health of faith, and the soundness of the Lord's dis-

cipline, accrue not easily to any unless patience sit by his side.[3] So is patience set over the things of God, that one can obey no precept, fulfil no work well-pleasing to the Lord, if estranged from it. The good of it, even they who live outside it,[4] honour with the name of highest virtue. Philosophers indeed, who are accounted animals of some considerable wisdom, assign it so high a place, that, while they are mutually at discord with the various fancies of their sects and rivalries of their sentiments, yet, having a community of regard for patience alone, to this one of their pursuits they have joined in granting peace: for it they conspire; for it they league; it, in their affectation of[5] virtue, they unanimously pursue; concerning patience they exhibit all their ostentation of wisdom. Grand testimony this is to it, in that it incites even the vain schools of the world[6] unto praise and glory ! Or is it rather an injury, in that a thing divine is bandied among worldly sciences? But let them look to that, who shall presently be ashamed of their wisdom, destroyed and disgraced together with the world[7] (it lives in).

CHAP. II.—GOD HIMSELF AN EXAMPLE OF PATIENCE.

To *us*[8] no human affectation of canine[9] equanimity, modelled[10] by insensibility, furnishes the warrant for exercising patience; but the divine arrangement of a living and celestial discipline, holding up before us God

---

[3] [Elucidation I.]
[4] i. e. who are strangers to it.
[5] Or, "striving after."
[6] Or, "heathendom"—sæculi.
[7] Sæculo.
[8] i.e. us Christians.
[9] i. e. cynical = κυνικός = dog-like. But Tertullian appears to use " caninæ" purposely, and I have therefore retained it rather than substitute (as Mr. Dodgson does) " cynical."
[10] i.e. the *affectation* is modelled by insensibility.

---

[1] [Written possibly as late as A.D. 202 ; and is credited by Neander and Kaye, with Catholic Orthodoxy.]
[2] " Nullius boni ;" compare Rom. vii. 18.

Himself in the very first place as an example of patience; who scatters equally over just and unjust the bloom of this light; who suffers the good offices of the seasons, the services of the elements, the tributes of entire nature, to accrue at once to worthy and unworthy; bearing with the most ungrateful nations, adoring *as they do* the toys of the arts and the works of their own hands, persecuting His Name together with His family; *bearing with* luxury, avarice, iniquity, malignity, waxing insolent daily:[1] so that by His own patience He disparages Himself; for the cause why many believe not in the Lord is that they are so long without knowing[2] that He is wroth with the world.[3]

CHAP. III.—JESUS CHRIST IN HIS INCARNATION AND WORK A MORE IMITABLE EXAMPLE THERE-OF.

And *this* species of the divine patience indeed being, as it were, at a distance, may perhaps be esteemed as among "things too high for us;"[4] but what is that which, in a certain way, has been grasped by hand[5] among men openly on the earth? God suffers Himself to be conceived in a mother's womb, and awaits *the time for birth;* and, when born, bears *the delay* of growing up; and, when grown up, is not eager to be recognised, but is furthermore contumelious to Himself, and is baptized by His own servant; and repels with words alone the assaults of the tempter; while from being "Lord" He becomes "Master," teaching man to escape death, having been trained to the exercise of the absolute forbearance of offended patience.[6] He did not strive; He did not cry aloud; nor did any hear His voice in the streets. He did not break the bruised reed; the smoking flax He did not quench: for the prophet—nay, the attestation of God Himself, placing His own Spirit, together with patience in its entirety, in His Son—had not falsely spoken. There was none desirous of cleaving to Him whom He did not receive. No one's table or roof did He despise: indeed, Himself ministered to the washing of the disciples' feet; not sinners, not publicans, did He repel; not with that city even which had refused to receive Him was He wroth,[7] when even the disciples had wished that the celestial fires should be forthwith hurled on so contumelious

a town. He cared for the ungrateful; He yielded to His ensnarers. This were a small matter, if He had not had in His company even His own betrayer, and stedfastly abstained from pointing him out. Moreover, while He is being betrayed, while He is being led up "as a sheep for a victim," (for "so He no more opens His mouth than a lamb under the power of the shearer,") He to whom, had He willed it, legions of angels would at one word have presented themselves from the heavens, approved not the avenging sword of even one disciple. The patience of the Lord was wounded in (the wound of) Malchus. And so, too, He cursed for the time to come the works of the sword; and, by the restoration of health, made satisfaction to him whom Himself had not hurt, through Patience, the mother of Mercy. I pass by in silence (the fact) that He is crucified, for this was the end for which He had come; yet had the death which must be undergone need of contumelies likewise?[8] *Nay,* but, when about to depart, He wished to be sated with the pleasure of patience. He is spitted on, scourged, derided, clad foully, more foully crowned. Wondrous is the faith of equanimity! He who had set before *Him* the concealing of Himself in man's shape, imitated nought of man's impatience! Hence, even more than from any other trait, ought ye, Pharisees, to have recognised the Lord. Patience of this kind none of *men* would achieve. Such and so mighty evidences—the *very* magnitude of which proves to be among the nations indeed a cause for rejection of the faith, but among us its reason and rearing —proves manifestly enough (not by the sermons only, in enjoining, but likewise by the sufferings of the Lord in enduring) to them to whom it is given to believe, that as the effect and excellence of some inherent propriety, patience is God's nature.

CHAP. IV.—DUTY OF IMITATING OUR MASTER TAUGHT US BY SLAVES. EVEN BY BEASTS. OBEDIENT IMITATION IS FOUNDED ON PA-TIENCE.

Therefore, if we see all servants of probity and right feeling shaping their conduct suitably to the disposition of their lord; if, that is, the art of deserving favour is obedience,[9] while the rule of obedience is a compliant subjection; how much more does it behove *us* to be found with a character in accordance with our Lord,—servants as we are of the

---

[1] See Ps. lxxiv. 23 in A. V. It is Ps. lxxiii. in the LXX.
[2] Because they see no visible proof of it.
[3] Sæculo.
[4] So Mr. Dodgson; and La Cerda, as quoted by Oehler. See Ps. cxxxi. 1 in LXX., where it is Ps. cxxx.
[5] 1 John i. 1.
[6] I have followed Oehler's reading of this very difficult and much disputed passage. For the expression, "having been trained," etc., compare Heb. v. 8.
[7] Luke ix. 51-56.

[8] Or, "yet had there been need of contumelies likewise for the undergoing of death?"
[9] "Obsequium," distinguished by Döderlein from "obedientia," as a more voluntary and spontaneous thing, founded less on authority than respect and love.

living God, whose judgment on His servants turns not on a fetter or a cap of freedom, but on an eternity either of penalty or of salvation; for the shunning of which severity or the courting of which liberality there needs a diligence in obedience[1] as great as are the comminations themselves which the severity utters, or the promises which the liberality freely makes.[2] And yet we exact obedience[3] not from *men* only, who have the bond of their slavery under their chin,[4] or in any other legal way are debtors to obedience,[5] but even from cattle,[6] even from brutes;[7] understanding that they have been provided and delivered for our uses by the Lord. Shall, then, *creatures* which God makes subject to us be better than we in the discipline of obedience?[8] Finally, (the creatures) which obey, acknowledge *their masters.* Do we hesitate to listen diligently to Him to whom alone we are subjected—that is, the Lord? But how unjust is it, how ungrateful likewise, not to repay from yourself the same which, through the indulgence of your neighbour, you obtain from others, to him through whom you obtain it! Nor needs there more words on the exhibition of obedience[9] due from us to the Lord God; for the acknowledgment[10] of God understands what is incumbent on it. Lest, however, we seem to have inserted *remarks* on obedience[11] as something irrelevant, (let us remember) that obedience[11] itself is drawn from patience. Never does an *im*patient *man* render it, or a *patient* fail to find pleasure[12] in it. Who, then, could treat largely (enough) of the good of that *patience* which the Lord God, the Demonstrator and Acceptor of all good things, carried about in His own self?[13] To whom, again, would it be doubtful that every good thing ought, because it pertains[13] to God, to be earnestly pursued with the whole mind by such as pertain to God? By means of which (considerations) both commendation and exhortation[14] on the subject of patience

are briefly, and as it were in the compendium of a prescriptive rule, established.[15]

CHAP. V.—AS GOD IS THE AUTHOR OF PATIENCE, SO THE DEVIL IS OF IMPATIENCE.

Nevertheless, the proceeding[16] of a discussion on the necessaries of faith is not idle, because it is not unfruitful. In edification no loquacity is base, if it be base at any time.[17] And so, if the discourse be concerning some particular *good*, the subject requires us to review also the *contrary* of that good. For you will throw more light on what is to be pursued, if you first give a digest of what is to be avoided.

Let us therefore consider, concerning *Im*patience, whether just as patience in God, so its adversary quality have been born and detected in our adversary, that from this consideration may appear how primarily adverse it is to faith. For that which has been conceived by God's rival, of course is not friendly to God's things. The discord of *things* is the same as the discord of their *authors*. Further, since God is best, the devil on the contrary worst, *of beings*, by their own very diversity they testify that neither works for[18] the other; so that anything of good can no more seem to be effected for us by the Evil One, than anything of evil by the Good. Therefore I detect the nativity of impatience in the devil himself, at that very time when he impatiently bore that the Lord God subjected the universal works which He had made to His own image, that is, to man.[19] For if he had endured (that), he would not have grieved; nor would he have envied man if he had not grieved. Accordingly he deceived him, because he had envied him; but he had envied because he had grieved: he had grieved because, of course, he had not patiently borne. What that angel of perdition[20] first was—malicious or impatient—I scorn to inquire: since manifest it is that either impatience took its rise *together with* malice, or else malice *from* impatience; that subsequently they conspired between themselves; and that they grew up indivisible in one paternal bosom. But, however, having been instructed, by his own experiment, what an aid unto sinning was that which he had been the first to feel, and by means of which he

---

[1] Obsequii.
[2] "Pollicetur," not "promittit."
[3] Obedientiam.
[4] "Subnixis." Perhaps this may be the meaning, as in Virg. Æn. iv. 217. But Oehler notices "subnexis" as a conjecture of Jos. Scaliger, which is very plausible, and would mean nearly the same. Mr. Dodgson renders "supported by their slavery;" and Oehler makes "subnixis" = "præditis," "instructis." [Elucidation II.]
[5] Obsequii.
[6] Pecudibus," i. e. tame domestic cattle.
[7] "Bestiis," irrational creatures, as opposed to "homines," here apparently *wild* beasts.
[8] Obsequii. For the sentiment, compare Isa. i. 3.
[9] Obsequio.
[10] See above, "the creatures . . . *acknowledge* their masters."
[11] Obsequii.
[12] "Oblectatur" Oehler reads with the MSS. The editors, as he says, have emended "Obluctatur," which Mr. Dodgson reads.
[13] See the previous chapter.
[14] See chap. i.
[15] [All our author's instances of this principle of the *Præscriptio* are noteworthy, as interpreting its use in the *Advs. Hæreses*.]

[16] "Procedere:" so Oehler, who, however, notices an ingenious conjecture of Jos. Scaliger—"procudere," the hammering out, or forging.
[17] Tertullian may perhaps wish to imply, in *prayer*. See Matt. vi. 7.
[18] Facere. But Fulv. Ursinus (as Oehler tells us) has suggested a neat emendation—"favere," favours.
[19] See Ps. viii. 4-6.
[20] Compare the expression in *de Idol.* iv., "perdition of blood" = "bloody perdition," and the note there. So here "angel of perdition" may="lost angel."

had entered on his course of delinquency, he called the same to his assistance for the thrusting of man into crime. The woman,[1] immediately on being met by him—I may say so without rashness—was, through his very speech with her, breathed on by a spirit infected with impatience: so certain is it that she would never have sinned at all, if she had honoured the divine edict by maintaining her patience to the end. What (of the fact) that she endured not to have been met alone; but in the presence of Adam, not yet her husband, not yet bound to lend her his ears,[2] she is impatient of keeping silence, and makes him the transmitter of that which she had imbibed from the Evil One? Therefore another human being, too, perishes through the impatience of the one; presently, too, perishes of himself, through his own impatience committed in each respect, both in regard of God's premonition and in regard of the devil's cheatery; not enduring to observe the former nor to refute the latter. Hence, whence (the origin) of delinquency, arose the first origin of judgment; hence, whence man was induced to offend, God began to be wroth. Whence (came) the first indignation in God, thence (came) His first patience; who, content at that time with malediction only, refrained in the devil's case from the instant infliction[3] of punishment. Else what crime, before this guilt of impatience, is imputed to man? · Innocent he was, and in an intimate friendship with God, and the husbandman[4] of paradise. But when once he succumbed to impatience, he quite ceased to be of sweet savour[5] to God; he quite ceased to be able to endure things celestial. Thenceforward, a creature[6] given to earth, and ejected from the sight of God, he begins to be easily turned by impatience unto every use offensive to God. For straightway that *impatience* conceived of the devil's seed, produced, in the fecundity of malice, anger as her son; and when brought forth, trained him in her own arts. For that very thing which had immersed Adam and Eve in death, taught their son, too, to begin with murder. It would be idle for me to ascribe this to impatience, if Cain, that first homicide and first fratricide, had borne with equanimity and not impatiently the refusal by the Lord of his own oblations—if he is not wroth with his own brother —if, finally, he took away no one's life. Since, then, he could neither have killed un-

less he had been wroth, nor have been wroth unless he had been impatient, he demonstrates that what he did through wrath must be referred to that by which wrath was suggested during this cradle-time of impatience, then (in a certain sense) in her infancy. But how great presently were her augmentations! And no wonder. If she has been the first delinquent, it is a consequence that, because she *has* been the first, therefore she is the only parent stem,[7] too, to *every* delinquency, pouring down from her own fount various veins of crimes.[8] Of *murder* we have spoken; but, being from the very beginning the outcome of *anger*,[9] whatever causes besides it shortly found for itself it lays collectively on the account of impatience, as to its own origin. For whether from *private enmities*, or for the sake of *prey*, any one perpetrates that wickedness,[10] the earlier step is his becoming *impatient of*[11] either the hatred or the avarice. Whatever *compels* a man, it is not possible that without *impatience of itself* it can be perfected in *deed*. Who *ever* committed *adultery* without impatience of *lust*? Moreover, if in females the sale of their modesty is forced by the price, of course it is by impatience of contemning gain[12] that *this sale* is regulated.[13] These (I mention) as the principal delinquencies in the sight of the Lord,[14] for, to speak compendiously, *every* sin is ascribable to impatience. "Evil" is "impatience of good." None *immodest* is not *impatient of modesty; dishonest* of *honesty; impious* of *piety;*[15] *unquiet* of *quietness*. In order that each individual may become *evil* he will be *unable to persevere*[16] in being *good*. How, therefore, can such a hydra of delinquencies fail to offend the Lord, the Disapprover of evils? Is it not manifest that it was through impatience that Israel himself also always failed in his duty toward God, from that time when,[17] forgetful of the heavenly arm whereby he had been ·drawn out of his Egyptian affliction, he demands from Aaron "gods[18] as his guides;" when he pours down for an idol the contributions of his gold: for the so necessary delays of Moses, while he met with God, he had borne with impatience. After the edible rain

---

[1] Mulier. See *de Orat.* c. xxii.
[2] 1 Cor. vii. 3; compare also 1 Pet. iii. 7.
[3] Impetu.
[4] Colonus. Gen. ii. 15.
[5] Sapere. See *de Idol.* c. i. *sub fin.*
[6] Homo.

[7] Matrix. Mr. Dodgson renders *womb*, which is admissible; but the other passages quoted by Oehler, where Tertullian uses this word, seem to suit better with the rendering given in the text.
[8] Compare a similar expression in *de Idol.* ii. *ad init.*
[9] Which Tertullian has just shown to be the result of *impatience*.
[10] i.e. murder.
[11] i.e. unable to restrain.
[12] i.e. want of power or patience to contemn gain.
[13] "Ordinatur;" but "orditur" has been very plausibly conjectured.
[14] Mr. Dodgson refers to *ad Uxor.* i. 5, *q. v. sub fin.*
[15] Or, "*unduteous* of *duteousness*."
[16] i.e. *impatient*.
[17] I have departed slightly here from Oehler's punctuation.
[18] Ex. xxxii. 1; Acts vii. 39, 40.

of the manna, after the watery following[1] of the rock, they despair of the Lord in not enduring a three-days' thirst;[2] for this also is laid to their charge by the Lord as impatience. And—not to rove through individual cases—there was no instance in which it was not by failing in duty through impatience that they perished. How, moreover, did they lay hands on the prophets, except through impatience of hearing them? on the Lord moreover Himself, through impatience likewise of seeing Him? But had they entered *the path of* patience, they would have been set free.[3]

CHAP. VI.—PATIENCE BOTH ANTECEDENT AND SUBSEQUENT TO FAITH.

Accordingly it is patience which is both subsequent and antecedent to faith. In short, Abraham believed God, and was accredited by Him with righteousness;[4] but it was patience which *proved* his faith, when he was bidden to immolate his son, with a view to (I would not say the temptation, but) the typical attestation of his faith. But God knew whom He had accredited with righteousness.[5] So heavy a precept, the perfect execution whereof was not even pleasing to the Lord, he patiently both heard, and (if God had willed) would have fulfilled. Deservedly then was he "blessed," because he was "faithful;" deservedly "faithful," because "patient." So faith, illumined by patience, when it was becoming propagated among the nations through "Abraham's seed, which is Christ,"[6] and was superinducing grace over the law,[7] made patience her pre-eminent coadjutrix for amplifying and fulfilling the law, because that alone had been lacking unto the doctrine of righteousness. For men were of old wont to require "eye for eye, and tooth for tooth"[8] and to repay with usury "evil with evil;" for, as yet, patience was not on earth, because faith was not either. Of course, meantime, impatience used to enjoy the opportunities which the law gave. That was easy, while the Lord and Master of patience was absent. But after He has supervened, and has united[9] the grace of faith with patience, *now* it is no longer lawful to assail even with *word*, nor to say "fool"[10] even, without

"danger of the judgment." Anger has been prohibited, our spirits retained, the petulance of the hand checked, the poison of the tongue[11] extracted. The law has found more than it has lost, while Christ says, "Love your personal enemies, and bless your cursers, and pray for your persecutors, that ye may be sons of your heavenly Father."[12] Do you see whom patience gains for us as a Father? In this principal precept the universal discipline of patience is succinctly comprised, since evil-doing is not conceded even when it is deserved.

CHAP. VII.—THE CAUSES OF IMPATIENCE, AND THEIR CORRESPONDENT PRECEPTS.

Now, however, while we run through the causes of impatience, all the other precepts also will answer in their own places. If our spirit is aroused by the loss of property, it is commonished by the Lord's Scriptures, in almost every place, to a contemning of the world;[13] nor is there any more powerful exhortation to contempt of money submitted[14] (to us), than (*the fact*) the Lord Himself is found amid no riches. He always justifies the poor, fore-condemns the rich. So He fore-ministered to patience "loss," and to opulence "contempt" (as portion);[15] demonstrating, by means of (His own) *repudiation* of riches, that *hurts* done to them also are not to be much regarded. Of that, therefore, which we have not the smallest need to seek after, because the Lord did not seek after it either, we ought to endure without heart-sickness the cutting down or taking away. "Covetousness," the Spirit of the Lord has through the apostle pronounced "a root of all evils."[16] Let us not interpret that *covetousness* as consisting merely in the concupiscence of what is another's: for even what *seems* ours *is* another's; for nothing is ours, since all things are God's, whose are we also ourselves. And so, if, when suffering from a loss, we feel impatiently, grieving for what is lost from what is not our own, we shall be detected as bordering on covetousness: we *seek* what is another's when we ill brook *losing* what is another's. He who is greatly stirred with impatience of a loss, does, by giving things earthly the precedence over things heavenly, sin directly[17] against God; for the Spirit, which he has received from the Lord, he

---

[1] i.e. the water which followed them, after being given forth by the smitten rock. See 1 Cor. x. 4.
[2] See Num. xx. 1-6. But Tertullian has apparently confused this with Ex. xv. 22. which seems to be the only place where "a *three-days'* thirst" is mentioned.
[3] Free, i.e. from the bondage of impatience and of sin.
[4] See Gen. xv. 6 ; Rom. iv. 3, 9, 22 ; Gal. iii. 6 ; Jas. ii. 23.
[5] i.e. the trial was necessary not to prove his faith to *God*, who knows all whom He accounts righteous, but " typically" to *us*.
[6] Gal. iii. 16.
[7] John i. 17 ; Rom. vi. 14, 15.
[8] Matt. vi. 38, and the references there given.
[9] Composuit.
[10] See Matt. v. 22 ; and Wordsworth *in loco*, who thinks it probable that the meaning is " apostate."

[11] Ps. cxl. 3 ; Rom. iii. 13 ; Jas. iii. 8.
[12] Matt. v. 44, 45.
[13] Sæculo.
[14] Subjacet.
[15] This appears to be the sense of this very difficult passage as Oehler reads it ; and of Fr. Junius' interpretation of it, which Oehler approves.
[16] 1 Tim. vi. 10. See *de Idol.* xi. *ad init.*
[17] De proximo. See above, c. v. *Deo de proximo amicus*, " a *most intimate* friend to God."

greatly shocks for the sake of a worldly matter. Willingly, therefore, let us lose things earthly, let us keep things heavenly. Perish the whole world,[1] so I may make patience my gain! In truth, I know not whether he who has not made up his mind to endure with constancy the loss of somewhat of his, either by theft, or else by force, or else even by carelessness, would himself readily or heartily lay hand on his own property in the cause of almsgiving: for who that endures not at all to be cut by another, himself draws the sword on his own body? Patience in losses is an exercise in bestowing and communicating. Who fears not to lose, finds it not irksome to give. Else how will one, when he has two coats, give the one of them to the naked,[2] unless he be a man likewise to offer to one who takes away his coat his cloak as well?[3] How shall we fashion to us friends from mammon,[4] if we love it so much as not to put up with its loss? We shall perish together with the lost *mammon.* Why do we *find* here, where it is our business to *lose?*[5] To exhibit impatience at all losses is the Gentiles' business, who give money the precedence perhaps over their soul; for so they do, when, in their cupidities of lucre, they encounter the gainful perils of commerce on the sea; when, for money's sake, even in the forum, there is nothing which damnation (itself) would fear which they hesitate to essay; when they hire themselves for sport and the camp; when, after the manner of wild beasts, they play the bandit along the highway. But us, according to the diversity by which we are distinguished from them, it becomes to lay down not our soul for money, but money for our soul, whether spontaneously in bestowing or patiently in losing.

CHAP. VIII.—OF PATIENCE UNDER PERSONAL VIOLENCE AND MALEDICTION.

We who carry about our very soul, our very body, exposed in this world[6] to injury from all, and exhibit patience under that injury; shall we be hurt at the loss[7] of less important things?[8] Far from a servant of Christ be such a defilement as that the patience which has been prepared for greater temptations should forsake him in frivolous ones. If one attempt to provoke you by manual violence, the monition of the Lord is at hand:

"To him," He saith, "who smiteth thee on the face, turn the other cheek likewise."[9] Let outrageousness[10] be wearied out by your patience. Whatever that blow may be, conjoined[11] with pain and contumely, it[12] shall receive a heavier one from the Lord. You wound that outrageous[13] one more by enduring: for he will be beaten by Him for whose sake you endure. If the tongue's bitterness break out in malediction or reproach, look back at the saying, "When they curse you, rejoice."[14] The Lord Himself was "cursed" in the eye of the law;[15] and yet is He the only Blessed One. Let us servants, therefore, follow our Lord closely; and be cursed patiently, that we may be able to be blessed. If I hear with too little equanimity some wanton or wicked word uttered against me, I must of necessity either myself retaliate the bitterness, or else I shall be racked with mute impatience. When, then, on being cursed, I smite (with my tongue,) how shall I be found to have followed the doctrine of the Lord, in which it has been delivered that "a man is defiled,[16] not by the defilements of vessels, but of the things which are sent forth out of his mouth." Again, *it is said* that "impeachment[17] awaits us for every vain and needless word."[18] It follows that, from whatever the Lord keeps us, the same He admonishes us to bear patiently from another. I will add (somewhat) touching the *pleasure* of patience. For every injury, whether inflicted by tongue or hand, when it has lighted upon patience, will be dismissed[19] with the same fate as, some weapon launched against and blunted on a rock of most stedfast hardness. For it will wholly fall then and there with bootless and fruitless labour; and sometimes will recoil and spend its rage on him who sent it out, with retorted impetus. No doubt the reason why any one hurts you is that you may be pained; because the hurter's enjoyment consists in the pain of the hurt. When, then, you have upset his enjoyment by not being pained, *he* must needs he pained by the loss of his enjoyment. Then you not only go

---

[1] Sæculum.
[2] Luke iii. 11.
[3] Matt. v. 40; Luke vi. 29.
[4] Luke xvi. 9.
[5] "Alluding to Christ's words in Matt. x. 39" (Rigalt. quoted by Oehler).
[6] Sæculo.
[7] Delibatione.
[8] i. e. money and the like. Compare Matt. vi. 25; Luke xii. 23.

[9] Matt. v. 39.
[10] Improbitas.
[11] Constrictus. I have rendered after Oehler: but may not the meaning be "clenched," like the hand which deals the blow?
[12] As Oehler says "the blow" is said to "receive" that which, strictly, the dealer of it receives.
[13] Improbum.
[14] Matt. v. 11, 12; Luke vi. 22, 23.
[15] Deut. xxi. 23; Gal. iii. 13. Tertullian's quotations here are somewhat loose. He renders words which are distinct in the Greek by the same in his Latin.
[16] Communicari—κοινοῦσθαι. See Mark vii. 15, "made common," i.e. profane, unclean. Compare Acts x. 14, 15 in the Greek.
[17] Reatum. See *de Idol.* i. *ad init.*, "the highest impeachment of the age."
[18] Matt. xii. 36. Tertullian has rendered ἀργόν by "vani et supervacui."
[19] Dispungetur: a word which, in the active, means technically "to balance accounts," hence "to discharge," etc.

unhurt away, which even alone is enough for you; but gratified, into the bargain, by your adversary's disappointment, and revenged by his pain. This is the *utility* and the *pleasure* of patience.

CHAP. IX.—OF PATIENCE UNDER BEREAVEMENT.

Not even that species of impatience under the loss of our dear ones is excused, where some assertion of a right to grief acts the patron to it. For the consideration of the apostle's declaration must be set before us, who says, " Be not overwhelmed with sadness at the falling asleep of any one, just as the nations are who are without hope."[1] And justly; or, believing the resurrection of Christ, we believe also in our own, for whose sake He both died and rose again. Since, then, there is certainty as to the resurrection of the dead, grief for death is needless, and impatience of grief is needless. For why should you grieve, if you believe that (your loved one) is not perished? Why should you bear impatiently the temporary withdrawal of him who you believe will return? That which you think to be death is departure. He who goes before us is not to be lamented, though by all means to be longed for.[2] That longing also must be tempered with patience. For why should you bear without moderation *the fact that* one is gone away whom you will presently follow? Besides, impatience in matters of this kind bodes ill for our hope, and is a dealing insincerely with the faith. And we wound Christ when we accept not with equanimity the summoning out of this world of any by Him, as if they were to be pitied. " I desire," says the apostle, " to be now received, and to be with Christ."[3] How far better a desire does *he* exhibit! If, then, we grieve impatiently over such as *have* attained the desire of Christians, we show unwillingness ourselves to attain it.

CHAP. X.—OF REVENGE.

There is, too, another chief spur of impatience, the lust of revenge, dealing with the business either of glory or else of malice. But " glory," on the one hand, is everywhere " vain;"[4] and malice, on the other, is always[5] odious to the Lord; in this case indeed most of all, when, being provoked by a neighbour's malice, it constitutes itself superior[6] in following out revenge, and by paying wickedness doubles that which has once been done. Revenge, in the estimation of error,[7] seems a solace of pain; in the estimation of truth, on the contrary, it is convicted of malignity. For what difference is there between provoker and provoked, except that the former is detected as prior in evil-doing, but the latter as posterior? Yet each stands impeached of hurting a man in the eye of the Lord, who both prohibits and condemns every wickedness. In evil-doing there is no account taken of *order*, nor does *place* separate what *similarity* conjoins. And the precept is absolute, that evil is not to be repaid with evil.[8] Like deed involves like merit. How shall we observe that principle, if in our loathing[9] we shall not loathe *revenge?* What honour, moreover, shall we be offering to the Lord God, if we arrogate to ourselves the arbitrament of vengeance? We are corrupt[10]—earthen vessels.[11] With our own servant-boys,[12] if they assume to themselves the right of vengeance on their fellow-servants, we are gravely offended; while such as make us the offering of their patience we not only approve as mindful of humility, of servitude, affectionately jealous of the right of their lord's honour; but we make them an ampler satisfaction than they would have pre-exacted[13] for themselves. Is there any risk of a different result in the case of a Lord so just in estimating, so potent in executing? Why, then, do we believe Him a Judge, if not an Avenger too? This He promises that He will be to us in return, saying, " Vengeance *belongeth* to me, and I will avenge;"[14] that is, *Leave* patience to me, and I will reward patience. For when He says, " Judge not, lest ye be judged,"[15] does He not require patience? For who will refrain from judging another, but he who shall be patient in not revenging himself? Who *judges* in order to *pardon?* And if he shall pardon, still he has taken care to indulge the impatience of a judger, and has taken away the honour of the one Judge, that is, God. How many mischances had impatience of this kind been wont to run into! How oft has it repented of its revenge! How oft has its vehemence been found worse than the causes which led to it!—inasmuch as nothing undertaken with impatience can be effected without impetuosity: nothing done with impetuosity fails either to stumble, or else to fall altogether,

---

1 I Thess. iv. 13, not very strictly rendered.
2 Desiderandus.
3 Phil. i. 23, again loosely rendered: *e. g.* ἀναλῦσαι = " to weigh anchor," is rendered by Tertullian " recipi."
4 See Gal. v. 26; Phil. ii. 3.
5 Nunquam non.
6 i.e. perhaps superior *in degree of malice.*

7 i. e. of the world and its erroneous philosophies.
8 Rom. xii. 17.
9 Fastidientes, i. e. our loathing or abhorrence of *sin.* Perhaps the reference may be to Rom. xii. 9.
10 Isa. lxiv. 6.
11 Isa. lxiv. 8; 2 Cor. iv. 7
12 Servulis.
13 Præsumpsissent.
14 Deut. xxxii. 35; Ps. xciv. 1; Rom. xii. 19; Heb. x. 30.
15 Matt. vii. 1; Luke vi. 37.

or else to vanish headlong. Moreover, if you avenge yourself too slightly, you will be mad; if too amply, you will have to bear the burden.[1] What have I to do with vengeance, the measure of which, through impatience of pain, I am unable to regulate? Whereas, if I shall repose on patience, I shall not *feel* pain; if I shall not feel pain, I shall not *desire* to avenge myself.

CHAP. XI.—FURTHER REASONS FOR PRACTISING PATIENCE. ITS CONNECTION WITH THE BEATITUDES.

After these principal material causes of impatience, registered to the best of our ability, why should we wander out of our way among the rest,—what are found at home, what abroad? Wide and diffusive is the Evil One's operation, hurling manifold irritations of our spirit, and sometimes trifling ones, sometimes very great. But the trifling ones you may contemn from their very littleness; to the very great ones you may yield in regard of their overpoweringness. Where the injury is less, there is no necessity for impatience; but where the injury is greater, there more necessary is the remedy for the injury—patience. Let us strive, therefore, to endure the inflictions of the Evil One, that the counter-zeal of our equanimity may mock the zeal of the foe. If, however, we ourselves, either by imprudence or else voluntarily, draw upon ourselves anything, let us meet with equal patience what we have to blame ourselves for. Moreover, if we believe that some inflictions are sent on us by the Lord, to whom should we more exhibit patience than to the Lord? Nay, He teaches[2] us to give thanks and rejoice, over and above, at being thought worthy of divine chastisement. "Whom I love," saith He, " I chasten."[3] O blessed servant, on whose amendment the Lord is intent! with whom He deigns to be wroth! whom He does not deceive by dissembling His reproofs! On every side, therefore, we are bound to the duty of exercising patience, from whatever quarter, either by our own errors or else by the snares of the Evil One, we incur the Lord's reproofs. Of that duty great is the reward—namely, happiness. For whom but the patient has the Lord called happy, in saying, " Blessed are the poor in spirit, for theirs is the kingdom of the heavens?"[4] No one, assuredly, is " poor in spirit," except he be humble. Well, who is humble, except he be

patient? For no one can abase himself without patience, in the first instance, to bear the act of abasement. " Blessed," saith He, " are the weepers and mourners."[5] Who, without patience, is tolerant of such unhappinesses? And so, to such, " consolation " and " laughter " are promised. " Blessed are the gentle:"[6] under this term, surely, the impatient cannot possibly be classed. Again, when He marks " the peacemakers "[7] with the same title of felicity, and names them " sons of God," pray have the impatient any affinity with " peace?" Even a fool may perceive that. When, however, He says, " Rejoice and exult, as often as they shall curse and persecute you; for very great is your reward in heaven,"[8] of course it is not to the *impatience* of exultation[9] that He makes that promise; because no one *will* " exult " in adversities unless he have first learnt to contemn them; no one will contemn them unless he have learnt to practise patience.

CHAP. XII.—CERTAIN OTHER DIVINE PRECEPTS. THE APOSTOLIC DESCRIPTION OF CHARITY. THEIR CONNECTION WITH PATIENCE.

As regards the rule of peace, which[10] is so pleasing to God, who in the world that is prone to impatience[11] will even *once* forgive his brother, I will not say " seven times," or[12] " seventy-seven times?"[13] Who that is contemplating a suit against his adversary will compose the matter by agreement,[14] unless he first begin by lopping off chagrin, hardheartedness, and bitterness, which are in fact the poisonous outgrowths of impatience? How will you " remit, and remission shall be granted " you,[15] if the absence of patience makes you tenacious of a wrong? No one who is at variance with his brother in his mind, will finish offering his " duteous gift at the altar," unless he first, with intent to " re-conciliate his brother," return to patience.[16] If " the sun go down over our wrath," we are in jeopardy:[17] we are not allowed to remain one day without patience. But, however, since Patience takes the lead in[18] every species of salutary discipline, what

---

[1] i. e. the penalty which the law will inflict.
[2] Docet. But a plausible conjecture, " decet," " it becomes us," has been made.
[3] Prov. iii. 11, 12 ; Heb. xii. 5, 6 ; Rev. iii. 19.
[4] Matt. v. 3.

[5] Matt. v. 4.
[6] Matt. v. 5.
[7] Matt. v. 9.
[8] Matt. v. 11, 12, inexactly quoted.
[9] Exultationis impatientiæ.
[10] i. e. peace.
[11] Impatientiæ natus: lit. "born for impatience." Comp. *de Pæniten.* 12, *ad fin.* " nec ulli rei nisi pænitentiæ natus."
[12] Oehler reads " sed," but the " vel" adopted in the text is a conjecture of Latinius, which Oehler mentions.
[13] Septuagies septies. The reference is to Matt. xviii. 21, 22. Compare *de Orat.* vii. *ad fin.* and the note there.
[14] Matt. v. 25.
[15] Luke vi. 37.
[16] Matt. v. 23, 24.
[17] Eph. iv. 26. Compare *de Orat.* xi.
[18] Gubernet.

wonder that she likewise ministers to Repentance, (accustomed as Repentance is to come to the rescue of such as have fallen,) when, on a disjunction of wedlock (for that cause, I mean, which makes it lawful, whether for husband or wife, to persist in the perpetual observance of widowhood),[1] she[2] waits for, she yearns for, she persuades by her entreaties, repentance in all who are one day to enter salvation? How great a blessing she confers on each! The one she prevents from becoming an adulterer; the other she amends. So, to, she is found in those holy examples touching patience in the Lord's parables. The shepherd's patience seeks and finds the straying ewe:[3] for *Im*patience would easily despise *one* ewe; but Patience undertakes the labour of the quest, and the patient burden-bearer carries home on his shoulders the forsaken sinner.[4] That prodigal son also the father's patience receives, and clothes, and feeds, and makes excuses for, in the presence of the angry brother's *im*patience.[5] He, therefore, who "had perished" is saved, because he entered on *the way of* repentance. Repentance perishes not, because it finds Patience (to welcome it). For by whose teachings but those of Patience is Charity[6]—the highest sacrament of the faith, the treasure-house of the Christian name, which the apostle commends with the whole strength of the Holy Spirit—trained? "Charity," he says, "is long suffering;" thus she applies patience: "is beneficent;" Patience does no evil: "is not emulous;" that certainly is a peculiar mark of patience: "savours not of violence:"[7] she has drawn her self-restraint from patience: "is not puffed up; is not violent;"[8] for that pertains not unto patience: "nor does she seek her own" if, she *offers* her own, provided she may benefit her neighbours: "nor is irritable;" if she were, what would she have left to *Im*patience? Accordingly he says, "Charity endures all things; tolerates all things;" of course because she is patient. Justly, then, "will she never fail;"[9] for all other things will be cancelled, will have their consummation. "Tongues, sciences, prophecies, become exhausted; faith, hope, charity, are permanent:" Faith, which Christ's patience introduced; hope, which man's patience waits for; charity, which Patience accompanies, with God as Master.

CHAP. XIII.—OF BODILY PATIENCE.

Thus far, finally, of patience simple and uniform, and as it exists merely in the *mind:* though in many forms likewise I labour after it in *body*, for the purpose of "winning the Lord;"[10] inasmuch as it is *a quality* which has been exhibited by the Lord Himself in bodily virtue as well; if it is true that the ruling mind easily communicates the gifts[11] of the Spirit with its *bodily* habitation. What, therefore, is the business of Patience *in the body?* In the first place, *it is* the affliction[12] of the flesh—a victim[13] able to appease the Lord by means of the sacrifice of humiliation—in making a libation to the Lord of sordid[14] raiment, together with scantiness of food, content with simple diet and the pure drink of water[15] in conjoining fasts *to all this;* in inuring herself to sackcloth and ashes. This *bodily* patience adds a grace to our prayers for good, a strength to our prayers against evil; this opens the ears of Christ *our* God,[16] dissipates severity, elicits clemency. Thus that Babylonish king,[17] after being exiled from human form in his seven years' squalor and neglect, because he had offended the Lord; by the bodily immolation of patience not only recovered his kingdom, but—what is more to be desired by a man—made satisfaction to God. Further, if we set down in order the higher and happier grades of bodily patience, (we find that) it is she who is entrusted by holiness with the care of continence of the flesh: she keeps the widow,[18] and sets on the virgin the seal[19] and raises the self-made eunuch to the realms of heaven.[20] That which springs from a virtue of the *mind* is perfected in the *flesh; and,* finally, by the patience of the flesh, does battle under persecution. If flight press hard, the flesh wars with[21] the inconvenience of flight; if imprisonment over-

---

[1] What the cause *is* is disputed. Opinions are divided as to whether Tertullian means by it "marriage with a heathen" (which as Mr. Dodgson reminds us, Tertullian—*de Uxor.* ii. 3—calls "adultery"), or the case in which our Lord allowed divorce. See Matt. xix. 9.
[2] i. e. patience.
[3] Luke xv. 3–6.
[4] Peccatricem, i. e. the *ewe.*
[5] Luke xv. 11–32.
[6] Dilectio = ἀγάπη. See Trench, *New Testament Syn. s. v.* ἀγάπη; and with the rest of this chapter compare carefully, in the Greek, 1 Cor. xiii. [Neander points out the different view our author takes of the same parable, in the *de Pudicit.* cap. 9, Vol. IV. this series.]
[7] Protervum = Greek περπερεύεται.
[8] Proterit = Greek ἀσχημονεῖ.
[9] Excidet = Greek ἐκλείπει, suffers eclipse.

[10] Phil. iii. 8.
[11] "Invecta," generally =moveables, household furniture.
[12] Or, mortification, "afflictatio."
[13] i. e. fleshly mortification is a "victim," etc.
[14] Or, "mourning." Comp. *de Pæn.* c. 9.
[15] [The "water vs. wine" movement is not a discovery of our own times. "Drink a *little wine*," said St. Paul medicinally; but (as a great and good divine once remarked) "we must not lay stress on the *noun*, but the *adjective;* let it be very little."]
[16] Christi dei.
[17] Dan. iv. 33–37. Comp. *de Pæn.* c. 12. [I have removed an ambiguity by slightly touching the text here.]
[18] 1 Tim. v. 3, 9, 10; 1 Cor. vii. 39, 40.
[19] 1 Cor. vii. 34, 35.
[20] Matt. xix. 12.
[21] Ad. It seems to mean flesh has strength given it, by patience, to meet the hardships of the flight. Compare the πρὸς πλησμονὴν τῆς σαρκὸς, of St. Paul in Col. ii. 23. [Kaye compares this with the *De Fuga*, as proof of the author's freedom from Montanism, when this was written.]

take[1] us, the flesh (still was) in bonds, the flesh in the gyve, the flesh in solitude,[2] and in that want of light, and in that patience of the world's misusage.[3] When, however, it is led forth unto the final proof of happiness,[4] unto the occasion of the second baptism,[5] unto the act of ascending the divine seat, no patience is more needed *there* than *bodily* patience. If the "spirit is willing, but the flesh," *without* patience, "weak,"[6] where, *save in patience*, is the safety of the spirit, and of the flesh itself? But when the Lord says this about the flesh, pronouncing it "weak," He shows what need there is of strengthening, it—that is by patience—to meet[7] every preparation for subverting or punishing faith; that it may bear with all constancy stripes, fire, cross, beasts, sword: all which prophets and apostles, by enduring, conquered!

CHAP. XIV.—THE POWER OF THIS TWOFOLD PATIENCE, THE SPIRITUAL AND THE BODILY. EXEMPLIFIED IN THE SAINTS OF OLD.

With this strength of patience, Esaias is cut *asunder*, and ceases not to speak concerning the Lord; Stephen is stoned, and prays for pardon to his foes.[8] Oh, happy also he who met all the violence of the devil by the exertion of every species of patience![9]—whom neither the driving away of his cattle nor those riches of his in sheep, nor the sweeping away of his children in one swoop of ruin, nor, finally, the agony of his own body in (one universal) wound, estranged from the patience and the faith which he had plighted to the Lord; whom the devil smote with all his might in vain. For by all his pains he was not drawn away from his reverence for God; but he has been set up as an example and testimony to us, for the thorough accomplishment of patience as well in spirit as in flesh, as well in mind as in body; in order that we succumb neither to damages of our worldly goods, nor to losses of those who are dearest, nor even to bodily afflictions. What a bier[10] for the devil did God erect in the person of that hero! What a banner did He rear over the enemy of His glory, when, at every bitter message, that man uttered nothing out of his mouth but thanks to God, while he denounced his wife, now quite wearied with ills, and urging

him to resort to crooked remedies! How did God smile,[11] how was the evil one cut asunder,[12] while Job with mighty equanimity kept scraping off[13] the unclean overflow of his own ulcer, while he sportively replaced the vermin that brake out thence, in the same caves and feeding-places of his pitted flesh! And so, when all the darts of temptations had blunted themselves against the corslet and shield of his patience, that instrument[14] of God's victory not only presently recovered from God the soundness of his body, but possessed in redoubled measure what he had lost. And if he had wished to have his children also restored, he might again have been called father; but he preferred to have them restored him "in that day."[15] Such joy as *that* —secure so entirely concerning the Lord—he deferred; meantime he endured a voluntary bereavement, that he might not live without *some* (exercise of) patience.

CHAP. XV.—GENERAL SUMMARY OF THE VIRTUES AND EFFECTS OF PATIENCE.

So amply sufficient a Depositary of patience is God. If it be a wrong which you deposit in His care, He is an Avenger; if a loss, He is a Restorer; if pain, He is a Healer; if death, He is a Reviver. What honour is granted to Patience, to have God as her Debtor! And not without reason: for she keeps all His decrees; she has to do with all His mandates. She fortifies faith; is the pilot of peace; assists charity; establishes humility; waits long for repentance; sets her seal on confession; rules the flesh; preserves the spirit; bridles the tongue; restrains the hand; tramples temptations under foot; drives away scandals; gives their crowning grace to martyrdoms; consoles the poor; teaches the rich moderation; overstrains not the weak; exhausts not the strong; is the delight of the believer; invites the Gentile; commends the servant to his lord, and his lord to God; adorns the woman; makes the man approved; is loved in childhood, praised in youth, looked up to in age; is beauteous in either sex, in every time of life. Come, now, *see* whether[16] we have a general idea of her mien and habit. Her countenance is tranquil and peaceful; her brow serene,[17] contracted by no wrinkle of sadness or of anger; her eyebrows evenly relaxed

---

[1] Præveniat: "prevent" us, before we have time to flee.
[2] Solo.
[3] [Elucidation III.]
[4] i.e. martyrdom.
[5] Comp. Luke xii. 50.
[6] Matt. xxvi. 41.
[7] "Adversus," like the "ad" above, note 21, p. 713.
[8] Acts vii. 59, 60.
[9] Job. See Job i. and ii.
[10] "Feretrum"—for carrying trophies in a triumph, the bodies of the dead, and their effigies, etc.
[11] Compare Ps. ii. 4.
[12] i. e. with rage and disappointment.
[13] Job ii. 8.
[14] Operarius.
[15] See 2 Tim. iv. 8. There is no authority for this statement of Tertullian's in Scripture. [It is his inference rather.]
[16] Si. This is Oehler's reading, who takes "si" to be = "an." But perhaps "sis" (= "si vis"), which is Fr. Junius' correction, is better: "Come, now, let us, if you please, give a general sketch of her mien and habit."
[17] Pura; perhaps "smooth."

in gladsome wise, with eyes downcast in humility, not in unhappiness; her mouth sealed with the honourable mark of silence; her hue such as theirs who are without care and without guilt; the motion of her head frequent against the devil, and her laugh threatening;[1] her clothing, moreover, about her bosom white and well fitted to her person, as being neither inflated nor disturbed. For *Patience* sits on the throne of that calmest and gentlest Spirit, who is not found in the roll of the whirlwind, nor in the leaden hue of the cloud, but is of soft serenity, open and simple, whom Elias saw at his third essay.[2] For where God is, there too is His foster-child, namely Patience. When God's Spirit descends, then Patience accompanies Him indivisibly. If we do not give admission *to her* together with the Spirit, will (He) *always* tarry with us? Nay, I know not whether He would remain *any longer*. Without His companion and handmaid, He must of necessity be straitened in every place and at every time. Whatever blow His enemy may inflict He will be unable to endure alone, being without the instrumental means of enduring.

CHAP. XVI.—THE PATIENCE OF THE HEATHEN VERY DIFFERENT FROM CHRISTIAN PATIENCE. THEIRS DOOMED TO PERDITION. OURS DESTINED TO SALVATION.

This is the rule, this the discipline, these the works of patience *which is* heavenly and true; that is, of Christian *patience*, not false and disgraceful, like as is that patience of the nations of the earth. For in order that in this also the devil might rival the Lord, he has as it were quite on a par (except that the very diversity of evil and good is exactly on a par with their magnitude[3]) taught *his disciples* also a patience of his own; that, I mean, which, making husbands venal for dowry, and teaching them to trade in panderings, makes them subject to the power of their wives; which, with feigned affection, undergoes every toil of forced complaisance,[4] with a view to ensnaring the childless;[5] which makes the slaves of the belly[6] submit to contumelious patronage, in the subjection of their liberty to their gullet. Such pursuits of patience the Gentiles are acquainted with; and they eagerly seize a name of so great goodness to apply it to foul practises: patient they live of rivals, and of the rich, and of such as give them invitations; impatient of God alone. But let their own and their leader's patience look to itself—*a patience* which the subterraneous fire awaits! Let us, on the other hand, love the patience of God, the patience of Christ; let us repay to Him the *patience* which He has paid down for us! Let us offer *to Him* the patience of the spirit, the patience of the flesh, believing as we do in the resurrection of flesh and spirit.

---

[1] Compare with this singular feature, Isa. xxxvii. 22.
[2] i. e., as Rigaltius (referred to by Oehler), explains, after the *two* visions of angels who appeared to him and said, "Arise and eat." See 1 Kings xix. 4–13. [It was the *fourth*, but our author having mentioned *two*, inadvertently calls it the *third*, referring to the "still small voice," in which Elijah *saw* His manifestation.]
[3] One is finite, the other infinite.
[4] Obsequii.
[5] And thus getting a place in their wills.
[6] i. e. professional "diners out." Comp. Phil. iii. 19.

ELUCIDATIONS.

I.

(Unless patience sit by his side, cap. i. p. 707.)

Let me quote words which, many years ago, struck me forcibly, and which I trust, have been blest to my soul; for which reason, I must be allowed, here, to thank their author, the learned and fearless Dean Burgon, of Chichester. In his invaluable *Commentary* on the Gospel, which while it abounds in the fruits of a varied erudition, aims only to be practically useful, this pious scholar remarks: "To Faith must be added *Patience*, the 'patient waiting for God,' if we would escape the snare which Satan spread, no less for the Holy One (*i.e.* in the Temp. upon the Pinnacle) than for the Israelites at Massah. And this is perhaps the reason *of the remarkable prominence* given to the grace of *Patience*, both by our Lord and His Apostles; a circumstance, as it may be thought, *which has not altogether attracted the attention which it deserves."* He then cites examples;[1] but a reference to any good concordance will strikingly exemplify the admirable comment of this "godly and well-learned man." See his comments on St. Matt. iv. 7. and St. Luke xxi. 19.

II.

(Under their chin, cap. iv. p. 709.)

The reference in the note to Paris, as represented by Virgil and in ancient sculpture, seems somewhat to the point·

> " Et nunc ille Paris, cum semiviro comitatu.
> Mæonia mentum mitra crinemq, madentem,
> *Subnixus*, etc."

He had just spoken of the *pileus* as a " Cap of freedom," but there was another form of *pileus* which was just the reverse and was probably tied by *fimbriæ*, under the chin, denoting a low order of slaves, effeminate men, perhaps *spadones*. Now, the Phrygian bonnet to which Virgil refers, is introduced by him to complete the reproach of his contemptuous expression (semiviro comitatu) just before. So, our author—" not only from men, *i.e.* men so degraded as to wear this badge of extreme servitude, but even from cattle, etc. Shall these mean creatures outdo us in obedience and patience?"

III.

(The world's misusage, cap. xiii. p. 716.)

The Reverend Clergy who may read this note will forgive a brother, who begins to be in respect of years, like " Paul the aged," for remarking, that the reading of the *Ante-Nicene Fathers* often leads him to sigh—" Such were they from whom we have received all that makes life tolerable, but how intolerable it was for them: *are we, indeed, such as they would have considered Christians?* " GOD be praised for His mercy and forbearance in our days; but, still it is true that " we have need of patience." Is not much of all that we regard as " the world's misusage," the gracious hand of the Master upon us, giving us something for the exercise of that Patience, by which He forms us into His own image? (Heb. xii. 3.) Impatience of obscurity, of poverty, of ingratitude, of misrepresentation, of " the slings and arrows" of slander and abuse, is a revolt against that indispensable discipline of the Gospel which requires us to " endure afflictions " in some form or other. ·Who can complain when one thinks what it would have cost us to be Christians in Tertullian's time? The ambition of the Clergy is always rebellion against God, and " patient waiting" is its only remedy. One will find profitable reading on this subject in Massillon,[2] *de l'Ambition des Clercs:* " Reposez-vous sur le Seigneur du soin de votre destinée: il saura bien accomplir, tout seul, les desseins qu'il a sur vous. Si votre élévation est son bon plaisir, elle sera aussi son ouvrage. Rendez-vous en digne seulement par la retraite, par la frayeur, par la fuite, par les sentiments vifs de votre indignité. . . c'est ainsi que les Chrysostome, les Grégoire, les Basil, les Augustin, furent donnés à l'Église."

---

[1] See—A *Plain Commentary* on the Four Gospels, intended chiefly for *Devotional Reading.* Oxford, 1854. Also (Vol. I. p. 28) Philadelphia, 1855.

[2] Œuvres, Tom. vi. pp. 133-5. Ed. Paris, 1824.

INDEXES.

TERTULLIAN.

PART FIRST.—APOLOGETIC.

INDEX OF SUBJECTS.

TERTULLIAN.

PART FIRST.—APOLOGETIC.

INDEX OF TEXTS.

TERTULLIAN.

PART SECOND.—ANTI-MARCION.

INDEX OF SUBJECTS.

TERTULLIAN.

PART SECOND.—ANTI-MARCION.

INDEX OF TEXTS.

TERTULLIAN.

PART THIRD.—ETHICAL TREATISES.

INDEX OF SUBJECTS.

TERTULLIAN.

PART THIRD.—ETHICAL TREATISES.

INDEX OF TEXTS.

COSIMO

COSIMO is a specialty publisher of books and publications that inspire, inform and engage readers. Our mission is to offer unique books to niche audiences around the world.

COSIMO CLASSICS offers a collection of distinctive titles by the great authors and thinkers throughout the ages. At **COSIMO CLASSICS** timeless classics find a new life as affordable books, covering a variety of subjects including: *Biographies, Business, History, Mythology, Personal Development, Philosophy, Religion and Spirituality,* and much more!

COSIMO-on-DEMAND publishes books and publications for innovative authors, non-profit organizations and businesses. **COSIMO-on-DEMAND** specializes in bringing books back into print, publishing new books quickly and effectively, and making these publications available to readers around the world.

COSIMO REPORTS publishes public reports that affect your world: from global trends to the economy, and from health to geo-politics.

FOR MORE INFORMATION CONTACT US AT
INFO@COSIMOBOOKS.COM

❋ If you are a book-lover interested in our current catalog of books

❋ If you are an author who wants to get published

❋ If you represent an organization or business seeking to reach your members, donors or customers with your own books and publications

COSIMO BOOKS ARE ALWAYS AVAILABLE AT ONLINE BOOKSTORES

VISIT COSIMOBOOKS.COM
BE INSPIRED, BE INFORMED

CPSIA information can be obtained
at www.ICGtesting.com
Printed in the USA
BVHW040952260321
603431BV00003B/56